GW00808259

THE HOLLYWOOD WHO'S WHO

The Actors and Directors in Today's Hollywood

The
HOLLYWOOD WHO'S WHO

The Actors and Directors in Today's Hollywood

Edited by Robyn Karney

CONTINUUM • NEW YORK

1993

The Continuum Publishing Company
370 Lexington Avenue, New York, NY 10017

Hardcover library edition distributed exclusively by Gale Research, Inc.

Printed in England by Clays Ltd, St Ives plc

Library of Congress Cataloging-in-Publication Data

The Hollywood Who's Who: the actors and directors in today's Hollywood
/ edited by Robyn Karney.
p. cm.
ISBN 0-8264-0588-6 (pbk). 0-8264-0632-7 (hardcover)
I. Motion picture actors and actresses — United States — Biography — Dictionaries. 2. Motion picture producers and directors — United States — Biography — Dictionaries. I. Karney, Robyn.
PN1988.2.W46 1993
791.43'028092'273 — dc 20
[B] 93-18636
CIP

CONTENTS

INTRODUCTION

The Who's Who Of Contemporary Hollywood has been written by a team of eleven journalists dedicated to film. They were given free rein to bring their own opinions and prejudices to bear on their subjects, to retain their own styles and approach and to express themselves at whatever length felt comfortable for a given entry.

The result is, we believe, a series of stimulating profiles, sometimes provocative, occasionally amusing and, where the subjects themselves are heavyweight, sharply analytical. Biographical details have been provided throughout, as have filmographies which were as complete as possible at the time of going to press. We thus hope to have filled a gap in the market for readers with a professional interest in having easy access to the facts, while, at the same time, offering entertaining and informative reading for movie lovers of all ages and tastes.

In making the selection, we chose to range across a wide spectrum of acting and directing talent that has dictated the identity of Hollywood as we know it over the past three decades. Naturally, the stars are here, but so are very many lesser known but equally important supporting players and character actors who are so often overlooked. We've attempted to capture the essence of the people we've written about, to define their work, and, in the case of actors, to remind the reader of faces they know whose names they have forgotten by discussing particular roles and performances.

The inclusions embrace the long-running and the short-lived, the old and the young, the overnight star, the newcomer and the infinitely durable: in short all those who, in our opinion, have made a significant contribution during the period covered, either through their own gifts or popularity, or because they symbolised a fashion or a trend in Hollywood filmmaking at a given moment. Only a handful of essays deal with people who are no longer alive, but whose omission would not seem appropriate (e.g. John Cassavetes and Lee Remick).

There are, alas, omissions which were unavoidable. Time and space controlled numbers, which left worthy contenders such as the now-veteran Piper Laurie, and busy character actor Steve Buscemi to fall by the wayside. Then, too, the print deadline meant that the manuscript had to go off sooner than, for example, Madeleine Stowe or director James Foley conclusively nailed their colours to the mast. Also, the escalation of newcomers in this post-studio, video age is so rapid that it sometimes seems impossible to keep track. Nevertheless, somewhere in here are, perhaps, the stars and major directors of tomorrow. Who knows?

But whether your interest is Gregory Peck or Adrian Pasdar, Madonna or Mel Gibson, George A. Romero or Julia Roberts, Woody Allen or Karen Allen, Elizabeth Taylor or John Turturro, Greta Scacchi or Arnold Schwarzenegger,

Jodie Foster or Stephen Frears, Corey Feldman or Corey Haim, Paul Verhoeven or Jean-Claude Van Damme, Hanks, Hulce, or Cruise, Spielberg, Stallone or Swayze, Jeroen Krabbe or Swoosie Kurtz, William Hurt or Anthony Hopkins, Spike Lee or Jack Lemmon, you'll find them among the nearly 600 people whose work is discussed here.

EDITOR'S NOTES AND ACKNOWLEDGMENTS

The actors and directors in this book, other than the entirely obvious and expected names, make up a necessarily subjective choice. Sometimes this was made on the basis of the sheer quantity of a person's output, at others quality or originality dictated inclusion. The book is intentionally eclectic in an attempt to capture the wide-ranging flavour of the most powerful and influential media industry in the world – thus, directors of acknowledged genius rub shoulders with purveyors of shock, those with a cult following are found side-by-side with filmmakers of no particular distinction or individuality other than the not inconsiderable ability to turn out blockbusting moneymakers. Several non-Americans, both actors and directors, the body of whose work is mainly British or European, are here for particular contributions they have made in Hollywood.

The gathering of factual data was anything but straightforward. Birth dates and places occasionally proved unobtainable or unverifiable and, for this reason, are missing from a handful of entries. Filmographies change at an alarming rate: on occasion somebody leaves a film after shooting has commenced, or a film itself is shelved or, having been completed as a theatrical feature, goes straight to video or, most infuriating of all, changes title before reaching the circuit or between one country and another. Consequently, discrepancies are bound to arise in the fullness of time since we could only compile filmographies on the basis of what seemed accurate at the time of going to press. The filmographies record feature films and feature-length documentaries dated, wherever applicable, from first American theatrical release, but exclude material known to be made-for-TV or video.

As usual with an undertaking of this size, the finished product was only possible with the help of certain individuals. My indefatigable researcher, David Oppedisano, a perfectionist of rare enthusiasm and commitment, never lost his good humour and capacity for hard work in the face of continual frustrations; without Angie Errigo's quick mind, sharp memory and exceptional journalistic skills at proof stage, we'd never have made it to the printer; Kathryn Kirby, aside from being a contributor and a valued sounding board, remained a tower of strength throughout the difficult copy edit; David McGillivray, in a consultant capacity, provided useful suggestions and helped kick-start the project with the provision of invaluable data; Clive Hirschhorn generously made his library available, and my long-standing colleague Ronald Bergan, in addition to being a major contributor of profiles, lent unwavering moral support, as did Kathy Rooney and Tracey Smith at Bloomsbury, and my agent Tony Peake. Last but far from least, Myriam Fisher and Lindsay Powell came to the rescue with their word processors when copy became unreadable.

All of the writing team were enthusiastic and supportive as well as hard-working, but special thanks are due to Trevor Willsmer who performed a monumental rescue operation, taking on nearly 100 pieces at short notice, and to Max Loppert who sacrificed some of his precious sabbatical to contribute eighteen masterly essays. Several people were immensely helpful in making it possible to view key films ahead of release and my gratitude is recorded to Katy Sumner at Frontline, Ros Kidd at PSA, Lucy Vinson at Columbia Pictures, Anka Zakula at Warner Bros., Graham Smith and his staff at DDA, Brian Burton at Rank, Patrick Humphries at Vox Magazine, Ed Lewis of the Riverside Studios cinema, Clive Robotham at MGM Fulham, Chris Hands, and my former colleagues Phil Thomas and Jo Berry at Empire Magazine.

Robyn Karney
London 1993

CONTRIBUTORS

RONALD BERGAN: born in South Africa and educated there, in England and the USA. Taught literature, theatre and film for ten years in Paris at the British Institute and the Sorbonne. Co-author of the *Bloomsbury Foreign Film Guide*, a biography of Dustin Hoffman and the authorised biography of Jean Renoir. Other books include *Glamorous Musicals, The United Artists Story, The Great Theatres of London* and *Beyond The Fringe . . . and Beyond*, a four-part biography of Jonathan Miller, Peter Cook, Dudley Moore and Alan Bennett, *The Life And Times Of Laurel And Hardy*, and *The Life And Times Of The Marx Brothers.*

JOANNA BERRY: educated at Bishop's Hatfield Girls' School. Trained as a writer/researcher at *Time Out* Publications, working extensively on their guides, notably the *Time Out Film Guide.* Subsequently a freelance film reviewer, editorial consultant, and staff writer/commissioning editor for *Empire* magazine.

TOM CHARITY: raised in Yorkshire and took his degree in English Literature and Film at Christ Church College, Canterbury. Combined a job at Rank Video Services with a freelance career as a film critic and feature writer and is a regular contributor to several publications including *Sight and Sound, Select* and *Time Out.*

ROBIN CROSS: Oxford law graduate and former publishing editor, is a full-time writer specialising in military history and the cinema. Has written for countless anthologies and is a regular contributor and editorial consultant on special projects for the *Telegraph* newspapers. His numerous books include *The Big Book of B-Movies,* or *How Low Was My Budget; Chronicle of Hollywood, Science Fiction Films, 2000 Movies of the 1950s, 2000 Movies of the 1960s, The Life And Times Of Charlie Chaplin* (with Robyn Karney), and *JFK: A Hidden Life*, a book about Kennedy for Bloomsbury.

ANGELA ERRIGO: born in Tacoma, Washington, convent-schooled in Marin County, California and took her degree in film and journalism at San Francisco State University. Resident in London since the 70s when, as a rock journalist, she contributed regularly to several publications including *New Musical Express* and *The Observer* newspaper. Spent much of the 80s as a leading film publicist and is now a reviewer, interviewer and staff writer for *Empire* magazine, *Premiere* and *Elle*, as well as a popular film broadcaster for GLR and the BBC's Kaleidoscope.

ROBYN KARNEY: born in South Africa, read Literature and Drama at the University of Cape Town. A former film, theatre and literary critic on the *Cape*

Times, and a script and story editor for TV and film in London, she subsequently edited some 20 film books, including the Octopus studio history series, *Glamorous Musicals*, Joel Finler's *The Hollywood Story*, and *Academy Award Winners*. Co-author of the *Bloomsbury Foreign Film Guide* and *The Life And Times Of Charlie Chaplin*, author of *Stars of the Forties*, and contributing editor of Bloomsbury's *Who's Who in Hollywood*, she is a regular contributor to magazines and journals.

KATHRYN KIRBY: born in Yorkshire but grew up in Spain, Mexico and the USA. Attended university in Manchester and London. After a brief stint as a reporter on the *Miami Herald*, returned to England and worked as a film journalist, becoming the editor of *Films and Filming*. Subsequently joined the *Sunday Telegraph*'s *7 Days* magazine, and now divides her time between freelance editing and film writing.

KAREN KRIZANOVICH: Born in Big Rock, Illinois, the daughter of a US Marshal, she graduated in philosophy which she taught before making her home in London in 1987. Since then she has made a career of freelance film and rock journalism. Has appeared on several television programmes, and writes for numerous publications including *Q, Blitz, Elle, Sky, Time Out, City Limits, The Observer* and *NME*.

MARK LeFANU: read English at Cambridge. He teaches at the National Film and Television School and is Deputy Editor of *Screen Finance*. He contributed to *The Movie Stars Story*, has written numerous articles on the cinema for the national press, was a presenter of BBC 2's Film Club and is the author of a study of Andrei Tarkovsky published in 1987.

MAX LOPPERT: a lifelong cinema fanatic, was born in Johannesburg and read for his BA in English at the University of the Witwatersrand. A post-graduate in music of York University, he is Chief Music critic of the *Financial Times* and associate editor of *Opera*.

TREVOR WILLSMER: A regular contributor to the Virgin *Film Yearbook*, he has been an avid cinemagoer since childhood. After a variety of jobs in local cinemas and at Twickenham Film Studios while in his teens, he worked his way up to historical researcher and rewrite man, and formed his own company, Lone Wolf Productions, for which he has written, produced and directed a series of shorts. He is also a distributor of feature movies on 8mm.

Abraham, F. Murray
(Fahrid Murray Abraham)
Actor
Born 24 October 1939
Pittsburgh, Pennyslvania

'It would be a lie if I told you I didn't know what to say, because I've been working on this speech for 25 years,' announced F. Murray Abraham as he collected his Best Actor Oscar for his portrayal of Antonio Salieri in *Amadeus* (1983). 'I never thought I had a shot at the Oscar. I am not a leading man. Let me tell you who is a leading man – Cary Grant.'

The actor is certainly no Grant in the looks department, being gaunt, pock-marked and hook-nosed, nor is he exactly a leading man. But for his fortuitous casting in Milos Forman's eight-Oscar winner, he might have remained relatively unknown to the world at large. He was selected to play Salieri to Tom Hulce's Mozart after a year of auditions of dozens of candidates. 'I didn't want someone familiar like Jack Nicholson or Donald Sutherland that audiences would recognize. So all of us agreed to cast F. Murray Abraham – who *is* Salieri,' explained Forman.

Abraham was certainly impressive as the religious court composer who cannot accept that God should have used the blaspheming, foul-mouthed Mozart as a vessel in which to pour musical genius, while giving him comparatively mediocre gifts. Abraham's achievement was in revealing an intelligence behind the malevolence, and in making the crazed figure into a tragic and sympathetic one. He is especially moving when first gazing at Mozart's sketches for the Requiem. 'Here was the very voice of God,' he proclaims with a mixture of adoration and envy.

Although born in Pennsylvania of Syrian and Italian parents, Abraham was raised in El Paso, Texas, and educated at the University of Texas before making his way to New York. His off-Broadway debut was in the long-running musical *The Fantasticks* in 1967, and his Broadway debut in Robert Shaw's play *The Man In The Glass Booth*, a year later. Other Broadway roles included the 'chubby chaser' (a homosexual who likes fat men) in *The Ritz*, set in a New York gay bath-house, a part he humorously repeated in the Richard Lester film version in 1976. His reputation on stage, mainly in the classics, led film critic Pauline Kael, in a review of *The Big Fix* (1978), to write: 'On the stage, Abraham probably gives audiences as much joy as any American actor of his generation, and some suggestion of his gift comes through in this small part. His satirical version of a student leader who has grown older and changed his ideas but is still all hopped up feels completely right, because his body is in character.'

Following his heady Oscar win, Abraham returned to the stage and worked as Professor of Theatre at Brooklyn College, appearing sporadically in movies. He was seen to effect as the fearsome bald-pated and bearded inquisitor, Bernardo Gui, in *The Name Of The Rose* (1985) and, in marked contrast, in Peter Yates' *An Innocent Man* (1989), playing a veteran convict who convinces his cell mate Tom Selleck to kill the black prisoner victimising him. Abraham was also convincingly egotistical as the mayor in Brian De Palma's controversial and poorly received *Bonfire Of The Vanities* (1990), though he was unbilled after a contractual row.

1971 They Might Be Giants **1973** Serpico **1974** The Prisoner Of Second Avenue **1975** The Sunshine Boys **1976** All The President's Men; The Ritz **1978** The Big Fix; Madman **1983** Scarface; Amadeus **1985** The Name Of The Rose **1988** Russicum/Russicum I Giorni Del Diavolo (Italy) **1989** An Innocent Man; Slipstream; La Nuit De Serail/The Favorite (Switzerland); Personal Choice **1990** Stockade; The Bonfire of the Vanities **1991** Mobsters; By The Sword

Abrahams, Jim
Director, screenwriter
Born 10 May 1944
Milwaukee, Wisconsin

On the principle that three heads are better than one, Jim Abrahams and the brothers Jerry and David Zucker became the cinema's first triple-directing team. But, according to Danny DeVito, who they directed in *Ruthless People* (1986), 'I really don't give a damn – there are normally nine directors on any set.'

All three grew up in Milwaukee, where their fathers were partners in a real estate business and planned a similar fate for their sons. But the boys had discovered the Marx Brothers and TV series like *Mission Impossible*. 'We'd laugh at that as it was just so stupid and was great to send up,' explained Abrahams. In 1972, after attending Wisconsin University, they moved to LA, where their first stage show, *Vegetables*, ran for two years. They called their second *My Nose*, hoping that some critic would say '*My Nose* will run a long time.' This led to their opening the Kentucky Fried Theater, later devising and writing the *Kentucky Fried Movie* (1977), which the trio enlisted John Landis to direct after seeing him on the Johnny Carson Show discussing his movie, *Schlock*. 'During production,' Jerry Zucker has said, 'We saw that directing was no great mystery. That encouraged us to direct ourselves.'

So they wrote, directed and produced *Airplane*! (1980) for Paramount, at a cost of $3.5 million, and made almost $80 million. It was an outrageous, undisciplined and often hilarious spoof on the *Airport* cycle of movies. Deciding against making *Airplane II: The Sequel* (1982), which was merely a rehash directed by Ken Finkleman, the triumvirate tackled the spy genre with *Top Secret*! (1984). Despite some good visual gags, (eg the stations and scenery move while a train stands still), most of the juvenile humour belied the age of the three directors.

They retained their box-office credibility with the comparatively 'straight' *Ruthless People* (1986), a huge commercial success and the first that they didn't write themselves. Significantly perhaps, for Dale Launer's screenplay gave them their best constructed movie. In fact, the various ingenious twists in the plot – based on the old comic idea of gentle kidnappers (Judge Reinhold, Helen Slater) and uncontrollable victim (Bette Midler) – were funnier than some of the unsubtle antics performed in it, although it was directed and acted with pace and verve.

In 1988 Abrahams went solo as director of *Big Business*, a hectic and strained comedy of errors featuring Bette Midler and Lily Tomlin as two sets of identical twins, and David Zucker was the only director of *The Naked Gun*, written by the threesome and based on their short-lived TV series *Police Squad*, with Leslie Nielsen repeating his role as the incompetent cop Frank Drebin. The jokes came thick and fast, some good, some bad, and mostly vulgar enough to please their fans – like the lovers practising safe sex by covering their whole bodies in giant contraceptives. But, like most of their movies, it began to run out of steam towards the end, deteriorating into nothing more than an old Abbott and Costello-style comedy.

Jerry Zucker's first solo 'straight' film, *Ghost* (1990), was a comedy-thriller-fantasy that had Patrick Swayze bumped off in the first reel and attempting, in spectral form, to solve his own murder. It is an old *Topper* film with modern special effects, and the sort of sentimentality that the brothers and friend used to satirise, and it emerged as 1990's biggest unexpected blockbuster, grossing a large fortune over a short period. As David Zucker said, 'Put your brains on the seat and have a good time.' Thus did he define the trio's comic mission.

1980 Airplane **1984** Top Secret! **1986** Ruthless People **1988** Big Business (Jim Abrahams only) **1988** The Naked Gun (David Zucker only) **1990** Ghost (Jerry Zucker only); Welcome Home, Roxy Carmichael (Abrahams only) **1991** The Naked Gun II½ (David Zucker only); Hots Shots (Abrahams only) **1992/93** Hots Shots II (Abrahams only)

Adams, Brooke

Actress
Born 8 February 1949
New York City

With her cute turned-up nose, turned-down mouth, wide eyes and sensual figure, it's surprising that Brooke Adams has appeared in no more than a dozen films since 1977. Neither has she been particularly well used. The daughter of actor parents, Adams made her professional stage debut at the age of six on Broadway in *Finian's Rainbow*, before going on to receive an education at New York's famed High School of Performing Arts, and at the Institute of American Ballet, as well as studying acting with Lee Strasberg. A period of work in summer stock and on television led inevitably to the movies.

It was only her second picture, Terrence Malick's *Days Of Heaven* (1978), set in the Texan Panhandle of 1916, that made her name. She was convincingly 'period' and perverse as the streetwise migrant worker who poses as the sister of her jealous boy-friend (Richard Gere) and attracts a young farmer (Sam Shepard). It was to the actress' credit that she didn't disappear in the lush imagery that overwhelms every frame of the film.

Philip Kaufman's dispiriting remake of *Invasion Of The Body Snatchers* (1978) was somewhat enlivened by Adams' presence as the married health worker who has the hots for her boss, Donald Sutherland, before she turns into a zombie. However, even her sparkle couldn't do much for a suspenseless heist movie, *A Man, A Woman And A Bank* (1979), in which she accompanied Sutherland again; nor could her sexiness lessen the sentimentality of *Tell Me A Riddle* (1980), directed by actress Lee Grant. However, fans relished the scene when, on breaking up with her boyfriend, she slips into purple tights and red shorts, and goes roller skating.

Almost You (1984) found her wonderfully crabby and wielding a mean crutch in the role of the wife who breaks her hip, only to discover her husband (Griffin Dunne) falling for her nurse (Karen Young). Top billed for the first time, it seemed as though Adams would be going on to bigger things. Instead, although convincing in David Cronenberg's *The Dead Zone* (1983), she had nothing to do other than express understandable distress at ex-boyfriend Christopher Walken's uncanny ability to predict future disasters. A pity that, in life, nobody advised the actress against appearing in the disastrous *Man On Fire* (1987), an appalling thriller with a plainly unhappy international cast among whom Adams had little to do but drift around gloomily in European settings. What a disappointment for a star whose looks provoked the line, 'You were the most exotic, breath-stopping creature I'd ever known,' spoken to her by Sean Connery in Richard Lester's *Cuba* (1979).

However, she had a cracking role as the waitress-mother of a recalcitrant Ione Skye in 1992's independent, low-budget *Gas, Food And Lodging* which demonstrated that she had matured into an attractive middle-aged and valuable presence.

1977 Shock Waves **1978** Days Of Heaven; Invasion Of The Body Snatchers **1979** Cuba; A Man, A Woman And A Bank **1980** Tell Me A Riddle **1983** The Dead Zone; Utilities **1984** Almost You; Key Exchange **1985** The Stuff (cameo) **1987** Man On Fire **1991** The Unborn **1992** Gas, Food And Lodging

Aiello, Danny

Actor
Born 20 June 1933
New York City

Diamond-in-the-rough character actor Danny Aiello had a first career which took him from Greyhound Bus driver to transport labour union official until an ugly dispute led to his dismissal. The tough New Yorker was surviving by working as a night-club bouncer and, occasionally, a self-confessed thief, when a chance stint as compère at an improvisational night spot revealed his ability as a performer. A regional theatre production of Jason Miller's Pulitzer Prize-winning *That Championship Season* won Aiello a Most Outstanding Newcomer award as he was entering middle age, and he made his screen debut shortly after in *Bang The Drum Slowly* (1973).

For more than 15 years he played a succession of hard guys, cops, ordinary Joes, slobs and brutes in films ranging from gangster classics (*The Godfather Part II*, 1974, *Once Upon A Time In America*, 1984) to horror (*Amityville II*, 1982, and *The Stuff*, 1985) to Woody Allen films (*The Purple Rose Of Cairo*, 1985, and *Radio Days*, 1987) before making a real impression on audiences as Cher's irresolute suitor in the critical and popular 1987 hit *Moonstruck*. In 1989, his up-front portrayal of the beleaguered racist pizza parlour proprietor in Spike Lee's controversial *Do The Right Thing* was rewarded with an Oscar nomination as Best Supporting Actor despite the Academy's snubbing of the film itself.

Aiello's strength is his undeniably intimidating presence, an innate authority that doubtless propelled his rise as a trade union activist and lends credence to his roles as a gritty guy who is best not messed with, while he is also persuasive as a toughie with a soft centre. Nearing 60, Aiello was at last rewarded with a leading role, and delivered a compelling central performance as Dallas club owner Jack Ruby in the 1992 J.F.K. assassination conspiracy thriller, *Ruby*.

Parallel to his many screen appearances, the actor has distinguished himself at regular intervals on the Broadway stage since 1976 (when he won a Theatre World Award for his debut, *Lampost Reunion*), and he has featured in a number of movies made for TV, most notably *Family Of Strangers*, for which he won an Emmy in 1981.

1973 Bang The Drum Slowly **1974** The Godfather Part II **1976** The Front **1977** Hooch **1978** Bloodbrothers; Fingers **1980** Defiance; Hide In Plain Sight **1981** Fort Apache, The Bronx; Chu Chu And The Philly Flash **1982** Amityville II: The Possession **1984** Once Upon A Time In America; Old Enough **1985** The Purple Rose Of Cairo; Key

Exchange; The Stuff; The Protector **1986** Death Mask aka Unknown **1987** Man Of Fire; Radio Days; The Squeeze; Moonstruck; The Pick-Up Artist **1988** Little Odessa; Crack In The Mirror; Russicum, Giorni Del Diavolo/ Russicum (Italy) **1989** The January Man; Do The Right Thing; Harlem Nights **1990** Jacob's Ladder **1991** The Closer; Once Around **1992** Ruby; Mistress; The Pickle **1992/93** The Cemetary Club; Three Of Hearts

Alda, Alan
(Alphonso D'Abruzzo)
Actor, director, writer
Born 28 January 1936
New York City

Someone once characterised Alan Alda as 'a subject for canonisation.' Happily married to the same wife, Arlene, for almost 30 years, and with three attractive daughters, he campaigns regularly for feminist and liberal causes. At six foot two, eyes of blue, and greying dark hair, Alda exudes boyish charm, intelligence and wit.

Although he has been in show business – on stage, in films, on TV – for over three decades, he is most widely known for, and associated with, one particular role – that of the anarchic and wise-cracking 'Hawkeye' Pierce in the long-running TV series of *M★A★S★H* (started in 1972). 'It's the only comedy show on TV that shows the results of war. It's humour with feeling,' Alda explained. In episode after episode, as the flip medic sewing up casualties during the Korean War, and trying to keep his sanity by doing crazy things, he delivered one-liners to perfection. He also wrote and directed many episodes, always trying to extend the limitations of the genre.

As a feature film director, Alda has proved rather more conventional. *The Four Seasons* (1981) was a well-observed, wry but unadventurous tale of three complacent, middle-aged married couples (he and Carol Burnett were one of them), though it made $26.8 million for Universal; *Sweet Liberty* (1985), in which he played an academic romancing Michelle Pfeiffer, ventured some familiar and tame satirical jabs at the movie industry; *A New Life* (1988) was a very predictable story of a marriage break-up between a grey-bearded Alda and Ann-Margret, with some good jokes and performances rising above the mire; and *Betsy's Wedding* (1990) was a mildly amusing 'Father Of The Bride' domestic comedy (with Alda, of course, the father) that contained an extraneous and unconvincing gangster subplot. All four films were let down by the soft-centred approach to subjects that needed more acerbity. As someone says of the constantly-smiling star in the latter film, 'You're a sweetie. A pussy cat.'

The satiric intentions of *The Seduction Of Joe Tynan* (1979), directed by Jerry Schatzberg, for which Alda wrote the screenplay and was cast as an ambitious liberal senator led into abandoning his principles, were undermined by the blandness of his playing. Seldom, whether in his own films or others, has he recaptured the biting humour he displayed in *M★A★S★H*. Only Woody Allen has managed to ignite a spark so lacking elsewhere. As Woody's brother-in-law in *Crimes And Misdemeanors* (1990), he was able to play a smarmy, egocentric TV personality and yet suggest enough charm to make audiences understand the reasons for his media fame and his success in wooing a reluctant Mia Farrow.

Until the Allen film, Alda had mainly brought a sympathetic but hangdog quality to many of his roles, such as his weak and 'mellow' Hollywood screenwriter in *California Suite* (1978), squabbling with his forceful New Yorker ex-wife, Jane Fonda, over their daughter. He managed to age convincingly from 27 to 47 years old in *Same Time, Next Year* (1978) while carrying out an adulterous affair, only meeting his lover (Ellen Burstyn) for a passionate weekend once every year. This film version of a two-handed Broadway play was distinctly cosy though not unlikeable, but Alda again seemed too restrained. Hardly what one would expect from someone whose Italian-born father's name was Alphonso Giuseppe Giovanni Roberto D'Abruzzo, later known as the actor Robert Alda.

Alan's first appearance was in his teens, at the Hollywood Canteen with his father, giving imitations of Abbott and Costello. He graduated from Fordham University, where he began studying medicine (perhaps of some use to 'Hawkeye' in later years), then took chemical analysis before switching to English literature. After studying acting at the Cleveland Playhouse, he spent a number of years appearing both off and on Broadway – he was nominated for a Tony as the best musical actor in *The Apple Tree* (1966) – and in TV series such as *Route 66*, *Bilko* and the American version of *That Was The Week That Was*.

Although he made a certain impression in

his screen debut as the liberal-minded son of a tyrannical Georgia plantation owner in *Gone Are The Days* (1963), he had to wait five years for his next screen role in *Paper Lion*, based on journalist George Plimpton's experiences with the Detroit Lions football team. In it, Alda displayed the right combination of physical ineptitude and witty objectivity necessary to the role.

Despite critics' reservations regarding his film career, Alan Alda has managed to retain his integrity. As he has said, 'There's plenty of money to be had and you can get the same amount by doing junk every week. By just showing up . . . But you also lose your soul. What's the pleasure in losing your self-esteem, your dignity?'

As actor only unless stated otherwise: **1963** Gone Are The Days aka The Man From C.O.T.T.O.N **1968** Paper Lion; The Extraordinary Seaman **1970** The Moonshine War; Jenny **1971** The Mephisto Waltz **1972** To Kill A Clown **1978** Same Time, Next Year; California Suite **1979** The Seduction Of Joe Tynan (also writer) **1981** The Four Seasons (also w/d) **1985** Sweet Liberty (also w/d) **1988** A New Life (also w/d) **1990** Crimes And Misdemeanors; Betsy's Wedding (also w/d) **1992** Whispers In The Dark **1993** Manhattan Murder Mystery

Alexander, Jane
(Jane Quigley)

Actress
Born 28 October 1939
Boston, Massachusetts

Educated at Sarah Lawrence and Edinburgh University before entering the acting profession, Jane Alexander made her first major impact in 1968, on Broadway, as the white girlfriend of a black boxing champ (James Earl Jones) in *The Great White Hope*. She reprised the role (again with Jones) on screen in 1970, giving a performance of memorable passion and pain. Since then, she has become a major star of the American theatre and TV (where her many impressive roles included a brilliant impersonation of Eleanor Roosevelt in *Eleanor and Franklin, Calamity Jane*, and Hedda Hopper opposite Elizabeth Taylor's Louella Parsons, in *Malice in Wonderland*).

Tall, aristocratic and contained, Miss Alexander is primarily a dramatic actress. If she remains more immediately familiar to Broadway theatregoers and TV audiences than to movie fans, this is more indicative of Hollywood's lack of imagination than of her striking presence and substantial gifts. Apart from her several Obie, Emmy and Tony nominations and awards, she is a four-time Oscar nominee, named in both Best Supporting (*All The President's Men, Kramer vs. Kramer*) and Best Actress (*The Great White Hope; Testament*) categories; those who saw her extraordinary performance as a mother watching the community and her children die in Lynne Littman's superb protest against nuclear war, *Testament* (1983), will not easily forget the film, or its star.

Married to the distinguished theatre director Edwin Sherin, she lives in New York state and involves herself in production as well as performance. Actor Jace Alexander is her son.

1970 The Great White Hope **1971** A Gunfight **1972** The New Centurions **1976** All The President's Men **1978** The Betsy **1979** Kramer vs. Kramer **1980** Brubaker **1982** Night Crossing **1983** Testament **1984** City Heat **1987** Sweet Country; Square Dance **1989** Glory

Allen, Karen

Actress
Born 5 October 1951
Carrollton, Illinois

In what must be characterised as a chequered career, Karen Allen is likely to be forever remembered as Indiana Jones' feisty sidekick/love interest, Marion, in Steven Spielberg's colossal hit *Raiders Of The Lost Ark* (1981), despite some solid work in the decade which followed that success. The daughter of an FBI agent, Allen did her drama training in Washington, D.C. and New York after attending university, and spent several years with an experimental theatre company while gaining experience in front of the camera in student films.

Along with a gang of newcomers that included Tom Hulce, Kevin Bacon and Stephen Furst, she too made her film debut in the wacky *National Lampoon's Animal House* (1977) and two years later appeared fleetingly in Woody Allen's *Manhattan* (1979). It was not until her seventh film, *Raiders*, that Allen made an impact, when she delighted as the spunky, freckle-faced leading lady with a big, lopsided grin, who packed a mean punch and could outdrink the men.

Subsequent roles, however, were less fortunate. She made an unlikely other woman, for whom Albert Finney was supposed to have left Diane Keaton in Alan Parker's affecting *Shoot The Moon* (1982), and it was not until *Starman* (1984) that she enjoyed another lead role in a well-received film – as the young widow whose dead husband seems brought back to life to host the alien being of enchanting extra-terrestrial Jeff Bridges.

After a three-year hiatus, Allen returned to the screen in an all too aptly named thriller, *Backfire* (1987), which flopped, but then found herself in a much more distinguished project – Paul Newman's screen version of the Tennessee Williams classic *The Glass Menagerie* the same year, turning in a touching performance as shy, lame Laura opposite Joanne Woodward. An able craftswoman who undertook considerable stage work in the 80s (her Broadway debut in 1982 as Helen Keller in *Monday After The Miracle* earned her a Theatre World Award), Karen Allen has been seen to best advantage as a gutsy goody or as vulnerable, wistful creatures, but lacks the power to carry less obviously appealing characters.

1977 National Lampoon's Animal House; The Whidjit Maker **1979** Manhattan; The Wanderers **1980** A Small Circle Of Friends; Cruising **1981** Raiders Of The Lost Ark **1982** Split Image; Shoot The Moon **1983** Strange Invaders **1984** Until September; Starman **1987** Backfire; The Glass Menagerie; Terminus aka End Of The Line **1988** Scrooged **1989** Animal Behavior **1991** Sweet Talker (Australia) **1992** Home Fires Burning **1993** King Of The Hill

Allen, Nancy

Actress
Born 24 June 1950
Yonkers, New York

The daughter of a policeman, Nancy Allen took dancing classes from the time she was four years old and continued to do so at New York's High School of Performing Arts. However, she became not a hoofer but a model, from the age of 15, and appeared in over 100 TV commercials. After a bit part in *The Last Detail* (1973) with Jack Nicholson attracted the attention of an agent, she moved to LA to make a movie career. Her break came when Brian De Palma cast her in *Carrie* (1976). As the bitchy high school girl who spearheaded the torment of Sissy Spacek (enlisting the aid of John Travolta) and met a violent end, she made an impression. Shortly afterwards she and De Palma married, and she continued to be victimised in her husband's films, notably in the controversial *Dressed To Kill* (1980) and the following year's *Blow Out*, co-starring with John Travolta, who was unable to save her from a particularly grisly fate at the hands of prostitute-killer John Lithgow.

Allen is pretty and wholesome but far from boring. She has an attractive energy, freshness and positive personality which should have served her career better than it has. Her mother, apparently, used to ask, 'When is Brian going to write a nice romantic part for you?' He didn't, and, perhaps to her ultimate benefit, she missed being the Meg Ryan of the 1970s. The De Palmas divorced during 1984, Nancy's most professionally prolific year, if not necessarily her most distinguished. She remarried and lives in Los Angeles where, from 1987, her career entered another phase, beginning with her policewoman – older, plumper, shorn of her beautiful hair and exuding sympathy – opposite Peter Weller in the interesting and well-regarded *Robocop*, and progressing to the lead in *Limit Up* (1989), a satire on the business world.

1973 The Last Detail **1976** Carrie **1978** I Wanna Hold Your Hand **1979** Home Movies; 1941 **1980** Dressed To Kill **1981** Blow Out **1983** Strange Invaders **1984** The Buddy System; Forced Entry aka The Last Victim; Not For Publication; The Philadelphia Experiment; Terror In The Aisles (presenter) **1987** Sweet Revenge; Robocop **1988** Poltergeist III **1989** Limit Up **1990** Robocop 2 **1992/93** Robocop 3

Allen, Woody
(Allen Stewart Konigsberg)

Actor, director, writer
Born 1 December 1935
Brooklyn, New York

There are many competent, technically sophisticated American film directors, there are a few genuinely original ones, there are a handful of creative visionaries, and there is Woody Allen. Of all the creative artists working in the post-studio system era, he has the most consistently displayed an originality of thought and a steady development and synthesis of themes that marks him as a true *auteur*. Across a quarter of a century he has honed his work, marking his territory with signposts that have grown familiar and indispensible.

To insist that Allen is the American cinema's towering figure of the post-war period may be to court ridicule: one can well imagine the wry, killingly funny one-liner put-down that might emerge from the writer himself as a response to the very epithet 'towering'. But the longer the list grows of films which he has written, directed or acted in (often all three at once), the more astoundingly rich that body of work appears to be. Though Allen, who first came into the spotlight as a funnyman, has perfected the felicities of his spiked, deadpan wit, it is perhaps time to assert for his genius its deep seriousness of purpose, not a whit the less so for being so inimitably imbued with the spirit of comedy. That he returns to particular subjects – New York past or present, Jewish family situations, the emotional and psychological difficulties of the individual and the sometimes tortuous intricacies of personal relationships, and the fear of death – and that his mode of artistic expression moves ever nearer the chamber musical, should not be allowed to deny his work its imposing stature. The criticism, sometimes heard, that his films confine themselves to the same few middle-class themes and subjects to their ultimate detriment, is as blinkered as any would be which reproached Jane Austen for writing only about tea parties and balls.

Allen is unique in that his own most personal and private problems and passions have provided the weapons for his creative armoury. His love affair with New York City has informed all of his work since *Annie Hall* (1977) and he could well be the chronicler of a city whose face is rapidly changing. Many of his films are paeans to the place, and it is another of his singular achievements that he has managed to get assorted 'goys' from all over the world to appreciate his essentially Jewish-Manhattan, middle-class (and now middle-aged) experience. His long and well-publicised years on the psychiatrist's couch have contributed to the flavour of his comedy and the often painful darts aimed at sex, love and marriage; and his deep regard for the European cinema, notably the work of Bergman and Fellini, has led him to pay them explicit homage in more serious works such as *Interiors* (1978) and *A Midsummer Night's Sex Comedy* (1982), and fuelled his satirical bent against pseudo-intellectual pretension as in *Manhattan* (1979), luminously photographed in black and white and using the music of Gershwin to wonderful effect. Indeed, the use of music is another of his hallmarks: an accomplished jazz musician himself, his spirit (and that of his films) is replete with the best of American 20th-century popular music, precisely selected to evoke precise resonances, as well as with the classical masters such as Schubert.

As a performer, Allen uses humour to deflate, confront or make bearable serious situations, be it unrequited love (*Crimes And Misdemeanors*, 1990), threat of death (*Hannah And Her Sisters*, 1985), or professional failure (*Broadway Danny Rose*, 1984). Short, balding, freckled and bespectacled, he is hardly the romantic or sexy hero, so that when he succeeds – through vulnerability and charm – in winning an attractive woman, it is the happy negation of some of the most basic of Hollywood's dream-peddling clichés. Gag-production was Woody's first professional activity, and it could fairly be said to be the technique from which his multiple gifts have gained their particular stylistic thrust. As in all the most important talents, there is a fertile paradox at the heart of Allen's creativity. In his case it has to do with the way he has developed far beyond his artistic beginnings while remaining demonstrably true to them. The core of his expression has been the one-line gag, New York-Jewish in tone and delivery. His first few efforts may be seen, not discourteously, as marvellously entertaining loose bundles of gags of all kinds, tied up by a single dominating strand of parody (as in the frenetic *Bananas*, 1971) or satire (eg *Sleeper*, 1973, cocking a snook at futuristic theorising).

While still a Brooklyn high school pupil, Woody found a way into the New York newspapers as a supplier of comic snippets for leading gossip columnists such as Walter Winchell and Earl Wilson, and was soon a hired gag-writer on a retainer of $25 a week. Having enrolled at NYU (and later CCNY), he was eventually suspended, with inattention to work given as one of the reasons for his dismissal; in his early 20s a TV writing course led him to contribute material for several notable funnymen, including Sid Caesar and Art Carney, and to collaborate with already established writers like Mel Brooks. With encouragement from agents Charles Joffe and Jack Rollins, who subsequently became his film producers, he himself finally ventured onto the stage of the Greenwich Village Duplex in 1961, as a stand-up comic. By the mid-60s, he had established a local reputation and a growing following and, in 1965, his first script, *What's New Pussycat?*, was filmed by Clive Donner. Though the leads went to Peters O'Toole and Sellers, there was a part for Allen that swiftly made his spectacles, freckles and deadpan stare familiar to an international public. (In fact, he was dissatisfied with the project and attempted to withdraw from it in midstream.)

The following year he experimented with re-editing a Japanese film and fitting it out with an entirely new script; the quirkily comic result, *What's Up Tiger Lily*, may be seen as groundwork for more radical experiments in the 1980s: *Zelig* (1983), in which new and old material is spliced together with understated comic brilliance to tell the tale of 'chameleon' Leonard Zelig, able to hobnob with and assume the physical persona of a mad assortment of historical characters including Hitler and the Pope; and the Pirandello-like *The Purple Rose Of Cairo* (1985), in which 'real' characters and ones that step off the screen-within-the screen crisscross each others' reality to make up a potent fantasy on the power of movies to enter the lives and minds of their spectators. (Filmic legerdemain has been every bit as important to Allen as verbal wit, and a constant in his work.)

Soon he was ready to make *Take The Money And Run* (1969), his first outing as director; and from then on, apart from Herbert Ross' screen version of Woody's Broadway play, *Play It Again, Sam* (1972), a 007 role in the Bond spoof *Casino Royale* (1967), a lead in Martin Ritt's *The Front* (1976), and his outing with Bette Midler in Paul Mazursky's 1990 *Scenes From A Mall*, he has invariably directed his own material, much of it commercially successful, some of it only critically so. *Annie Hall* and *Manhattan* scored on both counts, the former winning the Oscars for Best Film, Director and Actress; but others, like *Stardust Memories* (1980) and the string of serious films that began in 1978 with *Interiors*, have divided popular and critical opinion.

Allen has remained a marvellous comic actor. There is such a thing as the 'Woody Allen' character, recognisable as such from *Take The Money And Run* right through to the 'Oedipus Wrecks' episode of *New York Stories* (1989). The Woody figures – Virgil Starkwell in *Take The Money*, angst-ridden New Yorker Alvy Singer in *Annie Hall*, intellectual womaniser Ike Davis in *Manhattan*, beleaguered movie director Sandy Bates in *Stardust Memories* (1980), Leonard Zelig, smalltime vaudeville agent *Broadway Danny Rose*, personally and professionally harassed TV director Mickey in *Hannah And Her Sisters*, mother-fixated Sheldon Mills ('Oedipus Wrecks') and (perhaps the most fully developed extension of all these) Clifford Stern in *Crimes And Misdemeanors* – are each tested by similar dilemmas of psychological and sexual anguish, frequently with a regulation head-shrinker in attendance, but with thematic variants to which those dilemmas are subjected, supplying the films with an eternally self-renewing energy.

So, for instance, the portrayal of Sandy Bates, much harried by the side-effects – fans, hangers-on, publicity seekers – of his fame, allows the material to take on an unfamiliarly black tone and bitter edge, which is perhaps one reason why this film has been so widely under-rated. With Mickey in *Hannah*, desperately searching for the meaning of existence via hilarious flirtations with Catholicism and the followers of Hari Krishna, the philosophical dimensions of the character are given searching exploration; and in the shape of agent Danny Rose, with his string of deliciously dreadful night-club acts and unfailing knack of being two-timed, we meet perhaps the greatest of all Woody Allen losers.

From the first, Allen the writer-director had been ready to challenge and extend his own character by confronting himself with a range of enjoyable parts for women. This is a side of his work which has expanded extraordinarily far and wide, and it is, in this regard, of the greatest significance that the three actresses in his off-screen life should have served as his main muses. His second wife, Louise Lasser, appeared in two of his films, Diane Keaton in seven, and Mia Farrow – his longest-lasting partner (12 years) and the mother of his son Satchel – had made 13 by the beginning of 1992.

Even without knowing the ins and outs of the Allen biography, one can honestly sense that such films as *Annie Hall* (Keaton) and *The Purple Rose Of Cairo* (Farrow) function as particularly graceful and loving tributes to their leading ladies. Working magic on their screen personas and performances is, indeed, another of his gifts, which he has increasingly conferred on an ever-expanding circle of brilliantly chosen actresses over recent years: Charlotte Rampling (*Stardust Memories*), Julie Hagerty (*A Midsummer Night's Sex Comedy*) Gena Rowlands (*Another Woman*, 1988), Elaine Stritch (*September*, 1987), Anjelica Huston (*Crimes And Misdemeanors*) and, in several films, Dianne Wiest, who must owe the elevation of her screen career to Allen. One may perhaps speculate that it was Allen's deepening involvement with women, after the heady infatuations of youth, that encouraged him to branch out into those serious films which are dominated by the agonies of women (and in which, crucially, the Woody character plays no part): *Interiors, September, Another Woman*. Even in the ensemble pieces, which twine serious and comic episodes – *Hannah*, the delightful *Radio Days* (1986), *Crimes And Misdemeanors* – the cares, aspirations and disappointments of women form the bulk of the dramatic material.

The whole question of stylistic influence is one that has dogged discussion of Woody Allen's achievement. At first he was called self-indulgent for making revue-sketch films filled with jokes at the expense of favourite targets, alongside affectionate nostalgic tributes to movies past; then for making a parade of cultural references; thereafter for showing the influence of Bergman in the exquisitely sad and often elegiac family dramas, and Fellini (the $8^1/_2$-like display of grotesques and cascades of dazzling images in *Stardust Memories*); and subsequently for making a meal out of memories of youth (*Radio Days*). And at almost every stage he has been maligned for not being as funny as in a previous film or period. Then there are those who can only bear films in which he appears, and the others who can only tolerate those from which he is physically absent. In between these extremes is a large and growing body of devotees who appreciate that each stage of the work has been artistically necessary and highly rewarding; nothing has been lost, much of value learned and gained, and the adaptability of visual style to fit film topic is now matched by an incredible smoothness, depth and fluency in filmic handling.

It is surely no longer possible to divide Woody Allen's films into serious and funny: some are more of the one than of the other, but each new work proves wonderfully rich in the emotional ambiguities and contrasts of tone and mood that only a mature creative artist, one who has worked long and hard to fashion his own artistic language, can dare to essay. If one were to pick out a composite title, somewhat in the manner of Balzac's *La Comédie Humaine*, to group and sum up his *oeuvre*, either the early *Love And Death* (1975) or the much later *Crimes And Misdemeanors* could serve that function very well: for Woody Allen is the American cinema's supreme poet of the first, and its most acute observer of the second. It could only be hoped that his controversial, acrimonious and scandal-attracting split from Farrow, with one of whose adopted daughters he instituted an affair, would not impede the flow of his creativity or deny him the opportunities to exercise it. His last completed film at the time of the break in 1992, *Husbands And Wives*, would doubtless prove his last outing with his former partner.

(As actor, director and writer or co-writer unless stated otherwise): **1965** What's New, Pussycat? (actor, writer only) **1966** What's Up, Tiger Lily (co-writer, narrator only) **1967** Casino Royale (actor only) **1969** Take The Money And Run **1971** Bananas **1972** Play It Again, Sam (actor, writer only); Everything You Always Wanted To Know About Sex . . . But Were Afraid To Ask **1973** Sleeper **1975** Love And Death **1976** The Front (actor only) **1977** Annie Hall **1978** (w/d only) **1979** Manhattan **1980** Stardust Memories **1982** A Midsummer Night's Sex Comedy **1983** Zelig **1984** Broadway Danny Rose **1985** The Purple Rose Of Cairo (w/d only); Hannah And Her Sisters **1986** Radio Days (w/d and narrator only) **1987** September (w/d only) **1988** Another Woman (w/d only) **1989** New York Stories ('Oedipus Wrecks' episode); Crimes And Misdemeanors **1990** Alice; Scenes From A Mall (actor only) **1991** Shadows And Fog **1992** Husbands And Wives **1993** Manhattan Murder Mystery

Alley, Kirstie

Actress
Born 12 January 1955
Wichita, Kansas

Arguably one of the most superb comediennes since Lucille Ball, Kirstie Alley is one of the few actresses who seemed to make the successful transition from television to big-screen popularity. After studying drama in her native Kansas she was sidetracked into a career as an interior designer and enjoyed a protracted fling as a wild girl, biker chick and cocaine abuser before moving to California, cleaning up through a rehabilitation centre and discovering purpose and direction through Scientology, a controversial philosophy she still whole-heartedly espouses.

Making an adequate screen debut as Spock's Vulcan protégée, Savik, in *Star Trek II: The Wrath of Khan* Alley then seized the opportunity to display more histrionics as fanatical abolitionist Virgilia in the epic TV mini-series *North And South* and its sequel. Her real breakthrough came when she won the role of bar manageress Rebecca Howe in the top-rated, long-running TV comedy series *Cheers*. Despite the prediction of many that she (and the show) would flop after the departure of Shelly Long's Diane, Alley was an instant success as the epitome of the attractive but anxiety-ridden, ambitious and lovelorn 80s woman, constantly at odds with Ted Danson's Sam.

She has demonstrated competence and conviction in drama, lending a cool, athletic presence to *Shoot To Kill* (1988), in which she scaled the Northwest Rockies in the company of a psychopathic killer. But it is her exuberance and unselfconscious ability to clown, at amusing odds with her elegant, cover-girl looks, that have placed her on the A list for Hollywood comedies. In the autumn of 1989 she scored a unique double when the cute but unremarkable baby comedy *Look Who's Talking* was the No. 1 US box-office attraction and *Cheers* was the No. 1 TV programme. Teamed with John Larroquette for *Madhouse* (1990), the pair fired on all cylinders in an otherwise lame madcap comedy, and the sequel to *Look Who's Talking* performed reasonably. Top-billed in her 12th film, Carl Reiner's disappointing *Sibling Rivalry* (1991), this green-eyed actress continued to combine casual elegance with raunchiness and a touch of the hoyden.

Alley, who is married to TV actor Parker Stevenson, bought the 30-room mansion built for Al Jolson in the San Fernando Valley (a home shared with approximately 40 pets), confirming her reputation as a shrewd, no-nonsense businesswoman.

1982 Star Trek II: The Wrath Of Khan; One More Chance **1984** Blind Date; Champions; Runaway **1987** Summer School **1988** Shoot To Kill aka Deadly Pursuit **1989** Look Who's Talking; Loverboy **1990** Madhouse; Look Who's Talking Too; Sibling Rivalry

Alonso, Maria Conchita

Actress
Born 1957
Cuba

This stunning Cuban-born actress began her career not in the USA, but in Caracas, where she began appearing in films and commercials while still a child. Her family had emigrated from Cuba to Venezuela when she was five years old, and settled in the capital, where, at the age of 14, Maria won the title of Miss Teenager Of The World in a beauty contest. In 1975, this archetypal Latin beauty, a contemporary answer to the legendary Dolores Del Rio, became Miss Venezuela, combining a promising modelling career with acting, TV commercials, starring in four Venezuelan films and appearing in ten Spanish-speaking soap operas.

It was not until 1982, when she moved to the USA, that her acting career took off in the English-speaking world. Within a year she had her first American role, as a dancer in Abel Ferrara's *Fear City* (1984), and, although it was only a small part in a cast headlined by Tom Berenger and Melanie Griffith (neither of them yet stars), it was enough for her to be noticed and given a supporting role in the comedy-drama *Moscow On The Hudson* (1984), as the fiery girlfriend of Russian sax-playing defector Robin Williams. The film, though charming, was only a moderate success, but Maria showed she was a talent to reckon with, and it pushed her into co-starring status.

In *Touch And Go* (1986), the actress had an opportunity to show her versatility, switching from humour to drama in the course of the film. The story, of a young tearaway (Ajay Naidu) who brings an egotistical hockey player (Michael Keaton) and his independent-minded Latin mother (Alonso) together, made Maria the pivotal character in the plot, and also bestowed her with the honour of being the first woman to act a love scene with Michael Keaton on screen. Now experienced at playing alongside comic actors (Williams, Keaton), she went on to co-star with two more, Ted Danson and Howie Mandel, in the Blake Edwards slapstick *A Fine Mess* (1986). The film, alas, lived up to its title and proved the worst of Alonso's movie choices, but she could console herself with the fact that her next film, *The Running Man* (1987), would pit her alongside Arnold Schwarzenegger.

Based on a Richard Bachman (alias Stephen King) story, the film was an action-packed sci-fi adventure with Alonso one of the few cast members capable of giving a performance of some merit while running through a plethora of special effects in a lycra bodysuit. It may not have been Shakespeare, but *The Running Man*, like most of Schwarzenegger's films, was a box-office success. With a knack for getting herself cast opposite some of Hollywood's most desirable men, she went on to co-star with Nick Nolte in *Extreme Prejudice* (1987), and a year later played cop Sean Penn's lover in Dennis Hopper's gang-violence film *Colors* (1988). After enduring a few beatings in that film, she went on to play a threatened woman in the misguided horror flick *Vampire's Kiss* (1989), starring an over-the-top Nicolas Cage. The movie, about a man who believes he is a vampire in modern-day New York, was decidedly eccentric but the actress was singled out for praise as the only credible player present.

1984 Fear City; Moscow On The Hudson **1986** Touch And Go; A Fine Mess **1987** The Running Man; Extreme Prejudice **1988** Colors **1989** Vampire's Kiss **1990** Predator 2 **1991** McBain

Altman, Robert

Director, writer
Born 20 February 1925
Kansas City, Missouri

'Hollywood is afraid of me, I guess. I can't make the kind of films they want to make, and the kind of films I make, they just don't want to make,' said Robert Altman in the 80s. In the previous decade there were few hotter directors in Hollywood, although he was always something of a maverick. Unusual by American standards, he has refused to make formula pictures, trying to do something different with each film, and his individualism gained him the reputation for being a difficult man for producers to work with. (He was fired from *Ragtime* in 1981).

Altman comes from a German-Catholic family in Kansas where he went to a parochial school and attended military academy. After serving as a B-54 bomber pilot during World War II, he returned home to make industrial films. In 1956 he made *The Delinquents*, a 75-minute teenage genre picture shot in Kansas City. He stipulated it had to be edited in California. This was his 'escape clause' and, in August 1956, he left for Hollywood.

After directing three forgettable movies, Altman was offered *M⋆A⋆S⋆H* (1970) because, as he remarked, 'fourteen more acceptable directors turned it down.' It grossed $41 million and won the Cannes Grand Prix. Its iconoclasm struck a responsive chord in a disenchanted nation which saw its Korean War setting as a reference to Vietnam. Only two of his subsequent movies, *Nashville* (1975) and *Popeye* (1981), did well at the box office.

His formalism, experimental use of sound, imaginative concern with space on the CinemaScope screen, and his interest in mapping out areas where a group of people are brought together for a particular purpose, were noticeable from his earliest features. The simultaneous conversations and loudspeaker announcements in *M⋆A⋆S⋆H*, the eight-track sound system in *California Split* (1974) and the 16 tracks in *Nashville*, produce sounds heard, overheard, misheard and garbled. There is no music score in *Thieves Like Us* (1973) except the constant music from the radio. His innovative manipulation of 24 characters in *Nashville* and 40 in *A Wedding* (1978) required expert editing. However, the contents of many of these interestingly wrapped packages were often less admirable. The two boorish sexist heroes of *M⋆A⋆S⋆H*, riding roughshod over everybody, are accepted at face value; *Brewster McCloud* (1971) is a whimsical satire as dated as the flower-child philosophy it presents; *Images* (1972), made in Ireland with Susannah York, is a superficial, tricksily shot view of mental illness; much of *The Long Goodbye* (1972) reduces Raymond Chandler to a Hollywood party game; *Quintet* (1979) and *Health* (1980) are confused literary allegories. Yet *McCabe And Mrs Miller* (1971), though overburdened with contemporary allusions, is an effective, melancholy Western; and *Three Women* (1977) is a well-acted (Shelley Duvall, Sissy Spacek, Janice Rule), enigmatic and resonant piece based on a dream Altman had of three friends changing identities.

Out of step with the more bland Hollywood of the 80s, Altman moved to New York, formed the Sandcastle 5 company, and concentrated almost exclusively on brilliantly transforming modern American plays into films, using meticulous compositions and close-ups. The first and most successful was Ed Graczyk's *Come Back To The Five And Dime, Jimmy Dean, Jimmy Dean* (1982), which he had directed on Broadway. 'I was standing backstage one night watching the play and realised there were things on those actresses' faces which the audience couldn't see,' he said. In the movie, he cleverly shifted the two time zones – 1955 and 1975 – by means of computer-controlled lighting. In *Beyond Therapy* (1986), which deals with a bunch of New York neurotics, he was once again able to juggle adroitly a variety of interlocking characters, as in some of his earlier, bigger movies. On TV, he had a hit with *Tanner '88*, a sharp and funny satire on American politics, shot during the 1988 presidential campaign; and with the painterly and leisurely four-hour *Vincent And Theo* (1989), made for Central TV, but also released theatrically in a shortened version. Continuing to surprise, Altman also wrote the libretto for an opera based on Frank Norris' novel, *McTeague*, His great triumph however, was his scintillating critical and box-office comeback with *The Player* (1992). This masterfully crafted and wickedly funny film is a savage satire on the Hollywood film industry that took no prisoners, firing alike on studio executives, spoiled stars, hustling writers, shark-like agents and power players.

As director only unless stated otherwise: **1957** The Delinquents (w/d); The James Dean Story (co-director) **1968** Countdown **1969** That Cold Day In The Park **1970** M*A*S*H; Brewster McCloud **1971** McCabe And Mrs Miller (also co-writer) **1972** Images (w/d) **1973** The Long Goodbye **1974** Thieves Like Us (also co-writer); California Split **1975** Nashville **1976** Buffalo Bill And The Indians (also co-writer) **1977** Three Women (w/d) **1978** A Wedding (also co-writer) **1979** A Perfect Couple (also co-writer); Quintet (also co-writer); Health (w/d) **1982** Come Back To The Five And Dime Jimmy Dean, Jimmy Dean **1983** Streamers **1984** Secret Honor **1985** Fool For Love **1986** Beyond Therapy **1987** OC & Stiggs; Aria (Rameau's *La Boréades* episode) **1988** The Caine Mutiny Court-Martial **1989** Vincent And Theo **1992** The Player **1993** Short Cuts

Ameche, Don
(Dominic Felix Amici)

Actor
Born 31 May 1908
Kenosha, Wisconsin

If ever there were a reflowering of a career, it was Don Ameche's. Unlike many of his contemporaries at 20th Century-Fox – Alice Faye, Tyrone Power, Betty Grable, Jack Oakie and Sonja Henie – who faded or died many years previously, the debonair star of the 30s and early 40s was discovered by the kids of the 80s, who never knew that he had 'invented the telephone', a joke that went around for years after he had starred in *The Story Of Alexander Graham Bell* (1939). Ameche's breezy personality graced dozens of lightweight musicals, as well as a few sophisticated comedies, including *Midnight* (1939), opposite Claudette Colbert, and Ernst Lubitsch's *Heaven Can Wait* (1943), during Hollywood's heyday and still seen on TV 50 years later. After being at the top for almost 20 years, his film career faded in the 50s, although he appeared with success in a number of Broadway hits such as Cole Porter's *Silk Stockings* in 1955.

It was his role in John Landis' *Trading Places* (1983), an attempt to recapture the atmosphere of the screwball comedies of the 30s, that brought him back into the public eye. Grey and balding, in contrast with the head of distinctive jet-black hair of his halcyon days, but still retaining his slim and elegant figure, warm baritone voice and the pencil moustache that had been his trademark, he played one of a pair of Philadelphia blueblood brothers (the other was veteran Ralph Bellamy) who set the 'Prince and the Pauper' – type plot in motion.

He confirmed his return to Hollywood with a much larger role in *Cocoon* (1985), bringing authority and wit to the gerontophile rompings, for which he was rewarded with the Best Supporting Actor Oscar. It was appropriate to the newly-minted star that the tale was about the rejuvenation of a group of old people by alien forces. He repeated his role in the even soppier *Cocoon: The Return* (1988), this time miraculously conceiving a child with Gwen Verdon (aged 63). In the same year, he was given his best role since *Heaven Can Wait*, in David Mamet's *Things Change*. To the portrayal of Gino, the humble and naive Italian shoeshine man who agrees to go to jail in place of a Mafia hit-man he resembles, he brought so much charm and dignity that one happily suspends disbelief at the Capraesque fairy-tale.

1936 Sins Of Man; Ramona; Ladies In Love **1937** One In A Million; Love Is News; Fifty Roads To Town; You Can't Have Everything; Love Under Fire **1938** In Old Chicago; Happy Landing; Josette; Alexander's Ragtime Band; Gateway **1939** The Three Musketeers; Midnight; The Story of Alexander Graham Bell; Hollywood Cavalcade **1940** Swanee River; Lillian Russell; Four Sons; Down Argentine Way **1941** That Night In Rio; Moon Over Miami; Kiss The Boys Goodbye; The Feminine Touch; Confirm Or Deny **1942** The Magnificent Dope; Girl Trouble **1943** Something To Shout About; Heaven Can Wait; Happy Land **1944** Wing And A Prayer; Greenwich Village **1945** It's In The Bag; Guest Wife **1946** So Goes My Love **1947** That's My Man **1948** Sleep My Love **1949** Slightly French **1954** Phantom Caravan **1955** Fire One **1961** A Fever In The Blood **1966** Rings Around The Worls (docu); Picture Mommy Dead **1970** Suppose They Gave A War And Nobody Came; The Boatniks **1961** A Fever In The Blood **1966** Rings Around The World (docu); Picture Mommy Dead **1970** Suppose They Gave A War And Nobody Came; The Boatniks **1976** Won Ton Ton, The Dog Who Saved Hollywood (cameo) **1983** Trading Places **1985** Cocoon **1987** Bigfoot And The Hendersons **1988** Cocoon: The Return; Things Change; Coming To America **1991** Oscar **1992** Folks!

Andrews, Julie
(Julia Welles)
Actress, singer
Born 1 October 1935
Surrey, England

The archetypal English rose of popular myth, Julie Andrews began her musical career as a child and graduated to the theatre via Sandy Wilson's hit 1920s pastiche, *The Boy Friend*, in 1954. Two years later, she became a major theatrical star in London and New York when she played Eliza Doolittle in the original production of *My Fair Lady*. Unexpectedly, and unwisely, Hollywood cast Audrey Hepburn in the film version, but Miss Andrews' own screen opportunity came with *Mary Poppins* (1964), which won her the Best Actress Oscar. Her next major international success was as the irrepressible convent novice-turned-governess to the Von Trapp family in *The Sound Of Music* (1965), which elevated her to mega-stardom.

But, for all its popularity, *The Sound Of Music* confirmed the star's clean-living, sugarsweet, prim English image to her professional detriment. It is an image which has elicited much sneering comment, typical of which is the following: 'The limpid, over-enunciated coloratura soprano voice emanating from Julie Andrews' ample mouth is her own. She entered films as the apotheosis of English nannyhood in *Mary Poppins* (1964), went on to play a singing governess in the chocolate box-office hit, *The Sound Of Music* (1965) and, despite frantic efforts to change the colour of her hair and her insipid image, she remains essentially a girl guide in attractive costumes.' It is difficult to understand why Miss Andrews provokes such uncharitable reactions to her work and personality. She was pleasing in *The Americanization Of Emily* (1964), delightful in the 1920s flapper-era lampoon, *Thoroughly Modern Millie* (1967); and in the major flop, *Star*! (1968), which nearly scuppered her box-office rating forever, she was seriously miscast as the late Gertrude Lawrence, but her much reviled performance actually had some very good moments.

Audiences (and, more especially, critics) found it difficult to accept Julie Andrews in strong roles and the 1970s were a struggle for her. She was divorced from designer Tony Walton and married director Blake Edwards, for whom almost all her subsequent work has been done (and for whom she – shock, horror – bared her breasts on screen in *S.O.B.*, her husband's 1981 parody of life in the fast lane of the movie colony). She weathered a breakdown and her flagging career to do everything she does best in *Victor/Victoria* (1982), and succeeded in proving her dramatic credentials in *Duet For One* (1987), directed by Andrei Konchalovsky and dealing with the relationship between a violinist struck down by multiple sclerosis and the psychiatrist who attempts to help her. Still here in the 1990s, she started the decade filming opposite Marcello Mastroianni in *Tchin Tchin*.

1964 Mary Poppins; The Americanization Of Emily **1965** The Sound Of Music **1966** Torn Curtain; Hawaii **1967** Thoroughly Modern Millie **1968** Star! **1970** Darling Lili **1974** The Tamarind Seed **1979** 10 **1981** S.O.B. **1982** Victor/Victoria **1983** The Man Who Loved Women **1986** That's Life **1987** Duet For One **1991** Tchin Tchin aka Cin Cin (Italy)

Ann-Margret
(Ann-Margaret Olsson)
Actress
Born 28 April 1941
Valsjobyn, Sweden

Pocketful Of Miracles (1961) was the final film of Frank Capra, the legendary veteran director of Hollywood comedy, and Ann-Margret's first. The pretty, long-legged 20-year-old played Bette Davis' daughter, brought up in Spain in the belief that her mother, a poor apple-seller round Broadway, is a high-society lady. Her performance led to a role in 20th Century-Fox's musical remake, *State Fair* (1962), in which she exuded more zest and talent than the rest of the cast, especially in her big production number, 'Isn't It Kinda Fun'. Further proof of her singing and dancing abilities came the following year in *Bye Bye Birdie*, in which she crooned 'How Lovely To Be A Woman' and five other songs. She was equally impressive as Elvis Presley's sexy co-star in *Viva Las Vegas* (1963), and in a number of straight roles, especially that of Karl Malden's sluttish wife in *The Cincinnati Kid* (1965). But she only proved her credentials as a serious actress in Mike Nichols' *Carnal Knowledge* (1971), for which she was Oscar nominated. Her performance as the vulnerable and touching model no longer in the flower of her youth seemed to bode a turning point in her career.

However, this voluptuous and vivacious

entertainer preferred not to make too many films, but rather to star in TV specials and appear at top nightclubs in Las Vegas, where she was known as 'the hottest number on the strip'. But in 1972, her career, and even her life, might have ended when she fell 22 feet from a platform to a hardwood floor during a performance in Lake Tahoe. Miraculously – she herself puts it down to her Lutheran faith – she recovered, and was working again within a year, having undergone plastic surgery for facial scars.

Ann-Margret was five when she arrived in the USA with her parents from Sweden, none of them speaking English, and settled in Chicago where the young girl learned singing and dancing. It was comedian George Burns who discovered her at nineteen and put her into his Las Vegas act. In 1967, she married TV actor Roger Smith, who also became her personal manager. When they met, he helped her settle her large debts, and she helped him raise his three children from a previous marriage.

After her accident, Ann-Margret returned to the screen, looking as attractive as ever, in Ken Russell's *Tommy* (1975), for which she received her second Oscar nomination. As the mother of the eponymous rock star, played by Roger Daltrey, she brought some sanity to the wildly undisciplined proceedings. She has continued to be active, but has been unwise in the choice of some of her recent material. However, she was splendid in Alan Alda's *A New Life* (1988), as a bored housewife who ends up happily alone riding her motorbike, a symbol of her new-found freedom – and has distinguished herself in a number of TV movies.

1961 Pocketful Of Miracles **1962** State Fair **1963** Bye-Bye Birdie **1964** Viva Las Vegas; Kitten With A Whip; The Pleasure Seekers **1965** Bus Riley's Back In Town; Once A Thief; The Cincinnati Kid **1966** Made In Paris; Stagecoach; The Swinger; Murderers' Row **1967** Criminal Affair (Italy); The Tiger And The Pussycat **1970** C.C. And Company; R.P.M. **1971** Carnal Knowledge **1972** The Train Robbers; Un Homme Est Mort/The Outside Man (France) **1975** Tommy **1976** The Prophet (Italy); Folies Bourgeoises (France) **1977** Joseph Andrews; The Last Remake Of Beau Geste **1978** The Cheap Detective; Magic **1979** The Villain **1980** Middle Age Crazy **1982** Lookin' To Get Out; I Ought To Be In Pictures; Return Of The Soldier **1985** Twice In A Lifetime **1986** 52 Pick-Up **1987** A Tiger's Tale **1988** A New Life **1992** Newsies aka Newsboys

Apted, Michael

Director

Born 10 February 1941

Aylesbury, England

Michael Apted is one of the many British directors who left the barren fields of British cinema for the richer pickings of Hollywood. After having worked for nine years on British television, directing plays and documentaries, followed by four unremarkable features and an abortive movie with Bianca Jagger, he made it big in the USA with the impressive *Coal Miner's Daughter* (1980), as American a subject as one could tackle.

It was a great stroke of luck that gave Apted *Coal Miner's Daughter*. He was called in as a replacement for director Joseph Sargent, who refused to have Sissy Spacek in the title role as the 'Queen of Country' singer, Loretta Lynn. As it happened, Spacek went on to win the Best Actress Oscar out of the seven nominations the picture received. Apted, assisted by the superb Spacek and a fine team, carefully over-rode most of the cliches of the rags-to-riches biopic.

His first feature, *Triple Echo* (1972), a TV-sized drama, had sensitively handled a cross-dressing theme, and was a modest success. It was set in the England of 1942, where a lonely woman on a farm (Glenda Jackson) hides a young deserter by dressing him in drag. After *Stardust* (1974), an uninspiring pop musical, and *The Squeeze* (1977), a predictable and sleazy thriller starring American Stacy Keach, the director found himself caught in the vituperative behind-the-scenes squabbles of *Agatha* (1979). The script was rewritten daily, producer David Puttnam walked out because of Dustin Hoffman, who he called 'this worrisome American pest', and everyone ended up suing everyone else. The end product was a visually elegant but pretty sluggish, padded-out anecdote.

Gorky Park (1983), a spy thriller from Martin Cruz's bestseller, despite good performances and photography, needed to be tauter and less rambling – there are endless shots of people in fur hats following other people in fur hats – and the Moscow setting lacked authenticity (perhaps because it was shot in Helsinki). By contrast, Apted gave the touching and absorbing tale of Dian Fossey (Sigourney Weaver) and her primate friends in *Gorillas In The Mist* (1988) a great sense of authenticity by shooting on location in the Virunga mountains of Central Africa, and the film was marred only by an irrelevant love affair between Weaver and Aussie photographer Bryan Brown.

Apted directs a variety of movies which share neither a thematic link nor any particular personal stamp, but he displays noticeable craftsmanship, and an evident attempt to make his films look good.

1973 Triple Echo **1974** Stardust **1977** The Squeeze **1979** Agatha **1980** Coal Miner's Daughter **1981** Continental Divide **1983** Gorky Park **1984** First Born; 28 Up; Kipperbang **1985** Bring On The Night (documentary); **1987** Critical Condition **1988** Gorillas In The Mist **1991** Class Action **1992** Thunderheart; Incident At Oglala (docu)

Archer, Anne

Actress
Born 25 August 1947
Los Angeles, California

Anne Archer had begun her movie career 15 years before the public finally noticed her. Her lack of recognition was largely due to the string of entirely forgettable movies in which she seemed doomed to appear and from which, in 1985, she decided to retire in favour of motherhood. (She is married to a TV network producer of sports programmes).

The daughter of actress Marjorie Lord and actor John Archer, she always intended to follow in her parents' footsteps. After taking a degree in theatre arts, she toured in summer stock and won her first major stage role in the national tour of a play called *Glad Tidings*, co-starring with veteran actress Ann Sothern. Over the years she made several TV movies and a couple of mini-series, but failed to become a name.

The tide turned unexpectedly for Archer after two years of absence from the screen. Director Adrian Lyne, about to make a new picture, saw her in an episode of TV's *Falcon Crest* and offered her the seemingly thankless supporting role of a wife whose husband becomes involved with another woman. The film was *Fatal Attraction* (1987), the husband Michael Douglas, the other woman a deranged Glenn Close. Archer, dark, strikingly pretty, sensual and intelligent, seized the bit between her teeth to create a memorably perfect wife whose qualities contributed a substantive emphasis to the tone of Lyne's box-office smash. After that, she signed for *Wild Orchid* (1990) opposite Mickey Rourke, but walked out when she discovered that it was schlock and she was required to strip. Archer, however, has neatly avoided becoming a stereotype and had better luck as a reluctant murder witness, co-starring with Gene Hackman, in *Narrow Margin* (1990); and in Alan Rudolph's *Love At Large* the same year, she surprised as the breathless, ambiguous night-club singer. Confirming that her previously lacklustre career had taken on a new shine, she won the female lead (another perfect wife, this time also a surgeon) opposite Harrison Ford in the blockbuster thriller *Patriot Games* (1992).

1972 The Honkers; Cancel My Reservation **1973** The All-American Boy **1976** Lifeguard; Trackdown **1978** Paradise Alley **1979** Good Guys Wear Black **1980** Raise The Titanic; Hero At Large **1981** Green Ice **1982** Waltz Across Texas **1985** Too Scared To Scream; The Naked Face **1986** The Check Is In The Mail **1987** Fatal Attraction **1990** Narrow Margin; Love At Large **1991** Eminent Domain **1992** Patriot Games **1992/93** Nails **1993** Body of Evidence; Short Cuts

Arkin, Alan

Actor, director
Born 26 March 1934
New York City

Alan Arkin is a talented man. The author of several children's books, a song composer, a photographer whose work has been exhibited, a stage and screen actor of considerable range, and a director. Yet he is generally thought of as a rather manic comedy actor with a depressive streak. Most typical was his Yossarian, the sane airman struggling to be certified mad in *Catch-22* (1970), Mike Nichols' uneven adaptation of the Joseph Heller satirical bestseller.

He was certainly very funny as Neil Simon's middle-aged Jewish fish restaurateur trying to seduce three women in *Last Of the Red Hot Lovers* (1972); the lunatic chicano cop in *Freebie And The Bean* (1974); the dim-witted driving instructor in *Rafferty And The Gold Dust Twins* (1975); and the excitable hack film director of early Hollywood in *Hearts Of The West* (1975), for which he won a New York Critics Award. He also gave his familiar portrayal of frustration in *Improper Channels* (1979), as a father running up against hospital bureaucracy, but as the psychology professor brainwashed into thinking he is from another planet in *Simon* (1980), he ranted and screamed more and more, to less and less effect, as the film lost its way.

Less typical were his psychotic villain persecuting blind Audrey Hepburn in *Wait Until*

Dark (1967); his poignant Oscar-nominated portrayal of a deaf mute in *The Heart Is A Lonely Hunter* (1968); the nervously disenchanted Puerto Rican father of two small sons in Spanish Harlem in *Popi* (1969); and Freud on the verge of fame, working with Sherlock Holmes in the *Seven-Per-Cent Solution* (1976).

Arkin was born in Brooklyn of Russian-German-Jewish parents. He dropped out of college to join a folk-singing trio called the Tarriers before joining the Chicago Second City company, with whom he performed and directed revue sketches. In the early 60s he moved back to New York, where he made a number of off and on Broadway appearances, of which the role of Harry Berlin, the obsessively self-analytical New Yorker in Murray Schisgal's *Luv* in 1964, gained the widest approval. It led to his Hollywood debut in *The Russians Are Coming, The Russians Are Coming* (1966), playing the confused Soviet submarine commander stranded in the small resort of Nantucket on America's East Coast. It was a role which earned him most of the movie's laughs and his first Oscar nomination.

The actor appeared in John Cassavetes' last film, *Big Trouble* (1985), as an insurance salesman desperate to send his musical triplets to Yale, a spoof thriller rather in the comic manner of Arkin's own directorial attempts, *Little Murders* (1971) and *Fire Sale* (1977). The former, by Jules Feiffer, which Arkin had also directed on Broadway, was wryly amusing, while the latter was frantic and strained. His wife, Barbara Dana, who had a featured role in *Fire Sale*, wrote the screenplay for *Chu Chu And The Philly Flash* (1981); his son Adam was one of the writers on *Improper Channels*, and starred as a werewolf in Larry Cohen's *Full Moon High* (1982), with his father in a small role.

In 1989 Arkin was cast as the Jewish judge in Brian De Palma's *Bonfire Of The Vanities*, but in order to redress what was felt to be the racial bias of Tom Wolfe's novel, he was replaced by the black Morgan Freeman. This left him free to appear in Sydney Pollack's *Havana* (1990), set in pre-revolutionary Cuba, and to play the part of a suburban father in *Edward Scissorhands* (1990). Then, in the all- star male cast of *Glengarry Glen Ross*, Arkin delivered one of the film's most affecting performances as a desperate real-estate salesman.

1966 The Russians Are Coming, The Russians Are Coming **1967** Woman Times Seven; Wait Until Dark **1968** Inspector Clouseau; The Heart Is A Lonely Hunter **1969** The Monitors; Popi **1970** Catch-22 **1971** Little Murders (also dir) **1972** Deadheat Miles; Last Of The Red Hot Lovers **1974** Freebie And The Bean **1975** Rafferty And The Gold Dust Twins; Hearts Of The West **1976** The Seven-Per-Cent Solution **1977** Fire Sale (also dir) **1979** The Magician Of Lublin (Israel/Germany); The In-Laws; Simon **1981** Chu Chu And The Philly Flash; Improper Channels **1982** Deadhead Miles; Full Moon High; The Last Unicorn; The Return Of Captain Invincible **1985** Big Trouble; Bad Medicine; Joshua Then And Now **1989** Coup De Ville **1990** Havana; Edward Scissorhands **1991** The Rocketeer **1992** Glengarry Glen Ross **1993** Tamakwa

Arquette, Rosanna

Actress

Born 10 August 1959

New York City

Rosanna Arquette, an actress of distinctive, off-beat looks – prominently pouting mouth, enormous doe eyes, willowy frame – personality and talent, worked her way up to star status by 1985 when she starred in Susan Seidelman's unexpected hit, *Desperately Seeking Susan*. None of her subsequent films has showcased her quite as successfully, but she remains admired and sought after.

Show business runs in the Arquette family. Rosanna's father, Lewis, was a founder member of the improvisational theatre troupe, The Committee, and two of her siblings are in the profession. (Brother Alexis played the effeminate homosexual who meets a sticky end in *Last Exit To Brooklyn*, 1990). The Arquettes moved around a lot, and Rosanna lived in New Jersey, Chicago, San Francisco and Los Angeles (where she appeared on stage in *Metamorphosis* at the age of 17) before settling in Front Royal, Virginia, where she acted with local drama groups. It was there that a casting director noticed her and, before long, she was busily employed in some high-grade TV movies, appearing variously with Bette Davis, Tom Conti, Timothy Hutton and Judge Reinhold.

On record as saying she detests being labelled a 'kook', that is nonetheless what Arquette played, quite wonderfully, in Martin Scorsese's ironic parody of Manhattan life, *After Hours* (1985), had more or less played as the sexy dropout in Blake Edwards' parody of the Hollywood scene, *S.O.B.* (1981), and played again in Scorsese's segment of *New York Stories* (1989). But there was nothing kooky about her as the vulnerable girlfriend of murderer Gary Gilmore (Tommy Lee Jones) in *The Executioner's Song* (1982), a heavyweight made-for-TV movie whose quality later earned it cinema release. It was that film which really drew attention to her, and she next found herself top-billed by John Sayles in *Baby, It's You* (1984), a superior movie about the growing pains of high school kids. She was top-billed again, with Christopher Reeve, in *The Aviator* (1985), but the film bombed; most of her role in Lawrence Kasdan's *Silverado* (1985) ended up on the cutting-room floor, leaving *Desperately Seeking Susan* to bring her the star sobriquet. As the bored and bemused yuppie wife caught in a dizzy spiral of mistaken identity involving Madonna, Arquette was memorably funny, touching, and deft.

Arquette is a woman of pronounced views who has expressed disillusion with Hollywood's methods of treating film subjects and, more profoundly, with the failures of the democratic process in America. Divorced from composer James Newton Howard, she based herself in England in 1990, her talent and sense of humour both thankfully intact, and starred in Tom Kempinski's *Separation* for the BBC television although, as her filmography demonstrates, she is not lost to the movie industry in her home country.

1979 More American Graffiti **1980** Gorp; Off The Wall **1981** S.O.B **1982** The Executioner's Song **1984** Baby, It's You **1985** The Aviator; After Hours; Desperately Seeking Susan; Silverado **1986** Nobody's Fool; Eight Million Ways To Die; Fly Away Home **1987** Amazon Women On The Moon **1988** The Big Blue (France) **1989** New York Stories **1990** Black Rainbow; Flight Of The Intruder; Wendy Cracked A Walnut **1992** Fathers And Sons; The Linguini Incident **1992/93** Crossing The Line

Ashby, Hal

Director
Born 1936
Ogden, Utah
Died 27 December 1988

Hal Ashby was an idealistic liberal-minded director whose work sits squarely in the 1970s. His first job on leaving Utah State University was in the RKO mailroom. He gradually worked his way up to becoming a distinguished editor, winning recognition for his work on four Norman Jewison movies, including *In The Heat Of The Night* (1967) which brought him an Oscar as Best Film Editor. Jewison produced Ashby's first movie as director, *The Landlord* (1970), which dealt with a young white landlord (Beau Bridges) and his relationship with his black tenants. Like several of Ashby's films, this debut effort was flabbily radical under its rather anarchic satirical surface. *Harold And Maude* (1971), concerning the love affair between a death-obsessed young man (Bud Cort) and a life-obsessed 80-year-old woman (Ruth Gordon), was a black comedy covered by a syrupy idealism about youth and 'the young at heart' which, predictably, gained college-kid cult status.

The Last Detail (1973) turned out to be less soft-centred than many of his other films, mainly because the director (and Robert Towne's script) refused to linger over the pathos of the naive 18-year-old seaman (Randy Quaid) who is being escorted to the brig for stealing $40 from a charity fund. The film was an enormous success, although it ran into trouble with the American Navy for its unflattering depiction of sailors, and the puritanical lobby objected to its 'salty' language.

Ashby hit the jackpot again with *Shampoo* (1975), a reasonably amusing satire on Beverly Hills sexual mores which reflected the self-regarding personality of Warren Beatty, its producer, co-screenwriter and star. However, the film is slightly undermined by its fuzzy philosophy and weak attempt to bring in a political dimension. (It all takes place on 4 November 1968, the day of Nixon's election.)

Bound For Glory (1976), a hagiography of legendary folksinger Woody Guthrie, was decorated with all the trappings of the Depression. Much of the homespun philosophy, however, palled over 150 minutes, though it did have its heart in the right place and was another demonstration of the director's sympathy for the marginals of American society. At the time, Ashby became very ill, his lungs having filled up with dust inhaled during the long and arduous shooting of the $7.5 million picture. He recovered sufficiently to make *Coming Home* (1978), a film instigated by its star, Jane Fonda, who wanted to appear in a picture with built-in criticism of the US policy in Vietnam. Ashby treated much of the soapy love story between an army wife (Fonda) and a returning vet (Jon Voight), paralysed from the waist down, with discretion, but overplayed the tearjerking side, and much of the dialogue was drowned by unrelenting pop music on the soundtrack. The public did not rush to see it, but when Fonda and Voight won Oscars (Ashby was nominated), business boomed.

Thanks to Jerzy Kosinski's satirical screenplay and Peter Sellers' haunting performance, *Being There* (1979), turned out to be Ashby's best film, despite the inclusion of miscalculated farcical scenes when Shirley MacLaine (as excessive as Sellers was restrained) attempts to seduce the *naïf* gardener who involuntarily becomes a national celebrity. As the 80s dawned, so Ashby's star mysteriously waned. All four of his last features, apart from his documentary, *Let's Spend The Night Together* (1982), on the Rolling Stones 1981 American tour, were copper-bottomed flops. His final film, *Eight Million Ways To Die* (1986), a lethargic thriller with Jeff Bridges, was beset by arguments and the director was eventually locked out of the cutting room. At the time of his death, he was preparing to shoot the Truman Capote story, *Hardcarved Coffins*.

1970 The Landlord **1971** Harold And Maude **1973** The Last Detail **1975** Shampoo **1976** Bound For Glory **1978** Coming Home **1979** The Hamster Of Happiness aka Second Hand Hearts; Being There **1982** Lookin' To Get Out; Let's Spend The Night Together aka Time Is On Our Side **1985** The Slugger's Wife **1986** Eight Million Ways To Die

Assante, Armand

Actor

Born 4 October 1949

New York City

Suave and handsome in the 'Latin Lover' mould, Armand Assante is increasingly heavily employed in internationally seen TV movies and mini-series (he played the title role in *Onassis*), but his feature film career, despite promising sparks, has nevertheless failed to ignite.

After studying at the American Academy of Dramatic Arts, he soon landed a significant stage role in *Why I Went Crazy*, directed by Joshua Logan, before picking up a bit part (he can be seen in the final wedding party) as Sylvester Stallone's cousin in the New York movie *The Lords Of Flatbush* (1974). He then went on location to North Africa with a leading role in a film that went bankrupt after a month. Assante only recovered from this setback by reluctantly taking work in daytime soaps, including *How To Survive A Marriage* and *The Doctors*, but later acknowledged these series as a valuable training ground. More Broadway credits followed and, in 1977, the actor decided to try his luck with the movies again, this time on the West Coast. It was during his first job there, guesting on *Kojak*, that he ran into Stallone. The latter was casting the part of his own smarter older brother in *Paradise Alley* (1979) and, recognising his erstwhile 'cousin', immediately arranged a screen test. The film, a transposition of *Rocky* themes to New York's Hell's Kitchen circa 1946, failed to win audiences and met with a generally hostile response from the critics, but it was a major role for Assante and he carried it off with aplomb. The same year, *Prophecy*, a collaboration with John Frankenheimer, failed to fulfil expectations, while James Toback's *Love And Money*, filmed shortly afterwards, was held back for two years.

The hit that Assante needed came in the seemingly unlikely field of romantic comedy, when he co-starred with Goldie Hawn in *Private Benjamin* (1980). He was cast as a sophisticated continental lover – a role that Rossano Brazzi would very probably have played in the 1950s – and the movie, directed by Howard Zieff, became a world-wide hit. *Unfaithfully Yours* (1984), also directed by Zieff, called for a repeat performance, but with Assante playing second fiddle to Dudley Moore's jealous orchestra conductor. In between these frivolities, the actor turned in his most impressive work, in a film that should have established him as a heavyweight once and for all: *I, The Jury* (1982). As Mickey Spillane's sleazy private dick, Mike Hammer, Assante was irredeemably scuzzy – one could almost smell the sweat. It was a convincing portrayal of a mean, tough and none-too-bright guy, an anti-hero with no disclaimers. Sadly, the film proved an ill-fated venture. Screenwriter Larry Cohen was replaced in the director's chair by Richard T. Heffron a week into shooting, the movie's ending was a shambles, and the production company went bust shortly after completion, thereby undermining the American release. In the late 1980s, Assante's movies, among them *The Penitent* (1988), a powerful and sombre allegory, failed to gain wide distribution, but he went into 1990 working for Sidney Lumet and stealing the show in *Q & A* (1990), a cop corruption drama. *The Mambo Kings* provided a flashy role for him as an ambitious Cuban musician emigré to New York, and he played it with relish, all sexy magnetism and hypnotic appeal.

1974 The Lords of Flatbush **1979** Paradise Alley;

Prophecy **1980** Little Darlings; Private Benjamin **1982** I, The Jury; Love And Money (made in 1980) **1984** Unfaithfully Yours **1988** The Penitent **1989** Animal Behaviour **1990** Q & A; Eternity **1992** The Mambo Kings; 1492 – Conquest Of Paradise; Hoffa

Avildsen, John G.

Director
Born 21 December 1935
Oak Park, Illinois

'My films are about people who have dreams, because I'm prone to fairy-tales.' Thus John G. Avildsen on the subject of his own work, and those who have seen *Rocky* (1976) and the similar *The Karate Kid* (1984) will immediately know what he meant. He also tapped the public's vast enjoyment in seeing the triumph of the underdog.

Rocky, the story of how an over-the-hill heavyweight boxer gets a crack at the world title, more than satisfied the audience's need to believe in the American Dream and the happy ending. There was an exuberant feel to Avildsen's direction as the film built to the climactic fight, while the streetwise dialogue and Sylvester Stallone's self-mocking performance as the good-hearted pug made the simple, sentimental situations palatable. The picture, made for the modest sum of $1 million, became one of the biggest hits in 20 years, earned over $54 million, and won three Oscars, including Best Director and Best Picture (significantly, over such serious-minded American Nightmares as *Taxi Driver, All The President's Men* and *Network*).

A further hit of such proportions, or any proportion, eluded Avildsen for some time. 'I tell ya. If we beat the odds in New York, we can do anything – kiss the moon, turn the garbage into roses,' says Paul Sorvino, the plump and plain hero of *Slow Dancing In The Big City* (1978). The director failed to turn this shamelessly maudlin garbage into roses. Not coming up roses either was *The Formula* (1980), a dull thriller that not even Marlon Brando could save, and *Neighbors* (1981), a hectic comedy that failed at the box office despite John Belushi's much-publicised death from drugs a few months after its release.

Obviously nostalgic for the heady days of *Rocky*, Avildsen decided to make it again. Well, almost. *The Karate Kid* is an extended Charles Atlas comic strip told less economically. When young Daniel Larusso (Ralph Macchio) gets sand kicked in his face by a bully, he learns karate from Mr Miyagi (Noriyuko 'Pat' Morita), and overcomes his tormentor at the exaggerated teenage fantasy climax. The formula worked commercial wonders (it grossed $90.9 million), and it was followed by more of the same in two sequels, which similarly raked in the cash.

Avildsen's career has something of the American Dream about it. The son of a tool manufacturer in Chicago, he began working as a copywriter for an advertising agency before doing his military service as a chaplain's assistant. He started in films as an assistant director on low-budget features, as well as directing several shorts, commercials and a couple of 'sexploitation' movies. Then he made *Joe* (1970), the story of a hardhat (Peter Boyle), a reactionary bigot who hates 'niggers' and hippies. Although ostensibly critical of its 'hero', the film moved dangerously close to condoning him. Shot on a shoestring on location in New York, with the director as his own cameraman, it turned out to be the sleeper of the year. One of his few films to concern itself with failure, *Save The Tiger* (1973), provided Jack Lemmon with an Oscar-winning role, but not much pleasure for anyone else. Naive, overstated and implausible though they may be, many of Avildsen's films have nevertheless managed to attract a popular response.

1969 Turn On To Love; Sweet Dreams **1970** Guess What We Learned In School Today? (also co-writer); Joe **1971** Okay Bill (also writer); Cry Uncle aka Super Dick **1972** The Stoolie **1973** Save The Tiger **1975** W.W. And The Dixie Dancekings; Foreplay (co-director) **1976** Rocky **1978** Slow Dancing In The Big City **1980** The Formula **1981** Neighbors; The President's Woman **1983** A Night In Heaven **1984** The Karate Kid **1986** The Karate Kid: Part II **1987** Happy New Year; For Keeps (GB: Maybe Baby) **1989** The Karate Kid Part III; Lean On Me **1990** Rocky V **1992** THe Power Of One

Aykroyd, Dan

Actor, writer, director
Born 1 July 1950
Ottawa, Canada

The grandson of a Royal Canadian mountie, and the son of a Canadian government official, Aykroyd, who was raised in Quebec, demonstrated a rebellious tendency early in life, getting himself expelled from a seminary and other quality educational establishments. Bringing a measure of this rebellion to bear on his roles as a Hollywood screen actor, he has compensated for a rather limited range by applying an unmistakeable nose for the commercial to his choice of projects.

Aykroyd, Dan

Dan Aykroyd's career began on the Canadian nightclub circuit, where he performed as a stand-up comic and managed Toronto's Club 505 for three years in the early 70s. Moving to the US, he honed his writing and performing skills in the company of John Belushi, Chevy Chase and Bill Murray on the hit TV show, *Saturday Night Live*, thus beginning associations which would prove integral to his future advancement. He was with the show from 1975 to 1979, during which time he and Belushi created their most famous alter egos, Jake and Elwood Blues. The Blues Brothers were sharp-suited, deadpan R & B musicians – Belushi took the lead vocals, Aykroyd supplied acerbic wit and a hip temperament, and together they struck a chord.

When Belushi became a movie star, courtesy of the surprise monster hit *National Lampoon's Animal House* (1978), Dan was right behind him. They both appeared (though not as a duo) in Spielberg's desperate *1941* (1979), and then collaborated with John Landis on *The Blues Brothers* (1980). The result was an expensive, extravagant comedy with a wayward plot and musical contributions from the likes of Aretha Franklin, Cab Calloway and James Brown. Although the movie was originally counted a failure, it has proved enduringly popular with cult and video audiences. In contrast, *Neighbors* (1981) remains a curio, an adaptation of Thomas Berger's novel which perversely cast Belushi as a quiet, middle-class square and Aykroyd as an uninhibited wild man. It was Belushi's last film before his drug-induced death in 1982, and Aykroyd went on to play (relatively speaking) straight man to a variety of other famous partners: Eddie Murphy, Albert Brooks, Chevy Chase, Tom Hanks, Walter Matthau, John Candy and, of course, fellow 'ghostbusters' Bill Murray and Harold Ramis. (Aykroyd co-wrote the phenomenally successful *Ghostbusters* and its sequel). The results have frequently been amusing, especially in the screwball comedy *Trading Places* (1983), in which Aykroyd's buttoned-up stockbroker, victim of a bet, was forced to swap lifestyles with Eddie Murphy's street con-man.

Dan Aykroyd's slightly cynical and rather prissy persona has not, in spite of his successes, ever been able to carry a movie on the strength of his name alone; *Doctor Detroit* (1983) and *My Stepmother Is An Alien* (1988), for example, were both well-deserved flops. And with the emergence of a marked paunch and very much a supporting role – although one he played with a plomb, aging over a period of years – in the Oscar-winning *Driving Miss Daisy* (1989), his leading man days seemed to be drawing to a close as the 90s dawned. However, he began the decade making his first directorial sortie with *Nothing But Trouble*, written by him and starring himself and old mates Chevy Chase and John Candy.

1974 Love At First Sight (Canada) **1979** Mr Mike's Mondo Video; 1941 **1980** The Blues Brothers **1981** Neighbors **1983** Doctor Detroit; Trading Places; Twilight Zone – The Movie **1984** Ghostbusters; Indiana Jones And The Temple Of Doom; Nothing Lasts Forever **1985** Into The Night; Spies Like Us **1986** Dragnet **1988** The Couch Trip; Caddyshack II; The Great Outdoors; My Stepmother Is An Alien **1989** Ghostbusters II; Driving Miss Daisy **1990** Loose Cannons **1991** Nothing But Trouble **1991** My Girl **1992** This Is My Life; Sneakers; Charlie

B

Bacon, Kevin

Actor
Born 8 July 1958
Philadelphia, Pennsylvania

A thoughtful, experienced actor with range, Kevin Bacon seems to have come into his own on several occasions, but despite a number of appealing performances he had yet to break conclusively into the first division by the end of the 1980s. Trained at New York theatre schools from the age of 17, he made his professional debut off-Broadway at 20 and his screen debut soon after in *National Lampoon's Animal House* (1977), the cult comedy crammed with now-familiar young faces.

After a lot of parts in daytime soap operas and several so-so films, Bacon's first real chance came with his memorably intense performance as the wild, heavy-drinking boy with a death wish in Barry Levinson's impressive first feature, *Diner*, in 1982. But film roles proved elusive, even though he continued to work steadily on the stage, notably in the powerful *Slab Boys* with Sean Penn in 1983. Then in 1984 the actor starred as the fancy-stepping adolescent in the runaway teen hit *Footloose* and for the second time seemed set for the stardom that didn't come.

Nevertheless, he delivered a delightful turn as a cab driver who falls in love with one of his fares, a shy older woman, and pursues her relentlessly in the quirky *Enormous Changes At The Last Minute* (1985), which received critical acclaim but a limited theatrical release. Routine parts followed – including an uncredited cameo in John Hughes' *Planes, Trains And Automobiles* (1987) – when a string of leading roles in the late 80s again suggested Bacon was about to break.

Disappointingly, Hughes' much-anticipated first grown-up film, *She's Having A Baby* (1987), fell flat despite engaging work from Bacon, Elizabeth McGovern and Alec Baldwin. Both the psychological thriller *Criminal Law* (1988), in which Bacon played a psychopathic killer, and *The Big Picture* (1989), a first-rate leg-pull of Hollywood in which he played a hapless young film-maker, were long held up between production and release. Soon after, Bacon enjoyed hero status with the cult comic horror hit *Tremors* (1990), and, also in that year, a straighter leading man outing in *Flatliners* as one of a group of medical students conducting dangerous experiments with death. His critical standing was markedly enhanced by his excellent work in Oliver Stone's *JFK* as a homosexual convict informer.

Married to actress Kyra Sedgwick, Kevin Baker lives with his wife and young son in Connecticut. He starred in an off-Broadway revival of Joe Orton's black comedy *Loot* and completed several more films for release in 1991. Bacon's own assessment of himself as 'a workhorse actor' is apt, and his prediction that 'I'm here for the long haul' seemed likely to be fulfilled – the other side of the equation is that with his distinctive if unglamorous looks, his charm, presence and versatility, he has lasting properties.

1977 National Lampoon's Animal House **1979** Starting Over **1980** Friday The 13th; Hero At Large **1981** Only When I Laugh **1982** Diner; Forty Deuce **1984** Footloose **1985** Enormous Changes At The Last Minute **1986** Quicksilver **1987** Rites Of Summer; Planes, Trains And Automobiles; White Water Summer **1988** She's Having A Baby; End Of The Line; Criminal Law **1989** The Big Picture **1990** Tremors; Flatliners **1991** Queen's Logic; He Said, She Said; JFK **1992** A Few Good Men

Badham, John

Director
Born 25 August 1939
Luton, England

John Badham was already in his late 30s when he directed his second film, *Saturday Night Fever* (1977), although one would have thought that all that youthful disco-technical exuberance must have come from a younger man. Although the movie centred on the electrifying dancing of John Travolta, Badham, working with the choreographer and editor, staged the numbers with a flowing movement, a rhythm which he keeps up in some of the non-dancing scenes. When he was at Yale Drama School he was fervently devoted to staging musicals.

The son of an English actress, Mary Hewitt, Badham grew up in Alabama where his mother had her own TV talk show; his younger sister Mary played Gregory Peck's nine-year-old daughter in *To Kill A Mockingbird* (1962). After graduating from Yale in

1966, he took a humble job in the Universal Pictures mailroom, worked up to a tour guide for the studio, and was finally promoted to the making of trailers and to casting work. Gradually he got into television, where he directed episodes of series such as *The Streets Of San Francisco*, and was nominated for an Emmy for the tough TV movie *The Law* (1974), with Judd Hirsch.

The Bingo Long Traveling All-Stars And Motor Kings (1976), about an all-black baseball team barnstorming through Middle America in 1939, was an impressive feature film debut. Badham's 'cool' direction and the funky playing of Billy Dee Williams, James Earl Jones and Richard Pryor made it an entertaining social comedy. After the high of *Saturday Night Fever*, Badham suffered a box-office set-back with his handsomely mounted but bloodless *Dracula* (1979), in which Frank Langella repeated his Broadway performance, this time (less entertainingly) playing it straight.

Commercial success returned with *Whose Life Is It Anyway?* (1982), which he had directed with the remarkable Richard Dreyfuss on Broadway 'as a kind of rehearsal for the movie'. The hospital drama worked well when closest to the play, but came unstuck when it tried to open it out and move into flashback. Badham's pacy direction of *WarGames* (1983) proved that five-minutes-to-midnight fever could be just as big at the box office as the Saturday night kind. It was a suspenseful and satiric tale, which had a teenage computer wizard (Matthew Broderick) accidentally simulating a nuclear attack on the USA.

Badham continued his fascination with hi-tech in *Blue Thunder* (1983), featuring a souped up helicopter, and the rather broadly comic *Short Circuit* (1985), which revolved around a top-secret weapon-robot called Number Five. In both cases, the human element was reduced in interest, something the director made up for in *Stakeout* (1987), an efficient comedy-thriller, which once again placed the effervescent Richard Dreyfuss centre stage. *Bird On A Wire* (1990) was an old-style romantic chase movie with Goldie Hawn and Mel Gibson, which went in for unsubtle situations and easy laughs, none of which affected the big box-office takings, mainly stimulated by the various sightings of Mr Gibson's bare behind, while 1991's *The Hard Way* was a highly enjoyable bickering-buddies (Michael J. Fox, James Woods) entertainment.

1976 The Bingo Long Traveling All-Stars And Motor Kings **1977** Saturday Night Fever **1979** Dracula **1982** Whose Life Is It Anyway? **1983** WarGames; Blue Thunder **1984** American Flyers **1985** Short Circuit **1987** Stakeout **1990** Bird On A Wire **1991** The Hard Way **1993** The Specialist aka Nikita

Baker, Joe Don

Actor
Born 12 February 1936
Groesbeck, Texas

The Lone, Tall Texan in person, Joe Don Baker's imposing physique and surly visage, topped by a boyish lock of dark hair, have earned him many, if not varied, parts in film and television. He was educated at North Texas State College, then worked his way on to the New York stage en route to Hollywood, which had him pegged for a cowboy. But the sun was setting on the Western when Baker earned his spurs and, like the major stars of the genre such as Clint Eastwood, he had to switch to contemporary thrillers to keep up with the times.

It was in 1972 with *Walking Tall* that Joe Don really earned wider attention. The movie, in which he played real life sheriff Buford Pusser, taking a stick to Tennessee roughnecks, proved a controversial hit; in essence the film was a Western but, in its modern setting, it took on uneasy vigilante connotations. *Walking Tall* might well have made Baker a star but, as it turned out, the same year's *Charley Varrick* – an eccentric thriller from Don Siegel which featured him in a supporting role as a Mafia hit-man known as 'Molly' – was to prove more typical of his subsequent career. For a while, the actor persisted in taking leading roles, usually as cop or hard man, in sub-standard action movies like the nasty revenge thriller *Framed* (1975), or *The Pack* (1977), a rip-off of Hitchcock's *The Birds*, but with dogs running amok.

Baker decided to concentrate on TV work in 1978 and disappeared from the big screen for four years, re-emerging in Hollywood as a now solid character actor in some significant movies during the mid-80s. He tried his hand at comedy in *Fletch* (1985), but returned to home ground, on both sides of the law, in frequent thrillers, including *The Living Daylights* (1987), in which he played the villain opposite Timothy Dalton's James Bond. Then, 1992 saw a return in a grade-A featured support, turning in an immaculate performance as the detective in the otherwise over-the-top Scorsese remake of *Cape Fear.*

1967 Cool Hand Luke **1969** Guns Of The Magnificent Seven **1970** Adam At 6 am **1972** Junior Bonner; Wild Rovers; Walking Tall; Charley Varrick; Welcome Home, Soldier Boys **1973** The Outfit **1974** Golden Needles **1975** Framed; Mitchell **1976** Crash **1977** The Pack aka The Long Hard Night; The Shadow Of Chikara aka Wishbone Cutter; Speedtrap **1982** Wacko **1983** Joysticks **1984** The Natural; The Maltese Connection aka Final Justice **1985** Fletch; Getting Even aka Hostage: Dallas **1987** The Killing Time; Leonard Part 6; The Living Daylights **1988** Criminal Law **1990** The Children **1992** Cape Fear **1992/93** The Distinguished Gentleman

Baker, Kathy

Actress
Born 8 June 1950
Midland, Texas

One of the most promising actresses to have come to light during the 1980s, Kathy Baker carries an unmistakeable aura of intelligence and sensitivity which, together with non-stereotypical looks, distinguish her from the crowd. In a matter of six years and comparatively few films, she had already held her own with actors of the calibre of Robert De Niro, Ed Harris, Michael Keaton and Jack Lemmon.

Although Texas born, Baker grew up across the border in New Mexico, then crossed it again to study French at Berkeley, following which she spent two years in Paris. There, she trained as a Cordon Bleu cook while, at the same time, acting with amateur theatre groups. To help make ends meet she dubbed some French films for the American market. Back home again, she joined the Magic Theatre in San Francisco, where she originated the role of May in Sam Shepard's *Fool For Love*, sufficiently impressing Shepard with her performance to be asked to repeat it off-Broadway, where she and co-star Ed Harris both won Obie Awards. Her feature film debut was as an astronaut's wife – one of the uniformly excellent supporting performances that marked the quality of Philip Kaufman's *The Right Stuff* (1983), and she went on to star opposite Peter Weller in *A Killing Affair*. However, this film, directed by *Cocoon* novelist David Saperstein in 1985, has not been released to date and was only seen at the American Film Institute Festival in 1988.

Thus it was that Kathy Baker's breakthrough role came with *Street Smart* (1987), the film remembered for Morgan Freeman's extraordinary performance as a vicious pimp. Kathy played one of Freeman's hookers who, in attempting to help journalist Christopher Reeve and to break free from her professional bondage, gets herself killed. Her portrayal was one of vigorous conviction and sincerity, projecting both strength and vulnerability, and was duly appreciated by the National Society of Critics who voted her Best Supporting Actress. She graduated to 'detox' with her performance as Michael Keaton's love interest in *Clean And Sober* (1988), and was given an even better showcase (though in not nearly as good a film) for her particular strengths in *Jacknife* the same year. David Jones directed, with De Niro and Ed Harris as two Vietnam vets slugging it out for attention . . . but it was Kathy Baker, as the woman caught in the middle, who walked away with the picture.

1983 The Right Stuff **1985** A Killing Affair **1987** Street Smart **1988** Clean And Sober; Permanent Record; Jacknife; **1990** Dad; Mr Frost; Edward Scissorhands **1992** Article 99; Jennifer Eight; Mad Dog And Glory

Balaban, Bob (Robert Balaban)

Actor, director
Born 16 August 1945
Chicago, Illinois

Bob Balaban began performing with Chicago's famous Second City group while he was still in high school. Nonetheless, he went on to study at Colegate University, and even took classes at New York University while he was appearing in the original broadway production of Neil Simon's *Plaza Suite*.

Short and serious, Balaban was not an obvious movie star, but he strung together an impressive list of credits during the early 70s before getting his big break in Steven Spielberg's *Close Encounters Of The Third Kind* (1977). He played alongside François Truffaut (for whom he had played a small part in *Day For Night*, 1973) as one of the NASA scientists investigating UFO activities. It was a small but memorable supporting role in a movie that became a phenomenal hit, and Balaban's career developed accordingly. He was a boyfriend in *Girlfriends* (1978), but more often played white-collar professionals at the star's elbow in well-intentioned prestigious dramas: he was seen variously as a cop, as a doctor and an astronaut and, with William Hurt in Ken

Russell's *Altered States* (1980), as a scientist again.

None of those performances anticipated Bob Balaban's late forays behind the camera. For television he directed episodes of *Tales From The Darkside* and Spielberg's *Amazing Stories* and, when his feature film debut as director finally materialised, it displayed a similar bent to the fantastic. *Parents* (1989) was a stylish, gruesome black comedy about a young boy who suspects his parents might be cannibals. Balaban prepared for the task by apprenticing himself to Sidney Lumet for four months during the shooting of *Deathtrap*, then delivered a wildly impressive Wellesian movie that merited comparisons with David Lynch and the Coen brothers. Balaban summed it up as 'an expressionistic view of a typical American family', an understatement distinctly absent from the film itself.

1969 Midnight Cowboy; Me Natalie **1970** The Strawberry Statement; Catch-22 **1971** Making It **1973** La Nuit Américaine/Day For Night (France) **1974** Bank Shot **1975** Report To The Commissioner **1977** Close Encounters Of The Third Kind **1978** Girlfriends **1980** Altered States **1981** Prince Of The City; Absence Of Malice **1982** Whose Life Is It Anyway? **1984** 2010; **1988** End of The Line **1989** Dead Bang; Parents (director only)

Baldwin, Adam

Actor

Born 27 February 1962

Chicago, Illinois

Adam Baldwin, commonly but erroneously thought to be yet another of the acting Baldwin brothers (Alec, William, Stephen), started appearing in movies while still at high school. Large and beefy, the fact that he is also handsome has frequently been obscured by the dark scowl deemed appropriate to several of the characters he has been called upon to play. Equipped to become well-known and popular like Matt Dillon, with whom he acted in his debut film, *My Bodyguard* (1980), stardom has eluded him, perhaps because his films have not proved lucky vehicles for him.

He made his debut playing the title role in *My Bodyguard* (1980), an unpretentious teen film dealing in adult themes of extortion, protection and revenge, in which he portrayed a silent, scowling bully who turns out to be a traumatised victim of circumstance and, ultimately, a hero. It was not uninteresting, Baldwin was fine, and one of the co-stars was Matt Dillon, but the movie went nowhere. He was one of the crowd in his next three, which included a feeble comedy, *D.C. Cab* (1983), before landing another lead in *Bad Guys* (1986, not to be confused with the Sean Penn vehicle, *Bad Boys*). Unrecognisable thanks to a head of dyed bright-blond hair, he played a young cop who, suspended from duty, takes up wrestling, but not before a spell as a male stripper. The movie was abysmal and Baldwin unremarkable, but Kubrick nonetheless cast him in *Full Metal Jacket* (1987). In this excoriating vision of the Vietnam War, Adam turned up in the second half as Animal, a soldier who has to take over command of a platoon threatened by hidden snipers, only to make a hideous mess of the job. Role and performance were memorable, giving notice that here was a valuable candidate for portraits of derangement.

Cohen and Tate (1989), the directorial debut of Eric Red who wrote *The Hitcher* (1986), was a high-intensity, if low-brained, thriller with Cohen (Roy Scheider), an old pro at the assassination game, lumbered with redneck Tate (Baldwin) for a partner. Tate kills for thrills. Together they have to deliver a newly orphaned (they killed the parents) nine-year-old boy to the Mob, but the kid proves too smart for the redneck and too young for the pro. The movie showed Baldwin at his hulking, six-foot-four best, convincingly menacing, sulky, moronically joking, and subject to sudden and violent fits of rage. A nasty and compelling little movie, it was insufficiently widely shown to elevate Baldwin's status but, given his part in *Next of Kin* the same year, marked him for typecasting as a psychopathic killer.

1980 My Bodyguard; Ordinary People **1983** D.C. Cab **1984** Reckless **1986** Bad Guys; 3.15 **1987** Going All The Way; Full Metal Jacket **1988** The Chocolate War **1989** Cohen And Tate; Next Of Kin **1990** Predator 2 **1992** Radio Flyer; Where The Day Takes You **1992/93** Deadbolt

Baldwin, Alec

Actor

Born 3 April 1958

Massapequa, New York

Dark – thanks to dying his naturally fair hair – and clean-cut with cover-boy good looks, piercing blue eyes and a dazzling smile, Alec Baldwin was one of the most versatile younger actors to emerge in the late 1980s and quickly found himself on the way to becoming a star character actor.

One of six children (four of whom, including William, are actors), Alec swapped an early ambition to be a lawyer for an acting career. A notably hard worker, he combined studies at the Lee Strasberg Theatre Institute in New York with daytime appearances on a popular soap, *The Doctors*, and stage work at night in a production of *A Midsummer Night's Dream*.

After moving to Los Angeles, he kept busy in television, notably in *Knots Landing*, and made his big-screen debut in *Forever Lulu* (1986). He quickly displayed his virtuosity and versatility, disappearing under hair dye and dialect in a string of juicy and varied supporting roles: a spectral stooge to Michael Keaton's somewhat less than blithe spirit, Betelguese, in *Beetlejuice* (1987); the lecherous minor Mafioso, Tony 'Cucumber' DeMarco, in *Married To The Mob* (1988), too much of a 'wise guy' to survive the second reel; Melanie Griffith's roughneck cheating boyfriend in *Working Girl* the same year; Kevin Bacon's so-called best friend, a degenerate smoothie, in *She's Having A Baby* (also 1988). He ended the year as the station boss in Oliver Stone's *Talk Radio*, a more straightforward character, and, in 1989, via a not altogether successful portrayal of evangelist Jimmy Swaggart to Dennis Quaid's Jerry Lee Lewis in *Great Balls Of Fire!*, he found himself completing a remarkable 18 months of activity by stepping up a notch to play the dogged CIA analyst hot on the trail of a defecting Soviet nuclear submarine in *The Hunt For Red October* (1989), starring Sean Connery. Although Paramount wanted Baldwin to reprise his Jack Ryan role in the projected series of sequels, the industry was astounded when he passed on *Patriot Games* in order to play Stanley Kowalski in the 1991 Broadway revival of *A Streetcar Named Desire*. (He received a Tony nomination for his efforts.)

Baldwin showed indisputable star quality in *Miami Blues* (1989), cast as a crew-cut charmer and casual psychopath, whose chilling amorality recalled the fatal attraction of Robert Walker's Bruno Anthony in Hitchcock's *Strangers On A Train* back in 1951. It was a bravura portrayal of the chameleon con-man who, in turn, embodies the American myth of the infinitely transformable self, but now that Baldwin (who, by the 90s, was enjoying a publicised liaison with Kim Basinger, with whom he co-starred in the ill-received *The Marrying Man*, 1991) has made it to the big time he should take care take that his seductive smile does not become a self-satisfied smirk.

1986 Forever Lulu **1987** Beetlejuice **1988** Married To The Mob; Working Girl; She's Having A Baby; Talk Radio **1989** Miami Blues; Great Balls Of Fire!; The Hunt For Red October **1990** Alice **1991** The Marrying Man aka Too Hot To Handle; **1992** Prelude To A Kiss; Glengarry Ross **1993** Damages

Baldwin, William

Actor

Born ?

Massapequa, New York

William Baldwin is the brother of Alec, Daniel and Stephen. A graduate in political science from the State University of New York at Binghamton, he worked briefly on Capitol Hill but, inspired by Alec's success, soon decided to pursue a career in acting.

After a couple of years relying on advertisements for work, William attracted attention with his portrayal of Robert Chambers in the television docu-drama *The Preppie Murder*. Oliver Stone, for whom Alec Baldwin featured in *Talk Radio* (1989), gave William a small role in *Born On The Fourth Of July* (1989) as Baldy, a member of Ron Kovic's platoon. But it was *Internal Affairs* (1990) that provided him with his first substantial feature film role. As Van Stretch, Richard Gere's drug-addicted partner, Baldwin sketched a memorable portrait of emotional instability and mental confusion in a few brief scenes. He also shared in director Mike Figgis' best sequence, when Gere at once cradles Van Stretch and breaks his neck. A taller, slimmer, darker version of his brother Alec, the callowness of youth in his first roles, together with a wary reserve about the eyes, made him the more distinctive of the two physically. Joel Schumacher made good use of his ready sexuality and haunted, distracted demeanour in the ambitious but otherwise questionable *Flatliners* (1990). This trite science-fantasy was such a hit with youth audiences that William Baldwin's future looked very bright, and he subsequently co-starred with Kurt Russell and Robert De Niro in the firefighting saga *Backdraft* (1991), but Alec's stardom was not yet forthcoming for his striking sibling.

1989 Born On The Fourth Of July **1990** Internal Affairs;

Flatliners **1991** Backdraft **1992/93** Three Of Hearts **1993** Sliver

Bancroft, Anne
(Anna Maria Louisa Italiano)
Actress
Born 17 September 1931
New York City

When Anne Bancroft returned triumphantly to Hollywood and won the Best Actress Oscar for *The Miracle Worker* (1962) after five years on Broadway, it was difficult for filmgoers to believe that she was the same actress who had previously had such an undistinguished film career.

The daughter of Italian immigrants, she was educated at the American Academy of Dramatic Arts and the Actors' Studio. Under the name of Anne Marno, she appeared in TV dramas before taking up a contract with Fox in 1952. Discouraged by a string of routine gangster movies and Westerns, she returned to New York where she soon made a name for herself on Broadway in two William Gibson plays, *Two For The Seesaw* and *The Miracle Worker*. In both the stage and film versions of the latter, her performance as Annie Sullivan, the partially blind teacher to the deaf, dumb and blind Helen Keller, combined vitality with complexity to reveal the character's own psychological needs.

Other emotional roles came in *The Pumpkin Eater* (1964), as the child-bearing-obsessed woman trying to save her crumbling marriage, and the would-be suicide in *The Slender Thread* (1965). So it was a surprise when the actress, who had seldom played comedy, proved perfect in the role of Mrs Robinson, the alluring older woman who coolly seduces a fumbling Dustin Hoffman as *The Graduate* (1967), for which she was Oscar-nominated.

Curiously, for someone of her abilities, her output since has been extremely variable. Among the rare good parts was Jack Lemmon's yelling wife in Neil Simon's urban comedy nightmare, *The Prisoner Of Second Avenue* (1975); Shirley MacLaine's cattish friend-rival in the soap ballet film *The Turning Point* (1977); a mother superior in *Agnes Of God* (1985), for which she received another Oscar nomination, and Helene Hanff in *84 Charing Cross Road* (1986), tenderly and wittily writing letters from New York to London bookseller Anthony Hopkins.

In the early 70s Bancroft became the wife of Mel Brooks, her second marriage, and had a son, Max. (Her first marriage was to a real estate man between 1953 and 1957) As if to reassure Brooks' Yiddish momma, the former Miss Italiano played Israeli premier Golda Meir on Broadway, went over the top as the Jewish 'Ma' in *Torch Song Trilogy* (1988), and wore herself out as mama ministering to her difficult men in *Broadway Bound*, the third of Neil Simon's Brighton Beach memoirs.

1952 Don't Bother To Knock **1953** The Kid From Left Field; Tonight We Sing; Treasure Of The Golden Condor **1954** Demetrius And The Gladiators; Gorilla At Large; The Raid **1955** The Last Frontier; A Life In The Balance; The Naked Street; New York Confidential; **1956** Nightfall; Walk The Proud Land **1957** The Girl In Black Stockings; The Restless Breed **1962** The Miracle Worker **1964** The Pumpkin Eater **1965** The Slender Thread **1966** Seven Women **1967** The Graduate **1972** Young Winston **1975** The Prisoner Of Second Avenue; The Hindenburg **1976** Lipstick; Silent Movie **1977** The Turning Point; Jesus Of Nazareth **1979** Fatso (also w/d) **1980** The Elephant Man **1983** To Be Or Not To Be **1984** Garbo Talks **1985** Agnes Of God **1986** 'night Mother; 84 Charing Cross Road **1988** Torch Song Trilogy; Bert Rigby, You're A Fool **1992** Broadway Bound; Mr Jones; Honeymoon In Vegas **1993** The Specialist aka Nikita

Barkin, Ellen
Actress
Born ? 1954
The Bronx, New York

Ellen Barkin has all the equipment of a major star: presence, sex appeal, great instinct and technical skill. But the consistently high quality of her work and the calibre of her credits has thus far been rewarded with only one unqualified box-office success (1989's *Sea Of Love*) and a handful of *succès d'estimes*.

Barkin was born and raised in the New York borough of the Bronx. From the High School for the Performing Arts she went on to theatre studies at Hunter College and juggled subsequent drama training with jobs like waitressing for a few years before she had the confidence to accept the offer of an off-Broadway role. Her film debut came in Barry Levinson's first and highly regarded feature, *Diner* (1982), in which she appeared as the neglected young wife of obsessive record collector Daniel Stern. Work for prestigious directors quickly followed: another taken-for-granted, unhappy wife (to Timothy Hutton) in Sidney Lumet's absorbing but commercially doomed *Daniel* (1983); Oscar-winning Robert Duvall's estranged daughter in Bruce Beresford's *Tender Mercies* (1983); the sympathetic, pregnant girl-next-door to Paul Newman and Robby Benson in Newman's *Harry And Son* (1984). While these were well-drawn supporting characters, Barkin positively shone in a principal role as a loveless, hard-pressed but enduring young mother settling for the awkward courting of a dreary man after her husband has abandoned her in the low-budget minor gem *Enormous Changes At The Last Minute* (1983), an adaptation of three loosely connected feminist tales by Grace Paley, scripted by John Sayles with Susan Rice and directed by Mirra Bank and Ellen Hovde.

From put-upon housewives Barkin departed into bottle-swigging tough cookies, raucous hookers and sexually combustible floozies, providing memorable vignettes in films good – *Desert Bloom* and *Down By Law* (both 1986) – bad – *The Adventures Of Buckaroo Banzai Across The Eighth Dimension* (1984) – and indifferent – Alan Rudolph's *Made In Heaven* (1987). It was as the vulnerable, anxious, repressed and uncompromising assistant DA in Jim McBride's unusual and flavourful romantic thriller *The Big Easy* (1987), however, that she tightened her grip on the hearts of her devoted, if not yet massive, following. Playing uptight but undone by Dennis Quaid's easy charm, Barkin and her co-star delivered one of the steamiest clothed sex scenes in modern memory in a film treasured by a fervent minority.

An unhappy and troubled shoot for the unfortunate experimental supernatural thriller *Siesta* (1987) did nothing for this unusual looking actress' career, although she bore all the weight of a baffling picture and an unappealing character on her strong shoulders. She did, however, marry her leading man, Irish actor Gabriel Byrne, with whom she has a son, Jack.

Despite its implausibilities – could such a tempting and highly-toned blonde bomb need to look for men in the personal ads? – Barkin's seductive, enigmatic performance as the did-she-or-didn't-she-do-'em-in serial murder suspect in *Sea Of Love* (1989) pleased audiences and the accountants. Much vaunted as Al Pacino's 'comeback' vehicle, it was equally notable as Barkin's big-time 'arrival'. Testing her range further, Barkin played a male chauvinist reincarnated in the body of – what else but? – a smart, sexy blonde in Blake Edwards' unsuccessful *Switch* (1991) and, alas, went on to the female lead in one of 1992's major flops, *Man Trouble.*

1982 Diner **1983** Daniel; Tender Mercies; Enormous Changes At The Last Minute **1984** Eddie And The Cruisers; Harry And Son; The Adventures Of Buckaroo Banzai Across The Eight Dimension **1986** Desert Bloom; Down By Law **1987** Made In Heaven (unbilled); The Big Easy; Siesta **1988** Clinton And Nadine aka Blood Money, **1989** Sea Of Love **1990** Johnny Handsome **1991** Switch **1992** Man Trouble; Mac; Into The West

Barrymore, Drew (Andrew Barrymore)

Actress
Born 22 February 1975
Los Angeles, California

Acting is Drew Barrymore's birthright. When you consider her background, it is hardly surprising that she began her own career when she was 11 months old. Her actor father, John Jr, is the son of the legendary matinee idol John, making Lionel and Ethel, the other famous Barrymores, Drew's great uncle and aunt.

The child made her debut in a TV commercial when she was less than a year old, and followed this at the age of two-and-a-half with a part in the TV movie *Suddenly Love*, with Cindy Williams. She had to wait until she had reached the ripe old age of four before she broke into the movies, appearing as William Hurt's daughter in Ken Russell's excursion into psychedelia, *Altered States* (1980). It was her next role that hauled the by now seven-year-old into stardom, and demonstrated she had as much to offer as actors three times her age. The film was Steven Spielberg's *E.T. The Extra-Terrestrial* (1982), and young Drew could not have have had a better start to her career – the film was possibly the biggest grossing movie of the decade. Together with her young co-star, Henry Thomas, and the loveable alien himself, Drew stood out from the more seasoned actors and was singled out for praise as Gertie, the little girl who teaches E.T. to speak.

Next came *Irreconcilable Differences* (1984), in which she played the brattish daughter of a warring couple (Ryan O'Neal and Shelley Long) who decides to divorce her parents. The film aroused only the mildest flicker of interest, but at least the young actress was able to prove that she could play both adorable and irritating little girls with equal facility. Directly following on from these supporting roles she won her first lead, at the age of nine, in the horror flick *Firestarter* (1984), based on the Stephen King bestseller, and found herself in the company of such heavyweights as Martin Sheen, George C. Scott and Louise Fletcher. As a small girl with the power to set things alight by thought alone, Drew set the film on fire, but could not do enough to save it from adverse criticism. Undeterred, she returned to the big screen in another Stephen King adaptation, *Cat's Eye* (1985), a trio of horror shorts linked by a roaming cat, in which she appeared in the final episode. After a slew of bad reviews, the ten-year old actress retired until 1989, but she was by no means out of the limelight.

Numerous newspapers related her unfortunate slide into drug addiction, her subsequent rehabilitation, and her metamorphosis into a teenage sex siren, posing in revealing clothes at 14 years of age. Despite the bad publicity, the actress picked herself up and returned to films in 1989, first in a TV movie about drug abuse, *Fifteen And Getting Straight* (1989), and then as Jeff Bridges' daughter in the romance-drama *See You In The Morning* (1989). She entered the 90s hopefully set to continue the Barrymore succession.

1980 Altered States **1982** E.T. The Extra-Terrestrial **1984** Irreconcilable Differences; Firestarter **1985** Cat's Eye **1989** Far From Home; See You In The Morning **1992** Poison Ivy; Sketch Artist; Gun Crazy **1992/93** Doppelganger

Bartel, Paul

Actor, director
Born August 1938
New Jersey

'I'm very interested in doing eccentric, individual low-budget films,' said Paul Bartel early in his career, and he has not swerved from that intention. It was *Death Race 2000* (1975), a typical low-budget Roger Corman production, that gave the unknown Bartel the chance to make a name for himself. A campy, sci-fi comedy which, like the best comic-books, caricatured the horrors of contemporary society, the film involved a trans-American car race in which every pedestrian is fair game, the winner being determined by the quickest time and the highest body count. Although much of it was Corman's conception, many of the quirky, nasty bits were certainly Bartel's. It was a terrific hit with the Saturday night crowd, and as a result Corman gave him another car-crash movie, *Cannonball*, the following year. The comedy was broader but no less black than the first, and among the 'in' jokes were appearances by Corman (as a DA who wants to ban the cross-country race), Martin Scorsese, Sylvester Stallone and Bartel himself – bald, bearded and portly.

Bartel came to the movies after taking a four-year course in film and theatre at UCLA. On a Fulbright scholarship, he spent a year at the Centro Sperimentale film school in Rome, before returning to the States to make television commercials, as well as a couple of comic-erotic shorts, *The Secret Cinema* (1966) and *Naughty Nurse* (1970), and, in stark contrast, *Preludio Olímpico* (1968), a 12-minute introduction to the Olympic Games in Mexico City.

But what Bartel really wanted to do was make bad-taste sexual comedies on the lines of his first feature, *Private Parts* (1972), which told of a teenage runaway girl who takes refuge in a seedy San Francisco hotel inhabited exclusively by perverts. It took six years before he could raise the budget for another movie close to his heart. While he was serving on the jury of the 1979 Berlin Film Festival he wrote the initial script for *Eating Raoul*. Filming began in November 1980, a weekend at a time, and was finished over a year later.

'I wanted to make a film about two greedy, uptight people who are at the same time not so unlike you and me and Nancy and Ronnie, to keep it funny and yet communicate something about the perversity of these values,' Bartel explained. The director and Mary Woronov (from Andy Warhol's Factory) were Paul and Mary Bland – they had previously appeared together in *Hollywood Boulevard* (1976) and *Rock 'n' Roll High School* (1979) – who dream of buying a house in the country and opening their own restaurant. But the only way they can get it is by knocking off every sleazeball in Hollywood by means of a frying pan. The couple were played in a wonderfully straight manner that made all the funnier the fact that they were the only normal people in the movie aside from the incidental fact that they kill people. Black comedy is a difficult thing to carry off, but Bartel struck the right comic chord from the start, and there is not a drop of blood visible.

After this funny, off-the-wall satire on LA swingers, the director turned out a surprisingly tame comedy, *Not For Publication*, and a tiresomely camp B-Western spoof, *Lust In The Dust* (both 1984), before returning to the comicsadistic world of *Eating Raoul* with *Scenes From The Class Struggle In Beverly Hills* (1989). But, whereas the former film had a unity of tone, this was an unfocused, soft-focus, unamusing soap-opera lampoon, frenziedly trying to shock. 'You live long enough you're bound to do some weird shit,' says one of the characters, a remark that one need not dwell on. The movie ends with the Cole Porter song 'Let's Be Outrageous (Let's Misbehave)', something Bartel has done both well and badly over the last few years.

As actor only unless stated otherwise: **1969** Hi, Mom! (cameo) **1972** Private Parts (also director) **1975** Death Race 2000 (also director) **1976** Cannonball aka Carquake (also director); Hollywood Boulevard; Eat My Dust **1977** Grand Theft Auto; Mr Billion **1978** Piranha **1979** Rock 'n' Roll High School **1981** Heartbeeps **1982** Eating Raoul (w/d); Trick Or Treats; White Dog **1983** Heart Like A Wheel; Get Crazy **1984** Lust In The Dust (also director); Not For Publication (also director) **1985** The Longshot (also director); Into The Night (cameo); National Lampoon's European Vacation **1986** Chopping Mall; Killer Party **1988** Shakedown; Caddyshack II **1989** Scenes From The Class Struggle In Beverly Hills (also director) **1990** Gremlins 2: The New Batch **1991** The Pope Must Die **1992** Desire And Hell At Sunset Motel

Basinger, Kim

Actress
Born 8 December 1953
Athens, Georgia

The spotlight first fell on Kim Basinger as a model for Breck shampoo (like her mother before her), and for Ford in New York. She can also claim credit as a *Playboy* centrefold, and, for a time, pursued a singing career under the *nom-de-chant* Chelsea before breaking into TV work. Her lissom and uninhibited body and pronounced 'bee-stung' mouth have attracted a large male following – sufficiently so to keep her in work to date, but most of her roles could not be described as much more than decorative.

A native Southerner, Basinger can turn a mean Southern accent as so far used in at least four of her movies, *Hard Country* (1981, her debut), Sam Shepard's *Fool For Love* (1985, perhaps her best and most interesting performance), *No Mercy* (1985), in which she was fairly memorably dragged through a Louisiana swamp by Richard Gere, and Robert Benton's unconvincing comedy-thriller, *Nadine* (1987), in which she had some appealing moments opposite Jeff Bridges. But she is primarily noted for her sex appeal and became a name with *9½ Weeks* (1985), the mildly notorious pseudo soft-porn caper in which she willingly stripped for Mickey Rourke – after which she got uncontrollably drunk with Bruce Willis in the inordinately silly *Blind Date* (1987) and was little more than decorative as Vicki Vale, love interest of *Batman*, in 1989.

Basinger is one of a veritable explosion of long-haired blondes to make an impression during the 80s. To date, however, she has displayed limited talent and suffers from comparison with competitors such as Ellen Barkin, Meg Ryan and Michelle Pfeiffer. Nonetheless, her box-office clout outstrips them all and she herself has grown exceedingly rich, which doesn't displease her, and she's nothing if not canny with her money: besides giving the queen of Hollywood real-estate wealth, Jackie Bisset, something to think about, Basinger bought herself a town in her home state of Georgia! Not short of admirers, she went into the 90s involved in a close liaison with Alec Baldwin.

1981 Hard Country **1982** Mother Lode **1983** The Man Who Loved Women; Never Say Never Again **1984** The Natural **1985** Fool For Love; 9½ Weeks; No Mercy **1987** Blind Date; Nadine **1988** My Stepmother Is An Alien **1989** Batman **1991** The Marrying Man aka Too Hot To Handle **1992** Cool World; Final Analysis

Bates, Kathy

Actress
Born 28 June 1948
Memphis, Tennessee

But for director Rob Reiner's determination not to cast a star in *Misery* (1990), Kathy Bates might never have become one – not, at any rate, of the Hollywood variety. She would have continued, in all probability, to mix small parts in films and television shows with the considerably more substantial stage work that had given her her best roles. The daughter of a mechanical engineer, she graduated from the Southern Methodist University in Dallas before moving to New York in 1969 and eventually landing a blink-and-you'll-miss-it bit in Milos Forman's *Taking Off* (1971) and nothing else. Moving to Hollywood she was told, in no uncertain terms, that she wasn't attractive enough for movies and too fat for daytime TV. Only on stage, first in Virginia with 1973's *Virginia Folk Tales*, and later New York, was she allowed to show her talent with plays such as *The Fifth Of July*, *Come Back To The Five And Dime, Jimmy Dean, Jimmy Dean* (repeating her role in Robert Altman's 1982 film) and, best of all, her Tony-nominated role as the suicidal daughter in *'night, Mother* (1983), a considerably more substantial and moving portrayal than Sissy Spacek's in the later film version.

It wasn't until *White Palace* (1990) that she got a really noticeable film role (as James Spader's boss and confidante), but it was her Annie Wilkes in Reiner's *Misery* that was to earn her a place in the hall of fame – as well as a coveted Oscar for Best Actress. One of the most believable movie psychopaths of all time, her sweetly devoted fan of James Caan's injured novelist believes absolutely in the rationality and normality of her behaviour, unexpectedly exploding her resentment at her life's disappointments over little things, yet perfectly calm as she cripples the object of her affections without ever tipping the balance into laughable hysteria.

She continued in not dissimilar vein with the unsympathetic wife of missionary Aidan Quinn, uncomfortable with herself and the natives and ultimately driven to insanity – 'like Annie Wilkes' sister who went off and became a missionary' – in Hector Babenco's *At Play In The Fields Of The Lord* (1991), only to find the role Terence McNally wrote for her (and which won her an Obie Award in 1988) in *Frankie And Johnny At The Claire De Lune* going to Michelle ('I-hate-being-beautiful') Pfeiffer instead. But that was before the Oscar that made Kathy Bates an infinitely more attractive proposition to casting directors and which seemed certain to secure her at least some roles comparable to her stage successes.

1971 Taking Off **1978** Straight Time **1982** Come Back To The Five And Dime, Jimmy Dean, Jimmy Dean **1983** Two Of A Kind **1986** The Morning After **1987** Summer Heat **1988** Arthur 2: On The Rocks **1989** High Stakes; Signs Of Life **1990** White Palace; Men Don't Leave Misery **1991** At Play In The Fields Of The Lord; The Road To Mecca **1991** Fried Green Tomatoes At The Whistle Stop Café **1992** Shadows And Fog; Prelude To A Kiss; Used People **1993** A Home Of Our Own

Beals, Jennifer

Actress
Born 19 December 1963
Chicago, Illinois

Few recent film careers have commenced as promisingly as that of Jennifer Beals, whose debut in the lead of *Flashdance* (1983) shot her to instant celebrity status. (A previous film credit, 1980's *My Bodyguard*, was a walk-on appearance as an extra when she was still a high school student). Although Beals did not actually dance in the sleeper hit – hoofer Martine Jehan doubled for her in the film's arresting, gymnastic musical sequences – no one much cared as the romantic piffle about a girl steel welder in Pittsburgh aspiring to become a ballerina became one of the biggest grossing films of its time, with Beals striking a chord in audiences as something of a daintier Rocky, the poor kid who makes a dream come true.

Rather than immediately capitalizing on this overnight stardom, the academically motivated Beals returned to her degree course in American Studies at the prestigious Yale University, where she graduated with honours. To date, the momentum of her acting career which began with *Flashdance* has yet to be recovered.

In 1984 she took another break from university to star with singer and sometime actor Sting in a well-dressed, ill-conceived and shockingly received version of the horror classic *The Bride Of Frankenstein* as the eponymous gothic heroine of *The Bride* (1985). Three years later, she received second billing but had little to do as a bafflingly enigmatic fantasy figure in suspender belt and stockings who triggers Nicolas Cage's Draculean psychosis in the off-beat black tragi-comedy *Vampire's Kiss*, which was not released until 1990. As the obligatory love interest in a family melodrama, *Split Decisions* (1988), which starred Gene Hackman, she fared little better.

Her study of acting, directing, set design and playwriting suggested Beals was intent on a serious career, but her selection of roles to date has scarcely realised her ambitions. Since 1986, she has been married to Alexandre Rockwell, a writer-director with whom she was hoping to collaborate on a film.

1980 My Bodyguard **1983** Flashdance **1985** The Bride **1988** La Partita; Split Decisions **1989** Vampire's Kiss **1991** Doctor M; Tinikling aka La Madone Et Le Dragon (France); Blood And Concrete **1992** In The Soup **1992/93** Day Of Atonement

Beatty, Ned

Actor
Born 6 July 1937
Louisville, Kentucky

Ned Beatty is in many ways the archetypal American character actor – the actor who finds a character that suits him and simply shades it in with exuberance or restraint, as the film in question demands. For much of his screen career, Beatty has put his large build and deep voice in the service of a series of bullish oafs (the corrupt politician of *Switching Channels*, 1988) and idiots (Lex Luthor's incompetent sidekick in *Superman*, 1978) as well as more restrained performances in similar moulds – the crooked, but still very human cop of *The Big Easy* (1986) and the Oscar-nominated, coldly logical chairman of the board in *Network* (1976) among them.

Beatty originally intended to become a clergyman but caught the acting bug with a high school production of *Harvey*. By the age of 21 he was playing Big Daddy on stage in *Cat On A Hot Tin Roof* against actors five years older than him playing his children, but it was not until his appearance in the Broadway production of *The Great White Hope* that he was spotted by director John Boorman and made his movie debut.

Utterly convincing as probably the screen's first male rape victim in Boorman's *Deliverance* (1972), his assured and believable performance quickly made him one of the most sought-after supporting players in American movies in both comedy and drama, although an unfortunate side-effect of his first film was a later succession of windbags as part of Burt Reynolds' stock company, which left him little to do but make Reynolds look good. Like Michael Caine, with Beatty it is often a case of having to sit through four bad films and autopilot performances to find one good one – a price of his almost constant work, equally divided between film and TV – and while in later years casting directors seemed to forget just how very impressive he could be with good material, Ned Beatty has nevertheless proved one of the most durable and easily cast of actors, proving particularly beguiling as Irish tenor Josef Locke in the Anglo-Irish sleeper hit, *Hear My Song* (1991).

1972 Deliverance; The Life and Times of Judge Roy Bean **1973** The Thief Who Came To Dinner; White Lightning; The Last American Hero **1975** W.W. And The Dixie Dancekings; Nashville **1976** All The President's Men; The Big Bus; Network; Silver Streak; Mikey and Nicky **1977** Exorcist II: The Heretic; Alambrista!; The Great Bank Hoax aka Shenanigans; **1978** Gray Lady Down; Superman **1979** Promises in the Dark; 1941; Wise Blood **1980** Hopscotch; The American Success Company; Superman II **1981** The Incredible Shrinking Woman **1982** The Toy **1983** Stroker Ace; Touched; The Ballad of Gregorio Cortez **1985** Restless Natives **1986** Back To School; The Big Easy **1987** Rolling Vengeance; The Fourth Protocol; The Trouble With Spies; Shadows in the Storm **1988** The Unholy; Midnight Crossing; Switching Channels; Physical Evidence; The Purple People Eater; The Passage **1989** Time Trackers; Ministry of Vengeance; Tennessee Nights; Chattahoochee **1990** Dive! aka Submarine!; Repossessed; A Cry in the Wild; Big Bad John; Captain America **1991** Hear My Song; Black Creek **1992** Prelude To A Kiss

Beatty, Warren
(Warren Beaty)

Actor, director, writer
Born 30 March 1937
Richmond, Virginia

It is difficult to believe that Warren Beatty has made only 19 films in 30 years. He has always seemed to be in pictures or in the public eye since his screen debut as a randy adolescent in Elia Kazan's *Splendor In The Grass* (1961), a role he has been playing, on and off screen, ever since.

A millionaire many times over, he is, according to his older sister, Shirley MacLaine, 'very much into money'. He is also very much into women, and has had affairs with co-stars Natalie Wood (*Splendor In The Grass*), Leslie Caron (*Promise Her Anything* – her husband Peter Hall named Beatty co-respondent in their divorce), Julie Christie (*Shampoo*), Diane Keaton (*Reds*), Isabelle Adjani (*Ishtar*) and Madonna (*Dick Tracy*), as well as Susan Strasberg, singer-actress Michelle Phillips and Joyce Hyser, ex-girlfriend of Bruce Springsteen, to whom he was engaged for a short period. He seemed destined to remain a bachelor, and his inability to sustain a relationship, combined with his arrogant persona, led actress Mamie Van Doren to say, 'Warren is the type of man who will end up dying in his own arms.' But then came his famous tumble for *Bugsy* co-star Annette Bening, which led rapidly to fatherhood and a conversion to domestic stability.

But Beatty is not just a pretty face, even though his dark good looks, big brown eyes, laid-back sexuality and off-screen affairs have dominated the public's perception of him. He was the astute producer of the profitable *Bonnie And Clyde* (1967), *Shampoo* (1975), and *Heaven Can Wait* (1978) which he co-directed, and was the director-star of *Reds*

(1981) and *Dick Tracy* (1990). Having reached the age of 54, his production of *Bugsy* (1991) enjoyed huge critical and commercial success, garnering the Los Angeles Critics award for Best Picture, and a hefty ten Oscar nominations, including one for Beatty's performance – his best ever – as the charming, quixotic and vicious sociopath, Bugsy Siegel. Also, on second glance, one realises that many of the roles he has played have gone against his reputation as an insatiable Don Juan.

'I told you I wasn't no lover boy,' he says as the gangster Clyde, who is actually impotent (and whose incarnation was one of Beatty's best performances). In *Shampoo*, as George Roundy, the hairdresser who woos every desirable woman in Beverly Hills, he ends up as an exhausted, hollow wreck. One of the few ideas in the disastrous *Ishtar* (1987) was the casting of lover-boy Beatty as a nebbish, useless with women, and Dustin Hoffman as a character irresistible to the opposite sex. To emphasise this Beatty wears square clothes and woolly hats, and cannot pronounce 'schmuck' even though he is one. In the title role of *Dick Tracy*, he is again the sexual innocent, unconvincingly resisting seduction by Madonna.

He has, though, given ample display of sexual and heroic prowess in other movies. In his second film, *The Roman Spring Of Mrs Stone* (1961), he played the Italian gigolo from whom an ageing Vivian Leigh buys favours. At first Tennessee Williams, on whose novella the film was based, was opposed to the casting of Beatty, claiming he was too American, but the actor convinced the writer of his suitability by demonstrating his Italian accent to him. But he was more at home as the nihilistic stud in *All Fall Down* (1962), written by William Inge. Beatty had appeared previously on Broadway in Inge's *A Loss Of Roses*, before the playwright urged Kazan to cast him in his screenplay of *Splendor In The Grass*, thus setting him on the road to stardom.

With his sister, to whom he was not close, Beatty started acting as a child in amateur productions directed by their mother, a drama coach. He was a star footballer at Washington Lee High School in Arlington, Virginia – he later did his own stunt work in the commercially successful but feeble football fantasy, *Heaven Can Wait* – and, after a year at Northwestern University, he dropped out and did various manual jobs while taking drama lessons with Stella Adler.

Early on in his career Beatty took risks by appearing in two off-beat films – *Lilith* (1963), Robert Rossen's poetic and intelligent study of schizophrenia, in which he was the sensitive trainee therapist, and Arthur Penn's over-symbolic *Mickey One* (1965), in which he played the paranoid nightclub performer of the title. *Reds* was a courageous film to make, not only in Hollywood but in Reagan's America. (Beatty calls himself a liberal Democrat and has campaigned on behalf of John F. Kennedy, Eugene McCarthy and Gary Hart.) But this ambitious project, beautifully photographed by Vittorio Storaro, was directed with little pace, while its images of the Russian Revolution had been done better elsewhere; and the presence of 'actual witnesses' made one long for a documentary instead of the romantic Reds-on-the-bed guff that passed for truth. Beatty himself was too bland in the role of American Communist John Reed.

Blandness too, was a weakness in his weary portrayal of Dick Tracy in the loudly-hyped film referred to in the business as 'Warren's Dick'. Unlike many of the other characters, he wore no prosthetic mask, but looked as if ageing lines had been drawn over his still-handsome face. Although entertaining and visually striking, it was a mindless movie, with two-dimensional characters more applicable to the genre of the comic-book from which it derived.

Like Howard Hughes, the man he has always wanted to portray on screen, Warren Beatty prefers not to give too many interviews and tries to retain a mystique about his real character. Mainly because of this attitude, this unpredictable, enigmatic Hollywood personality remains fascinating to the public.

As actor only unless stated otherwise: **1961** Splendor In The Grass; The Roman Spring Of Mrs Stone **1962** All Fall Down **1964** Lilith **1965** Mickey One **1966** Promise Her Anything; Kaleidoscope **1967** Bonnie And Clyde **1970** The Only Game In Town **1971** Dollars; McCabe And Mrs Miller **1973** Year Of The Woman (docu) **1974** The Parallax View **1975** Shampoo (also co-writer); The Fortune **1978** Heaven Can Wait (also co-director, co-writer) **1981** Reds (also director, co-writer) **1987** Ishtar **1990** Dick Tracy (also director, co-writer) **1991** Truth Or Dare (GB: In Bed With Madonna) (docu); Bugsy

Bedelia, Bonnie

Actress
Born 25 March 1952
Yorkville, New York

The Hollywood career of Bonnie Bedelia has been rather a stop-go affair in terms of both frequency and importance of roles. Her noticeable absences from the screen were partly voluntary: she preferred to concentrate on family life for a few years, confining her acting work to the less strenuous demands on her time made by television. Nonetheless, for an actress of such innate quality to have been so under-used hints at a lack of perception, or persistence, on the part of producers.

The most major, high-profile and acclaimed role of her career came with *Heart Like A Wheel* (1984), Jonathan Kaplan's biopic about triple world champion drag-racer Shirley Muldowney. Bedelia's performance, spanning Muldowney's life from thrill-seeking teenager, through marriage and motherhood, to racing success in her 40s, honestly and eloquently revealed the multi-faceted development of the woman. For this actress is characterised by honesty and depth of interpretation, and by the well-judged restraint that makes less mean more.

God-given talent and the taste for using it were in evidence very early in Bonnie's life. She studied ballet from the age of four, won a scholarship to the School of American Ballet at eight, and appeared with the New York City Ballet over a period of three years in between acting, which she began at nine in a production of *Tom Sawyer*. She continued in summer stock and off-Broadway, had bit parts on television and, by the time she was 13, had landed herself a role in a daytime TV series, *Love of Life*. Contrary to what her schedule might indicate, she did go to high school, at the same time studying acting at Quintano's School for young pros. She later took classes with the distinguished Uta Hagen, but preferred working with what she termed 'creative' directors to being taught. By the time she was 18, she had four Broadway plays to her credit, including *My Sweet Charlie*, opposite Lou Gossett, for which she won the 1967 Theater World Award. She went to LA at the invitation of director Andre Gregory and continued her stage and TV work there, making her screen debut in John Frankenheimer's *The Gypsy Moths* (1969) as the girl in thrall to the daredevil air-circus feats of Burt Lancaster and Gene Hackman.

Soon after, Sydney Pollack cast Bonnie, who had been voted the Most Promising Personality of 1969, as Ruby, the pregnant and desperate marathon dancer, in *They Shoot Horses, Don't They*? (1970). However, far from graduating to big leads and star status thereafter, she had a catalyst role as Gig Young's about-to-be-married daughter in *Lovers And Other Strangers* (1970), reaped no benefits from *The Strange Vengeance Of Rosalie* (1972) or the Canadian *Between Friends* (1973), and virtually retired from the big screen but for an all too brief appearance as Richard Dreyfuss' ex-wife in *The Big Fix* (1978). Her television roles in the ten-year interim before *Heart Like A Wheel* were numerous but the vehicles largely unmemorable, and the Kaplan film came as something of a surprise to those audiences and critics who had all but forgotten her.

The resuscitation of Bedelia's Hollywood career seemed to be following much the same course the second time around. However, her appearance in *Die Hard* (1988) as Bruce Willis' estranged wife, a high-powered LA executive, familiarised her name to a new generation of cinemagoers. She brought the naturalistic conviction to her small role that connoisseurs had long admired in her, and Alan J. Pakula rewarded her with the smallish but pivotal and difficult role of Harrison Ford's betrayed wife in *Presumed Innocent* (1990). As Barbara Sabich, coping with the knowledge of her husband's affair with a glamorous female prosecutor and his subsequent trial for murder, her understated performance was masterly, her eyes truly the window of her soul, and she brought conviction to a denouement that strained credibility, daring one to query it.

1969 The Gypsy Moths **1970** They Shoot Horses, Don't They?; Lovers And Other Strangers **1972** The Strange Vengeance Of Rosalie **1978** The Big Fix **1984** Heart Like A Wheel **1986** Violets Are Blue; Death Of An Angel; The Boy Who Could Fly **1988** Die Hard; The Prince Of Pennsylvania **1989** Fat Man And Little Boy (GB: Shadowmakers) **1990** Die Hard 2; Presumed Innocent **1993** Needful Things

Begley, Ed Jr

Actor

Born 16 September 1949

New York City

The son of the noted and prolific (vaudeville, radio Broadway, films) character actor Ed Begley Sr, Jr has to date had a career along similar lines, with television standing in for radio (he made his debut at 17 in the series *My Three Sons*), and colleges and nightclubs taking the place of vaudeville when he busied himself on the stand-up comedy circuit.

After working briefly as a TV cameraman he returned to acting with guest roles in various hit TV shows (*Happy Days*, *Columbo*, *Starsky And Hutch*) while, in his film career, he graduated from small parts in Disney campus comedies where his tall, angular frame and over-zealously WASPish features earned him the odd line of dialogue, to slightly better roles in considerably better films that included *Stay Hungry* (1976), *Citizen's Band* (1977) and *Blue Collar* (1978).

It was with television's *St Elsewhere* that Begley Jr landed his best role and won public acclaim, as well as an Emmy nomination, as the flippant Dr Erlich, a full-time brown-noser with terminal foot-in-mouth disease yet with occasional moments of humanity. Since the series, he has worked fairly regularly in films, but without making much impact – although his son of the Invisible Man livened up *Amazon Women On The Moon* (1987), and he was horrifically funny as one of William Hurt's grocery-filing brothers in *The Accidental Tourist* (1988).

Begley had a major role in Susan Seidelman's version of *She-Devil* (1989), and proved a perfect choice for the ultimately wimpish husband of Roseanne Barr who leaves her for Meryl Streep, but the film was largely crucified by critics and virtually ignored by the public. Despite having worked for an impressive array of directors that includes Bob Rafelson, Jonathan Demme, John Carpenter, Jack Nicholson, Paul Schrader, Reiners Carl and Rob, Walter Hill, John Landis and Lawrence Kasdan, Ed Begley Jr seems most at home and best used on the small screen.

1972 Now You See Him, Now You Don't **1973** Charley And The Angel; Showdown **1974** Superdad **1976** Stay Hungry **1977** Citizens Band aka Handle With Care **1978** Goin' South; Blue Collar; The One And Only; Record City; Elvis **1979** The In-Laws; The Concorde – Airport '79; Hardcore (GB: The Hardcore Life) **1981** Buddy, Buddy; Private Lessons **1982** Cat People; Eating Raoul; Young Doctors In Love; An Officer And A Gentleman **1983** Get Crazy; The Entity **1984** Protocol; Streets Of Fire; This Is Spinal Tap **1985** Transylvania 6–5000 **1987** Amazon Women On The Moon **1988** The Accidental Tourist **1989** Scenes From The Class Struggle In Beverly Hills; She-Devil **1990** Meet The Applegates **1992** Dark Horse

Belushi, James

Actor, writer
Born 15 May 1954
Chicago, Illinois

Despite his much-dismissed talent, it is probable that the career of James (sometimes Jim) Belushi would not have developed so fully were it not for the death of his brother John at the height of his cult success. While not sharing John's slovenly image, James followed a similar professional vein via Chicago's famous Second City improvisational group and regular appearances on *Saturday Night Live*, although he diversified more with prestigious stage work (he got his degree in speech and theatre) in *The Pirates of Penzanee* and *True West*.

He made an excellent debut as the discreet, warm and matter-of-fact partner of James Caan's professional *Thief* (1981), although he attracted more attention as the party-loving goon whose gorilla suit is put to hideous use in *Trading Places* (1983) for the director of his brother's biggest hits, John Landis. He showed his talents to the full in 1986, reprising his stage role from David Mamet's *Sexual Peversity In Chicago* as the unromantic, uncommitted male chauvinist pig out for a good time in the movie version, *About Last Night . . .* and was utterly convincing as the callous sleazeball journalist who goes to *Salvador* to score drugs in Oliver Stone's relentless political thriller. Lead roles followed (and a surprising credit as the co-writer of the routine cop thriller *Number One With A Bullet*, 1987) but it was not until a couple of unlikely bad cop, worse cop pairings that he scored big at the box office – first as a Chicago policeman paired with Russian Arnold Schwarzenegger in *Red Heat* in 1988 and with a psychologically unsound German shepherd dog in *K-9* (1989).

Subsequent star vehicles have proved less successful, with both the high concept, low laugh *Taking Care Of Business* (1990) and the comedy fantasy *Mr Destiny* (1990, a non-musical virtual remake of *Damn Yankees*) relying too heavily on his charm and timing to cover the limitations of the scripts. Belushi's dramatic ambitions are still much in evidence, with Andrei Konchalovsky's *Homer And Eddie* (1989) and his venture into Italian cinema with *To Forget Palermo* (1990), but it is clear that the shadow of his brother's reputation keeps Hollywood's perceptions of his talents firmly in a comedic mould.

1981 Thief aka Violent Streets **1983** Trading Places **1985** The Man With One Red Shoe **1986** Salvador; About Last Night . . .; Little Shop Of Horrors; Jumpin' Jack Flash **1987** Number One With A Bullet (writer only); The Principal; Real Men **1988** Red Heat **1989** K-9; Who's

Harry Crumb?; Homer And Eddie **1990** Taking Care Of Business aka Filofax; Mr Destiny; Wedding Band; Di Menticare Palermo/To Forget Palermo (Italy/France) **1991** Only The Lonely **1991** Curly Sue **1992** Traces Of Red; Once Upon A Crime; Diary Of A Hit Man

Belushi, John

Actor
Born 24 January 1949
Wheaton, Illinois
Died 5 March 1982

With his peculiar brand of anarchic, excessive and sometimes menacing humour, John Belushi came to represent a new era in American comedy; with his untimely death in 1982, he became an American legend, leaving a legacy of only seven uneven films by which to remember him.

The son of an Albanian immigrant who was a struggling restaurateur, Belushi was born and raised in Wheaton, Illinois, one of a family of four children, another of whom, Jim, also became an actor. A popular teenager, John was a high school football player, drummer in a rock 'n' roll band and a promising and funny actor. After a season of summer stock in 1967, he enrolled at the University of Wisconsin at Whitewater with the intention of majoring in drama, but his family's financial hardship forced him to transfer to the college of DuPage. With two fellow students, Belushi formed a comedy group, the West Compass Players, and, after leaving college in 1970, the trio moved to Chicago, where Belushi came to the attention of a talent scout for the famous Second City comedy troupe. One-and-a-half years of performing improvisational stand-up comedy followed before Belushi's winning impersonation of Joe Cocker landed him an important role in the National Lampoon off-Broadway revue, *Lemmings*. The New York critics were full of praise for the rising young comedian and, after a brief stint performing, writing and directing on the *National Lampoon Radio Hour*, he joined the cast of a new comedy TV show that took to the air in 1975.

From its inception, *Saturday Night Live* was a runaway success – daring, experimental and offbeat. It became a fertile breeding ground for comic talent, spawning Chevy Chase, Gilda Radner, Bill Murray, Dan Aykroyd – and John Belushi. As the show gained in popularity, its players acquired a hip, cult status which aroused the interest of the Hollywood studios.

For Belushi, his big-screen debut in 1978 proved unsatisfying – and extremely brief. As a Mexican deputy sheriff in Jack Nicholson's curious Western, *Goin' South*, the actor had barely five minutes of screen time but, nevertheless, managed to draw critical approval and laughter. But it was his second film role, as the frat-house slob, Bluto, in John Landis' *National Lampoon's Animal House* (1978) that established the frenetic young comedian as a hot ticket. Millions flocked to see Belushi's gross and outrageous celluloid college capers, while his chubby jowls and wickedly arched eyebrows graced the cover of *Newsweek*, undeniable confirmation that a star was in the ascendant.

However, Belushi's next two projects were disappointing. The low-budget *Old Boyfriends* (1979) made shamefully little use of the actor's talent, casting him in a secondary role as one of Talia Shire's former lovers; and his volcanic over-the-top performance as a crazy bomber pilot in *1941* (1979), while more in keeping with the animal-like Bluto, was obscured by the over-produced excesses of the Spielberg fiasco.

But it was a character he was honing on *Saturday Night Live* that was to immortalise John Belushi: when he and fellow cast member and close friend Dan Aykroyd donned their Ray-Bans and pork pie hats to become the Blues Brothers they weren't just performing a skit, they were laying the foundations for a duo that would rapidly have a No. 1 selling album and a major movie to their credit. As the deadpan Jake Elwood, Belushi had free rein to indulge his love for rock 'n' roll and rhythm and blues; although no accomplished vocalist, his enthusiastic and energetic renditions proved irresistible, and the off-the-wall humour of *The Blues Brothers* (1980) was an enduring success.

A driven, self-destructive man who married his high school sweetheart, Judy, Belushi had from his earliest days partied with the famous and regularly used and abused drugs. His comedy style blatantly steamrollered the parameters of taste; yet the performer, whose idol was Marlon Brando, hankered after more heavyweight roles. He therefore agreed to play the 'normal' role of a Chicago newswriter in the romantic comedy *Continental Divide* (1980). The film, uneven at best, was a flop. Belushi, a man with a bear-like, overweight physique, was uncomfortable as a romantic lead, but the role was noteworthy in providing him with his only truly likeable screen character. His final film,

Neighbors (1980), which teamed him once again with Aykroyd, was a tiresome and disastrous black comedy – a sad coda for an actor whose talent had just begun to be tapped.

In 1982, aged only 33, John Belushi was found dead of a drug overdose in Hollywood. The circumstances surrounding his death led to a book, *Wired* which, in 1989, was made into a movie of the same title, starring Michael Chiklis as the doomed protagonist.

1978 Goin' South; National Lampoon's Animal House **1979** Old Boyfriends; 1941 **1980** The Blues Brothers **1981** Continental Divide; Neighbors

Bening, Annette

Actress
Born 1959?
Topeka, Kansas

Annette Bening's rise to fame was swift – from unknown to Hollywood star in the space of little more than a year. Prior to her breakthrough as the Marquise de Merteuil in Milos Forman's *Valmont* (1990), she had a very small part in *The Great Outdoors* (1988), following television work which included a few appearances in series such as *Miami Vice* and, more notably, in *The Spoils of War*.

Kansas-born Bening was raised in San Diego, California, the daughter of an insurance man who also taught selling techniques at the Dale Carnegie Institute. She began singing and acting lessons as a child, and grew up to become a stage actress. She developed a substantial repertory career with leading groups such as Washington's Arena Stage company before making the move to New York where she landed a role in *Coastal Disturbances* for which she won the Clarence Derwent Award for the most promising actress of the season.

It was the canny John Hughes who spotted her screen potential and cast her in the nitwit camping holiday comedy, *The Great Outdoors* (1988). Then, by a coincidence of choice and a misfortune of timing, *Valmont* found itself totally eclipsed by *Dangerous Liaisons* (1988), both of them screen adaptations of the same novel, and it died the death accordingly. However, as the scheming Marquise weaving a dangerous web of sexual intrigue (played by Glenn Close in the rival film), Bening gave notice that she was an actress to watch – attractive, skilful and with a strong, seductive presence. A cameo, but a significant one, dishing the dirt on Dennis Quaid to Meryl Streep in *Postcards From The Edge* (1990), confirmed her ability to use a sharp tongue and flashed her sensual presence briefly at a large audience, but it was *The Grifters* the same year (directed, ironically, by *Dangerous Liaisons*' Stephen Frears) that unleashed Bening's unbridled sensuality, and apprised a wider audience of her ability to portray ruthlessness and amorality without compromise. As female grifter Myra, getting her tentacles round lover Roy (John Cusack) and her knife into Roy's mother, Lily (a formidable Anjelica Huston), while planning scams and giving her body in lieu of rent, Bening – tall and sinuous, like a threatening queen spider – was chillingly believable. She was nominated for a Best Supporting Actress Oscar for her pains (losing out to Whoopi Goldberg) but, by then, she had already made *Regarding Henry* with Harrison Ford for *Postcards* director Mike Nichols and *Guilty By Suspicion* for Irwin Winkler (both 1991).

It was the latter film which demonstrated that Bening is, after all, capable of playing something other than bitches. If the movie doesn't altogether succeed, it is nonetheless a commendable exposé of the effects of McCarthyism and, as the schoolteacher ex-wife of a blacklisted screen writer (Robert De Niro) who rallies in support of her former husband, the actress exudes warmth, sympathy and kindness.

Following on her success with *The Grifters*, however, she was slated for two more major films designed to draw on her tough and sexy quality: Barry Levinson's *Bugsy* about the famous mobster (played by Warren Beatty) and, unsurprisingly, given her lissom build, the Cat Woman in *Batman Returns*. However, *Bugsy* (1991) changed her life when it resulted in Hollywood's most determined bachelor marrying her, and her famous pregnancy with Kathlyn Bening Beatty saw the role of Cat Woman go to Michelle Pfeiffer.

1988 The Great Outdoors **1990** Valmont; Postcards From The Edge; The Grifters **1991** Guilty By Suspicion; Regarding Henry **1991** Bugsy

Benjamin, Richard

Actor, director
Born 22 May 1938
New York City

When Richard Benjamin appeared as the college drop-out in love with a 'Jewish princess' (Ali MacGraw) in *Goodbye Columbus* (1969), he had never been seen on screen before – as an adult, that is.

Benjamin, who was educated at the New York High School of Performing Arts, played child roles in a few films of the 50s, including *Thunder Over The Plains* (1953), a Randolph Scott Western, and *Crime Wave* (1954), both directed by André de Toth. After schooling, he went straight into the professional theatre, performing in stock and touring companies until he established himself on Broadway in 1966 in Neil Simon's *The Star-Spangled Girl*. The following year, he and Paula Prentiss, his wife since 1961, were cast in the successful TV series *He and She*.

Prentiss had been in films for nine years before her husband got his Hollywood opportunity with *Goodbye Columbus*, based on Philip Roth's fresh and amusing novella of 50s Jewish lifestyles in the New York suburbs. In it, Benjamin immediately established himself as a comic no-goodnik, which he followed up with his insufferable go-getting lawyer in *Diary Of A Mad Housewife* (1970). He played a similar pre-yuppie part in *The Marriage Of A Young Stockbroker* (1971) before landing the title role in *Portnoy's Complaint* (1972), a limp film version of Roth's bestselling novel about a Jewish mother-dominated boy with masturbation problems. Benjamin did the best he could with the impossible screenplay, but mostly wandered through it with a pained expression. Subsequently, he was mainly confined to supporting roles, his best being the callow tourist at a theme park in *Westworld* (1973), pursued by manic robot Yul Brynner.

With little further satisfaction to be had from acting, Benjamin took up directing, his first film, *My Favourite Year* (1982), being his best to date. Set in 1954 'when TV was alive and comedy was king', it revolved hilariously around Peter O'Toole's boozy, rabble-rousing Hollywood star causing havoc in a TV studio. After that came a conventional and mediocre rites-of-passage drama, *Racing With The Moon* (1983); an unsubtle comedy *City Heat* (1984), in which Burt Reynolds and Clint Eastwood take themselves off; the slapstick yuppie nightmare *The Money Pit* (1985), starring Tom Hanks, and the puerile though commercially successful *My Stepmother Is An Alien* (1988), with Kim Basinger and Dan Aykroyd. However, all of them have certain zany moments that promise a return to the comic form of Benjamin's directorial debut movie, and he was the third and final choice made by Cher for *Mermaids* (1991), after two previous directors departed.

As actor: **1969** Goodbye Columbus **1970** Diary Of A Mad Housewife; Catch-22 **1971** The Marriage Of A Young Stockbroker **1972** Portnoy's Complaint **1973** The Last Of Sheila; Westworld **1975** The Sunshine Boys **1978** House Calls **1979** Love At First Bite; The Last Married Couple In America; Scavenger Hunt **1980** How To Beat The High Cost Of Loving; First Family; Witches Brew **1981** Saturday the 14th

As director: **1982** My Favourite Year **1983** Racing With The Moon **1984** City Heat **1985** The Money Pit **1988** My Stepmother Is An Alien; Little Nikita **1990** Downtown **1991** Mermaids **1992/93** Made In America

Benson, Robbie
(Robert Segal)

Actor, director
Born 21 January 1956
Dallas, Texas

Best known for his squeaky-clean all-American roles, baby-faced Robbie Benson has only occasionally managed to escape from this screen image. In fact, it was his very wholesomeness that led producers to put money into his first film as director, *Crack In The Mirror* (1988), about drug-taking in New York. Their only proviso was that he should play the lead of the Park Avenue yuppie in order to warn audiences that anyone, even someone as preppy and decent-living as Benson, could get hooked on the stuff – crack, to be precise, as the pun in the title suggests. Unfortunately, the film was more well meaning than well made, and Benson, as both actor and director, seemed a little out of his depth. The principal interest of the contrived and shallow film was that it was shot on Sony's high-definition TV system.

Benson had been in movies since he was 15 years old, making his debut in *Jory* (1972), an undistinguished thriller in which he played a boy turned revenge killer after watching his father murdered. More notice was taken of him in the title role of *Jeremy* (1973), a teenage love story to which he lent a gawky charm, saving the film from becoming overcute. He is a 'kinda goofy kid' who plays the cello as well as basketball, is mad about horses, reads poetry to his dog, and is in love with ballet student Glynnis O'Connor. Benson keeps saying 'Wow!', not something that could be said of this gentle little picture. Five years later, in *The End*, he had a hilarious encounter with Burt Reynolds, a man bent on suicide, who goes to church for his first confession in 20 years only to be faced with Benson as an adolescent novice priest who can only say 'Wow!'.

In *Ode To Billy Joe* (1976), the actor was a sawmill worker in a Mississippi backwater in the 50s, in love with a girl (once again Glynnis O'Connor) from the other side of the tracks. Based on a song by Bobbie Gentry about the suicide of a 17-year-old boy who leapt from the Tallahatchie Bridge, it was a box-office winner and Benson was praised for his ability to express the joys and anguish of the adolescent hero. There were even some 'daring' scenes where he got drunk and had a homosexual encounter.

One On One (1977), co-written with his father, ends with the Paul Williams song 'Nice Guys Finish First', which could be Benson's signature tune. The nice guy he played is a dedicated basketball star from a small town in Colorado, who accepts a sports scholarship from Western University. But at five feet ten he is dwarfed by his teammates and harrassed mentally and physically by the coach. The ending is the stuff (and nonsense) that dreams are made of when he scores the winning point of the championship, gets his own back on the martinet coach, gains the love of an attractive girl (Annette O'Toole) and obtains top grades. Somehow Benson managed to get away with it all.

Other films with sporting themes followed. In *Ice Castles* (1979), he portrayed an ice-hockey player inspiring a former ice-skating champion (Lynn-Holly Johnson) to triumph over adversity when she goes almost totally blind in an accident. The movie was another box-office winner in the disability stakes. *Running Brave* (1983) was the true story of soft-spoken Billy Mills, a Sioux who left the reservation on an athletics scholarship to the University of Kansas, and ran in the 10,000 metres at the 1964 Olympic Games. Of course he encounters racism on the way. In the lead, the young actor exuded niceness and was convincing as an exceptional runner.

Previously, a long-haired Benson, looking several shades darker than usual, was less convincing in *Walk Proud* (1979), playing Emilio, a tough chicano gang member in East Los Angeles; in *The Chosen* (1981) his pleasant features were hidden behind Hassidic Jewish locks and large hat as the son of rabbi Rod Steiger. This was one of several sentimental father-son dramas in which Benson was rather overwhelmed by his older star partners. Both *Tribute* (1980) and *Harry And Son* (1984) were mainly vehicles for Jack Lemmon and Paul Newman, respectively, to display their acting wares, though Benson was an effective filial foil.

In 1990, Benson, who teaches film-making at the University of Southern California, directed his second movie, *Modern Love*, starring Burt Reynolds and himself, and in the making of which he involved many of his students. His pleasant, well-spoken baritone voice has also given him a successful sideline, providing characterisations in animated work. Benson's is the voice of the popular TV cartoon hero, Prince Valiant, and the 'beastly' romantic lead in Disney's award-winning smash-hit feature, *Beauty And The Beast.*

1972 Jory **1973** Jeremy **1975** Lucky Lady **1976** Ode To Billy Joe **1977** One On One **1978** The End 1979 Ice Castles; Walk Proud **1980** Die Laughing; Tribute **1981** The Chosen **1982** National Lampoon Goes To The Movies **1983** Running Brave **1984** Harry And Son **1985** City Limits **1988** Crack In The Mirror (also director); Rent-A-Cop **1990** Modern Love (also director)

Benton, Robert

Writer, director
Born 29 September 1932
Waxahachie, Texas

Robert Benton is an interesting director who for one reason or another hasn't done as well as predicted. Commencing at about the same time as Coppola, Scorsese, Spielberg and the Movie Brats, he has always belonged to a somewhat different world, going his own way, following an idiosyncratic path. His best-known and most successful film – the Academy Award-winning *Kramer vs. Kramer*, starring Hoffman and Streep (1979, five Oscars, including those for best screenplay and best direction) – is in certain respects his least satisfactory. The morality is dull; you don't feel, at the end of the film, that either position (the husband's or the wife's) has been properly tested. His films are autobiographical in one sense (*Places in the Heart*, 1984, was shot in the town of his birth; *Nadine*, 1987, in Austin, Texas where he received his schooling), yet belong to such different genres that it becomes hard to extract the unifying factor that could turn this director into an *auteur*.

No films of his, perhaps, have been as powerful as the two movies he was associated with early in his career: *Bonnie and Clyde* (1967, written by Benton and partner David Newman, directed by Arthur Penn), and his directorial debut, *Bad Company* (1972). In both of these extremely violent works, death is looked at with fine coldness and clarity, a sense of its biting absurdity worthy of a great playwright like Beckett. *Bad Company* starts off like *Huckleberry Finn* but ends like a Jacobean tragedy. Death catches the protagonists by surprise. The look of disgust and sheer incredulity on the faces of the four youngsters as they meet their awkward end in a sort of ridiculous, upright, sitting position is as memorable a moment of screen horror as one can think of, and might have augured great things to come from the man who imagined it. But *Still of the Night*, for example, made ten years later – a clever, interesting film in many ways – is in essence 'only' a commercial thriller, with none of the metaphysical halftones that hover round the edges of *Bad Company*, giving it modelling and depth.

Benton was born into a moderately poor family background in Texas and spent the first years of young adulthood trying to put this past behind him. Success came in 1956 when he landed a job in *Esquire* magazine's head office in New York where he met his future writing partner, David Newman. Together they composed and became famous for a monthly column in *Mademoiselle* magazine over a period of ten years. The Academy Award-nominated script for *Bonnie and Clyde*, 1967's sleeper of the year, landed on 20 directors' desks before being taken up by Arthur Penn and turned into the legendary movie.

In the next year or two, very much in demand, Benton and Newman wrote scripts for Joseph L. Mankiewicz (*There Was A Crooked Man*, 1970) and the then highriding Peter Bogdanovich (*What's Up Doc?*, 1972) before Benton went solo with *Bad Company*. But the artistic success of that movie wasn't matched by a commercial one. His next film, a rather charming detective spoof, *The Late Show* (1977), with Art Carney and Lily Tomlin, wasn't made for another five years, and then only courtesy of director-turned-independent producer Robert Altman. So it was back to screenwriting (*Superman*, 1978, in collaboration with Mario Puzo). After which came *Kramer vs. Kramer*.

Once more, and for the second time in Benton's career, success at the box office failed to be built upon. His films of the 1980s are interesting but small-scale. *Still of the Night* (1982), a sort of Hitchcock genre exercise, has good performances from Roy Scheider and Meryl Streep, while its art-world/auction-room ambience is crisply imagined but, as thrillers go, it's only mildly compelling. In contrast to that film's icy clarity, *Places in the Heart* (1984) is distinctly emotional – perhaps the most autobiographical of Benton's films to date, taking its cue from a real-life incident, in which Benton's great-grandmother was left to cope by herself after her husband was shot dead on the railway tracks by the local drunk. The movie garnered a Best Actress Oscar for Sally Field as the feisty young widow, eking out a living with the help of a black cotton picker (Danny Glover), and Benton collected another screenplay nomination.

With *Nadine* (1987), the writer-director set out deliberately to make a lighter film – a 'divertimento', as he called it, in the manner of Truffaut (a movie like *Confidentially Yours*): a sort of skit on old B pictures, 'full of wild car chases and gaiety', but even the best efforts of Jeff Bridges and Kim Basinger couldn't save it from silliness. Neither of the Texas films in the event were box-office hits but they are worth seeing – apart from anything else because of their beautiful colour photography crafted by the great Cuban–Spanish cameraman Nestor Almendros (he also photographed *Still Of The Night* and *Kramer vs. Kramer*).

In these films you get as good a pictorial record of small-town Protestant America as you are likely to find. As Almendros noted: 'the most common places, such as a beauty salon, a photographer's office, an alley, a third-rate bar, a junk yard, were all transfigured, mythified by the camera – with almost no help from us.' Five years later (this longish gap between films being a feature of Benton's career), the director, working from an adaptation by Tom Stoppard, embarked on the film version of E.L. Doctorow's novel *Billy Bathgate*, starring Dustin Hoffman. Unfortunately, the finished project failed to live up to the scale of its ambition and was ill-received.

As writer and director unless stated otherwise: **1967** Bonnie and Clyde (co-writer only) **1970** There Was A Crooked Man (co-writer only) **1972** What's Up Doc? (co-writer only); Bad Company **1977** The Late Show **1978** Superman (co-writer only) **1979** Kramer vs. Kramer **1982**

Still of the Night **1984** Places in the Heart **1987** Nadine **1991** Billy Bathgate

Berenger, Tom

Actor
Born 31 May 1950
Chicago, Illinois

Quickly establishing himself as one of the more versatile of American leading men in recent years, Tom Berenger spent much of his early career as a perennial bridesmaid, always on the verge of stardom but always just missing out. Having studied drama at the University of Missouri he began his acting career with a college production of *Who's Afraid Of Virginia Woolf?*, originally intending to concentrate on a stage career only to find his good looks often counting against him (although he has a string of impressive theatrical credits, and is particularly familiar with the works of Tennessee Williams).

Enjoying the popularising process of the daytime soap *One Life To Live*, he survived his screen debut buying a flat that houses the gateway to hell at the end of Michael Winner's *The Sentinel* (1976) and soon made amends as the disturbed homosexual whose abortive one-night stand with Diane Keaton in *Looking For Mr Goodbar* (1977) ends in her murder. After bedding a cast that should have known better in *In Praise Of Older Women* (1978) he seemed poised on the edge of the big time with his engaging Butch Cassidy in the *Early Days* prequel (1979), complementing rather than imitating Paul Newman's performance but, as with his businesslike mercenary in *The Dogs Of War* (1980), the public did not catch on and the actor found himself relegated to so-so land. Even his witty interpretation of the former radical turned TV private eye in Lawrence Kasdan's *The Big Chill* seemed to do nothing to get things moving.

It took Berenger's realisation of the scarred psychotic/demonic sergeant who willingly gives in to atrocity in *Platoon* (1986) to bring him to the fore. It was a part that dispensed with his good-natured charisma, and turned his all-American looks against themselves to represent the ugliness under the surface of the 'hearts and minds' policy; and which was iconically mirrored in his Marine recruiting officer enticing Ron Kovic to Vietnam with his talk of elitism and honour in Stone's later *Born On The Fourth Of July* (1989). He was just as impressive, but very sympathetically and attractively so, as the downtown cop who falls for the uptown witness (Mimi Rogers) he is assigned to protect in Ridley Scott's *Someone To Watch Over Me* (1987), putting the torment and guilt back into on-screen extra-marital affairs; and a revelation as the decent, homespun Fascist murderer in Costa-Gavras' *Betrayed* (1988), getting to the root of the man's need to have an ethnic enemy in order to maintain his belief in his country. Now so firmly established that not even the laughably bad Mafia priest thriller *Last Rites* (1988, did you really need the money Tom?) did little damage to a career that has continued to attract directors as disparate as Jim Sheridan, Alan Rudolph, Wolfgang Petersen and Hector Babenco in between the more mainstream pleasures of *Shoot To Kill* (1988) and *Major League* (1989), and his career seems to have entered its most vital and varied phase.

1976 The Sentinel **1977** Looking For Mr Goodbar **1978** In Praise Of Older Women **1979** Butch And Sundance: The Early Days **1980** The Dogs Of War **1982** Beyond The Door **1983** Eddie And The Cruisers; The Big Chill **1984** Fear City **1985** Rustler's Rhapsody **1986** Platoon **1987** Someone To Watch Over Me **1988** Shoot To Kill aka Deadly Pursuit; Last Rites; Betrayed **1989** Major League; Born On The Fourth Of July **1990** Love At Large; The Field (GB) **1991** Shattered; At Play In The Fields Of The Lord **1992** Sniper

Beresford, Bruce

Director, writer
Born 16 August 1940
Sydney, Australia

When, in March 1990 at the 1989 Oscars, Master of Ceremonies Billy Crystal facetiously referred to *Driving Miss Daisy* as 'the movie that directed itself' the audience gasped appreciatively at his pointed acknowledgement of a breathtaking snub by the Academy. Rarely is the director of a Best Picture nominee himself cold-shouldered in the nominations. Insult was added to injury when *Daisy* went on to win the award for Best Picture.

The director in question was possibly less perturbed than his producers and supporters, since his career has been characterised by extreme highs and lows, raves and rants, kisses and blows. And it is hard to credit that Bruce Beresford, a keen film-maker from the age of 12, can turn out a character study such as *Tender Mercies* (for which he was nominated for an Oscar as Best Director in the Academy's 1983 Awards) and two powerful dramas that were high marks of the Australian cinema renaissance, *Breaker Morant* (1979) and *The Club* (1980), while also being the perpetrator of the leaden biblical-style epic disaster *King David* (1985), best remembered as the film in which Richard Gere danced in a diaper.

After obtaining a degree in philosophy at Sydney University, Beresford moved to London in 1961, where he worked first as a teacher, then as a film editor and producer. From 1966 to 1971 he served as Head of Production on the BFI Production Board. His subsequent return to Australia coincided with the Australian government's increasingly benevolent support of the indigenous film industry. Aided by a grant, he made his first feature, *The Adventures Of Barry McKenzie* (1971), a lowbrow comedy about a beer-swilling Aussie oaf. It was critically panned but a box-office hit. Three years later he made a follow-up, also poorly received. Then, in 1976, he stunned critics with one of the first films from the revitalised Australian industry to herald the New Oz Wave, *Don's Party*. A biting adaptation of a play by David Williamson, it was a potent black comedy of contemporary suburban mores, deftly realised by the director.

Beresford followed that in 1977 with a coming-of-age drama, *The Getting Of Wisdom*, which followed a young outback girl's progress at a posh girls' school. Beresford's treatment was sensitive and created a strong period feel. Two years later he co-wrote and directed what is still arguably his best film, *Breaker Morant* (1979), a taut courtroom drama inspired by the real court-martial of three Australian officers in South Africa during the Boer War. The picture deals strongly in notions of duty, honour, comradeship and political expediency, and features first-rate performances from Edward Woodward, Jack Thompson and Bryan Brown. Beresford's reward was international acclaim, several Australian Academy Awards and an Oscar nomination – his first – for the screenplay.

After another teenage tale in 1981, the pleasant but rather clichéd *Puberty Blues*, Beresford was lured to Hollywood, where he was off to a flying start with the winning *Tender Mercies* (1983), directing Robert Duvall to his Best Actor Oscar. Two years later, scorched by the *King David* disaster, he returned to Australia for a sentimental but worthy drama, *The Fringe Dwellers*, centring on an Aboriginal family's attempt to integrate in a middle-class white neighbourhood. Back in America, he took on an altogether more ambitious project with the Pulitzer Prize-winning play *Crimes Of the Heart* (1986). Despite good performances from Sissy Spacek, Jessica Lange and Diane Keaton, the oddball comedy-drama did not translate well to the big screen, with Beresford unable to strike a consistent tone. Two almost simultaneous releases of 1989 showcase Beresford's strengths and weaknesses. *Driving Miss Daisy* betrayed its stage origins and a contrived, overly sentimental premise, but the director once again elicited bravura performances from his principals (Jessica Tandy, Morgan Freeman) and struck a stylish period feel. *Her Alibi*, starring Tom Selleck, proved he was less adept with an inexperienced actress (Paulina Porizkova) and could conjure neither intrigue nor laughter out of a ho-hum script. He takes flight, it seems, when his heart is actively engaged and the material is superior, as in the sombre, spectacular Canadian missionary-in-the-wilderness epic, *Black Robe*. Otherwise, Bruce Beresford's output is that of a competent workhorse.

1971 The Adventures of Barry McKenzie **1974** Barry McKenzie Holds His Own **1976** Don's Party **1977** The Getting Of Wisdom **1978** Money Movers **1979** Breaker Morant (w/d) **1980** The Club 1981 Puberty Blues 1983 Tender Mercies **1985** King David **1986** The Fringe Dwellers; Crimes Of The Heart **1988** Aria (segment) **1989** Driving Miss Daisy; Her Alibi **1990** Mister Johnson **1991** Black Robe **1992** Rich In Love

Bergen, Candice

Actress

Born 8 May 1946

Beverly Hills, California

As a child, Candice Bergen had to suffer jokes about being the daughter of Charlie McCarthy, the famous ventriloquist's dummy forever paired with her father, Edgar Bergen. Although she spent some of her childhood in the show business surroundings of Hollywood where her father worked, she attended an exclusive finishing school in Switzerland and completed her education at the University of Pennsylvania.

At the age of 20, the tall, patrician-looking blonde was ideally cast as the Vassar graduate in Sidney Lumet's screen version of Mary McCarthy's bestselling novel, *The Group* (1966). Although her character, that of Lakey, the lovely lesbian (coyly referred to as 'Sapphic') suffered most from the attempt to cram as much as possible of the book into the screenplay, she nevertheless made an impact in her screen debut. In fact, out of the several bright new actresses introduced in the film, Bergen became the biggest star, despite a rather patchy subsequent filmography.

Immediately following *The Group*, she was co-starred with Steve McQueen in *The Sand Pebbles*, released the same year. But, with her hair in a tight bun, playing a missionary in China, she got lost in the over-long and sprawling epic. She was then able to use her French in Claude Lelouch's slick and specious *Vivre Pour Vivre* (*Live For Life*, 1967), as the American fashion model who has an affair with globe-trotting TV news reporter Yves Montand.

Three mediocre films later, she was effective in two 1970 movies: sharing some passionate love scenes with fellow student Elliott Gould in *Getting Straight* and, top-billed for the first time, in the gory Western, *Soldier Blue*, as the liberated fiancée of an army officer who sides with the Indians. Better performances, though, came in better films. She was the ravishing co-ed 'shared' by Jack Nicholson and Art Garfunkel in the bitter comedy of male sexual mores, *Cornal Knowledge* (1971), in which director Mike Nichols held her in rapturous close-up for some considerable time as she told a story. Pity, therefore, that her role was so abruptly truncated.

Having been kidnapped by outlaw Oliver Reed in the repellent *The Hunting Party* (1971), she was again abducted, this time by Berber bandit Sean Connery, in John Milius' splendid Kiplingesque adventure, *The Wind And The Lion* (1975). As the proper American widow who falls for her captor, she displayed the right mixture of cold and hot.

In the mid-70s Bergen became deeply involved in the feminist movement and tried to reflect her beliefs in her screen roles. In *Oliver's Story* (1978), the soppier sequel to the soppy *Love Story*, she was the beautiful, liberated rich woman with whom Ryan O'Neal finds consolation after the death of his wife. In *Starting Over* (1979), she played the wife of Burt Reynolds, who leaves him because marriage is getting in the way of her career. In *Rich And Famous* (1981), a remake of *Old Acquaintance*, co-starring another beauty, Jacqueline Bisset, she sported a broad Southern accent and transformed herself from conventional California housewife and mother into a glamorous and successful novelist. However, the film was so silly and soapy that any subtext on her character's growth of independence drowned in the suds.

Bergen had been an independent person from a young age, and had worked as a model and photojournalist. (In *Gandhi*, 1982, she featured as Margaret Bourke-White, the *Life* photographer who uncovered unique insights into the personality of the Indian saviour.) She has also written extensively for magazines and television, and is the author of an autobiography, *Knock Wood*, and a play, *The Freezer*.

In 1980, the actress married French director Louis Malle. After the wedding, which took place in a French country house that Malle had owned for 15 years, the couple returned to live in her Manhattan apartment. They now have a home in Hollywood, where she remains with their child, while he commutes between Paris and LA. Her top-rated TV series as newswoman *Murphy Brown*, made her an Emmy winner and, though Candice Bergen has made relatively few films over a long period of years, many of them hardly worthy of her talent, she is a screen actress to be reckoned with.

1966 The Group; The Sand Pebbles **1967** Vivre Pour Vivre/Live For Life (France); The Day The Fish Came Out **1968** The Magus **1970** The Adventurers; Getting Straight; Soldier Blue **1971** Carnal Knowledge; The Hunting Party; T.R.Baskin **1974** 11 Harrowhouse **1975** The Wind And The Lion; Bite The Bullet **1977** The Domino Principle; The End Of The World In Our Usual Bed In A Night Full Of Rain **1978** Oliver's Story **1979** Starting Over **1981** Rich And Famous **1982** Gandhi **1985** Stick

Bergin, Patrick

Actor

Born 1953

Dublin, Ireland

Handsome, strapping, six-foot-three Patrick Bergin had previously only appeared in small roles in two modest films made in Ireland before he burst onto the screen in the show-piece leading role in Bob Rafelson's ambitious, overblown epic, *Mountains Of The Moon*, in 1990. As the legendary Victorian explorer, adventurer and scholar Sir Richard Burton, Bergin cut a considerable dash, hacking his way across darkest Africa at the head of an ill-fated and gory expedition to find the source of the Nile. The film was not a success, but blue-eyed, black-haired Bergin was besieged by offers from the industry. Within a year he had filmed leading roles in four pictures before the public had even grasped who he was. These included the coveted role of Robin Hood in a version of the adventures of the bandit of Sherwood Forest, which unfortunately, proved a terrible failure, particularly in view of the Kevin Costner rival vehicle, *Prince of Thieves* (1991).

Bergin's father was a trade union activist in Ireland who started an agit-prop theatre group for his fitters' union. But the young Patrick did not seem destined for an acting career. At 17, he moved to London with few educational qualifications. He found employment at the British National Library and attended night classes to raise his school-leaving qualifications; after which, in his 20s, he obtained a degree in Education at North London Polytechnic. By this time he had founded his own experimental theatre group, trying his hand at acting, writing and directing. While teaching, he incorporated the use of videos and puppets into his remedial classes for truants.

Feeling burned out after five years of teaching, Bergin travelled around Europe before deciding to pursue an acting career. A stint in repertory theatre led to a few small television roles and he was featured in a 35-minute short film, *No Man's Land*, made for the British National Film School, which attracted some attention and won him his first film part in *The Courier* (1980), a bleak thriller about drug-running which was made in Dublin and starred Gabriel Byrne, to whom Bergin bears a distinct resemblance. He subsequently played second banana to another Irish name, Pierce Brosnan, in the dire thriller *Taffin* (1988). Far more memorable was his appearance the same year in a TV mini-series, *Act Of Betrayal*, in which he stood out and attracted rave reviews as an IRA informer. Given the poor reception of Robin Hood, it remained to be seen whether mass audiences would eventually embrace Bergin with the same fervour displayed so soon into his film career by the producers (who teamed him successfully, with Julia Roberts for *Sleeping With The Enemy* in 1991) and a lobby of critics in the wake of *Mountains Of The Moon*.

1988 The Courier; Taffin **1990** Mountains Of The Moon **1991** Sleeping With The Enemy; Highway To Heaven; Robin Hood **1992** Map Of The Human Heart; Love Crimes; Patriot Games

Bernsen, Corbin

Actor
Born 7 September 1954
Los Angeles, California

The son of actress Jeanne Cooper, Corbin Bernsen holds a BA in Theatre Arts from UCLA, where he also took his Masters in playwriting while serving as a teaching assistant. He went to New York in 1981 to study acting and, like Harrison Ford, supported himself by working as a carpenter. He was also engaged as a model for Winston cigarettes, an apt display case for his particular good looks – blond and lean, simultaneously smooth and macho.

Bernsen had acquired some minimal theatre experience, played a few small movie roles, and spent two years in a daytime soap when he landed the plum part of Arnie Becker, divorce lawyer extraordinaire and archetypal womaniser, in TV's superior series, *LA Law*. It was a case of a man finding his right time and place, for Arnie's humour and sexiness, his combination of high-powered ruthlessness and little-boy-lost charm – not to mention the glamorous clothes – fitted him like a glove.

Unfortunately, the big screen has not treated Bernsen well, confining him to playing off his persona as best he can in unchallenging second-rate films. A major role in *Major League (1989)*, with Tom Berenger and Charlie Sheen, should have enlarged his status, but this baseball comedy was quite awful and hinted at the actor's limitations; and again, *Disorganized Crime* the same year, an inferior caper, and the good but overlooked thriller, *Shattered*, made use of his looks and personality without advancing his career. Nonetheless, by 1990, married to English actress Amanda Pays and the father of a small son, Bernsen had undoubtedly become a household name on both sides of the Atlantic, and was gradually adding to his big-screen filmography.

1974 Three The Hard Way **1976** Eat My Dust; King Kong **1981** S.O.B. **1987** Mace; Hello Again **1989** Major League; Disorganized Crime; Bert Rigby, You're A Fool **1991** Shattered **1992** Frozen Assets **1992/93** Grey Night

Biehn, Michael

Actor
Born 31 July 1956
Anisten, Alabama

Best known as the second lead of three

science-fiction movies directed by James Cameron, *The Terminator* (1984), *Aliens* (1986) and *The Abyss* (1989), Michael Biehn grew up in Nebraska, where his father was an attorney. It is, in fact, not difficult to imagine Biehn as a lawyer himself, given that he possesses an undoubted physical presence which somehow tends to abstraction: he is tall and rangy, yet his (admittedly good-looking) face is none too easily retained by the mind's eye.

His first acting job came in the 1977 TV pilot for the short-lived sci-fi series *Logan's Run*, and he had minor roles in several feature films before returning to the genre as the adversary of Arnold Schwarzenegger's robotic villain in Paul Verhoeven's ambitious *The Terminator* (1984). He managed not to be eclipsed by this heavyweight competition, but was inevitably left somewhat on the sidelines, as happened again in *Aliens*, where Sigourney Weaver and the aliens themselves claimed the centre of attention. After being a good guy in these movies, he was provided with a rather meatier role, as a militaristic heavy, in *The Abyss*. Oddly enough, he played in that film an officer in the US Navy's 'Seals' division, an association extended in his next movie, a seagoing story of poor quality, unambiguously titled *Navy Seals* (1990). If the films between were, to say the least, unmemorable, the actor nonetheless continued to be a useful addition to the list of younger, but definitely adult, leading men.

1978 Coach **1980** Hog Wild **1981** The Fan **1983** The Lords of Discipline **1984** The Terminator **1986** Aliens **1988** In a Shallow Grave; The Seventh Sign; Rampage **1989** The Abyss **1990** Navy Seals; Nameless **1991** K-2 **1992** Timebomb **1993** Deadfall

Bigelow, Kathryn

Director, writer
Born 1952
San Carlos, California

With an in-your-face visceral style of film-making that taps into the violence inherent in American culture in a way that woman directors aren't supposed to, and a talent for subverting genres from within, former performance artist Kathryn Bigelow is one of the most striking of directors to emerge in the 80s, influenced as much by Kafka and Nietzsche as by Jim Thompson and James M. Cain. Raised in Northern California in a bucolic childhood that seems to belie her later films, she studied at the San Francisco Art Institute, drawn to art as a way to create a world from which she did not feel ostracized, and later moving on to the Columbia University film school. Her first short film, *The Set-Up* (1979), which replayed its initial ten-minute sequence of a bloody alley fight with a split-screen discussion on the nature of violence, set the tone for her later work by its assertion that violence was not a reaction to external events but an internal need looking for expression.

Her first feature, *The Loveless* (1983, co-directed by Monty Montgomery), dealt with the mounting tension caused by the arrival of a gang of bikers in an Edward Hopper-like small town and the violence that ultimately erupts, and similarly demonstrated her lean style – she likes things bare and simple with a clearly defined look – and the tendency towards fetishism with uniform that resurfaces in later work. After several years developing scripts for other companies on Walter Hill's recommendation, she teamed up with writer Eric Red to create the cult horror film *Near Dark* (1987), a virtual modern-day vampire version of *The Wild Bunch* (1969), with a bar-room massacre so relentless in its violence it was akin to the audience being raped by the director and told to enjoy it. There was no restraint or sense of directorial moral outrage at its undead nuclear family's killing spree – Bigelow admits that she never identifies with victims but is always drawn towards the locus of power – but despite, or perhaps because of, the bitter taste it left in the mouth, the film established her as an up-and-coming talent (its iconic visual images are striking) and caught the attention of overtly masculine film-makers Oliver Stone and James Cameron (to whom she was briefly married).

It was with Stone's backing as her producer that she was able to make the far more accomplished *Blue Steel* (1990). Through Jamie Lee Curtis' rookie cop romanced by a psychotic killer, Bigelow reinterpreted women's role in violence away from that of victim or avenger to that of participant. She establishes an attraction to violence for the power it bestows (normally the sole province of the male) and makes her woman in a man's world a reflection of her prey: 'You would do what I do if you knew yourself better' he tells her. Yet despite her tense handling of the many action scenes – concentrating on Curtis and moving only with her until she gains the confidence to control a situation – her opponent's conversations with God and his over-literal attempt to get inside her in a rape scene showed a tendency towards excess that was also prevalent in the philosophical interludes that punctuated the perfectly controlled, thrills 'n' spills action sequences of the Cameron-produced *Point Break* (1991); a tendency that one suspects could and should be eliminated at script stage if Katherine Bigelow's films are to become more than an impressive collection of set-pieces, all too loosely strung together.

As director only unless stated otherwise: **1983** The Loveless (co-director) **1987** Near Dark (also co-writer) **1990** Blue Steel (also co-writer) **1991** Point Break

Bisset, Jacqueline
(Winifred Jacqueline Bisset)
Actress
Born 13 September 1944
Surrey, England

Jacqueline Bisset is possessed of a great beauty. No one denies it. In 1977, *Newsweek* enthusiastically, if a little over-generously, voted her 'the most beautiful film actress of all time.' And as she stalked into middle age, her English Home Counties, bitch-goddess looks grew ever more daunting, ready to turn serried ranks of pink-faced stockbrokers to stone with her humourless, basilisk stare.

And yet a patina of grim anxiety clings to most of her work. Like another celebrated beauty, Kim Novak, acting has appeared to be somewhat of an ordeal for Bisset, and she has never really thawed out under the studio lights. Even with a wet T-shirt famously plastered to her luscious breasts (*The Deep*, 1977), or steamily bedding college boys under half her age (son Rob Lowe's best friend Andrew McCarthy in *Class*, 1983), she seems too dismayed by her own voluptuousness to let go, or even repay the audience with a smile of genuine warmth.

Of Scottish-French parentage (her father was a doctor), Jackie went to school at the French Lycée, and studied dancing from the age of three. She turned to modelling in her mid-teens, which fortuitously coincided with the explosion of 'Swinging London' in the mid-1960s. She was first noticed in *The Knack* (1965) – along with another quintessentially English beauty, Charlotte Rampling – and was caught teasingly by Roman Polanski as a clammed-up deb in *Cul-de-Sac* (1966). She soon moved to California, where her Hollywood career was given a kick-start opposite Frank Sinatra in *The Detective* (1968). On the whole, directors seemed content merely to photograph her: in *Bullitt* (1968, co-starring with Steve McQueen and providing a welcome relief from car chases), *The Mephisto Waltz* (1970), *Believe In Me* (1971), and, in 1972, *The Life And Times Of Judge Roy Bean* with Paul Newman, and *The Thief Who Came To Dinner*. But it was in Europe that she was helped to international stardom when François Truffaut skilfully exploited her basic insecurity as the neurotic leading lady in *Day For Night* (1973). The process of expanding her reputation which began there was completed by *The Deep*, which made of her a kind of dripping cinematic icon, and stamped her as one of the few remaining sex symbols in the post-Monroe era – an image which has continued to flourish, rather than diminish, as the decades roll by.

Her fame and strange remoteness made Bisset a natural choice to play Jackie Onassis in *The Greek Tycoon* (1978), but the result was as limp as most of the junk in which she appeared during the following decade: *Rich And Famous* (1981), a horribly botched remake of *Old Acquaintance* (1943), directed by a senescent George Cukor with Jackie and Candice Bergen subbing for Bette Davis and Miriam Hopkins; *Class*, in which an attempt to ruffle her opulent poise turned her into a cradle-snatching vamp; *Under The Volcano* (1984), the entire cast of which was buried by the lava flow of director John Huston's pretensions. In *Scenes From The Class Struggle In Beverly Hills* (1989), a frenetic black comedy directed by Paul Bartel, she unbent a little as a self-absorbed soap star planning a comeback, but was clearly unable to see any of the jokes. In the unpleasantly voyeuristic *Wild Orchid* (1990), co-starring with Mickey Rourke, she was cast as a near-hysterical businesswoman in a male-dominated world.

And, ironically, it is as a businesswoman that the actress has discreetly become a multi-millionaire. Her flair for the real-estate racket, apparently the fruit of a long relationship with a French tycoon (she remains unmarried), has made her one of the wealthiest women in Hollywood; rich and famous. But the inescapable conclusion is that Jacqueline Bisset, whose staying power can only be admired, has fared rather better as a ravishing property developer than as an actress of real accomplishment.

1966 Cul-de-Sac; Arrivederci, Baby (GB: Drop Dead,

Darling) **1967** Casino Royale; Two For The Road **1968** The Detective; The Sweet Ride; Bullitt **1969** The First Time; La Promesse/Secret World (France) **1970** Airport; The Grasshopper **1972** The Mephisto Waltz; Believe In Me; Stand Up And Be Counted; The Life And Times Of Judge Roy Bean **1974** The Thief Who Came To Dinner; La Nuit Americaine/Day For Night (France); Le Magnifique (France); Murder On The Orient Express **1975** Der Richter Und Sein Henker/End Of The Game (Germany) **1976** La Donna Dela Domenica/The Sunday Woman (Italy); St Ives **1977** The Deep **1978** Secrets (made in 1971); Who Is Killing The Great Chefs Of Europe?; The Greek Tycoon **1979** Amo Non Amo/I Love You, I Love You Not (Italy); The Day The World Ended **1980** When Time Ran Out aka Earth's Final Fury **1981** Rich And Famous **1982** Inchon **1983** Class **1984** Under The Volcano **1987** High Season **1989** Scenes From The Class Struggle In Beverly Hills **1990** Wild Orchid

Black, Karen
(Karen Ziegler)
Actress

Born 1 June 1942

Park Ridge, Illinois

With her appearances in two landmark road movies, *Easy Rider* (1969) and *Five Easy Pieces* (1970), Karen Black emerged at the same time as her co-star Jack Nicholson as a significant figure in the new Hollywood of the 70s. Her well-proportioned body, rather square face, generous mouth and slight squint have somehow condemned her to playing mostly vulnerable, bubble-headed bimbos.

The roles belie her education at Northwestern University, Illinois, and her beginnings on stage in off-Broadway satirical revues and her training at the Actors' Studio. She was acclaimed for her Broadway debut in *The Playroom* in 1965, but the play folded within a month. It was not long before the 26-year-old Francis Ford Coppola, making his first professional movie, cast her in *You're A Big Boy Now* (1967), a lively comedy set in New York, in which she was one of three women contributing to a young man's sexual education.

But it was as the acid-tripping whore in *Easy Rider*, and the dumb, red-haired waitress named Rayette, whom Nicholson picks up, gets pregnant and deserts in Bob Rafelson's *Five Easy Pieces*, that she really made her mark. (The latter brought her an Oscar nomination and the New York Critics Award for Best Supporting Actress.) The original script of *Five Easy Pieces*, of which Black approved, had her and Nicholson going over a cliff in their automobile, with only her surviving. In the climax as shown, he leaves her at a gas station and hitches a ride on a passing truck going to Alaska. The second ending became a point of contention between Black and Nicholson, although it didn't stop him putting her in his first film as director, *Drive He Said* (1971), a counter-culture campus comedy-drama in which she played a college professor's wife with whom the anti-hero student has an affair.

She was the best thing in the lamentable *Portnoy's Complaint* (1972) as an upper East side hillbilly, and in *The Great Gatsby* (1974) she was touching as Bruce Dern's mistress, killed by his wife's reckless driving. As the stewardess in *Airport 75* (1974), she bravely pilots down the stricken Jumbo 747, while being coached from the ground, and was the empty-headed extra in *The Day Of The Locust* (1975). None of these films was particularly distinguished, a situation rectified by Robert Altman's *Nashville* (1975), in which she played a would-be singer, and by Alfred Hitchcock's last film, *Family Plot* (1976), a twisted tale of kidnapping and jewel robbery, which cast her as one of the quartet of leads.

After further poor films with roles to match, Altman came to her rescue again by casting her in *Come Back To The Five And Dime, Jimmy Dean, Jimmy Dean* (1982). In company with Cher and Sandy Dennis, she excelled as the cool, elegant and mysterious husky-voiced stranger who intrudes on the meeting of the local James Dean fan club in a small Texas town, and then shocks everyone by revealing that she is really their friend Joe, who has undergone a sex change. This was followed by her portrayal of a neurotic wife going mad under the African sun in *The Grass Is Singing* (1983); and in the same year, a kook, convinced that she's being followed by her ex-husband, in Henry Jaglom's *Can She Bake A Cherry Pie?*. Perhaps due to the director's improvisatory techniques, she came over as irritatingly mannered, but she got to sing the blues quite well. She then resorted to appearing in schlock like *Out Of The Dark* (1988), in which she ran a phone sex business called Suite Nothings, and which was evidence that Hollywood frequently misuses its best actors.

1967 You're A Big Boy Now **1969** Hard Contract; Easy Rider **1970** Five Easy Pieces **1971** Drive He Said; A Gunfight; Born To Win **1972** Cisco Pike; Portnoy's Complaint **1973** The Pyx; Little Laura And Big John; The

Outfit **1974** Rhinoceros; The Great Gatsby; Airport 75 **1975**; Law And Disorder **1975** An Ace Up My Sleeve; The Day Of The Locust; Nashville **1976** Crime And Passion; Family Plot; Burnt Offerings **1978** The Rip-Off; Capricorn One; In Praise Of Older Women **1979** The Number; The Naked Sun; Killer Fish; The Last Word **1980** The Squeeze **1981** Separate Ways; Chanel Solitaire **1982** Come Back To The Five And Dime, Jimmy Dean, Jimmy Dean **1983** The Grass Is Singing; Can She Bake A Cherry Pie? **1984** Bad Manners; Killing Heat; Savage Dawn **1985** Cut And Run/Inferno In Diretta (Italy); Martin's Day **1986** The Blue Man; Flight Of The Spruce Goose; Invaders From Mars; It's Alive III: Island Of The Alive **1988** Out Of The Dark; Eternal Evil; The Invisible Kid **1990** The Children **1991** Rubin & Ed **1992** The Player (cameo) **1992/93** Return Of The Roller Blade Seven; Meantime; The Trust

Blades, Rubén

Actor, composer, singer, writer
Born 16 July 1948
Panama City, Panama

The Latin-American actor Rubén Blades is a man of several talents and an excellent actor whose abilities have not been best used. He has enjoyed a highly successful career as a musician since, in the mid-80s, recording 'Buscando Americana' ('Searching For America'), an album which broke new ground in salsa music. Subsequently he and his own band, Seis del Solar, have made several award-winning albums of South American music and given concert performances at venues throughout Europe, Central America and the US, where they've appeared at Carnegie Hall and Washington DC's Kennedy Center.

Blades' mother was a singer and radio actress, his father a percussionist who later became a detective. Their son opted for a degree in political science and law at the Universidad Nacional in Panama. After graduating, he worked on the legal staff of the Banco Nacional and as a legal adviser to a record company before furthering his studies with a Master's in law at Harvard. After all that, he chose to follow his dream of becoming a musician and based himself in Miami.

He began a parallel career as an actor in 1983, playing in a few low-budget movies, then graduating to decent supporting billing in more mainstream Hollywood ventures such as *Critical Condition*, starring Richard Pryor, and the Whoopi Goldberg vehicle *Fatal Beauty* (both 1987). Unfortunately, this pair of comedies was ill-received and did nothing for the new addition to the ranks of Latin screen actors. Indeed, Blades appears to have been seriously hampered by unlucky movies. Stocky, good-looking, and a player of efficiency and natural ease, he was pleasing as the sympathetic sheriff in Robert Redford's idealistic tale of struggling peasant farmers fighting off ruthless property developers, *The Milagro Beanfield War* (1988), but that one didn't arouse interest either. His biggest and best role, which fully unveiled the strength and charm of his screen persona, was as Diane Keaton's long-suffering, tolerant and supportive lover in her own production, *The Lemon Sisters* (1989). Alas for Rubén, this one was a monumental bomb, whose frequent disappearances (for re-editing), and brief reappearances (with nothing improved) made it something of a jokey legend by 1990, and in Spike Lee's *Mo' Better Blues*, Blades was way down the cast list, though doubtless happy to be performing in a jazz milieu.

1983 The Last Fight **1984** Beat Street **1985** Crossover Dreams (also co-writer); When The Mountains Tremble **1987** Critical Condition; Fatal Beauty **1988** Homeboy; The Milagro Beanfield War **1989** Disorganized Crime; Waiting For Salazar; The Lemon Sisters **1990** Mo' Better Blues; The Two Jakes **1990** Predator 2; The Super

Blair, Linda

Actress
Born 22 January 1955
St Louis, Missouri

The pudgy-faced, seemingly eternally youthful Linda Blair started her lengthy career as a model and actress on television commercials before delving into feature films. It is fair to say that the high point of her entire acting life to date was as the young girl possessed by the devil in *The Exorcist* (1977), a role for which she was nominated for the Best Supporting Actress Oscar at the tender age of 14. Both before and since, however, Blair has appeared in nothing but an endless line of exploitation movies – so much so that she has now become, whether by design or chance, the queen of that genre. Because of the immense impact of *The Exorcist*, she continued to receive top billing in a multitude of films, but most of them have been very poor and she often appears only in cameo or via edited pre-shot footage, as in the dreadful *Savage Island* (1985). Having battled with drug addiction, Blair headlined the recent *Exorcist* spoof, Repossessed (1990). Made in the mode of

Airplane!, it was not, alas, the comeback for which she had hoped.

It was already doubtful in the early 90s whether this still young actress would escape the trap of gratuitously violent, mindlessly sensationalist films with which she had become virtually synonymous. It is fair to add that her performance in *Savage Streets* (1984) which, for once, saw her as a 'nice' girl leading a high school group of 'goodies', was considered camp, delightful and, by exploitation film standards, respectable.

1970 The Way We Live Now **1971** The Sporting Club **1973** The Exorcist **1974** Airport '75 **1977** Exorcist II: The Heretic **1979** Roller Boogie; Hard Ride To Rantan; Wild Horse Hank **1981** Hell Night; Ruckus **1983** Chained Heat; Night Fighters **1984** Night Patrol; Savage Streets **1985** Red Heat; Savage Island; Nightforce **1988** Grotesque; SFX Retaliator; Silent Assassins **1989** Witchery; Aunt Millie's Will; The Chilling; Zapped Again; Bad Blood; W.B. Blue And The Bean; Moving Target; Up Your Alley **1990** Repossessed; Bedroom Eyes II **1991** Dead Sleep (Australia) **1992** Fatal Bond

Bochner, Hart

Actor
Born 3 October 1956
Ontario, Canada

The handsome, dark-haired son of veteran film and television character actor Lloyd Bochner, Canadian-born Hart Bochner obtained a degree in English literature at university in San Diego before finally determining to follow in his father's footsteps. Earlier, during a summer vacation while he was still in his teens, Bochner was spotted at an American Film Institute function by the wife of director Franklin Schaffner, who subsequently cast the youth in the unmemorable *Islands In The Stream* (1975).

After university, Bochner made a more promising start in a supporting role as one of the college-boy cycling rivals in Peter Yates' surprise success, *Breaking Away* (1979), and he made a suitably appetising 'younger man' for Jacqueline Bisset's brainy novelist in George Cukor's last film, *Rich And Famous* (1981). Subsequent features and his performances in them ranged from the unremarkable to the wooden, however, and Bochner fared better on television in adaptations of *East Of Eden* and *The Sun Also Rises.* His most noticeable success thus far came in the epic World War II TV mini-series *War And Remembrance*, from the Herman Wouk blockbuster, as the true-blue submariner heartthrob Byron Henry, replacing Jan Michael Vincent, who originated the role in *The Winds Of War*.

On the big screen Bochner has yet to make his presence felt: his smarmy, bearded yuppie businessman was bumped off less than halfway through *Die Hard* (1988). Two low-budget, independent productions abroad offered him rather more interesting opportunities. A bizarre Anglo-Argentinian chiller, *Apartment Zero* that same year gave him his best role to date as a seductive pathological killer, and the British period film *Fellow Traveller* (1989) cast him as a 50s Hollywood movie star destroyed by McCarthyism. His attractiveness notwithstanding, it seemed likely that he would prove most effective, like his father, as a capable if unexciting supporting player.

1975 Islands In The Stream **1979** The Band Of Four; Breaking Away; Terror Train **1981** Rich And Famous **1984** Supergirl; The Wild Life **1987** Making Mr Right **1988** Die Hard; Apartment Zero **1989** Fellow Traveller **1990** Mr Destiny **1992** Mad At The Moon

Bogdanovich, Peter

Director, producer, writer
Born 30 July 1939
Kingston, New York

Peter Bogdanovich belongs to the generation of film directors who emerged in the 70s, brought up on, and inspired by, the movies produced during the golden age of the major studios. In fact, the majority of his films are exercises in style – attempts to re-create the Hollywood past. In his documentary on John Ford, he disarmingly allows himself to be put down by the great man.

Not surprisingly, his two best films were shot in black and white, a practice that had already become rare in the previous decade. Both *The Last Picture Show* (1971) and *Paper Moon* (1973) lovingly invoke the spirit of Ford, William Wellman and William Wyler and, despite their allusiveness, they appeal to the non-film buff. The first of these, a fondly nostalgic look at 50s small-town America, cast Ben Johnson (a Ford favourite) as surrogate father to the town's youngsters, and owner of the movie house forced to close because of the advent of TV. For *Paper Moon*, Bogdanovich went back further into the past – the Depression – for a charming yet cynical picaresque tale of a father-daughter con team (Ryan and Tatum O'Neal) wheedling money out of widows.

Although Bogdanovich studied acting with Stella Adler, and both appeared in and directed a number of plays, he was always drawn to film. Before he worked as Roger Corman's assistant on *The Wild Angels* (1966), he had written several monographs of directors for the Museum of Modern Art, and books on Ford, Allan Dwan and Fritz Lang. Corman gave the tyro director the money to make *Targets* (1967), an extremely impressive debut movie, in which the octogenarian Boris Karloff played Byron Orlok, a horror movie star in danger from a sniper, and confronted by his own image (in Corman's *The Terror*) on the screen of a drive-in movie theatre.

When he was preparing *The Last Picture Show*, Bogdanovich discovered the 19-year-old fashion model Cybill Shepherd, whom he lovingly cast as the richest girl in town. It was not long before he would divorce his wife, Polly Platt, the splendid set designer on his first films and mother of his two children, and live with Shepherd. With her in mind, he directed *Daisy Miller* (1974), Henry James without the prose, which came in for a heavy lambasting from the critics and indifference from the public. 'Trying to make that little thing he's with into Daisy Miller was hilarious,' director Henry Hathaway cruelly remarked. Undeterred, Bogdanovich starred 'the little thing' (Shepherd) in *At Long Last Love* (1975), a flat-footed, off-key musical, co-starring Burt Reynolds. It was greeted with even greater scorn than the previous movie. This was followed by a third bomb, *Nickelodeon* (1976), a slapdash, slapstick and dubious homage to silent screen comedy. A few years previously, though, *What's Up, Doc?* (1972), a heavy homage to hectic 30s screwball humour, graced by Ryan O'Neal and Barbra Streisand, had grossed a healthy $28 million for Warner Bros.

After three years spent licking his wounds, Bogdanovich returned, helped by producer Corman, with *Saint Jack* (1979), a sincere attempt to get away from Hollywood in both senses. It has a splendid sense of locale (the red-light district of Singapore) but, set in a world of pimps and prostitutes, is too reminiscent of films like *The World Of Susie Wong* (1960). Among a cast headed by Ben Gazzara, the director himself played an unpleasant American mobster.

There was more drama in his private life when his girlfriend (the Shepherd liaison was over), *Playboy* Playmate of the Year Dorothy Stratten, was murdered by her husband after he learned of her affair with the director. Bogdanovich then married Stratten's younger half-sister, Louise Hoogstraten.

After another flop, *They All Laughed* (1981), an old-fashioned 'meeting cute' comedy, the former boy wonder regained some credibility with *Mask* (1985), a film that eschewed any resurrection of dead genres. Powered by Cher's strong performance as the drug-taking biker mother of a deformed child, the film gave the director the praise that had eluded him for so long. However, a hankering after the kind of acclaim he had enjoyed with *The Last Picture Show*, led him back to the same author (Larry McMurtry) and characters, played by many of the same cast, in *Texasville* (1990), but it proved singularly lacking in the same appeal or success. His necessarily stagey film of the theatre farce, *Noises Off*, drew on Bogdanovich's skill at orchestrating screwball antics, but it, too, failed to ignite.

As director only unless stated otherwise: **1968** Targets (w/d) **1969** Lion's Love (actor only) **1971** Directed By John Ford (docu; w/d); The Last Picture Show (also co-writer) **1972** What's Up, Doc? (also writer) **1973** Paper Moon; Vérité Et Mensonges (France; actor only) **1974** Daisy Miller **1975** At Long Last Love (w/d) **1976** Nickelodeon (also co-writer) **1979** Saint Jack (also actor) **1981** They All Laughed **1985** Mask **1988** Illegally Yours **1990** Texasville **1992** Noises Off

Boorman, John

Director, writer
Born 18 January 1933
Shepperton, England

One of the least prolific of the major British directors to emerge in the 60s, John Boorman has shown little evidence in his often stylised film work of his roots in documentaries (he started his career as a film editor at ITN). As documentary drama came to occupy the New Wave of British television, spawning directors such as Ken Loach and Michael Apted, he was put in charge of the BBC's documentary film unit in Bristol. The success of his series The Newcomers in 1964 led to his first feature film, *Catch Us If You Can*, which bore as much similarity to Richard Lester's *A Hard Day's Night* as its stars, the Dave Clark Five, did to the Beatles with its not altogether successful mixture of anarchy, irony and occasional documentary realism in the use of locations.

It was *Point Blank* (1967) that made Boorman's reputation as he turned what promised to be a standard revenge thriller with 'swinging 60s' overtones into a dreamlike, elemental, almost mythical quest set against the clash of its protagonists' contrasting codes of honour and behaviour – a virtual Sir Gawain and the Green Gangster. Its success was not repeated with *Hell In The Pacific* (1968), an intriguing and much imitated (*Enemy Mine*, *Crusoe*) World War II story of two enemies (Toshiro Mifune, *Point Blant*'s Lee Marvin) on the same island, told with a minimum of dialogue and playing at times like the best of silent cinema. Disastrously, the ending was clumsily changed and remained unseen for years, thus destroying the film's argument that it was the trappings of civilisation that fostered conflict.

A slightly different point of view was taken in the even more imitated *Deliverance* (1972) in which four city dwellers plan to take on nature during a backwoods canoeing trip which goes nightmarishly wrong as nature and the local rednecks turn on them, forcing them to strip away their values and become savages to survive – a drama ironically played out in a wilderness that is ultimately to be conquered by flooding instigated by business interests. The movie also offered plenty of opportunities for Boorman to indulge in his penchant for Arthurian imagery, with a hand breaking through the water, a shotgun taking the place of the sword in the yet-to-be filmed *Excalibur* (an image almost repeated when Sean Connery emerges in slow motion, gun first, from a pile of grain in *Zardoz* 1974).

It was not until 1981 that Boorman was able to wield *Excalibur* itself through the waters with a wonderful use of colour and light, showing his talent as a superb visual sensualist, capturing the very feeling of a moment while also providing ample proof that he is equally atrocious with words – some of the dialogue is funnier than *Monty Python And The Holy Grail* – while a parade of over-ripe performances and silly accents frequently detract from the picture's romanticism and emotional core. Similarly, the ecological protest of *The Emerald Forest* (1985) proved best when dealing with its more elemental aspects, with only the semi-autobiographical *Hope And Glory* (1987) showing much grasp of characterisation through dialogue.

Despite the twin disasters of *Zardoz* and *Exorcist II: The Heretic* (1977), neither of them as bad as their reputations, albeit with their moments of insight and originality swamped by heavy handed pretentiousness, Boorman has never made a completely worthless film (although 1990's *Where The Heart Is* is but a hair's breadth away) but by the same token has never achieved a truly great one. His body of work remains a series of great moments often lacking context and surrounded by self-indulgence.

As director only unless stated otherwise: **1965** Catch Us If You Can aka Having A Wild Weekend **1967** Point Blank **1968** Hell In The Pacific **1970** Leo The Last (also co-writer) **1972** Deliverance **1974** Zardoz (w/d) **1977** Exorcist II: The Heretic **1981** Excalibur (also co-writer) **1985** The Emerald Forest **1987** Hope and Glory (w/d) **1990** where The Heart Is (also co-writer) **1991** I Dreamt I Woke Up (Ireland) (w/d; also actor)

Bottoms, Timothy

Actor
Born 30 August 1949
Santa Barbara, California

With his kind-featured, all-American small-town looks, together with a fetching on-screen introverted awkwardness, Timothy Bottoms seemed likely to make more of his screen career than he did; he displayed such constant misjudgement that his good films have been more by accident than intent. After touring Europe with the Santa Barbara Madrigal Society in 1967, he was spotted in a production of *Romeo and Juliet* that led to his first screen role as the crippled soldier treated, literally, like a sideshow freak by the folks at home in Dalton Trumbo's *Johnny Got His Gun* (1971). While the actor gave it genuine emotion for the early and closing scenes, everything in between – including hip chats with a spaced out Jesus – was an embarrassing and pretentious mess, although he himself regarded it as an 'important and deep' film. Yet it was his touching portrait of the young Sonny, coming to terms with an affair with an older woman and the death of his friend Sam 'The Lion' (Ben Johnson) in the same year's *The Last Picture Show*, a film *he* regarded as trivial by comparison, that was both his most moving and best remembered screen work.

Bottoms followed with a series of interesting films: he was one of the shipwrecked whalers who exploits the Eskimos who save him in Philip Kaufman's 15-years-too-early *The White Dawn* (1974); he brought much emotional depth to one of the Czech assassins in *Operation Daybreak* (1975), giving a particularly moving death scene, but only *The Paper Chase* (1973) met with success, albeit doing more for director John Houseman's career than for Bottoms'. After his brooding saboteur in *Rollercoaster* (1977), he embarked on some of the worst films ever made, a few even proving unreleasable, and a few average TV movies. His return to mainstream cinema in the *Last Picture Show* sequel, *Texasville* (1990), was less than gracious – he did not want to make it 'because I don't like any of the people in it' – and his reputation for self-importance and cold shoulders seemed to indicate the return was only a passing visit.

1971 Johnny Got His Gun; The Last Picture Show **1972** Love and Pain and the Whole Damn Thing; Look Homeward **1973** The Paper Chase **1974** The Crazy World of Julius Vrooder aka Vrooder's Hooch; The White Dawn **1975** Operation Daybreak aka Price Of Freedom aka Seven Men At Daybreak **1976** A Small Town In Texas **1977** Rollercoaster; **1978** The Other Side of the Mountain II **1979** First Hello; Hurricane **1980** High Country **1984** Hambone and Hillie aka The Adventures of Hambone; The Census Taker; Secrets of the Phantom Caverns **1986** Invaders From Mars; In The Shadow of Kilimanjaro; The Fantasist; The Sea Serpent **1987** The Wind; Mio In The Land of The Faraway (Norway) **1988** The Drifter **1989** Return From The River Kwai **1990** Texasville; Istanbul: Keep Your Eyes Open

Boyle, Peter

Actor
Born 18 October 1933
Philadelphia

A busy, reliable character actor who has performed in comedies and drama with equal success, Peter Boyle was once a monk with the order of Christian Brothers. He left the cloistered life behind in the early 1960s to pursue an acting career, but has always retained a distinctively monkish hairstyle: closely cropped back and sides, bald pate.

After playing in several off-Broadway stage productions, Boyle enjoyed a spell with the Second City improvisational troupe before moving to Hollywood to seek out TV and film work. It was the height of the counter-culture and he soon scored a notable success in the title role of *Joe* (1969). As a blue-collar, redneck bigot who turns to extortion, the actor displayed a manic intensity that transformed a mediocre movie into something of an event, and a sequel, *Citizen Joe*, followed 17 years later. Curiously, Boyle also played New York racketeer Joe Gallo in *Crazy Joe* (1974), and infamous Senator Joe McCarthy in a 1977 TV movie called *Tail Gunner Joe*. Something of a fixture in liberal, or even vaguely radical, movies, Boyle was an anchor in straight drama like *The Candidate* (1972), with Robert Redford, but really cut loose in the comedies *Slither* (1973) and *Young Frankenstein* (1974), Mel Brooks' superior horror spoof. As the monster, Boyle had all the best moments, including a hilarious scene with Gene Hackman's blind monk, and singing 'Puttin' On The Ritz' in top hat and tails. In Scorsese's *Taxi Driver* (1976) and Paul Schrader's *Hardcore* (1978), this versatile actor contributed deft, witty cameos as, respectively, a philosophical cab driver and an ineffectual private eye.

During the 80s, the quality of the movies fell off somewhat, but Boyle continued to do good work in *Outland* (1981), *Hammett* (1982) and *The Dream Team* (1989). The latter film reunited him with *Slither* director Howard Zieff, and put him in the spotlight as the senior member of a quartet of mental patients (Michael Keaton, Christopher Lloyd and Stephen Furst were the others) on the loose in New York.

1968 The Virgin President; Medium Cool **1969** Joe **1970** Diary Of A Mad Housewife **1971** T.R. Baskin (GB: A Date With A Lonely Girl) **1972** Steelyard Blues; The Candidate **1973** Slither; The Friends Of Eddie Coyle; Kid Blue aka Dime Box **1974** Crazy Joe; Ghost In The Noonday Sun; Young Frankenstein **1976** Swashbuckler aka The Scarlet Buccaneer; Taxi Driver **1978** Hardcore aka The Hardcore Life; F.I.S.T. **1979** Beyond The Poseidon Adventure; The Brink's Job; In God We Trust **1980** Where The Buffalo Roam; **1981** Outland **1982** Hammett **1983** Yellowbeard **1984** Johnny Dangerously **1985** Turk 182! **1986** Citizen Joe **1987** Surrender; Walker **1988** Red Heat; The In-Crowd **1989** The Dream Team; Speed Zone **1990** Men Of Respect **1991** Rubin and Ed; Kickboxer 2: The road Back **1992** Nervous Ticks; Honeymoon In Vegas

Bracco, Lorraine

Actress
Born 1955
Brooklyn, New York

With relatively few American movies to her credit, Lorraine Bracco made a strong impression in her first substantial supporting role in *Someone To Watch Over Me* (1987). The strength of her screen personality and her evident intelligence led her, three years later, to the only female part of any size and importance in Scorsese's *GoodFellas*. As the Jewish girl who marries Irish-Italian mobster Ray Liotta and is sucked into a very different kind of close-knit family from that she has previously known, Bracco brought credibility and understanding to a difficult task.

Dark and attractive, she began her professional life as a fashion model in the States when she was 16, and continued the work in Europe. Successful in France, where she was featured on the covers of *Elle* and *Cosmopolitan* and made TV commercials, she diversified to become a Paris disc jockey, after which she produced and presented interviews for a French TV documentary special about the relationship between music and fashion. Having dipped her toe in the waters of screen acting with something called *Duo Sur Canape* (1970), she made a second French film, *Fais Gaffe à la Gaffe*, in 1981. Her next outing was Italian, under the aegis of Lina Wertmuller, who gave her a small featured role in *Camorra: The Naples Connection* (1985), and cast her again, four years later, in *Una Notte Di Chiara Di Luna*.

By then, Bracco had taken the plunge back in her native land, first in a small part as a hooker in *The Pick-Up Artist* (1987), then as policeman Tom Berenger's wife in Ridley Scott's *Someone To Watch Over Me*, which was her breakthrough. The movie was one of the most intelligent and attractive thrillers made during the 80s and, as the Queens housewife and mother in danger of losing her husband to a sophisticated and beautiful Manhattan heiress (Mimi Rogers), Bracco transformed what could have been a thankless role into one of considerable impact. The results began to show a couple of years later, although she was not ideally cast as a schoolteacher in the extremely mediocre *Sing* (1989). She fared better as the only noticeable woman in *The Dream Team* (1989) and, with the huge success of *GoodFellas* (1990), was established enough to rate the plum female lead opposite Sean Connery in the enjoyable hokum of the environmentally friendly jungle romance, *Medicine Man*.

In her private life this lady of diverse interests and accomplishments married Harvey Keitel, in three of whose films she has appeared, and opposite whom she made her New York stage debut in David Rabe's *Goose And Tom Tom,* co-starring Sean Penn and Madonna, at the Lincoln Center.

1979 Duo Sur Canape (France) **1981** Fais Gaffe à la Gaffe (France) **1985** Camorra: The Naples Connection **1987** The Pick-Up Artist; Someone To Watch Over Me **1989** The Dream Team; Una Notte Di Chiaro Di Luna/On A Moonlit Night (Italy); Sing **1990** GoodFellas; Stranger In The House; **1991** Switch; Talent For The Game **1992** Radio Flyer; Medicine Man; Traces of Red

Brandauer, Klaus Maria

Actor

Born 22 June 1944

Alt Aussee, Austria

Klaus Maria Brandauer, Austrian-born, a luminary of the German-speaking theatre, is an actor of undoubted leading-man stature. Bull-headed and stocky of physique, he cannot be described as conventionally handsome, yet with fierce bright eyes set in a face of high-cheekboned, slightly Slavic cast, he exerts a presence of extraordinary magnetism on both stage and screen. In past eras Hollywood would have captured him and moulded him into a star; but in spite of his success in *Out Of Africa* (1985), where his playing of Meryl Streep's charming aristocratic wastrel of a husband quite eclipsed that of the film's nominal male star, Robert Redford (and won him a Best Supporting Actor Oscar nomination), the modern American cinema seems to have been unable to set a suitable value on Brandauer – to its cost. Perhaps the reputation that he has developed for being moody and uncooperative on set has something to do with it.

He was educated in Germany, at the Stuttgart Academy of Music and Dramatic Arts, and subsequently worked his way up through the repertory theatre companies of Tübingen and Düsseldorf to reach the renowned Burgtheater in Vienna: by 1970 he had become a classical actor of considerable renown in all the leading German-speaking cities. His first experience of the camera came in the making of a French TV mini-series adapted from Romain Rolland's huge novel *Jean-Christophe*. As a feature film actor his debut was not a promising one: a Central European heavy in the mediocre thriller *The Salzburg Connection* (1972). This was a type he was to repeat opposite Sean Connery in the 1983 Bond thriller *Never Say Never Again*, and, again opposite Connery, a Russian scientist in the Le Carré adaptation *The Russia House* (1990). Brandauer's smoothly sinister Baron is a prime asset in the Anglo-American chiller *Burning Secret* (1988), but on the whole the list of his English-language roles is not an inspiring one.

It has been left to the three films he made with the Hungarian director István Szabó – *Mephisto* (1981), *Colonel Redl* (1985) and *Hanussen* (1988) – to demonstrate the actor's enormous breadth of range. Each of these films deals in a different way with the theme of betrayal; whether as the slippery actor-manager of *Mephisto*, rising to power and prestige along with the Nazis, the demonically driven, closet-homosexual Austrian officer of *Colonel Redl*, or the shady clairvoyant of *Hanussen*, Brandauer fleshes out the particular issues with a magnificent combination of dramatic intelligence, volatile temperament and sheer, screen-filling personality.

1972 The Salzburg Connection **1981** Mephisto **1983** Never Say Never Again **1985** Colonel Redl; Out Of Africa; The Lightship **1986** Streets of Gold **1988** Burning Secret; Hanussen **1989** Das Spinnenetz/The Spider's Web (Germany) **1990** La Liberté Ou La Mort/The French Revolution (France); The Russia House **1991** White Fang

Brando, Marlon

Actor
Born 3 April 1924
Omaha, Nebraska

Modern screen acting began with Marlon Brando. Unlike the stars of an earlier generation who generally adapted their roles to their personalities, Brando brought a new realism to the screen. No matter how mannered or misconceived some of his performances have been, he has invested an intelligence and intensity in each role. Even in films unworthy of his talents, there is always something electric happening when he is before the camera–and off it. Only Brando could have asked $3 million for his ten-minute appearance as The comic-book hero's father in *Superman* (1978) and got it, or have such a powerful – largely off-screen – presence as Colonel Kurtz in Francis Ford Coppola's *Apocalypse Now* (1979) to justify his top-billed, top-salaried apparition 15 minutes from the end of the two-and-a-half hour movie.

This symbol of rebellion was born into a middle-class family of French extraction (the name was once Brandeau). He was a difficult child, so his father sent him to a military academy in Minnesota from which he was expelled. Young Marlon drifted around for a while before joining his two older sisters, Frances and Jocelyn, in New York. His work with Elia Kazan at the Actors' Studio was crucial to his development as an actor, and it was Kazan who cast him as the inarticulate brutal slob, Stanley Kowalski, in Tennessee Williams' *A Streetcar Named Desire* on Broadway. He worked with Kazan again in the 1951 film version of the play, and, with the same director, in *Viva Zapatal* (1952) and *On The Waterfront* (1954), as the washed-up boxer Terry Molloy, for which he won an Oscar. His appearance as the hoodlum biker in *The Wild One* (1964), trading on his muscular handsomeness and animal magnetism, made him the leather-jacketed idol of the erotic-anarchic motor-cycle cult in the 50s.

The 60s was not Brando's best period, despite his English-accented Fletcher Christian in *Mutiny On The Bounty* (1962) or his closet homosexual major in *Reflections In A Golden Eye* (1967) opposite Elizabeth Taylor, and an excursion into directing with the brooding Western *One-Eyed Jacks* (1961). But in the 70s, he became a force to be reckoned with again with his meticulously delineated character performance as the old Don Corleone in *The Godfather* (1972), which won him his second Academy Award. (He repeated the role with his tongue in his padded cheeks in *The Freshman*, 1989.) At the Oscar ceremony, an Indian girl read a prepared statement on his behalf, rejecting the award in order to draw attention to the plight of the American Indian people, one of his many civil rights' concerns. He also caused controversy with his role as the anguished middle-aged American in Bernardo Bertolucci's *Last Tango In Paris* (1972), for which he was threatened with prosecution under Italian law for alleged indecencies committed on screen.

Brando's personal life has always been in the public eye. In 1957, he married Anna Kashfi, thinking she was Indian, but she was, in fact, of Irish descent. They separated a year later, after the birth of a son, Christian, and Brando later won custody of the child following a bitter wrangle. In 1960, he married the Mexican actress Movita, whom he had known for many years. But while on location for *Mutiny On The Bounty*, he met a Tahitian beauty called Tarita, with whom he had two children.

After nine years away from the screen, a bulky Brando returned to play the small but scene-stealing role of a liberal South African lawyer in *A Dry White Season* (1989), for which he gave his fee to the Anti-Apartheid Movement. Although he makes few films, everything he does still makes news. In 1989, he was thrust unwillingly into the headlines when his son, Christian, was arrested for the murder of his half-sister's boyfriend. He himself then turned in a curiously subdued portrayal of Torquemada in one of several Christopher Columbus quincentennial epics. One can only suppose he did it for the money.

1950 The Men **1951** A Streetcar Named Desire **1952** Viva Zapata! **1953** Julius Caesar **1954** The Wild One; On The Waterfront; Désirée **1955** Guys And Dolls **1956** The Teahouse Of The August Moon **1957** Sayonara **1958** The Young Lions **1960** The Fugitive Kind **1961** One-Eyed Jacks (also director) **1962** Mutiny On The Bounty **1963** The Ugly American **1964** Bedtime Story **1965** Morituri aka The Saboteur aka Code Name Morituri **1966** The Chase; The Appaloosa **1967** The Countess From Hong Kong; Reflections In A Golden Eye **1968** Candy **1969** The Night Of The Following Day; Queimada/Burn! **1971** The Nightcomers **1972** The Godfather; Last Tango In Paris (Italy) **1976** The Missouri Breaks **1978** Superman **1979** Apocalypse Now **1980** The Formula **1989** A Dry White Season; The Freshman **1992** Christopher Columbus: The Discovery

Bridges, Beau
(Lloyd Vernet Bridges III)
Actor
Born 9 December 1941
Los Angeles, California

One of the best known contemporary father-son dynasties in Hollywood is that of the Bridges – Lloyd, Beau and Jeff. Although Beau Bridges appeared in a number of films directed by friends of his father – Lewis Milestone (*No Minor Vices* and *The Red Pony*) and Abraham Polonsky (*Force Of Evil*) – when he was seven and eight, he had no ambitions to become an actor. He was much more interested in a sporting career, especially basketball, despite being only five-feet-nine-inches tall. But when he discovered, after his two years at UCLA, that he would be hard put to it to become a pro sportsman, he decided to follow in his father's footsteps.

Nevertheless, Beau appeared in a number of films with a sporting theme, giving dogged rather than inspired performances. He was the skiing champ 'Mad Dog' Buek, who helps and proposes marriage to a paralysed skier in the too self-consciously tear-jerky but successful *The Other Side Of The Mountain* (1975) but, as he was killed in an aircrash while hurrying to his sweetheart's side, he was unable to participate in the sequel. He then took to wheels in *Greased Lightning* (1977), a biopic on the first black stock car racer, in which he played a redneck driver; he was also the 'bad boy of international racing' in a stars-and-stripes helmet on a 500cc Suzuki in *Silver Dream Racer* (1980), and the drag-racing hero of Jonathan Kaplan's *Heart Like A Wheel* (1983), starring Bonnie Bedelia.

His very first role as an adult was in the low-budget *The Explosive Generation* (1961), playing a high school student who participates in an eerily silent basketball match (the students are on a silence strike) and, much later in his career, he was the innocent-seeming gym instructor in Sidney Lumet's *Child's Play* (1972), set in a Catholic boys' boarding school.

Bridges first came to the fore by convincingly portraying a couple of innocents abroad. First in *Gaily, Gaily* (1969), a period romp supposedly based on Ben Hecht's autobiographical tales, with the actor breathlessly playing Ben Harvey. 'You're so dumb', says prostitute Margot Kidder when he naively finds himself accommodation in a brothel, and the character and the film were likewise; and then as the well-meaning owner of a tenement in Brooklyn's black ghetto in Hal Ashby's *The Landlord* (1970), this time playing a similar role but with more subtlety.

Unfortunately, while his younger brother Jeff (eight years his junior) was beginning to appear in good films with good directors, Beau continued mostly in a series of duds, relieved only by the well-intentioned *Norma Rae* (1979), in which he played textile worker Sally Field's husband, complaining that she neglected her family for union activities. The film won a couple of Oscars, and Bridges bathed in reflected glory for a while. But it was not until *The Fabulous Baker Boys* (1989), in which he was paired with brother Jeff as sibling rivals for the attentions of lovely Michelle Pfeiffer, that he began to be taken seriously again. In the less flashy role of the more conservative and less talented member of the nightclub piano duo, the now portly Beau seemed inspired to deeper and more nuanced playing by the fraternal theme opposite his own, more charismatic, brother.

1961 The Explosive Generation **1965** Village Of the Giants **1967** The Incident **1968** For Love Of Ivy **1969** Gaily Gaily (GB: Chicago, Chicago) **1970** Adam's Woman; The Landlord **1971** The Christian Licorice Store **1972** Hammersmith Is Out; Child's Play **1973** Your Three Minutes Are Up **1974** Lovin' Molly **1975** The Other Side Of The Mountain (GB: A Window To The

Sky) **1976** One Summer Love aka Dragonfly; Swashbuckler; Two-Minute Warning **1977** Greased Lightning **1978** The Four Feathers **1979** The Runner Stumbles; Norma Rae; The Fifth Musketeer **1981** Honky Tonk Freeway **1982** Love Child; Night Crossing; Silver Dream Racer **1983** Heart Like A Wheel **1984** The Hotel New Hampshire **1987** The Wild Pair (also director) **1988** The Iron Triangle; Seven Hours To Judgement **1989** The Fabulous Baker Boys; Signs Of Life; The Wizard **1990** Daddy's Dyin' – Who's Got The Will? **1991** Married To It **1992/93** Sidekicks

Bridges, James

Director, writer
Born 3 February 1936
Paris, Arkansas

One of Hollywood's veteran workhorses, one-time actor James Bridges has been successfully employed in television, in theatre and in film since his youth, turning his hand to writing, directing and producing. While he has never quite been regarded as being among the first rank, much of Bridges' film work has commanded attention for good or ill, and his remarkably timely 1979 nailbiting drama, *The China Syndrome*, justly gave him a critical and commercial hit.

A product of Arkansas Teachers College and the prestigious University of Southern California, Bridges debuted as an actor at the age of 21 with a bit in the Ethel Barrymore vehicle *Johnny Trouble* (1957) and notched up around 50 appearances in television shows and a handful of feature films, most notably John Cassavetes' *Faces* (1968). Writing proved a more rewarding outlet for him, however: apart from his film work Bridges has written 16 plays and his television writing credits include 18 episodes for the late 1970s revival *Alfred Hitchcock Presents*. In the course of his career he has also directed theatrical productions in New York, Los Angeles, and at the Edinburgh Festival.

Bridges' first produced screenplay was for the moderately well-received *The Appaloosa* (1966), a moody character study Western starring Marlon Brando. The other three films he has scripted but not directed have been quite different and distinctive, if not entirely distinguished: *Colossus: The Forbin Project* (1970) was one of the first of a wave of computer-run-amok thrillers, and one of the most frighteningly plausible; *Limbo* (1972), co-written with Joan Micklin Silver, was one of the first American films to deal with the impact of the Vietnam War on those back home but proved a mediocre, melodramatic production; and, most recently, Bridges co-scripted *White Hunter, Black Heart* (1990) for Clint Eastwood, which met with sharply divided reactions.

As a film director he made his debut with *The Baby Maker* in 1970. It was a curious mixture of the tepid with the overwrought as a tiresome hippy (Barbara Hershey) agreed to produce a baby for a middle-class, childless couple. But like much of Bridges' subsequent work it displayed his savvy in anticipating movie trends, with the same subject still recurring in TV and feature movies. His second effort, *The Paper Chase* (1973), was a superior comedy-drama ensemble piece set at Harvard Law School that not only earned its maker an Oscar nomination for his screenplay but spawned a TV series and set the tone for countless imitative group interaction series and films. An original, if histrionic, slightly autobiographical film, *September 30, 1955* was a disappointing and long-in-coming follow-up in 1978 that has some minor cult status for tackling the phenomenon of movie star fanaticism via the extreme reaction of an Arkansas boy to the death of his hero, James Dean.

The high point of James Bridges' career is unquestionably *The China Syndrome* (1979), a taut, tense, intelligent drama succinctly played by Jack Lemmon and Jane Fonda that dealt not only with the sinister cover-up and aftermath of an accident at a nuclear plant, but with the role and responsibilities of television news. Released almost simultaneously with the real-life nuclear 'incident' at Three Mile Island in Pennsylvania, the film probably did as much as the true event to spark heated public debate about nuclear reactors. Bridges won several awards, Golden Globe nominations for direction and writing, and his second Oscar nomination for his contribution to the screenplay. Next was *Urban Cowboy* (1980), centred on John Travolta's performance as a young man struggling to live up to the machismo required in a Texan honky-tonk milieu. It wasn't in the same league but it was unusual, effective and well received.

Bridges then bombed through the 1980s. *Mike's Murder* (1984), only released after two years of editing and re-editing to no avail, pitted Debra Winger against a drugs murder mess; *Perfect* (1985) – Travolta again – was a risible attempt to explore contemporary mores through a *Rolling Stone* reporter's investigation of the aerobics scene; *Bright*

Lights, Big City (1988) was an unconvincing effort to translate the yuppie-falling-apart novel to the screen.

As writer-director unless stated otherwise: **1966** The Appaloosa (writer only) **1970** The Baby Maker; Colossus: The Forbin Project **1972** Limbo (co-writer only) **1973** The Paper Chase **1978** September 30, 1955 **1979** The China Syndrome (co-writer, director) **1980** Urban Cowboy **1984** Mike's Murder **1985** Perfect (co-writer, director) **1988** Bright Lights, Big City (co-writer, director) **1990** White Hunter, Black Heart (co-writer only) **1991** The Object Of My Affection

Bridges, Jeff

Actor

Born 4 December 1949

Los Angeles, California

Writing about *The Last American Hero* (1973), Pauline Kael observed that Jeff Bridges 'may be the most natural and least self-conscious screen actor that ever lived'. A pardonable exaggeration, perhaps, as Bridges has the rare quality of simply *being* the character he's playing – easy, relaxed, effortless, always himself and yet, almost paradoxically, always convincing.

Well-built, with a broad all-American grin and a thick thatch of very light brown hair, Bridges has a reassuring presence – a throwback to the great days of the studio system when stars like Barbara Stanwyck, Gary Cooper and James Stewart made screen acting seem so simple. It's not surprising, then, to discover that Bridges has celluloid in his veins. If not born quite to the Hollywood purple, he was certainly a Tinseltown princeling, son of Lloyd Bridges, a highly serviceable second-rank leading man, whose 1950s TV series *Sea Hunt* featured the child Jeff and his older brother Beau.

Jeff made his big-screen debut in *Halls Of Anger* (1970) and then came to the fore in Peter Bogdanovich's poignant ode to lost American innocence, *The Last Picture Show* (1971), playing the pivotal role of Duane Jackson, personification of the boy next door. The performance gained him an Oscar nomination for Best Supporting Actor, but the award went to another member of the cast, old-timer Ben Johnson. Either through luck or good judgment, Bridges then chose parts in some of the most interesting minor Hollywood films of the early 1970s: flexing his easy-going blend of bluff and bravado in Robert Benton's anti-Western, *Bad Company* (1972); excellent as the tanktown protégé of washed-up pug Stacy Keach in John Huston's *Fat City* the same year; and comfortably slipping into the character of Junior Jackson, moonshine runner-turned-demolition derby champ in Lamont Johnson's *The Last American Hero* (1973).

He easily held his own against Clint Eastwood in Michael Cimino's *Thunderbolt And Lightfoot* (1974) as the amiable young drifter recruited for a daring bank heist. Then, in 1975, he brought bags of shaggy-dog charm to two of the most charming comedies of the decade: Frank Perry's *Rancho Deluxe*, joining forces with Sam Waterston to rustle cattle in modern Montana; and Howard Zieff's *Hearts Of The West*, an affectionate tribute to the lower depths of Hollywood in the early 1930s, with Bridges playing a hick with literary ambitions who falls foul of incompetent con-men and ruthless B-Western producer Alan Arkin, the Erich von Stroheim of Poverty Row.

In Bob Rafelson's equally delightful *Stay Hungry* (1976), Bridges was the scapegrace heir to a Southern fortune, romancing pert Sally Field and sparring with Arnold Schwarzenegger's equally pert pectorals. He had an even bigger co-star in the disastrous Dino De Laurentiis remake of *King Kong* (1976) before being reunited with John Huston in *Winter Kills* (1979). This was one of Huston's acting assignments, in which he was Bridges' wicked old dad in a political conspiracy thriller typical of the period. However, Bridges' reunion with Michael Cimino in *Heaven's Gate* (1980) was less happy, although his performance holds up better than those of Isabelle Huppert, Christopher Walken and Kris Kristofferson.

Conspiracy stalked through Ivan Passer's *Cutter's Way* (1981), a bleak thriller in which Bridges was the complacent beach-bum bullied by his crazed Vietnam-vet friend (John Heard) into probing a sex-murder case. Then he metamorphosed into a sympathetic humanoid alien stranded on Earth and quizzically coming to terms with the puzzling behaviour of the people he finds there, in John Carpenter's beguiling *Starman* (1984). Taylor Hackford's *Against All Odds* (1984) was a bold shot at reworking the *noir* classic *Out Of The Past* (1948), but this time the actor seemed overawed by the languid shadow cast by Robert Mitchum, star of the original, and discomfited by the presence of two of Mitchum's co-stars, Jane Greer and Richard Widmark.

But, for all his popularity and constant

output of work, Jeff Bridges somehow never was thought of as a star of the first rank. That changed with Richard Marquand's smash-hit thriller, *Jagged Edge*, in 1985. Bridges' charm has always been at its most effective when mixed with moral ambivalence and here, co-starring with Glenn Close, he made a plausible psychopath in this fairly implausible but audience-grabbing exercise in 'intimate jeopardy'. This was followed by another thriller of sorts, *The Morning After* (1986), made by Sidney Lumet in what was clearly a moment of aberration. This time, the star played a redneck ex-cop befriending an alcoholic actress (Jane Fonda), who wakes up to find a murdered man in her bed. Then, in Francis Coppola's *Tucker* (1988), he evoked the bland optimism and visionary determination of 1940s car designer Preston Tucker who, in a neat cinematic joke, is betrayed by a politician played by Jeff's own father, Lloyd Bridges.

The next logical step was to co-star with brother Beau in *The Fabulous Baker Boys* (1990), as a bickering cocktail-lounge piano duo whose lives are turned upside down when they hire leggy chanteuse Michelle Pfeiffer to spice up the act. Inevitable bathos followed in *Texasville* (1990), Peter Bogdanovich's ill-conceived sequel to *The Last Picture Show*, in which Bridges' Duane Jackson returns to the scene of his youth as a rich, disillusioned oil man. The movie's failure, however, seemed unlikely to dent the reputation of Jeff Bridges – happily married, hard-working family man and irresistible box-office favourite – who gave one of his most striking performances teamed with Robin Williams in Terry Gilliam's splendid New York fable, *The Fisher King*.

1969 Halls Of Anger **1970** The Yin And Yang Of Mr Go **1971** The Last Picture Show **1972** Fat City; Bad Company **1973** The Last American Hero aka Hard Driver; The Iceman Cometh; Lolly-Madonna XXX **1974** Thunderbolt And Lightfoot; **1975** Rancho Deluxe; Hearts Of The West **1976** Stay Hungry; King Kong **1978** Somebody Killed Her Husband **1979** Success aka The American Success Company; Winter Kills **1980** Heaven's Gate **1981** Cutter's Way aka Cutter And Bone **1982** Tron; Kiss Me Goodbye **1984** Against All Odds; Starman **1985** Jagged Edge **1986** Eight Million Ways To Die; The Morning After **1987** Nadine **1988** Tucker **1989** Cold Feet; The Fabulous Baker Boys **1990** See You In The Morning; Texasville **1991** The Fisher King **1992** American Heart **1992/93** Joy Ride; The Vanishing

Broderick, Matthew

Actor
Born 21 March 1962
New York City

Although only 19 when he appeared in his first film, Matthew Broderick had already established a name for himself on stage, having developed a working relationship with playwrights Horton Foote and Neil Simon. He made his professional stage debut in 1979 in an off-off-Broadway production of Foote's *On Valentine's Day* with his father, James Broderick, in the lead, and later appeared in the film version. Foote also wrote the screenplay for *1918* (1983), and the play *The Widow Claire*, in which Broderick appeared off-Broadway.

The turning point in his youthful career came when he auditioned for both Neil Simon's Broadway production of *Brighton Beach Memoirs* and the film of Simon's *Max Dugan Returns* (1982), with Jason Robards and Marsha Mason. He landed both parts, winning a Tony for the former. He was later to star in both the stage and film versions of *Biloxi Blues* (1987), the sequel to *Brighton Beach Memoirs*. In addition, he won an Outer Critics Circle Award as best supporting actor and a villager Award for his performance in Harvey Fierstein's *Torch Song Trilogy*, in which he played the child adopted by the drag-queen hero. When it came to the 1989 film version, he played the too-good-to be true young boyfriend who is killed by muggers.

There is, in fact, something too good to be true about the fresh-faced innocent-looking Broderick, who first made a wide impact in John Badham's *WarGames* (1983), as the teenage computer wizard who inadvertently hacks in to the Pentagon defence system and almost causes World War III. In the same year, he was Philippe the Mouse in *Ladyhawke* (1983), part of the sword-and-sorcery cycle. As the young pickpocket in constant contact with God, the part provided him with some of the best lines and his comic playing brought light to the Dark Ages gloom.

In *Biloxi Blues*, he is the intelligent, sympathetic but rather blank narrator, and was even more vacant as Robert Gould in *Glory* (1989), a colonel leading the first platoon of blacks during the American Civil War. Sporting a little moustache and goatee, he seemed to have been, like the character he was playing, thrust unwillingly into the role. In Sidney Lumet's mish-mash *Family Business* (1989), he played the highly unlikely son of Dustin Hoffman and the grandson of Sean Connery, generating enough charm to get by as a graduate following in his family's felonious footsteps.

But Broderick's widest popularity came with the title role in John Hughes' *Ferris Bueller's Day Off* (1986), which spawned a successful TV series. As an anarchic teenage brat on a spree (24-year-old Broderick managing to pass for 16), he was cheekily amusing, flouting authority and getting away with it; although elements of over-cuteness were allowed to take over the character. 'When I started out, looking so young was a definite advantage. At the time there were so many good teenage roles about and though I was no longer a teenager, I would've hated to miss out on a part like Ferris,' he commented.

He played a *naif* again in *The Freshman* (1989), but this time acting his age as a country boy involved with Marlon Brando's Mafioso godfather. It says something for Broderick that he managed to move some attention away from the mammoth magnificence of Brando in their scenes together.

1982 Max Dugan Returns; 1918 **1983** WarGames; Ladyhawke **1985** On Valentine's Day **1986** Ferris Bueller's Day Off **1987** Project X; Biloxi Blues **1988** Torch Song Trilogy **1989** Family Business; Glory; The Freshman **1992** Welcome To Buzzsaw; Out On A Limb

Bronson, Charles
(Charles Bunchinsky)

Actor
Born 3 November 1921
Ehrenfeld, Pennsylvania

Charles Bronson's tough, craggy, broad-nosed, stone face has been his fortune, but he was in his late 40s and in foreign parts when true stardom was thrust upon him. It was as the taciturn, harmonica-playing unnamed stranger, an almost superhuman apparition, in Sergio Leone's *Once Upon A Time In The West* (1968), the apotheosis of the Spaghetti Western, that he became a world-wide screen hero.

At the moment of his breakthrough to stardom in 1968, he married British-born actress Jill Ireland, who would thereafter appear with him in almost all his films and with whom he had six children. (She died of cancer in 1990.) One of 15 children of a Lithuanian coalminer, Bronson went to work in the mines in his teens, despite being the only member of the family to have finished high school. After serving in World War II as a tail gunner aboard a B-29 bomber, he went to Philadelphia, where he studied art and joined an acting company. In 1949, he moved to California, where he joined the Pasadena Playhouse school, then gradually worked his way into movies, his brawny figure and pugilistic features getting him character parts, generally as a gangster. As Charles Buchinski or Buchinsky, he cropped up in various films, most significantly in Robert Aldrich's first two Westerns, *Apache* and *Vera Cruz* (both 1954), in which he played a Red Indian and a villain respectively.

As Charles Bronson, he continued to appear as Indians and heavies in a number of Westerns, until he was offered the title role in Roger Corman's first cheapo gangster movie, *Machine Gun Kelly* (1958). Much wider popularity came as one of *The Magnificent Seven* (1960), the John Sturges Western that also boosted the careers of Steve McQueen and James Coburn. By the time of *The Dirty Dozen* in 1967, he was a familiar face in action movies. Most of the films that followed were European co-productions dubbed in the countries of showing, including *Once Upon A Time In The West*, and in 1971 he received the Golden Globe as the world's most popular actor.

Returning to the USA in 1972, he continued to play similar thick-ear roles, the most successful of all in Michael Winner's *Death Wish* (1974), a brutish apologia for taking the law into one's own hands. Bronson played Paul Kersey, an average urban man transformed into a killer after his home is invaded by hoodlums, and his wife and daughter raped. Audiences cheered every time the star slaughtered another suspect without benefit of a trial, and thus he became an extremely dubious folk-hero. Three sequels followed, in which his performances hardly varied but his actions became less and less justifiable and more and more violent.

The message that came across in many of his other films during the 80s was that it's better to have Charles Bronson on your side than against you. Yet, as the 90s rolled around, it was difficult for the septuagenarian actor himself to believe he could continue to go around blasting people to bits, and he delivered an impressive character cameo in *The Indian Runner* (1991). However, this went completely unnoticed, leaving him on the verge of *Death Wish V*.

1951 You're In The Navy Now; The People Against O'Hara; The Mob **1952** Red Skies Of Montana; My Six Convicts; The Marrying Kind; Pat And Mike; Diplomatic Courier; Bloodhounds Of Broadway **1953** House Of Wax **1954** Miss Sadie Thompson; Crime Wave; Tennessee Champ; Riding Shotgun; Apache; Vera Cruz; Drum Beat **1955** Big House USA; Target Zero **1956** Jubal **1957** Run Of The Arrow **1958** Gang War; Showdown At Boothill; Machine Gun Kelly; When Hell Broke Loose **1959** Never So Few **1960** The Magnificent Seven **1961** Master Of The World; A Thunder Of Drums **1962** X-15; Kid Galahad **1963** The Great Escape; 4 For Texas **1965** The Sandpiper; Battle Of The Bulge **1966** This Property Is Condemned **1967** The Dirty Dozen **1968** Guns For San Sebastian; Villa Rides; Adieu L'Ami (France); Once Upon A Time In The West **1970** Twinky aka Lola; You Can't Win 'Em All aka The Dubious Patriots; Citta Violenta/The Family (Italy); De La Part Des Copains/Cold Sweat (France) **1971** Quelqu'un Derrière La Porte/Someone Behind The Door (France); Red Sun **1972** Joe Valachi aka The Valachi Papers; Chato's Land; The Mechanic **1973** Chino aka Valdez; The Halfbreed aka The Valdez Horses; The Stone Killer **1974** Mr Majestyk; Death Wish **1975** Breakout; Hard Times (GB: The Streetfighter) **1976** Breakheart Pass; St Ives; From Noon Till Three **1977** The White Buffalo; Telefon **1979** Love And Bullets; Cabo Blanco **1980** Borderline **1981** Death Hunt **1982** Death Wish II **1983** Ten To Midnight **1984** The Evil That Men Do **1985** Death Wish III **1986** Act Of Vengeance; Assassination; Murphy's Law **1987** Death Wish IV: The Crackdown **1988** Messenger Of Death **1989** Kinjite: Forbidden Subjects **1991** The Indian Runner

Brooks, Albert
(Albert Einstein)

Actor, director, writer
Born 22 July 1947
Los Angeles, California

The son of a comedian, Harry Einstein, Albert Brooks – whose real name, incredibly, is Albert Einstein – was destined for a career as a comic but briefly attended the Carnegie Institute of Technology before entering show business as a stand-up. Even earlier, when he was in his mid-teens, he had developed his writing interest with a sports reporting stint for a local radio station.

By 1969, Brooks was a comedic regular on Dean Martin's television variety series and a guest act on many other shows, including those of Ed Sullivan, Steve Allen and Flip Wilson. In 1975 his second comedy LP, 'A Star Is Bought', earned him a Grammy nomination and he had begun producing and directing short films for the popular comedy showcase *Saturday Night Live*.

Brooks made his feature film debut with a small but good appearance in Martin Scorsese's searing *Taxi Driver* (1976). In 1979 he wrote, directed and starred in *Real Life*, a mildly amusing extension of his funnier shorts and a development of his hustling jokester persona, in this case as a quasi-documentary maker. Between 'straighter' roles in other people's films he carried the jape further in his own *Modern Romance* (1981), playing a neurotic, only occasionally side-splitting film editor giving his girl a hard time of it. His 1985 film, *Lost In America*, was an unqualified rib-tickler, with Brooks firing on all cylinders as the 80s yuppie who persuades his wife (Julie Hagerty) to escape the rat race with him for a carefree life on the road that becomes a catalogue of wacky misfortunes.

His finest screen hour to date, however, has been in James L. Brooks' first-class comedy *Broadcast News* (1987). Brooks nearly stole the film from Holly Hunter and William Hurt, and gained an Oscar nomination for his appealing performance as the intelligent, cynical, heavy-sweating TV news reporter who's great with the wisecracks but runs a poor second to Hurt with the TV viewers and the girl. It was a role that perfectly suited his forte – a faster-talking, brainier version of Everyman, an obnoxious but likeable schmo. What a pity then, that his outing with Meryl Streep, *Defending Your Life* (1991), was a whimsical disaster.

1976 Taxi Driver **1979** Real Life (also director, co-writer) 1980 Private Benjamin **1981** Modern Romance (also director, co-writer) **1983** Twilight Zone The Movie **1984** Unfaithfully Yours **1985** Lost In America (also director, co-writer) **1987** Broadcast News **1991** Defending Your Life (also director, co-writer) **1993** I'll Do Anything

Brooks, James L.

Director, writer
Born 9 May 1940
North Bergen, New Jersey

The cinematic acclaim accorded intermittent producer and two-time director of motion pictures James L. Brooks is as nothing to his legendary television career, writing and producing multiple Emmy award-winning shows like *Rhoda* and the *Mary Tyler Moore Show* and going on to create and produce *Taxi* and *Cheers*. The shows were firmly character-based, using a basic location to assemble an ensemble cast of losers and undeserving winners, going against the overt sentimentality of the sit-com mindset of the day with cynical putdowns, while still harbouring a deep affection for the characters, a situation repeated in Brooks' films.

Brooks' screenplay for *Starting Over* (1979) didn't have a genuinely bad word for any of its characters as it went over the emotional debris of Burt Reynolds' divorce, only to go astray with an unlikely finale; while his colossally successful directorial debut, *Terms Of Endearment* (1983), simply used its snappy one-liners and Shirley MacLaine's hysterically pitched performance to hide its mawkish centre (although he did pull off a convincing and uncliched death scene) and, despite his two Oscars as writer-director, was more manipulative than accomplished, showing poor control over many of the cast. Conversely, *Broadcast News* (1987) was a genuine cause for celebration, an intelligent, almost-romantic comedy set against the internal politics of a prime-time TV newsroom where the talented are disposed of and the bland rewarded as news is manipulated and subjugated to appearances, with Brooks' Oscar-nominated script and direction catching the right tone for almost every moment.

Since, Brooks has concentrated his newfound movie muscle on nurturing other directors' projects through his Gracie Films production company – Cameron Crowe's *Say Anything* (1989), Penny Marshall's *Big 1988) and Taxi* star Danny De Vito's *War Of The Roses* (1989) – and found notoriety with TV's most anti-social animated family, *The Simpsons*. That he should have only two features to his credit, given their enormous success, remains an enigma, though a third, *I'll Do Anything*, a musical starring Nick Nolte, was announced for production in 1993.

1979 Starting Over (writer only) **1983** Terms Of Endearment (w/d) **1987** Broadcast News (w/d)

Brooks, Mel
(Melvin Kaminsky)
Actor, director, writer
Born 28 June 1926
Brooklyn, New York

The comic talent of Mel Brooks was forged during the hectic period in the early 50s when he was a full-time writer on Sid Caesar's hit TV programme, *Your Show Of Shows*. As part of a team that included Carl Reiner, Neil Simon, Woody Allen and Larry Gelbart, he was earning $5000 a week. Much of the humour in his film work has not strayed too far from those early days. Caesar was a father figure to him, and years later Brooks cast him as the studio chief in *Silent Movie* (1976).

His own father, a first generation Russian immigrant, died when he was two. 'I can't tell you what sadness, what pain it is, never to have known my own father,' Brooks has said. 'Maybe in having the male characters in my movies find each other, I'm expressing the longing I feel to find my father and be close to him.'

After a brief period of service in World War II, he became a drummer for a dance band, and then replaced the resident comic. It was then that he changed his name to Brooks, a shortening of his mother's maiden name of Brookman. Although working on *Your Show Of Shows* earned him money and some fame, the pressure turned him into a nervous wreck, and he left the show and sought psychiatric help. At the same time, his marriage to Florence Baum, a dancer with whom he had had three children, broke down, and he was living on unemployment benefit.

However, he was rescued from penury by 'The 2000-Year-Old Man', a routine he improvised, with Carl Reiner, at parties. It consisted of a series of interviews with a modern day Methuselah who reminisces hilariously about his meetings with Christ, Joan Of Arc, Shakespeare, Robin Hood etc. The sketches were made into three records and a cartoon. In 1963 he wrote and delivered the commentary of the Oscar-winning cartoon *The Critic*, an old man's reactions to the avant-garde images he sees on the screen. He then created several TV series, including *Get Smart* about a bungling spy.

The first feature Brooks directed was *The Producers* (1967), which played fast and loose with the concept of 'bad taste', using the idea of a producer hoping to make more money out of a flop than a hit. The wonderfully camp 'Springtime For Hitler' number is very funny, but not even the most unsophisticated New York Jewish audience could have seen it as other than a burlesque. This was further emphasised by turning the rest of the show into a corny Borscht-belt vaudeville routine. More consistently funny was the playing of Zero Mostel, as the producer, and Gene Wilder as his neurotic accountant. *Blazing Saddles* and *Young Frankenstein* (both 1974), both with Wilder, despite bad TV-fodder jokes and excesses, had enough belly laughs and were well enough made to display some feeling for the genres parodied. *High Anxiety* (1977), however, had virtually no feeling for, or understanding of, Hitchcock's work, which was used as the basis for low comedy. The *History Of The World Part I* (1981) was a tatty ragbag in which Brooks regressed to his early TV days and beyond to infancy, and *Spaceballs* (1987) heavily parodied *Star Wars* ten years too late. Perhaps because of the limitations imposed by no dialogue (except for the 'non' uttered by the ever-mute mime Marcel Marceau), *Silent Movie* turned out to be Brooks' funniest and best structured film.

In the 80s, he established Brooksfilms, producing 'straight' movies such as the admirable *The Elephant Man* (1980), and *84 Charing Cross Road* (1986) featuring his wife Anne Bancroft. He also had the chutzpah to produce (it was directed unstylishly by Alan Johnson) a completely dispensable and irrelevant remake of one of the cinema's great classics, Ernst Lubitsch's *To Be Or Not To Be* (1983), as a vehicle for Bancroft and himself. The best things in the film were in the original, the worst weren't. A naughty Jewish leprechaun, Mel Brooks is undoubtedly a very funny man who has yet to learn how far to go too far.

As actor, director and writer unless stated otherwise: **1967** The Producers (director only) **1970** The Twelve Chairs **1974** Blazing Saddles; Young Frankenstein (director only) **1976** Silent Movie **1977** High Anxiety **1979** The Muppet Movie (cameo only) **1981** History Of The World Part I **1983** To Be Or Not To Be (actor only) **1987** Spaceballs **1991** Life Stinks

Brown, Clancy

Actor
Born 5 January 1959
Urbana, Ohio

A tall, broad-shouldered hulk of a man, with a rough-hewn profile and thick, daunting features that wouldn't look out of place on Easter Island, Clancy Brown seems born to play bad guys. Hollywood, always happy to commit the sin of typecasting, would concur; most of his movies during the 1980s required him to play psychotics.

The son of an Ohio newspaperman, Brown came to acting via a drama programme at Northwestern University, outside Chicago. He was working as a bartender when he landed his first feature movie, *Bad Boys* (1983). Originally the producers considered the newcomer too old to play an inmate in a juvenile prison, but came back to him when the Christian fundamentalist parents of their 17-year-old first choice objected to the tough and violent script. The movie earned some attention as a breakthrough for its star, Sean Penn, and Brown himself proved memorably nasty as the baddest boy on the block. He capitalised on his success playing Frankenstein's monster in the otherwise disastrous *The Bride* (1985), then made *Highlander* (1986), a silly but stylish fantasy with Sean Connery and Christopher Lambert. The two stars and Clancy slugged it out as immortal foes across the centuries, and the film was best seen for the vigour and invention of Brown's villain, growling out 'New York, New York' as he mowed down the nth innocent bystander. *Shoot To Kill*, co-starring Tom Berenger and Sidney Poitier, had him as another psycho, though audiences were kept guessing for the first half-hour by the presence of another specialist in evildoers, Andy Robinson, as a red herring. With the onset of the 90s, Brown has attempted to break free of his image in Kathryn Bigelow's *Blue Steel*, and Chris Monger's *Waiting For The Light*, in which he essayed a gentle and reticent loner.

1983 Bad Boys **1984** The Adventures Of Buckaroo Banzai Across The 8th Dimension **1985** The Bride **1986** Highlander **1987** Extreme Prejudice **1988** Shoot To Kill (GB: Deadly Pursuit) **1989** Season Of Fear **1990** Blue Steel; Waiting For The Light **1991** Ambition; Mind Game **1992** Past Midnight; Pet Sematary II

Bujold, Genevieve

Actress
Born 1 July 1942
Montreal, Canada

Genevieve Bujold became an international star and was Oscar nominated for her role as a sweet and sprightly Anne Boleyn in *Anne Of The Thousand Days* (1968). She got the part on the strength of another title role, *Isabel*, released the same year, her first English-speaking performance. In this modest Canadian thriller (written, produced and directed by Paul Almond, her husband since 1967), she displayed many of the qualities that would become apparent in her cosmopolitan career over the next two decades – warmth, intelligence and a Bardot-like pouting sensuality, albeit her distinctive face is almost plain.

There was plenty of that sensuality in her

sex scenes with Yves Montand in *La Guerre Est Finie* (*The War Is Over*, 1966). The director, Alain Resnais, chose Bujold from many candidates for the role when she was on a visit to Europe. She remained in France to complete two further films, *Le Roi De Coeur* (*King Of Hearts*, 1966) and *Le Voleur* (*The Thief Of Paris*, 1967).

The daughter of a French-Canadian bus driver, the convent-educated Bujold studied at the Quebec Conservatory of Drama, paying her way by working as an usherette at a Montreal cinema. She made her screen debut in *The Adolescents* (1964) before being launched into stardom by Resnais. But the roles following *Anne Of The Thousand Days* gave her little chance to shine; as Cassandra in *The Trojan Women* (1971) she was in good company (Katharine Hepburn, Vanessa Redgrave, Irene Pappas) but a bad film, and as Cliff Robertson's kidnapped wife and her double in Brian De Palma's *Obsession* (1976), she lacked the mysterious allure Kim Novak had brought to *Vertigo* (1958), the film's model. Her best Hollywood role in the 70s was as the doctor in *Coma* (1978), desperately trying to discover why all the anaesthetics administered at her hospital proved terminal.

It was the director Alan Rudolph who rescued her from the idiocies of *Monsignor* (1981), in which she played a postulant nun in love with Superpriest Christopher Reeve, and the tawdry Clint Eastwood thriller *Tightrope* (1984). She stands out in three of Rudolph's kaleidoscopic group portraits: in *Choose Me* (1984) she is the sexually frustrated radio agony aunt; in *Trouble In Mind* (1985) she runs a café at the sleazy end of Seattle, and in *The Moderns* (1988), turbaned throughout, she is a canny art dealer in 1920s Paris. Returning to the medical thriller world of *Coma*, Bujold played the sexy *casus belli* of identical twins (both Jeremy Irons) in David Cronenberg's *Dead Ringers* (1988). In this bizarre, nasty but absorbing film, she skilfully moved from anger to understanding after discovering she has been making love not to one man, but two.

1964 The Adolescents/Les Adolescents (French Canadian) **1966** The War Is Over/La Guerre Est Finie (France); King Of Hearts/Le Roi De Coeur (France) **1967** The Thief Of Paris/Le Voleur (France) **1968** Isabel; Anne Of The Thousand Days **1970** Act Of The Heart/Acte Du Coeur (French Canadian) **1971** The Trojan Women; Journey **1974** Earthquake; Kamouraska **1976** Swashbuckler; Obsession; Alex And The Gypsy aka Love And Other Crimes **1977** Another Man, Another Chance/Un Autre Homme Une Autre Chance (France) **1978** Coma **1979** Murder By Decree **1980** Final Assignment; The Last Flight Of Noah's Ark **1981** Monsignor **1984** Tightrope; Choose Me **1985** Trouble In Mind **1988** Dead Ringers; The Moderns **1990** False Identity; Les Noces De Papier/Paper Wedding (French Canadian) **1991** Rue Du Bac (France) **1992/93** The Bottom Drawer; Oh What A Night aka Comfort Creek

Burstyn, Ellen
(Edna Rae Gillooly)

Actress

Born 7 December 1932

Detroit, Michigan

Ellen Burstyn's best work capitalises on her bruised good looks and the discomfiting cheerfulness her characters bring to hopeless prospects and dead-end lives. She excels as a woman on the edge, her round face at once both strong and doll-like, yet forever threatening a flood of bitter tears. It all came together for her in Bob Rafelson's *The King Of Marvin Gardens* (1972), in which she was shifty fantasist Bruce Dern's girlfriend, a frayed beauty desperately trying to overlook that he was inexorably moving in on her flaky daughter. The moment when reality breaks through her defences and she hacks her hair off in self-abuse is one of the most harrowing in memory.

Like many of the characters she has played, Burstyn, the daughter of middle-class Irish parents, came up the hard way. She left home at 18, first for Texas and then New York, calling herself just Edna Rae, and working as a waitress, store counter-girl, and other odd jobs while she struggled to break into show business. She began as a model, danced in the chorus of a Montreal nightclub under the name Keri Flynn, and took a screen test in the mid-50s as Erica Dean. She finally secured a role on Broadway, appearing in a comedy called *Fair Game* in 1957, as Ellen McRae. She retained that name until the mid-60s, while she worked busily in television (including the series *The Doctors*) and made her first two feature films, *For Those Who Think Young* and *Goodbye Charlie* (both 1964). She became Ellen Burstyn when she married her third husband (whom she later divorced).

After studying under Lee Strasberg at the Actors' Studio, Burstyn made an impression in Joseph Strick's *Tropic Of Cancer* (1969), in a small part as the disgusted wife of roistering expatriate writer Henry Miller (Rip Torn). She survived the Felliniesque ambitions of Paul Mazursky's *Alex In Wonderland* (1970), then stamped her authority (and collected a Best Supporting Oscar nomination) on Peter Bogdanovich's *The Last Picture Show* (1971); she was Cybill Shepherd's seductive Southern belle mother, kindling fond memories in Ben Johnson's Sam the Lion and offering an understanding bed for younger men. Although now clearly revealed as an actress to notice, she marked time (but collected a Best Actress nomination) in *The Exorcist* (1973), as Linda Blair's harassed mother, dodging jets of green vomit, and the charming *Harry And Tonto* (1974) in which her role was small.

Then, later the same year, came *Alice Doesn't Live Here Anymore*. Although directed by Martin Scorsese, the movie was very much Burstyn's personal project; she found the screenplay, reworked it, chose the cast (Kris Kristofferson was the man in the case) and director and sold it to Warners for ten per cent of the profits. As the newly-widowed Alice, setting off with child in tow on a voyage of self-discovery, the actress conveyed courage and confusion in equal parts, inviting compassion and admiration, and, when her efforts brought her the Best Actress Oscar, it was a well-deserved tribute to her gifts.

After this triumph, Alain Resnais' *Providence* (1977) found the actress stranded on a strange shore, uncomfortable in chic clothes and lost in a labyrinthine time scheme. She failed to regain her bearings in Jules Dassin's *A Dream Of Passion* (1978), playing an American jailed in Greece for infanticide in an overwrought parallel with Medea. *Same Time, Next Year* (1978) – the acceptable face of adultery – was the screen version of the Broadway hit which had won her a Tony award and which, on celluloid, brought her another Oscar nomination. It was a frippery which offered the nearest she had come to standard American entertainment and, thereafter, during the 1980s, she largely forsook film work for live theatre and television. In the latter medium she earned an Emmy nomination (and should perhaps have won) for *The People vs Jean Harris* (1981). Burstyn's performance as the unhappy and vengeful mistress who murdered Dr Herman Tarnower, inventor of the fashionable if somewhat fatuous Scarsdale Diet, was superb; uncompromising and affecting.

Her Hollywood performances have been sporadic, but she added some weight to *The Ambassador* (1985), a typically slick piece of Cannon fodder set in the Middle East, in which she was diplomat Robert Mitchum's wife, enmeshed in an improbably steamy affair with a PLO leader while her husband is up to his neck in the intractable problems of the region. It was hokum, but, five years later, this first-rate actress had the good sense to steer clear of *Texasville* (1990), Peter Bogdanovich's botched *recherche du temps perdu*.

1969 Pit Stop **1970** Tropic Of Cancer; Alex In Wonderland **1971** The Last Picture Show **1972** The King Of Marvin Gardens **1973** The Exorcist **1974** Harry And Tonto; Alice Doesn't Live Here Anymore **1977** Providence (France) **1978** A Dream Of Passion (Greece); Same Time, Next Year **1979** Resurrection **1981** Silence Of The North **1985** The Ambassador; Twice In A Lifetime **1988** Hanna's War **1991** Dying Young **1992/93** The Cemetery Club

Burton, Tim

Director
Born 1959
Burbank, California

Few new film-makers have enjoyed the kind of unbroken run of success that director Tim Burton experienced during the last half of the 80s. From the release of his 1985 debut feature film, *Pee-Wee's Big Adventure*, through to the 1989 blockbuster *Batman*, Burton's innovative and surrealistic style established him as one of the hottest young directors in LA.

Born and raised in Burbank, the heartland of the Hollywood film and TV industry, Burton was a withdrawn child who had trouble fitting in at school; his greatest pleasure lay in watching Vincent Price movies on TV. His father worked for the Parks and Recreations Department and his mother ran a gift shop. A talented artist, Burton won a scholarship to the California Institute of the Arts, where he studied animation. A job as an apprentice animator at Disney followed, but Burton's bizarre imagination and ideas were at odds with the Disney philosophy, and he later recalled, 'I was sort of treated like the special retarded child.' Nevertheless, during his time there, he made several shorts that launched his career, among them *Vincent*, an award-winning six-minute piece of animation narrated by his childhood hero, Vincent Price, and *Frankenweenie*, about a boy who reanimates his dead dog. Despite Disney's refusal to release *Frankenweenie*, the word of mouth about the 30-minute film was such that before long Burton was given his first feature film to direct.

Pee-Wee's Big Adventure is a fairy tale, a quest story in which the child-in-a-man's-body, Pee Wee (Pee Wee Herman alias Paul Rubens), goes in search of his stolen bike. In terms of its themes – childhood, alienation, belonging – and style – the surrealistic and stylised white-picket suburbia, the score by Danny Elfman, the obsession with gadgetry and the obvious cartoon-like quality – the film was indicative of Burton's unique stamp as a director. His second film, *Beetlejuice* (1988), was even more imaginative, anarchic – and successful. A comedy about a dead couple forced to call upon the services of the repulsive spirit Beetlejuice (Michael Keaton) in order to rid their house of the obnoxious new tenants, the film manages to be simultaneously grotesque and good-natured, and Burton allows Keaton's comedy full rein as the eponymous anti-hero.

Yet in his subsequent film, *Batman* (1989), the young director extracted a quietly intense performance from Keaton as the comic-book hero who, characteristic of Burton's main characters, is the archetypal outsider. Despite the $50 million film's mixed critical reception, Warner Brothers' confidence in their talented prodigy paid off: *Batman* went on to become one of the highest-grossing movies in history.

With such an impressive track record, Burton, who by then was married to German painter Lena Gieseke, was given *carte blanche* for his next feature, the much more personal project, *Edward Scissorhands* (1990). A Christmas fable about another outsider, a man-child with scissors instead of hands, the film draws on myth, fairy-tale and Gothic romance, and features the influential Vincent Price as Edward's benevolent but ailing creator. Despite its highly stylised look, the modestly successful film is, largely through the performances of Johnny Depp and Dianne Wiest, deeply moving.

Batman Returns (1992), a much-anticipated sequel, proved a mixed bag: set off-balance by an overdominant Danny DeVito as the repulsive penguin, it nevertheless titillated with its sexual frisson between Keaton's Batman and Michelle Pfeiffer's wonderfully schizoid Cat Woman. Stylistically darker, more expressionistic and baroque than any of Burton's previous work, it proved that a sequel could be more than just a re-hash.

1985 Pee-Wee's Big Adventure **1988** Beetlejuice **1989** Batman **1990** Edward Scissorhands **1992** Batman Returns; Buffy The Vampire Slayer

Busey, Gary

Actor

Born 29 June 1944

Goose Creek, Texas

The blonde and beefy Gary Busey most readily comes to mind as something of a shambling, rambling, good ole Texas boy, which to some extent he actually is. But he is also capable of thoughtful performances, and in middle age and at the leaner end of his weight spectrum, Busey cuts a mean and formidable figure as a heavy. It is interesting that it was in one of his unlikeliest roles physically, that of the comparatively weedy Buddy Holly, that Busey received an Oscar nomination as Best Actor, so successful was he in concealing his own substantial presence in a remarkable impersonation.

Busey's first love was rock 'n' roll, and after attending junior college in Texas, Kansas State College and the University of Oklahoma, he played drums with The Rubber Band between 1963 and 1970. He was quick to establish himself as an actor following his debut, in 1970, in an episode of TV's *High Chaparel*, but kept his hand in on the rock scene, guesting occasionally as a drummer with the likes of Leon Russell, Kris Kristofferson and Willie Nelson under the sobriquet Teddy Jack Eddy.

His film debut was in the 1971 biker road flick *Angels Hard As They Come*, a slightly satirical but formulaic affair that co-writer Jonathan Demme bewilderingly insisted was a motorcycle version of *Rashomon* (1951). For the next seven years Busey put in solid supporting performances in a string of varied films, mainly as backwoods boys, petty crooks and the odd car-racer, rocker or surfer – at one stage playing a third banana to Jeff Bridges in three consecutive films. With his literally electrifying performance in *The Buddy Holly Story* (1978), in which he did his own singing and guitar playing, Busey engrossed critics and audiences. The film itself was far superior to most rock 'n' roll musical biopics, and the actor's portrayal of Holly was a three-dimensional homage to the legendary young talent, himself a Texas boy and a youthful hero of Busey's.

Unfortunately, Busey was never really able to capitalize on this success. Although he starred in two very good films, as a carnival hustler opposite Jodie Foster in *Carny* (1980)

and the fireball sidekick of Willie Nelson in a colourful Western, *Barbarosa* (1982), they were pictures that got away, and he was lost in a couple of dumb comedies. Another biopic, *The Bear* (1984), in which he earnestly impersonated American football coaching legend 'Bear' Bryant, was a painfully old-fashioned nonsense, and by 1986 he was reduced to werewolf shlock and the sordid revenge flick *Eye Of The Tiger*. His most interesting role in this period was in Nicolas Roeg's startling adaptation of the Terry Johnson play *Insignificance* (1985) – consigned to the arthouse circuit – in which Busey put in a fascinating performance as an unnamed baseball star (clearly inspired by Joe Di Maggio) unhappily obsessed with his blonde bombshell movie star wife.

Busey showed some bounce – albeit in a supporting role – as a scumbag killer in *Lethal Weapon* (1987), then bombed again with ghastly canary-bleached hair in an inferior cop actioner, *Bulletproof* (1988). A scarcely seen creeper, *Hider In The House* (1989) did little for him; and his narrow escape from death in a motorcycle accident which put him out of action for a time was no help either. Recovered, he once again plunged into what seems a happy-go-lucky enthusiasm for any role that comes his way.

1971 Angels Hard As They Come **1972** Dirty Little Billy; The Magnificent Seven Ride **1973** The Last American Hero; Lolly-Madonna XXX **1974** Thunderbolt And Lightfoot **1976** The Gumball Rally; A Star Is Born; Alex And The Gypsy **1978** Big Wednesday; Straight Time; The Buddy Holly Story **1980** Foolin' Around; Carny **1982** Barbarosa **1983** D.C. Cab **1984** The Bear **1985** Insignificance; Silver Bullet **1986** Eye Of The Tiger **1987** Let's Get Harry; Lethal Weapon **1988** Bulletproof **1989** Hider In The House **1990** Act Of Piracy; Predator 2 **1991** Point Break; My Heroes Have Always Been Cowboys **1992** Under Siege **1993** Rookie Of The Year

Byrne, Gabriel

Actor
Born 1950
Dublin, Ireland

Off-screen, black-haired, blue-eyed Gabriel Byrne has retained his strong, lilting Irish accent but has seldom exercised it on screen, having creditably impersonated a succession of Englishmen, Americans, Spaniards, Italians and an Israeli. This facility is no doubt due, at least in part, to his ear for languages as well as to his striking if slightly askew classical features.

Byrne, who made his film debut as a randy, bellicose Uther Pendragon in John Boorman's ravishing Arthurian *Excalibur* (1981), came to acting late. After obtaining his university degree at Dublin's Trinity, he worked as an archaeologist for three years, then took a job teaching Spanish and Gaelic at a convent school for another four. There he started a drama class and, after a production in which he had taken part, one of the parents – a member of Dublin's prestigious Abbey Theatre – told him he could make a living as an actor. Byrne left his job at the end of the school year, and after a few roles in community theatre was himself accepted at the Abbey, where he remained for two years. In 1979, he joined London's Royal Court Theatre, long a showcase for new and politically committed work.

In the early 1980s Byrne found himself in demand for television miniseries, including *The Search For Alexander The Great*, *Mussolini* (as faithful son to George C. Scott's dictator) and the title role in *Christopher Columbus*. His second film appearance was in *Miami Vice* creator Michael Mann's outlandish World War II horror yarn, *The Keep* (1983), in which a remarkably distinguished cast made jackasses out of themselves as Nazis occupying an accursed Romanian fortress with a ghastly 'thingie' in the oubliette: a flop treasured by connoisseurs of trash horror.

Among the better things that subsequently beckoned were those that satisfied Byrne's personal taste for films with a political context. Costa-Gavras chose him to play a tough Israeli prosecuting attorney opposite Jill Clayburgh in *Hanna K* (1984) – dramatically disappointing but interesting for its sympathetic presentation of the Palestinian point of view. The same year, he turned in a very strong central performance as the determined British investigative journalist obsessed by a governmental cover-up in the first-rate political thriller *Defence Of The Realm*.

Byrne has been fortunate, however, in surviving a string of poorly received pictures, notably Ken Russell's particularly crazed *Gothic* (1986), a psychedelic account of life with the Shelley-Byron set, as a suitably 'mad, bad and dangerous to know' Lord Byron; the under-rated psychological thriller *Julia And Julia* (1987) opposite Kathleen Turner; and the catastrophic surreal mystery *Siesta* (1987), for which, at least, he was compensated for the role of a Spanish trapeze artist by meeting Ellen Barkin, whom he married in 1988.

Some of Byrne's best work has been done for modest, independent British films that met with little commercial success. *The Courier* (1988), an otherwise poor thriller about drug trafficking in Dublin, was noteworthy for the actor's unflinching portrayal of a cold, perverted crime boss, and in *Diamond Skulls* (1990), a dull affair loosely inspired by the Lord Lucan case, he gave a well-observed impersonation of an arrogant, hard-drinking British aristocrat.

Seized upon by the Coen brothers, Joel and Ethan, for their flamboyant gangster homage with a twist, *Miller's Crossing* (1990), Byrne had one of his best roles to date, playing in extremis what he seems to do better than anything – the smart, hard loner. Not a fan of what he calls 'coffee-table films' – nostalgic period pieces – or action movies, he nevertheless opted for Nils Gaup's pirate adventure, *Hakon Hakonsen* (1991) as a follow-up, seeing the opportunity to swash a buckle as a bit of fun and, he hoped, entertainment for his own small son, Jack.

1981 Excalibur **1983** The Keep **1984** Hanna K **1985** Defense Of The Realm **1986** Gothic **1987** Lionheart; Julia And Julia; Siesta; Hello Again **1988** The Courier; A Soldier's Tale **1990** Diamond Skulls; Miller's Crossing **1991** Shipwrecked **1992** Cool World; Into The West **1993** The Specialist aka Nikita

C

Caan, James

Actor
Born 26 March 1939
Bronx, New York

'I hardly ever go out. I spend most of my time upstairs in my bedroom wearing out one spot on the bed where I sit when I'm making phone calls.' So said James Caan in the mid-80s during a fallow period when people started to ask 'What ever happened to . . .?' After having been a top box-office star for a decade, a series of unhappy circumstances put him in the doldrums from which he has since emerged. It was not only a number of flops, such as *The Thief* (1981), *Kiss Me Goodbye* (1982) and his own competent directorial effort, *Hide In Plain Sight* (1980), that caused his temporary fading away, but the messy divorce from his wife Sheila Ryan was followed by the untimely death of his sister, Barbara. Then he had a motorbike accident and his house was nearly destroyed by a landslide. On top of all that, he was announced for *The Holcroft Covenant* (1985) but was replaced by Michael Caine before his friend Francis Ford Coppola gave him the lead in *Gardens Of Stone* (1987). Finding a new *gravitas*, Caan was utterly convincing as an embittered, stiff-necked sergeant, which he followed with a world-weary, alcoholic cop in the futuristic *Alien Nation* (1988). It all seemed a long way from the time when he rose to stardom in a couple of Howard Hawks movies as a cool and calculating young man – a daredevil racing driver in *Red Line 7000* (1965) and 'Mississippi', John Wayne's gunslinging sidekick, in *El Dorado* (1967).

The son of a kosher meat dealer, he had always been good at sports, and during school vacations supported himself as a lifeguard, nightclub bouncer and children's camp counsellor. His experience in New York's Neighborhood Playhouse led to roles off-Broadway before his first substantial role as a young thug terrorizing Olivia de Havilland in *Lady In A Cage* (1964).

Tough insouciance was his style, well-suited to his handsome but rather emotionless features. Not for nothing did Coppola cast him as the heir apparent to the Corleone family in *The Godfather* (1972). He is perfect as Brando's hedonistic, volatile elder son whose bloody ways end in his own death, thus preventing his appearance, save for a brief flashback, in *Godfather II* (1974). He was soon wallowing in violence again as the embittered hero of *Rollerball* (1975). Although presented as the moral centre of the film, the character is just as sadistic as everyone else around him, and more violence came his way as the brutal CIA man in Peckinpah's *The Killer Elite* (1975). From time to time, however, a certain vulnerability and warmth surfaces in Caan's persona, generally away from the male-dominated movies – in Coppola's *The Rain People* (1969), as the mentally-retarded football player opposite Shirley Knight; or in *Funny Lady* (1975) as Billy Rose, the gambling, philandering impresario husband of Barbra Streisand's Fanny Brice, and in *Comes A Horseman* (1978) teamed up with Jane Fonda against a load of baddies. Caan had been nicknamed 'The Jewish Cowboy', not only because of his regular appearances in Westerns, but also because of his participation in rodeos and ownership of a fine stable of horses.

By the 90s, Caan seemed en route to regeneration, following his cameo in *Dick Tracy* with the lead in Rob Reiner's *Misery* (1990), although the failure of *For The Boys* (1991), which teamed him with Bette Midler, could only be viewed as another setback.

1963 Irma La Douce (bit) **1964** Lady in A Cage **1965** The Glory Guys; Red Line 7000 **1967** El Dorado; Games **1968** Countdown; Journey To Shiloh; Submarine X-1 (GB) **1969** The Rain People **1970** Rabbit Run **1971** T.R.Baskin **1972** The Godfather **1973** Slither; Cinderella Liberty **1974** The Gambler; Freebie And The Bean; The Godfather Part II (cameo) **1975** Funny Lady; Rollerball; Gone With The West; The Killer Elite **1976** Harry And Walter Go To New York; Silent Movie (cameo) **1977** A Bridge Too Far (GB); Another Man, Another Chance aka Another Man, Another Woman/Un Autre Homme, Une Autre Chance (France) **1978** Comes A Horseman **1980** Hide In Plain Sight (also director) **1981** The Ins And The Outs; Thief (GB: Violent Streets) **1982** Kiss Me Goodbye **1987** Gardens Of Stone **1988** Alien Nation **1990** Dick Tracy (cameo); Misery **1991** The Dark Backward; For The Boys **1992** Honeymoon In Vegas

Cage, Nicolas
(Nicholas Coppola)
Actor
Born 7 January 1964
Long Beach, California

'In my Uncle Francis's imagination my role [in *Rumble Fish*, 1983] was very much like my father, so he had me sort of looking like him and that was uncomfortable. I was terrified, but at that time I didn't know how to say no. He wouldn't let me create my own thoughts for the character, so that was when I decided to change my name.' *Rumble Fish* was the first and last film which featured Nicholas Coppola because he didn't want to be judged in relation to his uncle, Francis Ford Coppola. With a new name taken from two off-beat Cages, comic-book hero Luke and composer John, Nicolas Cage burst onto the screen in *Valley Girl* (1983) where he played a sensitive street kid pursuing a desperate passion for a rich Pasadena girl whose snobby friends consider him a creep.

Nicolas was raised in Long Beach, California until he was 12, when his family moved to San Francisco. At 15, he enrolled in San Francisco's American Conservatory Theatre, where he appeared as the boxer hero in the school's production of *Golden Boy*, and then later moved to Beverly Hills High, where he was a classmate of Crispin Glover. He went on to study acting with the renowned drama instructor Peggy Feury, who was killed in a car crash in 1985. Cage's father, August Coppola, Dean of Creative Arts at San Francisco State University, was a great influence on his son, who also found inspiration from Marlon Brando, James Dean, and comedian Jerry Lewis, 'for his freedom, his craziness'.

There is certainly something frantically demented about most of Cage's work: as H. I. McDonnough, the doleful, maladroit thief trying desperately to settle down with a lady cop and a kidnapped baby in *Raising Arizona* (1987); as Ronnie Cammareri, the wild and tormented one-handed baker wooing Cher in *Moonstruck* (1984); as the nutty yuppie Manhattan bloodsucker in *Vampire's Kiss* (1987); and the snake-jacketed Sailor Ripley in David Lynch's *Wild At Heart* (1990), madly romancing Laura Dern in the voice of Elvis Presley while careening around the USA.

Although he detached himself from the family name, the actor made two films for Coppola after *Rumble Fish* (where he was outshone as a youth gang member by Mickey Rourke and Matt Dillon), but neither gave him much satisfaction. He was the psycho gangster 'Mad Dog' Dwyer (Richard Gere's kid brother) in the botched *The Cotton Club* (1984), and the slightly nerdy, nasal, blond-haired husband of time-traveller Kathleen Turner in *Peggy Sue Got Married* (1986). He was allowed more range in Alan Parker's *Birdy* (1985), playing the Vietnam war veteran buddy of the shell-shocked Matthew Modine. For the role, Cage had two teeth extracted to simulate shrapnel damage, an example of the lengths he sometimes goes to get to the truth of a character. ('They were baby teeth, so they'll come back,' he commented reassuringly.) Fortunately, he did not have his hand severed in a bread slicer for *Moonstruck*, though his raw romanticism was informed with veracity.

The actor with the 'sensitive wolf' looks, who divides his time between Hollywood and a Victorian home in San Francisco, is essentially a loner although he lived with actress Jenny Wright for two years. He is also a man of principle who turned down a part in *Top Gun* because he thought it too right wing, a gesture somewhat undermined by his lead role in *Firebirds* (1989), a *Top Gun* clone, in which he could do nothing much with the conventional role of gung-ho helicopter pilot. He is far more in his element in oddball roles.

The hairstyles and the voice may change with each movie, but the mournful aqua-blue eyes and the power and passion behind each performance remains, making Nicolas Cage a true heir to the anarchic actors of an older generation.

1983 Rumble Fish (as Nicholas Coppola); Valley Girl **1984** Racing With The Moon; The Cotton Club; Moonstruck; Birdy **1986** The Boy In Blue; Peggy Sue Got Married **1988** Raising Arizona; Vampire's Kiss **1989** Tempo Di Uccidere/Short Cut (Italy) **1990** Fire Birds (GB: Wings Of The Apache); Wild At Heart **1991** Zandalee **1992** Honeymoon In Vegas; Red Rock West **1993** Deadfall

Caine, Michael
(Maurice Micklewhite)
Actor
Born 14 March 1933
London, England

'I'm a sort of boy next door. If that boy has a

good script', Michael Caine once quipped. One of the English-speaking cinema's longest lasting and perennially popular stars, Caine could not have come from a more modest background. The son of a Billingsgate fish-market porter and a charlady, he was evacuated from London during World War II, returning to find his parents' tenement flat had been destroyed in the Blitz and that home would henceforth be a prefabricated shack. He left school at 15 and worked at Smithfield Meat Market by day to pay for drama classes taken at night. He had caught the acting bug a year earlier when he served tea in a London theatre. After a spell with the British army in Korea and Germany, he began playing small parts in provincial theatres and on British television.

Taking his name from the play *The Caine Mutiny Court Martial*, which was running in London's West End in 1956, he started his film career predictably playing cockney roles in a string of fairly dispensable features. 'I look at my early films and wonder how anyone could have thought I had anything,' he once truthfully remarked.

However, in 1964, his breakthrough performance came in *Zulu*, ironically not in the cockney role for which he tested, but as an effete, aristocratic British army officer battling to hold out against the black hordes at Rorke's Drift. Then came an even bigger break with his next film, *The Ipcress File* (1965), which successfully spawned two sequels, *Funeral In Berlin* (1966) and *Billion Dollar Brain* (1967). Caine was Harry Palmer, Len Deighton's dry, sarcastic, bespectacled spy (it was rare for a screen hero to wear glasses), an anti-James Bond, fairly minor in the organisation which employed him. The popularity of these films can be put down to the star's sharp and sardonically funny characterisation.

Caine was Oscar-nominated for his portrayal of *Alfie* (1985), the unscrupulous womaniser whose asides to the camera were so much a part of the characterisation, a role he won only because Terence Stamp turned it down. From his first Hollywood-made picture, opposite Shirley MacLaine in the heist comedy-thriller *Gambit* (1966), he continued to alternate between British and American movies, although his main home was in California with his Indian wife, Shakira, and two daughters. (The Caine family settled back in England in 1987.) Unfortunately, though he could afford to be selective, the workaholic actor has made many a mediocre film between the good ones, nearly all of them benefiting from his low-key, white-mousy snake-eyed presence and cockney wit.

His best performances have been in his best films – ingenious in various disguises as the lover of Laurence Olivier's wife in Joseph Mankiewicz's *Sleuth* (1972); playing laconically against the more flamboyant Sean Connery in John Huston's *The Man Who Would Be King* (1975); beautifully bitchy as Maggie Smith's gay antique-dealer husband in the best episode of *California Suite* (1978); icily murderous in Sidney Lumet's *Deathtrap* (1912); world-weary and boozy as the bearded academic in Lewis Allen's *Educating Rita* (1983); and, best of all, in Woody Allen's *Hannah And Her Sisters* (1986), as the perplexed husband, who, despite being married to the woman of his dreams (Mia Farrow), lusts after her sister (Barbara Hershey). Caine once said that he could play both Woody Allen and Clint Eastwood, and he proved it in *A Shock To The System* (1990), where he transforms himself from a nebbish executive into a murderer.

It is the quality of these performances that keeps reminding audiences of Caine's acting ability, and he has retained his popularity world-wide. 'I seem to have the capacity for survival, which, although I didn't know it when I came into the business, is now the most important quality,' he said. In 1992, he was awarded the CBE by the Queen for his contribution to the arts.

1956 A Hill In Korea **1957** How To Murder A Rich Uncle **1958** The Key; Blind Spot **1959** The Two-Headed Spy **1960** Foxhole In Cairo; The Bulldog Breed **1961** The Day The Earth Caught Fire **1962** Solo For Sparrow **1963** The Wrong Arm Of The Law **1964** Zulu **1965** The Ipcress File **1966** Alfie; The Wrong Box; Gambit; Funeral In Berlin **1967** Hurry Sundown; Billion Dollar Brain; Woman Times Seven **1968** Tonight Let's All Make Love In London (docu); Deadfall; The Magus **1969** Play Dirty; The Italian Job; The Battle Of Britain **1970** Too Late The Hero **1971** The Last Valley; Get Carter; Kidnapped **1972** Zee And Company; Sleuth **1974** The Black Windmill; The Marseilles Contract; The Destructors **1975** The Romantic Englishwoman; The Man Who Would Be King **1976** Peeper; Harry And Walter Go To New York; The Eagle Has Landed **1971** A Bridge Too Far; Silver Bears **1978** The Swarm; California Suite **1979** Ashanti; Beyond The Poseidon Adventure **1980** The Island; The Hand; Dressed To Kill **1981** Escape To Victory **1982** Deathtrap **1983** Educating Rita **1984** Beyond The Limit (GB: The Honorary Consul); Blame It On Rio **1985** Water; The Jigsaw Man; The Holcroft Covenant **1986** Hannah And

Her Sisters; Half-Moon Street; Mona Lisa; Sweet Liberty **1987** The Fourth Protocol; Jaws: The Revenge; Surrender; The Whistle Blower **1988** Dirty Rotten Scoundrels; Without A Clue **1990** A Shock To The System; Bullseye **1991** Mr Destiny **1992** Noises Off; Blue Ice; The Muppet Christmas Carol

Cameron, James

Director, writer
Born 16 August 1954
Ontario, Canada

Hailing from a little town called Kapuskasing, James Cameron became one of the few important directors to emerge in Hollywood during the 1980s, elevating hi-tech action movies to new heights of sophistication. His progressive genre pictures are distinguished by brilliantly orchestrated thrills, verisimilitude, originality, and strong, absorbing characters.

Like so many of America's most talented film-makers, Cameron began his career at Roger Corman's New World Pictures. Unusually, though, his credits were on the technical side: as miniature-set builder, process projection supervisor and art director on *Battle Beyond The Stars* (1980), the 'Seven Samurai' in outer space, scripted by John Sayles. Corman re-used the sets and special effects in countless cheapies, and gave Cameron his first shot at directing. The result was *Piranha II* (1981), the sequel to John Sayles' and Joe Dante's witty *Jaws* rip-off. Filmed chaotically, and forfeiting all the values of its predecessor, it must rate as one of the least auspicious debuts by a major director. In contrast, *The Terminator* (1984) was a boldly conceived, meticulously planned science fiction thriller; pitting man against machine (somewhat paradoxically, one of Cameron's favourite themes), it was suspenseful, clever and packed with action. The director co-wrote it with Gale Anne Hurd, who became his partner until the traumatic production of *The Abyss*, and who may well have been responsible for the feminist slant in their collaborations.

The Terminator was a breakthrough for Arnold Schwarzenegger as the robot assassin from the future (the film was a box-office smash) and the time-slip premise of the plot was much copied, but its director was the real discovery, and if his contribution to the script of *Rambo: First Blood Part II* (1985) was strictly for the boys, *Aliens* (1986) dispelled any doubts. While maintaining close links with Ridley Scott's original, Cameron's sequel is an infinitely more imaginative, thematically rich piece. In essence a patrol picture *manqué*, it explores concepts of heroism and loyalty in frighteningly unknown terrain, and crucially develops Sigourney Weaver's heroine, Ripley, with the introduction of a surrogate child and an alien mother for a climax as astonishing as it is simple. Weaver was Oscar nominated for her role, an unprecedented acknowledgement of an action movie by the Academy.

Even more ambitious was *The Abyss* (1989), an expensive ($50 million) deep sea adventure that spawned an entire fleet of imitators before it had finished filming. While the others replayed *Alien* underwater, Cameron emphasised suspense over shocks and came up with a sweaty, grimy version of *Close Encounters Of The Third Kind*, complete with friendly ETs and anti-nuke propaganda. It was a hugely flawed work and, like the other films in the school, it belly-flopped grandly. Nevertheless, the dialogue is authentically terse and the relationships genuinely dramatic; there are sequences as good as any Cameron has shown us to date: Ed Harris having to watch his estranged wife drown before his eyes, then desperately trying to revive her in a painfully prolonged scene . . . The problem with the picture is its soft heart, so at odds with the hardboiled attitude that permeates Cameron's work. In a film full of the fear of death, *The Abyss* ultimately opts for fantasy. The production was a troubled one, with a feud developing between the director and his actors (who nonetheless give A-grade performances), and the separation of Cameron and Gale Hurd mirroring events onscreen.

It is evident from James Cameron's filmography that he is not a man to rush into projects and, by 1990, his admirers were waiting for a sign of another film. If he still had something to prove, it was his versatility, but he could already claim two-and-a-half remarkable movies to his credit.

As director only unless stated otherwise: **1981** Piranha II – The Spawning aka Flying Killers (also co-writer) **1984** The Terminator **1985** Rambo: First Blood Part II (co-writer only) **1986** Aliens (also co-writer) **1989** The Abyss (also co-writer) **1991** Terminator 2: Judgement Day (also co-writer) **1992/93** The Crowded Room

Candy, John

Actor, writer
Born 31 October 1950
Toronto, Canada

As with Burt Reynolds, the bedrock of John Candy's career is not the quality of his films (generally low to middling) but his pure likeability, although he has run the risk of relying too heavily on it. Beginning acting in the 11th grade at school and originally intending to be a journalist, he got his first professional job as a member of a children's theatre group (much of his comedy is still good-natured juvenile knockabout stuff) before small roles in several low-budget Canadian films, including a number of straight dramatic roles, led to his coming to prominence in the famous Second City theatre, first in Chicago and then in Toronto. It was the SCTV television series, in which he wrote and performed (creating the infamous polka-playing Schmenges Brothers with Eugene Levy on route) between 1975 and 1983, winning two Emmys for his scripting in the process, that got him more visible roles in highly successful comedies, often alongside *Saturday Night Live* graduates – *1941* (1979), *The Blues Brothers* (1980), *Stripes* (1980) and *National Lampoon's Vacation* (1983).

Playing Tom Hanks' large-hearted, sex obsessed brother in *Splash* (1984) – and in particular a scene in which he masquerades as a Swedish scientist with phrases he has learnt from Scandinavian porno films – elevated the rotund actor to comic lead status, although with variable success, and it was not until 1987 that he chalked up another major winner. His fellow traveller from hell in *Planes, Trains And Automobiles* was the archetypal Candy character – terrifyingly annoying, completely oblivious to his horrifyingly anti-social habits, an unshakeable shaggy dog of a human being who is a victim of his own excessive good nature: the life and soul everybody tries to avoid at parties made flesh. It signalled the start of a successful partnership with writer-director John Hughes, following a simple formula of ordinary guy driven to distraction by hyperactive, good-natured slob (although in *The Great Outdoors*, 1988, Candy was the quiet one) that was to prove colossally successful with *Uncle Buck!* (1989). But John Candy still has to prove himself bankable away from the support system of Hughes or a big name co-star, with even his popularity unable to save the star-heavy *Nothing But Trouble* (1991) or the ghastly *Delirious* the same year, from sinking with remarkable speed.

Candy's attempts to extend his range in 1991 proved similarly ill-fated: his touchingly low-key performance in *Only The Lonely* outshone by the veteran Maureen O'Hara as his domineering mother; his dramatic role in *JFK* lost amid the all-star cast.

1971 Face Of The Lady **1973** Class Of '44 **1975** It Seemed Like A Good Idea **1976** Tunnelvision; The Clown Murders; Find The Lady **1978** The Silent Partner **1979** Lost And Found; 1941 **1980** The Blues Brothers; Double Negative **1981** Stripes **1982** It Came From Hollywood **1983** Going Berserk; National Lampoon's Vacation **1984** Splash; Brewster's Millions **1985** Sesame Street Presents: Follow That Bird; Summer Rental; Volunteers **1986** The Canadian Conspiracy; Armed And Dangerous; Little Shop Of Horrors; Three Amigos! **1987** Spaceballs; Planes, Trains And Automobiles **1988** The Great Outdoors **1989** Speedzone aka Cannonball Fever; Uncle Buck!; Who's Harry Crumb? (also co-writer) **1990** Home Alone; Masters Of Menace **1991** Nothing But Trouble; Delirious; JFK; Only The Lonely **1992** Once Upon A Crime

Cannon, Dyan
(Samille Diane Friesen)

Actress, director
Born 4 January 1939
Tacoma, Washington

In the late 1960s and early 1970s – long before Farrah Fawcett and Jane Fonda made aerobics and the anorexic look fashionable – Dyan Cannon's was the face that launched a million bimbos. Petite, pug-faced and mini-skirted, with a tumbling Bardot-like mane and sumptuously cantilevered bosom, she seemed the kind of sultry tease with whom an area sales manager might hope to get lucky at the fag-end of the office party. Not surprisingly, her heyday was studded with roles as a goodhearted slattern or the bored Mrs Available next door, eyeing up her husband's best friends.

The Washington-born actress attended the University of her home state, where she studied anthropology, before heading for Los Angeles where she worked as a model until spotted by writer-producer Jerry Wald. Wald gave Dyan her 'explosive' stage name, MGM took her up, and she eventually made her acting debut on TV's Playhouse 90 with Art Carney in *The Ding-A-Ling Girl*. She broke into films in 1960, billed as Diane Cannon and playing Wiggles, a member of a teenage gang in *This Rebel Breed*, and well down the cast list as a floozy briefly romanced by mobster Ray Danton in *The Rise And Fall Of Legs Diamond*. Subsequently she appeared on Broadway (with a young Jane Fonda) in *The Fun Couple*.

Thus far Cannon had made few waves, but everything changed when she met and moved in with Cary Grant. He was 65 and she was 27. In 1965 they were married, and three years later emerged from one of Hollywood's messier divorces during which Cannon alleged that Grant spent much of the time high on LSD and beat her in front of the servants.

She returned to the screen in 1969 in Paul Mazursky's directorial debut, *Bob & Carol & Ted & Alice*, winning a Best Supporting Actress Oscar nomination as Elliot Gould's well-stacked but uptight wife queasily contemplating a *ménage à quatre* with suburban swingers Robert Culp and Natalie Wood. The actress was very busy indeed in 1971. In *Doctors' Wives* she was a bored spouse on the prowl; *The Anderson Tapes*, a superior heist caper directed by Sidney Lumet, saw her as a high-class hooker keeping Sean Connery's bed warm; and in *The Burglars* she played a performer in a live sex show. In *The Love Machine*, a deliciously absurd screen version of a Jacqueline Susann schlockbuster, she heaved and panted as the nymphomaniac consort of a TV mogul. She concluded this celebration of sluttishness with Otto Preminger's tart black comedy, *Such Good Friends*, bedding down with her dying husband's best of same. In similar vein Cannon was ripely blowsy as Burt Reynolds' love interest in *Shamus* (1973), a mildly parodic send-up of the thick-ear school of detective thriller, and very funny as a bitchy Hollywood agent in the quirky murder mystery *The Last Of Sheila* (1974), submitting to intimate massage with a succession of burly deckhands.

Then, tired of being typed, Dyan Cannon withdrew into a period of characteristically fatuous Californian introspection during which she wrote, directed and produced an Oscar-nominated 48-minute documentary, *No. 1* (1976), which set out to explore the problems of childhood and sexuality. (It was more than a whim – she has made two more of her own films to date.) She emerged from self-imposed exile as a rather tiresome feminist – although still capable of throwing good old-fashioned star tantrums when the mood took her – but nevertheless turned in a series of performances which showed how good an actress she can be: touchingly trying to hang on to erring singer-husband Willie Nelson in *Honeysuckle Rose* (1980); playing a lethal, cuckolding wife in *Heaven Can Wait* (1981), which won her a second Supporting Actress Oscar nomination; as the kookily shopsoiled movie star Alice Detroit in *Author! Author!* (1982), coaxed onto Broadway by Al Pacino and consoling herself with champagne and aspirin cocktails; and, before she is bumped off, sharply amusing as Michael Caine's hysterically valetudinarian wife in *Death Trap* (1982).

1960 This Rebel Breed; The Rise And Fall Of Legs Diamond **1969** Bob & Carol & Ted & Alice 1971 Le Casse/The Burglar (France); The Anderson Tapes; Doctors' Wives; The Love Machine; Such Good Friends **1973** Shamus; The Last Of Sheila **1974** Child Under A Leaf **1978** Heaven Can Wait; Revenge Of The Pink Panther **1979** For The First Time (director) **1980** Coast To Coast; Honeysuckle Rose **1982** Deathtrap; Author! Author! **1988** Caddyshack II **1990** The End Of Innocence (w/d) **1992** The Pickle

Capshaw, Kate (Kathy Sue Nail)

Actress
Born 1953
Fort Worth, Texas

Kate Capshaw was just another pretty blonde model from Texas trying her hand at acting before Steven Spielberg cast her as the romantic interest in the second of the phenomenally successful Indiana Jones films, *Indiana Jones And The Temple Of Doom* (1984), which brought her international but fleeting recognition.

Capshaw is actually a woman of more substance than either her role (as a squealing, handwringing 'dame') or her earliest professional work in a daytime TV soap suggest. A graduate of the University of Missouri with a master's degree in learning disabilities, she was a teacher before going the Ford Agency model route to acting in New York. Her film debut came in a routine comedy-drama, *A Little Sex* (1982), and was little remarked, but her fortunes rose with a streak of four films in 1984, although these included the Dudley Moore dud *Best Defense* as well as the Spielberg 'Indy' smash and the entertaining sci-fi adventure *Dreamscape*, in which she played a sympathetic doctor/romantic lead to Dennis Quaid's gifted psychic.

Post-*Indiana Jones*, Capshaw predictably didn't come close to a vehicle with comparable commercial appeal although she was attractive and capable, particularly in a Louis L'Amour Western adaptation made for

America's HBO television, *The Quick And The Dead* (1987), and did well with her role as a night-club hostess in Ridley Scott's brutal but slick actioner *Black Rain* (1989), opposite Michael Douglas. She was one of several actresses under-used in Alan Rudolph's infuriating romantic *noir* thriller homage, *Love At Large* (1990), giving an intriguing performance as the guilty wife of a bigamist in her few scenes. Despite some dozen films to her credit, by the 90s Capshaw was undoubtedly still best known to the general public as the second wife of Steven Spielberg.

1982 A Little Sex **1984** Indiana Jones And The Temple Of Doom; Best Defense; Dreamscape; Windy City **1986** Power; Spacecamp **1988** Ti Presento Un'Amica Quite By Chance (Italy) **1989** Black Rain **1990** Love At Large **1991** My Heroes Have Always Been Cowboys

Carpenter, John

Director, writer
Born 16 January 1948
Bowling Green, Kentucky

John Carpenter is one of a generation of movie-crazy directors steeped in the films made under the studio system, especially the low-budget thrillers, serials and space movies of the 40s and 50s. From the tender age of eight he was shooting 8mm sci-fi shorts, and as a film student at the University Of Southern California he wrote and directed several shorts, one of which, *The Resurrection Of Broncho Billy*, actually won an Oscar in 1970. His first full-length feature, *Dark Star* (1974), began as a student project and cost $60,000. A witty science-fiction movie with a bouncing biped beach ball serving as an alien, it was a shoestring antidote to Stanley Kubrick's *2001*. Carpenter called the film, about the bored crew of a spaceship becoming prey to their own phobias, 'One big optical *Waiting For Godot* in space'.

Taking Howard Hawks' *Rio Bravo* as his model, *Assault On Precinct 13* (1976) was an exploitation movie made with bravura, creating a claustrophobic atmosphere as cops and cons are besieged by terrorists in a disused LA police station. *Escape From New York* (1981) saw the director moving into more expensive territory with cheaper thrills, although the story, set in 1997 when the entire Manhattan island has become a prison, had its fascination despite the patchwork of borrowings from elsewhere and a sense of anticlimax.

The huge box-office hit *Halloween* (1978) showed Carpenter suffering from Psychosis in which he used Hitchcockian shock cuts, a Bernard Herrmann-like theme (composed by the director), and Janet Leigh's daughter, Jamie Lee Curtis, as the intended victim of a mad killer, pursued relentlessly by a subjective camera on the cleverly used CinemaScope screen. Less interesting stylistically were the sequels, *Halloween II* (1981) and *Halloween III* (1982), which Carpenter only wrote and produced but didn't direct.

The Fog (1979), about a respectable coastal community threatened by ghosts of lepers, contained the seeds of a superb, subversive supernatural thriller, but Carpenter could not bring them to fruition. *The Thing* (1982) revealed too much, too soon and too unconvincingly to stand comparison with the subtle menace to be found in the 1951 Hawksian version of the same tale of a monster emerging from the icy wastes. There is some wry humour to alleviate some of the noisy violence in *Big Trouble In Little China* (1986), in which Kurt Russell fights against oriental supernatural forces, and the gloom of *Prince Of Darkness* (1987) is sometimes broken by laughs, some intentional and others not, but both films end up becoming the sort of movies they seem to be taking off.

Another film with a strong theme and central idea which fails to live up to its promise is *They Live* (1988). Carpenter expertly creates an alien milieu, in this case the world of an underclass whose members, when wearing special sunglasses, see the skulls beneath the faces of their rich oppressors in order to identify and eliminate them. But the apocalyptic vision deteriorates into a conventional, brutish thriller with an interminable fist fight and lousy acting. *They Live* is an example of Carpenter's many attempts to give horror science-fiction movies a new social slant, but succumbing about half-way through to the more exploitative aspects of the genre.

His first 90s outing, starring an attractively maturing Chevy Chase, also suffered from a lack of focus in the screenplay. However, *Memoirs Of An Invisible Man* is a triumph of special effects and boasts a screenplay of entertaining wit (to which William Goldman contributed). It marked a possible change of gear for the director.

As director only unless stated otherwise: **1974** Dark Star (also co-writer) **1976** Assault On Precinct 13 (w/d) **1978**

Halloween (w/d) **1979** The Fog (also co-writer) **1981** Escape From New York (also co-writer); Halloween II (writer only) **1982** The Thing; Halloween III (writer only) **1983** Christine **1984** Starman **1986** Big Trouble In Little China; The Boy Who Could Fly (cameo only) **1987** The Kid Brother (actor only); Prince Of Darkness (also writer under pseudonym) **1988** They Live; The House On Carroll Street (cameo only) **1992** Memoirs Of An Invisible Man

Carradine, David
(John Arthur Carradine)
Actor
Born 8 December 1936
Hollywood
CaliforniaThe eldest of John Carradine's three actor sons, David took after his gaunt, booming-voiced, eccentric father in being as thin, tall, and unpredictable. After graduating from San Francisco State University, he spent several years roaming the country, working as a labourer and giving concerts in which he played guitar and sang songs, some of them his own compositions. This restless background later made him perfect casting as the legendary hobo folksinger, Woody Guthrie, in Hal Ashby's biopic, *Bound For Glory* (1976).

In the mid-60s he was still a rebel, experimenting with hallucinogenic drugs and riding a motorbike while appearing in the Broadway production of *The Royal Hunt Of The Sun* (1965); in the title role in the short-lived TV Western series *Shane*; and as heavies in a number of feature Westerns, being shot at by the likes of Robert Mitchum in *The Good Guys And The Bad Guys* and *Young Billy Young*, and Glenn Ford in *Heaven With A Gun* (all 1969).

Carradine's career received a boost in 1972 when he was chosen to star in the popular TV series *Kung Fu*, at the time when chop-socky movies were all the rage. It was appropriate casting for a man who is an exponent of the martial arts. The same year, Martin Scorsese cast him as the male lead, a con-man, opposite Barbara Hershey, in *Boxcar Bertha*, the director's first professional feature. After performing in two unreleased films, *Around* and *A Country Mile*, the following year, the actor finally established himself as a counter-culture hero in two of Paul Bartel's crazy, futuristic road-race movies, *Death Race 2000* (1975) and *Cannonball* (1976), in both of which he was the hero behind the wheel of a monster car. Also for the Roger Corman factory came similar driving roles in *Thunder And Lightning* (1977), *Deathsport* (1978) and, with motorcycles this time, *Fast Charlie . . . The Moonbeam Rider* (1979), one of the many *Death Race* rip-offs.

Apart from the daredevil driver and the martial arts expert (*Circle Of Iron*, 1979, *Lone Wolf McQuade*, 1983 etc), and a couple of unsuccessful attempts at directing, Carradine was to be found floundering as the doom-laden American-Jewish trapeze artist in 1923 Berlin in Ingmar Bergman's first English-language film, *The Serpent's Egg* (1977). He was much more comfortable the year after, returning to the kind of tongue-in-cheek, kick-in-the-groin action movies in which he made his name.

1964 Taggart **1965** Bus Riley's Back In Town **1967** The Violent Ones **1968** Too Many Thieves **1969** The Good Guys And The Bad Guys; Heaven With A Gun; Young Billy Young **1970** Macho Callahan; The McMasters **1972** Boxcar Bertha **1973** Mean Streets (bit); **1975** Death Race 2000; You And Me (also director) **1976** Bound For Glory; Cannonball aka Carquake **1977** The Serpent's Egg; Thunder And Lightning **1978** Deathsport; Gray Lady Down **1979** Circle Of Iron aka The Silent Flute; Fast Charlie . . . The Moonbeam Rider; Cloud Dancer; The Mandate Of Heaven **1980** The Long Riders **1981** Americana (also director) **1982** Q; Safari 3000; Trick Or Treat **1983** Lone Wolf McQuade **1984** On The Line; The Warrior And The Sorceress **1986** Armed Response; P.O.W. The Escape **1987** Wheels Of Terror **1988** The Misfit Brigade; Crime Zone **1989** Wizards Of The Lost Kingdom II; Nowhere To Run **1990** Think Big; Future Zone; Sundown: The Vampire In Retreat; Bird On A Wire **1992** Roadside Prophets; Waxwork II: Lost In Time **1992/93** First Force

Carradine, Keith
Actor
Born 8 August 1951
San Mateo, California

While elder half-brother David made his name as an extrovert ace driver and kung fu specialist, Keith Carradine used his similarly angular features to portray more introverted, sensitive and tortured characters. However, like David, he is an accomplished guitarist and singer, and has a restless and rebellious nature.

Keith knew from childhood that he wanted to follow his father, John Carradine, into acting, and began appearing in plays at high school. Impatient with his theatre arts studies at Colorado State University, he left after one semester to seek professional acting jobs. A role in the 1969 LA production of the hippie musical. *Hair*, got him small parts in two Westerns in 1971, *A Gunfight* and, more significantly, Robert Altman's *McCabe And Mrs Miller*. It has been Carradine's association with Altman and Alan Rudolph, Altman's protégé and assistant on *Nashville* (1975), that has provided the actor with his best roles and his filmic identity.

He brought a tragic dimension to the part of the doomed young outlaw fleeing the cops with Shelley Duvall in Altman's *Thieves Like Us* (1974), more convincing than the fragile Farley Granger in *They Live By Night*, the 1948 version. Now established as a member of the Altman company, he stood out from a large cast in the kaleidoscopic *Nashville*, playing an unscrupulous country-and-western singer and becoming the first performer to win an Oscar for his own composition, 'I'm Easy', for which he wrote the music and lyrics.

In *Welcome To LA* (1976), the first of four films Carradine made for Alan Rudolph, he played a similarly egocentric rock musician, this time searching Tinseltown for some meaning to his life. He delivered more depth and variation in three further Rudolph movies: he was Mickey, the amorous escapee from a mental home in *Choose Me* (1984); Coop in *Trouble In Mind* (1985), abandoning his wife and child to join a maverick black gang, his hairdo becoming increasingly wild in the process; and in *The Moderns* (1988), he was perfectly in period as failed expatriate artist Nick Hart in 1920s Paris. As another kind of artist, a photographer, in Louis Malle's *Pretty Baby* (1978), he added charm and poignancy to the voyeuristic role of a man trying to capture the world of a turn-of-the-century New Orleans bordello through his lens.

Carradine showed a tougher side in two films by a tougher director, Walter Hill – grittily determined as a National Guardsman trying to survive a murderous trip through the Louisiana bayou in *Southern Comfort* (1981), and as one of the three notorious Wild West Younger brothers (the other two were played by David and Robert Carradine) in *The Long Riders* (1980). Keith continues to carry the Carradine name with distinction as witness his co-starring appearance with Vanessa Redgrave in *The Ballad Of The Sad Café* (1991).

1971 A Gunfight; McCabe And Mrs Miller **1973** Emperor Of The North Pole (GB: Emperor Of The North); Hex **1974** Thieves Like Us; Run, Run, Joe!; Antoine Et Sebastian (France) **1975** Idaho Transfer; Nashville; You And Me **1976** Lumiere (France); Welcome To LA **1977** The Duellists **1978** Pretty Baby; Sgt Pepper's Lonely Hearts Club Band **1979** An Almost Perfect Affair; Old Boyfriends; Take Two **1980** The Long Riders; A Rumour Of War **1981** Southern Comfort **1984** Choose Me **1985** Maria's Lovers; Trouble In Mind **1987** Backfire **1988** The Moderns **1989** Cold Feet; Daddy's Dyin' – Who's Got The Will? **1990** The Bachelor (Italy) **1991** The Ballad Of The Sad Café **1992** Crisscross

Cassavetes, John

Director, actor
Born 9 December 1929
New York City
Died 3 February 1989

'For years I claimed the artist's right not to be headed down by anything or anybody. I made films, got drunk, stayed away from home. I destroyed my wife yet she stood by me through child after child. So I made this film as a tribute to Gena for all the lousy things I'd done to her.' The film referred to was *A Woman Under The Influence* (1974) and Gena was Gena Rowlands, Cassavetes' wife since 1959. It was a typically up-front statement from a film-maker who was never afraid to expose his most private passions in public. Like jazz, which often accompanies his very personal movies, the films were made in an improvisational manner with the actors given a fairly free rein. Using *cinéma verité* techniques with vast close-ups, the characters/actors are revealed to the camera/psychoanalyst, generally depicting menopausal (male and female) emotional crises. The films are often painful and uncomfortable to watch, making some audiences feel voyeuristic, or merely embarrassed, by such unconstrained acting, while others recognise the power of the performances and the importance of Cassavetes' influence on younger film-makers to make independent movies outside the studio system.

Raised in the Bronx, the son of a wealthy, Greek-born, Harvard-educated businessman, Cassavetes made it as an actor on TV in the early 50s, principally as jazz-loving private eye Johnny Staccato, an apt nickname for him as actor and director. With $40,000 earned from the TV series, he made his first film, *Shadows* (1959), shot in 16mm on location in New York with a crew of four and a script based on the actors' improvisations. The film's raw vitality and racial theme won it the Critics Film Award at the 1959 Venice

Film Festival. Strangely, Paramount saw enough in the film's grainy texture and hand-held camera the antithesis of that studio's renowned polish – to offer the director a contract. But the two movies he made for them, *Too Late Blues* (with himself and Stella Stevens, 1961) and *A Child Is Waiting* (starring Judy Garland and Burt Lancaster, 1963), convinced him that there was no place for artistic freedom in the studio system.

From 1968, he was able to make independent films (only *Gloria*, 1980, his most approachable film, was financed by Columbia), working with his own group of technicians and actor-friends (Peter Falk, Ben Gazzara, Seymour Cassel), many of them on deferred salaries, and Gena Rowlands, a central figure in most of his work. However, there was no room for his wife in *Husbands* (1970), a self-indulgent 154 minutes of Falk, Gazzara and Cassavetes on a drunken spree in London. As an actor for other directors, his best known role was as Mia Farrow's heel of an actor-husband in *Rosemary's Baby* (1968), cast by Roman Polanski over Paramount's objections. Otherwise, he was frequently limited to playing unsmiling gangsters in violent movies such as Don Siegel's *The Killers* (1964), Robert Aldrich's *The Dirty Dozen* (1967) and Brian De Palma's *The Fury* (1978), in which he ended up splattered across the ceiling. He had a little more chance to show his acting talents as a modern-day Prospero in Paul Mazursky's *Tempest*, and again as a con-man (improvising with Falk) in Elaine May's *Mikey And Nicky* (1976), but both were dismal box-office flops.

John Cassavetes' premature death from cirrhosis of the liver represented a significant loss to a Hollywood short on original film-makers unafraid to venture out of the mainstream.

As actor: **1953** Taxi **1955** The Night Holds Terror **1956** Crime In The Streets **1957** Edge Of The City; Affair In Havana **1958** Saddle The Wind; Virgin Island **1962** The Webster Boy aka Middle Of Nowhere **1964** The Killers **1967** The Dirty Dozen; Devil's Angels **1968** Rosemary's Baby; Machine Gun McCain **1969** Bandits In Rome; If It's Tuesday It Must Be Belgium (cameo) **1975** Capone **1976** Two-Minute Warning; Mikey And Nicky **1978** The Fury; Brass Target **1981** Incubus; Whose Life Is It Anyway? **1982** Tempest **1983** Marvin And Tige **1984** Like Father And Son; I'm Almost Not Crazy. . . **1986** The Third Day Comes

As director: **1959** Shadows **1961** Too Late Blues (also actor) **1963** A Child Is Waiting **1968** Faces **1970** Husbands (also actor) **1971** Minnie And Moskowitz (also actor) **1974** A Woman Under The Influence **1976** The Killing Of A Chinese Bookie **1977** Opening Night (also actor) **1980** Gloria **1983** Love Streams (also actor) **1984** Big Trouble

Cassidy, Joanna

Actress

Born 2 August 1944

Haddonfield, New Jersey

Well-regarded and under-used could describe a number of actors; few more appropriately than Joanna Cassidy, a handsome woman of ability and presence. In more than 20 years in films she has had few roles to sink her teeth into, but when she has her work has been excellent.

At the age of 18, Cassidy entered Syracuse University to study art, but left after one year for an early marriage, which foundered. She moved to San Francisco, where she enjoyed a successful career as a model and made very fleeting appearances in two films shot there, the excellent *Bullitt* (1968) and the execrable *Fools* (1970). Her first real role came in one of many San Francisco police dramas, *The Laughing Policeman* (1974), which starred Walter Matthau and Bruce Dern. It was a small part but she looked at ease and confident on film – she was by then a veteran of several television commercials – and easily landed two more jobs that year. *The Outfit*, a 'mob melodrama' starring Robert Duvall, wasn't bad but did little for her; *Bank Shot*, a daft heist comedy caper starring George C. Scott, was good fun and gave her prominent billing, which seemed to promise big things.

But it was two years before Cassidy appeared again, further down in the supporting cast, in Bob Rafelson's *Stay Hungry* (1976), and a further six years of unmemorable roles in variable films before she made an impression in a real winner, Ridley Scott's *Blade Runner* (1982), as a statuesque android battling with Harrison Ford and blasted through a plate-glass window in a brutal, exciting set piece.

Cassidy finally had her day with a plum role in Roger Spottiswoode's outstanding political thriller, *Under Fire* (1983). She was superb as a news reporter compromising her professionalism by becoming emotionally involved in the Nicaraguan revolution, and made a plausible romantic lead caught between Gene Hackman and Nick Nolte. Unfortunately, strong women's roles are still so thin on the ground as to be the prerogative of a handful of Hollywood A-list actresses, and Cassidy's work through the remainder of the decade – a slight comedy, a couple of Cold War thrillers and straight woman to the special effects in *Who Framed Roger Rabbit?* – didn't provide much of a challenge, although her second outing with Hackman, as his smart, military officer ex-wife in *The Package* (1989) reconfirmed that she gives good value as an intelligent and capable woman 'of a certain age'.

1968 Bullitt **1970** Fools **1974** The Laughing Policeman; The Outfit; Bank Shot **1976** Stay Hungry **1977** Stunts; The Late Show **1978** Our Winning Season; The Glove **1980** Night Games **1981** Prime Time aka American Raspberry **1982** Blade Runner **1983** Under Fire **1986** Club Paradise **1987** The Fourth Protocol **1988** Who Framed Roger Rabbit? **1989** The Package **1990** Where The Heart Is **1991** The Real World; Don't Tell Mom The Babysitter's Dead; Lonely Hearts **1992** All-American Murder **1992/93** Landslide

Cates, Phoebe

Actress
Born 1964
New York City

The daughter of producer-director Joseph Cates, Phoebe was a dance prodigy and successful New York model before breaking in to movies. For some time, it was the latter talent rather than the former that was more evident in her performances. She can look like the proverbial girl next door (as Kate in *Gremlins*, 1984, for example), but there is also a beguiling hint of the exotic in her olive complexion and Eurasian features. Just as well, for there was little else remarkable about her debut in the Blue Lagoon rip-off, *Paradise* (1982), or her participation in the smutty Porky's-style *Private School* (1983).

Between these two forgettable misadventures Cates fared better in Amy Heckerling's *Fast Times At Ridgemont High* (1982), alongside future stars Sean Penn, Judge Reinhold, Jennifer Jason Leigh and Forest Whitaker. Reinhold and Cates (both only 20 years old at the time) got a taste of the big time in the Spielberg-produced blockbuster *Gremlins*, directed by Joe Dante. Cates may have suffered the indignity of being second-billed to a puppet show – but what a show! She followed it up with another home run, this time on the small screen. Shirley Conran's trashy but best-selling *Lace* became an immensely successful two-part TV mini-series, with Cates as a sex symbol in search of her parents. *Oedipus Rex* it wasn't; watched around the world it certainly was.

Marrying Kevin Kline, she took a break from acting to concentrate on her family. She came back in 1988 with a thankless role as the estranged fashion model wife of Michael J. Fox in *Bright Lights, Big City*, a film that even its star couldn't save. She showed a lighter touch in *Gremlins* 2 (1990), having already indicated in *Shag* and *Heart Of Dixie* the previous year that she had extended her range. If, in the past, Phoebe Cates had given in to the innocuous in token girl parts, she sparked as bright Southern belles in those two lively movies, both directed very much towards women.

1982 Paradise; Fast Times At Ridgemont High **1983** Private School **1984** Gremlins **1988** Bright Lights, Big City; Shag **1989** Date With An Angel; Heart Of Dixie **1990** Gremlins 2: The New Batch; I Love You To Death (unbilled cameo) **1991** Drop Dead Fred **1992/93** Bodies, Rest And Motion

Cattrall, Kim

Actress
Born 21 August 1956
Liverpool, England

After growing up in England, Kim Cattrall crossed the Atlantic to attend the American Academy of Dramatic Arts in New York and moved on to a stage career, first in Canada and then in Los Angeles. There, she impressed critics in plays such as *A View From The Bridge*, *Agnes Of God*, and *The Three Sisters*. (She has since played Chekhov again, in *Wild Honey* on Broadway.)

She had made her movie debut before that, in Otto Preminger's *Rosebud* (1975), in which she was cast as one of five rich young women kidnapped by the PLO, an overladen thriller that sank ignominiously. Her move to Canada proved more beneficial, bringing her to the attention of director Bob Clark, who gave her a supporting role in the Jack Lemmon tearjerker, *Tribute* (1980), which she followed with a memorable turn in the appallingly tasteless but very popular *Porky's* (1981). The female lead in the even more popular *Police Academy* (1984) cemented the impact she had made although, now nearing 30, she was perhaps growing a mite old for her constituency of adolescent fans. Subsequent vehicles misfired, including Bob Clark's *Turk 182!* (1985), and *Mannequin* (1987) typified what was going wrong with her career. In that irredeemably witless comic fantasy, Cattrall played a shopping-mall dummy by day and Egyptian princess by night, just waiting for the true love of young Andrew McCarthy to set her free. Confined to the market, the couple had little to do but sample fashion accessories, including each other, but the movie made money.

By refusing to participate in the lucrative sequels to either *Porky's* or *Police Academy*, Cattrall signalled her faith in herself but, by 1987, she seemed to have lost all forward momentum in a series of 'girl' parts that called for nothing more than a pretty face, which she effortlessly supplied. Then, in 1988, the actress changed her tactics, finally playing her age in straight dramatic roles. She was a bitchy adulteress in Bob Swaim's tortuous *Masquerade*, and an adulterous bitch in the even sillier *Midnight Crossing*. If the films were unworthy, Kim Cattrall still looked promising, and it was no surprise to find her in hot company with Tom Hanks, Melanie Griffith and Bruce Willis in 1990's *Bonfire Of The Vanities*.

1975 Rosebud **1977** The Other Side Of Midnight II **1980** Tribute **1981** Porky's; Ticket To Heaven **1984** Police Academy **1985** Turk 182; City Limits; Hold-Up **1986** Big Trouble In Little China **1987** Mannequin **1988** Masquerade; Palais Royale; Midnight Crossing; For Better Or For Worse **1989** The Return Of The Musketeers; Brown Bread Sandwiches **1990** Honeymoon Academy; The Bonfire Of The Vanities **1992** Split Second; Star Trek VI: The Undiscovered Country **1992/93** Double Vision

Caulfield, Maxwell

Actor

Born 23 November 1959

Glasgow, Scotland

British-born Maxwell Caulfield got off to a Hollywood career starring opposite Michelle Pfeiffer, herself still a new girl in town, in *Grease 2* (1982) playing, in effect, what amounted to the Olivia Newton-John role opposite Pfeiffer's talented but barely more credible John Travolta. The film failed to become the success that had been expected, but Caulfield picked up a similar role in the feeble *Electric Dreams* (1984), playing second fiddle to a computer.

The young actor's transatlantic career was beginning to look doomed from the start, but the following year's *The Boys Next Door* brought a complete transformation. Penelope Spheeris' extremely hard-hitting film cast Caulfield and Charlie Sheen as a couple of ordinary kids whose joyride to the city entails an escalating trail of casual violence and murder. The material trod a thin line between exploitation and expose, but Caulfield was a revelation, virtually unrecognisable with blond hair, an authentic American accent, and a latent psychotic streak. However, his next outing, *The Supernaturals* (1986), was a disaster and, deserting the movies for a while, he joined TV's *The Colbys* in a regular role which only re-emphasised his original soft-centred image.

Caulfield, who returned to the big screen for the vampire movie *Sundown*, in 1989, began his show business career dancing in a London nightclub. In 1978 he opted for the lure of New York, where he later won a Theatre World award for his work in *Class Enemy*. He lives on a ranch in Santa Barbara with British actress Juliet Mills, many years his senior, to whom he is happily married.

1982 Grease 2 **1984** Electric Dream **1985** The Boys Next Door **1986** The Supernaturals **1989** Sundown: The Vampire In Retreat; Mind Games **1990** Fatal Sky **1991** Dance With Death **1993** Inevitable Grace; Alien Intruder

Channing, Stockard (Susan Williams Antonia Stockard Channing Schmidt)

Actress

Born 13 February 1944

New York City

Small, square and almost chubby-faced, with a personality that can bubble or alarm with equal ease, Stockard Channing is a distinguished member of the Broadway stage fraternity who, from time to time, graces a Hollywood movie, generally in supporting character roles, and always to advantageous effect.

The daughter of a wealthy shipping executive, Channing was educated at Radcliffe, where she took a BA degree *cum laude* before joining an experimental group, The Theatre Company of Boston, where she started her stage career in the 60s. It was not too many years before she graduated to the New York big time, where she has appeared in more than 25 Broadway plays, received two Tony nominations, and the award itself for her performance in the harrowing *A Day In The Death Of Joe Egg*, playing the mother of a baby born a 'vegetable'. She began in films with a string of bit parts, as in *The Hospital* (1971) but, officially, her film debut was really marked by her appearance in director

Mike Nichols' *The Fortune* (1975), a spoof in which Channing (as Freddie Quintessa Bigard, 1920s heiress to a sanitary napkin fortune!) deftly held her own against the predatory presence of both Warren Beatty and Jack Nicholson, her inborn air of privilege imbueing the role with a credibility that few others could have matched. Aside from gaining popularity with her ballsy, show-stealing performance in the hit musical *Grease* (1978), Channing is a familiar face to American TV audiences for the several leads she has played in television movies – not all of them, it must be said, of the highest quality. Although the diminutive actress lacks conventional beauty – she was once memorably described as resembling 'a cross between Elizabeth Taylor and a chipmunk' – she is far from unattractive, and has specialised in keeping the comic tradition of the sexy, smart innocent alive in an age when it has not always been fashionable to do so.

However, hovering at the gates of middle age by 1990, Channing appeared to be coming into her own on the big screen after so many roles in disappointing, often ridiculous comedies (*Sweet Revenge* and *The Big Bus*, both 1976, for example), or giving her all in upmarket failures like the Meryl Streep-Jack Nicholson starrer *Heartburn* (1986). She had opportunities to shine – and grabbed them – in Michael Lehmann's *Meet The Applegates* and Lee Grant's *Staying Together* (both 1990), films which benefited from intelligent screenplays and solid casts, and went on to co-star with the splendid Ron Silver, as well as Beau Bridges and Cybill Shepherd, in Arthur Hiller's *Married To It*. After her acclaimed Broadway and London performance in the award-winning *Six Degrees Of Separation*, she was, at playwright John Guare's insistence, engaged to reprise her role in the screen adaptation.

1970 Comforts Of Home **1971** The Hospital **1972** Up The Sandbox **1975** The Fortune **1976** Sweet Revenge aka Dandy The All American Girl; The Big Bus **1978** The Cheap Detective; Grease **1979** The Fish That Saved Pittsburgh **1982** Rally aka Safari 3000 **1983** Without A Trace **1986** Heartburn; The Men's Club **1988** A Time Of Destiny **1990** Meet The Applegates; Staying Together aka A Boy's Life **1991** Married To It **1992/93** Six Degrees Of Separation

Chaplin, Geraldine

Actress
Born 31 July 1944
Santa Monica, California

As the daughter of Charles Chaplin and the granddaughter of Eugene O'Neill, Geraldine Chaplin had to struggle to come out from under their long shadows and make a name for herself. Her first appearance on screen was as an eight-year-old child seen in the street (with her younger brother and sister) in her father's *Limelight* (1952). The only other time she worked with him was a cameo appearance in his final film, *The Countess From Hong Kong* (1967).

Aside from the dominant figure of her famous father, there have been three other important men in her life, the directors Robert Altman, Alan Rudolph and the Spaniard Carlos Saura, the latter being her long-time inamorato with whom she made half a dozen films in Spain, most of them conceived as vehicles for her. It was Saura who revealed her to have a wider range and more passion than her somewhat wan and cold appearances in her English-language films had suggested. In a dual role in *Peppermint Frappé* (1967), she plays both a shy, plain nurse and a lively and attractive wife; and in *Ana And The Wolves* (1972), she is an English governess who becomes the object of the sexual desires of the three sons in the family.

This most cosmopolitan of actresses was first introduced to Spain during the lengthy location shooting on *Doctor Zhivago* (1965), in which she played Omar Sharif's long-suffering wife. She had been educated in Switzerland and studied ballet in England, where she became a member of the Royal Ballet for a period.

After appearing as the loquacious and irritating BBC journalist in Altman's *Nashville* (1975), she became part of his repertory company. For Altman, she played Annie Oakley in *Buffalo Bill And The Indians* the following year, and was the bossy caterer in *A Wedding* (1978). She was better served in a number of Alan Rudolph movies – emptily talkative in *Welcome To LA* (1977); furiously hellish in *Remember My Name* (1978), wreaking revenge on her ex-husband (Anthony Perkins); and notoriously man-eating as Nathalie de Ville in *The Moderns* (1988). Of the latter role, Rudolph commented, 'She plays the kind of character who is only alive when the light is on; she definitely comes and goes with the period. Geraldine makes it seem like a fun-house mirror being held up, and at the same time she has a bit of Goya in her.' Since the end of her relationship with Saura, this actress of singularly unconventional looks and personality has had a varied (and variable) career.

1965 Doctor Zhivago **1967** Stranger In the House aka Cop-Out; The Countess From Hong Kong (bit); J'ai Tué Rasputin/I Killed Rasputin (France); Peppermint Frappé (Spain) **1969** La Madriguera (Spain) **1970** The Hawaiians **1971** Sur Un Arbre Perché (France) **1972** Zero Population Growth aka ZPG; Innocent Bystanders; La Casa Sin Fronteras (Spain); Ana Y Los Lobos/Ana And The Wolves (Spain) **1974** The Three Musketeers; Verflucht Dies Amerika! (Germany); La Banda De Jaider (Spain) **1975** The Four Musketeers; Nashville **1976** Buffalo Bill And The Indians; Cria Cuervos/Raise Ravens (Spain) **1977** Welcome To LA; Roseland; Elisa, Vida Mia/Elisa, My Love (Spain); Noriot (France); In Memoriam (Spain); Une Page D'Amour (Belgium) **1978** A Wedding; Remember My Name; Los Ojos Vendados (Spain); L'Adoption (France) **1979** Mais Ou Et Donc Ormecar (France) **1980** The Mirror Crack'd **1982** Bolero **1983** La Vie Est Un Roman/Life Is A Bed Of Roses (France) **1984** L'Amour Par Terre/Love On The Ground (France) **1987** White Mischief **1988** The Moderns **1989** I Want To Go Home; The Return Of The Musketeers **1990** The Children **1991** Buster's Bedroom (Germany/Canada/Portugal) **1992/93** Charlie

Chase, Chevy
(Cornelius Crane Chase)

Actor
Born 8 October 1943
New York City

Dark haired and moderately handsome, with a cleft chin to rival Kirk Douglas', Chevy Chase has a smug, smart-aleck demeanour he constantly undercuts with pratfalls; it is a trademark which accounts for both his relative success as a comic actor and for his limitations: whether toned up or down, his have been basically one-note performances.

He burst onto the American television scene with a catchline that has since become famous – 'I'm Chevy Chase and you're not' – in a show that has since become legendary, *Saturday Night Live*. Hired as a writer (he'd already cut his teeth off-Broadway as a member of an underground video revue group lampooning television, the best sketches of which were filmed and released as *The Groove Tube*, 1974, and in National Lampoon's revue *Lemmings*), Chase nursed an ambition to appear before the cameras, and his campaign to convince the show's producer, Lorne Michaels, that this was a good idea quickly paid off for both. Along with other founder members like John Belushi and Gilda Radner, Chase became a hugely popular TV personality, winning two Emmys – as writer and supporting actor – in 1976.

Neither his background nor his education indicated that Chase would become a comic actor. The son of a publishing executive and a plumbing heiress, he was brought up in the privileged world of upper middle-class New York and received a degree in English from Bard College. However, from childhood he had always been a mischievous clown and something of a rebel and he gradually worked his way into the entertainment business through a series of jobs, one of the first of which was as an artist for the anarchic *Mad* magazine.

Having made a name for himself with *Saturday Night Live*, the three-times married Chase wasted no time in heading off to Hollywood. His feature film debut came in the moderately amusing but financially successful 1978 comedy *Foul Play*, in which he played it surprisingly straight as a cop protecting librarian Goldie Hawn from pursuing assassins, and the engaging pair teamed up more effectively in 1980's *Seems Like Old Times*. His filmography since then has consisted of a not inconsiderable series of predictable comedies, ranging from the amusing (*National Lampoon's Vacation*, 1983, the first and best of the sappy Griswold family romps) to the truly dreadful (William Friedkin's *Deal of the Century*, also 1983). Not surprisingly, he has maintained his links with the *Saturday Night Live* crowd, particularly Harold Ramis, who directed him in the first *Vacation* movie and in *Caddyshack*, (1980); and Dan Aykroyd, his co-star in *Spies Like Us* (1985) and *The Couch Trip*, (1988), and who directed him in 1991's *Nothing But Trouble*. His brand of comedy is neither sophisticated nor manic; as Chevy Chase himself knows only too well, his usually deadpan, middle-class and likeable if brash persona is best suited to the lowest-common denominator comedies he continues to make with such apparent effortlessness. However, in John Carpenter's uneven but interesting mélange of sci-fi, corruption and romance, *Memoirs Of An Invisible Man* (1992), the star displayed an attractive new maturity which augured well for a slight but welcome change of gear.

1974 The Groove Tube **1976** Tunnel Vision **1978** Foul Play **1980** Oh, Heavenly Dog!; Caddyshack; Seems Like Old Times **1981** Under The Rainbow; Modern Problems **1983** National Lampoon's Vacation; Deal Of The

Century **1985** Fletch; National Lampoon's European Vacation; Spies Like Us; Sesame Street Presents: Follow That Bird **1986** Three Amigos! **1988** The Couch Trip; Funny Farm; Caddyshack II **1989** Fletch Lives; National Lampoon's Christmas Vacation **1991** Nothing But Trouble; Home Run; LA Story (unbilled cameo) **1992** Memoirs Of An Invisible Man; Hero

Cheech and Chong
(Richard Marin and Thomas Chong)
Actors, writers, directors

Richard Marin

Born 13 July 1946

Los Angeles, California

Thomas Chong

Born 24 May 1938

Edmonton, Alberta, Canada

This inexplicably popular US comedy team stretched their one routine way past breaking point and, having realised it, failed to come with anything new to replace it. The Abbott and Costello of the drug set, they hit the jackpot impersonating a couple of amiable dopeheads whose endless search for 'good grass' took them through the byways of an LA sub-culture neglected by the mainstream but instantly recognisable nonetheless.

Tommy Chong was a guitarist in the Canadian rock groups The Shades and The Vancouvers before he founded the improvisational group City Works and met up with Richard Marin. Initially mixing comic repartee with music, the pair soon relegated the latter to the sidelines and concentrated instead on their rambling, spaced-out patter. Marin became Cheech, a kind of chicano 'wide boy' whose dogged pursuit of a score rarely pans out. He is as close as the duo get to a 'straight man'. Chong is even more out of it, mentally and physically becalmed except before the most direct stimulae: 'babes', 'grass' and the cops. Cheech and Chong built up a strong cult following on the concert circuit and through records before they made the low-budget *Up In Smoke* (1978). The first and best of their films, this established the formula by de-emphasising the plot in favour of way-out gags and long verbal digressions between the two stars (though neither of their vocabularies extends much beyond 'man', a noun, pronoun and exclamation without which no sentence is complete). The wit veers between the very, very dry and the very, very obvious, but their good-natured, laid-back personalities compensate for the banal passages to some extent.

Chong took over the directing chores with their second effort, *Cheech And Chong's Next Movie* (1980), and it soon became obvious that the partnership had nowhere much to go. While Marin's clowning and Chong's talent for mimicry should not be underestimated, their timing does not extend to film sequences, which are almost inevitably done to death in their pictures. Their ignorance, or rejection, of plot and structure led to increasingly incoherent pictures of which *Still Smokin'* (1983) marked the nadir. *The Corsican Brothers* (1984), an equally directionless parody shot in France, failed to revive their inspiration. Since then, California State graduate Richard Marin has pursued a moderately successful solo career working variations on the Cheech persona. He scored a notable chart hit with his fine Springsteen parody, 'Born In East LA', but when he adapted it into a movie, which he directed himself, the results were at best sketchy. Chong took a back seat until *Far Out Man* (1990), which he wrote and directed, and cast with his family and friends, including his daughter, Rae Dawn Chong, and son-in-law C. Thomas Howell. He was honest enough to label it 'A Tommy Chong Attempt', which is what it looked like. Non-relatives will do better with the pair's amusing contribution to Martin Scorsese's *After Hours* (1985): all you need to know about Cheech and Chong in about five minutes screen time.

As co-writers and actors unless otherwise stated: **1978** Up In Smoke **1980** Cheech And Chong's Next Movie (Chong director) **1981** Cheech And Chong's Nice Dreams (Chong director) **1982** Things Are Tough All Over; It Came From Hollywood (cameos only) **1983** Yellowbeard (actors only); Still Smoking (Chong director) **1984** The Corsican Brothers (Chong director) **1985** After Hours (actors only) **1986** Echo Park (Cheech only – actor) **1987** Born In East LA (Cheech only – actor, writer, director) **1989** Rude Awakening (Cheech only – actor); Ghostbusters II (Cheech only, cameo) **1990** Far Out Man (Chong actor, writer, director, Cheech cameo only)

Cher
(Cherilyn Sarkasian)
Actress, singer

Born 20 May 1946

El Centro, California

Cher began her professional life as a back-up singer for The Crystals and then The Ronettes, before teaming with her first husband, Sonny Bono (whom she later divorced). Sonny And Cher's first hit, 'I Got

You Babe', sold three million copies, and the couple appeared in two movies, *Wild On The Beach* (1965) and *Good Times* (1967). By 1969, the hit pop singer had a nightclub cabaret act put together, and by 1971 was signed by CBS for a TV series. But she didn't really register as an actress until 1982 when she made her stage debut, in New York, in *Come Back To The Five And Dime, Jimmy Dean, Jimmy Dean*, playing a member of a James Dean women's fan club who meet to mark the 20th anniversary of their idol's death. It was Robert Altman's film version of this a year later which announced that a new screen actress of note had appeared, an impression confirmed by her strong performance as Meryl Streep's passionately devoted friend in *Silkwood* (1983).

Fairly outrageous in her personal life, and notoriously flamboyant in her dress, the relative newcomer to Hollywood quickly fell prey to the reigning ethos of physical perfection and subjected her irregular but nonetheless striking and original features (her extraordinary origins include Armenian and Cherokee Indian) to plastic surgery. But the cosmetic overlay, if less interesting, did miraculously little harm, as was proved in *Mask* (1985). As the hard-living, drug-taking but devoted mother of a deformed 'elephant man' – type son, Cher demonstrated that she is a natural actress of the highest order – powerful, attractive, relaxed and truthful. Surprisingly, although she shared the award at Cannes with Argentinian actress Norma Aleandro (*The Official Story*), she was not even Oscar-nominated for *Mask*, an Academy oversight which they rectified by voting her Best Actress for the romantic comedy *Moonstruck* (1987) – a consolation prize which, although her performance as a shy, conformist, New York Italian ugly duckling who turns herself into a rebellious swan couldn't be faulted – should perhaps on that occasion have gone to Glenn Close, Holly Hunter or Sally Kirkland, co-nominees for some pretty weighty work.

There can, however, be little disagreement that Cher is one of America's best screen actresses, whose very presence tends to lend credibility to even run-of-the-mill commercial fodder. In *Suspect* (1987), for example, co-starring with Dennis Quaid, she played a defending attorney caught in a conspiracy of political corruption and murder with such flair as to make the film irresistibly enjoyable; while, in the more upmarket *The Witches of Eastwick* the same year, she was a superbly cast companion to Michelle Pfeiffer and Susan Sarandon. Unfortunately for filmgoers, this mother of two (Chastity, her daughter by Bono, and Elijah Blue from her short-lived marriage to rock star Greg Allman) returned solely to her music concert career for three years after *Moonstruck*, reportedly nervous of living up to the new expectations which Hollywood would have of her. She need not have worried. With *Mermaids* (1990), she discovered that she had entered the power-play stakes, with approval of everything from wardrobe and co-stars to director – a power she used to fire two directors in a row (Lasse Hallstrom, Frank Oz) before settling with Richard Benjamin, and to replace Emily Lloyd with Winona Ryder. Unfortunately, though, the much-hyped romantic comedy, about a kooky mother of two who finds happiness in the unlikely arms of Bob Hoskins, proved her least memorable screen foray to date.

1965 Wild On The Beach **1967** Good Times **1969** Chastity **1983** Come Back To The Five And Dime, Jimmy Dean, Jimmy Dean; Silkwood **1985** Mask **1987** Suspect; The Witches Of Eastwick; Moonstruck **1990** Mermaids **1992** The Player (cameo)

Chong, Rae Dawn

Actress
Born 1962
Vancouver, Canada

This fine black actress was much admired in her unusual film debut as a cave dweller in Jean-Jacques Annaud's *Quest For Fire* (1981), a prehistoric fable with language devised by Anthony Burgess, and Desmond Morris on hand for the body talk. But by this time, Rae Dawn Chong, daughter of comedian Tommy Chong (one half of Cheech and . . .) had already been acting for seven years, having made her debut in the TV show *The Whiz Kid Of Riverton*, at the age of 12. Rae Dawn's father cast her in his first directing effort, *The Corsican Brothers* (1984), which also featured other members of the Cheech and Chong dynasties, but by the end of 1985, she was probably more established than he. (She later appeared in his 1989 solo movie, *Far Out Man*).

Slim, attractive and intelligent, the young actress found almost immediate favour in Hollywood, graduating from Abel Ferrara's characteristic exercise in sleaze, *Fear City* (1984), which also boasted Melanie Griffith and Tom Berenger in the cast, to another kind of darkness for Alan Rudolph. Given an opportunity to shine in Rudolph's bitter-sweet *Choose Me* (1984), she turned in an impressive supporting performance as a poetic barfly, coping with a violent husband, who muses, 'I hope I get laid in my coffin', and took the lead in the Harry Belafonte-produced *Beat Street* the same year. Spielberg cast her in a supporting role in *The Color Purple* (1985), but it was in *Soul Man* (1986) that Chong really shone. In this witless film, which sabotaged its own interesting premise about a white boy (C. Thomas Howell, who she subsequently married) who blacks up in order to win a scholarship to Harvard law school, Chong was co-starred as a brilliant law student, struggling to work her way through while at the same time caring for her small child. Called upon to be tough, tender, acerbic, energetic and exhausted by turns, the actress more than delivered the goods, managing the incredible feat of overcoming the script to involve and move the audience.

Given the balance of her filmography to date – movies that can hardly be said to have had much impact – one is tempted to speculate on whether this excellent actress' colour has held back her career; but Rae Dawn Chong has played female leads in non-black films rather more often than *The Color Purple*'s better known Whoopi Goldberg.

1981 Quest For Fire **1984** Cheech And Chong's The Corsican Brothers; Fear City; Choose Me; Beat Street **1985** American Flyers; Commando; The Color Purple; City Limits **1986** Soul Man **1987** The Squeeze; The Principal **1988** Walking After Midnight **1990** Far Out Man **1991** Chain Dance; The Borrower **1992** When The Party's Over; Amazon

Cimino, Michael

Director, screenwriter
Born 1943
New York City

Michael Cimino's career in films could not have begun in a better fashion. A Yale graduate, he started making industrial documentaries and TV commercials in New York before moving to Hollywood in 1971. He immediately attracted attention as co-writer on the science-fiction picture *Silent Running* (1971) and (with John Milius) on *Magnum Force* (1973), the second Dirty Harry movie. Clint Eastwood was sufficiently impressed with Cimino's work to invite him to write and direct *Thunderbolt And Lightfoot* (1974). The film's appeal lay not in Cimino's derivative script about a bank heist carried out by macho buddy-buddies, though that was entertaining enough, nor in Eastwood's expressionless performance, but in the director's pictorial sense, the ability to shift comfortably from comedy to tragedy, the interplay between the characters, and Jeff Bridges' richly nuanced portrayal of Lightfoot. The movie made over $8 million at the box office and resulted in its first-time director being trusted with a huge budget to direct *The Deer Hunter* (1978), which won five Oscars.

Cimino's second feature exactly caught the mood of the time – the need of Americans to find some justification for the war in Vietnam. (The director had served with the Green Beret Training Unit in Texas.) *The Deer Hunter* focused on the lives of three Pennsylvanian steelworkers (Robert De Niro, Christopher Walken and John Savage) before, during and after combat duty. The set pieces, such as the wedding (almost a production number) and the deer hunt itself, were epically conceived. But the battles were no more convincing than Errol Flynn or John Wayne's heroics against the Japs, and the most famous and gripping scene, when the Americans are forced to play Russian Roulette by their captors, crudely depicted the Vietcong as the incarnation of evil. The homecoming, reminiscent of *The Best Years Of Our Lives* back in 1946, worked hard on audiences' emotions and sense of patriotism and, like temptation proved difficult to resist. Despite the adventure-magazine attitudes to the story of *The Deer Hunter*, at a running time of three hours, the structure is impressive.

With the Best Picture and Best Director Oscars on his mantelpiece, 36-year-old Cimino was on top of the world. He then had an idea for an epic Western based on the Johnson County War between the cattlemen and the immigrant farmers called *Heaven's Gate* (1981). The budget of this folly, the title of which became synonymous with expensive film failures, escalated from $11 million to over $35 million but only recovered about $1.5 million at the box office, becoming the most famous and expensive floperoo of all time.

Cimino and his expert cameraman, Vilmos Zsigmond, had plainly set out to make a masterpiece of monumental proportions. There was hardly a sequence without smoke, steam or clouds billowing by, or crowds striking postures. But the characters remained hazy and impersonal, lost in the virtuoso sweep of the panoramic ensembles, and the narrative was sprawling and confused. After a critical lambasting, the movie was reduced from 225 to 148 minutes and became even more incoherent.

Heaven's Gate virtually put an end to United Artists as a production company, and Cimino became the scapegoat. He didn't make another film for four years, when he returned with the Oliver Stone-scripted *Year Of The Dragon* (1985), which concerned the exploits of a racist Vietnam vet cop (Mickey Rourke) determined to clean up New York's Chinatown. The structure and attitudes are fairly simplistic, despite some visual coups, and the audience is asked too often to sympathise with some of the cop's more xenophobic hatred. But Cimino brought the movie in on time and within budget. However, his next outing was the portentous and stridently hagiographic *The Sicilian* (1987), in which the notorious bandit Salvatore Giuliano (an uneasy Christopher Lambert) is equated with Christ. Shorn of 27 of its 146-minute running time in the USA, it was greeted with scorn from the critics and was ignored by the public. Michael Cimino could only go up from there, though he showed little sign of it with his redundant remake of *Desperate Hours* and it remained doubtful whether he could ever regain the high of the year of the *Deer Hunter*.

1974 Thunderbolt And Lightfoot **1978** The Deer Hunter **1981** Heaven's Gate **1985** Year Of The Dragon **1987** The Sicilian **1991** Desperate Hours

Clark, Candy

Actress
Born 20 June 1947
Norman, Oklahoma

A singular presence whenever she has appeared, Candy Clark may well have been tempted to echo Orson Welles' self-appraisal, 'I started at the top and worked my way down.' Witness her marginal role as psycho Christopher Walken's woman in Jim Foley's intriguing thriller, *At Close Range* (1986) 14 years after her promising debut.

A skinny, waif-like creature when younger, with big intent eyes and a toothy grin, she was a successful New York model before landing an excellent part in John Huston's masterly study of downbeat boxers in Northern California, *Fat City* (1972). The following year she won a Best Supporting Actress Oscar nomination for her delightful dizzy blonde, cruising Modesto and chewing gum like there was no tomorrow, in George Lucas' influential *American Graffiti*. Clark was like a reborn Judy Holliday, with a little girl whine and quirky style that should have been infuriating but was, instead, irresistible. In *The Man Who Fell To Earth* (1976), Nicolas Roeg's absorbing, elliptical adaptation of a Walter Tevis novel, she was a small-town waitress who hitches up with David Bowie's alien genius. Touchingly vulnerable, but with the tough skin of someone who has known troubles, she gave her kooky character the kind of emotional depth that compares well with Theresa Russell's variations on the same child-woman theme in later Roeg films. She was so good that she was subsequently offered little else besides fantasy movies such as *Q* (1982), *Cat's Eye* (1985) and *The Blob* (1988), that hoped to tap a comparable cult audience.

Jonathan Demme's *Citizen's Band* (1977) marked Candy Clark's last substantial success to date – an appealing comedy in which she was second-billed to her *American Graffiti* co-star, Paul Le Mat. There was little to stretch her thereafter, and too few opportunities to demonstrate her oddball comic gifts, but she continued to brighten inferior fare, and made her off-Broadway debut in 1981.

1972 Fat City **1973** American Graffiti **1976** I Will, I Will . . . For Now; The Man Who Fell To Earth **1977** Citizen's Band aka Handle With Care **1978** The Big Sleep **1979** When You Comin' Back, Red Ryder?; More American Graffiti; National Lampoon Goes To The Movies **1982**Q (GB: Q – The Winged Serpent) **1983** Blue Thunder; Amityville 3-D **1984** Hambone And Hillie **1985** Cat's Eye **1986** At Close Range **1988** The Blob; Blind Curve **1992** Original Intent; Deuce Coupe

Clayburgh, Jill

Actress
Born 30 April 1944
New York City

'If they don't give me good parts in movies, I'm just not going to do them. And there's a time at which they just move on to the next person,' said Jill Clayburgh at the height of her fame in 1978. It was a prophetic statement, because Clayburgh, one of the brightest female stars of the 70s, found herself virtually forgotten in the following decade. Perhaps conservative Hollywood does not really know how to cope with an independent-minded actress who refuses to be pigeonholed and likes to take risks.

The daughter of a wealthy, socially prominent family, the tall blue-eyed blonde was educated at the exclusive Brearley School and Sarah Lawrence College. While at the latter, she began acting in summer stock and after graduating joined the Charles Street Repertory Theater in Boston. Moving to New York, she appeared in several off-Broadway productions, and then on Broadway in such musicals as *The Rothschilds* and *Pippin*, and the Tom Stoppard play *Jumpers*, while in the midst of a five-year relationship with Al Pacino.

But what really excited her was film acting. 'One of the things I like about the movies is the adventure of it; I like going to different places and I like doing a different scene every day.' After her debut screen appearance in Brian De Palma's apprentice first feature, *The Wedding Party* (1966), it took her some years to become a recognisable face. She had little to do as Ryan O'Neal's ex-wife in *The Thief Who Came To Dinner* (1973) or as the stripper murder victim of computer-brain George Segal in *The Terminal Man* (1974). Then Clayburgh was unexpectedly cast as Carole Lombard to James Brolin's Clark Gable in the stunningly banal *Gable And Lombard* (1976), from which only she emerged with any dignity. In fact, this actress has the kind of warmth and witty sophistication barely seen since Lombard or Jean Arthur, a special favourite of hers.

This was demonstrated in *Silver Streak* (1976), where she played the lady on a train who tangles with Gene Wilder, in an entertaining throwback to 30s comedy-thrillers; and in *Semi-Tough* (1977), as the beautiful, free-thinking woman living in a platonic threesome with footballers Burt Reynolds and Kris Kristofferson until one of them makes a pass. These carefree, liberated characters led Paul Mazursky to give her the lead in *An Unmarried Woman* (1978), her most famous role to date. (It was third time lucky because she had been turned down for two previous Mazursky films, *Blume in Love* and *Next Stop Greenwich Village*.) Here, in one film, she proved that she was equally adept at drama and comedy. As the woman making her life anew after being deserted by her husband, she overcame many of the more superficial aspects of the script by her ability to show strength and vulnerability. Her performance earned her the Best Actress Award at Cannes and an Oscar nomination. Also Oscar-nominated was her performance in Alan J. Pakula's *Starting Over* the following year, in which she played an unmarried woman again, but this time with a different emphasis: unmarried because she is a spinster schoolteacher who, having once been hurt, keeps involvement at bay by remaining deliberately dowdy. At the same time, she had seized the chance to work with Bernardo Bertolucci in Italy in *La Luna* (1979) as an internationally renowned opera singer who has an almost incestuous relationship with her teenage son. The film was rather impenetrable, but its star had all the strength and glamour required.

In the 80s, Clayburgh met with a singular lack of commercial success in the choices she made, although she was splendid in *It's My Turn* (1980) as a mathematics professor who has an affair with ex-baseball player Michael Douglas, and, as the first female judge appointed to the US Supreme Court in *First Monday In October* (1981). *I'm Dancing As Fast As I Can* (1982) was adapted by her playwright husband, David Rabe, from Barbara Gordon's autobiographical book about a cold turkey withdrawal from valium addiction. *Hanna K* (1983) found her as a lawyer involved in conflicting relationships with her Israeli ex-husband and a Palestinian attempting to reclaim his ancestral home. But her powerful performance was little seen in this least successful of Costa-Gavras' films. She then spent five years raising her family, and tending the garden of her seven-acre Georgian home in Mount Kisco, New York, reappearing on Broadway in *Design For Living* with Raul Julia, and on film as a journalist researching an article in the Louisiana bayou in Andrei Konchalovsky's over-the-top flop, *Shy People* (1987). You can't keep a good actress down on the farm for long.

1969 The Wedding Party **1971** The Telephone Book **1972** Portnoy's Complaint **1973** The Thief Who Came To Dinner **1974** The Terminal Man **1976** Gable And Lombard; Silver Streak **1977** Semi-Tough **1978** An Unmarried Woman **1979** La Luna (Italy); Starting Over **1980** It's My Turn **1981** First Monday In October **1982** I'm Dancing As Fast As I Can **1983** Hannah K **1986** Where Are The Children? **1987** Shy People **1990** Beyond The Ocean **1992** Rich In Love; Whispers In The Dark **1992/93** Day Of Atonement

Close, Glenn

Actress

Born 19 March 1947

Greenwich, Connecticut

At the end of 1989, when the Top Ten Box

Office Stars poll was taken in the film industry, by one of those bizarre anomalies that characterise the nature of Hollywood, only one woman was on the list (at No 10).

A real actress as opposed to a movie star, and with a distinguished provenance in the theatre, Glenn Close inhabits similar territory to Meryl Streep, both in appearance and in the style of her finely honed craft. In her case, though, it is not the technical transformation of self that displays her courage, but her fearless embrace of the sort of roles which, traditionally, are supposed to be box-office poison: a woman who offers the services of her own husband (Kevin Kline) to a friend wanting to become pregnant (*The Big Chill*, 1983), a ballsy yet vulnerable lawyer who makes a fool of herself falling for the wrong man (*Jagged Edge*, 1985), a murderously unhinged, man-eating executive (*Fatal Attraction*, 1987), and the cruelly manipulative Madame De Merteuil, whose decadent machinations lead others to death and destruction (*Dangerous Liaisons*, 1988).

It was the mega-success of *Fatal Attraction* that gave Glenn Close her star status, and her performance was one of uncompromising bravery. Her expertise, however, had long been acknowledged with Best Supporting Oscar nominations, all in a row, for *The World According To Garp* (1982), *The Big Chill*, and *The Natural* (1984, with Robert Redford). Best Actress Nominations followed for *Fatal Attraction* and *Dangerous Liaisons*, and it can only be a matter of time before she collects.

Educated at the College of William and Mary, where she studied anthropology as well as acting, and the possessor of a fine lyric soprano voice, Close began her career performing with a repertory theatre group calling itself Fingernails, before touring the country with a folk-singing group. (She can be seen in musical mode in her only really appalling film, *Maxie*, 1985.) She made her professional acting debut at New York's Phoenix Theatre in a season of plays that included English period classics (*Love For Love*) and Carson McCullers' *The Member Of The Wedding*, but it was her appearance in the Broadway hit musical *Barnum* which brought her first Tony nomination. She won the Tony Award itself in 1984, for Tom Stoppard's *The Real Thing*, in which she co-starred with Jeremy Irons. They were re-united on film for *Reversal Of Fortune* (1990) in which she played the ambiguous and ill-fated Sunny von Bülow – a role in stark contrast to her childless woman caught in the emotional spirals of adoption in *Immediate Family* (1989). Glenn Close is undoubtedly versatile, but continues to pursue the dangerous roles (Gertrude to Mel Gibson's prince in *Hamlet*, 1990, for example) with absolute clarity of dramatic purpose.

1982 The World According To Garp **1983** The Big Chill **1984** The Natural; The Stone Boy **1985** Maxie; Jagged Edge **1987** Fatal Attraction **1988** Dangerous Liaisons **1989** Immediate Family; Orders **1990** Reversal Of Fortune; Hamlet **1991** Meeting Venus

Coburn, James

Actor

Born 31 August 1928

Laurel, Nebraska

It didn't take James Coburn too long in pictures before his strong lean frame, handsome weather-beaten face, ready smile and greying hair became familiar to fans of Westerns and war films in the 60s. His first two films in 1959, *Ride Lonesome* and *Face Of A Fugitive*, saw him as a subtle baddie, hoping to gather the bounty meant for Randolph Scott in the first, and wonderfully nasty in the second, but it was as the knife-thrower in *The Magnificent Seven* (1960) that he really made an impression, though less so than Steve McQueen. He was overshadowed again by McQueen in his next two movies, *Hell Is For Heroes* (1962) and *The Great Escape* (1963). In 1965, he played sidekicks to Charlton Heston and Anthony Quinn respectively, as an Indian scout in Sam Peckinpah's *Major Dundee* and as a pirate in *A High Wind In Jamaica*, before becoming his own man at last, and a star, in *Our Man Flint* (1966). It was Coburn's suave, tongue-in-cheek presence that placed this espionage comedy-thriller a cut above the plethora of James Bond spin-offs at the time. It was so popular that there were hopes for a series, but *In Like Flint* (1967), a tired spoof, put an end to all that.

Coburn studied acting at LA City College, the University of Southern California, and with Stella Adler in New York. His stage debut was at the La Jolla Playhouse in *Billy Budd*. Following some TV commercials and live plays, he made his film debut. In the 70s, he projected a laconic laid-back sexuality and a rather frivolous personality, perfect for advertising Schlitz Light on TV. His passion for fast cars, his dabbling in Buddhism and mysticism, and his deserting his wife of many years in 1977 for the singer-songwriter Lynsey De Paul (he left her, too), kept him in the public eye.

On screen, the actor featured in a number of heavy-handed caper comedies, but was at his best in Westerns such as *Waterhole No. 3* (1967), in which he defined rape as 'assault with a friendly weapon'; and Sergio Leone's *Duck, You Sucker*! (1972) in which he sported a black Mexican moustache and an Irish accent as a brainy IRA dynamite expert. In *The Honkers* (1972), Coburn revealed some depth in his unsympathetic role as perennial drifter, philanderer and rodeo rider, an ageing cowboy trying to cope with the modern world. But he had to wait until Sam Peckinpah cast him as the famous sheriff who caught the famous outlaw in *Pat Garrett And Billy The Kid* (1973), to display a fine mixture of steel and warmth as he played the waiting game. The actor continued in a number of tough-guy roles, the best being the fight promoter in Walter Hill's debut movie, *Hard Times* (1975); a hard-bitten German soldier in Peckinpah's only war film, *Cross Of Iron* (1977), and Major Dannenberg, the defence counsellor in *Death Of A Soldier* (1985), trying to save the life of a GI accused of murder. However, James Coburn, one of the most famous faces on screen in the 60s and 70s, grew less visible in the following decade. Even hard men must slow down eventually, but the early 90s proved that he hadn't entirely disappeared from view.

1959 Ride Lonesome; Face Of A Fugitive **1960** The Magnificent Seven **1962** Hell Is For Heroes **1963** The Great Escape; Charade **1964** The Man From Galveston; The Americanization Of Emily **1965** Major Dundee; A High Wind In Jamaica; The Loved One **1966** Our Man Flint; What Did You Do In The War, Daddy?; Dead Heat On A Merry-Go-Round **1967** In Like Flint; Waterhole No. 3; The President's Analyst **1968** Duffy; Candy **1969** Hard Contract **1970** The Last Of The Mobile Hotshots aka Blood Kin **1971** Duck, You Sucker! aka A Fistful Of Dynamite; The Honkers; The Carey Treatment **1972** Pat Garret And Billy The Kid; The Last Of Sheila; Harry In Your Pocket **1973** A Reason To Live, A Reason To Die (Italy); The Internecine Project **1975** Jackpot; Bite The Bullet; Hard Times (GB: The Streetfighter) **1976** Sky Riders; The Last Hard Man; Midway **1977** White Rock (docu); Cross Of Iron **1979** Goldengirl; The Baltimore Bullet; Firepower **1980** Loving Couples; Mr Patman **1981** High Risk aka Big Bucks; Looker **1983** Digital Dreams **1984** Draw! **1985** Martin's Day; The Leonski Incident aka Death Of A Soldier **1990** Young Guns II **1991** Hudson Hawk **1992** The Player (cameo) **1993** Deadfall

Coen, Ethan

Producer, writer
Born 21 September 1957
Minneapolis, Minnesota

Coen, Joel

Director, writer
Born 29 November 1954
Minneapolis, Minnesota

Like Britain's Boulting brothers and Italy's Taviani brothers, Joel and Ethan Coen, known as the Coen brothers, are inseparable as a film-making unit. Self-contained, the sibling partners conceive, write, pre-plan every detail of their films at storyboard stage, produce, direct and oversee the editing and music in unison. Nominally, Joel, the elder of the two, directs, and the younger Ethan produces, but they are jointly involved in every aspect of production. Collaborators and their casts are wont to describe them as a double act, speaking in their own 'shorthand' and frequently completing each other's sentences. Each of their first three films has been an inspired *succés d'estime*, twisting time-honoured Hollywood genres – the *noir* thriller, the screwball comedy, the gangster picture – into contemporary delights, and the Coens must be seriously considered among the foremost film-makers to have emerged in the 1980s. As a Hollywood studio executive noted, although like Woody Allen's, the films of the Coens do not make mega-bucks, 'You want to be in business with the Joel and Ethans, the Spike Lees, and the Phil Kaufmans. These are the people who are going to make the great movies of our time.'

The Coens had an unremarkable, suburban middle-class upbringing and are the sons of a university professor of economics. Like many of their contemporaries, the boys made a few Super-8 films and saw a lot of movies, but gave little indication of their future careers. After attending private school in Massachusetts, Joel entered the film programme at New York University and Ethan took his degree in philosophy at Yale. Joel got his grounding in the industry doing odd jobs and editing horror films until Ethan joined him and the two started writing murder and mystery screenplays.

Their debut feature, *Blood Simple* (1984), made with a then virtually unknown cast on a tiny budget inveigled from small investors, provoked gasps of admiration from critics and of shock from rapt audiences. It was an audaciously stylish dark thriller of infidelity, deceit, misunderstanding and murder that wrung suspense out of letting the audience know much more than the characters, and held some bravura cinematic touches.

Raising Arizona (1987) was a madcap comedy of a daft kidnapping perpetrated by Holly Hunter in her first leading role and Nicolas Cage in his most engaging one, and a highly original, clever combination of zany slapstick, breakneck chase thrills and dry, sly satire. With *Miller's Crossing* (1990) and by their standards a luxurious budget – reportedly $9 million – the Coens remained style-conscious cinema buffs playing to an appreciative audience who love homages and abundant genre references, but they also brought to the screen a hypnotically intelligent character study of a cool enigmatic man, tough guys and a wise-cracking 'twist' who are all much more than they at first appear. It was a film in which sophisticated, literate adults could revel, full of electrifying dialogue and arresting images.

The Coens' fourth film, the black comedy, *Barton Fink* (1991), set in 40s Hollywood and centring on a screenwriter with writer's block, was written as a diversion by the duo when *they* had writers' block mid-*Miller's Crossing*. The film won the Palm D'Or and director awards at Cannes (as well as Best Actor for John Turturro) for the dazzling style of its execution, though the bizarre, surreal turn of the plot left some viewers cold. But it would be a major surprise if the Coen brothers do not go on to make some 'of the great movies of our time'.

1984 Blood Simple **1985** Crimewave (co-writers only) **1987** Raising Arizona **1990** Miller's Crossing **1991** Barton Fink **1993** The Hudsucker Proxy

Cohen, Larry

Director, writer
Born 20 April 1938
New York City

Larry Cohen has been one of the most prolific writer-directors at work in America, but his hostility to joining the ranks of mainstream Hollywood means that it is difficult to place him – indeed to keep up with him. His films hover between being pure underground exercises and appealing to a wider public (after all, the special effects on a work like *Q – The Winged Serpent*, 1982, must have been expensive). Very few of his features have found theatrical release in the United Kingdom, so that the *aficionado* must hunt them down, if he cares to, on video, and a couple have barely been seen in America. Against this, we have the conviction from eminent critic Robin Wood that Cohen is one of the most under-rated of contemporary directors, an artist with a peculiarly pure grasp of society's neuroses: a man prepared to use the horror genre to analyse (rather than sentimentalise) profound, in-built contradictions in American 'patriarchy'.

Is this all too solemn? It might be believed so. Cohen's apprenticeship (after a stint at film school) was in television where during the 1950s he wrote and produced numerous shows. That ability to take things on the run – not caring too much about aesthetic considerations – which he inherited from busy TV schedules, survived into his first feature films, beginning with *Bone* (1972), a rather hard-edged rape story. *Black Caesar* and *Hell Up In Harlem* (both 1973) are two 'blaxploitation' pictures that give a flavour of Cohen's intelligent opportunism – his homing in on a genre (black crime thrillers were popular at the time) and refashioning it for his own private purposes.

The same could be said about the three horror pictures that followed – *It's Alive* (1974), *It Lives Again* (1975, released 1978) and *God Told Me To* (aka *Demon*, 1976) – all of which owed something, in conception at any rate, to popular commercial horror successes like *The Exorcist*. But Robin Wood isn't the only critic to have felt that these films are not merely rip-offs, but complicated works of art in their own right, particularly in the way that they dramatise evil not as some external force, but as part and parcel of the good, embedded deeply in our human nature. As in the early 80s film *Q – The Winged Serpent*, the monster, if there is one, is invariably beautiful as well as vicious, feminine as well as masculine, caring/nurturing as well as predatory.

Cohen's other important film of the 70s is very different. *The Private Files of J. Edgar Hoover* (1976) is a movie which brings together in a distinctively original way political and psychological (or public and private) commentary. It is classically shot, not at all sensationalist, if anything too downbeat for popular appeal (Broderick Crawford is a somewhat dour FBI chief). The film shows how close this director can come to the mainstream if he cares to. But his films of the 80s, though numerous, are once again very small-scale and hidden away in non-prestigious genres (horror, parody, B-movie fare), an exception being *The Ambulance* (1989). This inexplicably little-released movie, starring Eric Roberts, is a 'medical' thriller in the *Coma* vein – taut, economical, frightening and funny – presenting a dark-toned and claustrophobic New York and some interesting social comment.

Some day, the critics will catch up with Larry Cohen, and decide whether he really is a genius or simply an energetic schlock merchant with a twinkle in his eye. Meanwhile, with something like 80 separate credits in film, television and theatre (as writer, producer, director, consultant) his productiveness, at least, can't be gainsaid.

As director and writer unless stated otherwise: **1966** I Deal In Danger (writer only); Return of the Seven (writer only) **1969** Daddy's Gone A-Hunting (writer only) **1970** El Condor (co-writer only) **1972** Bone aka Beverly Hills Nightmare; Black Caesar; Hell Up In Harlem **1974** It's Alive; God Told Me To aka Demon **1976** The Private Files of J. Edgar Hoover **1978** It Lives Again **1979** The American Success Company (writer only) **1981** I, The Jury (writer only) **1982** Q – the Winged Serpent **1984** Special Effects; Perfect Strangers aka Blind Alley; Scandalous (writer only) **1985** The Stuff **1987** Deadly Illusion (also co-writer); Best Seller (writer only); It's Alive III: Island of the Alive; Return to Salem's Lot **1989** Wicked Stepmother; The Ambulance **1991** So Help Me God (writer only); Maniac Cop 2 (writer only)

Coleman, Dabney

Actor
Born 3 January 1932
Austin, Texas

Dabney Coleman looks like everybody's idea of the typical all-American dad: thinning hair and a fleshy, seemingly friendly face adorned more often than not by a crooked moustache. Until his foray into comedy, the actor made his career by portraying deceptively ordinary bastards of the kind one finds lurking in every office, the slippery kind of fellow who is out to get what he can no matter what. In real life, the cigar-chomping Coleman is well known for his wit, giving talk-show heavyweights a hard time. There is more complexity to him, both as an actor and a man, than initially meets the eye.

A Texan (claiming descent from the famous Native American Indian squaw Pocohantas), Coleman attended a Virginia military school before studying law at the University of Texas between 1951 and 1957 (1953 to 1955 were spent in the US army). He then studied for the theatre at The Neighborhood Playhouse School before venturing to New York and Los Angeles. For nearly a decade, he played heavies, making an impression in supporting roles in *Downhill Racer* (1969), *Cinderella Liberty* (1973) and *The Towering Inferno* (1974), as well as earning a more prominent role in *The Other Side of The Mountain* (1975), playing the ski coach to Jill Kinmont (Marilyn Hassett) in the soapy but successful account of the crippled skier's life.

Although primarily employed as a character actor in TV series, films and made-for-TV movies which range from mediocre to moderately good, Coleman found fame on *Mary Hartman, Mary Hartman*, a spoof soap which became a landmark of alternative television. Tapping into his ability to express sharp-ended humour, he appeared in 1980's *Melvin And Howard* and, more noticeably, *Nine To Five* (which many rate as his best comedy performance) portraying the chauvinistic office boss on whom the misses Parton, Fonda and Tomlin wreak revenge; then a straight supporting role in *On Golden Pond* (1981) and back to comedy in *Tootsie* (1982). He also earned an Emmy nomination for his starring role in the outrageous TV series *Buffalo Bill* (1983–1984). In 1990, Coleman starred in the popular if improbable *Short Time* (portraying a policeman who, months before his retirement, thinks he has a terminal illness and tries to take advantage of his pension by attempting to get killed on duty) and was terrific as 'Aunt Bea' in Michael Lehmann's black and whacky *Meet The Applegates* the same year.

1965 The Slender Thread **1966** This Property Is Condemned **1968** The Scalphunters **1969** Downhill Racer; The Trouble With Girls **1970** I Love My Wife **1973** Cinderella Liberty **1974** The Dove; The Towering Inferno **1975** Bite The Bullet; The Other Side of The Mountain **1976** Midway **1977** Rolling Thunder; Viva Knievel!; Black Fist **1979** North Dallas Forty **1980** How To Beat The High Cost Of Living; Melvin And Howard; Nothing Personal; Nine To Five **1981** Modern Problems; On Golden Pond **1982** Tootsie; Young Doctors In Love **1983** WarGames **1984** Cloak And Dagger; The Muppets Take Manhattan **1985** The Man With One Red Shoe **1987** Dragnet; Guilty Of Innocence **1988** Hot To Trot **1990** Where The Heart Is; Meet The Applegates; Short Time **1992** Paydirt **1992/93** Clifford

Connery, Sean (Thomas Connery)

Actor
Born 25 August 1930
Edinburgh, Scotland

'His vitality may make him the most richly masculine of all English-speaking actors; that thick, rumbling Scotsman's voice of his actually transforms English – muffles the clipped edges and humanises the language,' wrote Pauline Kael. Whether playing an Arab chieftain in *The Wind And The Lion* (1975), the Irish-American policeman, Malone, in *The Untouchables* (1987), or unlikely father to Harrison Ford and Dustin Hoffman respectively in *Indiana Jones And The Last Crusade* and *Family Business* (both 1989), the distinctive tones resound on the soundtrack, deep, virile and warm as his screen persona. Although grown almost bald, with greying temples and moustache, and his handsome face now seamed with age, Connery entered second adulthood as a mature hero, standing (often literally) head and shoulders above most of his co-stars.

'He doesn't give a damn for the ancillary assets of being a star,' said Terence Young, who directed him in three James Bond movies, including *Dr No* (1962), the first 007 feature. It is that realism and integrity that made him shed his toupee and all the inhibitions to which sex objects and superstars are prey, and concentrate on character parts, laying to rest the alter ego that first made him a millionaire.

Perhaps his background as the son of a lorry driver and a charwoman in working-class Edinburgh, his spell with the Navy and various manual jobs, have kept his feet on the ground. While working on a building site, he spent much of his spare time body-building in gyms, which helped get him a job modelling swimming trunks in ads. Stage experience in the sailor chorus in the 1951 West End production of *South Pacific*, and work in rep, led him into films. After a run of insignificant roles in insignificant films, he was chosen from several contenders to create the screen James Bond. Ian Fleming, author of the original novels, saw David Niven in the Bond role, but the virtually unknown, tough Connery gave a more modern image to 007, licenced to kill. Fleming's Bond was an ultra-smooth gentleman spy, equally at ease in five-star restaurants and torture chambers, knowing precisely which fork or weapon to use. Connery's Bond was a somewhat rougher diamond, but in several ways a more sympathetic character since blessed with a wry sense of humour. In any event, *Dr No* was a sensation and the Bond pictures became the most durable of all the series in the history of cinema, still going strong after almost a quarter of a century. Connery starred as 007 seven times, and although there have been three other Bonds, he has remained the most popular.

Yet, because of the fear of typecasting, the actor determinedly made other, different kinds of films, establishing a reputation that would stand him in good stead after he had buried the super spy. In Alfred Hitchcock's *Marnie* (1964), he was coolly enigmatic as the rich man who marries the psychologically disturbed Tippi Hedren – a role in complete contrast to the rebellious inmate of a gruelling British military prison camp in North Africa in *The Hill* (1965), the first of five films he made for Sidney Lumet. He also gave a wonderfully eccentric performance as a bohemian poet in *A Fine Madness* (1966). *The Offence* (1973) was part of a deal made by United Artists with Connery, allowing him two pictures of his choice in exchange for reprising the Bond role for one last time in *Diamonds Are Forever* (1973). The failure of this murky melodrama, however, precluded a second movie, although it gave him the opportunity to play a brutal police inspector who finally has a nervous breakdown after a suspect dies from a beating. Thereafter, with Roger Moore successfully taking over Bond, Connery was free to tackle a variety of roles for different studios.

Three of his best were the Arab brigand Raisuli who kidnaps an American woman (Candice Bergen) in John Milius' *The Wind And The Lion* (1975); Michael Caine's companion in adventure in John Huston's *The Man Who Would Be King* (1975), and an embittered, grizzled Robin Hood recovering his ideals through a renewal of his love for Maid Marian (Audrey Hepburn) in Richard Lester's autumnal *Robin And Marian* (1976). After a few less than exciting ventures, he returned for his valedictory performance as Bond in the aptly titled *Never Say Never Again* (1983), a virtual rerun of *Thunderball* (1965), from which he donated his $1 million fee to a charitable organisation which he had founded for deprived Scottish children.

'I wish I had met me ten years and 20 lb ago,' he says in a wavering Irish accent as Malone, the incorruptible Irish-American cop in Brian De Palma's overblown gangster movie, *The Untouchables* (1987), for which he won the Best Supporting Actor Oscar. As the sturdy, mature mentor to Kevin Costner's FBI investigator, Eliot Ness, Connery brought authority to the role of a retired policeman who has no hesitation in saying 'wop' or 'dago', and who gets shot dozens of times but still manages to crawl around and speak the name of his killer. His next big hits were as Harrison Ford's father in *Indiana Jones And The Last Crusade*, as the idealistic Russian submarine commander in *The Hunt For Red October* (1990), who defects to the West during pre-glasnost days, and as a publisher who becomes a reluctant spy and falls for Michelle Pfeiffer in *The Russia House* (1990).

Connery is very much his own man. There is hardly a studio he hasn't sued in the last 25 years and he has built an incomparable reputation for driving a hard bargain. He waged a famous battle against former accountant Kenneth Richards which ended with the star being awarded £23.8 million. But treat him fairly and he will deliver the goods every time. His ten-year marriage to actress Diane Cilento, which produced a son, Jason, an actor in his own right, ended in 1973, and he has been happily married to his second wife, Micheline, for many years. In 1989 he went into hospital for an operation on some throat nodules. It was widely and falsely reported that he had cancer. 'I was terrified. I faint at the sight of needles and can collapse having a blood test,' remarked this most macho of actors.

1956 No Road Back **1957** Hell Drivers; Time Lock; Action Of The Tiger **1958** Another Time, Another Place **1959** Darby O'Gill And The Little People; Tarzan's Greatest Adventure **1961** The Frightened City; On The Fiddle **1962** The Longest Day; Dr No **1963** From Russia With Love **1964** Marnie; Woman Of Straw; Goldfinger **1965** The Hill; Thunderball **1966** A Fine Madness **1967** You Only Live Twice **1968** Shalako **1970** The Molly Maguires **1971** The Red Tent (USSR/Italy); The Anderson Tapes; Diamonds Are Forever **1973** The Offence **1974** Zardoz; Murder On The Orient Express **1975** Ransom aka The Terrorists; The Wind And The Lion; The Man Who Would Be King **1976** Robin And Marian; The Next Man **1977** A Bridge Too Far **1978** Meteor **1979** The First Great Train Robbery; Cuba **1981** Outland; Time Bandits **1982** Five Days One Summer; The Man With The Deadly Lens aka Wrong Is Right **1983** Never Say Never Again **1984** Sword Of The Valiant **1986** The Name Of The Rose; Highlander **1987** The Untouchables **1988** The Presidio; Memories Of Me **1989** Indiana Jones And The Last Crusade; Family Business; **1990** The Hunt For Red October; The Russia House **1991** Robin Hood: Prince Of Thieves (cameo); Highlander II **1992** Medicine Man **1993** Rising Sun

Coppola, Francis Ford

Director, writer, producer
Born 7 April 1939
Detroit, Michigan

The career of Francis Ford Coppola has been a switchback affair. Not only has he always been torn between two extremes of film-making – the massive, epic form, and the small, intimate picture – but he has fluctuated between mammoth and modest hits and mammoth and modest disasters.

There is a belief that Francis Coppola's middle name was taken from the director John Ford, but actually he was born in the Ford Hospital in Detroit, and his Italian immigrant father, Carmine, was first flautist with the Detroit Symphony Orchestra and official arranger for the *Ford Sunday Evening Hour*. (Carmine has composed the music for many of his son's features.) As befits someone whose films have often concerned themselves with the workings of the family, particularly siblings, Francis has a close relationship with his elder brother August (father of Nicolas Cage) to whom he dedicated *Rumble Fish* (1983): 'My first and best teacher'. His younger sister, the actress Talia Shire, was Connie Corleone in *The Godfather* cycle of films; his second son, Roman (named after Polanski), works as a producer for his father, and daughter Sofia, who appeared as Diane Lane's younger sister in *Rumble Fish* and – disastrously – *The Godfather Part III*, was the co-writer on *Life Without Zoë* in *New York Stories* (1989). Tragically, his eldest son, Giancarlo ('Gio'), was killed in a speedboat accident in 1986, aged 22.

Coppola developed an early interest in amateur film-making and took a film degree at UCLA, where he studied with former director Dorothy Arzner, who encouraged him, and attended lectures given by Jean Renoir. At university he produced, wrote and directed a nudie movie called *Tonight For Sure* (1961) – two stories, one about a voyeur and the other about a drunken cowboy who sees naked girls instead of cows. At the same time, he wrote a screenplay, *Pilma Pilma* ('pure Tennessee Williams', he says) which won the Samuel Goldwyn Award in 1962 but was never produced.

His first professional job was as writer and assistant to Roger Corman, who enabled him to direct his first feature movie, a gruesome cheapie called *Dementia 13* (1963), made in a few days in Ireland. Set in a Gothic castle, it dealt with a gathering of a family, one of whom is a mad axe murderer, prefiguring much of the director's future obsession with the family as a source of drama. In the same year, he married artist Eleanor Neil.

Warner Bros. released Coppola's first commercial venture, *You're a Big Boy Now* (1967), a lively comedy set in New York about a young man's sexual education. It was shot on a limited budget in under a month, with the crew and actors volunteering their time. 'Andy Hardy gets hit by the New Wave,' in Coppola's description. It was very much a movie by a 26-year-old of the mid-60s, with techniques derived from Richard Lester's Beatles films. But it proved to Warner Bros. that he was a man to watch. His second film for them, however, the screen version of the Broadway musical *Finian's Rainbow* (1968), failed in almost every respect. The indigestible Irish whimsy, interspersed with songs and platitudes, might have worked better on a smaller scale and in a studio setting. *The Rain People* (1969) was shot on location across America, from New York to LA, but wasn't very sure of where it was going. Well-acted, and influenced by European cinema, this view of an alienated America was weighed down with flashbacks and an unsubtle play on the emotions.

As the decade ended, Coppola opened his own studio, American Zoetrope – literally, Greek for 'life in movement' – in an office in San Francisco with George Lucas. He wanted to establish a studio 'run by the creative talents, free of businessmen and bureaucrats'. *The Conversation* (1974), made for Zoetrope, was an intriguing post-Watergate thriller about a professional eavesdropper (Gene Hackman at his best) being bugged himself, that moved edgily from the physical to the metaphysical. Although it gained critical favour, winning the Palme D'Or at Cannes, it had only minor commercial success. However, *The Godfather* (1972) made the public an offer it couldn't refuse. This long (175 mins) and leisurely apotheosis of the Mafia and the Family built up a rich pattern of relationships, meticulously detailing the rituals of an enclosed group. The film, only tenuously linking the Mafia with American society as a whole, was laudatory and romantic. *The Godfather Part II* (1974) was more complex in its structure and attitudes, even attempting to establish an objective viewpoint through an outsider played by Diane Keaton.

The Godfather parts I and II proved that Coppola was a man who could handle big themes and big budgets, but the 16 months' filming in the Philippines of *Apocalypse Now* (1979) were fraught with difficulties, including an earthquake that destroyed $1 million worth of sets, almost doubling the original budget of $12 million. *Apocalypse Now* assaulted the senses and numbed the mind with some extraordinary set pieces. The director wanted to 'give its audience a sense of the horror, the madness, the sensuousness and the moral dilemma of the Vietnam war,' and the quest to find Marlon Brando in 'the heart of darkness' by river (it is loosely based on Conrad's short novel), is like a nightmarish Disneyland ride. Unfortunately, at the end of the journey, audiences were forced to listen to the muddled mumblings of the crazed Brando.

Coppola then conceived of a picture that would recapture the heyday of the musical. *One From The Heart* (1982), which the director called a 'fantasy about romantic love, jealousy and sex', cost $25 million and was filmed in a huge and impressive set built entirely at Zoetrope. Unfortunately, the over-elaborate production suffocated the plot about a couple (Frederic Forrest and Teri Garr) who, after a quarrel, go off temporarily with new and anonymous partners (Nastassia Kinski and Raul Julia). The film's monumental failure virtually put Zoetrope out of business.

On a smaller scale, he shot *The Outsiders* and *Rumble Fish* back to back in Tulsa in 1983, both based on novels by S.E. (Susie) Hinton. Full of (relevant) golden sunsets and sunrises, *The Outsiders* is a full-blown romantic film about a group of young men from the wrong side of the tracks called greasers. With hardly an adult in sight, Coppola wholeheartedly enters the world of semi-tough youths, raptuously concentrating on the pubescent faces of up-and-coming stars like Matt Dillon, Ralph Macchio, C. Thomas Howell, Tom Cruise, Rob Lowe, Patrick Swayze and Emilio Estevez. Dillon appears to even better effect in *Rumble Fish*, the darker side of *The Outsiders*, filmed in monochrome, with intermittent use of colour. Two of his best and most personal films, they failed at the box office, as did *The Cotton Club* (1984), a misconceived and muddled attempt to recapture Harlem night life during Prohibition, although some of the numbers were well performed and staged.

It is quite likely that the director, having

taken a number of severe beatings over the last years, identified closely with the independent spirit of Preston Tucker, the hero of *Tucker: The Man And His Dream* (1988), who tried to get his revolutionary 1948 automobile accepted by the industrial establishment. Beautifully photographed and designed with browns dominating, Coppola caught the atmosphere of the period in this good old-fashioned biopic. Jeff Bridges, splendid in the title role, commented, 'Maybe Francis is the Tucker of our day.'

Coppola, hungry to recover his past success, finally embarked on *The Godfather Part III* (1990) with several of the original cast, despite having refused to direct another *Godfather*. 'I would just take the story and tell it again, which is what they do on these sequels. I'm not really interested in gangsters any more.' However, the director succeeded in creating a powerful, if uneven, coda to the Corleone family saga and the public were still interested enough in gangsters to pay millions to see it.

As writer and director unless stated otherwise: **1961** Tonight For Sure **1963** Dementia 13 (GB: The Haunted And The Hunted,) **1966** This Property Is Condemned (writer only); Is Paris Burning? (writer only) **1967** You're A Big Boy Now **1968** Finian's Rainbow (director only) **1969** The Rain People **1970** Patton (writer only) **1972** The Godfather **1974** The Great Gatsby (writer only); The Conversation; The Godfather Part II; **1979** Apocalypse Now **1982** One From The Heart **1983** The Outsiders (director only); Rumblefish **1984** The Cotton Club **1986** Peggy Sue Got Married (director only) **1987** Gardens of Stone (director only) **1988** Tucker: The Man And His Dream (director only) **1989** New York Stories ('Life Without Zoe' episode) **1990** The Godfather Part III; Hollywood Mavericks (actor only) **1992** Bram Stoker's Dracula

Corman, Roger

Director, producer
Born 5 April 1926
Los Angeles, California

For the last two decades Roger Corman has been known as the genial godfather and mastermind behind a vast range of creative talents, using his great skills as a promoter and consolidating his reputation as 'King of the Z-movies'. The list of those to whom he first gave opportunities to direct would make a who's who of contemporary cinema in itself. Suffice it to say that Martin Scorsese, Peter Bogdanovich, Francis Ford Coppola, Monte Hellman, and later John Sayles, Joe Dante and Jonathan Demme owe a great deal to Corman. 'You can see right away that the guy's a superior producer,' said Jack Nicholson, who appeared in five Corman movies. 'He's the best producer I've met in the business. The man carried me for seven years. I feel tremendously indebted to him.' But to pre-70s cinemagoers, Corman – responsible in his producer capacity for some 200 films – was an *auteur* in his own right.

He was educated at Leland Stanford University where he took an engineering degree and then did a year's graduate work in English Literature at Oxford University. After three years in the Navy, he entered the movies as an errand boy at Fox in 1948. By 1953, he had set up Roger Corman Productions, and began directing two years later. His filmography can be roughly divided into three groups: 1) The quickies (1955–1960) 2) The Edgar Allan Poe series (1960–1964) 3) The mainstream experiments (1966–1970). In the first period, on a tiny budget and in rented studios, he produced and directed such Z-movies as *She-Gods Of Shark Reef* (1956), *Attack Of The Crab Monsters* (1957) and *Teenage Cavemen* (1958). They were aimed at the drive-in-movie youth market with its taste for science-fiction horror and rock 'n' roll, who enjoyed the tatty special effects, cut-price monsters and unknown casts.

In the early 60s, for American International, he went more upmarket with a series of adaptations from Poe, a favourite writer of his since childhood. Using the team of designer Daniel Haller writer Richard Matheson and cameraman Floyd Crosby, he created garish, camp and amusing shockers, taking their tone from Vincent Price's sibilant, ghoulish hamming. They were sometimes referred to as 'Late Wife' movies because, in most of them, Price had a deceased wife lying around a castle. Taking only 15 days to shoot, they contained scenes and sets interchangeable from one film to the next, but they were vastly popular and gathered a cult following.

A departure from the horror genre of the period, and one of Corman's favourites, was *The Intruder* (1961), a gritty social drama in which a rabble-rouser (William Shatner) arrives in a southern town to disrupt racial integration in the schools. His taste for updated American Gothick was more strongly evident in the biker movie *The Wild Angels* (1966), which featured actual members of Californian Hell's Angels, and *The Trip*

(1967), an indulgent plunge into psychedelia, both starring Peter Fonda, who went on to produce the Corman-influenced *Easy Rider* (1969), a combination of the two movies.

Corman's vivid blood-splattered re-creation of 1928 Chicago in *The St Valentine's Day Massacre* (1967) was more tightly controlled and wordier than his usual product, with impeccable performances from Jason Robards as Al Capone and Ralph Meeker as Bugs Moran. In the cold-eyed and unromantic *Bloody Mama* (1970), Shelley Winters let rip as Kate Barker, the plump and murderous matriarch of a gang of outlaws. Both these gangster films were bigger budget commercial successes, but Corman gave up directing in 1971 after *Von Richthofen And Brown* nose-dived at the box office. The trouble was that neither the direction and screenplay nor the performances could make the characters anything but cardboard figures. (Phoney German accents were dubbed in against Corman's wishes.) However, the dog fights, actually filmed in the air, gave the World War I flying sequences authenticity. (A stunt flyer died during the shooting.)

Corman's reasons for retiring as a director were manifold: he had made around 26 films in ten years and felt the need of a rest; he also complained that when he made cheap films nobody tinkered with them, but as a big-budget director everyone seemed to think they had a right to maul his work. Also, he was getting married for the first time.

In 1974, he set up his own company called New World and continued to produce exploitation formula pictures for the youth market, abiding by the extremely profitable philosophy of 'make 'em quick, make 'em cheap and make 'em popular'. Then, in 1990, he sat down in his director's chair again and made *Frankenstein Unbound*, which proved he could still spin a gory tale, though alas, without the success of yesteryear.

As director and producer only unless stated otherwise: **1955** Five Guns West; Apache Woman **1956** The Day The World Ended; Swamp Woman; The Oklahoma Woman; Gunslinger; It Conquered The World **1957** Not Of This Earth; The Undead; Naked Paradise; Attack Of The Crab Monsters; Rock All Night; Teenage Doll; Carnival Rock; Sorority Girl; The Viking Woman And The Sea Serpent **1958** War Of The Satellites; The She-Gods Of Shark Reef; Machine Gun Kelly; Teenage Caveman **1959** I Mobster; A Bucket Of Blood; The Wasp Woman **1960** Ski Troop Attack; The House Of Usher (GB: The Fall Of The House Of Usher); The Little Shop Of Horrors; The Last Woman On Earth; The Creature From The Haunted Sea; Atlas **1961** The Pit And The Pendulum; The Intruder (GB: The Stranger); The Premature Burial **1962** Tales Of Terror; Tower Of London; The Young Racers; The Raven; The Terror **1963** 'X'-The Man With The X-Ray Eyes; The Haunted Palace; The Secret Invasion; The Masque Of The Red Death **1964** The Tomb Of Ligeia **1966** The Wild Angels; A Time For Killing (bit part as actor only) **1967** How To Make It (GB: Target Harry); The St Valentine's Day Massacre; The Trip **1968** De Sade (part-director only) **1969** Bloody Mama; Gas-s-s-s (GB: Gas!) **1970** Von Richthofen And Brown (GB: The Red Baron) **1974** The Godfather Part II (acting cameo only) **1982** The State Of Things (actor only) **1984** Swing Shift (acting cameo only) **1990** Frankenstein Unbound **1991** The Silence Of The Lambs (actor only)

Cort, Bud
(Walter Edward Cox)
Actor

Born 29 March 1950

New Rochelle, New York

A small, owlish flower child who represented for a while the confused aspirations of his young generation, Bud Cort was a star for a year or so, then he disappeared, to re-emerge on our screens a mature character actor nearly ten years later.

The son of middle-class parents (both merchants, though his father was also a pianist, and his mother a reporter), Cort attended the School of Arts at New York University between 1967 and 1969. He also studied with Bill Hickey and Groucho Marx, among others. His first experience of film-making came as an extra in *Up The Down Staircase* (1967); he also had two lines in Bob Fosse's *Sweet Charity* (1969), before landing a supporting role in the bizarre fable *The Travelling Executioner* (1970). But it was his night-club act that earned Cort his biggest break. Writing and performing stand-up material – and singing too – he was spotted in a New York club by director Robert Altman, who promptly cast him in *M⋆A⋆S⋆H* (1970). The role was small (he is Private Boone), but the film was a smash hit, and Altman entrusted the nervous 20-year-old with the title role in his next picture, *Brewster McCloud* (1970). A scattershot contemporary satire and a mythical fable, the film was not well received at the time, though it is certainly an intriguing oddity today. Brewster is a modern-day Icarus, tied to the earth by sex and by society. Altman uses Cort's absurdly delicate frame and quirky compulsiveness as the embodiment of hippy utopianism weighed down by the world, though the best lines go to the other actors: Shelley Duvall, Sally Kellerman, Rene Auberjonois, John Schuck and Michael Murphy.

Two other films in what was a frantic year for Cort suggested that he was the man of the moment, though both were disappointments. Roger Corman's *Gas-s-s-s!* (1970) was a crazy science-fiction comedy about the hijinks of the flower children after everyone over the age of 30 has been poisoned. Cort was a pilgrim along for the ride, and his wide-eyed *faux-naïf* style was well suited to this ramshackle, occasionally pointed venture. Corman blamed re-editing for the mixed results (they cut out at least one major character, he says), but it is unlikely that we were deprived of a masterpiece. *The Strawberry Statement* (1970) was an eagerly awaited, soon discarded treatment of the riots at Columbia University, another dud from Hollywood's flirtation with the counterculture, the demise of which may have put paid to Cort's career as a sort of late 60s Andy Hardy drop-out. Before that happened, he found one role that finally vouchsafed his place in the affections of cult movie devotees everywhere. *Harold And Maude* (1971) took 11 years to go into the black, but it played almost continually on campuses and in repertory cinemas throughout those years. An oddball romance between Cort's kooky kid with a penchant for suicide and Ruth Gordon's wacky old woman with a lust for life (both with a passion for attending funerals), this is the cult film *par excellence*: anti-establishment, outrageous, funny, lyrical and over-rated. Cort is at his best here, sweet and innocent in the quite moving love scenes, and gloriously deadpan during the hilarious black comic sequences.

For reasons that remain vague, Cort dropped out of sight after *Harold And Maude*, with only the Canadian drama *Why Shoot The Teacher?* (1977) to his credit in the 70s. He also played the lead in *Hitler's Son*, completed in 1978 but as yet unreleased. He made his Broadway debut in *The Wise Child*, and made a number of stage appearances in Los Angeles, winning a Dramalogue award for *Endgame*. Television credits were infrequent after his debut in *The Doctors*. It was a pleasant surprise when Cort returned to film-making in the 80s as a versatile character actor, often in independent productions. He made an oily villain in *Die Laughing* (1980), played a director in Robert Dornhelm's *She Dances Alone* (1981), and was the voice of the computer in *Electric Dreams* (1984). Slipping from comedy (*The Secret Diary Of Sigmund Freud*, 1984), to sensitive dramas (*Love Letters*, 1983, *Maria's Lovers*, 1985), to schlock horror (*Brain Dead*, 1990), Cort was clearly in control of his career. A first film, (*Love In Venice*), as writer and director was in the offing in 1991.

1969 Sweet Charity **1970** The Travelling Executioner; M*A*S*H; Gas-s-s-s!; The Strawberry Statement; Brewster McCloud **1971** Harold And Maude **1977** Why Shoot The Teacher? **1978** Hitler's Son (unreleased) **1980** Die Laughing **1981** She Dances Alone (Austria/US) **1983** Hysterical; Love Letters **1984** The Secret Diary Of Sigmund Freud; Electric Dreams **1985** Maria's Lovers **1986** Invaders From Mars **1987** Burnin' Love **1988** The Chocolate War **1989** Out Of The Dark **1990** Brain Dead **1991** Love In Venice (also director, writer)

Costa-Gavras, Constantin
(Konstantinos Gavras)

Director
Born 12 February 1933
Athens, Greece

Politics and its direct effect on human lives is so rarely treated in mainstream cinema that Costa-Gavras, whose theme it has been in every one of his films except his first, is to be warmly welcomed.

The son of a bureaucrat in the conservative Greek government, Costa-Gavras received a strict Orthodox education. Already on the left and unhappy with the Greek regime, he rebelled against his background and went to settle in France at the age of 18 to study at the Sorbonne, where he took a degree in literature. He then attended the Institut des Hautes Études Cinématograph, before becoming assistant director to Yves Allégret and René Clément, both socially aware directors.

There was not a whiff of his political preoccupations in his directorial debut, *The Sleeping Car Murders* (1965), a taut whodunnit starring Yves Montand and Simone Signoret, but an ability to stir the emotions was already apparent. After *Shock Troops* (1967), a harrowing film about the French Resistance, he gained an international reputation with *Z* (1969), a very slick and effective condemnation of the colonels' regime in Greece, although the country was not named. He then continued in France to make movies with political subjects, though he was not so much drawn to the ideas as to the dramatic effect of events.

So impressed were Paramount with his work that they approached him to direct *The Godfather* (1972), but he turned it down because he felt it glorified the Mafia. Nine years passed before he made his first American film, *Missing* (1981). It told of a father's anguish when his son is arrested by the military junta in Chile in 1973. Ricardo Aronovich's camera work chillingly captured the atmosphere of a police state and the message was unequivocal – the CIA were largely to blame for the coup. He also managed to create a domestic drama in which the conservative father (Jack Lemmon) is reconciled with his liberal-minded daughter-in-law (Sissy Spacek) in a shared tragedy. However, the personal and the political, the fiction and the fact, were unbalanced in *Hanna K* (1983), which uneasily used the Palestinian question as a background for a romance and as entertainment, while offering only some tentative stabs at the audience's conscience. *Betrayed* (1988) gradually reveals the dark side of Americana, showing right-wing, racist middle-Americans as ordinary clean-living, God-fearing citizens who just happen to go hunting 'niggers' for sport. The film created tension by seldom switching from the viewpoint of the FBI agent (Debra Winger), but moved rather too far from the political context into pure thriller, thus diminishing its central theme.

Then, in *Music Box* (1989), the director seemed to be more interested in a father-daughter struggle than the war-crimes trial that forms the basis for the plot. Nevertheless, although politics is more complex than the political thrillers of Costa-Gavras suggest, *Music Box* provided meaty roles (Jessica Lange and Armin Mueller-Stahl are superb), intriguing ambiguities and food for thought, as the best of his films always have.

1965 The Sleeping-Car Murders (France) **1967** Shock Troops (France) **1969** Z (France) **1970** The Confession (France) **1972** State Of Siege (France) **1975** Special Section (France) **1979** Clair De Femme (France) **1981** Missing **1983** Hanna K; Conseil De Famille (France) **1988** Betrayed **1989** Music Box

Costner, Kevin

Actor
Born 18 January 1955
Lynwood, California

Kevin Costner crept quietly up on the movie industry through the 80s, to arrive into the 90s as a megastar, power-playing producer and Oscar-winning director. Very good looking in a quietly macho, comforting sort of way, he had been variously hailed as the new Gary Cooper, the new James Stewart and the new thinking woman's sex symbol – all of which indicates the difficulty of describing the quality of his attractive presence. The labels are consonant, too, with the actor's own sentiments that, 'I was born 30 years too late for the kind of cinema I'd like to do.'

Those words, however, were spoken before the 1991 Academy Awards ceremony from which he walked away with seven Oscars, including Best Director and Best Picture, for his debut directing effort, *Dances With Wolves* (1990). The three-hour spectacle (four in its complete version), handsomely photographed and audaciously using the Lakota Sioux language with subtitles where appropriate, took lead position in that small list of 'conscience' movies with which Hollywood has tried to atone for the White Man's sins against the Native Americans, and it took the US by storm.

The film's director-cum-star was educated at California State University where he majored in marketing before taking a job suitable to his degree. It lasted only a month before he decided on an actor's life. Costner's previous experience had consisted of working with a community theatre group called South Coast Actors' Co-op while he was at college, and his haul to the top proved no easy matter. He made his debut in a forgotten film called *Shadows Run Black* (1981), and his early appearances included a low-budget exploitation movie called *Sizzle Beach*, and one line in *Frances* (1982). However, he was certainly noticeable as a distraught young husband and father in the nuclear drama *Testament* (1983), married to an equally unknown Rebecca De Mornay. Cast in Lawrence Kasdan's *The Big Chill* (1983), together with a dazzling line-up of future stars (Kline, Close, Hurt, Goldblum, Berenger), his entire part landed on the cutting-room floor. Additional misfortunes included rejection for roles in *The Killing Fields* (1984) and *Mask* (1985), and for the lead in 1987's *Raising Arizona* (it went to Nicolas Cage); and he displayed a severe failure of judgement in turning down both *Jagged Edge* (1985), which upped the ante for Jeff Bridges instead, and *Platoon* (1986), leaving the showy part of the brutal sergeant to Tom Berenger.

Kasdan made it up to Costner by making him the hero in *Silverado* (1985), but this affectionate return to the Western made little impression on the box office, leaving the actor still relatively unrecognised when Brian De Palma gave him Eliot Ness, the special investigator sent to break Al Capone, in *The Untouchables* (1987). As scripted, Ness was clean-living, humourless and bland and, in his fidelity to the character, Costner bordered on the boring. Nonetheless, although the honours went to Sean Connery and the fireworks to Robert De Niro, the film somehow put Costner on the map, and he made a more than adequate and appealing leading man in the same year's *No Way Out*, a political conspiracy thriller which found him in a steamy clinch with Sean Young that signalled his sex appeal. But it was with his performance as a faded baseball star, a loner with literary leanings, opposite Susan Sarandon in the raunchy and original baseball movie *Bull Durham* (1988), that he really showed his range. This was followed by another, and very different, baseball movie, *Field Of Dreams* (1989), in which the star's confident charm and down-to-earth presence made it possible to swallow the fantasy fable of a farmer instructed by the ghost of 'Shoeless Joe' Jackson to turn a cornfield into a baseball diamond.

In 1989, the actor formed his own company and served as executive producer on *Revenge* (1990) – a severe financial failure. As a not very nice man locked into a violently lustful affair with his best friend's wife, Costner left his image – a man of integrity, bravery, family values and moral uplift – firmly behind, embarking on a rougher, tougher road which led, not to a series of morally questionable roles, but the cut-and-thrust of getting *Dances With Wolves* made, and made without compromising his vision.

Showing his remarkable business savvy, Costner followed his *Dancer* triumph with dramatically different back-to-back roles. As a lanky Yankee *Robin Hood* he drew hoots of derision from some critics, but the Sherwood Forest romp was a huge commercial hit. As the central character – persistent New Orleans D.A. and Kennedy assination investigator Jim Garrison – in Oliver Stone's controversial *JFK*, he added another string to his bow. He was again a rather bland if obstinate Mr Clean, but in the climactic courtroom scene Costner showed more depth and feeling than one had come to anticipate from him.

Married to his childhood sweetheart, Cindy, with whom he has three children, Kevin Costner lives in California.

1981 Shadows Run Black; Chasing Dreams **1982** Table For Five; Night Shift; Frances **1983** Stacy's Knights; St Louis Square; Testament **1984** The Gunrunner (released 1989) **1985** American Flyers; Fandango; Silverado **1987** No Way Out; The Untouchables **1988** Bull Durham **1989** Field Of Dreams **1990** Revenge **1990** Dances With Wolves (also director) **1991** Robin Hood: Prince Of Thieves; Truth Or Dare (GB: in Bed with Madonna) (cameo); JFK **1992** The Bodyguard

Cox, Alex

Director, writer
Born 15 December 1954
Cheshire, England

Alex Cox is in the younger guard of British directors who have sought to make their reputation in America, and has attempted, with only intermittent success, to inject a punk sensibility into commercial film-making.

He began his training as a film student at Bristol and progressed to the film studies department at UCLA. His first feature, *Repo Man* (1984), was made on a low budget in the US and got him off to a cracking start in his profession. The movie was a rapid-fire collage of urban chaos and absurdist behaviour, held together by a deliberately artificial yet tightly wound narrative, complete with sci-fi overtones, acknowledging that *Invasion Of The Bodysnatchers* (1956) is one of Cox's favourite movies. The story concerned the misadventures of a new recruit (Emilio Estevez) to the ranks of 'repo' men – free-lance operators who snatch back cars from hire purchase defaulters – and, as the the anti-hero's bleary mentor, Harry Dean Stanton imported a whiff of downbeat humanity: 'Ordinary people', he sneers toward some harmless bystanders. 'I hate 'em'.

The offhand attack of this movie was not to be found in its British-made successor, *Sid And Nancy* (1986). Its subject, the ill-fated affair between the degenerate punk rock musician Sid Vicious and his lover, Nancy Spungeon, might have seemed to provide plenty of potential for provocation. But the movie that emerged seemed incongruously glossy, even academic, with its measured pace and flashback construction, despite being centred on a graphic performance by Gary Oldman. Much worse was to come, however, with the self-indulgent silliness of

Straight To Hell (1987), an incoherent spoof of Spaghetti Westerns, performed by an assortment of rock musicians and hangers-on. Something of the same spirit infected and eventually undid Cox's next film, *Walker*, the same year; but for about half its length this exaggerated, non-realistic account of the colonialist activities in mid-19th century Nicaragua of the American adventurer William Walker (Ed Harris) managed to convey a bizarre sort of commitment. Cox returned to Britain to direct another dramatised case history, this time that of the now legendary Craig-Bentley murder case of the early 1950s but, in the event, the highly acclaimed *Let Him Have It* (1991) was directed by Peter Medak.

Flitting between the US and Britain, Alex Cox has managed to retain the air of an outsider in both countries, but sometimes in rather the wrong sense of the word and, by 1992, seemed in danger of disappearing altogether.

1984 Scarred (assist. dir) Repo Man (w/d) **1986** Sid and Nancy (w/d) **1987** Straight to Hell (w/d); Walker

Coyote, Peter
(Peter Cohon)
Actor
Born 1942
Englewood, New Jersey

Describing himself as 'a Zen Buddhist student first – an actor second', Peter Coyote makes up for the conventional villainy of most of his screen characters with a vengeance off screen. Born into money, the son of an investment banker, he changed his name in 1967 as the result of a vision induced by taking the drug peyote and, after studying with the San Francisco Actors Workshop, joined a prominent mime troupe that toured with an anti-Vietnam piece. He continued the 60s in a similar vein, joining an improvisational group, Diggers In The Haight, and proclaimed the death of the dollar while setting up free food programmes and medical clinics. Appointed to the California Arts Council in 1975–83, he proved instrumental in gaining massive increases in the state's arts funding budget while finding time to act in several TV films and mini-series.

Best remembered as E.T.'s nemesis in the 1982 blockbuster, he managed to give surprising depth to the role. At first sinister and threatening, he is ultimately revealed as a sympathetic, rather sad shadow of the boy Elliott – he is what the boy would have become had he never found the alien, a man who has been wishing for something all his life only to inadvertently smother it with the science that has taken the place of his innocence. Coyote's tendency to change convincingly his characters' spots is a feature of many of his performances – the charming, decent teacher who turns out to be a murderous renegade spy in *Outrageous Fortune* (1987), his very weird cop in *Heart Of Midnight* (1989) – but he has often been limited both by his parts and his erratic choice of films, frequently being called on to do nothing much. However, this tall, dark, gangling actor can be outstanding with the right material, particularly when required to be sinister (as in *Jagged Edge*, 1985). Coyote, attractive but uncontrollably creepy, seems destined to play oddballs and psychopaths – certainly, his romantic lead for Diane Kurys in *A Man In Love* (1987) was a major factor in sinking the movie. To date, the high spot of his career is still the ice-cold, megalomaniacal film director, subjugating reality to his obsessive desire to control all aspects of his players' lives, in the intriguing and too-little seen *Strangers Kiss* (1984).

1979 Die Laughing **1980** Tell Me A Riddle **1981** Southern Comfort; The Pursuit Of DB Cooper aka Pursuit **1982** Out; E.T. The Extra-Terrestrial; Endangered Species; Partners **1983** Timerider: The Adventure Of Lyle Swann **1983** Cross Creek; Strangers Kiss **1984** Slayground; Heartbreakers **1985** Jagged Edge; The Legend Of Billie Jean; Troupers **1987** Stacking aka Season Of Dreams; A Man In Love; Outrageous Fortune **1988** Heart Of Midnight **1990** The Man Inside **1991** Crooked Hearts **1992** Bitter Moon

Craven, Wes
(Wesley Earl Craven)
Director, writer
Born 2 August 1939
Cleveland, Ohio

Like many directors associated with the horror genre, Wes Craven – the true begetter of the 'nightmare scenario' – has often expressed a wistful desire to direct a love story. But his own obsessive love affair with the relationship between the 'normal' and the 'monstrous', and between dreams and 'reality', has taken his switchback Hollywood career along a different road.

Craven grew up in Cleveland, Ohio, the child of strict Baptist parents who forbade cinemagoing. He took a BA in education and psychology at Wheaton College, and an MA in philosophy and writing at John Hopkins University. In 1981 he recalled: 'I had no film background. I was teaching literature when I did my first film with some students and was so happy with the experience, if not the result, that I just decided to go to New York and get into the film business.'

Joining forces with producer-director Sean Cunningham (of subsequent *Friday The 13th* fame) Craven made a pseudo-documentary porno film, *Together* (1970), whose modest success encouraged their backers to give them $90,000 to make 'a knock-down, drag-out horror movie'. The result was an extraordinary reworking of Ingmar Bergman's *The Virgin Spring* (1959) entitled *Last House On The Left* (1972), in which a Mansonesque gang rapes and tortures two girls to death only to meet horrific justice themselves. In a climax of disturbing resonance and gruesome violence, the gang, now posing as solid members of the middle class, are unmasked and then butchered by the parents of their victims.

The film flopped under its first two titles, *Krug and Company* and *Sex Crime Of The Century*, deservedly perhaps, but hit the jackpot with the evocative *Last House On The Left*, chosen by a canny publicist. It was greeted with outrage, uproar, and brisk business at the box office, while Craven attempted to disarm some of the more virulent criticism with the claim that the movie was 'a reaction on my part to the violence around us, specifically to the Vietnam War.'

The underlying theme of *Last House On The Left* – the subverting of the American middle-class 'ideal' by colliding it with its nightmarish mirror image – resurfaced in *The Hills Have Eyes* (1977), whose inspiration lay in the 17th-century tale of Sawney Bean, a real-life flesh-eating outlaw, whose gang preyed on hapless travellers in Scotland. His modern successors are a grotesque family of cannibalistic backwoodsmen whose victims are middle-American campers.

In *Deadly Blessing* (1981), the director abandoned gore for an atmospheric exploration of American rural gothic, in which terror, both natural and supernatural, besets a fanatical Hittite community and its neighbours. The terror is all the more effective for taking place in the full light of day. Less impressive were *Swamp Thing* (1981), a celebration of 50s comic culture with a suitably 1980s 'green' monster, and *The Hills Have Eyes II* (1983), which revived Craven's terrible family on a somewhat bigger budget than the original.

Craven had always been fascinated by dreams – as a student he carefully catalogued his own – and has claimed that the scenario for *The Hills Have Eyes* sprang fully formed from one of them. And dreams played the central, driving role in his most perfectly realised excursion into the fantastique, *A Nightmare On Elm Street* (1984). The original idea for the movie came from a news item Craven saw about Laotian refugees in California who suffered from terrible nightmares, told family and friends that they were afraid to risk dreaming again and subsequently died in their sleep from unknown causes. Craven transplanted the notion of 'people being killed from inside their dreams' to the 'teen terror' scenario beloved of exploitation film-makers, and in the process created the most outrageous anti-hero of the 1980s, razor-taloned Freddy Krueger, a cackling bogeyman who exploits the perverse logic of nightmares to pursue his teenage victims down the corridors of their unconscious. In spite of *A Nightmare On Elm Street*'s low budget – Craven could interest none of the majors in the project, which had been conceived in 1979 – the film's special effects are striking, notably a sequence in which a bed swallows up its slumbering occupant and then shoots a huge jet of blood into the air. Craven had no qualms about plagiarising some of his earlier films, notably *Last House On The Left* and *Deadly Blessing*, for shocks, and the result is a fantasy located somewhere between *Halloween* (1978) and the hallucinatory *Videodrome* (1983).

Elm Street's creator has been directly involved in only one of the four sequels, as co-writer and producer of the third in the money-spinning series, *A Nightmare On Elm Street 3:Dream Warriors* (1987), in which Freddy terrorises the teenage inmates of a psychiatric hospital. The film's release was accompanied by a barrage of criticism from self-appointed guardians of public morality, who feared that an outbreak of 'copycat' teenage suicides would follow Freddy's celluloid exploits. But this hysterical reaction was at odds with the almost jokey style which the series had by then assumed.

Having lost control of Freddy Krueger, Craven seemed to lose control of his career. He was frustrated in his attempts to join the big-studio club: *Deadly Friend* (1986), for Warners, was a misfiring variation on the Frankenstein theme, filled with the trademark bad-dreams sequences which have characterised all of the director's films since *Last House On The Left*; and *The Serpent And The Rainbow* (1988), for Universal, was a listless voodoo chiller set in Haiti, zombie capital of the world. Like many a hero of the exploitation movie, Craven's powers waned as his budgets waxed. The director has commented, 'As a film-maker you just cringe at what they can do to your films after you have made them.' Seeking greater control, he withdrew from the mainstream in the late 1980s, signing a multi-picture deal with the small Alive Films arm of the Island music group.

As director only unless stated otherwise: **1972** Last House On The Left (also co-writer) **1977** The Hills Have Eyes **1981** Deadly Blessing (w/d); Swamp Thing (w/d) **1983** The Hills Have Eyes: Part II (w/d) **1984** A Nightmare On Elm Street (w/d) **1986** Deadly Friend **1987** A Nightmare On Elm Street Part 3: Dream Warriors (co-writer only); Flowers In The Attic (co-writer only) **1988** The Serpent And The Rainbow **1989** Shocker (w/d) **1991** The People Under The Stairs (w/d)

Crichton, Michael
(John Michael Crichton)

Director, writer
Born 23 October 1943
Chicago

The son of the executive editor of *Advertising Age*, Michael Crichton graduated *summa cum laude* from Harvard, continuing at the university until he received his MD degree. Before he came to films, Crichton had made a name (or names) for himself as a writer of thrillers under the *noms-de-plumes* of John Lange, Michael Douglas (in a collaboration with his younger brother Douglas) and Jeffrey Hudson. He also published a number of science-fiction novels under his own name, two of which, *The Andromeda Strain* (1970) and *The Terminal Man* (1974), were turned into films. It was his disappointment in these which prompted him to go behind the cameras himself.

After writing the script for *Extreme Close-Up* (1973), a soft-porn movie on voyeurism, he directed *Westworld*, his first feature film, the same year. (He had already directed *Binary*, a 1972 TV movie from his own novel.) *Westworld* was an ingenious and enjoyable Western with a difference, in which tenderfoot tourist Richard Benjamin takes on automaton Yul Brynner in a gunfight at a fake cowboy holiday resort, the latter having been encouraged to play a robotic version of his character in *The Magnificent Seven* (1960).

Crichton's medical studies must have helped when it came to directing and writing his second feature, *Coma* (1977), based on a Robin Cook novel. A huge hit, it was set in a hospital where a series of fatal anaesthetics take place. Crichton adeptly built up the tension as Doctor Genevieve Bujold fled for her life while trying to uncover the secret behind the deaths.

The novel and screenplay (both by Crichton) of *The Great Train Robbery* (1979) were based on the actual 'first robbery from a moving train' which took place in the London of 1855. The director, with the help of cinematographer Geoffrey Unsworth, gave it an authentic mid-Victorian look, and though the picture took a while to work up steam, it had an exciting climax with Sean Connery (without a stunt man or back projection) clambering along the top of a speeding train.

There was a return to familiar sci-fi territory with *Looker* (1981), the title being an acronym for Light Ocular Oriented Kinetic Energy Responsers, and involved James Coburn as a tycoon experimenting with subliminal TV commercials. *Runaway* (1984) took place in the near future, and had cop Tom Selleck tracking down murderous machines. Crichton's interest in manipulative technology found less of an outlet in *Physical Evidence* (1988), an extremely lacklustre courtroom thriller, starring Burt Reynolds and Theresa Russell. The failure of this attempt led him to hand over the directorial reins of his bestsellers, *Jurassic Park* and *The Rising Sun* to Spielberg and Philip Kaufman respectively. Crichton's best movies are futuristic tales of atmospheric menace, though he has, to date, failed to reach the standard of his first two films.

As director and writer unless stated otherwise: **1973** Extreme Close-Up (writer only); Westworld **1977** Coma **1979** The Great Train Robbery (GB: The First Great Train Robbery) **1981** Looker **1984** Runaway **1988** Physical Evidence (director only) **1993** Jurassic Park (writer only)

Cronenberg, David

Director, writer
Born 15 May 1943
Toronto, Canada

'I could conceive of a beauty contest for the

inside of the human body where people would unzip themselves and show you the best spleen, the best heart, the best-looking viscera . . .' David Cronenberg once stated. And, indeed, his films *are* visceral, in both the literal and figurative sense.

Cronenberg studied Biochemistry at Toronto University, but didn't like the way it was taught, so switched to English Language and Literature. Film already interested him at that time, and he made two surreal shorts while still a student. His first feature, *Crimes Of The Future* (1969), was shot in Toronto in 35mm for $15,000, and presaged his future obsessions. Set in the Institute for Neo-Venereal Disease, it dealt with genetic mutilation. Thus began the exploration of the theme of the fraught relationship between mind and body and the fascination with physical decay and mutilation which would inform his future work. *Stereo*, of the same year, showed a group of youngsters working for the Canadian Academy of Erotic Inquiry on a scientific experiment, which increases their powers of telepathic communication.

All Cronenberg's films, with the exception of *Fast Company* (1979), a B-picture about car racing, have been in the sci-fi and horror genres. In his first commercial feature, *Shivers* (1975), a luxury block of flats becomes an inferno of manic promiscuity when black, phallic, slug-like parasites pass from one tenant to another, another allegory of VD; and in *Rabid* (1976), a girl with a penile sting on her armpit infects others. These films got the director dubbed 'The King Of Venereal Horror'.

Inspired by his own bitter divorce, *The Brood* (1979) concerned a woman under the influence of a new psychotherapy that produces murderous offspring, while *Scanners* (1981) has twin brothers as telepathic victims of institutionalised science engineering in, literally, a mind-blowing battle, a theme revisited in *Dead Ringers* seven years later. In *Scanners*, Cronenberg used special effects more predominantly than hitherto, especially skilfully in the scenes of heads blowing up and faces becoming grotesque. These low-budget exploitation movies, though glorifications of gore, had a certain coherence and aesthetic control. *Videodrome* (1982), however, moved too far into the tawdry media world it began by satirising when the hero has a video machine implanted in his stomach so that he can generate his own hard-core pornography.

The Dead Zone (1983) was the first film Cronenberg neither wrote nor co-wrote. Adapted from a Stephen King story about a man who has premonitions after a car accident, it is his most conventional movie in style and plot, and rather tame in terms of his *oeuvre*. But it does have an intriguing plot and the director, as usual, draws good performances from his cast (Christopher Walken, Brooke Adams, Martin Sheen). Although *The Dead Zone* was Cronenberg's first Hollywood film, it was shot, like all his features, in Canada, where he feels most at home.

Cronenberg saw *The Fly* (1986) as a metaphor for ageing. 'In time, we all turn into monsters of one kind or another,' he has said. The problem is that the story of scientist Seth Brundle (a frenetic Jeff Goldblum), whose genes are fused with those of a fly, loses its impact by piling one more horrific special effect upon the other. A very literal-minded director, Cronenberg leaves nothing to the imagination, lingering over the grotesque distortions and violations of the body. *Dead Ringers* (1988) tells of telepathically close twin gynaecologist brothers (Jeremy Irons times two) whose relationship is disturbed by the intervention of a childless actress (Genevieve Bujold) who has three cervixes. It is a clinical film in two senses. The decor is modern, hard and cold, reflecting the cold and misanthropic view of the director, although his unflinching regard for bodily decay with sexual connotations, and the aesthetics of surgical instruments, exert a morbid fascination, as do most of Cronenberg's fundamentally unlovable films. His ambitious attempt to film the unfilmable – William Burroughs' seminal drug experience novel *The Naked Lunch* – was more psychedelic than psychological and only a limited *succès d'estime*.

As director and writer unless stated otherwise: **1969** Crimes Of The Future; Stereo **1975** Shivers aka They Came From Within aka The Parasite Murders **1976** Rabid **1979** Fast Company; The Brood **1981** Scanners **1982** Videodrome **1983** The Dead Zone (director only) **1985** Into The Night (actor only) **1986** The Fly (director and co-writer) **1988** Dead Ringers (director and co-writer) **1990** Nightbreed (actor only) **1991** The Naked Lunch **1993** M. Butterfly

Crouse, Lindsay

Actress
Born 12 May 1948
New York City

The daughter of playwright Russel Crouse, and educated at Radcliffe, Lindsay Crouse began her professional life as a modern and jazz dancer (she also studied piano and flute) before settling on an acting career. Throughout her stage, and all but her most recent screen, work she has shown a loyalty to New York liberalism and 'alternative' films within the mainstream – most notably in her trio of appearances for Sidney Lumet. Despite the film's three-hour running time, much of her role in *Prince Of The City* (1981) hit the cutting-room floor, but impressed the director enough to cast her as a key witness in *The Verdict* (1982, scripted by her then husband, David Mamet), still her most emotionally powerful screen work, and as the Ethel Rosenberg-like martyred communist mother of *Daniel* (1983).

Mamet directed her in his debut film, *House Of Games* (1987), in which she (untypically) gave the most outstandingly bad performance of her screen career. Often somewhat cold on-screen in the past, as the emotionally regulated psychiatrist drawn into Joe Mantegna's psychological con-games she seriously miscalculated the character's control mechanisms, reading dialogue with a lifeless precision that simply seemed inept; although she did make amends with a recurring role in several episodes of *Hill Street Blues*, pseudonymously written by Mamet.

Communion (1989) and, to a lesser extent, Michael Cimino's *Desperate Hours* (1990, in which her DA is saddled with lesbian tendencies seemingly more for box-office than artistic reasons) showed a move towards more mainstream, apolitical films in what seemed in many ways an agent-inspired attempt to instill some box-office success into her CV, yet both proved only that Lindsay Crouse's name, sadly, meant more to discerning critics than to average cinemagoers.

1976 All The President's Men **1977** Between The Lines; Slap Shot **1981** Prince of the City **1982** The Verdict **1983** Daniel **1984** Iceman; Places in the Heart **1987** House of Games **1989** Communion **1990** Desperate Hours

Cruise, Tom
(Thomas Cruise Mapother IV)
Actor
Born 3 July 1962
Syracuse, New York

While teen 'stars' of the 80s came and went, Tom Cruise matured easily and gracefully into a bona fide international superstar, possessed – as David Puttnam described it – with more 'want to be' about him than any other American movie star in years. (Men want to be him; women want him.) In the same year that he received real recognition as an actor and an Oscar nomination for his committed and touching performance as paralysed Vietnam veteran Ron Kovic in Oliver Stone's *Born On The Fourth Of July* (1989), Cruise was also being crowned The Sexiest Man Alive by a leading American consumer magazine, confirming his position as the hottest hero in Hollywood.

Christened Thomas Cruise Mapother IV and raised with four sisters by his mother, Cruise was drawn to acting in school plays. He skipped the drama classes and stage training route, appearing in a supper-club production of the pop opera *Godspell* before he was spotted by an agent who got him a little television work after leaving school. His film entrée came with a minor role in the 1981 Franco Zeffirelli turkey, *Endless Love*. Dubious break though this might have been, Cruise looked good enough on screen to rate a meatier supporting role in *Taps* (1981) and made a strong impression with his gung-ho, crew-cutted, beret-sporting military cadet who goes blood-crazy. It proved a more memorable character than the nicer boys assigned to the two juvenile leads billed above him: Timothy Hutton and, in his first film, Sean Penn.

Matt Dillon got most of the attention in *The Outsiders* (1983), and Cruise, well down the cast list of future stars, had little to do, but he was unequivocally the star of a pleasant enough teens-on-the-tiles escapade, *Losin' It* (1983). His giant leap at the box office came in *Risky Business* (1983), Paul Brickman's superior and quite original teen satire, in which Cruise delighted as the obedient son and good student run wild and embroiled in a prostitution ring while left in charge of the family home. He followed that with a nice portrayal of a down-to-earth, ambitious high school footballer in *All The Right Moves* the same year, winding up his youth movie period as he himself turned 21.

The only glitch in Cruise's career to that date came in the shape of Ridley Scott's extravagant *Legend* (released in 1985), a fairytale fallen flat in which a limp script did not support the actor's attempt at a romantic fantasy hero. All the more surprising then, was his spectacular ascent via *Top Gun* (1986) for Ridley Scott's directing brother, Tony. To critics it was little more than a slick recruitment video for the US Navy aviation programme, but it was one of the top-grossing films of its day as audiences responded to the aerial stunts and Cruise in Ray-Bans as a cardboard stud.

The rising star's next move was a great stroke artistically and commercially, co-starred with Paul Newman in Martin Scorsese's attractive *The Color Of Money* (1986). Despite an unsatisfactorily written second half, the sequel to *The Hustler* was a fine showcase both for Newman – rewarded at last with his Oscar – and Cruise, flashing the smile and style every bit as disarming as those of Newman in his youth. Indeed, Cruise's progress has certain parallels with the career of Newman, something of a mentor figure to his heir apparent. Clearly no fool, the younger man has interspersed fluff (*Cocktail*, 1988) and tailor-made action (*Days Of Thunder*, 1990) with gradually more demanding dramatic roles (*Money, Rain Man* and *Fourth*), and has revealed himself as co-operative and eager to develop with quality directors and experienced stars like Newman and Dustin Hoffman. While the major awards showered on *Rain Man* (1988) made no acknowledgement of Cruise, there can be no argument that his presence attracted a vastly wider audience than the film would otherwise have reached, and his performance as the sharp, selfish young brother to Hoffman was stylish, impressively energetic and fluid, and certainly underrated. Electing to follow his triumph in *Born On The Fourth Of July* with a self-conceived hobby horse, *Days Of Thunder*, may be considered something of a self-indulgence, but although the stock-car racing entertainment failed to live up to over-expectation in a summer packed with macho action films, it performed creditably and not unprofitably.

Tom Cruise's first, three-year marriage to actress Mimi Rogers ended in 1990, and he married his *Days Of Thunder* co-star, Australian actress Nicole Kidman, teaming with her in *Far And Away* (1992). With so much of himself invested in this epic-that-wasn't, his judgement stood in question, though his personal appeal remained untarnished.

1981 Endless Love; Taps **1982** Losin' It **1983** The Outsiders; Risky Business; All The Right Moves **1985** Legend **1986** Top Gun; The Color Of Money **1988** Rain Man; Cocktail **1989** Born On The Fourth Of July **1990** Days Of Thunder **1992** Far And Away; A Few Good Men **1993** The Firm

Cryer, Jon

Actor

Born 16 April 1965

New York City

Born into a theatrical family – father David an actor, mother Gretchen a songwriter and actress – Jon Cryer studied in Massachusetts at the Stagedoor Manor Performing Arts Training Center, and spent a term at RADA in London. He began his career by starring in Neil Simon's autobiographical *Brighton Beach Memoirs* on Broadway, then appeared in Harvey Fierstein's *Torch Song Trilogy*. He beat both of them to Hollywood, however, when Robert Altman, who had spotted him in the latter, cast him in *O.C. & Stiggs* (1984).

Slightly built, cutesy and goofy in both looks and personality, Cryer was then given the lead – a lovesick, snap-happy teenager who falls in love with 'older' woman Demi Moore and helps make her a star – by Jerry Schatzberg in *No Small Affair* later the same year. A part-turgid, part-charming teen pic, it allowed the young actor ample room to reveal his aforesaid goofy, somewhat smart-ass persona, which the ever astute John Hughes picked up on for the popular *Pretty In Pink* (1986). As humble Ducky, brash on top but sensitive below, loyal best pal and lovesick would-be swain to wrong-side-of-the-tracks Molly Ringwald's heroine, he was nuttier than ever and displayed a whirlwind comic energy that was positively exhausting to watch. Hughes originally gave him the gal at the final fade, but Cryer's manic charm failed to win over preview audiences, who felt that Molly deserved solemn rich boy Andrew McCarthy. Hughes obliged, and Cryer's subsequent career failed to yield a hit to date, despite high-profile participation in *Superman IV* (1987), and films for directors such as Penelope Spheeris (the amusing 1987 punk Western, *Dudes*) and Arthur Penn (*Penn And Teller Get Killed*, 1988).

Not to everybody's taste, Jon Cryer is nonetheless a distinctive comic presence as his TV series, *The Famous Teddy Z*, demonstrated.

1984 O.C. & Stiggs; No Small Affair **1986** Pretty In Pink **1987** Superman IV: The Quest For Peace; Hiding Out; Dudes; Morgan Stewart's Coming Home aka Homefront **1988** Penn And Teller Get Killed **1991** Hot Shots

Crystal, Billy

Actor

Born 14 March 1947

Long Island, New York

With the blockbusting success of Rob Reiner's *When Harry Met Sally* in 1989, Hollywood found itself a new and unlikely romantic leading man in Billy Crystal. As the guy who meets Meg Ryan at college and spends the next ten years trying to convince her that a man and a woman can't have a friendship without sex getting in the way, Crystal was at once witty, brash, trendy and, although without conventional good looks, attractive.

He was born into the entertainment business. The Crystal family owned the Commodore jazz record label and his father, Jack, produced jazz concerts. Billy was educated at New York University and worked with the Alumni Theatre Group at Nassau Community College before teaming up with two friends to form a comedy act. Calling themselves 'Three's Company', they toured colleges and coffee-houses, and it was from there that he branched out on his own to become a stand-up comedian – indeed, one of America's top three, alongside Eddie Murphy and Robin Williams. Appearances in *The Rabbit Test* in 1978 and *This Is Spinal Tap* in 1984 were minor digressions in a career which was bringing him nationwide fame for his role as the gay son in TV's long-running parody on soaps, *Soap*. He began nurturing a movie career in 1986, starting with *Running Scared* (1986), a Peter Hyams police farrago in which he played a smart-ass Chicago detective partnering Gregory Hines. His strong personality rose above the material and he went on to the lead in Danny DeVito's directorial debut, *Throw Momma From The Train* (1987). The movie, a black comedy about a creative writing teacher who is desperately trying to produce a novel and is pipped to the post by one of his students (DeVito), was something of a major enough vehicle for the comedian-turned-actor to attract attention.

The following year saw Billy, heavily disguised, playing a Jewish (which he is) miracle man in the delightful Rob Reiner fantasy, *The Princess Bride*, but sinking in the tedious mire of a sentimental father-son drama, *Memories Of Me*, which he co-wrote and co-produced for the directorial debut of TV star Henry Winkler. It could have marked the beginning of a downward spiral, but Harry came to the rescue. *City Slickers* (1991), conceived by Crystal and tailor-made by writers Lowell Ganz and Babaloo Mandel to fit the actor's masterly delivery of smart one-liners was another joyous hit, prompting Crystal to devise, produce, direct and star in the life story of a miserable old comic, *Mr Saturday Night*, again written by Ganz and Mandel.

1978 The Rabbit Test **1984** This Is Spinal Tap **1986** Running Scared **1987** Throw Momma From The Train **1988** The Princess Bride; Memories Of Me **1989** When Harry Met Sally **1991** City Slickers **1992** Mr Saturday Night (also director)

Curtis, Jamie Lee

Actress

Born 21 November 1958

Los Angeles, California

Of the major female stars working in Hollywood, Jamie Lee Curtis boasts a singular androgyny that lends her versatility and unique attractiveness. Cool and detached at one moment, she is capable of enveloping warmth the next; spiky and strong, she can also be very funny.

A true Hollywood child, Jamie Lee is the daughter of Tony Curtis and Janet Leigh (whose most famous role as the murder-in-the-shower victim of *Psycho* offers an extra umbilical connection to her daughter's early success). She bears a distinct resemblance to her blonde and pretty mother, but is less glamorous and much tougher. Indeed, she has curiously asymmetrical looks, her jaw a little too pronounced and causing this undoubtedly sexy and fetching woman to look almost plain from certain angles; her voice is low and distinctive, she has 'attitude'. The ambiguity prevails in her body, too, which is muscular and athletic and which she often uses with a masculine rather than a feminine grace. Her athleticism is ingrained and genuine. Trained as a dancer, she appeared as an acrobat on CBS Television's *Circus Of The Stars*, and her physical strength and fluidity became a theme of James Bridges' *Perfect* (1985), in which she played an aerobics and dance instructor romanced by investigative journalist John Travolta. Her numerous TV appearances included *Operation Petticoat*, *Quincy* and *Charlie's Angels*, but her career was determined by Universal Studios who signed her to a contract in 1977.

Famous since the 30s as the home of horror, Universal seemed bent on carrying on the tradition and chose Jamie Lee for the female lead in *Halloween* (1978). It was a fortuitous debut. Written and directed by John Carpenter, the movie was a massive international hit, spawning several sequels, and securing Carpenter's reputation. Fundamentally a piece of ludicrous teen-horror schlock, deathly slow and scripted in giggle-making clichés, it was nonetheless made with an expertise in creating tension that was irresistible. It also carried not uninteresting undercurrents of social comment on teenage mores, with Jamie Lee marked as the morally and intellectually superior 'outsider' and the only kid on the block to survive the blood-letting. Her matter-of-fact, throwaway style was in evidence, as was her capacity for warmth, but it was the placing of the character which served her so well. In any event, *Halloween* brought her an immediate following among sci-fi and horror freaks. She won the Best Actress Award given by the International Society of Science Fiction, Horror and Fantasy, and was paid the same compliment at the eighth Science Fiction Film Festival in Paris, having by then appeared in Carpenter's far more stylish and interesting *The Fog* (1979).

If her work was patently growing in assurance with each new film, Curtis nonetheless seemed for a time destined to an ultimate fate as the queen of modern horror. Fortunately, John Landis perceived her wider potential and cast her as the hooker who unhooks Dan Aykroyd in his screwball satire, *Trading Places* (1983). Wearing a trendy haircut and few clothes, Curtis unveiled her sexuality and her flair for a certain kind of abrasive comedy, but a stream of undistinguished movies followed in which even her presence, as in Randal Kleiser's messy *Grandview USA* (1984), could do little more than relieve the tedium. She was excellent playing against type as the broadcaster disastrously in love with a married man in *Love Letters* the same year, but proved miscast and uncomfortable in the small role as Peter Coyote's possessive wife in *A Man In Love* (1987), an altogether catastrophic English-language venture by French director Diane Kurys; and if she effortlessly displayed her repertoire in *Dominick And Eugene* (1988), it did nothing to elevate her status. The major breakthrough came later that year with the surprise success of the Anglo-American comedy *A Fish Called Wanda*, in which Curtis hilariously and expertly romanced John Cleese for nefarious purposes. Suddenly a new audience and another stratum of critics sat up and took notice.

By 1990, Jamie Lee Curtis who, in private life is married to actor and director Christopher Guest (*The Big Picture*, 1990) and is the mother of a small daughter, had established herself fully as an actress who could deliver the goods. In Kathryn Bigelow's *Blue Steel* (1990), the double image of her as a uniformed New York cop, fearless and drawn to the power of the gun, while at the same time vulnerable to the sexual attraction of a man by whom she is menaced, offered an impressive synthesis of the qualities which had distinguished her screen persona since her debut 12 years earlier.

1978 Halloween **1979** The Fog **1980** Terror Train; Prom Night **1981** Road Games; Halloween II **1983** Trading Places **1984** Grandview USA; Love Letters **1985** Perfect **1986** Eight Million Ways To Die **1987** Amazing Grace And Chuck (GB: Silent Voice); A Man In Love **1988** Dominick And Eugene (GB: Nicky And Gino); A Fish Called Wanda **1990** Blue Steel **1991** Queens Logic; My Girl **1992/93** The Rest Of Daniel

Cusack, Joan

Actress
Born 11 October 1962
Evanston, Illinois

Dark-haired Joan Cusack, sister of the talented John, is an off-beat and versatile actress, tending to specialise in character comedy, who proved one of the delights to emerge from Hollywood in the 1980s.

Educated at the University of Wisconsin, she became a member of Ark, an improvisational comedy group based in Madison, and cut her acting teeth in a series of plays with the Riven Theater Workshop. Joan's screen career was slow to get off the mark: four fleeting appearances before she was cast in a co-lead in *The Allnighter* (1987). It was a cretinous youth movie about the lives and loves of three girls sharing a beach house; savaged by the critics, it died a swift death. Cusack, however, who had spent the 1985–6 season as a regular on TV's *Saturday Night Live*, emerged intact and collected some complimentary notices such as 'only Cusack manages to bring some life to her part via some spontaneous goofiness'.

The goofiness was very soon to become her trademark, but tempered by her obvious gift for characterisation and flexibly manipulated to suit the occasion. Her hysterical, put-upon production assistant to Holly Hunter in *Broadcast News* (1987) was memorable, and you couldn't fail to notice her among the gaggle of Mafia wives in *Married To The Mob* (1988), albeit the role was minute. She was promoted to Daniel Day Lewis' love interest, likeable computer expert Irene Stein, in *Stars And Bars* the same year, but the film was a failure and did nothing to raise the actress' profile. But she ended the year giving a stand-out performance as Melanie Griffith's secretary friend, all eyeshadow and hair, in *Working Girl*, and was rewarded with a Supporting Actress Oscar nomination for her pains, losing out to Geena Davis (*The Accidental Tourist*).

Joan Cusack proved her versatility with a cameo role in her brother's starring vehicle, *Say Anything*, in 1989. It was a finely observed performance as his sister, loving and supportive in spite of the struggle of her own life as an unmarried mother. The movie was a huge success but Joan, unbilled at her own request and virtually unrecognisable, passed largely unnoticed. When mainstream Hollywood cast her as a lawyer, with Steve Martin, in *My Blue Heaven* (1990), it seemed that she was finally being given her due but, alas, the movie was a dog and her role, although acquitted with her usual excellence, didn't allow her to shine. Nonetheless, it had become clear to connoisseurs that Joan Cusack was an actress to watch for during the 90s.

1980 My Bodyguard **1983** Class (bit) **1984** Grandview USA; 16 Candles **1987** The Allnighter; Broadcast News **1988** Married To The Mob; Stars And Bars; Working Girl **1989** Say Anything **1990** Men Don't Leave; My Blue Heaven **1991** The Cabinet of Dr Ramirez **1992** Toys; Hero **1992/93** Pure Heart

Cusack, John

Actor
Born 26 June 1966
Evanston, Illinois

The son of documentary film-maker Richard Cusack and his theatrically-minded wife, Nancy, John was an active member of the River Theatre Workshop from the age of nine. While he was still in high school he appeared in industrial films and commercials, and 'cornered the 12-year-old market for voice-overs'. In addition, he wrote and staged two musical comedies that reached cable TV. He still lives in Chicago, and continues to work in the theatre there, where he has produced *The Day They Shot John Lennon* and directed the satirical plays *Alagazam . . . After The Dog Wars* and *Methusalem*.

John Cusack presents a beguiling mixture; he is both earnest and wacky, sincere and a joker, and palpably intelligent. The dichotomy is in his thin, long face: the straight eyebrows and high forehead give a goofy twist to his clean-cut good looks – or should that be a *Droopy* twist? There's something of the cartoon star in him. He made his film debut in *Class* (1983), and was fortunate to coincide with a boom in teen movies, many based in Chicago, John Hughes' home town. Comic supporting roles in *Grandview USA* and Hughes' *Sixteen Candles* were both shot during his school holidays and released in 1984 (the latter also featured his wonderful sister, Joan). A year later he had graduated to lead roles. As the glib, affable student in Rob Reiner's witty teenage variation on *It Happened One Night*, *The Sure Thing* (1985), Cusack found the perfect showcase for his talents. 'Have you ever considered a sexual encounter so intense it could conceivably change your political views?', he demanded of strait-laced Daphne Zuniga. He was sharp, up for anything, but appealing and sensitive in the quieter moments.

He followed this with what became his standard pattern: a drama and an off-the-wall comedy. *The Journey Of Natty Gann* (1985) showed that he was equally at ease in a low register, and, unlike the hipsters of the Brat Pack, in a period setting. *Better Off Dead*, also 1985, was the first of a series of silly, energetic youth comedies in which Cusack seems to blow off steam. Not even the best of them, *Tapeheads* (1989), amounted to much, but the actor clearly delighted in their left-field anarchy.

On the other hand, Cusack's work with serious, liberal film-makers like John Sayles, Roland Joffé and Stephen Frears in the period dramas *Eight Men Out* (1988), *Fat Man And Little Boy* (1989) and *The Grifters* (1990), reveals a committed, rather old-fashioned (in the best sense) star. He does not lose himself in a part, but *uses* himself. He is instinctive and straightforward, closer to James Stewart than James Dean. No matter what he does, even as the con-man Roy Dillon in *The Grifters*, Cusack always endows his characters with an innate decency, an innocence at odds with his surroundings. Others may have the meatier roles, but he invariably becomes the moral focal point of the film.

There was a suspicion, confirmed by *The Grifters*, that Cusack was still wet behind the ears, although it was not surprising that his subtle performance was overshadowed by the imperious Anjelica Huston; more surprisingly, however, Annette Bening also came out of the movie with a higher profile than he did (and an Oscar nomination to boot). But he is still a young man, and his superb, relaxed performance in the acclaimed teen movie *Say Anything* (1989), which for once exploited both his comic and dramatic impulses, proved that John Cusack really was coming of age.

1983 Class **1984** Grandview USA; Sixteen Candles **1985** The Sure Thing; The Journey Of Natty Gann; Better Off Dead **1986** Stand By Me (cameo); One Crazy Summer **1987** Hot Pursuit; Broadcast News (cameo) **1988** Eight Men Out **1989** Tapeheads; Say Anything; Fat Man And Little Boy aka Shadowmakers **1990** The Grifters **1991** True Colors **1991** Shadows And Fog **1992** The Player (Cameo as himself); Glengarry Glen Ross; Bob Roberts (Cameo); The Last Of The Mohicans; Map Of The Human Heart **1992/93** American Dreamers; Roadside Prophets

D

Dafoe, Willem

Actor
Born 22 July 1955
Appleton, Wisconsin

Few actors have spent so much of their careers being compared to other actors – Richard Widmark for his lean looks and early baby-faced villains, Kirk Douglas for his tendency towards superficially unsentimental issue movies, Brando, with his affection for crucifixion imagery and taking a good beating. Yet Willem Dafoe has, throughout, remained his own man, ultimately defying typecasting and attracting some of the industry's top directors (Scorsese, Stone, Parker, Lynch, Milius) along the way.

Expelled from college for making a 'mildly pornographic' video, he joined Milwaukee's avant-garde Theatre X before moving, in 1977, to New York and the Wooster Group, whose brand of performance-orientated theatre he returns to between movies. After a false start as one of the cockfighting immigrants in *Heaven's Gate* (1980, but only in the uncut version) he was cast as the iconic Brandoesque biker in Kathryn Bigelow's hymn to leather, *The Loveless* (1982), in which he sullenly haunted the Edward Hopper middle American small-town landscape like the Grim Reaper looking for some action. But Dafoe soon got bogged down in skeletal villainy – to startling effect in *Streets Of Fire* (1984) and as the demonic forger perishing in a hellish inferno in William Friedkin's *To Live And Die In LA* (1985) – until landing the role of the good sergeant in Oliver Stone's *Platoon* (1986). Cast against the attractive Tom Berenger as his satanic counterpart, he was chosen both for his corrupted – almost unformed – appearance and cynical manner that made his unforced righteousness both credible and muscular. His death scene, kneeling, arms outstretched amid a hail of bullets, paying for the sins of others, proved a canny signpost for his next and most controversial role.

'This is the face of a murderer, not of Our Lord!' cried Sergio Leone on seeing the actor's tortured Messiah in *The Last Temptation of Christ* (1988) while much of middle America cried blasphemy, labelling director Martin Scorsese the Antichrist or the False Prophet and Dafoe the Whore of Babylon (as well as whipping up anti-Semitic protests against the distributors for good measure). Yet his was the most convincing screen portrait of Jesus to date, alive, emotive, with an arresting immediacy both of His time and all time. Filled with doubt, this Christ attempts to relate to people a message they continually misunderstand, struggling to comprehend a destiny initially resisted but ultimately joyfully (even triumphantly) accepted with his crucifixion. Despite the damnation that met the film, for a while Dafoe seemed typecast on the side of the angels, with his idealistic, impractical federal agent in *Mississippi Burning* (1988) and his concentration camp boxer in *Triumph Of The Spirit* (1989, too proud and resilient to ring entirely true), but he returned spectacularly to villainy with the psychotic black angel Bobby Peru, unforgettable in accidentally blowing his own head off in *Wild At Heart* (1990).

But while his malevolent presence is ideal for such roles, Willem Dafoe lacks the quality to carry a star vehicle such as *Off Limits* (1988, and one of his many return trips to Vietnam), which also revealed his inadequacy as a romantic lead, and is generally at his best with meaty, ambiguous roles, such as his obnoxious and bitter paraplegic trading atrocities with Tom Cruise in *Born On The Fourth Of July* (1989). He was compelling in Paul Schrader's *Light Sleeper* (1992) as the 40-year-old insomniac drug peddlar forced to seek a new career; but – through no fault of his own – adrift in the impossibly convoluted thriller, *White Sands*, the same year.

1980 Heaven's Gate **1983** The Loveless; The Hunger; New York Nights **1984** Roadhouse 66; Streets Of Fire; The Communists Are Comfortable (And Three Other Stories) **1985** To Live And Die In LA **1986** Platoon **1988** Off Limits aka Saigon; The Last Temptation Of Christ; Mississippi Burning **1989** Born On The Fourth Of July; Triumph Of The Spirit **1990** Wild At Heart; Cry-Baby **1991** Flight Of The Intruder **1992** Light Sleeper; White Sands

D'Angelo, Beverley

Actress
Born 1954
Columbia, Ohio

The daughter of a bass player and a violinist

(she herself plays the piano and guitar, possesses a fine voice and has written songs for some of her films and recorded her own LPs) Beverley D'Angelo attended school in Europe, lived for a time in Italy, and began her career as a cartoonist at Hanna-Barbera before singing in Canadian coffee-houses and appearing with a rock band, Elephant. Moving into theatre via the Charlotte Town Festival Company, she made her Broadway debut as Ophelia in the rock musical *Rockabye Hamlet*, and an inauspicious movie debut as Sylvia Miles' girlfriend in Michael Winner's *The Sentinel* (1977).

Her career got a major boost when she played Geoffrey Lewis' sweet girlfriend in Clint Eastwood's orang – utang comedy, *Every Which Way But Loose* (1978), and the female lead in the belated movie version of *Hair* (1979), before her outstanding performance as Patsy Cline in *Coal Miner's Daughter* (1980) showed that she could rise to strong dramatic material which, apart from the role of Stella in a television version of *A Streetcar Named Desire* (1984), has not been forthcoming. The impetus did not last and some major box-office failures such as *Honky Tonk Freeway* (1981, in which she gave what was to become a typically eccentric performance as a small-town nymphomaniac) soon gave way to a succession of undistinguished movies with only the *National Lampoon* 'Vacation' series (in 1983, 1985 and 1989) scoring financially, although throughout the 80s the actress was kept constantly employed in films and television.

Despite working for some major directors – John Schlesinger, Richard Lester, Neil Jordan, John Cassavetes – D'Angelo has failed to live up to her early promise, often, at best, only livening up a few moments in otherwise dull films, and seems to have settled into the role of jobbing actress, with even her long overdue return to drama in *The Miracle* (1991) offering little to inspire.

1977 The Sentinel; First Love; Annie Hall **1978** Every Which Way But Loose. **1979** Hair **1980** Coal Miner's Daughter **1981** Honky Tonk Freeway; Paternity **1983** National Lampoon's Vacation **1984** Finders Keepers; Highpoint (made in 1979) **1985** National Lampoon's European Vacation **1986** Big Trouble **1987** Aria (Rigoletto sequence); Maid To Order; The Woo Woo Kid aka In The Mood **1988** Trading Hearts; High Spirits **1989** National Lampoon's Christmas Vacation aka National Lampoon's Winter Holiday; Cold Front **1990** Daddy's Dyin', – Who's Got The Will? **1991** The Miracle; The Pope Must Die; Lonely Hearts **1992** Man Trouble

Daniels, Jeff

Actor
Born 1955
Georgia

Tall and clean-cut, but with too prominent a jaw and too narrow a mouth to qualify him as glamorously good-looking, Jeff Daniels is nonetheless attractive, and boasts an invaluably flexible personality which switches from four-square, regular-guy roles, through drama, to romantic comedy, with consummate ease and no apparent tricks. It is perhaps this versatility, combined with the fact that not all the films in which he has starred were destined for popularity, which made his name lesser known than it ought to have been, until 1990 when he became an increasingly familiar presence in the leading man listings.

Raised in Michigan where his father ran a lumber business, Daniels was educated at the University of Central Michigan, after which he went to New York and, like many distinguished actors, served his acting apprenticeship with the Circle Repertory. He built up a solid body of credits in the live theatre, and won an Obie for *Johnny Got His Gun* off-Broadway, but it was his role in *The Fifth Of July*, as an embittered young veteran of the Vietnam war (he later repeated the performance for a TV movie version), which won him wider recognition.

His Hollywood debut was prestigious insofar as he appeared in Milos Forman's beautifully crafted and sensitive adaptation of E.L. Doctorow's *Ragtime* (1981). However, his role was small and the film a commercial failure, and Daniels' next film role was three years coming. This time he was associated with an enormous Oscar-laden box-office success, James L. Brooks' *Terms Of Endearment* (1984), in which he played the complex and unsympathetic part of Debra Winger's husband and got himself noticed. Next, thanks to Woody Allen, he found himself with a strong lead, co-starring with Mia Farrow in *The Purple Rose Of Cairo* (1985). As the screen character who steps out of his celluloid confines into the material world, he was at once naively defiant, amusing and charming and, if some still couldn't put a name to his face, Allen followers certainly took note of his individualistic persona. Later the same year, he switched gear decisively to play the corrupt and conscienceless state law officer of Tennessee, attempting to use Sissy Spacek as a cover-up, in

Marie. It's a true story, and the actor was striking in the role but, once again, the film was seen by the few rather than the many.

It was Jonathan Demme's *Something Wild* (1986), in which he was a delightful yuppie *naïf* abducted by Melanie Griffith for a series of outrageous adventures, sexual and otherwise, that brought the actor popular recognition, after which he played in some hideously mediocre to poor movies (Meryl Streep's editor in *Heartburn*, the FBI man tangled with Kelly McGillis in *The House On Carroll Street*, the neurotic businessman of *Checking Out*), but always managing to bring some credibility to his characters even if he couldn't save the films. By the 90s, however, Jeff Daniels was firmly established, with several glossy movies in either the can or the pipeline, all serving to demonstrate his continuing versatility and maturing gifts.

1981 Ragtime **1984** Terms Of Endearment **1985** The Purple Rose Of Cairo; Marie **1986** Something Wild **1987** Heartburn; Radio Days **1988** Sweet Heart's Dance; The House On Carroll Street **1989** Checking Out **1990** Arachnophobia; Welcome Home Roxy Carmichael; Love Hurts **1991** No Place Like Home; The Butcher's Wife **1992** Paydirt

Danner, Blythe

Actress
Born 3 February 1944
Philadelphia, Pennsylvania

Blonde, but the opposite of dizzy, Blythe Danner, like Jane Alexander and Stockard Channing, is a Broadway star who all too rarely graces a Hollywood movie. The daughter of a bank president, she was raised in privileged circumstances, attending a private school and spending a year in Berlin where she became fluent in German. While there, she performed in American musicals with a local theatre group, then took a BA in drama at New York's Bard College before embarking on her acting career. She spent her first working years with repertory companies in New York and other East coast cities, playing a wide range of parts in everything from Shakespeare to musicals before her Broadway breakthrough in *Butterflies Are Free*, which won her the Best Supporting Actress Tony in 1970. Since then she has enjoyed an unbroken record of stage success, appearing in numerous prestigious productions such as Harold Pinter's *Betrayal*, and has been seen in quality TV movies.

Danner's movie career, however, has followed a curious pattern. Almost from the beginning she was cast in major roles with well-known co-stars and never failed to distinguish herself, but the films to which she brought her strong personality and pretty face were on the whole forgettable: she graduated from a charming belle in the musical *1776* to being paired with Alan Alda in *To Kill A Clown* (both 1972) as a couple menaced by a killer, but the film rated zero; she had the title role in Sidney Lumet's *Lovin' Molly* (1974), spanning four decades as a woman involved with two brothers (Beau Bridges, Anthony Perkins) but eschewing marriage to either in pursuit of independence. She rose to the challenge but the movie was ponderous and diffuse; *Hearts of The West* (1975), a gentle satire on 30s Hollywood starring Jeff Bridges, fared better but Danner's role was smaller; she was splendid in *The Great Santini* (1979), a powerful drama about a fighter pilot (Robert Duvall) who, unable to adjust to peacetime domesticity, drives his wife (Danner) to despair. Looking wonderful with her tall, angular body, candy-floss hair and huge blue eyes, Blythe Danner displayed the full strength of her toughness and brought distinction to *Man, Woman And Child* (1983); portraying a wife coping with the discovery that her husband (Martin Sheen) has a child by another woman, she turned in a terrific performance in a weepie that disappeared from all but video view.

Then the pattern changed. Approaching middle age, Danner moved into supporting roles (including an unlikely Jewish mother in *Brighton Beach Memoirs*, 1986) and made, perhaps, her biggest impression to date on movie audiences. As Joanne Woodward's best friend who suffers a breakdown in *Mr And Mrs Bridge* (1990), she was absolutely superb – at once witty, abrasive and tragic – and, with only a few scenes as Mia Farrow's down-to-earth, world-weary lawyer sister in Woody Allen's *Alice* (1990), and Nick Nolte's long-patient wife in *The Prince Of Tides* (1991), Blythe Danner once again proved her worth.

1972 To Kill A Clown; 1776 **1974** Lovin' Molly **1975** Hearts Of The West **1976** Futureworld **1979** The Great Santini aka The Ace **1983** Man, Woman And Child **1986** Brighton Beach Memoirs **1989** Another Woman **1990** Mr And Mrs Bridge; Alice **1991** The Prince Of Tides

Danson, Ted

Actor

Born 29 December 1947

San Diego, California

Tall, good-looking, clean-cut, square-jawed Ted Danson had made a few movies before he became a household name as the womanising, affable bar-owner, Sam Malone, in the tremendously popular TV sit-com *Cheers*, which began way back in 1982 and continued on a very long run. He wasn't around long enough to make much of an impression in his debut movie, *The Onion Field* (1979), in which he played the LA cop murdered by two hijackers he tries to arrest. But the memory of the character lingered on because of the guilt his surviving partner (John Savage) carries about his death. As William Hurt's bespectacled lawyer-friend in Lawrence Kasdan's *Body Heat* (1981), Danson was a far cry from the satiric superstud image he would later project. It was his TV fame that allowed him to follow Shelley Long, his sexual sparring partner in *Cheers*, into starring roles on the big screen.

The son of an archaeologist, he grew up without a thought of being an actor, or anything else, for that matter. 'I was interested in fooling around, that's all,' he commented. It was at Stanford University that he discovered acting because a girl he fancied was a member of the dramatic society. He later married architectural designer Casey Coats who, in 1980, suffered a stroke as she gave birth to their first child. Doctors said she wouldn't walk again, but with her husband's constant assistance, she was back to normal two years later, and gave birth to another child.

Danson's work in films, post *Cheers*, began with *Just Between Friends* (1986), in which he played the adulterous husband of Mary Tyler Moore, who has an affair with Christine Lahti before getting himself killed. However, his undoubted charisma failed to come across, and it was difficult for audiences to understand how he had inspired the love of two women and the deep loyalty of his friend (Sam Waterston). In the same year he got top billing in the well-named *A Fine Mess*, only this time most of the blame was apportioned to Blake Edwards, who directed the frantically unfunny proceedings. Danson played a movie extra, known as 'Sex Machine Spence', chased by cops, the mob, and angry ex-girlfriends.

The hunky star is described as 'one giant gland' by his two friends (Tom Selleck and Steve Guttenberg) in *Three Men And A Baby* (1987), the inferior remake of Coline Serreau's *Three Men And A Cradle* (1985), but it was as big a hit as his previous two films were flops. With his hair slicked back, Danson played an egocentric actor in commercials (changed from the airline pilot in the French original) and the bachelor father of the baby dumped by the mother on him and his flatmates. He had his moments in this smooth, predictable package, changing from Macho Man to New Man and beginning to live up to his paternal/maternal responsibilities. In the even softer sequel, *Three Men And A Little Lady* (1990), Danson, Selleck and Guttenberg continued to play dad to the now five-year-old.

He was far better served in Joel Schumacher's *Cousins* (1988), another American remake of a French comedy hit. A more attractive personality than Victor Lanoux in *Cousin, Cousine* (1975), he played a semi-Bohemian, trumpet-playing, ballroom-danc ing teacher who gradually moves into having an affair with Isabella Rossellini because of his wife's infidelity with the latter's husband. 'He's a failure in everything except life,' comments his uncle (Lloyd Bridges) in the movie that gave Danson the opportunity to display the kind of laid-back charm he had revealed in *Cheers*.

In contrast, his role in *Dad* (1989) was that of a rather stiff Wall Street broker who has to comfort his 78-year-old father Jack Lemmon when his mother suffers a heart attack. Although he managed the sob stuff quite well, it was plainly Lemmon's film, but it proved that Ted Danson could play dramatic as well as comic and romantic leads.

1979 The Onion Field **1981** Body Heat **1982** Creepshow **1986** Just Between Friends; A Fine Mess **1987** Three Men And A Baby **1988** Cousins **1989** Dad **1990** Three Men And A Little Lady **1992/93** Made In America

Dante, Joe

Director

Born 28 November 1946

Morristown, New Jersey

Joe Dante's rampantly subversive sense of humour and virtuoso technique made him one of the liveliest directors working within the Hollywood system – though that conflict has not always been to the benefit of his pictures, which teetered precariously between anarchy and banality in the late 1980s.

Dante, a *cinéphile* even by the standards of his own Movie-Brat generation, learned his trade at Roger Corman's New World studio. Sat down in front of a Movieola in the trailer department he taught himself to edit. He and Allan Arkush worked on previews for the likes of *Big Bad Mama*, *Street Girls* and *TNT Jackson* ('TNT Jackson, she'll put you in traction'). It was a result-orientated training ground, and Corman's influence remained evident in Dante's predilection for comic-edged horror and science fantasy genre films. (The *de rigueur* presence of Corman star Dick Miller may be an acknowledgement of the debt; it has become Dante's signature). Dante and Arkush were granted their shot at directing with *Hollywood Boulevard* (1976), made in a matter of days on a miniscule budget. Incorporating stock footage from other Corman pictures, and all the requisite exploitation elements, the directors and writer Patrick Hobby nevertheless came up with something different by setting their story in a New World-style film studio, Miracle Pictures ('If it's a good picture, it's a Miracle!'). This off-the-cuff self-parody is surprisingly witty, overflowing with clever sight gags, in-jokes and throwaway lines. Paul Bartel steals the film as a pretentious exploitation director, anxious to 'spice up the crucifixion scene'.

Arkush went on to direct *Rock 'n' Roll High School* (1979) and various television episodes; Dante found a new collaborator in John Sayles. Corman brought them together for *Piranha* (1978), an effectively tongue-in-cheek *Jaws* rip-off, and they followed it with *The Howling* (1981), a hip contemporary satire in the framework of a sometimes scary werewolf movie. With a bigger budget than Corman could provide (he has a cameo as a money-pincher) Dante proves himself a vivid, imaginative stylist, but his sense of humour remains well to the fore. Though, like a number of his pictures, the film has its structural problems, it ends memorably, with pretty WASP newscaster Dee Wallace Stone transforming into a wolf on air, only for a cynical viewer to comment, 'It's amazing what they can do with special effects these days.'

Rather to his surprise, Dante was invited to direct an episode of *Twilight Zone – The Movie* (1983) by Steven Spielberg. It was an unlikely partnership, not least because Dante's work is in direct opposition to Spielbergian homilies and platitudes, and often parodies his style quite explicitly, but it proved lasting and fruitful nonetheless (and Dante on his part speaks of Spielberg the producer with nothing but praise). In the *Twilight Zone* movie, while Spielberg sentimentally turned old folks into children, Dante's 'It's A Good Life' presented a truly monstrous kid. A visual and imaginative tour de force, deliriously executed in homage to animators Tex Avery and Chuck Jones, the piece is only marred by an unwarranted, sugary ending. (Jones is another important influence on the film-maker, and he has cameos in a number of Dante's subsequent pictures.) *Gremlins* (1984), written by Chris Columbus and again sponsored by Spielberg, establishes a Christmassy small-town community out of *It's A Wonderful Life* (1946), introduces cuddly E.T.-like creatures, and then gleefully watches the ensuing havoc as they transform into malicious devils. It is no coincidence that the local cinema is showing 'A Boy's Life' and 'Watch The Skies', two working titles for *E.T.*, or that the gremlins go crazy for Disney, for Dante goes out of his way to trash Spielberg's backyard.

Explorers (1985) failed to repeat its predecessor's commercial success, but it's Dante's most fully realised film. The story of three intrepid youngsters who make contact with aliens, again it evokes Spielberg only to subvert him ('To them we must seem horrible,' muses one kid. 'Horrible? Us!'). It transpires that the aliens only know about Earth from television airwaves, and can only communicate in the clichés of that medium . . . worse, they turn out to be junior aliens, who have borrowed their dad's spaceship. If it sounds silly, it isn't. *Explorers* is the first post-modernist sci-fi children's movie, and something like a masterpiece.

The failure of this cherished project led Dante to a period of artistic retrenchment. He contributed a number of light-hearted sketches to the campy *Amazon Women On The Moon* (1987), namely: Hairlooming; Bullshit Or Not; Critic's Corner; Roast Your Loved One and Reckless Youth. *Innerspace* (1987) had a cartoonish energy but no subtlety. It was an eccentric mainstream film, but it lacked the subversive edge and highly recognisable personality of his earlier films. *The 'Burbs* (1989) was a rushed production that sent mixed messages: amid some broad comedy and before a studio-inflicted cop-out ending, there are a number of incisive sequences – particularly an integral speech from Tom Hanks, locating menace not in the alien but in the very heart of American suburbia itself, perhaps the key speech in Dante's work to date.

Gremlins 2 (1990), for which Dante was reputedly granted complete artistic control, virtually dispensed with narrative tension in favour of an anarchic comic satire on conglomerates, modern architectural design, big-city life, genetic experimentation and, not least, itself (John Glover's composite of Ted Turner and Donald Trump even discusses the possibility of merchandising the mogwai doll at the end of the movie). While there are signs here that Dante's satire is reaching out beyond *cinéphile* in-jokes and truly engaging with the outside world, he does seem to be caught in a fantasy-film vacuum. Given studio backing, and some self-discipline, he looked well capable of breaking free and taking his place beside Jonathan Demme as one of the foremost directors of his generation, although he seemed to be lagging behind in silence as the 90s got underway.

1976 Hollywood Boulevard (co-director) **1978** Piranha **1980** The Howling **1983** Twilight Zone–The Movie (co-director) **1984** Gremlins **1985** Explorers **1987** Amazon Women On The Moon (co-director); Innerspace **1989** The 'Burbs **1990** Gremlins 2: The New Batch **1992** Sleepwalkers (Cameo) **1993** Matinee

Davidovich, Lolita

Actress
Born July 1961
Ontario, Canada

Lolita Davidovich burst onto the scene amid much hype as the Louisiana stripper Blaze Starr, mistress of Governor Earl Long (Paul Newman) in Ron Shelton's likeable romance, *Blaze* (1988). Though the film did not perform as well as hoped, Lolita was a match for her venerable co-star at his wiliest, in a role that called for her to be innocent, sexy, funny, mature and loving.

With her feisty, independent humour, Davidovich might be a rather more voluptuous Katharine Hepburn, but her mix of statuesque sex appeal and down-home charm also suggests Ava Gardner's sweet country cousin. But appearances can be deceptive. Despite an intensive milkshake diet, the actress was the first to admit that she had 'fake everything. Fake hair, fake eyelashes and fake breasts.' She made it all seem natural, however, and carried off the strip routines with aplomb.

Lolita Davidovich didn't quite come from nowhere, but close to it. Her parents, who were divorced when she was ten (she remained with her mother) were Yugoslavian and she grew up speaking Serb-Croat. Determining to become an actress, she moved to Chicago where she took classes, found some stage work and, eventually, billed as Lolita David, began to pick up bit parts in the likes of *Adventures In Babysitting* (1987) and *The Big Town* the same year in which, strangely, she also played a stripper. After six months of auditions and in the face of fierce competition, she landed her lead in *Blaze*. She said that it 'wasn't until ten weeks went by on the movie that I realised I didn't have to do my own laundry'. After her supporting role alongside John Malkovich and Andie MacDowell in *Object of Beauty* and the female lead in Konchalovsky's *The Inner Circle* (both 1991), it seemed unlikely that she would have to worry again on that score. Indeed, her major role as Tom Hulce's wife driven to despair and suicide in the latter, revealed an actress of considerable dramatic potential.

1986 Recruits (bit); **1987** Adventures In Babysitting (GB: A Night On The Town – bit); The Big Town **1990** Blaze **1991** Object Of Beauty **1992** The Inner Circle; Raising Cain **1992/93** Leap Of Faith **1993** Money Men; Younger And Younger

Davis, Brad
(Robert Davis)

Actor
Born 6 November 1949
Tallahassee, Florida
Died 8 September 1991

Brad Davis was proof that the light that burns twice as bright burns half as long. Winning a music talent contest at 17, he worked his way through theatre in Atlanta, Georgia into off-Broadway shows (via the Academy of Dramatic Art in New York) before winning roles in the prestigious mini-series *Roots* and, more significantly, *Sybil* in 1976 which, re-edited and released theatrically in Europe, brought him to the attention of the producers of *Midnight Express* (1978).

As the young American sentenced to a Dante-esque Turkish prison for drug smuggling, he was given the unenviable task of keeping a human focus amid the film's catalogue of atrocities while keeping the audience's sympathy as he himself is drawn into them – at one point biting out an informant's tongue and shaking it between his teeth like a rabid dog. While the film made the careers of director Alan Parker, producer David Puttnam, British actor John Hurt and screenwriter Oliver Stone, Davis was unable to build on his ferociously elemental performance – *A Small Circle of Friends* (1980) was so bland in its nostalgia that it barely got a release and his lack of star quality rendered his cameo in *Chariots Of Fire* (1981) a non-starter.

The turning point in his career was when, against all advice that it was an act of occupational suicide, he took the lead in Fassbinder's vividly stylised gay melodrama, *Querelle* (1983). A deserved critical and commercial disaster, Davis' appearance – more window dummy in a sailor suit than tortured soul discovering his true sexual identity – made him unemployable in mainstream cinema, relegating the actor to small parts in sporadic and largely unmemorable foreign films (when Percy Adlon's quirky 1989 movie, *Rosalie Goes Shopping*, is your best screen credit in a decade, you know your career is in some trouble) and the odd minor TV series. Nonetheless, Brad Davis, especially in maturity, was a pleasing and efficient screen presence, tragically robbed of a future by his premature death from Aids. A brief cameo in *The Player* (filmed shortly before his death) seemed to serve as a fleeting footnote of quality to a career that never managed to fulfil its true potential on the big screen.

1978 Midnight Express **1980** A Small Circle Of Friends **1981** Chariots Of Fire **1983** Querelle **1987** Heart **1988** Cold Steel **1989** Rosalie Goes Shopping; The Rainbow Warrior Conspiracy **1991** Hangfire **1992** The Player (cameo)

Davis, Geena
(Virginia Davis)

Actress
Born 21 January 1957
Wareham, Massachusetts

Although now known for her screen performances this tall, striking actress has also worked as a successful model, starred in her own TV comedy series, *Sara*, in 1985, and is an accomplished musician who plays the flute, piano and organ. Geena Davis' career began after she attended Boston University, where she went on a professional Actor's Training Programme in 1979. From there, she joined the Mount Washington Repertory Company in New England. Her first acting role for the cameras was in an episode of the TV series *Buffalo Bill*, which she also wrote. Then she appeared in a few TV movies before landing a small supporting role in the Oscar-winning comedy *Tootsie* (1982), sharing the on-screen dressing room of Dustin Hoffman's Dorothy.

After this stroke of good fortune she went on to play Chevy Chase's girlfriend in the mystery-comedy *Fletch* (1985). With a background of comic roles behind her, the actress then won another comedy part in the horror spoof *Transylvania 66–5000* (1985), which starred Jeff Goldblum (whom Davis later married). The couple were reunited for *The Fly* (1986), which proved to be one of the most successful horror films of the 80s with Geena playing the girlfriend of scientist Seth Brundle (Goldblum), who finds himself turning into a human fly after an experiment goes wrong. It was a refreshing change to see a strong-minded heroine in place of the usual hysterical bimbo, and Davis' performance was believable enough for her to be asked to appear in the sequel three years later.

With a mixture of roles behind her, ranging from comedy to horror, she met her strangest character yet as a recently deceased woman (married to also-dead Alec Baldwin) in the hilarious Tim Burton bio-exorcist comedy, *Beetlejuice* (1987). It was certainly her most original character to that date, and she admirably stood her ground against scene-stealing Michael Keaton as Beetlejuice himself. The film was a huge success, despite the story being almost indescribable and decidedly off-centre, and the actress began to acquire something of a name in Hollywood.

Her next role, as a Valley Girl who falls in love with an alien (Jeff Goldblum) in Julien Temple's *Earth Girls Are Easy* (1988), was just as wacky, but did not have the wide audience appeal of *Beetlejuice*. With her off-beat screen personality firmly established, it came as no surprise when she won the role of Muriel, the long-fingernailed, dizzy dog-trainer who falls in love with travel writer William Hurt in the romantic comedy *The Accidental Tourist* (1988). She proved that the rule that actors should never compete with children and animals doesn't always hold, working with both in this instance and coming out on top. Her truthful, sensitive and funny portrayal of Muriel won her a deserved Best Supporting Actress Oscar.

Davis died within a few seconds of giving birth at the beginning of *The Fly II* (1989) and the actress, now separated from Goldblum, returned to play a lead in a conventional comedy, as Bill Murray's long-suffering girlfriend in *Quick Change* (1990). But it was in Ridley Scott's feminist comedy-adventure-drama, *Thelma And Louise*, that Geena Davis, sharing the honours (and Oscar nominations) with Susan Sarandon, proved she had become a formidable leading lady for the times. This status was emphasised by her co-starring role with Dustin Hoffman and Andy Garcia in Stephen Frears' *Hero*.

1982 Tootsie **1985** Fletch; Transylvania 6–5000 **1986** The Fly **1987** Beetlejuice **1988** Earth Girls Are Easy; The Accidental To/urist **1989** The Fly II **1990** Quick Change **1991** Thelma And Louise **1992** A League Of Their Own; Hero

Davison, Bruce

Actor
Born 28 June 1946
Philadelphia, Pennsylvania

When Bruce Davison received his Oscar nomination for a heart-wrenching performance in *Longtime Companion* (1990), the first 'mainstream' feature film to deal with the tragic subject of AIDS, it marked something of a return from the wilderness for the thin blonde actor who made an impressive film debut more than 20 years earlier but has since had a fitful screen career.

Davison, educated at Pennsylvania State University and New York University, trained for the theatre at NYU's highly regarded School of the Arts and made his stage debut on Broadway at the age of 21 in *Tiger At The Gate*. While he has never made much of an impact on cinemagoers, his theatrical career has been a fruitful one and he has distinguished himself in works ranging from Shakespeare to American classics and provocative modern dramas. His performance as the pitiably deformed John Merrick in the Broadway production of *The Elephant Man* earned him a Dramalogue Award, as did his work in Los Angeles productions of Larry Kramer's AIDS play, *The Normal Heart*, and *Streamers*, which also brought him Los Angeles Critics Awards.

It was in 1969, in the powerfully disturbing *Last Summer*, that Davison had his first film role, as one of four teenagers (the others were played by Barbara Hershey, Cathy Burns and Richard Thomas) coming of age in a chillingly evil manner, and he was quite good as the 'bad boy'. However, despite making roughly a film each year since, these have been a largely ho-hum string of credits. Prior to *Longtime Companion*, Davison ironically had his biggest success as the weird but touching boy with his rats in the box-office hit *Willard* (1971) and by the mid-80s he was relegated to negligible roles in Ken Russell's *Crimes Of Passion* (1984) and the goofy espionage spoof *Spies Like Us* (1985). In 1978, he received an Emmy nomination for his performance as an escaped POW in the poignant TV movie *Summer Of My German Soldier*, and subsequently notched up a number of television appearances in the 80s, in which, as on film, he has shown to best advantage when playing sensitive souls, victims of circumstance and a caring, sharing kind of guy. His longest-running popular success, however, has been as Dad in the TV spin-off sitcom of *Harry And The Hendersons*.

1969 Last Summer **1970** The Strawberry Statement **1971** Willard **1972** The Jerusalem File; **1973** Ulzana's Raid **1974** Mame **1975** Mother, Jugs And Speed **1977** Grand Jury; Been Down So Long It Looks Like Up To Me **1978** Short Eyes; Brass Target; French Quarter **1981** High Risk **1982** A Texas Legend; Kiss My Grits **1983** Lies **1984** Crimes Of Passion **1985** Spies Like Us **1986** The Ladies Club; The Misfit Brigade **1990** Longtime Companion **1991** Steel And Lace; Oscar **1993** Short Cuts

Day Lewis, Daniel

Actor
Born 29 April 1958
London, England

The son of the distinguished British poet Cecil Day Lewis and the actress Jill Balcon, Daniel Day Lewis was born into intellectually privileged circumstances, and was educated at the progressive private school, Bedales. His background perhaps accounts, at least in part, for his evident intellectual capacity, but his dazzling range as an actor of accomplishment is his own gift, and one which he evidently continues to hone.

Very tall, very dark, very slim, with slightly aquiline features and burningly expressive eyes, he is perhaps closest in general type to another British actor of international repute, Jeremy Irons, but has more distinctive looks and an unpredictable and interesting personality, both on and off the screen. For a time, Day Lewis thought he wanted to be a cabinet-maker, but instead of pursuing that course or attending a university when he finished school, he spent a year doing a succession of manual labourer's jobs, including loading lorries, before enrolling at the Bristol Old Vic drama school. On completing his studies, he began building a stage career in Britain, working at the Bristol Old Vic, the Royal Shakespeare Company, the National Theatre and in London's West End, where he played Guy Bennett in *Another Country*. His first substantial appearance in front of a camera (at the age of 12 he had essayed a ruffian scratching cars with broken bottles in *Sunday, Bloody Sunday*) was as the lead, a young officer in conflict with his superiors during World War I, in Moira Armstrong's feature-length BBC TV film, *How Many Miles To Babylon?* It was an impressive debut, and although more TV and a couple of small screen roles in which he got lost in the vast cast followed, it wasn't until 1985 that Day Lewis commenced what appeared to others to be a meteoric rise.

Cast by James Ivory to play Cecil Vyse, the effete and waspish monocled fiancé of Helena Bonham–Carter in *A Room With A View*, the young actor seized the showy opportunity with both hands, and made a strong impression in a period British film that beguiled America. Audiences could hardly believe it was the same actor when, later that year, he played a gay cockney, hair streaked blond under a cloth cap, seducing an Indian lover in *My Beautiful Laundrette*. If this outrageous, somewhat low-budget and deeply English film, directed by Stephen Frears from a screenplay by the anarchic Hanif Kureishi, was not to everybody's taste, it was nonetheless garlanded with critical praise and became an art-house hit on both sides of the Atlantic. Day Lewis won the New York Critics Award for Best Supporting Actor, jointly for both films, and was now a name with which moviegoers were positively acquainted. He went to France to make Connie Templeman's *Nanou* (1986) before being invited to play the lead in Philip Kaufman's screen version of the Milan Kundera novel *The Unbearable Lightness Of Being* (1988).

Co-starred with Sweden's Lena Olin and France's Juliette Binoche, two outstanding beauties who are also first-class actresses, the actor was virtually never off screen in an epic East European romance with heavily political undertones, and his portrayal of a womanising doctor, stripped of his position after the Prague Spring, was devastating in its application of cold intelligence and simmering sexuality. After that, of course, there was no holding him, but Day Lewis picks his projects carefully and if *Stars And Bars* (1988) turned out to be something of a mistake, his performance the following year as Christy Brown, the disabled child born to a poor Irish family, who turns out to be a gifted writer, was a tour de force and acknowledged as such by critics and audiences everywhere, including the Academy, who gave him the Best Actor Oscar. As the 1990s got under way, it was clear that the film industry had found a British actor with international appeal and rare versatility whose presence, it was to be hoped, would periodically continue to add a touch of class to American movies.

1982 Ghandi **1984** The Bounty **1985** A Room With A View; My Beautiful Laundrette **1986** Nanou **1988** The Unbearable Lightness Of Being; Stars And Bars **1989** My Left Foot; Eversmile, New Jersey **1992** The Last Of The Mohicans **1992/93** The Age Of Innocence

De Mornay, Rebecca

Actress

Born 29 August 1961

Santa Rosa California

After a childhood spent abroad which gave her a European education – she completed her schooling in Austria – Rebecca De Mornay trained as an actress at the Los Angeles branch of the Lee Strasberg Institute. She was then taken on as an apprentice at Coppola's ill-fated Zoetrope Studios and was around during the making of *One From The Heart* (1982) in which she was an understudy – a highly unusual job in the film industry. No doubt, with her heart-shaped face, communicative eyes, provocative sexuality and stunning body, she was shadowing Nastassia Kinski.

Her rise was steady rather than meteoric, but she has qualities that belie her better-known credentials. Her physical attributes, combined with a carapace of toughness and a cool and knowing expression, first showed themselves in *Risky Business* (1983). She played a hooker who organises a brothel for high school boys in the home of innocent Tom Cruise's parents, while initiating him in the joys of physical love. The movie was a sexy teen caper in which Cruise's toothy wholesomeness and De Mornay's upfront sophistication combined to highly enjoyable effect. And it was doubtless this performance which led Roger Vadim to choose her for his American remake of *And God Created Woman* (1988). The film was really rather absurd and

De Mornay no Bardot, but she brought energy and conviction to the role of a jailbird who seduces a respectable Vincent Spano into marriage in order to get her parole, and then withholds her substantial favours from him.

But if De Mornay's name was initially best known to audiences whose preference is for the mildly prurient, she has proved to have a much wider range which, by the end of the 1980s, hadn't yet had a vehicle of sufficient note to make her a household name. Her debut appearance in the nuclear holocaust movie *Testament* (1983), had her as a young wife (to a then unknown Kevin Costner) whose adored tiny baby is one of the first victims of fallout. It was a small role, but one in which she was very affecting; she was also pretty without giving a clue as to her sex symbol possibilities. And in Andrei Konchalovsky's unusual adventure-cum-moral tale about the penal system, *Runaway Train* (1985), she disguised her physical attributes in the service of her role as a female railway worker, unrecognisable with matted mousy hair, dungarees and dirt-covered, freckled face. She began her second decade of work in the firefighting drama, *Backdraft*, with Kurt Russell; but it was as the deranged nanny in *The Hand That Rocks The Cradle* (1992), a deserved runaway hit, that Rebecca De Mornay finally got her big opportunity, relishing every monent given her by the excellent screenplay.

1983 Testament; Risky Business **1985** The Slugger's Wife; Runaway Train; The Trip To Bountiful **1987** Beauty And The Beast **1988** Feds; And God Created Woman **1989** Dealers **1991** Backdraft **1992** The Hand That Rocks The Cradle **1993** Beyond Innocence

De Niro, Robert

Actor
Born 17 August 1943
New York City

For many *the* actor of his generation, Robert De Niro has become, through his absolute dedication to the Method, the natural heir to Brando, Dean and Montgomery Clift. Like these iconic predecessors, De Niro has come to personify the spirit of his times. From the mid-70s to the early 80s the best movie-makers in the world came to him; together they made the most considerable films of the period.

Robert De Niro senior was a painter and a poet. Virginia De Niro also painted; it was with her that two-year-old junior lived when the couple divorced. The junior De Niro grew up in New York's Little Italy district, just a few blocks from his future friend and collaborator Martin Scorsese. By the time he was 16, the boy had already decided to become an actor. He studied at the Dramatic Workshop, the Luther James Studio, the Stella Adler Studio and later at the Actor's Studio. Appearances off-off Broadway followed, and a spell on the TV soap *Search For Tomorrow*, but De Niro's future was to be in the cinema. In 1965 he had a walk-on part in Marcel Carné's *Trois Chambres À Manhattan*, but in fact he had acted in a student film the previous year, *The Wedding Party*, co-directed by Brian De Palma. The film was not edited until 1966, and not released for a further three years, but De Palma came back to De Niro with one of the leads in his independent film *Greetings* (1968), and starred him in the equally anarchic follow-up, *Hi, Mom!* (1970), with De Niro wildly flamboyant as voyeur Jon Rubin. Other assistance came from Shelley Winters, who picked him for a supporting role in his first studio picture, Roger Corman's *Bloody Mama* (1969). A clutch of minor movies followed, then, in 1973, two breakthrough roles: *Bang The Drum Slowly* and *Mean Streets*.

Although John Hancock's baseball weepie, *Bang The Drum Slowly*, is a low-key affair, it was well received at the time as a serious drama, and it was the actor's first starring role in a mainstream picture. He played a catcher dying of Hodgkin's disease, who only wants to play ball. The scenario is sentimental, but De Niro plays against this, essaying an amiable but none too bright character. Stories of his obsessive preparation for a role and total immersion in his character began with this film – for which he won the New York Critics Circle Award as Best Supporting Actor.

Mean Streets was even more significant. An urgent, edgy look at the lower echelons of gangsterdom in New York's Little Italy, it brought together the fledgling actor with up-and-coming director Martin Scorsese. Although the main role went to Harvey Keitel, De Niro's brash Johnny Boy commanded top billing. He is a loud-mouthed, small-time hustler, a gambler and a womaniser, with the fastest grin on the block. Shooting at the lights of the Empire State, boogie-ing in the street, and relishing the sidestreets and alleyways of Italian-American patois, Johnny Boy is intensely alive, but implacably set on a course for self-destruction. The cross-currents and undertows at work in the unparalleled collaboration of Scorsese and De Niro began here, with the director's kinetic, ostentatious camera style and syncopated editing techniques bouncing off De Niro's exploratory delivery, his lightning mood changes, his charm and his danger.

Francis Ford Coppola's *The Godfather Part II* (1974) was a production sufficiently prestigious to validate De Niro's emerging credentials. Entrusted with the responsibility of playing the young Vito Corleone, he re-created Brando's stiff formal postures and measured gestures; the hands masking the chin, the head held back, still, like a python ready to strike. The body language was eloquent, the dialogue, in Italian with only a smattering of English, delivered with Brando's throaty purr. De Niro beat two of his co-stars to win the Best Supporting Actor Academy Award. Inevitably he became the 'new Brando', a sobriquet that stuck to him through collaborations with Coppola, Bertolucci and Kazan – the three directors who had got the best out of Brando. But both *1900* (1976) and Kazan's *The Last Tycoon* (1976) proved disappointingly top heavy, though in the latter De Niro gave a hauntingly interior account of the title role.

If at this stage De Niro was more of a leading actor than he was a star, *Taxi Driver* (1976) changed that. The film was at one with the times, and Travis Bickle, perhaps ironically, became the first of his roles to catch the public imagination. Ironically because, as written by Paul Schrader, Bickle is an empty man, an existentialist cipher dressed up in *film noir* motifs and scrambled through mid-70s angst (Vietnam, Nixon, and urban violence). The taxi cab is a coffin and New York a cesspool. Between Scorsese's hallucinatory visuals and the seduction and bombast of Bernard Herrman's score, De Niro's anti-hero becomes chillingly powerful.

Michael, in *The Deer Hunter* (1978), was a far more mature, subtle study of a similarly alienated character (both might have been inspired by John Wayne's Ethan in *The Searchers*). While director Michael Cimino loses the measure of his material in the Vietnam sequences, the long, beautifully realised first act makes it clear that the roots of disaffection lie in the heartlands, in the unresolved three-way love story and Michael's 'one shot' mentality. De Niro by this time had cast approval (and helped to launch both Meryl Streep and Christopher Walken), and, granted enviable space by his director, he turned in one of his most detailed performances, for which he was nominated for the Best Actor Oscar in 1978.

Before this rigorously repressed characterisation, De Niro cut loose as sax-man Jimmy Doyle in Scorsese's unexpected, under-rated *New York, New York* (1977). Doyle is an irresistible egoist who woos and wows Liza Minnelli's Francine Evans. Funny and furious by turns, he revels in the opportunity to exhibit his range and humour without sacrificing emotional authenticity – the breakdown of their relationship takes the musical into new ground.

But *Raging Bull* (1980) remains this partnership's greatest accomplishment. De Niro urged his friend to take on the project, and together they transformed the story of 1950s boxing champion Jake La Motta into a devastating critique of male frustration, aggression, and the codes that engender them. De Niro's La Motta is the ultimate expression of the Method, his protean qualities taken to incredible physical extremes so that the ageing, paunchy character of the film's conclusion is unidentifiable with the actor who plays him (De Niro put on more than 60 lb over his normal body weight; he also learned to box, and actually contested three genuine fights). Paradoxically, the very lengths to which he went to hide himself ensured his high profile as a chameleon-actor. He was rewarded with the Oscar for Best Actor.

Raging Bull is widely regarded as the best film of the 80s, and its virtuosity tends to overshadow the austere *King Of Comedy* (1982), in fact an anti-comedy, and something of a masterpiece without an audience. This financial disaster unjustly overshadowed Scorsese's career for most of the next decade, and De Niro did not work with him again until *GoodFellas* in 1990. (He passed up Jesus in *The Last Temptation Of Christ* because he could not relate to the role.) The conservative climate in Hollywood after *Heaven's Gate* (1980) was not conducive to the kind of ambitious film-making De Niro had pursued, but in truth the actor did relax after La Motta. Perhaps, like Brando after *Last Tango In Paris* (1973), he had little more of himself to give; or perhaps he felt that he could go no further with his project for absolute authenticity; conceivably he was simply exhausted . . . but De Niro's acting displayed less urgency in the mid-80s; his roles didn't plug into America the way they used to. He gave polished, wonderfully crafted star turns in *Brazil* (1984), *Angel Heart* (1987) and *The Untouchables* (1987); courted the box office in *Falling In Love* (1984) and *Stanley And Iris* (1990), and put himself in the hands of English directors Alan Parker, Roland Joffe and David Jones. *The Mission* (1986) and Neil Jordan's *We're No Angels* (1990) were the first evidence of a limit to his range (coincidentally he was a reprobate who donned a priest's cassock in both), while in *Jacknife* (1989) it was sad to see him repeating himself to no great purpose. The one commercial hit of this period, *Midnight Run* (1988), was a breathtakingly ingenious comic adventure that revealed the star at his brightest – even so, this was coasting. Only Sergio Leone's magnificent *Once Upon A Time In America* (1983) rekindled the passion, the scale and the sheer bravura of past triumphs, with De Niro aging 30 years as a gangster returning to New York to reconcile himself with his past.

Although Robert De Niro is only the second lead, *GoodFellas* reclaims the high ground; so too does *Awakenings* (1990), in which he gives a touching performance as a man who wakes up after a 30-year sleep-like state. He began the 90s with a schedule booked solid for at least a couple of years. His senenth collaboration with Scorsese saw him over the top and down the other side as the cunning tattooed psychopath, Max Cady, in *Cape Fear* (1991), and won him another Oscar nomination. His own TriBeCa building in Lower Manhattan comprises a restaurant, film centre, and office space to let, and it will be De Niro's headquarters for his next big challenge: a promised move behind the camera, to produce and direct.

1965 Trois Chambres À Manhattan **1966** The Wedding Party **1968** Greetings **1969** Bloody Mama **1970** Hi, Mom! **1971** Jennifer On My Mind; The Gang That Couldn't Shoot Straight; Born To Win **1973** Bang The Drum Slowly; Mean Streets **1974** Sam's Song aka The Swap; The Godfather Part II **1976** Taxi Driver; 1900; The Last Tycoon **1977** New York, New York **1978** The Deer Hunter **1980** Raging Bull **1981** True Confessions **1982** The King Of Comedy **1983** Once Upon A Time In America **1984** Brazil; Falling In Love **1986** The Mission **1987** Angel Heart; The Untouchables **1988** Midnight Run **1989** Jacknife **1990** Stanley And Iris; We're No Angels; GoodFellas; Awakenings **1991** Backdraft; Guilty By Suspicion; Cape Fear **1992** Mistress; Mad Dog And Glory; Night And The City **1992/93** This Boy's Life; A Bronx Tale (also director)

De Palma, Brian

Director
Born 11 September 1944
Newark, New Jersey

By the late 1970s the critical jury on Brian De Palma was still out; by the mid-80s he was in process of being found guilty with mitigating circumstances; with the 90s under way there was no plea-bargaining with the arbiters of taste as they variously accused him of voyeurism and sensationalism and pursued him with cries of pornographer and, worse, misogynist (a charge that took root in 1980 when feminists picketed the cinemas showing *Dressed To Kill*). On the artistic front, De Palma came to be regarded as a shamelessly derivative stylist, even while his technical expertise was acknowledged, and many a raised eyebrow greeted the news that he was to direct Tom Wolfe's scathing satire of New York life, mores and morals, *The Bonfire Of The Vanities* (1990).

In short, few major mainstream commercial directors arouse such strong hostility. Undoubtedly a master of both the pacing and construction of the (generally bloody) set-pieces within his films, De Palma is clearly fascinated by violence, both criminal and sexual, and it is indeed difficult on occasion to defend the director against certain accusations. In *Body Double* (1984) for example, the climactic blood-letting takes the form of eviscerating a woman with a large electric drill – a sequence presented with graphic brutality and nauseating gloss. And the film, as a whole, degenerates from a promising premise (the pull and danger of voyeurism) into an untidy muddle that offers little justification for what has gone before. Then, too, in *Blow Out* (1981), Nancy Allen (De Palma's then wife) not only keeps a rendezvous, intended for his entrapment, with a psychopathic sex killer, but is allowed to die moments before her rescuer (John Travolta) reaches her. If this downbeat ending can be read as cruelty to women, it might also, with some validity, be interpreted as a daring refusal to make a fairy-tale concession to the demands of commercialism. In fact, De Palma subverts the function of the mythical hero with genuinely unnerving results.

The director openly admits to his numerous borrowings from Hitchcock (notably the shower scene and the continuous art gallery take with Angie Dickinson in *Dressed To Kill*), and his 'homage' to Eisenstein (the so-called 'Odessa Steps' sequence in 1987's *The Untouchables*), which have led to his numerous detractors calling him a hollow and superficial film-maker, resorting to second-hand and inferior versions of the techniques and vision that marked his models as geniuses of the cinema. Technically, the expertise of his swooping camera and a predilection for split-screen techniques – which first made its mark in *Sisters* (1973), considered by many to be his best film – are undeniably effective in the 70s collection of occult-laden subjects in which it seemed he would specialise (*Phantom Of The Paradise*, 1974, *Obsession* and *Carrie* in 1976, *The Fury*, 1978).

Brian De Palma was originally one of a select group of tyro directors who were dubbed the Movie Brats – the others were Spielberg, Scorsese, Coppola and George Lucas. He began by making shorts while a student at Columbia University, then, continuing his studies at Sarah Lawrence College, he persuaded a wealthy female student to finance a feature. Shot in black and white at a cost of $100,000, it was called *The Wedding Party* (1963), never found distribution but for one New York theatre in 1968, and starred two young unknowns named Robert De Niro and Jill Clayburgh. After college, De Palma settled into the New York scene, doing odd jobs and making documentaries, one of which earned sufficient to finance his second independent feature, *Murder À La Mod* (1967), which suffered a fate similar to that of the first. In 1968 he teamed up with Charles Hirsch, a young producer, and made *Greetings* for only $43,000. Improvisatory in style and suffering visually from its lack of budget, the movie nonetheless struck lucky. It found a distributor and became a modest hit, recouping its cost several times over and paving the way for *Hi, Mom!* (1969). Both movies, starring De Niro, dealt in contemporary themes and concerns of the young such as the draft and sexual matters, with *Hi, Mom!* satirical in tone. They were counter-culture movies that mirrored their time and place, and boded well for De Palma.

By 1970 he was in Hollywood with a contract to make *Get To Know Your Rabbit*, a droll, rather fey affair about a bored businessman who becomes a magician. The movie starred Tommy Smothers and Orson Welles, with Katharine Ross supplying the female interest, and De Palma handled the whole thing with tongue-in-cheek deftness. But nothing resulted from the movie which was ill-treated by the distributors and has since become a minor cult on TV, and De Palma found himself back in New York making *Sisters*, an inexpensive thriller which started him on the next phase of his career. From *Sisters* through to *Body Double* the movies, ever more technically proficient, progressed from the bloodiness of *guignol* to that of the slasher school, interrupted only by the much-maligned baroque – some would say overblown – remake of *Scarface* (1983) starring Al Pacino and revealing Michelle Pfeiffer as an actress to watch. (De Palma has always had a superb eye for casting, though many feel it deserted him with his choice of Tom Hanks for *Bonfire's* Sherman McCoy.)

After *Body Double*, it seemed that the director might be looking to expand his horizons. First came *Wise Guys* (1984), a wacky comedy about a couple of bumbling mobsters. It starred Danny DeVito and was quite unlike the director's previous efforts. *The Untouchables*, inspired, like the TV series of the same name, by the work of FBI special agent Eliot Ness, was a period (20s Chicago) cops 'n' robbers tale of epic proportions which showcased Kevin Costner, reunited De Palma with De Niro (a memorable Al Capone), co-starred Sean Connery, gave Andy Garcia his first prominent role, and showed De Palma as a superb architect and choreographer of operatic bloodshed.

Coming perhaps too late in the spate of Vietnam revelation movies, *Casualties Of War* (1989) made less impact than it should have done, and unleashed a new stream of venom against De Palma in the wake of the movie's rape scene – handled, in fact, without a trace of salaciousness. Like the war it depicts and the events on which it focuses, the film is uncompromisingly nasty, and all the more powerful for that, but is badly marred by a hamfisted and ludicrously sentimental epilogue for which there is no accounting.

It is indisputable that De Palma's work displays little interest in offering moral directives; neither do the films proffer love, loyalty or dignity as recipes for salvation. There *is* no salvation, at best there is revenge. The recipe is not pretty, but it is never boring, sometimes interesting and often gripping. However, with Brian De Palma stranded in the ruins of *Bonfire Of The Vanities*, and savage opprobrium heaped gleefully on his head from all quarters, it was difficult to predict what route this controversial director would take next. In the event, he opted for a return to what, arguably, he does best, applying spellbinding imagery to a demented thriller, *Raising Cain* (1992).

1967 Murder À La Mod (w/d) **1968** Greetings (also co-writer); The Wedding Party (made in 1963; co-writer, co-director) **1969** Hi Mom! (co-writer) **1972** Get To Know Your Rabbit (made in 1970) **1973** Sisters (w/d) **1974** Phantom Of The Paradise (w/d) **1976** Obsession; Carrie **1978** The Fury **1980** Dressed To Kill **1981** Blow Out **1983** Scarface **1984** Body Double **1987** The Untouchables **1989** Casualties Of War **1990** Bonfire Of The Vanities **1992** Rasing Cain (w/d)

DeLuise, Dom

Actor
Born 1 August 1933
Brooklyn, New York

Chubby, and now, in middle age, rotund, Dom DeLuise is a gifted, energetic comic actor with a range from the highest of camp to the lowest of scoundrels. A veteran of stage, TV and film, he is best known for the work he has done with actor-directors Mel Brooks, Burt Reynolds and Gene Wilder.

Born in Brooklyn to Italian parents, he nursed an early ambition to become an actor, attending New York's High School of the Performing Arts (immortalised in Alan Parker's *Fame*, 1980) before moving on to Tufts University. From there he progressed to his first professional engagements at the Cleveland Playhouse, where he spent two seasons. But despite the success of his burgeoning theatre career he chose instead to enrol at Brooklyn College in order to become a biology teacher and it was only the offer of a part he couldn't resist, in the off-Broadway play *The Jackass*, that coaxed him back to acting. He went on to appear in other theatrical comedies, including the show *Another Evening With Harry Stoones*, featuring newcomer Barbra Streisand, and before long had launched his TV career by playing a bumbling magician, Dominick the Great, on *The Garry Moore Show*. He quickly found himself a much-in-demand television performer, appearing in programmes such as *The Tonight Show* and *The Dean Martin Show*, and was given his own TV special, *The Bar-Rump Bump*.

It was just a matter of time before the rising young funnyman made the crossover into films but, ironically, when he did it was in a straight role. Appearing alongside Henry Fonda and Walter Matthau, DeLuise played Seargeant Collins, the man who sells the plans for destroying the Air Force in Sidney Lumet's tense drama *Fail-Safe* (1964). But it was in humorous roles that he was best served, and his facility for broad, slapstick comedy found a perfect outlet in some of the better Mel Brooks films. The two first met, and immediately became friends, when Brooks cast the actor in *The Twelve Chairs* (1970), a mediocre comedy elevated by DeLuise's delightful performance as the main rival to impoverished nobleman Ron Moody. Their collaboration continued, with the actor gracing such spoofs as the hilarious *Blazing Saddles* (1974), the less effective *Silent Movie* (1976) and the sporadically side-splitting *History of the World – Part I* (1981, in which he portrayed a gloriously debauched Emperor Nero) with his over-the-top, hammy persona; he also lent his voice to 1987's *Spaceballs*. Doubtless because of his frendship with Brooks and his wife Anne Bancroft, DeLuise was cast as the lead in Bancroft's 1980 directorial debut, *Fatso*. In a tailor-made role, the actor portrayed Dominic DeNapoli, an obese man attempting to lost weight after the death of his equally fat cousin. The film, however, was an uneasy blend of laughs and drama revealing a tendency in both writer-director and actor towards sentimentality. The previous year, DeLuise had had more success directing his own film (a feat he has to date not repeated) *Hot Stuff*, a nice little movie in which he plays a Miami cop assigned to an underworld 'sting' and which also featured his three sons by his actress wife, Carol Arthur.

For another Brooks collaborator, Gene Wilder, the actor has also provided hilarious support. In *The Adventure of Sherlock Holmes' Smarter Brother* (1975) he played a florid opera singer, and livened up 1977's *The World's Greatest Lover*; and he appeared in drag as Great Aunt Kate in the otherwise abysmal *Haunted Honeymoon* (1986). As for his working relationship with Burt Reynolds, it got off to a cracking start with the *The End* (1978). An outrageous black comedy, it starred Reynolds (who also directed) as a man who decides to kill himself when he learns he is dying of cancer; but it is DeLuise, playing the cheerful schizophrenic Reynolds befriends in a sanitarium, who really steals the show. None of their four subsequent partnerings in any way compared, although the substandard *Cannonball Run II* (1984) did give DeLuise the chance to show off his remarkable talent for mimicry when he sent up Marlon Brando's 'Godfather'.

His substantial filmography notwithstanding, the actor has throughout his career maintained his stage and television work, including his own series, *Lotsa Luck*. In the late 80s, although he seemed to be favouring voice work (on such animated films as *An American Tale*, 1986, *Oliver and Company*, 1988, and *All Dogs Go to Heaven*, 1989), his appearance opposite Gene Hackman and Dan Aykroyd in 1990's *Loose Cannons*, as low-life witness-to-murder Harry 'The Hippo' Gutterman, indicated that he planned to keep 'em laughing for a good while to come.

1964 Fail-Safe; Diary of a Bachelor (bit) **1966** The Glass Bottom Boat **1967** The Busy Body **1968** What's So Bad About Feeling Good? **1970** The Twelve Chairs; Norwood **1971** Who Is Harry Kellerman And Why Is He Saying Those Terrible Things About Me? **1972** Every Little Crook and Nanny **1974** Blazing Saddles **1975** The Adventure of Sherlock Holmes' Smarter Brother **1976** Silent Movie **1977** The World's Greatest Lover **1978** The End; The Cheap Detective; Sextette **1979** Hot Stuff (also director); The Muppet Movie (cameo) **1980** The Last Married Couple in America; Wholly Moses; Smokey and the Bandit II; Fatso **1981** History of the World – Part I; The Cannonball Run **1982** The Best Little Whorehouse in Texas **1984** Cannonball Run II; Johnny Dangerously **1986** Haunted Honeymoon **1987** My African Adventure; Tassinaro A New York/A Taxi Driver in New York (Italy) **1990** Loose Cannons **1991** Autobahn
d)

Demme, Jonathan

Director
Born 22 February 1944
Baldwin, New York

While many of his contemporaries moved into films via advertising, at least Jonathan Demme (who originally trained to be a vet) had the virtue of starting off in film publicity through a chance meeting with Joseph E. Levine. Soon he was cutting trailers (which taught him both visual economy and what he should and should not shoot), writing his first script, *The Hot Box* for Roger Corman's New World Pictures in 1972, and directing *Caged Heat* in 1974, courtesy of the maestro's keen eye for talented newcomers who would work cheaply and quickly. Despite schlock titles, low budgets and tight schedules, these ventures allowed Demme the freedom to hint at the panache for quirky characterisation and wry satire on blue-collar social conventions that came to the fore with his often delightful, Capraesque *Citizens Band* (1977) and the very wonderful *Melvin And Howard* (1980).

The latter avoided the obvious temptations to exploit Howard Hughes' eccentricities and celebrated the trials and tribulations of perennial loser Melvin Dummar (Paul Le Mat) with real warmth and affection for his failings as well as his successes; throughout his work, Demme has been one of the few modern directors to really *like* his characters without, for the most part, sentimentalising them or smoothing away their rougher edges. The critical and modest commercial success of the film gave him a second chance at the mainstream (the first, the excellent but slightly too Hitchcockian 1979 thriller *Last Embrace*, ironically, quickly found itself the supporting feature to *Motel Hell*), but the result, *Swing Shift* (1984) was fairly disastrous. Halfway through shooting, the stars, Goldie Hawn and Kurt Russell, fell in love and suddenly the director's homage to women war workers turned into a romantic comedy over which he had no control.

Two concert movies later, he made an impressive comeback with the dangerous romantic comedy, *Something Wild* (1986), that went beyond the screwball opening to show the pain and despair beneath the regulated conformity (Jeff Daniels) and outrageous zaniness (Melanie Griffith) of its characters, en route to a surprisingly dark ending that left some critics and many audiences cold – one wag complained that it was like halfway through a fun date having your girlfriend pull a gun on you. The production company, Orion, stood behind Demme and the studio became his home, allowing him final cut and artistic freedom and receiving prestigious, successful films in return. He chose to begin the new decade producing *Miami Blues* (1990) before making the stunning and deeply unsettling *The Silence Of The Lambs*, changing gear to a narrative-driven style of directing that surprised those in the industry who had felt him miscast with such an intense psychological thriller, and winning all four major Academy Awards (Picture, Director, Actor, Actress) in the process.

1974 Caged Heat aka Renegade Girls (w/d) **1975** Crazy Mama **1976** Fighting Mad (w/d) **1977** Citizens Band aka Handle With Care **1979** Last Embrace **1980** Melvin And Howard **1984** Swing Shift; Stop Making Sense **1986**

Something Wild; Swimming To Cambodia **1988** Married To The Mob **1991** The Silence Of The Lambs **1992** Cousin Bobby

Dempsey, Patrick

Actor

Born 1966

Lewiston, Maine

This eager-faced actor seems to have cornered the market in loveable, off-beat characters, playing a series of incorrigible youngsters who have a way with women. Although most people will remember him for his roles in comedies such as *Can't Buy Me Love* (1987) and *Loverboy* (1989), that only require a beguiling smile and comic timing, the actor has an impressive list of performing credits stemming back to his high school years in Maine.

As well as becoming the state downhill skiing champion, Patrick Dempsey earned a reputation for being a clown around school, giving impromptu displays of juggling, puppetry and magic, and later performing at Elks clubs and community organisations. He also won second prize at the 1981 International Jugglers Competition, and from there took a turn away from undiluted comedy to be cast by the Maine Acting Company in their interpretation of *On Golden Pond*. He continued in theatre, winning roles in acclaimed plays that included *Torch Song Trilogy* in San Francisco, and then joining a touring company performing Neil Simon's *Brighton Beach Memoirs*.

In 1985, Dempsey made his film debut in a small role in the comedy about Catholic school life in 1960s Brooklyn, *Heaven Help Us* (1985), alongside seasoned actors like Donald Sutherland, and up-and-coming players Kevin Dillon and Andrew McCarthy. From here he moved to the small screen, debuting in a made-for-TV movie (*A Fighting Chance*), and then, in 1986, joining the cast of the series *Fast Times At Ridgemont High*, based on the film of the same name. Dempsey was nominated for an Emmy during the year he acted on the show, and he then returned to feature films, making a few brief appearances before he was cast in the lead role in *The Woo Woo Kid* (1987). Directed by Phil Alden Robinson (who later made *Field Of Dreams*), the movie told the true-life story of Sonny Wisecarver, a 14-year-old who bigamously married two married women in their 20s during World War II. This charmingly off-beat tale indicated the type of roles at which Dempsey would later excel, that of an open-mouthed innocent who does it all for love, without often thinking of the consequences. His engaging performance led to more of the same, most notably a comic performance in *Can't Buy Me Love* (1987), as nerdy Ronald, the boy who pays the prettiest girl in town to be his date for a month and then undergoes a dramatic transformation into the hunk of the school; and as pizza delivery boy Randy in Joan Micklin Silver's *Loverboy* (1989). This hilarious comedy-farce was Dempsey's most successful role to date, although really the film was just an 80s update of *The Woo Woo Kid* story, with Randy a teenager trying to earn enough money to return to college by romancing lonely Beverly Hills housewives who give him $200 tips when they order his 'pizza'. Dempsey was the undoubted star of the show, despite competition from a female line-up that included Kirstie Alley, Barbara Carrera and Carrie Fisher, and the film confirmed him as a young talent to watch. The actor has used the fact that he does not have classic good looks to his advantage, and has established himself in comic roles that seem to suit his personality and allow him to put some of his juggling and performing skills to good use.

1985 Heaven Help Us aka Catholic Boys **1987** Meatballs III; The Woo Woo Kid aka In The Mood; Can't Buy Me Love **1988** In A Shallow Grave; Some Girls **1989** Happy Together; Loverboy **1990** Coupe De Ville **1991** Run; Mobsters: The Evil Empire **1992** R.S.V.P. **1992/93** Face The Music

Dennehy, Brian

Actor

Born 9 July 1939

Bridgeport, Connecticut

'I think also he enjoyed himself immensely and won't go back to playing New York cops again, he'll want big, juicy parts,' commented Peter Greenaway, director of *The Belly Of An Architect* (1987), which cast Brian Dennehy as Stourley Kracklite, a celebrated American architect in Rome dying from cancer of the stomach. It proved that a supporting actor of Dennehy's considerable talents could command a whole film when given the chance, and revealed a hitherto unsuspected range. Nevertheless, he did go back to playing cops (and heavies), something he was built to do.

Dennehy's commanding bulk, authoritative manner and powerful personality had gained him notice, even in the smallest of roles, since his screen debut as a football player in *Semi-Tough* (1977). He had started acting while a student at Columbia University in New York. After graduating, he was conscripted into the Marine Corps, serving in Vietnam from 1965 to 1966. During that period, he broadcast as the Dear America voice to the home front. Back in the USA, he completed his studies at Yale, paying his way with odd jobs, from working on the Stock Exchange to driving a truck.

Theatre work came in off-off Broadway plays, before he got a big break on Broadway in *Streamers*, the David Rabe play set in an army training camp. He then moved on to TV, appearing in more than 25 films, as well as gradually climbing up the cast list in the movies, from the sympathetic barman listening to Dudley Moore's problems in *'10'* (1979) to the bullyboy sheriff Teasle, who makes the mistake of running Rambo out of town in *First Blood* (1982). In the same year, in *Split Image*, he was permitted to reveal a more vulnerable side for the same director, Ted Kotcheff, when he played the father of a son brainwashed by a religious sect. This was followed by his iron-fisted American policeman abroad in *Gorky Park* (1983), and other imposing roles – pursuing outlaws in *Silverado* and as a very down-to-earth extraterrestrial in *Cocoon* (both 1985). He took two contrasting leads in two contrasting films in 1987, the aforementioned *The Belly Of An Architect* – especially magnificent in a drunken scene at an open-air restaurant where he confronts two women eating a meal and exposes his huge belly, saying 'Feel it, it's not eating you but it's eating me' – and the LA detective and crime novelist Dennis Meachum in *Best Seller*, finding himself in an uneasy relationship with a sleazy hit man (James Woods).

Although Dennehy soon disappears in *Miles From Home* (1988) by dying, he made a deep impression as the owner of an Iowan farm greeting Khrushchev. Then he was back to playing cops again; in the small but important role of Harrison Ford's superior in *Presumed Innocent*, and top-billed again in *The Last Of The Finest* (both 1990), giving a powerhouse performance as a veteran LA cop in the narcotics unit, disillusioned by the compromises and corruption that have invaded his once honourable profession.

1977 Semi-Tough; Looking For Mr Goodbar **1978** F.I.S.T.; Foul Play **1979** '10'; The Jericho Mile; Butch And Sundance – The Early Days **1980** Little Miss Marker **1982** First Blood; Split Image **1983** Gorky Park; Never Cry Wolf **1984** Finders Keepers; The River Rat **1985** Cocoon; Silverado; Twice In A Lifetime **1986** F/X: Murder By Illusion; Legal Eagles; The Check Is In The Mail **1987** Best Seller; The Belly Of An Architect; Lion Of Africa; The Man From Snowy River Part II **1988** Miles From Home; The Artisan; Cocoon: The Return **1989** Seven Minutes **1990** Presumed Innocent; The Last Of The Finest (GB: Blue Heat) **1991** FX 2: The Deadly Art Of Illusion **1992** Gladiator **1992/93** Triumph Of The Heart; Foreign Affairs

Dennis, Sandy
(Sandra Dale Dennis)

Actress
Born 27 April 1937
Hastings, Nebraska
Died 2 March 1992

Having played a supporting role to Natalie Wood and Warren Beatty in Kazan's *Splendor In The Grass* (1961), Sandy Dennis won the Academy Award for Best Supporting Actress in only her second film, *Who's Afraid Of Virgina Woolf?* (1966). The five-year gap is explained by the fact that Dennis was primarily a stage actress, whose substantial Broadway career had already won her two Tony Awards in two successive years (1963 and 1964) for *A Thousand Clowns and Any Wednesday*.

She began her acting career in local stock companies in Nebraska before becoming a student at the Actors Studio in New York, from which she emerged as an archetypal exponent of the Method – intense and nervy, and having perfected a distinctive and, in the opinion of some, intensely irritating, vocal delivery in the stammer-mumble style which made her success in stage comedy somewhat surprising. Her neurasthenic personality, however, has proved capable of adjusting itself to roles both tough and vulnerable over the years and, if it is too extreme to have guaranteed major screen stardom, it has also proved ideal for her best vehicles, beginning with the bewildered young academic wife of George Segal, enduring the Burton-Taylor onslaught in *Virginia Woolf*.

That Oscar-winning success was followed with some substantial lead roles in the 60s, notably as a teacher in a rough New York school in *Up The Down Staircase* (1967). She was a young woman alone and pregnant in a damp and misty London in the British-made adaptation of a Margaret Drabble novel, *A Touch Of Love* (1969); and an unexpected but successful choice for the screen version of D.H. Lawrence's *The Fox* (1968), locked in a lesbian relationship with Anne Heywood. But neither of these films scored for her (although *The Fox* made money for its producer), and her screen career began gradually to fade away during the 70s and, even more so, the 80s – although she began the decade with a substantial role in Alan Alda's *The Four Seasons* (1981), and followed that immediately, alongside Cher and Karen Black, with Altman's *Come Back To The Five And Dime, Jimmy Dean, Jimmy Dean* (1982).

Thereafter, Sandy Dennis virtually disappeared off the Hollywood map – until, that is, Woody Allen gave her the part of Gena Rowlands' long-lost friend in *Another Woman* (1988). The once-youthful honey blonde was now a slightly blowsy middle-aged woman, her distinctive qualities intact but aged in the wood, and she delivered one of her best screen performances in her cameo appearance as an embittered, heavy-drinking actress. She subsequently appeared in Bob Balaban's *Parents*, and as the nagging mother in *976 Evil*, directed by Robert 'Freddy Krueger' Englund.

In 1991, despite her battle with cancer, she made a cameo appearance as Charles Bronson's wife in *Indian Runner* for first-time director Sean Penn, before her sad death at the age of 55.

1961 Splendor In The Grass **1966** Who's Afraid Of Virginia Woolf? **1967** Up The Down Staircase **1968** The Fox; Sweet November **1969** That Cold Day In The Park; A Touch Of Love aka Thank You All Very Much **1970** The Out-Of-Towners **1971** The Only Way Out Is Dead **1975** Mr Sycamore **1976** Nasty Habits; God Told Me To **1977** Demon; The Three Sisters **1981** The Four Seasons **1982** Come Back To The Five And Dime, Jimmy Dean, Jimmy Dean **1988** Another Woman; Parents **1989** 976 Evil **1991** Indian Runner

Depp, Johnny

Actor, singer
Born 9 June 1963
Owensboro, Kentucky

'He's the kind of guy that every girl wants, but shouldn't marry!!' read the posters of John Waters' *Cry-Baby* (1989). As Wade 'Cry-Baby' Walker, the most feared and revered tough guy in the schoo', Johnny Depp made an impression beyond the teeny-bopper crowd that had previously known him only as a pop idol. In his leather jacket, his hair in a DA with a kiss curl, he not only sang (ironically, lip-synching to someone else's voice) and danced dynamically in Waters' kitschy 50s homage, but played the role to the hilt. He was especially effective telling his girlfriend (Amy Locane) from the other side of the tracks why he only produces a single tear from one eye.

Kentucky-born Depp moved to Miramar, Florida when he was six, arriving at the age of 20 in Los Angeles, intent on becoming a rock musician. It didn't take him long before he found himself voted by *US* magazine one of the 'Ten Sexiest Bachelors In The Entertainment Industry'. His transition from rocker to actor came at the urging of his friend Nicolas Cage, who advised him to meet his agent. Depp took his advice and was very soon cast in Wes Craven's *A Nightmare On Elm Street* (1984), as one of the teenagers terrified to fall asleep lest mad Freddy materialises. This was followed by the small role of a young and innocent soldier in Oliver Stone's *Platoon* (1986).

Alternating singing with acting, he was nominated as one of *Rolling Stone* magazine's 'Hot Faces of 1988' while appearing as Officer Tom Hanson in the TV series *21 Jump Street*. John Waters, who had never heard of Depp, came across a photo of the baby-faced, good-looking pop idol in the pages of a teen magazine, and knew immediately that he had found the star of his next picture. It was on the strength of *Cry-Baby* that *Batman* director Tim Burton offered Depp the title role in *Edward Scissorhands* (1991). The young star, playing opposite his girlfriend Winona Ryder, brought an effective little-boy poignancy to the part (originally offered to Tom Cruise) of an innocent Frankenstein monster of the suburbs, with ten-inch scissors for hands.

1984 A Nightmare On Elm Street **1986** Platoon **1989** Cry Baby **1990** Edward Scissorhands **1992** American Dreamers **1992/93** Benny And Joon

Derek, Bo
(Mary Cathleen Collins)

Actress
Born 20 November 1955
Long Beach, California

There was a joke going around at the time of the release of '*10*' (1979) that went: 'What is 10, 9, 8, 7, 6 . . .?' Answer: 'Bo Derek ageing.' However cruel, the crack was accurate, since all her roles have, to date, consisted of little more than just looking her ravishing, voluptuous, statuesque, blonde, blue-eyed self in various stages of *déshabillée*. In fact, her career dipped into virtual non-existence as she passed the dangerous age of 30. Her husband, John Derek, 29 years her senior, had also seen his film career wane as he lost his prettyboy looks but, for one short moment in '*10*', the display of Bo Derek in her one-piece bathing suit and Afro-plaited hair brought her international fame.

She met and married John Derek while in her teens. He became her manager, and refused script after script as unworthy of her talents until Blake Edwards offered him *'10'*. (She had only appeared once previously, in a minor part in *Orca – Killer Whale* in 1977.) In '*10*' she played Dudley Moore's ideal woman, the ten out of ten of the title. Her seduction of Moore takes place against the background music of Ravel's Bolero, which she refers to as 'the most descriptive sex music ever written'. He cannot rise to the occasion, she pulls his hair painfully, her braids get in his face and the love-making is variously interrupted by his having to put the record of Bolero back to the beginning, to unstick the record and say 'hi' to her hospitalised husband on the phone. The scene is the highlight of the movie because of the incongruous spectacle of the maladroit, dwarfish Moore trying to make love to the beautiful blonde giantess.

She reprised her dreamgirl image in a snide and less funny comedy, *A Change Of Seasons* (1980), based on an Erich Segal script about a married college professor (Anthony Hopkins) who takes a mistress (Derek). For those interested, she has a revealing scene in a bathtub.

When *Tarzan, The Ape Man* (1981) was advertised with the slogan 'The most exciting pair in the jungle', we were back to the days of Jane Russell and Jayne Mansfield when posters advertising their films carried such *doubles entendres*. Certainly Bo's Jane was one of the first to match her jungle mate chest for chest. She herself produced, and her husband directed and photographed this utterly silly 'Playboy' version of the classic tale, which concentrated on the leading lady rather than on the king of the jungle, played with an air of bemusement by muscular Miles O'Keeffe.

'I'm still a virgin,' she claims as Jane, and she continued to keep her maidenhead intact in the even more risible *Bolero* (1984), in which she played a wealthy young girl travelling the world to find a man worthy enough to receive the sacrifice of her virginity. Again directed and photographed by John Derek, and produced by its star, the film managed to display her body but very little was seen of her acting abilities and, indeed, there is some doubt as to whether she possesses any. Certainly, her career to date is distinguished by the paucity of her appearances, as well as that of her performances.

1977 Orca Killer Whale **1979** '10' **1980** A Change Of Seasons **1981** Tarzan, The Ape Man **1984** Bolero **1990** Ghosts Can't Do It

Dern, Bruce

Actor

Born 4 June 1936

Chicago, Illinois

From his first appearance on the big screen in Elia Kazan's *Wild River* (1960) as a thuggish yokel who beats up Montgomery Clift, it was clear that he was not only a really nasty piece of work but a nutter as well. Mind you, he always got what was coming to him in the end. He had his head bashed in by a poker after attempting rape in Alfred Hitchcock's *Marnie* (1964) and his hands chopped off after persecuting Bette Davis in *Hush . . . Hush Sweet Charlotte* (1965). He was a psychotic cretin in a series of Westerns – killed by John Wayne in *The War Wagon* (1967), hunted by Clint Eastwood in *Hang 'Em High* (1968) and outwitted by James Garner in *Support Your Local Sheriff!* (1969). In two Roger Corman movies, *The Wild Angels* (1966) and *The Trip* (1967), he had the wild look of someone on speed, drugs and bikes, and in *Psych-Out* (1968), from the Corman stable, he played another acid-head whose death is his ultimate trip.

Bruce Dern's high-powered background could not be further from the overheated world he inhabits on screen. His grandfather had been governor of Utah and he was the nephew of Roosevelt's Secretary of War, and the distinguished poet-playwright Archibald MacLeish. Marching to his own drum, he dropped out of college and took up acting, studying with Lee Strasberg and Elia Kazan at the Actors's Studio. 'Method acting enables you to find the things which will relax you, unlock you, and let all the private emotion come out,' he commented. 'It has to do with being able to recall the emotions and sensations of a particular incident, but it takes about five years of total concentration to learn how to do it.'

He didn't have to wait too long before he began getting supporting roles on stage and TV, and his angular features and combustible energy soon cast him as scrawny heavies. But by the early 70s his persona was translated into the counter-culture of the day. When his friend Jack Nicholson made his directorial debut with *Drive He Said* (1971), Dern was effectively cast as the bullying, latent homosexual basketball coach who wants to win at all costs. He was able to extend his range further by giving a detailed performance as Nicholson's hustler brother in *The King Of Marvin Gardens* (1972). One of his most prestigious roles was as filthy-rich cad Tom Buchanan in *The Great Gatsby* (1974). Unfortunately, the film was a glossy vacuity, and Dern played it on one note – unpleasant and scowling.

As a refreshing break between the nastiness, Dern showed a gift for sharp comedy in Michael Ritchie's satire *Smile* (1975) as 'Big Bob' Freelander, a mobile-home dealer and chief judge of a beauty contest. He was also an amusing cab-driver con-man in Hitchcock's last film, *Family Plot* (1976). But he was soon back to villainy in *Black Sunday* (1977) as the fanatic pilot of an airship threatening the annihilation of 80,000 spectators at a football match, and continued to chill as the creepy cop pursuing Ryan O'Neal in *The Driver* (1978). More satisfying was his Best Supporting Actor-nominated role in *Coming Home* of the same year, although as Jane Fonda's disturbed hawkish war vet husband, he showed little development from the macho character who goes off to war and the casualty who returns.

In the 80s, while less in demand, Dern's by then grey and sepulchral presence was a great plus to films like *Tattoo* (1980), as a tatooist who kidnaps a girl, decorates her with his needle and forces her to have sex with him. Not nice at all. He was also Kiefer Sutherland's gung-ho father in *1969* (1988), took himself off wonderfully as a crazed army man in *The 'Burbs* (1989), and was back to creepy villain, all teeth and smiles, in *After Dark, My Sweet* (1990), manipulating Rachel Ward and Jason Patric. Carrying on the family tradition is the talented Laura Dern, his daughter from his marriage to Diane Ladd, with whom he appeared in *The Wild Angels*.

1960 Wild River **1964** Marnie **1965** Hush . . . Hush Sweet Charlotte **1966** The Wild Angels **1967** The St Valentine's Day Massacre; Waterhole No.3; The Trip; The War Wagon **1968** Psych-Out; Will Penny; Hang 'Em High **1969** Support Your Local Sheriff!; Castle Keep; Number One; They Shoot Horses, Don't They? **1970** Cycle Savages; Bloody Mama **1971** Drive He Said; The Incredible Two-Headed Transplant **1972** The Cowboys; Silent Running; The King Of Marvin Gardens **1973** The Laughing Policeman (GB: An Investigation Of Murder) **1974** The Great Gatsby **1975** Smile; Posse **1976** Family Plot; Won Ton Ton – The Dog Who Saved Hollywood; Folies Bourgeoises (France) **1977** Black Sunday **1978** Coming Home; The Driver **1980** Middle Age Crazy; Tattoo **1981** Harry Tracy **1982** That Championship Season **1984** On The Edge **1987** The Big Town aka The Arm **1988** 1969 **1989** The 'Burbs **1990** After Dark, My Sweet **1992** Diggstown

Dern, Laura

Actress

Born 10 February 1966

Santa Monica, California

When David Lynch's eagerly awaited stew of sex, violence and flouting of conventional mores, *Wild At Heart* (1990), was unveiled at the Cannes Film Festival, where it captured the Palme D'Or, Laura Dern, aged 23, became a name. A visual feast in the typically macabre Lynch vein, the movie starred Dern as Lula Pace Fortune, an uninhibited Southern sex-bunny, hedonistic, headstrong yet vulnerable, who sparks a heady chemistry with her lover, Sailor Ripley (Nicolas Cage). It was the young actress' opportunity to break free of the virginal roles she had previously played and to blossom into full womanhood, and she seized it with both hands, surprising those who had overlooked the evident promise of her early performances.

Laura Dern, intelligent, articulate and doggedly committed to her own choices, was born into the acting profession and, although discouraged from following it by her parents, Bruce Dern and Diane Ladd (who played Lula's deranged mother in Lynch's film), was intent on emulating them from a ridiculously early age. She was five when she watched a replay of *Hush . . . Hush Sweet Charlotte* (1964) and saw Bette Davis fling her daddy's decapitated head down a flight of stairs, thus learning what he did for a living, but it was Diane who was unwittingly responsible for seducing Laura into Hollywood ambitions. After Ladd and Dern divorced, the little girl lived with her mother and accompanied her on many visits to film sets, thus collecting her first walk-on at the age of six in *White Lightning* (1973). Then director Martin Scorsese cast her in *Alice Doesn't Live Here Anymore* (1975); it was a tiny role but one which required her to eat a banana ice-cream cone – 19 times before the take was perfect.

Afterwards, Scorsese told her mother that any child who could do that without throwing up *had* to be an actress.

The aspiring actress won her first featured role in Adrian Lyne's mediocre *Foxes* (1980). She did so by engineering her own audition and passing herself off as being in her mid-teens. She was actually 11 and, three years later, with a couple of further films behind her, she was attending classes at the Lee Strasberg Institute, transporting herself there on a push-bike since her disapproving parents refused to drive her.

Dern's leggy frame, cascading flaxen locks and strange, almost homely face combine to give her a credibility on film that those with more obvious beauty lack. Until *Wild At Heart*, she was associated, by those who could recognise her by name, with a kind of virginal innocence that served her extremely well in *Mask* (1985), touchingly playing the blind girl in love with Eric Stoltz's hideously disfigured hero. By then, she had already embarked on the Method approach of doing extensive homework for her roles: for Arthur Hiller's *Teachers* (1984) she checked into a private clinic under the pretence of pregnancy so as to observe how young women really handle abortion; for *Mask* she spent a fortnight entirely blindfolded.

Although Joyce Chopra's *Smooth Talk* (1986) won the actress the prestigious Los Angeles Film Critics New Generation Award for her impressive performance, opposite Treat Williams, as a moody, sullen and rebellious teenager caught in the darker terrors of sexual awakening (a far cry from Mask, announcing her versatility), it was David Lynch's *Blue Velvet* (1986) that, thanks to Molly Ringwald's mother rejecting the role for her daughter, primed Dern for fame. Her character, Sandy, the film's girl-next-door to Kyle MacLachlan (with whom she had an off-screen relationship for four years), didn't begin to plumb her talents and she was somewhat eclipsed by Isabella Rossellini. But it established her within the director's circle of 'reuseable' actors. When it came time for him to cast the wild female leading role in *Wild At Heart* (1990), Dern was his first choice.

Able to claim Tennessee Williams as a cousin and the poet-playwright Archibald MacLeish as a great-uncle, Dern's provenance is a distinguished one. After *Wild At Heart*, she turned down a role in Hector Babenco's *At Play In The Fields Of The Lord* (1991) and the part went to Daryl Hannah. Opting for a small, gentle period drama in *Rambling Rose*, Dern was enchanting as a simultaneously gauche, graceful, innocent, brazen, sexually provocative country girl – and was rewarded with an Oscar nomination for Best Actress. (In a unique double Dern's mother, Diane Ladd, was also an Oscar nominee for her performance in the film.) Clearly confident enough to take decisions, she looked set for major stardom while biding her time and nurturing her own future.

1973 White Lightning **1974** Alice Doesn't Live Here Any More **1980** Foxes; **1984** Teachers; **1985** Ladies And Gentlemen: The Fabulous Stains; Mask; Smooth Talk; **1986** Blue Velvet; **1988** Haunted Summer; **1989** Fat Man and Little Boy (GB: Shadow Makers); **1990** Wild At Heart **1991** Rambling Rose **1993** Jurassic Park

DeVito, Danny

Actor, director
Born 17 November 1944
Asbury Park, New Jersey

Danny DeVito was once described as looking like 'a coarse, out-of-shape pea who has accidentally left the pod and gone for a walk'. Round, squat and balding, he has relished playing nasty little toads, with a wicked tongue and temper. It was a character that he perfected during his years on the popular TV series *Taxi*, as the irascible Louis, throwing insults at the drivers from his cage. In the world of bland family sit-coms, it came as a welcome breath of foul air. His films as director have also shown a vicious acerbity and no-punches-pulled black humour.

At 18 DeVito got his first real job, working as a hairdresser for a year at his sister's beauty salon, something for which he had trained at the Wilfred Academy of Hair and Beauty Culture. No beauty himself, he resorted to humour in most situations, and had the customers giggling under the driers. Despite his looks, he was determined to try an acting career. After studying at the American Academy of Dramatic Arts, he began to get theatre work from 1969, including with the New York Shakespeare Festival and a role in the 1971 off-Broadway production of *One Flew Over The Cuckoo's Nest*, Dale Wasserman's stage adaptation of the

Ken Kesey novel with William Devane in the lead. His performance as Anthony Martini, one of the patients in the mental hospital, led to his being cast in the Milos Forman movie version four years later. He and Devane had previously made *Lady Liberty* (1972), an Italian comedy starring Sophia Loren.

A number of small roles followed until Jack Nicholson, a friend since *One Flew Over The Cuckoo's Nest*, asked him to play Hog, riotously partnered by the gross John Belushi, one of Nicholson's gang members in *Goin' South* (1978). *Taxi* then took up most of his time from 1979 to 1983, although he did make *Going Ape* (1980), an unamusing diversion with Tony Danza, one of his partners from the TV series. DeVito, sporting a Mexican moustache, was fourth-billed as Lazlo, helping out Danza as a millionaire's son who can only inherit if he can keep his father's orang-utans happy for five years.

With *Taxi* over, DeVito began to get bigger roles in better films, such as the cackling villain pitted against Michael Douglas and Kathleen Turner in the ripping tongue-in-cheek yarn *Romancing The Stone* (1983), and its sequel, *The Jewel Of The Nile* (1985). In *Ruthless People* (1986), he played a despicable little creature who wants rid of his loud-mouthed wife (Bette Midler), and is thrilled when she is kidnapped. DeVito, who made even Midler seem demure, went amusingly over the top.

A wittier and more subtle performance came in Barry Levinson's *Tin Men* (1987), in which the actor portrayed an aluminium siding salesman locked in a bitter feud with Richard Dreyfuss. As the less socially privileged of the two, and with his rival falling for his wife (Barbara Hershey), the sawn-off runt managed to gain audience sympathy over the taller but nevertheless short Dreyfuss. However, the physical incongruity of DeVito and Arnold Schwarzenegger as *Twins* (1988) – 'only their mother can tell them apart' – is about the only joke in a movie which wears thin when violence and sentimentality take over, with DeVito, uncharacteristically, colluding in the proceedings.

His first film as director, *Throw Momma From The Train* (1987), revealed real flair and promise. He himself played a funny bug-like man with a horrendous mother he would like to see dead. When he hears Billy Crystal announcing a similar desire (albeit rhetorically) about his ex-wife, DeVito decides that they swap murders à la *Strangers On A Train*. Some clever jump cuts and fantasy flash-ins showed a certain interest in narrative experiments, and the abrasive humour was kept ticking over even though it avoided real pain.

There is no such cop out in *The War Of The Roses* (1990), a vitriolic anatomy of the breakdown of a marriage that makes Strindberg's *The Dance Of Death* seem tame. DeVito, the director, was restrained as the narrator-lawyer who uses the passive listener device to tell the story of Michael Douglas' manic desire to remain married to Kathleen Turner. She refuses to compromise and, thankfully, neither does the film. DeVito has himself been happily married for some years to Rhea Perlman, one of the stars of the long-running TV sit-com *Cheers*. Publicly, his profile was raised again by the huge success of *Batman Returns* in which he featured unforgettably as the Penguin.

As actor only unless stated otherwise: **1972** Lady Liberty aka La Mortadella (Italy) **1975** One Flew Over The Cuckoo's Nest **1976** Deadly Hero; Car Wash **1977** The Van; The World's Greatest Lover **1978** Goin' South **1980** Going Ape **1983** Romancing The Stone; Terms Of Endearment **1984** Johnny Dangerously **1985** Head Office; The Jewel Of The Nile **1986** Ruthless People **1987** Wise Guys; Tin Men; Throw Momma From The Train (also director) **1988** Twins **1990** The War Of The Roses (also director) **1991** Other People's Money **1992** Batman Returns; Hoffa **1992/93** Jack The Bear

Dickinson, Angie
(Angeline Brown)

Actress

Born 30 September 1931

Kulm, North Dakota

Although never an absolutely top-rank star, Angie Dickinson long carved a niche as the fantasy mate of many a middle-aged film critic. They grew older with her, but she lasted the course better, retaining a cool, self-possessed beauty as she approached her 60s. For many people she is TV's *Police Woman* rather than a serious actress, perhaps because her screen career has not been well served by most of her material, but she seems sanguine about some of the dross in which she has appeared and in which she was never less than utterly assured.

Dickinson, who took her name from her first husband, a college football star (she later married and then parted from composer-musician Burt Bacharach), began in the old-fashioned way in the dying days of the studio system. The winner of a beauty contest, she broke into the movies as a starlet in a Doris Day musical, *Lucky Me* (1954), and for several years played bits and small roles in movies exemplified by *Man With The Gun, Tennessee's Partner* (both 1955), and *Tension At Table Rock* (1956). She came to life as a half-caste in *China Gate* (1957), a typically rough-hewn anti-Communist actioner directed by Sam Fuller; and as girlfriend to maniac Rod Steiger in *Cry Terror* (1958). This last led to *Rio Bravo* (1959), in which she played the warm, intelligent, female component of the oddly assorted 'family' which lawman John Wayne gathers round him. *Rio Bravo's* director, Howard Hawks, once remarked that he liked women who looked young but seemed older. Dickinson's Feathers fitted the bill perfectly, completely attuned to the Hawksian world of male camaraderie and ensemble playing, a woman moving easily in a man's world without disturbing any of the conventions. The sensual rapport between Dickinson and Wayne, some 24 years her senior, seemed the most natural thing in the world.

She repeated the role in the considerably less substantial *Ocean's Eleven* (1960), a self-satisfied crime caper featuring Sinatra's rat pack. The same year she then played a nurse hopelessly in love with Richard Burton in *The Bramble Bush*. This seemed to typecast her as a crisply starched object of desire: she was a missionary nurse in the Congo in *The Sins Of Rachel Cade* (1961); a midwife lusted after by the menfolk of an Italian village in *Jessica* (1962); assistant to army psychiatrist Gregory Peck in Captain *Newman M.D.* (1963).

Things improved. Dickinson was both beautiful and treacherous in Don Siegel's *The Killers* (1964), suffering the indignity of a vicious slap in the face from a washed-up Ronald Reagan in his last screen role. A touching performance as the wife of sheriff Marlon Brando in *The Chase* (1966) was followed by the part of the dangerous decoy in John Boorman's excellent *Point Blank* (1967) in which, for most of the movie, she remains unfazed by Lee Marvin's bull-headed machismo. Subsequently she displayed a sumptuous pair of breasts to a somnolent Burt Reynolds in *Sam Whiskey* (1969) and clearly enjoyed herself as a raunchy bank robber in *Big Bad Mama* (1974), which her nude scenes have made a cable TV favourite.

However, her big screen appearances began to tail off thereafter, though she made an impression and aroused the interest of a new generation of moviegoers when she was cast as the cool, beautiful and mature victim of Brian De Palma's calculated misogyny, messily murdered in an elevator in his gory homage to Hitchcock, *Dressed To Kill* (1980).

1954 Lucky Me **1955** Man With The Gun **1956** Gun That Man Down **1957** China Gate **1958** Cry Terror **1959** Rio Bravo **1960** The Bramble Bush; Ocean's 11 **1961** The Sins Of Rachel Cade; Fever In The Blood **1962** Rome Adventure; Jessica **1964** Captain Newman M.D.; The Killers **1965** The Art Of Love **1966** The Chase; Cast A Giant Shadow **1967** Point Blank; The Last Challenge **1969** Sam Whiskey; Young Billy Young; Some Kind Of A Nut **1971** Pretty Maids All In A Row; The Resurrection Of Zachary Wheeler **1973** The Outside Man (France) **1974** Big Bad Mama **1979** Labyrinth; The Angry Man **1980** Klondike Fever; Dressed To Kill; Charlie Chan And The Curse Of The Dragon Queen **1981** Death Hunt **1987** Big Bad Mama II

Dillon, Kevin

Actor
Born 19 August 1965
Mamaroneck, New York

Like his elder brother Matt, Kevin Dillon enjoyed major roles from the start of his career, but took longer to convince critics of his ability and his range. Also like Matt, he has the features of a bruised angel, a rueful strength about the eyes, though physically he is much the slighter of the pair.

Dillon's debut came in 1985, supporting Donald Sutherland and John Heard (teachers) alongside Andrew McCarthy (pupil) and Mary Stuart Masterson (girl), in *Heaven Help Us*, a nostalgic rites-of-passage comedy set in a Catholic school for boys circa 1965. This was cosy fare, not without its amusing moments, but Dillon grew up fast in Oliver Stone's *Platoon* (1986), touted as the essential Vietnam movie. His sharply convincing portrayal of the gung-ho grunt gone rabid propelled him into leading roles in *Remote Control* (fantasy thriller), *The Rescue* (kiddie Rambo), *The Blob* (sci-fi), and *War Party* (as a modern-day native American Indian) – all released in 1988. *Immediate Family* (1989), however, was a welcome sign of his being accorded emotional maturity, in the impressive company of director Jonathan Kaplan, producer Lawrence Kasdan, and fellow leads Glenn Close, James Woods and Mary Stuart Masterson. If the latter compared report cards with Dillon over their five-year careers, they must both have read 'Progress satisfactory'. If there was room for improvement,

Kevin Dillon then appeared in Oliver Stone's high-profile Jim Morrison biopic, *The Doors*, and could point to solid work in the theatre – including *The Dark At The Top Of The Stairs* – in his defence.

1985 Heaven Help Us aka Catholic Boys **1986** Platoon **1988** Remote Control; The Rescue; The Blob; War Party **1989** Immediate Family **1991** The Doors **1992** A Midnight Clear

Dillon, Matt

Actor

Born 18 February 1964

New Rochelle, New York

Ten years after his film debut, pretty boy Matt Dillon finally came of age on screen with his gritty, credible performance as a junkie and robber in *Drugstore Cowboy* (1989). The resulting praise heaped upon his head must have come as a relief to one whose long-term career prospects were looking decidedly shaky, despite early prominence as a teenage pin-up.

Dillon was discovered at the age of 14 when casting agent Vic Ramos – subsequently his manager – visited his school on a quest for boys to play the frighteningly young 'rebels without a cause' in the disturbing alienation-in-the-suburbs drama *Over The Edge* (1979). By the time he was 18, Dillon had shot well to the fore of Hollywood's high-profile Brat Pack, with an army of ardent female fans and industry recognition as a headliner. He was the glamorous hoodlum star and was made the most of in Francis Ford Coppola's highly-stylised adaptation of S.E. Hinton's problem-teen bestseller *The Outsiders* (1983). Ironically, several other members of the ensemble – which included Tom Cruise, Patrick Swayze, Rob Lowe, Emilio Estevez and Ralph Macchio – went on to major star status or at least massive box-office hits, leaving the smoulderingly handsome star with his Greek-god features way behind.

Despite a good, surprising light comedy performance in *The Flamingo Kid* (1983) and a handsome, mumbling brood through Coppola's *Rumble Fish* (1984), things began to go awry. *Target* (1985), the young actor's entry into mainstream fare as a grown-up, teamed him with Gene Hackman but the far-fetched thriller met a cool reception. Then he chose to do a wretched low-budget Australian musical drama, *Rebel* (1986), set in World War II, in which he wanly played a Yankee deserter inconceivably smitten with a low-rent club chanteuse. A formulaic outing in *The Big Town* (1987) as a crapshooting hotshot was an all too poor man's *Hustler/Cincinatti Kid*, and Dillon looked decidedly out for the count by 1988, when he partnered Andrew McCarthy as yet another teen tearaway in the dreadful *Kansas*.

With *Drugstore Cowboy*, Matt Dillon appeared at last to have put behind him the moody male model period of his career. Undeniably, he has always been watchable, with a natural intensity accompanying his bad-boy sex appeal. In 1991 this was acknowledged with an unusual accolade for such a young actor: a retrospective of his films at Britain's National Film Theatre.

1979 Over The Edge **1980** Little Darlings; My Bodyguard **1981** Liar's Moon **1982** Tex **1983** The Outsiders; The Flamingo Kid **1984** Rumble Fish **1985** Target **1986** Rebel; Native Son **1987** The Big Town **1988** Kansas **1989** Bloodhounds Of Broadway; Drugstore Cowboy **1991** A Kiss Before Dying **1992** Singles **1992/93** Mr Wonderful; The Saint Of Fort Washington

Dillon, Melinda

Actress

Born 13 October 1939

Hope, Arkansas

Melinda Dillon is somebody who can generally be relied upon to elevate even the smallest and most ill-written of roles into something special, noticed by critics and collectors of finely judged performances while her name remains unfamiliar to the public. Her counterpart during the late 1980s and early 90s might be said to be Laurie Metcalf.

The actress launched a distinguished Broadway career with her appearance as Honey in the original production of *Who's Afraid Of Virginia Woolf?* (the role taken by Sandy Dennis in the screen version). Although hardly plain, Dillon is no beauty and, perhaps because of this, movies were slow to come her way. But for a bit part in *The April Fools* (1969), she had to wait until 1976 for a break that came when Hal Ashby cast her as the first – and in the film, most prominent – Mrs Woody Guthrie in his excellent *Bound For Glory*. A small supporting role in the Paul Newman ice-hockey drama, *Slap Shot* (1977), as a player's wife who transfers her affections to another woman, won critical notice; her distraught mother in Spielberg's *Close Encounters Of The Third Kind* the same year, probably her best-known screen role, earned her an Academy Award nomination for Best Supporting Actress. She was nominated again for what *Variety* described as 'a beautiful display of understated acting in a small but pivotal role' in Sidney Pollack's strongly cast issues movie, *Absence Of Malice* (1981), but she's been seen only intermittently since, with her appearance in *The Prince Of Tides*, as Nick Nolte's disturbed sister, both fleeting and silent.

Dillon has shown taste in choosing her projects (Alan Rudolph's 1984 *Songwriter*, for example, in which she was another estranged wife), but has largely had to be satisfied with wife/mother parts in which, but for her exceptional gifts, she might be considered interchangeable with Jobeth Williams or Dee Wallace Stone: good actresses of a certain age.

1969 The April Fools (bit) **1976** Bound For Glory **1977** Slap Shot; Close Encounters of The Third Kind **1978** F.I.S.T. **1981** Absence of Malice **1983** A Christmas Story **1984** Songwriter **1987** Harry And The Hendersons aka Bigfoot And The Hendersons **1989** Staying Together; Captain America **1991** The Prince Of Tides

Divine
(Harris Glenn Milstead)

Actor
Born 19 October 1945
Baltimore, Maryland
Died 8 March 1988

Divine fulfilled the dream of all drag artists by becoming a genuine movie star. Weighing in at 294 lbs, the self-styled Queen of Trash was born plain Harris Milstead in suburban Baltimore. Fortunately, he went to school with future director John Waters, and they became inseparable, thanks to their shared love of schlocky Hollywood movies and camp actresses.

While still a hairdresser (his initial profession), Milstead appeared in two 8mm amateur films, *Roman Candles* (1966) and *Eat Your Makeup* (1968), directed by Waters. Reborn as Divine, a name befitting a screen goddess, 'she' was to become the prima donna of all Waters' features, starting with the well-named *Mondo Trasho* (1969). To the background of songs from the 50s, the decade to which the star and the director were most attuned, Divine lugged around the lifeless body of Mary Vivian Pearce, whom 'she' has run over with her Cadillac convertible. In the same year, Divine further exercised extremely bad taste in *Multiple Murders*, in which 'she' played a mass murderer and, in 1972, made claim to being 'the most disgusting person alive' in *Pink Flamingos* by putting two pieces of dog turd in 'her' mouth.

The corpulent star was raped in both *Female Trouble* (1974) and *Desperate Living* (1977), in the former by 'herself' in male form, and in the latter, by a 15-foot long lobster. *Polyester* (1981), the first Divine-Waters film to gain wide distribution outside the late-night drive-in crowd, was a mock soap opera, in which 'she' played a Baltimore housewife temporarily finding romance in the arms of Tab Hunter. As in the other collaborations, Divine's grotesque parody of womanhood had a certain surreal comic edge to it, helping to raise the film above the dim-witted, but juvenile excesses outweighed any sophistication. However, in Waters' jaunty *Hairspray* (1988), 'she' was amusing and likeable as the fat mother of a fat teenage girl, for once not playing the heroine.

Just when 'her' act was beginning to become a drag, it was a revelation to see the performer playing a nasty racketeer (male) in Alan Rudolph's *Trouble In Mind* (1985), and an LA cop in Michael Schroeder's *Out Of The Dark*, Divine's last role before dying of a heart attack. Who knows, he/she might well have had a new career as a fine character actor/actress.

1969 Mondo Trasho; Multiple Maniacs **1972** Pink Flamingos **1974** Female Trouble **1977** Desperate Living **1981** Polyester **1985** Lust In The Dust; Trouble In Mind **1988** Out Of The Dark; Hairspray

Donaldson, Roger

Director
Born 15 November 1945
Ballarat, Australia

Born in a rural part of Australia, Roger Donaldson emigrated to New Zealand in 1965 where he established a stills photography business. Developing a desire to see his pictures move, the non-existent state of New Zealand's film industry meant that he could only do so through television commercials and the documentaries which served as his apprenticeship for seven short dramas called *Winners And Losers*. In 1977, he managed to raise enough to produce his first motion picture, *Sleeping Dogs*, a confused political drama set in the near future that was New Zealand's first feature film in 15 years, as well as the first to be shown in American cinemas. Although credited with helping to create the country's Film Commission, it was not until 1982's *Smash Palace* that Donaldson was able to direct for the big screen again. A darkly comic examination of marital breakdown, the movie shared the uncertainty of tone evident in its maker's debut, and was at its best when viewing events through the eyes of the couple's seven-year-old child; but it earned much acclaim and some limited commercial success in the States and, most surprisingly, the chance for Donaldson to helm *The Bounty* (1984) for Dino De Laurentiis when original director David Lean fell out with screenwriter Robert Bolt.

The director's most outstanding and accomplished film, *The Bounty* eschewed the hero-and-villain approach of previous versions in favour of mostly historically accurate revisionism. It laid the blame for the mutiny not in events but in the psychology of the sexually repressed Bligh (Anthony Hopkins) and the weak-willed Christian (Mel Gibson), with both their friendship and their lives destroyed by their inability to cope with the conflict between the liberation of the islanders and the rigorous social order of the cramped 'Bounty'. Despite a difficult shoot Donaldson drew incredible performances from his leads and showed an impressive visual eye, but the film's brooding atmosphere, combined with poor distribution in many territories, scuttled it at the box office. His next feature, again for De Laurentiis, *Marie* (1985), a drama starring Sissy Spacek that spent as much time on it's heroine's domestic problems as her fight against parole-board corruption, followed it without making a ripple.

It was not until 1987's *No Way Out*, an excellent remake of *The Big Clock* (1948) transported from the newsroom to Reagan's Pentagon, that he finally scored big at the box office (and then mainly due to the sudden popularity of its star, Kevin Costner and the infamous sex scene in the back of a limo with Sean Young). To much surprise, the glossy, lightweight, highly improbable and frequently embarrassing Tom Cruise vehicle, *Cocktail* (1988), which was enlivened only by Bryan Brown's winningly cynical performance, made twice as much and gave Donaldson, always an ambitious director, clout – just about the only valid reason for making it. He was able to instigate *Cadillac Man* (1990), returning to the car dealing world, though American-style, of *Smash Palace*. (The director's father was a car salesman). Dismissed as 'Tin Men on a Dog Day Afternoon' and a speedy box-office disappointment after back-to-back hits for both the director and star (Robin Williams), the film nevertheless had much to recommend it, with a winning way with characters, but was judged more on expectations than on its own merits. Sharing the mood shifts of Donaldson's films, it showed that Hollywood is more interested in him as a helmer of well-crafted, one-tone star vehicles than as an individual talent. However, his ambitious but incomprehensibly complicated thriller, *White Sands*, was a step in the wrong direction.

1977 Sleeping Dogs **1982** Smash Palace (also writer) **1984** The Bounty **1985** Marie **1987** No Way Out **1988** Cocktail **1990** Cadillac Man **1992** White Sands

Donner, Richard

Director
Born 1939
New York City

Richard Donner, who moved from low-budget films to commanding $5 million a picture, began his career as an off-Broadway actor, getting work in the then New York based TV industry, working at one point with Martin Ritt in a TV version of *Of Human Bondage*. Moving to California in 1958 to direct commercials, industrial films and documentaries, he made his TV debut behind the camera during the 1959 season of the Steve McQueen Western series, *Wanted:Dead Or Alive*, quickly becoming one of the industry's top directors. He was less lucky with films – his debut feature, *X-15* (1961), did little to boost the up-and-coming Charles Bronson while 1969's *Twinky* positively hindered him when he made it, and although *Salt And Pepper* the previous year did well enough to prompt a sequel, Donner was replaced by Jerry Lewis – and went back to the small screen with episodes of *Get Smart* and *Kojak* as well as some successful TV movies.

The director's ability to work within a low budget without the limitations showing won him *The Omen* (1976), a much derided but hugely successful devil movie that still contains most of his best work. Despite the extravagance and imagination of its deaths, the film was paced as a thriller rather than a horror movie and focused as much on the human dilemma facing its hero as on its apocalyptic overtones. With its impressively constructed set-pieces and a superb use of CinemaScope to combine disparate visual elements into a gradual perversion of normality, subtly defining the threat to the family unit, the movie propelled Donner to the rank of major director – although he only got his next film after almost every other director had turned it down.

Superman (1978) was 'two years of hell, seven days a week with maybe four hours of sleep a night – if I was lucky'. The budget went out of control and the crew divided into factions, blaming either the director or the producer, and Richard Lester had to be brought in as 'associate to the producers' to mediate, but despite everything the film was a huge success. Donner was able to bring to a decidedly iffy project a sense of dignity, grandeur, mysticism and humanity, treating its superhero with respect and managing moments of deep compassion in its early scenes that none of the sequels even attempted to match. Despite the fabulous box-office returns he was unceremoniously fired from 1981's *Superman II* (even though he had shot much of it) and replaced amid much personal acrimony by Lester; ironically, Donner was to do the same himself ten years later with *Radio Flyers*.

For a while he deliberately made smaller scale films, such as the low-budget, brooding human drama *Inside Moves* (1981) and the dismal *The Toy* (1982), a part of Hollywood's ongoing misguided attempts to remake French comedies and the first example for those unfamiliar with TV's *Get Smart* of his hopelessly unsubtle approach to comedy. After his pet project, the medieval romantic fantasy *Ladyhawke* (1985), showcasing Michelle Pfeiffer and Rutger Hauer, proved more successful in its attempt to update epic conventions to 80s sensibilities, his work began to lose passion. When *Lethal Weapon* (1987) provided him with his third blockbuster, its fast pace and glossy feel were more the trademarks of producer Joel Silver and seemed to confirm that Donner had simply become a talented journeyman – an impression certainly not challenged by the lacklustre *Scrooged* (1987) – while its even more successful sequel seemed little more than a string of set-pieces held together by watered down re-runs of the original star turns. Even his move back into drama, *Radio Flyers* (1990), seemed marred by Donner's determination not to delve too deeply into the darker elements of the million-dollar script. The result was his first major box-office disaster, although he was quick to restore his commercial credibility with the formulaic *Lethal Weapon 3*.

1961 X-15 **1968** Salt And Pepper **1969** Twinky **1976** The Omen **1978** Superman **1981** Superman II (as co-director, uncredited); Inside Moves **1982** The Toy **1985** Ladyhawke; The Loonies **1987** Lethal Weapon **1988** Scrooged **1989** Lethal Weapon 2 **1992** Lethal Weapon 3; Radio Flyer

Douglas, Kirk
(Issur Danielovitch, later Isidore Demsky)

Actor, director
Born 9 December 1916
Amsterdam, New York

It has been said by more than one of his directors that Kirk Douglas' problem was that he always wanted to be Burt Lancaster (a frequent co-star), with the result that he seemed to discard an impressive, often hard-hitting career in favour of extrovert barnstorming that frequently turned him into a self-parody. The son of Russian immigrants, he worked as a waiter to pay his way through university, where he excelled at wrestling, taking it (and a variety of menial jobs) up professionally to put himself through the American Academy of Dramatic Arts. His fledgling stage career was interrupted by the war, but on his return from the Navy he managed to land some larger Broadway parts than his 1941 debut had provided, as well as doing radio work.

From his 1946 screen debut in *The Strange Love Of Martha Ivers*, a powerful *noir* drama starring Barbara Stanwyck, Douglas got substantial parts in important films, but it took his unscrupulous boxer in *Champion* (1949) to make him a star and establish his image – aggressive, selfish, intense and an often deeply unsympathetic victim of his own anger, ultimately driven to cathartic revulsion at his own actions, as demonstrated by his ambitious newspaperman in Billy Wilder's relentlessly cynical *Ace In The Hole*, his pathologically driven detective in William Wyler's *Detective Story* (both 1951), or his rapist in Otto Preminger's *In Harm's Way* (1965).

The exhibitionistic side of the actor's temperament was readily apparent in *20,000 Leagues Under The Sea* (1953) and *Ulysses* (1955, for which he was one of the first major American stars to work in Italy) as well as his many Westerns, but it was kept in check, unlike his characters with a penchant for self-mutilation (a finger in *The Big Sky*, 1951, an ear in *Lust For Life*, 1955, an eye in *The Vikings*, 1958), and was bracketed by his commitment to important, challenging films alongside them. Through Bryna, his own production company (named after his mother) formed in 1955, he was able to produce the powerful anti-war drama *Paths Of Glory* (1957), banned for nearly three decades in France, and the literate, passionate epic *Spartacus* (1960), two of Stanley Kurbrick's finest and most emotional films, as well as smaller subjects such as *Lonely Are The Brave* (1961). His personal integrity was much in evidence, too, with his insistence on hiring blacklisted writers such as Dalton Trumbo and giving him screen credit despite studio objections, and his decision to appear in Anthony Mann's *The Heroes Of Telemark* (1965) to make up for firing that director from *Spartacus*. He didn't win all his battles (trying for several years to bring *One Flew Over The Cuckoo's Nest* to the screen to universal disinterest, only to see his son Michael produce it and give the lead to Jack Nicholson) but he was one of the most passionately involved actors of his time.

By the late 1960s, Kirk Douglas' scallywag persona began to get the better of him as the scripts began to pale and the films to become more ragged around the edges: of his 70s films, only the political Western *Posse* (1975, which he also directed) and Brian De Palma's *The Fury* (1978) were in any way accomplished, with nothing to compare to the anguish he gave his Vincent Van Gogh in *Lust For Life*, the passion of *Spartacus* or the pure bile of *Ace In The Hole*'s unscrupulous newshound. While his son Michael's star rose in the 80s, Kirk waned in films that wasted their premises and surrounded their star with embarrassing dialogue. Indeed, when he walked out on a film for the first time in his career after bitter arguments on *First Blood* (1982) there seemed nowhere to go but the round of mini-series, chat shows and published autobiography that old movie stars retreat into towards the end. Even a pleasing return to his best comic form opposite his *OK Corral* croney Lancaster, as a couple of ageing ex-cons in Touchstone's amiable *Tough Guys* (1986) failed to make much impact. Yet despite that, and a helicopter crash that he miraculously survived in 1991, Douglas still kept a high profile in the 90s. He wrote a novel, enjoyed a rapprochement with Stallone to appear as his gangster father in John Landis' comedy *Oscar* (1991) and basked in the glory of a prestigious revival of the restored version of *Spartacus*, probably the major achievement of a generally impressive body of work.

1946 The Strange Love Of Martha Ivers **1947** Mourning Becomes Electra; Out Of The Past aka Build My Gallows High **1948** I Walk Alone; The Walls Of Jericho; My Dear Secretary **1949** A Letter To Three Wives; Champion **1950** Young Man With A Horn aka Young Man Of Music; The Glass Menagerie **1951** Along The Great Divide; Ace In The Hole aka The Big Carnival; Detective Story **1952** The Big Trees; The Big Sky **1953** The Bad And The Beautiful; The Story Of Three Loves; The Juggler **1954** Act Of Love; 20,000 Leagues Under The Sea **1955** The Racers; Ulisse/Ulysses Italy; Man Without A Star; The Indian Fighter **1956** Lust For Life **1958** Paths Of Glory; The Vikings **1959** Last Train From Gun Hill; The Devil's Disciple **1960** Strangers When We Meet; Spartacus **1961** The Last Sunset; Town Without Pity **1962** Lonely Are The Brave; Two Weeks In Another Town **1963** The Hook; The List Of Adrian Messenger; For Love Or Money **1964** Seven Days In May **1965** In Harm's Way; The Heroes Of Telemark **1966** Cast A Giant Shadow; Paris Brule-t-il/Is Paris Burning? (France) **1967** The Way West; The War Wagon **1968** A Lovely Way To Die; The Brotherhood **1969** The Arrangement **1970** There Was A Crooked Man The Light At The Edge Of The World; A Gunfight; Catch Me A Spy **1972** Un Uomo Da Rispettare/Hearts And Minds (Italy) **1973** Scalawag (also director) **1975** Once Is Not Enough; Posse (also director) **1977** Holocaust 2000 aka The Chosen **1978** The Fury **1979** Home Movies; The Villain aka Cactus Jack; **1980** Saturn 3; The Final Countdown **1983** Eddie Macon's Run; the Man From Snowy River **1986** Tough Guys **1991** Oscar; Veraz

Douglas, Michael

Actor, producer

Born 25 September 1944

New Brunswick, New Jersey

An Oscar-winning producer long before he became a box-office star, Michael Douglas was 40 by the time he attained the kind of film celebrity his father, Kirk Douglas, enjoyed in the 1950s. In short order Kirk's blue-eyed boy superceded his father, taking the Best Actor Oscar for his performance in *Wall Street* (1987) and, by 1991, commanding a reported $15 million dollars for *Basic Instinct*. Currently one of the most 'wantable' of Hollywood leading men, and long acknowledged as a savvy industry businessman, Douglas has steered himself through a career remarkable by anyone's standards.

Born of Kirk's marriage to British actress Diana Dill, Michael was raised in Westport, Connecticut, after his parent's divorce, when he was eight. During vacations from his military academy he was a frequent visitor to his father's film locations and while still in his teens he began acquiring experience as an assistant director, first on *Lonely Are The Brave* (1962). After some drama study at the University of California he bummed around, 60s fashion, for a while, returned to drama training in New York and appeared off-Broadway before making his film debut in a poor Vietnam-era family drama *Hail, Hero!* (1969). A couple of unremarked dramas later, he was befriending Jodie Foster in the Disney family fare *Napoleon And Samantha* (1972) and engaging television viewers as the youthful sidekick to Karl Malden in the long-running cop series *The Streets Of San Francisco*. Before quitting the show in 1975 he also directed two episodes.

Years before, Kirk Douglas had scored a success on Broadway playing Randall P. McMurphy in the stage version of Ken Kesey's novel *One Flew Over The Cuckoo's Nest* and he bought the film rights. He could never get the project off the ground, however, and handed it over to the enthusiastic Michael. Tenaciously raising the finance and bringing on board Czech director Milos Forman and Jack Nicholson for the role of McMurphy, Douglas saw the 1975 film become only the second in Academy history to that date to sweep the 'Big Five' Oscars (Best Picture, Direction, Actor, Actress (Louise Fletcher) and Screenplay (Laurence Hauben).

Returning to the screen in Michael Crichton's effective thriller *Coma* (1978), Douglas made a handsome doctor and lover to heroine Genevieve Bujold while nicely suggesting he might be part of the murderous hospital conspiracy dealing in organs for transplants. The next year he put together his second major production, the prestigious and timely *The China Syndrome* (1979), a tense nuclear accident cover-up drama directed by James Bridges, in which Douglas co-starred with Jack Lemmon and Jane Fonda as the independent TV news cameraman urging Fonda's reporter to act on her conscience. It was another critical and commercial hit.

Still driven to make his mark as an actor, however, he took leads in three modestly budgeted dramas, none of them popular, although his performances – particularly as a young judge determined to uphold justice and drawn into a high-powered legal conspiracy in *The Star Chamber* (1983) – were creditable. Summoning up the roguish genes he inherited from his father, Michael surprised with his next production choice: *Romancing The Stone* (1984), a sly, knowing, action-packed romantic escapade in which he proved both sexy and funny as the caddish, second-rate adventurer saddled with a wistful but plucky Kathleen Turner and a screwball buried-treasure plot. The film delighted audiences and made Douglas an unqualified international star. Sir Richard Attenborough's film version of the phenomenal Broadway success *A Chorus Line* (1985) did little for him as a follow-up, stuck as he was in the theatre stalls through much of the uninspired proceedings, but he was attractive as the auditioning stage director. Bowing to obvious commercial temptations he produced a charmless but financially successful sequel to *Stone, The Jewel Of The Nile* (1985), re-teaming with Turner and old buddy Danny DeVito and exhausting himself with the double act of starring and producing in difficult North African locations.

Douglas bounded back with a breathtaking one-two in 1987, demonstrating that there may be few in the business with a better instinct for a winning script than he, and setting aside production responsibilities to immerse himself in two strong, contrasting roles. In *Fatal Attraction*, directed by Adrian Lyne and written by James Deardon, Douglas (starred opposite Glenn Close) was almost unreasonably sympathetic as a basically goody-goody lawyer whose thoughtless, lusty fling makes him the prey of the psychotic stalker woman. For the most part a shockingly clever table-turning sex thriller, it proved one of the most sensational hits of the year, despite feminist protests. Straight after that, the actor was brilliantly bad-assed as arch-villain despoiler Gordon Gekko in Oliver Stone's indictment of the grasping yuppie ethos of the 80s, *Wall Street*, living up to Stone's hunch that the son of Kirk Douglas must have in him the capacity for a dark and belligerent characterisation. Ironically, Douglas' performance not only won him the Oscar but was so stylishly compelling it inspired 'wannabe' Gekkos in the world's financial capitals to embrace his cinematic sartorial style of slicked-back hair and braces.

Douglas is never better than as a you-can't-help-but-warm-to-him heel, and he was perfect paired for the third time with a magnificently enraged Kathleen Turner for

Danny DeVito's very black, vicious comedy, *The War Of The Roses* (1989), arguably the most audaciously sour Battle of the Sexes ever filmed in Hollywood and, at least partly, excruciatingly funny. With director Ridley Scott he then turned in a plausible hard guy in every contemporary leading man's required tough-action thriller, *Black Rain* (1989). Apparently pacing himself to plan, Douglas followed another break with back-to-back pictures for 1992, the romantic spy thriller *Shining Through* with Melanie Griffith as his leading lady, and *Basic Instinct*, directed by Paul Verhoeven – famous before it even went into production as the script Joe Eszterhas sold for a record-shattering $3 million, only for him to quit the project when Douglas was cast and requested changes to the screenplay. Admirers may have been disappointed to see Douglas playing low and dirty as a misogynist jerk, but the explicit sex scenes propelled the critically booed thriller to international box-office success. And since Douglas' script sensibilities have more often than not been uncannily sound for more than 15 years, it was reasonable to suppose he would hold his high ground for some time to come.

1969 Hail, Hero! **1970** Adam At 6 A.M. **1971** Summertree **1972** Napoleon And Samantha **1978** Coma **1979** The China Syndrome; Running **1980** It's My Turn **1983** The Star Chamber **1984** Romancing The Stone **1985** A Chorus Line; The Jewel Of The Nile **1987** Fatal Attraction; Wall Street **1989** The War Of The Roses; Black Rain **1992** Shining Through; Basic Instinct **1992/93** Falling Down

Dourif, Brad
(Bradford C. Dourif)

Actor
Born 18 March 1950
Huntington, West Virginia

With his slight build and fragile features, blue-eyed, mousey-haired Brad Dourif possesses an innate air of tensile energy that has lent itself well to roles as diverse as a gentle, mentally-disturbed patient and a perverse murderer.

Dourif was born in West Virginia to an art collector father. He attended Marshall University before spending a three-year apprenticeship with the Circle Repertory in New York. A student of the renowned drama coach Sanford Meisner, he was 25 when he landed his first feature film role in the powerful, award-winning drama *One Flew Over the Cuckoo's Nest* (1975). The young actor's superb portrayal of Billy, the vulnerable stutterer, was rightly nominated for an Oscar, and secured Dourif's step in the Hollywood door.

And so, after playing an ill-fated driver in the chilling *Eyes of Laura Mars* (1978), he landed his first leading role, as the obsessed preacher of the Church Without Christ, in John Huston's adaptation of the Flannery O'Connor story *Wise Blood* (1979). Despite critical acclaim, the film did poorly at the box office, a pattern which would continue to dog the actor's career. A supporting part in Michael Cimino's notorious flop, *Heaven's Gate* (1980), followed before he went on to portray the sensitive renegade WASP fighting the establishment on behalf of blacks in *Ragtime* (1981). It was a substantial role, beautifully acted, but the film, directed by Milos Forman, failed to draw the public in spite of largely favourable reviews. The actor responded by taking a three-year break from movies, during which time he taught acting and directing at New York's Columbia University.

He returned before the cameras for a supporting part in David Lynch's inauspicious *Dune* (1984), and his career (with the exception of a minor role in 1986's *Blue Velvet*) continued along a desultory path of B movies until he hit the jackpot with *Mississippi Burning* (1988). In Alan Parker's shocking tale of racism and murder in the Deep South, Dourif excelled himself with his portrayal of the bigoted, wife-beating deputy sheriff of a small town, and the movie, despite provoking heated controversy, proved both a commercial and critical success.

An exciting actor whose performances are characterised by an unpredictable edginess, Dourif has become a favourite with maverick directors and, as the 90s got underway, he looked likely to build on his reputation as one of Hollywoods' most talented actors.

1975 One Flew Over the Cuckoo's Nest; W.W. and the Dixie Dancekings **1978** Eyes of Laura Mars **1979** Wise Blood **1980** Heaven's Gate **1981** Ragtime **1984** Dune **1985** Impure Thoughts **1986** Blue Velvet **1987** Fatal Beauty **1988** Child's Play; Mississippi Burning **1990** The Exorcist III; Hidden Agenda; Grim Prairie Tales; Stephen King's Graveyard Shift; The Horseplayer **1990** Spontaneous Combustion; Sonny Boy; Child's Play 2 **1991** Chaindance (Canada); Scream Of Stone (Canada); Body Parts; Jungle Fever **1992/93** Diary Of The Hurdy-Gurdy Man **1993** Trauma

Down, Lesley-Anne

Actress
Born 17 March 1954
London, England

A dark-haired, blue-eyed decorative English actress who found a little niche for herself as the love interest in a handful of light transatlantic productions – and even clocked up a couple of strong roles – Lesley-Anne Down has, on the whole, looked more at home on the small screen.

She began her professional career early, appearing in *The Smashing Bird I Used To Know* and *All The Right Noises* (both 1969), when she was only 15, and later gaining nationwide popularity as the aristocratic daughter in TV's *Upstairs Downstairs*. From supporting roles in British horror movies, she graduated to supporting roles in American movies made on location in Europe: Kirk Douglas directed her in *Scalawag* (1973), she appeared with John Wayne in *Brannigan* (1975) and with the Queen of Hollywood herself, Elizabeth Taylor, in the ambitious but ill-fated screen version of Sondheim's *A Little Night Music* (1976). She was at her most strikingly lovely, and her professional best, as the famous stripper in the TV movie *The One And Only Phyliss Dixey* in 1978, but was overstretched in lead roles on the big screen – in *Hanover Street* (1979) as a married World War II Red Cross nurse involved with Harrison Ford, and in the archaeology caper, *Sphinx* (1980) – which cruelly exposed her limited range. She seemed much happier in heist movies such as *The Great Train Robbery* (1978), cavorting with Sean Connery or, similarly, with Burt Reynolds in *Rough Cut* two years later.

The 1980s saw a falling off in Lesley-Anne Down's career, perhaps partly caused by a disastrous marriage to director William Friedkin. They were later divorced, leaving a distinct possibility – yet to be realised by the beginning of the 90s that she would re-emerge on her own account.

1969 The Smashing Bird I Used To Know; All The Right Noises **1970** Sin Un Adios (Spain) **1971** In The Devil's Garden aka The Assault aka Tower Of Terror **1972** Countess Dracula; Pope Joan **1973** From Beyond The Grave; Scalawag **1975** Brannigan **1976** A Little Night Music; The Pink Panther Strikes Again **1978** The Betsy; The Great Train Robbery aka The First Great Train Robbery **1979** Hanover Street **1980** Rough Cut; Sphinx **1981** Off Beat **1985** Nomads **1992/93** Heartfelt

Downey Jr, Robert

Actor
Born 4 April 1965
New York City

A flip, hip young actor with plenty of credibility but no commercial hits to his name, Robert Downey Jr made his screen debut at the age of five in his father's independent film *Pound* (1970). Playing a puppy, his first line on film was 'Got any hair on your balls?'. Downey senior is the cult director of *Putney Swope* (1969) and other anarchic low-budget comedies. His son has also made cameo appearances in *Greaser's Palace* (1972), *Up The Academy* (1980); *America* (1985), *Rented Lips* (1988), and *Too Much Sun* (1990).

Officially, Downey Jr's debut is John Sayles' *Baby, It's You* (1983), though when three weeks work was cut down to one brief glimpse, his friends dubbed the picture 'Maybe It's You'. In the midst of the mid-1980s boom in teen pictures the young actor slowly worked his way up the cast list with variations on his zany punk self. He met his long-time girlfriend Sarah Jessica Parker on the set of *Firstborn* (1984); had a few scenes in *Weird Science* (1985), and began to get noticed with his wild man act in Rodney Dangerfield's *Back To School* (1986) and appearances on the TV series *Saturday Night Live*. His first leading role, as a cocksure Casanova in the misfiring Molly Ringwald vehicle *The Pick-Up Artist* (1987), showed him at his most assured, hustling and cajoling with boundless energy and finesse. His expressive face and live-wire physicality easily stole the picture from Ringwald; then Downey pulled off the same trick against Andrew McCarthy and Jami Gertz in the dreadful adaptation of Bret Easton Ellis' *Less Than Zero* (1987). His Beverly Hills addict Julian – whose disintegration becomes the emotional core of the film – was the one asset this otherwise bankrupt project could boast. A manful performance, it showed his range extended from comedy to drama, and paved the way for future roles.

Just as people were beginning to take notice of his talent, Downey seemed to be everywhere, with three pictures released in the space of five months. Ernest Thompson's *1969* (1988) made few sparks, but he was handsome and appealing as the romantic lead opposite Cybill Shepherd and Mary Stuart Masterson in the deft comic fantasy *Chances Are* (1989), and even more impressive as the idealistic young law graduate (his first absolutely straight character) who teams up with cynical James Woods in the superior thriller *True Believer* (1989). He and Woods shared excellent rapport; it was unfortunate that more people did not see it. Despite this sound body of work, Downey was still without a popular hit, and it was a surprise to see him get equal above-the-title billing with Mel Gibson for *Air America* (1990). All the more ironic that the movie should bomb. His rookie pilot Billy Covington showed some of the strain the actor must have been feeling; unusually, he forces his natural charisma down our throats, plays it broadly and – like the film itself – misses. Rumours in 1991 that he was up for Sammy Glick in the adaptation of Budd Schulberg's legendary and seathing satire on Hollywood, *What Makes Sammy Run?*, and the challenging title role of Charlie Chaplin in Richard Attenborough's biopic suggested that the best was yet to come.

1970 Pound **1972** Greaser's Palace **1980** Up The Academy **1982** Baby, It's You **1984** Firstborn **1985** Tuff Turf; Weird Science; To Live And Die In LA **1986** Back To School; America aka This Is America The Movie, Not The Country **1987** The Pick-Up Artist; Less Than Zero **1988** Rented Lips; **1989** Johnny Be Good **1989** Chances Are; True Believer aka Fighting Justice **1990** Air America; Too Much Sun **1991** Soapdish **1992** Charlie **1993** Short Cuts

Dreyfuss, Richard

Actor
Born 29 October 1947
New York City

Chubby, freckled, short and frequently bespectacled, Richard Dreyfuss seems an unlikely candidate for star status. But the Dreyfuss case is a good example of the aesthetic change that began in American films in the mid-60s, so it was logical that Steven Spielberg should have chosen him as the representative ordinary mid-Western guy, who takes off with the little green men in their flying saucer, in *Close Encounters Of The Third Kind* (1977).

Before leaving for stellar regions, this lawyer's son had spent his childhood in Brooklyn and Queens where he had started performing at nine, and had acted at the Beverly Hills Jewish Center when his family moved to LA. After some work on Broadway, and stage and TV parts in California, the 19-year-old was momentarily glimpsed in *The Graduate* (1967) as a Berkeley student with one line: 'Shall I get the cops. I'll get the cops!' while Dustin Hoffman is making a row in the lodging house. However, his burgeoning acting career was interrupted when he registered as a conscientious objector during the Vietnam War, which required him to work for two years in an LA hospital as alternative service.

Back in movies, Dreyfuss created an impression as Baby Face Nelson in John Milius' *Dillinger* (1973), the most destructive member of the gang led by Warren Oates. In the same year, he played the role that was to make him a star – the energetic, smart-talking intellectual among the kids (including Ron Howard, Candy Clark, Paul LeMat and Harrison Ford) of a small Californian town in 1962 in George Lucas' *American Graffiti*, one of the key Hollywood films of the 70s. Two performances in 1975 contrasted his bubbling extrovert side with his more neurotic, introvert screen persona: the title role in *The Apprenticeship Of Duddy Kravitz* demonstrated his range of bouncy mannerisms as a go-getter; and in *Inserts* he was more restrained and intense as Boy Wonder, a film director forced to make porno movies in his own home.

In two Spielberg films he found himself somewhat eclipsed – in *Jaws* (1975) by 'Bruce' the shark machine, and in 1977's *Close Encounters Of The Third Kind* by the dazzling special effects but his nervy, comic technique and manic laugh was given full rein in the Neil Simon-scripted *The Goodbye Girl* (1977), which made him, at 29, the youngest man to that date to win a Best Actor Oscar. As an egocentric off-Broadway actor unwillingly having to share a small Greenwich Village apartment with an ex-hoofer (Marsha Mason) and her precocious daughter (Quinn Cummings), Dreyfuss managed to make an irritating character endearing. The scene of a misconceived production of *Richard III*, in which he is asked to play the king as a screaming queen, was a comic high spot.

One of the star's most relaxed performances was as Moses Wine, a 'would-be Marxist gumshoe' in *The Big Fix* (1978), a man who has left his radical ideals behind him at Berkeley in the 60s, which prompted the critic Pauline Kael to comment that he was 'like a puppy who wants petting after every scene'. He was far less cuddly but extremely convincing in *The Competition* (1980), as an ageing *wunderkind* pianist having a last shot at winning a San Francisco contest and falling for his main rival (Amy

Irving). But it was as the paralysed patient desperately wanting to die in *Whose Life Is It Anyway?* (1981) that Dreyfuss proved he had more talent in his head alone than many actors have in their whole bodies. Brilliantly negotiating the thin line between comedy and tragedy, he conveyed the defensive sardonic wit of a once-active sculptor who has lost the use of his limbs.

Unfortunately, after the acclaim he received for the role, on stage and on film, his life fell apart due to, in his own words, 'stupidity, fear and good old-fashioned American hedonism'. In October 1982, he was involved in a car crash that led to an arrest on drug charges. 'I was doing two grammes of cocaine, twenty Percadon pills and about two quarts of alcohol a day. The only difference between John Belushi and me is that he's dead and I'm not.' However, with the assistance of a group of supportive people, he conquered his drug dependency, and in 1983 he married Jeramie Rain, a TV producer, with whom he had two children.

Among his best comeback roles were the unscrupulous salesman with the cadillac in Barry Levinson's *Tin Men* (1986), who steals Danny De Vito's wife (Barbara Hershey); and the coat-hanger tycoon who welcomes tramp Nick Nolte into his beautiful home with disastrous results in Paul Mazursky's *Down And Out In Beverly Hills*, the same year, As the grey-haired, grey-bearded, overworked lawyer in *Nuts* (1987), he was content to play second fiddle to Barbra Streisand, but was back hogging the limelight in *Stakeout* (1987), John Badham's slick comedy-thriller that relied heavily on the star's charm and versatility in the role of a brash cop assigned to watch the house of a girl in case her escaped con boyfriend arrives.

After a short break from films, during which he played an AIDS sufferer in Larry Kramer's *The Normal Heart* on stage, he accepted another showy role for Mazursky in *Moon Over Parador* (1988), portraying an actor on location in a Central American republic who impersonates the country's dictator, but all his best efforts at manic cheekiness couldn't save this undisciplined farce. For his third film for Spielberg, *Always* (1989), he was 30s screwball for most of the time, even when a ghost, but delicately handled the pathos of the deceased pilot allowing his lover (Holly Hunter) to put him behind her and start a new romantic life. His performance in Tom Stoppard's *Rosencrantz And Guildenstern Are Dead* (1990) proved conclusively that he is one of Hollywood's most intelligent actors.

1967 Valley Of The Dolls (bit); The Graduate (bit) **1968** The Young Runaways **1969** Hello Down There **1973** Dillinger; American Graffiti **1975** The Apprenticeship Of Duddy Kravitz; The Second Coming Of Suzanne **1975** Jaws **1976** Inserts **1977** Close Encounters Of The Third Kind; The Goodbye Girl **1978** The Big Fix; **1980** The Competition **1981** Whose Life Is It Anyway? **1984** The Buddy System **1986** Down And Out In Beverly Hills; Stand By Me; Tin Men **1987** Nuts; Stakeout **1988** Moon Over Parador **1989** Always; Let It Ride **1990** Once Around; Rosencrantz And Guildenstern Are Dead; Postcards From The Edge **1991** what About Bob? **1992/93** Lost In Yonkers

Dukakis, Olympia

Actress
Born 20 June 1931
Lowell, Massachusetts

After 23 years of minor appearances in a cross-section of largely undistinguished films (including *John And Mary*, 1969, as Dustin Hoffman's militant mother), Olympia Dukakis struck pay dirt. Cousin Michael's campaign for the presidency of the United States already had the family name on everybody's lips when the previously unknown Olympia found herself the recipient of the Best Supporting Actress Oscar for her finely judged performance – warm, poignant and humorous – as Cher's mother in the romantic hit *Moonstruck* (1987). Since then, necessarily confined by virtue of her age, appearance and style to supporting character roles, she has made an impression in a variety of parts from the tight-lipped personnel officer in *Working Girl* (1988) to the archetypal comic 'Jewish mother'-type parent of Kirstie Alley in *Look Who's Talking* (1989) and the acid-tongued Clairee Belcher, trading a a salvo of one-liners with Shirley MacLaine in *Steel Magnolias* (1989).

It is probable, looking at Dukakis' career, that her ambitions never lay in the direction of Hollywood. A Master of Fine Arts from Boston University, she has a distinguished record in the theatre as actress, director, teacher and guiding light in the profession. She is a founder member of the Charles Playhouse, Boston, where she worked from 1957 to 1960 and has taught acting at New York University and at Yale. Married to actor Louis Zorich, she and her husband have been the artistic inspiration behind the Whole Theatre in Monclair, New Jersey; she has adapted plays for the company and has directed dinner theatre there and at summer festivals elsewhere in the US. In addition to her formidable cultural contribution to students and theatre companies, she has herself appeared in more than 100 plays on and off Broadway, as well as in various regional theatres across the country. Olympia Dukakis will never be a Hollywood movie star, but she went into the 90s as something of a fixture and very definitely a name.

1964 Lilith **1969** John And Mary **1971** Made For Each Other **1973** Sisters **1974** Death Wish; Twice A Man **1979** Wanderers; Rich Kids **1980** The Idolmaker **1983** National Lampoon Goes To The Movies **1985** Flanagan aka Walls Of Glass **1987** Moonstruck **1988** Working Girl **1989** Steel Magnolias; Look Who's Talking **1989** Dad **1990** In The Spirit; Look Who's Talking Too **1992** Over The Hill **1992/93** Ruby Cairo

Dunaway, Faye

Actress
Born 14 January 1941
Bascom, Florida

Faye Dunaway has played Evita Perón, Aimee Semple McPherson and Wallis Simpson on television, and Joan Crawford and Bonnie Parker on film. 'These women all had something in common. They had tremendous force of will and they were determined to make their own destinies,' explained the tall, statuesque, green-eyed blonde actress. 'And they were also passionate people.'

The daughter of a career army officer, Dunaway was raised and educated in various American and European towns. After attending the University of Florida and the School of Applied Arts at Boston University, she headed for New York and an acting career. From 1962 until 1967, she appeared in a number of plays, including *A Man For All Seasons*, and in Elia Kazan's production of Arthur Miller's *After The Fall*, as the thinly-disguised Marilyn Monroe character. Her screen debut in *The Happening* (1967), as a member of a band of beachcombing vagrants who accidentally kidnap a top Mafia gangster (Anthony Quinn), only gave an inkling of what was to come in the same year.

As Bonnie Parker, the Southern small-town girl who pairs up with gangster Clyde Barrow (Warren Beatty) in *Bonnie And Clyde*, she was naive, sexy, perverse and tragic at the same time. Arthur Penn's influential amoral movie became a smash hit and earned its virtually unknown female star an Oscar nomination. The simple frocks and black beret she wore as Bonnie gave way to a series of chic gowns for her role as a high-flying insurance investigator, on the trail of Boston tycoon Steve McQueen, in *The Thomas Crown Affair* (1968), Norman Jewison's glossy thriller. In a series of sexually charged set-pieces, she was dazzling.

Continuing to look stunning, she had meatier roles in two overheated dramas: Kazan's *The Arrangement* (1969), in which she played Kirk Douglas' liberated mistress, and *Puzzle Of A Downfall Child* (1970), in which she portrayed a successful photographic model who retreats to an isolated beach house to avoid mental breakdown. Unfortunately, she inappropriately carried her Park Avenue allure into the role of Katie Elder, the prostitute whom Doc Holliday (Stacy Keach) wins in a poker game way out west in *Doc* (1971). But in *Oklahoma Crude* (1973), with her hair dyed black, she was credible as the man-hating shrew tamed by boozy George C. Scott, who helps her defend her oilwell from nasty Jack Palance.

The actress was at her most icily glamorous in Roman Polanski's *Chinatown* (1974), for which she gained a second Oscar nomination. As the classic *film noir* mysterious woman who hires private eye Jack Nicholson to shadow her errant husband, she is revealed to have been concealing the darkest of secrets. After the picture was completed, Polanski stated publicly that 'she was a gigantic pain in the ass. She demonstrated certifiable proof of insanity', adding to Dunaway's reputation for being difficult. It is certainly the case that many people who have worked with her have come away bruised.

Frequently an implacable bitch in her films, the actress was superb as the ruthless TV programming executive in Sidney Lumet's *Network* (1976), a character whose obsession with the ratings even extends to her talking about them while making love to male menopausal William Holden. Her sharp-edged performance, for which she was rewarded with the Best Actress Oscar, gave the Paddy Chayefsky script the rapier-thrust it required.

Directors such as Penn, Polanski and Lumet had managed to check her tendency to overact, but she was allowed to go over the top in jackboots and a monocle in *Voyage Of The Damned* (1976), and was given free rein in *The Eyes of Laura Mars* (1978) as a fashion photographer who has premonitions of her beautiful subjects being brutally murdered. Although she had to pull out all the stops as Joan Crawford in *Mommie Dearest* (1981), Dunaway merely created a campy caricature of the earlier Hollywood mistress of melodrama, whom she resembles. Crawford had been dead some four years before the unflattering biopic depicting her stormy relationship with her daughter Christina hit the screens, but she had written in her autobiography that 'of all actresses, to me only Faye Dunaway has the talent and the courage to make a real star'.

Whatever Dunaway does, however, whether good or bad, she brings to it a sense of excitement and style, even in Michael Winner's vulgar remake of *The Wicked Lady* (1983). Though she did not erase memories of Margaret Lockwood as the aristocrat-highwaywoman, she played the role with wit and conviction. In *Burning Secret* (1988), she was the half-Austrian wife of an American diplomat who takes her asthmatic son to a mountain spa in post-World War I Austria. She was beautifully costumed again in the sort of role that Joan Crawford would have filled in the past, and into whose shoes Faye Dunaway seemed firmly to have stepped.

1967 The Happening; Hurry Sundown; Bonnie And Clyde **1968** The Thomas Crown Affair **1969** The Extraordinary Seaman; The Arrangement; Gli Amanti/A Place For Lovers (Italy) **1970** Little Big Man; Puzzle Of A Downfall Child **1971** Doc **1972** The Deadly Trap **1973** Oklahoma Crude **1974** The Three Musketeers; Chinatown; The Towering Inferno **1975** The Four Musketeers; Three Days Of The Condor **1976** Voyage Of The Damned; Network **1978** Eyes Of Laura Mars **1979** The Champ **1981** Mommie Dearest **1983** The Wicked Lady **1987** Barfly **1988** Midnight Crossing; Burning Secret **1989** In Una Notte Di Chiaro Di Luna/On A Moonlit Night (Italy/France) **1990** The Handmaid's Tale **1991** Scorchers **1992** American Dreamers **1992/93** The Temp **1993** Double Edge (US/Israel); Even Cowgirls Get The Blues

Dunne, Griffin

Actor
Born 8 June 1955
New York City

Since leaping to cinema folklore as a decomposing corpse advising his best friend on the most humane way to commit suicide in *An American Werewolf In London* (1981), Griffin Dunne has had a more-than-a-little erratic screen career, although he has shown an amusing take on New York Jewish yuppie angst. The nephew of John Gregory Dunne and the son of producer-writer Dominick Dunne, he studied acting at the Neighbourhood Playhouse with Uta Hagen, soon developing a career that at times seemed an indeterminate hotchpotch of film, stage and TV acting and occasional production. (He formed his own film production company, Double Play Productions, with Amy Robinson.)

After being seriously underemployed in films, his deft comic touch found a marvellous showcase in his undead American tourist in *American Werewolf* ('I'm not having fun here. Have you ever talked to a corpse? It's bor-ing!' he opines), but seemed to flounder in the undernourished scripts that followed. Aware of this, and having previously produced *Baby, It's You* for John Sayles in 1983, he set up his best starring role as the sane but increasingly manic computer programmer caught up in an ever escalating comic nightmare journey across New York in Martin Scorsese's *After Hours* (1985), but once again found himself with little to do on screen elsewhere, to the extent of accepting a highly derivative role in the Madonna fiasco *Who's That Girl?* (1987).

Since, Dunne has alternated between solely producing – as with Sidney Lumet's *Running On Empty* (1989) – and combining the task with acting, the latter quite impressively in a TV movie account of the Vanunu 'nuclear spy' affair, *Secret Weapon* (1990), but without making quite the impact he deserves.

1975 The Other Side Of The Mountain **1980** Head Over Heels aka Chilly Scenes Of Winter **1981** The Fan; An American Werewolf In London **1984** Cold Feet; Almost You; Johnny Dangerously **1985** After Hours **1987** Who's That Girl?; Amazon Women On The Moon **1988** The Big Blue **1989** Me And Him/Ich Und Er (Germany) **1991** Once Around; My Girl **1992** Stepkids; Straight Talk; The Pickle

Durning, Charles

Actor
Born 28 February 1933
Highland Falls, New York

One of the most readily recognisable supporting players in modern film, the burly Irish-American actor Charles Durning made his debut in a touring stage production of *The Andersonville Trial* in 1960, working his way through Shakespeare and daytime TV (such as the soap *Another World* in 1964) until his film debut in 1965's *Harvey Middleman, Fireman*. However, it was not until 1973 that he made an impact with featured roles in De Palma's *Sisters* and the first of many Irish American cops (a franchise he and Kenneth McMillan seemed to share for the next two decades) in *The Sting*.

Since then, Durning has rarely been off the screen – though seldom on the side of the angels – and has racked up some impressive credits en route. He was the sympathetic policeman trying to control *Dog Day Afternoon* (1975), the honourable President who allows himself to be assassinated in *Twilight's Last Gleaming* (1977), a politically ambitious priest in *True Confessions* (1981) and a misguided, well-intentioned one in *Where The River Runs Black* (1986), but his sordid and sweaty private eye in *Cat Chaser* (1989) was perhaps more characteristic. His best, and most moving, performance was as the simple-hearted farmer who unwittingly falls in love with Dustin Hoffman in *Toootsie* (1982): the scene where he proposes to 'her' is the most outstanding, yet understated and natural in his career, and more than makes up for the occasional duff performance, such as his over-the-top comic-strip villain in *Stick* (1985).

1965 Harvey Middleman, Fireman **1970** I Walk The Line **1972** Dealing or The Berkeley-to-Boston Forty-Brick Lost-Bag Blues **1973** Sisters; The Sting **1974** The Front Page **1975** Dog Day Afternoon; The Hindenburg **1976** Breakdown Pass; Harry And Walter Go To New York **1977** Twilight's Last Gleaming; The Choirboys; An Enemy Of The People **1978** The Greek Tycoon; The Fury **1979** Starting Over; The Muppet Movie; When A Stranger Calls; Die Laughing; North Dallas Forty; Tilt **1980** The Final Countdown **1981** True Confessions; Sharkey's Machine **1982** Tootsie; The Best Little Whorehouse in Texas; Deadhead Miles; **1983** Two of a Kind; To Be or Not To Be **1984** Mass Appeal; Hadley's Rebellion **1985** The Man With One Red Shoe; Stick; Stand Alone **1986** Where The River Runs Black; Tough Guys; Solarbabies (aka Solarwarriors); Big Trouble **1987** Happy New Year; The Rosary Murders **1988** A Tiger's Tale; Cop; Far North **1989** Etoile (Italy); Brenda Starr; Cat Chaser **1990** Fatal Sky; Dick Tracy; Project: Alien **1991** Warshawski

Duvall, Robert

Actor, director
Born 5 January 1931
San Diego, California

'I love the smell of napalm in the morning,' says Robert Duvall as the mad, warloving Colonel Kilgore in Francis Coppola's *Apocalypse Now* (1979). Kilgore is certainly a caricature of the American military, but Duvall gave him a terrifying reality. Presenting a man only as insane as the war around him, his brief appearance was central to the film and full of impact.

The son of a rear-admiral, Duvall, with his stern features, fixed gaze and gleaming forehead, seemed born to play psychotic soldiers, gangsters and cops. There has always been a recognition in American films that the line between the military, the mobsters and the police is a fine one, and Duvall walks it with perfect equilibrium. Among his roles in uniform were the disturbed soldier in *Captain Newman M.D.* (1964); the military doctor literally driven crazy by the boorish heroes of *M*A*S*H* (1969), and the Nazi officer plotting to kidnap Churchill in *The Eagle Has Landed* (1976). His portrayal in *The Great Santini* (1979) of a peacetime officer unable to think outside the military code even when it comes to his relationship with his family, a toned-down version of Kilgore, won him his first Best Actor Oscar nomination.

Duvall did two years of military service after being educated at Principia College, Illinois. He then joined the Neighborhood Playhouse in New York, gaining particular recognition for his portrayal of longshoreman Eddie Carboni in *A View From The Bridge* in 1965. He had already made his screen debut as the simple-minded Boo Radley in *To Kill A Mockingbird* (1963), and continued in supporting roles such as the Southern cuckold of Janice Rule in Arthur Penn's *The Chase* (1965), until he was cast in the title role of George Lucas' first film, *THX-1138* (1970), an Orwellian nightmare in which the shaven-headed Duvall was a social rebel fleeing androids.

His reputation became firmly established in Coppola's *The Godfather* (1971), and its 1974 sequel, in which he played the sharp lawyer, Tom Hagen, go-between, confidant and retainer to the all-powerful Corleone family. His strong, discreet performance held the family, and indeed, the two films together. He was less restrained but still effective as a psychotic Jesse James in Philip Kaufman's *The Great Northfield Minnesota Raid* (1971) and, remaining out west in *Joe Kidd* (1972), an unscrupulous rancher who hires equally unscrupulous Clint Eastwood to kill a Mexican bandit. Duvall continued to be a nasty piece of work as an avenging ex-con *in The Outfit* (1973), and in Sam Peckinpah's *The Killer Elite* (1975) he was head of an enemy organisation out to kill a Taiwanese politician opposed by buddy James Caan on the CIA side.

Even when playing cops, ostensibly on the right side of the law, the actor brought moral ambiguity into roles such as the New York detective in *Badge 373* (1973), an unpleasant thriller based on the exploits of Eddie Egan, the man who inspired the better *French Connection* movies; and in *True Confessions* (1981), he was the tough, dedicated detective counterpointing Robert De Niro's ambitious priest, a film which makes the point that the cop has the instinct of the priest and vice versa.

After all these variations on evil, Duvall stated that he wanted a chance to portray a good person. The result was his Best Actor Oscar-winning role in *Tender Mercies* (1983). Superb as the rejuvenated over-the-hill country-and-western singer, he not only sang competently but was able to generate a warmth denied him for most of his previous career. Continuing to diversify, he turned director, investing almost $1 million of his own money and three years of his time on *Angelo, My Love* (1984), a gentle, sympathetic tale of a gypsy boy growing up in New York, with a non-professional cast of real gypsies. He had previously directed a documentary called *We're Not In The Jet Set* (1975), about the Nebraska farm people he met while making Coppola's *Rain People* (1969).

As an actor, apart from his tender role in *Tender Mercies*, Duvall has managed to move into areas away from cops and hoodlums. He was an excellent Dr Watson, complete with English accent, to Nicol Williamson's Sherlock Holmes in *The Seven Per Cent Solution* (1976), a far cry from the usual bumbler; and (over)played a foppish Southern dandy in Jerzy Skolimowski's allegorical *The Lightship* (1986), pitted against Klaus Maria Brandauer's sea captain. But he is still at his best in the sort of roles that brought him fame, such as the weary, streetwise LA cop in Dennis Hopper's *Colors* (1988). He exuded a paternal protectiveness towards Sean Penn's arrogant rookie, as he did towards Tom Cruise in *Days Of Thunder* (1990), bringing a finely tuned performance into the formula racing-car movie. And his kindly, paternal Southern gentleman, alongside the formidable duo of Diane Ladd and Laura Dern in *Rambling Rose*, was a marvellous turn.

Duvall is no believer in the Method, likening the technique to walking on crutches when you have two good legs of your own. His style comes from acute observation of people, his long stored-up memories of individual quirks which he calls upon to enrich his characters.

1963 To Kill A Mockingbird **1964** Captain Newman M.D; Nightmare In The Sun **1965** The Chase **1966** Fame Is The Name Of The Game **1967** Cosa Nostra; An Arch Enemy Of The FBI **1968** Countdown; The Detective; Bullitt **1969** True Grit; Rain People; M*A*S*H **1970** The Revolutionary **1971** THX-1138; Lawman **1972** The Godfather; The Great Northfield Minnesota Raid; Joe Kidd; Tomorrow **1973** Badge 373; Lady Ice; The Outfit **1974** The Godfather Part II; The Conversation **1975** Breakout; The Killer Elite; We're Not In The Jet Set (docu; director only) **1976** The Seven Per Cent Solution; Network; The Eagle Has Landed **1977** The Greatest **1978** The Betsy **1979** The Great Santini; Apocalypse Now **1981** True Confessions; The Pursuit Of D.B. Cooper **1983** Tender Mercies **1984** The Natural; The Stone Boy; Angelo, My Love (director only) **1986** The Lightship **1987** Hotel Colonial; Let's Get Harry **1988** Colors **1990** Days Of Thunder; The Handmaid's Tale **1991** Rambling Rose; Convicts **1992** Newsies (GB: The News Boys) **1992/93** Falling Down, The Plague/La Peste (France/GB/Argentina)

Duvall, Shelley

Actress
Born 7 July 1949
Houston, Texas

Apart from her role in Stanley Kubrick's *The Shining* (1979), and a few small parts in other films, Shelley Duvall has appeared solely in the movies of Robert Altman, the director who discovered her at a party in her home town of Houston. Although she had never acted outside high school, Altman cast the tall, gangling, toothy 19-year-old in *Brewster McCloud* (1970). The following year she made a brief appearance in *McCabe And Mrs Miller*, before Altman gave her the co-lead in *Thieves Like Us* (1974), as the simple daughter of the farmer who helps incompetent bank robber Keith Carradine escape the law. It was an extremely touching and engaging performance, lending a poetic quality to the drama set during the Depression.

Taking a short breathing space between Altman movies, Duvall was most amusing in a sequence in *Annie Hall* (1977) as one of Woody Allen's disastrous dates, a pseudo-hip rock critic from *Rolling Stone* magazine, whose cultural attitudes are anathema to Woody's. Then it was back with Altman, who cast her as an empty, loquacious physical therapist who becomes mentor to her room-mate (Sissy Spacek) at a Palm Springs motel in *Three Women* (1977). Making the vapid character varied and entertaining in this compelling, dream-like drama won her the Best Actress award at Cannes.

'The wonderful thing about Shelley is her eccentric quality – the way she talks, the way she moves, the way her nervous system is put together,' Stanley Kubrick commented about her performance as Wendy Torrence in his spine-chiller, *The Shining* – although she didn't have to do very much more than look terrified and react to her husband, Jack Nicholson, gradually going off his head in an isolated hotel in the Colorado mountains.

Few actresses could have been better cast as Olive Oyl than the gawky Duvall. With her blackened hair in a bun, she was perfect as the plain girlfriend of the famous spinach-eating sailor (Robin Williams) in Altman's *Popeye* (1980). With the director's departure from Hollywood to New York-based independent productions, the actress' career faded. Only making occasional appearances, she has been generally wasted in roles such as Daryl Hannah's friend in *Roxanne* (1987) but she was wonderful in Tim Burton's acclaimed short film, *Fraukenweenie* the same year. Perhaps her looks and talents are rather too specialised to fit easily into the many formula films that characterise the turnover in Hollywood.

1970 Brewster McCloud **1971** McCabe And Mrs Miller **1974** Thieves Like Us **1975** Nashville **1976** Buffalo Bill And The Indians **1977** Annie Hall (cameo); Three Women **1979** The Shining **1980** Popeye **1981** Time Bandits **1987** Roxanne **1991** Suburban Commando

E

Eastwood, Clint

Actor, director
Born 31 May 1930
San Francisco, California

Despite the trappings of stony-faced violence that set him apart from his initial contemporaries, Clint Eastwood is very much the last movie star of the old school, with a style of direction informed by classic directors such as Anthony Mann and his acting by stars like William Holden (the lead in *Breezy*, 1973) whose surface solid professionalism tended to hide the light of their passion under a bushel during their lifetimes. Unlike them, Eastwood has been able to see his reputation grow in his own lifetime (albeit while his box-office appeal wanes), largely through his determination to make one personal project for every commercial one, but it is a position won by much paying of dues and a long apprenticeship.

After a rootless Depression childhood following his petrol pump attendant father along much of the West Coast, many menial jobs and a spell in the army as a swimming instructor, a chance introduction by a friend after he had completed a business administration course resulted in a contract with Universal-International in the mid-50s. After being run through their 'charm school' and being given few bit parts (he spent 1955 as an absent-minded scientist losing a laboratory mouse in his top pocket in *Revenge Of The Creature* and napalming a giant spider in *Tarantula*) he was fired because, according to Burt Reynolds who was fired the same day, 'he wasn't goodlooking enough and his Adam's apple stuck out too much'. Then Eastwood spent eight seasons as the amiable, fresh-faced sidekick Rowdy Yates in the Western TV series *Rawhide* where his ambition to direct first surfaced, and he left the show when the producers reneged on a promise to let him helm an episode. His fortunes seemed to be on the downturn when he accepted a low-budget Western whose Italian director was unable to afford James Coburn, but the film, *A Fistful Of Dollars* (1964), and its two sequels, *For A Few Dollars More* (1965) and the epic *The Good, The Bad And The Ugly* (1966), proved sensational successes, turning the convention of the genre on its head and inspiring an exodus of second feature players to try their fortunes in Italy.

Despite the shockingly casual violence of the actor's monosyllabic, cigar-chewing gun for hire, his tarnished angel's romantic past owed as much to the Western's long tradition of disillusioned heroes as the first film did to the plot of Kurosawa's *Yojimbo* (a situation that kept all three in legal limbo in the US for a couple of years), but more than simply establishing Eastwood's screen persona, they were the first films to realise the power of his face. Director Sergio Leone's style, varying from the sweepingly operatic to giant close-ups, was partially responsible, but it was the star, who discarded most of his dialogue and rewrote what remained, who knew that he could say far more by simply moving a cigar from one side of his mouth to the other than with any monologue – particularly one written by an Italian with a poor grasp of the English language. Leone tried to give his Man-With-No-Name a final send-off in the opening sequence of *Once Upon A Time In The West*, alongside his Bad and Ugly co-stars Lee Van Cleef and Eli Wallach, as the three hired killers gunned down by Charles Bronson at the railway station, but Eastwood – alienated from the director after he blew up a bridge he had just crossed in *The Good, The Bad And The Ugly* to get a better shot – failed to see the joke.

The films finally reached the States and Eastwood's subsequent American Western, *Hang 'Em High* (1968), gave Universal its quickest pay-off in their history. Then Don Siegel's transposition of the genre onto the cop thriller in *Coogan's Bluff* (1968) proved equally successful, and the actor's career really took off. Hollywood's initial response was to put him in big-budget roadshow pictures like *Where Eagles Dare* (1969), but his horror at the runaway expenditure on the musical *Paint Your Wagon* (1969) and his bitter disappointment over the re-editing of *Kelly's Heroes* (1970), its anti-war satire and Vietnam parallels passed over in favour of more explosions and burning bridges, led to him taking more control of his career. Through his own Malpaso production company he produced all his subsequent films, keeping a tight rein on budgets and building up a reliable stock company of both actors and technicians and finally making his directorial debut with the psychological thriller

Play Misty For Me (1971). Predating *Fatal Attraction* by a decade and a half, it cast the macho star as a DJ victimised by an unbalanced female fan (Jessica Walter) to good effect, but the actor's direction was less certain, veering at times towards over-obvious symbolism (there are an awful lot of knives in an awful lot of scenes).

He had actually directed one scene on his previous film, Siegel's *Dirty Harry* (1971), and it was the character of Harry Callahan, the cop whose major difference from the psychopath he pursues is his badge, that was to dominate the next phase of his career and inspire a series of much imitated catchphrases – 'Do you feel lucky, punk?', 'Go ahead, make my day.' and, most pointedly, 'A man's gotta know his limitations.' Over the next two decades, Harry was to take on vigilantes, terrorists and Mafiosi in four increasingly episodic and sensationalist sequels that turned the character into a superhero and, along with his orang-utan comedies *Every Which Way But Loose* (1978) and *Any Which Way You Can* (1980), proved the financial backbone of his career but lacked Siegel's uneasy undercurrents. Perhaps aware of this, Eastwood tended to undercut his meal ticket in his other cop movies, parodying Harry with the dumb 'patsy' Shockley in *The Gauntlet* (1977) and delving even further into the dark side of his psyche with his most disturbing film, *Tightrope* (1984). His Detective Wes Block needs to control relationships and distance himself emotionally by his use of handcuffs during sex in a plot that turns his profession, his private vices and his current case in on each other until, at one point, even he cannot say immediately that he is not the killer he is seeking: what at first appears to be an interview with a witness turns out to be a liaison with a prostitute, just as what at first appears to be the crimes of a pervert turn out to be someone deliberately mirroring his sexual desires. No other star even approaching Eastwood's stature would have touched the part, but he turned it into something of a triumph (although not with feminists, who picketed the film).

Constantly examining and exploring his screen persona elsewhere, Clint went beyond the Man-With-No-Name in his increasingly rare subsequent Westerns that shared only that anti-hero's laconic nature (he frequently gives his own lines to other actors). The Western 'ghost' stories, *High Plains Drifter* (1973) and *Pale Rider* (1985), cast him as the mystical avenger of his own death, while perhaps his most accomplished film, *The Outlaw Josey Wales* (1976, which he took over from Phil Kaufman), was a touching journey back to life for a man whose soul had been killed by the atrocities of the Civil War; as with Anthony Mann's *The Far Country* (1955), it is a tale of revenge redeemed by love (and marked the start of his long-term affair with actress Sondra Locke that ended in his divorce from his wife, sensational headlines and litigation, but didn't prevent him from famously becoming the mayor of Carmel). Like Mann, Eastwood frequently gave his Western heroes some physical scar or stigmata to overcome, and sharing, too, Mann's feeling for landscape and his leaning towards night scenes and low lighting as his own directorial confidence developed.

While his direction of his commercial vehicles – the awful *Sudden Impact* (1982) and the dire *The Rookie* (1990) in particular – showed an increasing lack of imagination, his personal projects became more interesting and ambitious in their subversion of his image. *Bronco Billy* (1980) was an engaging comedy about a group of losers, led by Eastwood's former shoe salesman, making their dreams come true in a travelling Wild West show; and in *Honky Tonk Man* (1982) he cast himself almost heroically against the spirit of the times as a consumptive country-and-western singer on the road to Nashville with his estranged son. He showed his European sensibilities (that had their more embarrassing roots in Vittorio De Sica's episode of *The Witches*, 1967) by following an emotional rather than a narrative line with his much lauded pet project *Bird* (1989), the story of his childhood hero, jazz musician Charlie Parker (wonderfully played by Forest Whitaker). Around this time, Eastwood seemed more valued in Europe than on his home ground: *White Hunter, Black Heart* (1990), boasting one of his most interesting performances as a John Huston-like director obssessed with killing an elephant because 'it's the only sin you can buy a licence to commit', took more money in France than in America. His freedom to make the films that earn him that esteem, despite their genuine economy in an era of spendthrift productions, seemed resting rather precariously on his ability to restore his box-office popularity with the kind of action films he no longer seemed to want to make by the 1990s. The worry was dispelled with the extraordinary critical and commercial success of *Unforgiven* (1992), a script

Eastwood had acquired some ten years earlier and waited to 'age into'. Dedicated to 'Sergio and Don', it rewrote the language of the Western while adhering to its structures. In many ways an inversion of *Josey Wales*, with its killer journeying from redemption back into hell, it is striking for its willingness to confront the effects of violence on both those who commit it and those who suffer it, and for the sense of the characters' awareness of their own mortality.

A personal triumph that for once was not lost on the critics, *Unforgiven* also seemed to allay increasing rumours that Clint Eastwood was planning to retire to the other side of the camera.

As actor only unless stated otherwise: **1955** Revenge Of The Creature; Lady Godiva; Tarantula **1956** Never Say Goodbye; The First Travelling Saleslady; Star In The Dust **1957** Escapade In Japan **1958** Ambush At Cimarron Pass; Lafayette Escadrille **1964** Per Un Pugno Di Dollari/A Fistful Of Dollars (Italy) **1965** Per Qualche Dollari In Piu/For A Few Dollars More (Italy) **1966** Il Buono, Il Brutto, Il Cattivo/The Good, The Bad And The Ugly (Italy) **1967** Le Streghe/The Witches (Italy) **1968** Hang 'Em High; Coogan's Bluff **1969** Where Eagles Dare; Paint Your Wagon **1970** Two Mules For Sister Sara; Kelly's Heroes **1971** The Beguiled; Dirty Harry; Play Misty For Me (also director) **1972** Joe Kidd **1973** High Plains Drifter (also director); Breezy (director only) **1974** Thunderbolt And Lightfoot **1975** The Eiger Sanction (also director) **1976** The Outlaw Josey Wales (also director); The Enforcer **1977** The Gauntlet (also director) **1978** Every Which Way But Loose **1979** Escape From Alcatraz **1980** Any Which Way You Can; Bronco Billy (also director) **1982** Honky Tonk Man (also director); Firefox (also director) **1983** Sudden Impact (also director) **1984** Tightrope; City Heat **1985** Pale Rider (also director) **1986** Heartbreak Ridge (also director) **1988** The Dead Pool **1989** Pink Cadillac (also director); Bird (director only) **1990** White Hunter, Black Heart (also director); The Rookie (also director) **1992** Unforgiven (also director) **1993** In The Line Of Fire

Edwards, Anthony

Actor
Born 19 July 1962
Santa Barbara, California

Tall and slim, with blond hair and boyish good looks, Anthony Edwards has an unusually diverse filmography for one of his generation. Keeping one foot firmly planted in downmarket teen pap, he moved forward with the other to participate in quality productions such as *Mr North* (1988).

Between the ages of 12 and 17 Edwards acted in more than 30 plays before training in London in 1980. He also did a stint of drama at USC, but this did not prevent him from making his feature film debut in 1982 in one of the talent spotters' favourite teen pics, *Fast Times At Ridgemont High*. He then played the kid brother of Shirley Muldowney (Bonnie Bedelia) in Jonathan Kaplan's serious *Heart Like A Wheel* (1984), before co-starring with Robert Carradine in the not-so-subtle *Revenge of The Nerds* the same year. He made a brief but telling appearance as a drunken, manic, indeed seemingly demented, high school graduate in Rob Reiner's *The Sure Thing* (1985), and followed that with a geeky but likeable kid in *Nerds* director Jeff Kanew's *Gotcha*; then came Goose, the most personable of the Aryan wannabees in Tony Scott's flashy hit *Top Gun* (1986).

But Edwards seemed altogether better suited to Danny Huston's gentle, old-fashioned Thornton Wilder adaptation, *Mr North* (1988). As the eponymous white-bread hero, Edwards succeeded in making virtue incarnate less boring than it might have been. His naturally light touch was augmented by a charge of static electricity, enough to keep old-timers Robert Mitchum and Lauren Bacall on their toes. In the British film *Hawks*, also in 1988, the actor was a bearded dying American football player – though the movie was marred by its conspicuous vulgarity, it was a meaty role, a coming of age that laid the way for a couple of impressive thrillers, *Miracle Mile* (1988) and *Downtown* (1990).

1982 Fast Times At Ridgemont High **1984** Heart Like A Wheel; Revenge Of The Nerds **1985** The Sure Thing; Gotcha **1986** Top Gun **1987** Summer Heat; Revenge of The Nerds 2: Nerds In Paradise(cameo) **1988** Mr North; Hawks; Miracle Mile **1989** How I Got Into College **1990** Downtown **1992** Pet Sematary II **1992/93** Delta Heat

Edwards, Blake
(William Blake McEdwards)

Director, producer, writer
Born 26 July 1922
Tulsa, Oklahoma

There are two stars that most people immediately associate with the films of Blake Edwards – Peter Sellers and Julie Andrews. Sellers because the British actor created his most famous role as the bumbling Inspector Clouseau in seven Pink Panther movies; Andrews because she has starred in over half-a-dozen of the director's films since her marriage to him in 1970.

Before graduating to directing, Edwards served a long apprenticeship as a writer for radio and television, acted in several films in the 40s, and co-wrote the screenplays for six Columbia movies from 1952 to 1957, all directed by his friend Richard Quine. His first directorial efforts were two breezy Frankie Laine musicals (Quine had also directed two similar vehicles for the popular portly singer of the 50s), and three light Tony Curtis pictures, almost indistinguishable from Quine's efforts. It was *Breakfast At Tiffany's* (1961), a sugary version of the Truman Capote story, that brought Edwards' name into greater focus. The charm of Audrey Hepburn as kooky callgirl Holly Golightly, and the pleasant Oscar-winning Henry Mancini-Johnny Mercer song 'Moon River', made it a box-office hit.

In direct contrast to everything he had done previously, the director embarked on a couple of dramas starring the lovely Lee Remick in 1962. *Days Of Wine And Roses*, a social comedy that turns into a surprisingly black, realistic portrayal of alcoholism, gave Jack Lemmon his meatiest role so far as Remick's advertising executive husband who gets hooked on drink, with his wife following suit. *Experiment In Terror* was a shadowy atmospheric tale of bank teller Remick, whose life is threatened by an anonymous asthmatic telephone caller. The quality of these non-comedies makes one ponder on how much better (though less wealthy) Edwards might have been had his development not been arrested by Inspector Clouseau.

The Pink Panther (1964) began one of the most commercially successful cycle of comedies in the history of cinema. The maladroit French detective created by Peter Sellers was unable to cross a room without breaking something, had a continuous battle with inanimate objects, and a singular accent which caused communication problems. With his broad-belted trench-coat, tweed hat, small moustache and large magnifying glass, the character fitted in well with the animated credit titles. Clouseau made his first encore, in the same year, in *A Shot In The Dark*, but disappeared for 11 years, until Edwards, after a number of flops, brought him back a further five times. Such was the director's obsession with Clouseau that, despite the death of Sellers in 1980, he wasn't deterred from making *The Trail Of The Pink Panther* (1982), starring the deceased star, by maladroitly piecing together leftovers and clips from previous Panther films. Lynne Frederick, Sellers' widow, gained a settlement from United Artists after suing for their unauthorised use of the material.

For Edwards, Sellers also played an accident-prone Indian actor in *The Party* (1968). This plotless comedy, really a series of gags in the Jacques Tati manner, had some funny episodes, but many of them were milked dry by the end. Edwards' passion for slapstick was also evident in *The Great Race* (1965) which told of an improbable race from New York to Paris via Siberia and Ruritania in 1918 in wildly improbably cars but deteriorated into an unfunny takeoff of *The Prisoner Of Zenda* and Victorian melodrama, with Tony Curtis as the hero and Jack Lemmon the villain. The film was dedicated to 'Mr Laurel and Mr Hardy', but only rarely touched the genius of its dedicatees. Over 25 years later, Edwards made the frantic and dispiriting *A Fine Mess* (1986), starring Ted Danson, also inspired (if that's the word) by Laurel And Hardy.

While Sellers fell about, as did many audiences, the director took a couple of pratfalls himself with two spy capers starring his wife – *Darling Lili* with Rock Hudson (1970) and *The Tamarind Seed* with Omar Sharif (1974). His fidelity to Julie continued with *'10'* (1979), though she didn't have much to do other than wait for Dudley Moore to have scruples about Bo Derek and return to her for the soppy happy ending. The film, a mellow, male-menopausal Californian comedy, made $60 million, and was the director's last big hit to date. Hoping for another *'10'*, Edwards and Dudley Moore got together again a few years later for *Micki And Maude* (1982), a painfully contrived, intermittently funny farce about bigamy.

Away from the more farcical films, Edwards went in for a number of bitter comedies with autobiographical elements. *S.O.B.* (1981) was a bile-filled satire on Hollywood, in which the director played against his wife's Mary Poppins image, though it revealed more of his sour grapes than her slightly bigger bared breasts. He admitted that the rancorous, self-pitying, hypochondriac character played by Jack Lemmon in *That's Life!* (1984) was based on himself. This costly home movie was shot in the Edwards' home in Malibu, and the cast included Mrs Edwards, her daughters Jennifer Edwards and Kate Walton (from her previous marriage), and Lemmon's wife (Felicia Farr) and son, Chris, as well as real-life friends.

He was on safer ground with *Victor-Victoria* (1982) which, apart from some anachronistic vulgarities and a timid ending, was a pleasantly gay (in both senses) musical comedy with Julie Andrews looking convincing as a woman pretending to be a man pretending to be a woman. *Sunset* (1988), too, was a pleasant light comedy about Hollywood Westerns in the silent era with Bruce Willis as Tom Mix and James Garner as Wyatt Earp, an advisor on the set, making a good team. Then Edwards was back to the world of mid-life crisis with *Skin Deep* (1989), a title that might tempt the critic to sum up much of his erratic *oeuvre*, before making another attempt to resurrect the *Pink Panther* with Roberto Begnini in the Clouseau role.

1955 Bring Your Smile Along **1956** He Laughed Last **1957** Mister Corey **1958** This Happy Feeling **1959** The Perfect Furlough; Operation Petticoat **1960** High Time **1961** Breakfast At Tiffany's **1962** Experiment In Terror (GB: The Grip Of Fear) **1963** Days Of Wine And Roses **1964** The Pink Panther; A Shot In The Dark **1965** The Great Race **1966** What Did You Do In The War Daddy? **1967** Gunn **1968** The Party **1970** Darling Lili **1971** Wild Rovers **1972** The Carey Treatment **1974** The Tamarind Seed **1975** The Return Of The Pink Panther **1976** The Pink Panther Strikes Again **1978** Revenge Of The Pink Panther **1979** *'10'* **1981** S.O.B. **1982** Victor-Victoria; The Curse Of The Pink Panther; The Trail Of The Pink Panther **1983** The Man Who Loved Women **1984** Micki And Maude **1986** That's Life!; A Fine Mess **1987** Blind Date **1988** Sunset **1989** Skin Deep **1991** Switch **1993** Son Of The Pink Panther

Eichhorn, Lisa

Actress
Born 4 February 1952
Reading, Pennsylvania

Lisa Eichhorn is a beautiful and intelligent actress, American by birth and upbringing but equally at home on the other side of the Atlantic and in playing Englishwomen's roles. Her training was at RADA, which she attended after graduate study in literature at St Peter's College, Oxford (she had previously been an undergraduate in Canada). So England, or Englishness, is part of her artistic make-up. In fact, the first role she played in cinema (for which she won London's *Evening Standard* Actress of the Year Award and a Golden Globe nomination) was as a young Yorkshire girl who falls for handsome American airman Richard Gere in John Schlesinger's *Yanks* (1979). In *The Weather In The Streets* (1983), Gavin Millar's adaptation of the famous Rosamund Lehmann novel, she was faultless as the 1930s upper-class English heroine, Olivia, suffering from the oppressive sexual conventions of the time. 'Why do men make women cry?' the unsatisfactory lover, Michael York, muses somewhere in the course of the film (it seems to be what the story is about).

Eichhorn has done quite a lot of crying – suffering, anyway – in her film career. She has an inwardness, an intensity, a broodiness to counterbalance her classical, healthy good looks. One of her most memorable film roles was as the alcoholic wife, Mo, in Ivan Passer's strange and effective thriller, *Cutter's Way* (1981), where she is married to the bitter Vietnam vet John Heard, but secretly lusting after his blue-eyed friend Jeff Bridges. She has the stamp of education about her – a certain haughtiness and elegance that makes her first choice in adaptations of the classics. Twice she has played in Henry James adaptations, once on screen in James Ivory's *The Europeans (1979)*, and again on television in the serial *The Wings Of The Dove*. She has done a fair amount of television in her time and a lot of very distinguished stage acting, excelling in Shakespeare, Ibsen and Brecht. Altogether, she is a fascinating and lovely actress, rather under-used in cinema, which only makes her increasingly rare appearances on the big screen the more valuable, though the standard of the projects themselves seem to have deteriorated.

1979 Yanks; The Europeans **1980** Why Would I Lie? **1981** Cutter's Way, aka Cutter And Bone **1983** The Weather In The Streets **1984** Wild Rose **1987** Opposing Force **1990** Moon 44; Grim Prairie Tales **1992/93** As Long As You're Alive **1993** King Of The Hill

Elizondo, Hector

Actor
Born 22 December 1936
New York City

A distinguished Hispanic-American actor who studied with both the Actors' Studio and, more surprisingly, the Ballet Arts Company of Carnegie Hall, Hector Elizondo has appeared regularly on the live stage throughout his career, and has brightened up most of the pictures he has featured in with colourful, exquisitely turned supporting performances.

If Hollywood did not deem him leading man material, Elizondo at least knew the value of his gap-toothed grin and high forehead; it did not take him long to find a niche for himself as a character actor in the classical Hollywood tradition of Elisha Cook and Thomas Mitchell. He is an everyday Joe to the core, one of the working stiffs, one of us . . . but he also exhibits a certain dry panache, he can be flashy and deadpan all in the twinkling of an eye, and can turn his hand to suavity with effect. He makes a wonderful detective of the Columbo dirty mac brigade; in Paul Schrader's *American Gigolo* (1980) he was the only character who *breathed*. In the 80s Elizondo concentrated on comedies, to which he brings an air of class no matter what's going on around him. Director Garry Marshall is obviously a fan, having cast him in virtually all of his films from *Young Doctors In Love* (1982) through *The Flamingo Kid* (1984), in which he played Matt Dillon's dad, to *Pretty Woman* (1990) and *Frankie And Johnny* (1991).

Marshall's smash-hit romantic comedy, *Pretty Woman*, brought Elizondo a new kind of recognition from audiences hitherto ignorant of his name. As the snooty hotel manager whose disdain for Julia Roberts' hooker turns to admiration and affection, he was one of the movie's more than incidental pleasures. In 1992 he was rewarded with the plum role of lawyer Sandy Stern in the TV mini- series of Scott Turow's bestseller, *Burden of Proof.*

1971 Pocket Money; Born To Win; Deadhead Miles **1972** Stand Up And Be Counted; One Across, Two Down **1974** The Taking Of Pelham One, Two, Three **1975** Report To The Commissioner **1977** Thieves **1979** Cuba **1980** American Gigolo **1981** The Fan **1982** Young Doctors In Love **1984** The Flamingo Kid **1985** Private Resort **1986** Nothing In Common **1989** Leviathan **1990** Pretty Woman **1991** Frankie & Johnny; Necessary Roughness; Final Approach; Samantha

Elliott, Sam

Actor

Born 9 August 1944

Sacramento, California

A grizzled, rough-necked man's man, Sam Elliott only came into his own as he passed into his 40s and acquired the grace and wisdom a few flecks of grey hair naturally bestow. Not that he lacked success before that, but it was his television career that supported a few intermittent stabs at campy Rod Taylor territory on the silver screen.

A graduate of the University of Oregon, Elliott made his debut as a card player in *Butch Cassidy And The Sundance Kid* (1969), featuring his future wife, Katharine Ross. The TV series *Mission: Impossible* established his leading-man credentials (he was with the show through 1970–71), but neither *Frogs* nor *Molly And Lawless John* (both 1972) suggested much hope for cinema stardom. Television movies followed, including *The Blue Knight* (1973) with William Holden, which merited a theatrical release in Europe. *Mask* in 1985 completely changed the complexion of Elliott's career. Peter Bogdanovich's sentimental but effective tale of a heavily disfigured boy and his biker mum struck a chord, and if Cher and Eric Stoltz commanded most of the attention, Elliott's charismatic, genial Hell's Angel was a revelation to some. With his distinctive gruff voice, long unkempt hair and lanky physique it seemed obvious there was a new sheriff in town. *Fatal Beauty* (1987), *Shakedown* (1988) and *Prancer* (1990) were verification enough, and the British title for *Shakedown, Blue Jean Cop*, sums up the actor's appeal.

Sam Elliott even retained his credibility as the old dog teaching young pup Patrick Swayze new tricks in the macho flick *Roadhouse* (1989), though his sardonic demeanour and surly integrity were too good for the movie that capitalised on these qualities.

1969 Butch Cassidy And The Sundance Kid **1970** The Games **1972** Frogs; Molly And Lawless John **1976** Lifeguard **1978** The Legacy **1985** Mask **1987** Fatal Beauty **1988** Shakedown (GB: Blue Jean Cop) **1989** Road House **1990** Prancer; Sibling Rivalry **1992** Rush

Englund, Robert

Actor

Born 6 June 1949

Glendale, California

The peculiar conventions of the horror film have created some intriguingly unusual stars: among them a mild-mannered, cadaverous, cricket-loving Englishman, born William Henry Pratt in Dulwich, but later long resident in Hollywood as Boris Karloff; or former Hungarian matinée idol Arizstid Olt, better known to his legion of fans in the 1930s as the sleekly menacing Bela Lugosi, immortal incarnation of Count Dracula.

However, there have been few more unlikely members of the horror hall of fame than Robert Englund, who might pass unnoticed in a busy street but stops the traffic when he turns up to open a shopping mall in the grotesque make-up of Freddy Krueger, the ghoulish anti-hero of the *Nightmare On Elm Street* films. Involved in theatre from the age of 12 (he joined a children's theatre programme), Englund later attended the University of Oakland and UCLA, then studied acting at the Michigan Academy Of Dramatic Arts. He enjoyed a busy theatre career which kicked off with a production of *Godspell* in Cleveland and found fame after a creditable but unspectacular career as a supporting player in more than 30 feature and made-for-TV films. Potato-faced and balding, he was the kind of actor you might dimly recognise on a late-night movie show, usually cast in the kind of self-effacing role which required an early exit – the third astronaut on the left, who's always the first one to be killed by the alien monster. Ironically, it was while playing a sympathetic alien in the TV series *V* that Englund was spotted by director Wes Craven, who cast him as Freddy Krueger in *A Nightmare On Elm Street*
(1984). By the mid-1980s the teen movie market, awash with gore and gleefully attuned to the glint of razor-sharp knives, was ready for Freddy, 'bastard son of 100 maniacs', the child murderer who was burned to death after escaping conviction on a technicality. Twenty years later, hamburger-faced and razor-taloned, he returns to Elm Street to infiltrate the dreams of its teenage inhabitants. They begin to share common nightmares about being stalked and killed by a weird figure in a striped sweater and a porkpie hat who wields a set of wickedly curved blades at the ends of his fingers. With these he can literally carve his way into their homes and their subconscious. As the nightmares become ever more horrifying, so the teenagers succumb to their nocturnal tormentor and are found dead in their beds, their bodies savagely mutilated. Like some ghastly combination of Peter Pan and the Pied Piper, Freddy made sure they never grew up. Four sequels followed but, although these displayed a remarkable visual inventiveness, their tone became increasingly laboured as ever more waggish ways were found for Freddy to dispose of his hapless victims. However, Englund's Freddy Kreuger (does anyone know he's Robert Englund?), billed sixth on the first one, quickly rose to above-the-title star status, confirming his graduation from sleazy bogeyman to all-round cult hero. In *A Nightmare On Elm Street Part 3: Dream Warriors*
(1987), one glorious scene has him interrupting a TV chat show to lurch crazily towards a fatuously wittering Zsa Zsa Gabor! Bursting the bonds of any individual film, Freddy achieved an iconic niche in the pantheon of screen monsters, enabling Englund to reap the benefits of a huge marketing drive which spewed forth T-shirts, books, models and rubber and plastic imitations of Freddy's taloned glove. He even appeared on TV, Alfred Hitchcock-style, as the host of a particularly tacky anthology show, *Freddy's Nightmares*. At his peak in the late 1980s, Freddy eclipsed *Friday The 13th*'s Jason, *Halloween*'s Michael and *Texas Chainsaw Massacre*'s Leatherface to achieve a psychopathic superstardom matched only by *Psycho*'s Norman Bates. Horror stardom gave Englund his opportunity to broaden his horizons and direct a movie. The result was *976-Evil*
(1988), in which a teenager discovers that his telephone provides a hot-line to Hell. The actor then indulged himself in the title role of the *Phantom Of The Opera*
(1990). However, unlike his great horror predecessors Lon Chaney and Karloff he was quite unable to suggest that, under the make-up, was a living breathing, suffering creature.

1974 Buster And Billie **1975** Hustle **1976** Death Trap aka Starlight Slaughter aka Eaten Alive; St Ives; A Star is Born; Stay Hungry **1978** Big Wednesday; Blood Brothers; The Great Smokey Roadblock aka The Last Of The Cowboys **1980** The Fifth Floor **1981** Dead And Buried; Galaxy Of Terror **1982** Don't Cry, It's Only Thunder **1984** A Nightmare On Elm Street **1985** A Nightmare On Elm Street Part 2: Freddy's Revenge **1986** Never Too Young To Die **1987** A Nightmare On Elm Street Part 3: Dream Warriors **1988** A Nightmare On Elm Street Part 4: The Dream Master; 976-Evil (director only) **1989** A Nightmare On Elm Street Part 5: The Dream Child; Phantom Of The Opera **1990** The Adventures of Ford Fairlane **1991** A Nightmare on Elm Street Part 6: Freddy's Dead

Estevez, Emilio

Actor, writer, director
Born 12 May 1962
New York City

The eldest son of actor Martin Sheen, Emilio

Estevez took his father's original Spanish surname and, indeed, looks more Hispanic than either his father (who is half Irish) or his brother Charlie. Estevez was one of the numerous teen stars who got their break via youth novelist S.E. Hinton. He and Matt Dillon were in the first Hinton adaptation, *Tex* (1982), and he had a small part in Francis Ford Coppola's *The Outsiders* (1983) alongside Ralph Macchio, Patrick Swayze, Rob Lowe, Tom Cruise, C. Thomas Howell and Dillon again. The Brat Pack was born. Surprisingly, Estevez, with his slight build and sometimes rodent-like face, was to become its unofficial leader.

In 1984–85 he scored a one-two hit that showed him equally at ease as anarcho-punk Otto in the demented *Repo Man* (1984), and as a middle-class jock in John Hughes' very straight *The Breakfast Club* (1985). It was a range that served him well, and allowed him to escape the endless locker-room comedies that feature so heavily in his co-stars' filmographies. *St Elmo's Fire* (1985) was the sort of presumptuous nonsense that did nobody any favours, but Estevez had the momentum to carry past his mistakes and the enterprise. He wrote the script for *That Was Then, This Is Now* (1985) from the S.E. Hinton novel, and did a fair job of it. He also turned in one of his most authentic portrayals as an alienated adolescent trying to get a grip on the world.

Neither Stephen King's directorial debut, *Maximum Overdrive* (1986), nor Estevez's own *Wisdom* (1986) worked out, but they were honourable efforts. In the case of *Wisdom*, which Estevez wrote and directed as well as starred in, he was certainly overreaching himself. The film, co-starring his then fiancée, Demi Moore (she left him shortly afterwards and married Bruce Willis), starts out in realist vein, but turns in to a *Bonnie And Clyde*-cum-*Robin Hood* fantasy. As an actor, Estevez is a shrewd observer, but it remains to be seen if he has anything to tell us as a writer.

In the hands of John Badham and Touchstone Pictures, Estevez re-established his commercial appeal in *Stakeout* (1987) – a conventional cop buddy movie with Richard Dreyfuss. Estevez's moustache was the only real surprise, but the movie had the requisite quota of thrills and laughs, and the double act with Dreyfuss was fun. *Men At Work* (1990), which he directed and co-starred in with his brother Charlie, hardly resolved doubts about his ability behind the camera, but as Billy the Kid in *Young Guns* (1988) and its sequel, *Young Guns II* (1990), he still looked the natural leader of the pack, aging 70 years in the second film, and carrying some extra weight with aplomb. With his cackling laugh and ironic catch-phrase ('I'll make you famous!') Estevez plays the part to the hilt, and compares favourably with Paul Newman's interpretation of the role in *The Left Handed Gun* (1958).

1982 Tex **1983** Nightmares; The Outsiders **1984** Repo Man **1985** The Breakfast Club; St Elmo's Fire; That Was Then, This Is Now (also writer) **1986** Maximum Overdrive; Wisdom (also w/d) **1987** Stakeout **1988** Young Guns **1989** Never On Tuesday **1990** Young Guns II; Men At Work (also w/d) **1992** Freejack; The Mighty Ducks **1992/93** Bombay; National Lampoon's Loaded Weapon

F

Fahey Jeff

Actor
Born 1954?
Olean, New York

One of 13 children of an Irish-American family, Jeff Fahey, after the traditional restlessness and odd jobs – crewman on a fishing boat, ambulance driver in Germany, kibbutznik in Israel – began his career with three years in the Joffrey Ballet, subsidised by jobs as a vacuum cleaner and encyclopaedia salesman. His appearances in musical revivals led to a two-and-a-half year stint on the daytime soap *One Life To Live* and a full-blown acting career. His movie debut as a villainous landowner in *Silverado* (1985) was a competent but inconsequential performance, and along with his unrestrained, sleazy dementia in *Psycho III* (1986), gave little indication of a talent to watch, an impression denied by his off-Broadway work and his energetic and powerful performance opposite Albert Finney in the London production of *Orphans* (a role he lost to Matthew Modine in the subsequent film). His screen roles were either uninspiring – he spends much of *Backfire* (1988) as a vegetable – or hidden in derivative (*Split Decisions*, 1988) or disappointing (*Impulse*, 1990) films until his skilful, thinly veiled portrait of Peter Viertel in *White Hunter, Black Heart* (1990).

Serving as a Cassandra-like chorus, putting the film's moral arguments forward so that Clint Eastwood's self-possessed John Huston figure can trample on them to serve his own deification and damnation, Fahey provided the sole voice of reason in an unreasonable world, a man grounded in reality as we know it, set against an irrational obsession and ultimately retreating impotently to the sidelines. A remarkably restrained performance and by far his most confident screen work, it showed the actor's intelligence and won him some critical acclaim – but, alas, by 1991, none of the better parts he needed to follow up the impression he had made. The surprise success of the 'Virtual Reality' horror fantasy, *The Lawnmower Man* (1992), however, in which he starred as a technologically updated version of Frankenstein's monster, gave Fahey a big hit to sustain his career.

1985 Silverado **1986** Psycho III **1988** Backfire; Split Decisions **1989** Outback; True Blood **1990** Impulse; White Hunter, Black Heart; Last Of The Finest aka Blue Heat; Iron Maze **1991** Body Parts **1992** The Lawnmower Man; Sketch Artist

Falk, Peter

Actor
Born 16 September 1927
New York City

Peter Falk's famous squint, as if continually looking through the barrel of a gun, comes from the fact that he lost an eye at the age of three, and his down-to-earth personality derives from his tough New York upbringing. One of his first jobs was as a cook with the merchant marines, during which time he studied Social Research and Public Administration, obtaining degrees from Syracuse University. Bored with his job as an efficiency expert for the Budget Bureau of the State of Connecticut, he became interested in amateur dramatics and in 1955 turned pro with the encouragement of the actress Eva Le Gallienne, attracting attention in an off-Broadway production of Eugene O'Neill's *The Iceman Cometh*. This led to Broadway, television and films.

Given his looks, it was inevitable that Hollywood would cast him as a gangster in a number of his early pictures, including the Oscar-nominated supporting role of big-time racketeer Abe Reles in *Murder Inc.* (1960). In Frank Capra's *A Pocketful Of Miracles* (1961) he lightened the hoodlum characterisation with comedy, his Runyonesque persona being well suited to playing bootlegger Glenn Ford's sidekick, for which he received a second Oscar nomination. His comic gifts were further demonstrated in Blake Edwards' slapstick *The Great Race* (1965), in which he portrayed arch villain Jack Lemmon's cackling assistant. In a different farcical vein, Falk rescued erstwhile mate Lemmon from suicide in *Luv* (1967), in order to palm his wife (Elaine May) off on him.

It was not until his friend John Cassavetes gave him really meaty parts in *Husbands* (1970) and *A Woman Under The Influence* (1974) that Falk was able to prove his ability as a dramatic actor. In the former, he, Cassavetes and Ben Gazzara revealed the sadness, ugliness and emptiness of three middle-aged husbands on a spree in London in a futile attempt to forget the death of a friend. In *A Woman Under The Influence*, he played the lower middle-class father of three kids, driven to violent anger by the irrational behaviour of his alcoholic wife (Gena Rowlands).

A return to comedy saw him giving a fair imitation of Humphrey Bogart as, respectively, private-eyes Sam Diamond and Lou Peckinpaugh in two wildly undisciplined parodies directed by Robert Moore – *Murder By Death* (1976) and *The Cheap Detective* (1978). After hamming through two forgettable comedy-thriller capers, *The Brink's Job* (1978) and *The In-Laws* (1979), he was excellent in Robert Aldrich's *All The Marbles* (1981), as the wise-guy fast-talking manager of a glamorous female wrestling tag team.

Narrating gloomily in English, Falk appeared in Wim Wenders' piece of German whimsy, *Wings Of Desire* (1987). He played himself, in Berlin to star in a film about the Nazis and, would you believe it, turns out to be a fallen angel. Far better was his splendid performance as a jewel thief in some wonderfully convincing disguises in John G. Avildsen's *Happy New Year* (1987), a tepid remake of Claude Lelouch's *La Bonne Année* (1973). Continuing on the wrong side of the law in Susan Seidelman's rather laboured *Cookie* (1989), the actor played Dominick 'Dino' Capisco, an ex-con who has to contend with a wife (Brenda Vaccaro) he hates and an illegitimate daughter (Emily Lloyd) he doesn't know.

Whatever Peter Falk's range and talent in the movies, it will always be his fate to be associated with one character, that of Columbo, the dogged, quizzical private eye in the grubby raincoat who has been exposing murderers on television since 1971.

1958 Wind Across The Everglades **1959** The Bloody Brood **1960** Pretty Boy Floyd; Murder Inc.; The Secret Of The Purple Reef **1961** Pocketful Of Miracles **1962** Pressure Point **1963** The Balcony; It's A Mad Mad Mad Mad World **1964** Robin And The Seven Hoods **1965** The Great Race **1966** Penelope **1967** Luv **1968** Machine Gun McCain; Anzio (GB: The Battle For Anzio); Too Many Thieves **1969** Castle Keep **1970** Husbands **1974** A Woman Under The Influence **1976** Murder By Death; Mikey And Nicky **1978** The Cheap Detective; The Brink's Job **1979** The In-Laws **1981** All The Marbles (GB: The California Dolls) **1985** Big Trouble **1987** Der Himmel Uber Berlin/Wings of Desire (West Germany); Happy New Year; The Princess Bride **1988** Vibes **1989** Cookie **1990** In The Spirit **1991** Tune In Tomorrow (GB: Aunt Julia And The Scriptwriter) **1992/93** In Weiter Ferne, So Nah (Germany)

Farrow, Mia

Actress

Born 9 February 1945

Los Angeles

The metamorphosis of Mia Farrow's looks can serve as a shorthand guide to her development as a film actress. At the start of her career she was a blonde, huge-eyed waif, often cast for the fey fragility of her face and frame – most successfully so in *Rosemary's Baby*, Roman Polanski's celebrated 1968 thriller of supernatural possession. In the 1980s, as the most recent (and longest-surviving) of the women who have played Muse, off-screen as well as on, to Woody Allen's creative genius, she blossomed into one of the most radiant and affecting presences in the English-speaking cinema. It's a developmental process that has undergone many twists and turns, and quite a few hiccups, on the way to what, at the start of the 1990s, looked very much like a Happily Ever After conclusion.

Third of seven children born to the noted director John Farrow and the even more celebrated Irish-born actress Maureen O'Sullivan, Mia was a Hollywood native in more sense than one. Serious childhood illnesses left her with a delicate physique and constitution, which did not deter her from launching into acting (in a 1963 off-Broadway production of *The Importance Of Being Earnest*) while still in her teens. Her screen debut in the 1964 British-colonial action film *Guns At Batasi* and her stint in the long-running 60s television soap *Peyton Place* won Farrow some attention; but it was her marriage to Frank Sinatra in 1966 – she was his third wife, and 30 years his junior – that gained her most publicity.

They were divorced two years later, by which time she had already made *Rosemary's Baby* (a highly skilful piece of audience manipulation in which Farrow is unwittingly impregnated by the Devil in the guise of her own husband) and played an unstable child-woman clinging to Elizabeth Taylor's raddled prostitute, in Joseph Losey's absurd Gothick melodrama *Secret Ceremony* (1968). In both, Farrow's pinpoint acting skills create an aura of strangeness on which Polanski and Losey both capitalize: such frail characters, treading a thin line between sanity and madness, certainly appeared to be her forte.

Tackling other material, however, whether opposite Dustin Hoffman in the Peter Yates comic-romantic two-hander *John*

And Mary (1969), or opposite Robert Redford in Jack Clayton's disappointing film version of *The Great Gatsby* (1974), she seemed a somewhat mannered performer of limited emotional range. At the start of the 1970s Farrow had married the internationally renowned conductor André Previn. He was music director of the London Symphony Orchestra at the time and, as a result, she chose to spend much of the decade in England, rearing children (adopted as well as natural-born), acting on the London stage, and making a few largely forgettable films. As the marriage (which ended in 1979) entered a period of strain, she returned to a series of 'prestige' small roles in such disparate film assignments as Robert Altman's *A Wedding* (1978) and *Death On The Nile*, the 1978 Agatha Christie adaptation.

At this time there seemed not much shape or form to Farrow's performances, nor much sense of direction to her career. Then Woody Allen invited her to take an important part in his Bergmanesque ensemble piece, *A Midsummer Night's Sex Comedy* (1982), marking for her the beginning of a new creative phase (as well as a 12-year relationship with Allen and the birth of their child Satchel). With each successive Allen film – he is the only director with whom she has worked since 1982 – she has given the impression of becoming ever more stretched, more fully herself, on screen. He has demanded from her a range of characterisation hardly suspected before. In *Zelig* (1983) she is the bespectacled psychiatrist who cures the chameleon-personality hero; in *Broadway Danny Rose* (1984), a brassy, gum-chewing Mafia widow; in *The Purple Rose Of Cairo* (1985), a downtrodden small town waitress named Cecilia, more in love with movies than real life; in the 'Oedipus Wrecks' episode of *New York Stories* (1989), Allen's non-Jewish girlfriend, finally scared off by his mother's hilarious guerilla tactics. Of all of these, Cecilia is perhaps Farrow's richest portrayal: pathos, her stock-in-trade, is now balanced by an acutely judged art of discreetly sending herself up, so that the character draws audience smiles as well as pity.

Allen also encouraged the actress to take risks. This is most notable in the Chekhovian *September* (1987), where she makes a complex and disquieting figure out of the daughter of a self-absorbed ex-film star (Elaine Stritch); this tear-drenched loser is by no means played entirely for sympathy. Even in those other Allen ensemble pieces – *Hannah And Her Sisters* (1985), *Radio Days* (1987), *Crimes And Misdemeanors* (1990) – which cast her as a relatively straightforward object of male affections, her ability to distinguish the character by means of unexaggerated expressive nuances sheds a luminous grace on each one. It may be to Allen's credit that we owe the emergence of such an actress, but it is to Mia Farrow's that with each new film her art seems fine and valuable.

Regrettably, mid-1991 saw a sensationally public and acrimonious split between the couple, in the wake of which her admirers could only hope that she would find new avenues in which to shine.

1964 Guns At Batasi **1968** A Dandy In Aspic; Rosemary's Baby; Secret Ceremony **1969** John And Mary **1971** See No Evil (GB: Blind Terror) **1972** Follow Me (GB: The Public Eye); Docteur Popal aka The Scoundrel in White (France) **1974** The Great Gatsby **1975** Trikimia aka The Tempest (Greece) **1977** Full Circle aka The Haunting of Julia **1978** Avalanche; A Wedding; Death On The Nile **1979** The Hurricane **1982** A Midsummer Night's Sex Comedy **1983** Zelig **1984** Broadway Danny Rose **1985** Hannah And Her Sisters; The Purple Rose Of Cairo **1987** Radio Days; September **1989** Another Woman; New York Stories ('Oedipus Wrecks' episode) **1990** Crimes And Misdemeanors; Alice **1991** Shadows And Fog **1992** Husbands And Wives

Fawcett, Farrah

Actress
Born 2 February 1946
Corpus Christi, Texas

Although 50 years ago Farrah Fawcett would have found her natural level as a B-movie queen, churning out brisk programmers for RKO or Columbia, in her own era she has never made it to the big time – not as an actress at any rate. A small-boned blonde of slightly anxious mien, her top-of-the-range, all-American cover-girl good looks – wonderful hair, sparkling eyes, healthy teeth – found her fortune through her face during the 1970s.

The daughter of a Texas oil contractor, she was voted one of the ten most beautiful girls while a freshman at the University of Texas. Becoming a model, she switched on her taut grin for more than 100 TV commercials and dozens of magazine cover shots before moving into films. At first it was something of a struggle. In 1970, she was arrested twice for shoplifting, and she made little impact in the films in which she appeared: the French-made *Love Is A Funny Thing* (1969), *Myra*

Breckinridge, Logan's Run (both 1970). However, a single season of toothsome crime-busting in the anodyne TV series *Charlie's Angels* transformed her into a nationwide pin-up and eventually led to a starring role in Richard C. Sarafian's sloppy but enjoyable *Sunburn* (1979), in which she posed as the wife of insurance investigator Charles Grodin in order to crack a murder case in Acapulco.

Although distinctly underpowered as an actress, Fawcett is nontheless quite effective when under pressure or threatened, and there was plenty of the latter in *Saturn 3*, a science-fiction thriller in which she was hotly pursued by a lustful robot whose filaments are set fizzing by her trim body. She decorated the gormless Burt Reynolds chase movie *Cannonball Run* (1981) – the one in which Dean Martin and Sammy Davis Jr play priests – and made a brave and reasonably successful stage debut off-Broadway as a rape victim in *Extremities*. It was perhaps her most substantial achievement, and she repeated the role on screen in 1986. Also during the 80s, Fawcett displayed a touching vulnerability and unsuspected strength in the made-for-TV *Between Two Women*, rising to the challenge of her co-star, the magnificent Colleen Dewhurst, whose persecuted daughter-in-law she played.

Since then, however, her big-screen career has depreciated even further. She appeared briefly as Jeff Bridge's ex-wife, aptly a successful model, in Alan J. Pakula's *See You In The Morning* (1989); but her part in *Funny About Love* (1990), a romance starring Gene Wilder and Christine Lahti, ended up on the cutting-room floor.

During her marriage to actor Lee Majors, the actress was billed as Farrah-Fawcett Majors, but reverted to Farrah Fawcett when the couple divorced. She later became the longtime partner of Ryan O'Neal, with whom she has a son.

1969 Un Homme Qui Me Plait/Love Is A Funny Thing (France) **1970** Myra Breckinridge **1976** Logan's Run **1978** Somebody Killed her Husband **1979** Sunburn **1980** Saturn 3 **1981** The Cannonball Run **1986** Extremities **1989** See You In The Morning

Feldman, Corey

Actor
Born 16 July 1971
Reseda, California

This diminutive actor managed to build up an impressive resume of screen credits by the time he was in his late teens. Hardly surprising, perhaps, when one considers that Feldman has been in the business since the age of three, starring in more than 60 television commercials by the time he was seven. After such a prolific beginning, it also comes as no surprise to discover that Corey Feldman became known as a workaholic around Hollywood, making more than 11 movies in as many years, as well as a string of appearances on television (including a recurring role in the series *Mindy And Mork*).

After graduating from TV to film, Feldman spent the years 1978 to 1983 (with time off to go to school), playing small roles as the archetypal 'cute kid' in such films as the H. G. Wells saga, *Time After Time* (1979), and the abysmal *Born Again* (1978) that dealt with the religious rebirth of Nixon aide Charles Colson. Bit parts followed, most notably in two of the *Friday The 13th* films as one of the few characters who survive, and as the pesky kid who spills water on a Mogwai (causing the creature to multiply) in the hit movie *Gremlins* (1984).

Perhaps his best performance to date came in Rob Reiner's classic account of growing up, *Stand By Me* (1986). It was in this film, as the unfortunate kid whose father had burnt his ears as a punishment, that Feldman outshone other equally talented and competent young actors (including Oscar nominee River Phoenix), and it was also the first time he displayed a talent for playing somewhat off-beat and often weird characters. In another teen movie of the late 80s, Joel Schumacher's *The Lost Boys* (1987), Feldman played one of the two Frog brothers, a distinctly strange pair who take it upon themselves to rid Santa Carla of vampires, despite being scared out of their minds.

Following that, he took on a couple of supporting roles alongside his friend Corey Haim, and then got to play with older and more established actors in Joe Dante's satire on suburban America, *The 'Burbs* (1989). Abandoning 'cute' for a more trendy adolescent image (complete with Heavy Metal T-shirt and teenage slang), Feldman came away as one of the only credible characters in a decidedly incredible film.

Unfortunately, Corey Feldman's impressive workload took its toll, and he was twice arrested for cocaine possession in 1989 and 1990. Not one to rest during his rehabilitation, the young actor kept busy by supplying the voice to Donatello, one of the

Teenage Mutant Ninja Turtles (1990) in the movie of the same name.

1978 Born Again **1979** Americathon; Time After Time **1984** Friday The 13th Part IV: The Final Chapter; Gremlins **1985** Friday The 13th Part V: A New Beginning; The Goonies **1986** Stand By Me **1987** The Lost Boys **1988** License To Drive **1989** Dream A Little Dream (also choreographer); The 'Burbs **1991** Rock 'N' Roll High School Forever **1992** Meatballs 4 **1992** Blown Away; Round Trip To Heaven

Ferrara, Abel

Director
Born 1952
The Bronx, New York

Abel Ferrara is an independent New York film-maker whose rough, tough low-budget forays into sleazy backstreets and their often even sleazier inhabitants have a kind of contradictorily baroque immediacy reminiscent of certain underground styles. He started nibbling at the mainstream, however, with *Cat Chaser* (1989), adapted from an Elmore Leonard novel and set far away from Manhattan in Leonard's favourite milieu, palm-fringed Florida. Brilliantly casting Peter Weller as the outsider-hero, Ferrara made an efficient enough job of the movie, capturing the strange, tenuous world of the characters but unable to translate them into something sufficiently involving – except in a set-piece of violence which surprised in its suddenness, shocked with its uncompromising brutality, and impressed with its execution.

That this should have been the case was to be expected, for violence is the currency in which Abel Ferrara trades, usually placing it in contexts so off-centre, and depicting it with such thoroughgoing casualness, as to have made him something of an *auteur* and certainly a cult figure.

He was born in the Bronx, but his family later moved to the suburb of Peekskill where Abel became friends with Nicholas St John and John McIntyre, who later become his screenwriter and sound engineer respectively. The youthful trio played around with making 8mm movies, then went their separate ways until the mid-70s when they got together and formed Navaron Films. Their first feature, *Nine Lives*, described as a 'contemporary love story with an element of fantasy', was released on the independent cinema circuit in New York in 1975 before disappearing from view.

Four years later the notorious *Driller Killer* (1979) brought Ferrara attention, and not necessarily of the kind most directors would welcome. The story concerns a struggling artist, Reno Miller (played by the director under the pseudonym Jimmy Laine), sharing a dank apartment with two girls, fending off debt, and spending a lot of time observing the derelicts in the streets outside who clearly both attract and repel him. The obviously unstable Reno is finally driven into psychopathic violence by the noise of a rock band who move into the building. His uncontrollable rage is not, however, directed at the musicians, but at the vagrants whom he proceeds to murder at night by means of a portable electric power drill. The movie chalks up no fewer than 13 of these gory episodes while, in between times, the largely handheld camera and inadequate lighting find their way through the physical and moral murk of the movie's milieu to dwell on as many disgusting images of decay and degeneration as possible. Quickly deemed a video nasty, perhaps *the* video nasty, *Driller Killer* is extremely crude at every level – viewed some 12 years later, it had lost its capacity to shock and seems almost boring, and occasionally even funny, while still able to provoke a certain disgust.

But the movie established a distinct style which Ferrara continued to pursue and even to polish somewhat, and which he used to really rather powerful effect on *Ms 45 – Angel Of Vengeance* (1981) and *China Girl* (1987). The first is genuinely shocking as a mute garment worker (the wonderfully named Zoe Tamerlis) is raped in a back alley on her way home, only to encounter a further rapist in her apartment. Filching his gun, she kills him, cuts up his body and freezes the pieces for easy disposal, and embarks on an orgy of revenge killings, growing madder by the victim. This stomach-churning film, however, is not without a curious morality and exerts a hypnotic fascination on the viewer; paradoxically, this is partly achieved by the fairly primitive quality of the film's technique. *China Girl* offers a strong contrast. Here, the bloodletting and violence spring from the ethnic gang warfare in Chinatown and Little Italy which Ferrara uses to frame yet another version of *Romeo And Juliet* as a Chinese girl and an Italian boy fall in love with tragic consequences. Once again, the movie is raw, crude (but less so) and atmospheric, but the love story is genuinely tender and moving and the piece as a whole shows its maker capable of a more solid structure than the earlier work had indicated. Interestingly, the director took exception to the inevitable *West Side Story* (1961) comparisons, claiming Shakespeare as the true provenance of the piece. Between making his features, Abel Ferrara has carved a niche in television, bringing his obvious gifts for realising tough and violent situations to bear on series such as *Miami Vice*, whose producer Michael Mann also entrusted him with the two-hour pilot for *Crime Story*, which enjoyed limited theatrical release. Perhaps TV is responsible for Ferrara's graduation to glossy pictures, fully unveiled with *King Of New York* (1990). Starring a charismatic Christopher Walken, the movie is a brilliantly shot and edited account of gang warfare among drug dealers, with an ambiguous hero-villain at its centre. But it is, finally, a noisy, overblown and hollow exercise. For true followers of Ferrara's work (and granted, a strong stomach is needed for such allegiance), it left the rueful suspicion that, in going big-budget, this unique chronicler of the Manhattan underbelly had lost some of his particular vision and power.

1975 Nine Lives **1979** Driller Killer **1981** Ms 45 – Angel Of Vengeance **1984** Fear City **1986** Crime Story **1987** China Girl **1989** Cat Chaser **1990** King Of New York **1992** Bad Lieutenant; Body Snatchers 3

Field, Sally

Actress

Born 6 November 1946

Pasedena, California

Unfortunately always remembered for her toe-curling 'You like me, you really like me!' acceptance speech for her second Oscar that effectively shattered her credibility as a serious actress, Sally Field, while sometimes rather too winsome for comfort, has a lot more talent than most people are willing to admit. Despite a career constantly crippled by the hurdles of other people's prejudices – and as the stepdaughter of ex-Tarzan Jock Mahoney, longtime companion of Burt Reynolds and star of TV's *Gidget* and *The Flying Nun* she has a lot to live down – she has not only livened up some bad films but also shown her mettle when given tough, realistic roles. It was the part of Gidget that earned her her first movie role (in *The Way West*, 1967) but, despite taking acting classes at Columbia studios and studying at the Actors' Studio for two years (1973–75), it was the fallout of two years of *The Flying Nun* that kept her off the big screen (the producers of *True Grit* refusing even to allow her to audition) until Bob Rafelson's *Stay Hungry* (1976) in which she shone against some stiff competition with a pleasingly natural performance. The pert, perky and pretty little actress showed good comic timing as the runaway bride in *Smokey And The Bandit* (1976), but the success of the film and her very public affair with its star led to her being branded a 'Burt Reynolds actress' – an appealing but not outstanding distraction in blue-collar romps. That all changed with Martin Ritt's *Norma Rae* (1979) and her convincing progress from housewife and textile worker to committed trade unionist, a performance as aware of the domestic as the commercial exploitation of her character. It secured her a well-deserved Oscar (accepted very quietly that time) but few good roles, with even her reporter blinded and exploited by her ambition in Sidney Lumet's *Absence Of Malice* (1981) with Paul Newman not entirely devoid of an absence of logic. She had to wait until 1984 to get another meaty part – and that second Oscar – with *Places In The Heart* and her utterly convincing and deeply moving portrait of a small-town widow struggling to keep her home and family together in the Depression. Despite that success giving her enough influence to form her own production company, she was still cast in most studios' minds as a comedienne, with her subsequent films offering more to her male co-stars than herself – possibly one of the reasons she accepted the somewhat unsuitable role of Julia Roberts' mother in the female dominated *Steel Magnolias* (1989). An attempt to return to drama with the true story of a mother trying to rescue her kidnapped child from her estranged husband in Iran in *Not Without My Daughter* (1991) quickly fell victim to the Gulf War and Sally Field returned once more to comedy as the daytime TV star with only a fleeting acquaintance with reality in the satire *Soapdish* (1991).

1967 The Way West **1976** Stay Hungry **1976** Smokey And The Bandit **1977** Heroes **1978** The End **1979** Beyond The Poseidon Adventure; Norma Rae **1980** Smokey And The Bandit II **1981** Back Roads; Absence Of Malice **1984** Places In The Heart **1986** Murphy's Romance **1987** Surrender **1988** Punchline **1989** Steel Magnolias **1991** Not Without My Daughter; Soapdish

Finney, Albert

Actor

Born 9 May 1936

Lancashire, England

Albert Finney, an actor of larger-than-life presence on stage and screen, has spent most of his career surprising the public. Tipped to become England's most significant leading man since Laurence Olivier (whom he understudied as Coriolanus for the Royal Shakespeare Company at Stratford in the 50s), he has pursued a zigzagging course in both the cinema and the theatre with (it seems) the avowed intention of avoiding that fate: he has steered clear of type-casting, regular work, and any suggestion of the predictable in his portrayals.

The son of a North Country bookmaker, from an early age he excelled equally at athletics and acting. A scholarship to the London Royal Academy of Dramatic Arts made him classmates with Peter O'Toole and Alan Bates, and won him early notice as a player of leading classical roles. He joined the Birmingham Repertory Company in 1956, and shortly afterwards made debut appearances in the West End and at Stratford. A small part in the screen version of John Osborne's play *The Entertainer* (1960) led immediately to the film which revealed Finney as a vital new force in the new-realist mood that overtook the English cinema in the early 1960s: with his Lancashire accent, blunt good looks and burly ebullience in dominating the screen, he created a perfect anti-hero for the times in Karel Reisz's *Saturday Night And Sunday Morning* (1960). In the same style, if in a different period of costume, was Tony Richardson's riotous adaptation of Fielding's *Tom Jones* (1963): the title role showed Finney as a goodhearted young man of rumbustious charm and rich comic resource – the eating scene with Joyce Redman has become a classic of comic suggestiveness – and gained him the first of four Oscar nominations.

Yet instead of attempting to capitalise on those huge international successes, or a few years later on the popularity that followed his first Hollywood venture, the light-comedy pairing with Audrey Hepburn in *Two For The Road* (1967), Finney automatically did something different – a habit which became a trademark. Since this 'different' has involved long periods devoted exclusively to the theatre and to the production company he formed in the mid-60s, interspersed with periods of pure escape (he spent a year sailing the South Pacific), the cry of unrealised potential is one that has come to dominate criticism of this actor's work. But since Finney regularly springs back with performances of arrestingly original quality – in *Charlie Bubbles* (1967, the only film he has himself also directed), as the hilarious, touchingly raddled old mountebank Sir in *The Dresser* (1983), more recently as an Irish crime boss in the Coens' *Miller's Crossing* (1990) and an unhappy Irish policeman obsessed with the village beauty in *The Playboys* (1992)– it has proved distinctly unwise to write him off. Occasionally the choice of character roles involving heavy make-up and a foreign accent has lured him over the top: in his Hercule Poirot in *Murder On The Orient Express* (1974) and Daddy Warbucks in John Huston's musical, *Annie* (1982), the relish is spread rather thick. Likewise, not everyone found convincing his participation in Alan Parker's American domestic drama *Shoot The Moon* (1982) opposite Diane Keaton. But his gift for comedy and his ability to rise with raw power and cool intelligence to a challenge he has set himself ensure that, in the best sense, no one can be certain what Finney will come up with next. This must be the reason why Hollywood, so often blamed for a lack of vision in its handling of actors, has been content to pursue him as often as it has. He has kept his private life private; for a period in the 1970s he was married to the elegant French actress Anouk Aimée.

1960 The Entertainer; Saturday Night And Sunday Morning **1963** Tom Jones; The Victors **1964** Night Must Fall **1967** Two For The Road; Charlie Bubbles (also director) **1969** The Picasso Summer **1970** Scrooge **1971** Gumshoe **1973** Alpha Beta **1974** Murder On The Orient Express **1976** Adventures Of Sherlock Holmes Smarter Brother (cameo) **1977** The Duellists **1980** Loophole; Looker **1981** Wolfen **1982** Annie; Shoot The Moon **1983** The Dresser **1984** Under The Volcano **1987** Orphans **1990** Miller's Crossing **1992** The Playboys **1992** Rich In Love

Fisher, Carrie

Actress

Born 21 October 1956

Los Angeles, California

Best known on-screen as Princess Leia in *Star Wars* (1977) and its two sequels, Carrie Fisher is appreciably better known for the publicity attaching to her private life, as retailed in the book and the film later drawn from it, *Postcards From The Edge* (1990). Her association with scandal began early: her first public appearance was in a *Life* magazine photograph when she was a toddler in the arms of her mother, actress Debbie Reynolds, and if both looked upset it was because the child's father, Eddie Fisher, had just run off with Elizabeth Taylor.

Carrie and her brother were brought up by their mother, and, at 16, she began professional life as a chorine in the Broadway revival of *Irene* in which Debbie starred. She subsequently studied for a time at the Central School of Speech and Drama in London, and then was launched into a very different milieu, first with a small part in the Warren Beatty starrer, *Shampoo* (1975), then in the blockbusting hit of *Star Wars*. Money and fame seemed to exacerbate her personal problems; a lengthy relationship with singer-songwriter Paul Simon led to a brief (1982–84) marriage. She became addicted to drugs, a subject she discussed frankly in the 'semi-autobiographical' *Postcards*. The book achieved widespread popularity and attention, and was filmed by Mike Nichols from Fisher's screenplay, focusing on a difficult mother-daughter relationship, though Fisher stringently denied that Shirley MacLaine's character was in any way modelled on Debbie. She has subsequently authored another equally frank volume, *Surrender the Pink*, but also maintains a periodic acting career, playing sleek supporting roles in movies as disparate as Woody Allen's *Hannah and Her Sisters* (1986), *Appointment With Death* (1988) and *When Harry Met Sally* (1989) in which, as the tough, manhunting best friend of Meg Ryan, she beats her pal to the altar.

In characteristic salty vein, she has opined that acting engenders and harbours qualities best left behind in adolescence . . . (like) 'ingratiating yourself with people you wouldn't fucking spit on if they were on fire'.

1975 Shampoo **1977** Star Wars **1978** Mr Mike's Mondo Video **1980** The Empire Strikes Back; The Blues Brothers **1981** Under the Rainbow **1983** Return of the Jedi **1984** Garbo Talks **1985** The Man With One Red Shoe **1986** Hannah and Her Sisters **1987** Hollywood Vice Squad; Amazon Women on the Moon; The Time Guardian **1988** Appointment With Death **1989** The 'Burbs; When Harry Met Sally; Loverboy; She's Back **1990** Postcards From the Edge (writer only); Sibling Rivalry **1991** Soapdish **1992** This Is My Life

Fonda, Jane

Actress
Born 21 December 1937
New York City

The stages in Jane Fonda's acting career have been many, varied, and – though sometimes confusingly overlapped – all closely tied in to developments in her personal life, culminating in her publicly announced retirement from acting when she became engaged to Ted Turner. She has been an ingénue (*Tall Story*, 1960, *A Period Of Adjustment*, 1962), a bubbly sex-kitten (*Any Wednesday*, 1967, *Barbarella*, 1968), an employee of the French New Wave cinema (Jean-Luc Godard's *Tout Va Bien*, 1972), a serious American actress with a commitment to feminist and other new-realist themes (*Klute*, 1971, *Steelyard Blues*, 1973, *Julia*, 1977, *Coming Home*, 1978), and finally a Hollywood veteran reconciled to such middlebrow crowd-pleasers as *On Golden Pond* (1981) and *Old Gringo* (1989).

These may seem staggering developments for any one actress to undergo, but it has been, after all, a pretty staggering personal life. The daughter of the actor Henry Fonda, one of the most esteemed and loved figures in the history of the American cinema, she had a turbulent childhood, scarred by the tragedy of her mother's suicide when she was 12, and subsequently followed by youthful rebellion, numerous liasions, three marriages (to French film director Roger Vadim, 1967–73, American left-wing political activist Tom Hayden, 1973–89 and Turner, billionaire proprietor of CNN, who she married in 1992) and the espousal of various anti-Establishment political enthusiasms – the most notorious of which, her support for the Viet Cong during the Vietnam war, turned her at the time into Middle America's favourite hate figure and gave her the nickname 'Hanoi Jane'.

It is something of a miracle that she has survived it all, let alone flourished – which, by her 50s, she appeared to be doing in grand style, having made big money out of a hugely successful series of keep-fit videos while simultaneously making her peace with the American mainstream. Perhaps the secret of that survival is to be traced to her possession of natural gifts – intelligence, sharp wits, courage, candour and, not least, fine-honed physical beauty – which have stood her in such good stead across three decades of continuous film-making.

All the same, it's possible to feel that the

development of Jane Fonda the actress has not kept pace with that of Jane Fonda the superfit mature woman. In the 1970s, and above all in *Klute*, which won her the first of two Best Actress Oscars, admirers of great film acting thought they were at last able to salute the latest in the line of the really powerful American film actresses – the unflinching Hepburn and Davis breed, who dig deep into themselves and find there a kind of dramatic honesty and vitality that requires neither camera tricks nor cosmetic glamorising to make the screen blaze. In this complex New York psychological thriller, directed by Alan J. Pakula (who was also to work with Fonda on *Comes A Horseman*, 1978, and *Rollover*, 1982), she is Bree Daniels, a high-class, highly intelligent call-girl whose life is being threatened by a crazed former client; and she creates a minutely detailed portrait of a woman snappily brittle on the outside and painfully fragile within, whose relationship with Klute (Donald Sutherland), the private detective called in to protect her, exposes in the character a naked emotional intensity very rarely caught in the detective-thriller genre.

This special dramatic flame, hard, bright, fiercely burning, had already been felt in the first of Fonda's 'serious' American undertakings, the 1969 *They Shoot Horses, Don't They*?, in which she plays one of the entrants in a Depression-era dance marathon; and it was to be kindled again in several other 70s pictures, notably *Julia* (in which Fonda takes the part of the playwright Lillian Hellman), *Coming Home* (the story of a war-hero's wife falling in love with a paraplegic Vietnam war-victim which won her that second Oscar) and the 1979 nuclear-disaster thriller *The China Syndrome*.

But in the following decade, Fonda's work-list began to be filled out with such 'feel-good' dramas as the glutinous weepie *On Golden Pond* (it was the first film Fonda made with her father, his last, and the agent of their personal reconciliation after years of estrangement), *Agnes Of God* (1985) and *Stanley And Iris* (1991). The flame seemed to be flickering. *Stanley And Iris*, which transplants the gritty working-class realist novel *Union Street* from its original Belfast setting to the poorer parts of Toronto, fails to capitalise on its big-name partnering of Fonda and Robert De Niro, mainly because it's almost impossible to believe in this sleek-bodied, lustrous-looking woman as a downtrodden, widowed bakery-worker from the wrong side of town. When she has attempted something outside the strong-woman-with-a-mission type – as the bespectacled doormat-turned-kidnapper opposite Lily Tomlin and Dolly Parton in the feminist office-politics comedy *Nine To Five* (1980), or in the visually spectacular *Old Gringo*, which the actress herself masterminded and produced – the performances have been characterized by curious limitations of range and style. Only in the off-beat, wildly uneven *The Morning After* (1986), a Sidney Lumet thriller in which a failed, semi-alcoholic actress wakes up to find a dead body in her bed, does one sense a return of the old, powerful Fonda. It would, of course, be absurd to presume that she will not be seen and heard of again in the years to come; but it does seem to be the case that the return to the fold of Jane Fonda the prodigal daughter marked the dulling of her artistic edge. Whether she would grow bored with retirement, and emerge for a second career in her latter years, was a matter for speculation by 1993.

1960 Tall Story **1962** A Walk On The Wild Side; The Chapman Report; Period Of Adjustment **1963** In The Cool Of The Day **1964** Sunday In New York; Les Félins/The Love Cage aka Joy House (France); La Ronde (France) **1965** Cat Ballou **1966** The Chase; La Curée/The Game Is Over (France); Any Wednesday **1967** Hurry Sundown; Barefoot In The Park **1968** Histoires Extraordinaires/Spirits Of The Dead (France); Barbarella **1969** They Shoot Horses, Don't They? **1971** Klute **1972** Tout Va Bien (France) **1973** Steelyard Blues; A Doll's House **1976** The Blue Bird **1977** Fun With Dick And Jane; Julia **1978** Coming Home; Comes A Horseman; California Suite **1979** The Electric Horseman; The China Syndrome **1980** Nine To Five **1981** On Golden Pond **1982** Rollover **1985** Agnes of God **1986** The Morning After **1987** Leonard Part 6 **1989** Old Gringo **1990** Stanley And Iris

Fonda, Peter

Actor, writer, director
Born 23 February 1939
New York City

Henry's son and Jane's brother, Peter Fonda cannot match those reputations. Even so, simply taken on his own terms, Fonda's always erratic career appears to have slipped alarmingly out of control in recent years. Peter, like Jane, had a troubled childhood, but decided at an early age that he wanted to become an actor. He studied at the University of Omaha, and had his first success on the boards as the lead in *Harvey*. He made his Broadway debut in 1961, in *Blood, Sweat And Stanley Poole*, and two years later began to pick up straight leads in quite anaemic Hollywood fluff such as *Tammy And the Doctor* (1963) with Sandra Dee (Fonda was the doctor). Presumably his surname was not a drawback.

In 1966, *The Wild Angels* provided a complete change of image for the young star. In a time of counter-culture, when institutions such as Hollywood were found wanting, Fonda turned away from his father's sphere of influence, in effect dropped out, and went to Roger Corman's independent set-up for his hit biker picture, variously described as 'the most explicitly nihilistic movie ever made' (Paul Taylor) and 'OK after about 24 beers' (Maltin's Guide). Despite this low-budget, drive-in success, Fonda was less integrated in the 'alternative' film scene of the 60s than his friends Dennis Hopper and Jack Nicholson. The three worked in various capacities on Roger Corman's acid movie *The Trip* (1967), but Peter only made one other true hippie picture, the most influential, popular film of the period, *Easy Rider* (1969). About two bikers' odyssey across America, the film focused on the tensions of the time with such raw clarity and scope that its more indulgent passages were readily overlooked. Innovative editing and the groundbreaking use of current acid rock made an immediate impact, and Fonda's Captain America became one of the generation's icons of martyrdom: tall, thin and cool in black leathers and shades, with an unruly shock of dark hair and a quiet watchfulness into which you could read any intelligence you wanted. Fonda also produced and wrote the screenplay with his co-star Dennis Hopper, Hopper directed, and Nicholson replaced Bruce Dern at the last minute as a boozy lawyer. A phenomenal success, *Easy Rider* will ensure Peter Fonda's place in the history of the movies. Nevertheless, despite many imitators, it proved a false trail for Hollywood; a one-off. Hopper's follow-up, *The Last Movie* (1971), was too demanding for American tastes, while Fonda's own quite capable shot at directing, *The Hired Hand* (1971), was too modest for fans of Captain America. Like his later effort, *Wanda Nevada* (1979), this was a slow, thoughtful Western concerned with an independent woman in a man's world.

As the cycle of counter-culture movies dried up, Fonda picked up a few reasonable parts in low-rent properties like *Race With The Devil* and *92 In the Shade* (both 1975), but his cool, laid-back style now looked simply cold and bored. Whether out of choice or necessity, he continued to work in independent, low-budget productions, often for a drive-in circuit that barely exists anymore (hence the number of co-productions and international films in his credits). A few of these tie in with the politics of the late 1960s (*Peppermint Freedom*, 1982; *The Rose Garden*, 1989); most are simply redneck fodder, some of which were shot in South Africa (*Mercenary Fighters* 1986). As an actor, Peter Fonda was always limited; his best performances, after *Easy Rider*, are probably to be found in (dubbed) Continental pictures; his films as director have been sound rather than inspired; nevertheless, his record over the 80s was bewilderingly poor. His daughter, Bridget, emerging at the end of that decade, seemed set for brighter things.

1963 Tammy And The Doctor; The Victors **1964** Lilith; The Young Lovers **1966** The Wild Angels **1967** The Trip **1968** Histoires Extraordinaires/Spirits Of The Dead (France/Italy) **1969** Easy Rider (also writer) **1971** The Hired Hand (also director); The Last Movie **1972** Two People **1974** Dirty Mary Crazy Larry; Race With The Devil; 92 In The Shade; Killer Force aka The Diamond Mercenaries **1976** Futureworld; Fighting Mad **1977** High-Ballin'; Outlaw Blues **1979** Wanda Nevada (also director) **1981** The Cannonball Run **1982** Peppermint Freedom (Germany); Split Image **1983**. All Right, My Friends aka Daijobu My Friend (Japan); Dance Of The Dwarfs aka Jungle Heat; Spasms **1985** Certain Fury **1986** Mercenary Fighters; Hawken's Breed **1987** A Time Of Indifference; Long Voyage **1988** Fatal Mission; **1989** The Rose Garden (West Germany) **1990** Enemy; Fatal Mission (also co-writer) **1992/93** South Beach **1993** Deadfall

Ford, Harrison

Actor

Born 13 July 1942

Chicago, Illinois

One of the biggest stars in the Hollywood firmament from the early 1980s onwards, Harrison Ford had an inauspicious early career. He began acting while at Ripon College in Wisconsin, after which he spent a brief time working in summer stock before taking himself off to Hollywood. Once there, he was signed up by Columbia – one of the last contract players to a studio system which was in its death throes – but found himself relegated to small, unnoticed roles. Indeed, his debut film, *Dead Heat On A Merry-Go-*

Round (1966), saw him as a bellboy with precisely one line of dialogue to deliver in those flat, quiet tones which were to become so familiar.

The parts didn't get much bigger either on screen or on TV, where he played fairly anonymous cowboys in series such as *Gunsmoke* and *The Virginian*, and the aspiring actor, growing depressed at his lack of prospects, left the profession and became a carpenter. Then a casting director friend helped him to a role in *American Graffiti* (1973). Although the part, a wise-guy racer, was not big, Ford was finally noticed, and in a film which was itself successful. (He played an unbilled cameo as a motorcycle cop in the sequel six years later.) But the big break came with the part of space pilot Han Solo in *Star Wars* (1977) and Ford, already 35 years old, found himself in a blockbusting hit which changed the course of his career, even though he made several more undistinguished movies before *The Empire Strikes Back* (1980) started him on an unbroken run of successes.

Square-jawed, with soft brown hair, and sympathetic eyes which can turn on a steely glint when required, Ford is undeniably good-looking and, not the same thing, very attractive. But his physical appearance also has an ordinariness about it which makes his image accessible and has doubtless contributed to his popularity with both sexes. As an actor he performs in the laid-back, do-nothing, speak-softly style. All in all, he was not necessarily the obvious choice for the role he made his own, that of 1930s archaeologist-adventurer Indiana Jones whose battered hat and bullwhip became icons for a generation of cinemagoers, eclipsing the glamour of Superman's cape. (*Magnum* star Tom Selleck was apparently the film-makers' first choice for the role of Indy; however, his contractual obligations to his successful TV series prevented him from taking the part and the rest, as they say, is history.) *Raiders Of The Lost Ark* (1981), Steven Spielberg's artful and joyous homage to the movie serials of a bygone age, all thrills and spills, archetypal hero pitted against archetypal villain, saw Ford's 'Indy' routing a bunch of Nazis in fine style. His persona gelled perfectly with the ethos of the movie and his successful creation of the hero was acknowledged in the titles of the sequels, which all carry Indiana Jones' name.

By the time of Indy's last outing in 1989, Ford had starred in a variety of other films of some note. As the tough but vulnerable investigator picking his way through the miasma of Ridley Scott's nightmarishly futuristic LA in *Blade Runner* (1982), the actor established himself as a screen personality of quietly compelling presence; in Peter Weir's *Witness* (1984), a classy and original thriller-cum-love story, he sought refuge in a closed religious community and nursed his unspoken affection for Kelly McGillis with dignity and strength. Then, in Mike Nichols' Capraesque comedy of modern Wall Street manners, *Working Girl* (1988), Harrison was seen in a new guise – light romantic comedy, the part Cary Grant would have played back in the 40s – and made a wonderful foil for Melanie Griffith and Sigourney Weaver. But it was as Rusty Sabich, public prosecutor accused of murder in *Presumed Innocent* (1990), that the actor came of age. Sober-suited and looking his 48 years, he allowed himself a range of emotions – passion, frustration and anger – that lent the necessary authenticity to the screen incarnation of novelist Scott Turow's protagonist.

Harrison Ford, whose several television movies included *The Court Martial Of Lt William Calley*, about the officer held responsible for the infamous Mai Lai massacre in Vietnam, is the father of two grown-up sons by his first wife. He is happily remarried to screenwriter Melissa Mathison (*E.T. The Extra-Terrestrial*), and they live, with their small son and daughter, on an 800-acre ranch in Wyoming, far from the machinations of Hollywood which Ford, a private man, consciously eschews.

Nonetheless, in 1992, the fortuitous casting of Ford as Tom Clancy's Cold Warrior Jack Ryan in the superior action thriller, *Patriot Games*, resulted in an unprecedented deal for the star: $50 million over 10 years to reprise the role in five more Clancy screen adaptations.

1966 Dead Heat On A Merry-Go-Round **1967** A Time For Killing **1968** Journey To Shiloh **1970** Zabriskie Point; Getting Straight **1973** American Graffiti **1974** The Conversation **1977** Star Wars; Heroes **1978** Apocalypse Now (cameo); Force 10 From Navarone **1979** More American Graffiti (unbilled cameo); Hanover Street; The Frisco Kid **1980** The Empire Strikes Back **1981** Raiders Of The Lost Ark **1982** Blade Runner **1983** Return Of The Jedi **1984** Indiana Jones And The Temple Of Doom **1985** Witness **1986** The Mosquito Coast **1988** Working Girl; Frantic **1989** Indiana Jones And The Last Crusade **1990** Presumed Innocent **1991** Regarding Henry **1992** Patriot Games

Forman, Milos

Director
Born 18 February 1932
Caslav, Czechoslovakia

In 1968, just before the Soviet tanks rolled into Czechoslovakia to put an end to the 'Prague Spring', Milos Forman left his country for America. However, the US Immigration Board, acting on a complaint from the Screen Directors' Guild, nearly prevented him from working in the USA, but Sidney Lumet, Paddy Chayefsky, Mike Nichols and others pleaded his case. As a result, Forman made a successful leap from European cinema to Hollywood.

Forman, whose parents were killed by the Nazis when he was eight, studied at the Prague Film School. His first two films, short documentaries on a talent contest and a band competition, revealed a keen eye for the minutiae of human behaviour and a taste for gently mocking simple people's pleasures. Using mostly non-actors, a *cinema verité* technique and slight plots, his first two feature films, *Peter And Pavla* (1963) and *A Blonde In Love* (1965), both about young people in conflict with their elders, had a comic freshness. *The Firemen's Ball* (1967), which grossly satirised the firemen of a small town, brought him into disfavour with the authorities.

The exiled director cast the same sardonic eye on American middle-class families in his first Hollywood film, *Taking Off* (1971), with amusing results. Yet he was disappointed when this generation-gap comedy failed commercially, and with the threats of expulsion hanging over him he came close to a nervous breakdown. 'This showed me that it's much more comfortable to slip into a state of acute depression in America than back home.' It was then that he was approached to direct *One Flew Flew Over The Cuckoo's Nest* (1975), taken from Ken Kesey's 1962 counter-culture bestseller. Although the State Mental Institution in which it is set still stood as a metaphor for a comformist society, the film replaced the novel's drug-induced subjectivity with a more realistic stance, and Forman managed to bring his humour and sharp observation to bear on most of the picture. It was only when the story turned from bitter comedy to tragedy that he lost some of his grip. But wonderful performances were obtained from Jack Nicholson as the grinning anti-hero fighting the system as represented by Nurse Ratched, played with chilling authority by Louise Fletcher. The picture, made at a cost of $3 million, earned over $56 million, making it one of the all-time box-office bonanzas. It was also the first movie since *It Happened One Night* (1934) to win all five top Oscars (film, director, actor, actress, screenplay).

After this hymn to non-conformity, and given his record of films about adolescents, Forman seemed a logical choice to direct the screen version of *Hair* (1979), the hippiedom stage musical hit of 1967. But the Age of Aquarius seemed long over, and its Flower Power paraphernalia had withered and died. Detached from the relevance, urgency and joyful liberation of the original, Forman and choreographer Twyla Tharp offered no more than vigorous dancing through the streets and parks of New York, some uninhibited playing from young performers and a touch of nostalgia for the over twenty-fives. Much of Forman's special intimist talent was submerged when tackling the 'big subjects' of *Ragtime* (1981), an impressive but not altogether coherent panoramic survey of America at the beginning of the century. He concentrated on the specific episode of racism from the E. L. Doctorow novel, but the film was a severe box-office failure.

Forman returned to his home town, Prague, to shoot most of *Amadeus* (1983). He had seen Peter Shaffer's play about the rivalry between Mozart, the musical genius but childish buffoon, and Antonio Salieri, the dignified but far less talented court composer, and immediately let the playwright know through a mutual agent that he wanted to film it. Veering dangerously close to an old-fashioned Hollywood biopic in a manner the play had never suggested, and ironing out its more subtle elements, the film was nevertheless a sumptuous visual spectacle, empowered by wonderful music and with an uninhibited, giggling performance from Tom Hulce in the title role. It won five Oscars, including Best Director.

Remaining in the 18th century, Forman embarked on *Valmont* (1989), an adaptation of *Les Liaisons Dangereuses*. It flopped, not only because it followed too directly on the heels of Stephen Frears' excellent version starring Glenn Close and John Malkovich, *Dangerous Liaisons* (1988), but because, although sumptuous to look at, it lacked the irony to make this perverse tale work. It was another example of Milos Forman's formidable talents showing a tendency to go awry.

1964 Peter And Pavla (US: Black Peter; Czechoslovakia) **1965** Blonde In Love (US: Loves Of A Blonde; Czechoslovakia) **1967** The Firemen's Ball (Czechoslovakia) **1971** Taking Off **1973** Visions Of Eight ('High Jump' and 'Decathlon' Episodes) **1975** One Flew Over The Cuckoo's Nest **1979** Hair **1981** Ragtime **1983** Amadeus **1989** Valmont

Forrest, Frederic

Actor
Born 23 December 1938
Waxahachie, Texas

While Frederic Forrest's chance for major stardom seems to have been and gone, he remains a valuable supporting player with the occasional ability to bring distinction to the films in which he appears. Hailing from the same quaintly named home town as writer-director Robert Benton, he studied acting with Sanford Meisner and Lee Strasberg before beginning his career off-Broadway and moving into experimental theatre, including with Tom O'Horgan's La Mama troupe which gave him his first taste of film with the screen version of their show *Futz* (1969). While appearing in a show in LA he was approached for the role of a young Indian befriended by an ageing rodeo star in *When The Legends Die* (1972); his performance attracted much attention and a Golden Globe nomination as Best Newcomer.

He was soon busy for some impressive directors, but the films were generally disappointing and it was not until 1979 that he renewed his initial promise with his roles as the 'cook' in *Apocalypse Now* and as Bette Midler's lover in the rock drama *The Rose*, for which he was Oscar nominated. Coppola, for whom he had first worked on *The Conversation* (1974), signed him up as the first and most important of his contract players at the new Zoetrope Studios but any hopes for the big time were dashed by the chaos surrounding the filming of *One From The Heart* (1982) and *Hammett* (1983). The latter, started with one supporting cast and finished with another, was dominated by Forrest's striking impersonation of the phlegmatic, cynical novelist but proved one of his few lead roles. For the remainder of the decade he played burnt-out cases disappearing within themselves, punctuated by some impressive TV work such as *Lonesome Dove* and Stephen Frears' *Saigon, Year Of The Cat*.

He made an impression at the decade's end with his pathetic private eye in *Cat Chaser* (1989) and was at his best as the prosecutor trying to expiate his domestic guilt through his pursuit of a Nazi war criminal in *Music Box:* for the role he observed several trials at the court of his brother-in-law (a Texas judge) to understand the way lawyers use their voices and bodies. With one of the more believable performances in Jack Nicholson's failure, *The Two Jakes* (1990), to his credit, Frederic Forrest seemed to have foregone any ambitions for more prominent roles, setting comfortably into his niche as a striking character actor.

1969 Futz **1972** When The Legends Die **1973** The Don Is Dead aka Beautiful But Deadly **1974** The Dion Brothers aka The Gravy Train; The Conversation **1975** Permission To Kill **1976** The Missouri Breaks **1978** It Lives Again! **1979** Apocalypse Now; The Rose **1982** One From The Heart **1983** Hammett; Valley Girl **1984** The Stone Boy; The Return: A Case Of Possession **1986** Valentino Returns **1987** Stacking aka Season Of Dreams **1988** Tucker: The Man And His Dream **1989** The Dead Can't Lie aka Gotham; Cat Chaser; Music Box **1990** The Two Jakes **1992** Falling Down; Twin Sisters **1993** Trauma

Fosse, Bob

Director, choreographer, actor, dancer
Born 23 June 1927
Chicago, Illinois
Died 23 September 1987

Once a svelte, simpering, boyish blond dancer in 1950s film musicals such as *Give A Girl A Break* (1953) and *My Sister Eileen* (1955), and prize-winning choreographer of the Broadway musicals *The Pajama Game* (1955), *Damn Yankees* (1958) and *How To Succeed In Business Without Really Trying* (1967), Bob Fosse won an Oscar for *Cabaret* (1972), only his second film as director.

Fosse had made his stage debut in vaudeville at the age of 13. After the war, he teamed up with his first wife, Mary-Ann Niles, to form a dancing duo. In 1953, he went to Hollywood to choreograph and appear in the MGM musical *Kiss Me Kate*, and met and married the dancer Joan McCracken. His third wife was the Broadway musical star Gwen Verdon, whom he directed in a number of stage shows, beginning with *Redhead* in 1959.

For his first movie as director, Fosse chose *Sweet Charity* (1969), the musical he had directed and choreographed on Broadway starring Verdon as the New York taxi dancer who dreams of love, the role taken in the film by Shirley MacLaine, giving her all. Despite his having choreographed for the screen, Fosse's over-reliance on stage structure and his strident direction showed inexperience of the medium. *Cabaret* was far more successful because he wisely jettisoned most of the stage musical and refused to 'open out' the numbers, keeping the sleazy night-club at the centre of the film. The excellent colour photography, the editing, and the lively performances, headed by Liza Minnelli, almost eliminated the suspicion that a slick musical is not the best vehicle to comment on the rise of Nazism.

Lenny (1974), also set in the world of cabaret, was a powerfully effective biography of the outrageous cult night-club comedian Lenny Bruce, superbly played by Dustin Hoffman. Through the use of Bruce Surtees' sharp black-and-white photography, the *cinema verité* camerawork sometimes straining after documentary realism, the film managed to serve the function of Bruce's humour: to shock audiences into questioning their prejudices. However, there are far too few laughs in what is, after all, the life of a comedian.

Prior to the film's release, Fosse, who had recently directed two Broadway shows, *Pippin* and *Liza With A Z* (ie Minnelli), and had been simultaneously rehearsing the musical *Chicago*, suffered a severe coronary condition. 'I did cocaine and a lot of Dexedrine,' he explained. 'I'd wake up in the morning, pop a pill. After lunch, when I couldn't get going, I'd pop another one, and if I wanted to work all night, still another one. There was a certain romanticism about that stuff. There was Bob drinking and smoking and turning out good work. Still popping and screwing around with the girls . . . I probably thought I was indestructible.'

Fosse used his heart attack and his relations with his wife, mistress and daughter as the basis for *All That Jazz (1979)*, a two-hour long cynical, clinical, razzle-dazzle, Felliniesque, extended production number. But the brilliant cutting and dancing could not prevent it from being a self-indulgent, self-pitying wallow. The sour side of fame and success was explored again in his last film, *Star 80* (1983), the story of ill-fated *Playboy* model Dorothy Stratten (Mariel Hemingway), who had a short career before being murdered by her jealous husband. Superficial, sordid and flashy, it was a sorry valediction from an extremely talented but self-destructive man, whose films were both condemnations and celebrations of his profession and whose epitaph could read: 'There's no business *but* show business.'

1953 Kiss Me Kate (actor only); Give A Girl A Break (actor only) **1955** My Sister Eileen (actor only) **1958** Damn Yankees (dancer only) **1969** Sweet Charity **1972** Cabaret **1974** Lenny **1979** All That Jazz (also co-writer) **1983** Star 80 (w/d)

Foster, Jodie

Actress, director
Born 19 November 1962
Los Angeles, California

The career of Jodie Foster, Hollywood's youngest survivor, seems to be a long fight against the perception of her as a victim off screen as well as on since John Hinckley Jr decided to show his admiration for her by taking potshots at the President. (Ironically, in the film that 'inspired' him, Robert De Niro tries to kill a political candidate to impress Cybill Shepherd). But Foster has fought back with the determination and savvy that once buried her Disney film roots with worldly wise and sexually provocative screen teens. Her mother divorced before she knew she was pregnant with Jodie, who followed her elder brother into commercials at the age of three and then TV series like *Gunsmoke*, *Ironside* and *The Partridge Family* when she developed the ability to read and comprehend scripts at the age of five (a gifted child, she attended LA's bilingual Lycée Français, making one film in France and dubbing her own films there).

Appearing opposite Michael Douglas and a lion that on one occasion savaged her between takes, she made her movie debut in *Napoleon And Samantha* (1972) and continued in Disney (*One Little Indian*, 1973) or Disneyesque (*Tom Sawyer*, 1973) vein, briefly taking on the mantle of Tatum O'Neal in the short-lived *Paper Moon* TV series until she went against type as the wine-swigging alley cat in Scorsese's *Alice Doesn't Live Here Anymore* (1975) and, the following year, as the drug-addicted 12-year-old prostitute immune to affection who inspires Robert De Niro's violent 'rescue mission' in *Taxi Driver*. Disney's response was to put her in the family comedies *Freaky Friday* (1977) and *Candleshoe* (1978) to prove that she was a 'nice girl' after all, but others capitalised on the controversy – the lyrics to Tallulah's song in *Bugsy Malone* (1976) made it quite clear what she was selling, while she played a murderess in *The Little Girl Who Lives Down The Lane* (1977) and a fairground con-artist in *Carny* (1980).

By the 80s her career was in sharp decline, and despite maturing fast on screen she had lost her controversial edge and was unable to make the transition to adult parts. Hinckley gave her new currency and her career an image it had lacked in its somewhat aimless period (she had taken time out to go to Yale when the incident happened), yet the role of victim soon turned into a straitjacket – gang rape, lesbianism and incest in *The Hotel New Hampshire* (1984), fending off the unwelcome attentions of an unbalanced admirer in *Five Corners*, a suicide in *Stealing Home* (both 1988) – hence her determination to land roles where she could fight back.

Her rape victim set on making sure the outrage is not plea-bargained away despite the additional assaults launched on her by a trial in *The Accused* (1988) was the beginning of this highly intelligent young woman's renaissance. It earned her a Best Actress Oscar and put her back on the A-list for the first time in a decade, but it was a part she had to fight for, as was her even more impressive Clarice Starling in Jonathan Demme's *The Silence Of The Lambs* (1991), a role the director originally intended for Michelle Pfeiffer. As FBI trainee Starling, silencing her personal demons by her attempts to stop others from becoming victims and thus give herself some measure of peace, Foster's performance featured some telling and emotional close-ups that conveyed a world of pain which seemed to be beyond acting, winning her a second Best Actress Oscar (and led to charges from some of the more dense journalists that she was simply exploiting the history foist upon her). Her directorial debut, *Little Man Tate* (1991), which starred her as the single mother of a gifted seven-year-old (a part not, one suspects, a million miles away from her own formidable mother, Brandy), was a thoughtful, touching, funny and *nice* picture that confirmed this gifted woman is having the most fruitful career of any former child star.

1972 Napoleon And Samantha; Kansas City Bomber **1973** Tom Sawyer; One Little Indian **1975** Alice Doesn't Live Here Anymore **1976** Echoes Of Summer; Taxi Driver; Bugsy Malone **1977** Freaky Friday; The Little Girl Who Lives Down The Lane; Il Cosotto (Italy) Moi, Fleur Bleue (France) **1978** Candleshoe **1980** Carny; Foxes aka Ladies Of The Valley **1983** O'Hara's Wife **1984** The Hotel New Hampshire; Le Sang Des Autres (France) **1986** Mesmerized (New Zealand) **1987** Siesta **1988** Five Corners; Stealing Home; The Accused **1990** Catchfire aka Backtrack **1991** The Silence Of The Lambs; Little Man Tate (also director); Shadows And Fog **1992/93** Sommersby

Fox, Michael J.

Actor
Born 9 June 1961
Alberta, Canada

When Michael J. Fox was cast as time-travelling teenager Marty McFly in the biggest box-office success of 1985, *Back To The Future*, he was already 23 years old and an Emmy-award-winning household name, thanks to seven years in the top-rated TV sitcom *Family Ties*. In that series, he played Alex P. Keeton, the reactionary yuppie son of liberal parents and, in time, became the virtual star of the show.

After finishing high school, Fox was given a role in a Canadian television series and then took off for California to pursue his acting ambitions. Less than a decade later, the perennially baby-faced, five-feet-four-inches tall actor had married actress Tracy Pollan, fathered a son, and amassed a personal profit in the region of $40million from the *Back To The Future* trilogy. Unusually, in an age of inferior sequels, Parts II and III were almost as popular as the original, as Marty continued to shunt back and forth through time as a consequence of his friendship with mad inventor Christopher Lloyd. (In the first movie he journeys back to the 50s and engineers the marriage of his own parents.) Clearly, the formula touched a romantic and nostalgic nerve in audiences, and Fox became the emblem of their escapist satisfaction.

But, by the time of *Back To The Future III* (1990), it was clear that, coming up for 30, he could no longer remain the nation's favourite teenager – a slight problem perhaps, since his forays into more serious roles had in the main failed. True, the spoof *Teen Wolf* (1985), released after *Back To The Future*, did well enough riding on his name, while *The Secret Of My Success* (1987), about a young man trying to make his way up the ladder, similarly scored. But as another young man on the climb, this time falling prey to cocaine-sniffing, in *Bright Lights, Big City* (1988), he failed to attract an audience for what was a boring and inept version of Jay McInerney's best-selling novel. His most adult venture to date was Brian De Palma's *Casualties Of War* (1989), which gave him a serious role (although one well in keeping with his Mr Clean persona) but the public didn't want to see a film about rape in the Vietnam War.

With the 1990s under way, Fox quickly abandoned his dreams of becoming another Hoffman or Pacino to settle for what he could get: 'I'm not a comedian. I'm just an actor who doesn't take myself too seriously.' Like so many of the new breed of actor, he set up a production company and plans to direct. He is known to be hardworking and diligent, and his natural charm and simple sincerity won him the world-wide adoration of teenagers and the liking of their parents. However, acknowledged maturity and the death of the 'Back To' series marked a falling off, and neither his outing with detective James Woods in *The Hard Way* or the sentimental *Doc Hollywood* were of blockbusting proportions.

1980 Midnight Madness **1982** Class Of 1984 **1985** Teen Wolf; Back To The Future **1987** Light Of Day; The Secret Of My Success **1988** Bright Lights, Big City **1989** Back To The Future Part II; Casualties Of War **1990** Back To The Future III **1991** The Hard Way; Doc Hollywood

Frankenheimer, John

Director
Born 19 February 1930
Malba, New York

It is strange now to recall that three decades ago John Frankenheimer was seen as a key talent in the American cinema. The sad fact is that, after a string of interesting films in the 1960s, his work, though he has continued to be quite prolific, has slumped drastically in quality.

Frankenheimer, who had earlier been attached to a film unit in the air force, became an alumnus of the 'golden age' of live TV drama in the 1950s, when imagination had to go hand in hand with quick thinking and organisational skill. After directing a large number of plays of every sort, notably in the *Playhouse 90* series, he made his first theatrical feature at the then youthful age of 26. This was *The Young Stranger* (1959), a sharply observed study of the generation gap; but it made no great impact and he subsequently returned to television, to be really launched into films a few years later.

The movie that made his name was *The Manchurian Candidate* (1962), a satirically angled conspiracy thriller of much wit and originality, with Laurence Harvey as a Korean War brainwashing victim. This, and its even more striking because less showy successor, *Seven Days In May* (1964), with Burt Lancaster as a renegade general planning a political coup, translated Frankenheimer's evident fascination with the mechanics of visual storytelling into the very substance of his work. The Mephistophelean thriller *Seconds* (1966), in which a middle-aged businessman achieves an illusory new life amid the California beach set, was a still more impressive exercise in tension, though the blockbuster motor-racing movie *Grand Prix*, the same year, amounted to little more than a hymn to high-powered cars. There were still one or two more good movies to come (an off-beat comedy, *The Extraordinary Seaman*, made in 1967 but only released two years later; a downbeat small-town drama, *I Walk the Line*, in 1970), but his work seemed quite suddenly to fall away into a variety of misfires, most inexplicably in the case of *Black Sunday* (1977), a disaster movie with the sort of jigsaw plot that had once been the director's natural habitat.

One or two of his later films, such as the Elmore Leonard adaption, *52 Pick Up* (1986), are reasonably good thrillers in a minor key, and some critics have even claimed that *The French Connection II* (1975) improved on William Friedkin's original, on the strength especially of the harrowing 'cold turkey' ordeal undergone by Gene Hackman's Popeye Doyle. But it was depressing indeed that *The Holcroft Covenant* (1985), a complex espionage melodrama, should resemble nothing so much as a botched variant on the routine spy movies to which Frankenheimer's 1960s work stood in sophisticated contra-distinction; its effect was to make the director's halcyon days seem to belong irrevocably to the past – an impression not alleviated by the feeble efforts that followed from 1989 onwards.

1957 The Young Stranger **1961** The Young Savages **1962** All Fall Down; Birdman of Alcatraz; The Manchurian Candidate **1964** Seven Days in May; The Train **1966** Seconds; Grand Prix **1968** The Fixer **1969** The Extraordinary Seaman (made 1967); The Gypsy Moths **1970** I Walk the Line **1971** The Horsemen **1973** L'Impossible Object/Impossible Object (France); The Iceman Cometh **1974** 99 and 44/100 per cent Dead aka Call Harry Crown **1975** The French Connection II **1977** Black Sunday **1979** Prophecy **1982** The Challenge **1985** The Holcroft Covenant **1986** 52 Pick Up **1989** Dead Bang **1900** The Fourth War **1991** Year of the Gun

Frears, Stephen

Director

Born 20 June 1941

Leicester, England

Stephen Frears' film-making career was slow to take off: between his first feature, *Gumshoe* (1971), and his runaway success of the 1980s, *My Beautiful Laundrette* (1985), a vast amount of television work intervened. (And in fact *Laundrette*, like an earlier Frears film, *Bloody Kids*, had been originally made for television.) But since then, the cinema has kept him continually in action, with the happy result that each new Frears film seems to follow hard on its predecessor, and in the process bears out his reputation as the most interesting, most socially observant and most 'personal' British film director of his generation. He is, indeed, a very British director, as *Laundrette* above all shows. An ear-to-the-ground comedy of manners and morals in which some highly industrious (in criminal as well as above-board business matters) Asian immigrants are thrust among the layabout natives in a down-at-heel corner of London, it stands as one of the country's key products of the Thatcherite 80s, a sly satire, witty and at the same time oddly compassionate, that is literate in its talk yet utterly and economically 'filmic' in its movement. It is, indeed, this last combination – a Frears film has its own distinct visual style no less acutely judged than its verbal – that must be a significant factor in the success of the two non-British films to date, *Dangerous Liaisons* (1988) and *The Grifters* (1990), that have done so much to enhance the director's international reputation. A Cambridge law graduate, Frears became an apprentice director at the Royal Court, one of London's most celebrated 'committed' theatres. This led him to assist Karel Reisz, Lindsay Anderson, and Albert Finney on the making of the films *Morgan* (1966), *If . . .* (1969) and *Charlie Bubbles* (1968) respectively. It was to Finney that Frears turned with his *Gumshoe* project – wisely, since this affectionate send-up of the Philip Marlowe private-eye genre transplanted to the unlikely setting of Liverpool offered the actor one of his most enjoyable leading roles. All the Frears trademarks are already present in this funny, elegant fantasy-thriller – the wryly knowledgeable (but never self-advertising) references to film classics, the unwasteful evocation of place and mood, the sympathy with outsiders (in later films, sexual as well as social), the gift of drawing tight, sharp-edged acting performances.

But *Gumshoe* was not a box-office success; and for the next decade it was in British television drama that Frears gained further experience, making many highly praised dramas written by Tom Stoppard, Alan Bennett and Christopher Hampton among others. (The close collaboration with these and other important British playwrights has borne cinematic fruit: Bennett wrote the screenplay for the 1987 *Prick Up Your Ears*, the screen biography of the playwright Joe Orton and his lover-murderer, Kenneth Halliwell; and Hampton adapted for Frears his play version of the classic novel *Les Liaisons Dangereuses* by the 18th-century Frenchman Choderlos de Laclos.) But, unlike many other television drama directors, Frears never lost or diluted his sense of the potency of visual imagery: even in such relatively unsuccessful pieces as the thriller *The Hit* (1984) or *Sammy And Rosie Get Laid* (1987), a more violent and 'extreme' follow-up to the social satire of *Laundrette*, an *auteur*'s feeling for the marriage of visual style and dramatic tone provides compensation for dramatic quirks and discontinuities.

In terms of filmic achievement *Dangerous Liaisons* must count as a breakthrough for Frears. It was his first big-budget film and his first costume drama, yet its strengths lie in precisely the way he used the material to relate worlds past and present. The choice of American actors – John Malkovich, Glenn Close, Michelle Pfeiffer – to portray Laclos' *ancien régime* aristocrats was an act of daring that paid off handsomely: the performances are sumptuously period in look yet coolly modern in delivery, confronting the spectator with the uncomfortable modernity of the subject matter. The focus on polished surfaces (mirrors, glass, gilt edges) and doors constantly opening creates eloquent thematic leitmotifs and formal structures out of a novel told entirely in letters: a game of sexual partners with a cruel yet strictly satisfying conclusion.

In *The Grifters* it is the same ability to construct unobtrusive yet taut cinematic forms out of fiction – in this case a relentlessly cynical thriller by Jim Thompson – that lends the film its downbeat fascination. The fates of three hardbitten, selfish minor criminals maimed by life and by family and emotional ties are woven against a marvellously underplayed Californian background; the pace and timing of *Gumshoe* (and, no less,

Frears' affection for the *film noir* genre) are allied to the elaborate yet economical sexual patterning of *Dangerous Liaisons*, and the leading performances of Oscar nominated actresses Anjelica Huston and Annette Bening, and John Cusack are among the finest Frears has ever inspired and for which he rightly received a Best Director nomination from the Academy.

1971 Gumshoe **1979** Bloody Kids **1984** The Hit **1985** My Beautiful Laundrette **1987** Sammy And Rosie Get Laid; Prick Up Your Ears **1988** Dangerous Liaisons **1990** The Grifters **1992** Hero

Freeman, Morgan

Actor
Born 1 June 1937
Memphis, Tennessee

In the long struggle of black American actors and entertainers to free themselves from the shackles of stereotyping, Morgan Freeman has, alongside James Earl Jones, been one of the most successful of the pre- Richard Pryor-Eddie Murphy-Spike Lee generation. Indeed, from 1971 to 1976, he was the 'Easy Reader' in the popular kids' TV programme *The Electric Company*, and it was this that made him a national figure well before his screen career got under way.

Educated at LA Community College, he served in the US Air Force from 1955–59 before studying acting. His first role, in the off-Broadway production *The Niggerlovers* quickly led to his Broadway debut in the all-black version of *Hello Dolly!* opposite the great Pearl Bailey. It was the beginning of a distinguished stage career which has embraced everything from Shakespeare to Brecht and, to date, has brought him a Drama Desk Award, a Clarence Derwent Award, and three Obies – one for *Driving Miss Daisy*, in which he created the role of the chauffeur-turned-loving friend and comfort to a difficult, wealthy Jewish lady in Alabama. The part required reserves of dignity, charm, humour and sympathy, all of which Freeman displayed in generous measure, earning himself a Best Actor Oscar nomination for the film version.

Versatility combined with refinement of his craft is the keynote of Morgan Freeman's success which, in Hollywood, was a long time in coming. But he took off like a rocket with *Street Smart* (1987) for which he won the Best Supporting Actor Award from both the New York and LA critics and the National Board of Review. As the powerful pimp who controls an empire of New York prostitutes with a combination of ruthless violence and unstable psychopathic charm, Freeman was hypnotically brilliant. He's been getting his quota of good guys since then, although they're never less than interesting, and gave an impressive performance in *Lean On Me* (1989) as a committed but rigidly disciplinarian school principal. In both *The Bonfire of The Vanities* and *Robin Hood*, he essayed roles for which he was unexpected: subbing for Tom Wolfe's original Jewish judge in the first; written in to a previously rigidly Anglo-Saxon context in the second.

Clearly, this fine actor is excited by challenge, and undaunted by controversy, and entered the director's arena for the first time with a South African subject – *Bopha* (1993).

1971 Who Says I Can't Ride A Rainbow! **1980** Brubaker **1981** Eyewitness (UK: The Janitor) **1984** Harry And Son; Teachers **1985** That Was Then, This Is Now; Marie **1987** Street Smart **1988** Clean And Sober **1989** Lean On Me; Driving Miss Daisy; Glory; Johnny Handsome **1990** The Bonfire of The Vanities **1991** Robin Hood: Prince of Thieves; Hit Man **1992** Unforgiven; The Power Of One **1993** Bopha (director)

Friedkin, William

Director
Born 29 August 1939
Chicago, Illinois

A leading member of the so-called group of early 70s Whiz Kids, William Friedkin is undoubtedly one of Hollywood's most technically skilful directors, with a pronounced gift for creating suspense and handling action. Alas, he has also proved, over the years, a film-maker of dubious taste and motives, whose most effective work leaves the viewer distinctly uncomfortable at having been entertained by morally questionable films in which sleaze triumphs over substance.

Friedkin's career began, humbly, as a teenager employed in the mailroom of Chicago's WGN station. He was still in his teens when he began directing live TV and, by the time he was 20, he'd directed an hour-long documentary for the small screen. He had chalked up countless television shows and several documentaries by 1966, when he met Sonny Bono who invited him to direct *Good Times* (*1967*), starring the singer and his then wife and professional partner, Cher. The film languished in semi-obscurity, but the word was out that Friedkin was a young director with know-how and United Artists gave him *The Night They Raided Minsky's* (1968), a re-creation of the vaudeville era which offered an authentic atmosphere and some well-handled set-pieces, but little more. Certainly, there was not yet an indication of the Friedkin trademarks.

These began to emerge in the next two films. In 1968 he grafted an overlay of thriller-style suspense onto Harold Pinter's stage play *The Birthday Party* (not a success); then came the first hint of prurience with *The Boys In The Band* (1970), another stage play adaptation which eavesdropped on a homosexual birthday gathering and traded in camp stereotypes and viciousness (also not a success). Then, by what must be ascribed to good fortune, *The French Connection* (1971) landed in Friedkin's lap.

Starring Gene Hackman as the now famous Popeye Doyle, tough-guy cop on the trail of heroin dealers, *The French Connection*, filmed on location in New York City, demonstrated the director's high ability with action sequences, suspense and atmosphere – all delivered with an expertise that glossed over the lack of moral perspective or characterisation, won a slew of Oscars, including Best Picture and Best Director, made a fortune, and set the tone of cop movies for the next decade and more.

Friedkin then achieved unprecedented success with *The Exorcist* (1973), which spared nothing in its accomplished visual and aural articulation of horror, gore and suspense. Cold, questionable and manipulative, the film set out to shock and succeeded triumphantly. Since then, the director's filmography has been neither prolific nor distinguished (and, in the case of 1977's *Sorcerer*, a pointless and over-budget remake of Clouzot's *The Wages Of Fear*, 1953, disastrous) and has aroused little interest. The exceptions are *Cruising* (1980), which attracted attention only for its prurient and exploitative approach to homosexuality under the guise of a murder hunt, and *To Live And Die In LA* (1985). This last named is hard-hitting, stylish and skilful but, once again, the glossy expertise of Friedkin's work (and that of a cast which included William Petersen, Willem Dafoe and Dean Stockwell) only served to emphasize the sleaziness and moral rot of a sadistic cop thriller in which each side is as bad as the other, and the female angle points to a fascination with the sordid.

Friedkin was married to French actress Jeanne Moreau for a brief time; his next wife was Lesley-Anne Down, a liaison that ended, unhappily, in a welter of public recrimination.

1967 Good Times **1968** The Birthday Party; The Night They Raided Minsky's **1970** The Boys In the Band **1971** The French Connection **1973** The Exorcist **1977** Sorcerer **1979** The Brink's Job **1980** Cruising; Deal Of The Century **1985** To Live And Die In LA **1988** Rampage **1990** The Guardian (also co-writer)

G

Gallagher, Peter

Actor
Born 19 August 1955
Yonkers, New York

With yuppiedom peaking at the end of the 80s, Peter Gallagher, a talented young actor with saturnine good looks and intense, brooding dark eyes, made a huge impression as the shallow, thrusting yuppie lawyer in *sex, lies and videotape* (1989), Steven Soderbergh's acclaimed comedy of sexual manners. 'It was the least interesting and toughest role, as written,' Soderbergh has explained. 'Peter came up with a lot of things on his own that made John much more three-dimensional.' And, indeed, Gallagher succeeded in making audiences enjoy watching his very unsympathetic character – a lawyer having an affair with the sister (Laura San Giacomo) of his wife (Andie MacDowell) – get his comeuppance.

Gallagher studied at Tufts University outside Boston where he worked with local theatre troupes every summer. After graduating in 1977, he got a singing and dancing part in the Broadway revival of the musical *Hair*, which propelled him into the lead role of Danny Zuko in *Grease*, another Broadway revival. Still with his hair greased down in 50s fashion for his film debut, *The Idolmaker* (1980), he was a more than acceptable Fabian lookalike in a tale based on the career of Bob Marcucci, who groomed such pop singers of the past.

This led to top billing in only his second picture, *Summer Lovers* (1982), in which he portrayed a rich and thoroughly unpleasant young stud who rents a villa on a Greek island with his girlfriend, Daryl Hannah, and becomes attracted to a female archaeologist (Valerie Quennessen). This vacuous movie decided Gallagher to leave films for a while in order to give preference to more worthwhile TV dramas and the stage. Satisfaction came from playing Jack Lemmon's alcoholic son in Jonathan Miller's production of Eugene O'Neill's *Long Day's Journey Into Night* on Broadway in 1986, for which he received a Tony nomination. On television he was again cast opposite Lemmon, as the accused murderer in *The Murder Of Mary Phagan*, as well as playing Lieutenant Commander John Challee in Robert Altman's TV movie of *The Caine Mutiny Court-Martial* (1988).

During that period, the actor returned to the big screen once in *Dreamchild* (1985), portraying a New York journalist seeking an exclusive interview with the aged Alice Hargreaves (Coral Browne), who had been the inspiration, as a child, for Lewis Carroll's Alice. Gallagher was ideal as a go-getter of whom it is observed that 'You can always tell when he's talking about money. His lips go all wet.'

It was after appearing as Brother John in Neil Jordan's *High Spirits* (1988), about to take his final vows and trying to resist the attractions of Jennifer Tilly, that he was cast in *sex, lies and videotape*. Gallagher described his role in *Late For Dinner* (1991) as 'an ambitious pig of a real-estate developer who wants to raze Sante Fe and put up another sweaty, bulging LA'. More advantageous was his role in Altman's critically acclaimed *The Player*, in which his ambitious, thrusting studio power player added to the troubles of Tim Robbins' beleagured executive.

1980 The Idolmaker **1982** Summer Lovers **1985** Dreamchild **1986** My Little Girl **1988** High Spirits **1989** sex, lies, and videotape **1990** Tune In Tomorrow (GB: Aunt Julia And The Scriptwriter) **1991** Late For Dinner; The Cabinet Of Dr Ramirez **1992** The Player; Bob Roberts (Cameo) **1993** Short Cuts

Garcia, Andy

Actor
Born 12 April 1956
Havana, Cuba

With the exception of a few early bit parts, the career of the sheepish, soft-spoken but quietly dangerous Andy Garcia has been steeped in crime and punishment – even his screen debut was in the pilot episode of *Hill Street Blues*. Detached from and suspected by his colleagues in *Internal Affairs* (1990), destroyed in an alien environment in *Black Rain* (1989), the illegitimate heir apparent carving his way into the family in *The Godfather Part III* (1990), Garcia is very much the outsider on film, often projecting the easygoing manner of one who has spent much of his life deflecting prejudice and who saves his anger for extreme cases. It's a persona which seems to owe much to his own childhood (as an immigrant whose family fled Castro's Cuba to Florida, his difficulties with the language there left him isolated at school).

Determined not to accept parts unless he believed in them, his early career was sporadic – regional theatre, appearances at the Comedy Store, some improvisational work, the odd TV part and the mainstay of the acting profession, waiting on tables – until his electric performance in *Eight Million Ways To Die* (1986). As the slightly idiosyncratic drug dealer, his scenes were the only reason for watching the otherwise muddled and overwrought film and he caught the eye of Brian De Palma, who offered him the part of a sadistic hit man in his next film. Wary of repeating himself, Garcia managed to talk him into giving him a different role as one of *The Untouchables* (1987). Taking a leaf out of Clint Eastwood's book, he pared down his dialogue to the minimum to create his quiet man of action, managing both to hold the screen opposite some formidable opposition (Connery, Costner, De Niro) and getting the attention of the major studios; while he was playing the likeable, earnest cop in *Black Rain*, *Internal Affairs* was being written with him in mind. It was with that portrait of another, very different cop, whose morality and sanity are torn apart by a corrupt colleague's manipulation of his sexual insecurity, that he really arrived. When he won the role of Vincent in *The Godfather Part III* it was without competition and in recognition that he had enough screen presence for a character who was a challenging amalgam of the qualities of James Caan, Al Pacino (to whom he has often been compared), Marlon Brando and John Cazale in the previous films. Previously very much a supporting player, his success in the film marked his imminent ascension to leading man as decisively as the two preceding chapters confirmed Pacino and De Niro, and, by 1992, he was in a new league, co-starring with Dustin Hoffman and Geena Davis for Stephen Frears in *Hero*.

1983 Blue Skies Again **1983** A Night In Heaven **1984** The Lonely Guy **1985** The Mean Season **1986** Eight Million Ways To Die **1987** The Untouchables; Stand And Deliver **1988** American Roulette aka Latin Roulette **1989** Black Rain **1990** A Show Of Force; Internal Affairs; The Godfather Part III **1991** Dead Again **1992** Jennifer 8; Hero

Gardenia, Vincent
(Vincente Scognamiglio)
Actor
Born 7 January 1922
Naples, Italy
Died 1992

The paternal, sometimes sad-faced Vincent Gardenia, like Karl Malden or Danny Aiello, was a man with considerable talent for both drama and comedy. Although not exactly a household name, Gardenia was one of Hollywood's most familiar character actors. Specialising in Italian-Americans (Italian was his first language), he became one of American cinema's stalwarts: he turned in consistently fine performances, irrespective of the quality of the script, and audiences knew him well, even if they couldn't always put a name to the face.

Moving from Naples to New York at the age of two, Gardenia performed in his father's Italian-language theatre company, leaving school at 14 to devote more time to the task. He continued to appear, although at increasingly long intervals, with the company until 1960. During World War II he spent two years as a private in the US army before rejoining his father's theatre. Very active in New York's Italian theatrical scene, Gardenia did not embark on his considerable film career until he had reached his mid-30s. He was, however, soon marked out as a heavyweight in the character field and, although his filmography contains more than a fair share of undistinguished movies, he could also claim to have been integral to several successes including, early on in his film career, a supporting role in *The Hustler* (1961), Robert Rossen's superb pool-room drama starring Paul Newman. In 1973, Gardenia earned the first of two Best Supporting Actor Oscar nominations for his performance in *Bang The Drum Slowly* (1973), with Robert De Niro. The second came 14 years later for Norman Jewison's *Moonstruck*. His performance as an outwardly grumpy, inwardly soft paterfamilias, sparring with his wife and daughter (Olympia Dukakis and Cher) was a delight and displayed a range of nuance from funny to serious. Then, aged almost 70, the now veteran actor turned in a characteristically solid performance opposite Joe Pesci in *The Super* (1991).

In between screen performances, Vincent Gardenia enjoyed a successful Broadway career, bringing conviction and craftsmanship to a range of parts, winning several

Obies, and a Tony Award for *The Prisoner Of Second Avenue*.

1958 Cop Hater **1960** Murder Inc. **1961** The Hustler; Mad Dog Coll **1962** A View From The Bridge **1965** The Third Day **1970** Where's Poppa?; Jenny **1971** Little Murders **1972** Hickey And Boggs **1973** Bang The Drum Slowly **1974** Lucky Luciano; Death Wish; The Front Page **1975** The Manchu Eagle Murder Caper Mystery **1976** Il Grande Racket/Big Racket (Italy) **1977** Fire Sale; Greased Lightning **1978** Heaven Can Wait **1979** Firepower; Home Movies **1980** The Lost Flight Of Noah's Ark **1983** Death Wish II **1985** Movers And Shakers **1986** Little Shop Of Horrors **1987** Moonstruck **1989** Skin Deep; Born Dumb **1991** The Super

Garner, James
(James Baumgarner)

Actor
Born 7 April 1928
Norman, Oklahoma

If there were a 'Mr Congeniality' award made for screen personae, James Garner could have few rivals for it. Tall, dark, pleasing and a shrewd businessman, Garner was one of the biggest earners in town within a decade of hitting Hollywood, and if he never quite made it into the top ranks of film superstardom one has to suspect that was more by choice than bad luck.

Garner was a school dropout who left Oklahoma to enlist in the merchant marines as soon as he was 16. A few years later he joined the US Army, seeing action in Korea, where he was wounded and received the Purple Heart. He subsequently returned to Oklahoma, where he attended university for a time and went through a typically odd string of odd jobs, from salesman to model. When an old schoolfriend who had become a theatrical producer offered him a bit part – without dialogue – in the Broadway play *The Caine Mutiny Court Martial* in 1954, Garner chanced upon his *métier*. Personable and willing, he had little trouble getting television roles that grew bigger and bigger. By 1957 he was a star in the hit TV Western series *Maverick*, and had broken into films as a graceful, natural supporting player in Westerns, drama and comedy. His first leading role in a film came when Warners – producers of *Maverick* – fell out with Charlton Heston and substituted Garner as the World War II commander in *Darby's Rangers* (1958).

One high point for Garner was 1963, when he fitted like a hand in a glove the character of devil-may-care Canadian RAF man Hedley in the thrilling World War II POW camp adventure *The Great Escape*. He was delightful as the con-man/scrounger, fast-talking German guards and pilfering an incredible array of escape necessities from 'don't ask' where, and was one of the most popular elements of a huge hit. Three comedies quickly followed, two of them with the reigning box-office queen, Doris Day, for whom he was a charming sparring partner. Thereafter he fell into a none-too-distinguished string of Westerns, thrillers and average comedies in which he was reliably likeable but made no great effort to reveal depth or range. From the late-60s, his previously high box-office stock went into rapid decline although he was one of the highest-salaried stars and had his own production company, Maverick. By 1969 he had to fight for a role he wanted, as Raymond Chandler's detective, Philip Marlowe, in the screen version of *The Little Sister* that was retitled *Marlowe* (1969), but had far greater commercial success in a slight bit of fun he produced, *Support Your Local Sheriff* (1969).

Like his contemporary Rock Hudson, Garner regained his star status on television in the 70s. He headlined in a series called *Nichols* for Warner Bros, reteamed with *Maverick* co-star Jack Kelly for a *Return Of . . .* reunion adventure, and, to massive international success, played the laid-back, beach-dwelling private detective of *The Rockford Files*. The actor's few films in this era were average affairs, but in 1985 he came back with a wonderful performance for Martin Ritt in *Murphy's Romance*. All his easygoing charm intact, Garner delighted as the small-town pharmacist smitten by a young divorcée (Sally Field) and he was rewarded with his first Oscar nomination.

In 1986, Garner produced and starred in a movie for television, *Promise*, as an unfettered single man forced, on the death of his mother, to take care of his schizophrenic brother. He bravely cast a brilliant James Woods as his co-star, the pair played beautifully together and the film was a multiple Emmy winner, including the award for Outstanding Special.

Heart surgery in the late 80s curtailed Garner's activities, but his presence on the screen is always welcome, as was re-affirmed by his engaging Wyatt Earp in the so-so comedy *Sunset* (1988).

1956 Toward The Unknown; The Girl He Left Behind

1957 Shoot-Out At Medicine Bend; Sayonara **1958** Darby's Rangers **1959** Up Periscope **1960** Cash McCall **1962** The Children's Hour; Boys' Night Out **1963** The Great Escape; The Thrill Of It All; The Wheeler Dealers; Move Over Darling **1964** The Americanization Of Emily **1965** 36 Hours; The Art Of Love **1966** A Man Could Get Killed; Duel At Diablo; Mister Buddwing; Grand Prix **1967** Hour Of The Gun **1968** How Sweet It Is; The Pink Jungle **1969** Marlowe; Support Your Local Sheriff **1970** A Man Called Sledge **1971** Support Your Local Gunfighter; Skin Game **1972** They Only Kill Their Masters **1973** One Little Indian **1974** The Castaway Cowboy **1979** Health **1981** The Fan **1982** Victor/Victoria **1984** Tank; The Glitter Dome **1985** Murphy's Romance **1988** Sunset **1993** Fire In The Sky

Garr, Teri

Actress
Born 11 December 1949
Lakewood, Ohio

Teri Garr is a versatile actress with her own distinctive style: bright, charming, up-beat, yet with a vulnerable streak just below the surface, and often touched with real pathos. Her looks, pretty without being too individual (she once described herself as having 'this American pie face'), and her light touch with pace and timing help to conceal the considerable art that goes into her art – which, though particularly well suited to comedy, embraces serious roles with no less skill. Strangely and (some would say) sadly, Hollywood has yet to build around her the vehicle that could make the most of all these qualities. When not wasted on such mediocrities as the caper-comedy *Miracles* (1986), opposite Tom Conti, she tends to be cast as second fiddle to other leading ladies – Jessica Lange in *Tootsie*, Rosanna Arquette in *After Hours*, Shirley Maclaine in *Waiting For The Light*; yet at the end of the film it is usually her contribution that has lodged most firmly in the memory.

Born to a showbiz family (her father the actor Edward Garr, her mother a dancer), Teri made her screen debut in the late 60s, in the experimental pop-music fantasy *Head* (1968), although it was in television that she gained most of her early experience, becoming in particular a fixture on *The Sonny And Cher Show* as Cher's friend Olivia. Francis Ford Coppola picked her to play Gene Hackman's girlfriend in *The Conversation* (1974): eight years later he cast her opposite Frederic Forrest in *One From The Heart* (1982). This self-indulgent semi-musical romance whose huge cost and subsequent failure at the box office broke Coppola's Zoetrope Studios, offered her one of her few big chances, as partner in a marriage temporarily under strain during a fourth of July weekend in Las Vegas, and she made the most of it.

But it was in the earlier *Tootsie*, the film which won her a Best Supporting Actress Oscar nomination, that Teri gave the most appealing account of a type she understands so well – Dustin Hoffman's often-stood-up girlfriend Sandy, a rueful loser whom an audience can simultaneously sympathise with and laugh at (just a little, anyhow). And perhaps her most remarkable achievement came in another New York comedy, much darker in tone: Scorsese's *After Hours* (1985). She plays a lonely cocktail waitress with absurd ambitions as an artist and an apartment full of weird objects: and she proves one of the most alarmingly hilarious of the waifs, strays and lunatics Griffin Dunne encounters on his unwilling voyage of discovery in the city's lower depths.

1968 Head **1969** Changes **1970** The Moonshine War **1974** Young Frankenstein; The Conversation **1975** Won Ton Ton, The Dog Who Saved Hollywood **1977** Oh God!; Close Encounters Of The Third Kind **1978** Mr Mike's Mondo Video **1979** The Black Stallion **1980** Witches' Brew **1981** Honky Tonk Freeway **1982** The Escape Artist; Tootsie; One From The Heart **1983** The Black Stallion Returns; Mr Mom (GB: Mr Mum); The Sting II **1984** Firstborn **1985** After Hours **1986** Miracles **1988** Full Moon In Blue Water **1989** Out Cold; Let It Ride **1990** Waiting For The Light; Short Time **1991** Convicts **1992** The Player (Cameo); Mom And Dad Save The World

Gere, Richard

Actor
Born 31 August 1948
Syracuse, New York

The sullen lips, the slanted, heavy dark eyes and muscular body of Richard Gere made him one of the hunkiest heart-throbs of the 80s. His emergence as a stud in *American Gigolo* (1979) and *An Officer And A Gentleman* (1982) coincided with the time when it became acceptable for women to ogle men.

Born into a staunchly Methodist middle-class family, Gere loved music from an early age, and at school he mastered several instruments – the trumpet, piano, guitar, banjo and sitar – and composed scores for end-of-term productions. (He played his own cornet solos in Francis Ford Coppola's *The Cotton Club*, 1984.) Following an unsuccessful attempt to launch his own rock group, the young performer landed the lead as Danny Zuko in the London production of the musical *Grease* in 1973, and stayed on in England to work at the Young Vic, where he was seen as Christopher Sly in *The Taming Of The Shrew* (1974).

After making his film debut in the small role of a pimp in *Report To The Commissioner* (1974), Gere continued to alternate between stage and screen, getting rave revues in an off-Broadway production of Sam Shepard's *Killer's Head* (1975). Shepard costarred with Brooke Adams and Gere in Terrence Malick's overly aesthetic *Days Of Heaven* (1978); the trio respectively played wealthy young farmer, migrant worker and jealous boyfriend posing as her brother. The limited box-office receipts of the film did little to promote Gere's career, although he had made an impact the year before in *Looking For Mr Goodbar*. In the role of Tony Lopanto, he was chilling as the self-proclaimed 'greatest fuck of your whole life' whom Diane Keaton picks up in a bar and who terrorises her.

A powerhouse return to the stage in the Broadway production of *Bent* (1979), Martin Sherman's play about homosexuals in a Nazi concentration camp, was followed by his breakthrough into superstardom. As Julian Kay, the high-class Californian stud-for-hire in Paul Schrader's *American Gigolo*, a role that John Travolta had pulled out of, he preened and strutted with panache. Switching from the sexual service of rich females and the wearing of stylish Italian suits in *American Gigolo* to military service and the crisp white uniform of *An Officer And A Gentleman*, Gere was even more alluring to female audiences. He played the loner during 13 weeks of relentless training at the Naval Aviation Academy, a tough guy with a touch of vulnerability; witness his bedroom scene with Debra Winger. There was more nudity in *Breathless* (1983), the crass remake of Jean-Luc Godard's 1959 *Nouvelle Vague* classic, in which he gets by on bullish charm as a car thief who fills his life with booze, fast driving and the music of Jerry Lee Lewis.

As the doctor in Argentina trying to trace his missing father in *Beyond The Limit* (1983) – played in an acceptable English accent – and then looking extremely uncomfortable as the biblical *King David* (1985), stripped down to what resembled adult diapers, Gere found that his move away from the stud roles that made him famous put his career on hold for a while. After two more flops in the 80s (a smooth media consultant to American political hopefuls in Sidney Lumet's *Power*, 1986; a farmer turned outlaw in *Miles From Home*, 1988), Gere re-entered the big time with two films in 1990. In *Internal Affairs*, he played a corrupt and violent policeman under investigation by fellow officer Andy Garcia, effectively using a veneer of charm to hide his psychotic malevolence. Then, venturing into romantic comedy for the first time in *Pretty Woman*, Gere elegantly portrayed a millionaire mogul who plays Pygmalion to a hooker (the delicious Julia Roberts). The movie became a box-office hit world-wide, and the actor's performance a reasonable stab at moving into territory vacated by Cary Grant; as was his psychiatrist caught up in love, murder and mystery in the Hitchcockian thriller, *Final Analysis* (1992). The years had barely altered Gere's handsome features, now framed by a very becoming head of grey hair, and he proved that sex symbols can mature and still remain sex symbols.

1975 Report To The Commissioner (GB: Operation Undercover) **1976** Baby Blue Marine **1977** Looking For Mr Goodbar **1978** Days Of Heaven; Blood Brothers **1979** Yanks; American Gigolo **1982** An Officer And A Gentleman **1983** Breathless; Beyond The Limit (GB: The Honorary Consul) **1985** King David **1986** Power **1988** Miles From Home **1990** Internal Affairs; Pretty Woman **1992** Final Analysis **1992/93** Mr Jones

Gertz, Jami

Actress
Born 28 October 1965
Chicago, Illinois

Jami Gertz won a nationwide talent contest for her role in the TV comedy series *Square Pegs*. So much for the nation's talent. Meryl Streep she is not. After the series, Gertz studied at New York University's Drama School and did some theatre work in LA, picking up bit parts the while in a Hollywood obsessed with teen movies.

The parts improved with *Mischief* (1985), and she was the female lead in *Quicksilver*, *Crossroads* and *Solar Warriors* (all 1986). It was *The Lost Boys* in 1987 that provided her first hit. In Joel Schumacher's teen vampire adventure Gertz was an eye-catching gypsy siren. Her wild ringlets and lacy bodice were enough to provoke the fervent attention of Kiefer Sutherland and Jason Patric, and to distract audiences from the increasingly blatant realisation that, beyond shaking her locks and flashing her eyes, the actress had no idea how to behave on camera. To date, she has given little evidence that she can even walk convincingly, let alone talk. Able to purse her mouth into a convincing sneer, when she opens it the results are, alas, less than zero. In a straight dramatic role there is no avoiding her inadequacy – a supporting part in the thriller *Renegades* (1989) almost killed the film on its feet, and it is no surprise that most of her movies have bombed. In short, Jami Gertz is that sporadic Hollywood phenomenon, a screen actress with no apparent qualifications for the job, who nevertheless continues to work.

1981 On The Right Track; Endless Love **1984** Alphabet City; Sixteen Candles **1985** Mischief **1986** Quicksilver; Crossroads; Solar Warriors **1987** The Lost Boys; Less Than Zero **1989** Silence Like Glass; Renegades; Listen To Me **1990** Sibling Rivalry; Don't Tell Her It's Me **1992** Jersey Girls (GB: Jersey Girl)

Gibson, Mel

Actor
Born 3 January 1956
Peekskill, New York

Mel Gibson's screen career has been so identified with men driven to madness – be they Mad Max, Fletcher Christian, suicidal cop Martin Riggs or latterly Hamlet – that his talents have been overlooked as often as his origins have been misrepresented. Born in America, Gibson moved with his family to Australia when he was 12 because of his father's determination to keep his older brothers from being sent to Vietnam, and he only developed an Australian accent as a result of constant 'bagging' by other kids at school there. Originally planning on a career in journalism, he attended the National Institute of Dramatic Art in Sydney and was so nervous in his first play there that he was unable to stand and had to play the part sitting down. Following his film debut in 1977 (a low-brow comedy called *Summer City* for which he never got paid his $20 fee) and graduation he joined the South Australia Theatre Co, where he appeared in small roles in *Oedipus, Henry IV, Romeo And Juliet, Waiting For Godot* and *Death Of A Salesman*.

A street fight that left the good-looking future heart-throb's face badly bruised for his audition with director George Miller gave him the look that landed him the role of *Mad Max* (1979), the highway cop in a world where society is fraying apart, but the film made little impression outside Australia and, despite a strong, enthusiastic performance as a retarded young man in *Tim* the same year, Gibson quickly found himself relegated to clumsy guest spots on sit-coms and TV shows. It was not until the phenomenonal world-wide success of the second *Mad Max* film, closely followed by his charismatic supporting performance as one of the idealistic young recruits in Peter Weir's *Gallipoli* (1981) that his career took off.

He was interesting as the inexperienced journalist with no clear moral sense in Weir's *The Year Of Living Dangerously* (1983), but it was *The Bounty* (1984) that was to prove the real revelation. With an impeccable English accent and aided immensely by Robert Bolt's penetrating script, Gibson's Fletcher Christian was no romantic idealist but weak-willed, easily manipulated by the crew, and as in thrall to his emotions as Bligh was repressed by his, with his act of piracy, as it was in real life, a moment of terrifying blind rage almost akin to an epileptic fit. The film proved an undeserved flop, a fate shared by his first American films, *The River* and *Mrs Soffel* (both 1984, the latter directed by Australia's Gillian Armstrong), in which his characters were kept firmly to the sidelines by leading ladies Sissy Spacek and Diane Keaton respectively. Once again it was up to *Mad Max* to restore his drawing power, although the pressures of five long back-to-back shoots took their toll on Gibson, leaving him with a reputation for bad behaviour that clung to him for the rest of the decade.

The cop thriller *Lethal Weapon* (1987) provided him with his first hit without a number after the title, although the inevitable and even more successful sequel in 1989 dispensed with the character's dark psychosis in favour of formulaic set-pieces and one-liners. He showed a more amoral side with his not-entirely-reformed drug dealer romancing gorgeous Michelle Pfeiffer in *Tequila Sunrise* (1988) and his CIA pilot running guns on the side in *Air America* (1990), but it was his *Hamlet* (1990) – cast after director Franco Zeffirelli saw a mirror to the famous soliloquy when Gibson attempts to commit suicide in the original *Lethal Weapon* – that attracted the most attention, if not the most money. Bringing an energy and masculinity to the part, hiding his anger at his own indecision with outbursts of physical activity and delivering his dialogue with considerable precision and aplomb in what was in many ways ideal casting ('He's mad and he kills five people' Gibson pointed out), he was able to make the piece both accessible and alive. While this initially made his return to formula film-making with *Lethal Weapon 3* (1992) seem all the more disappointing, its success gave him the freedom to make a challenging directorial debut, also starring as a former child abuser, in *The Man Without A Face*.

1977 Summer City **1979** Tim; Mad Max **1980** Attack Force Z **1981** Mad Max 2 aka The Road Warrior; Gallipoli **1983** The Year Of Living Dangerously **1984** The Bounty; The River; Mrs Soffel **1985** Mad Max Beyond Thunderdome **1987** Lethal Weapon **1988** Tequila Sunrise **1989** Lethal Weapon 2 **1990** Bird On A Wire; Air America; Hamlet **1992** Lethal Weapon 3; Forever Young **1992/93** The Man Without A Face (also director)

Gilliam, Terry

Director, writer, actor, animator
Born 22 November 1940
Minneapolis, Minnesota

Even without the knowledge that Terry Gilliam had been the brilliant animator of the surreal cartoon sequences in the madcap *Monty Python's Flying Circus* BBC TV series in the 70s, one would be immediately aware from a few scenes from his films that this was an artist with a remarkable eye for the striking, humorous and disturbing image.

Gilliam's first solo directing job was *Jabberwocky* (1976), which painted a darkly comic picture of pestilential medieval life to encompass the absurdities of Lewis Carroll's nonsense poem. In *Time Bandits* (1981), a vividly realised children's fantasy, with excellent special effects and effective special guest stars, six dwarfs capture a small boy and whizz him through the history of the world. A bizarre Orwellian world was masterfully created for *Brazil* (1985), while the wildly extravagant *The Adventures Of Baron Munchausen* (1988) continued in the phantasmagoric vein. This impressive tall (and long) tale failed miserably at the box-office and almost bankrupted its Anglo-German producers.

Three years later, the American-born and educated Gilliam (resident in England since 1967), returned to the USA for a less expensive but no less ambitious film, *The Fisher King* (1991). The first of his pictures to be based on another's screenplay, it still has his singular personality stamped upon it. Set in a nightmarish New York, not unlike the futuristic city portrayed in *Brazil*, *The Fisher King* has a medieval quest theme underlying it. Two down-and-outs (Jeff Bridges and Oscar-nominated Robin Williams) – a modern knight and his Fool – go on a metaphorical and even literal search for the Holy Grail that will liberate them from their disquieting pasts. Although reality and illusion sometimes jostle awkwardly, and the symbolism often overreaches itself, the film has more warmth than hitherto in Gilliam's work and concentrates more on the performances. The roles are superbly served, not only by the two always watchable men, but by Amanda Plummer (as Williams' chronically shy girlfriend) and by Mercedes Ruehl (Best Supporting Actress Oscar), the passionate lover-protector of the wino Bridges.

Whether Gilliam makes films in Hollywood or Britain, he will indubitably continue to bring his very special animator's eye-view to bear on further strange voyages into storybook territory.

1971 And Now For Something Completely Different (co-writer, actor, animator) **1975** Monty Python And The Holy Grail (co-director, co-writer, actor, animator) **1976** Jabberwocky (w/d); Pleasure At Her Majesty's (actor only) **1979** Monty Python's Life Of Brian (actor, co-writer, animator) **1981** Time Bandits (w/d) **1983** Monty Python's The Meaning Of Life (actor, co-writer, animator) **1985** Brazil (w/d); Spies Like Us (cameo only) **1988** The Adventures Of Baron Munchausen (w/d) **1991** The Fisher King (director only)

Gish, Annabeth

Actress
Born March 1971
Albuquerque, New Mexico

Fresh, pretty and natural, ingenue actress Annabeth Gish looks set, on the basis of her early work, for a maturing career. Born in New Mexico but raised in Cedar Falls, Iowa, Gish is the daughter of a university professor of English and a teacher of gifted children – her mother – who enjoyed amateur theatricals and introduced their daughter to acting in children's theatre in Waterloo, Iowa, when Annabeth was eight. An artistic child who enjoyed singing and studied piano, Gish appeared in a number of amateur, children's and college stage productions by the time she was 11, when she began modelling in advertisements.

In her early teens, Gish impressed at a casting call in Minneapolis that eventually led to her winning the central role in *Desert*

Bloom (1986) opposite Jon Voight. A modest, low-budget production written and directed by Eugene Corr, who had been helped to develop the project by Robert Redford's Sundance Institute, the film centred on a 13-year-old girl's coming-of-age in a troubled family and was evocatively set in Nevada during the early 50s atomic testing programme. Gish's poignant, sensitive performance stood out in a strong ensemble cast that included Voight and Ellen Barkin.

A predictably silly teen comedy with Jon Cryer, *Hiding Out* (1987), followed, but a slight little sleeper of 1988, *Mystic Pizza*, scored with audiences thanks to the excellent work of its trio of young leading ladies – Gish, Julia Roberts and Lili Taylor – as three girls seeking different escape routes from slinging pizzas in Mystic, Connecticut. In *Shag* (1988), another 'girls growing up' comedy set in the 50s Deep South, Gish shared billing and screen time with three other actresses (Phoebe Cates, Bridget Fonda, Paige Hannah) but again shone as the dumpy one who – surprise, surprise – blossoms and wins the titular dance contest. A formula 'brothers' comedy drama, *Coupe De Ville* (1990) did little for her, but Gish's unaffected manner and appealing quality stand her in good stead. (She is not, incidentally, related to the legendary Lillian.)

1986 Desert Bloom **1987** Hiding Out **1988** Mystic Pizza; Shag **1990** Coupe De Ville

Glenn, Scott
(Theodore Scott Glenn)
Actor
Born 26 January 1942
Pittsburgh, Pennsylvania

Tall, rangy and at times almost gaunt, Scott Glenn stalks the territory between character actor and leading man. Where he lacks the dash to cut much of a romantic lead, he is a man's man enough to pose intimidating heavies of the lean and lupine type, and commanding authority figures. He is also capable of a subtlety that has invested some of his bigger roles with unlooked-for dimension.

Born in Pittsburgh but raised in West Virginia, he attended the College of William and Mary in Virginia, one of the oldest universities in America. Afterwards he served his required military stint in the US Marine Corps, then accepted a job as a cub reporter in Kenosha, Wisconsin. By the mid-60s he had decided a career as a newspaperman was not for him and in 1967 he moved to New York City to pursue his interest in acting. There he trained at Lee Strasberg's Actor's Studio – of which he remains an associate – and did odd jobs from bricklaying to managing a burlesque club to support himself, but by 1968 was already beginning to meet with some heavyweight success off-Broadway in productions such as *Long Day's Journey Into Night*, *Fortune In Men's Eyes*, *Collision Course* and *The Impossible Years*. Most recently he appeared in the Broadway production of *Burn This*.

In 1970 Glenn made his film debut with a supporting role in James Bridges' first feature film, *The Baby Maker*. He then spent several years on the bikers/revenge flick/road movie route with the Fonda-Carradines-Busey brigade. Among the more noteworthy exceptions were Robert Altman's *Nashville* (1975), in which he played a small but key role in the dazzling kaleidoscope of character sketches. Glenn, more attractive as he matured, entered a more rewarding prime with the 1980s: a formidable rival to John Travolta in *Urban Cowboy* (1980); the manipulative athletics coach in *Personal Best* (1982); an above-par martial arts hero in John Frankenheimer's action drama *The Challenge* (1982), in which he starred with the great Japanese actor Toshiro Mifune.

One of Scott Glenn's finest moments was his portrayal of astronaut Alan Shepard – the first American in space – in Philip Kaufman's thrilling *The Right Stuff* (1985), a characterization that conveyed machismo, humour and envy. Laurence Kasdan later starred him in an exciting attempt to revive the Western – *Silverado* (1985) – alongside the Kevins Kline and Costner, but the film failed, although it has something of a mystique now. Starred as a 20th-century sheriff-turned-gunman in *Verne Miller* (1988), however, he was flat and uninspired.

More recently Glenn particularly impressed in the comedy drama *Miss Firecracker* (1989) as the lonely town drunk who was the only person sensitive enough to see the beauty in Holly Hunter's absurd and pitiful misfit. In an ensemble of oddly cast stars, he characteristically cut a more persuasive figure as the US submarine commander capably carrying out *The Hunt For Red October* (1990) before finding himself in classy company as Jodie Foster's boss in *The Silence Of The Lambs*.

1970 The Baby Maker **1971** Angels Hard As They Come

1973 Hex **1975** Nashville **1976** Fighting Mad **1978** More American Graffiti **1979** Apocalypse Now; She Came To The Valley **1980** Urban Cowboy **1981** Cattle Annie And Little Britches **1982** Personal Best; The Challenge **1983** The Right Stuff; The Keep **1984** The River **1985** The Wild Geese II; Silverado **1987** Man On Fire **1988** Off Limits aka Saigon; Verne Miller **1989** Miss Firecracker **1990** The Hunt For Red October **1991** Home Grown; The Silence Of The Lambs; Backdraft; My Heroes Have Always Been Cowboys **1992/93** Rope Of Sand **1993** Slaughter Of The Innocents

Glover, Crispin

Actor
Born 1964
New York City

'Eccentric' doesn't begin to do justice to Crispin Glover's extraordinary acting style. He speaks with a whispery intensity that verges on the demented; he approaches a line as if it were a three-point turn and rounds it off with the manic cackle that's the only legitimate brake for his sing-song voice. Then there are the gestures: whether he is speaking or listening, Glover will emphasise the scene with zen/karate movements that carve up the air and endanger his co-stars. It's the Method taken to Expressionist extremes; Glover and Nicolas Cage are (to date) its only known exponents.

Glover's mother was a dancer and his father, Bruce, an actor and teacher of acting. At 14, Crispin played Friedrich Von Trapp in *The Sound Of Music* on stage at LA's Dorothy Chandler Pavilion. Four years later he made his feature film debut in *My Tutor* (1982) and soon attracted attention with his personal style. By 1984 he was in regular work and had a supporting part in *Racing With The Moon* (with Nicolas Cage), then got a big break in the Spielberg production *Back To The Future* (1985). Glover's caricatured wimp, George McFly, looked right at home with the gee-whiz comic-strip action orchestrated by Robert Zemeckis; but he was the only leading player from the original film not to return in the sequels – except in footage rerun from the first movie.

Ostensibly, the actor was unavailable for the series due to previous commitments, but it is not impossible that Spielberg and co were running scared from the increasingly dangerous personality Glover was cultivating both an and off the screen. He co-starred in two of the darkest teen movies of the decade, *At Close Range* (1986) and *River's Edge* (1987), his presence a deeply disturbing (some might say intensely irritating) component of both, and his contribution to the latter was especially controversial. 'A great performance ... as Widow Twanky' bitched one critic. In a film that constantly teetered between black comedy and nihilist exposé, Glover and Dennis Hopper were more on edge than most. Glover seemed to stay in character for television appearances at the time, publicising two bizarre books he had edited and republished (*Rat Catching* and *Concrete Inspection*); and he almost kicked David Letterman in the head during a live TV broadcast.

The parts dried up for a while, but Crispin Glover returned with a vengeance in 1990. He released an album featuring lyrics by Charles Manson ('The Big Problem = The Solution. The Solution = Let It Be'). He had a significant role in the cult comedy *Twister*, played a homosexual fashion designer in John Boorman's *Where The Heart Is*, and relished a cameo in David Lynch's Palme D'Or winner, *Wild At Heart*. As 'Dingle' Dell, who stuffs cockroaches down his pants and has a penchant for midnight sandwiches, he proved one of the few genuine delights in the film, his by-now-familiar lunacy coming into its own.

1982 My Tutor **1984** Teachers; Friday The 13th – The Final Chapter; The Orkly Kid; Racing With The Moon **1985** Back To The Future **1986** At Close Range **1987** River's Edge **1990** Twister; Wild At Heart; Where The Heart Is **1991** Little Noises; Rubin & Ed; The Doors (cameo)

Glover, Danny

Actor
Born 22 July 1947
San Francisco, California

A serious, dignified actor, Danny Glover did not come to the movies until his 30s, and was surprised by vast popular success at 40. He attended San Francisco University, then trained at the Black Actor's Workshop prior to an acclaimed career on the stage. Among many theatrical credits, Glover has starred in the Broadway productions of Athol Fugard's *The Island*, *Sizwe Banzi Is Dead*, *The Blood Knot* and *Master Harold And The Boys* – for the latter he won a New York theatre award.

Glover had bit parts in Don Siegel's prison drama, *Escape From Alcatraz* (1979), the moronic comedy *Chu Chu And The Philly Flash*

(1981) and Fred Schepisi's *Iceman* (1984). He fared better in the delicate and pivotal role of Moze the farm-worker in Robert Benton's Oscar-winning *Places In The Heart* (1984), in the prestigious company of Sally Field, Lindsay Crouse, Ed Harris, Amy Madigan and John Malkovich. Glover stayed on the farm for two other directors: Lawrence Kasdan cast him as one of the four amigos in his recycled western, *Silverado* (1985) (Glover's presence a rather self-conscious spot of revisionism perhaps); and Steven Spielberg saw him as Whoopi Goldberg's oppressive husband in his first stab at 'Serious Cinema', *The Color Purple* the same year. Although feminists criticised the shading of this role – somewhat softened from Alice Walker's book – it was a tour de force of economy and sensitivity, suggesting the man's inadequacy as well as his violence. Glover also had a supporting role as a murderous cop in the Peter Weir-Harrison Ford hit *Witness*, making 1985 a watershed year in his film career – indeed, a year that suggested him as the belated middleman between Sidney Poitier and Denzel Washington.

Nevertheless, no one, least of all Danny Glover, anticipated the scale of the commercial success of *Lethal Weapon* (1987). A formula buddy cop movie, with ingeniously contrived set pieces in place of a cohesive plot, it was held together by a handful of gimmicks, to which Glover's Cosby-style middle-class black family was central. On one level a positive role model, which sits readily enough with the one-dimensional vilification of South African diplomats in *Lethal Weapon 2* (1989), on another this is a curiously empty character – unthreateningly bourgeois, and essentially a straight man to Mel Gibson's reactionary hero. However, it was enough to make 40-year-old Glover a leading man in action pictures, a status that brought him the unexpected challenge of filling Arnold Schwarzenegger's shoes for the 1991 sequel to *Predator* (1987) and, more importantly, the power to help get Chester Himes' novel *A Rage In Harlem* (1990), on which he was executive producer, and Charles Burnett's *To Sleep With Anger* (1990) to the screen.

1979 Escape From Alcatraz **1981** Chu Chu And The Philly Flash **1984** Iceman; Out; Places In The Heart **1985** Witness; The Color Purple; Silverado **1987** Lethal Weapon **1988** Bat-21 **1989** Lethal Weapon 2 **1990** Predator 2; To Sleep With Anger **1991** Flight Of The Intruder; A Rage In Harlem; Pure Luck; Grand Canyon **1992** Lethal Weapon 3 **1992/93** The Saint Of Fort Washington **1993** Bopha

Goldberg, Whoopi (Caryn Johnson)

Actor
Born 13 November 1949
New York City

Cackling comedienne Whoopi Goldberg, first popularly known as an outrageous stand-up comic, met the praise that greeted her performance in the 1990 megahit *Ghost* with the objection, 'Comeback? I didn't know I'd been away.' If so, she was the only one, as her five-year, seven-film film career, off to such an important start with *The Color Purple* (1985), had been in steady decline. *Ghost* not only raised her stock at the box office, it also won her a Best Supporting Actress Oscar.

A precocious child, Goldberg began performing at the age of eight at the Helena Rubenstein Children's Theater in New York and was enrolled in the Hudson Guild children's arts programme. Later she was a student at the celebrated High School for the Performing Arts (of *Fame* fame). After a move to California, Goldberg became a founder member of the San Diego Repertory Theatre, where she furthered the serious side of her work with roles in dramas such as Brecht's *Mother Courage*. Subsequently she joined the improvisational group Spontaneous Combustion and moved on from there to the fringe drama in Berkeley, California, at the Blake Street Hawkeyes Theatre.

Goldberg created her solo satirical act, The Spook Show, in the early 1980s, first in San Francisco and then taking the developing show on the road around the US and Europe. In 1983 director Mike Nichols was sufficiently captivated by her arresting shtick to direct her one-woman show on Broadway (where in her teens and early 20s she had played small roles in the musicals *Hair*, *Pippin* and *Jesus Christ Superstar*). She won both Drama Desk and Theatre World awards for her work.

Steven Spielberg's controversial adaptation of Alice Walker's novel *The Color Purple* (1985) provided Goldberg with a remarkable showcase role in which to make her dramatic screen debut. Despite criticisms that the film was a sprawling, overly sentimental picture of black life in the deep South, spanning over 40 years, it was undeniably emotional as well as ravishing to look at. Goldberg herself displayed dignity, pathos, humour and keen intelligence in a bravura performance that won her the Golden Globe for Best Actress and an Oscar nomination.

The same year the actress won a Grammy award for Best Comedy Recording for the album of her Broadway show. Unfortunately, her comedic talents proved less successful on-screen as a quartet of stinkers threatened to sink her career. While she was funny in *Jumpin' Jack Flash* (1986) as a computer programmer embroiled in an espionage caper, the slight vehicle – Penny Marshall's directorial debut – was second-rate. In *Burglar* (1981) – as a cat burglar, *Fatal Beauty* (1987) – as a narcotics policewoman, and *The Telephone* (1988) – as a neurotic, out-of-work actress, Whoopi's mugging began to take on a desperate-to-amuse air and fell flat. She was much better as a warm-hearted Jamaican housekeeper in the otherwise bland melodrama *Clara's Heart* (1988), which restored credibility to her talent but didn't help her at the box office.

Comparatively restrained as fake medium Oda Mae Brown in *Ghost* (1990), Goldberg reminded audiences she can be hilarious; unquestionably she took the acting honours in what was a cute but unsensational entertainment, the surprise $200 million-plus hit of the year. Returning to drama and co-starred with Sissy Spacek in the civil rights-set, two-handed character study *The Long Walk Home* (1991), Goldberg was again strong and watchable and could look forward to worthwhile projects, of which Robert Altman's *The Player* (1992) was notably the first.

Parallel to her screen career, Whoopi Goldberg has been active in the American Comic Relief charity projects, has performed award-winning solo shows (including *Living On The Edge Of Chaos* in the US, Canada and Australia), and has done well on television. She was Emmy-nominated for a guest role in *Moonlighting* and starred with Jean Stapleton in the TV series *Bagdad Café*.

1985 The Color Purple **1986** Jumpin' Jack Flash **1987** Burglar; Fatal Beauty **1988** The Telephone; Clara's Heart **1989** Homer And Eddie **1990** Ghost **1991** Wisercracks (docu); The Long Walk Home; Soapdish **1992** Sister Act; The Player; Sarafina **1993** The Pagemaster

Goldblum, Jeff

Actor

Born 22 October 1952

Pittsburgh, Pennsylvania

Tall, dark and nobody's idea of handsome, Jeff Goldblum effected a startling screen transformation from perennial gawky geek to personable leading man in the 1980s, an impression boosted off screen by the presence on his arm of gorgeous second wife Geena Davis (from whom he parted after four years). Long a bit-part player and frequently a comic one, Goldblum first really made his mark in Lawrence Kasdan's hugely enjoyable ensemble piece *The Big Chill* (1983), in which he held his own in such company as William Hurt and Kevin Kline, as a hustling, wise-cracking journalist, so memorably pitching a 'Lost Hope' story concept to his editor: 'What do you mean you don't like it? You'd love it if it was The Lost Hope Diet!'

Goldblum trained for the stage at Sanford Meisner's highly-regarded Neighborhood Playhouse in New York City, where he has worked both on and off-Broadway since the 1970s in productions ranging from Shakespeare through theatrical revue to musicals. He made his feature film debut at the age of 22 in Michael Winner's brutal, enormously successful vigilante film starring Charles Bronson, *Death Wish* (1974), unremarked and unlamented as one of the many muggers unwise enough to cross Bronson's retributory path. Between many negligible appearances, Goldblum made the most of near-cameo characters in some superior films, among them Robert Altman's kaleidoscopic *Nashville* (1975) and Paul Mazursky's semi-autobiographical evocation of Greenwich Village in the 1950s, *Next Stop, Greenwich Village* (1976). He is also to be glimpsed fleetingly as a very LA party guest in Woody Allen's *Annie Hall* (1977) but enjoyed a bigger break the same year as one of Joan Micklin Silver's virtually unknown young cast in the little gem *Between The Lines* as one of the principal staffers of a financially and ideologically embattled Boston underground newspaper.

His real leap to recognition came in 1983 – from the absurd cartoon-like government dork who was half of an always-one-step-behind-events Mutt and Jeff team in Philip Kaufman's space race celebration *The Right Stuff*, to *The Big Chill*'s witty commentator on his peer group's times and mores. He was even more engagingly off-beat as the hapless and unlikely hero accidentally prompted to save Michelle Pfeiffer from sinister foreign killers in John Landis' comic caper *Into The Night* (1985), and gave a good account of himself as a slick gambler and snake in Kasdan's ambitious, boisterous but unsuccessful Western, *Silverado* (1985). Commercially, Goldblum scored a personal triumph as the star of David Cronenberg's wildly lucrative, spectacularly horrific *The Fly* (1986) with a quite remarkable if disgusting performance as the obsessed scientist tragically and sick-makingly transforming into 'Brindelfly'. Unfortunately, he followed this with Robert Altman's worst bomb, *Beyond Therapy* (1987), and a couple of only marginally interesting flops. His performance in *The Tall Guy* (1989), however, was a delight; he played a gangling American actor in London propelled to stardom in a sidesplittingly ludicrous musical version of *The Elephant Man.* Between film roles Goldblum has also done some excellent work in a fistful of television movies, notably the prestigious BBC production *Life Story* (1987) in which he presented a driven, zealous James Watson, a winner of the Nobel Prize for his work on the structure of DNA.

1974 Death Wish; California Split **1975** Nashville **1976** Special Delivery; The Sentinel; Next Stop, Greenwich Village **1977** Annie Hall; Between The Lines **1978** Remember My Name; Thank God It's Friday; Invasion Of The Body Snatchers **1981** Threshold **1983** The Right Stuff; The Big Chill **1984** The Adventures Of Buckeroo Banzai Across The Eighth Dimension **1985** Transylvania 6–5000; Into The Night; Silverado **1986** The Fly **1987** Beyond Therapy **1988** Vibes **1989** Earth Girls Are Easy; The Tall Guy; El Sueno Del Mono Loco/The Mad Monkey **1990** Mister Frost **1992** The Favour, The Watch And The Very Big Fish; Deep Cover; Fathers And Sons **1993** Jurassic Park

Goodman, John

Actor
Born 20 June 1952
St. Louis, Missouri

A character actor notable for his appearances as best friends, slobs and cons since the mid-80s, big John Goodman (six foot three inches and up to around 300 pounds at his heaviest) finally attained headlining status with the so-so 1991 comedy *King Ralph*, as a likeable Las Vegas schmo who inherits the British throne. It was doubtless his great popularity as working-class good-guy Dan in the TV series *Roseanne* that finally brought major audience recognition his way, but his ability and presence had already won him admirers, and non-stop employment in a string of valuable supporting roles. While he plays comedy well, Goodman is not restricted to good-natured fat men, having persuaded as tough guy, killer and troubled soul.

Born and raised in St Louis, Goodman entered Southwestern Missouri State University on a football scholarship. When injury sidelined him he concentrated on his drama studies, alongside classmates Kathleen Turner and Tess Harper. In 1975 he moved to New York, where he has worked off-off-Broadway, off-Broadway and on Broadway (in the Mark Twain-inspired musical *Big River*, and *Loose Ends*) and in TV commercials.

Eddie Macon's Run (1983) marked Goodman's film debut, a very brief appearance in a dull chase adventure, followed by bits in disparate duds. The roles grew bigger with the sassy, romantic thriller starring Dennis Quaid, *The Big Easy* (1985), in which he amused as a deceptively clownish bent cop who, it emerged, was nothing to laugh at. He was a revelation – if a minor one – as a tenacious escaped convict, both in the Coen brothers' madcap comedy *Raising Arizona* (1987) and a much tamer effort, *The Wrong Guys* (1988). Reunited with buddy Dennis Quaid in *Everybody's All-American* (1988) he turned in a realistic, sad and seedy supporting performance as a college football star whose failure in the real world brings ruin and tragedy. Then, in *Sea Of Love* (1989) he held his own on screen with Al Pacino as the detective's wisecracking partner; and in the funny, scary *Arachnophobia* (1990) he stole the film with his comic portrayal of a know-it-all, professionally proud pest exterminator, and completed his second leading role in the Coen brothers' *Barton Fink* the following year.

1983 Eddie Macon's Run; The Survivors **1984** Revenge Of The Nerds; C.H.U.D.; Maria's Lovers **1985** Sweet Dreams **1986** The Big Easy; True Stories **1987** Blind Date; Raising Arizona; Burglar **1988** The Wrong Guys; Punchline; Everybody's All-American **1989** Sea Of Love; Stella; Always **1990** Arachnophobia **1991** King Ralph; Barton Fink **1992** The Babe **1992/93** Born Yesterday; Matinee

Gossett Jr, Lou
(aka Louis)
Actor
Born 27 May 1936
New York City

A prodigious performer, Lou Gossett has played basketball professionally, sung in nightclubs, and earned an Emmy and an Oscar for his television and film acting respectively. He was educated at New York University and then lent his towering physique to the Knicks (he's well over six feet tall, with powerful, broad shoulders) – though he had already begun to act. He made his stage debut at the age of 17.

When Lorraine Hansberry's play *A Raisin In The Sun* was filmed by Daniel Petrie in 1961, Louis Gossett weighed in with a supporting role behind Sidney Poitier and Ruby Dee. It proved a rare opportunity to explore black experience on the screen, and Gossett did not pick up on a film career again until the 1970s. He continued with theatre work however, and even sang in nightclubs for a time. Hal Ashby cast him as a tenant in his first film, *The Landlord* (1970), and a year later Gossett co-starred with James Garner in the spot-on comic Western *Skin Game*. On the face of it, they were master and slave, but in fact that was the scam; here was equality, two partners in crime, ripping off slave merchants. Gossett was to return to this period in more serious vein. He won an Emmy for his performance in the groundbreaking TV drama *Roots*, and also starred in the *Gideon Oliver* series.

Prior to that, he appeared in George Cukor's film of *Travels With My Aunt* (1972), and remained aloof from the period's fashion of Blaxploitation. He did sound work in the 70s – including films with Philip Kaufman and an off-form Robert Aldrich – but, ironically, his most hackneyed role provided Gossett with his Oscar and public recognition. *An Officer And A Gentleman* (1982) was an expertly manipulative update of the old-fashioned war propaganda picture, neatly coinciding with the Reagan era. Gossett was accounted the year's Best Supporting Actor for his by-the-numbers portrayal of the loudmouth sergeant, thus joining the risibly elite group of black Oscar winners. It was clever casting: Gossett made a formidable adversary for star Richard Gere, but his performance hardly rates among his finest. It set the tone, however, for a series of bread-and-butter tough guy roles, in *Jaws 3-D* (1983), *Iron Eagle* (1986), *The Principal* (1987) and *The Punisher* (1990); but the actor's most complex accomplishment was *Enemy Mine* (1985), an allegorical science-fiction movie with Dennis Quaid as a sort of astral Robinson Crusoe, and Gossett an alien Friday. Initial antipathy gives way to grudging respect and even love, and Gossett ends up giving birth to a son! It is a moving, subtle piece of acting, as good as he has shown us. It is also hidden beneath layers of reptilian make-up.

1961 A Raisin In The Sun **1970** The Landlord; The Bushbaby **1971** Skin Game **1972** Travels With My Aunt **1973** The Laughing Policeman aka An Investigation Of Murder **1976** White Dawn; J.D.'s Revenge; The River Niger **1977** The Deep **1978** The Choirboys **1982** An Officer And A Gentleman **1983** Jaws 3-D **1984** Finders Keepers **1985** Enemy Mine **1986** Iron Eagle; Firewalker **1987** The Principal; Iron Eagle II; Beyond The Flag **1990** The Punisher **1991** Toy Soldiers **1992** Aces–Iron Eagle III; Diggstown **1992/93** Keeper Of The City; Genghis Khan

Gould, Elliott
(Elliott Goldstein)
Actor
Born 29 August 1938
Brooklyn, New York

As a past master of laid-back comedy and following George Segal as one of the first openly Jewish leading men (until the 60s the formula for screen comedy had always been write Jewish, cast WASP), it comes as quite a surprise to discover that Elliott Gould began his career studying ballet and appearing in the chorus line of *Irma La Douce* when it was still a stage musical. He won his first stage lead on Broadway with *I Can Get It For You Wholesale*, in which he began to develop his neurotic, sometimes manic but amusingly self-critical persona and which co-starred him with Barbra Streisand, who he married in 1963 only to divorce five years later as her career skyrocketed while his star dimmed. (His debut film, *Quick, Let's Get Married*, made in 1964, sat on the shelf until 1971.)

The actor gained some ground with *The Night They Raided Minsky's* (1968), but it was *Bob And Carol And Ted And Alice* (1969) that brought him an Oscar nomination (for Best Supporting Actor) and fame, the latter cemented by his exuberantly cynical Trapper John in the amazingly successful M★A★S★H (1970). He quickly became an iconic figure, summing up a generation's disillusionment with the Norman Rockwell vision of America and determined not to buy into the establishment (most embarrassingly in the finale of 1970's *Getting Straight*, where his English teacher rejects academic doubletalk for personal commitment to change by jumping onto a table and insulting F. Scott Fitzgerald and all his works while a riot rages outside). With the exception of the blacker-than-night comedy *Little Murders* (1971). Gould followed M★A★S★H with a couple of bombs that all but killed his career, culminating in his obnoxious performance in Ingmar Bergman's *The Touch* the same year; and he went from being one of America's top box-office stars to a nervous breakdown, making him unemployable until Robert Altman rescued him with *The Long Goodbye* in 1973. The actor returned the favour with his finest performance, playing Chandler's Philip Marlowe as a burnt-out radical, pursuing a case with the same world-weariness as his futile attempts to persuade his cat to eat a different brand of cat food.

Soon his career settled into a routine of odd, good little films – *Busting*, *California Split* (both 1974), *The Silent Partner*, *Capricorn One* (both 1978) – amid total disasters – *Harry And Walter Go To New York* (1976), *Matilda* (1978) – suggesting that Gould was better at reading cheques than scripts. Despite fairly constant work, his contribution to the cinema of the 80s went almost entirely unnoticed, with several films too bad even for video release outside the States and Gould just seemed to be going through the motions – and sometimes not even that, as with his totally inept performance in *The Naked Face* (1984) where he hardly even reacts when he gets shot. His cameo in *The Big Picture* (1989) as one of the stars of a student film directed by an agent's son seemed sadly indicative of his career, which showed little likelihood of re-scaling its early heights: the legendarily bad *The Lemon Sisters* (1990) spent more time on the shelf than in the theatres (though Diane Keaton must shoulder the blame) while his supporting role in *Russian* (1991) passed unnoticed by the advertising campaign, proof that a man once regarded as a box-office certainty had become a box-office liability.

However, hope of regeneration came with *Bugsy* (1991). In the Barry Levinson/Warren Beatty blockbuster, a now very middle-aged, overweight Gould gave a skilful and moving character performance as a less-than-brainy, doomed sidekick in the Mafia.

1964 Quick, Let's Get Married; The Confession **1968** The Night They Raided Minsky's **1969** Bob And Carol And Ted And Alice **1970** M★A★S★H; Getting Straight; Move; I Love My Wife **1971** The Touch; Little Murders **1973** The Long Goodbye **1974** Busting; S★P★Y★S; California Split **1975** Who?; Nashville (cameo); Whiffs (aka C★A★S★H) **1976** Mean Johnny Barrows; I Will, I Will . . . For Now; Harry And Walter Go To New York **1977** A Bridge Too Far **1978** The Silent Partner; Capricorn One; Matilda **1979** The Last Flight Of Noah's Ark; The Lady Vanishes; Escape To Athena; The Muppet Movie (cameo) **1980** Dirty Tricks; Falling In Love Again **1981** The Devil And Max Devlin **1983** The Muppets Take Manhattan (cameo) **1984** The Naked Face; Over The Brooklyn Bridge aka My Darling Shiksa **1986** Inside Out; The Myth; Boogie Woogie **1988** The Telephone; Dangerous Love **1989** The Big Picture (cameo) **1990** Dead Men Don't Die; The Lemon Sisters; **1991** Russian; Company Business; Bugsy

Grant, Lee
(Lyova Rosenthal)

Actress, director
Born 31 October 1927
New York

Lee Grant's background is in the theatre. She made her film debut in William Wyler's *Detective Story* (1951) as a frightened shop-lifter – a part she previously played on stage. Although this was quite a small role, she played it to the hilt, and was recognised with an award at the Cannes film festival and an Oscar nomination. Shamefully, her movie career was nipped in the bud when she refused to testify before HUAC against her husband, playwright Arnold Manhoff. Blacklisted by the major studios, Lee Grant made only two more motion pictures in the 1950s: Cornel Wilde's *Storm Fear* (1956) and Delbert Mann's *Middle Of The Night* (1959), adapted from a Paddy Chayefsky play.

With an impressive body of theatre work behind her, the actress re-established her film career in the late 60s with a series of strong character roles, often with a neurotic twist, including an Oscar-nominated turn in Hal Ashby's *The Landlord* (1970). She specialised in tough, attractive older women who know what they want and how to get it. In *Shampoo* (1975) – again directed by Ashby – Grant is the one woman who looks capable of handling Warren Beatty, even if she doesn't quite. (She won a Best Supporting Actress Academy Award though.) Denied by age the leading roles that should once have been hers, Grant spent most of the 70s making cameo appearances in top-heavy productions like *Airport '77* (1977); *Damien – Omen II* (1978); *The Swarm* (1978) and *The Voyage Of The Damned* (1976) – for which she was again nominated by the Academy in the supporting actress category.

While she has coasted on her talents as a movie actress, since 1980 Lee Grant has put more effort into a career behind the cameras, with some success. Her first film as director was a sensitive adaptation of Tillie Olson's poignant novella *Tell Me A Riddle* (1980), with Lila Kedrova as a dying housewife and Melvyn Douglas as her husband of 40 years. This was followed by the documentary *Willmar Eight* (1980) and eventually by *Staying Together* (1989), a sharp, unpretentious family drama, well acted and quietly affecting.

As actress only unless stated otherwise: **1951** Detective Story **1956** Storm Fear **1959** Middle Of The Night **1963** The Balcony **1964** An Affair Of The Skin; Pie In The Sky **1966** Terror In The City **1967** Divorce, American Style; In The Heat Of The Night; Valley Of The Dolls **1968** Buona Sera, Mrs Campbell **1969** The Big Bounce; Marooned **1970** The Landlord; There Was A Crooked Man **1971** Plaza Suite **1972** Portnoy's Complaint **1974** The Internecine Project **1975** Shampoo **1976** Voyage Of The Damned **1977** Airport '77 **1978** Damien – Omen II; The Mafu Cage; The Swarm **1979** When You Comin' Back, Red Ryder? **1980** Tell Me A Riddle (director only); Wilmar Eight (docu; director) **1981** Charlie Chan And The Curse Of The Dragon Queen; The Fright **1982** Visiting Hours **1984** Trial Run; Constance; Teachers **1987** The Big Town **1989** Staying Together (director only) **1991** Defending Your Life

Grant, Richard E.

Actor
Born 5 May 1957
Swaziland, Southern Africa

Tall, lean-faced Richard E. Grant (who avidly read about Donald Sutherland to keep his spirits up during long stretches of unemployment) is not typical leading man material but quickly carved a niche for himself with large roles in small-budget films and small roles in large-budget ones. After school, he was educated at Cape Town University, attending its drama school, and he co-founded the multi-racial Troupe Theatre Company with fellow students in 1977. However, he quickly became disillusioned with the theatre's inability to effect social change: 'In the theatre, blacks and whites could mix, but at the end of the day, they went one way and I went another.'

Arriving in London in 1982 with two suitcases, no agent and no contacts, a chance meeting with Jonathan Miller got Grant his first job, at the Donmar Warehouse – sweeping the stage. Two years on the stage in fringe and repertory earned him a nomination from *Plays and Players* magazine as 1984's most promising newcomer as well as some TV work, including the acclaimed improvised satire on advertising, *Honest, Decent And True*. That in turn led to his first film role, in which the teetotal non-smoker played the unsanitary, self-absorbed, scrounging, ranting, substance-abusing (any substance) Withnail of *Withnail And I* (1987) in a performance that enabled him to display his passion for the taste of furniture. He encored with three consecutive disasters, including even more fever-pitched ranting in the dire *How To Get Ahead In Advertising* (1989), but made amends with his heroic Scottish witch-hunter in *Warlock* (1989), revealing commendable comic aplomb in the delivery of lines such as 'Over my rotting corpse!' to an airline hostess who asks if she can take his lightning conductor for the duration of the flight.

Grant's talents seem most readily appreciated in America, where he quickly built up an impressive array of prominent supporting roles in increasingly important films, such as the duplicitous Oliphant in Bob Rafelson's *Mountains Of The Moon* (1990) and the confused, kind and cuckolded American banker husband of Anaïs Nin (Maria De Medeiros) in Philip Kaufman's *Henry And June* (1991). If his cartoon baddy in the turkey *Hudson Hawk* (1991) did little for him, his marvellous double act (with Dean Stockwell) as a hustling screenwriter in Altman's *The Player* (1992) was a highlight of the film.

1987 Withnail And I; Hidden City **1989** How To Get Ahead In Advertising; Killing Dad; Warlock **1990** Mountains Of The Moon; Henry And June **1991** Hudson Hawk; LA Story **1992** The Player; Bram Stoker's Dracula

Grey, Jennifer

Actress
Born 1960
New York City

The petite and vivacious Jennifer Grey, daughter of Oscar-winning *Cabaret* Master of Ceremonies and Broadway star Joel Grey and his dancer wife, Jo, scored a big hit in one of the biggest surprise smashes of the 1980s, *Dirty Dancing* (1987). Unfortunately, her career seemed to go nowhere subsequently, and the numerous delays, false starts and question marks over the proposed *Dirty Dancing 2* made even Grey ponder whether it would see the light before she becomes too old to reprise the role of Baby.

Grey trained extensively in dance as a child in her native New York and her first work in the industry was as a dancer in television commercials. A graduate of New York's Neighborhood Playhouse School of Theatre, her stage work includes the off-Broadway show *Album*, a stint at San Francisco's acclaimed American Conservatory Theatre and the Williamstown Theatre in Massachusetts. She has also appeared in TV movies, most recently in the well-received civil rights drama *Murder In Mississippi* (1990). Her feature film debut came in 1984 with a small role in yet another alienated youth picture, *Reckless*, followed rapidly by another minor appearance in Francis Ford Coppola's Harlem nightlife homage, *The Cotton Club*. She was more noticeable in John Milius' risible tale of small-town teens taking on the invading Russkies, *Red Dawn* (also 1984), as one of an up-and-coming cast that also featured future *Dirty Dancing* star Patrick Swayze, Charlie Sheen and C. Thomas Howell.

The actress' performance in John Hughes' engaging hit chronicling *Ferris Bueller's Day Off* (1986) was something of a minor revelation; her comedic playing as the suspicious, enraged sister of Ferris (Matthew Broderick, her then boyfriend off screen) made for some of the funniest scenes in the caper. *Dirty Dancing*, which started off terrifically as a sharply funny slice of early 60s life before it deteriorated into hard corn, propelled Swayze to superhunk status, but Grey took the acting honours with a perfectly charming portrayal of the bright ingénue smitten with the Bad Boy. The absence of a suitable follow-up for her was a disappointment.

1984 Reckless; The Cotton Club; Red Dawn **1985** American Flyers **1986** Ferris Bueller's Day Off **1987** Dirty Dancing **1989** Bloodhounds Of Broadway **1992** Wind

Griffith, Melanie

Actress
Born 9 August 1957
New York City

With a career that encompasses both strong, likeable performances and others so lightweight you could blow them away, Melanie Griffith has constantly proved to be an interesting actress who is only as good as her director. Her early career was more notorious than notable, with her real-life role as Tippi Hedren's daughter gaining her more mileage in the gossip columns than on the screen.

Her debut, mostly sans clothes (her career is still punctuated by some wildly contrived nude scenes), in Arthur Penn's *Night Moves* (1975) set the tone for many of the dumb, breathy blondes that followed in a career that seemed to self-destruct with the world's most expensive home movie, *Roar* (1981), a plotless box-office catastrophe set among her family's own collection of lions and other assorted wild animals, in which she gave a performance that gave new meaning to the expression 'space cadet'. Yet three years later, as Brian De Palma's Hitchcockian *Body Double* (1984), she gave a shining performance and added some depth to an underwritten role, showing a real talent that was fulfilled with Jonathan Demme's *Something Wild* (1986). Griffith managed to convey the two different faces of her character – the carefree, promiscuous adventuress and the girl next door with a violent husband – showing the interdependence with considerable skill, but it was not until *Working Girl* (1988) that she found her way onto the A-list, and the Academy Awards nominations. (She won the Golden Globe.)

As the office Cinderella of Mike Nichols' modern-day fairytale, she was a convincing and affecting blue-collar heroine trying to bluff her way through the class barriers, yet the impetus it gave her career did not lead to more consistency in her work. Despite a compelling portrayal as the harassed, upwardly mobile householder in *Pacific Heights* (1990), she followed with an over-the-top caricature in De Palma's cartoonish version of *The Bonfire Of The Vanities* (1990), going along with the director's distillation of her character's redeeming features, admittedly against her better judgment, because 'he's having a hard enough time without me making any waves'. Her touching performance in *Paradise* (1991) opposite her husband Don Johnson, went as unremarked as the fine, sensitive film. Her roll of bad luck accelerated with the poor reception for the romantic WWII spy hokum, *Shining Through* (with Michael Douglas); and the universal derision accorded *A Stranger Among Us* in which the kittenish Griffith was hopelessly miscast as a tough homicide cop.

1975 Night Moves; Smile; The Drowning Pool **1977** The Garden/Hagan (Israel); One On One; Joyride **1981** Roar! **1984** Body Double; Fear City **1986** Something Wild **1988** Cherry 2000; The Milagro Beanfield War; Stormy Monday; Working Girl **1990** Pacific Heights; In The Spirit; The Bonfire Of The Vanities **1991** Shining Through; Paradise **1992** A Stranger Among Us aka Close To Eden **1992/93** Born Yesterday

Grodin, Charles

Actor

Born 21 April 1935

Pittsburgh, Pennsylvania

From only his second film role, in *Rosemary's Baby* (1968), Charles Grodin got the reputation for being able to play perfect jerks. In the Roman Polanski Satanic thriller, he was the obstetrician Mia Farrow trusts to deliver her child, only to have him think her paranoid. He was no less of a jerk in *Catch-22* (1970) as Aarfy Aadvark who sleeps with a girl, throws her out of the window and then explains, 'A lot of people get killed during war. What's everyone getting so excited about?'

Grodin's interest in acting was awakened when he saw Montgomery Clift in *A Place In The Sun* (1951) so, after attending the University of Miami, he studied drama under Uta Hagen and Lee Strasberg and began acting at the Pittsburgh Playhouse. He made his Broadway debut in *Tchin-Tchin* in 1962, in which Anthony Quinn starred. In films, he was given his first lead by his friend and mentor Elaine May in *The Heartbreak Kid* (1972), her second and most successful movie as a director. Neil Simon's funny and biting screenplay gave Grodin a splendid role as a Jewish schmuck on his honeymoon in Miami with godawful Jeannie Berlin (May's daughter). While his bride is confined to her hotel room with severe sunburn, he falls in love with WASP Cybill Shepherd, a girl he meets on the beach. There is a delightful scene when Grodin asks Shepherd's father (Eddie Albert) for his daughter's hand, explaining that the one hitch is that he is on his honeymoon.

A part as good as this has rarely come Grodin's way since. He was to get more satisfaction from writing, directing and playing on stage. In fact, he passed over the Richard Dreyfuss role of the ichthyologist in *Jaws* (1974) because he was directing Herb Gardner's play *Thieves* on Broadway. This over-whimsical comedy-drama was filmed in 1977, with Grodin as the principal of an exclusive private school at odds with his slum schoolteacher wife (Marlo Thomas). In 1975, he created the role of George in Bernard Slade's Broadway hit, *Same Time, Next Year*, opposite Ellen Burstyn, but Alan Alda played the role in the film version.

Hollywood reclaimed him for the remake of *King Kong* (1976), in which he exuded nastiness as the 'environmental rapist' leading the expedition to the island to find oil, but instead coming across the giant gorilla, which he also exploits. Then he and Dyan Cannon brought some much-needed black comedy into Warren Beatty's rather limp fantasy, *Heaven Can Wait* (1978), but he could do little with the private eye in *Sunburn* (1979) who hires Farrah Fawcett to pose as his wife while he investigates a murder. Goldie Hawn and Chevy Chase got all the attention in *Seems Like Old Times* (1980) although Grodin caught exactly the stiffness of Hawn's nerdish district attorney husband, unaware that his wife is hiding her ex in his house.

Although only in supporting roles, his were the best comic performances in *The Woman In Red* (1984), in which he played Gene Wilder's best friend who turns out to be gay, and in Elaine May's disastrous *Ishtar* (1987) where he was a corrupt CIA man trying to get saps Dustin Hoffman and Warren Beatty to work for him. He was also very funny in Michael Ritchie's *The Couch Trip* (1987) as a famous radio sex therapist who has a nervous breakdown. But his most rewarding role for some years came in *Midnight Run* (1988), playing the nervous, straight-faced, bail-jumping accountant, taken overland from New York to LA (he is allergic to flying) by Robert De Niro. His subdued, subtle performance created a delightful counterpoint to De Niro's more extrovert character. Grodin wrote an autobiography called *It Would Be So Nice If You Weren't Here*, something audiences seldom say about one of Hollywood's finest comic character actors.

1964 Sex And The College Girl **1968** Rosemary's Baby **1970** Catch-22 **1972** The Heartbreak Kid **1974** 11 Harrowhouse **1976** King Kong **1977** Thieves **1978** Heaven Can Wait **1979** Sunburn; Real Life **1980** It's My Turn; Seems Like Old Times **1981** The Incredible Shrinking Woman; The Great Muppet Caper **1984** The Woman In Red; The Lonely Guy **1985** Movers And

Shakers (also writer) **1986** Last Resort **1987** Ishtar; The Couch Trip **1988** Midnight Run **1990** Taking Care Of Business **1992** Beethoven **1993** Dave

Guttenberg, Steve

Actor
Born 24 August 1958
Brooklyn, New York City

As a pleasant-faced light comedian, Steve Guttenberg is the stuff of Hollywood's A-list, tickling the vast audiences of commercial smashes from the *Police Academy œuvre* to the *Three Men And . . .* movies. But he is less well suited to drama, proving, for instance, an uninspiring besieged hero in the would-be Hitchcockian thriller *The Bedroom Window* (1987). He can play slapstick, sweet or smarm; he can't play suave, sophisticated or seductive.

Guttenberg, the son of an electrical engineer, attended New York's fabled School of the Performing Arts prior to university in Albany, New York, and went on to drama training under the great John Houseman at the prestigious Juilliard School. He also studied with Uta Hagen and Lee Strasberg and made his professional debut with a role in an off-Broadway production of *The Lion In Winter*. After moving to California Guttenberg won his first screen role, a supporting part in the outstanding tearjerker made for television, *Something For Joey* (1977).

Among Guttenberg's more noticeable early appearances on film was his role in *The Boys From Brazil* (1978), as the young, impetuous Nazi-hunter whose discovery and murder set off the international search for Hitler clones. He also endured the dubious distinction of starring in one of the most desperate clinkers of the era, the Village People pop-music showcase, *Can't Stop The Music* (1980). He was redeemed by a good performance in Barry Levinson's acclaimed sleeper *Diner* (1982) but found real celebrity, if not critical approbation, in the tasteless but good-natured *Police Academy* (1984) as a pratfalling, prank-playing and randy police rookie, a role he reprised in three successful if dire sequels. In *Cocoon* (1985) and its 1988 sequel, Guttenberg was more or less second fiddle-cum-straight man to the aliens and geriatrics, while in *Three Men And A Baby* (1987) and its 1990 sequel he and Ted Danson took a back seat to Tom Selleck's chief of the trio. Nevertheless, Steve Guttenberg has nearly always been deft and assured, an audience pleaser. In Neil Jordan's uneven Irish spooks spoof, *High Spirits* (1988), he (and his leading lady Beverly D'Angelo) proved capable of carrying a patchy comedic load with good timing and determined energy.

1977 The Chicken Chronicles; Rollercoaster **1978** The Boys From Brazil **1979** Players **1980** Can't Stop The Music **1982** Diner **1983** The Man Who Wasn't There **1984** Police Academy **1985** Police Academy 2: Their First Assignment; Cocoon; Bad Medicine **1986** Short Circuit; Police Academy 3: Back In Training **1987** Surrender; The Bedroom Window; Police Academy 4: Citizens On Patrol; Three Men And A Baby; Amazon Women On The Moon **1988** High Spirits; Cocoon II: The Return **1990** Three Men And A Little Lady; Don't Tell Her It's Me

Haas, Lukas

Actor
Born 16 April 1976
West Hollywood, California

With the looks of every parent's ideal child, the saucer-eyed, big-eared Haas has managed to amass a more impressive array of credits than most child players, with a reputation for attention to detail that goes back to the age of four, when he crawled the entire mile of an LA parade as a spider to stay in character. The precocious youngster soon made his professional debut as Jane Alexander and William Devane's youngest son in *Testament* (1983) after his kindergarten principle brought him to the attention of a casting director – and delivered a genuinely wrenching and un-cute performance as a victim of nuclear fall-out.

His best-remembered child role came two years later as the small Amish boy who is *Witness* (1985) to a murder. Managing the not inconsiderable feat of projecting innocence without resorting to sentimentality, and remaining an identifiable enough figure to hold the first 15 minutes of the film which are seen through the wide eyes of his character, almost unaided, he was soon much in demand. Aside from the risible *Solarbabies* (1986), he opted for lead roles in small, left-of-centre films such as the under-rated ghost story *The Lady In White* and the low-key emotional drama *The Wizard Of Loneliness* (both 1988), before moving on to more overtly serious roles. In *Music Box* (1989) he was the unquestioningly loving grandson of a suspected Nazi war criminal while on television he played Ryan White, a child AIDS victim, further extending his range by joining Steve Martin and Robin Williams in Mike Nichols Broadway revival of *Waiting For Godot*.

This surprisingly far-sighted variety displayed by Lukas Haas paid dividends with *Rambling Rose* (1991), an impressive performance, opposite Laura Dern, as a teenager coming to terms with his developing sexuality. It seemed a conscious farewell to child roles and a clear statement of his intent to establish a career that would outlast short trousers.

1983 Testament **1985** Witness **1986** Solarbabies (aka Solar Warriors) **1988** The Lady In White; The Wizard of Loneliness **1989** See You In The Morning; Music Box **1991** Convicts; Rambling Rose **1992** Alan And Naomi **1992/93** Leap Of Faith

Hackman, Gene

Actor
Born 30 January 1931
San Bernadino, California

With his lined potato-face, high forehead and a frame like a baggy suit, it has often been remarked that Gene Hackman looks more like a character actor than a star. If so, it is in the American sense of an actor with character, a familiar face on the edge of the screen, not the British notion of a chameleon who loses himself in a variety of contrasting parts. For all the diversity of his films, what Hackman brings to them does not change that much. He is the epitome of the troubled man. In the 20-plus years he has been a star, he has always been middle-aged, and inevitably that is the condition he explores. What does change, and it is the quality that makes him one of the premier movie actors in the world, is the register of the performance. Hackman is no composer, but he is a finely-tuned instrument, a virtuoso, and a conductor.

Considering his immense productivity – according to American TV's *Entertainment Tonight*, he was the busiest movie star of the period 1985 to 1990 – there are remarkably few Hackman tics. One does not associate him with specific gestures or expressions (a squint perhaps, and an unamused chuckle) so much as underlying traits: thoughtfulness (sometimes impotent), authority, integrity. One can only talk of an actor's integrity in terms of work that bears the mark of honesty, no matter if it is a question of verisimilitude or something instinctive. Whatever the genre, Hackman will always dig out the human sub-text in a sequence; like Spencer Tracy, he never stops listening. He is not simply *in* a scene, he's *inside* it.

He is so sensitive to mood it can transform his co-stars. Talking about *Lilith* (1964), Hackman's second film, Warren Beatty has admitted: 'I suddenly woke up when I was talking to [Gene]. It was like I had been in some sort of trance before that, in the previous week's work. And when I put him in

Bonnie And Clyde, it was so he would make me good . . . All I know is that it's impossible for me to be bad in a scene with Gene Hackman.' His Buck Barrow in *Bonnie And Clyde* (1967) was a turning point for Hackman: he was nominated for a Best Supporting Actor Academy Award, but he was already 35 years old when he made the film. He had lived half a life before he was established as an actor.

At 16 he lied about his age and joined the Marines. It was a move he soon came to regret, and he left as soon as his three-year stint was up. He drifted through a number of deadend jobs – truck driver, shoe salesman, soda jerk, doorman – and took courses in journalism and art. Acting was always at the back of his mind, however, and having worked as an announcer for radio and television, he decided to enrol at the Pasedena Playhouse. Legend has it that he and a classmate were voted the 'two least likely to succeed'. The classmate was Dustin Hoffman.

For a few years Hackman worked steadily on Broadway, predominantly in comedies. (His comic gifts have never been properly exploited in film, though he made very funny contributions to *Young Frankenstein*, 1974, and *Superman*, 1978.) In a period when the top box-office attractions were Paul Newman, Steve McQueen and Clint Eastwood, Hackman seemed to have little chance of becoming a star. When he took the leading role opposite Melvyn Douglas in *I Never Sang For My Father* (1970) he suffered the double-edged honour of another Oscar nomination – in the category of *supporting* actor. He was the sixth choice for the role of Popeye Doyle in *The French Connection* (1971). At the time, Hackman had no great hopes for this violent, seedy cop movie. To his surprise, it was both a critical and box-office hit, the harbinger of a new, realistic mode of thriller. His own anti-heroic performance ('Did you ever pick your feet in Poughkeepsie?') took the Best Actor Academy Award, though he modestly credits it to director William Friedkin. *The Poseidon Adventure* (1972) confirmed the actor's new stature, and he followed it with two of the best movies he has made: Jerry Schatzberg's *Scarecrow* (1973) and Francis Ford Coppola's *The Conversation* (1974). *Scarecrow* is an actor's film (and Hackman's personal favourite), with Al Pacino and Hackman as a couple of bums who establish a tenuous friendship; a modern variation on Steinbeck's *Of Mice And Men*. *The Conversation* is an ironic paranoia thriller about Harry Caul, 'the best bugger on the West Coast'. It is a fine example of Hackman's appeal. Caul is an intensely lonely, private man, yet the actor reveals him to us in all his complexity, and without a hint of affectation or sentimentality.

The commercial failure of these two projects left Hackman disillusioned. As he tells it, he decided, 'I'll do films that will definitely make money and I'll just make a load of dough'. The results were mostly awful (and still did not make money); a string of flops that included *Bite The Bullet* (1975), *Lucky Lady* (1975) and *March Or Die* (1977). The only exceptions were *French Connection II* (1975) and the under-rated *Night Moves* (1975), in which he supplied fresh evidence of his consummate technique and dogged screen presence. Taken together, Harry Caul and *Night Moves*' Harry Moseby tell us everything about a stagnant time in American history: the Nixonian hangover from the 1960s. It is hardly surprising they failed at the box office. Hackman exacerbated his declining situation by turning down such projects as *One Flew Over The Cuckoo's Nest*, *Close Encounters Of The Third Kind* and *Network*. After his lucrative role in *Superman* (1978) he decided to call a halt, and went into semi-retirement for two years.

When he returned it was with a new maturity. He is at the peak of his powers in *Eureka* (1982), *Under Fire* (1983) and *Mississippi Burning* (1988) – his fourth Oscar nomination, some 17 years after the last one. Hackman's special mixture of toughness and sensitivity really comes into focus in these films. Even in what are little more than cameo roles he dominates *Another Woman* (1989) and *No Way Out* (1987), and was noticeably superb on the sidelines in *Postcards From The Edge* (1990). Nevertheless, whatever it is that drives him to keep making movies has also produced a dismaying number of dull films (*Superman IV*, 1987; *Split Decisions*, 1988). The question must be asked, to what extent do second-rate vehicles detract from a great actor? In terms of the history of cinema, perhaps not much. After all, Welles, Olivier, Cagney and Tracy all made any number of forgettable, and subsequently forgotten, films. Whether these make-weight efforts may not compromise the genuinely worthwhile work is more problematic, and in 1990 an exhausted Hackman suffered a near heart attack and angioplasty surgery. He might reflect on a career in which at best one in four of his pictures has merited his presence. Hesitant plans to direct (*The Silence Of The Lambs* at one stage) could add yet another twist to this already circuitous tale: meanwhile his brutal sheriff in Clint Eastwood's *Unforgiven* (1992), was one of the richest elements of this dark, complex piece.

1961 Mad Dog Call **1964** Lilith **1966** Hawaii **1967** A Covenant With Death; First To Fight; Banning; Bonnie And Clyde **1968** The Split **1969** Riot; The Gypsy Moths; Downhill Racer; Marooned **1970** I Never Sang For My Father **1971** Doctor's Wives; The Hunting Party; The French Connection **1972** Cisco Pike; Prime Cut; The Poseidon Adventure **1973** Scarecrow **1974** The Conversation; Zandy's Bride; Young Frankenstein **1975** French Connection II; Bite The Bullet; Night Moves; Lucky Lady **1977** March Or Die; The Domino Principle; A Bridge Too Far **1978** Superman – The Movie **1980** Superman II **1981** All Night Long; Reds **1982** Eureka **1983** Misunderstood; Under Fire; Uncommon Valor **1985** Target; Twice In A Lifetime **1986** Power; Hoosiers (GB: Best Shot) **1987** No Way Out; Superman IV: The Quest For Peace **1988** Full Moon In Blue Water; Split Decisions; BAT 21; Mississippi Burning **1989** Another Woman; Loose Cannons; The Package **1990** Narrow Margin; Postcards From The Edge **1991** Class Action; Company Business **1992** Unforgiven

Hagerty, Julie

Actress
Born 15 June 1955
Cincinnati, Ohio

When Julie Hagerty made her Hollywood debut at the age of 25, she had already studied drama for six years in Ohio, then with William Hickey in New York, and had attended the Juilliard School. In short, she prepared for her chosen profession with the utmost earnestness, only to make her name as a comedienne. The term, however, fails to convey the deep core of seriousness that underscores the laughter, or to indicate the vulnerability and pain that lurk at the heart of her work.

Prior to her Hollywood debut, she had done some modelling work and pursued a stage career that began with her brother Michael's theatre group, the Production Company, based in Greenwich Village. Cast as the girlfriend of passenger-forced-to-turn-pilot Robert Hays in *Airplane*! (1980), Julie found herself in almost the biggest comedy hit of the decade and, in the much less successful 1982 sequel, was back again, in charge of the plane's computers, and hilariously dizzy. But, as so often in the fortunes of unusual and gifted American actresses, it was Woody Allen who saw the true potential of this gaunt, angular, doe-eyed and highly individualistic actress. *A Midsummer Night's Sex Comedy* (1982) was an elegant fable of love and life concerning a group of six people weekending in the country during a 1900 summer, and pursuing illicit passions for each other's partners. The odd man – or woman – out, was Hagerty's Dulcie, a warm, ingenuous nurse, uncomplicatedly free with her sexual favours, who turns out to have a sharper, more perceptive grip on reality than her more educated companions; so much so that José Ferrer's grand old man of science and letters dies in her embrace. Hagerty was, quite simply, sensational, portraying her character with a mix of unselfconsciousness, humour, mild vulgarity as befitted her difference of class, and unexpected depths of feeling.

Another comedy *auteur*, Albert Brooks, followed in Woody's footsteps, and co-starred himself with her in his good-natured road movie, *Lost In America* (1985), about a couple who abandon the materialistic life and set out, in a beautifully equipped camper van, to seek simplicity. As the former LA executive who has difficulty disciplining herself to her husband's unrealistic ideals, Hagerty was by turns ebullient, bewildered, and deftly comic. Her other major performance of note was in Robert Altman's frankly bizarre exploration of Freud and contemporary mores, *Beyond Therapy* (1987), in which the actress contrived to bring absolute conviction and sincerity to a role that, as written, was all clever surface. Then, in 1990, she contributed a surprise element to *Reversal Of Fortune*, giving a totally straight and unbilled cameo as Claus Von Bülow's mistress.

1980 Airplane! **1982** Airplane II: The Sequel; A Midsummer Night's Sex Comedy **1985** Lost In America; Goodbye New York; Bad Medicine **1987** Beyond Therapy **1988** Aria **1989** Bloodhounds Of Broadway; Rude Awakening **1990** Reversal Of Fortune (unbilled cameo): **1991** What About Bob? **1992** Noises Off

Haim, Corey

Actor
Born 23 December 1972
Toronto, Canada

One of a group of young actors who became prominent in the late 1980s, Corey Haim established a career for himself by playing the boy next door in a collection of teen comedies and horror movies.

The young, baby-faced actor began his career at the tender age of ten, starring in a slew of television commercials before becoming a regular on a Canadian television show for children *The Edison Twins* (1983). However, it was in the film *Firstborn* (1984) that his acting talent was first put to use, as one of two boys whose mother is trying to cope with bringing up her children alone. Here, he had the opportunity to prove he was more than just an average child actor, and it also brought him to the attention of director David Seltzer, who cast the 14-year-old Corey in the title role of *Lucas* (1986). Surrounded by a cast of young actors (including Charlie Sheen and Winona Ryder) who were soon to make their own mark in Hollywood, Haim shone as a precocious boy who develops a crush on an older girl. Unlike most other youth films of the time that tended only to depict teenage rebellion, *Lucas* painted the portrait of a young boy confused with life around him, who desperately wants to conform and be like the other kids. The actor's depth of sensitivity in this role (especially in a scene where young Lucas decides to play football for the school team despite being half the size of the other players) helped make the film a sleeper hit.

With few such roles being available to one of his age and type, he subsequently found himself in a collection of more mainstream teen films, in company with other younger stars like Kiefer Sutherland and Corey Feldman. In *The Lost Boys* (1987) he displayed comic talent as the boy who discovers his brother is hanging around (literally) with a group of young and trendy vampires. It was this role that brought him to the attention of teenage girls, who were impressed by his character's wit, dress sense and obsession with MTV. His teenage appeal has since brought him leads in such light and inconsequential films as *License To Drive* (1988), the unfrightening horror film *Watchers* (1988), and the disappointing *Dream A Little Dream* (1989). Although apparently confined to more commercial projects by the 1990s, Corey Haim's appealing performances seemed to have guaranteed him a large following.

1984 Firstborn **1985** Murphy's Romance; Secret Admirer; Silver Bullet **1986** Lucas **1987** The Lost Boys **1988** License To Drive; Watchers **1989** Dream A Little Dream **1991** Fast Getaway; Prayer Of The Roller Boys **1992** Oh, What A Night aka Comfort Creek; Blown Away **1992/93** OO Kid

Hall, Anthony Michael

Actor

Born 14 April 1968

Boston, Massachusetts

Anthony Michael Hall was only 14 when he appeared in his first film, *Six Pack* (1982). Intended as a vehicle for country-singing star Kenny Rogers, whose first theatrical release it was, *Six Pack* is a twee comedy about a stock-car racer who inherits six mischievous orphans. Diane Lane was one. Anthony Michael Hall was another.

Thereafter, Hall balanced school with a movie career. He was the first (and best) incarnation of Rusty Griswold in *National Lampoon's Vacation* (1983), opposite Chevy Chase, Beverly D'Angelo and Randy Quaid. He and Chase (as loyal son and beleagured father) shared some of the more subtle moments in this frenetic but quite funny Harold Ramis picture. If Hall was the only member of the family not to reprise his role in the inferior *National Lampoon's European Vacation* (1985) it was only because screenwriter John Hughes had taken him off to bigger and better things by then. In *Sixteen Candles* (1984), Molly Ringwald is a schoolgirl with a crush on a senior and a family that forgets her 16th birthday. Hall was the most prominent of the secondary characters, turning in an astonishingly complete account of 'the geek': a weedy, obnoxious nerd. With his braces, slight frame and freckled complexion Hall certainly looked the part, but he acted it too, accentuating his lispy delivery and adolescent clumsiness, his rather morose features perking up at the slightest hint of sex.

Reviewers singled out Hall's efforts in the film, but more importantly, so did John Hughes himself. Not only did he give Hall the girl in the end, he also gave him two more opportunities to explore the persona they had created together. *The Breakfast Club* (1985) was a stab at a more serious teen movie, with five 'types' stuck in detention together for a day: a princess, a jock, a punk, a nut and a swot (Hall). Hall did not come out so well here. As the youngest of the performers, the competition was particularly stiff, and Hughes gave him less to play with. However the others changed, you could not help feeling the swot was still a bore. If this was disappointing for the actor, the movie itself was a big hit, and renewed some critical interest in the genre. In contrast, *Weird Science* (1985) was a complete disaster. A compendium of all the lapses in taste and sexist attitudes Hughes had ever let slip, this schoolboy's 'Bride Of Frankenstein' had none of the usual compensations, and with Anthony Michael Hall as its leading man he bore the brunt of the stick.

The relationship with Hughes came to an end. They both hoped to grow up. Fearing, rightly, that the audience for adolescent nerds was strictly limited, Hall set about transforming his image. After a brief stint on TV's *Saturday Night Live* he appeared in Richard Tuggle's *Out Of Bounds* (1986), a thriller about an Iowa farm kid who comes to LA and finds himself hunted by the police and murderous drug dealers within 24 hours of his arrival. This attempt at action heroics was generally considered unwatchably stupid, as was *Johnny Be Good* (1988), a return to teen comedy, which posited Hall as 'the hottest high-school quarterback in the nation', courted by colleges and girls alike. Despite pandering to the lowest common denominator (in the US, Orion released a video version with 'new, sexually explicit footage') the film was another commercial failure for Hall. However, with his mature and convincingly unlikeable performance as Winona Ryder's boyfriend in *Edward Scissorhands* (1990), the now well-built and adult-faced former nerd looked set to tackle adult roles with requisite competence.

1982 Six Pack **1983** National Lampoon's Vacation **1984** Sixteen Candles **1985** The Breakfast Club; Weird Science **1986** Out Of Bounds **1988** Johnny Be Good **1990** Up World; Edward Scissorhands **1992** Into The Sun; Who Do I Gotta Kill?

Hamill, Mark

Actor
Born 25 September 1952
Oakland, California

Synonymous world-wide for his *Star Wars* persona, Luke Skywalker, actor Mark Hamill has to date been unsuccessful at forging any significant alternative screen identity for himself.

Born into the family of a US navy captain, Hamill was one of nine siblings; due to his father's postings he had a somewhat nomadic upbringing, living in New York, California, Virginia and even Japan. He was struck by the acting bug at an early age, and went on to study drama at the Los Angeles City College, during which time he made his professional debut in a 1970 episode of TV's *The Bill Cosby Show*. After graduation, Hamill's career followed a slow but steady path: he had a regular slot on the daytime soap *General Hospital*, appeared in various TV movies, including *Sarah T.* and *In Circumstantial Evidence*, and starred in the ill-fated series *The Texas Wheelers*. However, his feature film debut in the phenomenon that was George Lucas' *Star Wars* (1977) transformed his career – albeit temporarily – from that of a modestly successful TV actor to that of an immediate international name.

Hamill's features – the baby face, blue doe eyes and dark blonde hair – suggested just the right quality of callow innocence and earnestness for his role as the young hero. Whether learning to harness 'the force' from the venerable Obi Wan Kenobi (Alec Guinness) or battling to save Princess Leia (Carrie Fisher) from the clutches of the evil Darth Vader, he combined very effectively the qualities of impetuousness and idealism that form the basis of Luke Skywalker's character. In the film's two sequels the actor seized the opportunity to expand upon his increasingly mature part, most notably in *The Empire Strikes Back* (1980), the darkest and most impressive of the *Star Wars* trilogy, in which Luke learns the shattering truth about his parentage.

Sadly, however, Hamill's non-galactic career failed to get lift-off. Aged 26, he played a high-schooler looking for his stolen car and falling for aspiring prostitute Annie Potts in the mediocre teenage yarn *Corvette Summer* (1978). His starring role as a soldier under the command of Lee Marvin in the World War II drama *The Big Red One* (1980) did him little service either; the film was well received critically but sank without trace at the box office. And *The Night The Lights Went Out in Georgia*, made the following year, did more for co-star Dennis Quaid's career than it did for Hamill's: with the exception of a cameo in *Britannia Hospital* (1982) and the third *Star Wars* instalment, *Return of the Jedi* (1983), it was eight years before he made his next film. Another sci-fi adventure, *Slipstream* (1989) cast Hamill as a swashbuckling hero but it was in every sense light years away from George Lucas' trilogy.

Nevertheless, Hamill, who is married and has a child, has enjoyed a productive theatre career; he made his Broadway debut in the title role of *The Elephant Man*, played Mozart in a production of Peter Shaffer's award-winning *Amadeus*, and in 1987 starred as an architect whose life becomes chaos in *The Nerd*. As he approached his 40s, it appeared that, with three films underway, he was finally determined to pick up the threads of his uneven Hollywood career.

1977 Star Wars **1988** Corvette Summer (GB: The Hot One) **1980** The Big Red One; The Empire Strikes Back **1981** The Night The Lights Went Out in Georgia **1982** Britannia Hospital (cameo) **1983** Return of the Jedi **1989** Slipstream **1991** Black Magic Woman

Hamilton, Linda

Actress

Born 26 September 1957

Salisbury, Maryland

Educated at Washington College, Maryland, and trained for her chosen profession at Lee Strasberg's Actors' Studio in New York, Linda Hamilton is an interesting actress, much underused by Hollywood. Most of her career has flourished in television where she has appeared in many series for CBS and ABC, notably as the girl in the oddball *Beauty And The Beast*, and she has made numerous TV and video movies.

A glance at her filmography shows it to be both sparse and confined to forgettable schlock. However, nobody who saw the complex and ambitious sci-fi movie *The Terminator* (1984) is likely to forget her. As the intended victim of Schwarzenegger's cyborg, rescued by Michael Biehn by whom she is to bear the hero-child of a post-nuclear future, Hamilton delivered a performance of range and sympathy, maturing from slightly tacky working girl to earth mother with naturalness and conviction. A year later, she was practically unrecognisable – her hair dyed black, her personality voluptuous, vulgar and tough – as a neurotic dropout turned high-powered car thief in *Black Moon Rising*. She was a weighty match for co-star Tommy Lee Jones in this off-beat thriller which, like *The Terminator*, was darkly disturbing although not in the same class of imagination and ambition. However, the movie demonstrated Hamilton's versatility and it is surprising that she disappeared from the big screen for five years until the blockbusting *Terminator 2* in 1991.

1982 T.A.G: The Assassination Game **1984** The Stone Boy; The Terminator; Children Of The Corn **1985** Black Moon Rising; Sexpionage **1986** King Kong Lives **1991** Terminator 2: Judgment Day

Hanks, Tom

Actor

Born 9 July 1956

Concord, California

Hollywood has a tendency to make facile and often pointless comparisons between its younger crop of stars and the big names of yesteryear. When, however, it comes to defining the subtle and diverse strengths of Tom Hanks, it is perhaps appropriate to mention him in the same breath as Jack Lemmon: perennially youthful, lacking conventional leading man looks and sporting a distinctively scooped out nose, possessed of a superb gift for comedy, yet capable of being romantically appealing.

By the end of the 1980s, Hanks had become one of the newly crowned kings of romantic comedy, largely on the strength of two major hits, *Splash* (1984) and *Big* (1988). He possesses an uncanny ability to bring a combination of boyish sensitivity, warmth and humour to the big screen so effortlessly that one forgets he is acting at all. His failing has been to select material which does no favours to his talent, but he has nonetheless imbued each of his roles with a sense of friendly intimacy and openness to which audiences immediately respond. He acts *with* the camera, not *at* it.

Tom's parents divorced when he was five. He endured a peripatetic childhood, travelling extensively in Northern California with his father, an itinerant cook. Raised 'like lion cubs', Hanks and his sibling were subjected to constant changes of schools, religions, and stepmothers. Finally settling in Oakland, he participated in high school dramatics and eventually enrolled at California State University, Sacramento, where he was immersed in college productions. In 1978 he moved to New York, eked out a living and started a family with actress-producer Samantha Lewes, whom he married after the birth of their son.

It wasn't until 1979 that Hanks scored his first feature film role (and $800) in *He Knows You're Alone*, a cheap but moderately chilling slasher movie. By 1980, the young actor was in LA where he grabbed at the leading role in *Bosom Buddies*, a short-lived TV sit-com in which he appeared, more often than not, in drag. Sporadic work in other TV series such as *Taxi* and *Family Ties*, and the made-for-TV movie *Mazes And Monsters* helped him gain a reputation as an all-rounder. It was this profile which brought him his breakthrough lead (after it had been turned down by Michael Keaton among others) in the Disney comedy *Splash!*, which became the sleeper hit of 1984. Daryl Hannah's sexy mermaid made the magazine covers, but Hanks' exquisitely balanced performance as a romantic maladroit turned hero gained him huge critical and popular acclaim. That same year, the workaholic actor appeared in *Bachelor Party*, a rather rough pre-nuptial comedy made before *Splash!* and suitably eclipsed by it. Despite a good cast and the best efforts of leading man Hanks as a violinist caught up with the CIA, *The Man With One Red Shoe* (1985) was a desperately unfunny remake of the French film, *The Tall Blond Man With One Black Shoe*; and the same year's *Volunteers* had the actor braving a script that only worked for the first 50 minutes. (However, during filming he met Rita Wilson, who was to become the second Mrs Hanks after his divorce in 1987.)

Between 1986 and 1988, Tom Hanks participated in a long string of mainly unfunny comedy experiments in which his own consistently high-quality work was almost buried in the mire around him. Then, in *Nothing In Common* (1986), he was given the golden opportunity of playing a dramatic lead opposite the ailing Jackie Gleason in a tale of father-son reconciliation. The role mirrored Hanks' experiences with his own illness-plagued father and, although it was a box-office failure, it became the actor's personal favourite. He co-starred with Dan Aykroyd in *Dragnet* (1987), but this parody on the TV series of the same name was no more than a predictably absurd cop romp through LA.

It was *Big*, directed by former TV star Penny Marshall, that finally gave the actor a clear run. A superb script, subtly directed to avoid the pitfalls of a plot in which a boy in a man's body becomes, among many other things, romantically involved with a grown woman (Elizabeth Perkins), helped Hanks to charm the socks off audiences of all ages. His attempt to eat a baby ear of corn at a cocktail party, attacking it as if it were a large corn-on-the-cob, was memorable, his romance with Perkins magical, and the movie proved one of 1988's biggest hits.

Yet again, success was followed by disappointment. The actor gave his all as the bitter comedian in *Punchline* (1988), a sardonic account of the jungle warfare of stand-up comedy, co-starring Sally Field, but the screenplay didn't quite hang together; neither did Joe Dante's imaginative but uneven black comedy *The 'Burbs* (1989), which had been crippled by the writers' strike and studio walkouts. And although Hanks made his role as a bachelor cop in *Turner And Hooch* (1989) both interesting and brilliantly funny, the ever-drooling dog who was his co-star stole the show. *Joe Versus The Volcano* (1990) was another kind of dog: an odd, uneasy fable about life which left audiences puzzled as Meg Ryan and even Hanks appeared to sleepwalk through their respective roles.

Nonetheless, Tom Hanks' star status rose high when he was cast as the lead in the screen version of Tom Wolfe's bestseller, *Bonfire Of The Vanities*, co-starring Bruce Willis and Melanie Griffith. Alas, for all concerned, Brian De Palma's troubled production was universally and justifiably castigated, with its star taking a lot of the flak which he would have to overcome thereafter.

1980 He Knows You're Alone **1983** Bachelor Party **1984** Splash **1985** The Man With One Red Shoe; Volunteers; The Money Pit **1986** Nothing In Common; Everytime We Say Goodbye **1987** Dragnet **1988** Big; Punchline **1989** The 'Burbs; Turner And Hooch **1990** Joe Versus The Volcano **1990** Bonfire Of The Vanities **1992** A League Of Their Own; Radio Flyer

Hannah, Daryl

Actress
Born 1960
Chicago, Illinois

Recent years have not been kind to Daryl Hannah, as her reputation has gone from watchable actress to annoying, wisp-like flake. Certainly, there is a sense of her not being entirely present in her later work, making her casting as a ghost in *High Spirits* (1988) somewhat ideal, although she has little of substance in most of her performances to indicate that this may not be her own fault.

Starting her career as a classical dancer, she studied acting in Chicago and later with Stella Adler, being picked out for a small role in *The Fury* (1978) while she was still at school. Subsequent parts were as uninspiring as the films they inhabited – the sister of Kim Basinger (the actress she most resembles, though Hannah's prettier) in *Hard Country* (1981), one of the many victims meeting a genuinely unpleasant end in *The Final Terror* (1981), and one third of the *ménage à trois* in the heavily market-researched *Summer Lovers* (1982), but she was getting her face known. Her breakthrough came as Pris, the gymnastic punk replicant in *Blade Runner* (1982) and as the innocent (but not naive) mermaid in Manhattan in *Splash* (1984) with Tom Hanks.

Her attempts to build on her success, most notably with her own production of the world's first feminist caveman movie, *Clan Of The Cave Bear* (1986), were less than successful and she occupied her own personal twilight zone in the mediocre *Legal Eagles* (1986, in which she lost a lot of credibility with a piece of performance art she devised herself); and her not unappealing *Roxanne* (1987) ultimately appeared too self-obssessed to be worthy of Steve Martin's Cyrano De Bergerac figure. Even when working with major directors such as Oliver Stone and Neil Jordan, Hannah has been relegated to bimbo roles, and took a rather irritating shot at character playing in *Steel Magnolias* (1989), admittedly an altogether irritating film. But, intent on proving that her head is not an echo chamber (a case not helped by 1990's *Crazy People*), she continues to take small roles in prestigious films like *Crimes And Misdemeanors* (1989) and *At Play In The Fields Of The Lord* (1991, a disaster), and a rather larger one, for which she was well-cast and sympathetic, opposite Chevy Chase in *Memoirs Of An Invisible Man*.

1978 The Fury **1981** Hard Country; The Final Terror aka Campsite Massacre aka Three Blind Mice **1982** Summer Lovers; Blade Runner **1984** Reckless; The Pope Of Greenwich Village aka Village Dreams; Splash **1986** The Clan Of The Cave Bear; Legal Eagles **1987** Wall Street; Roxanne **1988** High Spirits **1989** Steel Magnolias; Crimes And Misdemeanors (cameo) **1990** Crazy People **1991** At Play In The Fields Of The Lord **1992** The Memoirs Of An Invisible Man

Harmon, Mark

Actor
Born 2 September 1951
Burbank, California

Mark Harmon grew up in Hollywood. His Father, Tom Harmon, was a football star. His mother, Elyse Knox, was an actress. At UCLA, where he took a BA in communications, Mark followed in his father's footsteps, becoming a star quarterback, but eventually he gravitated towards an acting career. With his athletic physique, sandy hair and penetrating eyes, Harmon broke into the movies in his late 20s, with small roles in *Comes A Horseman* (1978) and *Beyond The Poseidon Adventure* (1979). This proved something of a false start however. It was on television that the young aspirant established himself.

NBC's *St. Elsewhere*, a cross between *General Hospital* and *Hill Street Blues*, found in Harmon their Daniel J. Travanti – the thinking young woman's sex symbol. Harmon was California-cool to the bone, but it was pleasant that he did not try to push it, and that furrowed brow might easily be taken for intelligence. One publication dubbed him 'The Sexiest Man Alive'. It was clearly time to give the movies another shot.

Carl Reiner's *Summer School* (1987) paired him with another television star, Kirstie Alley from *Cheers*. Harmon was a delinquent high school teacher forced to spend his vacation teaching delinquent kids. Unsurprisingly, they get on like a house on fire; more surprisingly, they learn something in the process. This was determinedly lowbrow fare, and Harmon could play a beach bum in his sleep, but it was likeable enough. *The Presidio* (1988) was a more serious try for the Hollywood mainstream. A thriller that owed something to *No Way Out*, at one stage Tony Scott was set to direct, and Marlon Brando had been approached for a supporting role. In the event, Jack Warden played the part, and Peter Hyams directed, with Harmon and Sean Connery as the grudgingly teamed investigators whose mutual antipathy centres on Meg Ryan, Connery's wild daughter. Despite some effective sequences, *The Presidio* was sunk by a hackneyed script that did no favours to Harmon, and his relationship with Ryan was given particularly short shrift. Connery was reportedly unimpressed with his co-star, but it is unlikely that even a Kevin Costner would have made much impression with this material.

Stealing Home (1988) was an even bigger let-down. Harmon played a 'thirtysomething' nobody who could have been a somebody. Going home for the funeral of his best friend, he recollects the past – his potentially major league baseball career, and the accident that changed everything. For the first time, the actor was stretching himself beyond his winning television persona. Unfortunately, he had little to do but look doleful and unshaven, and cue flashbacks to his younger days, personified by William McNamara. It was McNamara who took on most of the dramatic moments, the comedy, and all the embarrassingly trite scenes with the film's leading lady, Jodie Foster. Of the string of baseball movies of the late 80s (*Bull Durham,*

Field of Dreams, Major League) *Stealing Home* was the only one not to get past first base. With two strikes against him, Harmon seemed to lower his sights a little, opting for the low farce (*Worth Winning* 1989) he can carry with ease. By the beginning of the 1990s the actor had yet to imprint his personality on the big screen.

1978 Comes A Horseman **1979** Beyond The Poseidon Adventure **1987** Summer School **1988** The Presidio; Stealing Home **1989** Worth Winning **1991** Till There Was You **1992** Cold Heaven

Harper, Tess

Actress

Born 1952

Mammoth Spring, Arkansas

Tess Harper's Hollywood career to date has not brought the opportunities which her debut seemed to promise, even though her quality has been frequently reconfirmed.

She got off to a terrific start, playing opposite an Oscar-winning Robert Duvall in Bruce Beresford's touching *Tender Mercies* (1983). As the young Vietnam war widow, struggling to run her Midwestern farm and raise her young son, whose life is changed for the better by the arrival of Duvall's 'hired help', the blonde, blue-eyed young actress gave an appealing performance, combining strength and vulnerability in equal parts. Beresford remained loyal, using her again in *Crimes Of The Heart* (1986). In a supporting role as the brassy, bigoted and venomous cousin to the Southern belles (Diane Keaton, Jessica Lange and Sissy Spacek) at the heart of the drama, Harper flounced, bridled and spat with deft conviction, proving herself capable of far more than 'nice' girls, and winning a Best Supporting Oscar nomination. Sadly, during the 80s, she was otherwise confined to tiny supporting roles (a factory worker in *Silkwood*, 1983; Tom Selleck's suburban sister-in-law in *Her Alibi* 1989), or appeared in box-office failures such as the catastrophic *Ishtar* (1987) and Sam Shepard's *Far North* (1988).

In between times, Tess Harper, who was educated in Missouri and cut her teeth on children's theatre, dinner theatre and commercials in Texas, has made TV movies and mini-series.

1983 Tender Mercies; Amityville 3-D; Silkwood **1984** Flashpoint **1986** Crimes Of The Heart **1987** Ishtar **1988** Far North; Criminal Law **1989** Her Alibi **1990** Daddy's Dyin' – Who's Got The Will? **1991** My Heroes Have Always Been Cowboys; The Man In The Moon **1992** Home Fires Burning; My New Gun

Harris, Ed

Actor

Born 28 November 1950

Tenafly, New Jersey

The explosive quality that lurks in the childlike eyes of Ed Harris is rarely seen in blonde, blue-eyed character leading men, but Harris, no pretty boy, has intensity along with his stocky solidity.

Harris, who played American football for two years while he was a student at New York's Columbia University, took up acting classes and wet his feet in summer stock after his transfer to Oklahoma State University. From there he removed to the California Institute of the Arts, and after graduation worked extensively in the West Coast theatre. His first screen outings were for television, including a supporting role in *The Amazing Howard Hughes* (1977).

After a few bit parts Harris starred in an unusual cult film from horror meister George Romero, *Knightriders* (1981), as one of a travelling group who stage jousts on motorcycles and aspire to a latter-day Arthurian code of chivalry. His film career really began to take off in 1983, however, when he impressed in two contrasting roles. In Roger Spottiswoode's first-rate political thriller *Under Fire*, which centred on journalists in Nicaragua played by Nick Nolte, Joanna Cassidy and Gene Hackman, Harris presented a chilling, cheerful American mercenary killer. In Philip Kaufman's thrilling adaptation of Tom Wolfe's *The Right Stuff*, the story of America's Mercury space programme astronauts, Harris was at once commanding and touching as the gung-ho Marine pilot-turned-American icon, John Glenn.

More than a dozen films followed in rapid succession, Harris always making a mark whether as Goldie Hawn's unpleasant, cuckolded sailor husband in the Jonathan Demme misfire, *Swing Shift* (1984), or the small-town Lothario in *Places In The Heart* (1984). He also turned in some memorable leads, notably as a beleagured Texan fisherman venting his rage hatefully on Vietnamese immigrants in *Alamo Bay* (1985), in which he starred with his wife, Amy Madigan, and as the lovestruck but over-macho, frustrated, heavy-drinking husband of country-and-western singing star Patsy Cline, played by

Jessica Lange, in *Sweet Dreams* (1985). His performance of the unhappy Charlie, from cocky seducing barfly to dazed, heartbroken widower was a beautiful piece of work.

While Alex Cox's doomed and damned *Walker* (finally released in 1988 after being held for some time) sank, Harris was arresting as the real-life 19th-century American mercenary who made himself the president of Nicaragua. In 1989 he provided a stolid central hero in James Cameron's spectacular, wildly overblown underwater saga, *The Abyss* (for which the actor endured months of discomfort filming underwater in a converted nuclear plant), and held his own brilliantly with Robert De Niro as a haunted Vietnam veteran in the under-appreciated *Jacknife*. In a supporting role among the starry male ensemble of *Glengarry Glen Ross* he impressed yet again as one of the foul-mouthed, ruthless, desperate real estate salesmen.

1978 Coma **1980** Borderline **1981** Knightriders **1982** Creepshow **1983** Under Fire; The Right Stuff **1984** Swing Shift; A Flash Of Green; Places In The Heart **1985** Alamo Bay; Sweet Dreams; Code Name: Emerald **1988** Walker; To Kill A Priest **1989** Jacknife; The Abyss **1990** State Of Grace **1991** Paris Trout **1992** Glengarry Glen Ross **1993** Needful Things

Hauer, Rutger

Actor
Born 23 January 1944
Breukelen, Holland

The Dutch actor Rutger Hauer, tall, Viking-blond, strikingly handsome and the possessor of a pair of piercing, startlingly blue eyes that can be turned to intensely sinister account, is an international movie star who has increasingly graced the American screen.

The son of drama teachers, Hauer grew up in Amsterdam but ran away to sea when he was 15 and spent a year scrubbing decks aboard a freighter. Returning home, he worked variously as an electrician and a carpenter for three years, at the same time attending drama classes at night school. He went on to join an experimental acting troupe, with whom he stayed for five years, before getting a part as a swashbuckler in a Dutch TV series. His career changed course when director Paul (*Robocop, Basic Instinct*) Verhoeven, making his own screen debut, gave him the lead in *Turkish Delight* (1973), an aggressive, alienating and erotic movie in which Hauer portrayed a rebellious, promiscuous sculptor. Due almost certainly to the daringly full-frontal sexual element, the movie found box-office favour abroad as well as at home and within two years its virile star was invited to make his English-language debut in *The Wilby Conspiracy* (1975). The late Ralph Nelson's mediocre film, set in South Africa and starring Michael Caine and Sidney Poitier, was an action melodrama focusing on apartheid for its conflict, and found Rutger essaying an Afrikaner playboy, helped to authenticity by his Aryan mien and Dutch accent. However, the supporting role was hardly enough to establish him in Hollywood's eyes and he returned to European film-making for several years.

It was in the Sylvester Stallone vehicle, *Nighthawks* (1981), that Rutger Hauer finally made his American debut proper. Cast as a much-wanted, psychopathically cold-blooded terrorist, he was a chilling antagonist in this cop drama and made a strong impression which was confirmed by a major role the following year as the chief android pitted against Harrison Ford in Ridley Scott's bleak vision of the future, *Blade Runner*. Hauer's build and looks, those extraordinary eyes and the accent came magnificently into their own, and he worked continuously thereafter in movies of variable quality. He was the adventurer courting Gene Hackman's daughter (Theresa Russell) in Nicholas Roeg's poorly received *Eureka* (1983), and the handsome knight paired with Michelle Pfeiffer in the well-received medieval romance, *Ladyhawke* (1985). But, good or bad, Hauer's movies sank with little trace, although the actor himself continued to make an impression. And no more so than in the terrifyingly sinister *The Hitcher* (1986), in which he was the mysterious stranger, calmly and uncompromisingly intent on massacring C. Thomas Howell's lone motorist, and anyone who crossed his path *en route*.

It was left to the distinguished Italian director Ermanno Olmi to mine the gentler, more mystic and soulful side of Hauer's personality in *The Legend Of The Holy Drinker* (1989), the story of a lost soul who dies of drink in Paris while attempting to pay a debt of honour in a church; and Philip Noyce attempted to capitalize similarly, but far less successfully, on the actor's spiritual qualities in the martial arts action adventure, *Blind Fury* (1989). By the early 90s Hauer was as well-known for his humorous appearances in mystifying Guinness commercials as for his screen roles.

1973 Turkish Delight **1973** Pusteblume/Dandelion aka Hard To Remember (W. Germany) **1975** The Wilby Conspiracy; Keetje Tippel/Cathy Tippel (Holland); Amulett Des Todes (W. Germany) **1976** Cancer Rising (Holland); Max Havelaar (Holland) **1978** Femme Entre Chien Et Loup (Belgium) **1979** Soldaat Van Oranje/ Soldier Of Orange/Survival Run (Holland); Grijpstra En De Gier (Holland; released in USA in 1983 as Outsider In Amsterdam); Mysteries (Holland) **1980** Spetters (Holland) **1981** Chanel Solitaire (France); Nighthawks **1982** Blade Runner **1983** Eureka; The Osterman Weekend **1984** A Breed Apart **1985** Ladyhawke; Flesh And Blood **1986** The Hitcher **1987** Wanted: Dead Or Alive **1989** The Legend Of The Holy Drinker (Italy/France); Salute Of The Jugger; Bloodhounds of Broadway; In Una Notte Di Chiaro Di Luna/On A Moonlit Night (Italy); Up To Date; Blind Fury **1992** Past Midnight; Split Second (GB); Buffy The Vampire Slayer

Hawke, Ethan

Actor

Born 6 November 1971

Austin, Texas

By the age of 20 Ethan Hawke was already a well known, seven-year film veteran and considered among the most promising actors of his generation. Born in Texas and raised in Princeton, New Jersey, Hawke made his film debut at 14 in Joe Dante's charming and imaginative science-fiction fantasy *Explorers* (1985) alongside River Phoenix as the boys who construct a spacecraft out of bits of junk. Between acting classes at Princeton's McCarter Theatre, in England with the British Theatre Association and at Carnegie Mellon University in Pittsburgh, he turned in an impressive range of youth roles, including the shy student Todd, movingly encouraged to open up and express himself by Robin Williams in *Dead Poets Society* (1989), Ted Danson's son and Jack Lemmon's grandson in *Dad* (1989), the leads in Jack London's classic Alaskan adventure story *White Fang* (1991), the romantic comedy *Mystery Date* (1991) and the fine World War II drama *A Midnight Clear* (1992) as the intelligent young platoon leader. He followed that with a small but key supporting role as the confrontational high school student, Price, to Jeremy Irons' troubled history teacher in *Waterland* (1992). Grown into a tall, slender, pale and intense young man, Hawke was not short of good juvenile parts as he reached 21, but was still awaiting a quality lead role.

1985 Explorers **1989** Dead Poets Society; Dad **1991** White Fang; Just Another Night aka Mystery Date **1992** A Midnight Clear; Waterland; Rich In Love; Alive

Hawn, Goldie (Goldie Jean Studlendgehawn)

Actress

Born 21 November 1945

Washington DC

Ever since Goldie Hawn's appearances as a saucer-eyed, giggling dizzy blonde on Rowan and Martin's TV *Laugh-In* (1968–1973), she has been associated with that image. *Life* magazine described her at the time as having 'the sex appeal of Lolita and the innocence of Charlie Brown,' and despite a few attempts to change, she has carried this characterisation into most of her screen roles.

Describing her own childhood as 'suburban, conventional and traditional Jewish', this daughter of a musician was encouraged from an early age to attend ballet and tap classes. When studying drama at American University in Washington, she paid her fees by managing a dance studio, and it was while dancing in TV's *Andy Griffith Show* that she was spotted by an agent who put her into the comedy series *Good Morning World* (1967–1968), which led to her long stint on *Laugh-In*.

Naturally, she was cast as a kook in her first films: the Greenwich Village mistress of bachelor dentist Walter Matthau in *Cactus Flower* (1969), bringing zest to the dull comedy for which she gained a Supporting Actress Oscar nomination; Peter Sellers' latest 'bit on the side' in *There's A Girl In My Soup* (1970); and the hooker who pairs up with Warren Beatty in *Dollars* (1971) to deprive a safe deposit box of $1 million. She was touching and funny as the girl who falls for a blind young man in *Butterflies Are Free* (1972), but it was Steven Spielberg, with his first feature, *The Sugarland Express* (1973), who really gave her a chance to prove she was an actress capable of a wider range than first supposed. The part was that of a woman who helps her husband escape from prison because she needs him to help keep her baby and fight the forces who want to put the child up for adoption.

She continued to bring sparkle to a number of comedies, including *Shampoo* (1975), in which she played one of hairdresser Warren Beatty's client-lovers, and she was a saloon singer partnered with George Segal in a vulgar spoof Western, *The Duchess And The Dirtwater Fox* (1976). Much better was *Foul*

Play (1978), a protracted but amusing comedy-thriller, in which she portrayed a recently divorced librarian called Gloria Mundy, who gets caught up in a plot to murder the Pope on a visit to San Francisco, while getting involved with nonchalant detective Chevy Chase. The partnership with Chase worked well and they were teamed again in *Seems Like Old Times* (1980), a Neil Simon comedy in which Goldie hides ex-hubby Chase, on the run from the police, in her house without her buttoned-up husband (Charles Grodin) knowing.

Hawn's big blue eyes were wider than usual in the title role of *Private Benjamin* (1980), a Jewish princess who joins the army. The jokes came thick, fast and predictable, but the star, who also co-produced, gave an engaging performance and gained a Best Actress Oscar nomination. But Oscar nominations notwithstanding, her best role to date was in *Swing Shift* (1984), a change of pace from the typical slick sit-com packages she usually appeared in by anonymous directors. Jonathan Demme's film, set in the early 40s, showed Hawn as one of the many women working to build fighter aircraft while their husbands were away at war. For once suppressing her kookie side, she was impressive in demonstrating the shift from average housewife to liberated woman. The affair at the centre of the film was between Hawn and trumpet player Kurt Russell, Hawn's boyfriend in real-life. (She was first married to Gus Trikonis, and later to Bill Hudson, member of the Hudson Brothers rock-comedy group.)

The star played against type as the shrewish heiress who falls *Overboard* (1987) from her yacht and loses her memory, before reverting to her usual dippy-blonde broad manner when Kurt Russell convinces her she's his wife. After a three-year break in order to spend time with her four young children, and hungry for a hit that had eluded her since *Private Benjamin*, she returned in *Bird On A Wire* (1990), a popular but formula vehicle for her and Mel Gibson, in which she overdid her squealing, shrieking and cuteness. The majority of her parts belie her statement that 'I have fought all my life, and am still fighting, for validity as a person who has a brain.' In order to prove it, however, Goldie Hawn was back to more substantial material in *Crisscross* (1991), directed by Chris Menges, about a mother and son deserted by a returned Vietnam vet, followed by the indifferent conspiracy thriller, *Deceived* (1991) in which she had nothing to giggle at, and the romantic comedy *Housesitter* (1992) in which she essayed a compulsive liar opposite a hapless Steve Martin.

1968 The One And Only Genuine Original Family Band **1969** Cactus Flower **1970** There's A Girl In My Soup **1971** Dollars (GB: The Heist) **1972** Butterflies Are Free **1973** The Sugarland Express **1974** The Girl From Petroka **1975** Shampoo **1976** The Duchess And The Dirtwater Fox **1978** Foul Play **1980** Private Benjamin; Seems Like Old Times **1982** Best Friends **1984** Swing Shift; Protocol **1985** Wildcats **1987** Overboard **1990** Bird On A Wire **1991** Deceived **1992** Crisscross; Housesitter; Death Becomes Her

Headly, Glenne

Actress

Born 13 March 1955

New London, Connecticut

Glenne Headly is a respected and experienced stage actress who, like her ex-husband John Malkovich, came to the movies through her long-term association with Chicago's acclaimed Steppenwolf Theatre Company. Unlike Malkovich, however, she had to cut her teeth in small supporting parts over several years before she began landing meatier roles in the late 80s.

A native of Connecticut, Headly is a graduate of New York's High School of the Performing Arts. She studied at the Herbert Berghof Studios before spending a year at the American College of Switzerland. Upon her return to the States she joined Chicago's New Works Ensemble, moving on later to Steppenwolf, where she met and married Malkovich. Her performances there brought her acclaim and four Jefferson Awards (for *Say Goodnight, Gracie, Balm in Gilead*, directed by Malkovich, *The Miss Firecracker Contest* and *Coyote Ugly*). In addition, she has directed the play *Canadian Gothic* and has also appeared off-Broadway in *Arms and The Man*, co-starring Raul Julia and Kevin Kline, and on Broadway in a production of *Extremities* with Susan Sarandon.

On screen, though, it wasn't until 1988's *Dirty Rotten Scoundrels* that Headly made an impact. Prior to that, she had provided modest but adept support in a variety of films, including a brief appearance in 1985's *Fandango*, small parts in two Malkovich starrers, *Eleni* (also 1985) and *Making Mr Right* (1987), and a supporting role alongside fellow Steppenwolf actress Laurie Metcalf in the poorly received *Stars and Bars* (1988). But in Frank Oz's Riviera-set comedy Headly really came into her own. An actress of chiselled features and thin lips, she bears more resemblance to Katharine Hepburn or Irene Dunne than to her many pouting, tousle-haired contemporaries; in addition, she has a surprisingly gentle, girlish voice and the overall demeanour of a guileless ingenue that doesn't, however, conceal her underlying intelligence. It was these innate qualities that Headly brought to bear so effectively in her performance as an apparently naive and vulnerable American 'soap heiress' who seemingly falls prey to arch con-men Michael Caine and Steve Martin, only to later turn the tables on the pair. Although the movie itself was an uneven affair, it is to Headly's credit that she was never overshadowed by the outrageous antics of Caine and, especially, Martin, and was vivid and delightful throughout.

Doubtless in part because of her old-fashioned traits, Headly was cast in such films as Woody Allen's Depression-era *The Purple Rose of Cairo* (1985), the poor 1950s-set comedy *Nadine* (1987) which she enlivened with a painfully funny-sad performance as Jeff Bridges discarded amour and the Western TV special *Lonesome Dove* (1989). Doubtless, too, those qualities led to her being chosen as Tess Trueheart, fiancée to the eponymous hero of Warren Beatty's *Dick Tracy* (1990). Gloriously designed and executed, the comic-strip adaptation received mixed critical reception and only respectable box-office takings, some of the blame for which must go to Beatty's tediously wooden performance as Tracy. Headly, however, with relatively little to work on, was a breath of fresh air, bringing a well-needed human angle into the curiously passionless enterprise. Through her portrayal of a patient, girl-next-door type she provided the film with a few moments of real emotion and proved the most fully-rounded character in the film.

1981 Four Friends **1983** Doctor Detroit **1985** Fandango; Eleni; The Purple Rose of Cairo **1986** Seize The Day **1987** Nadine; Making Mr Right **1988** Stars and Bars; Paperhouse; Dirty Rotten Scoundrels **1990** Dick Tracy **1991** Mortal Thoughts

Heard, John

Actor
Born 7 March 1946
Washington, D.C.

Handsome John Heard, professionally a product of New York and Chicago theatre, threatened to become an A-list leading man with a succession of troubled, moody and charming romantic leads in the late 1970s. However, despite definite screen charisma, respect for his acting ability among colleagues and within the industry, and admirers for whom he is a cult heart-throb, major stardom never quite happened. In recent years, though, Heard has brought weight and appeal to many supporting roles in drama, comedies and thrillers.

This actor's considerable theatre work began with the Organic Theatre, with whom he attracted attention in the Chicago and New York productions of *Warp*. In 1977 he won a Theater World Award for his performance in *Streamers*, and in 1979 he was awarded an Obie for two disparate off-Broadway roles, in *Othello* and *Split*. Meanwhile, Heard had made his fortuitous film debut in Joan Micklin Silver's off-beat gem *Between The Lines* (1977) as the star reporter and feckless Romeo of the underground radical paper. A few films later, Silver starred him again as the alternately infuriating and charming obsessive wooer in *Head Over Heels* (1979). The same year he made a riveting job of the guilty-sinner minister in a prestigious production of *The Scarlet Letter* mounted for America's highbrow-oriented Public Service Television.

Free spirits and tormented souls, though not without their appeal, followed and probably undid Heard's headway with mainstream audiences. He was in distinct danger of drowning in duds, although he continued to work on the stage, including a sensitive portrayal of the 'gentleman caller' in the 1983/4 Broadway revival of *The Glass Menagerie*. Keen Heard spotters were taken aback by his hefty weight gain when he reappeared on screen in a cameo as the bartender in Scorsese's bizarre comic nightmare *After Hours* (1985), but, weight down, he carried on in mainly worthwhile projects.

After the hiccup of the ghastly Whoopi Goldberg boo-boo *The Telephone* (1988) Heard made a likeable reluctant hero figure in Robert Redford's enchanting ensemble piece, *The Milagro Beanfield War* (1988), playing a disenchanted cynic whose ideals are forced back into play in a community crisis. In *Big* (1988) he was fun as the sneaky, envious toy company rival to Tom Hanks' little-boy-in-a-man's-body, and within the same year persuasively played a calculating FBI operative for Costa-Gavras in *Betrayed* and squared off with the overpowering Bette Midler in the women's weepie *Beaches*. His first completely heinous villain, a US Army colonel masterminding a political assassination, was equally, disturbingly credible opposite Gene Hackman in *The Package* (1989), and he has continued to work non-stop.

1977 Between The Lines; First Love **1978** On The Yard **1979** Head Over Heels aka Chilly Scenes Of Winter **1980** Heart Beat **1981** Cutter's Way aka Cutter And Bone **1982** Cat People **1983** Best Revenge **1984** Violated; C.H.U.D. **1985** Heaven Help Us; Too Scared To Scream; After Hours; The Trip To Bountiful **1986** Violated **1988** The Telephone; The Milagro Beanfield War; The Seventh Sign; Big; Betrayed; Beaches **1989** The Package **1990** Awakenings; Home Alone; Mindwalk; The End Of Innocence **1991** Deceived; Rambling Rose **1992** Radio Flyer; Home Alone 2: Lost In New York; Waterland (GB); Gladiator

Heckerling, Amy

Director, writer
Born 7 May 1954
New York

Amy Heckerling's only real distinction as a director is her sex. As one of the very few women film-makers working in Hollywood, her output merits some attention on those grounds alone. Ironically, Heckerling's mostly mediocre comedies tend to reinforce chauvinist stereotypes and occasionally fall into more or less explicit sexism.

She was educated at New York's School of Art and Design, then went on to study film and television at New York University. Sponsored by the American Film Institute, she made three short films on 16mm: *Modern Times*, *High Finance* and *Getting It Over With*. This last in particular persuaded Hollywood to trust her with *Fast Times At Ridgemont High* (1982), a look at high school life based on Cameron Crowe's factual book. The movie purported to 'tell it like it is', and Heckerling may have got the job to emphasise the project's credibility. In the event, however, this is only a step above 'Porkys' style exploitation; if the movie is to be believed, caricatures not characters populate American high schools. That said, this is probably Heckerling's most spirited film, and it introduced an enviable number of young actors. It was Sean Penn's breakthrough role, Jennifer Jason Leigh and Phoebe Cates also made an impression, and it was the first film for Anthony Edwards and Eric Stoltz. A couple of sex scenes were handled awkwardly, but from a female perspective.

After she helped produce a *Fast Times* television series spin-off, Heckerling made the lame gangster movie parody *Johnny Dangerously* (1984) – which resembled a TV comedy itself, but without a laugh track. Meanwhile her husband, Neal Israel, made *Bachelor Party* (1984), a tacky sex comedy starring Tom Hanks. *National Lampoon's European Vacation* (1985) was another feeble effort, far inferior to both the first and third in the series. Limply trailing from one European country to another, the movie looked like it was improvised en route, and Heckerling's travelogue direction recalled equally dull pictures from the early 60s. Farcical attempts to rev up the flagging pace are all too transparent – and a handful of sequences are astonishingly sexist.

A cameo role in John Landis' *Into The Night* (1985) and an assignment on the *Twilight Zone* TV series confirmed the director's mainstream status, but it was not until 1989 that she made another feature, *Look Who's Talking*. Her own screenplay was a high concept, one-joke affair, but it proved an irresistible come-on to audiences. Through Bruce Willis' voice-over we are made party to baby talk – and even baby think. While the production is cosy enough, agreeably performed by John Travolta and Kirstie Alley, it is a hackneyed piece that soon overplays its hand. The story of a single mother and her child in search of a suitable father, this is clearly anti-feminist. At least Alley is afforded a few privileged moments that reveal an alternative perspective for virtually the first time in Heckerling's career. A sequel and a TV series followed.

1982 Fast Times At Ridgemont High **1984** Johnny Dangerously **1985** National Lampoon's European Vacation **1989** Look Who's Talking (w/d) **1991** Look Who's Talking Too (w/d)

Hemingway, Mariel

Actress
Born 22 November 1961
Ketchum, Idaho

Mariel Hemingway never knew her celebrated grandfather, Ernest. He shot himself four months before she was born, but her name is seldom dissociated from that of the great novelist. When her elder sister,

Margaux, became a top model, she was accused of using the Hemingway tag to advance her career, but Mariel's advance towards fame came about almost reluctantly. When Margaux got top billing in *Lipstick* (1976), the 13-year-old Mariel accepted the role of the giggling younger sister for 'a lark'. The part called for her to lure the man (Chris Sarandon) who raped her sister into a trap. The unpleasant, over-theatrical movie did nothing for the careers of anyone connected with it, but it gave Mariel a certain taste for acting.

Three years later, while preparing to go off to summer camp, she got a call from Woody Allen asking her to appear opposite him in *Manhattan* (1979). What the director/actor wanted was a very young, unspoiled girl to play Tracy, the teenage drama student with whom the middle-aged Woody falls in love. At 42, he worries about the age difference though she takes it in her stride. 'When I was your age I was being tucked in by my grandparents,' he explains. Mariel's performance, for which she won a Best Supporting Actress Oscar nomination, was pleasantly natural, radiating innocence mixed with a certain knowingness.

Having grown into an alluring woman, she returned to the screen as an Olympic pentathlon contender in Robert Towne's *Personal Best* (1982). Being a good tennis-player and skier, the athletic, five-feet 11-inches tall Mariel enjoyed training for almost a year for the part, developing and toning her muscles. However, her acting abilities were not greatly stretched in this trite tale of a lesbian relationship between Mariel and a rival track star (Patrice Donnelly).

When she applied to Bob Fosse for the role of the ill-fated *Playboy* pin-up Dorothy Stratten in *Star 80* (1983), the director told her she wasn't glamorous or sexy enough. Determined to prove him wrong, she had silicone implants to enhance her breasts, and then turned up at his apartment provocatively dressed. Although the film was not a success, Hemingway gave a sensitive and charming performance as a woman torn between her hustling husband (Eric Roberts), her film director lover (Roger Rees) and *Playboy* magnate Hugh Hefner (Cliff Robertson).

Her film career since has progressed in little hops rather than leaps and bounds: roles as a woman threatened by a psychopathic killer in *The Mean Season* (1985), and as the daughter of the owner of the *Daily Planet* in *Superman IV* (1987), vainly making advances to Clark Kent (Christopher Reeve), did little to enhance it. She had a more intriguing part in Blake Edwards' *Sunset* (1988), in which she played a butch, male-suited hostess at the Candy Store, a pleasure palace where celebrities indulge their fantasies, and again demonstrated her ability to combine sexiness with innocence. Mariel Hemingway has claimed that her best role is as the wife of restaurateur Steve Grisman, whom she married in 1984 and with whom she has run Sam's Café in Los Angeles.

1976 Lipstick **1979** Manhattan **1982** Personal Best **1983** Star 80 **1985** Creator; The Mean Season **1987** The Suicide Club; Superman IV **1988** Sunset **1992** Falling From Grace; Delirious

Herman, Pee Wee
(Paul Rubenfeld aka Paul Rubens)

Actor, writer
Born 27 August 1952
Peekskill, New York

It was inevitable that the 1960s men's suit *in extremis* would come back into fashion at some point, but no one could have predicted the tremendous appeal of Paul Rubens' self-generated alter ego, Pee Wee Herman. Skinny, short-haired, whiny, nervy, selfish yet soft-hearted, Herman is a hyperactive oxymoron – a hip nerd. With his polyester suit (several sizes too small), red bow tie, white socks and heavy, almost funereal make-up, Herman arose as *the* whacky, outrageous hero of the late 1980s, spawning two successful comedy films, *Pee Wee's Big Adventure* (1985) and *Big Top Pee Wee* (1988), the latter less satisfying as the rather artificially androgynous boy falls in love.

Rubens (his preferred professional name) was raised in Sarasota, Florida, where his parents ran a lamp store. He was educated at Boston University and the California Institute Of The Arts before he debuted as Pee Wee (named after a tiny harmonica) in 1978 at the Los Angeles improvisational theatre, Groundlings. A groundswell of popularity on the college and club circuit peaked with the live *The Pee Wee Herman Show* which sold out for five months at an LA rock club and was taped for a national cable TV special. Guest appearances on *Late Night With Dave Letterman* and other TV shows (where he did hilarious tricks with, among other things, a pair of very large men's Y-fronts) catapulted Pee Wee into stardom. Outside of the Pee Wee movies, Rubens created, co-directed and co-wrote the Emmy-winning children's show *Pee Wee's Playhouse*. By 1990, the live show was in its fifth season, with its subversive, surreal quality maintaining a large cult following among adults. This entertainer's diverse talents (he provided the voice for Max in 1986's *The Flight Of The Navigator*), outlandish imagination and box-office clout were fully expected to be a source for more alternative comedy ventures as the decade progressed.

Pee Wee rode out a minor sex scandal to reappear, as Paul Rubens, as Penguin's Father in *Batman Returns* (1992).

1980 The Blues Brothers (as Paul Rubens) **1980** Cheech & Chong's Next Movie (as Pee Wee Herman) **1985** Pee Wee's Big Adventure (also co-writer) **1988** Big Top Pee Wee (also co-writer) **1992** Batman Returns; Buffy The Vampire Slayer

Hershey, Barbara
(Barbara Herzstein)
Actress
Born 5 February 1948
Hollywood, California

It is scarcely surprising that beautiful brunette Barbara Hershey, having been born in Hollywood, found her way into a television series (country family saga *The Monroes*) as a teenager and was featuring in films as a seductive nymphet in short order. What is interesting is that she survived a much-publicised and much-derided free-spirited period during which she was consort to David Carradine, changed her name to Barbara Seagull and bore a son she named Free to re-emerge, Hershey once more, as a respected actress.

Her teen film debut was as a member of Doris Day's chaotic household in *With Six You Get Eggroll* (1968). But it was with her performance as a teasing, taunting, perfectly evil little bitch in the powerful and disturbing drama *Last Summer* (1969) that she made people sit up and notice her. Her looks and the times then marked her as the archetypal swinging chick in a string of variable efforts, among the best known the irritating *The Baby Maker* (1970) for James Bridges, in which she played a hippy up to no good when she agrees to procreate for a childless couple and literally comes between them. Martin Scorsese's first studio film, *Boxcar Bertha* (1972), was a bit more exciting, with Hershey and Carradine paired as something of a rail-riding version of Bonnie and Clyde, and it was during the making of this film that the actress drew Scorsese's attention to the novel *The Last Temptation Of Christ*, a pet project they were to see realised 15 years later.

While continuing to work, Hershey had a low-profile presence, with the roles for which she was wanted none too thrilling. Then in 1978 she appeared in an outstanding, dark send-up of moviedom, *The Stunt Man*, as a neurotic leading lady, and seemed back on track. *The Entity* (1981), remembered as the picture in which she was repeatedly raped by an invisible 'thingie', was so notoriously exploitative it might have undone her, but she followed it with a sympathetic and strong showing in *The Right Stuff* (1983) as the wife of legendary test pilot Chuck Yaeger and a brief but effective turn as a seductive psychotic serial killer plugging Robert Redford in *The Natural* (1984). Since then, Hershey has been on a roll with attractive, well-regarded and well-judged performances in several quality films, notably Woody Allen's *Hannah And Her Sisters* (1986), Barry Levinson's *Tin Men* (1987) and, her finest hour to date, the excellent and moving portrayal – based on a true story – of an anti-apartheid journalist in South Africa, *A World Apart* (1988), for which she was a Best Actress winner at the Cannes Film Festival for a second year running, following her backwoods woman of *Shy People* (1987). After finally playing Mary Magdalen for Scorsese, Barbara Hershey startled fans, and readers of tabloid columns, by her apperance opposite Bette Midler in *Beaches* (1988) with collagen-injected lips giving her a spectacularly unfamiliar pout.

She won an Emmy for her performance in Stephen Gyllenhaal's made-for-television feature *A Killing In A Small Town*, and her face settled down again, was equally impressive in his *Paris Trout* (1991), which enjoyed critical acclaim on its theatrical release outside the USA.

1968 With Six You Get Eggroll **1969** Heaven With A Gun; Last Summer **1970** The Liberation Of L.B. Jones; The Baby Maker **1971** The Pursuit Of Happiness **1972** Dealing; Boxcar Bertha **1974** The Crazy World Of Julius Vrooder **1975** Love Comes Quietly **1976** The Last Hard Men; Dirty Knights' Work **1978** The Stunt Man; A Man Called Intrepid **1981** The Entity **1983** The Right Stuff **1984** The Natural **1986** Hannah And Her Sisters **1987**

Hoosiers aka Best Shot; Tin Men; Shy People **1988** A World Apart; The Last Temptation Of Christ; Beaches **1990** Tune In Tomorrow (GB: Aunt Julia And The Scriptwriter) **1991** Paris Trout; Defenseless **1992** The Public Eye **1992/93** Swing Kids; Falling Down

Hill, George Roy

Director
Born 20 December 1922
Minneapolis, Minnesota

George Roy Hill arrived at film directing late, and left early; since in the 1980s he made only three features, and spent time teaching drama at Yale University, it seems proper to consider him semi-retired. The main body of his work fits neatly into two decades, and is studded with commercial successes (the knack of creating which seemed to desert him after *The Sting*, 1973); but at his best, while never a powerfully original film-maker, Hill showed a particular flair in drawing snappy, sizeable performances from his actors and in keeping his subjects (particularly the comedies and the action pictures) light, fast-moving, and free of portentousness.

Hill made his first film, a screen adaptation of the Tennessee Williams stage comedy *Period Of Adjustment* (1962), at the age of 40. Having studied music, at Yale and then in Dublin, he had started his professional life as an actor (first in Ireland, later on tour in the US and off-Broadway) – a career interrupted by pilot service in both World War II and Korea. It was as a writer (and later director) for television that he first established himself thereafter, moving on in 1957 to direct the first of several Broadway plays.

The Williams comedy and Hill's second film, the 1963 *Toys In The Attic* (another play adaptation, this time from William Inge's fairly ludicrous New Orleans family melodrama), provided a natural transition between media; and though neither made any great impact at the box office, Jane Fonda's performance in the first and the sisters played by Geraldine Page and Wendy Hiller in the second demonstrated Hill's gift of encouraging strong acting. *The World Of Henry Orient* (1964), an amusing but overlong New York comedy following two teenage girls as they dog the private life of a famous concert pianist, did more of the same for Peter Sellers, Angela Lansbury, and Paula Prentiss; and while the 20s Flapper Age musical *Thoroughly Modern Millie* (1967) may seem over-inflated for its substance and style (according to Hill an extra 20 minutes that he himself had cut from the film was reinstated on studio insistence), it drew delightful performances from Julie Andrews, Mary Tyle, Moore, Carol Channing, and (briefly but memorably) Beatrice Lillie.

This was a huge commercial success. So was the next Hill film, *Butch Cassidy And The Sundance Kid* (1969), which, with *The Sting*, its sequel in casting terms if not in subject matter, achieved something bolder than the director had previously attempted. In retrospect one might even suggest that with them he helped to define the new mood of the early 70s, in which the Love-And-Peace beliefs of the 60s were becoming darkened by cynicism. Each film shows a pair of attractive male Robin Hood figures bonded by their strong individuality; in the end they may lose out to the forces of law and order, but their way of doing so grapples the audience's sympathies. It's no coincidence that both films, exploiting the pairing of Paul Newman and Robert Redford, notched those actors' highest popularity watermarks; Hill's infusion into these Hollywood vehicles of free-wheeling camera styles and techniques learnt from the European New Wave of the preceding decade is what lent both films, and both leading men, their special freshness. *Butch Cassidy* picked up four Oscars in secondary categories; *The Sting*, however, confirmed its director's standing by capturing Best Picture and Best Director among its impressive seven.

After that, unfortunately, the Hill formula appeared to lose its potency. Certainly, his use of Redford without Newman, in *The Great Waldo Pepper* (1975), a 20s flying film, and Newman without Redford, in *Slap Shot* (1977), a loudmouthed ice-hockey comedy, failed to repeat their joint success; each is a disjointed whole brought intermittently to life by some excitingly paced action sequences. It seems sad that this director's most creative period should have been of brief duration, and that his most recent film to date should be the witless 1988 Chevy Chase comedy, *Funny Farm*.

1962 Period Of Adjustment **1963** Toys In The Attic **1964** The World Of Henry Orient **1966** Hawaii **1967** Thoroughly Modern Millie **1969** Butch Cassidy And The Sundance Kid **1972** Slaughterhouse Five **1973** The Sting **1975** The Great Waldo Pepper **1977** Slap Shot **1979** A Little Romance **1982** The World According To Garp **1984** The Little Drummer Girl **1988** Funny Farm

Hill, Walter

Director

Born 10 January 1942

Long Beach, California

Walter Hill's first films established him as one of the most forceful and interesting personalities in American cinema, a reputation which he later seemed to be doing his utmost to destroy.

Hill studied history and English literature at Michigan University before spending ten years writing screenplays. The only one of which he was proud was Sam Peckinpah's *The Getaway* (1972), a precursor of his own second feature as director, *The Driver* (1978), a taut, black road movie that followed the pursuit of Ryan O'Neal by cop Bruce Dern across a stark landscape.

Though Hill tried too hard for mythic qualities against a background cluttered with period detail, his debut film, *Hard Times* (1975), provided enough evidence that the director was an American parable-maker. It concerned Charles Bronson (an archetypal movie loner) surviving during the Depression by taking on all comers in bare-knuckle fights. The director's handling of allegorical material was more assured in *The Warriors* (1979), based on Xenophon's *Anabasis*. Set mainly in the New York subways, it told of one night's odyssey of a street gang, on their way back to their own territory. It is one of the few teenage subculture movies that do not have middle-class, middle-aged perceptions imposed upon it, although there are unconvincing sections when the characters, none of whom is over 20 years old (the cops are shadowy figures), become too self-aware.

Another example of the director's interest in revising genre pictures was *The Long Riders* (1980), yet another Western about the James gang. Hill injected new life into old material with the symbolic treatment of the outlaws' existence, and by casting four sets of real brothers in the main roles (two Guests, three Carradines, two Quaids, two Keaches), to underline the theme of kinship. There is also male bonding in *Southern Comfort* (1981), in which the Louisiana bayou is hostile territory through which a platoon of National Guardsmen must find their way. A laconic, claustrophobic (it seldom leaves the swamps) and violent tale, it echoed the war in Vietnam.

With *48 HRS.* (1982), Hill left the off-beat and stepped right into the mainstream, gaining big box-office returns and becoming less interesting. Nick Nolte and Eddie Murphy (in his film debut) were a cop and a criminal on parole (for two days), tracking down the latter's former associates. The streets of San Francisco and the subway system provided the background to the hectic cops 'n' robbers action, occasionally brutal but salted with humour. *Streets of Fire* (1984) tried to return to *The Warriors* territory, but this rock fantasy of street gangs, set in downtown Chicago in the early 50s, lacked the depth and coherence of the earlier film. A couple more flops followed: the ill-judged remake of *Brewster's Millions* (1985), Hill's first attempt at a full-blown comedy, and *Crossroads* (1986), an affectionate but superficial tribute to the blues, starring Ralph Macchio as a musical prodigy with a guitar.

Hill was back to excessive brutality with *Extreme Prejudice* (1987), a virtual remake of Peckinpah's *The Wild Bunch*, updated to include Vietnam vets, and *Red Heat* (1988), featuring Arnold Schwarzenegger as a Russian policeman in the USA teamed with Chicago cop James Belushi on the trail of a Soviet pusher. The location work in Moscow was interesting, but once Stateside it became too familiar. In 1990, he delivered *Another 48 HRS.*, a dull re-tread of the Nolte-Murphy hit, and *Johnny Handsome*, a more interesting crime yarn in which Mickey Rourke, hideously disfigured and semi-articulate, plans a robbery, is double-crossed and wreaks vengeance after plastic surgery.

In his best movies, Walter Hill has shown a striking visual sense, usually reducing narrative and dialogue to essentials. However, too much reliance on locale, and a tendency to over-simplification and under-characterisation have marred his later work.

1975 Hard Times (GB: The Streetfighter) **1978** The Driver **1979** The Warriors **1980** The Long Riders **1981** Southern Comfort **1982** 48 HRS. **1984** Streets Of Fire **1985** Brewster's Millions **1986** Crossroads **1987** Extreme Prejudice **1988** Red Heat **1990** Johnny Handsome; Another 48 HRS. **1992** Alien 3 (co-writer only) **1992/93** Trespass aka The Looters

Hiller, Arthur

Director

Born 22 November 1923

Alberta, Canada

Arthur Hiller's particular distinction as a director is to have produced one enormous winner – *Love Story*, the 1970 adaptation of Erich Segal's celebrated novel, which brought together Ryan O'Neal and Ali McGraw for Hollywood's most famous and weepiest death scene since Bette Davis staggered blindly up the stairs at the end of *Dark Victory* (1939). Alongside this smash hit can be found a handful of moderate critical successes (*The Americanization of Emily*, 1964, *The Out-Of-Towners*, 1970, *Plaza Suite*, 1971, *The Hospital*, 1971, *Silver Streak*, 1979), not all of them equally successful at the box office, and a whole host of mediocrities, among which the film version of the Broadway Don Quixote musical, *Man Of La Mancha* (1972), with Peter O'Toole and Sophia Loren, defines the lowest level.

For a veteran Hollywood film-maker who has been kept hard at work for more than three decades, this is a curious record. The linking factor in Hiller's career seems to be that he exercises no artistically convinced or decisive command over his material but is, rather, in the nature of a professional packager. When the contents of the package are intrinsically valuable, or (in the case of *Love Story*) put together according to an unbeatably powerful commercial formula, well and good; otherwise, the results, while often glossy to look at, tend to be flabby, uncertainly paced and timed, and lacking in identifiable artistic purpose. The 1982 romantic drama *Making Love* is a case in point: one of Hollywood's rare attempts to deal unsensationally, even sympathetically, with the subject of homosexuality, it sinks in a welter of sentimental clichés.

A Canadian by birth, Hiller gained his early experience in Canadian television before moving to the US and working on such well-regarded and durable 50s and early 60s television programmes as *Playhouse 90*, *Alfred Hitchcock Presents* and *Gunsmoke*. His early films were comedies, by and large; those with a hard edge of cynicism, such as *The Americanization Of Emily*, a World War II satire written by Paddy Chayefsky, which made expert use of James Garner's light touch as an attractive heel and gave Julie Andrews a rare chance to be unsugary, tended to come off better. In a similar vein, if somewhat less sure of aim, are *The Out-Of-Towners*, an over-the-top comic view of the diverse horrors of New York that befall Jack Lemmon and Sandy Dennis during a one-day visit, and *The Hospital*, another Chayefsky screenplay, in which the sheer manic energy of George C. Scott as doctor-in-charge compensates for the increasingly uncontrolled broadness of the satire.

Silver Streak, a send-up of the classic thriller unfolding on a glamorous cross-country train journey, gets good work from Gene Wilder and Richard Pryor; this is a comic duo which offered Hiller a good deal of mileage. Nearly a decade later, the chase-comedy *Outrageous Fortune* (1987) pairs Bette Midler and Shelley Long as two wildly dissimilar actresses in search of the same two-timing lover (Peter Coyote), who turns out to be wanted even more urgently by the CIA. Yet in both comedies Hiller seems not to have known how and where to prune his material – it's a special pity that in *Outrageous Fortune* the cops-and-robbers elements get stretched out far beyond their intrinsic worth, to the point of tedium.

1957 The Careless Years **1963** Miracle Of The White Stallions; The Wheeler Dealers **1964** The Americanization of Emily **1966** Promise Her Anything; Penelope **1967** Tobruk; The Tiger Makes Out **1969** Popi **1970** The Out-Of-Towners; Love Story **1971** Plaza Suite; The Hospital **1972** Man Of La Mancha **1974** The Crazy World Of Julius Vrooder **1975** The Man In The Glass Booth **1976** W.C. Fields And Me; Silver Streak **1979** The In-Laws; Nightwing **1982** Author! Author!; Making Love **1983** Romantic Comedy **1984** The Lonely Guy; Teachers **1987** Outrageous Fortune **1989** See No Evil, Hear No Evil **1990** Taking Care Of Business **1992** The Babe

Hines, Gregory

Actor
Born 14 February 1946
New York City

While there is nothing wrong with his acting – the same cannot be said of some of the dramas in which he has been employed – it is the flying feet of Gregory Hines, one of America's foremost contemporary tap dancers, that have rendered some otherwise dubious material highly watchable.

The son of dancer-actor Maurice Hines, Gregory made his entry into showbusiness at the tender age of two as the most junior member of the family dance act. By the time he was five, Gregory and brother Maurice Jr were appearing in nightclubs as the Hines Kids, then, in their teens, as the Hines Brothers. From 1963 to 1973 the dance trio Hines, Hines and Dad was wowing audiences on the cabaret circuit and television. Meanwhile, Gregory had long since made his Broadway debut, at the age of eight, in the 1954 musical *The Girl In Pink Tights*. His adult stage credits include

Sophisticated Ladies, *Eubie*, for which he won a Theater World Award and one of his three Tony nominations, and *Twelfth Night*. He gave up the dance act in 1973 and went on to form his jazz-rock band, Severance. (He has also recorded a solo singing album, called, simply, 'Gregory Hines', released in 1988.)

Hines made his feature film debut in 1981, not as a hoofer but as a coroner, and proved a scene-stealer in Michael Wadleigh's well-regarded surreal mystery *Wolfen*, which starred Albert Finney. He has competently played comedy, drama and action in a dozen films since, but it is the opportunities he has had in an almost musical-free era to dazzle with his stylish dancing that stand out: Francis Ford Coppola's *The Cotton Club* (1984), for which he also served as choreographer, as a 1920s street dancer who becomes a star; Taylor Hackford's *White Nights* (1985), in which his dancing was contrasted with Mikhail Baryshnikov's (and which featured one remarkable sequence of Hines' American soldier, defected to the USSR, recounting his life story through dance), and the celebratory treat *Tap* (1989).

1981 Wolfen; History Of The World – Part 1 **1983** Deal Of The Century **1984** The Muppets Take Manhattan; The Cotton Club **1985** White Nights **1986** Running Scared **1988** Off-Limits aka Saigon **1989** Tap **1991** Eve Of Destruction; Rage In Harlem; Undercover

Hoffman, Dustin

Actor
Born 8 August 1937
Los Angeles, California

After eight years of struggling to scratch a living from his chosen profession, the 30-year-old Dustin Hoffman was at last beginning to make a name for himself as a character actor in the New York theatre when Mike Nichols offered him a screen test for *The Graduate* (1967). Hoffman told Nichols, 'I don't think I'm right for the role. He's a kind of Anglo-Saxon, tall, slender, good-looking chap. I'm short and Jewish.' During the screen test he forgot his lines, tried to look tall, was nervous and clumsy. But it was just what Nichols was looking for: 'He had a kind of pole-axed quality with life, but great vitality underneath.'

Hoffman was convincing as the 20-year-old Benjamin Braddock in *The Graduate*, becoming the 60s anti-hero of middle-class kids who identified with his rejection of his parents' values and a job in plastics. His hilarious seduction of Mrs Robinson (Anne Bancroft), the mother of his girlfriend (Katharine Ross), struck a blow for 'short and Jewish' looks against the 'walking surfboard' type. With his greasy hair, pallid complexion, bad teeth and gammy leg, his petty con-man, Ratso Rizzo, in *Midnight Cowboy* (1969) proved that 'I was a character actor, not just this nebbish kid that Nichols found.' His achievement was to make this ostensibly repellent character warm, comic and ultimately tragic.

As the 121-year-old Jack Crabb, Cheyenne by adoption and last survivor of Custer's Last Stand in Arthur Penn's *Little Big Man* (1970), Hoffman reminisces entertainingly over his long life under a 14-piece latex mask which took five hours a day to apply. Playing his own age in *Straw Dogs* (1971), he was a mild man forced into bloody revenge against those who gang-raped his wife (Susan George) in a village in Cornwall. The nervy intensity of his performance made audiences face up to the potential violence in themselves. Chameleon-like, Hoffman reappeared in *Papillon* (1973) as a timid, thickly bespectacled Louis Dega, 'the best counterfeiter in France', opposite the contrasted Steve McQueen in the title role. As the controversial night-club comedian Lenny Bruce in Bob Fosse's *Lenny* (1974), the actor's tour-de-force performance got to the heart of the entertainer without giving a straight imitation.

After Hoffman had deprived himself of sleep for two days for a sequence in John Schlesinger's tawdry thriller, *Marathon Man* (1976), Laurence Olivier, his co-star, was prompted to ask 'Why doesn't the boy just act?' But audiences are aware that Hoffman's celebrated striving for perfection, the meticulous research and 'living' of his parts, generally pays off handsomely. It was his education (after he had given up his ambition to become a concert pianist) at the Pasadena Playhouse with a Stanislavsky-influenced teacher, and his Method sessions with Lee Strasberg at the Actors' Studio, that laid the foundation for the type of actor he was to become.

Straight Time (1978) was to have marked his directorial debut, but he found the pressures of being on both sides of the camera too great. With a moustache, sideburns and deeper voice, he was compelling as a tough ex-con battling to go straight in an unjust world. It was a flop, but worse came with *Agatha* (1979), in which the short (five foot six inches) and sensuous Hoffman rather ludicrously played opposite the tall, cool Vanessa Redgrave. But he came back with a bang in the same year with *Kramer* vs. *Kramer*, at last winning his first Best Actor Oscar. (He had been nominated for *The Graduate, Midnight Cowboy* and *Lenny*.) As a successful Madison Avenue man, whose wife (Meryl Streep) ups and leaves him alone with their six-year-old son (Justin Henry), Hoffman drew on the personal pain he had recently suffered from his own divorce from dancer Anne Byrne, to infuse Ted Kramer with truth.

His portrayal of a 'real woman', Dorothy Michaels, in *Tootsie* (1982), one of the best cross-dressing film performances of all time, was based loosely on his mother, 'an earthy, gutsy woman with a great sexual sense of humour'. It was a brilliantly deft comic double, self-mocking as a pretentious, out-of-work avant-garde actor, and instantly likeable as Dorothy, whom he creates to get a part in a day-time soap. For his superb Willy Loman in *Death Of A Salesman* (1985), a sad, irritating and shrivelled little man (he shed pounds for the part), he drew on his memories of his salesman father.

Never one to do things by halves, Hoffman was co-starred with Warren Beatty in one of the cinema's biggest box-office disasters, *Ishtar* (1987), a $43 million stinker. Undeterred, he then spent over a year researching the behaviour of autistic people. The result was his meticulous, touching and funny performance in *Rain Man* (1988) – the lack of eye-contact, the lopsided walk, the repetitive talk – and it won him his second Oscar. Refusing to rest on his laurels, the actor took on Shakespeare, presenting a subtle Shylock in *The Merchant Of Venice* on stage in London and New York in 1989, before returning to play the gangster Dutch Schultz in *Billy Bathgate* (1991) – a sadly unsuccessful adaptation of E.L. Doctorow's novel.

For years Hoffman and Steven Spielberg searched for a collaboration, which finally materialised with *Hook* (1991), a story predicated on what might have happened if Peter Pan had grown up. Delivered in a reasonably convincing English upper-class accent, Hoffman's portrayal of Captain Hook was amusing, and often charming, but lacked the necessary menace. Nonetheless, Spielberg's movie provided an arena new to the star, that of films for children, thus allowing yet another generation to discover him.

More than any other of the 'new breed' of leading men in the late 60s and 70s, Hoffman is a character actor star who has continued to be a force in the following decades, appearing with Tom Cruise (*Rain Man*), John Malkovich (*Death Of A Salesman*), Matthew Broderick (*Family Business*, 1989) and Bruce Willis (*Billy Bathgate*), stars of a younger generation. Until he came along, the ideal male stars were handsome action men like Rock Hudson and Tab Hunter, or brooding non-conformists like Marlon Brando or James Dean. Hoffman was not afraid to play a nebbish, a man more sinned against than sinning, a loser in a success-struck society. He set a precedent, since when the names and faces of Hollywood stars have reflected more accurately the diversity of ethnic groups in America.

1967 The Tiger Makes Out; The Graduate; Madigan's Millions **1969** John And Mary; Midnight Cowboy **1970** Little Big Man **1971** Who Is Harry Kellerman And Why Is He Saying Those Terrible Things About Me?; Straw Dogs **1972** Alfredo Alfredo (Italy) **1973** Papillon **1974** Lenny **1976** Marathon Man; All The President's Men **1978** Straight Time **1979** Agatha; Kramer vs. Kramer **1982** Tootsie **1985** Death Of A Salesman **1987** Ishtar **1988** Rain Man **1989** Family Business **1990** Dick Tracy **1991** Billy Bathgate; Hook **1992** Hero

Hooper, Tobe

Director
Born 1943
Austin, Texas

Few of the independent horror *auteurs* of the 1970s have come a greater cropper at the hands of Hollywood (and his own limitations) than Tobe Hooper. Since his triumph with *The Texas Chainsaw Massacre* (1974), his career has lurched from one botched project to the next. By the end of the 1980s he was reduced to directing the video pilot for the tacky *Freddy's Nightmares* TV series.

Hooper grew up in the domestic no-man's land of Texan hotels – his father was an hotelier-cum-entrepreneur who claimed to have coined the word 'motel'. He also owned a cinema, where the young Tobe spent much of his adolescence gorging himself on films. He made his way in documentary and television before coming to controversial prominence with *The Texas Chainsaw Massacre*, a grisly tale of travellers in rural Texas who fall into the blood-boltered hands of a hellish inversion of the classic all-male American family – three ghoulish brothers and their bloodsucking skeleton of a grandfather. Like *Psycho* (1960) and *Deranged* (1974), *Chainsaw* owed something to the real-life career of the 'Wisconsin Ghoul', mass murderer Ed Gein, but it derived its visceral power from Hooper's assured camerawork and editing (the movie's reputation for gore belied the fact that there was very little on-screen bloodletting) and a distinctly unsettling *musique concrète* score which the director co-wrote with Wayne Bell.

No mere 'splatter' movie, *Chainsaw* is in part a heavily ironic comment on the perversion of the 'pioneer' ethic so beloved of Americans: the deranged latter-day 'frontiersmen' who decorate their remote cabin with severed limbs (an 'armchair' is literally just that) now hunt humans rather than buffalo.

The director's subsequent work displayed similar black humour, but with rapidly diminishing effect. The 1976 *Eaten Alive* was an intermittently droll piece of Grand Guignol in which swampland hotelier Neville Brand whiles away the time by feeding disagreeable guests to the crocodile he keeps in the front yard, muttering 'you gotta do what you gotta do' at chow-time while the radio plays a country-and-western ditty with the refrain 'Oh, the cowboy's a god-fearin', hard-workin' man'. In *The Funhouse* (1981) two reckless teenagers spend an ill-advised night in the sleazy carnival attraction of the title and pay the price of their libidinous behaviour when they encounter a real-life family of grotesques among the monstrous exhibits.

But disaster followed. *Poltergeist* (1982), a Steven Spielberg production, ended with a squabble over credits and the precise extent of Hooper's contribution as director, and a full-page ad was taken out by Spielberg in *Variety* to counter rumours of 'creative differences'. Then Hooper was sacked from *Venom* (1982), which subsequently became an unintentionally (at least, one presumes so) camp classic in the hands of Piers Haggard. Then the increasingly hapless film-maker turned to the baroque science fiction convolutions of *Life Force* (1985) in which vampires from outer space, led by a sumptuously naked voluptuary, take control of London. This was followed by *Invaders from Mars* (1986) a high-tech remake of William Cameron Menzies' small 1950s masterpiece of unease. However, unlike other remakes of sci-fi classics, notably *Invasion Of The Body Snatchers* (1978) and *The Thing* (1982), Hooper's *Invaders from Mars* remained in thrall to the original – down to the studied evocation of Menzies' dreamily effective sets – and ends in bathos.

All that remained was a sad return to Texas and the self-parodic *Chainsaw Massacre 2* (1986) in which Hooper's horrible family join the enterprise culture, opening a fast-food joint whose prize-winning chili contains only the choicest cuts. Their nemesis, and possibly Tobe Hooper's, is God-crazed Texas Ranger Dennis Hooper.

1974 The Texas Chainsaw Massacre (also co-writer) **1976** Eaten Alive aka Death Trap aka Starlight Slaughter aka Legend Of The Bayou aka Horror Hotel **1981** The Funhouse **1982** Poltergeist **1985** Life Force **1986** Invaders From Mars; The Texas Chainsaw Massacre 2 **1990** Spontaneous Combustion (also co-writer) **1992** Sleepwalkers (cameo actor only)

Hopkins, Sir Anthony

Actor
Born 31 December 1937
Port Talbot, South Wales

Once hailed as the new Olivier but initially displaying the more self-destructive tendencies of Richard Burton, Anthony Hopkins has managed to emerge from both formidable shadows as one of the most impressive of the less-is-more school of acting. The son of a master confectioner and baker, Hopkins entered the Cardiff School of Music and Drama with an initial interest in the piano but, after his two years national service in the Royal Artillery, he found himself more drawn towards acting. Following two years at RADA he acted in rep, earning a place at the National Theatre by showing his 'bloody nerve' to director Laurence Olivier (who he later mimicked perfectly when called upon to redub his lines in the restored version of *Spartacus*) by auditioning with a piece from *Othello* which Olivier was then performing. Working with the cream of British theatre directors (Olivier, Tony Richardson, Lindsay Anderson), he progressed to leads and a strong film debut as the angry, unbalanced homosexual, Richard the Lionhearted, in *The Lion In Winter* (1968).

His progress through films was fairly steady, and he was even touted as another potential James Bond with his first lead in *When Eight Bells Toll* (1971). He became a household name as Pierre in the prestigious BBC adaptation of *War And Peace* the following year, but he seriously impeded his advancement with Burtonesque bouts of heavy drinking which made him particularly obnoxious and unreliable on stage, rendering him almost unemployable in England, causing the break-up of his first marriage, and facilitating his move to America with the Broadway production of *Equus* in which he played the psychiatrist. His career got off to a strong start in America with his role as the distinguished doctor accused of war crimes in the first TV mini-series *QBVII*, and as the weak Bruno Hauptmann in *The Lindbergh Kidnapping Case* TV movie in 1976, but quickly became mired in a succession of lesser roles in films and television (despite his Emmy Awards for his Yitzhak Rabin in *Victory At Entebbe* and his Hitler in *The Bunker*). Things began to turn around with his third collaboration with director Richard Attenborough (they later fell out over the actor's refusal to play the eponymous lead in *Gandhi*) in *Magic* (1978), both chilling and pathetic as the ventriloquist who pours all his scorn and disappointment into his dummy. The movie's huge box-office success and its star's decision to give up drinking led to a decade of more interesting parts and an eventual, initially reluctant, but triumphant return to Britain's National Theatre in the mid-1980s, where his roles included Shakespeare's Antony in *Antony and Cleopatra*, and Lear; while on Shaftesbury Avenue he starred in *M. Butterfly*.

Hopkins' at first dispassionate but later decent and self-doubting surgeon in *The Elephant Man* (1980) was a performance of quiet strength (even in his worst films he has stolen scenes with stillness while others chew the scenery around him) but *The Bounty* (1984) was a real breakthrough. His Bligh was no larger-than-life villain but a man tortured by his own inadequacy, his repressed passions horrified by the sexual liberation of the islanders that undermines the rigorous social status quo of his ship, a man with stubborn bluster in his voice but terror in his eyes. The actor conveyed an awesome degree of passion in the film's many close-ups of his face as he fights his inner demons without actually appearing to do anything. He was equally superb as the bitter divorcé taking his revenge through another man's custody battle in *The Good Father* (1986), and unostentatiously affecting in *84 Charing Cross Road* (1987), although it was only in the 1990s that he made it spectacularly onto the A-list.

Hot on the heels of his wildly misjudged Vietnam veteran whose family is terrorised in Michael Cimino's remake of *The Desperate Hours* (1990, his worst performance), he vindicated himself and terrified America with his Hannibal Lecter in Jonathan Demme's *The Silence Of The Lambs* (1991). As with his best performances, it is not so much what 'Hannibal the cannibal' does – in fact very little – as what the actor does not do that makes the part so interesting, and which overshadowed Brian Cox's superb but very different portrayal of the same character in *Manhunter* (1987). Completely at odds with the described atrocities with which Lecter is credited, Hopkins plays against the physical aspects of the role, emphasising the intelligence, using the Tom Wolfe-like voice to ingratiating effect: that he never needs to manifest his undenied violence, allied with his supreme inner confidence, only makes him more unnerving. Eschewing the Method approach or intense research in favour of just thinking about the look of the part and playing the scenes, Hopkins created a character that earned him the epithet 'the most feared man in America' as well as the Oscar for Best Actor, and cemented his position as one of the few British actors able to pick and choose his parts. He was Knighted in 1993.

1968 The Lion In Winter **1969** Hamlet **1970** The Looking Glass War **1971** When Eight Bells Toll **1972** Young Winston **1973** A Doll's House **1974** The Girl From Petrovka; Juggernaut **1975** All Creatures Great And Small **1977** Audrey Rose; A Bridge Too Far **1978** International Velvet; Magic **1980** A Change Of Seasons; The Elephant Man **1984** The Bounty **1986** The Good Father **1987** 84 Charing Cross Road **1988** The Dawning **1989** A Chorus Of Disapproval **1990** The Desperate Hours **1991** The Silence Of The Lambs **1992** Howard's End; Spotswood; Free-Jack; Charlie; Bram Stoker's Dracula **1992/93** The Innocent; Remains Of The Day

Hopper, Dennis

Actor, director
Born 17 May 1936
Dodge City, Kansas

The mid-1980s return to grace and favour of one of Hollywood's great modern outlaws was a remarkable comeback by most standards: the once-detested and unemployable Dennis Hopper received his first Oscar nomination – for *Hoosiers* (1986) – and made more than a dozen films within three years.

An actor since his teens, Hopper was a moody James Dean acolyte (and supporting player to Dean in both *Rebel Without A Cause* and *Giant*) who contributed a brooding presence in a number of minor roles in features but made himself unpopular with several veteran directors and producers who pronounced him difficult, argumentative and violently temperamental. From 1958 through 1963, he appeared in only four films and was in danger of sinking into complete obscurity, recollected occasionally to play a grubby gunslinger or participate in an oddity like the space vampire weirdie, *Queen Of Blood* (1966). Hopper was tenacious enough to turn up in small roles in some major films (*Cool Hand Luke* in 1967, *True Grit* in 1969), but a younger, hipper generation of film-makers and audiences in the late 1960s saw him as a star when the cycle of dope and biker movies kicked off. Roger Corman's seminal acid flick *The Trip* (1967) cast Hopper with Peter Fonda. The duo – no strangers to the grape or to the weed – together conceived, wrote, raised the finance for and starred in *Easy Rider* (1969) with Hopper directing.

Easy Rider, the alienated youth-road movie of its era, electrified a generation and made icons of Hopper and Fonda on their motorcycles. They made the film for $400,000 and it took over $16 million, to the chagrin of the industry which had not taken Hopper seriously and which now desperately tried to emulate him by churning out a stream of tacky, imitative pictures with equally loud rock soundtracks. Hopper, meanwhile, was out of control. After writing and starring in an autobiographical documentary, *The American Dreamer* (1971), he decamped to Peru with a cast and crew for a self-penned, directed and edited fiasco, *The Last Movie* (1971). This set the seal on his reputation as the most flipped-out man in movies, and in Hollywood terms he spent the next 15 years in the wilderness of foreign films, highly personal projects and low-budget art-house or exploitation movies. The quality of these veered wildly, but Hopper turned in one of his most memorable performances in Wim Wenders' fascinating adaptation of Patricia Highsmith's *Ripley's Game*, *The American Friend* (1977) as the enigmatic, homicidal title character. He also put in a good-value appearance in Francis Ford Coppola's startling Vietnam epic, *Apocalypse Now* (1979), and was a commanding 'elder statesman' amid the Brat Pack cast of Coppola's *Rumble Fish* (1983) – few of whom can aspire to hold a candle to Hopper as an iconoclastic talent or hell-raiser. In 1983, at the age of 47, Hopper also finally directed his third feature, *Out Of The Blue*, a very effective, tense and disturbing drama about a family well outside the middle-American mainstream.

The renaissance of Dennis Hopper and a new regard for him as an actor came in 1986 with his thoroughly astonishing portrayal of a full-tilt psychopath in David Lynch's controversial, riveting *Blue Velvet*. The actor's crazed drug dealer 'kidnapper' sadist was the most distressing but compelling element in a thoroughly audacious film, and he followed it immediately with an antithetically subdued and touching performance as an ashamed alcoholic loser in *Hoosiers* (1986). In six films in one year he ranged from a left-wing media terrorist in *The American Way* (1986) to a Texan tycoon bumped off by his wife in *Black Widow* (1987); from a mad ex-biker with his own strangely moral code in *River's Edge* (1987) to American princess Molly Ringwald's dad in *The Pick-Up Artist* (1987). In 1988, Hopper directed Robert Duvall and Sean Penn in a violently realistic cops-versus-street-gangs drama, *Colors*, released to a debate over whether the film reflected or exacerbated intense gang conflicts in the city, but in the event neither particularly exciting or exceptional. A worse fate met his next directorial effort, *Catchfire* (1990), in which he starred with Jodie Foster as, respectively, kidnapper and responsive victim. Released in a cut and edited version of which he did not approve, the film, at Hopper's insistence, was attributed to the pseudonym favoured by enraged American film directors who wish to disown a project: Alan Smithee.

What sounded like a good idea for *Flashback* (1990) – erstwhile 60s radical activist gone 'underground' Hopper is apprehended by Mr Clean FBI agent Kiefer Sutherland – was disappointingly dull and obvious, but at 54, off alcohol and drugs, Hopper was looking as slim, trim and arresting as ever, and already had several other films lined up.

1955 I Died A Thousand Times; Rebel Without A Cause **1956** Giant; The Steel Jungle **1957** Gunfight At The O.K. Corral; The Story Of Mankind **1958** From Hell To Texas **1959** The Young Land **1960** Key Witness **1963** Night Tide **1964** Tarzan And Jane Regained Sort Of **1965** The Sons Of Katie Elder **1966** Queen Of Blood aka Planet Of Blood **1967** Cool Hand Luke; The Trip; The Glory Stompers; Panic In The City **1968** Hang 'Em High **1969** Easy Rider (also director, co-writer); True Grit **1971** The American Dreamer (also writer); The Last Movie (also director, co-writer) **1972** Crush Proof **1973** Kid Blue **1975** The Sky Is Falling **1976** Mad Dog Morgan; Tracks **1977**

Les Apprentis Sorciers (France); The American Friend; Couleur Chair (France) **1978** L'Ordre Et La Sécurité Du Monde (France) **1979** Apocalypse Now **1981** King Of The Mountain; White Star **1982** Human Highway; Reborn **1983** Out Of The Blue (also director); The Osterman Weekend; Rumble Fish **1984** Slagskampen **1985** My Science Project **1986** Blue Velvet; Hoosiers aka Best Shot; The Texas Chainsaw Massacre 2; The American Way **1987** Black Widow; O.C. And Stiggs; River's Edge; Straight To Hell; The Pick-Up Artist **1988** Colors (director only) **1989** Chatahoochee **1990** Blood Red; Catchfire aka Backtrack (also director, credited as Alan Smithee) **1990** The Hot Spot (director only); Flashback **1991** Paris Trout; Indian Runner **1992** Eye Of The Storm; Nails; Red Rock West

Hoskins, Bob

Actor
Born 26 October 1942
Bury St Edmunds, England

Burly, earthy Brit Bob Hoskins, with his short, stocky frame and cockney working man's persona, may not be the stuff of which leading men conventionally are made, but his capacity to convey warmth, passion and sensitivity endears him to audiences. Parallel to his distinguished career on stage, screen and television in Britain, he has impressed American audiences as a gangster, a straight man to a cartoon rabbit and an ardent swain to Cher.

Hoskins was raised in the North London area of Finsbury Park and laboured as, among other things, a porter and a steeplejack before a chance encounter in a pub drew him into a fringe theatre production on the premises when he was in his mid-20s. By the age of 30 he had established himself as a useful character player able to tackle classical and avant-garde work. His many theatre credits range from Shakespeare to Shaw, from Pinter to Sam Shepard, and he has appeared at Britain's most prestigious theatre companies, the Royal Court, the Royal Shakespeare Company, and the National Theatre where he delighted as Nathan Detroit in *Guys And Dolls* and exploded in Shepard's *True West*.

His film debut came in the British hospital satire *The National Health* (1973), but his two key breakthrough roles of the 70s were as the tragic little Depression era Everyman, Arthur the sheet music salesman, in Dennis Potter's original television serial musical drama *Pennies From Heaven* (later made into an unsuccessful film starring Steve Martin), and as the embattled gangland boss in John Mackenzie's tough, compelling contemporary London drama *The Long Good Friday* (1980). Hoskins' US film debut was less felicitous, casting him as a South American police chief tailing Richard Gere in Mackenzie's poorly-received *The Honorary Consul* (1983), but his facility with an American accent brought him work in the States. As the nightclub owner in Francis Ford Coppola's striking albeit uneven *The Cotton Club* (1984) Hoskins' Mutt and Jeff double act with big Fred Gwynne provided the only really appealing characterisations of the film; and Alan Alda's movie-making comedy *Sweet Liberty* (1986) was enlivened by Hoskins' amiably desperate-to-succeed screenwriter. The same year the actor delivered his finest portrayal to date, as the fall guy and ex-con turned driver for a beautiful, manipulative hooker in Neil Jordan's dark drama, *Mona Lisa* (1986), a beautiful piece of work as a hard nut with a good heart who is betrayed by love and devotion, and a performance rewarded with an Oscar nomination for Best Actor.

Hoskins has been continually in demand since, commuting from his London home to star in such disparate films as the colossally successful live-action-animation comedy *Who Framed Roger Rabbit?* (1988), as the third-rate private eye who takes the 'toon's case, *Heart Condition* (1990), as the bigoted LA cop who receives the heart and haunting companionship of slain lawyer Denzel Washington, and *Mermaids* (1991), as Cher's kindly, determined small-town suitor. The largely self-educated Hoskins also co-wrote and directed a feature, the Central European gypsy tale *The Raggedy Rawney* (1988), an ambitious failure which had only a limited release. His abundant TV leads include the title role in *Mussolini: The Decline And Fall Of Il Duce*.

1973 The National Health **1975** Royal Flash **1976** Inserts **1979** Zulu Dawn **1980** The Long Good Friday **1982** Pink Floyd – The Wall **1983** The Honorary Consul aka Beyond The Limit **1984** The Cotton Club; Lassiter **1985** Brazil **1986** Sweet Liberty; Mona Lisa **1987** A Prayer For The Dying; The Lonely Passion Of Judith Hearne **1988** Who Framed Roger Rabbit?; The Raggedy Rawney (also director, co-writer) **1990** Heart Condition; Mermaids; Shattered **1991** The Cherry Orchard; Hook **1992** The Inner Circle; The Favour, The Watch And The Very Big Fish; Passed Away **1992/93** Super Mario Brothers

Howard, Ron

Director, actor
Born 1 March 1954
Duncan, Oklahoma

In some quarters Ron Howard is still best known as little Opie, or as Richie Cunningham, from *The Andy Griffith Show* and *Happy Days*, the popular television series he starred in as a child and as a young adult actor respectively. Howard was the boy next door, prone to jams, perhaps a little gauche, but fundamentally a good kid. It is an impression his subsequent work as a feature film director tends to sustain.

Ronny Howard made his stage debut with his parents, Rance and Jean, at the age of two. Two years later he appeared in *The Journey* (1959), the first of half-a-dozen movies as a child actor, which were to lead to his long stints as a television star. He had a bit part in George Lucas' *American Graffiti* (1973), and after *Happy Days* he starred in the sequel, *More American Graffiti* (1979), but the audience had moved on – by 1979 they were flunking out at *Animal House*. In any case, Howard was already more interested in a directing career (his only other adult appearances were in the superior TV movie *Bitter Harvest* in 1981, and in *Channel 99*, 1988). He had been allowed behind the camera for the odd episode of *Happy Days*, and directed his first feature as early as 1977. Co-written with his father Rance, *Grand Theft Auto* (1977) is often handily overlooked in Howard's filmography. His guilty secret is actually a thuddingly banal car-crash action picture, vividly described by John Conquest as 'an automotive snuff movie . . . like something Peckinpah might have made as a boy'. Rather more in character, *Skyward* (1980) was a TV movie about how a former stunt pilot, played by Bette Davis (!), and an airport watchman, Howard Hesseman, help a teenaged paraplegic learn to fly a plane. The story was written by Anson Williams from *Happy Days*, and the results helped propel Howard into mainstream Hollywood.

Night Shift (1982) took seedy subject matter and made it delightfully appealing. An amiable farce, it cast Henry 'Fonz' Winkler (also of *Happy Days*) as a timid morgue attendant with girl troubles, Shelley Long as a prostitute, and introduced Michael Keaton as the manic hustler who brings the two together. Howard gave the picture an unfussy, low-key ambience that allowed his actors every chance to shine, and showed himself adept at light comedy. *Splash* (1984) was equally attractive, and found a wider audience with its romantic pairing of Tom Hanks and mermaid Daryl Hannah (Howard has a good record for spotting up-and-coming talent; John Candy also made waves with this film). *Gung Ho* (1986), a corporate farce contrasting American and Japanese work ethics, was the third Lowell Ganz-Babaloo Mandel script Howard brought to the screen, and the first that failed to skirt questions of taste entirely satisfactorily. It was a step back for Howard; he was now in the big league, having pulled off the tricky blockbuster *Cocoon* (1985). Like Steven Spielberg's episode in *Twilight Zone: The Movie* (1983), this was a fantasy about senior citizens discovering the fountain of youth. Although Spielberg's influence was much in evidence, Howard's is in fact the better effort, charming without becoming cloying, with lively performances from Don Ameche (who won the Best Supporting Actor Oscar), Hume Cronyn, Jessica Tandy and Gwen Verdon.

Made for George Lucas, *Willow* (1988) was an underrated romp through medieval mythologies. The director was not fazed by a comparatively epic scale and a plethora of special effects; he kept things quick and funny, and for once hit on an ending that really worked. In the late 80s he moved into producing with the ill-fated comedy *Vibes* (1988) for David Puttnam's Columbia Pictures, and the drug rehabilitation movie *Clean And Sober* (1988) – with Michael Keaton in his first serious role. *Parenthood* (1989), which he directed with Steve Martin as the star, was probably the closest Howard got to a personal film. Ostensibly based on his own experiences as a father (and those of his friends), the picture was only too keen to elicit audience sympathies, underscored by a streak of sentimentality a mile wide. More surprisingly, this most retiring of directors revealed pretensions to artistry with a couple of embarrassingly literal cinematic effects. It was amusing though, and its heart was in the right place. Nice.

Backdraft (1991) proved Howard could handle big-scale special effects excitingly, though the drama itself was shallow and cliched; as it was in the $60 million would-be Tom Cruise epic, *Far And Away* (1992), from which one was tempted to conclude that growing up on and in television has not equipped this director for work of any great depth.

As director only unless stated otherwise: **1977** Grand Theft Auto (also co-writer, actor) **1979** More American Graffiti (actor only) **1982** Night Shift **1984** Splash **1985** Cocoon **1986** Gung Ho **1988** Willow **1989** Parenthood **1991** Backdraft **1992** Far And Away

Howell, C. Thomas

Actor

Born 7 December 1966

Los Angeles, California

By 1990 C. Thomas Howell was already a seasoned professional before the cameras, with more than 20 years experience under his belt. He was a regular on the television series *Little People* at the age of four! Other series followed in due course (*Two Marriages; Into The Homeland*), and he made his feature film debut when he was only 16. The film was *E.T. The Extra-Terrestrial* (1982).

Spielberg cast Howell in a supporting role as one of the neighbourhood kids; the film's box office went down in the record books, and Howell moved up to better things. Francis Ford Coppola gave him the lead in his film of *The Outsiders* (1983). Appreciating the youngster's extraordinary prettiness, Coppola saw him as Ponyboy, author S.E. Hinton's alter-ego (Hinton was only 16 when she wrote the novel). Ponyboy was a 'greaser', from the wrong side of the tracks, but he was also shy and sensitive. Howell, a former junior rodeo circuit champion, proved he could supply both sides of this character, and he was the right age. *The Outsiders* introduced a host of teenage stars, including Emilio Estevez, Tom Cruise, Matt Dillon and Ralph Macchio, but in their subsequent careers they rarely looked their character's age as they do here.

After Spielberg and Coppola, Howell worked with another of the so-called Movie Brat directors, John Milius. In *Red Dawn* (1984) America is invaded by the Soviet Union, but Howell, Patrick Swayze (an older cast member of *The Outsiders*) and a handful of kids mount guerilla attacks from the hills to repel the enemy. It was a sharp concept, but the results were mostly embarrassing, full of macho posturing and jingoistic nonsense. Howell really was not cut out for this sort of thing, drinking deer's blood and the like. In his best action movie, *The Hitcher* (1986), he is the prey (to Rutger Hauer's psychopathic killer), not the hunter. But he was altogether more at home in the gentler but very mediocre *Grandview USA* (1984), again with Swayze, and *Tank* (1984) which probably appealed to him as a spoof on *Red Dawn*. Neither fared well with the public however. *Secret Admirer* (1985) hit on Howell's forte. A light, witty farce structured around crossed love letters, it was equally appealing to grown-ups and their teenage offspring. Howell's clean good looks made him a natural young romantic lead, and he displayed a sure sense of timing and a bent for slapstick. *Soul Man* (1986), although it was based on the downright tacky notion of a young man blacking up to win a minority scholarship to Harvard, still had its moments and co-star Rae Dawn Chang who Howell married. *A Tiger's Tale* (1988) at least thought it was a comedy, and *Far Out Man* (1989) certainly should have been, but it was clear by this time that Howell's career was caught in a downward spiral.

Kid (1990) tried to tap the audience that made *The Hitcher* Howell's biggest international hit, but this juvenile reworking of *High Plains Drifter* (1973) cast Howell as the killer and, try as he might, with a slick coat, a permanently furrowed brow, and a hint of tough-guy stubble, the young actor resembled a sulky male model rather more than he did an embryo Clint Eastwood. *Side Out* (1990), with our hero seduced by the world of beach volleyball in California, was evidently more in his line.

1982 E.T. The Extra-Terrestrial **1983** The Outsiders **1984** Red Dawn; Grandview USA; Tank **1985** Secret Admirer **1986** The Hitcher; Soul Man **1988** A Tiger's Tale; The Young Toscanini (unreleased) **1989** Return Of The Musketeers; Far Out Man **1990** Kid; Side Out **1992** Nickel And Dime; That Night; Tattle Tale **1992/93** First Force

Hughes, John

Director, writer

Born 1950

Lansing, Michigan

Just as the Beach Party flicks of the early 1960s fostered the belief among teenagers the world over that American youth of the day was exclusively engaged in surfing or gyrating on sandy beaches, the clean, sweet and frequently funny 80s youth entertainments written, produced and mostly directed by John Hughes presented the world with kids whose preoccupations flew in the face of sickening reality. Hughes' teen tales were all set in his native Chicago suburbs, depicted as archetypal but mythic white bread, milk-and-cookies Midwestern communities, where the concept of poverty and struggle is not having $650 for a perfect prom dress.

Hughes tapped into the American youth market by contemporising standard romantic comedy plots and universal problems of self-absorbed adolescents, adding to their appeal with hip, 'happening' soundtracks and creating new icons with fresh young faces like Molly Ringwald. One of America's most prolific film-makers, with 16 films in his first seven years in the industry, Hughes' more adult-oriented works have generally been equally popular, and his 1990 production, *Home Alone*, written by Hughes and directed by Christopher Columbus, rapidly captivated audiences of all ages.

Hughes' early aspirations of being a writer were initially stymied by economic realities, when his early marriage and parenthood necessitated his accepting employment as an advertising copywriter – an experience he recalled when he graduated from teen themes to twentysomethings with the enjoyable but comparatively poor-performing *She's Having A Baby* (1988). His eventual entrance into films saw his first two produced screenplays, *Mr Mom* and *National Lampoon's Vacation*, both hits in 1983, empowering him to direct his own script, *16 Candles* (1984), with a teen ensemble that included Miss Ringwald, Anthony Michael Hall and the gifted Cusack siblings, John and Joan. *The Breakfast Club* (1985) – something of a junior *Big Chill* – the tasteless *Weird Science* (1985), *Pretty In Pink* (1986) – with Molly as the Poor Girl who gets Mr Right, directed not by Hughes but by Howard Deutsch – *Some Kind Of Wonderful* (1987) – with Eric Stoltz as the Poor Boy who gets Miss Right, again directed by Deutsch – and *Ferris Bueller's Day Off* (1986) – teen Mr Big triggers a fast-paced farce – followed. Producing and collaborating with other directors, Hughes also wrote *The Great Outdoors* (1988) – a lame vacation caper for Dan Aykroyd and John Candy – and the further instalments of Chevy Chase's tumultuous holidays in the *National Lampoon's Vacation* series.

Although it received mixed reviews, Hughes' *Planes, Trains & Automobiles* (1987), a cheerful and at times sweet disaster farce starring Steve Martin and John Candy, demonstrated in his feeling for the characters that he was maturing as a film-maker. The same was true of *She's Having A Baby*, with Kevin Bacon and Elizabeth McGovern, and the enormously successful *Uncle Buck* (1989), a tremendous vehicle for Hughes regular John Candy. *Uncle Buck* also gave the world Hughes' discovery, Macaulay Culkin, who would swiftly become the youngest of multimillionaire superstars. Inconsistent and inevitably rendered tedious at times by Hughes' love of plots laden with comic screw-ups and wearying farce, they nevertheless possess sensitive and sentimental themes and 'caring, sharing' characters who appeal.

Home Alone (1990) presented one of Hughes' richest screenplays, full of spot-on childlike observations alongside grown-up gags. He was probably wise to hand over the direction to Columbus, who is at least as adept at Hughes at setting up wheezes and rather better at giving small incidents and set-ups the sensation of big, exciting action. Starring young Culkin, the film revived the fortunes of 20th Century-Fox and, by the end of 1992, was the highest-grossing, most successful comedy ever!

Hughes entered the new decade with a stream of forthcoming projects from his production company, including the self-penned and directed *Dutch*, starring Candy.

1983 Mr Mum aka Mr Mom (writer only); National Lampoon's Vacation (writer only) **1984** 16 Candles (w/d) **1985** Weird Science (w/d); The Breakfast Club (w/d); National Lampoon's European Vacation (writer only) **1986** Pretty In Pink (writer only); Ferris Bueller's Day Off (w/d) **1987** Some Kind Of Wonderful (writer only); Planes, Trains & Automobiles (w/d) **1988** The Great Outdoors (writer only); She's Having A Baby (w/d) **1989** National Lampoon's Christmas Vacation (writer only); Uncle Buck w/d **1990** Home Alone (writer only) **1991** Driving Me Crazy (writer only); Career Opportunities (writer only); Curly Sue (w/d) **1992** Home Alone 2: Lost In New York (writer only)

Hulce, Tom

Actor
Born 6 December 1953
White Water, Wisconsin

If the sweet, open-faced looks of Tom Hulce have prevented him from maturing on screen into a conventional romantic leading man or a plausible heavyweight, he has made one indelible mark with his performance as the giggling, vulgar, brilliant Mozart in Milos Forman's multiple Oscar-winning film of Peter Shaffer's *Amadeus* (1984), while to the cult of National Lampooners he is forever the definitive college fraternity nerd, Flounder, of *National Lampoon's Animal House* (1978).

Set on acting from an early age, Hulce left

home in his mid-teens to train at the New York School of Arts. At 17 he was engaged to understudy Peter Firth in the lead role of the boy in love with horses in Shaffer's play *Equus* on Broadway, and went on to take over the part. He has continued to work in theatre, notably in recent years in the lead in Larry Kramer's play about AIDS, *The Normal Heart*, in London's West End. Like Dennis Quaid, Hulce made his film debut as one of the small-town youths affected by the death of James Dean in the unusual James Bridges drama *September 30, 1955* (1978). He was billed as Thomas Hulce, as he was in *Animal House* and the under-appreciated, superior little comedy-drama *Those Lips, Those Eyes* (1980) in which he played a starry-eyed would-be actor in a 1950s ropey repertory company.

The sumptuous, literate hit *Amadeus* – for which the actor received an Oscar nomination for Best Actor (won by his co-star F. Murray Abraham) – proved a tough act to follow, but he subsequently acquitted himself capably in a couple of less-than-terrific thrillers, a rather delightful off-beat comedy – *Echo Park* (1986) – and as part of the familial ensemble in the hit *Parenthood* (1989). Arguably his finest performance to date, however, was his four-hankie portrayal of the sweet, innocent retarded Dominick in the wildly sentimental but affecting *Dominick And Eugene* (1988), while he brought an appropriate vulnerability to the role of Stalin's projectionist whose starry-eyed adulation of his master leads to tragedy in Konchalovsky's interesting failure, *The Inner Circle* (1992).

1978 September 30, 1955; National Lampoon's Animal House **1980** Those Lips, Those Eyes **1984** Amadeus **1986** Echo Park **1987** Slam Dance **1988** Dominick And Eugene aka Nicky And Gino; Shadowman **1989** Parenthood **1990** Black Rainbow **1992** The Inner Circle **1993** Joy Ride

Hunt, Linda

Actress

Born 2 April 1945

Morristown, New Jersey

For all her celebrated stage and film work, Linda Hunt and her remarkable talents only became evident to the general public in director Peter Weir's *The Year Of Living Dangerously* (1983). Co-starring with Sigourney Weaver and Mel Gibson, the then unknown actress astonished audiences with her performance as the photographer Billy Kwan, a male Indonesian dwarf who functions as a kind of spiritual guide during that country's civil uprising. The role earned her a well-deserved Oscar for Best Supporting Actress. Her tiny size and irregular, rather wizened looks disguise the fact that Hunt is one of America's most versatile and skilled character actresses: a pocket-sized dynamo capable of holding her own in the best company.

Raised in Westport, Connecticut, Hunt was inspired to act at the age of six after seeing Mary Martin in a production of *Peter Pan*. Drama lessons began at 13 and although she adored performing, she was persuaded to study directing as a safeguard in the event that her unusual appearance would keep her from all but the quirkiest parts. At Chicago's prestigious Goodman Theatre School, she majored in directing. Several years spent in New York stage managing, directing and doing the odd bit of acting brought her back to performing, especially in alternative theatre with companies such as La Mama and the Open Theatre. After years of slogging in bit parts and directing for a children's theatre, she finally found her feet and won two Obie awards and a Tony nomination.

After *The Year Of Living Dangerously*, Hunt earned critical raves in James Ivory's *The Bostonians* (1984), playing with Vanessa Regrave, and *Eleni* (1985), yet she is equally at home with comedy as with drama: she was a singular saloon-bar manageress in the Old West in Lawrence Kasdan's *Silverado* (1985) and a splendid accomplice for Roseanne Barr in Susan Seidelman's unfairly maligned *She-Devil* (1989). She began the 90s featured in *Kindergarten Cop* – a limited supporting role but one in which she nevertheless survived the presence of the star, Arnold Schwarzenegger.

1980 Popeye **1983** The Year Of Living Dangerously **1984** The Bostonians; Dune **1985** Eleni; Silverado **1987** Waiting For The Moon **1989** She-Devil **1990** Kindergarten Cop; **1991** If Looks Could Kill **1993** Younger And Younger

Hunter, Holly

Actress

Born 20 March 1958

Conyers, Georgia

One of a slew of actresses from the South (Frances McDormand, Kim Basinger, Julia Roberts to name but three) to emerge during the 1980s, Holly Hunter, the youngest in a family of seven, grew up on a large cattle and hay farm in Georgia. She moved to New York City to pursue an acting career, studied at the Carnegie Mellon Institute, and enjoyed success in the theatre, largely in a series of plays by Beth Henley (including *Crimes Of The Heart* and *The Miss Firecracker Contest*).

Hunter's screen debut passed unnoticed – a bit part in one of the most awful schlock horror movies made to date, *The Burning* (1981) – and small roles in three more, including the aircraft factory worker whose husband is killed in action in Jonathan Demme's nostalgic *Swing Shift* (1984). Then, in 1987, having been suggested by her friend Frances McDormand, the young actress found herself co-starring with Nicolas Cage in the Coen brothers' screwy, anarchic black comedy, *Raising Arizona*. As the Southern prison wardress who runs off with an ex-con to live a life of wedded bliss, marred only by her obsessional desire for a baby which leads to the theft of one, Hunter delivered the goods with a feisty wallop, her tiny frame quivering with abrasive energy.

The actress' highly individual qualities resurfaced almost immediately in *Broadcast News* later the same year. Her driven TV executive, combining woman-in-a-man's-world ballsy defiance with personal wistfulness won her the Best Actress vote from the New York and Los Angeles Film Critics and the National Board of Review, as well as an Oscar nomination. (That was the year everybody lost out to Cher for *Moonstruck*.)

The diminutive Hunter (five feet two inches), no glamour girl, is not easy to cast, but *Miss Firecracker* (1989, from the Beth Henley play), in which she played a small-town girl who desperately wants to follow in the footsteps of her glamorous cousin (Mary Steenburgen) and win the local beauty contest, was – although a mediocre movie – an excellent vehicle for her talents.

1981 The Burning **1984** Swing Shift **1985** Animal Behavior (released 1989) **1987** End Of The Line; Broadcast News; Raising Arizona **1989** Always; Miss Firecracker **1990** Once Around **1992** Crazy In Love **1992/93** The Piano Lesson (working title)

Hunter, Tim

Director, writer
Born ?
From ?

Alienated youth is the speciality of director Tim Hunter, who co-wrote (in one case) and directed (in the other) two of the most disturbing pictures of kids gone wrong made in America in the last decade, *Over The Edge* (1979) and *River's Edge* (1986).

Hunter's straightforward, realistic style reflects his concern with true events. The perceptive *Over The Edge*, which Hunter scripted in collaboration with Charlie Haas and which was directed by Jonathan Kaplan, was inspired by the new wave of crime statistics in the 1970s, when a phenomenal rise in arrests of juveniles under the age of 18 for vandalism and other crimes was reported. Almost invariably, these were occuring in depressed urban centres or in pre-planned suburban communities – the American equivalent of Britain's 'new towns' – where a disproportionately young population had few, if any, recreational facilities, sporting or social centres. A surge in aimless, motiveless crime was a scarcely surprising but nevertheless shocking result. Powerful and well made, *Over The Edge* spotlighted the problem, although unfortunately it could do little towards solving it, and among the young adolescent rebels without a cause in the good cast were Vincent Spano and a 14-year-old Matt Dillon.

Hunter made his directorial debut with *Tex* (1982), adapted from the novel by S.E. Hinton and the first of her books – enormously popular with American teenagers – to reach the screen (followed by *The Outsiders, Rumble Fish, That Was Then This Is Now* and *Wisdom*). Small, direct and appealing, it starred Matt Dillon as the deprived, loveless boy coming of age, and provided a 19-year-old Emilio Estevez with his first feature film role. Less likeable was the more routine girl-and-her-horse yarn *Sylvester* (1985) with the young veteran Melissa Gilbert and some nice equestrian scenes, but little else to excite.

The director's reputation, however, rests on his 1986 feature, *River's Edge*, written by Neal Jiminez with many parallels to *Over The Edge*. Triggered by a true and shocking case that occurred in Milpitas, California, the film tells of a senseless, passionless murder of a schoolgirl by her boyfriend, who brings his curious but detached friends to view the body. A wild Crispin Glover led the gang of youngsters who try on but cannot feel emotional or even appropriate responses to the event. The film-maker's concern and stance is ironically presented through Dennis Hopper – in a superb performance – as a permanently out-of-it, crippled biker relic of the 60s who initially is willing to help the kids but ultimately is horrified and angered by their lack of *any* code, any values, any feeling. As an indictment of society's devaluing of education, culture and community it was terrifying, truthful and deeply disturbing.

Hunter's subsequent lack of output is mystifying; at the end of the decade he joined the team of directors occupied with the weird and wonderful soap 'noir', *Twin Peaks* and, in 1991, directed *Lies Of The Twins*. This intriguing psycho-thriller romance, starring Isabella Rossellini and Aidan Quinn as good and bad psychoanalyst twins was made for cable TV in the USA, and went straight to video in Britain.

1979 Over The Edge (co-writer only) **1982** Tex **1985** Sylvester **1986** River's Edge **1992/93** The Saint of Fort Washington

Hurt, John

Actor

Born 22 January 1940

Chesterfield, England

Few actors live up to their name on screen quite so consistently as John Hurt who, throughout his career, has been hung for crimes he did not commit, sent to a Turkish prison, survived cancer and deformity, been a hopeless drunk, a victimised homosexual and given birth to aliens (twice); while, off screen, the tabloid press' determination to portray him (inaccurately) as a philandering, hard-drinking hellraiser in the Burton-Harris tradition has caused him no little grief as well. The wiry, freckled clergyman's son with the voice that seems forever on the verge of breaking, going up and down like an Innsbruck ski jump (gracing animated features such as *Watership Down*, 1978, *The Plague Dogs*, 1982 and *The Black Cauldron*, 1985) studied painting before attending RADA and making his stage and screen debuts in 1962. Following his role as the ambitious Rich in *A Man For All Seasons* (1966), Hurt began his regular process of being 'discovered' every five years, filling in the interims with stage and minor film work.

His second 'discovery' was as the weak and boastful Timothy Evans in *10 Rillington Place* (1970), the first of his string of pathetic and bewildered losers and victims of society to make it to the big screen. Yet it was his mid-70s TV roles as the outrageous Quentin Crisp in *The Naked Civil Servant* and his demented, tormented Emperor Caligula in *I, Claudius* that made the greatest impression on the public and casting directors alike, with Hurt making the most of the movie opportunities it gave him. His sordid, drug-addicted prisoner in *Midnight Express* (1978) won him an Oscar nomination, while his role as unwitting surrogate mother in *Alien* (1979, which he parodied eight years later in Mel Brooks' *Spaceballs*) made his face so well known across the world that his career was one of the few to escape *Heaven's Gate* (1980) unblemished. However, his most impressive screen excursion hid his face under layers of prosthetic make-up as *The Elephant Man* (1980, his second Oscar nomination), the deformed John Merrick, treated as a freak by Victorian society but whose romantic soul – and incidental vanity – is brought out by a sympathetic surgeon (Anthony Hopkins). The subtle and heartbreaking nuances of Hurt's extraordinary performance reached through the latex in a way that no actor had managed since Lon Chaney.

Much of the remainder of his work during the 80s was inconsistent – a few so-so films from great directors mixed with parts that seemed to have been accepted simply to remain visible. Although both his heroic jockey, *Champion* (1983), and Stephen Ward in the dismal *Scandal* (1989) offered him the opportunity for centre-stage suffering, he has been edged more and more towards supporting character roles and voice-overs for some of the better known household products, with parts such as his Irish village idiot in the John Mills tradition in *The Field* (1990), although finally convincing, seeming to marginalise rather than exploit the energy and sympathy he can give to a performance.

1962 The Wild And The Willing **1963** This Is My Street **1966** A Man For All Seasons **1967** The Sailor From Gibraltar **1968** In Search Of Gregory **1969** Before Winter Comes; Sinful Davey **1970** 10 Rillington Place **1971** Mr Forbush and The Penguins; The Pied Piper **1974** Little Malcolm And His Struggle Against The Eunuchs; The Ghoul **1976** East Of Elephant Rock; Stream Line The Shout; Midnight Express; The Disappearance **1979** Alien **1980** Heaven's Gate; The Elephant Man **1981** History Of The World – Part 1; Partners **1982** Night Crossing **1983** The Osterman Weekend; Champion **1984** The Hit; Success Is The Best Revenge **1985** After Darkness **1986** Jake Speed **1987** Spaceballs **1988** White Mischief **1989** Scandal **1990** Roger Corman's Frankenstein Unbound; Windprints; The Field **1991** King Ralph **1992** Memory; Memoire Traquée/Memory (France) **1993** Even Cowgirls Get The Blues

Hurt, Mary Beth
(Mary Beth Supinger)
Actress
Born 26 September 1948
Marshalltown, Iowa

Educated at the University of Iowa and New York University's School Of The Arts, this excellent actress takes her professional name from that of her ex-husband (from 1972–1982), William Hurt. Interestingly, she flexed her acting muscles with the well-known London amateur theatre the Questors, in Ealing, when she and William spent a year in the city. Her professional debut followed back home with the New York Shakespeare Festival in 1972, and she continued a successful stage career for the next nine years, earning a Tony nomination for *Trelawney Of The Wells* and winning two Obie awards, one for *Crimes Of The Heart.*

Woody Allen was responsible for the actress' screen debut. Having seen her at work in the theatre, he cast her in his Bergmanesque *Interiors* (1978). As the youngest of the three sisters in a fraught household, her portrayal of a failed artist and actress in the grip of creative impotence and guilt for hating her mother won her critical acclaim and the co-lead in Joan Micklin Silver's funny and touching *Head Over Heels* the following year.

Since *Interiors*, Mary Beth Hurt, whose distinctive looks have a period flavour reminiscent of say, Mary Astor, has made regular if not frequent screen appearances, proving her ability in a wide range of material, from D.A.R.Y.L. (1985), in which she fostered a child who turns out to be a robot, to a more conventional if no less stressed mother in Bob Balaban's *Parents* (1988). She is married to writer and director Paul Schrader, for whom she appeared as a psychic counsellor to Willem Dafoe in *Light Sleeper* (1992).

1978 Interiors **1979** Head Over Heels aka Chilly Scenes Of Winter **1980** Hide In Plain Sight (uncredited); A Change Of Seasons **1982** The World According To Garp **1985** Compromising Positions; D.A.R.Y.L. **1988** Parents **1989** Slaves of New York **1991** Defenseless **1992** Light Sleeper

Hurt, William
Actor
Born 20 March 1950
Washington DC

William Hurt is an actor in the world heavyweight class who combines in a highly individual way the old and the new aspects of the Hollywood leading man. He is blessed with classic American good looks – blond hair, handsome, clean-cut features at once collegiate and patrician, sportsman's physique – and, in addition, a quality of 'breeding' that can be traced to his upper-crust ancestry and privileged upbringing in affluent surroundings. And yet, from the first, he has taken pains to avoid the vehicles that openly court popularity and fame, or that might stamp him in a too easily identifiable character mould. Indeed, he has excelled at playing a wide range of outsiders, loners, losers, and moral equivocators. It seems typical of this actor's peculiar integrity that, against physical type, he should have sought out and made such an extraordinary success of Molina, the effeminate homosexual Latin-American jail-bird in *Kiss Of The Spider Woman* – the role which won him the 1985 Best Actor Oscar.

A feeling of sometimes tortured emotional intensity boiling up behind a cool facade is a Hurt characteristic. This has been mirrored, it seems, in his private life: in 1989, during a court case for palimony initiated by the dancer Sandra Jennings, his companion of the early 80s, it was alleged that he was an alcoholic prone to fits of violence and self-loathing; in 1986 he spent time drying out at the Betty Ford Clinic, where he met his second wife, Heidi Henderson. Another notable characteristic is a readiness to alter his features to the point of near-unrecognisability if it will serve the film. Both the turbanned, eyebrow-plucked Molina and Hurt's brilliantly executed cameo role as a bearded, spaced-out would-be assassin in the comedy *I Love You To Death* (1990) prove the point beyond question. To himself he is clearly an actor first and a leading man second; but to the cinema audience it is the balance struck between both those categories that makes him so fascinating to watch.

Hurt's father was a high-ranking US State Department official in charge of foreign aid programmes, and much of the actor's early childhood was spent in various parts of the South Pacific. His parents having divorced, his mother married Henry Luce III, the son of the founder of *Time* magazine when Hurt was ten; he went to school in Massachusetts, and thence to Tufts University, where he started as a theology major but switched to acting in his third year, rounding off his training at the New York Juilliard School.

After time spent on Australian sheep farms and motorcycling across the US, he plunged into the theatre. His career took off swiftly, and included Shakespeare opposite Meryl Streep at the New York Shakespeare Festival (where he met his first wife, the actress Mary Beth Hurt) and membership of the off-Broadway Circle Repertory Company, as well as several plum parts on television.

Hurt's first cinema roles were leads, in Ken Russell's production-troubled *Altered States* (1980) and Peter Yates's *Eyewitness* (1981). In the first, he played a scientist absorbed in psychedelic experiments which go wrong, in the second, a bespectacled night-shift janitor; both characters are private people, emotionally off-centre, increasingly revealed as obsessives. But it was in his third assignment, with Kathleen Turner as leading lady and Lawrence Kasdan as director and scriptwriter, that the full force of Hurt's magnetism was unleashed. *Body Heat* (1981) proved to be an 80s revival of the 40s *film noir* genre, with the difference that Kasdan did not shrink from filling the screen with the overt sexual jousting that had of necessity to be left latent in the era when the Hays Office view of morals and manners still held sway over Hollywood. In a beautifully evoked Florida sea-coast setting glistening with sweaty heat and big-money luxury, the director rubbed Hurt and Turner up against each other – the small-time lawyer Ned, big on brawn and flip chitchat but slow on the uptake, the bored wife Matty, plotting to murder her rich husband – and sat back while their combustion scattered showers of erotic sparks. It's a marvellous pairing, cool-hot, sweet-sour; and both actors drew out of it endless variations on the theme of amoral minds in highly attractive bodies. Hurt's ability to suggest his character's woozy soft centre no less than his steamy physical appeal showed courage as well as considerable artistry.

Although he has said that he follows the axiom 'Go for good projects, never good parts', thus far Hurt's work-list is full of both. The 1983 *Gorky Park* might be thought a comparative failure, though the actor's contribution to it was trim and disciplined. In the 1988 *A Time of Destiny* he seemed perhaps a little uncomfortable as the black sheep of a Californian immigrant family, and he was surprisingly wooden as Mia Farrow's adulterous husband in *Alice*. But such misfires are relative, and have been few. Collaboration with Kasdan has brought him a ripe variety of parts. In sustaining the leisurely chamber music of *The Big Chill* (1984). Hurt's damaged Vietnam War veteran, a drug-taker in hip dark glasses, plays a notable part; in *The Accidental Tourist* (1988) his portrait of a divorcé straitjacketed by his own emotional passivity and pulled between two determined (and very different) women, Kathleen Turner and Geena Davis, is a masterly study in understated comic-dramatic shading; and in the already-mentioned *I Love You To Death*, he achieves the certainty of comic aim strangely missed by the films principals, Tracey Ullman and Kevin Kline.

In other directorial hands he has shown no less versatility. He can underplay sympathetically (as the teacher of the hearing-handicapped in *Children Of A Lesser God*, 1986, and the cancer-stricken surgeon in *The Doctor*, 1991, both for director Randa Haines) or with fine irony (as the good-looking, intellectually unreliable TV smoothie in *Broadcast News*, 1987); as he made clear in *Kiss Of The Spider Woman*, he can also paint in unashamedly bold lines and exotic colours when the situation demands it. Hurt's is, in sum, a talent at once complex, formidable and flexible, and as he moved into his 40s its potential seemed greater than ever.

1980 Altered States **1981** Eyewitness aka The Janitor; Body Heat **1983** Gorky Park **1984** The Big Chill **1985** Kiss Of The Spider Woman **1986** Children Of A Lesser God **1987** Broadcast News **1988** A Time Of Destiny; The Accidental Tourist **1990** I Love You To Death; Alice **1991** The Doctor; Until The End Of The World **1992/93** The Plague/La Peste (France/GB/Argentina)

Huston, Anjelica

Actress

Born 9 July 1951

Los Angeles, California

Anjelica Huston for a long time was a successful *Vogue* model, which may be surprising if one considers her mainly as a character actress. Certainly she is striking, and classy, but her looks are not conventional or classical. In 1980 she was involved in a bad car accident in which her nose (already slightly too prominent) was broken in four places; even after repairs, the odd bump or two remains.

She is tall and big-boned, with a terrific figure, but somewhat masculine and authoritative in her body language (appropriately, she plays a lion-tamer in Bob Rafelson's 1981 remake of *The Postman Always Rings Twice*).

Her acting career started late, if one ignores the single teenage part she played under the direction of her father, John Huston, in 1969; as a result, she has missed out on the soft, pretty ingénue roles in which a Hollywood actress traditionally makes her reputation. Despite her pedigree background – perhaps because of it – she has suffered from lack of confidence and has had to work hard to establish herself as an actress in her own right rather than being spoken of, as she was for many years, as the appendage of Jack Nicholson. (The couple broke up in 1989 after a 17-year romance.) Undoubtedly the Academy Award as Best Supporting Actress in *Prizzi's Honour* (1985) changed her dramatically, and since the mid-80s she has taken some glorious parts, effectively establishing her as one of the best and most original of contemporary actresses in Hollywood.

Anjelica was brought up in County Galway, Ireland, the daughter of the legendary director John Huston and his second wife, ballet dancer Ricki Soma. An idyllic country childhood was broken at the age of 11 when her parents separated, and she followed her mother to London. London in the 60s (and in the wealthy circles in which Anjelica mixed) provided an adolescence of glamour and fast living that in due course led to problems of rebellion, and of drug-taking. The modelling assignments got her through this rough patch, giving her confidence and a place in the world.

Her first screen roles, in the 1970s, were few and undistinguished (she had a small part in Kazan's sketchily-conceived *The Last Tycoon*, 1976, starring Robert De Niro). It wasn't until meeting the famed and sympathetic acting coach, Peggy Fleury, at the beginning of the 1980s (when Huston was already 30) that her career and her inner life came together properly.

She had tiny parts in the biopic *Frances* (1982) and in Bob Reiner's gloriously funny rock music parody, *This Is Spinal Tap* (1984). In *Prizzi's Honour*, directed by her father, she shone playing a vengeful Mafia princess whose stunning looks belie the coarsest Brooklyn language. The following year, by contrast, in the last of her father's films, the elegiac *The Dead* (taken from a tale by James Joyce), she was wistful, tender and melancholy as the wife Gretta – never more than in the beautiful moment when she is spied by her husband on the staircase in a gesture of profound inner thoughtfulness (she has said about this, a bit thespianly: 'I just had to look at my father and think of Ireland . . . it was all there.') She was in one of Coppola's less successful films, *Gardens Of Stone* (1987) and played a butch American aviatrix in one of the better Evelyn Waugh adaptations, *A Handful Of Dust* (1988). Two excellent roles followed: in Paul Mazursky's *Enemies, A Love Story* and Woody Allen's *Crimes and Misdemeanors* (both 1989), in both of which she plays women scorned and abandoned by, respectively, a husband and a lover – prophetically so since it was shortly after these films that Nicholson, in her private life, deserted her for a 26-year-old waitress. After this shakeup, Huston starred with much success in Nicolas Roeg's sinister confection *The Witches* (1989), and scored more critical plaudits (including a Best Actress Oscar nomination) as a tough, fatalistic con artist in Stephen Frears' film *The Grifters* (1990), where she was astonishingly effective in a blonde wig and, indeed, walked away with the film, thanks to a virtuoso performance.

Obviously Anjelica Huston relishes not being typecast. Her pleasure in adapting to different roles drawn from a wide social spectrum has had her compared, at times, to Hollywood's other great impersonator – or character actress – Meryl Streep; but she is more tender than Streep and ultimately more sympathetic (you never feel with her that virtuosity springs from technique). In private she is witty and fast-talking, apparently a marvellous letter-writer. She is a bold horsewoman and still rides with the Galway Blazers. A childhood friend, the novelist Joan Juliet Buck, speaks of there being at least four Anjelicas: the Beauty, the Wit, the Drama Queen, the Self-Mocking Loon. There is flattery in that, but also shrewdness. Plainly, she is flamboyant – histrionic and theatrical by nature. But she is far too clever to take the more pretentious aspects of her profession seriously. She is very much her own person, and by the turn of the decade into the 90s was enjoying a peak of creativity.

1969 A Walk With Love And Death **1976** Swashbuckler (GB: Scarlet Buccaneer); The Last Tycoon **1981** The Postman Always Rings Twice **1982** Frances **1984** This Is Spinal Tap; The Ice Pirates **1985** Prizzi's Honour **1987** The Dead; Gardens Of Stone **1988** A Handful of Dust; Mr North **1989** Enemies, A Love Story; Crimes And Misdemeanors; The Witches **1990** The Grifters **1991** The Addams Family **1992** The Player (cameo as herself) **1993** Manhattan Murder Mystery

Hutton, Lauren
(Mary Laurence Hutton)
Actress
Born 17 November 1943
Charleston, South Carolina

Despite having worked for directors of the calibre of Alan Rudolph, Robert Altman, Karel Reisz and Paul Schrader, and starred opposite some of Hollywood's most desirable leading men – including Richard Gere, Robert Redford, Tom Selleck and Burt Reynolds – Lauren Hutton remains more famous as a model than as an actress.

Born in South Carolina, she spent just one year at the University of Florida before becoming a Playboy bunny in New York and moving, unsuccessfully at first, into modelling. As legend has it, Hutton was finally signed by top agent Eileen Ford only when she agreed to have her slightly bumpy nose and gappy front teeth fixed; in point of fact they were to become her trademark and her fortune. A healthy looking, carefree beauty, she gradually established herself as one of the world's top models and became the epitome of the 70s woman during her decade as *the* Revlon model.

It was while still a model that Hutton began her career as an actress, debuting opposite Alan Alda in the well-received *Paper Lion* (1968). She worked for Alan Rudolph and Robert Altman, playing supporting roles in *Welcome to LA* (1976) and *A Wedding* (1978) respectively, and played opposite Burt Reynolds three times, in *Gator* (1976) – Reynold's directing debut – *Paternity* (1981) and *Malone* (1987). She has, however, had her fair share of duds throughout her career, including Karel Reisz's *The Gambler*, *Lassiter* (both 1974), *Once Bitten* (1985), in which she played a vampiress, and the excruciatingly dreadful *Viva Knievel* (1977).

A competent rather than inspired actress, Hutton is best in roles that draw on her glamorous earthiness and sex appeal. She was thus cast to great effect in Paul Schrader's steamy *American Gigolo* (1980) and her sensual performance as the politician's wife bedded quite explicitly by Richard Gere is probably her best remembered role to date.

Aside from appearing in the off-Broadway play *Extremities* and in the CBS TV movie *Sins*, Lauren Hutton featured as a literary agent to psychic Ally Sheedy in *Fear* (1990).

1968 Paper Lion **1970** Pieces of Dreams; Little Fauss and Big Halsey **1972** Rocco **1974** The Gambler **1976** Gator; Welcome to LA **1977** Viva Knievel **1978** A Wedding **1980** American Gigolo **1981** Zorro, The Gay Blade; Paternity; Hecate Et Ses Chiens (France) **1982** Tout Feu, Tout Flamme (France) **1983** Lassiter **1985** Once Bitten; Flagrante Desir/Flagrant Desire (France); Bulldance **1986** From Here To Maternity **1987** Malone Leben Und Sterben In Der Society/Blue Blood (West Germany) **1989** Scandalous **1990** Fear **1991** Guilty As Charged; Miliardi (Italy)

Hutton, Timothy
Actor
Born 16 August 1960
Malibu, California

When Timothy Hutton, at the age of 19, became the youngest actor ever to win an Oscar – as Best Supporting Actor for his heartwrenching performance in Robert Redford's tremendous directorial debut, *Ordinary People* (1980) – he could not have guessed he would spend the next decade mainly playing sensitive wimps. Possessed of the same open, pleasant, fresh-faced looks of his late father, Jim Hutton, who starred in a string of romantic comedies in the 1960s and later played television's Ellery Queen, the younger Hutton has consistently sought heavyweight projects and intelligent drama, with variable results.

Raised in Berkeley by his mother after his parents' divorce, Hutton appeared in high school plays and in a touring production of *Harvey* with his father during a summer vacation. After leaving school he went to live with his father in Southern California and obtained roles in several TV films – notably *Friendly Fire* (1979) and *Young Love, First Love* (1979). Shortly after his father's early death from cancer, Redford cast him in the pivotal role of the tormented teenager Conrad, whose guilt and suicidal depression after the death of his brother forces his parents (Donald Sutherland, Mary Tyler Moore) to confront the realities of their marriage in *Ordinary People*. His was a beautiful portrayal. The attention, acclaim and Oscar triumph that greeted it promised great things to come. Briefly, Hutton was regarded as head and shoulders above a crowd of second-generation Hollywood kids dubbed the Brat Pack.

Hutton's second major vehicle, *Taps* (1981), in which his head-boy character led an armed rebellion at a military academy, was only a fair drama with a predictably tragic climax, although he was fine as an earnest youth driven by an illusory code, despite some of his thunder being stolen by supporting players Tom Cruise and – in his debut – Sean Penn. Sidney Lumet's *Daniel* (1983) was a superior, thought-provoking and brave film exploring the consequences for their children of a couple's passionate political commitment, and Hutton was very strong as the son coming to terms with his heritage. But the film was a box-office disaster, withdrawn in days because its leftist orientation repelled Americans during a hot incident in the Cold War (the film opened when a passenger plane was shot down near North Korea).

Fred Schepisi's first-rate sci-fi venture *Iceman* (1984) provided Hutton with another good, involving role as a sympathetic scientist, but it was not a hit. Another prestigious misfire, John Schlesinger's *The Falcon And The Snowman* (1985), based on the real story of two young and affluent Americans jailed for their attempts to sell government secrets to the USSR, again saw Hutton as a sensitive character with depth. But neither he nor the script succeeded in illuminating the young man's motives or real mind, and co-star Sean Penn outshone him as his nervy, drugged-up sidekick. The same year the young actor proved ill-suited to an off-beat, clumsy comedy, *Turk 182!* and entered a five-year career crisis of regular but disappointing film work (including a blink-and-you'll-miss-it, non-speaking moment in Costa-Gavras' *Betrayed*) and an ultimately failed marriage to Debra Winger (with whom he has a son, Noah). Alan Rudolph's *Made In Heaven* (1987) was a plodding, cultish fantasy; Gregory Nava's *A Time Of Destiny* (1988) was a major disappointment with uninspired performances from both Hutton and his co-star William Hurt as wartime buddies trapped in a tragic, senseless family vendetta; in Taylor Hackford's *Everybody's All-American* (1988) Hutton was yet again an earnest, sensitive soul and very much second banana to a brash Dennis Quaid and a terrific Jessica Lange; and things appeared to be taking a desperate turn with Hutton miscast as a Russian aristocrat torn between Nastassia Kinski and Valeria Golino in Jerzy Skolimowski's handsome but tedious Turgenev adaptation, *Torrents Of Spring* (1990). His moody brooding was better suited to Sidney Lumet's tough, gritty law and corruption thriller *Q&A* (1990), although inevitably his naive, truth-seeking rookie prosecutor was upstaged by Nick Nolte's ruthless, sadistic bad cop.

Having made his New York stage debut in 1984 in *Orpheus Descending*, Timothy Hutton returned to a Broadway lead in 1990, taking over from Alec Baldwin in the hit romantic fable *Prelude To A Kiss*. Critics sniffed that he was not as sexy in the role as Baldwin (who reprises the role in the film version), but Hutton's performance was charming and revealed a lighter touch than he had thus far been able to demonstrate on screen. He has also dabbled in direction, with an episode of NBC TV's *Amazing Stories* and the extremely popular Cars pop video, 'Drive' (1984), to his credit.

1980 Ordinary People **1981** Taps **1983** Daniel **1984** Iceman **1985** The Falcon And The Snowman; Turk 182! **1987** Made In Heaven **1988** A Time Of Destiny; Everybody's All-American aka When I Fall In Love **1990** Torrents of Spring; Q&A **1992/93** The Temp

Hyams, Peter

Director, writer
Born 26 July 1943
New York City

One of the premier craftsmen of the thriller genre and a director who knows his way around a set-piece and a 'Scope lens, Peter Hyams, the son of a Broadway publicist, began his progress towards films as a precocious child (sculpture at four, music at nine), studying both music and art before pursuing a jazz career as a drummer, playing with Bill Evans and Maynard Ferguson among others. Joining the CBS news staff in New York he went on to become an anchorman before going to Vietnam as a war correspondent for the network. He learned cinematography and made several documentaries on his return to the States, and joined Paramount as a writer in 1970. He sold his first screenplay, *TR Baskin*, the following year, and moved on to ABC to direct TV movies such as *The Rolling Man* and *Goodnight My Love* (both 1972) before making his big-screen directorial debut with *Busting* (1974). One of the many buddy cop thrillers of the 70s, it was distinguished by a superb and much-imitated cat-and-mouse chase in a supermarket, but angered the gay community with its jovial depiction of its two heroes staking out a public toilet. No one needed to picket the cinemas showing *Peeper* (1976), a truly dire Bogart spoof with little to recommend it, while Hyams was fired from the Charles Bronson thriller *Telefon* (1977) and replaced by Don Siegel early in production.

He managed to arrest his decline with the

ingenious conspiracy thriller *Capricorn One* (1978), in which NASA's faking of a Mars landing provided a strong framework for a series of exemplary action sequences, his superb use of cross-cutting heightening the tension of the unwilling astronauts' getaway by interspersing it with a NASA press conference announcing their 'deaths'. A modest commercial success, any ground it gained for Hyams was lost by his determinedly old-fashioned World War II romance *Hanover Street* (1979), while his tense and intriguing sci-fi version of *High Noon* crossed with *The French Connection*, *Outland* (1981) – somewhat weakened by a breathless central chase sequence that made the film's climax look tame by comparison – failed to live up to box-office expectations. Then *The Star Chamber* (1983), a fairly gripping and unusual movie, starring Michael Douglas and one of the few vigilante thrillers to confront the moral implications of its hero's actions, quickly disappeared.

Some box-office lustre was restored to Hyams' CV by *2010* (1984), yet, despite being a highly professional and sometimes atmospheric piece of work, the film lacked the epic grandeur of Kubrick's esteemed predecessor, *2001: A Space Odyssey* (1968). Unlike Kubrick, Hyams seemed to lack the confidence for extreme long shots and long takes. Indeed, throughout much of his work, Hyams the cinematographer (he shoots his own films to save time) has proved less impressive than Hyams the director, with his good eye for 'Scope composition somewhat compromised by his limited palette when it comes to the use of colour (a deficiency most notable in *Narrow Margin*, 1990).

Running Scared (1986), very much a highly formulaic *Busting* for the 80s, proved the director's biggest hit, but once again he failed to capitalise on it with the under-developed *The Presidio* (1988), throwing away a promising premise for by-the-number scripting and, opening car-chase aside, lacklustre direction, with even Sean Connery uncomfortably cast. By comparison, his excellent and much under-rated remake of *Narrow Margin* (1990) showed that, with strong material, Hyams could keep audiences on the edge of their seats, but the audiences stayed away, thus highlighting the essential paradox of his career: despite being one of the best directors of mainstream movies, his films continually fail to make it commercially, and despite Peter Hyams' great technical ability and his ear for snappy dialogue, he looked set by the 90s to become a director who would be more appreciated on the small screen in years to come than on the big one in years past.

As writer-director unless stated otherwise: **1971** TR Baskin (writer only) **1974** Busting; Our Time **1976** Peeper (also co-writer) **1977** Telefon (co-writer only) **1978** Capricorn One **1979** Hanover Street **1980** The Hunter (co-writer only) **1981** Outland **1983** The Star Chamber **1984** 2010 **1986** Running Scared (director only) **1988** The Presidio (director only) **1990** Narrow Margin (w/d) **1992** Stay Tuned (director only)

I

Irons, Jeremy

Actor
Born 1948
Cowes, Isle of Wight, England

Slim and elegant, with a distinctive, rich, deep voice, Jeremy Irons is the American ideal of a Great British Thespian. In Britain his stock is not quite so high, perhaps, with the hipper element regarding him as in the old-fashioned line of rather precious, 'actory' actors, most at home in period pieces or the camouflage of meticulously prepared character roles.

The well-bred Irons was educated at the exclusive Sherborne and trained at the Bristol Old Vic School (as did, coincidentally, 1989's Oscar-winning Best Actor, Daniel Day-Lewis), joining the Bristol Old Vic Company after two years. His traditional repertory stint with the company gave him experience in work ranging from Shakespeare to Joe Orton. In 1971 Irons came to London and worked at odd jobs from housecleaner and gardener to street busker before winning the role of John the Baptist in the hit stage musical *Godspell*.

Irons flourished both in the West End theatre and on television, and made his film debut in *Nijinsky* (1980) as the choreographer Fokine. But it was his starring role as Charles Ryder in the prestigious TV serial adaptation of Evelyn Waugh's *Brideshead Revisited* that brought Irons to the attention of an international audience and made him sought after as a romantic, velvet-voiced leading man. He consolidated this appeal with an attractive performance opposite Meryl Streep in the well-received *The French Lieutenant's Woman* (1981), but it was in Jerzy Skolimowski's original, poignant and at times very funny *Moonlighting* (1982) that Irons broke type and showed that he is capable of more than brooding handsomely. As the beleaguered foreman of a group of Polish workmen stranded in London he delivered a wonderful performance full of irony, anxiety and pathos. Harold Pinter's *Betrayal* (1983) gave him another interesting role as the lover in a long-lived triangle but the film itself came over as too contrived and stagey, and he was back sighing heavily while impeccably dressed in a screen version of Ibsen's *The Wild Duck* (1983), and Volker Schlondorff's adaptation of Marcel Proust's *Remembrance of Things Past* as a far too coolly obsessed *Swann In Love* (1984).

The actor's Broadway debut in 1984 opposite Glenn Close in Tom Stoppard's *The Real Thing* brought more acclaim, and after a long and difficult period filming Roland Joffé's *The Mission* (1986) – in which he held his own opposite Robert De Niro with a fine, sensitive performance as the saintly Jesuit martyr Father Gabriel – Irons took a self-imposed hiatus from film work in favour of classical theatre. Joining his wife, Sinead Cusack, whom he married in 1978, at the Royal Shakespeare Company, he took leading roles in *The Winter's Tale, The Rover* and *Richard II* to mixed reviews. While he unquestionably has the looks, voice and technical equipment of a major classical actor, at this stage he seemed to lack something of the robustness and the ability to convey real emotional depth that mark the great.

During this period Irons took the opportunity for a lighter bit of fun to star with the elder of his two sons, Sam, and his father-in-law, Cyril Cusack, in a charming adaptation of Roald Dahl's children's story, *Danny The Champion Of The World* (1987), and to record the role of Professor Higgins to Kiri Te Kanawa's Eliza Doolittle for a popular album version of *My Fair Lady*.

Despite a mixed reception for the film *Reversal Of Fortune* (1990), Irons was universally praised for his interpretation of a cold, enigmatic Claus von Bülow, the international playboy tried and acquitted of the attempted murder of his comatose wife, Sunny, a role that reteamed Irons with Glenn Close and won him the Oscar for Best Actor. One cannot help but feel that Irons' performance – painstaking, thoughtful and impressive though it was – was the sort of thing he can do standing on his head, and that the award was almost a retrospective apologia from the American Academy for its failure to acknowledge his earlier work in David Cronenberg's *Dead Ringers* (1988), for which he was awarded Best Actor by the New York Critics. His most chilling and uncharacteristic work to date, Irons was seriously disturbing in the difficult dual role of loony loverboy twin gynaecologists. But one must presume this was too kinky and nasty for middlebrow tastes.

Following *Reversal Of Fortune*, Jeremy Irons opted for his third thriller on the trot, taking the title role in *Kafka* (1991) the interesting but poorly received follow-up of *sex, lies and videotape* director Steven Soderbergh. With his first British production in some time – and the first film in which he starred with his wife – *Waterland* (1992), he was widely acknowledged to be the glue that held together the jigsaw pieces of a difficult work, delivering a profoundly moving portrayal of a man coming to terms with his long-suppressed, painful past.

1980 Nijinsky **1981** The French Lieutenant's Woman **1982** Moonlighting **1983** Betrayal; The Wild Duck **1984** Swann In Love **1986** The Mission **1987** Danny The Champion Of The World **1988** Dead Ringers; A Chorus Of Disapproval **1989** Australia **1990** Reversal Of Fortune **1992** Kafka; Waterland **1992/93** Damage; M. Butterfly

Irving, Amy

Actress

Born 10 September 1953

Palo Alto, California

Tall and pretty, with frizzy, light brown hair, Amy Irving projects an air of frailty offset by an underlying suggestion of robustness. The robustness came somewhat to the fore in what is, to date, her most rewarding screen role, that of the Jewish girl confronted with a matchmaker's choice of a pickle merchant (Peter Riegert) as a suitor in the romantic comedy *Crossing Delancey* (1988).

Born into a theatrical family – her mother is actress Priscilla Pointer, her brother David directs – Amy trained at San Francisco's American Conservatory Theatre and in London. She subsequently acted in the theatre, and continues to do so, winning an Obie award for her performance in the New York production of Athol Fugard's *The Road To Mecca* in 1988. She has also enjoyed a decent TV career, notably as the star of the internationally popular mini-series, *The Far Pavilions*, but her Hollywood career has proved somewhat more elusive.

She made her film debut, deceptively youthful at 23, as the most sympathetic of the schoolgirl plotters against Sissy Spacek's telekinetic loner in Brian De Palma's *Carrie* (1976): it is her wrist that the dead Carrie's hand reaches from the grave to grasp in the concluding nightmare sequence. She went on to make a feisty impression, again for De Palma, in *The Fury* 1978). This time, Amy was the young woman possessed of telekinetic powers, which she ultimately used to reduce John Cassavetes' arch-villain to smithereens. Amy Irving is probably most famous among the public at large for having married Steven Spielberg and for subsequently obtaining a gigantic settlement when the liaison ended in divorce. However, she was nominated for a Best Supporting Actress Oscar for her performance as Barbra Streisand's temporary 'wife' in *Yentl* (1983), in which she was both pretty and touching and, although her wealth meant she need never work again, it was to be hoped that she would continue to lend her fresh presence to feature films.

1978 Carrie **1979** The Fury; Voices **1980** Honeysuckle Rose **1989** The Competition **1983** Yentl **1984** Micki And Maude **1987** Rumpelstiltskin **1988** Crossing Delancey **1990** Show Of Force

Ivory, James

Director

Born 7 June 1928

Berkeley, California

If you are an *habitué* of drive-ins rather than arthouses and a devotee of 'stalk and slash' or 'tits and terror', it is unlikely that you will be familiar with the work of James Ivory. If, however, your taste runs to the studied evocation of exotic locations, literary adaptations handled with the greatest care and deliberation, understated actorly performances from such as Denholm Elliott and Maggie Smith, handsome young men palely loitering in late Victorian dusks and exquisitely tailored linen suits, and other discreetly insistent feats of *mise en scène*, then you will almost certainly pencil in the latest Ivory offering.

Elegant, modestly profitable and critically acclaimed, the best of Ivory's films are both admirable and agreeable, but the feeling lingers that they are the cinematic equivalent of those chain stores which specialise in carefully constructed retro-chic, selling reproduction William Morris wallpaper by the yard and discreetly distressed Victorian washstands by the dozen. In short, both products – the films and the washstands – exhibit an obtrusively tasteful diffidence which, after a time, can pall.

After studying fine art at the University of Oregon with the aim of becoming a set designer (a clue to his abiding eye for period detail), Ivory enrolled in the film department of the University of Southern California. He cut his teeth on a documentary made in Europe (*Venice: Theme And Variations*) and another in New York (*The Sword And The Flute*, based on an Indian miniature) before being commissioned in 1960 to make a documentary about India.

It was a significant event. Ivory remained in India for several years, forming a partnership with Indian producer Ismail Merchant, and the novelist Ruth Prawer Jhabvala, who had been born in Germany of Polish-Jewish descent and had married an Indian architect. They remain a remarkable trio: Ivory, the quietest of Americans; Jhabvala, the mysteriously reclusive cosmopolitan; and Merchant, the ebullient entrepreneur, charming backers off the trees and counting every penny of their modestly budgeted productions.

Their first collaboration was *The Householder* (1963), adapted by Jhabvala from her own novel and a touching story of a young couple's first months of marriage. *Shakespeare Wallah* (1965), the one that began to make Ivory's name, had an original screenplay by Jhabvala and was a delicate and funny portrait of a forgotten byway of British imperialism – a travelling theatre company – which embodied one of the recurring themes of their films, the contrast between the resources of Western and Eastern culture. Ivory's next two films, *The Guru* (1969) and *Bombay Talkie* (1970), reflected similar preoccupations but did not fully express his ability to divine the essence of place and depict eccentric characters without patronising them. He then returned to the USA to make his first American film, *Savages* (1972), an ambitious allegory about the birth and death of civilisation set in a deserted mansion in upstate New York.

The movie was a failure and its maker reverted to Indian themes the following year, before embarking on a disastrous venture with AIP, *The Wild Party* (1975), a period piece based loosely on the Fatty Arbuckle scandal which rocked Hollywood in the 20s. AIP's mangled final cut was disowned by Ivory, who thereafter decided to maintain his independence and steer well clear of the Hollywood mainstream. Subsequently, Merchant-Ivory productions have followed a similar pattern. They are shot on location with sizeable casts which skilfully combine well-known faces and newcomers, and rarely exceed a budget of $3 million. This paradox is made possible by Merchant's ceaseless fund-raising and the willingness of big names like Vanessa Redgrave and Christopher Reeve (*The Bostonians*, 1984) to work at reduced salaries plus percentage.

The late Lee Remick starred in *The Europeans* (1979), a meticulous adaptation of Henry James' tale of the invasion of a prim 19th-century New England family by two exotic foreign cousins. Its theme – an outsider's perceptions of an alien culture – runs through later Merchant-Ivory offerings. *Heat And Dust* (1983), adapted by Jhabvala from her prizewinning novel, explored the discovery of India by two Englishwomen (Julie Christie, Greta Scacchi) separated in time by more than 60 years. In their greatest critical and commercial success, the 1986 adaptation of E.M. Forster's *A Room With A View* (eight Oscar nominations and numerous other awards), a group of repressed northerners (British, of course) discover happy release when they take a draught from the warm beaker of the South (Italy). In *Maurice* (1987), based on Forster's anguished tale of homosexual love, written in 1941 but withheld from publication until 1971, well-bred Oxford undergraduate James Wilby finds comfort in the arms of a gamekeeper in a closet variation of *Lady Chatterley*. Then it was back to America, unsuccessfully again, for *Slaves Of New York* (1989), adapted from Tama Janowitz's best-selling book. It had its moments, but the director of fine period pieces was clearly less at ease with youthful New York society of the early 80s.

James Ivory has observed that, 'People have to face up to what they are and devise some way of living in a happy and dignified way with themselves.' This, precisely, is one of the themes of *Mr And Mrs Bridge* (1990), brilliantly starring Paul Newman and Joanne Woodward as an Establishment couple growing old together in the American Midwest. It's a charming film, with which James Ivory was clearly more comfortable than that of Miss Janowitz's milieu, but, nonetheless, together with his formidable writer and producer, it was followed by a return to the fertile ground of E.M. Forster (*Howards End*) which has served them so well.

In August, 1992, a deal was announced between Merchant-Ivory and unlikely bedfellows Disney Studios. The *New York Times* characterised the proposed partnership as 'relentlessly commercial versus relentlessly highbrow', under the terms of which Disney would provide substantial finance for the pair, and guarantee them total creative control – on films costing less than a very modest $12 million.

1963 The Householder **1965** Shakespeare Wallah **1969** The Guru **1970** Bombay Talkie **1972** Savages **1973** Helen – Queen Of The Nautch Girls; Mahatma And The Mad Boy **1975** The Wild Party **1976** Sweet Sounds **1977** Roseland **1979** The Europeans **1981** Quartet; Jane Austen In Manhattan **1983** Heat And Dust **1984** The Bostonians **1986** A Room With A View **1987** Maurice **1989** Slaves Of New York **1990** Mr And Mrs Bridge **1992** Howards End **1992/93** Remains Of The Day

J

Jackson, Glenda

Actress
Born 9 May 1936
Lancashire, England

Scrubbed, unvarnished, and sometimes distinctly harsh in character, Glenda Jackson is one of the post-war era's most obstinately truthful actresses, in the theatre (her first home) and on film equally. These characteristics are, of course, a reflection of her own off-stage and off-screen personality and convictions, which are strongly held, always forcefully expressed, and intentionally lacking in glamour; and they are supported by a formidable arsenal of technical accomplishments (her voice, fascinatingly low in pitch, is a powerful instrument capable of the most subtle variations of timbre, and her ugly-but-striking looks and unremarkable physique serve her as a canvas on which to paint an extraordinarily wide range of complex emotions).

Herein lies the secret of some of her finest achievements: as, for instance, Gudrun in Ken Russell's 1969 adaptation of the D.H. Lawrence novel *Women In Love* (the film which won her the first of two Best Actress Oscars), a blunt-tongued, blunt-featured Nottinghamshire heroine blazingly alive to the extremes of passion, searing in moments of cruelty and hatred toward Oliver Reed's uncomprehending bull of a Gerald. At other times, however, she has shown uncertain taste in her choice of projects (comedies included) or else her actual portrayals (in *The Music Lovers* 1971, her second collaboration with Russell, it was no doubt the plethora of directorial excesses that pushed her into self-caricature as the unstable nymphomaniac wife of the homosexual Tchaikovsky). Where another actor or actress of similar stature might through technical sleights-of-hand attempt to disguise discomfort with the basic material, it seems to be almost an article of faith with her not to play tricks of prettification or concealment on the watching public. One may even hazard a guess that this remarkable woman – a 'rather glum tigress', one film-writer in the London *Guardian* called her – has become impatient with the whole overblown business of cinema; in the 1980s she allowed her film career to tail off to almost nothing, devoting herself instead to the spoken theatre and British politics.

The daughter of a bricklayer, she was raised in a strict North Country Presbyterian household, and left school at the age of 16 with the aim of becoming an actress. After study at the London Royal Academy of Dramatic Art in the early 50s she spent a hard but crucially formative decade in provincial British repertory theatres, supporting herself between plays as, among other things, an assistant in Boots, the chain of pharmacies. Her big break came from Peter Brook, who cast her first in his 1964 'Theatre Of Cruelty' revue and then as Charlotte Corday in his famous theatre staging, subsequently filmed, of Peter Weiss' play *The Persecution And Assassination Of Jean-Paul Marat As Performed By The Inmates Of Charenton Under The Direction Of The Marquis De Sade* (*Marat/Sade* for short). From here to the two Ken Russell films was a short step; but soon after all this unbuttoned (indeed, unclothed) extremism, and a shrewish Elizabeth I opposite Vanessa Redgrave in the lifeless *Mary Queen Of Scots* (1971), came a welcome enlargement of range in the form of John Schlesinger's *Sunday, Bloody Sunday* the same year and then *A Touch Of Class* (1973), her first American film. The former, about a young bisexual (Murray Head) involved in an emotional triangle whose other points are a Jewish doctor (Peter Finch) and a businesswoman (Jackson), showed that she could underplay with grace and even tenderness; the latter, a minor but pleasant comedy of romantic manners, struck surprising sparks from her partnership with George Segal, and won her a second Oscar.

Little that she has tackled since then – a disappointing pairing with Michael Caine in Losey's mannered *The Romantic Englishwoman* (1975), off-key comedy collaborations with Walther Matthau (*House Calls*, 1978) and, again, George Segal (*Lost And Found*, 1979), a preposterous cigar-chewing fixer in Robert Altman's bungled satire *Health* (1979) – has proved worthy of her. *Stevie* (1978), an affectionate portrait of the eccentric English poet Stevie Smith, was one of the exceptions to that rule; and in *Business As Usual* (1987), an unsubtle British drama about workers' rights in a Liverpool dress shop, she at least threw all her convictions into the subject. Significantly, this last and the 1989 *Doombeach*, an 'ecological' drama funded by the Children's Film Unit, were among her few cinema ventures of the 1980s.

In April, 1992, Jackson, a passionate and articulate member of the Labour Party, was elected Member of Parliament for Hampstead and took her seat in the House of Commons.

1966 Marat/Sade **1968** Tell Me Lies; Negatives **1969** Women In Love **1971** The Music Lovers; Sunday, Bloody Sunday; Mary, Queen of Scots; The Boy Friend **1973** Triple Echo; A Bequest To The Nation aka The Nelson Affair; A Touch Of Class **1974** The Maids **1975** The Romantic Englishwoman; The Devil Is A Woman; Hedda **1976** The Incredible Sarah; Nasty Habits **1978** House Calls; Stevie; The Class Of Miss MacMichael **1979** Lost And Found; Health **1980** Hopscotch **1987** Business As Usual; Salome's Last Dance **1989** Doombeach; The Rainbow

Jaglom, Henry

Director, actor
Born 26 January 1943
London, England

Admirers of Henry Jaglom's films point to the fact that he is one of the rare 'autobiographical' film-makers working in America, building stories out of his own personal life-crises, notably divorce and its aftermath. These are explored in films from *Can She Bake A Cherry Pie?* (1983) through *A Lonely Ride* (1984), and *Always* (1985), up to *Someone To Love* (1987) and beyond. Yet his detractors would reply this is so much self-indulgence. Jaglom has gone on record saying (in answer to a questionnaire) 'I am the quintessential expression of the 60s', and with that, it has to be admitted, goes a certain extreme tendency to examine his navel. The proof of the pudding (or the cherry pie) is in the eating: his films are formless and crudely made. They lack savour and variety of colour. Much of the dialogue is improvised, but instead of that leading (as it does in film-makers like Robert Altman or the late Jean Eustache) to genuinely dangerous and unforeseen communication between the actors, it tends to peter out in whimsy and maudlin hippy 'mateyness'. His films show the vice of extreme tolerance – an inability to focus on anything with a moral passion; to distinguish, in life, between the interesting and the banal.

It has to be said: Jaglom is a bit of a fraud. His long association with Orson Welles is riddled with uncertainty and equivocation. He claimed he was Welles' lifeline in his latter years. But others saw him more as a parasite, battening on the old man's prestige while futilely organising projects that could never in the nature of things have come off. It is a sad story in certain respects. Nonetheless, his films do have their moments. *Sitting Ducks* (1978) – perhaps his best known – has the lovely actress Patrice Townsend, who lights up every scene she is in; yet in the end she is thrown away mercilessly by the ineptitude of the movie.

Jaglom grew up in Manhattan, where his family had moved from England. He studied acting, writing and directing at the University of Pennsylvania; he also attended the Actors' Studio and took classes with Lee Strasberg. He had parts in some off-Broadway plays before moving to California where he appeared in TV series such as *Gidget* and *The Flying Nun*. During the Six Day War in Israel he started making a documentary which he subsequently converted into a three-hour silent movie. His first association with serious cinema was as an actor: indeed, he has kept this up and regularly appears in his own films, without however managing to generate anything of the necessary power of objectivity given to greater talents like Orson Welles or Woody Allen. Actually, his soft, emollient features are part of these films' irritating narcissism.

He was assistant editor on *Easy Rider*, and edited his debut movie as director, *A Safe Place*.

1968 Psych-out (actor only) **1969** The Thousand Plane Raid (actor only) **1971** Drive, He Said (actor only); The Last Movie (actor only); A Safe Place (w/d) **1972** The Other Side Of the Wind (actor only) **1977** Tracks (w/d) **1979** Sitting Ducks (w/d, also actor) 1982 National Lampoon's Movie Madness (co-director only) **1983** Can She Bake A Cherry Pie? (w/d) **1984** A Lovely Ride (w/d) **1985** Always (w/d, also actor) **1987** Someone To Love (w/d, also actor) **1989** New Year's Day (w/d) **1990** Eating (w/d) **1993** Venice/Venice (w/d)

Jarmusch, Jim

Director, writer
Born 22 January 1954
Akron, Ohio

When Jim Jarmusch went to Paris in the early 70s, he was under the influence of beat writers like Allen Ginsberg, Jack Kerouac and William Burroughs, and his ambition was to be a poet. But his discovery of the treasures of the Cinémathèque Francaise changed his perspective on life. After taking a BA at Columbia University, he became teaching assistant to director Nicholas Ray at New York University Graduate Film School. Sadly, his mentor died before Jarmusch shot his first picture, *Permanent Vacation* (1982), in 16mm at a cost of $12,000. It was about an alienated youth (played by 16-year-old punk Chris Parker) who wanders the deserted New York streets, meeting a variety of people including sax player John Lurie. The film already contained some of the director's hallmarks: off-the-wall humour, minimalist camerawork, and a loose screenplay constructed of a series of episodes, in which an outsider moves through an alien environment.

Laurie, a musician of Lounge Lizards fame, had the leading role in *Stranger Than Paradise* (1984), playing reluctant host to his young female cousin who has arrived in America from Hungary. The black-and-white film, which cost $150,000, was a revelation, and Jarmusch immediately established himself as a new *auteur* on the American scene. Ironic and laconic, and shot in static long takes; the film conjured up a view of the USA rarely seen by native directors. The observational style was influenced by Japanese cinema, and the sensibilities seemed closer to Europe than America.

Down By Law (1986) also had a foreign innocent confronted by American cynicism. The Italian Roberto Benigni meets up with John Lurie and Tom Waits in a New Orleans jail, and leads them to freedom. Without being camp or cinéphilic, Jarmusch's humorous and poignant picture made pointed reference to prison movies and *films noirs*. It opens with right-to-left/left-to-right tracking shots cut together to a song by Tom Waits, filmed by Robby Müller, the favourite cameraman of Wim Wenders, a director with whom Jarmusch has been compared. Although their restless wandering heroes have much in common, Jarmusch is far more abstemious with his camera, which seldom moves unless the characters do.

Just as *Down By Law* made New Orleans look less than enticing, *Mystery Train* (1989), Jarmusch's first colour film, presented Memphis as a crummy town, the background to three stories which cleverly take place simultaneously, all of them in and around a dump of a hotel. The first is a touching and comic study of two young Japanese tourists, but the second, concerning an Italian girl who sees Elvis Presley's ghost, and the third which tells of an Englishman on the run after shooting a liquor-store owner, are rather hollow. Linking the episodes are Screamin' Jay Hawkins, whose 'I Put A Spell On You' featured prominently in *Stranger Than Paradise*, and Cinqué Lee (Spike Lee's brother) as the Arcade Hotel's night clerk and bellboy, their performances enriching the film.

Night On Earth (1992) took a similar premise even further, with the globe itself a cosmic backdrop for five simultaneously occurring short tales set in taxis in LA, New York, Paris, Rome and Helsinki. With an international cast (Winona Ryder, Gena Rowlands, Armin Mueller-Stahl, Béatrice Dalle, Giancarlo Esposito, Roberto Benigni) playing out random encounters of varied mood as cab drivers and their fares, the film exploited its writer-director's offbeat hip sensibilities to the full. On the evidence of only a handful of movies, Jim Jarmusch can make claim to being among the few original American directors to have emerged in the 80s.

1982 Permanent Vacation (w/d) **1984** Stranger Than Paradise (w/d) **1986** Down By Law (w/d) **1989** Mystery Train (w/d) **1992** Night On Earth (w/d)

Jason Leigh, Jennifer

Actress

Born 1962

Los Angeles, California

Jennifer Jason Leigh had been in films for almost a decade before she made a name for herself in *Last Exit To Brooklyn* (1990), as the hard-as-nails peroxide blonde female hustler whose heart has been ripped out by the spiritual and material poverty of her existence. She had laid down the markers for the role in Randal Kleiser's fairly dreadful film *Grandview USA* (1984), in which she impressed as a faithless wife, similarly peroxided, deserting husband Patrick Swayze for the dubious arms of an ageing Troy Donahue.

But Jason Leigh has a somewhat Jekyll-and-Hyde screen persona. Her first prominent role, in the seminal teen movie *Fast Times At Ridgemont High* (1982), unveiled her as a mousy haired, sweet-faced, slightly chubby girl who gets herself pregnant by a heel but keeps on believing in true love; in *The Hitcher* (1986) she was still mousy, but slimmed down and grown up a little. She brought warmth, conviction and a splendid Southern accent to the diner waitress who tries to help C. Thomas Howell escape from Rutger Hauer's psychotic clutches, only to fall victim herself, and was delightful in Christopher Guest's charming and gentle send-up of the movie industry, *The Big Picture* (1989).

The daughter of actor Vic Morrow (tragically killed while filming *Blue Thunder*), and TV writer Barbara Turner, Jennifer studied at LA Valley College, where she won the school's best actress award for her performance in the stage play *The Shadow Box* in 1979. She has made a few appearances in TV movies but, not surprisingly since her powerful performance in *Last Exit*, the demand for her services in Hollywood began to show a sharp increase, and she shared billing with Alec Baldwin and Fred Ward in *Miami Blues* (1990). She then got to have a sex scene – atop a fire engine – with another Baldwin (William) in *Backdraft*, before delivering a harrowing portrayal of a drug-addicted undercover policewoman in *Rush* (1991), and an impressive performance in *Single White Female* (1992).

1981 Eyes Of A Stranger **1982** Fast Times At Ridgemont High; Wrong Is Right **1983** Easy Money **1984** Grandview USA **1985** Flesh And Blood **1986** The Men's Club; The Hitcher **1987** Under Cover **1988** Sister, Sister **1989** Heart Of Midnight; The Big Picture **1990** Last Exit To Brooklyn; Miami Blues **1991** Backdraft; Crooked Hearts **1991** Rush **1992** Single White Female **1993** Short Cuts; The Hudsucker Proxy

Jewison, Norman

Director
Born 21 July 1921
Toronto, Canada

Norman Jewison is probably the best known of the Canadian film directors, operating for the major part of his career from a Hollywood base, making films – to the extent that they are high-grade (and high-gloss) entertainment – of international appeal. Still, Canada is important to him: he returned to live there in 1979 after an absence of 19 years divided between Hollywood and London, and was honoured by his government which made him Officer of the Order of Canada (Canada's highest civilian decoration) in 1982. While happy in his own career to keep up links with Hollywood (a seven-picture deal with Warners, for example), he has declared himself anxious that Canada continue to be a distinctive presence on the world film map. In 1986, he founded the Canadian Centre for Advanced Film Studies to encourage young film-makers and native film scholars. As a producer, he has also been active in the US, giving, for example, his editor Hal Ashby his first directing opportunity with *The Landlord* (1970). He is very much an 'important personage', a returning hero, on his home patch – as befits a director whose movies have garnered nine Academy Awards and no fewer than 30 Oscar nominations.

His career began, like that of so many other film-makers of his generation, in television. Educated at the University of Toronto, he worked, after a brief overseas stint with the BBC, as a drama director with the Canadian Broadcasting Corporation between 1953 and 1958, before moving to the United States where he specialised in one-off celebrity shows centred on entertainment personalities like Judy Garland, Danny Kaye and Harry Belafonte. (Three Emmy awards came out of this stage of his career.) His early shots at feature films were all more or less undistinguished comedies. It wasn't until his fifth effort, *The Cincinnati Kid* (1965), starring Steve McQueen and Tuesday Weld, that he began to be noticed by a wide audience. He followed this film up with the cumbrously titled but in fact amusing comedy, *The Russians Are Coming, The Russians Are Coming* (1966); and then the first of his major hits, a double Academy Award winner (Best Picture and – in Rod Steiger – Best Actor) *In The Heat Of The Night* (1967), about racial bigotry in a steamy Southern town.

Thereafter (and with the tremendous commercial success of *The Thomas Crown Affair* a year later), he has had a string of pictures, an average of nearly one every year, which can be divided roughly speaking between pure entertainments (*The Thomas Crown Affair*, 1968, *Jesus Christ Superstar*, 1973, *Fiddler On The Roof*, 1971), and more 'serious' films that come across with a strong liberal message (*F.I.S.T.* 1978, . . . *And Justice For All* 1979, *A Soldier's Story*, 1984, *Agnes Of God*, 1985). But it is the serious films which sometimes present a problem for the critic. Jewison clearly has deeply felt political and intellectual pretensions, but not always the rigour to give them the biting edge or coherent centre they require. Thus, films such as . . . *And Justice For All*, in which Al Pacino plays a DA whose integrity is at odds with the system, call forth accusations of speciousness; while the faintly apocalyptic vision of *Rollerball* (1975) doesn't quite come off.

Yet Jewison himself is graciously unpretentious: 'I'm just a storyteller', he claims. He likes films that have 'a beginning, a middle and an end'. He is not afraid of sentiment, or even sentimentality. *Fiddler On The Roof* is schmaltz, but the best quality on offer. For the successful comedy-romance *Moonstruck* (1987), starring Cher and Nicolas Cage, he wanted to resurrect the idea of a modern fairy-tale of love at first sight in the manner of Lubitsch, Capra or Sturges. Happiness, unfashionably, is important to him: each character, in the same film, was designed to have his or her moment of glory (or 'glow' as Jewison puts it) like soloists in an orchestra. Such humanism is essential and can reconcile the viewer to quite large sections of banal or uninspired *mise-en-scène*. Characters, in Jewison films, never quite cease being actors, and this is finally a limitation of his art. No matter: his record speaks for itself, an honourable effort to provide high-grade entertainment over a period of 25 years. Few directors have demonstrated such stamina or cheerfulness.

1963 Forty Pounds Of Trouble; The Thrill Of It All **1964** Send Me No Flowers **1965** The Art Of Love; The Cincinnati Kid **1966** The Russians Are Coming, The Russians Are Coming **1967** In The Heat Of The Night **1968** The Thomas Crown Affair **1969** Gaily Gaily **1971** Fiddler On The Roof **1973** Jesus Christ Superstar **1975** Rollerball **1978** F.I.S.T. **1979** . . . And Justice For All **1982** Best Friends **1984** Soldier's Story **1985** Agnes Of God **1987** Moonstruck **1989** In Country **1991** Other People's Money

Johnson, Don

Actor
Born 15 December 1950
Flatt Creek, Missouri

Despite some attractive work and his celebrated 'drop-dead gorgeous' looks, Don Johnson seems fated never to regain via the big screen the widespread popularity and heart-throb status he enjoyed from the long-running television series *Miami Vice*, in which his police detective Sonny Crockett was impossibly swoonsome dressed in pastel Armani threads and commanding the steering wheel of a Porsche or Ferrari. It is slightly mystifying that, unlike other TV heroes of the 80s – Bruce Willis, Tom Selleck, Ted Danson – Johnson should have had so little luck in feature films, particularly since he has been striving for it since his teens.

Johnson made his film debut at the age of 16 in an all-but-forgotten piece called *Good Morning . . . And Goodbye* (1967). As a well-set-up youth with long blonde hair he was the archetypal late 60s California Boy and was cast as druggy, sexy, reckless-driving youths in the odd trippy flick or hip college picture. Among the more noteworthy of these curiosities is the distinctly off-beat rock Western *Zachariah* (1971) and the sex, truths and university tale *The Harrad Experiment* (1973), which co-starred Tippi Hedren and provided her daughter, a 14-year-old Melanie Griffith, with a day's work as an extra. Even in Hollywood the subsequent liaison between the 22-year-old Johnson and the teenybopper caused 'tsks' and unease, but the relationship in this Phase One was surprisingly long-lived, culminating in a brief young marriage. Meanwhile the actor starred in a sci-fi satire ignored on release but loved by a small cult, the adaptation of a popular Harlan Ellison novella, *A Boy And His Dog* (1975), in which Johnson's post-nuclear holocaust survivor scavenged sustenance and sexual partners thanks to his clever, telepathic mutt. His film career completely stalled after *Return To Macon County* (1975), notable only as the film debut of Nick Nolte, who was soon to be a star.

Television work was more consistent, with several TV movies added to Johnson's credits, along with some theatre roles, before *Miami Vice* shot him to prominence. Among his better roles was that of a haunted Vietnam veteran in the earnest drama *Cease Fire* (1984), while on TV he was suitably smouldering in the role that made Paul Newman a screen star, as the incendiary drifter in *The Long Hot Summer*. Since the end of *Miami Vice* and his remarriage to Melanie Griffith, Don Johnson has proved appealing on screen, but unfortunate in his choice of vehicles. He and co-star Susan Sarandon were delights in the comedy drama *Sweet Heart's Dance* (1988) but the script was frankly tedious, while *Dead Bang* (1989) was merely more unpleasant than most cop action thrillers and Dennis Hopper's *noir*ish *The Hot Spot* (1990) went awry. Fast approaching the age of no return, Johnson sought to develop a project in which he and Griffith would co-star, but *Paradise* (1991), although a fine, well-acted film, did not find favour at the box-office. Still looking for a formula that would click for them, the couple embarked on a remake of *Born Yesterday*, with Griffith recreating the late

Judy Holliday's unlettered moll, Johnson as her tutor (originally played by the late William Holden) and John Goodman as the uncouth sugar daddy.

1967 Good Morning. . . . And Goodbye **1970** The Magic Garden Of Stanley Sweetheart **1971** Zachariah **1973** The Harrad Experiment **1975** A Boy And His Dog; Return To Macon County **1982** Melanie; Soggy Bottom, USA **1984** Cease Fire **1988** Sweet Heart's Dance **1989** Dead Bang **1990** The Hot Spot **1991** Harley Davidson And The Marlboro Man; Paradise **1992/93** Born Yesterday **1993** Beyond Innocence

Jones, James Earl

Actor
Born 17 January 1931
Arkabutla, Mississippi

A formidable black actor whose girth and resonant, bassy voice have sometimes threatened to overshadow his range, James Earl Jones has worked steadily in both film and theatre to considerable acclaim.

Jones' father was a prizefighter turned actor. He raised his son in Michigan, where James Earl attended University and graduated in drama. His professional stage debut came in 1957, off-Broadway, and he soon came to prominence as a classical actor in New York Shakespeare Festival productions, including *Othello* in 1964. That same year he made his screen debut in Stanley Kubrick's devastating film, *Dr Strangelove* (he was one of Slim Pickens' flight crew). He concentrated on the theatre however, where quality work was more forthcoming, and in 1969 he won a Tony for the performance that made his name, as heavyweight champion Jack Jefferson in *The Great White Hope*. A film version followed in 1970, directed by Martin Ritt, with Jones and Jane Alexander, as his white mistress, repeating their stage roles. It was an important part for Jones, and he played it with power and conviction. He was nominated for an Academy Award and won the Golden Globe.

Despite this success the actor remained at a remove from Hollywood, lending his weighty voice to the documentaries *King* (1970) and *Malcolm X* (1972), but participating in only a handful of features. Joseph Sargent's *The Man* (1972) was originally made for television but got a theatrical release. In the title role, Jones was a black senator who becomes President of the United States when a freak accident removes the chief executive. It is more interesting as a side note than as a film. *Claudine* (1974) was a moderately realistic comedy about the romance between garbage-man Jones and mother-of-six Diahann Carroll, but director John Berry short-changed the material's more serious edge.

In 1976, he mounted his first sustained campaign on Hollywood, more than doubling his film credits in just two years. He appeared in as many failures as hits; among the former, *Swashbuckler* (1976) and *Exorcist II: The Heretic* (1977) were particularly ill-advised; of the successes, *The River Niger* (1976) was an intelligent look at black family life, and *Star Wars* (1977) was a box-office smash to which Jones contributed the voice of Darth Vader. Somewhere in between came *The Bingo Long Traveling All-Stars And Motor Kings* (1976), a lively comic look at the black baseball scene in the late 30s, with Billy Dee Williams and Richard Pryor, and *A Piece Of The Action* (1977) with Bill Cosby and Sidney Poitier, who also directed.

On stage, James Earl Jones continued to do good work. He won another Tony award in 1987 for his powerhouse performance as a frustrated baseball player in August Wilson's *Fences*, but when he returned to Hollywood in the mid-80s it was with a similar confusion of indiscriminate workaday jobs and occasional challenging films. He seemed content to bluster his way through too many of them (*Conan The Barbarian* 1983; *Allan Quatermain And The Lost City Of Gold* 1987; *Best Of The Best* 1989), though he impressed in Francis Ford Coppola's *Gardens Of Stone* (1987), and as the Salinger-like author in *Field of Dreams* (1989) – probably his most subtle, gentle performance of the decade.

1964 Dr Strangelove **1967** The Comedians **1970** King (doc); End Of The Road; The Great White Hope **1972** Malcolm X (narration); The Man **1974** Claudine **1976** Deadly Hero; The River Niger; The Bingo Long Traveling All-Stars And Motor Kings; Swashbuckler **1977** The Greatest; Exorcist II: The Heretic; The Last Remake Of Beau Geste; Star Wars (voice only); A Piece Of The Action **1989** The Bushido Blade **1982** Blood Tide **1983** Conan The Barbarian **1985** City Limits **1986** Soul Man; My Little Girl **1987** Allan Quatermain And The Lost City of Gold; Gardens Of Stone; Matewan **1988** Coming To America **1989** Three Fugitives; Field Of Dreams; Best Of The Best **1989** The Ambulance **1990** The Hunt For Red October; Grim Prairie Tales **1991** Scorchers; True Identity; Convicts **1992** Patriot Games; Excessive Force **1992/93** The Meteor Man; Somersby

Jones, Tommy Lee

Actor
Born 15 September 1946
San Saba, Texas

Highly intelligent and reflective, with a brooding machismo that often comes across as a dark refraction of the good ol' boy mentality, Tommy Lee Jones makes both a convincing villain and a credible hero. His background is similarly contradictory, with the young Jones working on oil fields before studying acting at Harvard where he was taking a degree in English. Following a small role in *Love Story* (1970) and some harrowing stage work, he started to scrabble his way up to larger film roles, but despite a couple of classic exploitation movies and a superb performance as the pushy but vulnerable husband to Loretta Lynn (Sissy Spacek) in *Coal Miner's Daughter* (1980), it is for two highly acclaimed TV dramas – subsequently released theatrically – that he became best known.

As *The Amazing Howard Hughes* (1977) he made a convincing transformation from dashing but insufferable egomaniac to haggard, paranoid eccentric; but it was as murderer Gary Gilmore, a role originally intended for Clint Eastwood, in Norman Mailer's *The Executioner's Song* (1982) that he found his most electrifying role. Jones was at once chilling and tragic as he drifted between redemption – in the form of Christianity, Buddhism, love and his crusade for the death penalty for his crimes – and damnation, catching the very soul of a wasted and aimless life.

He continually proved less lucky with his film roles – curiously cast as a romantic lead in the Harold Robbins melodrama *The Betsy* (1978) and a swashbuckling adventurer in *Nate And Hayes* (1983) – often appearing in movies with strong female characters but finding himself relegated to supporting parts that promised much but squandered his talents; both his American mobster expanding into the UK in *Stormy Monday* (1988) and his assassin in *The Package* (1989), though impressively menacing and hinting at darker things, are thrown away by writers. Jones constantly distinguishes the films he appears in, and won Academy recognition with a nomination for his outstanding performance as enigmatic, alleged conspirator Clay Shaw in *JFK* (1991). But he remains at his best in the more prestigious TV work (such as *Lonesome Dove*, and *Cat On A Hot Tin Roof* opposite Jessica Lange) that allows him fully developed roles.

1970 Love Story **1973** Life Study **1975** Elizah's Horoscope **1976** Jackson County Jail **1977** Rolling Thunder; The Amazing Howard Hughes **1978** The Eyes of Laura Mars; The Betsy **1980** Coal Miner's Daughter **1981** Back Roads **1982** The Executioner's Song **1983** Nate And Hayes aka Savage Islands **1984** The River Rat **1986** Black Moon Rising **1987** The Big Town **1988** Stormy Monday **1989** The Dead Can't Lie aka Gotham; The Package **1990** Wings Of The Apache aka Firebirds **1991** JFK **1992** Blue Sky; Under Siege **1992/93** House Of Cards **1993** Heaven And Earth

Julia, Raul

Actor
Born 9 March 1940
San Juan, Puerto Rico

Educated at the University of Puerto Rico, Raul Julia spent much of his early working life in theatre and television before Hollywood's awareness of the growing native Hispanic audience helped boost his movie career in the mid-80s. Studying theatre with Wynn Handman in the US, he made his New York debut in a Spanish play in 1964 and two years later began his long and fruitful association with Joseph Papp and the New York Shakespeare Festival. Despite making his movie debut in 1971 with the last of Sidney Poitier's Mr Tibbs movies, *The Organization*, followed by Jerry Schatzberg's *Panic In Needle Park*, it was five years before he returned to the big screen, and it was left to theatre and TV to build his reputation – Shakespeare by night, *Sesame Street* by day.

Several Tony nominations for his work in Broadway musicals such as *Nine* and *The Threepenny Opera* marked the end of his leaner days (and looks) and he came to the attention of Francis Ford Coppola who had bought a studio and was looking for stars for his ill-fated Zoetrope stock company. Pairing Julia with Teri Garr, Coppola tried to make him a revisionist Latin lover for the 80s in the over-produced *One From The Heart* (1982), but he was much more interesting as the Mayor's borderline psychotic son in Caleb Deschanel's muddled *The Escape Artist* the same year. Wearing his moments of calm and normality like a suit that he's unable to decide whether he likes or not, and changing his mood as often as the film changes tone, his performance showed the first warning signs of his tendency towards ham that became increasingly noticeable after his angry performance in *Kiss Of The Spider Woman* (1985) propelled him to below-the-line stardom (his billing is usually just after the title or as a prominant 'and').

This broad overplaying, though frequently proving fatal in the actor's attempts at screen comedy, is often not without its compensations – it at once ruins the careful mood of the first two-thirds of *Tequila Sunrise* (1988), yet it increasingly becomes the only thing worth watching as the script self-destructs. But Raul Julia, smooth, handsome and deeply Latin, is at his best when underplaying in drama, as in *Presumed Innocent* or *Havana* (both 1990), where he is able to give the impression of restrained power and passion without throwing it away with mannered eruptions. Although he carried the title role of the ill-fated archbishop *Romero* (1989) with force and dignity, and was amusingly hammy as the head of *The Addams Family* in 1991, it seemed that he would continue, on screen at least, to find his best opportunities in good supporting roles.

1971 The Organization; Panic in Needle Park **1976** The Gumball Rally **1977** Been Down So Long It Looks Like Up To Me **1978** Eyes Of Laura Mars **1982** One From The Heart; The Escape Artist; Tempest **1985** Compromising Positions; Kiss of the Spider Woman **1986** The Morning After **1988** The Penitent; Moon Over Parador; Tequila Sunrise; Trading Hearts; Tango Bar (Argentina) **1989** Mack the Knife aka The Threepenny Opera; Romero **1990** Presumed Innocent; Havana; The Rookie; Frankenstein Unbound **1991** The Addams Family **1992/93** The Plague/La Peste (GB/France/Argentina)

K

Kahn, Madeline

Actress
Born 29 September 1942
Boston, Massachusetts

Although she considers herself an actress rather than a comedienne it is for her delightful and distinctive comic talent that redheaded Madeline Kahn became best known. Her name might not be a household word, but few could forget her hilarious performance as the Dietrich-like café singer Lili Von Shtupp in Mel Brooks' outrageous Western spoof, *Blazing Saddles* (1974), or her portrayal of an uptight, peevish fiancée to Ryan O'Neal in the screwball comedy *What's Up Doc*? (1972).

Comedy, however, is but one of her artistic gifts. A trained opera singer – she studied music and drama at Hofstra University – the Boston-born Kahn embarked on a career in nightclubs and musicals, making her Broadway debut in the revue *Faces Of 1968*. Her appearance in the classic Ingmar Bergman parody short, *The Dove*, notwithstanding, Kahn made her feature film debut in Peter Bogdanovich's *What's Up Doc?* and was duly rewarded for her efforts when the director cast her in his subsequent movie, *Paper Moon* (1974). Co-starring once again with Ryan O'Neal, she received a Best Supporting Actress Oscar nomination for her funny-painful performance as the carnival dancer Trixie Delight, desperately in search of a man to love her.

Thus established, Kahn, with her shrewish voice and a face that alternates between vampish and deceptively vacant, successfully graced many 70s comedy hits, most memorably as a Mel Brooks 'regular' (alongside such other comedians as Gene Wilder, Dom DeLuise and Marty Feldman) in films like *Blazing Saddles* (for which she received her second Oscar nomination), *Young Frankenstein* (1974) and *High Anxiety* (1978). Even her appearance in less effective features like the Gene Wilder-directed *The Adventure of Sherlock Holmes' Smarter Brother* and the Bogdanovich musical flop *At Long Last Love* (both 1975) gave her the chance to display her considerable singing talents on screen. However, the 80s proved a different story, with a succession of comedies ranging from the merely so-so (*Simon*, 1980, *Clue*, 1985) to the truly inept (*Wholly Moses*!, 1980, *Yellowbeard*, 1983). Disappearing from the big screen for the last half of the decade, the actress made a welcome, if enforcedly somewhat low-key comeback as the mother of the bride in Alan Alda's otherwise disappointing *Betsy's Wedding* (1990).

But however indifferently used on the big screen after the 70s, she found challenging work elsewhere. Aside from various appearances in television specials and movies – one of which, *Wanted: The Perfect Guy* (1986), brought her an Emmy Award – she starred in her own programme, *Oh Madeline* (1983–84) and played opposite George C. Scott in the series *Mr President* (1987–88). She has also performed in such operas as *La Bohème* for the Washington Opera Society and *Candide* for the New York Philarmonic. Most satisfying however, has been her stage career. As long ago as 1973 she proved her versatility in a Tony and Drama Desk Award-nominated dramatic role in David Rabe's *In the Boom Boom Room*, and in 1978 she received her second Tony nomination for her performance as a quirky movie queen in the musical *On the Twentieth Century*. More recently, she was nominated for the third time for her star turn in the Broadway revival of *Born Yesterday* (1989), in the role immortalised by Judy Holliday – the comedienne Madeline Kahn perhaps most closely resembles.

1972 What's Up Doc? **1973** Paper Moon **1974** Blazing Saddles; Young Frankenstein **1975** At Long Last Love; The Adventure of Sherlock Holmes' Smarter Brother **1976** Won Ton Ton – The Dog Who Saved Hollywood **1977** High Anxiety **1978** The Cheap Detective **1979** The Muppet Movie **1980** Simon; First Family; Happy Birthday, Gemini; Wholly Moses! **1981** History of the World, Part 1 **1983** Yellowbeard **1984** City Heat; Slapstick of Another Kind **1985** Clue **1990** Betsy's Wedding

Kane, Carol

Actress
Born 18 June 1952
Cleveland, Ohio

With her large, dark-rimmed eyes set in a pale, Pre-Raphaelite face, Carol Kane was perfectly cast as Gitl, the young Yiddish-speaking Jewish girl from 'the old country' adapting to the American way of life in

Hester Street (1974). This intelligent and gentle story, set in New York at the turn of the century and directed by Joan Micklin Silver, centred upon the blossoming of the wan and shy wife, who gradually divests herself of her strict orthodox upbringing and learns English and a certain independence. Kane received an Oscar nomination for the role that has remained her best to date.

Educated at the Professional Childrens' School, New York, Kane began a stage career in her teens, making her Broadway debut as a schoolgirl in *The Prime Of Miss Jean Brodie*. On film, she was first noticed in *The Last Detail* (1973), as a touching young prostitute who has an encounter with Jack Nicholson. In *Annie Hall* (1977), she played the small but memorable part of Allison Porshnik, a political activist whom Woody Allen meets at an Adlai Stevenson fundraiser. She makes him so political that he can't sleep with her for trying to sort out the Kennedy conspiracy possibilities. In the same year, she had a role in Ken Russell's *Valentino*, and, coincidentally, played Gene Wilder's wife with an obsession with Rudolph Valentino in *The World's Greatest Lover*.

Her slightly off-beat looks and humour were given a further chance to shine in *The Mafu Cage* (1978), in which she played a dotty girl incestuously in love with her doting older sister (Lee Grant) and dead father. However, leading roles became thin on the ground, though she continued to make a few brief but welcome appearances in a number of films, including the raucous Jewish comedy *Over The Brooklyn Bridge* (1984), aggressively trying to seduce Elliott Gould; and in *Scrooged* (1988) she made an amusing Ghost of Christmas Present, got up as a traditional Christmas tree fairy, but with a nifty pair of fists. Her biggest and best role in years came in *The Lemon Sisters* (1989), as the driving force behind a trio of singers Kane, Diane Keaton, Kathryn Grody) who try to run a night-club. It showed off her multiple talents in a cracking performance but, alas, the movie was a barely released failure. For the rest, the delightful Carol Kane has largely been wasted in aging ingenue roles.

1969 Blood Of The Iron Maiden **1970** Is This Trip Really Necessary? **1971** Desperate Characters; Carnal Knowledge **1972** Wedding In White **1973** The Last Detail **1974** Hester Street **1975** Dog Day Afternoon **1976** Harry And Walter Go To New York **1977** Annie Hall; The World's Greatest Lover; Valentino **1978** The Mafu Cage **1979** The Muppet Movie; The Sabina; When A Stranger Calls **1981** Strong Medicine; Keeping On **1982** Pandemonium aka Thursday The 12th; Norman Loves Rose **1983** Can She Bake A Cherry Pie? **1984** Over The Brooklyn Bridge; Racing With The Moon; The Secret Diary Of Sigmund Freud **1985** Transylvania 6–500 **1986** Jumpin' Jack Flash **1987** Ishtar **1988** Sticky Fingers; Licence To Drive; The Princess Bride; Scrooged **1989** The Lemon Sisters **1990** Joe Versus The Volcano; My Blue Heaven; Flashback **1991** Lost In Venice; Goodbye Supermom **1992** In The Soup

Kaplan, Jonathan

Director, actor
Born 25 November 1947
Paris, France

Jonathan Kaplan's past as a film-maker was independent and unconventional, but with the polished and controversial rape drama *The Accused* (1988, which won the Oscar for Jodie Foster) from the stable of producers Sherry Lansing and Stanley Jaffé (their follow-up to the commercial success *Fatal Attraction*), it looked as if he had reconciled himself to moving increasingly over into mainstream Hollywood, perhaps with Academy Award aspirations. He is a second generation protégé of Roger Corman, through Corman's own protégé Martin Scorsese, under whose tutorship Kaplan studied at New York University Film School in the early 1970s. It was Scorsese who recommended Kaplan to Corman's AIP outfit, a break which led in due course to Kaplan helming a number of exploitation movies that packed beneath their surface (for those who were interested) a characteristically radical punch, and have become in their way minor cult classics.

Kaplan comes from a radical background. His father, the composer Sol Kaplan, was blacklisted in 1954, and the family was forced to move from Hollywood to New York. A child actor who performed on stage under such distinguished directors as Elia Kazan and Elaine May, Kaplan had his education interrupted when he was expelled from the University of Chicago for student activism in 1967, at the height of the anti-Vietnam War protests.

But he was always ambitious and a worker: while still at NYU (under Scorsese's eye) he got editing experience at PBC and in television commercials, as well as organising lighting rigs for rock concerts. Now and again, especially after the commercial failure of his teenage-violence picture, *Over The*

Edge (1979), he has been unable to find feature film work in the industry but, undaunted, he has turned back vigorously to TV. 'I'm a director,' he said on one occasion. 'I want to direct movies. I have been doing television movies because that's where I'm getting the best chance to find different material. Also, I don't mind the fast schedules.'

The uneven, on-the-run artistic quality of his work is made up for by energy and a certain quirky toughness that sees through genres to the possible life beneath. *White Line Fever* (1975, his first 'personal' film) has engaging echoes of *On The Waterfront* in its tale of truck drivers battling a corrupt industry. The documentary authenticity of *Over The Edge* was such that its release was delayed for fear of riots in the movie theatres; based on a true-life incident, it tells the story of vicious teenage gangs on a sort of suburban rampage. *Heart Like A Wheel* (1983) was another artistic success but commercial setback (it has since become critically recognised). Its feminist message – about woman racing driver Shirley Muldowney (Bonnie Bedelia) who takes on men at their own game and wins – was challenging in that it issued from a proletarian, rather than middle-class, milieu. ('In terms of Hollywood's approach to women's pictures – should Jill Clayburgh run off with Alan Bates or buy the best town house in Manhattan – it's very different', he remarked. 'It's a film about real choices, not upper-middle-class problems masquerading as feminism.') Some of that same intransigence survives in *The Accused*. It remained to be seen if greater proximity to Hollywood slackens or accentuates his radicalism, with the eagerly awaited inter-racial story *Love Field*, starring Michelle Pfeiffer to come.

As director only unless stated otherwise: **1972** Night Call Nurses **1973** Student Teachers; The Slams **1974** Truck Turner **1975** White Line Fever (w/d) **1976** Cannonball (actor only); Hollywood Boulevard (actor only) **1977** Mr Billion (w/d) **1979** Over The Edge **1980** The Howling (actor only) **1983** Heart Like A Wheel **1987** Project X **1988** The Accused **1989** Immediate Family **1992** Unlawful Entry **1992/93** Love Field

Kasdan, Lawrence

Director writer
Born 14 January 1949
Miami Beach, Florida

Had Lawrence Kasdan never taken up directing he would still have gone down in Hollywood legend as the screenwriter of some of the greatest popular successes of all time with the second and third films of the *Star Wars* trilogy – *The Empire Strikes Back* (1980) and *The Return Of The Jedi* (1983) – and the ultimate 'Boys Own' action adventure, *Raiders Of The Lost Ark* (1981). He is also a man who had kept bouncing back from 67 letters of rejection before selling his first script, ironic perhaps for a director whose best work has dealt with disappointed dreams and lost hope.

Born in Florida and raised in West Virginia, Kasdan took a Master's degree in Education at the University of Michigan (the alma mater of his reunited college friends of *The Big Chill*), intending to teach and write screenplays. Surprised and frustrated by his inability to obtain a teaching post he accepted a position he came to loathe, as an advertising copywriter, for five years. His first script sale never materialised on the screen, but his second became a likeable, albeit so-so vehicle for John Belushi as a Chicago newspaperman, *Continental Divide* (1981), whose executive producer was Steven Spielberg. Kasdan struck a chord with Spielberg, who in turn introduced him to George Lucas with three phenomenal hits resulting from the teaming.

The clout Kasdan acquired from *Empire* and *Raiders* provided him with the opportunity to direct, and his debut was the stylish, steamy, contemporary *noir* thriller *Body Heat* (1981), which was notable not only for its labyrinthine twists and fine performances (in particular from William Hurt) but for the sensational screen debut of Kathleen Turner, and the lush and menacing Florida locations. His second film, the entertaining *The Big Chill* (1983), beloved of thirtysomethings everywhere, detailed a weekend of confidences, regrets and couplings shared among a group of embourgeoised 60s student activists reunited in the 80s by the suicide of a classmate. The much-talked-about corpse, Alex, was played by Kevin Costner, whose entire 'flashback' role was cut when Kasdan concluded that the scenes jarred with the tone and pace of the film, but the intact screen ensemble presented a dream team the likes of which few could afford to reassemble even a few years later: William Hurt, Kevin Kline, Glenn Close, Jeff Goldblum, Tom Berenger, Meg Tilly, JoBeth Williams and Mary Kay Place. While praised chiefly for the actors' work, Kasdan showed a good eye for the details of their disparate lifestyles and a sure hand in interweaving the characters' concerns, mixing social satire with character study and wittily deploying a classic Motown soundtrack.

Kasdan's ambitions exceeded his grasp with his attempt to revive the full-scale Western in *Silverado* (1985). Teaming Kline and Costner with Danny Glover and Scott Glenn as wrong-righting buddies to the indifference of audiences, it was a sprawling affair, with a gaping plot tear through which miscast leading lady Rosanna Arquette virtually disappeared, but it was also handsome, rootin', tootin' entertainment that rightly became more favoured on the repertory, late-night and TV circuit as its stars became more of a draw.

Disappointed by the film's lack of success, its creator took some time before getting another project off the ground. In 1985 he was among many directors to be spotted by film buffs enacting cameos in John Landis' chase caper *Into The Night*, and he produced a slight, engaging romantic comedy, *Cross My Heart*, in 1987, directed by Armyan Bernstein and starring Martin Short.

Up to this point Kasdan's films had been considered – by many if not all – too derivative for him to be viewed among the first rank. His *Empire* and *Raiders* screenplays were obvious and well-constructed tributes to traditional Westerns and adventures, with all the staple elements of classic action films and popular Saturday serial escapades. *Body Heat* revelled in 40s *noir* conceits, and *The Big Chill*, critics sniffed, in concept and plot closely resembled John Sayles' earlier, well regarded but less widely seen *The Return Of The Secaucus 7* (1980). With his third film with William Hurt, *The Accidental Tourist* (1988), the director's delightful and moving adaptation of a quirky Anne Tyler novel won him more respect for the maturity and subtlety with which he handled the material. It also drew an inspired performance from Hurt and an Oscar-winning, captivating one from Geena Davis. (High-grade, imaginative casting is one of Kasdan's strong suits.)

Opting to try his hand at directing a script he had not originated, Kasdan fared less well with the odd black comedy *I Love You To Death* (1990), based on a bizarre real-life case of a philandering husband and his furious wife's bungling attempts to bump him off. Despite the comedic skills of Kevin Kline and Tracey Ullman and a rather remarkable supporting cast that included William Hurt, the humour was too off-kilter to find wide favour. Thus far, Kasdan's real strength evidently lies in tackling contemporary crises and middle-class, middle-age anxieties with his tongue just slightly in cheek. His most ambitious work, *Grand Canyon* – for which he and his wife Meg received screenwriting Oscar nominations – was just such a kaleidoscopic assault on the urban hell of Los Angeles, which trod the line between humour and despair, and featured another distinguished ensemble cast headed by Kasdan stalwart Kline.

1980 The Empire Strikes Back (co-writer) **1981** Raiders Of The Lost Ark (writer); Body Heat (w/d); Continental Divide (writer) **1983** Return Of The Jedi (co-writer); The Big Chill (director, co-writer) **1985** Into The Night (cameo); Silverado (director, co-writer) **1988** The Accidental Tourist (director, co-writer) **1990** I Love You To Death (director only) **1991** Grand Canyon (director, co-writer)

Kaufman, Philip

Director, writer
Born 23 October 1936
Chicago, Illinois

Now in his 50s, maverick American director Philip Kaufman has made only nine films, none of them commercial hits, but he is one of the most interesting writer-directors outside the Hollywood mainstream. And although he did not direct them he was instrumental in the development of two colossal money-spinners, *Star Trek: The Motion Picture* (1979) and *Raiders Of The Lost Ark* (1981).

Born in Chicago and educated at the University of Chicago and Harvard Law School, Kaufman became greatly influenced by the writings of Henry Miller, dropped his studies and took his wife and son to California where he met Miller and attempted to write his own novel. While writing he did odd jobs, moved to Europe and survived by teaching English and maths. The novel remained uncompleted, but back in Chicago in the early 1960s he transferred his attention to his first film, *Goldstein* (1964), a low-budget, distinctly odd satire centred on the prophet Elijah and a sculptor, co-directed with Benjamin Manaster. It won them a critics' prize at Cannes. In 1965 he wrote and directed another satire, *Fearless Frank*, starring a then unknown Jon Voight as a murder victim come back to life with super powers. Unreleased until 1967, it was regarded variously as a dud and a curio.

Kaufman fared better in overturning

Western clichés with his outlaw homage to the James-Younger gang, *The Great Northfield Minnesota Raid* (1972), distinguished by some imaginatively realised shoot-'em-up scenes and good performances from a cast including Cliff Robertson and Robert Duvall. Ever seeking to do things with a difference, he then set Warren Oates, Timothy Bottoms and Lou Gossett in an unpredictable whaling yarn adventure, *The White Dawn* (1974), in which the 19th-century trio unattractively busied themselves exploiting Eskimos. But the director's real breakthrough came with his weird, scarey and in-joke-strewn remake of *Invasion Of The Body Snatchers* (1978). Its reasonable reception went some way towards compensating Kaufman for several setbacks and disappointments. Engaged to write and direct *The Outlaw Josey Wales* (1976) for Clint Eastwood, Kaufman and the star did not see eye-to-eye and Kaufman was fired shortly after shooting commenced. Eastwood took over direction himself, but Kaufman retained a co-writing credit. He also worked with George Lucas on *Raiders* for some time during this period, expecting to direct the film. But by the time it was ready to be made he saw Steven Spielberg take the reins.

The cult classic of Kaufman's work to date remains his 1979 kaleidoscopic picture of 1960s Bronx teenagers, *The Wanderers*, a vivid and original period piece appreciated by the critics and still alive and well on the repertory circuit. Stretching for the epic, Kaufman realised his most impressive project, however, with the thrilling adaptation of Tom Wolfe's *The Right Stuff* (1983), combining awesome space flight sequences with a celebratory but irreverent and ironic portrait of the Mercury astronauts and the political scene around them. Nominated for eight Academy Awards, including Best Picture, the film won four, and was one of the most memorable (and certainly one of the most off-beat) Big Pictures of the decade.

Evidently at his most successful when mixing political and human elements, Kaufman's 1988 adaptation, *The Unbearable Lightness Of Being*, from the novel by Milan Kundera, was a sexy and cerebral, beautifully made portrait of a young Czech doctor whose womanising and emotional, intellectual crises coincide with the turmoil of the Prague Spring. Notable also for the striking performances of Daniel Day-Lewis, Lena Olin and Juliette Binoche, the film won Kaufman a BAFTA award, the US National Society of Film Critics award for Best Picture and the Orson Welles Award.

Not known as a fast worker – Kaufman prepared *The Right Stuff* over four years and *Lightness Of Being* over three – his most recent film, *Henry And June* (1990), was the fruit of his more than 30-year fascination with Henry Miller and Anaïs Nin. After a huge censorship controversy in America, where the film first received the now discarded kiss-of-death X certificate, it proved curiously unerotic and detached, though a stylish, intelligent and well-acted exploration of the Millers' introspective adventures in Paris in the 1930s. As ever, Philip Kaufman made the film in close collaboration with his wife Rose and son Peter (who acted as producer), an inseparable trio known to friends as Peter Rosenphil.

1964 Goldstein (co-w/d) **1967** Fearless Frank (w/d) **1969** The Great Northfield Minnesota Raid (w/d) **1974** The White Dawn **1976** The Outlaw Josey Wales (co-writer only) **1978** Invasion Of The Body Snatchers **1979** The Wanderers; Up Your Ladder (also co-writer) **1981** Raiders Of The Lost Ark (co-writer only) **1983** The Right Stuff (w/d) **1988** The Unbearable Lightness Of Being (also co-writer) **1990** Henry And June (w/d) **1992/93** The Rising Sun (w/d)

Kavner, Julie

Actress

Born 7 September 1951

Los Angeles, California

A TV and theatre actress *per se*, Julie Kavner has been modestly successful in the cinema. Born and raised in Los Angeles, the dark-haired and somewhat plain Kavner was a natural comic who had set her sights on an acting career by the time she graduated from high school. After majoring in theatre at San Diego State University, the 23-year-old actress promptly landed a role that was to secure her five years of recognition and acclaim – the part of New Yorker Brenda Morgenstern, Valerie Harper's younger sister in the TV series *Rhoda*. Kavner appeared in a variety of other series and television movies and was several times nominated for Emmys before making her less-than-auspicious big-screen debut in the appalling parody, *National Lampoon Goes to the Movies* (1981). The film was never given a general release and it was four years before Kavner made another movie, the similarly ill-fated *Bad Medicine* (1985), a comedy with Steve Guttenberg about medical students in a banana republic.

It wasn't until Woody Allen and *Hannah and Her Sisters* (1986) came along that Kavner was given a movie vehicle worthy of her comic talents. In her small but beautifully realised part as the reassuring assistant to hypochondriac TV producer Allen, Kavner so impressed the film-maker that he cast her, this time as his Jewish mother, in the nostalgic *Radio Days* (1987). Allen later called upon her to play the role of Treva, the hilarious but touching pseudo-medium who is given the maternal seal of approval in 'Oedipus Wrecks', his contribution to *New York Stories* (1989).

By the beginning of the 90s, still busy in theatre and television and with a warm supporting role as a nurse in *Awakenings* (1990) and the lead in Nora Ephron's debut feature, *This Is My Life* Kavner looked likely to continue to build on her to date small but distinctive movie career. Meanwhile, she was delighting millions as the voice of endlessly patient Marge Simpson in the hit animated TV sitcom, *The Simpsons*.

1981 National Lampoon Goes To The Movies **1985** Bad Medicine **1986** Hannah And Her Sisters **1987** Radio Days; Surrender **1989** New York Stories **1990** Awakenings; Alice (cameo) **1992** This Is My Life; Shadows And Fog **1993** I'll Do Anything

Keach, Stacy

Actor
Born 2 June 1941
Savannah, Georgia

In director John Huston's *Fat City* (1972), Stacy Keach proved how well he could do his job as an actor: his performance as the small-time, over-age boxer who fights against the odds and loses was both complex and poignant. Despite his vast array of films and his solid, football-star looks (enhanced by a hare-lip and a low-key attitude), Keach has remained a sadly underrated actor. A capable director (his 1971 short, *The Repeater*, was an award-winner, and he has tackled Pirandello's intricate classic, *Six Characters In Search Of An Author*, for TV) and an often-used narrator, his career seemed to peak with his starring role in the TV detective series of the 1980s, *Mike Hammer*. Sadder still, he is probably most widely known for serving a nine-month prison sentence in Britain after being stopped at Heathrow Airport Customs in 1984 with 31 grams of cocaine concealed in a tin of shaving foam.

The son of a moderately successful actor and dialogue director, Keach grew up in Los Angeles and was encouraged to study law to avoid the insecurities of show business. But Keach Jr (as he was listed in his official film debut in 1968's *The Heart Is A Lonely Hunter*) soon switched to drama. He shone at the Yale Drama School and earned a Fulbright Scholarship to study for a year at the London Academy of Music And Dramatic Art. In New York, rave reviews abounded for his performances in classical roles and the young actor pursued his ambition to become the American theatre's answer to Laurence Olivier until he realised, at 30, that America didn't *want* one.

During this time he continued to make movies, taking part in various Italian-made farragos and such mediocre ventures as Pia Zadora's debut vehicle, *Butterfly* (1981), with *Road Games* (1981) and *That Championship Season* (1982) being almost the only exceptions. After the disappointment of 1980's *The Long Riders* (which he co-produced, co-wrote and co-starred in with his brother James), TV mini-series became his salvation. *Princess Daisy* and *Mistral's Daughter* finally offered him the leading man status he craved. When the opportunity arose to play Mickey Spillane's classic tough-guy detective, Mike Hammer, Keach approached it 'as seriously as I approached Hamlet'.

Having served his sentence and kicked the cocaine habit, Stacy Keach wrote a book and narrated a film about drug addiction. Married to Polish actress Malgosia Tomassi (his fourth wife), it was to be hoped that he might renew his mark on serious acting which, according to him, he has always taken to 'like a duck to water'.

1963 Island Of Love **1968** The Heart Is A Lonely Hunter **1969** End Of The Road **1970** The Travelling Executioner **1970** Brewster McCloud **1971** Doc; The Repeater (short, director) **1972** Fat City; The Life And Times Of Judge Roy Bean; The New Centurions; Goodnight, Mike **1974** The Dion Brothers aka The Gravy Train; Luther; Watched **1975** Conduct Unbecoming **1976** The Killer Inside Me; Gli Escutori/ Street People aka The Sicilian Cross (Italy) **1977** The Squeeze; Il Grande Attacca/The Greatest Battle (Italy) **1978** Gray Lady Down; Deux Solitudes/Two Solitudes (Canada); Up In Smoke; La Montagna Del Dio Cannibale/Primitive Desires aka Mountain In The Jungle aka Prisoner Of The Cannibal God (Italy) **1979** Twinkle, Twinkle; Killer Kane aka The Ninth Configuration **1980** The Long Riders (also co-writer) **1981** Road Games; Butterfly; Cheech n' Chong's Nice Dreams **1982** That Championship Season **1990** False Identity; Class of 1999 **1992/93** Sunset Grill

Keaton, Diane
(Diane Hall)

Actress

Born 5 January 1946

Los Angeles, California

Shut your eyes and think of the 70s, and it's not entirely improbable that one film performance will immediately swim into view. In the title role of Woody Allen's *Annie Hall* (1977), Diane Keaton was more than a player of a part. The look (faintly wacky hat, scarf, shoulder bag, baggy trousers), the manner (wide stares, stop-start delivery spaced with loveably breathless interjections of 'um', 'gee', and 'oh wow') and the character (independent-minded yet unsure of direction, with an oddly vulnerable, poetic centre) – all were achieved with a touch so natural, a charm so unforced that in the best way it seemed impossible to judge where Diane Keaton ended and Annie Hall began. There were, of course, correspondences between Life and Art: Hall is the actress' real surname, she and her director-leading man were lovers at the time, and events and characters were borrowed from both their families and past histories. But the result, far from being archly knowing or mannered, was a film suffused with wry tenderness, an affectionate and graceful tribute to the woman at its centre; and, possibly as a result, possibly because of her own innate qualities, she seemed to embody the spirit of the age. This bittersweet comedy, in a genre and style not normally favoured for big Hollywood honours, scooped up the 1977 Oscars – Best Picture, Best Director, Best Screenplay, and Keaton as Best Actress.

Annie Hall, the third of her six Woody Allen films (seven if you include her lovely little cameo in the 1987 *Radio Days*), has marked the high point of Diane Keaton's career so far. And there's the rub. The end of her relationship with Allen did not by any means spell the end of her career; she continued to work throughout the 80s, on big projects and meaty roles. But few of them struck the right chord, and none of them suggested that her development as an actress had continued without interruption. To suppose that she is not an actress at all, but rather a dated single-note personality, is manifestly unjust. She has tackled a variety of serious parts seriously, and in some cases successfully – the kindergarten teacher of *Looking For Mr Goodbar* (1977), whose sexual adventures lead to her violent death; the plucky, headstrong journalist Louise Bryant in *Reds* (directed by Warren Beatty, with whom she had a brief liaison); Albert Finney's abandoned wife in *Shoot The Moon* (1982); and the most neurotic of a trio of Mississippi sisters (co-starring with Jessica Lange and Sissy Spacek) in Bruce Beresford's *Crimes Of The Heart* (1986).

Even in the Allen series, there were variations on the theme of Keaton as winsome kook: in *Interiors* (1978), the first of that director's serious films, she was Renata, the least attractive of another trio of sisters, whose pretentiousness and narcissism she conveyed with sober precision. More often than not, however, the post-*Annie Hall* period revealed limitations of range, style and even technique from which she seemed unable to break free; and too often the Annie Hall character was sensed hovering in the background – wistfully, or, when something more substantial was called for (as in the Le Carré thriller adaptation *The Little Drummer Girl* or the 19th-century prison drama *Mrs Soffel*, both 1984), inappropriately.

A native Californian raised in Santa Ana, Keaton started off in summer stock. In 1968 she understudied in the Broadway hippie musical, *Hair*, soon taking over one of the leading roles. Her first encounter with Woody Allen was in his 1970 Broadway play *Play It Again, Sam*, a role she would repeat when he came to film it two years later. But her first significant film role was the non-Italian girl with whom Al Pacino falls in love in *The Godfather* (1972) – the relationship was continued, through marriage, divorce and parenthood, in Parts II, 1974, and III, 1990. In the last years of the 80s she branched out into producing her films (the disastrous *The Lemon Sisters*, 1989, with Carol Kane and Kathryn Grody) and directing others (the documentary *Heaven*, 1987, a handful of pop videos, a 1990 episode in the David Lynch television soap, *Twin Peaks*), and has also published two collections of photographs. It would be unwise to write this intelligent, energetic and unstuffily attractive woman off entirely; but on the available evidence it was hard to see exactly where her acting career could go. However, 1993 saw a return to Woody Allen

1970 Lovers And Other Strangers **1972** The Godfather; Play It Again, Sam **1973** Sleeper **1974** The Godfather Part II; **1975** Love And Death **1976** I Will I Will . . . For Now; Harry And Walter Go To New York **1977** looking For

Mr Goodbar; Annie Hall **1978** Interiors **1979** Manhattan **1981** Reds **1982** Shoot The Moon **1984** The Little Drummer Girl; Mrs Soffel **1986** Crimes Of The Heart **1987** Radio Days; Baby Boom **1988** The Good Mother **1989** The Lemon Sisters **1990** The Godfather Part III – The Continuing Story **1991** Father Of The Bride **1993** Manhattan Murder Mystery

Keaton, Michael (Michael Douglas)

Actor
Born 5 September 1952
Coraopolis, Pennsylvania

Until the late 80s, Michael Keaton had been neatly pigeonholed as a relatively well-known comic actor, exuberant and motor-mouthed. But his controversial performance as a disturbing and introverted Batman, immediately followed by other even darker roles, revealed an unsuspected and promising dramatic talent.

One of seven children, Keaton (who had to change his surname for obvious reasons) was a class clown who opted for speech studies at Kent State University, only to drop out two years later. A variety of odd jobs followed, including driving an ice-cream van, while he struggled to launch himself as a stand-up comic. After a three-year stint working as a TV technician, the would-be performer moved to Hollywood where an erratic television acting career followed, with small parts on *The Tony Randall Show* and *Maude*. His big break came in 1982, with Ron Howard's *Night Shift*. Keaton's frenetic 'lurve broker', Billy Blaze, stole the show from Henry Winkler and Shelley Long, and pitched him into his own leading role as a hapless house-husband in the successful *Mr Mom* (1983). By now a star on the rise, the already divorced, mischievous-faced actor then went on to make a series of poor choices that resulted in forgettable movies. His run of bad luck was compounded when Woody Allen fired him during the filming of *The Purple Rose Of Cairo*.

What brought Keaton back on track was his manic, iconoclastic performance as a rent-a-ghoul in Tim Burton's *Beetlejuice* (1988). By then 37, the actor put aside his characteristic playfulness and gave an unprecedentedly mature performance in Glenn Gordon Caron's downbeat *Clean And Sober* the same year. With his pleasant 'Mr Average' – but slightly worn – appearance, Keaton convinced as an unlikeable substance abuser who undergoes a drug rehabilitation programme. An enigmatic and subdued performance in *Batman* (1989) continued his pursuit of more complex roles, which bore further fruit with his threatening portrayal of a tenant who sets about ruining the lives of his landlords, Matthew Modine and Melanie Griffith, in John Schlesinger's *Pacific Heights* (1990).

Despite Michael Keaton's occasional return to lightweight comic roles, as in the disappointing *The Dream Team* (1990), the actor's determination to continue developing his dramatic potential was apparent in the dark *Batman Returns* (1992) and his subsequent acceptance of a role in Kenneth (*Henry V*) Branagh's second Shakespearean screen venture, *Much Ado About Nothing*.

1982 Night Shift **1983** Mr Mom **1984** Johnny Dangerously **1986** Touch And Go; Gung Ho **1987** The Squeeze **1988** Beetlejuice; Clean And Sober **1989** The Dream Team; Batman **1990** Pacific Heights **1991** One Good Cop **1992** Batman Returns **1993** Much Ado About Nothing

Keitel, Harvey

Actor
Born 13 May 1947
New York City

One of the most intense and impressive of supporting actors, specialising in playing edgy, sometimes manic outsiders hiding in positions that instil self-importance (usually gradually eroded), Brooklyn-born ex-Marine Harvey Keitel studied acting under Frank Corsalo, Stella Adler and Lee Strasberg, becoming a member of the Actors' Studio (to which he has returned many times).

Following his Broadway debut opposite George C. Scott in a revival of *Death Of A Salesman*, he took the lead in his first film, Martin Scorsese's New York University thesis project, *Who's That Knocking At My Door* (1968), in which his hung-up streetwise Catholic in 'Little Italy' proved very much a dress rehearsal for the same director's *Mean Streets* (1973). It was that film's small-time hood coping with the pressures of his Catholic upbringing, a difficult family and an irresponsible friend (De Niro) that put Keitel on the map, and he went on to notch up impressive credits, albeit in smaller roles, with Scorsese's *Alice Doesn't Live Here Anymore* (1975) and *Taxi Driver* (1976), playing Jodie Foster's pimp. Although firmly associated with Scorsese, their relationship has proved volatile, with the actor walking off *The King Of Comedy* (1981–3), declaring it a disaster, and not returning to the fold until his sympathetic, zealous Judas in *The Last Temptation Of Christ* (1988).

Around the early 80s, Keitel made a concerted effort to enter the mainstream, but his total belief in his characters – usually intense obsessives such as the voyeuristic detective in *Bad Timing* (1980) or the fanatical protagonist of Ridley Scott's *The Duellists* (1977, a role he honestly believed was the hero of the film) – often led to fireworks, as when he refused to re-record his dialogue for *Saturn 3* (1979) following script changes, and had to be dubbed by Roy Dotrice. Since then, he has tended to be attracted more by directors than scripts, often bringing presence and conviction to even the slightest of roles – witness the corrupt patrolman of *The Border* (1982) or the mobsters of the inconsequential *Wise Guys* (1986) and *The Pick-Up Artist* (1987). After much continental work, particularly in Italy (including playing Pontius Pilate in the intriguing post-resurrection Biblical thriller *The Inquiry*, 1987), the furore surrounding *The Last Temptation* seems to have returned Harvey Keitel to mainstream American films; he gives one of the few restrained performances in *The Two Jakes* (1990–as the second Jake, and was reunited with director Ridley Scott on *Thelma And Louise* (1991) as the sympathetic arm of the law. By contrast, he gave a bristling performance as Bugsy Siegel's foul-mouthed LA sidekick in *Bugsy* (1991), twitching with belligerent energy and receiving an Oscar nomination for his efforts.

1968 Who's That Knocking At My Door? **1973** Mean Streets **1975** Alice Doesn't Live Here Anymore; That's The Way Of The World **1976** Taxi Driver; Mother Jugs And Speed; Buffalo Bill And The Indians **1977** Welcome To LA; Shining Star; The Duellists **1978** Fingers; Blue Collar **1979** Saturn 3; Health; Eagle's Wing **1980** Bad Timing; La Mort En Direct/Deathwatch (France) **1982** Exposed; The Border; Un Pierre Dans La Bouch (France); The New World **1983** Order Of Death **1984** Falling In Love; Dream One **1985** Un Complicato Intrigo Di Donne, Vicoli E Delitti/Camorra: The Naples Connection (Italy); Off Beat; El Caballero Fel Dragón/ Star Knight (Spain); La Sposa Americana/The American Wife (Italy) **1986** Corsa In Discesa/Downhill Race (Italy); The Men's club, Wise Guys **1987** L'Inchiesta/The Inquiry (Italy); Blindside; The Pick-Up Artist **1988** The Last Temptation Of Christ; Caro Gorbaciov/Dear Gorbachev (Italy) **1989** The January Man **1990** The Two Jakes; Due Occhi Diabolici/Facts In The Case Of Mr Valdemar aka Black Cat (Italy) **1991** Thelma And Louise; Mortal Thoughts; Bugsy **1992** Reservoir Days; Sister Act; Bad Lieutenant

Kellerman, Sally

Actress

Born 2 June 1936

Long Beach, California

A tall, quirky blonde, Sally Kellerman became a star with her bravura performance as Major 'Hot Lips' Houlihan in Robert Altman's *M★A★S★H* (1970), but like Altman himself she was too distinctive a talent to fit into Hollywood's preconceived notions of what makes a leading lady.

Kellerman attended Hollywood high school, and became stagestruck after appearing in a play there. She took acting classes at the Actors' Studio West, then with Jeff Corey, and finally at the Actors' Studio, New York. She made her screen debut in the B movie *Reform School Girl* (1957), but struggled for ten years to pick up more than bit parts. *M★A★S★H* came out of nowhere. A vitriolic black comedy set in the Korean war but made in the midst of Vietnam, its lunatic irreverence seemed not only justifiable but *de rigeur* at the time. Its cynical surgeons, Hawkeye and Trapper John, were the epitome of hip, in perpetual combat with the forces of self-righteousness: God, the Army and the Government. Asked where she hailed from, Kellerman's 'Hot Lips' Houlihan replied 'I like to think of the Army as my home'. As a military square, and a repressed woman to boot, 'Hot Lips' was fair game twice over, and most of her role consists of humiliation and frustration. It is an angle that badly dates Robert Altman's sometimes inspired feature, but Kellerman herself is a delight, her tall, blonde good looks never overshadowing the fierce pride she brings to the part. Despite everything, she is one of the movie's heroes. It brought her an Oscar nomination.

Kellerman stuck with Altman for one more film, the bizarre allegory-cum-spoof, *Brewster McCloud* (1970). Brewster (Bud Cort) is a virgin born with the potential to fly. Louise (Kellerman) is his guardian angel; mother, teacher, protector. Digressive and determinedly oddball, the film failed to capitalize on the popular success of *M★A★S★H*, but is not without a quirky appeal of its own. Kellerman is especially fine, and curiously affecting. Her words may spell out 'loopy', but her deep, throaty voice betokens dignity and intelligence.

Unfortunately, having established herself as star material, Kellerman proceeded to waste her talents on a series of aimless, scrappy features that largely put paid to any big league aspirations. *Last Of The Red Hot Lovers* (1972) remains one of the tawdriest Neil Simon adaptations, *A Reflection Of Fear* (1973) was a secondrate thriller, and *Lost Horizon* (1973) was nothing short of disastrous, an ill-advised, sloppy, soppy remake of Frank Capra's utopian fantasy. Kellerman did her best work in a pair of likeable throwaway comedies. In Howard Zieff's *Slither* (1973) she was one eccentric golddigger among many; in Dick Richard's *Rafferty And The Gold Dust Twins* (1975) she was just hitching a ride nowhere in particular. These warm, off-beat performances prefigure most of Kellerman's subsequent career, which has alternated between increasingly lowbrow comedies (cameos in Rodney Dangerfield's *Back To School*, 1986, *Meatballs III*, 1987), a handful of mediocre dramas (*Foxes*, *Loving Couples*, both 1980), and a couple of arthouse projects that probably reflect her own temperament more accurately: *Welcome To LA* (1976), directed by Altman protégé Alan Rudolph, and Henry Jaglom's *Someone To Love* (1987), in which she played an approximation of herself with world-weary charm.

1957 Reform School Girl **1962** Hands Of A Stranger (made 1960) **1965** The Third Day **1968** The Boston Strangler **1969** The April Fools **1970** M*A*S*H; Brewster McCloud **1972** Last Of The Red Hot Lovers **1973** Lost Horizon; Slither; A Reflection Of Fear **1975** Rafferty And The Gold Dust Twins aka Rafferty And The Highway Hustlers **1976** The Big Bus; Welcome To LA **1979** A Little Romance **1980** Foxes; Loving Couples; Serial; Head On aka Fatal Attraction **1985** Moving Violations **1986** Back To School; That's Life **1987** Meatballs III; Three For The Road; Someone To Love **1988** You Can't Hurry Love **1989** Limit Up; All's Fair **1992** The Player (cameo); Boris And Natasha **1993** Younger And Younger

Kidder, Margot

Actress

Born 17 October 1948

Yellow Knife, Canada

People associate Margot Kidder with her most well-known and successful role to date, that of Lois Lane in the *Superman* films, which first appeared on the big screen in 1978, but this dark, attractive (albeit somewhat toothsome) actress has appeared in more than 20 other films, and many TV movies.

She left school at the age of 16 to become an actress and made her debut in a production of *Oliver*. Then she was cast in a seemingly endless number of parts which required her to portray archetypally deranged teenagers and neurotic or fallen women before she appeared in a TV series where she played a group of people all interviewed by psychiatrists. The series won critical acclaim, and Kidder decided to try her luck in Toronto, where she appeared in some TV commercials and tried her hand at an assortment of other jobs, including film editing (as an apprentice) and modelling.

She was spotted on the cover of *McLean's Magazine* by director Norman Jewison who cast her in her first feature, with Beau Bridges, the comedy *Gaily Gaily* (1969), based on Ben Hecht's memories of being a junior cub reporter on a Chicago paper. She then co-starred with Gene Wilder in the rather absurdly titled *Quackser Fortune Has A Cousin In The Bronx* (1970), but the comedy didn't have as much staying power as the title, so she accepted a few television jobs which included guest spots on *Barnaby Jones* and *Hawaii Five-O*. She came back to the big screen with some impact, working for up-and-coming director Brian De Palma, and playing both lead roles (twins, one good and one evil) in his thriller *Sisters* (1973). Proving she could scream with the best of them, the actress then appeared in the thriller *Black Christmas* (1974), followed by a part in the adventure film *The Dion Brothers* (1974) with Stacy Keach.

None of these films pushed her to the forefront, but she was effective in her brief appearance in *The Great Waldo Pepper* (1975) with Robert Redford – the first of her films to become at least something of a box-office success. Kidder then quit movies after making *92 In The Shade* (1975) with Peter Fonda, and returned to college, studying film at the University of British Columbia. Her first role when she returned to acting was that of Superman/Clark Kent's girlfriend, Lois, in *Superman* (1978).

There was a danger, thereafter, that she might be typecast, but all notions that she was just Lois Lane were dispelled when she appeared in *The Amityville Horror* (1979), as the woman who moves with her family into a house where a brutal mass murder took place years before. After *The Omen* and *The Exorcist*, this was one of the most popular horror flicks of the 90s and spawned two sequels (one in 3-D), although Kidder only appeared in the original. She returned to the arms of Clark Kent for *Superman II* (1980), which was considered by some critics to be better than the original. Before returning to Lois yet again in *Superman III* (1983), the actress appeared in a few minor films, most notably the quirky female buddy movie *Heartaches* (1981).

Subsequent work has done nothing to help Kidder break away from her cartoon-character image, although she has appeared with Richard Pryor (*Some Kind Of Hero*, 1982) Burt Lancaster and Ted Danson (*Little Treasure*, 1985). Her films have remained widely unseen, while her personal life seems to have grabbed more attention. She married and divorced writer Tom McGuane, then married actor John Heard whom she also divorced after a brief time. She has also appeared in the tabloids speaking vehemently about her anti-war stance, most notably during the first days of the Gulf War in January 1991.

1969 Gaily Gaily **1970** Quackser Fortune Has A Cousin In The Bronx **1973** Sisters aka Blood Sisters **1974** Black Christmas; A Quiet Day In Belfast; The Dion Brothers aka The Gravy Train **1975** The Great Waldo Pepper; The Reincarnation Of Peter Proud; 92 In The Shade **1978** Superman **1979** Mr Mike's Mondo Video; The Amityville Horror **1980** Miss Right; Superman II **1981** Willie And Phil; Shoot The Sun Down; Heartaches **1982** Some Kind Of Hero **1983** Superman III; Trenchcoat **1984** Louisiana **1985** Little Treasure; Speaking Our Peace **1986** The Canadian Conspiracy **1987** Keeping Track; Superman IV: The Quest For Peace **1989** Mob Story **1990** White Room

Kidman, Nicole

Actress
Born 1966
Hawaii

Nicole Kidman was born in Hawaii to Australian parents. She studied ballet as a child, and persuaded her parents to enrol her in drama school when she was ten. She went on to study acting at the St Martin's Youth Theatre in Melbourne, and in Sydney at the Australian Theatre for Young People, and the Philip Street Theatre, under the direction of Peter Williams.

She got her first break at 14 when a casting director spotted her in a small production playing a 50-year-old American talking about sex. This landed Nicole her first film role in *Bush Christmas* (1982). A leading part in the children's movie *BMX Bandits* followed in 1983. She was a supermarket check-out girl who teams up with a couple of lads on BMX bikes when they become embroiled in a planned bank heist. It was a stunt film really, a child's variation on such mature, grown-up fare as *Convoy* and *Mad Max*, but Kidman was a feisty participant in the action. She continued her studies in between films, which she picked up at a rate of one a year: *Wills And Burke* (1985); *Windrider* (1986); *The Big Part*(1987). But she found greater public recognition on television, where she was voted the Australian Film Institute's Best Actress in a mini-series for *Vietnam* (1988) – an award she recaptured a year later with her sterling account of a woman in dire straits at the *Bangkok Hilton*. Her stint in *Vietnam* led the Australian public to vote her Best Actress of the Year. She was also nominated as Best Supporting Actress in 1989 for the film *Emerald City*. On the stage, she also won awards, and the Sydney Theatre Critics called her the best newcomer of the year for her portrayal of the doomed Southern belle in *Steel Magnolias*. The freckle-faced waif had grown into a beautiful, intelligent young woman. Her slightly pinched features, thin lips, pale cheeks and a petite nose are offset by her crystal-clear eyes and striking frizzy hair.

International acclaim soon followed with Kidman's memorable plucky performance as Ray in *Dead Calm* (1989). It was a major studio film, directed by Phillip Noyce, produced by *Mad Max*'s George Miller, from a novel by Charles Williams. Orson Welles had filmed it once before, as *The Deep*, but he never finished it. The action is restricted to two boats in the middle of the ocean. On one, married couple Kidman and Sam Neil are enjoying a holiday away from it all. The other is sinking, with psychotic Billy Zane and a crew of corpses on board. Zane succeeds in swapping places with Neil, so it's up to Ray to save herself and her husband. It's a thrilling scenario, expertly handled by Noyce, but Kidman gives the film its resonance. At the start she is a timid, vulnerable girl-woman haunted by nightmares from her past; but over the course of events she finds self-reliance and ingenuity she didn't know she possessed. While she exploits her natural beauty to entrap Zane, she must also outwit him – and challenge his physical authority. From this perspective, *Dead Calm* becomes one of the most positive woman-in-peril thrillers.

Duly impressed, Tom Cruise and producers Simpson and Bruckheimer cast

Kidman in their *Days Of Thunder* (1990). If this was *Top Gun* on Wheels, then Kidman got the Kelly McGillis role. As Dr Claire Lewicki, she won Cruise's heart on-and off-screen (they married on Christmas Eve, 1990). It was a slim part though, no more than a love interest with a highbrow profession as a fob to feminism. Though good opposite Dustin Hoffman in *Billy Bathgate* (1991) the film failed, thus doing little to enhance her prospects, while the over-blown immigrant saga vehicle for Mr and Mrs Cruise, *Far And Away*, was quite simply laughable.

1982 Bush Christmas **1983** BMX Bandits **1985** Wills and Burke **1986** Windrider **1987** The Big Part **1989** Emerald City; Dead Calm **1990** Flirting; Days of Thunder **1991** Billy Bathgate **1992** Far And Away

Kilmer, Val

Actor
Born 31 December 1959
Los Angeles, California

Val Kilmer, who got the big push for his exceptionally convincing portrayal of 60s icon and Lizard King, Jim Morrison, in Oliver Stone's celebration of the artist and the era *The Doors* (1991), began his career in the film industry seven years previously and had done sound if unsensational work in comedy, action and suspense. Born and raised in the San Fernando Valley, he entered the prestigious Juilliard School's drama programme in his teens and made his professional debut on the stage. Among his theatre credits was the off-Broadway production of *Slab Boys* with Sean Penn. He remains involved in theatre and in 1988 played Hamlet at the Colorado Shakespeare Festival.

Kilmer made his film debut with the leading role of a rock star caught up in a nutty espionage caper in Zucker-Abrahams-Zucker's silly but amiable spy spoof, *Top Secret* (1984), and extended the joke by recording some rock tracks under the guise of the movie's character, Nick Rivers. (His good baritone voice was to be put to even more impressive use in *The Doors*, for which he performed all the live concert material.) After appearing fairly prominently as Ice Man, one of the handsome, macho stud pilots in dark glasses in Tony Scott's box-office giant of 1986, *Top Gun*, Kilmer was starred in Ron Howard's *Willow* (1988). The lavish fantasy adventure in the *Star Wars* vein, in which, naturally, he played the handsome, swashbuckling goody-goody hero, received a lukewarm reception but paired Kilmer with one of Britain's hottest young actresses, Joanne Whalley, who in short order became Joanne Whalley-Kilmer. In 1989 the couple starred in a low-budget, rather tongue-in-cheek *film noir, Kill Me Again*, as *femme fatale* and smitten patsy, but the so-so picture did not enjoy a wide release.

After an engaging impersonation of gunslinger Billy the Kid for television, Kilmer campaigned relentlessly for the role of Jim Morrison and won it only after doorstepping Oliver Stone, making his own video singing and reciting Morrison's work and, reportedly, having a mole removed from his face to increase his already definite resemblance to the dead rock demi-god. While the film's appeal was primarily confined to existing Doors fans it was superior to most rock biopics and Kilmer's intense, meticulously prepared portrayal could scarcely be faulted. Subsequently Kilmer, who has also published a volume of poetry, was said to be considering his own recording deal while taking a role considerably removed from Morrison – that of an FBI agent rediscovering his Native American roots in Michael Apted's *Thunderheart*.

1984 Top Secret **1985** Real Genius **1986** Top Gun **1988** Willow **1989** Kill Me Again **1991** The Doors **1992** Thunderheart **1993** The Real McCoy; True Romance

Kinski, Nastassia
(Nastassja Naksynski; sometimes Nastassja/Nastasia)

Actress
Born 24 January 1961
Berlin, Germany

Nastassia Kinski's staggeringly beautiful looks have been both the making and undoing of her screen career, at once attracting great film-makers while at the same time blinding them as to quite what to do with the actress other than let the camera fall in love with her. The daughter of the considerably less than beautiful German actor Klaus Kinski, she was educated in Rome, Munich and Caracas, moving to America in her early teens to study English and take drama courses with Lee Strasberg. Her screen career began with a small role as a juggler in Wim Wenders' *Wrong Movement* (1975) but she got far more attention with the first of her many nude scenes in Hammer's disappointing final film *To The Devil A Daughter* (1976) and the limp German sex comedy *Passion Flower Hotel* (1978). It took Roman Polanski and *Tess* (1979) to make her a star, proving one of the few films to frame her beauty with both a strong story and a substantial characterisation as Thomas Hardy's innocent country girl corrupted and discarded by polite society.

Soon she was popping up and stripping off everywhere – a circus performer in Coppola's overblown *One From The Heart*, a none-too-convincing small-town Midwesterner mixed up in modelling and terrorism in *Exposed* (both 1982), a lesbian in a bear suit in *The Hotel New Hampshire* (1984) – while stories of her falling in love on every set and a poster of the naked actress with a snake made her America's favourite sexual fantasy. Only Paul Schrader's confused *Cat People* (1982) attempted to explore the inherent mixture of innocence and otherworldly sexuality where most directors were content to stand back and worship. The phenomenon did not go unnoticed by Wenders, however, who kept her behind a coin-operated glass screen that rendered even her fictional ex-husband Harry Dean Stanton a voyeur in *Paris, Texas* (1984).

Kinski's career soon reached a crisis when overwork and marital problems led to a breakdown, while her films flopped with astounding regularity – none more spectacularly than Hugh Hudson's woefully misconceived *Revolution* (1985). Since then, her film work has been sporadic – and decidedly continental – and met with less fanfare than the very public collapse of her marriage and subsequent custody battles.

1975 Falsche Bewegung/Wrong Movement (W. Germany) **1976** To The Devil A Daughter (UK–W. Germany – dubbed) **1978** Leidenschaftliche Blumchen/ Passion Flower Hotel (W. Germany) **1979** Cosi Come Sei/Stay As You Are (Italy); Tess **1982** Reifezeugnis/For Your Love Only (W. Germany); Cat People; One From The Heart **1983** Frühlingssimfonie/Spring Symphony (W. Germany) aka Symphony Of Love; Exposed; La Lune Dans Le Caniveau/The Moon In The Gutter (France) **1984** Unfaithfully Yours; The Hotel New Hampshire; Paris, Texas **1985** Maria's Lovers; Revolution; Harem (France) **1987** Maladie D'Amour/ Malady Of Love (France) 1988 Stille Nacht/Silent Night (W. Germany) **1989** Torrents Of Spring (Italy); In Una Notte Di Chiaro Di Luna/On A Moonlit Night (Italy); Magdalene **1990** Il Segreto/The Secret (Italy); Il Sole Anche Di Notte/Night Sun (Italy)

Kirby, Bruno
(real name Bruce Kirby, Jr)
Actor
Born ?
New York City

In the time-honoured tradition of character actors, Bruno Kirby had a promising beginning in his extreme youth – when, billed as B. Kirby, Jr he made a delightful young Little Italy hood, Clemenza, opposite Robert De Niro's young Vito Corleone in *The Godfather Part II* (1974) – only to be subsequently lost in bit parts and bombs for over a decade before his face and name became recognisable and his presence a pleasure to audiences.

The son of actor Bruce Kirby, Kirby Jr was born and raised in New York City, where he studied drama with Stella Adler and the late Peggy Feury. His career first took off in television with a regular role in a popular series, *Room 222*, and he has appeared in a number of TV movies, including *Some Kind Of Miracle, A Summer Without Boys, All My Darling Daughters* and *Million Dollar Infield*.

Kirby's film debut came in Mark Rydell's bittersweet romance *Cinderella Liberty* (1973), followed quickly with his good role in Coppola's Academy Award-winning sequel to *The Godfather*. Predictably, the film work was downhill afterwards, with Bruno (as he later called himself) turning up in the odd bonehead comedy (*Almost Summer*, 1978), a formulaic Charles Bronson actioner (*Borderline*, 1980), and Paul Verhoeven's gory mess of an American debut, *Flesh And Blood* (1985). But he also had a comic cameo in the hilarious Rob Reiner rock satire, *This Is Spinal Tap* (1984), and work with Alan Parker and Albert Brooks to his credit.

The actor really began to make an impression in 1987 as the uptight, idiotic lieutenant unsuccessfully trying to command respect and laughs from his insubordinate subordinants at the Armed Forces Radio station in Saigon in *Good Morning, Vietnam* (1987), a role in which he was sickeningly funny as a man with no sense of humour. The same year he exhibited another aspect of his gift for characterisation as the sweaty, servile nark in Barry Levinson's *Tin Men* then, reteamed with Rob Reiner for the smash hit *When Harry Met Sally* (1989), he offered first-rate support as Billy Crystal's best friend, whose courtship of Carrie Fisher neatly counterpointed that of the principals. In the under-rated, original comedy *The Freshman* (1990), Bruno Kirby's hustling, 'wannabe' mafioso threatened in his scenes to steal the picture from a surprisingly funny Marlon Brando, who subsequently raved about Kirby with uncharacteristic enthusiasm.

1973 Cinderella Liberty **1974** The Godfather Part II **1978** Almost Summer **1980** Borderline; Where The Buffalo Roam **1981** Modern Romance **1984** This Is Spinal Tap; Birdy **1985** Flesh And Blood **1987** Tin Men; Good Morning, Vietnam **1989** Bert Rigby, You're A Fool; When Harry Met Sally; We're No Angels **1990** The Freshman **1991** City Slickers

Kirkland, Sally

Actress
Born 31 October 1944
New York

The elusive screen career of Sally Kirkland – some 30 movies, many of them dreadful, in which she has played mainly cameos, small supporting parts or blink-and-you'll-miss-her bits – might have passed entirely unremarked were it not for *Anna* (1987). Kirkland's expert and moving performance deservedly captured her an LA Critics Best Actress award, a Golden Globe and an Oscar nomination but, alas, seemed to lead her nowhere. Not that she necessarily wished to be led anywhere, given her unconventional life and career as a 60s underground figure and a stage actress, of some note in both fields.

Dubbed 'the Isadora Duncan of nudo-thespianism' and 'the Helen Hayes of off-Broadway', Kirkland may have been classified as a hippie upstart early in her career but, unlike many of her peers of that era, she survived into the 90s with her ideas and style intact. The daughter of a well-bred scrap-iron merchant and a fashion editor of the influential *Life* magazine (a woman who was often surrounded by luminaries of the day like Jean Shrimpton, Verushka and Jackie Kennedy), Kirkland would often appear in *Vogue* and other magazines as a celebrity model, thanks to her mother's contacts.

After finishing high school, Sally joined the Actors' Studio to study with Uta Hagen and Lee Strasberg, then found work off-Broadway and off-off-Broadway where her appearance in *Sweet Eros* gained her quite some notoriety. (The production required the young actress to sit onstage for 45 minutes, tied up and nude.) The avant garde attracted her, as did the drug scene, a fatal attraction which resulted in a suicide attempt in 1964. Recovered from the crisis, she turned to yoga and painting as a means of therapy, before a spate of work in underground films notably for Andy Warhol (including *The Thirteen Most Beautiful Women* in 1965) led her to Hollywood. There, her talents were largely wasted, as she found herself mainly confined to the role of marginal girlfriend, prostitute, wife or passer-by, and if she worked in company with some big star names (Dennis Hopper, Redford, Streisand, Goldie Hawn), her off-screen associations were rather more noticeable – among those to whom she has been romantically linked are Bob Dylan, Robert De Niro amd Raul Julia.

Opting out of the acting scene in 1983, she founded the Sally Kirkland Acting Workshop, a travelling seminar which espoused the benefits of meditation and yoga for the theatrical arts. Four years later she returned to New York and *Anna* for director Yurek Bogayevicz. In this poignant tale of a middle-aged Czech actress who struggles in America after enjoying a brilliant career in her native country, Kirkland exhibited a Czech accent that would have shamed Meryl Streep, and gave a performance of depth and subtlety as the one-time starlet who helps another (Paulina Porizkova) to succeed where she cannot.

Kirkland tends to turn up wherever something potentially off-beat or interesting is happening, but the potential is seldom realised, as with the Robbie Benson flop about drug abuse, *Crack In The Mirror* (1988), or the Kevin Costner vehicle *Revenge* (1990), where she was one of the few actors who bravely attempted to lend depth to cardboard characters. She turned her hand to comedy with personal if not box-office success in the tacky and appalling *Bullseye!* (1990), in which she was the ex-lover of both Michael Caine and Roger Moore (and the mother of a daughter who is the child of one of them). After so many years in the business, she has refused to allow her age to prevent her from playing seemingly youthful women. Sally Kirkland is a unique bundle of energy, who uses her off-beat attraction, kooky grace and undoubted skill to offer unexpected performances in every aspect of the medium, from cable TV to feature films.

1964 The Thirteen Most Beautiful Women **1968** Blue

1969 Coming Apart; Futz! **1970** Brand X **1971** Going Home **1973** The Young Nurses; The Way We Were; The Sting; Cinderella Liberty **1974** Candy Striper Nurses; Big Bad Mama **1975** Bite The Bullet; Crazy Mama **1976** Breakheart Pass; A Star Is Born; Pipe Dreams **1979** Hometown USA **1980** Private Benjamin **1981** The Incredible Shrinking Woman **1982** Fatal Games; Human Highway **1983** Talking Walls; Love Letters **1987** Anna **1988** Crack In The Mirror **1989** Cold Feet; Best Of The Best; High Stakes **1990** Paint It Black; Revenge; Bullseye! **1991** Primary Motive; JFK **1992** The Player (Cameo); In The Heat Of Passion; Forever; Hit The Dutchman

Kline, Kevin

Actor
Born 24 October 1947
St Louis, Missouri

Kevin Kline's acting skills are prodigious in quantity and dazzling in quality. He is a comedian who can go the whole route from delicate suggestion to hilariously over-the-top farce – from the financially successful host of a group of old college friends in *The Big Chill* (1983) to the paranoid-lunatic burglar with woefully misconceived intellectual pretensions and a taste for live fish in *A Fish Called Wanda* (1988), the film which won him a Best Supporting Actor Oscar. In serious drama his range is similarly wide, with the brilliant but pathologically unbalanced husband of Meryl Streep's Auschwitz survivor (*Sophie's Choice*, 1982) marking one end of the spectrum and the sober portrait of the South African newspaper editor Donald Woods (*Cry Freedom*, 1987) marking the other, and both ends connected by a bold approach to dramatic scale and timing. He can sing and dance with athletic flair, as he has done in the Broadway musical *On The Twentieth Century* (1978) and the Broadway version of the Gilbert and Sullivan operetta *The Pirates of Penzance* (1980), the latter subsequently preserved on film (1982); he can play the piano. And he has a leading man's dashing good looks – dark hair, dark eyes, romantic profile, trim figure – which he can turn to the benefit of all genres: in *I Love You To Death* (1990), his swaggering Italian philanderer cuts a ludicrous figure precisely because he is credibly sexy.

For the moment, though, Kline remains a theatre star and a not-quite-categorizable cinema property. It may be the independent cast of his mind that is responsible for this curious state of affairs – he regularly returns to New York to play the classics (in 1991 *Hamlet*, which he also directed). Or perhaps it is the sense of real seriousness and even humility that filters through such ebullient versatility and professionalism: he is patently not out to be a film star regardless of cost. Whatever the cause, his talents have only been adumbrated on screen, rather than fully exploited; and whether the situation will change in the future is anyone's guess.

Born in St Louis, and educated there at a school run by Benedictine monks, Kline went to Indiana University as a music student but later switched to drama studies, which after graduation he rounded off at the New York Juilliard School. After several years playing the classics with John Houseman's travelling Acting Company, he made his Broadway debut in the musical *The Robber Bridegroom*. Tony Awards for *On The Twentieth Century* and *The Pirates Of Penzance* preceded Alan J. Pakula's *Sophie's Choice*, a remarkably complex and testing first assignment by any standards. After the *Pirates* film, *The Big Chill* marked his first screen encounter with Lawrence Kasdan, a director who brings out the best in good actors and who uses his favourites (such as Kline and his friend and *Big Chill* co-star, William Hurt), repeatedly. Their next collaboration, *Silverado* (1985), proved to be a fascinating but ultimately unsuccessful attempt to create a multi-faceted modern Western, part homage, part satire, period in dress and cool 1980s in tone; at the head of a strong cast (containing Kevin Costner, Jeff Goldblum, Danny Glover, Bryan Dennehy, Linda Hunt, and John Cleese in a cameo role) Kline's dashing hero did as much as any single actor could to hold the film together. The same could be said for his sympathetic, nicely balanced serio-comic performance as the affluent, well-meaning lawyer beset with crises in Kasdan's even more ambitious (and more successful) mosaic of life in disintegrating Los Angeles, *Grand Canyon* (1991). His third Kasdan film, *I Love You To Death*, is in some ways the least rewarding, for, though, the ingredients of the leading male role are supplied with Kline's wonderful feeling for comedy with an almost burlesque edge, the director's unexpected failure to sustain pace and tone the whole way through leaves the character with little room for development.

But whatever minor reservations one may have, and even in the Kline films that went wrong at the box office (*Silverado*), artistically (*I Love You To Death*), or both (the New York detective thriller *The January Man*, 1989), he himself is never less than compellingly watchable: a genuine American original. He is married to the actress Phoebe Cates.

1982 Sophie's Choice **1983** The Pirates of Penzance; The Big Chill **1985** Silverado **1986** Violets Are Blue **1987** Cry Freedom **1988** A Fish Called Wanda **1989** The January Man **1990** I Love You To Death **1991** Soapdish **1991** Grand Canyon **1992** Charlie **1992/93** Consenting Adults **1993** Dave

Konchalovsky, Andrei
(Sometimes Andre; Andrei Mikhalkov-Konchalovsky)
Director, writer
Born 20 August 1937
Moscow, USSR

Andrei Konchalovsky was born into an artistic Muscovite family. His mother was a poet, and his brother the well-known actor-director Nikita Mikhalkov. Although he trained as a musician at the Moscow conservatory, he switched to studying film under the distinguished director, Mikhail Romm. After graduating, Konchalovsky was involved in two films that suffered official disapproval, his second directorial effort, *Asya's Happiness* (1967), and Andrei Tarkovsky's *Andrei Rublev* (1966), which he co-wrote. The latter had to wait until 1971 for release, but the former was shelved for 22 years. What upset the Soviet establishment might have been the director's unheroic view of the peasant, and a heroine who has no wish to marry the man who has made her pregnant.

Lacking the freedom to make the kind of films he wanted, Konchalovsky directed worthy adaptations of Chekhov and Turgenev before *Siberiade* (1979), a stunning epic not unlike a saga of the American West. It was his last Russian film before he went to America, where he spent five fruitless years until he was able to make *Maria's Lovers* (1984), an elegiac and earthy romance that further emphasised certain similarities between Russian and American rural dramas. It told of the return of a soldier (John Savage) from World War II to his small home town in Pennsylvania, where he woos and weds Maria (Nastassia Kinski), but is unable to satisfy her sexually.

Runaway Train (1985), taken from an idea by Akira Kurosawa, could as easily have been set in Siberia as Alaska. Full of pulsating action, but simultaneously weighed down by some heavy philosophising, it starred Jon Voight (who first invited Konchalovsky to America), Eric Roberts and Rebecca De Mornay (the men are escaping convicts) caught on a train hurtling through the winter landscape without a driver.

The hopes raised by Konchalovsky's interesting first two films in the West were dashed by his next pictures: *Duet for One* (1986), a rather awkward opening out of the successful two-handed stage play about a gifted violinist (Julie Andrews suffering nobly) suddenly becoming a victim of multiple sclerosis; and *Shy People* (1987), an unintentionally amusing melodrama set in the Louisiana bayou involving rape and voodoo, although Chris Menges' photography redeemed it somewhat. Any residue of Andrei Konchalovsky's past disappeared with *Tango And Cash* (1989) which saw him fully integrated into the Hollywood mainstream. A cop yarn which co-starred Sylvester Stallone and Kurt Russell crashing and quipping their way towards victory over international mobster Jack Palance, it was competent, mildly entertaining, and depressingly free from this gifted and intelligent Russian's trademarks – some of which reemerged in the patchily successful *The Inner Circle* (1991), which starred Tom Hulce as Stalin's private movie projectionist.

1965 The First Teacher (USSR) **1967** Asya's Happiness (USSR) **1969** A Nest Of Gentlefolk (USSR) **1974** Uncle Vanya (USSR); The Romance Of Lovers (USSR) **1979** Siberiade (USSR) **1984** Maria's Lovers **1985** Runaway Train **1986** Duet For One **1987** Shy People **1989** Homer And Eddie; Tango And Cash **1991** The Inner Circle

Kotcheff, Ted
(William Theodore Kotcheff)
Director
Born 7 April 1931
Toronto, Canada

Ted Kotcheff served his apprenticeship with CBC in his native country before Sydney Newman, a fellow Canadian and then executive producer of the pioneering and prestigious Armchair Theatre play series for Britain's ITV, invited him to London in the late 1950s. Newman's series, once pejoratively nicknamed 'Armpit Theatre', specialised in topics of social importance, and Kotcheff's best-known TV productions included *Hot Summer Night* by Ted Willis, about race relations, though he also ranged widely and directed a strikingly imaginative adaptation of Scott Fitzgerald's *The Last Tycoon*.

In 1962 the still young director entered the cinema. His first three films were made in England. Only *Life At The Top* (1965), the sequel to *Room At The Top*, made any impact, although it was generally regarded as a pale shadow of its forerunner, dealing to rather laboured effect in the social realism discovered by British movies a few years earlier. About the only notable feature of *Two Gentlemen Sharing* (1969), despite its potentially 'daring' treatment of race relations and homosexuality, was the length of time it took to achieve even a token release. After that, Kotcheff went off to Australia to make *Wake In Fright* (1971), a movie both incisive and powerful in depicting outback mores, and involving violence, both implied and actual, through the eyes of a young teacher stranded in a one-horse town. The Australian critic Brian McFarlane, wrote of it, 'Kotcheff's exploration of the myths of mateship and macho camaraderie has not been surpassed by any of the native forays into this field.'

Sadly, none of Kotcheff's later films achieved this standard, although the Canadian-made *The Apprenticeship Of Duddy Kravitz* (1974), set in 1940s Montreal with Richard Dreyfuss in the title role, was an attractively mounted and reasonably entertaining version of Mordechai Richler's novel. Despite lacking the bite of its source material, it proved to be the first international hit to emerge from the Canadian film industry, a fact which augured well for its director. However, his subsequent American projects have mainly comprised an assortment of comedies and action pictures. In the former genre, *Fun With Dick And Jane* (1977), starring Jane Fonda and George Segal, was a passable bedroom comedy; but *Switching Channels* ten years later, despite some incidental liveliness and effective playing by Burt Reynolds and Kathleen Turner, foundered to a large extent on the ill-advised premise of updating the classic newspaper play, *The Front Page*, to a TV news operation. As for the vulgar low farce of *Weekend At Bernie's* (1989), involving a corpse taken out on the spree and ostensibly engaging in waterskiing as well as more intimate activities, probably the less said the better. It is an odd reflection on Kotcheff's variability that this rowdy picture should come out shortly after *Winter People* (1988), a stodgily melancholy study of hillbilly folk in the 1930s, with Kelly McGillis and Kurt Russell marooned in an understandably unconvincing love affair amid the fussing and feuding.

Among the action movies he has made, Ted Kotcheff achieved his greatest popular success with *First Blood* (1982). An efficiently made thriller, it reprised the small-town setting of *Wake In Fright*, this time in the lush green American West, but its claim to fame is that it introduced to the screen, in the person of Sylvester Stallone, the character of disillusioned Vietnam veteran John Rambo who, in the sequels, Stallone was to promote into a dubious sort of new American superman. The Vietnam legacy theme, transported back to Asia, recurred in *Uncommon Valor* (1983), a larger-scale but less cogent undertaking, which found Gene Hackman taking rescue and revenge into his own hands.

Kotcheff has proved indisputably that he is a very reliable journeyman director, and that he can watchably rise to an effective screenplay when one comes his way. Unfortunately, his work seems unable to assume a consistent personality and, in the main, the variety of his output lacks much in the way of compensatory spice.

1962 Tiara Tahiti **1965** Life At The Top **1969** Two Gentlemen Sharing **1970** Wake In Fright **1971** Outback **1973** Billy Two Hats **1974** The Apprenticeship Of Duddy Kravitz **1977** Fun With Dick And Jane **1978** Who Is Killing The Great Chefs Of Europe? **1979** North Dallas Forty **1982** First Blood **1983** Uncommon Valor **1985** Joshua Then And Now **1987** Switching Channels **1988** Winter People **1989** Weekend At Bernie's **1992** Folks!

Kotto, Yaphet

Actor
Born 15 November 1937
New York City

Getting a taste for acting from dance lessons with his aunt (whose students also included James Dean and Marlon Brando) and voice lessons from Juanita Hall, the powerfully built, often soft-spoken but assertive Yaphet Kotto regards himself as 'an American actor' rather than a black one, and has generally managed to avoid racial typecasting although not always the wrath of black pressure groups. Coming to prominence via stage work when he took over the lead in a semi-professional production of *Othello* at the age of 19 after the principal actor fell ill, he entered films in the late 1960s when the civil rights movement made it cool to be black on screen, but strenuously avoided the 'blaxploitation' market for more substantial roles, preferably where his colour was irrelevant (such as his thief in *The Thomas Crown Affair*, 1968).

By 1972 his face was well enough known for him to write and direct, as well as appear in, *Time Limit* and go on to play a larger-than-life Bond villain in *Live And Let Die* (1973), a considerably less restrained performance than his norm and with none of the quiet menace of his other brushes with cinematic crime and punishment. Despite making good films, there have been few good roles – although his auto worker in *Blue Collar* (1978) is certainly one of them – but Kotto excels in filling out his characterisations with a good eye for the small details that make them real, as with his FBI man trying to stop smoking in *Midnight Run* (1938) who habitually steals suspects' cigarettes, but he has the good sense not to make an issue of them. They're just there and they work. Continually returning to the stage (to the extent of writing his own play, *Big Black*) for reasons that should be obvious from the majority of his recent films, Kotto remains a consummate, unmannered professional who is constantly better than his material.

1964 Nothing But A Man **1968** The Thomas Crown Affair; Five Card Stud **1970** The Liberation Of LB Jones **1972** Man And Boy; Bone; Time Limit (also w/d); Across 110th Street **1973** Live And Let Die **1974** Truck Turner **1975** Report To The Commissioner; Sharks' Treasure; Friday Foster **1976** Drum; The Monkey Hustle **1978** Blue Collar **1979** Alien; Brubaker **1982** Hey Good Lookin'; Death Vengeance aka Fighting Back **1983** The Star Chamber **1985** Warning Sign **1986** Eye Of The Tiger **1987** Terminal Entry; Prettykill; The Running Man **1988** Midnight Run **1989** A Whisper To A Scream; Ministry Of Vengeance **1990** I Love You To Death; Tripwire **1991** Freddy's Dead: The Final Nightmare **1992** Intent To Kill

Krabbé, Jeroen

Actor

Born 5 December 1944

Amsterdam, Holland

A heavy-set, dour Dutch actor, Jeroen Krabbé pursued a successful international career throughout the 80s, working as often in Europe as in Hollywood. No matter where he works though, he is most often typecast in villainous roles.

The offspring of a family of painters, and the grandson of a Dutch impressionist of note, Krabbé spent a year at Holland's Academy of Fine Arts, but at 17 he switched to acting, becoming the youngest pupil ever accepted at the Amsterdam Academy of Performing Arts. Not content with just acting, he went on to found a touring theatre company, design costumes, translate plays into Dutch, and direct – most successfully a new stage adaption of *The Diary of Anne Frank*, in which he also played Otto Frank. Something of a Renaissance man, Krabbé is also a widely exhibited painter (after three years of acting by night, painting by day, he graduated from the Fine Arts Academy in 1981); in Holland he hosted his own television chat show and a music programme on radio, and he is the author of *The Economy Cookbook*.

The Little Ark in 1972 brought Krabbé his first experience in film-making, though his was only a small role in this average children's movie. A more significant breakthrough came with *Soldier Of Orange* (1979), a drama tracing the effects of the German occupation of the Netherlands in 1940. Second-billed to Rutger Hauer, Krabbé turned in a typically moody performance and went to work with director Paul Verhoeven twice more. In the ribald *Spetters* (1983) he only made a cameo appearance, but was the lead in *The Fourth Man* (1983), playing Gerard, a Catholic, alcoholic homosexual writer prone to delirious hallucinations, who meets his match in Renee Soutendijk's sexy hairdresser-cum-witch. Krabbé was concentrating on film and television work by now, but the success in America of this extraordinary, eye-catching black comedy from Holland propelled him to follow Rutger Hauer to international film stardom (Verhoeven wasn't far behind them).

Supporting roles in the British fable *Turtle Diary* (1985) and the lame Whoopi Goldberg vehicle *Jumpin' Jack Flash* (1986) paved the way for Krabbé's memorable gang boss, Losado, in the otherwise disappointing Richard Gere vehicle *No Mercy* (1986). With his hooked nose and rugged, leathery face, the actor might be caricatured as a vulture; indefatigable moroseness is his forte, and his wily, seductive accent makes him a superb bad guy. Small surprise then that villains and shady characters have dominated his career since 1986, not only in features but also in a clutch of television movies in America and the UK. Even in Joan Micklin Silver's gentle romantic comedy, *Crossing Delancey* (1988), Krabbé's charismatic author turns out to be an unpleasantly egotistical chauvinist – a character expanded, oiled and upgraded, for

Barbra Streisand's egomaniacal musician husband in *The Prince of Tides* (1991). A criminal mastermind in the Bond film *The Living Daylights* (1987), a spy in *Scandal* (1989), and a mafia boss in *The Punisher* (1990), Krabbé has, to date, only found morally ambiguous roles in the British films *A World Apart* (1988) – as a Communist on the run from the South African authorities – and *Melancholia* (1989), in which he starred as a German art critic living in London, who is asked to renew his radical ideals and assassinate a South American torturer visiting the city. A communist and a killer – these are the heroes of Krabbé's work.

1982 The Little Ark **1979** Soldier of Orange (Holland) **1981** Een Vlucht Regenwulpen/A Flight of Rainbirds (Holland) **1983** Spetters (Holland); Die Vierde Man/The Fourth Man (Holland) **1985** Turtle Diary **1986** In De Scadur Van De Overwinning/In The Shadow Of Victory (Holland) Jumpin' Jack Flash; No Mercy **1987** The Living Daylights **1988** A World Apart; Crossing Delancey **1989** Scandal; Melancholia **1990** The Punisher **1991** The Prince of Tides; Kafka; Robin Hood (GB)

Kristofferson, Kris

Actor, singer, songwriter
Born 22 June 1936
Brownsville, Texas

A singer and prolific songwriter of considerable success before – and since – he became an actor, square-jawed, gravelly-voiced Kris Kristofferson has an unusual background. The son of an army general, he grew up in Texas and from an early age was a fan of country music; he began writing songs when he was just 11 and proceeded to major in creative writing at Pomona College, where he also excelled in (American) football and boxing. In 1958, he attended Oxford on a Rhodes scholarship, where he survived a short-lived and ill-fated attempt by a British promoter to turn him into a rock star. Returning to the United States, he followed in his father's footsteps and joined the army, which assigned him to Germany and later to West Point, where he taught English. But country music continued to exert its pull on the budding balladeer and before long he traded in his uniform for the precarious life of a struggling singer-songwriter in Nashville. He earned money doing a variety of jobs including bartending and working as a janitor until, in the mid-60s, the hits 'Vietnam Blues' and 'Me And Bobby McGee' brought him to the public's attention. By the time of his film debut in 1971's *The Last Movie*, he had for several years been enjoying a successful career as a top country-and-western performer.

An attractive, usually bearded, man with twinkling blue eyes, a wicked grin and an undeniably sexy presence, Kristofferson has mostly been cast according to his type, in recurring 'rugged' roles like that of singer, cowboy and soldier. It didn't require great imagination to see why, after his brief appearance in *The Last Movie*, Dennis Hopper's disastrous follow-up to *Easy Rider* (1969) for which he also wrote the music, Kristofferson was given the lead as the eponymous ex-rock star blackmailed by Gene Hackman in *Cisco Pike* (1972), for which he again supplied the music. Similarly, legendary director Sam Peckinpah sought to exploit the rising actor's 'tough hombre' demeanour and during the 70s cast him in three of his movies: 1973's uninspired retelling of *Pat Garret And Billy The Kid* (also starring Kristofferson's second wife, country singer Rita Coolidge) in which he played Billy; the brutal *Bring Me The Head of Alfredo Garcia* (1974), in which he had a supporting role; and as the lead, opposite Ali MacGraw, in 1978's *Convoy*, a noisy and excessively destructive tale about folk hero Kristofferson leading fellow truckers on a state-hopping run from a pursuing sheriff. Other 70s films trading on the actor's manly, somewhat leathery image included *Vigilante Force* (1976), in which he played a Vietnam veteran brought in to protect a California town from violence; *Semi-Tough* (1979), an amiable football movie co-starring Burt Reynolds; and *A Star is Born* (1976), Barbra Streisand's much maligned update of the classic showbiz story, for which Kristofferson was beautifully suited (if somewhat under-used) as John Norman Howard, a self-destructive rock star in decline who finds himself unbearably emasculated by his wife's meteoric success. While always a competent actor, in the hands of a good director and script, the sometimes charismatic Kristofferson can really shine, as he proved in both Paul Mazursky's examination of modern marriage, *Blume In Love* (1973), and Martin Scorsese's highly acclaimed *Alice Doesn't Live Here Anymore* (1975), in which he gave an unexpectedly tender performance as the well-intentioned man attempting to woo Ellen Burstyn's single mother trying to start a new life.

Come the 80s however, his acting career appeared to slide, starting in 1981 with a double dose of lamentable movies, *Heaven's Gate* and *Rollover*. The former, Michael Cimino's legendary Western disaster, had Kristofferson in the lead, which by association did nothing for the actor's box-office reputation, and the latter, an ill-conceived Alan J. Pakula drama, starred Jane Fonda as a rich heiress and a seriously miscast Kristofferson as a clean-shaven, unconvincingly urbane, trouble shooting banker. Since then, he has made movies only sporadically, most notably for director Alan Rudolph (*Songwriter*, 1985 and *Trouble in Mind*, 1986), preferring instead to concentrate on his musical talents. Despite a more active period at the end of the decade in such inferior movies as *Millenium* and *Welcome Home* (both 1989) it looked unlikely that Kristofferson would repeat the on-screen success he enjoyed in the 70s.

1971 The Last Movie aka Chinchero (bit, also music) **1972** Cisco Pike (also music) **1973** Pat Garrett And Billy The Kid; The Gospel Road; Blume In Love **1974** Bring Me The Head of Alfredo Garcia **1975** Alice Doesn't Live Here Anymore **1976** The Sailor Who Fell From Grace With The Sea; Vigilante Force; A Star is Born **1977** Semi-Tough **1978** Convoy; Freedom Road **1981** Heaven's Gate; Rollover **1985** Songwriter **1986** Trouble in Mind **1988** Big Top Pee-Wee **1989** Welcome Home; Millennium **1990** Perfume Of The Cyclone

Kubrick, Stanley

Director writer
Born 26 July 1928
The Bronx, New York

One of the few directors who has always been able to get the films of his choice made, Stanley Kubrick has a reputation which rests as much on his exclusivity – four films since 1971 – as his past triumphs. Encouraged as a child by his father to take up photography, he worked his way up to staff photographer on *Look* magazine by the time he was 17, but his abiding passion was always for moving pictures where the camera was not frozen to a single point of view. Quitting in 1950, he made and sold a short documentary, *Day Of The Fight*, to RKO for a $100 profit, as with 1951's *The Flying Padre*, which he directed, produced, wrote, photographed and edited – a pattern he was to repeat when he borrowed enough money from friends to make his feature debut, *Fear And Desire* (1953).

But Kubrick enthusiasts trace the beginning of his development as a film-maker to *Killer's Kiss* (1955), a B-movie thriller with stark visuals (he photographed that one, too) and a final fight sequence amid shop-window dummies that seemed to pre-figure the stylised violence and look of *A Clockwork Orange* (1971). *The Killing* (1956, the beginning of his partnership with producer James B. Harris) seemed similarly an exercise in visual stylistics, although grafted onto a strong B-movie plot, and showing a tendency to relegate characterisation to directorial signatures.

Those weaknesses were conspicuous by their absence from his two films with Kirk Douglas. *Paths Of Glory* (1957) remains one of the most striking anti-war films of all time (easily overshadowing his later cinematic foray to Vietnam), its production designed to enhance the emotion rather than, as in so many later cases, obscuring it. Dealing with the court martial of three French soldiers for cowardice, a futile attack designed to further a weak-willed general's career that ends in their inevitable and politically expedient execution (one of them still in his stretcher), it caused outrage in France where it was banned and only broke even elsewhere. By contrast, *Spartacus* (1960), the story of a failed slave rebellion against Rome made at the height of the Civil Rights movement, was a success on all counts, scoring impressively at the box office and heralding the thinking man's epics of the 60s. Brought in as a replacement for Anthony Mann during the early days of filming, Kubrick provided direction which was not only imaginative – note the scene where gladiators Douglas and Woody Strode eye each other nervously as another combat is heard off screen while they wait their turn, their duel itself simply a background for the political backbiting of its Roman audience – but passionate as well: its extended finale, with Spartacus (Douglas) killing his best friend to take his place on the last of the crosses that pave the road to Rome, where his freed wife shows him his son for the first time and begs him to die quickly, is one of the most intensely moving moments in cinema, and certainly the most emotive in Kubrick's career. But the director was unhappy with the film, publicly disowning it due to post-release editing (later restored) and producer Douglas' refusal to allow him to rewrite the script.

The desire to assume total control over his films that led him to England was realised soon after the success of his black comedy about the accidental end of the world, *Dr Strangelove Or: How I Learned To Stop*

Worrying And Love The Bomb (1964). Like the Douglas films and his watered-down version of Nabokov's satirical *Lolita* (1962), *Strangelove* was firmly anti-Establishment, with the preconceptions and prejudices of society leading to tragedy, in this case as technology renders humanity obsolete, a theme mirrored in *2001: A Space Odyssey* (1968). As with *Strangelove*, which was populated entirely by caricatures, it marked Kubrick's growing distrust of and coldness towards humanity, which, from earliest evolution, requires the stimulus of an outside force (a monolith) to inspire thought and development, a notion somewhat vindicated by the ultimate product of that thought, the Hal 9000 computer (perversely, the film's most human character) determining humans a liability to the task they have set him. In many ways the film was a turning point for Kubrick, moving away from the constraints of narrative and wallowing in a love of technology both on screen and off. And its three-year production period set him on a path of prolonged, meticulous perfectionism (one shot of Scatman Crothers crossing a road in *The Shining*, 1980, took 96 takes) at the cost of emotional spontaneity.

A Clockwork Orange, his most controversial film (which Kubrick, not the censor, removed from British cinemas), while improving on elements of Anthony Burgess' novel, fell prey to designer pessimism, its examination of society's attitudes and responses to violence compromised by the sheer premeditation inherent in every carefully composed shot. As with previous films – the generals in their museum-like headquarters sedately overlooking the deaths of their men in the rat-like trenches far away in *Paths Of Glory*, the murder of Quilty amid shrouded works of art in *Lolita* – it showed the implacability and incongruity of art when contrasted with human suffering, seeming to set it against life as a background for acts of violence: here, sex crimes committed to the strains of Beethoven, but this time the coldness seemed Kubrick's own, as though he were similarly set against the human race.

A human centre was also missing from his ornate, visually exquisite period piece, *Barry Lyndon* (1975), while *The Shining*, at times a virtual advert for Steadicam with its constant prowling shots of hotel corridors, was overwhelmed by the degeneration of Jack Nicholson's characterisation into a prime display of ham, as if the increasingly reclusive director had forgotten what real human behaviour was like. *Full Metal Jacket* (1986) at first seemed to be an answer to the criticism, its first 40 minutes charting the dehumanisation that was, and still is, an integral part of the army training process, only for the resultant killing machine (like Hal 9000) to turn on his drill sergeant, easily among the best of Kubrick's work. Yet the remainder of the film was tired clichés more akin to a late 40s World War II movie than one about Vietnam (recreated with uncanny accuracy in London's Docklands). It was padded out with incessant Steadicam tracking shots that, for all their technical precision and initial effect, lacked the hand-held documentary immediacy of the attack on the airbase in *Dr Strangelove*.

Now controlling all aspects of his films to an unprecedented degree, through his unique deal with Warner Bros., Stanley Kubrick – silent from 1986 to date – is free to take as much time as he likes to bring his work to the screen. But for all his technical ability, one cannot help but feel that his passion is spent by the time his material actually reaches the screen and that his work could benefit from a shorter gestation period.

1953 Fear And Desire (w/d) **1955** Killer's Kiss (w/d) **1956** The Killing (w/d) **1957** Paths Of Glory (also co-writer) **1960** Spartacus **1962** Lolita **1964** Dr Strangelove Or: How I Learned To Stop Worrying And Love The Bomb (also co-writer) **1968** 2001: A Space Odyssey (also co-writer) **1971** A Clockwork Orange (w/d) **1975** Barry Lyndon (w/d) **1980** The Shining (also co-writer) **1986** Full Metal Jacket (also co-writer)

Kurtz, Swoosie

Actress
Born 6 September 1944
Omaha, Nebraska

Named after an airplane her father (a colonel in the American Air Force) flew in World War II, Swoosie Kurtz had the advantage of a memorable name when she entered the entertainment business in the late 60s. Before that, she attended the University of Southern California, followed by a drama school in England. She made her acting debut in a series of regional theatrical plays before appearing in an off-Broadway production of *The Effects Of Gamma Rays On Man-In-The-Moon-Marigolds* in 1970. She won an Obie for her performance, one of several awards she has received for her stage work, including a Tony, a Drama Desk award and an Outer Critics' Circle Award for her performance as Gwen in Lanford Wilson's play *Fifth Of July*. Numerous other honours followed for her impressively varied roles, and the actress was finally spotted by Hollywood, who first signed her up for a part in the TV series *Love Sydney*, for which she won an Emmy award. Her first film was *Slap Shot* (1977), a moderate success starring Paul Newman as the champion player of an ice-hockey team, and even though Swoosie's role was small, it was enough to get her noticed.

The romance *First Love* (1977), with William Katt and Susan Dey, was a flop that quickly vanished, as did the sequel to *Love Story* (1970), *Oliver's Story* (1978) starring Ryan O'Neal, in which she had a small supporting role. Critics continually pointed her out as the best thing in a bad movie, and her determination paid off when she returned to the big screen four years later in the movie adaptation of John Irving's novel starring Robin Williams, *The World According To Garp* (1982). Although not a winner at the box office, the film was well-received by the critics, with Kurtz in great company alongside Williams, Glenn Close (in her feature debut), John Lithgow and Jessica Tandy.

The actress' next few films were not great critical successes, but she appeared with some big-name stars, and her performances continued often to be the only noteworthy ingredient. She was in company with heart-throb Jeff Bridges in Taylor Hackford's misguided tale of obsessional love, *Against All Odds* (1984), and rose to co-star status with Goldie Hawn in *Wildcats* (1986), the comedy about a woman who decides to coach a junior varsity football team. Her choice of roles was distinctly varied, one minute playing a straight comedy role, and the next appearing in the bizarre Talking Heads film *True Stories* (1986).

As Kurtz's movie outings became more frequent, she was offered more substantial roles. In 1988 she was in two mildly successful films and one that was highly acclaimed. First, she hammed it up with Judge Reinhold and 11-year-old Fred Savage in the body-swap comedy *Vice Versa* (1988), then she turned to more serious matters as the older woman a drugged-out Michael J. Fox turns to in the drama based on Jay McInerney's novel *Bright Lights, Big City* (1988). But it was her third role of that year that was the best in her movie career to date, that of the mother of virginal Uma Thurman in Stephen Frears' masterly evocation of French intrigue, *Dangerous Liaisons* (1988). It was certainly a part to boost her career, and, in a cast that included Glenn Close, John Malkovich and Michelle Pfeiffer, she was praised for her portrayal of a strictly moral 18th-century French aristocrat.

Since her performance in that film, the actress has been cast with other critically acclaimed stars – Robert De Niro and Jane Fonda in 1990s tedious *Stanley And Iris* (the only member of the cast not performing purely to win an Oscar nomination) and the same year Michael Caine in the unfunny satire *A Shock To The System*. If the vehicles to date have been unworthy of her talents, her record seemed, nonetheless, to ensure that Swoosie Kurtz would continue to produce quality performances.

1977 Slap Shot; First Love **1978** Oliver's Story **1982** The World According To Garp **1984** Against All Odds **1986** Wildcats; True Stories **1988** Vice Versa; Bright Lights, Big City; Dangerous Liaisons **1990** Stanley And Iris; A Shock To The System

L

Ladd, Diane
(Rose Diane Ladner)
Actress
Born 29 November 1939
Meridian, Missouri

Three times an Academy Award nominee, noted stage actress, ex-wife of actor Bruce Dern, mother of Laura, cousin of Tennessee Williams, writer and popular motivational lecturer on her pet subjects of holistic medicine and 'Balance – Mental, Physical and Spiritual – from the point of view of an Actress', Diane Ladd is an overwhelming bundle of energy. From a biker chick in *The Wild Angels* (1966) to the sassy waitress of *Alice Doesn't Live Here Any More* (1975) to the monster mom of *Wild At Heart* (1990), the latter two performances earning her Oscar nominations, she has displayed palpable dynamism.

Born and raised in Missouri, Ladd ventured to New York as a teenager, working as a model and a dancer at the Copacabana nightclub before making her New York stage debut in Williams' *Orpheus Descending*. In 1961 she made her film debut in the melodrama *Something Wild* (1961), which starred Carroll Baker, but she was more successful in the theatre, to which she has regularly returned over 30 years. After marrying Dern, with whom she appeared in *The Wild Angels*, she worked sporadically in Hollywood, but didn't really hit her stride until her work as tough cookie Flo in Martin Scorsese's *Alice* brought her Oscar, Golden Globe and BAFTA nominations. Her subsequent work in the television spin-off from the film, *Alice*, brought her a TV Golden Glove. After raising her daughter and while pursuing her many other interests, Ladd, who resides in Sedona, Arizona, found herself bankable and very much in demand in middle-age for very diverse mother roles. Her vengeful schemer in David Lynch's provocative *Wild At Heart* (1990), playing her real daughter's mother, was florid and mad, while her genteel, free-spirited Southern 30s intellectual in *Rambling Rose* (1991) opposite Robert Duvall and, once more, daughter Laura, was the warm and nurturing reverse. Ladd's and Dern's nominations, respectively, for Best Supporting Actress and Best Actress in the 1991 Oscars for the film made Academy Award history as a unique mother-daughter double and indicated that the prime of Miss Diane Ladd was not past. During late 1992, she was developing her own project, in which she hoped to star as the colourful Martha Mitchell, indiscreet wife of Richard Nixon's disgraced Attorney General.

1961 Something Wild **1966** The Wild Angels **1969** The Reivers **1970** Macho Callahan; Rebel Rousers aka Limbo; WUSA **1971** The Steagle **1973** White Lightning **1974** Chinatown **1975** Alice Doesn't Live Here Anymore **1976** Embryo; The November Plan **1981** All Night Long **1983** Something Wicked This Way Comes **1987** Black Widow **1988** Plain Clothes **1989** National Lampoon's Christmas Vacation **1990** Wild At Heart **1991** A Kiss Before Dying; Rambling Rose

Lahti, Christine
Actress
Born 4 April 1950
Birmingham, Mississippi

Although she has been seen in fewer than a dozen films and her public recognition factor is virtually zero, the tall and strikingly attractive Christine Lahti, when given the chance, has consistently proved herself a screen actress of outstanding ability and depth.

Educated at the University of Michigan, she trained for the stage with the legendary Uta Hagen at the Herbert Berghof Studio. She is also an accomplished mime artist and has performed in mime at Edinburgh's Traverse Theatre. Lahti made her debut as an actress on the New York stage in 1978 in *The Woods* and shortly after was cast opposite Al Pacino for a very attractive and promising film debut in Norman Jewison's biting judicial system satire *And Justice For All* (1979), written by Barry Levinson and Valerie Curtin. She was excellent as Richard Dreyfuss' doctor in *Whose Life Is It Anyway?* (1981) and in a supporting role in *The Executioner's Song* (1982), and simply wonderful as Goldie Hawn's friend and co-worker in the botched World War II women-at-war drama Jonathan Demme would like to forget, *Swing Shift* (1984).

Unfortunately, Lahti's invariably terrific character studies have almost always been in run-of-the-mill, here-today-gone-the-next releases or under-appreciated films. As a leading lady she was mesmerising in Bill Forsyth's gentle, poignant *Housekeeping* (1987), playing the irresponsible, free-spirited aunt whose two orphaned nieces are put in her unconventional care; and intensely believable as a wanted former college radical of the 1960s raising her children underground and on the run in Sidney Lumet's moving *Running On Empty* (1988). Married to director Thomas Schlamme, Lahti was seen in a cameo in his debut feature, *Miss Firecracker* (1989), as Holly Hunter's neighbour (holding the newborn Schlamme baby). *The Doctor* (1991) – in which she played taken-for-granted wife to William Hunt's arrogant surgeon stricken with cancer, at least gave her a presence in a mid-level hit mainstream film.

1979 . . . And Justice For All **1981** Whose Life Is It Anyway? **1982** The Executioner's Song **1984** Swing Shift **1986** Just Between Friends **1987** Housekeeping; Stacking aka Season Of Dreams **1988** Running On Empty **1989** Miss Firecracker; Gross Anatomy **1991** Funny About Love; The Doctor **1992** Leaving Normal; The Fear Inside

Lambert, Christopher

Actor
Born 29 March 1957
New York City

Frenchman Christopher (or Christophe when he's at home) Lambert's combination of good-looking physicality and cultivated background made him an apt choice for lost lordling raised in the jungle Tarzan in Hugh Hudson's ambitious, handsome, downbeat reworking of the Edgar Rice Burroughs favourite, *Greystoke: The Legend Of Tarzan, Lord Of The Apes* (1984).

Born in New York to French parents – his mother a psychologist and his father then working at the UN – Lambert was brought up in Geneva, and spent a brief period working at the London Stock Exchange at his parents' behest before following his own inclination and entering the National Conservatory in Paris to study drama. Expelled in his third year, he promptly landed a small role in *Le Bar Du Telephone* (1980) and was on his way in French cinema. Three films later he made his English language debut in *Greystoke* and attracted a lot of attention in the hunk stakes. But his subsequent films in English have brought mixed fortunes: Russell Mulcahy's somewhat crazed and definitely silly *Highlander* (1986) cast the French-accented Lambert as a Scottish immortal battling his way from the 16th-century Highlands to 20th-century New York under the tutelage of a Scots-accented Sean Connery as a Spanish immortal. It was not a particular hit, but spawned a sequel in 1991. *The Sicilian* (1987) from footage fetishist Michael Cimino was even more dubious, with Lambert more wooden than winning in the title role as Sicily's post-war secessionist hero Salvatore Giuliano.

Despite his pin-up status in France, Lambert has yet to fulfill his early build-up as the new Depardieu. His most arresting appearance to date came in Luc Besson's *Subway* (1985), starred with Isabelle Adjani as a literally underground (it's set in the metro) and stylish New Wave criminal in an original if ultimately aimless thriller. Lambert is married to the young American actress Diane Lane, with whom he starred in the murder-in-the-world-of-master-chess mystery, *Knight Moves* (1992), playing the suitably enigmatic is-he-or-isn't-he-the-serial-killer chess master.

1980 Le Bar Du Telephone (France) **1981** La Dame De Coeur (France) **1982** Legitime Violence (France) **1984** Greystoke – The Legend Of Tarzan, Lord Of The Apes **1985** Paroles Et Music/Love Songs (France); Subway **1986** Highlander **1987** The Sicilian **1988** To Kill A Priest **1989** Priceless Beauty at a Love Dream; Apres Le Pluie/After The Rain (France) **1989** Why Me? **1991** Highlander II – The Quickening **1992** Knight Moves; Fortress

Lancaster, Burt

Actor
Born 2 November 1913
New York City

Handsome, strapping Burt Lancaster with his big, flashing grin and athlete's physique was the epitome of a *Boys' Own* screen hero in the 1950s, when he popularly played a succession of swashbucklers, gunmen and irresistible rogues. Unlike many of his contemporaries, Lancaster's charisma aged well, and long after he had proven himself to be more than just prime beefcake he brought the weight of his presence and the intact twinkle to some very fine films in his sunset years.

The son of a postal worker, he distinguished himself solely in sports at school and at 17 joined a circus acrobatics troupe, partnering buddy Nick Cravat, who was later to appear as Burt's sidekick in films like *The Crimson Pirate* (1952). Ten years and some lean times later, Lancaster was reduced to employment in the lingerie department of

Chicago's Marshall Fields' department store. When America went to war Lancaster served in North Africa and got a taste for acting and dancing in army shows. Fresh from the service and back in New York in 1945, he got a role in a Broadway play, a big agent in Harold Hecht, and a Hollywood contract with Hal Wallis.

Scarcely knowing what he was doing, Lancaster made his film debut at the age of 33 in the *noir* classic *The Killers* (1946), inspired by the Ernest Hemingway short story. Surely by happy accident, his beauty and evident physical strength made for a memorable contrast with his character's passivity – ensnared by temptress Ava Gardner and embracing death as a willing victim. Lancaster learned what he was doing as he went along, and he did not become a real star until he embarked on his string of romantic action adventures with *The Flame And The Arrow* (1950) and *The Crimson Pirate* (1952). But his *noir* period apprenticeship yielded, ironically, some of his most interesting appearances. His rugged looks set him up as a tough guy, but the perversity of his playing weak patsies and masochistic mugs dominated by women – Barbara Stanwyck in *Sorry, Wrong Number* (1948), Yvonne De Carlo in *Criss Cross* (1949) – made the drama even darker.

Four years of studio hopping on loan-outs between Universal and Paramount to play cons and ex-cons fuelled the actor's desire to take control over his career, although he was not deprived of worthy projects – *All My Sons* (1948) gave him a good opportunity as Edward G. Robinson's embittered son in a solid adaptation of Arthur Miller's riveting family drama. It is a commonplace now for actors to form their own production companies, but Lancaster broke new ground and played a significant part in bringing down the old studio system when, in 1948, he and Harold Hecht formed what was to become (with James Hill) Hecht-Hill-Lancaster Productions. Not only did Lancaster thus gain control over his own vehicles, he and his partners were responsible for a number of strong films, notably two Paddy Chayefsky dramas, *Marty* (1951), which won the Oscar for Best Picture, Actor (Ernest Borgnine), Screenplay and Direction (Delbert Mann), and *The Bachelor Party* (1957).

As dashing heroes go, Lancaster never bettered his tongue-in-cheek performance in *The Crimson Pirate*, a thoroughly delightful character in a terrific, amusing spoof adventure full of zest. Juggling action men and romantic leads with serious character roles like the quiet, rigid husband who explodes in alcoholic rage in *Come Back Little Sheba* (1952), the actor and producer had become a very big man in Hollywood – one with popularity and power.

Taking himself very seriously as an actor, Lancaster grew blustery, hamming heavily in roles that were commanding enough: witness his scenery chewing in *The Rainmaker* (1956), which is not without charm. It comes as more of a surprise, then, to watch his tightly restrained, chilling performance – arguably the greatest of his career – in *Sweet Smell Of Success* (1957) as J.J. Hunsecker, gossip columnist. In this, his most sinister characterisation, Lancaster is icy, tyrannical and deeply disturbing. But it was for *Elmer Gantry* (1960), back in his barnstorming element, that Lancaster won the Oscar for his fast-talking con-man evangelist. Then he was capable, in *Bird Man Of Alcatraz* (1962), of a delicate, sensitive portrayal as the real-life prison inmate who became a self-taught authority on birds.

Ageing well and artistically still ambitious, Lancaster had one last greatly impressive leading man performance in him for Luchino Visconti's masterpiece, *The Leopard* (1963), before the predictable decline into starry ensemble pieces, routine thrillers and dramas that are the lot of most stars over 50. (Though he made another, *Conversation Piece*, for Visconti in 1975, and featured in Bertolucci's *1900* in 1976.) His production company wound up, although it had an unusually long and successful life span, and Lancaster seemed a spent force. Then, when he was nearing 70, Louis Malle cast him as an elderly petty hood on the lam in *Atlantic City* (1980), a majestic 'comeback' such as few aged stars can dream of. In 1983, he delighted again as the dotty oil tycoon in Bill Forsyth's enchanting *Local Hero*, and he was set for the lead in Hector Babenco's *Kiss Of The Spider Woman* (1985) when ill health finally brought him down and the film had to be postponed. William Hurt subsequently took the role and won an Oscar, but Babenco credits Lancaster's enthusiasm and support for helping the project get made.

In 1986 he bounced back, reunited with his old friend (and co-star of seven films) Kirk Douglas, for *Tough Guys*, a disappointing formula film about two grey crooks, but joyously watchable for fans of both old pros. And, in 1989, he was lured back onto the screen to play a saintly second banana to a new generation's heart-throb, Kevin Costner, in *Field Of Dreams*, contributing to the film's celebratory 'old Hollywood' magic. It was a lovely swansong for a legend.

1946 The Killers **1947** Brute Force; Variety Girl (cameo); Desert Fury; I Walk Alone **1948** All My Sons; Sorry, Wrong Number; Kiss The Blood Off My Hands **1949** Criss Cross; Rope Of Sand **1950** The Flame And The Arrow; Mr 880 **1951** Ten Tall Men; Vengeance Valley; Jim Thorpe – All-American **1952** The Crimson Pirate; Come Back, Little Sheba **1953** South Sea Woman; From Here To Eternity; Bad For Each Other; His Majesty O'Keefe **1954** Apache; Vera Cruz **1955** The Kentuckian (also director); The Rose Tattoo **1956** Trapeze; The Rainmaker **1957** Gunfight At The OK Corral; Sweet Smell Of Success **1958** Run Silent, Run Deep; Separate Tables **1959** The Devil's Disciple **1960** The Unforgiven; Elmer Gantry **1961** The Young Savages; Judgement At Nuremberg **1962** Bird Man Of Alcatraz **1963** Il Gattopardo/The Leopard (Italy); A Child Is Waiting; The List Of Adrian Messenger **1964** Seven Days In May; The Train **1965** The Hallelujah Trail **1966** The Professionals **1968** The Swimmer; The Scalphunters **1969** Castle Keep; The Gypsy Moths **1970** Airport; The Lawman **1971** Valdez Is Coming **1972** Ulzana's Raid **1973** Scorpio; Executive Action **1974** The Midnight Man (also co-director, co-writer) **1975** Gruppo Di Famiglia In Un Interno/Conversation Piece (Italy) **1976** Novecento/1900 (Italy); Buffalo Bill And The Indians **1977** The Cassandra Crossing; Twilight's Last Gleaming; The Island Of Dr Moreau **1978** Go Tell The Spartans **1979** Zulu Dawn; Cattle Annie And Little Britches **1980** Atlantic City **1983** Local Hero **1986** Tough Guys **1989** Field Of Dreams

Landau, Martin

Actor
Born 20 June 1931
Brooklyn, New York City

Martin Landau fits Julius Caesar's description of Cassius in having 'a lean and hungry look . . . such men are dangerous.' A supporting actor for many years, more often than not as a heavy, he has almost always made an impression even in small roles. After three decades of sterling service in the lower ranks, he was finally rewarded with a substantial, Oscar-nominated role in a prestigious film: the adulterous opthalmologist Judah Rosenthal, who kills his mistress (Anjelica Huston), in Woody Allen's *Crimes And Misdemeanors* (1989). He made a tortured Dostoevskian figure, one of the most flawed and tragic character's in Allen's *oeuvre*.

Landau was a cartoonist with the *New York Daily News* for a number of years, attending the Actors' Studio at the same time. After several appearances on stage and television, he stood out in his second film, Alfred Hitchcock's *North By Northwest* (1959), as the gaunt and sinister sidekick to villain James Mason. After toga roles in *Cleopatra* (1963) and *The Greatest Story Ever Told* (1965, as Caiaphas), Landau co-starred with his wife, Barbara Bain, in the TV sci-fi series *Mission Impossible* (1966–68). He continued to play a variety of baddies in Westerns and gangster films, until given the lead as Roderick Usher in a low-budget, low-level version of *The Fall Of The House Of Usher* (1980). Aside from his role for Woody Allen, his best opportunity to shine came in Francis Coppola's *Tucker: The Man And His Dream* (1988). Third-billed as Abe Karatz, the businessman who helps finance the car factory of Preston Tucker (Jeff Bridges), he revealed a warmth, vigour and humour rarely present in the characters he so skilfully plays, and was duly awarded a Best Supporting Actor Oscar nomination.

1959 Pork Chop Hill; North By Northwest **1960** The Gazebo **1962** Stagecoach To Dancer's Park **1963** Cleopatra **1965** The Greatest Story Ever Told; The Hallelujah Trail **1966** Nevada Smith **1970** They Call Me MISTER Tibbs; Operation SNAFU **1971** A Town Called Hell; Under The Sign Of Capricorn **1972** Black Gunn **1976** Tony Saitta/Tough Tony (Italy); **1977** Strange Shadows In An Empty Room aka Blazing Magnum **1978** Meteor **1980** The Fall Of The House Of Usher; The Return aka The Alien's Return; Without Warning **1982** Alone In The Dark **1983** The Being **1984** Access Code **1987** Cyclone; Empire State; Sweet Revenge **1988** Tucker: The Man And His Dream **1989** Crimes And Misdemeanors **1990** Paint It Black **1991** Treasure Island/ Ile Au Trésor (France); Firehead **1992** Mistress

Landis, John

Director, writer
Born 30 August 1950
Chicago, Illinois

Were it not for several notable exceptions within his filmography, it would be only too easy to dismiss John Landis as the American box office's equivalent to fast food – overladen with non-essentials, lacking in basic substance, yet instant and wildly popular. That however, is only part of the story. For, lurking within the director synonymous with excess and gross-out anarchic humour, is a gifted, intelligent film-maker of verve and wit who occasionally gets the upper hand.

Like his contemporaries Steven Spielberg and Joe Dante, Landis is a child of the movies; aged seven, he attended a screening of *The Seventh Voyage of Sinbad* (1958) which established his ambition to enter the film business, a path from which he has never diverged. Born in Chicago, he was a baby when his family moved to Los Angeles and just a little boy when his father, Marshall, an interior decorator, died. Landis dropped out of high school at 17 and became a mail boy at 20th Century-Fox studios before heading off to Yugoslavia and talking his way into a job as a gaffer and, later, a production assistant, on *Kelly's Heroes* (1970). It was the age of spaghetti Westerns in Europe and he found work on an impressive 70 features – mainly as a stunt man – before making his way back to the States. The Hollywood he returned to was in a state of economic crisis and, work being impossible to find, the enterprising Landis (aged 21) and his stunt man cohort Jim O'Rourke decided to make their own feature. *Schlock* (1972), written, co-produced by, and starring Landis (as the monster), was a crude but effective spoof of B-movie horror films which became a cult classic and led to what eventually became *Kentucky Fried Movie* (1977). Working with film-makers Jim Abrahams and David and Jerry Zucker, with whom Landis later collaborated on the best-forgotten parody *Amazon Women On The Moon* (1987), the team produced *Kentucky Fried*, a largely vulgar and outrageous series of skits which became a surprise hit and caused Universal, who were looking for a young director to helm a campus comedy they had in production, to come calling.

National Lampoon's Animal House (1977) was the result, a slapstick, anarchic and rude spoof of student life in the 60s, which, thanks in large part to John Belushi's gross antics as Bluto the slob (one highlight sees him spurting out a mouthful of pudding in an imitation of an exploding zit), in a performance the director encouraged the rising young star to improvise, proved one of the most popular comedies of all times.

By now dubbed 'Hollywood's resident lunatic' Landis was then prevailed upon to orchestrate the proceedings of the Belushi-Dan Aykroyd starrer *The Blues Brothers* (1980). The film was a witty journey through a variety of situations, many of them involving such musical talents as Aretha Franklin, Ray Charles and Cab Calloway, as the brothers (characters Belushi and Aykroyd had originally created on the TV comedy show *Saturday Night Live*) tried to raise money to salvage the orphanage where they grew up, and ending in a vast ocean of destroyed cars. Expensive, self-indulgent and excessive, it nevertheless had some hilarious moments and has since become a cult classic.

Together, Landis' first two Hollywood movies revealed a lack of proper narrative grasp, as well as a failure to discipline and channel his leading actors; yet they also proved him to be a director firmly plugged into the all-important youth market. However, his next venture, which he also scripted, was a different story in all respects. A dynamite mixture of gory horror and clever comedy, the self-explanatory *An American Werewolf In London* (1981) was a small-budget movie that rightly proved a critical if not a commercial hit, thanks to its well-structured script, firmly delineated characters, and startlingly effective make-up from the Oscar-winning Rick Baker (who originally worked with Landis on *Schlock*). The director's next film, one of the four episodes which make up *Twilight Zone – The Movie* (1983), is remembered more for the tragedy it caused than the modest merits of the less-than-intriguing feature which was based on the classic TV series. During the filming of Landis' sequence, a helicopter accident caused the deaths of actor Vic Morrow and two children, and Landis and four of his colleagues were charged with involuntary manslaughter. In the five years that it took to be found not guilty, the director continued to work regularly, with both greater and lesser success than hitherto. *Trading Places* (1983) was the old environment vs heredity debate updated and injected with a racial angle as poor con-man Eddie Murphy swaps lives with privileged, stuffy commodities broker Dan Aykroyd. It was an uneven effort not aided by a ridiculous subplot, but the excellent performances from Murphy, Aykroyd and Jamie Lee Curtis helped make it a winner at the box office. As in many of his films, Landis rounded up several of his director friends, including Paul Mazursky, Roger Vadim, David Cronenberg and Amy Heckerling, for the enjoyable caper *Into The Night* (1985). Made all the more enjoyable by the presence of actors Jeff Goldblum and Michelle Pfeiffer, the story of a nerdy man in LA helping a beautiful woman escape from the killers on her trail scored no points commercially but remains one of Landis' cleverest and most stylish films to date. Ever one for drawing on movies themselves for inspiration, he took a shot at the Hope-Crosby *Road* movies with 1985's *Spies Like Us*, and missed. This inane and overblown parody starring Chevy Chase and Dan Aykroyd still managed to pull in the audiences, as did the likeable but essentially one-joke musical Western comedy, *Three Amigos!* (1986).

Away from the big screen, Landis co-wrote Michael Jackson's mammoth 1983 video, *Thriller*, as well as directing a documentary about the making of it, and filming a video with bluesman BB King in 1985. He also produced – and directed the first episode of – the disarming adult TV sex comedy series, *Dream On*. He has made guest appearances in other directors' movies (as well as in four of his own), including one for Steven Spielberg in his gargantuan flop, *1941* (1979). Whereas Spielberg learned the hard way that massive self-indulgence (at the expense of a proper plot and characterisation) doesn't necessarily reap massive returns, Landis has yet to absorb the lesson. Hence he spent vast sums of money allowing an ego-driven Eddie Murphy to show how many different roles he could play in *Coming To America* (1988), in what was an otherwise lame and flat story about an African prince disguised as a poor man, who goes looking for a wife in New York. And, however, substandard, the film was a big hit.

It seems that, whatever the obvious talents Landis has as a film-maker, the public's continued willingness to flock to see his movies, many of which are undisciplined and second-rate but undeniably commercial, has lulled him into a sense of canny complacency from which he all too infrequently emerges to surprise us.

As director only unless stated otherwise: **1972** Schlock (also writer, actor) **1973** Battle For The Planet Of The Apes (bit only) **1975** Death Race 2000 (bit only) **1977** Kentucky Fried Movie; National Lampoon's Animal House **1979** 1941 (bit only) **1980** The Blues Brothers (also co-writer, cameo) **1981** An American Werewolf In London (w/d) **1983** Trading Places; Twilight Zone – The Movie (w/d of segment) **1984** The Muppets Take Manhattan (cameo) **1985** Into The Night (also cameo); Spies Like Us **1986** Three Amigos! **1987** Amazon Women On the Moon **1988** Coming To America **1991** Oscar **1992** Sleepwalkers (cameo only); Innocent Blood

Lane, Diane

Actress
Born 22 January 1965
New York City

The daughter of drama coach Burt Lane, Diane was a child actress who made the transition to adult roles with ease. She first appeared on stage at the age of six with the prestigious New York experimental group, Cafe La Mama, and later toured Europe with them in productions of *Medea*, *Electra*, and *The Trojan Women*. For Joseph Papp she appeared in *The Cherry Orchard* and *Agamemnon* at New York's Lincoln Center, and in 1978 she won rave reviews for her leading role in *Runaways*, but turned down the opportunity to take the play to Broadway in favour of her first film part, opposite Laurence Olivier, in *A Little Romance* (1979). She was 14 years old.

Playing a young American in Paris, Lane already possessed beautiful hair down to her elbows, pale, unblemished features, and those striking eyebrows – like acute accents over her rather suspicious eyes. In George Roy Hill's engaging film, she runs off with a French boy chaperoned by a rogueish Olivier. In *Cattle Annie And Little Britches* (1980) Amanda Plummer and Lane (Britches) were orphans who headed West in search of adventure, joined the dilapidated Doolin-Dalton gang (headed by Burt Lancaster), and inspired them to pull off a few more heists. Neither of these films made waves – still less *Touched By Love* (1980), in which Lane played a cerebral palsy victim with Elvis for a pen pal, or the Kenny Rogers vehicle *Six Pack* (1982) – but they provided ample evidence of the actress' range and promise.

Lane also had a couple of TV movies under her belt when she first met Francis Ford Coppola while visiting a friend on the set of *One From The Heart*. A few months later, she was in Atlanta filming *Six Pack* when she saw TV spots announcing casting for Coppola's adaptation of *The Outsiders* (1983). Ten days after a single interview Lane found herself in Tulsa, surrounded by the male contingent of what would become the Brat Pack. At 17 she was both glamorous and sweet, though there was no avoiding the sentimentality that swamps the film. *Rumblefish* (1983) – shot back-to-back – was much more interesting, and Lane impressed as a high school siren who dumps dumb Rusty James (Matt Dillon) in favour of cunning Nicolas Cage. Coppola cast his daughter as Diane's sister, and it was clear he was something of a father figure to the up-and-coming actress. Her work for him has a more relaxed, personable quality that borders on the flirtatious. There is also a humour in her acting that is not always her trademark. In interviews, Lane jokes that Coppola treats her like a Madonna off screen and a whore on it; though, in fact, her young vamp in *The Cotton Club* (1984) is sympathetically conceived. The role was adapted to suit her age, and Lane, her hair platinum blonde à la Jean Harlow, makes an ambivalent heroine, even if a little more focus would have been welcome in the later stages. She also contributes a couple of fine torch songs to the film.

Another singing role immediately preceded this one. Walter Hill's *Streets Of Fire* (1984), a rock'n'roll fantasy out of Greek mythology, cast her as a pop singer-cum-Helen of Troy. It was a 'hot' role, all it lacked was character – and Lane's attempts to inject some fell foul of her director's hyper-macho instincts. The film's failure was the second setback in Lane's career. The first was also concerned with a female rocker: *Ladies And Gentlemen, The Fabulous Stains*. Produced as a major attraction in 1981 with Lane in the lead role, the film was barely released theatrically.

Since *The Cotton Club*, Lane's film career languished somewhat. *Lady Beware* (1987) was an interesting prospect that ran into production difficulties when director Karen Arthur was required to spice up her footage, and *The Big Town* (1987) proved an all too familiar excursion into *Cincinnati Kid* territory. Lane's nymphomaniac stripper lacked conviction, nor did her passion for Matt Dillon's dice player convince – perhaps because personal relations between the two were said to be chilly. Then, too, in her first film opposite her husband, Christopher Lambert, the intriguing *Knight Moves* (1992), she was not too plausible as a psychologist assisting the hunt for a serial killer, and the chemistry between the two leads not too apparent.

1979 A Little Romance **1980** Cattle Annie And Little Britches; Touched By Love aka To Elvis, With Love **1981** Ladies And Gentlemen, The Fabulous Stains **1982** Six Pack **1983** The Outsiders; Rumblefish **1984** Streets Of Fire; The Cotton Club **1987** Lady Beware; The Big Town **1990** Vital Signs **1991** Priceless Beauty **1992** Knight Moves; Charlie; My New Gun **1993** Tamakwa

Lange, Jessica

Actress
Born 20 April 1949
Cloquet, Minnesota

Few actresses have so triumphantly surmounted their inauspicious beginnings as has Jessica Lange, going from gorilla's girlfriend to one of the hottest (though far from the most bankable) dramatic actresses in the business. Despite studying mime in Paris and dancing for several months in the chorus of the Opera Comique, it was through modelling (which she took up to afford alimony to her ex-husband) that she got her big break and was launched onto the screen amid much fanfare in Dino De Laurentiis' lavish remake of *King Kong* (1976). Regardless of the film's poor reputation, it proved a big hit at the box office, but that was no thanks to Lange. She looked good but acted atrociously, giving a performance that had 'I-am-a-brainless-bimbo-imitating-Marilyn-Monroe' written all over it. Her attempts to get subsequent roles were complicated by her seven-year contract with the producer and it was not until 1979 that she returned to the screen as the Angel of Death in Bob Fosse's self-indulgent *All That Jazz*. Along with the lame comedy *How To Beat The High Cost Of Living* the same year, it showed that she could be a competent actress but still had some way to go. Serious-minded and acutely intelligent, she was aware of this, and returned to her acting studies.

Then Lange caused a sensation with her sexually charged, convincingly sleazy performance in Bob Rafelson's *The Postman Always Rings Twice* (1981) and even though the film was not a success it made producers take notice. She followed it with roles as two very different actresses – the pleasant starlet who confides her problems with men to Dustin Hoffman in *Tootsie* (1982) and, more harrowingly, as the tragic, lobotomised 30s film star Frances Farmer (to whom she bears a striking resemblance) – earning Oscar nominations for both. Despite her impressive, emotionally draining performance in *Frances* (1982), it was for the former that she won the statuette as Best Supporting Actress in what many felt was a consolation prize for losing out to Meryl Streep for the main award, but either way it made her more than a star: it made her a force.

Her next film, as one of that year's many strong-willed farmer's wives keeping the farm together in the first of the mid-80s farm-of-the-week movies, *Country* (1984), drew praise for her believable performance (she spent much of her childhood travelling the rural Midwest as her father changed jobs) but much criticism in her capacity as co-producer for her relentless perfectionism that moved the budget into the $30m bracket. *Sweet Dreams* (1985), in which she played country-and-western singer Patsy Cline with superb conviction was an altogether more modest affair, but it marked the beginning of another downfall in her fortunes, with the ill-conceived female star vehicle *Crimes Of The Heart* (1986, a surprising reunion with producer De Laurentiis and one of her weakest performances) neither a critical nor a commercial success. There was little, too, to recommend *Far North* (1988), written and directed by her *Crimes* and *Country* co-star and off-screen love, Sam Shepard, with Lange depressingly one-note throughout; although she gave a strong, bittersweet performance as the housewife going from cheerleader to businesswoman as her marriage deteriorates in *Everybody's All American* (1989), the film was mostly remembered for her constant running battles with director Taylor Hackford ('That son of a bitch is scum' she said in one of her quieter moments on the subject).

It was not until Costa-Gavras' *Music Box* (1989) that she came back into the spotlight. She created a clear and wholly believable character amid the film's moral debate, through the changes in her very different relationships with the other (almost exclusively male) characters, matching their various perceptions of her as mother, daughter, sister, and lawyer while only allowing herself one specific moment (when she inadvertently catches sight of her reflection in a mirror) to be none of those things. Earning her a fourth Oscar nomination and much well-deserved praise, it showed just how much Jessica Lange can do within a strong framework and with a good director – a perception reinforced by her believable, beleaguered wife in Scorsese's otherwise hard-to-swallow *Cape Fear* remake (1991), and a Broadway run as Blanche Dubois opposite Alex Baldwin's Stanley Kowalski in *A Streetcar Named Desire*, the same year.

1976 King Kong **1979** All That Jazz; How To Beat The High Cost Of Living **1981** The Postman Always Rings Twice **1982** Tootsie; Frances **1984** Country **1985** Sweet Dreams **1986** Crimes Of The Heart **1988** Far North; Everybody's All American aka When I Fall In Love **1989** Music Box **1990** Men Don't Leave **1991** Cape Fear **1992** Night And The City; Blue Sky

Le Mat, Paul

Actor
Born ?
New Jersey

Paul Le Mat first came to the public's attention as John Milner, the uneducated stay-at-home pitched against Richard Dreyfuss' ambitious wanderer, in George Lucas' now classic *American Graffiti* (1973). He was a credible small-town outsider, expressing himself through hot-rodding and a cool persona that was grounded firmly in the realities of small town life: he doesn't stand up to cops but quietly mumbles his subservience to them like a child caught misbehaving. While the rest of *Graffiti*'s cast went on to better things, Le Mat only went on to reprise his role in the less successful sequel, and to turn in two marvellous portraits of small-town losers for Jonathan Demme in *Citizen's Band* (1977) and *Melvin And Howard* (1980) before his career seemed to peter away onto the small screen.

A tough, workmanlike no-nonsense actor who served in Vietnam (and later put much of his resentment against Jane Fonda in the unashamedly Republican *Hanoi Hilton*, 1987) and who for a time thought of turning professional boxer (he trained for the 1972 Olympics team), Le Mat belies his somewhat proletarian image, coming to the screen from a pedigree training at the Mitchell Ryan Actors' Studio and the American Conservatory Theatre in San Francisco. Yet he is still at his most convincing in ordinary, everyday roles, with his Melvin Dummar in the Demme film remaining his most outstanding showcase. It was, too, his most likeable – a portrayal of a regular guy living, none too successfully, from day to day with his stripper wife (Mary Steenburgen), only to find his life turned upside down when he is named in Howard Hughes' will. (His reaction to the sudden media attention is to climb a tree and hide!)

This actor seemed best served by the cult movies which dried up for him after 1983's *Strange Invaders*. As television took up the blue-collar concerns that Hollywood abandoned in favour of 'high-concept' product in the 80s, Paul Le Mat has continued to produce his best work for the small screen, as with his Golden Globe-nominated performance as Farrah Fawcett's wife-beating husband in *The Burning Bed* (1980), where his unobtrusive professionalism keeps him in demand.

1973 Amercian Graffiti **1975** Aloha, Bobby And Rose **1977** Citizen's Band aka Handle With Care **1979** More American Graffiti aka After American Graffiti aka American Graffiti II aka Purple Haze **1980** Melvin And Howard **1982** Jimmy The Kid; Death Valley; **1983**

Strange Invaders **1986** PK And The Kid (made in 1982) **1987** The Hanoi Hilton; PI: Private Investigations **1989** Veiled Threat; Puppet Master; Easy Wheels **1990** Grave Secrets **1992** Deuce Coupe; Wishman

Leachman, Cloris

Actress
Born 30 April 1926
Des Moines, Iowa

Despite making one of the most startling entries in film history – running naked but for an ill-fitting raincoat into the headlights of Mike Hammer's car in *Kiss Me Deadly* (1955), only to be sadistically murdered a reel later – Cloris Leachman has a film career that was late in developing, largely due to her desire to raise a family, but she made up for it with a vengeance in the early 70s. Beginning her professional life with an advice show on local radio, she started performing (after-becoming Miss Chicago and a finalist in 1946's Miss America pageant) with her TV work on *Lassie* and the *Mary Tyler Moore Show* (and her own spinoff, *Phyllis*), adding character to her face and taking her into middle age, when her talent came into its own with her Oscar-winning performance in *The Last Picture Show* (1971).

Her tall and bony frame enhanced the pathos she communicated, not so much through dialogue as with her eyes, in her portrayal of the forlorn coach's wife finding temporary solace with one of her husband's pupils. 'I played it with my own body, my skin, my face. I wanted that scorned look to come out through my skin rather than my mouth.' The finest of her few dramatic roles, she spent almost the entirety of the period between the character's revival in the ill-fated sequel, *Texasville* (1990), in broad comedy, showing a particular empathy for the *oeuvre* of Mel Brooks: she was unforgettable as the sado-masochistic whip-cracking nurse in *High Anxiety* (1977) and the housekeeper, Frau Blucher, in *Young Frankenstein* (1974), the mere mention of whose name sends distant horses into terrified whinnies.

Throughout the 1970s and 80s, Leachman appeared in many highly variable TV movies, netting three Emmys in the process, and while it is probably true that she has remained one of those performers not readily recognised by the public at large, she has become, perhaps for that very reason, a stalwart addition to the ranks of feature players.

1955 Kiss Me Deadly **1956** The Rack **1962** The Chapman Report **1969** Butch Cassidy And The Sundance Kid **1970** Lovers And Other Strangers; The People Next Door; WUSA **1971** The Steagle; The Last Picture Show **1973** Charley And The Angel; Dillinger; Run, Stranger, Run aka Happy Mother's Day . . . Love, George **1974** Daisy Miller; Young Frankenstein **1975** Crazy Mama **1977** High Anxiety **1979** The North Avenue Irregulars aka Hill's Angels; The Muppet Movie; Scavenger Hunt **1980** Foolin' Around; Yesterday; Herbie Goes Bananas **1981** History Of The World – Part One; This Time Forever **1986** Shadow Play **1987** Walk Like A Man; Hansel And Gretel **1989** Prancer **1990** Love Hurts; Texasville

Lee, Spike
(Shelton Jackson Lee)

Director, writer, actor
Born 20 March 1956
Atlanta, Georgia

Intense, arrogant, driven and flagrantly talented, Spike Lee – christened Shelton Jackson Lee – is the angry young man of contemporary American cinema. With his first four films he elicited raves and jeers, was denounced as a racist and advocate of violence, won awards and distinguished friends, and made powerful enemies. His response to both extremes has seemed equally indifferent.

Quickly regarded as the most significant of black American film-makers, Lee is no disenchanted, disenfranchised child of the ghetto but the well-educated, articulate product of a cultivated, creative and intellectual middle-class family. Born in Georgia but raised in Brooklyn, New York, where he still lives, he was the third generation of his family to obtain his university degree from Morehouse College in Atlanta, which has turned out generations of the *crème de la crème* of African-American communities. His mother is a teacher, his father a jazz musician and composer of some note who scores Lee's films. After leaving Morehouse, Lee did a summer internship at Columbia Pictures and returned to New York, where he began to receive recognition while he was still at NYU Film School. His student film, *Joe's Bed-Stuy Barbershop: We Cut Heads* (1982), was the first student work ever selected for showing in Lincoln Center's long-established 'New Directors, New Films' showcase, won a student award from the American Academy of Motion Pictures Arts and Sciences, and brought him offers from the biggest agents in the film industry. It was a long time, however, before Hollywood was to take him seriously. Not one to hang about,

Lee hustled, wheedled and borrowed $175,000 to produce his first professional feature, *She's Gotta Have It* (1986). Rough-edged but street-smart, fresh and wittily observed, the film centred on a sassy independent young woman (Tracy Camilla Johns) and three disparate men vying for her affections. One of these, manic, chattering Mars Blackmon, was played by Lee and delivered the film's most memorable, oft-quoted catch-phrase: 'Pleasebaby, pleasebaby, pleasebaby, babybabyplease'. Original, offbeat and very sexy, it won the Prix Jeunesse at the Cannes Film Festival and served notice that Lee was a talent to be reckoned with. As a companion piece to the film, its maker penned *Inside Guerrilla Film-making*, a shrewd textbook for the school of 'We can do things we want to do' thought.

Predictably, Lee went through the second film syndrome. *School Daze* (1988), a seriocomic fable with music, set on a black American college campus *à la* Morehouse, had a vastly bigger budget than its predecessor (which made $10 million) and ambitious, provocative ideas, but was written off by many critics. Lee, however, could shrug off the knocks since the film found a ready audience in black and white 'happening' young trendies. *Do The Right Thing* (1989) was a far more controversial work, one which won over a number of influential critics who acclaimed it as a masterpiece, and enraged others who viewed it as condoning racial violence. It was undeniably a vibrant, dynamic picture, confronting racial tensions as they really are without pretending to offer a conventional or pleasing resolution. The absence of the film in Oscar nominations apart from Danny Aiello's Best Supporting Actor nod and one for Lee's screenplay was generally perceived throughout the industry as a deliberate snub to a work that owed little to Hollywood formulae or values.

Undeterred, the director provoked even greater wrath with his jazz film, *Mo' Better Blues* (1990), in which the protagonist, Bleek (a role written for its star Denzel Washington), is a two-timing, immature egoist but a brilliant musician. It met with mixed critical reactions, generally cool towards the surprisingly sentimental themes of redemption through the love of a good woman and wonderful family, but did break ground in depicting black sexual relationships on screen that were at times tender and charming – something hard to recall in any mainstream American film. Jewish rights organisations mounted an aggressive attack on the movie, though, for its portrayal of two Jewish characters (club owners) as a 'highly dangerous form of anti-Semitic stereotyping', to which Lee responded by contending that the characters are historically valid.

His next film, *Jungle Fever*, (1991) addressed an interracial relationship, a first from Lee. Subsequently he undertook his most ambitious project yet in *Malcolm X* – starring Washington – which, predictably, set off heated debate even before filming commenced. Over budget, and defiant in the face of Hollywood executive objections to the shape the film was taking, Lee turned to prominent black artists, entertainers and athletes to raise additional finance. Initially greeted as 'a young, black Woody Allen', Spike Lee is now firmly established as a highly individual talent, an iconoclast and a *provocateur*.

As director, writer and actor: **1986** She's Gotta Have It **1988** School Daze **1989** Do The Right Thing **1990** Mo' Better Blues **1991** Jungle Fever **1992** Malcolm X

Lehmann, Michael

Director
Born 1958
San Francisco, California

Michael Lehmann's thesis film for his degree at the University of Southern California caused quite a stir. *Beaver Gets A Boner* may, as claimed, have 'followed all the George Lucas formulas strictly' but it also managed to invert them. An outrageous black comedy, centring on an impoverished student who applies for a scholarship to pay off his drug debts, it was good enough to tip Lehmann for Hollywood's new flavour of the month and secure him an agent (at William Morris no less). Two more black comedies later, and Lehmann's style and approach were clear: he uses acute but uncommon observations of modern family life and adolescent troubles, taking the perceived behaviour and lifestyles to extremes. The results were fresh, funny, hyper-realistic movies that created a kind of alternative and absurd universe.

The son of a psychiatrist and an artist, Lehmann studied painting at New York's School of Visual Arts before switching to a major in philosophy at Columbia University. After graduating, he studied in West Germany and came close to deciding on an academic career. In an about-face, he applied to film schools and snapped up a job as a project manager for the video department at Coppola's ill-fated Zoetrope studios. Just as Zoetrope went under, an application made three years earlier by Lehmann to USC and subsequently 'misplaced', was found and accepted.

Two hundred pages of a screenplay, 'unreadable, unfilmable and one of the funniest, strangest scripts' became the aspiring director's first feature-length film, *Heathers* (1989). A foul-mouthed, macabre and blackly funny comedy starring Winona Ryder and Christian Slater, it played upon the angst experienced by two odd-ball teens who murder their snobby peers and transform the homicides into apparent suicides. Subverting the social and sexual iconography of the John Hughes-style teen film, it was much admired by those critics and audiences who got the joke, but was destined to misfire with those viewers who 'didn't get it'. 'They said that you can't, just can't, make a studio film in which high school girls go around saying, "Fuck me gently with a chain saw"'. Then, in *Meet The Applegates* (1990), which he co-scripted, Lehmann married the scourge of the average American family to xenophobia and took the whole kaboodle to the ultimate extreme. Stockard Channing, Ed Begley Jr, Cami Cooper and Bobby Jacoby starred as giant insects disguised as America's most average family (in fact, they win an award for being so). Meanwhile, dad's real mission is to undermine the local nuclear facility. Brightly coloured sets and a script popping with rash acts and parody turned *The Applegates* into a cult hit.

How far Michael Lehmann could continue to mine the vein of his particular subversion with any profit remained to be seen. Certainly, on paper at least, his third film sounded as if it might be a different kettle of fish with its multi-million dollar budget, a major box-office star (Bruce Willis), and a plot concerning a cat burglar and a massive money conspiracy. However, Lehmann's sense of humour exploded in his face when *Hudson Hawk* was derided as 'Hudson The Duck' and 'Hudson The Turkey' before going down in flames as a self-indulgent disaster; and it can't have helped his status when his refusal to work with juvenile star Macaulay Culkin resulted in his dismissal from *The Good Son* (1993).

1989 Heathers **1990** Meet The Applegates **1991** Hudson Hawk

Lemmon, Jack
(John Uhler Lemmon III)

Actor

Born 8 February 1925

Boston, Massachusetts

Comedy with a human face: this is the clue to Jack Lemmon's success as a film actor, but it is by no means the whole story of his career, since the same qualities that made him one of the world's great film comedians have also allowed him a remarkable extension into straight drama and even tragedy. The face itself is the secret, and the source of all his strengths: that appealing but not especially characterful face, with its middle-class WASP features capable of being twisted and turned inside out with elastic facility and split-second timing. This is the classic Nice Guy face, a canvas upon which the artist can paint myriad shades of confusion, frustration, irritation, double-take and slow burn, myriad strokes of emotional definition from the lightest to the boldest.

And, because Lemmon is such an intelligent, formidably equipped and (at his best) powerfully focused actor, the stylistic modulation from funny to serious that such a range permits him carries absolute conviction. In his most memorable screen performances – which must include the jazz-musician-turned-transvestite on the run from the mob in *Some Like It Hot* (1959), the PR man succumbing to alcoholism in *Days Of Wine And Roses* (1962), the crisis-ridden garment manufacturer in *Save The Tiger* (for which he won the 1973 Best Actor Oscar), and the father battling the Chilean dictatorship to find his abducted son in *Missing* (1982) – the portraits of a reasonable man plunged into disarray (and, in the serious films, thrown to his downfall) by an unreasonable world are all closely related. The wholly unsympathetic figure, the out-and-out villain do not figure among them; if that suggests the limits of his range, it also explains why he has been a much-loved as well as much-admired actor throughout his career.

Born into a wealthy East Coast family (his father was the director of a doughnut company), Lemmon went to Harvard and thence into the navy for World War II service. Radio, television and various Broadway assignments preceded his film debut, in the comedy *It Should Happen To You* (1954), the first of two he made with the brilliantly gifted dumb-blonde comedienne Judy

Holliday. His fourth film, *Mr Roberts*, won him the 1955 Best Supporting Actor Oscar for his fly, wisecracking Ensign Pulver; and for a while it was this sort of character that kept Lemmon's career blossoming, with only the silly but enjoyable tropical smuggling melodrama *Fire Down Below* (1957), opposite Robert Mitchum and Rita Hayworth, and the lively off-beat Western *Cowboy* (1958), with Lemmon in the unlikely role of Frank Harris, to hint at the actor's wider possibilities.

It was the director Billy Wilder who divined and brought to full flower his comic persona. This happened first in *Some Like It Hot*, which the mixture of Lemmon, Tony Curtis and Marilyn Monroe, and particularly the 'love match' between Lemmon's saxophonist-in-drag 'Daphne' and the besotted old Florida millionaire Osgood (Joe E. Brown), made into one of Hollywood's comedy classics; and then immediately afterwards in *The Apartment* (1960), in which Lemmon plays a put-upon office softie who loans the boss his apartment for affairs. The latter, with its rueful sweet-sour relationship between two losers, Lemmon and Shirley MacLaine, was in some ways the more revelatory, since it sounded for audiences those tender, touching notes of pained humanity that later he and Lee Remick were to develop so effectively as the husband-and-wife alcoholics of Blake Edwards' *Days Of Wine And Roses*.

For Wilder he went on to make several more comedies, not all of them equally successful; in *The Fortune Cookie* (1966) he was introduced to the actor with whom he has formed perhaps the most enduring of his screen partnerships, Walter Matthau. In the 1968 film adaptation (directed by Gene Saks) of Neil Simon's play *The Odd Couple*, the contrast and combination of these two superbly gifted funny-men struggling (and failing) to achieve domestic harmony as they live together in Matthau's apartment, amounted to artistic matchmaking of rare felicity.

Not all of Lemmon's comic partnerships have been so rewarding, nor all their subjects so well chosen to polish up new facets of his talents. In fact, a surprising amount of uneven work, most of it made bearable by its leading man's imperishable energies, can be found in the 70s and 80s. The 1971 comedy *Kotch*, starring Matthau, and Lemmon's wife, Felicia Farr, gave him a promising start in directing that, owing to a lack of success at the box office, was never followed up.

But in three dramas – *Save The Tiger*, the 1979 nuclear-disaster thriller *The China Syndrome* (with Lemmon as the chief engineer of a damaged nuclear-power plant), and *Missing* – Lemmon was encouraged to dig deep into himself, and into his acting skills, and the result was a new economy, a newly mature insight into the characters that gave each film its special depth. In this latter part of his career the theatre has claimed a higher proportion of his time; the late-80s Broadway and London revival of the O'Neill masterpiece *Long Day's Journey Into Night* won him showers of praise for his account of the inflexible, uncomprehending, touchingly vulnerable paterfamilias James Tyrone. Both this play and *Dad*, the 1989 film comedy of families and generations (though the latter grossly sentimentalises the appeal of Lemmon's approach to old age), suggest that, with luck and the right choice of material, the actor's 'final period' could be his golden one. In fact, the baggage of his stardom detracted somewhat from his appearance as a frightened informant in *JFK* (1991), but *Glengarry Glen Ross* (1992), teaming Lemmon with Al Pacino, was a gift to the actor's ability to express the anxiety of an ageing salesman desperate to prove he still has what it takes.

1954 It Should Happen To You; Phffft **1955** Three For The Show; Mister Roberts; My Sister Eileen **1956** You Can't Run Away From It **1957** Fire Down Below; Operation Mad Ball **1958** Cowboy **1959** Bell Book And Candle; It Happened To Jane; Some Like It Hot **1960** The Apartment; Pepe; The Wackiest Ship In The Army **1962** The Notorious Landlady; Days Of Wine And Roses **1963** Irma La Douce; Under The Yum Yum Tree **1964** Good Neighbour Sam **1965** How To Murder Your Wife; The Great Race **1966** The Fortune Cookie **1967** Luv **1968** The Odd Couple **1969** The April Fools **1970** The Out-Of-Towners **1971** Kotch (director only) **1972** The War Between Men And Women; Avanti! **1973** Save The Tiger **1974** The Front Page **1975** The Prisoner of Second Avenue **1976** The Entertainer; Alex And The Gypsy **1977** Airport '77 **1979** Tribute; The China Syndrome **1981** Buddy Buddy **1982** Missing **1985** Maccheroni/Macaroni (Italy) **1986** That's Life **1989** Dad **1991** JFK **1992** The Player (Cameo); Glengarry Glen Ross **1993** Short Cuts

Lester, Richard

Director

Born 19 January 1932

Philadelphia

Richard Lester, an American who has lived in England since the mid-1950s, came to prominence in the following decade, and in many ways seems a highly representative commercial-cinema director of that period. He made the first two Beatles' films, *A Hard Day's Night* (1964) and *Help!* (1965); and their dazzling visual style, fast-paced, self-con sciously zany, dependent on quirky, highly skilful tracking and cutting, proved closely in sympathy with the new pop mood of the 60s exemplified by the famous four. Indeed, while the second Beatles film proved marginally less of a smash hit than the first, both established Lester's directorial trademarks. With hindsight one may fairly suggest that their world-wide success trapped him into stylistic traits which in later efforts too often came to seem empty self-indulgences. This could well be the reason why in the subsequent decades, though he continued to work (far less frequently in the 1980s), the formula for renewed success proved elusive.

Lester's first professional experience was in American television in the early 1950s; having settled in England, he was soon in demand for television commercials and comedy there. It was in this latter medium that he first worked with Peter Sellers and Spike Milligan, famous British comedians (and original members of the Goons radio team) whose influence was to be felt in the eccentric, wittily made English comedies that Lester also trademarked around the time of his Beatles collaborations – *The Knack* (1965), *How I Won The War* (1967), and the 1969 film version of the Milligan-John Antrobus play *The Bed-Sitting Room*. Not all of these 60s products have worn equally well, but certainly they are a great deal more interesting to re-visit than most of the Lester films that succeeded them.

Robin And Marian (1976), an unexpectedly graceful piece of cinematic nostalgia in which Sean Connery and Audrey Hepburn play the middle-aged versions of the Robin Hood couple, can be accounted an exception to that general rule; by contrast, *The Ritz* (also 1976), an ill-judged detective-caper comedy unfolded largely in a New York gay bathhouse, marks probably the nadir of Lester's artistic achievement. His involvement with the *Superman* series – he was producer of the 1977 original and director of its 1980 and 1983 sequels – kept him active thereafter, but as a whole the career seems a classic example of a sizeable and singular talent that simply failed to develop.

1962 It's A Trad Dad! aka Ring-A-Ding Rhythm **1963** The Mouse On The Moon **1964** A Hard Day's Night **1965** The Knack . . . And How To Get It aka The Knack; Help! **1966** A Funny Thing Happened On The Way To The Forum **1967** How I Won The War **1968** Petulia **1969** The Bed-Sitting Room **1974** The Three Musketeers; Juggernaut **1975** The Four Musketeers; Royal Flash **1976** Robin And Marian; The Ritz **1979** Butch And Sundance: The Early Days; Cuba **1980** Superman II **1983** Superman III **1985** Finders Keepers **1989** The Return Of The Musketeers **1991** Get Back (docu)

Levinson, Barry

Director, writer
Born 2 June 1942
Baltimore, Maryland

In an era in which the emphasis has so often been on action adventures, fantasy and genre pictures, Barry Levinson has distinguished himself with small-scale, character-driven films. Both as a screenwriter and as a director much of his work can be faulted for story weaknesses, but his strengths, whatever the subject or style, are that he is very good with actors, presents characters with humanity and humour, and is particularly gifted at illuminating male relationships.

Levinson was born and raised in Baltimore, where he attended Forest Park High School and hung out at Brice's Hilltop Diner, like the young male ensemble drawn from his memories in his directorial debut feature, *Diner* (1982). After brief spells at the Community College of Baltimore and American University in Washington, DC, he found work as a floor manager for a Washington TV station. In the early 1970s he moved to California and found an outlet for his sense of the absurd in a stand-up comedy act with Craig Nelson and Rudy DeLuca. A spot on a local TV show drew the trio to the attention of 'superagent' Michael Ovitz, who got them onto a national variety programme. Levinson and DeLuca continued their association as a comedy writing team, most notably for Carol Burnett, winning two Emmy awards for their work on her shows. He spent some time in London during the early 70s, honing his writing and producing skills before another customer, Mel Brooks, commissioned the duo to contribute to his screenplay for *Silent Movie* (1976) and cast them in bit parts. As an 'actor', Levinson's most memorable screen appearance is as the loopy hotel bellboy who attacks Mel Brooks with a rolled-up newspaper in the *Psycho* (1960) shower scene parody of *High Anxiety*

(1977), for which he and DeLuca again provided some gags.

Collaborating with his first wife, actress-writer Valerie Curtin, Levinson wrote several produced screenplays, but the pair's dramas were unremarkable. Their comedy *Best Friends* (1982) received a particularly starry treatment at the hands of Norman Jewison for leads Burt Reynolds and Goldie Hawn, but the autobiographically inspired tale of a screenwriting couple was disappointingly lacklustre. The best of their projects was the very black judicial satire . . . *And Justice For All* (1979), also directed by Jewison, which veered uncomfortably between savage humour and real tragedy, a course that could not be negotiated with complete success even by first-rate actors Al Pacino, Jack Warden, Lee Strasberg and Christine Lahti.

In 1982 Levinson got his chance to direct the self-penned *Diner*, as he had often been urged to do by Mel Brooks when recounting stories of his friends and days as a Baltimore youth. Filmed on location with a then virtually unknown cast – Mickey Rourke, Steve Guttenberg, Daniel Stern, Kevin Bacon and Ellen Barkin among them – and made with obvious love, *Diner* celebrates the youth, enthusiasms and comradeship of its male protagonists while conveying both amusement and regret at their incomprehension of women and the inability of some to move on. With many incidents inspired by real life – including the character, based on Levinson's cousin, who made his fiancée pass a test on his football team before setting the wedding date – the script was Levinson's first in which comedy and pathos were really persuasively joined.

Levinson's other two 'Baltimore pictures' (the only other ones he has both written and directed to date) are also informed by affectionate remembrance. The aluminium-siding salesmen of *Tin Men* (1987) were fellow denizens of Brice's Diner in 1963. Once again the film-maker's brand of comedy worked well with Richard Dreyfuss and Danny DeVito at odds with each other and life, but it did not mesh entirely satisfactorily with the drama elements. The back-to-back successes Levinson made subsequently out of other writers' screenplays (*Good Morning, Vietnam* in 1987 and *Rain Man* in 1988) gave him the clout to realise his most ambitious and most personal film, *Avalon* (1990). Based on his own family, with the character of the child Michael representing Levinson himself, *Avalon* follows the fortunes of a family across half a century, from the arrival of the Russian immigrant grandfather in 1914. Beautifully made and performed (Armin Mueller-Stahl and Joan Plowright portrayed the grandparents, Aidan Quinn and Elizabeth Perkins the parents), the film is a touching, funny and penetratingly observed picture of aspiration, cultural assimilation and family disintegration in American society.

While Levinson plans further Baltimore movies, his biggest commercial successes have come with directing-only assignments. The first of these, *The Natural* (1984), about a ball-player, proved he could handle a big league cast (Robert Redford with Robert Duvall, Glenn Close, Kim Basinger and Barbara Hershey in support) and epic imagery (achieved by the superb cinematographer Caleb Deschanel) although the material was unwieldy and too lovingly dwelt upon. *Young Sherlock Holmes* (1985), written by Chris Columbus and executive-produced by Steven Spielberg, was an entertaining and very atmospheric Victorian romp in which the director characteristically seized upon small touches amid the special effects and elicited fine 'buddy' performances from his teenaged Holmes and Watson.

Good Morning, Vietnam (1987), inspired by real-life Armed Forces Network disc jockey Adrian Cronauer's stint in Saigon in 1965, is notable for a *tour de force* performance from Robin Williams. The side of the film which attempted to portray him as a caring, sharing guy with the Vietnamese is contrived, but Williams credited Levinson's direction – always marked by calmness and a desire for spontaneity from actors – with drawing out his memorably hilarious, wild 'routines'. The film's take of $200 million represented a colossal hit, but Levinson's follow-up, *Rain Man* (1988) was a $500 million-earning, Oscar-strewn phenomenon. Considered by mainstream Hollywood and audiences a perfect Hollywood film, *Rain Man* was essentially a small, scantily-plotted road movie with the difference that one of the two standard 'mismatched males' was an unstandard character, an autistic 'savant'. Dustin Hoffman received the Oscar for Best Actor and Levinson won Best Director for what, it may be argued, is his least 'directed' picture, so utterly does it devolve on the obsessive Hoffman character and Tom Cruise's reactions to him. (The film also won Oscars for Best Picture and the screenplay by Ronald Bass and Barry Morrow). Levinson himself appears at the end of the film as a psychiatrist.

Bugsy (1991), was another multiple Oscar nominee in which Warren Beatty gave his best-ever performance (surrounding a clutch of superb supporting players) as the notorious psychopathic killer, rapist and drug-pusher, Bugsy Siegel. If the morality of the film was questionable in portraying Bugsy sympathetically as a man of vision and a fool for love, it was nonetheless grand old Hollywood entertainment, making interesting points about the mutual attraction between Hollywood and the underworld, and displaying some very clever directorial flourishes.

Barry Levinson and his second wife Diana, who met during the filming of *Diner*, reside in Los Angeles but retain close links to Baltimore where they also have a home.

As director only unless stated otherwise: **1976** Silent Movie (co-writer, actor) **1977** Silent Movie (co-writer, actor) **1977** First Love (co-writer) **1979** And Justice For All (co-writer) **1980** Inside Moves (co-writer) **1982** Diner (w/d) **1984** The Natural **1985** Young Sherlock Holmes **1987** Tin Men (w/d); Good Morning, Vietnam **1988** Rain Man **1990** Avalon (w/d) **1991** Bugsy

Liotta, Ray

Actor
Born 18 December 1955
Union, New Jersey

In a film career that was, strictly speaking, still in its infancy at the beginning of the 1990s, Ray Liotta had already established himself as one of those rare actors (like Willem Dafoe) who earn critical raves even in small roles. Tall – and good-looking in spite of a sallow and unusually blemished complexion – Liotta has extraordinary blue eyes that can glitter with icy menace or shine with sincerity; his curiously changeable features and mobility of expression help him in bringing credibility to a range of contrasting characters, all of whom he has appeared to portray with equal ease. Possessing vulpine grace, this actor is one of the few who have come close to capturing the essence of the troubled, sensitive, sometimes violent young men who marked the early career of Marlon Brando.

Of Italian-Irish heritage, Liotta obtained his degree in theatre and fine arts at the University of Miami. Within six months of residence in New York, he found work in commercials as well as bit parts on stage and television (including a three-year stint in a popular daytime soap). The big break came when, through his old friend Melanie Griffith, he captured the key supporting role of Ray Sinclair in Jonathan Demme's black comedy *Something Wild* in 1986. His portrayal of the ex-con, brutally possessive of his one-time wife (Griffith), was richly chilling and won him a Golden Globe nomination.

After that explosive beginning, Liotta was put on simmer for a while. He went straight to a lead, opposite Tom Hulce and Jamie Lee Curtis in *Dominick And Eugene* (1988), playing a highly sympathetic role as a medical student looking after his retarded brother, but the movie was sub-standard and failed to make an impression; then he appeared as a beguiling Shoeless Joe Johnson, the tarnished baseball hero back from the dead in *Field Of Dreams* (1989), but despite the film's enormous groundswell of popularity, it was star Kevin Costner whose name was on everybody's lips. Then Martin Scorsese cast him in the sensational *GoodFellas* in 1990 (apparently at the suggestion of Robert De Niro, who had noticed him in *Something Wild*). He played Henry Hill (the real-life mobster on whose memoirs the movie is based), an Irish-Italian kid who succeeds in his youthful ambition to become a wealthy gangster, only to have his position slowly erode until it almost destroys him.

Ray Liotta's mercurial impersonation of this complex character deservedly elevated him to something of star status, and created keen interest in his next appearance, the post-Vietnam drama *Article 99*, co-starring Kiefer Sutherland, Forest Whitaker and Kathy Baker, while *Unlawful Entry* (1992) earned him a rapturous critical reception.

1986 Something Wild **1988** Dominick And Eugene (GB: Nicky And Gino) **1989** Field Of Dreams **1990** GoodFellas **1991** Article 99 **1992** Unlawful Entry

Lithgow, John

Actor
Born 19 October 1945
Rochester, New York

Twice nominated for Academy Awards, and an Emmy and Tony award winner, the bulky blonde six-foot-four-inches tall John Lithgow was hailed by at least one highbrow 80s critic as the film actor of his generation. Certainly he was one of the most useful character actors on the screen in the last decade, but it is really in the theatre that Lithgow's enormous presence has made its mark.

A Fulbright scholar before he took up acting, Lithgow won the Tony with his Broadway debut performance in *The Changing Room* and subsequently met with much acclaim for his charismatic work in *Requiem For A Heavyweight*, *The Front Page* and *M. Butterfly*. He made his film debut in Brian De Palma's suspense thriller *Obsession* (1976), and was more memorably recalled by De Palma for the role of the appallingly plausible psychopathic killer in the disturbing *Blow Out* (1981). The actor has invariably proved persuasive, whether as a fire and brimstone preacher in the youth dance flick *Footloose* (1984), a haughty theatre director in *All That Jazz* (1979) or a queasy scientist in space as in *2010* (1984); and he has frequently given a lift to daft and dire material. His Oscar nominations for Best Supporting Actor were for his warm, wise transsexual Roberta Muldoon in *The World According To Garp* (1982) and his diffident, touching suitor of Debra Winger in *Terms Of Endearment* (1983), but he is perhaps most memorable for clinching all attention in *Twilight Zone – The Movie* (1983) as the horrifyingly panic-stricken airline passenger who alone sees a monster up to no good on the wing in the scarifying remake episode of *Nightmare At 20,000 Feet.*

John Lithgow has been used less advantageously in recent years, with a curious New Zealand production of *Mesmerized* (1986), a 19th-century period piece co-starring him opposite Jodie Foster, scarcely even seen. In addition to his stage hits, he has done major TV work and received an Emmy for a performance in the series *Amazing Stories*. With *Ricochet* (1992) he pulled out all the stops as a crazed psycho-killer stalking paragon-of-virtue Denzel Washington, and continued to mine the lunacy vein with a more subtle display of multiple personalities for Brian De Palma in *Raising Cain* (1992).

1976 Obsession **1979** All That Jazz; Rich Kids **1981** Blow Out **1982** The World According To Garp **1983** Twilight Zone – The Movie; Terms Of Endearment **1984** Footloose; The Adventures Of Buckeroo Banzai Across The Eighth Dimension; 2010 **1985** Santa Claus – The Movie **1986** Mesmerized (New Zealand); The Manhattan Project **1987** Bigfoot And The Hendersons **1991** At Play In The Fields Of The Lord **1992** Ricochet; Raising Cain **1993** Cliffhanger

Lloyd, Christopher

Actor

Born 22 October 1938

Stamford, Connecticut

Reclusive character actor Christopher Lloyd has remained an unfamiliar name to the general public despite having created several unforgettable roles in some of the movies' all-time blockbusters.

A late starter by Hollywood standards, Lloyd, whose wife Kay is also an actress, made his feature film debut in *One Flew Over the Cuckoo's Nest* (1975) when he was 37. He was also an Obie-award-winning veteran of the New York stage, having moved to the Big Apple from his native Connecticut after a teenage apprenticeship in summer stock. Coaching from Sanford Meisner at the Neighborhood Playhouse led to the young actor's first role on Broadway in *Red, White and Maddox* in 1969. A successful career, both on and off Broadway, followed, in such productions as *Kaspar* (1973), *Macbeth* (1974) and *In the Boom Boom Room* (1974), until Hollywood came calling.

With his elongated, skull-like face, manic eyes and mobile facial expressions, Lloyd was a very effective mental patient in *Cuckoo's Nest*, and it wasn't long before he had accumulated an impressive list of supporting roles in such minor league successes as *Goin' South* (1978), *The Onion Field* (1979) and *Mr Mom* (1983). However, it was his three-year stint (1979–1983) as the wacky Reverend Jim in the successful TV series *Taxi* which brought him into the major league, as well as winning him two Emmy awards.

A short time afterwards, Lloyd was making movie history in Robert Zemeckis' phenomenally successful time-travel comedy, *Back to the Future*. As Doc Brown, the crazy, wild-haired scientist who triggers off the film's madcap action, Lloyd made an indelible impression on audiences world-wide, and later resurrected the winning role in both of the less successful sequels. Lloyd's talent for portraying larger-than-life caricatured characters was made further use of by Zemeckis, who also directed him in an episode of *Amazing Stories* (1987), and later that year extracted an uncharacteristically evil performance from him as Judge Doom in the runaway hit, *Who Framed Roger Rabbit?*

In between his fruitful collaborations with Zemeckis, Lloyd made several smaller budget films, notably Nicholas Roeg's *Track 29*

(1988), in which he played a train-mad doctor unhappily married to Theresa Russell, and a rare straight role in *Eight Men Out* (1988).

While it might be unfair to pigeonhole Lloyd as Hollywood's rent-a-wacko, the actor's body of work throughout the 80s consisted almost entirely of off-the-wall roles, coming full circle in 1989 with his performance as an institutionalised character obsessed with orderliness in the disappointing *The Dream Team* – although, as the crazed uncle Fester, he was the highlight of a nest of eccentrics in the largely tedious though stylish reincarnation of *The Addams Family*.

1975 One Flew Over The Cuckoo's Nest **1977** Three Warriors; Another Man, Another Chance **1978** Goin' South; Midnight Express **1979** The Lady In Red; The Onion Field; Butch And Sundance: The Early Days **1980** The Black Marble; Pilgrim Farewell; Schizoid **1981** The Legend Of The Lone Ranger; The Postman Always Rings Twice; National Lampoon Goes To The Movies **1983** Mr Mom; To Be Or Not To Be **1984** Star Trek III: The Search For Spock; The Adventures Of Buckaroo Banzai; Joy Of Sex **1985** White Dragon; Clue; Back To The Future **1987** Amazing Stories; White Dragon; Miracles; Walk Like A Man **1988** Who Framed Roger Rabbit?; Eight Men Out; Track 29 **1989** Why Me?; Back To The Future II; The Dream Team **1990** Back To The Future Part III **1991** Suburban Commando; The Addams Family **1992/93** Dennis The Menace **1993** The Pagemaster

Lloyd, Emily
(Emily Lloyd Pack)

Actress
Born 29 September 1971
London, England

Emily Lloyd was barely 16 when she captivated audiences at the Cannes Film Festival with her performance as a defiant, disrespectful and sexually precocious teenager (favourite phrase, 'Up yer bum') in David Leland's *Wish You Were Here* (1987). In the words of British film writer George Perry, 'Her combination of rebellious scorn and childish innocence accounted for the most astonishing first appearance since Carroll Baker and *Baby Doll* in 1956.' The movie was a smash hit in New York and Emily was voted best actress of the year by America's National Board of Review.

British actor Roger Lloyd Pack and his first wife divorced when Emily was three and she was brought up by her mother. She laid down her markers early, displaying talent in the junior school plays as well as the behaviour of the naturally rebellious which resulted in more time spent outside the classroom door than within. Eventually her parents sent her to the Italia Conti stage school, but she still didn't knuckle down to discipline, and it was fortuitous that her father's agent suggested she audition for Leland.

It was the Americans who took advantage of the teenager's instant stardom and bright, spunky personality. Susan Seidelman co-starred her with Peter Falk and Dianne Wiest in *Cookie* (1989), a lightweight but pleasing tale of the relationship between a mobster and his defiant daughter. With admirable aplomb, Emily learned to drive a stretch limo, smoke cigarettes, and chew gum with conviction, but for all her efforts with a Brooklyn accent, she came across more like a London punk and the startling freshness and charm of the Lloyd personality was marginally less effective the second time around. Director Norman Jewison took her into new territory with *In Country* (1989) as the rural Kentucky girl living with her Vietnam vet uncle (Bruce Willis). Emily's only partly successful attempt to turn herself into a convincing Southerner seemed to limit her spontaneity and she failed to convince, but she was British again – and growing up a little – in the English movie (co-starring Kiefer Sutherland), *Chicago Joe And The Showgirl* (1990), based on the true story of a young couple during World War II who swap fantasies and commit senseless murder.

As a screen personality, Emily Lloyd is a true original – so much so that it may prove to be her undoing unless she develops range in the coming years. Her return to adopted American identity as a hoydenish reluctant bride in Louisiana swamp country in the abysmal *Scorchers*, however, did not augur well for her.

1987 Wish You Were Here **1989** Cookie; In Country **1990** Chicago Joe And The Showgirl **1991** Scorchers **1992/93** Husbands And Wives; A River Runs Through It

Locke, Sondra

Actress, director
Born 28 May 1947
Shelbyville, Tennessee

Sondra Locke's career and private life became so closely identified with Clint Eastwood that it is easily forgotten that she was Oscar nominated as Best Supporting Actress in

1968 for her first film, *The Heart Is A Lonely Hunter*, a role she earned via early community theatre work. Her touching performance as a troubled young girl who befriends a deaf mute and her impressive interaction with co-star Alan Arkin boded well for her future, but her career has left that promise unfulfilled. With the exception of the rat movie *Willard*, (1971) most of her early films have been forgotten and are best left that way, and it is probable that, but for her role in *The Outlaw Josey Wales* (1976), she would have proved as unmemorable.

Harking back to her debut, her role in *Josey Wales*, as the innocent young girl who becomes a part of the surrogate family that tempts Eastwood back to a world of emotions, seemed a mirror of what was happening off-screen. He cast her again in *The Gauntlet* (1977), this time as a foul-mouthed and hard-nosed prostitute – the best of her later roles – and left his wife for her, much to the anger of his fans, to whom she remained resolutely unlikeable. This impression was regrettably reinforced by her tendency to be at her best when aggressive; as soon as her characters mellow, as in *Bronco Billy* or *Any Which Way You Can* (both 1980), they become completely unconvincing. She was even unable to summon any sympathy as the rape victim in *Sudden Impact* (1983) and showed little evidence of dramatic range elsewhere.

Perhaps aware of this fact, Sondra Locke attempted to broaden her horizons in 1986 with her directorial debut, the very bizarre *Ratboy* (inspired by happy memories of *Willard*, perhaps?), which seemed at best to be a tax-break for Eastwood's Malpaso Co. Following their acrimonious split after many years together, her career floundered, with her second stab at directing, the promisingly premised thriller *Impulse* (1990), starring Theresa Russell, coming out a muddled disappointment, and her acting career sadly stalled by cancer and a bitter palimony suit against her ex-partner that made frequent excursions to the tabloids.

1968 The Heart Is a Lonely Hunter **1969** Cover Me, Babe **1970** Run, Shadow, Run; The Lovemakers **1971** Willard **1972** The Second Coming of Suzanne **1973** A Reflection of Fear aka The Daughter **1974** Death Game aka Death Trap aka The Seducers **1976** The Outlaw Josey Wales; Wishbone Cutter; The Shadow of Chikara **1977** The Gauntlet **1978** Every Which Way But Loose **1980** Bronco Billy; Any Which Way You Can **1983** Sudden Impact **1986** Ratboy (also director) **1990** Impulse (director only)

Loggia, Robert

Actor

Born 3 January 1930

New York City

For the most part of his screen career, Robert Loggia has specialised in playing the kind of people who not only know where Jimmy Hoffa is buried but probably put him there as well. Studying with Stella Adler at the Actors' Studio in New York, he made his Broadway debut with *The Man With The Golden Arm* in 1955 before launching a film career in the following year's *Somebody Up There Likes Me* that ground to a halt in 1965 as one of the many actors who'd like to forget he was in *The Greatest Story Ever Told* (1965, as Joseph).

He maintained a high profile by constant TV work in many hit shows, even directing some episodes of *Quincy*, *Magnum* and *Hart To Hart*, as well as appearing in numerous TV movies – playing an Israeli general in the theatrically released *Raid On Entebbe* (1976) – and mini-series such as *A Woman Called Golda*, in which he played Sadat to Ingrid Bergman's Golda Meir. Roles as big-time, small-morals crooks in several *Pink Panther* movies as well as his malicious drug baron in *Scarface* (1983) gave him an equally high profile on his return to the big screen and he has barely been off it since, averaging at least two films a year in addition to TV work (including his own series, *Mancuso FBI*). Even when the films haven't been good – and there are more than his fair share of turkeys on his CV – Loggia has always been value for money, with particularly outstanding contributions to *Jagged Edge*, for which he earned an Oscar nomination as Glenn Close's foul-mouthed private eye, and a joyously likeable performance as the department store head in *Big* (1988). He was rewarded with a prominent supporting role in the Auschwitz drama *Triumph Of The Spirit* (1990), noticed by critics and audiences alike.

1956 Somebody Up There Likes Me **1957** The Garment Jungle **1958** Cop Hater; The Lost Missile **1959** The Nine Lives of Elfego Baca **1963** Cattle King **1965** The Greatest Story Ever Told **1976** Raid On Entebbe **1977** First Love; The Three Sisters **1978** The Revenge Of The Pink Panther; Speedtrap **1980** The Ninth Configuration aka Twinkle, Twinkle Killer Kane **1981** SOB **1982** An Officer And A Gentleman; The Trail Of The Pink Panther **1983** The Curse Of The Pink Panther; Psycho II; Scarface **1985** Jagged Edge; Prizzi's Honor **1986** That's Life; Armed And Dangerous **1987** Over The Top; Hot Pursuit;

Gaby – A True Story; The Believers **1988** Big **1990** Triumph Of The Spirit; Opportunity Knocks **1991** The Marrying Man **1992** Gladiator; Necessary Roughness; Innocent Blood **1992/93** First Force

Lone, John

Actor
Born 1952
Hong Kong

John Lone is one of those rare Asian actors in American films who managed to break away from the Oriental stereotype and become a star in his own right. After training for the stage from the age of ten at the monastery-like Chin Chiu Academy in Hong Kong, Lone came to the USA to study at the American Academy of Dramatic Arts in Pasadena. In 1980, he made his professional stage debut, off-Broadway, in *F.O.B.* (Fresh Off The Boat), which he also choreographed. He continued to act in and choreograph a number of shows in New York, before Michael Cimino gave him his first screen role of any consequence in *The Year Of The Dragon* (1985), in which he received second billing to Mickey Rourke. He played Joey Tai, the powerful young crimelord of New York's Chinatown, which Rourke's cop is sent to clean up. Unfortunately, the script did not allow the character as much scope to develop as his white American adversary, but Lone was able to bring enough subtleties to his performance to make an impression. This did not stay the protests of Asian-American organisations who picketed cinemas, claiming that the film was racist.

But the Hong-Kong born actor could never have dreamed of a bigger and better role than he was given in Bernardo Bertolucci's sumptuous epic *The Last Emperor* (1987). He was superb as Pu Yi, the last man to ascend China's Dragon Throne, having to age from his early 20s to his 50s, and shift from imperial brat through empty international playboy, effete Japanese puppet, pathetic prisoner and, finally, to emerge a 're-educated' gardener in the New China.

In Alan Rudolph's *The Moderns* (1988), his range was extended in a part where his 'Orientalism' was irrelevant. As the malevolent self-made millionaire and art collector Bertram Stone in the Paris of the 20s, he was compelling. 'If I pay less, it would be less beautiful,' he says in a key line from the film, whose plot revolves around art dealing. It seems that the days of hiring Caucasian actors under thick make-up to play Asians now seem almost buried, thanks to the emergence of actors of John Lone's calibre.

1976 King Kong **1984** Iceman **1985** Year Of The Dragon **1986** Promises To Keep **1987** Shadows Of The Peacock; The Last Emperor **1988** The Moderns **1989** Echoes In Paradise **1990** Shadow Of China (Japan)

Long, Shelley

Actress
Born 29 August 1949
Fort Wayne, Indiana

Despite getting off to an appealing start in her screen career (and since burning her bridges in leaving her Emmy award-winning role in TV's *Cheers*, 1982–88), Shelley Long has failed to establish a workable screen persona, opting instead for caricatures and stereotypes with no identifiable humanity. A former TV model and spokesperson, she went on to write, direct and produce industrial and educational films as well as performing with the Second City improvisational troupe. There she was discovered by producers Bernie Kukoff and Jeff Harris, who brought her to Hollywood to do a TV pilot, *That Thing On ABC*. The show failed, but she guested in episodes of *M★A★S★H* and *The Love Boat* and co-hosted, co-wrote and associate-produced *Sorting It Out* in Chicago.

She was cute and likeable in *Caveman* (1980) and, even if not entirely convincing as a hooker in *Night Shift* (1982), displayed good comic timing, going on to relieve Tom Cruise of his virginity as the divorced housewife in *Losin' It* (1983). But it was as Diane Chambers, the intellectually pretentious, emotionally unstable barmaid in *Cheers* that she made her name, crossing swords and raising sparks with Ted Danson for six seasons. On the big screen she was fine in a more controlled role, watching her relationship with Tom Hanks disappear as their house falls to pieces in *The Money Pit* (1986); however, it was the success of her pairing with Bette Midler in a part not a million miles away from Diane in *Outrageous Fortune* (1987) that decided her on leaving the TV show.

Her first solo film, *Hello Again* (1987), a high-concept variation on *Blithe Spirit*, was a rare failure for Touchstone with Long trying too hard; and *Troop Beverly Hills* (1989) was an absolute disaster, with the actress over-zealously telegraphing the not very funny jokes well in advance in a part that felt like it had been written for Midler. As her performance in *Don't Tell Her It's Me* (1990) reveals, Long lacks the personality to carry a star vehicle and the depth to flesh out a screen role.

1980 A Small Circle Of Friends **1981** Caveman **1982** Night Shift **1983** Losin' It **1984** Irreconcilable Differences **1986** The Money Pit **1987** Outrageous Fortune; Hello Again **1989** Troop Beverly Hills **1990** Don't Tell Her It's Me **1992** Frozen Assets

Lowe, Rob

Actor
Born 17 March 1964
Charlottesville, Virginia

One cannot help but feel that someone would be doing Rob Lowe and his career a favour by breaking his nose. Despite having played drama, comedy, mystery and suspense, sometimes with nearly plausible conviction, and despite his highly-publicised sexual adventures, Lowe is so prettily boyish it is difficult to buy him as anything other than a middle-class or preppie lightweight.

Lowe was among the juvenile heart-throbs-in-the-making who comprised the cast of Francis Ford Coppola's adaptation of S.E. Hinton's alienated youth tale *The Outsiders* (1983), making his debut in the small role of middle brother between Patrick Swayze and C. Thomas Howell. He moved straight into star billing in his second feature, *Class* (1983), a comedy-drama distinctly short on same, as an affluent, bright and lively boarding-school boy whose wimpy room-mate has a furtive – not to say unlikely – affair with Lowe's screen mother, Jacqueline Bisset. Trying hard to register something resembling an emotion, Lowe was attractive but uninteresting opposite superior young actresses Jodie Foster and Amanda Plummer in Tony Richardson's baffling but game adaptation of John Irving's *The Hotel New Hampshire* (1984). He was no more than engaging in the light student romance *Oxford Blues* (1984) and downright dull in the lame hockey soap *Youngblood* (1986), but his performance in Joel Schumacher's slick 'young adults' cross of *The Breakfast Club* and *The Big Chill*, *St. Elmo's Fire* (1985) offered starrier charisma, with Lowe cutting considerably more dash than his co-starring Brat Packers as the immature, feckless, reckless saxophonist. *About Last Night . . .* (1986), the emasculated adaptation of David Mamet's *Sexual Perversity In Chicago*, was a success for Loew and leading lady Demi Moore and the actor was again pleasant, handsome and earnest without revealing any depth. Pulling all the stops out he impersonated a mentally handicapped youth in *Square Dance* (1987) to moving effect, possibly inspired by the distinguished company of Jane Alexander, Jason Robards and impressive ingénue Winona Ryder, and won unqualified praise from critics. Sadly for him, multitudinous thumbs down greeted his portrayal of a ruthless cad in a would-be Hitchcockian thriller of sexual intringue and murder, *Masquerade* (1988), a role which saw him very fetching in sailing apparel but betrayed his shortcomings since it demanded a young Cary Grant's combination of charm and deceit.

Throwing himself energetically into the Democratic support camp during the 1988 US Presidential election campaign, Lowe was a popular draw at rallies and was beginning to put himself over as a concerned, intelligent young man when the biggest Hollywood sex scandal in years broke over his head and a pirated videotape allegedly showing Lowe and an under-aged night-club habituée *in flagrante* became much-in-demand viewing.

Rather than destroying Lowe's career, the bad-boy publicity gave him an edge previously missing. Ironically, he had already been cast in the part of a seductive villain in the psychological thriller *Bad Influence* (1990), a film which makes provocative use of sexually compromising videotapes, and his resulting performance carried more weight than otherwise might have been the case.

1983 The Outsiders; Class **1984** The Hotel New Hampshire; Oxford Blues **1985** St Elmo's Fire **1986** Youngblood; About Last Night **1987** Square Dance **1988** Illegally Yours; Masquerade **1990** Bad Influence **1992** Wayne's World; The Finest Hour

Lucas, George

Director, writer, producer
Born 14 May 1944
Modesto, California

After George Lucas had directed *Star Wars* (1977), one of the biggest money-making movies of all time, he could sit back, enjoy its profits, and never have to exert himself as a director again. Subsequently, he emerged as a powerful producer, completing the Star Wars trilogy with *The Empire Strikes Back* (Irvin Kershner, 1980) and *The Return Of The*

Jedi (Richard Marquand, 1983), and backing the Steven Spielberg-directed *Indiana Jones* pictures (1981, 1984 and 1989). Not only was he head of Lucasfilms, but he had also set up the Industrial Light And Magic special effects company, responsible for many of the technical developments in films of the past decade.

Lucas studied film at the University of Southern California before becoming assistant to Francis Ford Coppola on *Finian's Rainbow* (1968). With Coppola, he founded American Zoetrope in an office in San Francisco in 1969. The company produced Lucas' first movie, *THX-1138* (1971), a small-scale Orwellian sci-fi tale shot mainly in San Francisco's unfinished subway system. It starred Robert Duvall as an individual in a comformist society where sex is forbidden and all heads are shaven. The idea was not fully explored, but the use of sound and machines showed technical know-how.

His second film, the box-office smash *American Graffiti* (1973), was a dreamy vision of adolescent life in a small Californian town in 1962, before Vietnam and the drug scene. Using the rock 'n'roll hits of the day on the soundtrack and with Haskell Wexler's brilliant hyper-realist photography, the film created a finger-lickin' golden past, and gave a boost to the careers of Richard Dreyfuss, Ron Howard, Paul Le Mat, Harrison Ford and Cindy Clark.

If *American Graffiti* drew on memories of teen-pix of the 50s, *Star Wars* echoed elements from every kiddie matinee serial of the 30s and 40s, but for all its barrage of technical show-offs, it had none of the menace, atmosphere or intelligence of its sources. However, the simple metaphor of Good vs Evil ('May The Force Be With You') and the fairy-tale characters – young hero Luke Skywalker (Mark Hamill) rescuing a princess (Carrie Fisher) from the evil clutches of Lord Darth Vader (David Prowse dubbed by the deep voice of James Earl Jones) with the help of wise wizard Ben Kenobi (Alec Guinness) and C3P0 and R2D2 (Anthony Daniels, Kenny Baker), a comic couple of robots – struck a chord with millions of children and adults alike. Lucas summed up his career best: 'I like action, adventure, chases, things blowing up. I like comic books.'

In March 1992, the Academy awarded this wizard of modern cinema a special Oscar in recognition of his achievements.

1971 THX-1138 (also co-writer) **1973** American Graffitti (w/d) **1977** Star Wars (w/d) **1983** The Return of The Jedi (co-writer only)

Lumet, Sidney

Director
Born 25 June 1924
Philadelphia, Pennsylvania

Sidney Lumet was one of a new breed of directors – among them Robert Mulligan, John Frankenheimer, Delbert Mann and Arthur Penn – who emerged in the mid-1950s from the forcing bed of television drama. Many of his contemporaries have fallen by the wayside, although Frankenheimer is still in there slugging away like a game old street fighter rolling with the punches and Arthur Penn is husbanding his fires. In contrast, Lumet has proved a remarkable survivor, although the bewildering range of his work suggests a notably efficient technician rather than an *auteur*.

He is, nevertheless, an extremely clever handler of actors, as is demonstrated by the tidy choreography of films as diverse as *Twelve Angry Men* (1957) and *Murder On The Orient Express* (1974), although this skill is sometimes undercut by a portentous and cold style. The director himself has fenced away at criticism with the candid admission: 'I never analyse why I say yes to a movie. I don't hold much with the cult of the director . . . We're just humble toilers in the vineyard. We've simply got to do the best we can.' It is as simple an explanation as any of the busy, multi-faceted mixing of directorial personality which has characterised his career.

The son of a noted American Yiddish actor, Lumet began as a child radio and stage performer, and in 1939 appeared in a movie, *One Third Of A Nation*, in which Sylvia Sidney starred as a poor girl trying to escape from her New York tenement. It was an oddly prophetic debut as Lumet has returned to the twin themes of social conscience and the gritty streets of New York – so much more 'real' than the palm-fringed boulevards of Hollywood – throughout his career.

After war service, he worked as a director in off-Broadway productions and summer stock before moving into live TV drama. His debut movie was one of the more glib transpositions from the small screen, *Twelve Angry Men* (1957), an assignment he was given on the insistence of the picture's star, Henry Fonda. Lumet skilfully sketched in the differing characters of the twelve jurors around whom the drama revolves, but the movie's dour high-mindedness makes it heavy going today.

After *Stage Struck* (1958), a remake of the Katharine Hepburn hit *Morning Glory* (1932), he spent time concentrating on adaptations from the stage: *The Fugitive Kind* (1960), *A View From The Bridge* (1961) and *Long Day's Journey Into Night* (1962). These are careful, sombre films in which great actors – Marlon Brando, Katharine Hepburn, Ralph Richardson – are faithfully filmed and superbly photographed by cameraman Boris Kaufman, a longtime associate of the director. These ventures, too, were indicative of an intellectual striving that comes periodically, though unevenly, to the surface of Lumet's ambitions.

Then Lumet plunged into the anguished nuclear cliffhanger *Fail-Safe* (1964), whose release was overshadowed by Stanley Kubrick's *Doctor Strangelove* (1964). If *Fail-Safe* had a hand on its liberal heart, then both hands were sweatily clutched to the balls of *The Pawnbroker* (1965), in which concentration camp survivor Rod Steiger thrashes about in a welter of grainy flashbacks. Switching again, he climbed *The Hill* (1965), set in a wartime military prison and punctuated with manically precise tracking shots as the prisoners slog up and down the punishment course of the title. This was followed by *The Group* (1966), adapted from Mary McCarthy's novel about a generation of Vassar girls which boasted a strong cast of then unknown actresses – Joan Hackett, Shirley Knight, Jessica Walter, Candice Bergen and Joanna Pettit.

From the mid-60s, it becomes increasingly difficult to tease out any sense from the switchback Lumet has ridden. His hard-won success was jeopardised by a long string of unadulterated clinkers, starting with the aptly named John Le Carré adaptation *The Deadly Affair* (1966) and including a cack-handed version of Chekhov's *The Seagull* (1968), *The Appointment* (1969), a dreary romance aping the 1966 Lelouch hit *A Man And A Woman*, and a misfiring Tennesse Williams adaptation, *The Last of the Mobile Hot Shots* (1970), based on *Seven Descents of Myrtle* and sunk by James Coburn's grinning complacency.

Lumet hauled himself back with *The Anderson Tapes* (1972), a watchable thriller with an electronic surveillance theme which prefigured Coppola's brilliant *The Conversation* (1974). Then he struck paydirt with the powerful *Serpico* (1973), the story of undercover New York cop Al Pacino's attempt to expose corruption in the NYPD. It was based on a true story, as was the more powerful *Dog Day Afternoon* (1975), also starring Pacino as a homosexual loser who holds up a Brooklyn bank to get the money for his lover John Cazale's sex-change operation. Humming with nervous energy and set in Lumet's favourite New York locations, both movies were huge box-office successes and nominated for Oscars. Also nominated a year later was *Network* (1976), Paddy Chayefsky's blackly outrageous satirical expose of television, whose comic-strip structure and explosive performances from Faye Dunaway and Peter Finch were kept creditably in control by Lumet's tentative naturalism.

A thuddingly literal adaption of Peter Schaffer's *Equus* (1977) and *The Wiz* (1978), a modern black musical version of *The Wizard of Oz* (1939, suggested that the director's successes of the mid-70s were merely the sudden tic of his social conscience, but he returned to the theme of corruption and ambivalent justice in *Prince of the City* (1981) in which Treat Williams played a divided hero in the *Serpico* mould; *The Verdict* (1982), splendidly starring Paul Newman as a washed-up attorney redeeming himself in the cold light of a Boston dawn; and *Daniel* (1983), adapted from the E.L. Doctorow novel *The Book of Daniel*, in which the children of a couple patterned on the Rosenbergs must come to terms with their parents' painful legacy.

Of *Daniel*, Lumet observed that his principal concern was not with the politics but with 'who pays for the commitment, what are the costs of passion, how many generations does it carry on?' In *Running On Empty* (1988) the costs are paid by the two young sons (notably the elder of the two, played by River Phoenix) of 60s activists Judd Hirsch and Christine Lahti, who have been living 'underground' for years, pursued by the FBI since an attack on a napalm plant went horribly wrong. There is a liberal wistfulness about *Running On Empty*, a lingering regret for the long-lost causes of yesteryear. In similar fashion, Lumet celebrated the raw ethnic diversity of New York in the generation-gap comedy-drama *Family Business* (1989); it featured a melting-pot of mourners gathering on a rooftop to sing 'Danny Boy' and say farewell to petty crook

Sean Connery against a big-city skyline that was redolent of the director's early work.

Sidney Lumet's record is, to put it mildly, uneven, his work veering from the gripping (*The Verdict*, for example) to *The Morning After* (1986), a third-rate and incoherent thriller whose presence in his filmography is inexplicable; and *A Stranger Among Us* (1992), a murder mystery set in a New York community of Hassidic Jews, which emerged as a muddled amalgam of *Witness* with *Fiddler On The Roof.* Nonetheless, the sincerity of his cultural, intellectual and liberal pretensions is not to be doubted, even if the quality of their expression has frequently let him down.

1957 Twelve Angry Men **1958** Stage Struck **1959** That Kind of Woman **1960** The Fugitive Kind **1962** Vu Du Pont/A View From The Bridge (France/Italy); Long Day's Journey Into Night **1964** Fail-Safe **1965** The Pawnbroker; The Hill **1966** Braverman; The Seagull **1969** The Appointment **1970** The Last of the Mobile Hot Shots **1971** The Anderson Tapes **1972** Child's Play **1973** The Offence; Serpico **1974** Lovin' Molly; Murder On The Orient Express **1975** Dog Day Afternoon **1976** Network **1977** Equus **1978** The Wiz **1979** Just Tell Me What You Want **1981** Prince Of The City **1982** The Verdict **1983** Daniel **1984** Garbo Talks **1986** Power; The Morning After **1988** Running On Empty **1989** Family Business **1990** Q & A (w/d) **1992** A Stranger Among Us aka Close To Eden **1993** Beyond Innocence

Lundgren, Dolph
(Hans Lundgren)
Actor
Born 3 November 1959
Stockholm, Sweden

At a time when other action men like Sylvester Stallone and Arnold Schwarzenegger were trying to discard their muscle-bound images, Dolph Lundgren, who came to prominence as the man who dated the androgynous Grace Jones, sprang up as an heir (along with Steven Seagal) to the Rocky/Rambo/Conan throne.

What sets Lundgren apart is his superior education. The actor received a Masters of Arts at the Royal Institute of Technology in his native Stockholm, and later attended Washington State University and the prestigious Massachusetts Institute of Technology. Not surprisingly, given his muscular build and square jaw, he was best remembered for his physical achievements: in 1979 he competed as part of the Swedish national karate team in Japan, won the European Championship in 1980, and also became a kick-boxing champion. With such an impressive list of credits for bodybuilding, he made a workout video called *Maximum Potential*, and it was on the strength of this that he was cast in the James Bond film *A View To A Kill* (1985) alongside his later companion, Grace Jones.

From this beginning, he went on to star alongside the man to whom he was later compared, Sylvester Stallone, in the boxing drama *Rocky IV* (1985), playing the superhuman Russian fighter who forces Rocky Balboa to defend his title. Now established as an up-and-coming action man, Lundgren was from there on no longer offered supporting roles. His career grew with his elevation to superhero parts like the comic-strip character He–Man in the nonsense film *Masters Of The Universe* (1986), and the leather-clad, revenge-driven protagonist of the futuristic *The Punisher* (1990). Lundgren seemed to have perfected the shoot-first ask-questions-later stereotype, roles which require little speech and a lot of muscle. This persona was probably best put to use in the simply awful *Dark Angel* (1990), where the words of dialogue could be counted on one hand, but since there is a market for this type of material he has continued to be successful, with his films often developing (in the case of *Red Scorpion*, *The Punisher* and *Dark Angel*) a cult following. His teaming with 'The Muscles from Brussels', Jean-Claude Van Damme, for the bigger-budget sci-fi actioner, *Universal Soldier*, boded well for his future as a prettier version of the Terminator.

1985 A View To A Kill; Rocky IV **1986** Masters Of The Universe **1989** Red Scorpion **1990** The Punisher; Dark Angel aka I Come In Peace **1991** Showdown In Little Tokyo; Cover Up **1992** Universal Soldier

Lurie, John
Actor, composer, musician
Born 1952
Boston, Massachusetts

John Lurie is first and foremost a musician and composer. The son of Welsh parents, he studied the alto sax in Boston, while his younger brother Evan took up the piano. In 1979 the two of them moved to New York, where they formed The Lounge Lizards, a freeform jazz combo that also introduced guitarist Marc Ribot, among others. The Lounge Lizards stretched avant-garde jazz to the realms of punk, but did so on the basis of outstanding musicianship. The group was welcomed by the 'alternative' art scene, and achieved some popular success too, especially as John's profile grew with his involvement in increasingly notable films.

Lurie directed and appeared in his own Super-8 films from 1977 onwards (*Men In Orbit*; *Hell Is You*) and acted in many of the New York Super-8 films that cropped up in the early 80s (*Underground USA* 1980; *Subway Riders* 1981). He also scored *The Offenders* (1980) and the independent features *The Vortex* (1981), *The Loveless* (1982), *City Limits* and *Variety* (both 1983), and *du-BEAT-e-o* (1984); sleazy snatches of discordant jazz interspersed with extended quieter passages are Lurie's signature. But most importantly he acted in and scored Jim Jarmusch's first feature-length film, *Permanent Vacation* (1982). It was to become a most fruitful collaboration. Lurie starred in Jarmusch's breakthrough film, *Stranger Than Paradise* (1984), as a cool, laconic but terminally bored hipster (a portrait Lurie has honed and refined in each subsequent film). He also put together a score that somehow linked Screamin' Jay Hawkins and Bartok. Jarmusch's brave deconstruction of the American film tradition was completed with the aid of German director Wim Wenders, who then himself cast Lurie in the small role of Nastassia Kinski's pimp in *Paris, Texas* (1984). Back in New York the musician actor played a similar role in Susan Seidelman's *Desperately Seeking Susan* (1985), then went down to the bayou with Jarmusch and Tom Waits for *Down By Law* (1986); a funny, minimalist prison-break picture.

While John Lurie has an appealingly deadpan cool and a face that is always interesting even when passive (which is most of the time, after all), there is no range to his acting, and he is the first to insist the music comes first: 'Imagine being an actor' he told an interviewer. 'Working two months a year and spending the rest thinking "What do I do with my life? . . . Better to treat it like a throwaway and just do it." Even so, he has worked with a range of the world's best directors that any career actor would envy. He had cameos in Scorsese's *The Last Temptation Of Christ* (1988) and David Lynch's *Wild At Heart* (1880), and he is in Wim Wenders' epic, *Until The End Of The World* (1991). Meanwhile, his soundtracks have grown in resonance and subtlety. *Mystery Train* (1989) – again for Jim Jarmusch – is his best yet, a charmingly spare, funny culture clash with a rhythm-and-blues riff out of Osaka – delicately Oriental, with quirky banjo pickings courtesy of Marc Ribot, and Lurie on guitar and harmonica. With The Lounge Lizards going their separate ways, Evan Lurie has also turned his hand to film scoring, with an apt series of South American tangos for Maggie Greenwald's *film noir*, *The Kill-Off* (1989).

As actor only unless stated otherwise: **1981** The Vortex (music only); Subway Riders **1982** The Loveless (music only); Permanent Vacation (music also) **1983** City Limits (music only); Variety (music only) **1984** du-BEAT-e-o (music only); Stranger Than Paradise (music also); Paris, Texas **1985** Desperately Seeking Susan **1986** Down By Law (music also) **1988** The Last Temptation Of Christ; Il Piccolo Diavolo (Italy) **1989** Mystery Train (music only) **1990** Wild At Heart **1991** Until The End Of The World

Lynch, David

Director, writer
Born 20 January 1946
Missoula, Montana

The film-maker who Mel Brooks once described with brilliant accuracy as 'Jimmy Stewart from Mars', David Lynch is a completely individual but very specifically American bundle of contrasts and ironies. While he and his work are consistently characterised as weird and he has revelled in eccentricities – such as his well-known penchant for eating exactly the same meal every day for years – Lynch is evidently a clear-sighted, pleasant, nice, politically conservative man whose work both celebrates and parodies banal Americana as much as it highlights sex, perversion and violence.

Born in Montana, the son of a US Department of Agriculture scientist, Lynch was raised in the Pacific Northwest and Virginia, where he had a stereotypically ordinary middle-class upbringing, was unremarkable at school and showed no special interest in cinema. He became interested in art, however, and after dropping out of the Boston Museum School journeyed to Europe with the idea of studying with the Expressionist painter Oskar Kokoschka. Overwhelmed by culture shock he went home to his parents in less than two weeks. After drifting through several aimless jobs he finally settled down at the Pennsylvania Academy of Fine Arts in Philadelphia, where he became fascinated with stylish and stylised images of corruption and urban decay. By 1970 he had made two short films, removed to the American Film Institute in California and over a period of five years made *Eraserhead*. Completed in 1976 and released in 1978, *Eraserhead* was a highly surreal, deeply unpleasant art-house horror centred on an odd couple and their freakish infant. In addition to acquiring mythic status as a cult film, it brought Lynch an unlikely mentor in the shape of Mel Brooks, who assigned him to the comparatively straight, prestigious drama production *The Elephant Man* (1980). What might have been utterly harrowing viewing in the dramatisation of hideously deformed John Merrick's tragic life was rendered compulsively watchable. This was thanks in large part to a heartbreaking performance from John Hurt and nicely judged, sympathetic support from Anthony Hopkins, but Lynch was wonderfully assured in balancing a mainstream treatment with experimental touches. Aided by stunning black-and-white cinematography from Freddie Francis, the director provided a vividly atmospheric picture of the Victorian period and its mores, for which he was rewarded with Oscar nominations for direction and screenplay and a $40 million budget from Dino de Laurentiis to realise the sci-fi epic *Dune* (1984).

After a long and tortuous shoot, *Dune*, from Frank Herbert's novel, emerged in release as a dark, grim and tedious work despite some marvellous visuals and attractive performances. Viewers unfamiliar with the novel were understandably at a loss to unravel the narrative, and the film was a financial disaster. Subsequently the put-out Lynch was able to reassemble the film with 50 minutes of footage hacked out by the studio for a TV edition (attributed to the fictitious and oft-credited director 'Alan Smithee'). The experience prompted him to create and control his own work again.

Graphic sexual violence and a shocking performance from Dennis Hopper as a sadistic psychopath provoked a storm of controversy around his dark, disturbing mystery *Blue Velvet* (1986), but the film earned Lynch another Oscar nomination and the Best Picture award from the National Society of Film Critics. Lynch's depiction of the cruelty, sickness and horror just under the surface of nice, clean, Middle America – the thrust of all his original work – is neither subtle nor particularly new. But in *Blue Velvet* it is remorselessly riveting, stylish and bold, a detached, surreal excursion into small-town American life in the guise of a detective thriller.

Nineteen-ninety was the year of David Lynch. The supposed iconoclast won the top prize at the Cannes Film Festival with hot 'n' nasty young lovers Nicolas Cage and Laura Dern deliriously on the run from convention, parental viciousness and a hit man in *Wild At Heart*, graced the covers of prestige magazines and disarmed prime-time television with the soap *noir, Twin Peaks*. More freewheeling and abstract than *Blue Velvet, Wild At Heart* disappointed in comparison, its provocative sexiness and determinedly bizarre digressions working to a less pointed end. Though *Twin Peaks* mania proved shortlived after a feverish period as the inescapable dinner-table topic, Lynch and co-creator Mark Frost's series was as superior as any of his film work at overturning American themes and sending up the clichés of popular culture and entertainment. Although it rapidly became a minority taste, *Peaks* received a staggering 14 Emmy nominations. Not recognising when enough was enough, Lynch took the joke too far with a lurid and incoherent feature film 'prequel' to the *Peaks* saga, *Fire Walk With Me* (1992).

In addition to his film-making, Lynch has continued to paint, produced the documentary series *American Chronicles*, and wrote the lyrics for the Julee Cruise album 'Floating Into The Night'. With *Twin Peaks* music composer Angelo Badalamenti he wrote and devised Industrial Symphony No. 1, premiered in New York at the end of 1989. He has long been developing a proposed film production with the working title *Ronnie Rocket* about a midget with an extraordinary voice. Twice married and divorced, Lynch had a four-year relationship with *Blue Velvet* star Isabella Rossellini and was subsequently linked with his *Wild At Heart* leading lady Laura Dern for a time. His daughter Jennifer, following in her father's footsteps, embarked on her own directorial career with *Boxing Helena* (1991).

1978 Eraserhead (also writer) **1980** The Elephant Man (also co-writer) **1984** Dune (also co-writer) **1986** Blue Velvet (also co-writer) **1988** Zelly And Me (actor only) **1990** Wild At Heart (also co-writer) **1992** Twin Peaks: Fire Walk With Me (also co-writer, actor)

Lynch, Kelly

Actress

Born ?

La Jolla, California

A hard-bitten, self-assured actress-turned-model-turned-actress, Kelly Lynch has brought some grit to a handful of underwritten sexpot roles, and impressed mightily in her one really good part. Nevertheless, she has yet to establish herself as an actress to reckon with.

Lynch was born into a family struggling on the lower echelons of show business. Her mother toured with the 'Aqua Follies' synchronised swimmers, and her father was a piano player who owned a drag club. He left when Kelly was still a child. She took to acting early – her first public appearance was at the age of four. As a teenager in Minneapolis, she studied dance and worked as an apprentice at the Guthrie theatre. At 21, she broke both her thighs in an accident, but she made a full, if slow, recovery.

As a drama student in New York, Kelly got into the same lift as the head of the Elite model agency. Tall and slim, with arrestingly up-front features, she made $250,000 in her first year as a model. Turning back to acting, she appeared in episodes of the television series *Miami Vice* and *The Equaliser* among others, and then took a small role as the blonde pick-up in *Bright Lights, Big City* (1988). Strictly speaking this may not have been Lynch's big screen debut; she has admitted to making eight films, 'some of which played just one night in Bangkok' but it is the first in her official filmography. *Cocktail* (1988) offered much the same blonde bimbo role. As Bryan Brown's sexy wife, the actress got more exposure but no more depth, and consequently looked dreadfully inept. Not that her co-stars fared any better; everyone looked like an ex-model in this travesty. *Roadhouse* (1989) was an improvement, but only fractionally. Lynch had the female lead this time, playing a doctor who *does not* stitch up bouncing bruiser Patrick Swayze (he does it himself). The sexual politics may have been prehistoric, but Lynch acquitted herself well enough.

Anxious to avoid the stereotypes that had so far been her lot, she accepted the leading role in the independent film *Warm Summer Rain* (1989), about a woman recovering from a suicide attempt, then co-starred with Matt Dillon in Gus Van Sant's off-the-wall take on drug addiction, *Drugstore Cowboy* (1989). This superbly controlled film proved the perfect antidote to the parsimonious 'Just Say No' campaign of the late 80s. It brooked no easy answers, refused to moralise, and brought its desperate group of addled criminals to memorable life with a good deal of humour along the way. As Dianne, Lynch is a revelation. The blonde, tanned look is forgotten; more than anything, Dianne is *normal*. Where she brought a fundamental toughness to her bimbo roles, here Lynch finds vulnerability under a tough skin.

1988 Bright Lights, Big City; Cocktail **1989** Roadhouse; Warm Summer Rain; Drugstore Cowboy **1991** Desperate Hours; Curly Sue **1992** The Linguini Incident; R.S.V.P. **1992/93** Three Of Hearts

Lyne, Adrian

Director

Born 1941

Peterborough, England

One of the more interesting of the British commercials directors in Hollywood, Adrian Lyne is still a long way from being a great film director. Able to create striking images and give the impression of substance to individual scenes, he is essentially a manipulator, selling the look over the ideas or reality of a situation.

The son of a schoolteacher, he went into advertising and worked his way up the ladder, ultimately forming his own company in 1971 to enable him to direct commercials. Twice winning the Palme D'Or at the Cannes Commercials Festival in 1976 and 1978, he is perhaps best known for the influential Cointreau 'an' de ahyce meldts' adverts that remain a favourite of parodyists (as well as being the forerunner of the Gold Blend coffee couple). Although he had directed two shorts, *The Table* (1970) and *Mr Smith* (1974), in Britain, he looked to America for his cinema career, albeit via fellow British advertising refugee David Puttnam's first stateside picture, the ill-fated *Foxes* (1979). It took a rather clichéd look at a quartet of valley girls (Jodie Foster and Laura Dern among them), and Lyne's interest in their lifestyles rather than their lives made for uninspiring drama.

Filling the time and his bank account with commercials for Levi and Pepsi among other big brands, he proved ideal raw material for 'total film-makers' Simpson and Bruckheimer: a director with no personal vision but much visual flair who they could manipulate to instil their own personality into a picture, in this case *Flashdance* (1983). Hugely successful, it was more rock video than film and drew the most flak of any of the ads-to-films directors' movies of the day, setting the mold for its producers but doing nothing for Lyne's reputation. *9½ Weeks* (1986) did little to elevate it. An uninvolving, misogynistic tease about a destructive sexual relationship between Kim Basinger and Mickey Rourke, it was more controversial (thanks to self-conciously exploitational marketing) than financially successful, but his second attempt at dangerous sexuality hit just the right nerve.

Glenn Close's good-time girl who becomes an unstoppable killer after a one-night stand with married man Michael Douglas in *Fatal Attraction* (1988) became the embodiment of audiences' new-found fear of AIDS (or more appropriately, AIDS hysteria): irrational, sucking away the adulterer's life and security, threatening his innocent family, but with the reassuring release of a hastily refilmed ending which allowed the human virus to be despatched by the Good Wife. If real life isn't that simple, the film was, nevertheless, what people wanted to believe and it earned vast sums of money and Lyne an ill-deserved Oscar nomination. Yet for all its occasional moments of menace, the success of *Fatal Attraction* owed more to its performances than its direction, which featured some of the most blatant continuity errors ever seen in a major movie.

Lyne's new-found position on the A-list was quickly compromised by *Jacob's Ladder* (1990), which he very publicly reshaped from its original concepts of heaven and hell on earth due to his dislike of special effects (and, in particular, of losing visual control to those who execute them), only to be unable to live up to the original script's high reputation. Yet, for the first time, there was the feeling that he was interested in more than just the immediate visual effect although there was still much striking imagery in its nightmarish vision of a man (Tim Robbins) trapped between the netherworlds of sanity and madness and life and death. Disturbing, but ultimately quite moving and reassuring, it was a victim of audience expectations (it was sold as a horror movie), but did promise better things to come from this highly visible director.

1979 Foxes aka Ladies Of The Valley **1983** Flashdance **1986** 9½ Weeks **1988** Fatal Attraction **1990** Jacob's Ladder **1992/93** Indecent Proposal

M

Macchio, Ralph

Actor
Born 4 November 1962
Long Island, New York

The deceptively young looks of Ralph Macchio have made both his fortune and his name and, conversely, hampered his career by marginalising him in largely teenaged roles.

A native of Long Island, Macchio comes from a family which owns a trucking business. He started his entertainment career as an adolescent, appearing as a singer and dancer in local musical productions before he began work in television commercials at the age of 16. While still in high school he auditioned for director Robert Downey and shortly afterwards was given a part in his wild and crude military school comedy, *Up The Academy* (1980). It was three years, interspersed with work on the TV series *Eight Is Enough*, before Macchio followed up his film debut, this time for director Francis Ford Coppola. *The Outsiders* (1983), a seminal teenage movie told in epic style, is as famous for its tale (from the book by S. E. Hinton) about 'Socs' and 'Greasers', rival teenagers in 60s Oklahoma, as it is for marking the birth of the Brat Pack. Co-starring alongside Matt Dillon, C. Thomas Howell, Rob Lowe, Tom Cruise, Patrick Swayze and Emilio Estevez, Macchio gave an intelligent and moving performance as Johnny, and seemed set for a promising future.

The Karate Kid, which he made the following year, certainly seemed to offer that. Grossing more than $100 million at the American box office, the film, from *Rocky* (1976) director John G. Avildsen, was in many ways a teenage version of the Stallone hit and in every way a shameless crowd pleaser. Macchio stars as Daniel, a New Jersey adolescent whose move to California with his mother marks the start of persecution at the hands of some unpleasant martial-arts-trained youths. With the help of the apartment handyman, the delightful and wise Noriyuki 'Pat' Morita (whose performance was nominated for an Oscar), Daniel learns the lessons of life as well as the art of karate. Macchio, with his pretty Italian looks and his credible performance as a decent but impetuous teenager, impressed audiences and critics alike, and unsurprisingly, the movie spawned two sequels (1986 and 1989), both inferior and neither allowing the character of Daniel the opportunity to mature beyond the age of 18.

The phenomenon of *The Karate Kid* aside, the actor made a handful of unremarkable movies, all of which cast him in youthful roles: the high school black comedy *Teachers* (1984), *Crossroads* (1986), in which he played a convincingly cocky young musician involved with a legendary bluesman, and *Distant Thunder* (1988), an unimpressive story about yet another Vietnam veteran, which features him as the young son who goes in search of his long lost ex-soldier father (John Lithgow), and *My Cousin Vinny* (1992), as a college boy requiring the services of his inexperienced lawyer cousin, Joe Pesci.

Off the big screen, Macchio has been offered more challenging and rewarding work, most notably as a boy dying from a rare ageing illness in the 1984 TV movie *The Three Wishes Of Billy Grier*, and in 1986 opposite Robert De Niro on Broadway in *Cuba And His Teddy Bears*, for which he received good notices. But, as the 90s got underway, Macchio's movie career was hanging in the balance: a married man entering his 30s cannot go on playing a kid forever.

1980 Up The Academy **1983** The Outsiders **1984** The Karate Kid; Teachers **1986** Crossroads; The Karate Kid Part II **1988** Distant Thunder **1989** The Karate Kid Part III **1992** My Cousin Vinny

MacDowell, Andie
(Rose Anderson MacDowell)

Actress
Born 1958
Gaffney, South Carolina

A familiar face in hundreds of magazines and TV commercials (she modelled for Calvin Klein among others), Andie MacDowell was already a photographic model of the first rank when she made her inevitable movie debut in 1984 as Jane in *Greystoke: The Legend Of Tarzan*. It was not an auspicious beginning. The decision was made to give the character an English accent and Andie was later dubbed – by American Glenn Close. That was one of the chief limiting factors in an unimpressive performance, and Andie was critically dismissed as just another model masquerading as an actress.

She went on to make a couple of appearances on Italian TV before Joel Schumacher dropped her into the Brat Pack line-up for *St Elmo's Fire* (1985), as a doctor over whom Emilio Estevez suffers unrequited love. It was a bland performance, but not without a hint of sympathy, and she looked good in a remote, soft-focused way. Nonetheless, it did little for her fledgeling career, and certainly didn't prepare anybody for the film in which she suddenly became a name, *sex, lies and videotape* (1988). Herself a daughter of the South, MacDowell had a superb grasp of the stereotyped, sexually confused and repressed wife in Stephen Soderbergh's square dance of neurosis and deception, and she found herself nominated as Best Actress at Cannes in company with Meryl Streep (who won).

Married to actor Paul Qualley and the mother of two sons, this former South Carolina tomboy, one-time billboard girl and Paris model continued to earn a hefty sum under contract to L'Oréal, and was thus able to afford the luxury of choice in her screen career. After her huge success in *sex, lies and videotape*, she clearly decided to exercise it, confining herself to only two movies by the end of 1990, both co-starring her with heavyweights: Gérard Depardieu in Peter Weir's *Green Card*, and John Malkovich in *Object Of Beauty*. Jane had left the jungle for more cultivated pastures.

1984 Greystoke: The Legend Of Tarzan **1985** St Elmo's Fire, **1989** sex, lies and videotape **1990** Green Card **1991** Object of Beauty; Hudson Hawk **1992** The Player (cameo as herself); Ruby Cairo **1992/93** Groundhog Day **1993** Short Cuts

MacLachlan, Kyle

Actor
Born 22 February 1959
Yakima, Washington

With his handsome chiselled face and clean, clipped speech, Kyle MacLachlan would meet most people's requirements for a conventional romantic leading man. But he has spent most of his film career to date perceived as something of a screen alter ego to director David Lynch, who has most regularly kept him in employment, from the ambitious *Dune* (1984) debacle to TV's *Twin Peaks*.

MacLachlan, like Lynch, is a native of the Pacific Northwest. From acting in school productions, he took his degree in Fine Arts at the University of Washington in Seattle, played Romeo at the Oregon Shakespeare Festival and worked in rep and summer playhouses before a national casting search for the young lead in *Dune* brought him to Lynch's attention. A fan of the novel since adolescence, MacLachlan was thrilled to be cast as Paul Atreides and like everyone else was disappointed by the film's failure to flesh out the characters. When both had recovered from the clinker experience the director again turned to MacLachlan to play the naive youth fascinated then ensnared in the macabre relationship between Dennis Hopper's crazed kidnapper/killer and Isabella Rossellini's terrorised cabaret singer in *Blue Velvet* (1986).

Away from Lynch, MacLachlan proved both delightful and well-built for action as the extra-terrestrial 'lawman' disguised as a human FBI agent in the off-beat sci-fi horror thriller *The Hidden* (1987), an entertainment ignored at the cinema but subsequently popular with video renters. After some more ordinary TV fare, the actor responded to Lynch's call to become *Twin Peaks*' FBI Special Agent Dale Cooper, the caring, sensitive, cherry-pie connoisseur whose epigrams and appreciation of a 'damn fine cup of coffee' became catch-phrases with the serial's fanatical following. Although the role made MacLachlan a household face and brought him a lucrative sideline plugging 'darn good' potato crisps in TV ads, it was with professional and personal relief that he won a role in Oliver Stone's *The Doors* (1991) as an unrecognisably bewigged and bespectacled Ray Manzarek, the band's keyboard player. With a credit from America's *other* hippest director under his belt, MacLachlan could reasonably expect a boost in his film fortunes, and he was duly cast, with Albert Finney, in Bruce Beresford's *Rich In Love*..

1984 Dune **1986** Blue Velvet **1987** The Hidden **1990** Don't Tell Her It's Me **1991** The Doors **1992** Rich In Love; Where The Day Takes You; Twin Peaks: Fire Walk With Me **1992/93** The Trial

MacLaine, Shirley (Shirley MacLaine Beatty)

Actress
Born 24 April 1934
Richmond, Virginia

When writing about Shirley MacLaine, the

finger instantly trembles over the letter 'k' on the keyboard: 'k' for 'kooky', 'krazy' or just plain 'kracked'. With her formidable reputation for 'out of body experiences' as well as her equally formidably preserved actual body, MacLaine is an actress whose idiosyncracies invite a condescending sneer. But that is to ignore her versatility, force of personality, and the sheer fact of her survival in the face of several acting aberrations and the torrent of self-absorbed psycho-babble to which she subjects journalists and chat-show hosts. Not only has she staying power, but a capacity for renewal amply demonstrated in the 1980s.

The older sister of Warren Beatty, Shirley was propelled into show business by her drama-teacher mother. The big break came in classic backstage musical myth style in 1954, when she was understudying Carol Haney in the Broadway production of *The Pajama Game*. The star got sick and the understudy was spotted by producer Hal Wallis, who offered her a contract.

She made her screen debut in Alfred Hitchcock's black comedy *The Trouble With Harry* (1955), impish and Bohemian as a young widow whose gamine hair perfectly matched the ravishing colours of the New England fall. Her first leading role came in Mike Todd's *Around The World In 80 Days* (1956), woefully miscast as an Indian princess. After *The Matchmaker* (1958), *Hot Spell* (1958) and *The Sheepman* (1958), in which she was a delightfully tomboyish foil for dogged Glenn Ford, she hit the big time in Vincente Minnelli's *Some Came Running* (1959), playing the small-town floozie yearning for Frank Sinatra and pleading 'You gotta remember, I'm only human'. It was a performance at once funny and heartbreaking.

In *Ask Any Girl* (1959) she was charming as the husband-hunting provincial who arrives in New York to find that most men's plans do not extend to matrimony. In the leaden *Can-Can* (1960) she reaffirmed her cherished origins as a chorus-line gypsy, championing the cause of the legendary French dance and struggling with a succession of unflattering costumes. Then came Billy Wilder's *The Apartment* (1960), in which she was funny and touching as the elevator girl Fran Kubelik whose ill-advised affair with Park Avenue executive Fred MacMurray leads to an attempted suicide and a final back-projected dash into the arms of Jack Lemmon's neurotic nebbish C. C. Baxter.

If Fran's self-destructive urges seemed a little strong for the conventional happy ending, the movie captivated millions and made MacLaine's status that of star. But there were now signs of self-indulgence creeping into her work. In the early 1960s her choice of parts, and her playing of them, wavered between the casual and the calamitous: self-consciously pathetic as the Greenwich Village cutie in *Two For The Seesaw* (1962), curiously paired with Robert Mitchum; excellent as a lesbian teacher in love with Audrey Hepburn in an ill-fated screen version of Lillian Hellman's *The Children's Hour* (1962); a movie star masquerading as a geisha girl in *My Geisha* (1962), produced by her then husband Steve Parker, an impresario based in Japan; and as a French prostitute in Billy Wilder's coarse-grained *Irma La Douce* (1963), delivering the deadpan *double entendre*, 'I never remember a face'.

The actress was off the screen for nearly two years before returning in a turkey, *John Goldfarb Please Come Home* (1965), and *Gambit* (1966), a mildly amusing caper movie co-starring Michael Caine, in which she played a Eurasian. She essayed seven roles in *Woman Times Seven* (1967) – about six too many – and then played the golden-hearted whore again in *Sweet Charity* (1969), Bob Fosse's musical version of Fellini's *Nights Of Cabiria* (1957) and a big Broadway hit, straining too hard for sympathy as a taxi-dancer in a sleazy Manhattan nightspot, but pleasing her legion of fans.

Politics now took up a lot of MacLaine's time, and she campaigned for Bobby Kennedy in 1968 and George McGovern in 1972. She also published a candid memoir, *Don't Fall Off The Mountain*, starred in her own TV series, *Shirley's World*, co-produced and directed a documentary about China after a visit in 1973 and wrote a book about the experience (*You Can Get There From Here*).

Her screen career semed to be winding down, and in 1976 she returned to the stage in a one-woman show, *A Gypsy In My Soul*. However, she was sufficiently attracted by the earnestness of Herbert Ross' disastrous *The Turning Point* (1977) to take the part of a former ballerina who has given up the stage for domesticity and a daughter now embarking on her own dancing career. She weathered the mid-life crisis and saw off Bo Derek in *A Change Of Seasons* (1980) and then cannily set about cornering the market in those rare but pivotal roles in which an overbearing middle-aged woman is caught up in a complicated relationship with a daughter. Gone were the warmhearted slatterns and klutzy artists' molls of the first half of her career, although there was more than a hint of them in the character she played in *Terms Of Endearment* (1983): an eccentrically glamorous Houston widow and grandmother finding a creaky coupling with horny ex-astronaut Jack Nicholson ('fan-fucking-tastic') and coping with the terminal cancer of daughter Debra Winger. As Aurora Greenaway she let untended roots whiten her hair and, in the best Hollywood tradition, won the Best Actress Oscar, an honour that many, including the recipient, considered long overdue.

She put on 20lb for *Madame Sousatzka* (1988), as the eponymous piano teacher nurturing a precocious talent. This was *The Corn Is Green* territory in which you are supposed to warm to a curmudgeonly tyrant, but in the hands of MacLaine and director John Schlesinger you just wanted to give the old bat a boot up the backside, a reproach many might have been tempted to administer to her crusty Ouiser Boudreaux in *Steel Magnolias* (1989) and confirmation that she is more dependent than most on a tight script and firm direction. But neither of these films prepared audiences for *Postcards From The Edge* (1990), adapted from Carrie Fisher's semi-autobiographical novel. MacLaine was magnificent as the indomitable old trouper Doris Mann, fighting to keep her actress daughter Meryl Streep from sniffing her future up her nose and both shocking and moving in the hospital scene which follows a car accident. In pitiless close-up she sits in her bed, scrub-faced and balding, while Streep patiently applies her warpaint, piece by painful piece, so that she can once more face the press. For a woman who claims that 'my juices didn't even get going until I was 40', MacLaine clearly has a lot more to give.

1955 The Trouble With Harry; Artists And Models **1956** Around The World In 80 Days **1958** The Sheepman; The Matchmaker; Hot Spell **1959** Some Came Running; Ask Any Girl; Career **1960** Ocean's 11 (cameo); Can-Can; The Apartment **1961** All In A Night's Work; Two Loves **1962** The Children's Hour; My Geisha; Two For The Seesaw **1963** Irma La Douce **1964** What A Way To Go!; The Yellow Rolls Royce **1965** John Goldfarb Please Come Home **1966** Gambit **1967** Woman Times Seven **1968** The Bliss of Mrs Blossom **1969** Sweet Charity **1970** Two Mules For Sister Sara **1972** The Possession Of Joel Delaney **1973** The Year Of The Woman (docu) **1974** Desperate Characters **1977** The Turning Point **1979** Being There **1980** Loving Couples; A Change Of Seasons **1983** Terms Of Endearment **1984** Cannonball Run II **1988** Madame Sousatzka **1989** Steel Magnolias **1990** Waiting For The Light; Postcards From The Edge **1992** Used People

Madigan, Amy

Actress
Born 1957
Chicago, Illinois

In the scheme of things, Amy Madigan is not a name to which average cinemagoers can instantly put a face because she has been mainly cast in secondary, and even tertiary, supporting roles, delivering discreet and acute performances as people's sisters, best friends, neighbours and wives. This is somewhat surprising, given that Madigan made her debut in a cracking great lead in *Love Child* (1982), in which she was never off the screen. She played a young inmate of a corrective prison who becomes pregnant by a warder (Beau Bridges) and goes to law to fight for the right to keep the child. It was a dramatisation of a true story and Madigan, waif-like and defiant, was first-class in the kind of role that Sissy Spacek has almost invariably tended to play. But if her work was striking, the movie was too downbeat to take the box office by storm. The same fate befell several more of her films, such as Louis Malle's *Alamo Bay* (1984), in which she starred with her husband, Ed Harris, while successes such as the same year's *Places In The Heart* failed to benefit the excellent supporting players like Madigan and Lindsay Crouse, since the spotlight was so firmly on Sally Field.

The daughter of a Chicago TV commentator, convent-educated Madigan began acting at school and also commenced studying classical piano at the Chicago Conservatoire of Music, a training she continued for nine years. After finishing her schooling, she spent a decade travelling the country with various all-girl bands – among them the quaintly named Alice Stone Ladies Society Orchestra! She then decided to exchange music-making for acting and enrolled at the LA branch of the Lee Strasberg Institute.

Amy Madigan, no glamour girl, is perhaps more of a premier character actress than a Hollywood leading lady, and has fared better on television, where her numerous appearances have included the internationally acclaimed nuclear holocaust drama, *The Day*

After (1983), and the dramatisation of the real-life abortion issue drama, *Roe vs. Wade* (1989). She is a convincing performer who excels in roles with which younger middle-class women can identify, playing characters who demand a basic ordinariness which she supplies, but to which she brings that little extra something, as with her sympathetic wife to Kevin Costner's man possessed with a vision in *Field Of Dreams* (1989).

1982 Love Child **1984** Alamo Bay; In Our Hands; Streets Of Fire; Places In The Heart **1985** Twice In A Lifetime; Love Letters **1987** Nowhere To Hide **1988** The Prince Of Pennsylvania **1989** Field Of Dreams; Uncle Buck **1992/93** The Dark Half

Madonna
(Madonna Louise Ciccone)
Actress, singer
Born 16 August 1958
Bay City, Michigan

Still best known for her phenomenal success as a pop singer, this outspoken and controversial icon of the 80s (and doubtless the 90s) has also managed to carve out a reasonably successful acting career in between million-selling records and sell-out concert tours.

Madonna, one of eight children in an Italian immigrant family, was, from an early age, devoted to ballet and absolutely determined to become a star. After studying modern dance, jazz and ballet for a brief period at the University of Michigan, she left for Paris where she made a living singing in clubs until she decided to make her way to New York. During her French sojourn she learned to play the drums, the guitar and keyboards, and teamed up with an aspiring producer, John 'Jellybean' Benitez, who helped put together her first album, 'Madonna', that spawned the hits 'Holiday' and 'Lucky Star'. By this time, Madonna had created an image for herself, that of a vamp outrageously sporting a crucifix, and with a penchant for wearing little more than underwear and jewellery in her pop videos and concert performances. This strength of character and its consequent notoriety won her a small role in the film *Vision Quest* (1985) as a bar-room singer, and led to a co-lead in Susan Seidelman's film *Desperately Seeking Susan* (1985). Madonna here came into her own, almost playing herself as the wild girl living on the edge whose main objective is to have a good time. The film's success was increased by the popularity of the song, 'Into The Groove', that she lent to the soundtrack.

Never one to shy away from publicity, the entertainer continued to court controversy with such songs as 'Like A Virgin', and paid homage to her idol, Marilyn Monroe, in the video for her hit 'Material Girl'. It was on the set of this video that she met actor Sean Penn, who later married her in a bizarre wedding ceremony photographed by numerous newshounds flying overhead in helicopters. Her husband's explosive temper generated pages of tabloid news over the months to come, and the couple did nothing to help matters when they appeared together in the dismal *Shanghai Surprise* (1986). Cast against type as a missionary, the star was held responsible for the film's lack of success, even though its premise, direction and script were quite clearly as much to blame.

Madonna's next foray into the movies was to supply the haunting theme 'Live To Tell' for the film *At Close Range* (1986) starring husband Penn. Then, fans had to content themselves with a string of hits from the albums 'True Blue' and 'Like A Prayer', news of her divorce in the papers, and the video release of a 'lost' Madonna film, *A Certain Sacrifice* (1982). The next legitimate movie of her career was *Who's That Girl?* (1987), an attempt to re-create the comedies of the 40s which bombed with a thud, and the equally awful Damon Runyon adaptation, *Bloodhounds Of Broadway* (1989) which, while claiming to star Madonna, had her in a small role as 1920s showgirl Hortense Hathaway. The film had little to recommend it, and was confined to a video release. The singer-actress came in for further criticism for her stage performance in the Broadway production of David Mamet's *Speed The Plow* in 1988, in which she battled valiantly to act in the brilliant company of Joe Mantegna and Ron Silver. Not surprisingly, she returned to music.

It was not until Warren Beatty cast her in the role of platinum-blonde vamp Breathless Mahoney in *Dick Tracy* (1990) that she found a niche as a songstress-cum-*femme fatale*. As well as surprising all the critics who thought that her performance in *Desperately Seeking Susan* would prove to be a one-off, Madonna also collaborated with Stephen Sondheim and produced an acclaimed soundtrack for the film.

Thus far best displayed in roles that are extensions of her pop personae, Madonna was captured with striking, almost naively obnoxious candour in the 1991 documentary *Truth Or Dare* (aka *In Bed With Madonna*) before putting in little more than a cameo as a circus seductress in Woody Allen's *Shadows And Fog* (1992), devouring John Malkovich with relish. Then came an adequate wisecracking turn in the women's baseball comedy, *A League Of Their Own* (1992) – not *too* stretched as team slut 'All-the-way Mae'. She was regularly said to be set for the on-off screen version of *Evita*, while a mega-deal with Time Warner has provided her with the backing to produce projects tailored to her own not inconsiderable ambitions.

Tough, beautiful, extremely shrewd and undeniably charismatic, it would be foolish to bet against her prevailing as a superstar.

1982 A Certain Sacrifice **1985** Desperately Seeking Susan; Vision Quest aka Crazy For You **1986** Shanghai Surprise **1987** Who's That Girl? **1989** Bloodhounds Of Broadway **1990** Dick Tracy **1991** Truth Or Dare (GB: In Bed With Madonna (docu) **1992** Shadows And Fog; A League Of Their Own **1993** Body Of Evidence

Mahoney, John

Actor
Born 20 June 1940
Manchester, England

A distinctive-looking and prematurely grey-haired character actor, John Mahoney only made his screen debut in middle-age but within a couple of years had portrayed a number of memorable and key characters ranging from salesman to diplomat, from farmer to professor. The British-born Mahoney (he went to the US when he was 19, having already worked as a juvenile stage actor) was in his mid-30s, living in Chicago and employed as the editor of a medical journal, when he experienced the mid-life identity crisis undergone by many but acted upon by few as dramatically. Always interested in acting, he signed up for classes at a local theatre co-founded by playwright David Mamet. Selected from the class for a role in a Mamet work, *Water Engine*, he left his job for the part and next to no money.

Subsequently, Mahoney joined Chicago's celebrated Steppenwolf Theatre at the urging of John Malkovich, and his more than 30 theatre credits include his Tony-award winning performance in *House Of Blue Leaves* on Broadway (for which he also won a Clarence Derwent Award) and the lead in *Orphans* in the Chicago and Broadway productions, which earned him a Theatre World Award. Still resident in Chicago, he has continued his association with Steppenwolf.

His major screen breakthrough came with Barry Levinson's popular comedy *Tin Men* (1987) in which he played the aluminium-siding sales partner of Richard Dreyfuss. He was an appropriately sinister judge in the entertaining thriller *Suspect* (1987) which starred Cher, but made a greater impact in her Oscar-winning turn, *Moonstruck* (1987), as the ageing, *bon vivant*, womanising university professor taking a shine to mumsy Olympia Dukakis in the action-packed Italian restaurant.

Working without pause, Mahoney has defied typecasting, delivering solid and varied work in films as diverse as Roman Polanski's Hitchcockian thriller, *Frantic* (1988, as the ineffectual American consul) and Cameron Crowe's superior coming-of-age comedy-drama, *Say Anything* (1989), as Ione Skye's over-devoted father at the centre of the plot. Mahoney's television work has included the role of White House Chief of Staff in *Favorite Son* and a reprise of his stage role in *House Of Blue Leaves*.

1982 Mission Hill **1985** Code of Silence **1986** The Manhattan Project **1987** Streets of Gold **1987** Tin Men; Suspect; Moonstruck **1988** Frantic; Betrayed; Eight Men Out **1989** Say Anything **1990** Love Hurts; The Russia House **1991** Article 99; Barton Fink

Malick, Terrence

Director, writer
Born 30 November 1943
Waco, Texas

The directorial debut of Terrence Malick in 1973 was an event of some significance and excitement for he at once demonstrated impressive intellectual and stylistic gifts outside the Hollywood mainstream. A Rhodes scholar who earned his living as a journalist and a philosophy lecturer, Malick wrote *Pocket Money* (1972), a modern Western for director Stuart Rosenberg, before turning his attention to directing his own work.

He based his first film on the true story of a youthful pair of delinquents in the Midwest of the 1950s who embark on a Bonnie and Clyde-type orgy of killing. The result was *Badlands* (1973) which showcased the talents of the then youthful Martin Sheen and Sissy Spacek, against a painterly visual landscape in direct counterpoint to the subject matter. Malick's protagonists, unlike Bonnie and Clyde, are seemingly unmotivated; they inhabit a world of tawdry dreams, fuelled by a passion for James Dean movies and low-grade magazines, which infects their minds, and such thoughts as they have are conveyed by the device of using the girl's banal, cliché-ridden diary as a narrative voice. The movie demonstrated the director's fine sense of irony and his literary feel, as well as his devastating eye for colour and composition. These qualities were again in evidence, six years later, in *Days Of Heaven*, in which Nestor Almendros' Oscar-winning camera captured the power of elemental disasters. Set in 1916, and starring Richard Gere, Sam Shepard and Brooke Adams, the movie dealt with economic crisis and sexual intrigue among migrant farm-workers, but proved a somewhat overblown and incoherent piece, less successful than its predecessor.

The power and beauty of Malick's work, however, has never been seen again. After *Days Of Heaven* the director left Hollywood for Paris and has not made another film. Rumour has it that scripts continue to arrive for his perusal, but none has tempted him. As the years rolled on, the hope that he would eventually re-emerge, his original vision and considerable gifts intact, began to fade, marking a significant loss to the American film industry.

1972 Pocket Money (writer only) **1973** Badlands (w/d) **1979** Days Of Heaven (w/d)

Malkovich, John

Actor
Born 9 December 1953
Benton, Illinois

One of the foremost theatre actors of his generation, John Malkovich is at first glance an unlikely – and evidently reluctant – heart-throb, but there is something of a dangerous animal in him that appeals deeply to women.

Raised in a large, noisy, argumentative, intellectual family in Benton, Illinois, Malkovich was the high school fat boy whose single-minded pursuit of a desired end is illustrated by his claim that he shed the unwanted weight by a self-imposed dietary regime of nothing but jelly for months.

At 22 he became a member of the fledgling Steppenwolf theatre company in Chicago, an intense, avant-garde young group whose hard-hitting, sometimes shocking early work made an impact felt throughout contemporary American theatre, in which the company is now renowned. Malkovich's many theatre credits include modern classics such as Tennessee Williams' *The Glass Menagerie*, Arthur Miller's *Death Of A Salesman*, Harold Pinter's *The Caretaker* and Lanford Wilson's award-winning plays *Fifth Of July* and *Burn This*, in which Malkovich originated the role of the explosive Pale in Los Angeles in 1987, took it to Broadway and in 1990 on to London, a sensational stage portrayal that electrified audiences. The actor has also directed numerous theatre productions and frequently turned his hand to set and costume design.

He made his film debut as a gutsy war photographer in Roland Joffé's emotive true-life Cambodian drama, *The Killing Fields* (1984), and received an Oscar nomination for his second film performance, that of the blind lodger in *Places In The Heart* the same year. Assuming him to be a stereotypical 'method' actor, the producers dispatched him daily to an institute for the blind to prepare for the role; explaining 'That's not what I do' he eventually confessed he'd spent the time driving about looking around car showrooms. The resulting performance was plausible enough to persuade a number of viewers he was actually blind.

Malkovich's next screen roles were less fortunate: *Eleni* (1985), Peter Yates' film of *New York Times* journalist Nicholas Gage's heart-wringing return to his native Greece to learn the truth about his mother's mysterious death misfired, with Malkovich's Gage rather too much the detached, rational journalist to engage the emotions; as both a misfit scientist and his alter-ego android creation in Susan Seidelman's comedy *Making Mr. Right* (1987) he had fun and delivered many good moments, but the film was very hit-or-miss. Malkovich was more effective as a cunning, cold-hearted POW American pilot determined to survive the Japanese occupation of China in World War II in Spielberg's production of J.G. Ballard's remarkable autobiographical novel *Empire Of The Sun* (1987), a characterisation that provided a sharp and nicely sour contrast to the largely British and better-behaved ensemble of the prison camp.

His biggest screen challenge to date, *Dangerous Liaisons* (1988), Stephen Frears' screen version of Christopher Hampton's play, was met with the most wildly mixed reviews an actor could dream of or agonise over. Cast (or as some had it, miscast) as an aristocratic French rake of the 18th Century, Malkovich may not have been pretty but made a coldly thrilling, seductive snake of a scheming despoiler. He was equally intense in Bernardo Bertolucci's less fortuitous adaptation of Paul Bowles' *The Sheltering Sky* (1990) as a soulful, feverish adventurer, but the film foundered in the sands of Morocco. Between stage and screen roles John Malkovich's interest in design has prompted him to take to the catwalk on occasion as a stylish clotheshorse, and his behind-the-scenes ambitions saw him as a producer of *The Accidental Tourist* (1988).

1984 The Killing Fields; Places In The Heart **1985** Eleni **1987** Making Mr Right; The Glass Menagerie; Empire Of The Sun **1988** Dangerous Liaisons **1990** The Sheltering Sky **1991** Object Of Beauty; Queen's Logic Shadows And Fog **1992** Jennifer 8; Of Mice And Men **1993** In The Line Of Fire

Malle, Louis

Director, Writer
Born 30 October 1932
Thumeries, France

'I'm always interested in exposing something, a theme, a character or situation which seems to be unacceptable. Then I try to make it work,' Louis Malle has said. More often than not, the French film director does make it work. He has tackled adultery (*The Lovers*, 1958), incest (*Dearest Love*, 1971) and child prostitution (*Pretty Baby*, 1978) sympathetically; lifted the lid on French collaboration during the Occupation (*Lacombe Lucien*, 1973), and racism in the USA (*Alamo Bay*, 1986). He has dealt sensitively with anti-Semitism (*Au Revoir Les Enfants*, 1987) and alcoholism (*Le Feu Follet*, 1963), made a fantasy that included a talking unicorn (*Black Moon*, 1975), and filmed 110 minutes of two people having a dinner conversation (*My Dinner With André*, 1982). *The Lovers* caused a scandal by its amoral attitude to adultery, but it made a star of Jeanne Moreau, with whom the director was romantically involved. Malle courted scandal again with *Dearest Love*, a social comedy about the sexual education of a young boy who, with disarming naturalness, is taken to bed by his attractive mother (Lea Massari).

Born into one of France's wealthiest families (their fortune came from sugar in the French West Indies), Malle was sent to a Carmelite boarding school in Fontainebleau during the Nazi occupation, a period which he dramatised in his most autobiographical work, *Au Revoir Les Enfants*. He was a student at film school in Paris when Jacques Cousteau picked him to make a voyage on the 'Calypso' because Malle had done underwater photography. The young man stayed with Cousteau for four years, and received co-director's credit on *The Silent World* (1956), the celebrated Oscar-winning underwater documentary.

Twenty-five-year-old Malle's first solo feature, *Lift To The Scaffold* (1957), gave a conventional thriller plot psychological depth and a dark atmosphere, and its use of Paris locations made it one of the first films of the *Nouvelle Vague*. After becoming established as one of France's most versatile directors, Malle decided to try his luck in Hollywood. His first American movie, *Pretty Baby*, was a loving recreation of a turn-of-the-century New Orleans brothel where a 12-year-old girl (Brooke Shields) is brought up. The director avoided sensationalism by viewing the prostitutes as part of a bustling, vibrant, tragi-comic community.

The old and the new, the past and the present, the values of the old and the young were captured with a subtle eye for detail and lives lived in *Atlantic City* (1980). Burt Lancaster, as a petty crook from another age trying to survive on lies as walls collapse around him, carried the movie, strikingly assisted by Susan Sarandon. In the same year, Malle, divorced and the father of two children, married actress Candice Bergen, and began living a great deal of the time in California, where he embarked on his most commercial Hollywood movie, *Crackers* (1984). A remake of the successful Italian heist comedy *I Soliti Ignoti* (1958), with Donald Sutherland and Sean Penn among the bumbling gang of thieves, it was shallow and whimsical, and flopped. *Alamo Bay* failed for a different reason. Malle's worthy attempt to expose the racism working against the Vietnamese in the fishing community along the Texas coast was too simplistically plotted. He was much happier on his return to his French roots with *Milou In May* (1990), a satirical family comedy set during the events of May 1968, but continues to be one of the very few post-war French directors who has enjoyed success in both Europe and Hollywood.

1956 Le Monde Du Silence/The Silent World (docu, co-director) **1957** Ascenseur Pour L'Echafaud/Lift To The Scaffold (US: Frantic) **1958** Les Amants/The Lovers **1960** Zazie Dans Le Métro/Zazie **1962** La Vie Privée/A Very Private Affair (also co-writer) **1963** Le Feu Follet/Will O' The Wisp (US: The Fire Within) (w/d) **1965** Viva Maria!

(also co-writer) **1967** Le Voleur/The Thief Of Paris (also co-writer) **1968** Histoires Extraordinaires/Spirits Of The Dead ('William Wilson' episode) (also co-writer) **1969** Calcutta (docu) (w/d) **1971** Le Souffle Au Coeur/Dearest Love (US: Murmur Of The Heart) (w/d) **1972** Humain Trop Humain (docu) (w/d) **1973** Lacombe Lucien (also co-writer) **1975** Black Moon (also co-writer) **1978** Pretty Baby (also co-writer) **1980** Atlantic City **1982** My Dinner With André **1984** Crackers **1985** God's Own Country (docu) 1986 Alamo Bay **1987** Au Revoir Les Enfants (w/d) 1990 Milou En Mai/Milou In May (US: May Fools) (w/d) **1992/93** Damage

Mamet, David

Director, writer
Born 30 November 1947
Chicago, Illinois

David Mamet had established himself as one of America's leading modern playwrights before he brought his colourful use of language, vivid creation of low-life characters and elaborate plotting to films, first as a screenwriter and then as director of his own scripts.

Mamet comes from a Russian-Jewish family; his father was a labour lawyer and his mother a teacher. He first worked backstage at the Hull House Theatre in his home town of Chicago, then moved on to Goddard College and acting studies at the Neighborhood Playhouse in New York. He subsequently returned to Goddard as artist-in-residence, where he formed what was to become the St Nicholas Theatre Company.

Among his more celebrated plays have been *A Life In The Theatre, American Buffalo, Sexual Perversity In Chicago* and *Glengarry Glen Ross*, for which he was awarded the coveted Pulitzer Prize and the Tony Award in 1984. Of his plays, Mamet has said, 'My characters are trapped in the destructive folds of the public myths of my country. The obsessive search for success and individuality has led to the abandonment of a sense of community and collective social goals.'

The best of Mamet's screenplays for other directors has been *The Verdict* (1982), for Sidney Lumet, a taut courtroom drama out of which a few surprising rabbits were pulled, though the characterisations (Paul Newman and James Mason as adversaries) lent the film its prime quality. On the whole, he tends to over-egg his plots, as in *House Of Games* (1987), his debut as a director, in which, as screenwriter, he manipulated his main characters, Lindsay Crouse (his then wife) and Joe Mantegna, through a rigidly plot-bound script of games that loses its way when the twists in the tale become highly implausible. Mamet's considerable strength as a writer is his sharply humorous use of the vernacular and his penetration of closed worlds: in *House of Games*, for example, he leads us into the sub-culture of the conman.

Things Change (1988), though also too concerned with plot, was an extremely amiable, gently amusing, whimsical and touching fable. It told how an elderly shoeshine 'boy' (Don Ameche) is contracted to take the rap for a Chicago gangster whom he resembles. The cast, including the inestimable Ameche, Mamet favourite Joe Mantegna, and many of his stage regulars, was splendidly directed. If Mamet does become a notable movie director, he will be one of the few active playwrights in film history to have done so, though his handling of *Homicide* (1991) seemed to lose its way halfway through in both script and direction.

As writer only unless stated otherwise: **1981** The Postman Always Rings Twice **1982** The Verdict **1987** House Of Games (w/d); The Untouchables **1988** Things Change (w/d) **1991** Homicide (w/d) **1992** Glengarry Glen Ross; Hoffa

Mann, Michael

Director, writer
Born 5 February 1943
Chicago, Illinois

Michael Mann's fascinating, commercially unsuccessful feature films are inevitably coloured by his highly influential but comparatively superficial television work. As the producer and stylist of the designer cop show *Miami Vice*, Mann created one of the definitive images of the 1980s. The first drama series to latch on to the MTV phenomenon, the show was slick, modish, middle-of-the-road fantasy; cool, violent, and enormously popular. Ironically, the series that revived Mann's career and made his reputation is little more than a hollow parody of his genuinely arresting thrillers *Thief* (aka *Violent Streets*, 1981) and *Manhunter* (1986) – films that neatly book-end his spell in 'Miami'.

Mann was educated at the University of Wisconsin, then studied at the London International Film School. Between 1965 and 1972 he gained experience making television documentaries and commercials in Britain – he might be compared (favourably) with such British advertising graduates as Alan Parker, Hugh Hudson, Adrian Lyne and the brothers Scott. His short film *Jaunpuri* won a Jury prize at the Cannes film festival. After returning to the United States, Mann contributed to the scripts of such prime-time TV shows as *Starsky And Hutch*, *Vegas* and *Police Story*. He also did uncredited work on the Dustin Hoffman movie *Straight Time* (1978), before breaking into directing with *The Jericho Mile* (1979). A prison film about an inmate (Peter Strauss) who runs to Olympic standard, it should have been a very ordinary TV movie, but Mann gave it a gritty, committed feel (his documentary experience well to the fore), and extracted searing performances from amateurs and actors alike, so that the results were quite outstanding, and the film was released theatrically to excellent reviews outside the States.

Thief, his first film for the cinema, was far more personal and ambitious, a modernist, existential thriller, no less. James Caan starred as the expert burglar of the title – but the director goes out of his way to de-emphasise personality (the writing is clipped and the acting understated) in favour of a nihilistic vision that calls to mind James Cameron's 'Tech-Noir' club and French thrillers like *Rififi* (1954) and *Touchez Pas Au Grisbi* (1953). He doesn't try to get under the actors' skins, but instead coolly observes what they do and how. He is obsessed with precision, so much so that the authorities wondered if this film's tour-de-force 20-minute bank robbery sequence couldn't serve as a blueprint for copycat crimes. Ultimately though, *Thief* was so true to its existential credentials that it failed as a thriller, and audiences stayed away. *The Keep* (1983) went further down the same road. A mystical confrontation between Nazi fascism and ancient evil in a desolate Romanian castle during World War II, it is a film quite unlike anything else Hollywood produced in the 80s. Not quite a horror movie, it works best almost abstractly, in its awesome expressionist surfaces and dank, grey atmospherics. Not surprisingly, it flopped, and only *Miami Vice* saved Mann's career.

Manhunter (1986) retained that show's pulsating score and high-tech ambience, but used them subversively, to plunge us into a terrifying, psychotic world where the cop hero (William Petersen), who tracks his man by identifying with him mentally, must question not only his own humanity but his very sanity. Among other things, this adaptation of Thomas Harris' *Red Dragon* is a rare study of voyeurism that never becomes voyeuristic itself. It is Mann's most subtle and unnerving film; its commericial failure, especially in the light of the success of the Demme adaptation of Harris' *The Silence Of The Lambs*, can only be attributed to unfortunate distribution problems.

1981 Thief aka Violent Streets (w/d) **1983** The Keep (w/d) **1986** Manhunter (w/d) **1992** The Last Of The Mohicans (w/d)

Mantegna, Joe

Actor

Born 13 November 1947

Chicago, Illinois

Joe Mantegna is not only an actor who knows how to talk, he is also an actor who knows how to listen – although he has specialised in characters who only do the latter for their own predetermined ends. There is little overtly sexual about his appeal despite his strong physical presence and the seductive quality of his voice: his love is the words his master craftsmen characters use to force those who oppose them to deal on his characters' own terms, be they sleazy (his plumber in *The Money Pit*, 1986), malicious (his don in *The Godfather Part III*, 1990) or, at his best, manipulative (*House Of Games*, 1987).

The Chicago-born actor made his stage debut there in the 1969 production of *Hair*, becoming a member of the city's Organic Theatre Co and making his Broadway debut with *Working* in 1978. He co-wrote the award-winning play *Bleacher Bums* the following year, although it was a guesting role on TV's *Soap* that was instrumental in getting his face known. Back in Chicago he joined the Goodman Theatre where he began his long association with playwright David Mamet that led to his Tony Award-winning role in *Glengarry Glen Ross* in 1983. It was also Mamet who was to set him on the cinematic map (until then he had only had a few small roles in screen comedies) when he cast him as the con-man who uses the emotional confidences he worms from Lindsay Crouse's psychiatrist against her self control to manipulate events in the writer's directorial debut, *House Of Games* (1987); then Mamet and his star turned the set-up on its head the following year with Mantegna's small-time Mafioso who is dragged along in the wake of Don Ameche's innocence in *Things Change*.

At his best with Mamet – again demonstrated in the intelligent thriller *Homicide*

(1991), in which he played a tough Jewish cop plunged into a crisis of conflicting loyalties – his delivery perfectly catching the rhythms of the writer's distinctive colloquial dialogue (not a physical actor, he acts with his voice and hands, occasionally adding a walk at moments of dominance), Mantegna is in some danger of allowing his screen persona to be defined by the writer – yet he has the ability to make more mundane writing work. The dialogue in *Suspect* (1987) conforms to Hollywood prosecutor tradition, but he injects it with a force *behind* his words: when he speaks, you listen. When given enough to work with, Joe Mantegna can hold the screen, and while there is little likelihood of his ever becoming a great romantic lead, he has quickly found himself working for most of the top directors in the business as one of the most quietly powerful of major supporting players.

1978 Towing **1983** Second Thoughts aka You Bastard **1985** Compromising Positions **1986** The Money Pit; Off Beat; Three Amigos! **1987** Critical Condition; House Of Games; Weeds; Suspect **1988** Things Change **1989** Wait Until Spring Bandini (France/Italy/US/Belgian) **1990** Alice; The Godfather Part III **1991** The Marrying Man; Queens Logic; Homicide; Bugsy **1992** Radio Flyer; Family Prayers **1992/93** Searching For Bobby Fischer

Marshall, Garry

Director, writer, actor
Born 13 November 1934
New York City

To date a director of largely formulaic mainstream comedies and comedy dramas, Garry Marshall was suddenly promoted to top rank with the surprise world-wide success of 1990's *Pretty Woman*. It is a position which, although he hardly deserves it artistically, is unlikely to faze a man who for many years created some of the most popular comedy shows on American television.

Born in New York City, Marshall is the son of an industrial film-maker father and dance teacher mother. Before a stint in the army he studied journalism at North Western University and went on to become a reporter on the *New York Daily News*, as well as playing drums in a jazz band. Shortly afterwards, he began writing television scripts for such programmes as the *Joey Bishop Show*, but it was his teaming with writer Jerry Belson that brought him into the big league. Together, the prolific duo created sit-coms such as *The Lunch Show* and *The Odd Couple*, as well as penning the screenplays to the movies *How Sweet It Is* (1968) and *The Grasshopper* (1970), both of which also featured Marshall in small roles. (Although not primarily an actor, he has made regular, if brief, appearances in movies throughout his career, including Albert Brooks' 1985 film *Lost In America*, and his sister Penny's directorial debut feature, *Jumpin' Jack Flash*, the following year.) After he and Belson went their separate ways in the mid-70s, he created and produced such phenomenally successful shows as *Happy Days*, *Mork And Mindy* and, starring Penny, *Laverne And Shirley*.

Given his TV background, it is not surprising that in his first feature film venture, *Young Doctors in Love* (1982), he drew on the small screen for inspiration. A spoof of daytime soap operas, the film is a madcap hospital comedy about an unlikely group of medics, television actors Dabney Coleman and Michael McKean (a *Laverne And Shirley* co-star) among them, which was a childish and too infrequently funny affair. *The Flamingo Kid* (1989), Marshall's second feature which he also co-wrote, was far more effective, a winning little coming-of-age story set in the early 60s which starred Matt Dillon as a working-class Brooklyn boy with a job at a beach club. However, his teaming of an irascible Jackie Gleason and a self-centred Tom Hanks (an excellent performance) as the father and son forced to come to terms with each other in the comedy-drama *Nothing in Common* (1986) was something of an overlong misfire with a touch too much calculated poignancy. Like all of Marshall's films to date, it also featured the wonderful Hector Elizondo in the cast.

A director with a sure hand for breezy, lightweight subjects, (usually) brisk pacing and a canny eye for attractive, audience-pleasing actors, Marshall nevertheless frequently displays a weakness for pathos, which, given the general lack of depth of his characters, results instead in sentimentality. It is a weakness which spoilt the likeable but unremarkable *Overboard* (1987), starring Goldie Hawn and Kurt Russell, and added a strong dose of suds to the already soapy *Beaches* (1988), a woman's friendship story of the 'you laugh-you cry' variety in which Bette Midler, as a talented performer, shamelessly upstages her terminally ill friend, Barbara Hershey.

And then came *Pretty Woman*. Originally intended as a dark, gritty tale with a downbeat finale, the project was lightened up and given a happier ending before being entrusted to Marshall's direction. The result is a flimsy, sparkling Cinderella-cum-Pygmalion story which blithely glosses over the sordid realities – prostitution, drug-taking – of its context, while positively revelling in its own wish-fulfilment fantasy. That it proved such an extraordinary success owed less to the director's slick packaging than to the fortunate match of a suave, handsome Richard Gere (who at the time had been all but written off the Hollywood map) and the splendid, irresistible and, although hard to believe now, little-known Julia Roberts, whose gawky beauty and hyena-like laugh bewitched cinemagoers the world over. Riding high in the wake of *Pretty Woman*, Garry Marshall next went on to a rather more heavyweight project – the screen version of the play *Frankie And Johnny In The Clair De Lune* (1991) starring the highly regarded Michelle Pfeiffer, and no less an actor than Al Pacino. Whether Marshall would be able to maintain his newly-elevated position in the 90s, remained to be seen, but one thing is for sure: although his films may not be 'art' they are as crowd-pleasing, undemanding and watchable as the best television sit-coms.

1968 How Sweet It Is (co-writer, actor only); Psych-Out (actor only) **1970** The Grasshopper (writer only) **1982** Young Doctors In Love (also bit) **1984** The Flamingo Kid (also co-writer, bit) **1985** Lost in America (actor only) **1986** Nothing in Common (also bit); Jumpin' Jack Flash (bit only) **1987** Overboard (also bit) **1988** Beaches **1990** Pretty Woman **1991** Frankie & Johnny; Soapdish (actor only)

Marshall, Penny

Actress, director
Born 15th October 1944
New York City

Although she likes to claim 'I'm from the negativity and depression school' Penny Marshall's work, both as an actress and director, is characterised by an engaging combination of great warmth and humour.

Born and raised in the Bronx by a film-maker father and a dance teacher mother, Marshall was predisposed to a life of show business. She began tap-dancing at the age of three and by the time she reached her mid-teens she and a group of friends had hot-footed their way onto *Ted Mack's Amateur Hour* and *The Jackie Gleason Show*. She went on to spend six years at the University of New Mexico in Albuquerque before making the move to Hollywood, where the buck-toothed actress landed small parts in such movies as *The Savage Seven* (1968) and *The Grasshopper* (1970), and made TV appearances on many shows, including *The Odd Couple, The Mary Tyler Moore Show* and *Happy Days*. But it was her brother, Garry Marshall, then a TV producer, who created the role with which she became synonymous – Laverne, in the hit series *Laverne and Shirley*. As the lovably goofy Milkwaukee factory worker, Marshall entertained audiences from 1976 to 1983; the fact that she was married to Rob Reiner, himself a star in the successful TV series *All In The Family*, only helped increase her growing celebrity clout.

However, Marshall's career as a movie actress never really took off, and with the exception of the odd cameo in such films as *Movers and Shakers* (1985), by the 1980s she had set her sights on an entirely new role – directing. By this time divorced from Rob Reiner, she cut her teeth on the occasional TV movie and *The Tracey Ullman Show*, before making her debut as a feature film director in 1986 with *Jumpin' Jack Flash*. The film was a comedy about spies starring Whoopi Goldberg and, in supporting roles, Marshall's brother Garry and her daughter, Tracy, from her first marriage to Michael Henry. Despite a good cast and a lively pace, the movie's silly script led to a very poor reception from critics and audiences alike.

However, Marshall's fortune was to undergo a radical reversal with her follow-up feature. With its simple title and guileless star turn by Tom Hanks, as a little boy who wakes up to find himself in the body of a 30-year-old man, *Big* (1988) charmed and delighted audiences world-wide. The tyro director had hit the movie jackpot.

It was more than two years before Marshall, now in demand, made another feature, this time a drama. *Awakenings* (1990) had been on the back boiler at 20th-Century Fox for years and Marshall had a struggle on her hands to get the film made until the casting of her friends Robert De Niro and Robin Williams secured a go-ahead. Taken from the journals of neurologist and author Dr Oliver Sacks, the film is a true story about a doctor's attempts to bring postencephalitic patients out of long-term states of vegetation. The director's confident handling of the potentially downbeat subject ensured that *Awakenings* was a delightful, bittersweet film boasting astounding acting from both Williams and De Niro; it garnered three Oscar nominations including one for Best Picture, but suprisingly, Marshall herself was overlooked by the Academy.

A League Of Their Own (1992) was less commercially and critically successful, despite re-uniting Marshall with her *Big* star, Tom Hanks, playing the drunken, uncouth coach of an all-female baseball league formed during World War II. Despite the film's energy and a stunning central performance from Geena Davis, it is swamped by sentimentality and contrivance.

Nevertheless, Penny Marshall is a courageous and often sure-handed director, who has been served well by her acting background: her particular skill lies in extracting performances from her actors that are moving and curiously innocent but never mawkish; and her trademark is lightness without levity. As the 90s unfolded, the former ditzy actress had firmly established herself as a Hollywood director of good calibre, and one of the few women succeeding in a traditionally male domain.

As actress only unless stated otherwise: **1968** The Savage Seven; How Sweet It Is **1970** The Grasshopper **1975** How Come Nobody's On Our Side **1979** 1941 **1985** Movers and Shakers **1986** Jumpin' Jack Flash (director only) **1988** Big (director only) **1990** Awakenings (director only) **1991** The Hard Way (cameo) **1992** A League Of Their Own (director only)

Martin, Steve

Actor, writer
Born 18 August 1945
Waco, Texas

'Wild and crazy guy' Steve Martin, since his film breakthrough with *The Jerk* (1979), has been the most consistently funny man in movies. Off screen a serious and artistically ambitious person, Martin has seldom equalled *The Jerk's* financial success in his subsequent films, but has instead won international acclaim and been stretched well beyond his early, completely manic persona.

A native of Texas, Martin had moved to Southern California with his family and was employed after school hours from the age of 10 for eight years as an assistant in Merlin's Magic Workshop at Disneyland when he came under the spell of ex-vaudevillian Wally Boag, who conjured animal shapes out of balloons. While reading logic at Long Beach State University he was an adept balloon twister, juggler and magician who also played the banjo and performed with an amateur drama group. His professional entry was as a TV comedy writer for *The Smothers Brothers*, Glenn Campbell and *The Sonny And Cher Show*, and although he won an Emmy for his work for Tom and Dick Smothers, Martin reasoned that he should be using his comic material himself. For several years he paid his comedy dues as a wacky warm-up act for country rock group The Nitty Gritty Dirt Band, and the Carpenters. A nightclub headliner in the early 70s, Martin's star rose with regular (starting in 1973) and hilarious spots on the national *Tonight* show hosted by Johnny Carson and *Saturday Night Live* in 1976. His first Grammy award-winning comedy album, 'Let's Get Small', sold an unprecedented one-and-a-half million copies, in 1977 he brought in a million dollars at the box office for a sold-out 50-city tour of his one-man show, and he received an Oscar nomination for his short film, *The Absent-Minded Waiter.*

While making guest appearances in a few films Martin was shopping around the screenplay that became *The Jerk* (1979), directed by Carl Reiner in the first of their four collaborations. Using shticks from Martin's stage routines, the movie was quite idiotic (more Mel Brooks than Oscar Wilde) but tickled audiences. Made for less than $5 million, it took more than 40 – at the time making it the 36th biggest money-spinner *ever*. Unfortunately, his follow-up in 1981 was the disastrously received film adaptation of Dennis Potter's *Pennies From Heaven*, a tragi-comedy with musical numbers on a spectacular scale not seen in years. A pefect example of 'second film syndrome', it cost over $20 million to make and grossed less than $4 million.

The disappointed but tenacious Martin reteamed with Reiner for three comedies cherished by Martin aficionados as side-splitters which became video rental favourites. *Dead Men Don't Wear Plaid* (1982), with its insane plot, is a one-joke film but the joke is a good one, featuring Martin as a 40s private eye reacting to and interacting with a remarkably edited-in series of vintage clips from favourite *films noir*, gangster flicks and B-pictures. *The Man With Two Brains* (1983), every bit as ridiculous, posited Martin as brain surgeon Michael Hfuhruhurr, wed to faithless slut Kathleen Turner but madly in love with a brain in a jar given the voice of Sissy Spacek. The last Martin-Reiner effort,

All Of Me (1984), in which half of Martin's body is seemingly possessed by the spirit of a deceased Lily Tomlin, was written by Phil Alden Robinson and was more sophisticated in its humour, if uneven. But the brilliance of Martin's physical comedy as he simultaneously walked and talked as half-man, half-woman overwhelmed even his sternest critics, and won him both the National Board of Review's and the New York Film Critics' awards for Best Actor.

With other directors, Martin's work was only partially successful until he hit upon the idea of adapting *Cyrano De Bergerac* as a contemporary romantic comedy with himself as the hideously-hootered 'C.D. Bales'. *Roxanne* (1987), directed by the normally heavyweight Fred Schepisi and co-starring a sweet Daryl Hannah as the titular beloved, was a fantastic leap forward for the attractive, distinctively grey-haired actor, eschewing the crude zaniness of much of his previous work for a genuinely clever, affectionate and touching film. His performance, as poignant as it was funny, also revealed more depth than he had hitherto shown, and it was a major surprise that he was passed over for an Oscar nomination. The Los Angeles Critics named him Best Actor and the Writers' Guild honoured him for Best Screenplay.

Now sought after as an actor in his own right, Martin considerably enlivened two 'odd couple' capers. As the hapless traveller landed with John Candy by John Hughes for *Planes, Trains and Automobiles* (1987) Martin was, unusually, the straight man through much of the slapstick and gave a good characterisation of a man moved from frustration and fury to compassion. He was also pleasing as a crass con-man holding his own with a considerably more suave Michael Caine in the Riviera larceny comedy *Dirty Rotten Scoundrels* (1988). But the big Martin winner of the late 80s was *Parenthood* (1989), for director Ron Howard, in which he shone in leading a marvellous ensemble cast enacting the joys and horrors of parenting. Far less engaging were more 'odd couple' exercises, *My Blue Heaven* (1990), written by Nora Ephron and directed by Herbert Ross, which saw the star as a mobster in hiding with FBI twerp Rick Moranis, and *Housesitter* (1992) in which Martin played the bewildered dupe of Goldie Hawn's glib, wacky con-artist. Hoping to pick up where he left off with *Roxanne* as a writer-actor, Martin initiated *L.A. Story* (1991), a bittersweet romance in which he co-starred with his wife, British actress Victoria Tennant, whom he met on *All Of Me*, and went on to work for Lawrence Kasdan as the exploitation flick producer in *Grand Canyon* the same year.

In 1988 Martin made his Broadway acting debut in the ticket sensation of the season, starred with the other outrageous comic of his generation, Robin Williams, in *Waiting For Godot*, directed by Mike Nichols.

1978 Sgt. Pepper's Lonely Hearts Club Band **1979** The Kids Are Alright; The Muppet Movie; The Jerk (also co-writer) **1981** Pennies From Heaven **1982** Dead Men Don't Wear Plaid (also co-writer) **1983** The Man With Two Brains **1984** The Lonely Guy; All Of Me **1985** Movers And Shakers **1986** Little Shop Of Horrors; Three Amigos! (also co-writer) **1987** Roxanne (also writer); Planes, Trains And Automobiles **1988** Dirty Rotten Scoundrels **1989** Parenthood **1990** My Blue Heaven **1991** L.A. Story (also writer); Grand Canyon; Father Of The Bride **1992** Housesitter **1992/93** Leap Of Faith

Mason, Marsha

Actress

Born 3 April 1942

St Louis, Missouri

Four-time Oscar nominee Marsha Mason began her career in New York theatre and bit parts in films and TV shows such as *Dr Kildare* and *Love Of Life* before she moved to San Francisco for a brief revival of Noel Coward's *Private Lives* directed by Francis Ford Coppola for the American Conservatory Theatre. While on the West Coast, she visited LA and won a supporting role in *Blume In Love* (1973), but it was her repertory work on stage that convinced director Mark Rydell he had found his *Cinderella Liberty* the same year (much to the dismay of the studio, who wanted Barbra Streisand). As a hooker with an illegitimate black son who finds herself falling in love with a sailor on shore leave, she artfully mixed realism with romance, and a perfect sense of timing gained her rave reviews and her first Oscar nomination.

For a while, Mason seemed to be threatened with typecasting as troubled mothers – the problem of a possessed daughter in *Audrey Rose* (1977), a single parent forced to share her apartment with an unemployed actor (Richard Dreyfuss) in her husband Neil Simon's *The Goodbye Girl* the same year (a second nomination) – and her initial attempts to move away were less successful until *Chapter Two* (1980, third nomination), in which she played a character based closely on herself and her early relationship with Simon. Her performance as an alcoholic actress with a troubled relationship with her daughter in *Only When I Laugh* (1981, fourth nomination – some people just never win) showed a move back towards more dramatic roles, but after the failure of both *Max Dugan Returns* (1983) and her marriage she found her screen career stalled by the seeming inseparability of her work from her ex-husband's (they were later re-united); she was typecast as a 'Neil Simon actress' in much the same way Diane Keaton was declared a 'Woody Allen actress', and she returned to the stage and numerous TV movies. With the dearth of good female roles and an excess of bigger name actresses clamouring after them, Mason has since had to settle for small supporting roles in other people's lack-lustre star vehicles.

1966 Hot Rod Hullabaloo **1968** Beyond The Law **1973** Blume in Love; Cinderella Liberty **1976** Audrey Rose **1977** The Goodbye Girl **1978** The Cheap Detective **1979** Promises In The Dark **1980** Chapter Two **1981** Only When I Laugh aka It Hurts Only When I Laugh **1983** Max Dugan Returns **1986** Heartbreak Ridge **1989** Stella **1991** Drop Dead, Fred

Masterson, Mary Stuart

Actress
Born ?1966
From ?

In an industry packed with pretty ingénues Mary Stuart Masterson might have remained in the niche 'everybody's girlfriend' to which she had been consigned opposite one Brat Packer after another, were it not for a captivating performance as a mechanically-minded tomboy in *Some Kind Of Wonderful* (1987).

The daughter of actor-director Peter Masterson (who directed Geraldine Page to her long-overdue Oscar in his debut film, *The Trip To Bountiful*, in 1985) and Broadway star Carlin Glynn, Masterson grew up surrounded by actors and never considered another profession for herself. She made her film debut at the age of eight, as the daughter of Katharine Ross and her real father, Peter, in the creepy chiller *The Stepford Wives* (1975). Educated at prestigious private schools and interested in modern dance training, she put acting just off to one side, taking part in school productions.

After leaving the Dalton School in New York, where she was a straight-A student, Masterson spent a summer in workshop at Robert Redford's Sundance Institute, acquired an agent and played the first of her 'girlfriend' roles – Andrew McCarthy's – in the very funny Catholic boys' school reminiscence *Heaven Help Us* (1985). Appendage number two – Sean Penn's – was in the downbeat drama *At Close Range* (1986). Third time out she was D. B. Sweeney's sweetie in Francis Ford Coppola's *Gardens Of Stone* (1987), in which her parents appeared as her screen parents. *Some Kind Of Wonderful* (1987) gave her more to work with as a rock 'n' roll drummer/auto mechanic/boyish waif pining for 'best friend' Eric Stoltz and finally winning him away – to the vast relief of audiences – from the more glamorous girl (Lea Thompson).

The romantic fantasy *Chances Are* (1989) provided her only with a supporting role, but she shone and held her own in the company of James Woods and Glenn Close in *Immediate Family* (1989). Despite the general drubbing handed the film itself, Masterson received glowing notices for her performance as the young woman who agrees to provide a childless couple with a baby, then – surprise, surprise – changes her mind. She returned to comedy opposite Gene Wilder in *Funny About Love* (1990) before a temporary move to Texas while her husband – a childhood sweetheart – was completing his Masters degree at university, but seemed set for consolidating her career in the coming decade.

1975 The Stepford Wives **1985** Heaven Help Us aka Catholic Boys **1986** At Close Range **1987** Gardens Of Stone; Some Kind Of Wonderful **1988** Mr North **1989** Chances Are; Immediate Family **1990** Funny About Love **1991** Married To It; Fried Green Tomatos At The Whistle Stop Cafe **1992/93** Mad At The Moon; Benny And Joon

Mastrantonio, Mary Elizabeth

Actress
Born 17 November 1958
Oak Park, Illinois

Educated at the University of Illinois, Mary Elizabeth Mastrantonio trained as an opera singer, but ended up spending a summer singing and dancing at the Opryland Theme Park in Nashville – in her case, a sign of versatility rather than failure. An engagement as understudy and vacation replacement for Maria in a revival of *West Side Story* took her to New York where, before long, her career gathered momentum in shows as disparate as Peter Shaffer's *Amadeus* and Sondheim's *Sunday In The Park With George*.

Dark-haired, dark-eyed and unconventionally beautiful, Mastrantonio burst on to the screen as Al Pacino's cosseted young sister, whom he finally destroys in a hail of bullets, in Brian De Palma's *Scarface* (1983). Her depth and versatility were confirmed and proven with her second film, *The Color Of Money* (1986), in which she co-starred with Paul Newman and Tom Cruise as Carmen, the hard-headed manager girlfriend to Cruise's tyro pool player. Her next three films were unworthy of her exceptional abilities, but she was luminous as plainclothesman Kevin Kline's girlfriend in the run-of-the-mill serial-killer thriller *The January Man* (1989).

A change of both gear and geography took her to Ireland to make *Fools Of Fortune* (1990) with Julie Christie and Iain Glen. It seemed an odd decision (though she *was* the girlfriend of, and subsequently married, the director), given the abundance of gifted British actresses around, to import an American for the role of an English girl but, in the event, she proved the saving grace of a film that can best be described as elegant tedium. Sporting a remarkably authentic accent with an ease that would have given Meryl Streep pause for thought, Mastrantonio progressed from young womanhood to adult maturity in the course of the narrative, bringing a brand of conviction to the role which underlined that she is an actress to be taken very seriously despite the fact that her plucky Maid Marian in *Prince Of Thieves* was mainly a bit of fun, and she was stranded by poor writing in *White Sands*.

1983 Scarface **1986** The Color Of Money **1987** Slam Dance **1989** The January Man; The Abyss **1990** Fools Of Fortune **1991** Class Action; Robin Hood: Prince of Thieves **1992** White Sands **1992/93** Consenting Adults

Matlin, Marlee

Actress

Born 24 August 1965

Morton Grove, Illinois

It is quite an achievement to win a Best Actress Academy Award for your first film role, and probably even more so when you consider that Marlee Matlin is also the first deaf performer to be accorded the honour.

The beautiful Matlin did not start out wanting to act. She studied at John Hershey High School in Chicago, which had a special education programme for deaf students, and then went on to William Rainey Harper College to major in Criminal Justice. Throughout her school years she had acted as a hobby, performing at the Children's Theatre Of The Deaf in Des Plaines since the age of eight, but she had only appeared in one show as an adult before she took on a supporting role in the stage production of *Children Of A Lesser God* at Chicago's Immediate Theatre.

It was during the run of that production that her performance caught the eye of film director Randa Haines, who decided to cast Matlin in the lead role of Sarah in her screen version of the play. Starring opposite Oscar-winning William Hurt, she powerfully portrayed the frustration and anger of a young woman who, deaf since childhood, has given up on learning how to speak or communicate with hearing people. Life imitated art when Matlin and Hurt continued their relationship off the set, and he presented her with her trophy at the Oscar ceremonies.

She then appeared in small roles in a few TV series (including the award-winning *Moonlighting*) before making her second film, *Walker* (1987), directed by Alex Cox. The historical satire never really found an audience, so Matlin returned to the stage and also appeared in a TV movie *Bridge To Silence* in 1987. With such an impressive beginning and a clear talent, the actress seemed certain to continue to give quality performances well into the 90s, although her opportunities are necessarily limited by her disability, which she handles with courage and dignity.

1986 Children Of A Lesser God **1987** Walker **1991** The Linguini Incident; Homme Au Masque D'or/The Man In The Golden Mask (France) **1992** The Player (cameo) **1992/93** Danger Sign

Matthau, Walter (Walter Matuschanskavasky)

Actor

Born 1 October 1920

New York City

With his slouching posture and the growling, irascible bloodhound face of one whose whole life is a series of hangovers, Walter Matthau – despite beginning his screen career as a succession of heavies – is one of God's gifts to comedy writers. Reputedly the son of a Russian Orthodox priest who very quickly disappeared from his life, Matthau began his acting career at the age of 11 when he sold drinks during the intermissions at a Second Avenue Yiddish theatre and soon found himself playing bit parts there for 50 cents a show.

Excelling at drama at school, it wasn't until after World War II service in the Air Force as a radioman-gunner that Matthau enrolled at the New School for Social Research Dramatic Workshop and began acting in earnest. Upon graduation from summer stock to key roles in Broadway shows his success in 1955's stage production of *Will Success Spoil Rock Hunter?* led to a film career and soon he was whipping Burt Lancaster in *The Kentuckian* (1955), beating up Elvis in *Kid Creole* (1958) and molesting Barbara Rush in *Strangers When We Meet* (1960), even directing the low-budget *Gangster Story* (1960). There were some sympathetic roles, too (most notably Rush's rather more concerned neighbour in Nicholas Ray's *Bigger Than Life*, 1956), but it was not until *Lonely Are The Brave* (1962) that he really broke out of the bad guy mold as the laid-back small-town sheriff more interested in watching a cat cross a hot tin roof than in hunting down Kirk Douglas.

He remained in predominantly straight roles until 1965, when Neil Simon wrote *The Odd Couple* for him and caused a Broadway sensation that was the making of them both. Billy Wilder was the first to exploit his comic talents with *The Fortune Cookie* (1966), teaming him up for the first time with Jack Lemmon and earning him a Best Supporting Actor Oscar as the scheming shyster lawyer exaggerating his brother-in-law's minor injury into a million-dollar lawsuit (after shaking hands with him, people count their fingers to make sure they're all still there). Both actors struck gold again when Matthau repeated his stage success as the grouchy, slovenly sports reporter sharing his apartment with Lemmon's obssessively tidy divorcee in the film version of *The Odd Couple* (1967), going on to play the elderly *Kotch* (1971) in Lemmon's directorial debut, although subsequent pairings in Wilder's *The Front Page* (1974) and the dire *Buddy Buddy* (1981) met with less success. His unrelenting meanness stole *Hello Dolly!* (1968) but he was generally at his best in overtly cynical roles (the playboy planning to marry and murder mousy heiress Elaine May in *A New Leaf*, 1971, or the has-been baseball coach in *The Bad News Bears*, 1976) or attacking strong material (especially Simon's) with a worthy opponent, as with his on-screen feud with George Burns in *The Sunshine Boys* (1975, a role he took over from Jack Benny).

The 70s saw the actor well employed in the tough thrillers *Charley Varrick* and *The Laughing Policeman* (both 1973), with *The Taking Of Pelham One Two Three* (1974) getting the best of both worlds, calling on his dramatic skills as he negotiates with the ruthless subway hijackers, and using his hangdog expression as a safety valve for much of the tension, providing the movie with one of the all-time great closing shots. However, the turn of the decade saw a turn for the worse as writers and directors made him loveable with a capital L in the likes of *Casey's Shadow* (1978) and *Little Miss Marker* (1980, which at least afforded him some great Damon Runyon one-liners) and set his career on a downward spiral. He was marvellous as one of life's eternal losers in Michael Ritchie's under-rated satire *The Survivors* (1983) and showed a stirring return to obnoxious amoral form (throwing in a cockney accent for good measure) in Polanski's dismal and grotesque *Pirates* (1986). But he seemed merely a distracting side show in *The Couch Trip* (1988) and, since following Lemmon's lead by making a film in Italy, has been all too little seen – a fact that seems perhaps less disappointing than it should due to the industry's inability to best use his talents when they secure them.

1955 The Kentuckian; The Indian Fighter **1956** Bigger Than Life **1957** A Face In The Crowd; Slaughter On Tenth Avenue **1958** King Creole; Voice In The Mirror; Onionhead; Ride A Crooked Trail **1960** Gangster Story (also director); Strangers When We Meet **1962** Lonely Are The Brave; Who's Got The Action? **1963** Island Of Love; Charade **1964** Ensign Pulver; Fail-Safe; Goodbye Charlie **1965** Mirage **1966** The Fortune Cookie aka Meet Whiplash Willie **1967** A Guide For The Married Man **1968** The Odd Couple; The Secret Life Of An American Wife; Candy **1969** Hello Dolly!; Cactus Flower **1971** A New Leaf; Plaza Suite; Kotch **1972** Pete 'N' Tillie **1973** Charley Varrick; The Laughing Policeman aka Investigation Of A Murder **1974** The Taking Of Pelham One Two Three; The Front Page; Earthquake (billed under his real name) **1975** The Sunshine Boys **1976** The Bad News Bears **1978** Casey's Shadow; House Calls; California Suite **1980** Hopscotch; Little Miss Marker **1981** Buddy Buddy; The First Monday In October **1982** I Ought To Be In Pictures **1983** The Survivors **1985** Movers And Shakers **1986** Pirates **1988** The Couch Trip; Il Piccolo Diavolo/Little Devil (Italy) **1991** The Visitor **1991** JFK

May, Elaine
(Elaine Berlin)
Director, writer, actress
Born 21 April 1932
Philadelphia, Pennsylvania

With Mike Nichols, Elaine May made up the brilliant satirical cabaret duo in the 50s and early 60s. After the pair split up, she carried over much of the scathing wit of the double act into her plays, screenplays and film directing. Prior to teaming up with Nichols, she had studied for the stage with the veteran Russian-born actress Maria Ouspenskaya, and then made a reputation for sparkling improvisations in the Second City revues in Chicago.

In 1967, she made her first appearances on screen in two Broadway hits made into film flops, *Enter Laughing* and *Luv*, in which she was mildly amusing as a would-be actress and disposable wife respectively. Her first two films as director were among the most cruelly funny American comedies since the 30s. In *A New Leaf* (1971), May hilariously played a wealthy, frumpish, short-sighted, accident-prone botanist whom Walter Matthau must marry (and murder) in order to pay his debts. The film was successful in spite of May's row with Paramount for having taken it away from her when she went over budget. *The Heartbreak Kid* (1972), written by Neil Simon, cast Jeannie Berlin (May's own daughter) as a Jewish Princess who drives her husband (Charles Grodin) into the arms of a beautiful WASP (Cybill Shepherd) while on their honeymoon.

It took some years before the troublesome *Mikey And Nicky* (1976) was presented to the few audiences that bothered to see it. A *film noir* written for her friends John Cassavetes and Peter Falk (playing two small-time hoods), it suppressed May's greatest forte – humour. Bad lighting, cutting and sound ruined any enjoyment that may have derived from the performances, which had been created out of lengthy improvisations. The film went outrageously over budget and the director was constantly in conflict with Paramount, as she had been with them on *A New Leaf*, from which she tried to remove her name as director. Other examples that have added fuel to May's reputation for being an awkward customer can be cited. A Broadway play she wrote in 1962, *A Matter Of Position*, closed in Philadelphia because she refused to make changes, and, because of rows with Otto Preminger, she rejected the screenwriting credit on *Such Good Friends*, preferring to use the *nom de plume* of Esther Dale.

It was more than a decade after *Micky And Nicky* before she directed another movie. The result was *Ishtar* (1987), a $35 million turkey starring Warren Beatty and Dustin Hoffman as an untalented pair of singer-songwriter nerds on the road to Morocco. May's direction moved too slowly for comedy and failed to make the more spectacular scenes either exciting or eye-catching. If it had been called El Ishtar, it would have been a perfect anagram for Real Shit. It is not easy, even for someone as clearly talented as Elaine May, to rise again from a disaster on this scale.

1967 Luv (actress only); Enter Laughing (actress only) **1971** Such Good Friends (writer only); A New Leaf (w/d, actress) **1972** The Heartbreak Kid (director only) **1976** Mikey And Nicky (w/d) **1978** California Suite (actress only); Heaven Can Wait (co-writer only) **1987** Ishtar (w/d) **1990** In The Spirit (actress only)

Mayron, Melanie
Actress
Born 20 October 1952
Philadelphia, Pennsylvania

Melanie Mayron is probably best known for her role as Melissa in the hit TV series *thirtysomething*, for which she won an Emmy award in 1989, but the redheaded actress began her career almost 20 years before with her studies at the American Academy of Dramatic Arts. She trained for a theatrical career with Sandra Seacat and John Lehne before making her debut in a touring production of *Godspell* which ran for three years.

Melanie made her first screen appearance in a small supporting role in *Harry And Tonto* (1974), the Paul Mazursky comedy of an old man (Art Carney) and his cat taking a trip across country. After a brief spell performing in the Los Angeles production of *Gethsemane Springs* in 1976, she appeared in a few low-budget films, including *The Great Smokey Roadblock* (1977) with Susan Sarandon and Henry Fonda. In between supporting film roles, she had parts in numerous TV series, including *Lily Tomlin*, *Hustling* and *Rhoda*. She returned to the cinema to star in *Girlfriends* (1978), the story of a young woman photographer trying to cope with love and a career after her room-mate leaves to get married, a performance which won her the Best Actress Award at the 1979 Locarno Film Festival.

In the same year, she made her New York theatre debut, winning critical plaudits for her work in *The Goodbye People*. Then she played a robot in the misguided love story *Heartbeeps* (1980), and appeared in a couple of TV movies, including a supporting part in the award-winning drama *Playing For Time* (1980), about the women who survived Auschwitz by playing in an orchestra that set the pace for the inmates who were being marched to their deaths. Then came her best opportunity to date, with Jack Lemmon and Sissy Spacek in Costa-Gavras' drama *Missing* (1981).

More supporting parts followed, but the actress teamed up with a friend, Catlin Adams, to write and produce their own work. First came the buddy film *Sticky Fingers* (1988), about two girls (Mayron and Helen Slater) going on a spending spree with 'borrowed' money. Although the attempts at wacky comedy went a bit askew, the film heralded the way for more Mayron–Adams co-productions, which included two TV films the pair wrote, *Tunes For A Small Harmonica* and *The Pretend Game*. By this time, Mayron had been cast in *thirtysomething*, as the independent photographer Melissa; later, she was given the opportunity to direct her co-stars, including Ken Olin, Patricia Wettig and Peter Horton, in episodes of the series.

Now known for playing slightly dizzy women, Mayron seemed perfect for the role of Jeff Daniels' scatty wife in David Leland's *Checking Out* (1989). Unfortunately, and maybe due to her presence as well as the script (about middle-aged angst), the film came over as an extended (and not very good) episode of *thirtysomething* and was a failure. Avoiding the trap of typecasting, she returned undaunted to play a rigid police officer in the comedy about the mob, *My Blue Heaven* (1990), proving her versatility as an actress.

1974 Harry And Tonto **1976** Car Wash **1977** The Great Smokey Roadblock aka Elegant John And His Ladies; You Light Up My Life **1978** Girlfriends 1980 Heartbeeps **1981** Missing **1986** The Boss' Wife **1988** Sticky Fingers (also writer, co-producer) **1989** Checking Out **1990** My Blue Heaven

Mazursky, Paul
(Irwin Mazursky)

Director, writer, actor
Born 25 April 1930
Brooklyn, New York City

The leading character in *Next Stop, Greenwich Village* (1975) is a young actor trying to make it in the theatre in New York. He works in a health-food restaurant and gets a part as a juvenile delinquent in a movie. Paul Mazursky worked in a health-food restaurant, acted off-Broadway, hung around the Village, and had a small role as an unruly school pupil in *The Blackboard Jungle* (1955). After having been a nightclub comic, actor and writer of TV comedy (including *The Danny Kaye Show*), he wrote his first film script, *I Love You, Alice B. Toklas!* (1968). Despairing at the way the movie had been turned by its director (Hy Averback) and star (Peter Sellers) into a cliché-ridden depiction of Southern California's 'alternative lifestyles', Mazursky decided henceforth to direct his own scripts.

Bob And Carol And Ted And Alice (1969) was a teasing satire on the new sexual permissiveness, and although pretty tentative, the film grabbed the public's curiosity. The attempt at wife-swapping by the two couples (Natalie Wood and Robert Culp, Dyan Cannon and Elliott Gould) is aborted when they realize that love and fidelity are more important than sex and join the other characters and crew in a Felliniesque parade finale to the strains of Dionne Warwick's 'What the world needs now is love . . .', which could be taken as the director's theme song.

Mazursky's admiration for Federico Fellini was evident in his second film, *Alex In Wonderland* (1971), about a director (Donald Sutherland) trying to make his second film, which included a dream sequence in which Fellini himself appears. It was a failure on most counts, but it did get an 'art movie' out of Mazursky's system. However, still in thrall to European cinema, he made *Blume In Love* (1973), which had George Segal, who refuses to accept that his wife has left him, catching up with her in Venice, as various couples get together (including Aschenbach and Tadzio from *Death In Venice*). *Willie And Phil* (1982), was a whimsical *ménage à trois* inspired by François Truffaut's *Jules and Jim*, and *Down And Out In Beverly Hills* (1986) was loosely based on Jean Renoir's *Boudu*

Saved From Drowning. It started off as a sharp satire on the bourgeois Californian lifestyle led by Richard Dreyfuss and family, a life disrupted by tramp Nick Nolte, but the American movie ditched the anarchic ending of the original French film in preference for a comfortable toothless one.

More successful, critically and commercially, were *Next Stop, Greenwich Village*, an affectionate and funny 50s memoir teetering on the edge of sentimentality, and *Harry And Tonto* (1974), a touching and comic odyssey across the USA, which revealed the wisdom and pain of old age. Art Carney (Best Actor Oscar), an elderly New York widower, and his orange cat took the title roles. *An Unmarried Woman* (1977) continued in the line of gently satirical character studies, although this witty and observant portrait of a woman (Jill Clayburgh), making her life anew after being left by her husband, rings false when she meets the man of her dreams (Alan Bates).

A few flops followed, including *Tempest* (1982), a long (142 minutes), modern updating of Shakespeare with John Cassavetes and Gena Rowlands getting away from it all on a nicely photographed Greek island, and *Moscow On The Hudson* (1984), starring Robin Williams as a Soviet saxophonist who defects to the USA, both undermined by a too pussy-footing approach to the subjects of mid-life crisis and culture clashes, respectively. The director returned to form with *Enemies, A Love Story* (1989), based on the novel by Isaac Bashevis Singer, about the relationship between a concentration camp survivor (Ron Silver) and three women, two of whom are his wives. Admitting that he likes to work on the 'edge of corn', Mazursky's romantic humanist movies, with New York humour and sensibility filtered through Californian mellowness, often work against one's better judgement, although he failed to pull off the rather one-joke *Scenes From A Mall* (1991), despite a casting coup that paired Woody Allen and Bette Midler.

1953 Fear And Desire (actor only) **1955** The Blackboard Jungle (actor only) **1966** Deathwatch (actor only) **1969** Bob And Carol And Ted And Alice (director, co-writer) **1971** Alex In Wonderland (director, co-writer) **1973** Blume In Love (w/d) **1974** Harry And Tonto (director, co-writer) **1975** Next Stop, Greenwich Village (w/d) **1976** A Star Is Born (actor only) **1977** An Unmarried Woman (w/d) **1980** Willie And Phil (w/d) **1982** Tempest (director, co-writer) **1984** Moscow On The Hudson (director, co-writer) **1985** Down And Out In Beverly Hills (director, co-writer) **1988** Moon Over Parador (director, co-writer); Punchline (actor only) **1989** Scenes From The Class Struggle In Beverly Hills (actor only); Enemies: A Love Story (director, co-writer) **1991** Scenes From A Mall (director, co-writer) **1992** Man Trouble

McCarthy, Andrew

Actor

Born 29 November 1962

New Jersey

The somewhat bland Andrew McCarthy has many detractors who feel he sleepwalks through his roles which, largely, have required him to portray 'Mr Nice' in a number of youth movies, notably Joel Schumacher's *St Elmo's Fire* (1985, nursing an unrequited passion for Ally Sheedy) and John Hughes' *Pretty In Pink* (1986, the rich boy courting Molly Ringwald). However, to his admirers, his WASPish good looks and pensive air, suggesting a poet or an intellectual lurking beneath the surface, lend him an added edge. Indeed, this actor has specialised in illuminating portrayals of a sensible (and sensitive) youth on the cusp of adulthood, and it is a credit to his skills that he can breathe life into roles that, as written, offer no more than dull stereotypes.

McCarthy moved to New York in 1980 to study at New York University, and took acting classes. He was 18 when he was cast in his debut film, *Class* (1983), a curious variation on the teen movie genre, in which a poor and naive private schoolboy (McCarthy) is befriended by a rich and sophisticated private schoolboy (Rob Lowe), who encourages him to seek sexual initiation in the city. Pushed into this, he's picked up by a gorgeous *femme fatale* old enough to be his mother (Jacqueline Bisset) who, in turn, turns out to be Rob's mother. It was pretty schlocky stuff but quite effective, and an excellent and sympathetic showcase for McCarthy. The critically shredded but unexpectedly commercial *Mannequin* (1987) in which the actor woos a store dummy (Kim Cattrall) who comes alive after hours, increased his following if not his prestige (he himself considers it the most ridiculous script he's ever read), but in between a few other poor movies, he made two prestigious forays to Europe. In the unfortunately little-seen *Waiting For The Moon* (1987), a slow-moving but elegant period vignette about Gertrude Stein and Alice B. Toklas, the actor played a young American in Europe with grace and aplomb; and he returned to France for no less a director than Claude Chabrol (*Clichy Days*, 1989). Then it was off to Rome for the lead in John Frankenheimer's undistinguished *Year Of The Gun* (1991).

Off-screen, Andrew McCarthy is relaxed, articulate and engagingly modest. A keen stage actor, he has admitted to a desire to break the pattern of the 'nice guy' roles with which he's become identified on film, suggesting that the portrayal of 'a baby-faced killer' might be the ideal solution.

1983 Class **1984** Dear Lola **1985** St Elmo's Fire; Heaven Help Us **1986** Pretty In Pink **1987** Mannequin; Less Than Zero; Waiting For The Moon **1988** Boys aka Boys Life; Fresh Horses; Kansas **1989** Weekend At Bernie's; Jours Tranquilles A Clichy/Clichy Days (France) **1990** Dr M **1991** Year Of The Gun

McDormand, Frances

Actress
Born 1958
Illinois

As the British film writer James Cameron-Wilson so succinctly summed it up, 'Few other actresses have aired their versatility so rapidly, with such good material, but in so few pictures.' And, one might add, with so little public awareness of her name or face. The daughter of a Bible Belt preacher, Frances McDormand was educated at Bethany College in West Virginia and at Yale Drama School, and began her career in some heavyweight theatre productions around the country – Shaw's *Mrs Warren's Profession,* Chekhov's *The Three Sisters* and *All My Sons* by Arthur Miller, to name a few. Her movie career got off to an auspicious start when the Coen brothers gave her the female lead, a none-too-bright adulteress, in their debut feature, *Blood Simple* (1984). This latterday *film noir* rocketed its makers to fame, but the cast, although appreciated, was largely ignored. At McDormand's suggestion, her friend Holly Hunter landed the co-lead in the Coens' next outing, *Raising Arizona* (1986), another success, in which few people noticed that the prim-and-proper bespectacled mother of quins – a cameo role – was played by Frances.

Along the way, the actress appeared as Stella in a New York stage revival of *A Streetcar Named Desire*, winning a Tony nomination, and played a recurring role in TV's popular *Hill Street Blues*. She also made *Leg Work*, a low-grade TV cop drama, and seemed destined for obscurity, if not unemployment. Then Alan Parker cast her in *Mississippi Burning* (1988). Her beautifully controlled, indeed heartbreaking, performance as the loveless, conscience-stricken but fearful wife of the Klan-minded sheriff (Brad Dourif), who finally succumbs to Gene Hackman's persuasion to tell what she knows, earned her an Academy nomination as Best Supporting Actress. Co-starred opposite Gary Oldman in *Chattahoochee (1989)* and with Liam Neeson in *Darkman* (1990), and hired by Britain's Ken Loach for his highly controversial film about Northern Ireland, *Hidden Agenda* (1990), Frances McDormand and her skills finally began to get recognition.

1984 Blood Simple **1986** Raising Arizona **1988** Mississippi Burning **1989** Chattahoochee **1990** Darkman; Hidden Agenda; Miller's Crossing (unbilled cameo) **1991** The Butcher's Wife **1992** Passed Away; Crazy In Love **1993** Short Cuts

McGovern, Elizabeth

Actress
Born 18 July 1961
Evanston, Illinois

Possibly the most talented, and certainly the most underused, actress of her generation, the gorgeously moon-faced, brilliantly blue-eyed Elizabeth McGovern has only occasionally been able to overcome the typecasting that comes with her girl-next-door looks. The daughter of two teachers, she was discovered by agent Joan Scott in a production of Thornton Wilder's *The Skin Of Our Teeth* while still at school in North Hollywood and quickly landed the part of Timothy Hutton's girlfriend in *Ordinary People* (1980), giving an attractive sense of life and vitality to the film's sole non-angst-ridden character.

One year later Milos Forman's *Ragtime* gave her (still) her best role and earned her an Oscar nomination as Evelyn Nesbit, the showgirl whose millionaire husband's jealousy leads to 'the murder of the century'. Sporting a smile that could light up a room and a terminally short attention span, she grabbed at the part and stole the film, hovering on the spur of each moment as a woman with no sense of responsibility or commitment but whose energy and vivacity was undeniably magnetic. It should have been a starmaking part, but like her follow-up films *Lovesick* (1983) and *Racing With The Moon* (1984) that disappointingly put her back in innocent mould, it failed at the box office.

The film that really stunted a career that

seemed to be headed in the direction later taken by Winona Ryder and Julia Roberts (although McGovern always managed to steer clear of Brat-Packing when it came to parts) was Sergio Leone's *Once Upon A Time In America* (1984). As the ambitious actress worshipped by De Niro's gangster, so in love with the memories of her that sustained him in prison that he is unable to see that she has become a different person, the damage lay not so much in the fact that it was her weakest performance – despite the fact that the scene in which the then 23-year-old actress takes off her stage make-up to reveal a middle-aged woman is one of the finest things she has ever done – but because, rather perversely, she caught the full fury of the outcry over the film's controversial rape scene.

Concentrating on stage work for the next two years, on her return to film-making she tended to be pigeonholed in 'nice girl' roles in overtly commercial films that neither performed nor offered her her best opportunities, although she still made the most of those she had. It was not until 1990 that the actress was given some real meat to work on. Her rebellious lesbian in *The Handmaid's Tale* was her only opportunity to date to realise a character not defined by her relationship with a man; and with one of her extremely rare forays into television as a 1930s radical unwillingly seduced on a train by a stranger she doesn't even like in HBO's *Women And Men*, her resigned and ironic voice-over commentary demonstrated the strong comic timing and ability to feel her way through a line to the full in a way that her films continually fail to exploit. Both seemed to cry out for the stronger parts that have not, thus far, been forthcoming, despite her fairly constant screen work, and offered more than enough explanation for the frequent returns to the stage by this wonderful actress.

1980 Ordinary People **1981** Ragtime **1983** Lovesick **1984** Once Upon A Time In America; Racing With The Moon **1986** Native Son **1987** The Bedroom Window **1988** She's Having A Baby **1989** Johnny Handsome **1990** The Handmaid's Tale; A Shock To The System; Tune In Tomorrow (GB: Aunt Julia And The Scriptwriter) **1992** The Favor **1993** King Of The Hill; Fanny

McGillis, Kelly

Actress
Born 9 July 1957
Newport Beach, California

Although she was fired from *Bachelor Party* (1984) because the producers found her 'neither sexy nor pretty', Kelly McGillis, a member of the svelte glamour brigade, didn't have much of a struggle climbing the ladder of success. At 16, she enrolled at the Pacific Conservatory of Performing Arts where she spent three years before continuing her training at the prestigious Juilliard School in New York. After graduating, she stepped straight into *Reuben, Reuben* (1983), a mediocre comedy in which she was co-starred opposite Tom Conti. As luck would have it, her second film, the following year, was Peter Weir's original, intelligent and poignant thriller, *Witness*, in which a wounded cop (Harrison Ford) takes refuge in the closed, religious Amish community where the calendar seemed to have stopped 100 years earlier. McGillis was superbly cast as the young widow who nurses Ford back to health and falls in love with him while knowing that her religion forbids her to express her feelings, which clearly embrace the sexual.

The actress appeared destined for stardom and, indeed, in commercial terms, her next appearance, as the cool flying-school instructor with whom Tom Cruise has an affair in *Top Gun* (1985), did her commercial standing no harm. However, the tall, large-boned actress (who must have one of the longest pairs of legs in Hollywood) has not entirely fulfilled her promise and remains a star with a small 's'.

McGillis clearly needs to be cast in exactly the right vehicle for the right director; a succession of mediocre movies in which she was neither more nor less than merely adequate did little to enhance her career, while *The Accused* (1988), an interesting and provocative film about rape which won Jodie Foster the Best Actress Oscar for her performance as the victim, showed McGillis unable to add an extra dimension to the screenplay's sketchy characterisation in her co-starring role as Foster's defence lawyer.

The actress lives in New York and works, with some success, in the theatre in various East Coast cities. On screen in 1989, she was suitably mean and glamorous in *Cat Chaser*, adapted from Elmore Leonard's novel but, the same year, everything about the creaky melodrama *Winter People* was risible.

1983 Reuben, Reuben **1984** Witness **1985** Top Gun **1987** Made In Heaven; Dreamers **1988** Promised Land; The House On Carroll Street; The Accused **1989** Winter People; Cat Chaser **1992** The Babe

McNichol, Kristy

Actress

Born 11 September 1962

Los Angeles

CaliforniaKristy McNichol is probably best remembered for the tough, tomboy roles that she played when she was a teenager, at a time when stars like Matt Dillon and Jodie Foster were emerging, but in fact her career began much earlier when she started acting in commercials at age seven.

She made her TV debut in the 1974 series *Apple's Way*, and also guested on shows such as the comedy series *Love American Style* and the action adventure *The Bionic Woman*, alongside Lindsay Wagner. It was during this period that the 14-year-old actress was brought to the attention of Spelling-Goldberg productions (responsible for numerous series including *The Love Boat*), and she was subsequently cast as Buddy Lawrence, the daughter in a middle-class Los Angeles family in the TV drama series *Family* which ran from 1976 to 1980. Kristy won two Emmy awards (1976 and 1977) for her performance, and received a People's Choice Award in 1980.

In between filming series of *Family*, she played a couple of supporting roles (in *Black Sunday*, 1977, and the Burt Reynolds flop *The End*, 1978), before making a spate of TV movies, including *My Old Man* with Warren Oates and the Emmy award-winning *Summer Of My German Soldier* in 1979. Kristy was then offered her first major film role with Tatum O'Neal and Matt Dillon in *Little Darlings* (1980), as one of two girls who wager which one will be the first to lose her virginity at summer camp. The film was average, but McNichol's performance was favourably received.

Despite this promising appearance, the actress seemed relegated to B-movie roles, appearing in *The Night The Lights Went Out In Georgia* (1981) as the ambitious half of a brother-sister country music duo, with an as-yet-undiscovered Dennis Quaid as her brother. The film quickly vanished, but she had more success with the next, playing Marsha Mason's teenage daughter in the bittersweet Neil Simon comedy *Only When I Laugh* (1981), impressing with her fresh personality and obvious talent. But she seemed to have a knack for picking the wrong movie. *The Pirate Movie* (1982), a parody of *The Pirates Of Penzance*, was universally dismissed as a bomb, while Sam Fuller's controversial *White Dog* (1981), about an actress who takes in a white dog unaware that it has been trained to attack black people on sight, was attacked for being racist and was held back from general release.

Low-budget film after low-budget film followed, with McNichol often singled out for praise as the only thing worth watching in an otherwise dreadful picture. Most recently this occured with the disastrous *Two Moon Junction* (1988, from the makers of *9½ Weeks*), starring Sherilyn Fenn and Louise Fletcher. The film, quite rightly, was panned by most critics, but McNichol's performance as the ex-girlfriend/drifter of the hero was certainly the only character who was remotely convincing, succeeding in bringing the sorry enterprise briefly to life while she was on the screen. The film that followed, *You Can't Hurry Love* (1988), disappeared within days of release, with McNichol thus beginning the 90s as a superior but wasted talent, having to content herself with a co-starring role in the TV sitcom, *Empty Nest.*

1977 Black Sunday **1978** The End **1980** Little Darlings **1981** The Night The Lights Went Out In Georgia; Only When I Laugh (GB: It Hurts Only When I Laugh) **1982** White Dog; The Pirate Movie **1984** Just The Way You Are **1985** Dream Lover **1988** Two-Moon Junction; You Can't Hurry Love **1991** The Forgotten One

McTiernan, John

Director

Born ?

New York

John McTiernan established himself as one of Hollywood's most gifted and most profitable directors of suspense in the space of only four films.

The son of an opera singer, McTiernan worked backstage and played bit parts in his father's productions from the age of seven. On leaving school he designed, directed and acted in summer stock and regional theatre before returning to his studies, first at Juilliard and then on the film course at New York University, where he shot a couple of shorts. After he graduated from there, he became designer and technical director at the Manhattan School of Music. Supported by the American Film Institute, he made another short (*Watcher*), and some 200 television commercials before he wrote and directed his first feature, an intriguing fantasy-cum-horror film starring Lesley-Anne Down, Pierce Brosnan and Adam Ant.

Nomads (1985) was the story of a French anthropologist in LA who becomes involved with a band of strange street people. Despite tacky, underhand moments, some critics consider this McTiernan's most individual work, before his personality was submerged by the system. It was enough at any rate to put him behind the camera on Arnold Schwarzenegger's next picture, *Predator* (1987).

Between the twin summits of *The Terminator* in 1984 and *Total Recall* in 1990, *Predator* ranks as the best of Schwarzenegger's intermediate features. In essence a simple patrol movie, with Arnie leading a SWAT team on a rescue mission through the South American jungle, *Predator* adds a pinch of science fiction to the broth in the elusive shape of an invisible alien set on tearing them apart, and the whole thing comes out something like *Southern Comfort* meets *Friday The 13th*. Quite ridiculous of course and more credit then to McTiernan, who pushes all the right buttons and turns in an enjoyable, gripping adventure.

Sticking with volcanic action producer Joel Silver, the director then established Bruce Willis as a macho star in *Die Hard* (1988). A blockbuster in every sense, *Die Hard* pitted Willis against a group of Euro-terrorists in a deserted high-rise for an enthralling game of cat and mouse. Ingeniously linking state-of-the-art hi-tech with established character traits, McTiernan brings to each suspense situation a remorseless logic worthy of Hitchcock. Like Hitch, he is a brilliant manipulator – though unlike him, on available evidence he is little more than that. *Die Hard* is marred by its barely restrained reactionary underpinnings – its xenophobic, gun-law mentality not really mitigated by an attempt to introduce Willis as a 'new man'.

The Hunt For Red October (1990) actually toned down the Cold War trappings of Tom Clancy's bestseller for a reasonably even-handed treatment of nuclear paranoia. McTiernan steers ably through an overly complicated plot and again proves his aptitude with the mechanics of suspense – but his limitations are cruelly exposed whenever he tries to suggest any depth of character beyond the job at hand. *The Hunt For Red October* was another box-office hit, the only one of 1990's numerous submarine thrillers, but a comparison with the ambition and scope of James Cameron's immensely flawed *The Abyss* (1990) suggests the difference between a craftsman and an artist. *Medicine Man*, which reteamed McTiernan with *Red October* star Sean Connery, was another capable enough jaunt, but unsatisfactorily diminished its Save-the-Rain Forest theme with old-fashioned Bwana-in-the-jungle romantic antics.

1985 Nomads **1987** Predator **1988** Die Hard **1990** The Hunt For Red October **1992** The Medicine Man **1993** The Last Action Hero

Metcalf, Laurie

Actress
Born 16 June 1955
Illinois

Still best known for her role as Roseanne Barr's neurotic sister on US TV which allows her to display the comic timing most actresses would kill to possess, Laurie Metcalf gradually built up an impressive body of screen work in often less than impressive films, but has shown that, when given enough room, her dramatic talents are equally finely honed. Attending the Illinois State University where she met John Malkovich, Joan Allen and Gary Sinise, whose prestigious Steppenwolf Theatre Company she joined in 1977, she went on to win an Obie for her performance in *Balm In Gilead* during her eight years there.

With 'real live person' (as opposed to 'movie star') looks that can be both hard and optimistic and seem destined to relegate her to the ranks of supporting players, Metcalf has marked her career with an ability to fill in a character between her few lines of dialogue, often getting the desired effect by reading those few she has against the way they are written and by demonstrating an obvious attention to minor but revealing details; she never quite does anything exactly the same way from one part to the next, and never seems obtrusive. Like the rest of the impressive cast, she made the most of Susan Seidelman's dialogue in her film debut, *Desperately Seeking Susan* (1985), at least ensuring that her supercilious 'New Jersey princess' was not lost in the crowd, and fared better than most in the director's follow-up, *Making Mr Right* (1987), as the lab technician who falls in love with the android played by Steppenwolf colleague Malkovich. There was a certain clique-ish quality to *Stars And Bars* and *Miles From Home* (1988), their casts peppered with Steppenwolfers, and a lack of subtlety in the broad comic playing of her would-be vampish neighbour attempting to seduce John Candy's *Uncle Buck* (1989), but her subsequent role really allowed her to shine.

With minimal background in the script, she turned the role of Andy Garcia's sidekick in *Internal Affairs* (1990) into a *tour de force* example of building bricks from straw. As the only character fully in control of her own sexuality, revealed like so much else in the film by a telling and natural gesture, her immunity to the psychological undermining and misogynistic macho posturing of Richard Gere's manipulative, corrupt cop can be dealt with by him only in terms of violence. It was a performance that completely reinterpreted the tokenism of women's roles in the genre. *Pacific Heights* (1990) gave her less to work with as the yuppie couple's sympathetic but outmanouevred lawyer, more a dramatic neccessity than a part, and although she filled it well, it made clear that it would not be easy for her to establish herself in most people's minds in roles other than Roseanne's ex-cop sister Jackie, eternally between boyfriends and saying the wrong things yet never becoming a sit-com stereotype.

1985 Desperately Seeking Susan **1987** Making Mr Right; Candy Mountain **1988** Stars And Bars; Miles From Home **1989** Uncle Buck **1990** Internal Affairs; Pacific Heights **1991** Frankie & Johnny; JFK **1992** Mistress

Midler, Bette

Actress, singer
Born 1 December 1945
Honolulu, Hawaii

Bold, brassy, vulgar and loud, the Divine Miss M seems supremely miscast in the role of the Walt Disney Company's most bankable two-legged star – indeed, for a while it looked like her film career was doomed almost as soon as it began. Born and raised in Hawaii, it was a small role in George Roy Hill's 1965 epic named after the island that took her to Los Angeles. From there she moved to New York where, within months, she made her stage debut in *Cinderella Revisited* before going on to take over the role of Tzeitel, one of Tevye's daughters in the Broadway production of *Fiddler On The Roof*. However, it was her cabaret act as an increasingly outrageous singer and comedienne that was to make her name, particularly her record-breaking run at the Continental Baths in New York where her brand of camp and bitchy parody – very much a cruder version of Mae West – was a big hit with the gay clientele.

Records, tours and a TV special followed before her first major film role, a surprisingly dramatic, deservedly Oscar-nominated, performance as a self-destructive Janis Joplin-like singer in *The Rose* (1979), but Midler soon found herself with a bad reputation for off-stage behaviour that reached its nadir in her spectacular rows with co-star Ken Wahl and director Don Siegel on the aptly named and barely released *Jinxed!* (1982 – a rather one-sided reinterpretation of which turns up in a confrontation scene in Midler's later film, *Beaches*). By the end of shooting no one was talking to anyone else and Midler was branded an unemployable prima donna and box-office poison.

After much haggling over money, she returned to the screen as one of the trio of tarnished stars given a new sheen by the Touchstone treatment (then an untried commodity) in *Down And Out In Beverly Hills* (1986), co-starring with Nick Nolte and Richard Dreyfuss. The film proved a huge success, with most of the laughs going to Midler as the self-obsessed, apathetic rich bitch, a role she was to make her own with only subtle variations in a succession of lucrative comedies that earned her a much publicised exclusive contract with Touchstone/Disney. She was the world's most unpleasant kidnap victim in *Ruthless People* (1986), the tacky would-be actress and star of Ninja Vixens in *Outrageous Fortune* (1987) and the ruthless/neurotic separated twins of *Big Business* (1988). All tended to run out of venom towards the end as her characters became 'loveable' and learned 'human values' in the true Disney fashion, but offered enough raucous humour en route to compensate.

Towards the end of the decade, Midler – in private life the happily married mother of a daughter – began to reshape her image in line with the classic women's pictures and female stars of the 1940s, at first successfully mixing comedy and tearjerking drama in the pseudo-autobiographical *Beaches* (1989, based more on wishful thinking than reality) but went disastrously wrong with *Stella* (1990), an artificial and uninvolving remake of *Stella Dallas* (1937), purloining Roseanne Barr's co-star John Goodman for her romantic lead. Even her reunion with *Beverly Hills* director Paul Mazursky opposite Woody Allen in *Scenes From A Mall* (1991) failed to heal the damage either critically or financially, the fault lying in the one-joke screenplay rather than the actress' performance. Not unaware that her singing career was proving more lucrative than her recent films, she responded by custom-building a vehicle to encompass both her vocal and earthier comedic qualities with the USO comedy *For The Boys* (1991), only to find herself in conflict with her Touchstone mentors and taking the project, amid some acrimony, to Fox. An ambitious attempt to chart America's decline from idealism to cynicism through a USO double act spanning three wars, *For The Boys* had impressive moments but never quite made it, earning her a rather curious Best Actress Oscar nomination but little at the box office – and resulted in a plagiarism suit brought by her 40s counterpart, Martha Raye.

1965 Hawaii **1979** The Rose **1980** Divine Madness **1982** Jinxed! **1986** Down And Out In Beverly Hills; Ruthless People **1987** Outrageous Fortune **1988** Big Business **1989** Beaches **1990** Stella **1991** Scenes From A Mall; For The Boys

Miles, Sylvia

Actress
Born 9 September 1932
New York City

Sylvia Miles, increasingly bizarre in both style and appearance as the years rolled by, was never the girl next door. The hooker next door, perhaps, with the most fondly remembered image of the feisty actress – a woman of seemingly indeterminate years, large New York voice and impressive bosom – that of the ferociously painted Park Avenue *fille de joie* in *Midnight Cowboy* (1969), noisily pleasured by dumb Texan stud Jon Voight and then leaving him in no doubt that *he* has to pay her. Miles' seven-minute *tour de force* in *Midnight Cowboy* shot her to fame and a nomination for the Best Supporting Actress Oscar, but she had been around for a long time before taking that teetering walk with a frisky poodle.

Born and raised in New York's Greenwich Village, the actress made her theatrical debut in 1955 in *A Stone For Danny Fisher*. Subsequently she appeared in many Broadway and off-Broadway productions, including *The Iceman Cometh* with Jason Robards and a revival of Tennessee Williams' *The Night Of The Iguana* with Richard Chamberlain.

Her first film was *Murder Inc* (1960), followed by a small part in *Parrish* (1961), a Troy Donahue vehicle starring Claudette Colbert. Her screen appearances have been sporadic, but she has excelled in a number of off-beat roles which have mixed eccentricity, a waywardly blowsy sexuality and occasional vulnerability. Her originality and genuine talent have ensured that she has ridden her successes while surviving the stinkers unscathed. She was the has-been movie star slumming it with bovine Joe Dallesandro in *Heat* (1971), the Warhol Factory's engaging stab at *Sunset Boulevard* (1950); the alcoholic Mrs Florian, winning a second Oscar nomination for tipsily confiding in Robert Mitchum's ageing Philip Marlowe in *Farewell My Lovely* (1975); a crazed Teutonic zombie in *The Sentinel* (1977); a Danish trapeze artist and jewel thief in *Shalimar* (1979, a movie once seen never forgiven); the relentless real-estate wheeler-dealer Sylvie Drimmer in *Wall Street* (1987).

A major supporting role as the grasping harridan of a Jewish matchmaker to a resistant Amy Irving in *Crossing Delancey* (1988) verged on the grotesque, but the audacious vulgarity of the performance was pleasurably awesome. Then, sporting grey hair and a hospital nightgown, she turned up as Meryl Streep's foul-mouthed mother, escaping the confines of the 'Golden Twilight' rest home to embarrass her social-climbing daughter in *She-Devil* (1990). The film failed, but the ebullient Sylvia Miles, who likes to empty plates of food over critics who displease her, was outrageous and hilarious, leaving audiences to hope that she would grace the screen with more gems before her time is up.

1960 Murder Inc. **1961** Parrish **1963** Violent Midnight aka Psychomania **1964** Pie In The Sky **1966** Terror In The City **1969** Midnight Cowboy **1971** The Last Movie; Who Killed Mary What's Ername? **1972** Heat **1975** 92 In The Shade; Farewell My Lovely **1976** The Great Scout And Cathouse Thursday **1977** The Sentinel **1979** Shalimar (India) **1979** Zero To Sixty **1981** The Funhouse **1982** Evil Under The Sun; **1987** Wall Street; Critical Condition **1988** Spike Of Bensonhurst; Crossing Delancey **1990** She-Devil

Milius, John

Director, writer
Born 11 April 1944
St Louis, Missouri

John Milius' macho interests include surfing, the martial arts, hunting, guns, and motorcycles, many of which he has put into his films. After studying film at the University of California, he began writing scripts, receiving his first solo screenplay credit on *The Life And Times Of Judge Roy Bean* (1972), although John Huston, the director, and Paul Newman, in the title role, softened Milius' initial portrait of 'the hanging judge' as an embodiment of the manly virtues of the Old West. With Michael Cimino, Milius provided the script for the blood-letting *Magnum Force* (1973), the second of the 'Dirty Harry' series.

Extreme violence also pervaded Milius' first film as director, *Dillinger* (1973), a sardonic and romanticised crime thriller which played up the love-hate rivalry between cop (Ben Johnson) and crook (Warren Oates). *The Wind And The Lion* (1975), a Kipling-esque adventure told with wide-screen sweep, was a story for admirers of strong leaders and those with nostalgia for Empire. *Big Wednesday* (1978) might have seemed a meandering, mawkish mess of a movie to those who didn't share the surf-cult mystique or wave fixation of the three leading characters (Jan-Michael Vincent, William Katt and Gary Busey), but most audiences appreciated the splendid surfing sequences.

Milius moved into sword 'n' scorcery territory with *Conan The Barbarian* (1982), a muscle-bound muscle-man odyssey with Arnold Schwarzenegger as an Aryan hero out to avenge his father's murder. The director (who co-wrote with Oliver Stone) cluttered this simplistic stuff with pretentious anti-liberal gestures, which did no harm to the box-office takings. *Red Dawn* (1984) purported to be a serious enactment of what might happen if Cuban and Nicaraguan paratroopers, supported by 60 Soviet divisions, were to invade small-town America. According to the mindless screenplay, a group of intrepid high school kids would take to the hills and carry out successful raids on the invading army. This revival of Cold War rhetoric and gung-ho patriotism showed John Milius at his worst, feeding hawkish adolescent fantasies of heroism. The director, a self-styled 'Zen anarchist', who was denied entry to the US Marines on grounds of health, found compensation by making will-to-power allegories.

Filmed in difficult conditions in Borneo at a cost of $16 million, *Farewell To The King* (1988) was about a US marine (Nick Nolte) who becomes chief of a tropical island's headhunting tribe, a character reminiscent of Marlon Brando's in Francis Ford Coppola's *Apocalyse Now* (1979), which Milius co-wrote. Plodding and portentous, this action adventure did contain less violence and a little more irony than his previous work, but *Flight Of The Intruder* (1990) was a return to the Vietnam War, with the director continuing to take the hawkish stance that is so appealing to the many who share his views, or to those who just like slam-bang comic-book yarns.

1971 Evel Knievel (co-writer only) **1972** Jeremiah Johnson (co-writer only); The Life And Times Of Judge Roy Bean (writer only) **1973** Dillinger (w/d) **1975** The Wind And The Lion (w/d) **1978** Big Wednesday (also co-writer) **1979** Apocalypse Now (co-writer only) **1982** Conan The Barbarian (also co-writer) **1984** Red Dawn (also co-writer) **1988** Farewell To The King (w/d) **1991** Flight Of The Intruder (director only)

Minnelli, Liza

Actress, singer
Born 12 March 1946
Los Angeles, California

There is a story told by Liza Minnelli that as a small child she and her mother Judy Garland were trapped in a powder room by a frantic female fan who admonished Judy 'never to forget the rainbow'. Broke, exhausted but still able to bite back, Garland replied, 'Rainbow, honey, I've got rainbows up my arse'.

The rainbow always haunted Judy, just as she has cast her pixie-like shadow over her daughter's life. Comparisons are inevitable between two performers of such breathless intensity and delivery, whose shared talent for plaintive self-exposure has set the standard by which all showbiz confessionals must be measured. Liza's upbringing and artistic legacy, and the abiding urge of press and public to find a ghoulish echo, have ensured that she has forever been running after mother.

Like mother, she has courted personal disaster. There have been three messy marriages and the now obligatory spell in the Betty Ford Center. The French have identified her with another legendary member of the walking wounded, dubbing Liza 'la petite Piaf Américaine'. But, unlike Judy and Edith, it seems that Minnelli has always worked her emotional high-wire act with a safety net.

Garland and Liza's father, star MGM director Vincente Minnelli, named her after a Gershwin song, and even before she could walk she was inhaling the dangerously toxic fumes of the greasepaint life. She made her screen debut at the age of 18 months as Judy and Van Johnson's baby in the final shot of *In*

The Good Old Summertime (1949). Her parents were divorced in 1951, and by the time Liza was an adolescent she was coping with her mother's drink- and drug- sodden disintegration. Perpetually hauled up and down financial and emotional hillsides, she attended more than 20 schools, including the High School of Performing Arts in New York. However, her most influential teacher was her mother, who told her that singing was a form of acting and that she should 'never lose the thought behind the word'.

After leaving the Sorbonne she plunged into show business, appearing with her mother at the London Palladium in 1964, an occasion which yawed between mawkishness and naked rivalry. (After her death in 1969 from a drug overdose, mother was no longer available for a repeat performance, but Minnelli nonetheless reprised it in eerie fashion with a female impersonator famous for his Judy Garland impressions.)

But talent – if not taste – will out, and at the age of 19 Liza became the youngest actress ever to win a Tony Award, for her performance in *Flora The Red Menace*. Films beckoned and in 1967 she made *Charlie Bubbles*, Albert Finney's first as a director, wistful and charming as disillusioned writer Finney's secretary, evoking the sparrow-like gaiety of Judy at her best. However, of the bulk of her subsequent films it must be said that, if singing is acting, then as an actor Minnelli is a very good singer. Her easy talent, self-conscious soulfulness and predilection for kooky self-advertisement have often been her undoing: as the neurotic college girl Pookie Adams in Alan J. Pakula's *The Sterile Cuckoo* (1969); the shrill, facially and emotionally scarred misfit in Otto Preminger's *Tell Me That You Love Me, Junie Moon* (1970); lost under a ridiculous blonde wig in Stanley Donen's *Lucky Lady* (1975); and, perhaps saddest of all, adrift in the botched schmaltz of her father's *A Matter of Time* (1976), as a chambermaid in pre-World War I Europe, learning about life at the feet of aristocrat Ingrid Bergman. It might just have worked with Judy in 1946, but 30 years on it was a box-office disaster.

However, Bob Fosse brilliantly built *Cabaret* (1972) around her brashly nervous gifts. Of course, Minnelli was far too talented to suspend disbelief as Christopher Isherwood's Sally Bowles, a fifth-rate *emigrée* night-club singer in Weimar Berlin, but her show-stopping style won her a deserved Best Actress Oscar. And her edgy vitality and swimming spaniel eyes were perfect for the Sally she created, dancing uninhibitedly but vulnerable and gauche in fitful repose, hopefully hymning the praises of 'divine decadence, darling' to uptight Michael York.

Five years later she slipped back to her mother's heyday, the 1940s, in Martin Scorsese's flawed, fascinating *New York, New York* (1977), which was loosely based on an old Ida Lupino vehicle, *The Man I Love* (1946). She was overshadowed by Robert De Niro's glowering saxophonist Jimmy Doyle, but as his *chanteuse* wife she sang superbly, and in her rendition of the title number rekindled memories of her mother which were moving rather than morbid. Scorsese filmed her glowingly, and the resulting affair wrecked her marriage to Jack Haley, Jr, the son of *The Wizard Of Oz's* Tin Man.

There were no screen triumphs in the 1980s. She was wasted in a supporting role in *Arthur* (1981), as the working-class object of alcoholic playboy Dudley Moore's desire. She fared little better as Burt Reynolds' hooker helpmate in the dismal *Rent-a-Cop* (1988) and doggedly played feed again to Dudley Moore in the dire *Arthur 2: On the Rocks*.

She steered clear of the rocks, picking up the pieces and reassembling herself in the way she knows best, returning triumphantly to the warm embrace of a live audience and joining forces with director Lewis Gilbert on *Stepping Out* (1991) to play a former showgirl turned tapdance teacher in beautiful Buffalo, a movie described by Gilbert as a 'cross between *Rocky* and *A Chorus Line*', but greeted by audiences as an old-fashioned tap-dancing encounter group session.

1967 Charlie Bubbles **1969** The Sterile Cuckoo aka Pookie **1970** Tell Me That You Love Me, Junie Moon **1972** Cabaret **1974** That's Entertainment **1975** Lucky Lady **1976** A Matter Of Time; Silent Movie **1977** New York, New York **1981** Arthur **1988** Rent-a-Cop; Arthur 2: On The Rocks **1991** Stepping Out; Superstar (docu)

Mitchum, Robert

Actor

Born 6 August 1917

Bridgeport, Connecticut

One of cinema's most under-appreciated actors, the sleepy-eyed, almost insomniac, bear-like Robert Mitchum – once compared by Howard Hawks to a pay toilet because 'you don't give a shit for nothin'' – has often belied his supposedly belligerent screen image with surprisingly gentle and decent characterisations, as well as boasting a bruised vulnerability that made him one of the screen's most ideal victims in the age of *film noir*. After an uprooted childhood, his father dying while Mitchum was still an infant, he went through the Depression as a nightclub bouncer, coalminer, prizefighter, promoter for an astrologer and a hobo among other things, before marrying his high school sweetheart (and remaining with her) and settling down as a drop hammer operator at Lockheed Aircraft. Joining the Long Beach Theatre Guild in 1942 in his free time, he went on to appear in supporting roles in 18 films ranging from *Hopalong Cassidy* Westerns and war movies to dramas, and even Laurel and Hardy's *The Dancing Masters* in 1943. He gradually climbed the ladder from B to A movies and made a huge impression as the anti-heroic Lieutenant Walker in William Wellman's stark *The Story Of GI Joe* (1945) before being demoted to private in the real army when he was subsequently drafted and spent eight months in training.

After being demobbed, Mitchum found himself promoted to the ranks of lead players, his detached surface and laconic style perfectly suited to the post-war cynicism that found its expression in *film noir* classics like *Crossfire* and *Out Of The Past* (both 1947). The latter, like so many of his roles in the genre, cast him as a man led to inner destruction by his trust and love of a woman (the English title, appropriately enough, was *Build My Gallows High*). Amid many programmers, Mitchum's trodden-on romanticism found a perfect outlet in the weary rodeo rider of Nicholas Ray's *The Lusty Men* (1952), while the touching simplicity of his Billy Buck in *The Red Pony* (1949) and the marine in his personal favourite, *Heaven Knows, Mr Allison* (1957), was offset by his terrifying preacher stalking the innocent children in *Night Of The Hunter* (1955), his most outstanding and extrovert performance and the beginning of his penchant for wolves in priests' clothing (*Five Card Stud*, 1968, *The Wrath Of God*, 1972). By the 1960s, however, Hollywood had decided to make the actor larger than life, checking his talents with the star-turn limitations of *The Longest Day* (1961) and *Mister Moses* (1965) that were cheerfully subverted with *The List Of Adrian Messenger* (1963, in which, intentionally, he was completely unrecognisable under layers of latex make-up) and mirrored by his legendary gun turned town drunk in Hawks' *El Dorado* (1967).

Mitchum went against all expectations with his moving Irish schoolteacher, unable to provide the spark of excitement his wife needs and watching helplessly as she has an affair with a British officer, in David Lean's *Ryan's Daughter* (1970, a one-year shoot he compared to building the Taj Mahal with matchsticks) but was deeply disappointed by its reception – according to Peter Yates, who directed his extraordinary performance as a small-time crook in *The Friends Of Eddie Coyle* (1973), much of his well-known reticence in interviews comes from the fact that he cares too much about films the critics couldn't care less for. There were still some good parts to be had in the 70s – his private eye repaying a debt of honour in *The Yakuza* (1975), a thinly veiled Louis B. Mayer in *The Last Tycoon* (1976), his superb Philip Marlowe in *Farewell, My Lovely* (1975) and its dismal, updated Anglicised successor, *The Big Sleep* (1978), but the 80s were less kind to the ageing star, with only the alcoholic father of John Savage in *Maria's Lovers* (1984) offering him enough to work any magic with.

Instead, the decade was dominated by TV work, most notably the highly successful mini-series *The Winds Of War* (1983) and its considerably less accomplished $100m sequel, *War And Remembrance* (1989). Since then, Mitchum seems to have been stuck in the cameo rut – a rare chance for his comic abilities (he is also an excellent mimic) to shine as the charmingly pixillated network chief obsessed with TV programming for dogs in the otherwise dismal *Scrooged* (1988), the benevolent millionaire in *Mr North* (1988, a role he took over from John Huston) and, most intriguingly, a small role as a police detective in Martin Scorsese's remake of *Cape Fear* (1991) which, nearly 30 years earlier featured one of his most menacing preformances as the vengeful convict stalking lawyer Gregory Peck – but he still has one of the most impressive and undervalued list of credits of any actor of his generation.

1943 Hoppy Serves A Writ; The Leather Burners; Border Patrol; Follow The Band; Colt Comrades; The Human Comedy; We've Never Been Licked; Beyond The Last Frontier; Bar 20; Doughboys In Ireland; Corvette K-225; Aerial Gunner; Lone Star Trail; False Colours; The Dancing Masters; Riders Of The Deadline; Cry Havoc; Gung Ho! **1944** Johnny Doesn't Live Here Anymore; When Strangers Marry; The Girl Rush; Thirty Seconds Over Tokyo; Nevada **1945** West Of The Pecos; The Story Of GI Joe **1946** Till The End Of Time; Undercurrent; The Locket **1947** Pursued; Crossfire; Desire Me; Out Of The

Past aka Build My Gallows High **1948** Rachel And The Stranger; Blood On The Moon **1949** The Red Pony; The Big Steal; Holiday Affair **1950** Where Danger Lives **1951** My Forbidden Past; His Kind Of Woman; The Racket **1952** Macao; One Minute To Zero; The Lusty Men **1953** Second Chance; Angel Face; White Witch Doctor **1954** She Couldn't Say No; River Of No Return; Track Of The Cat **1955** Not As A Stranger; The Night Of The Hunter; Man With The Gun **1956** Foreign Intrigue; Bandido **1957** Heaven Knows, Mr Allison; Fire Down Below; The Enemy Below **1958** Thunder Road; The Hunters **1959** The Angry Hills; The Wonderful Country **1960** Home From The Hill; The Sundowners; The Night Fighters; The Grass Is Greener **1961** The Last Time I Saw Archie **1962** Cape Fear; The Longest Day; Two For The Seesaw **1963** The List Of Adrian Messenger; Rampage **1964** Man In The Middle; What A Way To Go! **1965** Mister Moses **1967** The Way West; El Dorado **1968** Villa Rides; Anzio aka Battle For Anzio; Five Card Stud; Secret Ceremony **1969** Young Billy Young; The Good Guys And The Bad Guys **1970** Ryan's Daughter **1971** Going Home **1972** The Wrath Of God **1973** The Friends Of Eddie Coyle **1975** The Yakuza; Farewell, My Lovely **1976** Midway aka Battle Of Midway; The Last Tycoon **1977** The Amsterdam Kill **1978** Matilda; The Big Sleep **1979** Breakthrough aka Sergeant Steiner **1981** Agency **1982** That Championship Season **1984** Maria's Lovers **1985** The Ambassador **1988** Mr North; Scrooged **1990** Presume Dangereux/Believed Innocent (France) **1991** Until The End Of The World; Cape Fear

Modine, Matthew

Actor

Born 22 March 1959

Loma Linda, California

At a time when most young actors were being relegated to Brat-Pack adolescent roles, Matthew Modine, with his less-than-obvious good looks and soft voice, managed to secure lead roles with top directors like Alan Parker, Stanley Kubrick and Jonathan Demme, and thus escape the problems of his contemporaries who were confined to typecasting.

Although born in Loma Linda, Modine spent most of his childhood moving from town to town because his father, a manager of drive-in theatres, was relocated every couple of years. After finishing school he travelled to New York in 1979, working as a salad chef while training as an actor with Stella Adler. A few theatre productions followed in plays such as *Our Town*, *Tea And Sympathy* and *The Brick And The Rose*, and some occasional appearances in TV commercials.

His big-screen debut came in the film *Baby It's You* (1983), in a small part alongside such other soon-to-be-discovered actors as Rosanna Arquette and Robert Downey Jr. A tale of romance between a Jewish girl and a Catholic boy in 1960s New Jersey, it disappeared quite quickly, but it was a superior teen movie and enough to win Modine a part in *Streamers* (1983), directed by Robert Altman. Set in an army barracks at the dawn of America's involvement in Vietnam, the film was highly acclaimed, with the entire cast winning the Best Actor award at the 1983 Venice Film Festival. Modine continued in meaty roles, most notably in Alan Parker's testament to the ravages of war, *Birdy* (1984). As the sensitive young man who retreats into a world of silence in an army hospital after Vietnam, Modine outshone the other cast members, including the impressive Nicolas Cage.

After playing an awkward romantic lead in the movie *Vision Quest* (1985), which was most notable for Madonna's brief performance as a bar-room singer, Modine returned to Vietnam (although the movie was filmed in an East London warehouse) for Stanley Kubrick's contribution to the genre, *Full Metal Jacket* (1987). At a time when Oliver Stone was being praised for *Platoon*, the film was regarded as a sub-standard copy, although the first half, set at a Marine base during basic training, was as harrowing as anything seen in Stone's Oscar winner, and the performances (especially from Modine and real-life drill sergeant R. Lee Ermey) were excellent.

After such sensitive roles, it was a marked change to see the actor in comic vein as the fumbling FBI agent who falls in love with the Mafia wife (Michelle Pfeiffer) he is watching in Jonathan Demme's *Married To The Mob* (1988). Although it was not a big box-office success, Modine obviously impressed someone with his comic talent, for he was subsequently given the lead role alongside Christine Lahti in the medical school comedy *Gross Anatomy* (1989). Not one to choose the star vehicle which carries a movie, he returned to an ensemble picture with the excellent *Memphis Belle* (1990), playing the captain of the plane that flew 25 successful bombing missions with its team of American pilots in World War II. After completing that one, Modine took on his most challenging role to date, alongside Melanie Griffith and Michael Keaton in John Schlesinger's thriller *Pacific Heights* (1990). Although Michael Keaton stole the show as the tenant who moves into Modine and Griffith's home and slowly intimidates them until they are driven away, Modine more than held his own in his portrayal of a young man who sees his life falling apart around him. It is perhaps his talent for conveying a variety of emotions that made this performance so convincing, and which has enabled him to work alongside such actors as Jodie Foster, Mel Gibson, Rob Lowe, Michelle Pfeiffer and John Lithgow, while retaining a theatre career of some distinction.

1983 Baby It's You; Private School; Streamers **1984** The Hotel New Hampshire; Mrs Soffel; Birdy **1985** Vision Quest aka Crazy For You **1987** Full Metal Jacket; Orphans **1988** Married To The Mob; La Partita/The Match (Italy) **1989** Gross Anatomy **1990** Memphis Belle; Pacific Heights **1992** Wind; Equinox **1993** Short Cuts

Moore, Demi
(Demi Guynes)
Actress
Born 11 November 1962
Roswell, New Mexico

Demi Moore, a girl-next-door type brunette with a distinctively husky voice, has a particular gift for bringing a sort of down-to-earth, throwaway conviction to whatever she does. It's an attractive quality that seldom provides fireworks but generally pleases in the context of the somewhat mediocre movies which have fallen to her lot.

She was only 15 when she went to LA, found work as a model and appeared in a couple of television series. Her break came with an ongoing role in the immensely popular TV soap *General Hospital*, in which she played for three years, from 1981 to 1983, winning public recognition but making little impression in her first four movies, none of which gave her anything noticeable to do. Her first lead role was that of a would-be singer, performing in seedy clubs, who becomes the object of teenager Jon Cryer's devotion in *No Small Affair* (1984). It was an absurd romantic comedy of little distinction, but Moore looked good, acquitted herself well, and attracted some attention. This led to her role in the college-graduate ensemble piece, *St Elmo's Fire* (1985), in which she played the wealthy, glamorous, sophisticated but suicidally unhappy member of the group; it was a showy part, marking a real change of gear, to which she brought an impressive measure of panache and strength. In *Wisdom* (1986), the writing and directing debut of Emilio Estevez, she co-starred as his girlfriend (which, at the time, she was in real life), bringing a welcome measure of conviction to the generally muddled and unbelievable proceedings; while in *About Last Night* (1986), a watered-down screen version of David Mamet's *Sexual Perversity In Chicago*, she was back to scrubbed simplicity and, although affecting, seemed somewhat lost beside the histrionics of co-star Rob Lowe and supporting players Elizabeth Perkins and James Belushi.

By 1991, Demi Moore was no longer part of the youth scene. Married to Bruce Willis, she became a mother and co-starred with her husband in her own production *Mortal Thoughts* (1991), having scored a success in the huge summer box-office hit, *Ghost* (1990), and played the female lead in Dan Aykroyd's poor directorial debut, *Nothing But Trouble* (1991). She has also worked occasionally in the live theatre and won a Theatre World award in 1987 for her performance in *The Early Girl* off Broadway. In 1991 her appearance – nude, radiantly beautiful and heavy with her second child – on the cover of *Vanity Fair* sparked an international controversy but did nothing to obstruct her career: she won the much-coveted female lead in the screen adaptation of the acclaimed Broadway drama, *A Few Good Men*.

1981 Choices; Parasite **1982** Young Doctors In Love **1984** Blame It On Rio; No Small Affair **1985** St Elmo's Fire **1986** Wisdom; One Crazy Summer; About Last Night **1988** The Seventh Sign **1990** We're No Angels; Ghost **1991** Mortal Thoughts; Nothing But Trouble; The Butcher's Wife **1992/93** A Few Good Men; Indecent Proposal

Moore, Dudley
Actor
Born 19 April 1935
London, England

'Isn't it incredible?' Dudley Moore said to a reporter after the little British comic-musician had been metamorphosed into a Hollywood Superstar in '*10*' (1979). 'It's something I've always wanted, but I never thought I stood a chance.' It was certainly a long way from his unpromising beginnings as the club-footed, five-feet-two-and-a-half-inches tall son of a railway electrician, born in an ugly housing estate.

Moore, who demonstrated musical ability at an early age, got a scholarship to Oxford University where he gained a music degree in 1958. His talents for jazz, musical pastiche and comedy, amply displayed in university revues and cabaret, brought him into contact with three other Oxbridge performers (Jonathan Miller, Alan Bennett and Peter Cook), and together they put on a little satirical show called *Beyond The Fringe*. It was the hit of the 1960 Edinburgh Festival, followed by long runs in the West End and on Broadway.

Moore's success continued as the shorter half of a comedy duo with Peter Cook that featured in a long-running TV show, *Not Only . . . But Also*, and in a number of movies, including Stanley Donen's *Bedazzled* (1967), a Faustian comedy in which Moore is given seven wishes in exchange for his soul by Cook's Mephistophelean character. When the partnership (and two marriages, to actresses Suzy Kendall and Tuesday Weld) broke up, Moore settled in California. In his first Hollywood movie, *Foul Play* (1978), he played a would-be swinger whom Goldie Hawn picks up in a singles bar while on the run from a hit man. It was little more than a comic set-piece cameo, but was the kind of role that gets noticed and the little Brit managed to be slightly touching, as well as very funny in it.

It was only after George Segal's departure from *'10'* that the director, Blake Edwards, cast Moore in the role of the successful 42-year-old composer-pianist who falls for the voluptuous Bo Derek, the ten out of ten of the title. The actor ran the gamut from melancholy middle-aged disillusion to sexually fixated lover, while nimbly negotiating the various slapstick situations that punctuate the movie. It gained him a female following and the nicknames of 'Cuddly Dudley' and 'the Sex Thimble'.

The actor-comedian soon found himself in an even bigger hit with *Arthur* (1981), a tale founded on the notion that a poor little rich man who is continually inebriated and infantile could win audiences' concern and affection. It was to the star's credit that against all the odds he succeeded in giving the essentially irritating character credence. Arthur, one of the actor's most original creations, is a memorable comic drunk whose guffaws at his own jokes diffuse any creeping bar-room boredom. The $100 million box-office winner earned him a Best Actor Oscar nomination, and new status as a box-office attraction that enabled his agent to negotiate four features in a row for him, none of them much above the mediocre.

In *Six Weeks* (1982), his only dramatic role to date, he was miscast as an American congressman romantically involved with Mary Tyler Moore, the mother of a girl dying of leukaemia. He co-starred with Mary Steenburgen as a playwriting duo in *Romantic Comedy* (1983), adapted from the Bernard Slade Broadway hit, but the film was neither romantic, nor a comedy, and certainly not a hit. Of two other films released in the same year, *Lovesick*, in which Moore played a New York psychiatrist, had a slight edge on *Unfaithfully Yours*, which lacked the style of the original Preston Sturges movie with Rex Harrison. But if 'Sexy Rexy' had been more convincing as an international conductor, 'Cuddly Dudley' handled the visual gags better.

The reunion with the man who made possible his first triumph in the movies, Blake Edwards, resulted in a rather strained farce, *Micki and Maude* (1984), in which Moore had to shuffle frantically between two wives (Amy Irving, Ann Reinking), and *Arthur 2: On The Rocks* (1988), an attempt to recapture the sweet smell of success of *Arthur* which, although mildly diverting, failed to draw the crowds. Still, despite the string of flops, there are only a handful of stars today who can boast two of the biggest box-office hits in movie history (*'10'* and *Arthur*), and no other comedian can claim to have sung in *The Mikado* (in Jonathan Miller's production at the LA Music Center, 1987), cut jazz albums and fronted a classical music series on British TV partnered by Sir Georg Solti.

1966 The Wrong Box **1967** 30 Is A Dangerous Age, Cynthia; Bedazzled **1969** Monte Carlo Or Bust; The Bed-Sitting Room **1972** Alice's Adventures In Wonderland **1977** The Hound Of The Baskervilles **1978** Foul Play **1979** '10' **1980** Wholly Moses! **1981** Arthur **1982** Six Weeks **1983** Unfaithfully Yours; Lovesick; Romantic Comedy **1984** Best Defence; Micki And Maude **1985** Santa Claus – The Movie **1987** Like Father, Like Son **1988** Arthur 2: On The Rocks **1990** Crazy People **1992** Blame It On The Bellboy (G.B.)

Moranis, Rick

Actor
Born? Toronto
Canada

This diminutive actor has established himself as the screen's archetypal nerd, following in the footsteps of comedians such as Stan Laurel and Pee Wee Herman, but far outstripping them in that department; equally, he has outstripped such macho actors as Sylvester Stallone, Mel Gibson and Arnold Schwarzenegger by appearing, in a 12-month period, in movies that earned a total of more than $500 million world-wide. Quite an achievement for an bespectacled comic.

Rick Moranis' story began with a TV show in his native Canada, which developed into the movie *Strange Brew* (1982), co-written, co-directed and co-starring the actor. Because the central characters, the beer-drinking McKenzie Brothers, originated from the show on SCTV, the movie seemed little more than an extended episode of the series, but it displayed the actor's versatility as writer and star. His next two films, *Streets Of Fire* (1984) and *The Wild Life* (1984) did little to set the world alight, with Rick simply perfecting his nerdy persona. Both movies disappeared almost instantly, with the actor commenting on *Streets Of Fire*, that '. . . my character spent the entire movie whining and wanting to be somewhere else, and that came so naturally because I wanted to be somewhere else too.'

It was his next role that pushed him into the big time, as the wimp tax accountant who gets caught up in paranormal goings-on in Manhattan in the most successful comedy to date, *Ghostbusters* (1984). With the comic trio of Bill Murray, Dan Aykroyd and Harold Ramis, the film was bound to be a sure-fire success, but no one foresaw just how successful, with *Ghostbusters* merchandise making almost as much money as the movie itself. After such prominent exposure as a supporting actor, Moranis was in danger of becoming typecast for secondary roles, but after a few minor parts in flops like *Head Office* (1985) and the Robin Williams vehicle *Club Paradise* (1986), his status was raised to that of star in the film version of the musical comedy *Little Shop Of Horrors* (1987). His ability to carry a movie was revealed, with leading actors Steve Martin, Bill Murray and James Belushi in cameo roles while Rick stole the show as the young florist's assistant who comes across a plant (Audrey II) that feeds on blood (voice supplied by Levi Stubbs). The film, a cult hit, also unveiled the actor's previously unseen talent for singing and dancing.

He then returned to a supporting role in the Mel Brooks spoof of *Star Wars, Spaceballs* (1987), and reprised his *Ghostbusters* role in the sequel, *Ghostbusters II* (1989). Like its predecessor, the film was a huge success, with all the original cast returning, and Moranis went straight on to appear in the highly popular *Parenthood* (1989), a comedy about the problems of child-rearing, directed by Ron Howard. Among a cast of heavyweights that included Jason Robards, Steve Martin, Dianne Wiest, Tom Hulce and Mary Steenburgen, the petite actor again stood out with his portrayal of a rigid egg-head father who teaches his pre-school daughter the wonders of long division.

The film grossed $118 million, but it was Moranis' next film, *Honey, I Shrunk The Kids* (1990), for Disney, that broke box-office records, bringing in $207 million. The story of a group of children accidentally shrunk by their inventor father (Moranis) to the size of pins and left to roam their jungle of a garden enchanted adults and kids alike and confirmed that, nerd or not, Rick Moranis' comic touch brought in as many cinemagoers as Eddie Murphy, Bill Murray, or his idol Steve Martin (with whom he appeared again in the FBI/Mafia comedy, *My Blue Heaven*, 1990).

It was not surprising, given the hectic pace he had maintained, that Moranis had to withdraw from the filming of *City Slickers* (1991) due to exhaustion.

1982 Strange Brew (also co-writer, co-director) **1984** Streets Of Fire; Ghostbusters; The Wild Life **1985** Brewster's Millions; Head Office **1986** Club Paradise **1987** Little Shop Of Horrors; Spaceballs **1989** Ghostbusters II; Honey, I Shrunk The Kids; Parenthood **1990** My Blue Heaven; Life Stinks; LA Story (unbilled cameo) **1992** Honey, I Blew Up The Baby

Murphy, Eddie

Actor, director
Born 3 April 1961
Hempstead, New York

The signature note of Eddie Murphy's meteoric rise from stand-up comic to cinema superstar was that unmistakable hiccupping cackle. Within five years of being hailed the number one box-office draw in the world, of enjoying *carte blanche* from deferential studio executives, and of squandering an enormous talent to please in some very poor projects, however, the most powerful black star ever to have emerged in Hollywood was being overtaken in importance by actors and directors like Denzel Washington, Spike Lee and Robert Townsend. The face-splitting grin and the yuk-yuks were wearing thin.

Murphy, the son of a policeman who died when Eddie was three, was a precocious comedy talent who debuted on the stage when he was a 15-year-old high school student in middle-class Long Island. He was a nightclub attraction with his fast-talking sass before long, and at 19 he was engaged as a regular on the popular television gag-fest *Saturday Night Live*, where he appeared for four years. Paramount Pictures struck gold when they cast the young, hip, magnetic Murphy opposite Nick Nolte in the comedy action thriller *48 HRS.* (1982), a genuinely sensational screen debut laughingly remembered for the routine in which Murphy's con scarifies the redneck denizens of a country-and-western saloon. The next year he was charming and a riot as a streetwise panhandler turned commodities wizard in the far-fetched but beguiling black-white identity swapping jape, *Trading Places* (1983). So high was Murphy's stock with Paramount already that he was paid a million dollars to bolster the Dudley Moore turkey *Best Defence* (1985) in a hurriedly-devised guest sub-plot, without which the film would undoubtedly have lost even more than it did. Meanwhile, the release of *Beverly Hills Cop* (1984) had made Murphy cock of the walk. Cast in an unremarkable cop action caper when Sylvester Stallone withdrew. Murphy made it his own with seemingly effortless timing and delivery, and conjuring laughs from ho-hum, four-letter-wordstrewn dialogue. A colossal hit, taking over $100 million in the US alone, the film made Paramount determine not to lose Murphy at any cost and they signed him to a five-picture deal reported variously as worth anything from four-and-a-half to eight-and-a-half million dollars per picture to him, plus percentages. With the clout, he had acquired tales of arrogance, contract flouting and an expensive entourage of Murphy hangers-on which belied the actor's breezy persona, but the bottom line was that his energetic appeal was the only explanation for the big box-office success of the risible *The Golden Child* (1986) and the flat, contrived sequels to *48 HRS.* and *Beverly Hills Cop*. Pushing the envelope, Murphy elected Robert Townsend to direct the ribald record of his stage act *Eddie Murphy Raw* (1987), which contained, along with some outrageously hilarious impersonations and routines, more than its share of lavatorial humour, racist, sexist and homophobic allusions. And at the box office it outstripped any previous comedy in concert ventures, including the popular Richard Pryor chronicles.

In 1988 Murphy surprised by eschewing some of his tough, cool machismo with a sweet performance in the light romantic comedy *Coming To America*, but subsequently found himself embroiled in one of the great legal hoo-hahs in Hollywood history when humorist Art Buchwald, a national institution, successfully sued Paramount for using a story he had written for the screenplay story attributed to Murphy. By this time Murphy's reputed ego had alienated previously obsequious industry figures, and it was entirely predictable that he was riding for a fall when he chose to produce, write (largely in expletives), direct and star in *Harlem Nights* (1989). A 1930s caper in which Murphy cast the idol of his youth, Richard Pryor, as a beleaguered nightclub owner with whom he takes on white mobsters, it was actually far from a farrago and grossed over $40 million, but it was sufficiently thin and disappointingly dull to get the cold shoulder from critics, and sneering abuse was poured on Murphy in proportion to the adoration he was receiving only a few years earlier. Released in a blur of competitive action blockbusters, *Another 48 HRS.* (1990) performed adequately but left Eddie Murphy with the challenge of regaining his early drawing power.

In 1992, older and wiser, Murphy bounced back with a delightful performance in *Boomerang*, assuming the mantle of a buppy Cary Grant as a suave, womanising executive undone by some take-charge women. This sex comedy of overturned stereotypes was a smart move for Murphy: a mid-level hit, it started the move away from his youthful motor-mouth persona and went some way to restoring the lustre to his career.

1982 48 HRS. **1983** Trading Places **1984** Beverly Hills Cop **1985** Best Defence **1986** The Golden Child **1987** Beverly Hills Cop II; Eddie Murphy Raw **1988** Coming To America **1989** Harlem Nights **1990** Another 48 HRS. **1992** Boomerang **1992/93** The Distinguished Gentleman

Murray, Bill

Actor

Born 21 September 1950

Chicago, Illinois

It is hard to imagine that the wacky comic actor Bill Murray began his post-school life not as a comedian, but as a pre-med student, training to be a doctor at Regis College. The hard and serious life of a medical student did not suit him for long, however, and he left his studies to join his brother, Brian Doyle-Murray, at Second City, the famous Chicago improvisation theatre that has witnessed and nurtured the talents of Chevy Chase, Dan Aykroyd and John and James Belushi. Bill teamed up with his brother and they performed as a duo on the *National Lampoon Radio Hour* and then in the subsequent 1975 off-Broadway revue, *The National Lampoon Show*, which spawned the successful series of National Lampoon films in the late 70s and early 80s.

Staying with radio, Murray provided the voice of Johnny Storm, The Human Torch, on Marvel Comics' radio show, *The Fantastic Four*. The big break came when he was heard by the producers of TV's *Saturday Night Live* (who had recruited other members from Chicago's Second City). The series, recognised for its cult status among teen and twentysomething viewers, had gained a reputation for showcasing new comic talent, with well-known stars like Chevy Chase and John Belushi getting their first major exposure on the show. Murray began making appearances on a regular basis from 1976, performing in a number of skits and also contributing to the writing, winning an Emmy award for *Saturday Night Live* in 1977. (He stayed with the show until 1980).

Although not formally trained, Murray has a natural sense of timing and an irrepressible sense of humour that suits him best when playing goofballs. This was first evident in his second film, *Meatballs* (1979), a Canadian slapstick comedy directed by his pal Ivan Reitman. Despite a small budget, the movie was a great success, and Bill's acting career was established. Although some of his choices were more miss than hit (his first, *Jungle Burger* in 1975; *Mr Mike's Mondo Video* in 1979), the actor managed to pick some movies that became major successes. *Loose Shoes* (1980), a collection of skits based on 'coming attractions' (the film's original title) like 'Skateboarders From Hell', 'Jewish Star Wars' and 'Darktown After Dark' was a minor success with some very funny sketches, but Murray's next film, *Caddyshack* (1980), directed by Harold Ramis, was a major success, with Bill hamming it up à la *Animal House* at a posh country club with Chevy Chase, Rodney Dangerfield, brother Brian and gophers galore.

Then came *Stripes* (1981), one of Murray's best-known and best-loved films. It heralded his second collaboration with Harold Ramis (acting and co-scripting) and Ivan Reitman (directing), with Murray as a loser who decides to join the army, more intent on meeting female army officers than serving his country. The film surprised everyone, not because it was hilarious, but because it broke box-office records and made millions. After that, its star was offered the pick of comedy films: he chose a small role in John Waters' intentionally disgusting venture (filmed in Odorama, with audiences given Scratch Sniff cards), *Polyester* (1981), in which he sang the theme song, 'The Best Things'. He followed this with mainstream comedy, playing Dustin Hoffman's roommate who has to put up with his cross-dressing problems in the Oscar-winning *Tootsie* (1982) and almost stealing every scene he was in.

With such wise choices and successful films behind him, the actor had earned the clout to choose his next project and opted for something serious to change his image. Unfortunately, *The Razor's Edge* (1984), the downbeat story (from Somerset Maugham's novel) of a man questioning his life after World War I, did not enamour critics, who found it too confusing, and even though Murray gave it his best shot (he also co-wrote the screenplay), his public were not prepared for him in serious guise.

It was the winning combination of old friends Ivan Reitman, Harold Ramis and Dan Aykroyd that gave him the boost he needed. The film was *Ghostbusters* (1984), and in box-office terms, it became, to date, the most successful comedy ever made. Much of the humour could be attributed to Bill, delivering deadpan one-liners as Peter Venkman, the goofy scientist and leader of the Ghostbusters, a team of weirdos making their living ridding Manhattan of the paranormal.

Following a cameo role as a masochistic patient of Steve Martin's dentist in *Little Shop Of Horrors* (1986), he returned to a lead role in the Richard Donner comedy *Scrooged* (1988), a disappointing remake of the Dickens tale *A Christmas Carol*. Then it was back with the boys for *Ghostbusters II* (1989), a rerun of the original, but with Murray taking less of a front-seat role.

Having proven himself an accomplished writer and comic, he then demonstrated that he is also a competent director–or, at least, co-director–making (and co-starring with Geena Davis and Randy Quaid) *Quick Change* (1990), the tale of a trio of inept thieves and their numerous attempts to leave

New York City. It seems, after destroying New York with slime and ghosts in the *Ghostbusters* films, the city was reluctant to let him go.

1975 Jungle Burger **1979** Meatballs; Mr Mike's Mondo Video **1980** Where The Buffalo Roam; Loose Shoes aka Coming Attractions; Caddyshack **1981** Stripes; Polyester **1982** Tootsie **1984** The Razor's Edge (also co-writer); Nothing Lasts Forever; Ghostbusters **1986** Little Shop Of Horrors **1988** Scrooged **1989** Ghostbusters II **1990** Quick Change (also co-director) **1991** What About Bob? **1992/93** Mad Dog And Glory; Groundhog Day

N

Neeson, Liam

Actor

Born 7 June 1952

Ballymeena, Northern Ireland

Rangily tall at six-feet four-inches. Liam Neeson is undeniably a big man, but he also projects the aura of a quiet man. There is a suggestion of vulnerability about him, so that it seems appropriate that he was discovered for the movies when director John Boorman saw him as Lenny, the gentle giant of Steinbeck's *Of Mice and Men*, in a stage production at the Abbey Theatre, Dublin.

Neeson grew up in Ballymeena, the son of a caretaker; he showed some early promise as an amateur boxer, and was bitten by the acting bug after being 'coerced' into a school play (in Irish, a language he did not speak). He progressed from amateur acting to the Lyric Players in Belfast and then to the illustrious Abbey, and after being spotted by Boorman was cast as Sir Gawain in *Excalibur* (1981). He went on to minor roles in big movies, among them *The Mission* (1986 – on which he professed himself much influenced by Robert De Niro's dedication to physical preparation), and leading parts in small British films like *Lamb* (1986), in which his capacity for understatedness showed to advantage in the role of an abashed young priest. With *Suspect* (1987), he was taken up by Hollywood, and given an attention-getting part as a deaf-mute Vietnam veteran who becomes a derelict and is on trial for his life – with Cher defending. In the film he was initially hardly recognisable beneath a mane of hair and beard, and this chameleon quality re-surfaced in such roles as the porno film director of *The Dead Pool* (1988) and the morose hillbilly (albeit with a rather odd accent) who dons an avenger's mantle but ends up dead in *Next of Kin* (1989). A very different role, as the sculptor unjustly accused of being a child-corrupter opposite Diane Keaton in *The Good Mother* (1988), had also come his way before he graduated to top billing in smaller films in both Britain (*The Big Man*) and Hollywood (*Darkman*) in 1990. His role in the former, as a Scots miner persuaded into the milieu of bareknuckle fighting, drew indirectly on his own previous boxing prowess and, more significantly, hinted at his ability to shoulder a 'working-class hero' image comparatively rare on the British screen. On the other hand, he contrived in *Darkman* to be more of a comic-book hero, playing what vaguely resembled a latterday variant on *Phantom of the Opera*. At the time of these films, Neeson claimed to feel 'a little embarrassed' at not having been on the stage for several years, but made no bones about being committed to building a movie career. It is perhaps a pity that, to date, few of the movies in which he has played have possessed intrinsic distinction, but his combination of versatility and physical presence is not to be readily overlooked.

1981 Excalibur **1983** Krull **1984** The Bounty **1985** The Innocent **1986** Lamb; The Mission **1987** Duet For One; A Prayer for the Dying; Suspect **1988** Satisfaction; The Dead Pool; The Good Mother; High Spirits **1989** Next of Kin **1990** Darkman; The Big Man **1991** Under Suspicion **1992** Shining Through; Ruby Cairo **1992** Husbands And Wives **1992/93** Leap Of Faith

Neill, Sam (Nigel Neill)

Actor

Born 1948

Northern Ireland

Gifted with a distinctive speaking voice that recalls James Mason to many, and at ease with British, American and antipodean accents, the quietly sexy and rather elegant Sam Neill is a good-value character actor and leading man with a busy career internationally in film and on television.

Born in Northern Ireland, he was transplanted with his family to New Zealand at the age of seven. After leaving the University of Canterbury, where he began acting, Neill joined New Zealand's National Film Unit as an actor but directed a number of shorts and documentary subjects. He moved to Australia in the 1970s and found work in the country's emerging film scene. He first caught the eye of international audiences as the handsome, proud young landowner smitten with the headstrong heroine of *My Brilliant Career* (1979), and remained in Australia long enough to play a tough commando sergeant under junior officer Mel Gibson in *Attack Force Z* (1980), a taut, above-average World War II adventure.

Neill's big American break was to have been in *The Final Conflict* (1981), in which he played a son of Satan, Damien Thorne, in the third instalment of the *Omen* saga. Unhappily for him, it proved poor even as chiller sequels go. He fared better in Britain, as a seductive 'older man' in a modest but good adaptation of Edna O'Brien's *The Country Girls* (1983) and as a dashing, devious anti-hero in the television series *Reilly – Ace of Spies*. In a sumptuous remake of *Ivanhoe* for television, however, he was far too sympathetic and attractive for the heinous baddie supposed to be repellent to Olivia Hussey.

Director Fred Schepisi did well by Neill, casting him as the Resistance hero Meryl Streep could't forget in *Plenty* (1985); and the same trio reunited more impressively for the dramatisation of the notorious Australian 'Dingo Baby Case', *A Cry In The Dark* (1988), in which Neill was powerfully moving as a devout man and devoted husband shaken to his core by the nightmarish events that overwhelmed the Chamberlins. (Neill still maintains a home in Australia and returns there regularly to work).

The actor impressed again as a Hitchcockian victim of circumstances in a cracking good nailbiter, *Dead Calm* (1989), in which he had his hands more than full saving himself and young wife Nicole Kidman from a psychopath. He followed that with a stirring, thoughtful impersonation of American War of Independence hero General Lafeyette in the lavish French Revolution epic *La Revolution Française* (1989), immediately put on pounds and a Russian accent for one of the better performances (second-in-command to Sean Connery) among the glamorous ensemble of *The Hunt For Red October* (1990), and delivered a chilling villain chasing Chevy in *Memoirs Of An Invisible Man* (1992).

1975 Ashes; Landfall **1977** Sleeping Dogs **1979** My Brilliant Career; The Journalist; Just Out Of Reach **1980** Attack Force Z; The Final Conflict; Possession; Enigma **1983** The Country Girls **1985** Robbery Under Arms; Plenty **1986** For Love Alone **1987** The Good Wife **1988** A Cry In The Dark **1989** Dead Calm; La Revolution Française **1990** The Hunt For Red October; Death In Brunswick **1991** Until The End Of The World **1992** The Memoirs Of An Invisible Man; Hostage (GB)

Nelson, Judd

Actor
Born 1959
Portland, Maine

A fringe member of the so-called Brat Pack, Judd Nelson was, nevertheless, the very core and catalyst of the group's key movie, *The Breakfast Club* (1985). In the superior teen comedy-drama, directed by John Hughes and focusing on the Saturday detention of a mixed ensemble (Molly Ringwald, Ally Sheedy, Emilio Estevez, Anthony Michael Hall), Nelson fairly galvanised the proceedings as the film's denim-clad rebel with an attitude problem. It was an aggressive, showy performance which made audiences sit up and take note, and Nelson's appearance in two other movies that year (*Fandango*, in which he plays a strait-laced student opposite the then little-known Kevin Costner, and Joel Schumacher's successful *St Elmo's Fire*, another ensemble piece which reunited him with Sheedy and Estevez and saw him as the former's unfaithful, ambitious young professional boyfriend) seemed to herald the arrival of a brash new talent headed for stardom. However, since the high spot of 1985, the actor's career progress proved disappointing.

Well-educated and of a privileged background, Nelson is the son of two lawyers; his mother also a Congresswoman for the family's home state of Maine. He attended Haverford prep school, where he began acting and playing in summer stock, before going on to study philosophy at Bryn Mawr College. After graduating he studied at the Stella Adler Conservatory in New York (during which time he appeared in two Pushkin plays) and then performed in several New York University student films. His feature film debut came in 1984 with the so-so youth comedy *Making The Grade*, in which his playing of a poor young hustler hired to sit college for a rich kid drew little attention.

Despite Nelson's WASP background, his strong and aggressive personality coupled with his dark hair and eyes, bold features and beaky nose, have led him to be cast (and typecast) as arrogant, chip-on-the-shoulder types. Having already established a potential mold in *The Breakfast Club* and *St Elmo's Fire*, the actor was then called upon to play inferior variations on the theme in subsequent films. Reunited for the third time with Ally Sheedy in the appalling *Blue City* (1986), he portrayed a foul-mouthed smartass searching for his father's murderer in Florida; he was yet more unlikeable as the shameless, ambitious lawyer defending convicted murderer John Hurt in the equally unsuccessful *From The Hip* (1987). He even portrayed a real-life killer, the dangerous, manipulative Joe Hunt, who took things too far in his control over a group of young LA society boys, in the television movie *The Billionaire Boys Club* (1987). But, however convincing Nelson's angry, unappealing characters, the limitations of his persona and the general poor quality of his late vehicles suggested that his feature film career in the 1990s was uncertain.

1984 Making The Grade **1985** Fandango; The Breakfast Club; St Elmo's Fire **1986** Blue City **1987** From The Hip **1989** Relentless; Never on Tuesday **1990** Far Out Man (as himself) **1991** New Jack City; Entangled; The Dark Backward **1992** Primary Motive **1992/93** Conflict Of Interest

Newman, Paul

Actor, director
Born 26 January 1925
Cleveland, Ohio

Paul Newman has it all. God never blew breath into a handsomer man, and in one of the most remarkable of all Hollywood careers he has gone from a mortifying toga-skirted debut in *The Silver Chalice* (1954) through his 'James Dean replacement' period to the status of the undisputed top leading man of the 60s and 70s and true eminence in his own 60s as one of the screen greats. In 1988 one of the few superstars who can in any measure claim to be in the same league with Newman, Robert Redford, spoke of having had dinner with Paul Newman and his wife Joanne Woodward at their Connecticut home not long before, and after enumerating Newman's blessings: his marriage, his career, his lifestyle, his face Redford concluded, 'God, I wanted to shoot myself.'

His obvious physical beauty apart, Newman's background was unsuggestive of fame and fortune as the definitive modern movie star. His father owned a sporting-goods store and Paul's school record was unexceptional except on the sports field. From school he went straight into World War II, serving as a radioman with the US Naval Air Corps in the Pacific. After the war he entered Kenyon College, a private men's college in Ohio, with an athletics scholarship, and read economics. Sidelined from sports by a knee injury, he discovered the drama programme and quickly found a place in a summer stock repertory company in Wisconsin. From there he went on to a company in Illinois, where he met and married actress Jacqueline Witt. On the death of his father Newman returned to Cleveland to help his brother run the family store, but decided to sell his half to his brother and enter the prestigious Yale School of Drama in Connecticut. In New York on a term break he was engaged for a television series, *The Aldrich Family*, and never returned to Yale.

Newman appeared on numerous TV shows, including the historical drama series, broadcast live, *You Are There*, where he met the fledgling director who was to elicit some of his best work on film, Sidney Lumet. In 1952 he auditioned successfully for the fabled Actors' Studio, where the Method was shaping a new breed of contemporary actor. In 1953 Newman was hired to understudy Ralph Meeker in the Broadway production of William Inge's *Picnic* but was upgraded to a principal role (as Alan) before opening night. Off stage he was captivated by the ingénue understudy Joanne Woodward. On the strength of his performance and his looks the actor was signed to a contract with Warner Bros., where they intended to hype him as a 'second Brando'. After unsuccessfully testing for Elia Kazan's *East Of Eden* alongside a startling rival in the shape of James Dean, Newman was launched and almost sunk in the po-faced religious melodrama of early Christian doings *The Silver Chalice*, opposite Pier Angeli. His own assessment of this as 'the worst motion picture filmed during the 50s' is something of an overstatement, but he was still sufficiently heated on the subject some years later to take a famous full-page ad apologising for the movie when it was broadcast on television.

Returning to Broadway to lick his wounds, Newman was well received in *The Desperate Hours* in the role of the escaped convict that Humphrey Bogart played in the film adaptation. Back in California he determinedly took on a string of roles in variable films, but it was in two roles earmarked for James Dean before his death in 1955 that Newman's capabilities began to be glimpsed. As real-life boxer Rocky Graziano in Robert Wise's first-rate *Somebody Up There Likes Me* (1956) he gave a compelling, convincing portrayal of the poor boy with the heart of a champion and scored a popular hit; as one in a long line of screen Billy the Kids in *The Left-Handed Gun* (1958) for Arthur Penn (adapted from a Gore Vidal teleplay in which Newman had starred in 1955) he was a glamorous, insolent gunslinger, although the film's psychological slant was a bit too deep for shoot-'em-up fans to make it a box-office winner.

Martin Ritt's *The Long Hot Summer* (1958), based on two William Faulkner stories, provided the first indelible Newman image: the smouldering Southern stud, a ne'er-do-well rolling stone, moving in on his soon-to-be bride (on screen and off) Miss Woodward, with the memorable promise 'You're gonna wake up in the mornin' smilin'.' His steamy performance as the cynical, situation-creating drifter won him the Best Actor prize at the Cannes film festival and the lead in *Cat On A Hot Tin Roof* (1958), Tennessee Williams' cleaned-up but still classic Southern sizzler in which Newman and Elizabeth Taylor, neither of them ever more gorgeous, had audiences gasping. The actor received his first Oscar nomination for his bitter Brick, and although Williams criticised the film he was so struck with Newman that the hottest boy in Hollywood was invited to originate the starring role in the Broadway production of *Sweet Bird Of Youth*, a privilege he had to pay for at Warners with a slick melodrama, *The Young Philadelphians* (1959), in his first turn as a lawyer. After that Newman bought out his contract and went his own route.

From The Terrace (1960) – his third film with Woodward – was a long-winded account of a social-climbing young man's rise, with the actor giving one of his more perfunctory performances, but it was a hit, as was the interminable *Exodus* (1960) in which Newman cut a rather unlikely if devastatingly attractive figure as an Israeli Irgun leader. Fate then dealt him, in a career milestone, one of the great characters of the modern cinema, the disillusioned, petty ante pool-room hotshot 'Fast Eddie' Felson in Robert Rossen's piercing adaptation of the Walter Tevis novel *The Hustler* (1961). Newman's portrayal of Eddie, from cocky con-man to sadder but wiser man exiting with some character, touched audiences, earned him respect from critics who were still inclined to view him as one of the 'male model' school of film stars, and gave him his second Oscar nomination.

Sweet Bird Of Youth (1962), which like *Cat*, was laundered for the screen, presented Newman again as a Southern Romeo, this time a loser gigolo kept by a drunken fading star (Geraldine Page). The drama lost its edge in transition to the screen not only because the suddenly happy ending was out of key with the tone of the whole piece, but because Newman's ill-concealed charm and glorious face were at some odds with his character's desperation and hopelessness. Much less appropriate, however, was a premature attempt to extend his range with a supporting character role as a punchy old boxer for Martin Ritt in *Hemingway's Adventures Of An Old Man* (1962). His second great role of the decade was the cold, amoral snake in Ritt's *Hud* (1963), a power-packed demonstration of values dwindled to zero in the person of an upstanding old rancher's dissolute, good-for-nothing son. *Hud* gave Patricia Neal her Best Actress Oscar for her performance as the slatternly housekeeper fleeing Hud's sneering attentions ('I'll remember you honey; you're the one that got away.') and Melvyn Douglas the Best Supporting Actor prize for his tragic old father. Newman, for his excellence, had to be content with a nomination. (His third.)

Several duds followed, with Newman as yet showing little flair for comedy opposite his wife in *A New Kind Of Love* (1963), Shirley MacLaine in *What A Way To Go!* (1964) or Sophia Loren in *Lady L* (1966). He fared better in the glossy spy caper *The Prize* (1963), but his biggest gamble of the mid-60s, reteamed with Ritt for a Western remake of *Rashomon* playing the Toshiro Mifune role as a Mexican bandito in *The Outrage* (1964) was derided. Despite such hiccups Newman regularly had the luck and the judgment to select as many hits as misses, and more superior vehicles than most major stars with a comparable output could claim. Hitchcock's *Torn Curtain* (1966) was an espionage thriller well below the Master of Suspense's best and it offered no chemistry at all between Newman and Julie Andrews, but it was a box-office pleaser; the Chandleresque *Harper* (1966) character of a broke, battered, wise-guy private eye, as written by William Goldman from Ross MacDonald's Lew Archer yarn *The Moving Target*, fitted Newman better with a portrayal he said he based on Humphrey Bogart and Bobby Kennedy; and his lucky streak with 'H' films continued with *Hombre* (1967), teamed yet again with Martin Ritt for an off-beat, entertaining Western in which, given those azure eyes, he was surprisingly credible as a part-Indian.

The star, for such he had indubitably become, completed his hat-trick of unforgettable characters of the decade with an inspired performance as incorrigible, irrepressible *Cool Hand Luke* (1967) in Stuart

Rosenberg's splendidly irreverent prison camp drama, best remembered for Luke's sickeningly funny egg-eating contest, and for which he racked up a fourth Oscar nomination. Critically, however, Newman created even more of a sensation with his surprise move behind the camera to direct his magnificent wife in the insightful and delicately handled portrait of a lonely spinster, *Rachel, Rachel* (1968). This time Newman's Oscar nomination was for Best Director and he took the New York Critics' directing award. He capped a golden decade with one of his most popular roles, and one of the screen's happiest pairings, as Butch to Robert Redford's Sundance in the highest-grossing Western in history, *Butch Cassidy And The Sundance Kid* (1969), a smart, sharp, delightful character study of two legendary but not terribly 'ept' bandits that set the style for countless imitative buddy pictures.

Despite the fact that Newman was by now completely at his ease when inhabiting the screen he was, in middle age, selecting more diverse roles and artistically ambitious (sometimes pretentious) projects in the 70s that came off less well for him. Having produced or co-produced some of his more personal enterprises he founded the production company First Artists with Steve McQueen, Barbra Streisand and Sidney Poitier, but the company foundered (along with so many other independents in the 70s) as the hits grew harder to come by. As an actor, his most notable performances came in *WUSA* (1970) as another cynical drifter, this time a snide disc jockey; in *The Life And Times Of Judge Roy Bean* (1973) for John Huston as one of the West's most 'ornery' characters; with Redford again in the Best Picture of 1973 as the ingenious con-man concoctor of *The Sting*; and in *Slap Shot* (1977) for *Butch* and *Sting* helmer George Roy Hill as an ageing, comically desperate ice-hockey team captain. More popularly than in most of these he teamed with Steve McQueen to save a dwindling band of frying stars from *The Towering Inferno* (1974) and reprised his world-weary Lew Harper in *The Drowning Pool* (1976). As a director he again brought his wife to the screen in a mature and interesting film, *The Effect Of Gamma Rays On Man-In-The-Moon Marigolds* (1972), adapted from a Pulitzer Prize-winning play, but it did not inspire the same critical excitement as *Rachel, Rachel*.

It was when Newman was approaching what for most people is retirement age that the still remarkably handsome star commanded kudos for a string of charismatic performances, starting with the beleaguered street cop of *Fort Apache, The Bronx* (1981) and, in the same year, the libelled innocent bent on getting his own back in the absorbing *Absence Of Malice* (roll up, Oscar nomination number five) for Sydney Pollack. Indeed, from the early 80s, it was evident that Paul Newman had matured into an actor of remarkable depth, strength and restraint, able to illuminate characters with the subtlest of telling touches. Directed by Sidney Lumet in *The Verdict* (1982) he arguably surpassed anything he had previously achieved as the Boston lawyer at rock bottom whose obsession with a medical negligence case reawakens his desire for justice. It was an electrifying portrayal of a loser's rediscovery of self-esteem, and there was widespread expectation that Newman's sixth Oscar nomination must at last bring him the statuette, but he was pipped by the virtually unknown Ben Kingsley for a once-in-a-lifetime role as *Gandhi*. *Harry And Son* (1984), starring and directed by the actor, was disappointingly ordinary, and in 1985 the American Academy, apparently writing him off as a spent force, presented Newman with an honorary Oscar for career achievement. The next year, the seventh time, was the lucky charm and the Academy bowed to the inevitable, naming Newman Best Actor for the return, after 25 years, of Fast Eddie Felson in a hard-edged sequel to *The Hustler*, *The Color Of Money* (1986), directed by Martin Scorsese and partnering Newman with his eager-beaver acolyte, on screen and off, Tom Cruise. Despite much talk of the 'well, they had to give it to him' sentiment, there is no denying this as one of Newman's 'must-see' performances that bears repeated viewing for his complete authority in a character thoroughly known and understood.

After directing a creditable adaptation of *The Glass Menagerie* (1987) because he wanted to have on record Miss Woodward's acclaimed stage performance in the Tennessee Williams classic, Newman continued, in his mid-60s, to turn in one riveting study after another: as bellicose General Groves, supervisor of the scientists developing the atomic bomb during World War II in *Fat Man And Little Boy* (1989); as randy, raucous Governor Earl Long in the underrated *Blaze* (1989), and, in his tenth screen pairing with his wife, quite brilliant and absurdly overlooked in the rush to praise

Miss Woodward, as the cold, dry, rigid husband in *Mr And Mrs Bridge* (1990). This was a performance of classic stature, considered, controlled, eloquent in its stillness, and looked to be the apotheosis of a career that had seen well over 50 film outings to date.

Off screen, Newman's too-good-to-be-true reputation is as enviable as his film career, though he has not been untouched by tragedy. With his wife a well-known espouser of liberal causes, Newman has for years been an energetic political activist and in 1978 was a delegate to a United Nations conference on nuclear disarmament. After the death of his only son Scott in 1978 from a drugs and alcohol overdose Newman and his former wife Jacqueline Witt established a foundation in his memory. A generous philanthropist, the profits from one of Newman's interests – his Newman's Own Spaghetti Sauce, Salad Dressing and snacks – fund the Hole In The Wall Gang charity, which provides holidays and care for sick children. Newman and Woodward are also active supporters and participants in drama programmes in Connecticut and at the Actors' Studio in New York.

1954 The Silver Chalice **1956** The Rack; Somebody Up There Likes Me **1957** The Helen Morgan Story; Until They Sail **1958** The Long Hot Summer; The Left-Handed Gun; Cat On A Hot Tin Roof; Rally Round The Flag Boys! **1959** The Young Philadelphians **1960** From The Terrace; Exodus **1961** The Hustler; Paris Blues **1962** Sweet Bird Of Youth; Hemingway's Adventures Of A Young Man **1963** Hud; A New Kind Of Love; The Prize **1964** What A Way To Go!; The Outrage **1965** Lady L **1966** Torn Curtain; Harper **1967** Hombre; Cool Hand Luke **1968** The Secret War Of Harry Frigg; Rachel, Rachel (director only) **1969** Winning; Butch Cassidy And The Sundance Kid **1970** King (doc: co-narrator); WUSA **1971** Sometimes A Great Notion aka Never Give An Inch (also director) **1972** Pocket Money; The Effect Of Gamma Rays On Man-In-The-Moon Marigolds (director only); The Life And Times Of Judge Roy Bean **1973** The Mackintosh Man; The Sting **1974** The Towering Inferno **1976** The Drowning Pool; Silent movie (unbilled cameo); Buffalo Bill And The Indians, Or Sitting Bull's History Lesson **1977** Slap Shot **1979** Quintet **1980** When Time Ran Out **1981** Fort Apache, The Bronx; Absence Of Malice **1982** The Verdict **1984** Harry And Son **1986** The Color Of Money **1987** The Glass Menagerie (director only) **1989** Fat Man And Little Boy aka Shadowmakers ; Blaze **1990** Mr And Mrs Bridge **1993** The Hudsucker Proxy

Nichols, Mike
(Michael Igor Peschkowsky)
Director
Born 6 November 1931
Berlin, Germany

Despite his early huge successes and his ability to attract great casts, Mike Nichols, the first million-dollar director, took much time to develop the sense of being a real film director rather than a man who works with the actors and leaves the camera to itself – for a long time an unfortunate legacy of his glittering stage successes.

He arrived in the States at the age of seven when his family fled Hitler's Germany; later, when the death of his father left the family destitute, he financed his further education through a series of odd jobs – post office clerk, janitor, delivery-truck driver – and developed a passion for performing while at the University of Chicago. Despite studying with Lee Strasberg in New York he was unable to find work as an actor and returned to Chicago to form an improvisational group with similarly unwanted performers Barbara Harris, Alan Arkin, Paul Sills and, most importantly, Elaine May. Together, Nichols and May formed a quick-witted satirical double act that earned them great acclaim and ended with a Broadway season in 1960–61. After his directorial debut with the Broadway production of Neil Simon's *Barefoot In The Park* in 1963 he became one of the hottest directors on stage with a near unbroken string of long-running, critically acclaimed smash hits (including many more Simon pieces such as *The Odd Couple*).

Nichols made an ambitious film debut with the screen version of *Who's Afraid Of Virginia Woolf?* (1966), where his insistence on a month's rehearsal paid dividends with a superb quartet of performances led by Taylor and Burton, although he relied too heavily on Haskell Wexler's black-and-white photography to give the film its look. He was more adventurous with *The Graduate* (1967), which, despite a certain superficiality and a definite misogyny, perfectly caught the mood of a rootless generation (represented by newcomer Dustin Hoffman) being screwed in more ways than one by their parents' generation, but here he was over-reliant on editing effects – flash frames or trick cuts from orgasms to flopping heads down on sunbeds. Nonetheless, the movie captured the Best Director Oscar. There was no shortage of ambition on his mammoth film of Joseph Heller's stunning *Catch 22* (1970), but Nichols made the disastrous mistake of reshaping the bitterly satirical and highly cinematic source material into an overly arty, overtly anti-war movie (with none too subtle allusions to Vietnam) and, in losing the novel's drastic mood swings, took away the sting of death. Only in one scene, in which Yossarian (Alan Arkin) berates the quietest and most respectable of the pilots (Charles Grodin) for the pointless murder of a whore, only to find himself arrested by disinterested MPs for going AWOL, played as written in the book, did the inherent absurdity the director was striving for come across.

Despite the modest success of *Carnal Knowledge* (1971), which stirred up some of *Virginia Woolf*'s controversy because of its frank language, Nichols quickly found himself sliding into oblivion. The ecological conspiracy thriller *The Day Of The Dolphin* (1973), while an amiable (and hugely expensive) B-movie, was a clinical affair directorially, with cold photography and an opening self-consciously stolen from *Patton* (1970); and his screwball comedy *The Fortune* (1975) was far too broad and manic, proving a box-office disaster despite starring Jack Nicholson and Warren Beatty. Another film was abandoned in mid-production, while his rather static film of Gilda Radner's live show was barely distributed.

Silkwood (1983) was hailed as his major comeback, but, despite fine performances from Meryl Streep and the supporting cast and an interesting decision to concentrate on the daily life of its blue-collar heroine, it ended at the point the real story began. Similarly, *Heartburn* (1986) took promising material – Nora Ephron's fictionalised account of the break-up of her marriage to Watergate reporter Carl Bernstein – but took it nowhere. Nichols had definite talents – a way with actors, crisp (sometimes cold) timing and a feel for a moment – but was unable to turn them into real cinema.

That all changed in 1988, first with his confident film of Simon's *Biloxi Blues* and, more importantly, with *Working Girl*. Suddenly everything came into place. Perhaps taking the energy of the 'thousand New Yorks' of the latter, he really began to use the camera to capture the feeling of place and the situation of his characters, finally learning how to express himself without words, best typified by the two magnificently cinematic helicopter shots that framed *Working Girl*. The first swoops around America's favourite symbol of hope and aspiration, the Statue of Liberty, to move into the Staten Island Ferry and its huddled masses yearning to be rich, to find among them its heroine, Tess (an Oscar-nominated performance from Melanie Griffith) who, despite the outrageous hair, secretary's uniform of socks and trainers over her stockings and her broad 'Noo Yawk' drawl, is very much an individual. At the end of Nichols' darkly shaded Cinderella story, she has only defeated the ugly sister and won the handsome prince by assuming the sister's wardrobe, hairstyle and diction, leaving friends and lover behind to take on a new persona. As the camera celebrates her moment of victory – her own office – it pulls back from her window to reveal her as just one of hundreds of office workers in just one of hundreds of offices in just one of hundreds of tower blocks, and even the upbeat theme song cannot hide the loss of her individuality. It is only through changing everything she is that she is allowed the success she deserves, and despite her jubilation, she knows it; as she tells Harrison Ford, 'Would you have listened to me if I was just a secretary?' and stifles his protestations with a bitter 'Think about it'.

He continued to demonstrate his newfound cinematic flair in *Postcards From The Edge* (1990) with a long take pulling back from Meryl Streep's final song, craning up past the watching crew to Shirley MacLaine in the gallery, wordlessly conveying the distance the relationship of its mother and daughter needs in order to be bearable. In the process, Mike Nichols was confirming not only his return to commercial viability but also his emergence as a genuine film director.

1966 Who's Afraid of Virginia Woolf? **1967** The Graduate **1970** Catch 22 **1971** Carnal Knowledge **1973** The Day Of The Dolphin **1975** The Fortune **1980** Gilda Live **1983** Silkwood **1986** Heartburn **1988** Biloxi Blues; Working Girl **1990** Postcards From The Edge **1991** Regarding Henry

Nicholson, Jack

Actor, director, writer
Born 22 April 1937
Neptune, New Jersey

Stardom came slowly to Jack Nicholson, but when it happened it put him among the biggest of box-office earners. He had played small parts in no fewer than 20 movies before both Rip Torn and Bruce Dern turned down the part of George Hanson, the soft-spoken, alcoholically befuddled Southern lawyer in Dennis Hopper's *Easy Rider* (1969). Although bikers Hopper and Peter Fonda were the leads, Nicholson made the most impression, especially in the scene where he smokes grass for the first time.

The son of a young unmarried woman, Nicholson was raised by his maternal grandmother, who, until quite late in his adult life, he believed to be his mother; his 'sisters' were in fact his natural mother and his aunt. Nicholson's 'father' (who was in fact his grandfather), an alcoholic sign painter, deserted the family home when Jack was still a child, so that it fell to his 'mother', who ran a beauty parlour, to raise him and his two 'sisters'. Visiting one of these 'sisters' in California, he landed a job as an office boy in the cartoon department at MGM; then, acquiring a taste for live-action cinema, he trained as an actor with a small group called the Players Ring. A number of TV assignments followed, almost entirely in soap operas, until his screen debut as a hoodlum in a Roger Corman-produced quickie called *Cry Baby Killer* (1958). Corman went on to direct him in *The Little Shop Of Horrors* (1961), in which he was a deliriously masochistic dental patient ('No Novocaine! It dulls the senses.'), and in two Edgar Allan Poe adaptations, *The Raven* and *The Terror* (both 1963), where he played ineffectual juvenile leads, the latter opposite his then wife, Sandra Knight (who retired from the screen soon after). There came a slight change of direction when Monte Hellman, one of Corman's protégés, cast the actor in four of his shoestring productions in a row, including the mildly experimental Westerns *The Shooting* and *Ride The Whirlwind* (both 1966).

After the success of *Easy Rider*, he was misguidedly cast as a wealthy hippy in Vincente Minnelli's equally misguided musical *On A Clear Day You Can See Forever* (1970), but his solo number was cut from the final print. Fortunately, this was followed by Bob Rafelson's *Five Easy Pieces* in the same year. Nicholson's characterisation of a middle-class drifter who both rejects and is rejected by the American Dream won him his first Oscar nomination. He was to work with Rafelson again in *The King Of Marvin Gardens* (1972) and *The Postman Always Rings Twice* (1981). In 1971, he played an insatiable womaniser in *Carnal Knowledge*, and directed his first film, *Drive He Said*. This was a counter-culture campus comedy-drama that tried too hard to be *the* statement about America during the Vietnam War, but there were some good anti-Jock moments. His second movie as director, *Goin' South* (1978), was a comedy Western which would have been more effective had some restraint been applied to his own acting and the mannered camerawork of Nestor Almendros. These films had a lot in common with his own energetic, nervous, quirky and chaotic acting persona.

As an actor, however, Nicholson was going from strength to strength, giving brilliantly varied performances for a variety of major directors, including Michelangelo Antonioni in the enigmatic *The Passenger* (1975). In Hal Ashby's *The Last Detail* (1973) he played a hell-raising but ultimately sensitive petty officer who discovers his own entrapment in the Navy mirrored in the fate of the young prisoner (Randy Quaid) he has been detailed to accompany to the brig. Nicholson received an Oscar nomination for this and for his superb playing of the small-time private eye J. J. 'Jake' Gittes in 30s LA in Roman Polanski's *Chinatown* (1974). He spent most of the movie with a white plaster concealing his nose, a prospect that might not have appealed to most actors, but it was a detail that people remembered and it helped turn him into a major star. (He came a cropper when he attempted to reprise the character in a follow-up movie directed by himself, *The Two Jakes*, in 1990.)

Nicholson was finally to secure his Oscar for his extraordinarily dynamic performance as the rebellious inmate of a mental hospital in Milos Forman's One Flew Over The Cuckoo's Nest (1975), whose anarchic attitude to the institution and to the staff cause him to be lobotomised. An extrovert performer, he has been inclined to go way over the top in roles such as the possessed axe-wielding family man in Stanley Kubrick' s *The Shining* (1980), the randy Beelzebub in *The Witches Of Eastwick* (1987) and, even more maniacally, the Joker in *Batman* (1989). Yet he displayed a great deal of subtlety and shading as astronaut Garrett Breedlove, Shirley MacLaine's crude and finally caring neighbour-lover in *Terms Of Endearment* (1983), and was convincing as a dim-witted Mafia hit man in *Prizzi's Honor* (1985). Directed by John Huston, it featured his daughter, Anjelica, with whom Nicholson had had a relationship since 1973. (They broke up in 1990 when he had a child by a young waitress.) The unconventional star was more recently at his powerful best as the drunken hobo in the otherwise disastrous *Ironweed* (1987), eschewing the hamminess that has marred some of his latter work. But whatever Jack Nicolson does, he is always certain to provide a fair amount of electricity with his midnight idol looks – vulpine, world-weary and diabolically charming.

1958 The Cry Baby Killer **1960** Little Shop Of Horrors; Too Soon To Love; Studs Lonigan; The Wild Ride **1962** The Broken Land **1963** The Raven; The Terror; Thunder Island (also co-writer) **1964** Ensign Pulver; Back Door To Hell **1966** Flight To Fury (also writer); The Shooting; Ride The Whirlwind (also writer) **1967** Hells Angels On Wheels; Rebel Rousers; The St Valentine's Day Massacre; The Trip (also writer) **1968** Psych-Out; Head (also co-writer) **1969** Easy Rider **1970** On A Clear Day You Can See Forever; Five Easy Pieces; Drive He Said (director and co-writer only) **1971** Carnal Knowledge; A Safe Place **1972** The King Of Marvin Gardens **1974** The Last Detail; Chinatown **1975** The Passenger; Tommy; The Fortune; One Flew Over The Cuckoo's Nest **1976** The Missouri Breaks; The Last Tycoon **1979** Goin' South (also director); The Shining **1981** The Postman Always Rings Twice; Reds; The Border **1983** Terms Of Endearment **1985** Prizzi's Honor **1986** Heartburn **1987** The Witches Of Eastwick; Ironweed **1989** Batman **1990** The Two Jakes (also director) **1992** Man Trouble; A Few Good Men; Hoffa

Nielsen, Leslie

Actor
Born 11 February 1926
Regina, Canada

Few people watching the earlier films of the tall, husky and now grey-haired Leslie Nielsen would have predicted that he would become known for his droll appearances in comedies such as *Airplane* (1979) in his 50s. However, what directors Jim Abrahams and the Zucker brothers saw in him, and which they exploited in their camp lampoons, was his bland, stolid and po-faced persona.

The former Canadian radio announcer, disc jockey and stage actor was third-billed in his screen-debut in *Ransom* (1956) as a policeman helping Glenn Ford and Donna Reed recover their kidnapped child. In the same year, and for the same studio (MGM), he played an astronaut whose spaceship invades the *Forbidden Planet* of Walter Pidgeon and his daughter Anne Francis, an entertaining sci-fi version of *The Tempest*; and he was one of the men mistakenly introduced into *The Opposite Sex*, a feeble musical remake of the all-female American classic, *The Women* (1939).

In 1957, Nielsen shared the title roles with Debbie Reynolds in *Tammy And The Bachelor*, the popular romantic comedy that spawned two inferior remakes without the original stars. He exuded a certain weary charm playing a wealthy pilot who crashes in Mississippi and is nursed back to health by backwoods girl Reynolds, but the widely-seen picture didn't help Nielsen to better things, and he plodded on in bread-and-butter roles for a number of years. These included the ineffectual lieutenant in the third (and worst) remake of *Beau Geste* (1966); the villain in *Gunfight In Abilene* (1967); and a man in jeopardy in a couple of disaster movies, *The Poseidon Adventure* (1972) and *City On Fire* (1979), which led to *Airplane*, a take-off of the very films he had been appearing in.

The success of Nielsen's performance in the latter, as the doctor on board the threatened airliner, derived from his playing it straight, as if he believed in the crazy goings-on. He continued in similar vein in horror movies such as *Prom Night* (1980), a *Halloween* rip-off with Jamie Lee Curtis, and in George A. Romero's *Creepshow* (1982), his acting style altering not one iota from the traditional dramas he had appeared in pre-*Airplane*. The laughs he gathered in *The Naked Gun* (1988) were enough to rescue it from complete crassness; his hilariously inept plain-clothes cop, Frank Drebin, reprised the role he had created in the shortlived TV series *Police Squad* and was such a hit he found himself playing it in a string of TV commercials for cider. It seemed, in 1992, that Leslie Nielsen might well continue to mine this new and lucrative seam in his career for several more years.

1956 Ransom; Forbidden Planet; The Vagabond King; The Opposite Sex **1957** Hot Summer Night; Tammy And The Bachelor (GB: Tammy) **1958** The Sheepman **1965** Night Train To Paris; Harlow; Dark Intruder **1966** Beau Geste; The Plainsman **1967** The Reluctant Astronaut; Gunfight in Abilene; Rosie **1968** How To Steal The World; Counterpoint; Dayton's Devils **1969** How To Commit Marriage; Change Of Mind **1971** The Resurrection Of Zachary Wheeler **1972** The Poseidon Adventure **1973** And Millions Will Die **1976** Project: Kill **1977** Amsterdam Kill; Viva Knievel; Day Of The Animals; Sixth And Main; Grand Jury **1978** Little Mo **1979** City On Fire; Riel; Airplane **1980** Prom Night **1981** The Creature Wasn't Nice **1982** Creepshow; Wrong Is

Right (GB: The Man With The Deadly Lens) **1987** Home Is Where The Hart Is; Nightstick; Nuts **1988** The Naked Gun **1990** Dangerous Curves **1991** Repossessed; The Naked Gun 2½: The Smell Of Fear; All I Want For Christmas

Nimoy, Leonard

Actor, director
Born 26 March 1931
Boston, Massachusetts

Despite classical training and experience, and a reasonably successful directorial career, Leonard Nimoy will forever be known as *Star Trek*'s Spock.

Prior to his incarnation on the bridge of the Starship Enterprise, Nimoy received a BA degree in Drama from Boston College and a Master's degree from Antioch College in Ohio. After completing his US military service he worked as a taxi driver, a pet shop clerk, a cinema usher and a soda jerk among other things, facilitating his continued drama study with Jeff Corey at the Pasadena Playhouse. While a drama teacher himself, he played the odd supporting role on television, and in films, which he had broken into in a small way in his student days in the early 50s. To his own amusement, however frustrating it was to become, Nimoy became an international celebrity in the guise of his pointy-eared, dry, superanalytical and unemotional 'Vulcan' character, Spock, in the television sci-fi series *Star Trek*. The series originally aired in the US from 1966 until 1969, but has been repeated continuously around the world since it went off the air and eventually gave birth to the popular series of *Star Trek* films from 1979.

Meanwhile, Nimoy starred in TV's *Mission Impossible* from 1969 to 1971, wrote three books on photography, published poetry and the autobiography *I Am Not Spock*, recorded an album and became a popular speaker on the American college lecture circuit. Between his many TV roles in the 70s he turned his hand to directing, notably for *Rod Serling's Night Gallery*.

Star Trek – The Motion Picture (1979) may have been spectacular hooey but it overjoyed the Trekkies of the world, who demanded a sequel. *Star Trek II: The Wrath Of Khan* (1982) was much better and ended with a tearjerking shock in the death of Spock. Not allowed to rest, however, Spock was eventually restored in *Star Trek III: The Search For Spock* (1984), an escapade made considerably more alluring for Nimoy by presenting him with his first feature film directing assignment. Like its immediate predecessor, *The Search For Spock* was in keeping with the tone of the original TV series and proved very enjoyable for fans and well handled by Nimoy, who had no trouble moving between the little human drama of the well-known characters and some spectacular special effects sequences. *Star Trek IV: The Voyage Home* (1986) was even better, with the surprising and delightful injection of comedy into an ecological theme, and Nimoy again emerged with great credit on the screen and from behind the camera. As an actor he put a brave face on *Star Trek V: The Final Frontier* (1989), the unintentionally hilarious and by far the weakest instalment in the film series in which the by now shockingly aged Enterprise crew was put through some sadly lame paces by William Shatner taking *his* turn at directing.

Nimoy could afford to be serene since he had at last escaped *Star Trek* to helm *Three Men And A Baby* (1987) for Touchstone Pictures. Essentially a one-joke film – and the joke was baby poo – Nimoy kept it moving brightly with the help of charming performances from Tom Selleck, Ted Danson and Steve Guttenberg. This remake was as enjoyable as the French original of 1985 and became the surprise monster hit of its year. *The Good Mother* (1988), in contrast, had little appeal in its heavy-handed treatment of a depressing subject: a lonely divorcée at last finds good sex and liberation but is taken to court for custody of her child because of her sexual liaison. Well cast, the film is noteworthy more for Diane Keaton's moving central performance than for the direction. Returning to comic material, Nimoy was unable to reprise the success of *Three Men And A Baby* with *Funny About Love* (1990) and may have regretted passing up the sequel *Three Men And A Little Lady* (1990). Despite the reception accorded *Star Trek V*, yet another reunion in *Star Trek VI: The Undiscovered Country*, was a super send-off to the longest-run space saga.

1951 Queen For A Day; Rhubarb **1952** Kid Monk Baron; Francis Goes To West Point **1953** Old Overland Trail **1958** Satan's Satellites **1963** The Balcony **1966** Deathwatch **1967** Valley Of Mystery **1971** Catlow **1978** Invasion Of The Body Snatchers **1979** Star Trek – The Motion Picture **1982** Star Trek II: The Wrath Of Khan **1984** Star Trek III: The Search For Spock (also director) **1986** Star Trek IV: The Voyage Home (also director) **1987** Three Men And A Baby (director only) **1988** The

Good Mother aka The Price Of Passion (director only) **1989** Star Trek V: The Final Frontier **1990** Funny About Love (director only) **1991** Star Trek VI: The Undiscovered Country

Nolte, Nick

Actor
Born 8 February 1941
Omaha, Nebraska

A powerful frame, a voice that drawls and growls with the gravelly masculinity of the Midwest, a laconic, ruggedly earthy temperament with an underlying hint (often dramatically realised) of the explosive, a willingness to dig into the guts of his material: these are just some of the attributes that have made Nick Nolte one of America's most individual and most important screen actors. He is convincing as both hero and anti-hero. He can be both big in scale and – as he has revealed in a handful of fine, subtle comic performances – small. He neither shirks the big physical challenge nor in the process sinks into the merely Hollywood-stereotypical; a Nolte performance is almost always interesting in detail as well as substantial in outline. With the football-player's physique and the blond hair and blue eyes that spell the great outdoors, he might have made an honourable career out of creating updated versions of the classic tough-guy archetypes. A glance at his work-list shows how much wider his range has been – which, in turn, explains why at the start of the 1990s he remained one of the modern cinema's busiest top-ranking actors.

The feeling of inner turbulence disciplined to the services of acting that one gains from a Nolte performance finds reflections in the actor's own life history. He has gone through rocky periods, with serious personal problems exacerbated by prolonged difficulties with drink (although a third marriage, to Rebecca Linger in 1984, and subsequent fatherhood seemed to have brought him unbroken contentment). But even at his most personally tormented, Nolte's commitment to his craft has never been doubted. An athlete at school, he attended five colleges (including Pasadena City College and Phoenix City College) in four years, in each case on a football scholarship.

It was in Phoenix that he was persuaded by a friend to try acting; in 1960 he joined the Actors' Inner Circle of Phoenix, and over an eight-year career (which also included summer stock in Colorado) took at least 160 roles. In 1968 he moved to the Old Log Theatre in Minneapolis, and three years later via New York (and a stint with the La Mama experimental theatre troupe) to Los Angeles. TV began to come his way, diverse series work included; but it was the 1976–77 mini-series based on Irwin Shaw's *Rich Man, Poor Man* that made the wider world sit up and take note. He was Tom Jordache, a hell-raiser with a scarred childhood with whom everyone could sympathise. It was a rough diamond of a portrayal, crude, fierce, delivered from the heart, and it raised a piece of melodramatic hackwork to the level of near-tragedy whenever Nolte was on screen.

By that time, he had already made a small appearance in a Disney film, *Feather Farm* (1970), and taken his first lead in the negligible *Return To Macon County* (1975). More followed: the Peter Yates adventure yarn *The Deep* (1977), which is now mainly remembered for the sight of Jacqueline Bisset emerging from the water in a clinging T-shirt; Karel Reisz's *Who'll Stop The Rain* (1978), in which he is caught up in drug-smuggling with murky consequences; and *North Dallas Forty* (1979), a raw, rambling football drama to which Nolte as troubled hero brought understandable, and intense, conviction.

From these and other roles of the time it was becoming clear that the American cinema had gained itself a distinctive new face, but it took a while longer before the special value of this acquisition began to be recognised. In this regard, *48 HRS.* (1982) must count as something of a milestone: a San Francisco police caper, it couples Nolte as a weatherbeaten white cop and Eddie Murphy as a fly black con-man sprung from jail to help solve Nolte's case. The modulation in the men's relationship from disdain through gruff respect to friendship may be utterly predictable, the stuff of buddy movies, but both actors played it with irresistible (and in Nolte's case unsuspected) comic relish, and so it all seemed fresh and new. The huge popular success of *48 HRS.* was easy to explain, unlike Nolte's decision to take part in its feeble 1990 sequel, *Another 48 HRS.*, which must count as one of his few serious career miscalculations.

Even more interesting was the film that followed *48 HRS.*, the complex and disturbing *Under Fire* (1983), in which three journalists – the other two are Gene Hackman and Joanna Cassidy – suffer moral dilemmas and emotional contortions while covering a

Central American political upheaval. This is Nolte at his best, a screen-filling action man who can with burning intensity portray inner disquiet. And so, in an entirely different way, are his brilliant character studies in *Down And Out In Beverly Hills* (1985) and in 'Life Studies', the Martin Scorsese episode of the tripartite *New York Stories* (1989). Both might be said to be a cunning inversion of the 'Nolte Man' as previously depicted. In *Down And Out* he is a tramp given refuge in Richard Dreyfuss' luxury Hollywood home, who soon proves to be the unhappy household's saviour, all things to all men (and women); in 'Life Studies' he is a famous avant-garde painter working toward a forthcoming exhibition, who uses the love tangles in his life as a spur to creativity. In both, the rough diamond comes to be exposed, in carefully graded stages, as a highly proficient emotional con-man; the effect is deliciously, and at the same time delicately, comic, above all because of Nolte's wonderfully disciplined underplaying. He does it with the eyes, the voice, the shoulders – but so deftly that in the best way one only notices the skills involved afterwards.

In 1991 Nolte scored a remarkable double, critically and popularly, with Martin Scorsese's controversial, overwrought *Cape Fear* – presenting a flawed, morally ambiguous 'victim' of psychopath Robert De Niro's campaign of terror – and Barbra Streisand's sentimental, sprawling screen translation of *The Prince Of Tides*. Whatever the film's problems, Nolte's Oscar-nominated performance is a true *tour de force*, conjuring the great long-suppressed torment of a sensitive but bluff failure coming to terms with his life and the women in it.

Nick Nolte has had his share of failures. Notable among them is the large-scale one of John Milius's *Farewell To The King* (1989), in which he plays a US World War II deserter who has become leader of the Borneo tribe with whom he had taken refuge – a turgid, incoherent mess which not even its hard-worked leading actor (who spent weeks of earnest pre-production research in the Borneo jungle) could rescue. But on balance few of today's cinema leading men have been more consistent in the quality of their work, or more impressive.

1970 Feather Farm **1975** Return To Macon County (GB: Highway Girl) **1977** The Deep **1978** Who'll Stop The Rain (GB: Dog Soldiers) **1979** North Dallas Forty; Heart Beat **1982** Cannery Row; 48 HRS. **1983** Under Fire **1984** Teachers; Grace Quigley aka The Ultimate Solution Of Grace Quigley **1985** Down And Out In Beverly Hills **1987** Extreme Prejudice; Weeds **1989** Three Fugitives; Farewell To The King; New York Stories ('Life Lessons' episode) **1990** Everybody Wins; Another 48HRS.; Q & A **1991** The Prince Of Tides; Cape Fear **1992/93** Lorenzo's Oil **1993** I'll Do Anything

Norris, Chuck
(Carlos Ray Norris)

Actor
Born 1939
Ryan, Oklahoma

In *Rambo: First Blood Part II*, Sylvester Stallone's psychopathic ex-Green Beret asks the loaded question, 'Do we get to win this time?'. The film career of Chuck Norris has been spent supplying an answer in the affirmative. Unsmiling, unassailed by inner doubt and, above all, unkillable, he has performed celluloid exorcisms of the psychic damage inflicted on mainstream America by defeat in Vietnam and repeated humiliations at the hands of Iranian hostage-takers, international terrorists and Latin-American drug barons. With straining sinews and insistently phallic weaponry he has represented a messianic military power combined, against all military logic, in a single individual.

Before the Gulf War, Norris' films were make-believe victories in the face of defeat which revived the guts-and-glory tradition personified in *The Sands Of Iwo Jima* (1949) by John Wayne, the hero of Chuck's childhood. But the devastating allied triumph of arms in the Middle East bore a curiously disquieting resemblance to the high kill ratio with which Norris' films reach their climax as he disposes of dozens of faceless adversaries. These orgies of wish-fulfilment anticipated, in comic-strip form, the slaughter of the Iraqi army, 'crushed like ants' by superior firepower.

Born to an English-Irish mother and a Cherokee father, Norris spent a tough boyhood in Los Angeles before joining the United States Air Force and serving in Korea, where he became obsessed with the karate practised by the natives. After discharge from the service in 1961, he made karate his career, retiring in 1974 as the undefeated professional middleweight champion of the world. He was then encouraged by Steve McQueen, who was one of his karate students, to try his hand at acting, and he made his screen debut in 1973, pitted against kung fu hero Bruce Lee in *Return Of The Dragon*.

Astutely exploiting the martial arts boom of the 1970s, Norris made a string of unpretentious but commercially successful actioners such as *Breaker! Breaker!* (1975), *A Force Of One* (1979), *The Octagon* (1980), *An Eye For An Eye* (1981), *Silent Rage* (1982), and *Lone Wolf McQuade* (1983) – in which his fists, feet and an increasingly fearsome range of hardware did most if not all of the talking. The critics were uniformly dismissive, but as his popularity with the public grew, the actor cut back on the kicks and chops to concentrate on building up his strong, silent screen persona. As he had already mastered aggressive impassivity, this did not place undue demands on his limited acting range. Moreover, the characters he played – special forces commanders, ex-CIA agents, Vietnam vets and maverick cops who made Dirty Harry seem a wimp – still conformed to a pattern which nostalgically recalled the 'Cowboy Code' of Gene Autry.

Gene would never slug anyone smaller than himself or take unfair advantage, would not smoke or drink, and would never kiss the leading lady. Times may have changed a little since Gene rode the range in the 1940s, but the spirit remained the same, as did Chuck who, like Gene, always plays himself. In Norris' own words: 'I do what people want to see. I'll never play a drug addict or an alcoholic. Whatever role I'm playing, in the kids' eyes it's Chuck Norris up there on the screen.'

The big breakthrough for Norris came with *Missing In Action* (1984), a simplistic, revisionist fantasy in which he played Colonel James Braddock, an ex-POW in Vietnam who returns to Asia to liberate American prisoners still held there ten years after the end of the war. The movie's slogan, 'The war's not over until the last man's home', was an invitation to rediscover honour from the mess of defeat and, with its crude critique of American impotence and its hymning of American individualism, it struck a deeply Reaganite chord. The huge success of *Missing In Action* propelled its leading man into a furious burst of film-making and a place in the box office top five. Against all the odds, this slight, leathery, humourless man in his mid-40s had become a major star.

In swift succession came a series of actioners stamped from the Norris mould and produced by Cannon on a minimum budget for maximum bangs. First, a prequel to *Missing In Action, Missing In Action II* (1985). Then, *Code Of Silence* (1985), in which the hero played a Chicago cop battling drug barons with the aid of the usual inscrutably stern expression and a remote-controlled mini-tank equipped with cannons, grenade launchers and machine-guns. Hard on its heels came the richly paranoid *Invasion USA* (1985), with Chuck cast as a former CIA agent fighting a singlehanded war against an army of terrorists. Next, *Delta Force* (1986), which begins amid the chaos of the abortive attempt to rescue the US hostages in Teheran in 1980 and ends with Norris' crack commando unit defying half the firepower of the Middle East.

Subsequently, attempts to tinker with Chuck's Cro-Magnon image proved unsuccessful. *Firewalker* (1986) was a clumsy attempt to relax a little, Indiana Jones style, with Norris cast as a bounty hunter chasing jungle treasure. In *The Hero And The Terror* (1986) he played a 'sensitive' cop struggling to exorcise inner demons while battling with hulking serial killer Jack O'Halloran. With his eye on the box office, and perhaps on Anno Domini, he returned to the gung-ho certainties of *Braddock: Missing In Action 3* (1987) and *Delta Force II: Colombian Connection* (1990), respectively dealing with sadistic North Vietnamese generals and 'untouchable' South American drug tsars in a cathartic blaze of exploding missiles and flying fists.

Clearly, Chuck Norris, his producers and his fans remained unmoved by the march of time – although, by the 1990s, it seemed he would have to yield to Jean-Claude Van Damme and Steven Seagal.

1968 The Wrecking Crew **1973** Return Of The Dragon; The Student Teachers **1975** Breaker! Breaker! **1978** Good Guys Wear Black; Game Of Death **1979** A Force Of One **1980** The Octagon **1981** An Eye For An Eye; Slaughter In San Francisco (made in 1973) **1982** Forced Vengeance; Silent Rage **1983** Lone Wolf McQuade **1984** Missing In Action **1985** Missing In Action II: The Beginning; Code Of Silence; Invasion USA (also co-writer) **1986** The Delta Force; Firewalker **1987** Braddock: Missing In Action III (also writer) **1988** Hero And The Terror **1990** Stranglehold: Delta Force II: Colombian Connection **1991** The Hitman **1992/93** Sidekicks (as himself)

O

O'Connor, Kevin J.

Actor
Born 1964
Chicago, Illinois

Not to be confused with Kevin O'Connor, the actor who played Humphrey Bogart in the biopic *Bogie* (1980), Kevin J. O'Connor is one of the most promising young character actors around, capable of playing romantic leads and providing comic support with equal aplomb – and, indeed, often shading the one with the other, so that nothing he does is without passion *and* irony.

The son of a Chicago policeman and a schoolteacher, O'Connor attended an all-boys Catholic school. Although it did not have a drama department, the neighbouring all-girls school did – and he appeared in two of its productions. In four years at the Goodman School of Drama, O'Connor was never cast in a romantic role, but just a month after graduation he auditioned for Francis Ford Coppola and landed the role of the high school rebel who turns Kathleen Turner's head in *Peggy Sue Got Married* (1986). This biker and would-be beat writer positively throbs with youthful intensity and picks the film up just when it looks like running out of ideas. This was the first of an unusual series of writers O'Connor has played. With his unruly, tousled hair, loose-limbed stances and obsessively fixed stare, O'Connor is the embodiment of the American artist: physical, arrogant, unmistakeably heterosexual. It is his saving grace that he characteristically deflates these posturings with such subtle equanimity.

In the indepedent film *Candy Mountain* (1987), he had the lead role as Julius, a songwriter who takes to the road in search of a legendary guitar-maker. Co-directed by Rudy Wurlitzer and Robert Frank, and populated by musicians like Tom Waits, Dr John, Leon Redbone and Joe Strummer, this was impressive company for a 22-year-old just out of drama school, and it is on the independent fringe that O'Connor has done most of his work. Robert Altman cast him as Lt. Kiefer (a writer) in his television movie *The Caine Mutiny Court Martial* (1988), and then – memorably – as the journalist Taggerty in his groundbreaking TV series, *Tanner '88*. Altman's former protégé, Alan Rudolph, then approached O'Connor to play Hemingway in his film *The Moderns* (1988). As scripted, the part consisted of just three lines, but O'Connor decided 'I was better off taking a chance on Alan Rudolph than getting my teeth fixed and doing a teen cop movie'. The gamble paid off. Rudolph's penchant for improvisation allowed O'Connor his freedom, and Hemingway – continually trying on aphorisms and prospective book titles for size – is one of the delights of the picture. The actor also stole the show from the impressive ensemble in *Signs Of Life* (1989), a rather precious piece of whimsy set in Easthasset, Maine, off-off Broadway. Arthur Kennedy, Beau Bridges, Will Patton, Kate Reid and Vincent Philip D'Onofrio were also involved. His cameo in Rudolph's *Love At Large* (1990) did not amount to much, nor did his role as Sammy – Daryl Hannah's husband – in the very mainstream *Steel Magnolias* (1989), but that was no fault of his own, and it looked to be only a matter of time before Kevin J. O'Connor would get the parts he deserves.

1986 Peggy Sue Got Married **1987** Candy Mountain **1988** The Moderns **1989** Signs Of Life; Steel Magnolias **1990** Love At Large **1992** Hero

Oldman, Gary

Actor
Born 21 March 1958
South London, England

One of the most arresting young stage actors to have emerged in Britain in the 1980s, Gary Oldman is a rarity for the ease with which he made the transition into mainly American films. While his range on screen was still being tested, it was the psycho-killers with which he was in danger of being most widely associated by 1990.

After experience in the Greenwich Young People's Theatre, Oldman won a scholarship to drama school and toured in repertory before joining Glasgow's prestigious Citizens Theatre in 1980. He made his name in London's West End with several standout performances, notably at the Royal Court in *Rat In The Skull*, *Women Beware Women* and *Serious Money*, and his work in *The Pope's Wedding* won him Best Actor and Best Newcomer awards in 1985. At the same time he appeared in some first-rate TV drama including *Honest, Decent And True* as an artist striving for greatness.

Oldman made his remarkable film debut with an utterly convincing, horrifying portrayal of Sex Pistol punk Sid Vicious in Alex Cox's striking *Sid And Nancy* (1986), for which he won the London *Evening Standard*'s Best Newcomer award. He was equally persuasive as playwright Joe Orton in another account of an obsessive relationship, Stephen Frears' film of *Prick Up Your Ears* (1987) before heading to America with director Nicolas Roeg for the blackly bizarre *Track 29* (1988). Offered the role of the sociopathic killer in *Criminal Law* (1989) he ended up happier playing the yuppie lawyer undergoing a crisis of conscience in defending Kevin Bacon's killer. The film was not a success but Oldman's American accent was, and after a sojourn back in England to play a convict in *We Think The World Of You* (1988) he returned to the US to play a combat veteran institutionalised in the so-so reform drama *Chatahoochee* (1990). *State Of Grace*, the same year, saw him holding his own on screen with Ed Harris and Sean Penn as one of an Irish-American hoodlum circle, but the film was another joyless affair. It was refreshing, then, to see him playing the philosophising innocent, Rosencrantz, to Tim Roth's sardonic if equally hapless Guildenstern in Tom Stoppard's screen adaptation of his play *Rosencrantz And Guildenstern Are Dead* (1991), far artier fare. Following his third portrayal of a real person, the poet Dylan Thomas, starring with his second wife, actress Uma Thurman, Oldman was Dallas-bound for an eerily effective impersonation far removed from the others – in the role of Lee Harvey Oswald for Oliver Stone, before being cast in the title role of Francis Coppola's awaited-with-curiosity version of *Dracula* (1992).

1986 Sid And Nancy **1987** Prick Up Your Ears **1988** Track 29; We Think The World Of You **1989** Criminal Law; Chatahoochee **1990** State Of Grace **1991** Rosencrantz And Guildenstern Are Dead; JFK **1992** Bram Stoker's Dracula **1992/93** Dylan **1993** True Romanc

Olin, Lena

Actress
Born 1955
Stockholm, Sweden

Lithe, intense Lena Olin is the only Swedish actress to have made a really significant splash in Hollywood since Ingrid Bergman, Oscar-nominated in only her second English language film and given Robert Redford for her leading man in her next.

Born in Stockholm to actor parents (father Stig starred in several early Ingmar Bergman films), Olin had a classical training and has long been a member of Sweden's Royal Dramatic Theatre, where she has distinguished herself in leading roles ranging from Shakespeare and Strindberg to contemporary work. She made her Swedish film debut while still at drama school and has appeared in two of Bergman's films: the Oscar-winning *Fanny And Alexander* (1983) and *After The Rehearsal* (1984), in a role Bergman created for her, as Anna, the actress taunting the Lothario director who rejected her mother. Olin has also done a four-hour TV film, *Hebriana*, with director Bo Widerberg.

The actress' English-language film debut came in Philip Kaufman's *The Unbearable Lightness Of Being* (1988) – from the Milan Kundera novel – in which her voluptuous and beautiful Czech artist, Sabina, made audiences sit up as she taught Daniel Day Lewis' randy young doctor some tricks you can do with a bowler hat. A year later she received an Academy Award nomination and a New York Film Critics award for her harrowing performance as beautiful, passionate, despairing Masha, the Russian survivor of a Nazi death camp in Paul Mazursky's highly acclaimed *Enemies, A Love Story* (1989). Inundated with offers she plumped for another tortured beauty, the well-heeled revolutionary for whom Robert Redford's roving gambler falls on the eve of the Cuban revolution in Sydney Pollack's *Havana* (1990). Sadly, what on paper was a major prestige Hollywood film emerged as a major disappointment, lacking the heartstopping chemistry between Redford and Olin that this hybrid of *Casablanca* (1942) and *Salvador* (1986) needed. Nevertheless, the actress, who still lives in Stockholm, retained her enthusiasm for characters whose personal conflicts are highlighted by politically strained circumstances.

1980 Kärleken **1983** Fanny And Alexander (Sweden); Gräsanklinger/Grass Widowers (Sweden) **1984** After The Rehearsal (Sweden) **1986** Flucht In Den Nordes/Escape To The North (Germany/Finland) **1987** På Liv Och Död/Matter Of Life And Death (Sweden) **1988** Friends (Sweden/Japan); The Unbearable Lightness Of Being **1989** Sly Glädjen (Sweden); Enemies, A Love Story **1990** Havana **1992** Mr Jones **1992/93** Romeo Is Bleeding

Olmos, Edward James

Actor

Born 24 February 1947

East Los Angeles, California

A fine Hispanic-American actor who came to movies late in life and soon took up production as an adjunct to performing, Edward James Olmos seems in his career decisions to have been guided more by social concerns than the extent of his own part.

Olmos was educated at California State University, then concentrated on a singing career, fronting the rock group Eddie James and the Pacific Ocean. From the early 70s onwards, he appeared in bit parts in television series such as *Kojak* and *Hawaii Five-O*; he also picked up a supporting role in the lower-case melodrama, *aloha, bobby and rose* (1975), billed as Eddie Olmos. *Alambrista!* (1977), a realistic look at the exploitation of Mexican 'wet-backs' north of the border, introduced the actor to director Robert M. Young, whose first film this was. They became friends and later partners in YOY (why oh why?) Productions. But it was the stage production of the musical drama *Zoot Suit* that made Olmos. A fascinating, stylised tale based on an incident in 1942 when members of a chicano gang were railroaded to San Quentin for murder, Luis Váldez wrote and directed, and his brother Daniel wrote the music and starred as the gang leader – but Olmos won the plaudits for his panache in the showy role of Daniel's zootsuited alter ego. He won the LA drama critics award, and then when the play transferred to Broadway, a Theatre World award and a Tony nomination. The stage version was filmed in 1981.

As a supporting actor, Olmos did colourful work in *Wolfen* (1981) and *Blade Runner* (1982), and reached a far wider audience as the moustached, wavy-haired Lt. Castillo, Crockett and Tubbs' boss in the flashy cop show *Miami Vice* (he won an Emmy for best supporting actor in 1985). Probably more important to him, though, are his collaborations with Young. First, and best, *The Ballad Of Gregorio Córtez* (1982), another true story, about a Mexican farm labourer who shot a Texan sheriff in self-defence, then eluded a posse of 600 for two weeks. Olmos played Cortez, assistant-produced, and served as composer and music adapter. It was a beautiful, haunting piece of work, if too slow for a wide audience. *Saving Grace* (1986) and *Triumph Of The Spirit* (1989), both directed by Young, were less successful, though no less sincere, but Ramon Menendez's *Stand And Deliver* (1988) was a triumph, especially for Olmos. His was a tour-de-force performance as a tough maths teacher in an East LA school who inspires his *barrio* pupils to unparalleled accomplishments. This was *Dead Poets Society* (1989) without the nostalgia and romanticism, and all the better for it. Olmos, with a high forehead, pock-marked complexion, a shuffling gait and carrying an extra 40lb, became one of the most unlikely heroes of 1988, and was subsequently Oscar nominated.

1975 aloha, bobby and rose **1977** Alambrista! **1980** Virus (Japan) **1981** Zoot Suit; Wolfen **1982** Blade Runner; The Ballad Of Gregorio Cortez **1986** Saving Grace **1988** Stand And Deliver **1989** Triumph Of The Spirit **1991** Talent For The Game **1992** American Me (also director, co-writer)

O'Neal, Ryan
(Patrick O'Neal)

Actor

Born 20 April 1941

Los Angeles, California

Now best known for his tempestuous relationship with his children Tatum (Mrs John McEnroe) and Griffin, the former lifeguard and amateur boxer was himself born into a movie family (his father was a novelist and screenwriter and his mother an actress) and proved just as troublesome as his own offspring, on one occasion earning a 51-day jail sentence for assault and battery. Moving into the business via work as a stuntman on the German TV series *Tales Of The Vikings*, Ryan O'Neal returned to America for regular roles in the Western series *Empire* and, more importantly, as the blonde, handsome boy next door in some 500 episodes of *Peyton Place*.

The popularity of the series secured him a small role as a marathon runner in one of Michael Winner's more tolerable films, *The Games* (1970), which he carried off with some authority, but it was the surprise success of the five-handkerchief weepie, *Love Story*, the same year that convinced producers they had found a new star and which earned him an Oscar nomination. Yet despite giving some depth to a paper-thin part, he lacked sufficient dramatic weight for other roles: he was overshadowed by William Holden's seasoned professionalism in *Wild Rovers* (1971); and while he was ideally cast as the professorial innocent in *What's Up Doc?*

(1972), and was suitably superficial as the con-man of *Paper Moon* (1973, a film stolen from him by his own daughter) he was at times perhaps a little too remote and vacuous as Kubrick's *Barry Lyndon* (1975) and his career soon found itself in the doldrums. He was unfairly criticised for his boy general in *A Bridge Too Far* (1977), a creditable performance despite being older and less colourful than the man he was playing; and although he attempted to change his image and turned in his best screen work as the impersonal, highly professional getaway *Driver* (1978) in Walter Hill's iconic modern-day Western, good roles seemed to go out of their way to avoid him.

There was clear desperation in the *Love Story* sequel, *Oliver's Story* (1978), and a lacklustre reteaming with Barbra Streisand on *The Main Event* (1979), and soon his personal life was getting more attention than his films. Never having had a solid career base or a discernible group of fans, as he got older he was unable to find a new niche for himself. He was too old for guileless roles in screwball comedies (although that didn't stop him making them), yet was so closely identified with the genre via his association with Peter Bogdanovich that he made an unconvincing tough guy. True, he was superb as the egomaniacal director (clearly based on Bogdanovich) making a Ciminoesque remake of *Gone With The Wind* in *Irreconcilable Differences* (1984), but the laughs in *Fever Pitch* (1985) and *Tough Guys Don't Dance* (1987) were entirely unintentional. They are two of the worst films ever made, and O'Neal's performance in the former as a compulsive gambler made the cast of *Reefer Madness* look like method actors while, although he did some interesting things with his voice in the latter, delivering Norman Mailer's deliriously inane and frequently irrelevant dialogue wasn't one of them and his horrified mantra of 'Oh man! Oh God!' at one point is one of the most hilariously inept moments ever acted on film.

By contrast, O'Neal was surprisingly professional and appealing in a supporting role in *Chances Are* (1989) but the film never found an audience and he found it almost impossible to get work; even his small role as Farrah Fawcett's lover in the mini-series *Small Sacrifices* only came about when the original actor fell ill. And it was only through real-life lover Fawcett's involvement that he was able to land the TV series *Good Sports* after two years of unemployment, providing a gift to the gossip columnists because of the strain it allegedly placed on their tempestuous relationship, but brought no joy to the viewers or network heads. A ratings disaster, it ended its first series amid much acrimony and with a future as bleak as that of its faded star; with few hits, fewer good performances and a difficult reputation, O'Neal went into the 90s in desperate need of a change in fortune if he wished to continue his acting career.

1969 The Big Bounce **1970** The Games; Love Story **1971** Wild Rovers **1972** What's Up Doc? **1973** The Thief Who Came To Dinner; Paper Moon **1975** Barry Lyndon **1976** Nickelodeon **1977** A Bridge Too Far **1978** The Driver; Oliver's Story **1979** The Main Event **1980** Circle Of Two **1981** Green Ice; So Fine **1982** Partners **1984** Irreconcilable Differences **1985** Fever Pitch **1987** Tough Guys Don't Dance **1989** Chances Are

O'Neal, Tatum

Actress
Born 5 November 1963
Los Angeles, California

The daughter of actor Ryan O'Neal and actress Joanna Moore, Tatum O'Neal shot to international fame in 1973 and became the youngest recipient of an Oscar (Best Supporting Actress) when she co-starred with her father in Peter Bogdanovich's comedy *Paper Moon* (1973). Her portrayal of a semi-abandoned orphan, well-versed in rough talk, cigarette-smoking and working scams was astonishing and has proved an enduring delight, ensuring the film continued re-showings. A three-year hiatus followed for the precocious actress, after which she earned $350,000 and 9% of the net profits from her next film, *The Bad News Bears (1976)*, thus becoming the highest-paid child actor in cinema history to that time.

Alas, since her appearance in *Nickelodeon* (1976), Peter Bogdanovich's tale of film's early days which again starred daddy Ryan, Tatum O'Neal's career has been both unremarkable and increasingly invisible. *International Velvet* (1978), the ill-advised remake of Elizabeth Taylor's famous 1944 vehicle, *National Velvet*, was a flat affair that ended up falling between two stools: it was neither an exciting girl-loves-horse story nor was it a sufficiently interesting tale of international sports intrigue. *Little Darlings* (1979) centred on two young girls who have a race to lose their virginity at summer camp. Far from being as sordid as it sounds, it was a silly teen movie which failed to make waves and Tatum was outclassed by her talented co-star, Kristy McNichol.

From the 80s, Tatum O'Neal, blonde and pretty, became better known for her marriage to controversial tennis superstar John McEnroe than as an actress. The couple had two young sons (Kevin and Sean) and their mother was frequently in the news as a spokeswoman defending their father's fiery outbursts. Indeed, until her brief appearance in *Little Noises* (1990), Jane Spencer's comedy starring Rik Mayall and Crispin Glover, it seemed evident that Tatum O'Neal had put her career on hold for family reasons. Whether she would return to films (she dipped her toe in the water with a made-for-TV movie in 1989) as a matured performer or, like the most famous child star of them all, Shirley Temple Black, she would opt for a different career, remained a matter for speculation in the early 90s.

1973 Paper Moon **1976** The Bad News Bears **1976** Nickelodeon **1978** International Velvet **1979** Little Darlings **1980** Circle Of Two **1985** Certain Fury **1991** Little Noises

O'Toole, Peter

Actor
Born 2 August 1932
Connemara, Ireland

Not long into his film career, Peter O'Toole hit the top, as the screen's most poetic-looking new romantic idol; 30 years later, he was back there again, as a character actor of acute and sometimes wonderfully eccentric distinction, particularly in comic roles. In between, there have been many ups and downs – rather more of the latter, in truth, caused by the actor's hell-for-leather lifestyle, and a reliance on drink and drugs from which for reasons of severe health depredation he finally and entirely freed himself. At those times, indeed, it seemed that he was on the point of artistic and physical burn-out (a London stage production of *Macbeth* in the early 1980s, a fiasco which drew huge audiences because of its leading man's manic weirdness, must represent the nadir of his acting achievements). Yet against all the odds he has survived, and in so doing refined the peculiar strengths of his talent. One might even suggest that the metamorphosis in his looks provides a graph curve of the process – the fine-featured glamour of youth has been replaced by a face that is lined, weather-beaten, shorn of all spare flesh, and remarkably interesting.

Born in Ireland but brought up in the North of England city of Leeds, he was the son of a bookmaker. This feature of parentage he has in common with Albert Finney; another coincidence is that the two were classmates at the Royal Academy of Dramatic Art, where, after a youthful stint as a cub newspaper reporter and a period of national service in the Royal Navy O'Toole had headed on a scholarship. In 1955, he joined the Bristol Old Vic theatre company, staying there for two-and-a-half years, and then proceeding to London's West End. In 1959, the year in which he was showered with praise for his stage performance in *The Long, The Short And The Tall*, a handful of small film parts came his way, followed by a now-legendary big break – the title role of David Lean's *Lawrence Of Arabia* (1962).

In many ways O'Toole could not have dreamed of a more auspicious launching – an epic of historical conflict made by one of the world's masters of the genre, set in a magnificently bleak landscape (the beauties of Lean's desert visions have been greatly enhanced by the reissue of the film, in a version substantially longer than the original), and with the central character surrounded by a galaxy of distinguished veterans: Alec Guinness, Anthony Quinn, Jack Hawkins, Anthony Quayle and José Ferrer, to name a few. The unknown Irish actor, tall, rangy, blondhaired, blue-eyed, was certainly an inspired choice; for with his startling, almost improbable good looks, and with a gift for shading in the fascinating psychological contradictions in Lawrence's personality by means of a highly individual acting vocabulary of verbal and visual nuances, he discovered in the role an ideal blend of daredevil virility and tortured introspection. *Lawrence*, not surprisingly, gained O'Toole the first of seven nominations for the Best Actor Oscar.

With hindsight, however, one can see how easily the fine-tuned high style of this portrayal could turn into mannerism in the succession of epics that followed. Henry II in *Becket* (1964), opposite Richard Burton, was a vivid confrontation of two sharp-profiled actors, but by the time he returned to portraying the same king in *The Lion In Winter* (1968), the style had begun to reveal worrying hints of self-repetition and even self-indulgence. From here the list of O'Toole films seemed to divide fairly evenly. On the one hand there are the heavyweight, prestige items, many of them unsuccessful at the box-office (*Lord Jim*, 1965, *The Bible*, 1966, *The Night Of The Generals*, 1966, *Great Catherine*, 1968, and two particularly leaden musicals – *Goodbye Mr Chips*, 1969, and *Man Of La Mancha*, 1971); on the other, there are the small number of lightly entertaining comedies (*What's New, Pussycat?*, 1965, *How To Steal A Million*, 1966) that showed O'Toole in a less unflattering light.

This was a useful portent, for it was comedy that rescued O'Toole from the decadent aristocrats (in *The Ruling Class*, 1972, the Mexican-Swiss disaster *Foxtrot*, 1976, and Tinto Brass' lamentable *Caligula*, 1977) and other misbegotten assignments (*Rosebud*, 1975, *Man Friday*, 1975, *Zulu Dawn*, 1979) which came his way in the 70s. In *The Stunt Man* (1978), his power-crazed film director at work on a World War I epic revealed a touch of self-caricature that was, one felt, intentional and, up to a point, enjoyable, and the film was a surprise success with US audiences. Even more refreshing was his account of a drunk cinema has-been weaving his way through the world of 1950s American television in Richard Benjamin's *My Favorite Year* (1982). A variant of this character, the obsessive Nobel Laureate scientist bent on an absurd project, allowed O'Toole to provide one of the positive features of Ivan Passer's uneven comedy-drama *Creator* (1985); in similar vein, as a down-at-heel Irish landowner scheming to gull rich American tourists with promises of ghosts in his castle, he was a saving grace of Neil Jordan's otherwise hopelessly botched comedy, *High Spirits* (1988). And, as a reminder that this actor's knack of creating larger-than-life eccentrics can, in the right circumstances, be turned to the good of more serious material, his contribution to Bertolucci's *The Last Emperor* (1987) – he is Reginald Johnston, Pu Yi's Scottish tutor – was not only exquisitely judged but thoroughly well timed.

What seems, indeed, to have been forged in the fire of O'Toole's artistic and personal vicissitudes is his own individuality as an actor; and it is now as strong and true as tempered steel.

1960 Ombre Bianche aka Les Dents Du Diable/The Savage Innocents (Italy); The Day They Robbed The Bank Of England; Kidnapped **1962** Lawrence Of Arabia **1964** Becket **1965** Lord Jim; What's New, Pussycat? **1966** The Bible; How To Steal A Million **1967** The Night Of The Generals; Casino Royale **1968** The Lion In Winter; Great Catherine **1969** Goodbye Mr Chips **1970** Country Dance aka Brotherly Love **1971** Murphy's War; Under Milk Wood **1972** The Ruling Class; Man Of La Mancha **1975** Rosebud; Man Friday **1976** Foxtrot aka Other Side Of Paradise **1977** Caligula **1978** The Stunt Man; Power Play **1979** Zulu Dawn **1982** My Favorite Year **1985** Creator **1987** The Last Emperor **1988** High Spirits **1990** The Rainbow Thief (Italy) **1991** Wings Of Fame; Isabelle Eberhardt (France/Germany/Australia); King Ralph **1992** Rebecca's Daughters

P

Pacino, Al

Actor
Born 25 April 1940
New York City

For much of the 1970s, Al Pacino went to considerable lengths to conceal himself: hiding behind poetically conceived hobo's tatters in *Scarecrow* (1973); assuming a cold-blooded mask as he tightened his grip on the reins of Mafia power in *The Godfather Part II* (1974); ducking and weaving behind an Old English sheepdog and a hippy hairdo in *Serpico* (1973); and donning a pair of designer shades in *Bobby Deerfield* (1977). Perhaps he was dismayed into concealment by his brooding good looks, choosing only to reveal himself on his own terms. When the going got tough in the mid-80s, he chose to disappear altogether.

Of Sicilian descent, he grew up in New York's South Bronx district, a stage and movie-struck kid who won a place at Manhattan's High School of Performing Arts (later well known to the public because of the TV series and movie *Fame*, 1980). Pacino dropped out when he was 17, but subsequently worked his way through Herbert Berghof's acting academy and into some small parts off-Broadway. After further studies at the Actors' Studio, he won an Obie for his performance as a psychotic punk in *The Indian Wants The Bronx*, following it with a Tony award for his portrayal of a strung-out junkie in *Does The Tiger Wear A Necktie?* – both of them roles that prefigured his first major screen appearance.

Pacino made his film debut as a gigolo in *Me, Natalie* (1969), with Patty Duke, but had to wait another two years before Jerry Schatzberg gave him the lead in *Panic In Needle Park* (1971) as a small-time Manhattan heroin dealer and addict, racing rapidly downhill with his girlfriend (Katy Winn). His performance, bristling with nervous intensity and an uncompromising interpretation of a dangerously disturbed psyche, attracted the notice of Francis Ford Coppola, who cast him as the war hero Michael Corleone, heir to Marlon Brando's mobster Don Vito, in *The Godfather* (1972). Pacino looked a good deal younger than his 30 years, initially wide-eyed and bashful and gently ribbed by The Family's 'soldiers'. Gradually, his Michael retreats into the controlled coldness and deadpan calculation which is put to bloody use in the service of The Family. It is Pacino's particular skill to suggest that this purposeful, unsentimental metamorphosis liberates the real man from the boy who came home from the war destined for 'legitimate' business. When he lights a cigarette after foiling an attempt on his father's life, he notices that his hands are rock steady. In *The Godfather Part II*, now in melancholy control of the Corleone empire, morbidity turns to malignance as the camera dwells in close-up on his murderous reveries.

In spite of the Oscars won by Robert De Niro and Brando for *The Godfather*, Pacino's is the dominating and pivotal performance. It won him an Oscar nomination and stardom. His next film, *Scarecrow*, again for Schatzberg, represented a rather 'actorly' switch – designed perhaps to show his versatility – as a drifter teaming up with another no-hoper, Gene Hackman. Then he scored a big hit (and gained another Academy nomination) in Sidney Lumet's *Serpico*, based on a true story. The actor played a whistle-blowing New York cop, deftly subverting Lumet's tepid realism with an idiosyncratic portrait of a loner undercover policeman turning into a maddeningly modish hippy with sheepdog in tow. Another Lumet movie based on a true story, *Dog Day Afternoon* (1975), brought his third Oscar nomination and a second chance to slip the leash of impassivity as a homosexual holding up a bank to pay for lover John Cazale's sex-change operation. Next came a dive, or rather a belly-flop, into the sentimental melodrama of *Bobby Deerfield*, as a Grand Prix racing driver romancing aristocratic Marthe Keller, who is dying of one of those discreetly fatal movie diseases that dare not speak its name and leaves absolutely no physical traces. Not surprisingly, the movie and Pacino's performance died too.

The actor finished the decade as a conscience-burdened DA in . . . *And Justice For All* (1979), a slick, specious but nonetheless quite absorbing Norman Jewison movie indicting the iniqities of the legal system. Still considering himself essentially a stage actor, Pacino tended to take great care over his choice of movie roles, but his judgement betrayed the introspection he brought to the task. It clearly deserted him when he accepted William Friedkin's *Cruising* (1980), again as an undercover cop but this time lost in a labyrinth of sado-masochistic homosexual ritual as he searches for a killer stalking gay bars. An attempt to let his hair down as a harassed playwright in Arthur Hiller's *Author! Author!* (1982) attracted little attention, but in Brian De Palma's *Scarface* (1983), an updated version of the 1932 Howard Hawks classic, he was once again married to the mob as criminal Cuban refugee Tony Montana, sitting on (and sniffing) a mountain of cocaine in Miami. It was a bravura display of hysterical malevolence in a widely under-rated movie.

Then disaster struck. The star was cast in more conventionally heroic mould in Hugh Hudson's *Revolution* (1985), a sprawlingly ambitious British attempt to tell the story of the American War of Independence, which was greeted with a universal critical lambasting that stopped it dead in its tracks. Pacino failed to convince as Tom Dobb, the fur trapper caught up in the rush of great events, given a disconcerting Scots-Bronx accent by the dialogue coach, and resembling a contemporary New York hustler who has just stepped groggily into a time warp. It remains one of the wilder pieces of miscasting since Frank Sinatra and Cary Grant wheeled a huge cannon through the Peninsular War in *The Pride And The Passion* (1957).

When the dust had settled, the actor withdrew from films. He consoled himself with stage work and, on his own admission, heavy drinking. He made his comeback five years later, playing the morose middle-aged cop cast adrift on *A Sea Of Love* (1989) with explosively sexy murder suspect Ellen Barkin. Fortunately, the movie was a big success, and he went on to the Oscar nominated role of Big Boy Caprice in *Dick Tracy* (1990), efforlessly out-Caponing De Niro's performance in *The Untouchables* (1987) and clearly enjoying himself hugely. Al Pacino then allowed Coppola to twist his arm – with $5 million and a percentage of the box office – to resume his portrayal of Michael Corleone in *The Godfather Part III*, proving, after all his years away, that he was still eminently bankable. And, as the touchingly lonely but persistent wooer of Michelle Pfeiffer in *Frankie And Johnny*, proving, too, that at 50-plus, he was still a highly attractive leading man.

1969 Me, Natalie **1971** Panic In Needle Park **1972** The Godfather **1973** Scarecrow; Serpico **1974** The Godfather Part II **1975** Dog Day Afternoon **1977** Bobby Deerfield **1979** . . . And Justice For All **1980** Cruising **1982** Author! Author! **1983** Scarface **1985** Revolution **1989** Sea Of Love **1990** Dick Tracy; The Godfather Part III **1991** Frankie And Johnny **1992** Glengarry Glen Ross; Scent Of A Woman

Pacula, Joanna

Actress

Born 1 January 1957

Tomazsow Lubelski, Poland

It is rare to find the qualities of exotic beauty and innate simplicity in the same person, but these are Joanna Pacula's characteristics: down to earth and out of this world. She trained at the Warsaw Academy Of Theatrical Arts and made her film debut with a small role in Krzysztof Zanussi's *Barwy Ochronne* (1976) – which was shown in the West in 1979 as *Camouflage*. Larger roles soon followed in films and television, and she attracted special notice for her role in the TV serial *Jan Serce* (1981). In December 1981, she was holidaying in Paris when martial law was declared in Poland. She remained in France and began an affair with another Pole in exile, Roman Polanski. He arranged some modelling work for her, and soon she left for the United States, where she was featured in *Vogue*.

It was Polanski who recommended her for the female lead in *Gorky Park* (1983), which she won even though she spoke no English. Michael Apted's adaptation of Martin Cruz Smith's bestseller (with a Dennis Potter screenplay) cast William Hurt as a Moscow policeman, Lee Marvin as a shady dealer, and Pacula as the femme fatale involved with both. Generally considered a disappointment, this thriller turned out to be rather old-fashioned, and Pacula's performance merited little comment, though it led to her top billing in her next film, *Not Quite Jerusalem* (1985). Lewis Gilbert's lacklustre love story, set on a kibbutz, toned down everything interesting about Paul Kember's play in favour of national stereotypes and touristic photography. Only Pacula's Israeli supervisor comes to life; the actress looked composed and confident with the language now, and hers was a feisty performance. She was back in the Middle East for the hackneyed *Death Before Dishonour* (1987), and in Paris for the romantic comedy *Sweet Lies* (1987), but her most impressive piece of work consisted of playing a glamorous, exotic aunt who comes from old Europe to pass on the family curse to her American niece. *The Kiss* (1988) did nothing with its *Cat People*-like premise, but Pacula was ferocious in the role, full-blooded and sexy. European actresses in Hollywood have not fared well in recent years (Kinski, Adjani, Kaprisky – they come and go): Pacula has the talent, the trick is to find the roles.

1976 Barwy Orcronne aka Camouflage (Poland) **1977** Nie Zaznasz Spokoju (Poland); Akcja Pod Arsenatem (Poland) **1979** Zerwane Cumy (Poland); Ostatnia Noc Milosci (Poland); Pierwsza Noc Wojny (Romania) **1981** Czule Miejsca **1983** Gorky Park **1985** Not Quite Jerusalem aka Not Quite Paradise **1987** Death Before Dishonour; Sweet Lies **1988** The Kiss **1989** Options **1990** Marked For Death **1992** Husbands And Lovers

Pakula, Alan J.

Director, Writer
Born 7 April 1928
New York City

Best known for his conspiracy thrillers, Alan J. Pakula, in his work as a producer-director, embraces a wider variety of subjects, including frequent forays into the romantic, but which is held together by the consistent theme of the individual embattled in an implacable society that feeds dreams and lies and is set against those who cannot fulfil or believe them.

The son of a print and advertising executive, Pakula studied drama at Yale before briefly working as an assistant on Warner Bros. cartoons in 1949, joining MGM as an apprentice in 1950 and going on the following year to become a production assistant and, later, an associate producer, at Paramount. He began a long association with director Robert Mulligan in 1957, producing the baseball drama *Fear Strikes Out* and continuing with *To Kill A Mockingbird* (1962), *Love With The Proper Stranger* (1963), *Baby, The Rain Must Fall, Inside Daisy Clover* (both 1965) and *Up The Down Staircase* (1967) before parting company with Mulligan after 1969's revenge Western *The Stalking Moon*, when he decided to direct himself.

Pakula's first film at the helm, *The Sterile Cuckoo* (1969), already showed his interest in society's need for conformity: it was an unusual love story in which Liza Minnelli's kookie non-conformist wins over but eventually loses Wendell Burton's shy freshman. The movie was fairly widely reviled, but was followed by the award-winning *Klute* (1971), another story of mismatched love, this time between Donald Sutherland's innocent private eye and Jane Fonda's emotionally detached hooker under threat. Here, the city is a morally corrupting influence that reduces everything to commerce – she treats him like a customer until, when she is finally able to give love rather than have sex, they leave the city – with a murderer's incessant replaying of tape-recorded conversations an uncanny premonition of the Watergate scandal that would give the director his biggest success in the shape of *All The President's Men* (1976). More intriguing was his variation on the Kennedy assassination in *The Parallax View* (1973), a deceptive and intricate thriller where journalist Warren Beatty thinks he is infiltrating a mysterious organisation only to find he has been setting himself up as a patsy for another assassination, a turn of events hinted at both in the opening shot, where the camera tracks slightly past a totem pole to reveal a tower block, and the title itself (a parallax is an apparent change in the position of an object caused by a change of position by the observer).

By contrast, *Rollover* (1981) was a racist and alarmist piece of tosh about vindictive Arabs destroying the Western economy just for the hell of it and, along with the director's other poorly received reunion with Fonda, the post-war land rights Western *Comes A Horseman* (1978), signalled a move away from politics back towards more emotional territory, most successfully in the archetypal martyred Meryl movie, *Sophie's Choice* (1982). Following a long period in the wilderness and the total mess of *Dream Lover* (1986) on his return, he only hit his stride intermittently, a situation attributed by many (including *President's Men* screenwriter William Goldman) to his inability to act decisively at times. The hugely expensive three-hander *Orphans* (1987) was better, by virtue of its performances rather than its direction, while *See You In The Morning* (1989) was a manipulative and considerably less successful return to the territory of his post-divorce romance *Starting Over* a decade earlier. But he was vindicated at the decade's turn by the huge box-office success of his adaptation of *Presumed Innocent* (1990), a solid, intelligent transferring of Scott Turow's bestseller, despite a tendency to concentrate on surface rather than substance.

As director only unless stated otherwise: **1969** The Sterile

Cuckoo aka Pookie **1971** Klute **1973** Love And Pain And The Whole Damn Thing **1974** The Parallax View **1976** All The President's Men **1978** Comes A Horseman **1979** Starting Over **1981** Rollover **1982** Sophie's Choice (w/d) **1986** Dream Lover **1987** Orphans **1989** See You In The Morning (w/d) **1990** Presumed Innocent (w/d) **1992/93** Consenting Adults

Paré, Michael

Actor
Born 9 October 1958
New York City

One of ten children, Michael Paré trained at the New York Culinary Institute and was working as a *sous-chef* at Cafe Europa on the Upper West Side when a modelling agent offered to promote his services. A friend suggested he try acting, and after two years studying with Uta Hagen and Marvin Nelson, he was hired to play *The Greatest American Hero* in a planned TV series. When the project fell through (it was eventually made without him) he landed the lead in a TV movie, *Crazy Times* (1981), alongside Ray Liotta, and then the title role in *Eddie And The Cruisers* (1983), Martin Davidson's cult rock 'n' roll picture.

Paré's hooded eyes and insolently curled lip recall the icons of the Method, but his stumbling delivery and stubbled jaw denote attitude more than insecurity. He tends to regard the movie camera rather like a mirror; he preens and parades before it in elaborate self-flattery. At least he does so with *intensity*. In cliched fare like *Eddie And The Cruisers* this is some compensation.

Walter Hill – riding high on the back of *48 Hours* – spotted Paré in the movie and immediately signed him up as the lone hero, Tom Cody, for his *Streets Of Fire* (1984), the first of a prospective Cody trilogy. Like Hill's most typical favoured actors, Nick Nolte and Powers Boothe, Paré presents a tough, physical persona: the trio share an inexpressiveness that is their greatest strength; they are Samsons who must never let down their hair. Unlike Nolte however, Paré has precious little personal charm, sensitivity or acting skill. *Streets Of Fire* was his one shot at the big time, and the film's box-office failure relegated him to a string of hokey B movies, often in the sci-fi genre (*The Philadelphia Experiment* 1984; *Space Rage* 1985; *World Gone Wild* 1988; *Moon 44* 1989). The first of these was the best (and showcased the actor's best performance, as a sailor transported from 1943 to 1984), but by 1989 he was cynically resurrecting the role of Eddie Wilson in *Eddie And The Cruisers 11: Eddie Lives*, despite the character's death in the first film. Michael Paré's career by 1992, had shown no signs of comparable resuscitation.

1983 Eddie And The Cruisers; Undercover **1984** Streets Of Fire; The Philadelphia Experiment **1985** Space Rage; Instant Justice **1987** The Women's Club **1988** World Gone Wild **1989** Moon 44; Eddie And The Cruisers 11: Eddie Lives **1991** Killing Streets; Chasing The Dragon; The Closer **1992** Into The Sun **1992/93** Midnight Heat

Parker, Alan

Director
Born 14 February 1944
London, England

Alan Parker is an important and, in certain quarters, somewhat disliked, director whose films have consistently attracted controversy. Everyone can see that they are powerful and well made, but not everyone approves of their morality. He has been accused of an unconscious racism and gratuitous violence, though he defends himself vigorously against these charges. Since he is a liberal in politics, such accusations must have stung; and there is a way in which it is true that (more perhaps than many Hollywood directors) he is on the side of the angels – or, at least, of the underdog.

Yet his work is rather uneven, so that his films, to be judged fairly, need to be taken individually. There is a recognisable 'Parker style' (or Parker rhetoric) about all of them, of which the only suitable comment is that sometimes it works, and sometimes it doesn't. *Mississippi Burning* (1989), for example, is not racist, but its peripheralising of the Southern blacks in what is, after all, their story, comes in the end to seem like bad taste: a fault of the film's inner construction. On the other hand, a movie like *Angel Heart* (1987), which on the surface is far more exploitative than *Mississippi* in its dabbling with voodoo themes and in its linking of sexuality, evil and blackness, forges in the end a sort of dramatic integrity that impresses. Perhaps it is about dreams and the unconscious and not, primarily, about society.

Might not the same thing be said about *Midnight Express* (1978)? The people who attacked this film claimed that it took a racist view of the Turks, but essentially it was only half about the Turkish prison system. Its 'real' subject was simply fear of otherness, fear of what is different from you – a universal affliction, part and parcel of being human.

Such comments may seem too metaphysical (or too casuistical). Parker is not an intellectual; he is, even, an anti-intellectual director. He has a suspicion of educated fools that issues from his working-class background and the battles he has had to fight to advance himself. His qualities are his sincere passion and (paradoxically) his kindliness – a kindliness that can tip over into sentimentality, for example in *Come See The Paradise* (1990), about ethnic Japanese internees caught up in World War II.

Birdy (1985), too, is sentimental in its glamorising of young Matthew Modine's madness; or rather, in not making a specific enough distinction between what it is like to be mad, and to be not mad. Still, like all Parker's work, the movie has its remarkable sequences (like the Steadicam bird flight over suburban Pittsburgh, an extraordinary visual tour de force).

Shoot The Moon (1982) suffers from a typically violent rhetorical ending (Albert Finney's savaging of his wife's lover's tennis court) but up until that moment it scarcely set a foot wrong. Maybe the least known of Parker's films, it is a subtle and powerful dissection of modern marriage, neither feminist nor anti-feminist, but sympathetic to both sides of the battle, and tremendously convincing in its depiction of the minutiae of bringing up families.

Actually, not the least of Parker's skills is his expertise in directing children. Of his first three films, two – *Bugsy Malone* (1976, a gangster parody) and *Fame* (1980) – have casts made up exclusively of youngsters. These movies share an absolutely beguiling *joie de vivre*, which reached a peak of entertaining, moving and original perfection over a decade later with *The Commitments* (1991). This vibrancy issues from what one is tempted to call Parker's adopted American optimism. He is one of those British directors who are more at home with American subjects than with native ones (*The Commitments* being, perhaps, something of an exception – but then the setting and characters are Irish), for in England he is constrained by class resentment, whereas in the United States (it is part of his liberalism) resentment vanishes in front of the wonderful fact of the melting pot. *Talent* is what counts: this being, in fact, the message of *Fame*, spelt out in varying degrees of explicitness. And he has the right instinct for talent in choosing casts without always falling for star names: Hackman and Willem Dafoe, the young Jodie Foster (*Bugsy*), Mickey Rourke (*Angel Heart*), Peter Weller (Diane Keaton's lover in *Shoot The Moon*), Brad Davis (*Midnight Express*), Frances McDormand (the pivotal sheriff's wife in *Mississippi Burning*).

Yet Parker still likes England and spends time there. One gets the impression that the 1960s, when he worked in London with David Puttnam, were genuinely happy times. From those days in advertising he retains his keen visual sense (Parker's movies, photographed by long-time associates like Michael Serresin and Peter Biziou, are always crisply elegant and look as if the right amount of money has been spent on them); also his ability to build up a scene economically. He is a natural storyteller – an artist– still, perhaps, waiting to make his masterpiece.

1971 Melody (writer only) **1976** Bugsy Malone (w/d) **1978** Midnight Express **1980** Fame **1982** Shoot The Moon **1983** The Wall **1985** Birdy **1987** Angel Heart (w/d) **1989** Mississippi Burning **1990** Come See The Paradise (w/d) **1991** The Commitments

Parton, Dolly

Singer, actress
Born 19 January 1946
Sevierville, Tennessee

When the rather disappointing *Steel Magnolias* (1989) opened, its major drawcard was a line-up of top actresses from the now veteran Shirley MacLaine to newcomer Julia Roberts, plus Oscar-winners Sally Field and Olympia Dukakis. The surprise was Dolly Parton, world-famous country-and-western singer, making only her fourth movie in nine years, in the key role of Truvy, whose hairdressing establishment in a small Southern town is at the heart of the women's lives.

Raised on a farm, Dolly was one of a family of 12 children; she married at 17 and claims the Pentecostal Church as her strongest influence. Given her almost hillbilly background and her musical career, which began on local radio when she was ten, she is something of an oddity in the lexicon of movie stars. Indeed, she herself said: 'They don't hire me to be a great actress, they hire me to do Dolly Parton – and I do a pretty good job.' Her frank and refreshing demeanour is one of her best assets.

Dolly made her screen debut in *Nine To*

Five (1980), teamed with no less than ace comedian-actress Lily Tomlin and major star Jane Fonda, to complete a somewhat unlikely trio of put-upon secretaries who take revenge on their male chauvinist boss. The film was a wildly improbable but not unappealing farce, in which Parton's lack of sophistication, patent acting deficiencies and good-natured ebullience made a large contribution to keeping audiences entertained. Her almost vulgarly abundant vital statistics, musical talents and sassy lack of inhibition fitted perfectly the role of the brothel madame seducing Burt Reynolds in *The Best Little Whorehouse In Texas* (1982). Both these films were, for all their weaknesses, hugely successful at the box office, auguring well for the singer-composer's new career, but it took a nosedive with the dreadful *Rhinestone* two years later. Paired with Sylvester Stallone at his most idiotic, Parton, in effect, played an exaggerated version of herself in outrageous candy-floss hairdo, kitsch cowgirl outfits and dripping jewellery, and was called upon to deliver lines such as 'there are two kinds of people in this world and you ain't one of them'. It was a tribute to her charm that she got away with it. The movie at least offered a terrific country-and-western score composed by none other than Dolly Parton.

Then, in *Steel Magnolias*, she returned after four years absence, looking as young as ever, noticeably slimmer and trimmer, and this time was required to harness her personality to a real character. She did so admirably, making one regret how seldom this true original has been seen on screen, although she has remained as energetic as ever in music halls and recording studios across the country. She was as likeable as ever in *Straight Talk* as a homespun radio phone-in personality, but this Cinderella romance – in which she was teamed with James Woods – was too weak to find favour.

1980 Nine To Five **1982** The Best Little Whorehouse In Texas **1984** Rhinestone **1989** Steel Magnolias **1992** Straight Talk

Pasdar, Adrian

Actor
Born 1965
Philadelphia, Pennsylvania

This young actor with brooding good looks hit the big time on his first attempt, when he auditioned for a role in *Top Gun* (1986) for director Tony Scott. The British director was sufficiently impressed with Adrian Pasdar to add in the character of Chippie, one of the pilots in the film, especially for him. It was certainly an auspicious start, especially for somebody who didn't originally want to be an actor.

Pasdar was an English literature major at the University of Florida, with a talent for football. Sadly, a car accident at the end of his freshman year ended any chance of continuing a sports career and he spent several months recuperating from his injuries. He returned to his home town of Philadelphia, where his father is a heart surgeon, and interned as a technician, building sets at The People's Light Theatre Company. Adrian was hit by bad luck again when his thumb was badly sliced at work, but the disability payments he received funded a move to New York, where, now an aspiring actor, he attended the Lee Strasberg Theater Institute, selling hot dogs on the street on his days off to pay his fees.

It was after he finished at the Institute that he auditioned for *Top Gun*. The part was small, with only a few lines, but it was enough for the actor to make an impression in what proved to be a mega-hit, and to win him a supporting role in *Solarbabies* (1986), a futuristic drama starring Richard Jordan and Jami Gertz that was barely released (probably because it was outdated and daft). Undeterred, he went on to audition successfully for a role in *Streets Of Gold* (1986), starring Klaus Maria Brandauer. He played a young street kid who trains to be a boxer under the tutelage of Russian coach Brandauer, and, although the film was regarded as no more than a rip-off of the *Rocky* saga, Pasdar was praised for his performance.

From here he was given the lead role by up-and-coming director Kathryn Bigelow in her distinctive and off-beat film *Near Dark* (1987). This story about Caleb (Pasdar), a young cowboy who falls in love with Mae (Jenny Wright) not knowing she is a vampire until after she has bitten him, became a cult classic, highly praised by critics who recognised not only the director, but her leading man as a talent to watch. His sultry good looks and strong screen presence were perfect for the role of the confused hick who is reluctant to drink blood and kill in order to survive, and the Western-vampire love story gave his career lift-off. A part in *Made In The USA* (1988) followed, and then a supporting role in the Susan Seidelman comedy *Cookie* (1989), starring Emily Lloyd and Peter Falk.

The tale of a Mafia boss trying to go straight with the help of his daughter was not a great success, but Adrian, as the stubborn Mafia chauffeur, came off well.

The actor then appeared in a string of theatre productions, most notably Tennessee Williams' classic *The Glass Menagerie*, and two TV movies, the avant-garde piece *Big Time* for American Playhouse Productions in 1989, and the well-received *The Lost Capone*, in which he played the brother of Al Capone who left the family and became a marshal in Nebraska. Pasdar also spent time in Paris during 1990, writing a screenplay based on the novel *Ask The Dust* by John Fante, which was optioned on his return to the USA. Then it was back to Hollywood, first as a medical student in the comedy-drama *Vital Signs* (1990) with Jimmy Smits and Diane Lane, and then in the Israeli romance-drama *Torn Apart* with Cecilia Peck, the same year.

1986 Top Gun; Solarbabies; Streets Of Gold **1987** Near Dark **1988** Made In The USA **1989** Cookie **1990** Vital Signs; Torn Apart aka Forbidden Love **1992** Just Like A Woman (GB) **1992/93** Grey Night

Patinkin, Mandy

Actor
Born 30 November 1952
Chicago, Illinois

Dark, muscular and possessed of a glorious singing voice, Mandy Patinkin has entranced Broadway audiences, to whom he is particularly notable as an interpreter of Stephen Sondheim – memorably in the title role of *Sunday In The Park With George*. Vibrant on screen, he has contributed a significant presence in several fine films, but few that took the fancy of a wide audience.

Educated at the University of Kansas, Patinkin trained in drama and music at New York's Juilliard, played extensively in regional theatre and has appeared at the late Joseph Papp's Public Theatre in the New York Shakespeare Festival. He made his film debut – flitting by as a swimming-pool cleaner – in the Richard Dreyfuss vehicle *The Big Fix* (1978) and popped up again in Jonathan Demme's *Last Embrace* (1979). What should have been his big break – as the Jewish immigrant and street artist who rises to riches as a film director in Milos Forman's screen version of E. L. Doctorow's *Ragtime* (1981) – amounted to little when the kaleidoscopic story was narrowed to one central plot with Patinkin's robust character shunted to the periphery. Sidney Lumet's *Daniel* (1983), an adaptation of another Doctorow novel showed what he was capable of in a powerful performance as a committed left-wing activist whose 'sins' are visited upon his children, and Patinkin was chosen by Barbra Streisand as a suitable object for her affections in *Yentl* (1983).

While he was deft in an old-fashioned screwball comedy *Maxie* (1985), Patinkin has attracted most attention to date with two of his unlikelier roles. He was terrific as a weird-looking alien partnered with human 'buddy' James Caan in the sci-fi cop thriller *Alien Nation* (1988) and a hammy delight as the moustachioed, swashbuckling Spanish swordsman in Rob Reiner's *The Princess Bride* (1988). Even less recognisable in *Dick Tracy* (1990), Patinkin then opted to make his British stage debut, in Peter Hall's ill-fated 1990 production of a musical version of Ionesco's *Rhinoceros* at Chichester, before reminding movie audiences of his wonderful screen presence in *Impromptu* – well-received but, alas, another for a minority following.

1978 The Big Fix **1979** Last Embrace; French Postcards **1980** Night Of The Juggler **1981** Ragtime **1983** Daniel; Yentl **1985** Maxie **1988** The House On Carroll Street; Alien Nation; The Princess Bride **1990** Dick Tracy **1991** Impromptu

Patric, Jason

Actor
Born 1966
Queens, New York

His grandfather is Jackie Gleason, his father is playwright Jason Miller, but Jason Patric is not the kind of actor who beats his own drum. He's a prodigious reader and a budding writer who rarely gives interviews and states that he dislikes talking about himself ('The truest you're ever going to see an actor is right on screen.') The clichéd sobriquet, tall, dark, and handsome, is entirely accurate for Patric, who looks not unlike a young Warren Beatty, albeit slightly coarser-grained and, who has, to date, displayed much promise in his still relatively brief film career.

Patric, who once remained voluntarily unemployed for a year-and-a-half because he said he couldn't find a 'worthy' project at the time, spices his portrayals with surprises, breathing life into characters with little, unexpected details which highlight them. In *After Dark, My Sweet* (1990), for example, a *film noir* directed by James Foley from the novel by the legendary crime writer Jim Thompson, Patric portrays 'Kid' Collins, an ex-boxer of ambiguous, childlike simplicity who is drawn into a dark web of passion and crime. He brings a heightened realism to the role, displaying a convincing naiveté that conceals a sophisticated relationship with violence. It's an attractive and compelling performance.

A native New Yorker, Jason Patric moved to Los Angeles at the age of 16, and gained valuable experience on stage and TV before his debut appearance in Mel Brooks' dreadful *Solarbabies* (1986), which was nothing more than a poor if lavish teen take-off of *Mad Max* (1979). The experience of *Solarbabies* was so disappointing that Patric refuses to discuss the film, and it is little wonder that his official debut is often listed as Joel Schumacher's cult hit *The Lost Boys* (1987), in which the actor rose above the fundamental nonsense of the screenplay to convince as a healthy, hunky young man infected with vampirism in a small Californian town. This was followed by a sensitive portrayal of a young Russian soldier seeing duty in Afghanistan in Kevin Reynolds' *The Beast* (1988), a sharp contrast to his even-handed Lord Byron in Roger Corman's *Frankenstein Unbound* (1990) and the moody danger of 'Kid' Collins, the same year.

It was clear from the diversity and quality of Patric's first performances that he had yet to tap the full depth of his talents, but *Rush* (1991), a drug drama directed by Lili Fini Zanuck, gave him the opportunity, and he seized it with conviction.

1986 Solarbabies aka Solar Warriors **1987** The Lost Boys **1988** The Beast; Loon **1990** Frankenstein Unbound; After Dark, My Sweet **1991** Rush

Patton, Will

Actor

Born 14 June 1954

Charleston, South Carolina

A strong, impressive actor, Will Patton has done consistently high calibre work on film and on the stage. The eldest son of a Lutheran minister, he attended the North Carolina School of the Arts, then made his way to New York, where he studied with Lee Strasberg at the Actors' Studio and Joseph Chaikin at the Open Theatre, and was soon winning parts on and off Broadway: *Kingdom Of Earth* 1976, *Heaven And Earth* 1977, *Scenes From Country Life* 1978. He won a best actor Obie for *Tourists And Refugees 2*, and again in 1982 for Sam Shepard's *Fool For Love*. He starred in another Shepard play, *A Lie Of The Mind*, at London's Royal Court theatre, and he was a member of the Winter Project, an experimental theatre group in New York.

Patton also appeared in the soap operas *Search For Tomorrow* and *Ryan's Hope* and the short underground film *Minus Zero* (1979), and in the early 80s he began to get parts from the New York independents, in *The Third Person* (1981), *King Blank* (1983), and *Variety* (1983). From here it was not a big leap to Susan Seidelman's *Desperately Seeking Susan* (1985) and, the same year, Martin Scorsese's *After Hours*. Seidelman was the first to exploit Patton's potential for menace. A tall, thick-jawed man, his hair is blonde almost to the point of white. He is a most convincing heavy. In *Susan* he is the mob assassin who mistakes Rosanna Arquette for Madonna. In *After Hours* he is Horse, Linda Fiorentino's leather-and-chains boyfriend. Other films have yielded similar supporting parts, sometimes with a comic edge (*Stars And Bars*, 1988), but he has not been lucky in his projects. Patton is likely to be best remembered for his chilling homosexual villain, Scott Pritchard, Gene Hackman's dedicated aide in the superior thriller *No Way Out* (1987).

1981 The Third Person **1983** King Blank; Variety; Silkwood **1984** Chinese Boxes **1985** Desperately Seeking Susan; After Hours **1986** Belizaire The Cajun **1987** No Way Out **1988** Stars And Bars; Wildfire **1989** Signs Of Life **1990** Everybody Wins; A Shock To The System **1991** The Rapture **1992** Cold Heaven; The Paint Job

Peck, Gregory

(Eldred Gregory Peck)

Actor

Born 5 April 1916

La Jolla, California

The liberal conscience of American cinema (and consequently 'former friend' of Ronald Reagan) and one of the most sincere and downright decent leading men in the movies, Gregory Peck has had little to do in the slap bang wallop have it all ways youth cinema of the 80s, making only three films in the entire decade, but with the move away from product to more human stories he seemed to find a reason to go back to work in the early 90s.

Having served his apprenticeship in regional theatre and making an impressive Broadway debut in 1942, the spinal injury that kept him out of the armed forces proved a boon to his career as Hollywood seized upon the tall, upright and handsome actor as a replacement for their many absent stars and, thanks to the war, he found himself a popular romantic leading man from the start of his screen career. Likeable, honest and above all believable, he proved an ideal hero, particularly in strong dramas such as *Gentleman's Agreement* (1947) and *Twelve O'Clock High* (1949) that allowed him to wear his heart on his sleeve without slipping into sermonising, as well as showing a more romantic side that graduated from respectfully courting runaway princess Audrey Hepburn in *Roman Holiday* (1953) and Sophia Loren in *Arabesque* (1966), to a slightly dubious relationship with Tuesday Weld in *I Walk The Line* – and roguishly stealing a sigh from Jane Fonda in *Old Gringo* (1989).

But his inherent decency sometimes proved a straitjacket, with villainous roles being few and far between – *Duel In The Sun* (1946) and his over-the-top but interesting Joseph Mengele in *The Boys From Brazil* (1978) being his most notable – while the shadow of doubt over his possible murderer in *Spellbound* (1945) suffered from his image as the nicest guy in Hollywood (although in his autobiography he did surprisingly admit to attacking a nurse when prescribed morphine). There were accomplished portraits of darker characters, such as his weary *Gunfighter* (1950) doomed by his reputation and his highly under-rated performance as the obsessed Captain Ahab in *Moby Dick* (1956) that was like a determined hymn to damnation, but Peck is most firmly fixed in the memory as his Oscar-winning lawyer Atticus Finch in *To Kill A Mockingbird* (1962) – solid, dependable, kind hearted, the kind of father everybody wishes they had had.

His career began to slow down in the late 60s and 70s as he became more active in charitable and political causes, as well as serving as President of the Academy of Motion Picture Arts and Sciences between 1967 and 1970. It became apparent that Hollywood was not entirely sure what to do with the ageing star (who briefly turned his hand to producing with *The Trial Of The Catonsville Nine*, 1972, and *The Dove*, 1974), even after his strong performance in *The Omen* (1976) was instrumental in elevating the satanic thriller into a quality film (and one of his biggest box-office successes). After a few less-than-successful films and some television work he seemed content to rest on his laurels rather than succumb to the old movie stars' disease of working just for the sake of it (cf Charlton Heston), although he did venture out to play the President in the anti-nuclear fantasy *Amazing Grace And Chuck* (1987) – 'a nice idea that just didn't work'.

He seemed likely to disappear again until landing at the last minute the role of writer Ambrose Bierce, journeying to Mexico to die a glorious death in the revolution in *Old Gringo* (1989). Although it was hard at times not to imagine Burt Lancaster in the role (he was ousted from the film when the producers could not get him insured; ever the gentleman, Peck would not take the role without Lancaster's blessing first), Peck made it what at first appeared to be a fitting epilogue to his career, albeit in an unworthy film. Drawing both on his own Western film heritage and the darker side of the man himself, and looking for a kind of redemption for a failed life through a meaningful death, he instilled each action with the sense of a man doing everything for the last time in a farewell to life. Surprisingly, the film proved not the end of the trail but a calling card for new work, with a prominent role in the satire *Other People's Money* (1991) and a somewhat embarrassing cameo alongside his more controlled 1962 co-star Robert Mitchum in Martin Scorsese's 1991 remake of the nightmarish 1962 revenge thriller *Cape Fear*, which had starred the two now veteran actors.

1944 Days Of Glory; The Keys Of The Kingdom **1945** The Valley Of Decision; Spellbound **1946** The Yearling; Duel In The Sun **1947** The Macomber Affair; Gentleman's Agreement **1948** The Paradine Case; Yellow Sky **1949** The Great Sinner; Twelve O'Clock High **1950** The Gunfighter **1951** Only The Valiant; David And Bathsheba; Captain Horatio Hornblower **1952** The Snows Of Kilimanjaro; The World In His Arms **1953** Roman Holiday **1954** Night People; The Million Pound Note aka Man With A Million; The Purple Plain **1956** The Man In The Gray Flannel Suit; Moby Dick **1957** Designing Woman **1958** The Bravados; The Big Country **1959** Pork Chop Hill; Beloved Infidel; On The Beach **1960** The Guns Of Navarone **1962** To Kill A Mockingbird; Cape Fear; How The West Was Won **1963** Captain Newman, MD **1964** Behold A Pale Horse **1965** Mirage; **1966** Arabesque **1969** The Stalking Moon; Mackenna's Gold; The Chairman aka The Most Dangerous Man In The World; Marooned **1970** I Walk The Line **1971** Shoot Out **1973** Billy Two Hats **1976** The Omen **1977** MacArthur aka MacArthur: The Rebel

General **1978** The Boys From Brazil **1980** The Sea Wolves **1987** Amazing Grace And Chuck aka Silent Voice **1989** Old Gringo **1991** Cape Fear; Other People's Money **1992** Painting Churches

Peckinpah, Sam

Director
Born 21 February 1925
Fresno, California
Died 28 December 1984

Born and brought up on a ranch in California Sam Peckinpah attended military school and had a spell in the Marines. His films reflected his background a masculine world where one's manhood and independence can only survive through violence. Hence the nostalgia for the 'Old West' where men were men and women were nowhere. No matter how unpalatable one may find this philosophy he expressed it with passionate intensity.

In the late 50s he established himself as a writer and director on classic Western TV series such as *Gunsmoke* and *The Rifleman* and the majority of his films were Westerns the last gasps of a dying genre. The recurring theme of 'unchanged men in a changing land' first appears in *Ride The High Country* (1962) with Randolph Scott and Joel McCrea as ageing gunfighters escorting a cargo of gold to the bank but the movie had more to do with the Old Western than the Old West. William Holden and his gang in *The Wild Bunch* (1969) in 1914 try to live as outlaws from another age although the scenes of carnage reflect the year the film was made particularly its final and famously bloody slow-motion climax. *The Ballad Of Cable Hogue* (1970) was another elegy for the West and Steve McQueen who tries to scrape a living as a rodeo rider in *Junior Bonner* (1972) rather touchingly feels an anachronism (like the director?) in the new-style West.

Peckinpah's Westerns splattered with symbols and blood do have a lyrical disenchantment. Sadly with the decline of the genre the director had to venture into areas in which he had less interest and his blood-dimmed vision lacked conviction away from the controlling mythology of the West. It is at its most unpleasant in *Straw Dogs* (1971) where the man of reason (Dustin Hoffman) is forced into violence against those who raped his wife (Susan George) exulting in the eye-for-an-eye slaughter with the complicity of the director and audience.

The Killer Elite (1975) which had a hollow complex script involving buddies James Caan and Robert Duvall on opposite sides of the law and *Convoy* (1978) one long expensive (it cost $11 million) pretentious chase on wheels through three states with Kris Kristofferson as the pursued and Ernest Borgnine the pursuer were raised above average by the director's flair for action and the creation of a claustrophobic world shorn of illusion.

Despite indiscriminate violence and too much lingering camerawork in *Bring Me The Head Of Alfredo Garcia* (1974) the Mexican backgrounds were vivid and there were effective blackly humorous sequences including one in which Warren Oates as a bounty hunter having carried out the imperative of the title has a conversation with Garcia's fly-covered decapitated head rolling around in the back of his car.

Ironically as much violence was done to Peckinpah's films as to his characters and throughout his career the director continued a running battle with producers and film companies whom he saw as the bad guys. Among the worst victims of manhandling by the studios were *Major Dundee* (1965) a rugged lengthy Western starring granite-faced Charlton Heston as a Cavalry officer pursuing Indians and *Pat Garrett And Billy The Kid* (1973) with James Coburn pursuing Kris Kristofferson.

His somewhat untimely death certainly robbed Hollywood of a colourful if controversial and inconsistent film-maker who whatever the results was always his own man.

As director only unless stated otherwise: **1956** Invasion Of The Body Snatchers (co-writer and actor only) **1961** The Deadly Companions; Ride The High Country (GB: Guns In The Afternoon) **1964** Major Dundee (also co-writer) **1965** The Glory Guys (writer only) **1969** The Wild Bunch (also co-writer) **1970** The Ballad Of Cable Hogue **1971** Straw Dogs (also co-writer) **1972** Junior Bonner; The Getaway **1973** Pat Garrett And Billy The Kid **1974** Bring Me The Head Of Alfredo Garcia (also co-writer) **1975** The Killer Elite **1977** Cross Of Iron **1978** Convoy **1983** The Osterman Weekend

Penn, Arthur

Director
Born 27 September 1922
Philadelphia, Illinois

In the 60s, Arthur Penn's strong sympathy with the outsider and his anti-Establishment stance struck a chord with the anti-draft, anti-Vietnam War, middle-class college students. However, since those heady days of revolt, his scanty film work has failed to gain much attention.

Penn, who was trained in watchmaking, his father's trade, was drawn to the theatre at an early age. After World War II service, he formed theatre groups and studied acting with Michael Chekhov, the nephew of the Russian playwright. It was not long before Penn was directing for TV and on Broadway. Among his successes were two plays by William Gibson, *Two For The Seesaw* (1958) and *The Miracle Worker* (1959), both with Anne Bancroft. The 1962 film version of the latter offered a vivid record of the stage performances of Bancroft and Patty Duke as teacher Annie Sullivan and Helen Keller, her blind, deaf and dumb pupil. The fascinating and moving study of the efforts to 'disinter the soul' of the child, gradually giving her the ability to communicate, came across strongly under Penn's direction.

But his career as a film director suffered a few setbacks – he was removed from *The Train* (1963) after a few days, and *Mickey One* (1965), a self-consciously arty study of paranoia with Warren Beatty as a night-club singer, received mostly hostile reviews. *The Chase* (1966), with Marlon Brando's fair-minded sheriff trying to stop the inhabitants of a small Texas town from lynching Robert Redford, prefigured, in its plodding way, the law/outlaw theme in *Bonnie And Clyde* (1967), one of the most influential movies of the last four decades. This was due to the film's amoral attitude to 'the outlaw' as seen from a modern psychological and social viewpoint, its meticulous re-creation of the Depression era, the playing of Warren Beatty and Faye Dunaway in the title roles, and Penn's controlled direction of a bloody tale that moves from black comedy ineluctably towards the much imitated ending – hundreds of bullets pumping into the miscreant pair who die in controversially glamorous slow motion.

The Depression is referred to in Woody Guthrie's songs heard in *Alice's Restaurant* (1969), in which Arlo Guthrie (Woody's son) played himself at a hippy haven of all-embracing love. The film's ballad form and improvisational technique, mixing fact and fiction, satire, whimsy and social comment, reflected the free-flowing lifestyle of the characters, and it was one of the first Hollywood products to express the draft-dodging feeling among the young.

Little Big Man (1970) consciously viewed the past from a modern standpoint, seeing the Cheyenne as 'ethnic' hippies contrasted with the brutality of white civilisation, and Custer's raid on an Indian village echoed the massacre by American troops at Mai Lai during the Vietnam war. But this rambling Western, starring Dustin Hoffman, shifted uneasily between broad comedy and epic tragedy. The process of the demystification of Western legends such as Custer had already begun in Penn's first feature, *The Left-Handed Gun* (1958), where Paul Newman played a crazy mixed-up Billy the Kid with Method mannerisms.

In another Western, the muddled *The Missouri Breaks* (1976), Brando proceeded to make Penn pander to his every whim, which included simulating an Irish accent and romping around outrageously in granny drag. Jack Nicholson seemed somewhat bemused opposite him as the ringleader of a gang of rustlers Brando has been hired to eliminate. This hot property turned into a cold turkey.

Gene Hackman, who had played Beatty's brother in *Bonnie And Clyde*, made a couple more movies with Penn: *Night Moves* (1975), a complicated but intriguing Post-Watergate thriller, and *Target* (1985), a rather conventional espionage yarn. Among the director's less successful efforts in the 80s were *Four Friends* (1982), a platitudinous portrait of those Significant 60s, and *Dead Of Winter* (1986), an old-fashioned piece of Gothic hokum. The start of the 90s saw Arthur Penn still searching for a vehicle that would return him to the forefront of American directors, a position he occupied for only a short period.

1958 The Left-Handed Gun **1962** The Miracle Worker **1965** Mickey One **1966** The Chase **1967** Bonnie And Clyde **1969** Alice's Restaurant **1970** Little Big Man **1973** Visions Of Eight (episode) **1975** Night Moves **1976** The Missouri Breaks **1982** Four Friends **1985** Target **1987** Dead Of Winter **1989** Penn And Teller Get Killed

Penn, Christopher

Actor

Born 1967

Los Angeles, California

Christopher Penn has attracted neither the intense admiration nor the flak his brother cannot seem to avoid. He resembles a beefier, heavier Sean, but his features are less striking and he has not shown the flashes of brilliance that distinguish even the more hamfisted efforts of the more notorious Penn.

From the age of 12, Christopher studied acting with his father, director Leo Penn, though he was also a keen athlete; his training in wrestling and karate led eventually to five professional fights as a boxer and a kick-boxer. At Santa Monica high school he became interested in the Vietnam War and wrote, directed and appeared in a Super 8 film inspired by his research, *Nobody's Heroes*. Acting lessons with Peggy Feury led to his debut in Francis Ford Coppola's *Rumblefish* (1983), soon followed by *All The Right Moves* (1983), with Tom Cruise. His role was more central in the hit musical *Footloose* (1984), in which Kevin Bacon memorably taught him to dance, but his star turn in *The Wild Life* (1984) proved to be nothing more than a shallow clone of Sean's stoned surfer in *Fast Times At Ridgemont High* (1982). Christopher looked like a follower, not a leader as was indicated by his strictly supporting role as Sean's on-screen brother in James Foley's *At Close Range* (1986). He seemed oddly distant, even disinterested, in the intense Oedipal drama going on around him. He was more at home in the action roles offered by *Pale Rider* (1985), *Return From The River Kwai* (1989) and *Best Of The Best* (1989) – in which he played karate champion Travis Brickley (in homage to the Penns' revered De Niro perhaps?).

1983 Rumblefish; All The Right Moves **1984** Footloose; The Wild Life **1985** Pale Rider **1986** At Close Range **1988** Made In USA **1989** Return From The River Kwai; Best Of The Best **1991** Mobsters: The Evil Empire **1992** The Pickle; Reservoir Dogs

Penn, Sean

Actor
Born 17 August 1960
Santa Monica, California

It is difficult to pinpoint or analyse the appeal of Sean Penn, who is best summed up in the title of the first movie in which he played a lead, *Bad Boys* (1983). For a time during the mid-1980s, he was as famous (or infamous) for his off-screen exploits as bar-room brawler and husband of Madonna as for the gallery of morally questionable youths he portrayed in a variety of movies. Stocky, verging on the bandy-legged, and possessed of a rough-hewn and irregular physiognomy that calls to mind the boxing ring, Penn created a succession of assorted outsiders and rebels, from the humorous semi-dropout ordering in pizza deliveries to the classroom in *Fast Times At Ridgemont High* (1982), through the violent delinquent of *Bad Boys*, to the professional drug-dealer abandoning his respectable origins in John Schlesinger's *The Falcon And The Snowman* (1985).

In spite of his image, however, Penn has a genuinely commanding screen presence and an unexpected degree of evident charm. Not that there was anything charming about his brutal sergeant, masterminding rape and murder in De Palma's *Casualties Of War* (1989), a substantial role which demonstrated that the dispossessed teenager had conclusively graduated to disturbed adulthood. Before that, in *At Close Range* (1986), his portrait of an aimless youngster betrayed by his psychopathically criminal father (a chilling Christopher Walken) and redeemed by his coming to terms with truth, was a sympathetic and complex undertaking which touched a hidden layer in his skewed persona.

He was born into the profession – his father Leo is a director, his mother is actress Eileen Ryan – and was drawn to acting early on. After graduating from Santa Monica High School, he spent two years with the Los Angeles Group Repertory Theatre as a general backstage dogsbody, as well as making a couple of minor appearances and directing a one-act play. He then took acting lessons and broke into television with a small part in an episode of the series *Barnaby Jones*. Several more small roles followed before the young actor crossed the coast to New York and found work on the Broadway stage. He made his movie debut as Timothy Hutton's room-mate in *Taps* (1981), set in a military academy and, although his film career advanced rapidly (overcoming a couple of disasters such as the 1986 *Shanghai Surprise* which co-starred him with his then wife, Madonna), he has continued to work on stage in both New York and LA.

An actor of natural ease, Penn displays a confidence in the dubious characters who are his stock-in-trade which is, quite simply, fascinating to watch. His foray into adult comedy – he was an escaped convict masquerading as a priest with his friend Robert De Niro in the mediocre *We're No Angels* (1990) – did nothing to enhance his career, but he displayed unflagging good humour throughout. By the end of the 1980s, Sean Penn, like several of his contemporaries, had decided to broaden his career into writing and directing. His first effort, *Indian Runner*, was an honourable one, if not a great success; but his claim to originality as a performer in contemporary Hollywood was well established.

1981 Taps **1982** Fast Times At Ridgemont High **1983** Bad Boys **1984** Crackers; Racing With The Moon **1985** The Falcon And The Snowman **1986** At Close Range; Shanghai Surprise **1988** Colors; Judgement In Berlin **1989** Casualties Of War **1990** We're No Angels; State Of Grace **1991** Indian Runner (w/d)

Perkins, Elizabeth

Actress
Born 18 November 1960
Queens, New York

Although born in Queens, Elizabeth Perkins enjoyed a comfortable New England upbringing in Vermont. She headed for Chicago and the Goodman School of Drama for her acting studies, then went to New York City where she was engaged almost immediately to join the national touring company of Neil Simon's *Brighton Beach Memoirs*. This was followed by theatre seasons both on and off-Broadway, and some Shakespeare in Central Park, before making her movie debut in *About Last Night* (1986).

She played a large supporting role as Demi Moore's best friend, an abrasive character with a chip on her shoulder, and delivered the goods with fidelity to the script and no false concessions to charm. The movie itself, although adapted from a David Mamet play, got stuck in the middle rung of the college graduate market, and it was not until Penny Marshall's *Big* (1988), in which Perkins was the immaculate New York executive who falls in love with Tom Hanks' boy-in-a-man's-body, that she made a solid impression, undamaged by the deadly *Sweethearts Dance* (1988), in which she was the only thing worth watching.

Elizabeth Perkins is a useful addition to her age group. She has an appearance of neatness which is reflected in her crisp acting style, but also exhibits a spirited quality which can be turned to comedic purposes and her slow start in movies began to accelerate from 1990 and to include work with the upper echelons of the industry. She was excellent as Aidan Quinn's wife in Barry Levinson's semi-autobiographical saga of Jewish life, *Avalon* (1990), but failed to benefit from a cracking lead in *Over Her Dead Body* (1991). As the ditzy peroxide-blonde, smalltown girl attempting to dispose of her sister's corpse, she was barely off the screen and displayed a new versatility which went for nought in the face of a truly awful film, but she co-starred to good effect with Kevin Bacon in *He Said, She Said* later the same year.

1986 About Last Night **1987** From The Hip **1988** Big; Sweethearts Dance **1990** Love At Large; Avalon **1991** Over Her Dead Body aka Enid Is Sleeping; He Said, She Said; The Doctor; Nothing But Trouble **1993** Tamakwa

Perrine, Valerie

Actress
Born 3 September 1944
Galveston, Texas

In 1974, in her third movie, Valerie Perrine made a Big Impression. Cast opposite Dustin Hoffman in *Lenny*, the biopic of comedian Lenny Bruce, she played Honey Harlowe, the stripper who became Bruce's wife, and remained loyal and loving in the face of doom. It was a heart-melting performance which won the actress a deserved Oscar nomination, and she seemed set for big things. Alas, the gorgeous and talented Perrine, in the event, became one of the many tipped for stardom who somehow never make it, being denied the opportunities to shine. During the 1970s, casting directors tended to choose her for her figure first and her intelligence second. Nonetheless, she breathed life – sexy, sweet, and sometimes scatty – into a number of characters that might easily have remained two-dimensional.

The daughter of an army officer and a showgirl, Perrine grew up in overseas army posts before attending both Arizona and Nevada universities with the intention of becoming a psychologist. Tall and well-proportioned, she had no trouble finding work as a topless showgirl in Las Vegas. After all, it was the 60s and dropping out was the thing to do – as were drugs and suchlike – all of which the lissom Perrine sampled, only to find herself on welfare in LA before winning her first film role in *Slaughterhouse Five* (1972), George Roy Hill's feature based on the Kurt Vonnegut novel. Since *Lenny*, however, the best roles in both television and feature films seem to have eluded this actress. Her role as Lex Luther's glamorous sidekick in both *Superman* (1978) and *Superman II* (1980) was a particular waste of her talents, but a pivotal (if scant) part as a materialistic wife in *The Border* (1981) gave her a chance to shine alongside Jack Nicholson; she was prominent in the satirical *Water* (1986) with

Michael Caine, but the movie bombed, and she shone in *Maid To Order* (1987), clearly enjoying herself as a vulgar wife whose maid (Ally Sheedy) is actually a poor little rich girl. Once again, however, the movie, though a pleasing enough entertainment, made barely a ripple, leaving Perrine's future hanging in the balance.

1972 Slaughterhouse Five **1973** The Last American Hero **1974** Lenny **1976** W.C. Fields And Me **1977** Mr Billion aka The Windfall **1978** Superman **1979** Agency; The Magician Of Lublin; The Electric Horseman **1980** Can't Stop The Music; Superman II **1983** The Border **1986** Water **1987** Maid To Order **1990** Bright Angel **1991** Riflessi In Un Cielo Scuro/Reflections In A Dark Sky (Italy) **1992** Diary Of A Hit Man

Pesci, Joe

Actor
Born 9 February 1943
Newark, New Jersey

Joe Pesci's Best Supporting Actor Oscar for his performance in *GoodFellas* (1990) was most appropriately awarded for his work for director Martin Scorsese. For although Pesci might as reasonably have been recognised for other outstanding characterisations, it was Scorsese who delivered him from obscurity and got his film career on a firm footing with a strong role in one of the most outstanding films of the last decade, *Raging Bull* (1980).

Pesci, who was born in New Jersey but raised in the Bronx, New York, was a child actor who first tasted celebrity at the age of four, showcased on the radio programme *Star Time Kids*. The son of a musician and singer, Pesci was encouraged by his father, who provided the boy with singing and acting lessons. As a grown-up, however, the young Pesci couldn't even get arrested, and after a disappointing period in Los Angeles unable to obtain acting work he turned his hand to a number of jobs, including ditch digging and doing heavy labour for a mason in Las Vegas. A sometime composer and record producer, in his 30s Joe was back in the Bronx managing an Italian restaurant.

In 1975 Pesci finally made his film debut in a stinker about petty hoods entitled *Death Collector*. Pesci as – what else but? – one of the Italian-American tough guys, was a standout, though, and interested one of the few people who saw it – Martin Scorsese. Five years later Scorsese cast Pesci opposite Robert De Niro as boxer Jake La Motta's loyal brother Joey, a role that brought him awards from the New York Film Critics and the National Society of Film Critics, and Golden Globe and Oscar nominations.

Variable films followed steadily, from Nic Roeg's odd *Eureka* (1981) to the amiable Rodney Dangerfield comedy *Easy Money* (1983) and the Sergio Leone masterpiece *Once Upon A Time In America* (1984), and the actor was consistently first rate. But he really came into his own in 1989 with a sensationally funny performance as the manically irritating crooked accountant placed under the not-very-reassuring 'protection' of Mel Gibson's wacko cop Martin Riggs in *Lethal Weapon 2*; since when he has distinguished each film he's done with high visibility and wholly appropriate support. Contrasting sharply with the brilliance of his foul-mouthed, explosive psychopath Tommy De Vito in *GoodFellas* (1990), Joe Pesci proved adept at slapstick as the malevolent pratfalling gnome of a burglar in *Home Alone* (1990), affirming that his lack of height belies his acting stature which revealed yet another dimension in JFK.

1975 Death Collector aka Family Enforcer **1980** Don't Go In The House; Raging Bull **1981** Eureka **1982** I'm Dancing As Fast As I Can **1983** Dear Mr. Wonderful; Easy Money **1984** Tutti Dentro aka Put 'Em All In Jail'; Once Upon A Time In America **1987** Man On Fire **1989** Lethal Weapon 2 **1990** GoodFellas; Betsy's Wedding; Catchfire aka Backtrack; Home Alone **1991** The Super **1991** JFK **1992** My Cousin Vinny; Lethal Weapon 3; Home Alone 2: Lost In New York

Peters, Bernadette (Bernadette Lazzara)

Actress, singer
Born 28 February 1948
Queens, New York City

A star of Broadway and Las Vegas, the multi-talented Bernadette Peters has not managed to carve a comparable niche for herself on the big screen.

Born into an Italian-American family – her father was a bread-truck driver – Peters (she assumed her stage name at the age of ten) followed the all-too-familiar path of the daughter of an avid stage mother: tap dancing and singing lessons long before she could read or write, followed shortly after by successful appearances on television talent shows. At only 11 years of age, her marked precocity led to her Broadway debut in *The Most Happy Fella*; two years later, she was touring as Baby June in the musical *Gypsy*.

However, once she reached adolescence, Peters abandoned the stage in favour of the more low-key life as a student at Quintano's School for Young Professionals in New York.

But by the age of 19, the actress was back treading – and tapping – the boards and quickly established herself as a Broadway musical favourite in such productions as *Curley McDimple* and *Dames at Sea*. Her 1973 film debut in the muddled, troubled Spielberg story *Ace Eli And Rodger of the Skies* was unremarkable and the riotous football antics of Burt Reynolds and co hogged centre field in her next venture, *The Longest Yard* (1974). It wasn't until 1979's *The Jerk* that the kooky charm of Peters, with her kewpie-doll-like features, O-shaped mouth and head of corkscrew curls, was given full display. In the uneven Carl Reiner cult comedy, the actress, playing an innocent cosmetologist, more than held her own against the manic antics of star Steve Martin (with whom she had a live-in relationship) and it was no surprise that the following year she became a highly-in-demand leading lady. However, the three films she made back-to-back during that period (all 1981) proved unmitigated disasters – *Tulips* because it was a substandard romance; *Heartbeeps* because its premise was two robots (Peters being one of them) falling in love; and *Pennies From Heaven*, again co-starring Steve Martin, because it was (undeservedly) poorly received by the critics and cold-shouldered by a public unwilling to see a favourite funny man as anything other than a jerk. A terrible pity for a film with some remarkable features, not least of which is a moving performance from Peters, as the teacher who is 'wronged' by Martin's travelling salesman.

Thereafter, with the exception of the expensive musical failure *Annie* (1982), the actress took a seven-year break from the movies, concentrating instead on TV appearances, night-club acts and ever-increasing success on Broadway: she stole the show in two Sondheim musicals, *Sunday In The Park With George* and *Into the Woods*, played a famous Peter Pan, and won a Tony Award for her star turn in Andrew Lloyd Webber's *Song And Dance*. Her return to motion pictures in the late 80s was a mixed blessing; although her off-beat presence was a pleasure to behold once again on screen, she was one of the very few good points about either *Slaves of New York* or *Pink Cadillac* (both 1989). She entered the 90s in a supporting role in the period piece *Impromptu* (1991), the debut feature from her *Sunday In The Park With George* director, James Lapine, and with every indication that cinema was likely to remain an occasional rather than continuous occupation for this busy and successful musical actress.

1973 Ace Eli And Rodger of the Skies **1974** The Longest Yard (GB: The Mean Machine) **1976** Silent Movie; W.C. Fields and Me; Vigilante Force **1979** The Jerk **1981** Pennies From Heaven; Tulips; Heartbeeps **1982** Annie **1989** Slaves of New York; Pink Cadillac **1990** Alice (cameo) **1991** Impromptu

Petersen, William
(sometimes William L.)
Actor
Born 1953
Chicago, Illinois

Despite some impressive work, William Petersen has not seen his career develop in the interesting avenues his earlier films suggested – partially due to a tendency, despite alternating keys with each role, to play characters with one note. Active in theatre in his native Chicago, Petersen helped found the now well-established Remains Theatre Group and chalked up a substantial body of stage work – setting up a company with John Malkovich in 1986 – that accounts for the sparsity of his film performances.

His first shot at big screen fame, as an obsessive government agent in William Friedkin's *To Live And Die In LA* (1985), was not a success, with the film stolen from under his nose by Willem Dafoe's demonic forger, but he sufficiently impressed Michael Mann (for whom Petersen had made his screen debut with a small role in *Thief*, 1981) to give him the considerably more important role of Will Graham in *Manhunter* (1986). Playing the cop with the mind of a psychopath, who is terrified of becoming one of the serial killers he reluctantly tracks down, he impressed as a man who has seen far too much of hell to forget and lead the normal life he longs for. Again, the film was stolen from him (this time by Brian Cox's blithe mass murderer), but it was still a memorable portrait of sustained angst.

The blandness of his father in *Amazing Grace And Chuck* (1987) was offset by his chronically unfaithful husband in *Cousins* (1989), a commendably assured comic and moody performance, but despite bringing some interesting insights to Pat Garrett in

Young Guns II (1990) – drawing on his difference in age and how little he has in common with his teenage co-stars to provide a motive for his betrayal of Billy the Kid – Petersen still seemed an actor best served by smaller character roles.

1981 Thief aka Violent Streets **1985** To Live And Die In LA **1986** Manhunter **1987** Amazing Grace And Chuck aka Silent Voice **1989** Cousins **1990** Young Guns II **1991** Hard Promises **1992** Passed Away

Pfeiffer, Michelle

Actress
Born 29 April 1959
Orange County, California

Cool, svelte and *soignée*, Michelle Pfeiffer is also capable of playing the guttersnipe or exuding a quality of genuine warmth, and has emerged as one of the few mega sex-symbols since Marilyn Monroe. With her compelling light blue eyes and perfect bone structure, she has been named by *Harper's Bazaar* as one of the world's ten most beautiful women (she finds the oft-discussd subject of her looks to be boring and burdensome), and now commands upwards of $1 million per picture.

Pfeiffer boasts an unexceptional background from which she more or less drifted into the movies. Uninterested in school, she preferred the frivolities of life at the beach with her boyfriends. Her first full-time job was as a supermarket checkout girl but, a year later, spurred on by winning the Miss Orange County beauty contest and the Miss LA title, she began to reassess life, auditioned for commercials and modelling assignments, and attended acting school. Her first speaking part consisted of one line in an episode of TV's *Fantasy Island*, after which a succession of bit-part bimbos followed before she finally broke into the movies with small roles. Her break came when she was cast as Stephanie in *Grease 2* (1982), a part which hinted at her erotic qualities and gave her an opportunity to display her budding talents as dancer, singer and actress.

But it was as Elvira, the gangster's moll who becomes Al Pacino's wife in Brian De Palma's *Scarface (1983)*, that Pfeiffer first showed what she was capable of achieving. Her portrayal of a woman, too intelligent for her fate, who takes refuge in cocaine was sharply observed and evidenced a hard-edged talent for characterisation; a seductive mix of mystery, kookiness and vulnerability surfaced in *Into The Night* (1984), a comedy thriller in which she co-starred with Jeff Goldblum, and which doubtless inspired Jonathan Demme to give her the lead in *Married To The Mob (1988)* with Matthew Modine and Dean Stockwell. As the Mafia wife who wants out and runs away to seek respectability for herself and her small son in the back streets of Manhattan, Pfeiffer, the famous blonde hair sacrificed to a wild dark wig, drew on her combined skills to wonderful effect. In *Tequila Sunrise* (1988), cast as a sophisticated restaurateur caught in the crossfire between Mel Gibson and Kurt Russell, she proved herself an expert at the witty one-liner, a gift which would serve her well in *The Fabulous Baker Boys* (1989). And as the lovely Katya in the screen version of John Le Carré's *The Russia House* (1990) Pfeiffer brought dignity, quiet intensity and a superb accent to her portrayal of a Russian mother acting as an intermediary in a complex web of espionage. By now established as a thoroughgoing modern, her appearance in *Dangerous Liaisons* (1988) as the ill-fated Madame de Tourvel, a religious innocent in 18th-century France who falls prey to the decadent machinations of John Malkovich's Valmont, came as something of a surprise. Essentially miscast, it was a measure of the actress' seriousness that her stab at the role was not without honour.

Purposeful, intelligent and solitary, Michelle Pfeiffer parted from her husband (*thirty something's* Peter Horton) and lives in Santa Monica. She entered the 1990s as an Oscar nominee for her performance in *The Fabulous Baker Boys*. As Susie Diamond, a small-time whore turned nightclub singer whose presence disturbs the long-time relationship between two piano-playing brothers (Jeff and Beau Bridges), Pfeiffer set the screen alight with her unbridled sensuality, while drawing once again on her comedic gifts, her toughness and her vulnerability. The movie itself failed to find the finishing post, letting down all its best ideas. And, indeed, looking back over the first decade of Pfeiffer's movie career, one concludes that she is an actress of superior gifts in search of a screenplay to match. An initially surprising choice for the worn, lonely, loveless waitress of *Frankie And Johnny* (1991), she was both believable and touching; while she was an outright delight as crazy, mixed-up *Cat Woman* in the otherwise debatable *Batman Returns* (1992). But, as director Demme said of this undoubted star,

'. . . she can do anything. We will be moved by her in a variety of ways over the years.'

1980 Falling In Love Again; Hollywood Knights **1981** Charlie Chan And The Curse Of The Dragon Queen **1982** Grease 2 **1983** Scarface **1984** Into The Night **1985** Ladyhawke **1986** Sweet Liberty **1987** The Witches Of Eastwick **1988** Married To The Mob; Dangerous Liaisons; Tequila Sunrise **1989** The Fabulous Baker Boys **1990** The Russia House **1991** Frankie & Johnny **1992** Batman Returns **1992/93** Love Field; The Age Of Innocence

Phillips, Lou Diamond

Actor
Born 1962
The Philippines

Lou Diamond Phillips is most often cast as an Indian or a Hispanic-American. In fact, he was born in the Philippines to a Filipino-Hawaiian-Chinese-Spanish mother and a Scottish-Irish-Cherokee father – or so he says. He was raised simply enough in Arlington, Texas, and caught the acting bug at the age of ten. He received a degree in theatre from the University of Texas at Arlington, then studied film technique with Adam Roarke at the Film Actor's Lab in Dallas. He was an assistant director and instructor at the Lab between 1983 and 1986, during which time he appeared in the plays *Whose Life Is It Anyway?*, *Doctor Faustus* and *Hamlet* in Dallas and Fort Worth.

A passionate advocate of the Texas film industry, Phillips appeared in a number of modest independent films there, most of which only saw the light of day after his rise to stardom. Between 1983 and 1987 he made *Angel Alley, Interface, Harley, Dakota*, and *Trespasses* which, typically, had to wait four years for its limited release in 1987. Phillips was increasingly taking control of his own career – he co-wrote *Trespasses*, a dull melodrama, and associate-produced *Dakota* – but his break came from Hollywood. After a nationwide talent hunt, Phillips was suggested for the part of Richie Valens' brother in the biopic *La Bamba* (1987). Impressed by his open, clean-cut good looks, director Luis Valdez offered him the starring role instead (Esai Morales became Richie's dissolute brother). A fair, likeable movie in the tradition of *The Buddy Holly Story* (1978), with Los Lobos recreating the Valens sound (Phillips mimes throughout) and notching up a transatlantic number one with the title song, *La Bamba* is nevertheless an anodyne tale, most notable for its sympathetic portrayal of Hispanic-American culture, hitherto largely ignored by Hollywood. The film's surprising popular success can be attributed to three factors: the music; energetic promotion by David Puttnam's Columbia Pictures, including the release of Spanish-speaking versions in targeted areas; and Lou Diamond's charismatic, idealised performance. He married the film's assistant director, Julie Cypher.

Stand And Deliver (1988) was made on a small budget before the Valens picture was released. Phillips took a supporting role as an east LA *barrio* kid who is surprised and even embarrassed to find himself inspired by his maths teacher (Edward James Olmos). Another unexpected hit, the film seemed to confirm the actor's golden touch and his status as a leading representative for the Hispanic community. But while Phillips is an articulate voice for liberal causes, he refuses to get caught up in the hopelessly entangled politics of racial minorities. He was an Indian and an honorary member of the Brat Pack in his next film, the youth Western *Young Guns* (1988). As Chavez, his presence looked suspiciously tokenistic in this so-so pastiche. While the film-makers jokily debunk the Tonto stereotype, they fail to give him any character beyond the joke. Fascinated by their culture, Phillips became a Cherokee blood brother in real life, but his performance is strictly Hollywood redskin: dour and humourless. The same is true of his performance in the sequel, and in the routine cop thriller *Renegades* (1989) – again as an Indian.

Nevertheless, Phillips has shown a lighter touch, and a wider range. His Puerto Rican villain in *A Show Of Force* (1990) was a gripping, extravagant piece of acting, and his hapless crook in the heist comedy *Disorganized Crime* (1989) had droll moments. With a more personal project in the offing (*Mind Game*, which he wrote), and the lead in a proposed series of films based on Tony Hillerman's Navajo detective books, produced by Robert Redford and beginning with *The Dark Wind* in which he again essayed an Indian – this time a loaner rookie cop on a Reservation – Phillips looked likely to prove more than just a pretty face.

1983–1987 Angel Alley; Interface; Harley **1987** Trespasses (also co-writer); La Bamba **1988** Dakota; Stand And Deliver; Young Guns **1989** Disorganized Crime; Renegades **1990** The First Power; Young Guns II; A Show Of Force **1991** Ambition (also writer); The Dark

Wind **1992** Shadow Of The Wolf aka Agaguk **1992/93** S.I.S.

Phoenix, River

Actor
Born 23 August 1971
Madras, Oregon

During the making, and with the release, of *Running On Empty* (1988), the beguilingly named and attractive River Phoenix, still in his teens, was given a deal of media hype. And his reviews, growing army of fans and a Best Supporting Oscar nomination all pointed to a big star in the making.

'He's never studied formally, but boy, does he know how to reach inside himself': so said Sidney Lumet, veteran director of *Running On Empty*, in which Phoenix played the son of 1960s anti-Vietnam activists who have been on the run with their family ever since they accidentally caused the death of a janitor. This peripatetic upbringing partly reflects River Phoenix's own background, which included periods spent with his hippy inclined parents in several parts of South and Central America, as well as Florida, before they finally settled in California, though 'when we moved on, it was because they couldn't pay the rent'. (Picturesquely enough, he was born in a log cabin.)

River broke into showbiz via a daytime TV series called *Fantasy*, in which he had a spot playing guitar and singing. Subsequently, he appeared in the series *Family Ties*, was given parts in a couple of miniseries and a secured a regular role in the TV version of *Seven Brides For Seven Brothers*. He made his movie debut in Joe Dante's underrated *Explorers* (1985), and really arrived with his second film, Rob Reiner's sleeper hit *Stand By Me*, the following year. With his fair hair, blue eyes and residual chubbiness, he projected a boyish appeal underpinned by an intimation of adult irony, appropriate to the way that the rites-of-passage story represents the recollections of the writer (Richard Dreyfuss) whom Phoenix's character is to become. He returned to Central America to play the unfortunate son of Harrison Ford's eccentric inventor in *The Mosquito Coast* (1986), the movie where he met his great friend and confidante, Martha Plimpton; and his on-screen relationship with Ford was amusingly extended when, for the prologue to *Indiana Jones And The Last Crusade* (1989), Phoenix was cast as the younger self of the screen character that made Ford's name.

The qualities of litheness and timing which the youthful actor brought to this 'guest star' appearance suggested that he possessed technical range as well as force of personality, and it seemed reasonably safe to assume that he would transcend the failure of Lawrence Kasdan's *I Love You To Death* (1990), in which he had a supporting role as an over-the-top youth infatuated with Tracey Ullman's unhappy wife, nursing murderous intentions towards her husband (Kevin Kline). Gus Van Sandt's offbeat arthouse character study-cum-fantasy of rent boys in the Pacific Northwest, *My Own Private Idaho* (1991), had critics in agreement on only one point – that Phoenix had made the transition to adult roles with a brave and remarkably affecting performance as a lonely, narcoleptic young hustler.

Odd though it may be, the actor's name is his own, and his siblings are comparably named: sisters Rainbow, Liberty and Summer; brother Leaf. They all seek performing careers, and his brother made some impact as Dianne Wiest's unhappy son in *Parenthood* (1989).

1985 Explorers **1986** Stand By Me; The Mosquito Coast **1988** A Night In The Life Of Jimmy Reardon (GB: Jimmy Reardon); Running On Empty; Little Nikita **1989** Indiana Jones And The Last Crusade **1990** I Love You To Death **1991** Dog Fight; My Own Private Idaho **1992** Sneakers **1992/93** Silent Tongue

Pitt, Brad
(William Bradley Pitt)

Actor
Born 1964
Oklahoma

With his James Dean looks, pouting lips and general air of overripe sexuality, Brad Pitt established himself as a pin-up of the 1990s in just a handful of movies and, more significantly, a commercial for Levi jeans, before revealing that he is rather more than just a pretty face. Raised in Springfield, Missouri, Pitt never considered acting as an option until wanderlust got the better of him at 19 and he headed off to seek his fortune in Los Angeles. Nine months of odd jobs and acting classes later, he landed his first role in the long-running TV series *Dallas*. Other bit parts and guest roles followed, including appearances in the series *Glory Days* and the high school slasher movie *Cutting Class*

(1989), but it was the Levi ad that first caused people to sit up and take notice. Then came *Thelma And Louise* (1991).

A sensational critical and commercial success, Ridley Scott's female road movie did as much for the careers of already established leads Susan Sarandon and Geena Davis as it did for that of Pitt. In the film he plays the aptly named JD, a charming, deferential young hitchhiker who takes the fancy of Thelma (Davis) and seduces her in passionately energetic manner, only to then take off with the two women's money. It was a brief but eye-catchingly strong and cheeky performance, which immediately conferred heartthrob status on the young actor. His follow-up film, *Johnny Suede* (1992), was a modest cult movie with Pitt cast in the title role as a Brando-style innocent, obsessed with the music of Ricky Nelson and sporting a spectacular quiff. Despite suffering from an excess of stylisation, the film was a good showcase for the actor's boyish charms and strong talent; it also demonstrated his keenness to opt for projects that fall outside of the mainstream and, with three other feature films in the can after *Johnny Suede*, Brad Pitt looked to be well on the way to living up to his ambition of 'proving myself as an actor, not just trading as a pretty boy'.

1989 Cutting Class **1991** Across The Tracks; Thelma And Louise **1992** Johnny Suede; A River Runs Through It; Cool World **1993** Kalifornia; True Romance

Place, Mary Kay

Actress
Born 23 September 1947
Tulsa, Oklahoma

Mary Kay Place was educated at the University of Tulsa and pursued a career in television. She worked in various production jobs for regional and national broadcasters. She was Tim Conway's assistant on his TV show, then became secretary to Norman Lear (doyen of TV series producers) on *Maude*, until she began to write for the show herself. As a writer, Place contributed to many of Lear's series, including *The Mary Tyler Moore Show*, *Phyllis*, and *M*A*S*H*. She also wrote many episodes of the hit situation comedy *Mary Hartman, Mary Hartman* in which she starred (and for which she won an Emmy for Best Comedy Actress).

It was not until she was approaching 30 that Place made her big screen debut, with a small role in the Woody Guthrie biopic *Bound For Glory* (1976). More substantially, Scorsese cast her in his musical drama *New York, New York* (1977) as Liza Minnelli's short-lived, small-voiced replacement in De Niro's band and bed. It was a brief but touching performance, the first (and possibly the best) of a series of supporting roles in which this actress was often a sensitive but rather wet girlfriend or sidekick. Pretty but not glamorous, Place was always the bridesmaid, never the bride. *The Big Chill* (1983) might have changed that, but did not. Lawrence Kasdan's witty ensemble piece gave her as much time and space as the likes of William Hurt, Glenn Close, Tom Berenger, Kevin Kline and Jeff Goldblum and she made the most of the opportunity. As Meg, the only one of the ex-radical friends who still works for the community, Place is immensely appealing. Her scenes talking to Glenn Close's daughter ring beautifully true, and she is cute facing up to a series of potential surrogate fathers. Guiltily stoned at the wake, fending off the attentions of Goldblum's sleazy Michael, and finally bedding Kline, Place is at the centre of some of the funniest moments too.

The Big Chill did not lead to major roles however. Instead it marked a different bridge in Place's career: her transformation from best friend to 'super mom', notably (and more complicated) to Laura Dern in *Smooth Talk* (1985). Cosily familiar and sweet natured, every boy and girl should have a mother like this. Even when she is on strike she is adorable. Place must show some steel to escape this typecasting; in the meantime her career continued to run smoothly on the small screen, in TV movies like *The Girl Who Spelled Freedom* (1986) and *Out On The Edge* (1989).

1976 Bound For Glory **1977** New York, New York **1979** More American Graffiti; Starting Over **1980** Private Benjamin **1981** Modern Problems **1983** The Big Chill; Waltz Across Texas **1984** For Love Or Money; Mom's On Strike **1985** Explorers; Smooth Talk **1987** Baby Boom **1988** A New Life **1990** Bright Angel **1991** Samantha **1992** Captain Ron

Plimpton, Martha

Actress
Born 16 November 1970
New York City

The then 14-year-old Martha Plimpton made an immediate impression with her debut film, *River Rat* (1984), in which she co-starred as the motherless daughter of a convict (Tommy Lee Jones), awkwardly reunited with her father on his release when he returns to the outlying river territory where she lives with her grandma. She was perfect casting for the character – a feisty, defensive yet vulnerable tomboy – most at home in boats. Thereafter, she moulded her precocious talents into a career which rested on a string of not dissimilar parts, moving progressively, in line with her age, through a succession of later teen roles. She continued to display a distinctive personality and talent, but retained the defensive, defiant edge of her expression to the point of being in danger of becoming unappealingly abrasive.

Highly intelligent, a committed vegetarian and witty beyond her years, Martha was the fruit of a non-marital union between actor Keith Carradine and actress Shelley Plimpton, a liaison which ended before she was born. She was raised by her mother, without benefit of luxury, on the Upper West Side of New York City at a time when unwedded motherhood was not easily accepted, but Plimpton considers her upbringing to be very normal, despite the lack of a father. She began working at her chosen profession in a film-acting workshop at the age of eight, and at 11 made a series of Calvin Klein commercials in which prepubescent girls spoke frankly about themselves directly to the camera. *River Rat*, a film she almost didn't audition for because she thought she looked too sophisticated, came along the next year.

After *River Rat*, Spielberg cast her in *The Goonies* (1985), but it was *The Mosquito Coast* the following year that raised her profile in spite of the fact that the film was not a box-office success. It was on that shoot that she met River Phoenix who became a close friend, with their relationship leading to speculation and gossip without, it seems, any foundation. She and Phoenix were reunited for Sidney Lumet's *Running On Empty* (1988), in which she played the troubled, independent-minded, big-mouth girlfriend to his troubled young man forced to a life on the run by his parents' political past. Plimpton gave her best performance to date as Gena Rowlands' stepdaughter in Woody Allen's *Another Woman* (1989), and her pregnant teenager in the earnest, starry but failed *Stanley And Iris* (1990) stretched her beyond the typically aggressive female roles she had been dealt before. But this highly talented young actress had every reason to wonder whether her strong personality was straitjacketing her into stereotypes, and it became clear that in order for Martha Plimpton to fulfil her original promise, there would have to be some changes made.

1984 River Rat **1985** The Goonies **1986** The Mosquito Coast **1988** Running On Empty; Stars And Bars; Shy People **1989** Another Woman; Parenthood **1990** Stanley And Iris **1991** Samantha **1992/93** Killer S.A.M.

Poitier, Sidney

Actor, director
Born 20 February 1924
Miami, Florida

Sidney Poitier was the first black actor to move into stardom by breaking away from the demeaning 'Negro' stereotypes of the past, looking forward to the cool and sassy superstars of the 80s and forming a link between Stepin Fetchit and Eddie Murphy. As a director he prepared the way for the likes of Spike Lee.

Born into a family of poor tomato growers in the Bahamas (his mother gave birth to him while on a trip to Miami), Poitier was forced to leave school at 13, and shortly afterwards moved to Miami, taking a variety of dead-end jobs before acting in an all-black production of the Greek classic, *Lysistrata* in 1946. In the 50s, he appeared to striking effect in a series of 'social problem' films highlighting racism: in Joseph L. Mankiewicz's *No Way Out* (1950), the actor played a doctor treating a bigoted Richard Widmark; Martin Ritt's *Edge Of The City* (1957) saw his friendship with John Cassevetes broken up by a racist; and Richard Brooks' *Something Of Value* (also 1957) had Poitier as a Kenyan caught between his people and his white friend (Rock Hudson) during the time of the Mau Mau rebellion. His gritty performance earned him an Oscar nomination in Stanley Kramer's *The Defiant Ones* (1958), which had a chain as the clanking symbol binding Poitier to racist Tony Curtis, both of them cons on the run. He widened his range in Otto Preminger's stagy *Porgy And Bess* (1959), as the touching crippled Porgy opposite the voluptuous Dorothy Dandridge, before becoming the first black performer to win an Oscar in 24 years (since Hattie McDaniel in *Gone With The Wind*) for his role in *Lilies Of The Field* (1963). As a cheerful footloose handyman inveigled by a group of East European nuns to build a new chapel for them, Poitier, with his charm and gift for comedy, just saved the picture from falling into all the sentimental traps. However, it was his dignified and passionate performance as Virgil Tibbs, a police detective from Philadelphia at odds with redneck Mississippi sheriff Rod Steiger in Norman Jewison's *In The Heat Of The Night* (1967) that advanced Hollywood's treatment of racial themes. (He reprised the supersleuth character in *They Call Me Mister Tibbs!*, 1970, and *The Organization*, 1971, to far less effect.)

In Stanley Kramer's sentimental comedy of miscegenation, *Guess Who's Coming to Dinner* (1967), he played the brilliant, handsome suitor of Spencer Tracy and Katharine Hepburn's daughter, too much of a paragon really to offer a challenge to the liberal-minded. (In 1976, Poitier married white actress Joanna Shimkus.) The first of the films he directed were aimed at a black middle-class family audience, the best being *Uptown Saturday Night* (1974) and *Let's Do It Again* (1975), two amusing buddy movies starring himself and Bill Cosby. Both were box-office smashes, as was *Stir Crazy* (1980), a frenetic and coarse prison farce with Richard Pryor and Gene Wilder. With a number of mediocre comedies and unremarkable roles as an actor in the 80s, Sidney Poitier has become just another director and actor which, in a way, is a tribute to his achievement in helping to eradicate prejudice.

As actor only unless stated otherwise: **1950** No Way Out **1952** Cry The Beloved Country; Red Ball Express **1954** Go Man Go! **1955** The Blackboard Jungle **1956** Goodbye My Lady **1957** Edge Of The City (GB: A Man Is Ten Feet Tall); Something Of Value; Band Of Angels **1958** The Mark Of The Hawk; The Defiant Ones **1959** Porgy And Bess **1960** All The Young Men; Virgin Island **1961** A Raisin In The Sun; Paris Blues **1962** Pressure Point **1963** Lilies Of The Field **1964** The Long Ships **1965** The Greatest Story Ever Told; The Bedford Incident; A Patch Of Blue; The Slender Thread **1966** Duel At Diablo **1967** In The Heat Of The Night; To Sir With Love; Guess Who's Coming To Dinner **1968** For Love Of Ivy **1969** The Lost Man **1970** King (docu); They Call Me Mister Tibbs! **1971** Brother John; The Organization **1972** Buck And The Preacher (also director) **1973** A Warm December (also director) **1974** Uptown Saturday Night (also director) **1975** The Wilby Conspiracy; Let's Do It Again (also director) **1977** A Piece Of The Action (also director) **1980** Stir Crazy (director only) **1982** Hanky Panky (director only) **1984** Fast Forward (director only) **1988** Shoot To Kill aka Deadly Pursuit; Little Nikita **1990** Ghost Dad (director only) **1992** Sneakers

Polanski, Roman

Director, actor
Born 18 August 1933
Paris, France

Roman Polanski was born in Paris of Polish-Jewish parents, who returned to Poland inopportunely two years before the war. They were sent to a concentration camp where his mother died, leaving their young son to fight for survival in the ghetto. No wonder his films, told with the absurdist humour that comes out of adversity, make little distinction between nightmare and reality. 'This is not a dream. It is reality,' Mia Farrow screams in *Rosemary's Baby* (1968) when she believes she has been impregnated by the Devil.

Polanski started as an actor on stage and in films (he appeared in Andrej Wajda's *A Generation*, 1954), before spending five years at the Lodz film school. His first short films *Two Men And A Wardrobe, The Fat And The Lean* and *Mammals* were influenced by Surrealism and the Theatre of the Absurd, a strain that continued into his feature films. Using a spare and subtle style in *Knife In The Water* (1962), his only Polish feature, he turned a simple tale of three people on a sailing trip into a tragi-comic drama of sexual rivalry and the generation gap. It offended the Polish authorities, but it gained him an Oscar nomination and immediate fame.

His first two films in England, *Repulsion* (1965), on sexual disgust, and *Cul-de-Sac* (1966), on sexual humiliation, were both memorably photographed in black and white by Gilbert Taylor – witness the 'reality' of Catherine Deneuve's breakdown as the walls of her room come alive and a man rapes her in the former, and the bleakness of Holy Island in the latter. *Rosemary's Baby*, from Ira Levin's novel, demonstrated the Polish exile's ability to adapt his style and vision to a Hollywood movie, brilliantly creating an atmosphere of evil without resorting to any graphic special effects. The totally realistic settings of cities: New York (*Rosemary's Baby*), London (*Repulsion*), Paris (*The Tenant* and *Frantic*; 1976 and 1988) and Los Angeles (*Chinatown*, 1974) gradually become horrifying deathtraps. Like the figure of K in Kafka's novels, the victim in each case uncomprehendingly believes himself to be partly responsible for his fate. Polanski played the tormented K character in *The Tenant*, shot in the *quartier* of Paris where he had lived in leaner times, and in *The Fearless*

Vampire Killers (1967) he is trapped in a Transylvanian castle with vampires, one of them played by Sharon Tate, whom he married the following year. In 1969, she was brutally murdered under macabre circumstances in their Hollywood home by the demonic disciples of Charles Manson. (He had been married to Polish actress Barbara Kwiatkowska from 1959–1961.)

Two years later, Polanski caused discomfort by showing the gruesome murders in *Macbeth* (1971) – filmed in England – one of the most blood-soaked of all Shakespeare's plays and one with an undercurrent of supernaturally evil forces. Some new light was thrown on the play by having the Macbeths played by a couple in their 20s (Jon Finch and Francesca Annis), and it was clear that 'Fair is foul and foul is fair' well expressed Polanski's world. *Chinatown* was a splendid reconstruction of a 40s *film noir* plot with Chandleresque detective Jack Nicholson trying to clear up a murky mystery involving a corrupt tycoon (John Huston) and his daughter (Faye Dunaway). It was the director's last big success to date.

In 1977, Polanski's private life hit the headlines again. He was arrested in LA and brought to trial accused of having drugged and raped a 13-year-old girl at the home of Jack Nicholson. He was found guilty of having sex with a minor, and allowed bail in order to go and shoot *Hurricane* in Tahiti. He never made the film, nor did he return to the States where he remains a fugitive from justice.

His next film, *Tess* (1979), a fairly faithful and attractive adaptation of the Thomas Hardy novel, was shot in France, since residence in Britain could have had him subpoenaed under an Anglo-American treaty. In 1981, Polanski returned to Warsaw where he directed and played the title role in *Amadeus* on stage. Then, in 1986, he made his first film in six years, *Pirates* (1986). Filmed in Tunisia with Walter Matthau starring, it was, alas, a rather top-heavy and very expensive amalgam of every swashbuckler ever made; while *Frantic*, which took the wandering director back to Paris, was little more than an efficiently entertaining Hitchcockian potboiler, which starred Harrison Ford and Polanski's new love, Emmanuelle Seigner.

By the 1990s, a definite question mark hovered over the creative future of the once brilliantly gifted Roman Polanski, and little reassurance was provided by the sexually bizarre and, to many, risible *Bitter Moon* (1992), his first outing of the decade.

1954 Pokolenie A Generation (actor only; Poland) 1962 Noz W Wodzie Knife In The Water (also co-writer; Poland) **1964** Les Plus Belles Escroqueries Du Monde The Beautiful Swindlers (episode; also co-writer; France) **1965** Repulsion (also actor and co-writer) **1966** Cul-De-Sac (also co-writer) **1967** The Fearless Vampire Killers aka Dance Of The Vampires (also actor and co-writer) **1967** Rosemary's Baby (w/d) **1971** Macbeth (also co-writer) **1973** What? (also actor and co-writer) **1974** Chinatown (also actor) **1976** The Tenant (also actor and co-writer) **1979** Tess (also co-writer) **1986** Pirates (also co-writer) **1988** Frantic (also co-writer) **1992** Back In The USSR (actor only); Bitter Moon

Pollack, Sydney

Director, actor
Born 1 July 1934
Lafayette, Indiana

One of Hollywood's most successful 'safe' directors, Sydney Pollack began his career as an actor in the New York Neighborhood Playhouse studying under Sanford Meisner before going on to guest roles in *Playhouse 90* and *Alfred Hitchcock Presents*. His friendship with John Frankenheimer, then a leading light in live television, brought him to Los Angeles where he spent the early 60s directing episodes of *Ben Casey* and the *Bob Hope-Chrysler Theatre* among many other shows, earning a clutch of Emmy nominations and making his motion-picture debut behind the cameras with 1965's *The Slender Thread*. Although he failed to make the most of his material, he handled the performances (Anne Bancroft, Sidney Poitier) well enough to land *This Property Is Condemned* (1966) on Robert Redford's recommendation (they had met as actors on 1962's *War Hunt*), thus beginning a seven-film working relationship that has been the backbone of the director's career.

After the enjoyable comedy-Western *The Scalphunters* (1968) and the eccentric anti-war drama *Castle Keep* (1969, a major influence on William Peter Blatty's later *The Ninth Configuration*), *They Shoot Horses, Don't They?* (1969) proved Pollack's breakthrough film; a gruelling drama about a Depression-era dance marathon and the destructive relationships of its participants and promoters (Gig Young and Jane Fonda among them) it earned him his first Oscar nomination. However, many critics complained that it watered down the unrelenting pessimism of

Horace McCoy's novel to make it more palatable for mass consumption, and it is true that Pollack has shown a tendency to take intriguing subject matter and turn it into product – as in *The Way We Were* (1973), where left-wing politics and McCarthyism are relegated to the background for a Barbra Streisand – Robert Redford weepie.

He is at his worst when wearing his heart on his sleeve – the potent image of Redford and horse lit up like a Christmas tree riding through Las Vegas is far more effective than the 90 minutes of eco-speeches and addresses to the nation *The Electric Horseman*'s (1980) two crusading stars (Jane Fonda is the other) follow it with. And it does seem hard to credit his belief that a set-piece where horse and rider outwit several police cars is really symbolic of the inadequacy of mechanisation over nature rather than just a good excuse for a chase scene that will add to the box office.

Much of his best work is attributable to others – *Jeremiah Johnson* (1972) feels like a more controlled version of one of screenwriter John Milius' films, favouring individuality over ecology, while Robert Towne and Paul Schrader's concerns of honour, redemption and cultural and social divides are more readily on view in the much underrated *The Yakuza* (1975). Even the impressive thriller *Three Days Of The Condor* (1975, obviously his year for thrillers), with its picture of an intelligence community unable to understand the past and wreaking havoc in the present with its wargaming projections of future crises, diluted much of the politics of the source novel. Yet if they lack bite, Pollack does make entertaining, accessible and visually polished films and is at his best with a good cast and a simple theme, as with the perfectly realised *Tootsie* (1982), in which the director cast himself as Dustin Hoffman's harassed agent. It was a nightmarish 18-month, $32million shoot that ended in Pollack and Hoffman throwing seperate wrap parties at the same restaurant.

Since the 1970s, almost all of Pollack's films have been love stories about wildly different people thrown briefly together by circumstance (Redford's standing response to each of their projects is 'How long do I get to keep the girl this time?'), and it is surely no accident that *Out Of Africa* (1985), little more than a simple romance beautifully played out against an epic canvas, proved his biggest hit and finally won him his Best Picture and Best Director Oscars. Yet when he attempted to mix politics and moral ambiguity more prominently into his *ouevre* with the $45million *Havana* (1990) he came up with the most spectacular failure of his career. Perhaps growing aware that his style of film-making may be going out of fashion, Pollack, always a nervous director on set, has moved more into prestigious producing credits – including *The Fabulous Baker Boys* (1989), *Presumed Innocent* (1990) and the much troubled *Dead Again* (1991).

As director only unless stated otherwise: **1962** War Hunt (actor only) **1965** The Slender Thread **1966** This Property Is Condemned **1968** The Swimmer (one scene only); The Scalphunters **1969** Castle Keep; They Shoot Horses, Don't They? **1972** Jeremiah Johnson **1973** The Way We Were **1975** The Yakuza; Three Days of the Condor **1977** Bobby Deerfield **1979** The Electric Horseman **1981** Absence of Malice **1982** Tootsie (also actor) **1985** Out of Africa **1990** Havana **1992** The Player (actor only); Death Becomes Her (actor only) **1992** Husbands And Wives (actor only) **1992/93** The Firm

Pryor, Richard

Actor, writer, director
Born 1 December 1940
Peoria, Illinois

Along with Eddie Murphy, whom he stars with in *Harlem Nights* (1989), Richard Pryor is one of the very few truly popular black stars in contemporary Hollywood, versatile as a writer as well as an actor, and capable of commanding very large paychecks. His career has been hectic and prolific, and pitched at an edge of danger that few other contemporary performers would be able – or indeed care to – emulate. The victim at different times of a bad burns accident, a much publicised drugs problem, two massive heart attacks (and, it has been rumoured, multiple sclerosis), it was a matter of prayer and speculation by the 90s how long he could remain in the public arena. A complex, driven and formidable personality, he burns the candle at both ends – as many fine black artists have done (notably in the jazz field).

Pryor is mainly known to the general public for his performances in a number of hugely successful box-office hits – comedies or lighthearted thrillers such as *Silver Streak* (1976), *Greased Lightning* (1977), *Stir Crazy* (1980), *Superman III* (1983) and *Brewster's Millions* (1985) – in which he waltzes suavely through the roles. But a deeper and more interesting personality – full of rawness and audacity – emerges from the three autobiographical concert films he made between 1979 and 1983, which took the whole question of race in contemporary America and subjected it (both the pieties of white liberals and the certitudes of militant blacks) to a withering and lyrical satire. Blacks like himself (whom he calls 'niggers') and whites – middle-class whites especially – are chided with Olympian impartiality, their pretentions pointed up and mocked devastatingly in some of the richest and most obscene language ever used in the cinema. But of course the only reason he can get away with this, what indeed gives his performances their authority, is the honesty and beauty of his self-scrutiny. He is the butt of his own jokes – about sex and death and domestic violence, reminding us in the process of certain universal constraints in the human condition. He belongs to the fraternity of great universal clowns, like Chaplin or (from another angle) Woody Allen, performers whose neuroses illuminate our own deepest vulnerabilities and bring us back, with humour, to an irreducible human solidarity.

Like the great jazz trumpeter Charlie Parker (whose riffs and improvisations have a certain spiritual affinity with Pryor's verbal techtronics), Pryor was born in the Midwest of fairly humble parentage. Passionate for music, at seven years old he was hanging round night-spots, sitting in to play drums with professionals, and observing the skills of visiting greats such as Count Basie and Duke Ellington. Unhappy at school, he left early to take jobs packaging meat at a beef plant, racking balls at his grandfather's pool hall and driving trucks for the small construction firm owned by his father. After a couple of years in the army he got into television, excelling as a stand-up comic, appearing in due course on the Johnny Carson, Merv Griffin and Ed Sullivan shows; and impressed, too, as a preparer of material for other people (eg Lily Tomlin, Flip Wilson). Pryor is extremely skilful with his pen, co-winner, with Mel Brooks, of the 1974 Writers Guild award for the script of *Blazing Saddles*. He is also a talented singer and has released albums of best-selling hits.

His early film career wasn't so distinguished. He first came to larger public notice with a 1972 jazz biopic, starring Diana Ross as Billie Holiday (*The Lady Sings The Blues*). He is convincing as a poor down-and-out stumbling into a rich man's dream in James B. Harris' odd but likeable *Some Call It Loving* (1973); and again as a rich dude ('Daddy Rich') preaching the cause of black capitalism in the charming and under-rated all-black comedy *Car Wash* (1976). The opening moments of Paul Schrader's dour but powerful film *Blue Collar* (1978) are enlivened by Pryor's rare verbal and kinetic energy. In general, this big-built, moustachioed, slightly coarse-grained man (no Denzel Washington physically) graces the films he appears in, without – unfortunately – owning them, as Chaplin and Woody Allen do. His best film of all is undoubtedly the first of the concert films, *Richard Pryor Live In Concert* (1979), where he reveals himself as one of the most complex and fascinating of late 20th-century film personalities.

As actor only unless stated otherwise: **1966** The Busy Body **1968** The Green Berets; Wild In The Streets **1969** The Phynx **1971** Dynamite Chicken; You've Got To Walk It Like You Talk It Or You'll Lose The Beat **1972** The Lady Sings The Blues **1973** Hit!; The Mack; Wattstax; Some Call It Loving **1974** Uptown Saturday Night; Blazing Saddles (co-writer only) **1975** Adios Amigo (also writer) **1976** The Bingo Long Traveling All-Stars and Motor Kings (also writer); Car Wash; Silver Streak (also co-writer) **1977** Greased Lightning (also writer); Which Way Is Up? (also co-writer) **1978** The Wiz; The Muppet Movie; Blue Collar; California Suite **1979** Richard Pryor Live In Concert (also writer); In God We Trust; Richard Pryor Is Back Live In Concert (also writer) **1980** Wholly Moses!; Stir Crazy (also writer); Bustin' Loose; Some Kind Of Hero **1982** Richard Pryor Live On The Sunset Strip (also writer); The Toy (w/d) **1983** Superman III; Richard Pryor Here and Now (w/d) **1985** Brewster's Millions; Jo Jo Dancer (w/d); Richard Pryor Live and Smokin' **1986** Critical Condition **1988** Moving **1989** See No Evil; Hear No Evil; Harlem Nights **1990** Another You; Look Who's Talking Too

Q

Quaid, Dennis

Actor
Born 9 April 1954
Houston, Texas

Dennis Quaid had been in the business for a dozen years before his role as Cajun cop Remy McSwain saw him persuading not only Ellen Barkin's uptight assistant DA but audiences who were entertained by *The Big Easy* (1987) that he was an irresistible force. Of the two acting Quaid brothers – Randy is 'the big one' – Dennis was merely 'the cute one' and the reputed possessor of the best abdominals in Hollywood, forever on the brink of recognition. Since his big breakthrough year of 1987, Quaid has enjoyed heart-throb status and had numerous showcases for both his mischievous leer and his dark side, but it has to be acknowledged that he has as yet failed to prove a real box-office draw.

As the punier little brother of Randy, Dennis took up drama at his Houston high school – the sissy substitute for one too small for football. Both brothers studied drama at the University of Houston and at 20 Dennis dropped out of college to follow his brother to California. He couldn't even get an agent for a year, when he plagued producers himself to cast him as one of the small-town youths in James Bridges' *September 30, 1955* (1978), after which he trod the youth flick/bar-room brawl scenario and athletic movie path before his first apparent big break with *The Right Stuff* (1983). Among the more noteworthy of his early credits were Peter Yates' *Breaking Away* (1979), which saw him as one of the aimless bicycling Indiana youths, and Walter Hill's handsome revisitation of the James gang Western myth, *The Long Riders* (1980), in which he and Randy played the Miller brothers in a cast packed with siblings (the Carradines, Keaches and Guests).

Philip Kaufman's thrilling celebration of the Mercury astronauts, *The Right Stuff*, presented Quaid with a dream role in cocky, cackling, crewcutted 'hot-dogging' pilot Gordo Cooper, and he was constantly working after that, although still not really 'happening'. From the dire *Jaws 3-D* (1983) to Wolfgang Petersen's *Enemy Mine* (1985) – a warm-hearted sci-fi yarn in which Quaid's earthling space warrior battles then befriends Louis Gossett Jr 's extraordinary lizard alien – to Joe Dante's sci-fi comedy diversion *Innerspace* (1987) Quaid put himself over nicely as a brash, boyish, attractive action lead with more twinkle than toughness. It was *The Big Easy*, with its steamy, clothed kiss-ups and Quaid's breezy charm, which established that he had the stuff of a romantic lead, and he was credibly magnetic to Cher's plucky public defender in the under-rated Peter Yates thriller *Suspect* (1987). He was less persuasive as a college professor poisoned in the garish remake of *D.O.A.* (1988) but terrific as a washed-up football star in the curiously neglected *Everybody's All-American* (1988) opposite a marvellous Jessica Lange.

One of the most hyped productions of 1989, *Great Balls Of Fire*, allowed Quaid to indulge his hellraising proclivities as rock 'n' roll wild man Jerry Lee Lewis, but the film suffered from terminal wackiness and arguably should have been left until after the demise of Mr Lewis if it was to have been a superior, balanced musical biopic. A more sensitive, sober performance as the distressed husband of a Japanese-American bride in Alan Parker's picture of the internment of victimised 'aliens' in World War II, *Come See The Paradise* (1990), unfortunately went virtually unremarked, but he was predictably attractive in a supporting role as a ruthless womaniser in *Postcards From The Edge* (1990) and was not short of employment despite the continuing quest for a genuine commercial hit. Previously married to actress P.J. Soles, Quaid married actress (and two-time co-star) Meg Ryan on Valentine's Day 1991. A keen musician, he has written songs for three of the films in which he has appeared: *The Night The Lights Went Out In Georgia* (1981), *Tough Enough* (1983) and *The Big Easy*, and had plans to record his own album.

1977 September 30, 1955; I Never Promised You A Rose Garden **1978** Our Winning Season; Seniors **1979** Breaking Away **1980** The Long Riders; Gorp **1981** All Night Long; Caveman; The Night The Lights Went Out In Georgia **1983** Tough Enough; Dreamscape; The Right Stuff; Jaws 3-D **1985** Enemy Mine; Nothing But The Truth **1987** Innerspace; The Big Easy; Suspect **1988** D.O.A.; Everybody's All-American aka When I Fall In Love **1989** Great Balls Of Fire **1990** Postcards From The Edge; Come

See The Paradise **1992/93** Undercover Blues; Wilder Napalm

Quaid, Randy

Actor

Born 1 October 1950

Houston, Texas

Gormless, dopey, clumsy, gangling, geeky. The words that spring to mind in association with Randy Quaid's persona are not flattering. His is an odd, rubbery face. The expression 'mealy-mouthed' is usually suggested by an individual's words, but in Randy Quaid's case it is as if his extravagantly apologetic nature has shaped his visage, mouth and all; his is a *mealy-mouthed face*. At six-foot-four inches tall he is a lumbering, gentle giant, too docile to have played the heavies, too lop-sided for romantic leads. But Quaid is a fine, subtle actor; at home both with farce and drama. He is a regular, welcome presence in supporting roles, and has been since 1971.

Quaid's first professional job was as part of a comedy duo with actor Trey Wilson in Houston (it does not take a divining rod to guess that Quaid was the straight man; the slow burn is one of his specialities). Meanwhile he took drama classes at the University of Houston. He was still a junior when Peter Bogdanovich cast him as Lester Marlow in *The Last Picture Show* (1971). Lester was one of Cybill Shepherd's fumbling beaux, a born loser destined to become a cuckolded, insolvent banker – as the belated sequel *Texasville* (1990) illustrated. Cameos in Bogdanovich's *What's Up Doc*? (1972) and *Paper Moon* (1973) were superceded by Quaid's marvellous Oscar-nominated portrayal of a naive young sailor escorted cross-country to the stockade by Jack Nicholson and Otis Young in Hal Ashby's *The Last Detail* (1973). The actor's aptitude for playing abject dim-wits encouraged film-makers to typecast him, and he did little else in the 70s, usually in brief character roles (though he was nearer the action in *The Missouri Breaks*, 1976, and more articulate in *Midnight Express*, 1978). In 1980, he co-starred with his brother Dennis in the fraternal Walter Hill Western, *The Long Riders*.

Another facet of Quaid's talents emerged in frequent appearances on the television series *Saturday Night Live*, and his witty characterisations of Presidents John F. Kennedy and Ronald Reagan opened the way for a renewed career in comedy. His redneck brother-in-law in *National Lampoon's Vacation* (1983) was a boorish, snickering tour de force; variations of it crop up in *Moving* and in *Caddyshack II* (both 1988). However, he is better used when the farce is tempered with sensitivity, as in *Quick Change* (1990) or *Bloodhounds Of Broadway* (1989), where clumsiness and loneliness are linked. Straight dramatic roles in the 80s broadened the Quaid persona. Having played *True West* off-Broadway in 1983 (his debut), Quaid appeared in Robert Altman's film of *Fool For Love* (1985); he was a detective with a rare commodity in *No Man's Land* (1987) – brains! And in Bob Balaban's *Parents* (1988), he starred in the meaty role of an anxious father with a suspicious son, adding menace to his repertoire. Nevertheless, Randy Quaid may feel that his best work has been restricted to television. He was perfect as Lenny in *Of Mice And Men* (1981), won plaudits for his flamboyant Lyndon Johnson in *LBJ: The Early Years* (1987), and an Emmy nomination for Mitch in *A Streetcar Named Desire* (1984).

1971 The Last Picture Show **1972** What's Up Doc? **1973** Lolly Madonna XXX aka The Lolly Madonna War; Paper Moon; The Last Detail **1975** Breakout; The Apprenticeship Of Duddy Kravitz; The Fortune **1976** The Missouri Breaks; Bound For Glory **1978** The Choirboys; Midnight Express **1980** Foxes; The Long Riders **1981** Heartbeeps **1983** National Lampoon's Vacation **1984** The Wild Life **1985** Fool For Love; The Slugger's Wife **1986** The Wraith **1987** Sweet Country; No Man's Land **1988** Moving; Caddyshack II; Parents **1989** Out Cold; National Lampoon's Christmas Vacation; Bloodhounds Of Broadway **1990** Texasville; Days Of Thunder; Quick Change; Martians Go Home **1991** Cold Dog Soup **1993** hideous mutant FREEKZ

Quinn, Aidan

Actor

Born 8 March 1959

Chicago, Illinois

With his distinctive colouring – pale-white skin, dark hair and startlingly blue eyes – it is no great surprise that Aidan Quinn is of Irish stock. The son of Irish parents living in the States, he was born in Chicago but spent many of his early years in Ireland, where he first became interested in acting. Aged 19, he returned to Chicago, working briefly as a tar roofer before he became involved in several local theatre groups. Debuting in a production of *The Man In 605*, Quinn went on to appear in such plays as *Scheherazade*, *The Irish Hebrew Lesson*, and *Hamlet*. He then took the logical step of moving to New York where he appeared for the first time off-Broadway in Sam Shepard's *Fool For Love*. Other well-received performances followed and it was only a short time before Quinn landed his first screen role, as the biker punk from the wrong side of the tracks who falls for nice girl Daryl Hannah, in James Foley's *Reckless* (1984). An acceptable but unremarkable film about alienated youth, *Reckless* was not the most promising vehicle for a talented and serious young actor, but two subsequent projects revealed the depth of his range and consolidated his on-screen career. First was Susan Seidelman's underground comedy *Desperately Seeking Susan* (1985), which offered Quinn a delightful supporting role as a love-struck projectionist. While the surprising box-office success of the film helped introduce him to audiences world-wide, his superb Emmy-nominated performance as the young lawyer struggling to confront his parents with the fact that he is gay and has AIDS in the television movie *An Early Frost* (also 1985) significantly raised his artistic kudos.

From there, Quinn went on to appear in a series of high-quality feature films. Though undeniably good looking, with a sensitive, expressive face and a captivating smile, he suggests, through his choice of roles, that he is more interested in challenging parts that build upon his marked versatility than in becoming a traditional leading man playing strictly likeable characters. He more than held his own in his all-too-brief appearance opposite heavyweights Robert De Niro and Jeremy Irons in Roland Joffé's *The Mission* (1986), was dangerously menacing as the criminal at large in *Stakeout* (1987) and carried the full weight of the film *Crusoe* (1989) very impressively, as the eponymous island castaway in Caleb Deschanel's uneven revisionist version of the Daniel Defoe classic. Although (with the exception of *Reckless*) this was his only true leading role to date, the actor has turned in very effective supporting performances in both *The Handmaid's Tale* (1990, in which he brings a mysterious ambivalence to the role of the commander's chauffeur, Nick) and most notably in Barry Levinson's ensemble piece, *Avalon* (also 1990), a nostalgic immigrant-family story, in which he portrays – beautifully – the role of Jules, the loving son, husband and father whose hard-earned efforts to build his own piece of the American Dream are sadly and senselessly crushed.

1984 Reckless **1985** Desperately Seeking Susan **1986** The Mission **1987** Stakeout **1989** Crusoe; The Lemon Sisters **1990** The Handmaid's Tale; Avalon **1991** At Play In The Fields Of The Lord **1992** The Playboys (Ireland) **1992/93** Benny And Joon

R

Rafelson, Bob

Director, writer
Born 1934
New York City

If any one scene from his often highly personal films sums up Bob Rafelson, it is the moment at the beginning of *Five Easy Pieces* (1970) when Jack Nicholson's oil rig worker goes to a piano mounted on a truck and plays a piece of classical music with perfect precision. In many ways the archetypal Rafelson film, it embodies his major preoccupations – family ties, non-conformity, emotional repression and the void between appearance and reality. Appearances are deceptive with Rafelson the man as well, with his filmography giving few hints of his previous lives as a rodeo rider, sailor, jazz drummer, forces DJ in Japan, playwright, philosophy student, spare–time explorer and even one of the creators of The Monkees. Indeed, it was the original prefab four that gave him his big-screen break – after writing and directing an award-winning play and adapting 34 stage plays for TV's Play of the Week in the 1950s – with the psychedelic celebration of the group's artificiality, *Head* (1968). Co-written by Jack Nicholson, it marked the start of their long collaboration, with Rafelson producing *Easy Rider* (1969) and the actor's directorial debut, *Drive, He Said* (1972), as well as directing two of his best performances, in *Five Easy Pieces* and *The King Of Marvin Gardens* (1972).

The two films dealt with the fragility of family relationships, a theme that constantly runs through the director's later work, be the family genetic or, as in *Stay Hungry* (1976) or Bogdanovich's *The Last Picture Show* (1971) which he co-produced, extended: Nicholson's intrusion into a family unit in his remake of *The Postman Always Rings Twice* (1981) results in a lust as much for the husband's place as for the man's sexy, errant wife, only for him to prove just as weak as the victim he deposes; while *Mountains Of The Moon* (1989) is a reinterpretation of the (probably homosexual) relationship of Victorian explorers Burton and Speke as family substitutes – Burton for the brother who won't accompany him, Speke for an absent father. Yet despite their needs, Rafelson's characters find it impossible to connect – Debra Winger's insurance invesigator in *Black Widow* (1986) needs Theresa Russell's killer to define and cultivate her self-image, even to the point of attempting to take her place against a projected slide, but is firmly separated by her different sense of moral values. The films are all marked by scenes where people are unable to communicate even the obvious: Nicholson's inability to persuade a waitress to depart minutely from the menu in *Five Easy Pieces* or to dissuade brother Bruce Dern from his crackpot financial schemes in *The King Of Marvin Gardens*, Burton and Speke's rivalry created out of each's refusal to talk to the other. Even when there *is* contact, it is only when response is impossible, as when Nicholson agonisingly pours out his heart to his dying father in *Five Easy Pieces*, or Burton's softening of the features on Speke's death Mask.

Yet despite his ability to get under the skin of a film and the boost his work has given to the careers of Sally Field, Arnold Schwarzenegger, Nicholson, Jessica Lange, Patrick Bergin and others, Rafelson's films have proved sporadic in recent years. The bitter experience of being fired from *Brubaker* (1980) days into production seemed to provoke him into more commercial projects such as *Postman*, *Black Widow* and *Air America* (1990), the screenplay for which he was instrumental in depoliticising before the writer's strike gave him the opportunity to make his pet project, *Mountains Of The Moon*, instead. Despite all that, it is his less obvious projects (all, admittedly, more appreciated in retrospect than at the time of their release) that have consistently proved the most successful and memorable, while his 1992 foray, *Man Trouble*, was a universally panned disaster.

1968 Head (also co-writer) **1970** Five Easy Pieces **1972** The King Of Marvin Gardens (also co-writer) **1976** Stay Hungry (also co-writer) **1981** The Postman Always Rings Twice **1986** Black Widow **1989** Mountains Of The Moon (also co-writer) **1992** Man Trouble

Raimi, Sam

Director, writer
Born 1959
Royal Oak, Michigan

Imaginative and off-beat, Sam Raimi is one

of the generation of film-makers who spent his Michigan childhood roping his brother, the family pets and the neighbourhood children into his countless 8mm home movies, experimenting with comedy, adventure and horror. Always bent on a directing career, he made an eye-catching feature debut with the low-budget horror *The Evil Dead* (1983) but has not found it easy to realise his obvious potential.

While at Michigan State University, Raimi formed a student film-makers' society with his brother Ivan and Robert Tapert, and eventually left college to form his own small independent production company, Renaissance Pictures, with Tapert and another longtime buddy, actor Bruce Campbell. After making a few shorts, he devised *The Evil Dead* on the theory – for which there is abundant evidence – that an exploitation horror film made for more bravado than budget would serve well as an industry calling card and stand a reasonable chance of distribution on the extensive thrill-seekers' circuit. With Tapert producing and Campbell starring, Raimi made a half-hour version of the film and the enterprising young team screened it at parties to well-heeled professionals, inveigling investment in a full-length version from dentists, lawyers and the like in Detroit. The result was a wild, sick-making stew of gross effects, intentional laughs at grisly clichés and heady, stylish photography in which hapless college kids were trapped, possessed and sliced-and-diced in an evil-mountain-cabin scenario. Critics appreciated Raimi's panache, and genre fans and late-night screamers delivered a handsome return while the film went on to centre in a massive British censorship flap in the video industry. Banned officially as a 'video nasty' for several years, the admittedly repellent but scarcely degenerate piece acquired legendary status.

Courted by studios, Raimi and his Renaissance partners were given the finance, facilities and ultimately unwanted interference in making a chaotic slapstick comedy, *Crimewave* (1985), co-written by the director and his chums Joel and Ethan Coen. While it was another highly stylised effort with some good touches and a good grotesque cast (which included Louise Lasser, Brion James and Campbell), it failed on most counts and is best remembered by trivia hounds for a cameo from the Coens as press photographers. After this setback, Raimi had nowhere to turn but the inevitable *The Evil Dead II: Dead By Dawn* (1987), a virtual remake of the original but funnier. His tenacity was rewarded with a proper theatrical release and reasonable commercial success for a more mainstream if still unusual horror-fantasy-thriller, *Darkman* (1990), which starred Liam Neeson as a mutilated avenger and was notable for some intricately creepy design and effects.

Joker Raimi has also popped up on screen, as a security guard in John Landis' silly *Spies Like Us* (1985), as Rubber Mask in *Thou Shalt Not Kill . . . Except* (1987), and as a baby-faced, machine-gun toting plainclothes cop in one of the gorier set-pieces in the Coen Brothers' *Miller's Crossing* (1990). On the cards is *Evil Dead III*.

1983 The Evil Dead (also co-writer) **1985** Crimewave (also co-writer); Spies like Us (cameo only) **1987** The Evil Dead II: Dead By Dawn (w/d); Thou Shalt Not Kill . . . Except (cameo only) **1989** Intruder (actor only) **1990** Darkman (also co-writer); Miller's Crossing (cameo only) **1992/93** Army of Darkness aka Evil Dead III (also co-writer); The Nutty Nut (co-writer only) **1993** Tamakawa (actor only)

Ramis, Harold

Writer, director, actor
Born 21 November 1944
Chicago, Illinois

In the early 70s a group of talented young comics emerged from the Second City Actor's Group in Chicago, among them well-known names like Bill Murray, Gilda Radner and John Belushi (the latter two both sadly now dead). Among them was a tall, quiet man, Harold Ramis, who wrote many of the sketches that they performed. He was educated at Washington University, where he took a BA in English in 1966, and, after dropping out of graduate school (after two weeks), he went to work as the St Louis associate editor of *Playboy* magazine. He remained there from 1968 to 1970, when he returned to his hometown of Chicago to write for Second City.

After a three-year stint as the group's head comic writer, Ramis moved to New York. He again teamed up with Second City's brightest stars for the *National Lampoon Radio Hour*, and later appeared and wrote for the theatre revue spin-off, *The National Lampoon Show* in 1974, with old friends Murray and Belushi. In 1976 he got his first screen break, alongside Rick Moranis, writing and acting on the television show *SCTV* until 1978. But it was not until the show was cancelled that

Ramis was able to put his comic talent to good use. He received the big break with his first movie, the hilarious *National Lampoon's Animal House* (1978), which he co-wrote. His talent for slapstick comedy writing was put to good use, and seen to its best advantage when the character Bluto (John Belushi) was on the screen. The film, about Delta House, the worst fraternity on campus, whose students indulge a penchant for all-night drinking and toga parties, was a great success for the stars and Ramis alike.

Keeping his links with the friends he made at Second City, he co-wrote *Meatballs* (1979) with Ivan Reitman. The movie showcased the talents of Bill Murray, and although it was a small budget, low-intelligence appeal film, it made millions, and gave Ramis the clout to not only write but also direct his next screenplay. The result was *Caddyshack* (1980), starring Bill Murray and Chevy Chase, with the successful plot of *Animal House* transferred to a golf country club. Certainly, from then on, Hollywood decided that Ramis could do no wrong, and he proved as much with his next three films. First came another Bill Murray vehicle, *Stripes* (1981), which Ramis acted in and co-wrote with Ivan Reitman. The film blitzed everything at the box office, and Ramis proved, as Murray's put-upon friend who reluctantly joins the army, that he could be as funny in front of the camera as behind it. After returning to televison as the producer and chief writer for *The Rodney Dangerfield Show* in 1982, he directed Chevy Chase and Beverly D'Angelo in *National Lampoon's Vacation* (1983), which detailed one family's odyssey across America as they try to reach their holiday destination despite a dead aunt and a series of hilarious mishaps.

Harold Ramis then scored the biggest success of his career, writing and acting in the most successful comedy to date, *Ghostbusters* (1984). As Egon, the serious scientist on the brink of making paranormal discoveries, he proved a skilful co-star for more established screen comics Bill Murray and Dan Aykroyd. Unfortunately, after enjoying so many successes, the writer-director suffered a leaner period between 1985 and the year *Ghostbusters II* hit the screens (1989). During that time, he co-wrote and directed the unsuccessful Robin Williams movie *Club Paradise* (1986), and co-wrote the Rodney Dangerfield movie *Back To School* (1986) which failed at the box office.

Before returning to act in and write *Ghostbusters II* (1989), Ramis appeared both in front of and behind the camera; his performances included the Diane Keaton baby movie *Baby Boom* (1987), where he provided much-needed humour in an otherwise dismal comedy, and a more serious supporting role in the nostalgic romance *Stealing Home* (1988). By the beginning of the 90s he had won critical acclaim for his acting and was clearly established as a film personality of several skills.

1978 National Lampoon's Animal House (co-writer) **1979** Meatballs (co-writer) **1980** Caddyshack (co-writer director) **1981** Stripes (co-writer, actor) **1983** National Lampoon's Vacation (director) **1984** Ghostbusters (co-writer, actor) **1986** Club Paradise (co-writer, director) **1986** Back To School (co-writer); Armed And Dangerous (co-writer) **1987** Baby Boom (actor) **1988** Caddyshack II (co-writer); Stealing Home (actor) **1989** Ghostbusters II (co-writer, actor) **1992/93** Groundhog Day (director)

Redford, Robert
(Charles Robert Redford Jr.)

Actor, director
Born 18 August 1937
Santa Monica, California

The dazzling smile of Robert Redford is one of the more glorious natural wonders preserved on film. Too gorgeous not to be a star once he had given up his intention of becoming a painter in favour of acting, Redford was literally the golden boy of American film, particularly through the 1970s. Even as the curtain (inevitably when he reached his 50s) was coming down on his reign as a romantic leading man, Redford has remained one of the biggest names in the business. A serious man known for his political activities and conservationist campaigning, and a director with three films to his credit, he has always been ill at ease about his looks. Director Sydney Pollack, who has made seven films with Redford from *This Property Is Condemned* (1966) to *Havana* (1990) describes him rather loftily but quite shrewdly as an interesting metaphor for America: a golden boy with a darkness in him.

The son of an accountant and blessed with a graceful athleticism, Redford won a baseball scholarship to the University of Colorado but left in 1957 to paint for a year in Paris and Florence. On his return he married his girlfriend Lola, and studied art at the Pratt Institute in New York, but was diverted by drama training at the American Academy of Dramatic Arts. In 1959 he made his professional debut on Broadway with a small role in the comedy *Tall Story* and by 1963 he was the popular star of Neil Simon's hit *Barefoot In The Park*, in the role he reprised on screen opposite Jane Fonda in 1967. He also racked up numerous TV credits, including a memorable appearance as Death in a classic *Twilight Zone* episode. His feature film debut, notable only for his participation, was made in a small, independent, anti-war film, *War Hunt* (1962).

The lead in *Barefoot* brought Hollywood offers and Redford showed a taste for diversity in roles: as a homosexual movie star dumping bride Natalie Wood in *Inside Daisy Clover* (1965); as a hunted convict in his first film with Jane Fonda, *The Chase* (1966, having turned down the role of the sheriff played by Marlon Brando); as a railroad man ill-advisedly falling for Natalie Wood in Pollack's pretty dire film version of Tennessee Williams' *This Property Is Condemned* (1966). None of these proved popular, but the Redford-Fonda teaming in *Barefoot In The Park* (1967) was sexy and delightful and scored a hit. Rejecting *The Graduate* because he thought he was too old for the part (Dustin Hoffman is the same age), the younger man role in *Who's Afraid Of Virginia Woolf?* because he didn't like it, and *Rosemary's Baby*, Redford seemed surprisingly relaxed about his career. But his judgement was vindicated when he accepted a role passed over by Brando, Beatty and McQueen: Paul Newman's sardonic partner-in-crime Sundance in the hip and hugely popular *Butch Cassidy And The Sundance Kid* (1969), the most commercially successful Western ever.

Able to write his own ticket after that, the star chose another round of interestingly varied but indifferently received projects: *Tell Them Willie Boy is Here* (1969) as a dogged, manhunting lawman; *Downhill Racer* (1969) as a self-centred prat of an Olympic skier, and *The Candidate* (1972), a first-rate political tale in which he was excellent as an idealistic liberal persuaded to run for a senatorial seat and disillusioned by the political machinery engaged to sell him. Teaming again with Pollack and hiding any hint of glamour behind a beard, he produced another fine performance, as rugged, reclusive mountain man *Jeremiah Johnson* (1972). It was only with the classy, poignant and penetrating love story *The Way We Were* (1973) that Redford blew audiences away as a romantic leading man, the outwardly perfect American Dreamboat drawn to a superb Barbra Streisand playing a feisty left-wing ugly duckling, ultimately proving a weakling and dumping her in an ocean of tears. Romantically flawed and fallen heroes then became his forte from *The Great Gatsby* (1974) to *The Natural* (1984).

His best work of the decade was a subtly fastidious, eager representation of *Washington Post* Watergate investigative journalist Bob Woodward to Dustin Hoffman's less couth, aggressive Carl Bernstein in the outstanding 'howdunnit' reportage thriller, *All The President's Men* (1976), produced by Redford's Wildwood company. His most popular was his reunion with Paul Newman in what became the Best Picture of 1973, the seven-Oscar winner *The Sting*, in which his sassy small-time con-man is steered by Newman's more experienced hustler through an elaborate and thoroughly entertaining swindle caper.

Still wearing well, Redford made no kind of an Englishman but a suitably dreamy love-of-her-life for Meryl Streep in Pollack's Oscar-winning romantic epic *Out Of Africa* (1985), and a surprisingly amusing, tap-dancing, junk-food chomping lawyer in the feeble comedy *Legal Eagles* (1986). After a four-year absence from the screen, however, the radiant smile was intact in a much coarsened face in Pollack's drastically disappointing *Havana* (1990), a shockingly dull if lavish account of a grand passion, set against the backdrop of the Cuban revolution, that failed to convince.

In addition to his well-known support for liberal and environmental causes, and his pursuit of outdoorsmanship, in 1980 Redford established the Sundance Institute on his resort property near Provo, Utah, providing practical workshops, development resources and support to promising independent film-makers. He is also a founder of the Institute for Resource Management, a forum to encourage land developers and environmentalists to work together.

Surprisingly, in view of the results, Redford has turned his hand to direction infrequently, and with his debut feature, *Ordinary People* (1980), picked up Oscars for Best Picture and Best Director. The most triumphant proof that he was more than just a pretty face, *Ordinary People* was a sensitive adapatation of the Judith Guest novel, set in an affluent Chicago suburb, which examined despair and loathing in the cosy middle class through one family's highly-charged emotional crisis. Told largely from the viewpoint of a tormented boy, beautifully played by 19-year-old Timothy Hutton, the powerful drama put Redford overnight into the front rank as a director. Perhaps anxious that there was no way to go but down, he did not make a follow-up until 1988's *The Milagro Beanfield War*. While it did not catch at the box office, it was a visually exquisite and utterly charming comic fable about a rural Hispanic community fighting the evil forces of property development. Boasting an offbeat ensemble cast including John Heard, Melanie Griffith, Christopher Walken, Sonia Braga and a scene-stealing pig, it was overlong and slow to build but full of delights, including Oscar-winning music from Dave Grusin.

One of the few career ambitions Redford has publicly acknowledged is his desire to make a third film with Newman. 'I'd love to make one more movie with him. Just one more, the two of us.'

1962 War Hunt **1965** Situation Hopeless – But Not Serious; Inside Daisy Clover **1966** The Chase; This Property Is Condemned **1967** Barefoot In The Park **1969** Butch Cassidy And The Sundance Kid; Downhill Racer; Tell Them Willie Boy Is Here **1970** Little Fauss And Big Halsy **1972** The Hot Rock; Jeremiah Johnson; The Candidate **1973** The Way We Were; The Sting **1974** The Great Gatsby **1975** The Great Waldo Pepper; Three Days Of The Condor **1976** All The President's Men **1977** A Bridge Too Far **1979** The Electric Horseman **1980** Brubaker; Ordinary People (director only) **1984** The Natural **1985** Out Of Africa **1986** Legal Eagles **1988** The Milagro Beanfield War (director only) **1990** Havana **1992** A River Runs Through It (director only); Sneakers **1992/93** Indecent Proposal

Redgrave, Vanessa

Actress
Born 30 January 1937
London, England

The tallest tree in a small forest of Redgraves, of whom her daughters, Joely and Natasha Richardson, are the latest to come into bud, Vanessa is a woman of great beauty and presence who has never been comfortably accommodated by a film business uneasy with her radical political beliefs.

Always an earnest seeker after truth, Vanessa Redgrave remains mesmerised by the redundant mumbo-jumbo of dogmatic Marxism. There is something both heroic and profoundly silly about it. Unlike Jane Fonda, her co-star in *Julia* (1977), she has stuck to her political guns, even though they are firmly pointed at her foot. A stalwart of the British Workers' Revolutionary Party, she is the La Passionara of the acting world, and one can imagine her as a grim cultural commissar, regretfully sending ideologically unsound artists to the firing squad, rather as she did in a fantasy sequence in *Morgan – A Suitable Case for Treatment* (1966). She has often been roughly handled by the press, a problem exacerbated by the extremely narrow limits she imposes on any interviewer. But as the years spread strain and broken veins across her lovely face, the intrusive press camera sometimes catches her in mid-rant, her commanding jaw and blazing eyes increasingly suggesting the rictus of those dotty old ladies who dedicate their lives to the neutering of stray cats. And yet for all this, Vanessa Redgrave, luminous, powerful, intense and courageous in her work as in her politics, is one of the greatest actresses, in the serious sense, of her generation.

She was born into the theatre, her arrival announced over the footlights of the Old Vic by Laurence Olivier, where her father Michael was playing Laertes to Larry's Hamlet. After studying at the Central School she made her stage debut, aged 20, in the seaside setting of the Frinton Summer Theatre. She made her London debut in 1958, starring opposite her father in *A Touch Of The Sun*, playing opposite him again in her first film, *Behind The Mask* (1958), a limp medical melodrama typical of the cultural dead zone of the late 1950s, which seemed to encourage her in a dismissive attitude towards the cinema.

By the time she returned to the screen eight years later in *Morgan – A Suitable Case For Treatment*, she had been recognised by critics and audiences alike as a classical theatre actress of rare quality. In *Morgan*, one of the quintessential 'Swinging London' films of the mid-1960s, she was enchanting as the millionairess reluctantly contemplating life without her unhinged artist husband (David Warner), a man in whose life gorillas and Karl Marx assume an equally large if somewhat hazy importance. After a teasing, non-speaking cameo appearance as Anne Boleyn in *A Man for All Seasons* (1966), her gawky, self-conscious beauty was brilliantly used by Michelangelo Antonioni in *Blow-Up* (1966) as the mystery woman caught in photographer David Hemmings' lens, nervously pacing around his trendy pad like a caged lioness.

Her marriage to director Tony Richardson explains her fleeting presence in three of his films, *The Sailor from Gibraltar* (1967), *Red And Blue* (1967) and *The Charge Of The Light Brigade* (1968), the first leading to the break-up of the marriage on the grounds of her husband's adultery with its star, Jeanne Moreau. Shortly afterwards, Vanessa claimed a new lover, on screen and off, in the form of Franco Nero, who played Lancelot to her Guinevere in *Camelot* (1967) and was the father of her illegitimate son.

She rose to the challenge of playing the legendary dancer Isadora Duncan in Karel Reisz's *Isadora* (1968) and then drifted through a hit-and-miss period. She imparted some of her political passion to her cameo role as the Suffragette leader Mrs Pankhurst in *Oh! What A Lovely War* (1969); romped around (with Franco Nero) in sexy black underwear in the Italian *A Quite Place In The Country* (1969); was impressive as Nina in Sidney Lumet's screen version of Chekhov's *The Sea Gull* (1969); played Andromache to Katharine Hepburn's Hecuba in *The Trojan Women* (1971), directed by Michael Cacoyannis; and seemed to relish the part of a deformed mother superior lusting after priest Oliver Reed in the lurid grotesquerie of Ken Russell's *The Devils* (1971).

After playing the title role in *Mary Queen Of Scots* (1971), the kind of part which MGM used to trundle out for Garbo, Redgrave's left-wing political activities led to the refusal of a US visa to make *Gone Beaver* with Bruce Dern. Thereafter, her film career stayed in the doldrums until *Julia* (1977), adapted from Lillian Hellman's wish-fulfilment autobiographical fragment, *Pentimento*. Jane Fonda impersonated Hellman and Vanessa was radiant in the title role, a mysterious and dignified patron saint of liberals, saving Jews in Nazi Germany. Her performace in *Julia* won her the 1978 Best Supporting Actress Oscar. At the awards ceremony she lectured the assembled bigwigs on the plight of some less fashionable victims, the Palestinians, the subject of her next film, *The Palestinian* (1977), a documentary which she produced and in which she appeared brandishing a Kalashnikov rifle.

Her outspoken anti-Zionism nearly got her fired from *Yanks* (1979), a John Schlesinger film about wartime Britain in which she stirred memories of Rosamund John in *The Way To The Stars* (1945), playing an uptight middle-class matron succumbing to the charms of the American soldiery. Then she was cast as the queen of mystery writers, Agatha Christie, in *Agatha* (1979), a slim tale built around the novelist's unexplained 10-day disappearance in the 1920s. Vanessa was an unlikely but affecting Agatha while Dustin Hoffman scuttled around at about her knee-height as the equally improbable American newshound on the trail of the big story.

One of the sadder aspects of Vanessa Redgrave's screen career is the inhibiting effect of her political convictions and a predilection for worthy films which often subside into pretentiousness. She did attempt to let her hair down in *Consuming Passions* (1988), a witless comedy in which she went wildly over the top as a sex-crazed Maltese harpy. But she seemed more at home as the feminist Olive Chancellor in *The Bostonians* (1984), a James Ivory adaptation of Henry James' novel; the schoolteacher living a life of quiet desperation in *Wetherby* (1986), David Hare's oblique critique of the Thatcher years; enjoying herself hugely in *Prick Up Your Ears* (1987), as yet another real-life character, Joe Orton's agent, the indomitable Peggy Ramsay; and as the haunted Miss Amelia Evans in Simon Callow's version of Carson McCullers' 'strange fairy-tale', *The Ballad of the Sad Café* (1990). She again shone, in the impressive ensemble cast of Merchant-Ivory's final E. M. Foster adaptation, *Howard's End* (1992), playing the ethareal wife, of Anthony Hopkins, whose bequeathement of her house causes it to become the titular property of dispute.

1958 Behind The Mask **1966** Morgan – A Suitable Case For Treatment; A Man For All Seasons; Blow-Up **1967** The Sailor From Gibraltar; Red And Blue; Camelot **1968** Tonight Let's Make Love In London; The Charge Of The Light Brigade; Isadora; The Sea Gull; Un Tranquille Posto Di Campagna/A Quiet Place In The Country (Italy) **1969** Oh! What A Lovely War **1970** Dropout **1971** La Vacanza (Italy); The Trojan Women; The Devils; Mary Queen Of Scots **1974** Murder On The Orient Express **1975** Out Of Season **1976** The Seven-Per-Cent Solution **1977** Julia **1979** Agatha; Yanks **1980** Bear Island **1983** Wagner **1984** The Bostonians **1985** Steaming; Wetherby **1986** Comrades **1987** Prick Up Your Ears **1988** Consuming Passions **1990** Diceria Dell'Untore/The Plague Sower (Italy) **1991** The Ballad Of The Sad Café **1992** Howard's End

Reeve, Christopher

Actor
Born 25 September 1952
New York City

In almost every interview Christopher Reeve has given, he has told a story of how his journalist mother and Yale professor father were mistakenly delighted at the thought that their son had been given a part in George Bernard Shaw's play *Man And Superman*.

Having as much brain as brawn, Reeve seemed already set for a career as a performer when a child. At school he studied piano and voice, sang with a madrigal group, was assistant conductor of an orchestra, and made his stage debut with a small Princeton theatre company at the age of nine. Graduating in English from Cornell, he enrolled at Juilliard's drama division and studied under John Houseman. After stints at London's Old Vic and the Comédie Française as part of his master's degree course, he returned to New York and accepted a role in a long-running TV soap opera, *Love Of Life*. This led to a Broadway play, *A Matter Of Gravity*, which ran for seven months and starred Katharine Hepburn, an actress who influenced him. 'What I learned from her was simplicity,' he has said, 'she's a living example that stardom doesn't have to be synonymous with affectation or ego.'

In 1978, the unknown Reeve was selected, after deals with the likes of Robert Redford and Paul Newman fell through, to incarnate the title role of *Superman*, the same year as his unremarkable screen debut as a crew member of a nuclear submarine marooned at the bottom of the ocean in *Gray Lady Down* (1978). Much of the success of the *Superman* movies was due to Reeve's charm, humour and sense of irony, never descending into knowing camp, and he also managed to wear the shining red cape and blue tights to the manner born, having built his body up for the role. Behind the corny, comic-book heroics lies the assumption that within every shy, fumbling male, a Man of Steel is bursting to get out. All four films gave Reeve the chance to appear as both sides of the masculine coin, the muscle-bound hero and his mild-mannered, bespectacled alter ego.

To prove that he was not a one-role actor, Reeve went out of his way, sometimes not very happily, to play as many different parts as possible on film and on stage. He was rather stiff as the playwright who goes back to 1912 in *Somewhere In Time* (1979), a rather feeble fantasy, and very good as a would-be playwright and psychotic homosexual in *Deathtrap* (1981). He was ill at ease as the corrupt priest in the dreadful *Monsignor* (1982), left in the air as the introspective pilot in *Aviator* (1985), another ignominious flop, and pushed into the background by Burt Reynolds and Kathleen Turner in *Switching Channels* (1987), the dreary fourth remake of *The Front Page*. On stage he played a gay amputee in Lanford Wilson's *Fifth Of July* on Broadway and was somewhat overshadowed by Superwoman Vanessa Redgrave and Superdame Wendy Hiller in *The Aspern Papers* on the London stage. But in another Henry James adaptation, opposite Redgrave again, in James Ivory's *The Bostonians* (1984) playing the reactionary lawyer struggling to gain the love of a young suffragette, Christopher Reeve demonstrated what a fine actor he could be in the right role and with the right director.

1978 Gray Lady Down; Superman **1979** Somewhere In Time **1980** Superman II **1981** Deathtrap **1982** Monsignor **1983** Superman III **1984** The Bostonians **1985** The Aviator **1986** Street Smart **1987** Switching Channels; Superman IV **1992** Noises Off; Change Of Heart

Reeves, Keanu

Actor

Born 1965

Beirut, Lebanon

Good-looking, dark-haired and with slightly oriental features, Keanu Reeves has fast established himself as one of the busiest 'hot' young actors around. Despite his particular and popular (at the box office) line of speciality in spaced-out teenagers (best typified by his performance as Ted, an engagingly mindless Californian high schooler rescued from flunking his history class by a preposterous time-travel device in the *Back To The Future* rip-off *Bill And Ted's Excellent Adventure*, 1989) he is a performer of some range and versatility, using his distinctive man-child qualities to portray anything from callow exuberant youths to amoral adolescents.

The son of a Hawaiian father – which accounts for both his exotic looks and first name – Reeves had an itinerant upbringing which took him from the Lebanon to Australia and New York before his family settled in Toronto. There, already an aspiring actor, he studied at the city's High School for the Performing Arts and later at the Second City Workshop. Aged just 16, he made a television commercial for Coca-Cola and, more significantly, landed a role in a Toronto TV show, *Hanging In*. The show was shortlived but before long Reeves appeared on stage, both in Toronto and

Pennsylvania, where he spent a season in summer stock. Several roles in some modest Canadian features followed, including the ice-hockey yarn *Youngblood* (1986), in which he played a small supporting part to stars Rob Lowe and Patrick Swayze. He first came to the attention of the American market in *River's Edge* (1987), Tim Hunter's chilling tale about how a group of adolescents in a small town react when one of their friends senselessly murders his girlfriend. Apathetic and disturbingly alienated, Reeves was excellent in the role and was subsequently cast in a very different part, that of a high school underachiever devastated by the suicide of his friend (Alan Boyce) in the drama *Permanent Record* (1988), for which he received rave reviews. He had fun portraying a series of teenagers – a high school nerd in *The Night Before*, an off-beat free spirit wooing an older woman (Amy Madigan) and sporting a bizarre haircut in *Prince of Pennsylvania* (both 1988) and as one of a pair of time travellers in *Bill And Ted's Excellent Adventure* (1989) – while simultaneously landing some plum supporting roles in successful movies by such well-known directors as Stephen Frears, Ron Howard and Lawrence Kasdan. While Howard's *Parenthood* (1989) rather typecast him (complete with a half-shaved head) as the good-natured but blithely unrealistic young boyfriend of Martha Plimpton, Kasdan's *I Love You To Death* (1990) gave him the opportunity to reveal more of his obvious gift for comedy in his portrayal of a virtually brain-dead would-be assassin; and *Dangerous Liaisons* (1988) saw him in a period piece as an idealistic young lover corrupted by Glenn Close's Marquise de Merteuil. But he remains at his best in contemporary roles, which capitalise on his looks and was busier at the beginning of the 90s than ever before. And if Keanu Reeves seemed overshadowed by River Phoenix in *My Own Private Idaho* (1991), this was more the role as written than as played.

1986 Flying; Youngblood **1987** River's Edge **1988** The Night Before; Permanent Record; Prince of Pennsylvania; Dangerous Liaisons **1989** Bill And Ted's Excellent Adventure; Parenthood **1990** I Love You To Death; Tune In Tomorrow (GB: Aunt Julia And The Scriptwriter) **1991** Point Break; My Own Private Idaho; Bill And Ted's Bogus Journey **1992** Bram Stoker's Dracula **1992/93** Much Ado About Nothing (GB) **1993** hideous mutant FREEKZ; Even Cowgirls Get The Blues

Reiner, Carl

Director, actor, writer
Born 20 March 1922
The Bronx, New York

One of the key figures in American television comedy during the 50s and 60s, a theatre and film actor, screenwriter and latterly a movie director, Carl Reiner is without doubt a man of remarkable talent, energy and diversity. In a business where trends are all-important, his timely ability to swap artistic hats seems to have been in large part the secret of his survival – but not necessarily the secret of success. For, as is the case with his colleague and friend Mel Brooks, Reiner's facility for anarchic, silly comedy is rarely enough, on its own, to sustain a film, resulting in an output of mainly slap-happy unevenness which at best is carried by performances from gifted comic actors and at worst deteriorates into an abysmal mess. Unfortunately, the latter rather than the former has been a characteristic of his recent work, most notably 1990's redundant leaden farce, *Sibling Rivalry*.

The son of a watchmaker, the young Reiner aspired to be a baseball player but, aged 16, he began his working life as a machinist's helper. He turned to studying acting at the WPA Dramatic Workshop shortly afterwards, and had played several roles when World War II broke out and he was drafted into the army. He spent a period teaching French, and a year-and-a-half entertaining the troops as part of the Special Services Unit. Upon his discharge, he quickly landed the central part in the touring musical, *Call Me Mister*, which he later performed on Broadway.

Reiner's television career began when, in 1950, he became a writer and actor – alongside stars Sid Caesar and Imogene Coca – on the now legendary comedy series *Your Show of Shows*. Reiner spent nine years with the programme, during which time he also collaborated with Mel Brooks on the no less legendary comic recordings featuring the beloved character, The 2000-Year-Old Man, before turning his hand to creating, producing, writing and acting in *The Dick Van Dyke Show* in the early 60s. Simultaneously with his extraordinarily successful television career (for which he was awarded an impressive 11 Emmys) Reiner was also appearing as a supporting actor in feature film comedies, two of which, *It's A Mad Mad Mad Mad World* (1963) and *The Russians Are Coming, The Russians Are Coming* (1966) offered him the opportunity to play major roles. But, as his two screenplay efforts (1963's *The Thrill Of It All* and 1965's *The Art of Love*, both of which he also appeared in) presaged, it was off camera where he was headed.

When, in 1967, Reiner did make his directorial debut it was aptly enough with *Enter Laughing*, based on a semi-autobiographical novel he had had published in the late 50s, and which had become a Broadway play. Blander than the theatrical production, the film was nevertheless a funny, overtly Jewish comedy about the experiences of a struggling young actor, and it augured well for the director. His second film, *The Comic* (1969), starring Dick Van Dyke as a silent movie comedian, aside from indicating Reiner's recurring interest in 'the entertainer' and rise-and-fall themes, revealed a tendency towards a not always successful blending of pathos and laughs, which later spoilt both *The One and Only* (1978) and *Bert Rigby, You're a Fool* (1989).

A deft hand at sight gags, Reiner is an ingenious but simplistic director best suited to unsophisticated, even broad comedy. Unsurprisingly, in view of his career experience, he has always gravitated towards actors who share his television comedy background – Dick Van Dyke, George Burns (*Oh God*, 1977), Henry Winkler (*The One And Only* 1978), John Candy (*Summer Rental*, 1985), Kirstie Alley (*Summer School*, 1987, *Sibling Rivalry*) – and, of course, Steve Martin. A felicitous pairing, the two collaborated on four films in five years. *The Jerk* (1979) was the first, and marked the comic performer's motion-picture debut as the adopted white son of poor black sharecroppers who makes it big, only to be sued by a director (played by Reiner himself) who has become cross-eyed thanks to one of Martin's inventions. A slight, cheap-looking film, *The Jerk* was certainly no masterpiece but its daft, rags-to-riches-to-rags plot was a great vehicle for the actor's engagingly absurd, physical style of comedy. So too was the terminally silly but frequently hilarious *The Man With Two Brains* (1983) in which Martin plays surgeon Dr Hfuhruhurr, who falls in love with some pickled grey matter despite being married to a seductive but wonderfully evil Kathleen Turner. The actor's best role was in 1984's *All Of Me*. Playing a put-upon young lawyer, he delivers a superbly schizoid *tour-de-force* performance when half his body is taken over by the spirit of a recently deceased, cantankerous millionaires (Lily Tomlin).

Looking back on their collaborations however, it was doubtless more the talent of Martin than of Reiner that made the films special – certainly their least effective joint effort, *Dead Men Don't Wear Plaid* (1982) was co-written by the director; like too many of his films, this one was little more than a collection of jokes which, though frequently funny, were not enough to support the whole enterprise. The technique was clever – intercutting *film noir* excerpts from the 40s to give the impression that private eye Martin was actually involved with stars like Bogart, Bergman and Stanwyck – but however well-meaning Reiner's frequent homages to past styles of entertainment, they do not always make for effective movies, and, in the case of *Bert Rigby, You're A Fool* (a sort of MGM-style musical featuring Robert Lindsay as an English miner who becomes a Hollywood star), which he also wrote, they are nothing short of embarrassing.

Happily married to his wife, Estelle, since 1943, Reiner is a father of three; both his sons, Rob and Lucas, are also film-makers. But while his directorial star has gone into decline, that of his son Rob has ascended to heady heights, a situation which Carl Reiner, although likely to continue working for some time to come, will probably never reverse.

As actor: **1959** Happy Anniversary **1960** The Gazebo **1961** Gidget Goes Hawaiian **1963** The Thrill Of It All (also writer); It's A Mad Mad Mad Mad World **1965** The Art Of Love (also writer) **1966** Don't Worry – We'll Think Of A Title (cameo); The Russians Are Coming, The Russians Are Coming, **1967** A Guide For The Married Man (cameo) **1969** Generation (GB: A Time For Giving) **1973** Ten From Your Show Of Shows (compilation TV film) **1978** The End

As director: **1967** Enter Laughing (also co-writer) **1969** The Comic (also actor, co-writer) **1970** Where's Poppa? **1977** Oh God (also actor) **1978** The One And Only **1979** The Jerk (also cameo) **1982** Dead Men Don't Wear Plaid (also co-writer) **1983** The Man With Two Brains **1984** All Of Me **1985** Summer Rental **1987** Summer School (also cameo) **1989** Bert Rigby, You're A Fool (also writer) **1990** Sibling Rivalry

Reiner, Rob

Director, actor, writer
Born 6 March 1945
New York City

The director of two of the most irresistible movies of the 80s, *Stand By Me* (1986) and *When Harry Met Sally* (1989), Rob Reiner is an unapologetic populist who is equally sure-handed with everything from children's fairy-tales to psychological horror, and the few traits common to his six directorial efforts to date form the essential components for any good movie: an excellent, witty script, inspired casting, and, not least, a lightness of touch.

Like his father, Carl, Rob Reiner is a multi-talented man who made a name for himself in television. Born in New York, he was 12 when his family transferred to LA where, after summers spent working on his father's sets and in local theatre, he enrolled at UCLA to study drama. From there he began working in improvisational comedy and made his way into TV through writing comedy scripts for such programmes as *The Smothers Brothers' Comedy Hour* and the occasional guest slot on a show, as well as appearing in his father's first two movies. In 1971 he began an acting stint as Michael 'Meathead' Stivic in the popular long-running sit-com *All In The Family*, a role which brought him fame and two Emmys. But although he continued working as a writer and appearing in programmes such as *The Beverly Hillbillies* (which brought him another Emmy) and the TV movie *More Than Friends* (a semi-autobiographical comedy he also scripted and which co-starred his then wife Penny Marshall), Reiner had his sights set on the bigger picture.

This Is Spinal Tap (1984), a spoof rock documentary, was his first feature film. A low-budget, intentionally amateurish-look ing affair (plenty of handheld camera shots), its parody of the excesses and egomania of the heavy metal world was made all the more hilarious by its 'straight' approach as it trailed English headbangers (wonderfully played by American actors and co-writers Michael McKean, Christopher Guest and Harry Shearer) on a tour of the US. Featuring original music (with choice lyrics and titles like 'Lick My Love Pump') and the bearded, balding Reiner himself as director-interviewer Marty DeBergi, the film became an immediate cult hit whose modest success provided the backing for his second venture, *The Sure Thing* (1985). More than a cut above the average teenage comedy, the film depicted the unlikely pairing of two college students, the square, uptight Daphne Zuniga and the fun-loving, sex-driven John Cusack, on a disaster-beset journey across the States. Not only did the film foreshadow the themes of *When Harry Met Sally*, it also revealed Reiner as an actor's director with an eye for spotting new talent and drawing out engaging and thoroughly credible performances from a script which, however lighthearted and slight, contained insight and some great lines.

However, it was his third film that brought his real commercial breakthrough. Based on the Stephen King short story *The Body*, *Stand By Me* (1986) was a warm and nostalgic slice of 50s Americana with a rites-of-passage theme that quickly became a minor classic of its kind. Reiner never patronising, coaxes beguilingly truthful performances from his young adolescent stars (including River Phoenix) as they go in search of a corpse, and the film is a thoroughly sympathetic study of childhood confusion, friendship and coming of age.

For his next venture, Reiner tried a more rambunctious, broad-comedy approach, the nearest in tone he has ever got to his father's brasher style of film-making. However, *The Princess Bride* (1987), adapted by eminent screenwriter William Goldman from his own novel, was a hilarious and vastly superior fantasy tale, with a storyteller framework, and complete with giants, witches, masked swordsmen, cunning Sicilians and villainous aristocrats. An adventurous, tongue-in-cheek romp through a world of dangerous cliffs, swamps and castles, it was a kid's movie for adults and tremendous good fun. Kevin Kline in particular, as the hell-bent avenger Inigo Montoya is unforgettable, and Billy Crystal turns in a scene-stealing cameo as the miracle man, Max.

It was Crystal, a very close friend and co-star (both in *All In The Family* and 1987's *Throw Momma From The Train*) to whom Reiner turned when he was casting his screen alter ego in *When Harry Met Sally* (1989). A semi-autobiographical film, the project came to life after Reiner's marriage to Marshall fell apart and he found himself back in the dating game. Always a man to pick the sharpest and most talented of screenwriters, Reiner entrusted the idea to Nora Ephron, whose script was based in large part on interviews with Reiner and his producing partner, Andy Scheinman. The film returned the director to the realm of adults as it traced the friendship of Meg Ryan's Sally and Crystal's Harry (who, as in *The Sure Thing*, first meet – and get off on the wrong foot – on a journey across the US), and posed the question: 'Can men and women be friends or . . . does the sex always get in the way?'. As with all the best romantic comedies the outcome is wonderfully predictable, but only reached after a full series of amusing ups and downs and situations illustrating the gulf between the sexes, as when 'high-maintenance woman' Sally challenges Harry (a man who believes in reading the final chapter of a book first in case he dies before he reaches the end) on his powers to distinguish real from fake as she pretends an orgasm in a crowded deli. The scene has, quite rightly, already become one of the screen's classic 'moments' (and, incidentally, the woman who utters the unforgettable riposte 'I'll have what she's having' is Reiner's mother, Estelle). Eminently accessible but also clever, witty and insightful, the film resulted in favourable comparisons being drawn between Reiner and Woody Allen which, however flattering, proved entirely inappropriate for his next venture, *Misery* (1990).

Another Stephen King adaptation (again by William Goldman), Reiner's sixth feature is a dark, claustrophobic horror tale and a complete departure from his usual airiness. Basically a two-hander, the story involves a writer of tawdry romantic novels (James Caan) who, injured in a car accident, is rescued by his 'number one fan' (Kathy Bates), a nurse who turns out to be a raving psychopath. It is a film about unhinged obsession with some exceedingly gruesome scenes which Reiner handles masterfully, and powerhouse performances from Caan and Bates, who was rewarded with a Best Actress Oscar. However different from his previous features – remarkable and compelling though it is, it certainly doesn't make for comfortable viewing – *Misery*, as we've come to expect from Reiner, also weaves in some delightfully comic moments especially through the characters of the local sheriff and his wife. But whether this gifted director would continue to explore a darker side or opt to lighten up again in his projects, remained to be seen, for, however consistently superior the quality of Rob Reiner's work, his choices are, happily, unpredictable.

Now married to photographer Michelle Singer, Reiner continues to act occasionally, recently making a cameo appearance as a movie producer is in *Postcards From The Edge*, and in *Spirit of '76* (both 1990), the directorial debut of his brother, Lucas.

As director only unless stated otherwise: **1967** Enter Laughing (actor only) **1970** Where's Poppa? (actor only) **1977** Fire Sale (actor only) **1984** This Is Spinal Tap (also actor, co-writer) **1985** The Sure Thing **1986** Stand By Me **1987** The Princess Bride; Throw Momma From The Train (actor only) **1989** When Harry Met Sally **1990** Spirit of '76 (actor only); Postcards From The Edge (cameo only); Misery **1992** A Few Good Men **1992/93** Sleepless In Seattle (actor only)

Reinhold, Judge

Actor

Born 1956

Wilmington, Delaware

Although early appearances – the student-cum-short-order cook in *Fast Times At Ridgemont High* (1982), a cadet in *The Lords Of Discipline* (1983) – placed him in company with several young actors, such as Sean Penn, who became collectively known as the Brat Pack, Judge Reinhold has escaped the label. This might in some part be due to his flair for the kind of light comedy that was more prevalent in previous decades than it is now – indeed, his physique, his soft good looks, and the ability to look appealingly bemused, are somewhat reminiscent of the young Ryan O'Neal.

Reinhold became interested in acting while at high school and took a drama course at the University of Virginia. He then joined the Burt Reynolds Dinner Theater in Florida before making the move to California where he secured a contract with Paramount Television. He made no particular mark in TV, and began his movie career with tiny parts in *Running Scared* (1980) and *Stripes* (1981) before his featured appearance in *Fast Times*. It was his supporting role as the sympathetic and gullible rookie plainclothesman in *Beverly Hills Cop* (1984) which brought him real attention; while in *Roadhouse 66* (1984) as a bewildered preppie caught, trapped and challenged by a bunch of Arizona roughnecks, he established that he could hold centre stage.

Later roles show Reinhold to have matured into a stylish and accomplished light comedy actor. It remains to be seen whether he has the capacity for stronger roles, but he is a very attractive and useful addition to a wide range of 'thirty-something' and other fare. He was an excellent foil to Bette Midler in *Ruthless People* (1986) and, especially, to Marianne Sägebrecht in *Rosalie Goes Shopping* (1989), where, as the young priest who serves as the outrageous Rosalie's despairing confessor, he used his gifts with true expertise. His subsequent output however, proved disappointing, his talents wasted in such witless tedium as *Over Her Dead Body*.

1980 Running Scared **1981** Stripes **1982** Pandemonium; Fast Times at Ridgemont High **1983** Lords Of Discipline **1984** Gremlins; Roadhouse 66; Beverly Hills Cop **1985** Head Office **1986** Ruthless People; Off Beat **1987** Beverly Hills Cop II **1988** Vice Versa **1989** Rosalie Goes Shopping **1990** Daddy's Dyin' . . . Who's Got The Will? **1991** Last Tangle In Paris; Zandalee; Over Her Dead Body

Remar, James

Actor
Born 31 December 1953
Boston, Massachusetts

One of the most extreme examples of typecasting among 80s actors, the physically foreboding James Remar seems destined to be one of filmland's favourite psychopaths, unable to escape the role even on television or the stage – his Broadway debut in *Bent* in 1979 was as a Nazi. Dropping out of (and later returning to) high school to tour with a rock band, he studied acting at New York's Neighborhood Playhouse with Sanford Meisner, entering movies via the stage as one of the many punks in the Joan Micklin Silver-produced *On The Yard* (1978). But it was his second movie, as Ajax, the lieutenant of *The Warriors* (1979) street gang who ends up handcuffed to a park bench by an undercover policewoman, that was to prove more important, not just because it gave him more screen time but because it marked the first of his three films with Walter Hill. The tribal trappings of the role did not go unnoticed either – both his subsequent roles for Hill were half-breed Indians, while his performance as the vengeful son in the native American drama *Windwalker* (1980, shot entirely in Crow and Cheyenne) earned him the honorary title 'Standing 20' from the Cheyenne tribe.

He was a compelling example of pure brute force at its most disturbed in Hill's *48 HRS.* (1982) and his breathtaking and horrifying outbursts of extreme violence made his Dutch Schultz in *The Cotton Club* (1984) one gangster no one would idolise; but the impetus it gave his career was quickly halted when a personal drug problem cost him the male lead in *Aliens* (1986) and put his screen work on hold for a while. Re-emerging towards the end of the decade, he was back in the black hat with his silent killer in *Rent-A-Cop* (1989, a part exploiting his physical presence rather than his acting talents) and his corrupt cop, in the same year's *Dream Team*, as well as a more telling, physically effacing and paradoxically sympathetic role in *Drugstore Cowboy*. Remar moved into the mainstream with TV, and the portmanteau horror flick, *Tales From The Darkside* (1990), as well as Randal Kleiser's rather de-clawed Disney version of *White Fang* (1991), in which the actor alone of the film's cast looked as if he could genuinely have taken on the wilderness.

1978 On The Yard **1979** The Warriors **1980** Cruising; The Long Riders; Windwalker **1982** Partners; 48 HRS. **1984** The Cotton Club **1986** Band Of The Hand; The Clan Of The Cave Bear; Quiet Cool **1989** Rent-A-Cop; The Dream Team; Drugstore Cowboy; (Germany) Zwei Frauen/Silence Like Glass **1990** Tales From The Darkside: The Movie **1991** White Fang; Night Visions

Remick, Lee

Actress
Born 14 December 1935
Quincy, Massachusetts
Died 2 February 1991

It seems somewhat surprising that Lee Remick, always attractive without being threatening, was initially promoted as America's answer to Brigitte Bardot, although following her debut as a sexy drum majorette in *A Face In The Crowd* (1957) promiscuity seemed to play a large part in her screen roles: the Southern temptress crying rape in Preminger's *Anatomy Of A Murder* (1959), Frank Sinatra's nymphomaniac wife in *The Detective* (1968), the American tourist setting out to seduce James Coburn's hitman in *Hard Contract* (1969), the nurse in the film of Joe Orton's *Loot* (1971).

The daughter of an actress, the former model and dancer got herself a job in summer stock, working her way up to Broadway (a five-day run in *Be Your Age*) before Elia Kazan spotted her in a TV play and cast her in *A Face In The Crowd.* A short-term contract with 20th-Century-Fox and further flirtatious roles followed, as did the elevation to leading roles in *Wild River* (1960) and the dismal bowdlerisation of William Faulkner's *Sanctuary* (1961), but it was not until she was released from her contract that good roles were forthcoming.

She proved a credible common-sense heroine in Blake Edward's taut thriller *Experiment In Terror* (1962) and quickly followed it with her performance as the wife who follows husband Jack Lemmon into alcoholism in the same director's *Days Of Wine And Roses.* Her portrayal of dignity and personality disintegrating in a way that had previously only been the province of male actors, had true shock impact and earned her an Oscar nomination. However, more substantial parts failed to materialise, and even when united with formidable directors and casts the results proved distinctly disappointing, leading to occasional returns to the stage (Sondheim's *Anyone Can Whistle*, the thriller *Wait Until Dark*).

Things seemed to perk up with Remick's nicely judged comic performance as George Segal's WASP girlfriend learning to be Jewish ('I've always said it's the only religion') to ingratiate herself with his domineering mother in *No Way To Treat A Lady* (1968), but still Hollywood didn't catch on, precipitating her move to England, where she met and married her second husband, assistant director William 'Kip' Gowans, while filming *A Severed Head* (1971). Occasionally commuting to America, she found stronger roles in television – most notably as Winston Churchill's mother in *Jennie* – and soon became a common face in mini-series on both sides of the Atlantic. Ageing gracefully and no longer so firmly typecast, her film roles became fewer – although she was impressive with her maternal instincts giving way to fear in *The Omen* (1976) and as one of *The Europeans* (1979) – as television took up more of her time until her career was brought to an unfortunate halt when she developed cancer. Despite a heroic fight, she suffered a relapse that caused her return to work in the mini-series *Young Catherine* in 1990 to be called to an abrupt halt in mid-production, and led to her untimely death in Los Angeles at the age of 55.

1957 A Face In The Crowd **1958** The Long Hot Summer **1959** These Thousand Hills; Anatomy Of A Murder **1960** Wild River **1961** Sanctuary **1962** Experiment In Terror aka Grip Of Fear; Days Of Wine And Roses **1963** The Running Man; The Wheeler Dealers (aka Separate Beds) **1965** Baby, The Rain Must Fall; The Hallelujah Trail **1968** No Way To Treat A Lady; The Detective **1969** Hard Contract **1971** A Severed Head; Loot; Sometimes A Great Notion aka Never Give An Inch **1973** A Delicate Balance **1975** Hennessy **1976** The Hunted; The Omen **1977** Telefon **1978** The Medusa Touch **1979** The Europeans **1980** The Competition; Tribute **1985** Emma's War

Reynolds, Burt
(Burton Leon Reynolds Jr)
Actor, director
Born 11 February 1936
Waycross, Georgia

A brief glimpse at Burt Reynolds' filmography shows a dispiritingly small number of good films – indeed, the best that can be said of most of them is that they are amiable. The star's days of glory were due more to personality than quality, and Reynolds has always had personality to spare. One of the screen's most appealing show-offs, his initial fame was due more to his witty appearances on talk shows (on one memorable occasion chatting up host Dinah Shore on air) and his infamous nude centrefold in the April 1972 issue of *Cosmopolitan* than any of the TV series or films he was promoting.

A car accident having shattered his pro-football ambitions, he switched to college dramatics and dropped out of school to head for New York and a stage career, finding immediate success as a dishwasher and nightclub bouncer before his stage debut opposite Charlton Heston in a 1956 revival of *Mister Roberts* led to a Universal contract. (He was subsequently fired by the studio the same day as Clint Eastwood.) Despite a few movie jobs, his career developed through recurring roles, often as Indian half-breeds (his grandmother was a Cherokee), in TV series such as *Riverboat* and *Gunsmoke* (1962–65) before he was given a short-lived cop show of his own, *Hawk* (1966–67), and the private eye series *Dan August* (1979–71), in which he gradually established his screen persona: serious when need be but generally flippant, and virile enough to appeal to a female audience without threatening the male viewers.

With the exception of his scene-stealing bandit in *100 Rifles* (1969) Burt's big-screen career took longer to mature, but the advent of *Deliverance* (1972) and his atypical performance as a macho businessman whose cocky self-assurance is destroyed by a hostile environment, saw him effortlessly steal the film from its nominal star, Jon Voight, and propelled him into the mainstream. It truly was effortless; for one of the more physically gruelling scenes, Voight asked for four minutes to prepare by running up a sweat and doing strenuous exercises. Reynolds simply asked for ten seconds to empty a bucket of water over his head and carried the scene.

Subsequent films, aside from Robert Aldrich's anti-Establishment prison satire, *The Mean Machine* (1974), were nothing to write home about, but the films weren't important – it was Reynolds the public was buying. Men wanted to be like him and women just wanted him, and it was his spontaneous blue-collar charm that made him

America's top box-office star for five consecutive years (a feat unequalled since Shirley Temple). Yet even in his heyday there were major flops like *Lucky Lady*, *At Long Last Love* (both 1975) and *Nickelodeon* (1976), so when the phenomenal success of *Smokey And The Bandit* (1976) offered a simple formula of 'fast cars plus country boys and the hell with the law equals big bucks', he stuck to it in a move that at once gave him greater control of his career and gradually eroded it as he worked the vein to death.

He followed Eastwood's example, establishing a stock company of regulars – almost exclusively personal friends such as Sally Field, Ned Beatty, Dom DeLuise, and Hal Needham (a great stuntman but a truly appalling director) – and moving into direction himself, yet failing to match the depth of his monosyllabic box-office rival; the films were far from personal, the shots generally loose, and it became increasingly apparent that those on set were having more fun that those in the aisles. He did attempt to broaden his appeal and range, effectively playing a divorcee still in love with his ex-wife in *Starting Over* (1977) but his public didn't want to know and he spent much of the 80s in a series of production-line star vehicles such as the ham-fisted *Cannonball Run* films (1980 and 1983) in which his cockiness began to veer towards the surly and obnoxious.

Indeed, the early part of the decade was littered with warning signals – John Boorman's departure from *Sharky's Machine* (1981, Reynolds last huge hit) prior to shooting, the sudden collapse of a big-budget film of *The Bourne Identity* in pre-production and a surprising number of folded projects – and by the time he appeared opposite Eastwood in the lacklustre and much troubled *City Heat* (1984) it seemed an acknowledgement on both stars' parts that the good old days when everything they touched to gold had gone. While his co-star had been establishing a critical reputation for his old age through a series of highly individual films, Reynolds moved to an increasingly dour series of thrillers that were quickly relegated to video outside the States.

No longer a box-office guarantee, the furore surrounding the production of *Heat* (1987) virtually turned him into a liability. As if working for Cannon were not disturbing enough, Reynolds and director R.M. Richards came to much publicised blows (Reynolds was successfully sued for $300,000), while the actor's temporarily failing health caught the full fury of a media circus that had just buried Rock Hudson's reputation and was looking for more fresh HIV positive blood, whether he had the disease or not (he didn't). Soon the gossip columns were full of 'close personal friends' speculating on whether or not he had AIDS, lines from previous movies (most particularly 1975's *W.W. And The Dixie Dancekings*) were quoted out of context and attributed to Reynolds as proof of his possible homosexuality and he became a feature of night-club comics' acts. Worse was to follow as spectacularly bad business investments drove him into debt to the tune of $20 million. Reynolds' star was already fading fast – partially because his 'good ol' boy' image was at odds with the 'new man' of the 80s; partially because in an age of Meryl's accents and De Niro's metamorphoses he never pretended to be anything other than Burt Reynolds, Movie Star; but largely because people just got tired of seeing him behind the wheel of a car and forgot he could do anything else – but the eventually discredited stories just added insult to injury. Even a pleasing return to comic form in *Switching Channels* (1988) was marred by the knowledge that he was only a last-minute replacement for a suddenly unavailable Michael Caine.

Ironically, it was precisely the downturn in his career that earned him his best screen role since *Deliverance*, as the greying safecracker of *Breaking In* (1989). A remarkably brave and sensitive performance – marked by his matter-of-fact revelation to his on-screen protégé (Casey Siemaszko) that he is unable to have a relationship with a woman who isn't a prostitute, delivered without any sense of irony or sentimentality – it should have heralded the start of a new career as a character actor, but poor distribution and director Bill Forsyth's kamikaze press interviews attacking both the film and its star with faint praise ensured its speedy disappearance. When Reynolds finally did rake up another hit that year, it was as the voice of a German shepherd in the animated feature *All Dogs Go To Heaven*.

It was his return to television that brought him back into the limelight, albeit after a few false starts. The sit-com *Evening Shade* proved that people still wanted to *see* Burt Reynolds even if they didn't want to pay to do it, and his easygoing, self-deprecating performance brought his career full circle to its small-screen roots.

1961 Angel Baby; Armored Command **1965** Operation

CIA **1967** Navajo Joe **1969** Sam Whiskey; 100 Rifles; Impasse; Shark! **1970** Skullduggery **1972** Fuzz; Deliverance; Everything You Always Wanted To Know About Sex . . . But Were Afraid To Ask; 173 Shamus; The Man Who Loved Cat Dancing; White Lightning **1974** The Mean Machine aka The Longest Yard **1975** W.W. And The Dixie Dancekings; At Long Last Love; Lucky Lady; Hustle **1976** Silent Movie; Gator (also director); Nickelodeon; Smokey And The Bandit **1977** Semi-Tough **1978** The End (also director); Hooper **1979** Starting Over **1980** Smokey And The Bandit II aka Smokey And The Bandit Ride Again aka Smokey And The Bandit Have A Baby; Roughcut; The Cannonball Run **1981** Sharky's Machine (also director); Paternity **1982** The Best Little Whorehouse In Texas; Best Friends **1983** Stroker Ace; Cannonball Run II; The Man Who Loved Women; Smokey And The Bandit III (cameo only) **1984** City Heat; Uphill All The Way (cameo only) **1985** Stick (also director) **1987** Heat; Malone **1988** Rent-A-Cop; Switching Channels **1989** Physical Evidence; Breaking In **1990** Modern Love **1992** The Player (cameo as himself); Cop And-A-Half

Rickman, Alan

Actor
Born?
England

It is quite ironic that this tall, precise, English actor, trained at RADA and renowned for his work with The Royal Shakespeare Company, should make his big-screen debut in, of all things, a big-budget action adventure. But Alan Rickman became known on both sides of the Atlantic in 1988 for his role in the Bruce Willis-starring box-office smash *Die Hard* (1988).

Although it was that film that catapulted the actor to fame, he had an equally impressive past beginning when, at the age of 26, he abandoned his career as a graphic designer in London to become an actor. He appeared in several productions including *The Devil Is An Ass* and *Measure For Measure* for the Birmingham Repertory Theatre Company and worked at the National Theatre before joining the Royal Shakespeare Company. It was there that he was cast as the Vicomte de Valmont in *Les Liaisons Dangereuses*, for which he won acclaim in London and on Broadway, receiving the 1987 Tony nomination.

In between his stage performances, Rickman found time to appear in TV series, including the BBC's adaptation of Zola's *Therese Raquin* in 1981 and the popular *Smiley's People* in 1982. After more than a decade of impressive work which included directing the play *Desperately Yours* in New York in 1980, he was offered the role of evil Hans Gruber in the phenomenally successful *Die Hard*. With almost as much screen time as hero Bruce Willis, Rickman excelled as the evil leader of a gang of terrorist-thieves who hold the staff of the Nagasaki building hostage while he attempts to steal millions of dollars in negotiable bonds from the building's vaults. It was an impressive entry into Hollywood, with Rickman displaying a frightening degree of menace.

Immediately after shooting ended, he went into *The January Man* (1989), a thriller starring Kevin Kline. As the eccentric painter caught up in Kevin Kline's investigation of serial murder, Rickman's part was very much a supporting one but, nonetheless, made an impression. Unfortunately the film was not a success and the actor returned to playing the bad guy in his next movie, this time alongside another heavyweight, Tom Selleck, in the Australian adventure-comedy *Quigley Down Under* (1990). The Western-style adventure enjoyed moderate success, and the actor returned to his home country to appear in two British features, including *Close My Eyes* (1991), directed by Stephen Poliakoff. Although Alan Rickman, with his English accent and demeanour seemed to be typed for 'bad guy' roles in international movies, he chose them well, and increased his standing with his appearance as a grotesque, deranged Sherriff of Nottingham in Kevin Costner's *Robin Hood: Prince Of Thieves* (1991).

1988 Die Hard **1989** The January Man **1990** Quigley Down Under; Truly, Madly, Deeply (GB) **1991** Close My Eyes; Robin Hood: Prince Of Thieves; Closet Land **1992** Bob Roberts

Riegert, Peter

Actor
Born 11 April 1947
New York City

Peter Riegert is one of those attractive 'ordinary men' who draws attention to himself with a particularly engaging performance at approximately five-year intervals and meanwhile carries on working steadily in unlikely places or completely unremarkable projects.

Along with half of Equity's membership who were approaching middle age by the 90s, Riegert made his film debut in *National Lampoon's Animal House* (1978) as one of the frat-house prats. In 1979 he first worked with Joan Micklin Silver in the downbeat drama *Head Over Heels*, but he had to wait until 1983 for a juicy role – in Bill Forsyth's disarming Scottish comedy *Local Hero* as the Yankee oil company employee enchanted by the canny villagers of the coastal beauty spot marked for development.

Riegert's has been a realistic presence as shit, sweetie or schlemiel in some interesting films, notably *The City Girl* (1984), the Argentina set thriller *The Stranger* (1987), and Diane Kurys' Italian-set English language debut film, *A Man In Love* (1987), in which he played harassed sidekick-cum-lackey to Peter Coyote's egomaniac movie star. His most delightful opportunity to cut a romantic figure came in Joan Micklin Silver's charming *Crossing Delancey* (1988) as the Lower East Side Jewish pickle-maker smitten by Amy Irving's reluctant uptown romantic, a proposition undermined only by the fact that in reality no such presentable bachelor would find a woman so hard to get in Manhattan. Riegert has also worked on television, most prominently as a lead in the immigrant saga mini-series *Ellis Island*.

1978 National Lampoon's Animal House **1979** Americathon; Head Over Heels aka Chilly Scenes Of Winter **1983** National Lampoon's Movie Madness aka National Lampoon Goes To The Movies; Local Hero; Grand Carnival **1984** The City Girl **1987** The Stranger; A Man In Love **1988** Sticky Fingers; Crossing Delancey **1990** A Shock To The System; Beyond The Ocean **1991** The Object Of Beauty; Oscar **1992** Passed Away; The Runestone

Ringwald, Molly

Actress
Born 14 February 1969
Sacramento, California

Red-haired Molly Ringwald, the million-dollar teenager, was the fastest-rising star of the 80s, and also one of the fastest to all but disappear. She began her career singing in her father's Great Pacific Jazz Band when only four years old, making her stage debut at five and recording her own jazz album, 'I Wanna Be Loved By You,' at six. TV's *The New Mickey Mouse Show* led to a supporting role in a West Coast production of *Annie* and the TV series *The Facts Of Life*, ensuring that Ringwald was already a seasoned pro by the time she made her film debut in Paul Mazursky's *Tempest* (1982). If the film sprawled, her performance was refreshingly to the point and it was her coltish charm, more than the Golden Globe she won for the part, that led writer-director John Hughes to write *16 Candles* (1984) for her, inspired by the picture of her he placed above his word processor as he worked.

The film was the first of a trio of likeable, good-humoured teen-orientated projects for Hughes and Ringwald, perfectly framing her appealing reality – her roles as girls who were not great beauties, not great brains and not particularly gifted were therefore perfectly identifiable – in a successful formula that culminated in the smash-hit high school Cinderella story *Pretty In Pink* (1986) that boasted a performance surprisingly conscious of social nuances. From there it was all downhill: dissuaded by her mother from taking the Laura Dern role in *Blue Velvet* (1986) and persuaded by producer Warren Beatty (who subsequently took his name off the film) to make James Toback's typically confused *The Pick-Up Artist* (1987), she continued to commit career hara-kiri with Godard's embarrassingly uneventful, directionless mess, *King Lear* (1987). She did enjoy moderate success as the pregnant teenager in *For Keeps* (1988), only for the backwoods *Pretty In Pink* clone *Fresh Horses* (1988) to earn her bad reviews (and even worse publicity for her behaviour on set), while *Loser Takes All* (1989) seemed content to stay on the shelf.

By the time she made a conscious effort to relaunch her career, playing the thankless role of the bride in Alan Alda's *Betsy's Wedding* (1990), the teen movies she excelled in had disappeared as grown-ups returned to the cinema, and she faced the 90s with the hard task of dispelling some unwelcome publicity creating a new niche for herself in character roles, and finding herself at the centre of a storm whipped up by family lawyers of Ted Hughes, the Poet Laureate, when it was mooted she would play his late wife, the poet Sylvia Plath.

1982 Tempest; PK And The Kid **1983** Spacehunter: Adventures In The Forbidden Zone aka Spacehunter: Adventures In The Creepzone **1984** 16 Candles **1985** The Breakfast Club **1986** Pretty In Pink **1987** The Pick-Up Artist; King Lear **1988** For Keeps aka Maybe Baby; Fresh Horses **1989** Loser Takes All aka Strike It Rich (unreleased) **1990** Betsy's Wedding

Ritchie, Michael

Director
Born 28 November 1938
Waukesha, Wisconsin

It was Robert Redford who gave Michael Ritchie his first crack at directing a feature.

The star had been so impressed by one of Ritchie's TV films that he asked him to direct *Downhill Racer* (1969). Ritchie, a Harvard graduate who had worked on TV for some years directing episodes of *Dr Kildare* and *The Man From U.N.C.L.E.* among others, used a semi-documentary style, mixing 16mm with 35mm, to give a rare insight into the sport of Olympic skiing for his debut picture. The laconic script and Redford's character bordered on the sententious, but it was in the downhill races that interest mounted. The director continued his theme of competition in *The Candidate* (1972) and *Smile* (1975), satires on Middle America. The first only dug a little deeper than the surface irony and realistic reconstruction of an election campaign, although Redford was well cast in the vapid title role. *Smile*, virtually a series of sketches following the fortunes of the 32 entrants in the annual Young American Miss competition, was often amusing despite the superior position adopted by the director towards the hokey beauty contest.

A much lighter touch was evident in *The Bad News Bears* (1976), a delightfully wry comedy containing the un-American message that winning isn't everything. The Little League baseball team was the most individualised bunch of kids since 'Our Gang', cute in the sense of smart, while Walter Matthau, as their misanthropic coach, never noticeably played for laughs nor tried to be lovable. *Semi-Tough* (1977), starring Burt Reynolds and Kris Kristofferson as footballers living in a platonic threesome with Jill Clayburgh until sex rears its head, had a witty, free-wheeling quality for most of the way with pro football only one target of the film's sharp jibes.

Ritchie continued to explore the ethics of competition in *An Almost Perfect Affair* (1979), a romantic comedy with Keith Carradine and Monica Vitti as producer and star at the Cannes film festival. Unfortunately, the dismal box-office takings of the movie drove Ritchie into making less interesting commercial products. These included *The Island* (1980), an unintentionally risible but intentionally gruesome modern pirate tale; *The Survivors* (1983), a surprisingly unfunny black comedy given that its stars were Walter Matthau and Robin Williams, and *The Golden Child* (1986), mystical Oriental guff featuring Eddie Murphy and a Chinese waif. No less awful were *Fletch* (1985) and *Fletch Lives* (1989), involving Chevy Chase in multiple disguises and silly situations, and *The Couch Trip* (1987), with over-the-top performances from Dan Aykroyd and Walter Matthau as a lunatic sex therapist and potential suicide respectively. A sad decline for a once highly promising director, with no indication of what was to come in the future.

1969 Downhill Racer **1972** Prime Cut; The Candidate **1975** Smile **1976** The Bad News Bears **1977** Semi-Tough **1979** An Almost Perfect Affair **1980** The Island; Divine Madness **1983** The Survivors **1985** Fletch **1986** The Golden Child **1987** The Couch Trip **1989** Fletch Lives **1992** Diggstown

Ritt, Martin

Director
Born 2 March 1920
New York
Died 8 December 1990

Martin Ritt was politically a man of the left – 'a complete reflection of the time I grew up, as most people are' – a liberal and a humanist whose views were formed by his apprenticeship to the highly politicised Group Theatre in the 1930s, under high-octane directors and teachers like Stella Adler, Harold Klurman and Elia Kazan. He switched from mainly acting to mainly directing after World War II, and was a prominent player in the first, golden age of live television drama – responsible between 1948 and 1951 for some 200 transmissions for CBS.

Disaster struck in 1950 when, in the wake of the HUAC proceedings and soon-to-be-rampant McCarthyism, he was dismissed from his New York-based job without compensation. There followed six years in the wilderness. Hard up, and with a young family to provide for, he nonetheless managed to spend a lot of time at Brooklyn's Jamaica racecourse (in later years of prosperity he owned a couple of race horses, and was known as the source of the best racing tips round Hollywood). Also, and importantly, he gave irregular teaching sessions among his old acquaintances at the Actors' Studio (Rod Steiger, Paul Newman and Joanne Woodward were among his pupils). Clifford Odets, an old friend who had 'squealed' at the McCarthy hearings (and in whose play *Golden Boy* Ritt had begun his stage career in 1937), hired him from time to time as an actor.

Ritt's lucky break back into the mainstream came in 1957 – relatively early for a blacklistee – when a screenwriter friend, Robert Alan Arthur, managed to get him a Hollywood directing ticket on what turned into a modest and successful thriller, *Edge Of The City*

(1956). Thereafter, Ritt was taken up by a rival studio, 20th-Century Fox, whose right-wing president Spyros Skouras was said to have admired the director's integrity.

Edge Of The City had a plot involving racial prejudice, a theme that was taken up in a number of Ritt's subsequent movies, most notably *Hombre* (1967), *Sounder* (1972), *Conrack* (1974) and *The Great White Hope* (1970, with James Earl Jones). Other contemporary areas of existence that interested Ritt included labour relations – from the side of unions, not management, of course – as in *The Molly Maguires* (1970) and *Norma Rae* (1979); also the theme of betrayal, explored in *The Spy Who Came In From the Cold* (1965) and in Ritt's intelligent comedy set in the McCarthy era, *The Front* (1976, starring Woody Allen). Not a writer himself, Ritt relied on collaboration with trusted screenwriters, notably the Ravetches, a famous husband-and-wife team.

Ritt's best known film remains the Academy Award-nominated *Hud* (1963), memorable for its fine performances by Paul Newman, Patricia Neal and Melvyn Douglas). But Richard Harris is equally as arresting in the lesser-known movie *The Molly Maguires*. In later years Martin Ritt came increasingly to stand for a certain strand of thoughtful, carefully crafted, subject-oriented movies: the antithesis of much of today's Hollywood product. Accordingly, the feisty and sensuous Sally Field becomes a favourite actress (*Norma Rae, Back Road* and *Murphy's Romance*). 'Conviction, good will, sense and sensitivity, an idiosyncratic narrative, discreet camerawork and strong performances mark the best of Ritt films', says Pat McGilligan, who interviewed Ritt for *Film Comment* in January 1986 – perhaps the best single article on this director, who died suddenly at the end of 1990 while in the midst of filming *Mr Jones* with Michael Keaton.

1957 Edge Of The City; No Down Payment **1958** The Long Hot Summer **1959** The Black Orchid; The Sound And The Fury **1960** Five Branded Women **1961** Paris Blues **1962** Hemingway's Adventures As A Young Man **1963** Hud **1964** The Outrage **1965** The Spy Who Came In From The Cold **1967** Hombre **1968** The Brotherhood **1970** The Molly Maguires; The Great White Hope **1972** Sounder; Pete'n'Tillie **1974** Conrack **1976** The Front **1978** Casey's Shadow **1979** Norma Rae **1981** Back Roads **1983** Cross Creek **1984** City Heat **1985** Murphy's Romance **1987** Nuts (also actor) **1990** Stanley and Iris

Ritter, John

Actor

Born 17 September 1948

Hollywood, California

Son of the late Tex Ritter (the fabled country-and-western star who sang the hit title song for *High Noon*), John Ritter is perhaps best known to American audiences as the supposedly (but not really – perish the thought!) gay flatmate of two girls in the supremely idiotic TV series of the late 70s and early 80s, *Three's Company*. Slender and brown-haired, with a somewhat triangular face, Ritter has virtually made a career out of playing hyperactive, rather foolish comedy characters.

After attending Hollywood High School, he graduated from the University of Southern California. Majoring in drama and minoring in psychology, his interest in acting led him to the theatre (his appearances included a production at the Edinburgh Festival), before he became familiar in a multitude of made-for-TV movies for which he earned both Emmy and Golden Globe nominations. Ritter's feature film break came with Disney's *The Barefoot Executive* (1971) which starred a chimp who goes on to become a corporate big shot. Although Ritter has no claim to straight dramatic gifts, his association with director Peter Bogdanovich in films such as *Nickelodeon* (1976) and *They All Laughed* (1981) proved fruitful ventures into romantic comedy. Director Blake Edwards gave him the lead in *Skin Deep* (1989), playing a hedonistic writer plagued by wine, women and song. It was quite a virtuoso performance but the film had only limited appeal, and it was the raucous *Problem Child* (1990), in which he was the beleaguered adoptive father of a juvenile monster, that finally furnished Ritter with the blockbuster that he badly needed to further his Hollywood career.

1971 The Barefoot Executive; Scandalous John **1972** The Other **1973** The Stone Killer **1976** Nickelodeon **1978** Breakfast In Bed **1979** Americathon **1980** Hero At Large; Wholly Moses **1981** They All Laughed **1987** Real Men **1989** Skin Deep **1990** Problem Child **1992** Noises Off; Stay Tuned; Problem Child II

Robards, Jason

Actor

Born 26 July 1922

Chicago, Illinois

Jason Robards is one of the best senior actors in Hollywood, indispensable for playing presidents, distinguished senators, and assorted citizens of pith and *gravitas*. His craggy face, rich deep voice, kind eyes and aura of calm authority have given class to numerous movies, especially in the later part of his career.

There is something ironic about this. The son of a notable actor (Jason Robards Sr) and himself, throughout the early part of his career, one of America's most valuable men of the theatre (known for a time as Robards Jr) he has, in the past, tended to speak of cinema disparagingly. It was 'piece work', undertaken to help him pay his alimony; his lifework was elsewhere, on the boards, playing modern classics like O'Neill, which everyone agrees he does consummately well. (He debuted with O'Neill's *The Iceman Cometh*; and three times has played brilliantly in *A Long Day's Journey Into Night*.) Even today, after he has acted in films under some of the most famous directors, he cultivates a somewhat insouciant disregard towards the art form – in public at least – liking to quote Spencer Tracy's description of the actor's duties: 'Be on time, know the jokes. Say them as fast as you can. Take the money and go home.' He may be, secretly, an intellectual; but he wouldn't like to be mistaken for one.

Of his early films in the 1960s, the only one he has really happy memories of is *A Thousand Clowns* (1965), directed by Fred Coe. Yet he also remembers some of the others not unkindly. 1967 saw him as a gangster in a Roger Corman quickie *The St Valentine's Day Massacre*, 'a quick, brisk, efficient little film' (shot in 11 days). The same year he played Doc Halliday in the John Sturges Western *Hour Of The Gun*. Westerns indeed, or quasi-Westerns, take up a significant part of his filmography: he has appeared in some very distinguished ones – notably, Leone's *Once Upon A Time In the West* (1968), and two superb Peckinpahs: *The Ballad Of Cable Hogue* (1970) and *Pat Garrett And Billy The Kid* (1972: he plays a world-weary Mexican provincial governor in a memorable evening scene on the verandah). Alan Pakula's *Comes A Horseman* (1978), in which Robards gets under the skin of a perverted cattle baron, remains one of the best – and most beautifully photographed (by Gordon Willis) – examples of the genre in the 70s.

Robards' major roles, as far as the general public is concerned, however, are the two parts for which, in two successive years (1976, 1977) he received Oscars for Best Supporting Actor: firstly, as *Washington Post* newspaper editor Ben Bradlee in Pakula's excellent Watergate drama, *All The President's Men*; next, as the boozy, mentally tortured crime writer Dashiell Hammett in Fred Zinneman's version of Lillian Hellman's autobiography, *Julia*. Both films are examples of superior Hollywood entertainment, treating audiences as intelligent adults; something that you can find again in a more recent movie, *Reunion* (1969), directed by Jerry Schatzberg from a script by Harold Pinter – the tale of a successful Jewish American professional who goes back on a trip to Germany. Here he relives an episode of boyhood friendship that ended (because of racial politics) in catastrophe. The role, although very small (the body of the film is flashback) is acted with typical thoughtfulness and depth of feeling.

Robards nearly died in a car crash on a mountain on a California highway in 1972 – he had no heartbeat on arrival at hospital. But two years later, he was back on Broadway in another O'Neill triumph, *A Moon For The Misbegotten* – his sixth Tony-nominated performance in 14 years. He opened Brooklyn's Opera House by directing himself in another production of *A Long Day's Journey* in 1978.

A grandfather, Robards married his fourth wife, Lois O'Connor, in 1970. He has six children. Two of his four sons follow the family tradition: Jason III, from his first marriage, and Sam Robards, from his third wife, Lauren Bacall.

1958 The Journey **1961** By Love Possessed; Tender Is The Night **1962** Long Day's Journey Into Night **1963** Act One **1965** A Thousand Clowns **1966** A Big Hand For A Little Lady; Any Wednesday **1967** Divorce – American Style; The St Valentine's Day Massacre; Hour Of The Gun **1968** The Night They Raided Minsky's; Once Upon A Time In The West; Isadora **1970** Julius Caesar; The Ballad Of Cable Hogue; Tora!Tora!Tora!; Fools **1971** Johnny Got His Gun; Murders In The Rue Morgue **1972** The War Between Men And Women; Death Of A Stranger; Pat Garrett And Billy The Kid **1975** Mr Sycamore; A Boy And His Dog **1976** All The President's Men **1977** Julia **1978** Comes A Horseman **1979** Hurricane; Capoblanco; Melvin And Howard (cameo) **1980** Raise The Titanic **1981** The Legend Of The Lone Ranger **1983** Max Dugan Returns; Something Wicked This Way Comes **1987** Square Dance; Bright Lights, Big City **1988** Dream A Little Dream; Reunion

1989 Parenthood; Black Rainbow **1992** Storyville **1992/93** The Trial

Robbins, Tim

Actor
Born 16 October 1958
Covina, California

This tall, tousled-haired actor has managed to move from small supporting roles to leads in the space of a few years during the late 80s winning critical acclaim along the way.

The son of a Greenwich Village folk-singer, Robbins grew up in New York and was bitten by the acting bug while still in high school. He began work as a lighting technician at an off-Broadway theatre, while spending his spare time acting in street theatre in different parts of the city. He then attended New York University, later transferring to UCLA through their theatre programme. After graduating with honours, he moved on to study with French actor George Bigot of the Theatre Du Soleil. Wanting to branch out on his own, he then formed, with a group of likeminded friends, the Actors' Gang, which quickly became one of Los Angeles' leading theatre companies.

Although best known for his acting talents, Robbins participated in all aspects of the Gang, writing, directing and financially aiding the productions. While working with the group, the actor managed to get himself some work in TV movies, and also guested in episodes of *St Elsewhere* and the cop drama series *Hill Street Blues*. Then, at the age of 26, he appeared in his first big-screen film, *Toy Soldiers* (1984), as one of a group who try to rescue their friends from captivity in a Latin-American country. A minor role in *No Small Affair* (1984) followed, but this romantic comedy, which starred Demi Moore and Jon Cryer, quickly disappeared from view.

It was the actor's next appearance that got him noticed, as the strait-laced driver with a penchant for endlessly singing show tunes who gives John Cusack and Daphne Zuniga a ride in Rob Reiner's *The Sure Thing* (1985). The film was a success, as was Tim Robbins, who displayed an appealing gift for comedy. Two small roles in disasters (*Fraternity Vacation*, 1985, *Howard The Duck*, (1986) came next, but he scored again, as one of the fighter pilots alongside Tom Cruise, in the hugely successful *Top Gun* (1986). He then co-starred with Jodie Foster, playing a civil rights worker in the little seen but highly regarded drama *Five Corners* (1988), and was reunited with friend John Cusack in the even less seen music video industry satire *Tapeheads* (1988).

The turning point for Tim Robbins came when he got to take the pitcher's mound as 'Nuke' Laloosh in *Bull Durham* (1988). A fan of The New York Mets, he fulfilled a lifelong ambition to play baseball, but, more important, he co-starred with actress Susan Sarandon (who later became his girlfriend) in a marvellously original and funny film which gave him full scope to show off both his dramatic and comic talents. Although Kevin Costner was top-billed, few who saw the film were likely to forget Robbins tied to a bed while Sarandon read him Walt Whitman's poetry, or the sight of him turning up to practice wearing one of her black lace garters for good luck.

His comic skills were required again for the Deep South comedy drama with Holly Hunter, *Miss Firecracker* (1989), and the Terry Gilliam extravaganza *Erik The Viking* the same year, in which he had the title role. It wasn't a commercial success, but his antics as the Viking opposed to rape and pillage won him the role of Larry, the crazed gunman who holds Robin Williams and his fellow car salesmen hostage in *Cadillac Man* (1990). The film, which was criticised for being overlong and without an adequate storyline, was saved by the (often improvised) banter between the two stars – Robbins proving an adequate match for seasoned comedian Williams.

The actor then did an about-face and returned to serious drama in Adrian Lyne's biblical-hallucinatory thriller *Jacob's Ladder* (1990). He displayed depth in his portrayal of Jacob, a Vietnam veteran suffering from hallucinations in which he is followed and tortured, but the film was too confusing and abstract for the general public, and although praised as innovative and gripping, it was not a success, and was saved only saved by Tim Robbins' sympathetic performance.

In 1992 Robbins really came into his own with a marvellous central performance as the eponymous thrusting young studio executive in Robert Altman's savagely witty indictment of Hollywood, *The Player*, which won him Best Actor at Cannes; and his man-of-the-moment status was further fuelled by his directorial bow with the political corruption satire, *Bob Roberts*, wearing his own liberal heart on his sleeve.

1984 Toy Soldiers; No Small Affair **1985** The Sure Thing; Fraternity Vacation **1986** Top Gun; Howard The Duck

1988 Five Corners; Tapeheads; Bull Durham **1989** Miss Firecracker; Erik The Viking **1990** Cadillac Man; Jacob's Ladder **1992** The Player; Bob Roberts (also director) **1993** Short Cuts; The Hudsucker Proxy

Roberts, Eric

Actor
Born 18 April 1956
Biloxi, Mississippi

Eric Roberts is the most infuriating of actors. Lithe, virile and attractive (he bears an unmistakeable resemblance to his younger sister, Julia, whose rise, unlike his own, was meteoric) he is also undoubtedly talented. However, this dark-haired, melting-eyed actor must undoubtedly be one of the most irritatingly mannered members of his profession. He appears to have taken the dangerous posturings and irregular speech patterns of the Method rather too much to heart, and even his spectacularly winning smile, displaying a mouthful of perfect teeth, soon engenders animosity in an audience, so often and so self-consciously (and, dare one say it, self-regardingly) does he use it. It is perhaps for these reasons that his career, though generally busy, is only intermittently successful, and in danger of being eclipsed by that of his sister who, ironically, got her first screen role thanks to his good offices. The result, *Blood Red*, made in 1986, was so poor it wasn't released, surfacing four years later to ride on the back of her subsequent stardom.

The son of parents involved in the founding and running of an actors and writers workshop in the Deep South, he himself first appeared on a stage at the age of five. When he was 17, he went to London and trained at the Royal Academy (RADA), and continued his studies at the American Academy of Dramatic Arts when he returned to the US. He made his stage debut in a play called *Rebel Women*, and has since worked fairly steadily in the theatre, TV and film, even taking over from John Malkovich in the highly successful Broadway production of *Burn This*.

Perhaps what Roberts needs is a director who won't let him get away with it, which is what one assumes must have been the case when he worked for Larry Cohen in *The Ambulance* (1989). His mega-lead hero role in the medical thriller was almost entirely successful, and the hip New Yorker (which one suspects Southerner Roberts longs to be) was kept well in control so that he proved both virile and sympathetic as a young man caught in a nightmare series of events involving the abduction of diabetic women for experimental purposes. Unfortunately – and it really *is* Roberts' misfortune rather than his fault – this excellent film has, quite inexplicably, barely been released.

The actor's disturbing technique, which leads him to over-dramatise too often and counter-productively to the character and situation, almost derailed Andrei Konchalovsky's intriguing *Runaway Train* (1985) and made co-stars John Voight and Rebecca De Mornay look better than they were; and in *The Pope Of Greenwich Village* the previous year, as an ill-fated, would-be crooked Italian waiter with an excruciatingly overplayed accent, he was eclipsed not only by the Oscar-winning expertise of the late Geraldine Page, but even by Daryl Hannah (whose simplicity scored) and Mickey Rourke, who at least bore a resemblance to a real character. It was impossible, by the 1990s, to predict which way this actor's career would go, and his appearance in *Final Analysis* as Kim Basinger's abusive husband passed virtually unremarked.

1978 King Of The Gypsies **1982** Raggedy Man **1983** Star 80 **1984** The Pope Of Greenwich Village **1985** The Coca-Cola Kid; The Runaway Train **1986** Nobody's Fool **1989** Best Of The Best; The Ambulance; Rude Awakening; Options (cameo); Blood Red **1991** By The Sword **1991** Lonely Hearts **1992** Final Analysis

Roberts, Julia

Actress
Born 28 October 1967
Atlanta, Georgia

The most popular film of 1990 on both sides of the Atlantic was *Pretty Woman*, Garry Marshall's Cinderella-cum-Pygmalion romance about an independent-minded LA hooker and the multi-millionaire tycoon she tangles with. It's a charming, funny, delightful, 'feel-good' movie, but the extent of its huge success was undoubtedly due to the presence of leggy, auburn-haired Julia Roberts, the most singularly enchanting young woman to hit the screen since Audrey Hepburn arrived in *Roman Holiday* way back in 1953.

A Southerner, she comes from a theatrically minded family. Her parents ran theatre workshops in Atlantic City and her elder brother – to whom the physical resemblance is unmistakable – is actor Eric. Always intent on an acting career, she took herself to New York right after high school, finally found an agent and tramped round audition rooms without particular success. A minor role in the mediocre *Blood Red*, a film starring her brother, did her no good as it wasn't released until late in 1990; but there followed in quick succession during 1988 her movie debut proper in *Satisfaction*, then a made-for-cable-TV movie and, finally, *Mystic Pizza*, the one that did the trick. As the sexy and rebellious one of three working-class girlfriends employed in a pizza parlour, whose charms seduce a wealthy Ivy-League college layabout, the newcomer packed a punch in the face of strong competition from Lili Taylor and Annabeth Gish. She won good notices and the attention of casting directors, and soon found herself in the company of Shirley MacLaine, Sally Field, Dolly Parton et al in the Southern comedy-weepie, *Steel Magnolias* (1989).

Roberts played Shelby, the Southern belle in the midst of wedding preparations and unaware of the tragedy that lies in wait for her. Her performance in this adaptation of the Broadway comic weepie garnered an Academy Award nomination for Best Supporting Actress and, her star status assured, Julia has had her pick of offers since, and progressed to more serious subject matter with Joel Schumacher's *Flatliners* (1990), which deals with a quintet of medical students experimenting with temporary death, *Sleeping With The Enemy* (1991) as an obsessed wife, and her first real audience turn-off, *Dying Young* (1991), in which she was romantically involved with a terminally ill patient. Her personal difficulties in the wake of her cancelled wedding to Kiefer Sutherland didn't help her performance as a prickly, mumbling Tinkerbell in *Hook* (1991); but she remained among the most sought-after leading ladies, as demonstrated by her cameo in Robert Altman's *The Player* as the star whose presence makes an otherwise doubtful film project viable.

1988 Satisfaction; Mystic Pizza **1989** Steel Magnolias **1990** Pretty Woman; Flatliners; Blood Red **1991** Sleeping With The Enemy; Dying Young; Hook **1992** The Player (cameo as herself)

Roberts, Tony

Actor

Born 22 October 1939

New York City

Despite his appearances in the tough thrillers *Serpico* (1973) and *The Taking Of Pelham One Two Three* (1974 – quietly stealing scenes as the unpopular mayor's cheerfully defeatist advisor), Tony Roberts remains best known as the curly-haired, self-obsessed straight man to Woody Allen. This is mainly due to the nature of Roberts' film work away from Allen, sporadic, and generally in movies rated B or below.

The son of an actor and a cousin to Everett Sloane (himself best known for his association with one director, Orson Welles), Roberts studied drama at Northwestern University but got off to a slow start professionally. One of his more interesting early credits is as art director on one of the archetypal British 'dirty raincoat' movies of the 60s, *The Naked World of Harrison Marks* (1967). The actor's ability to convey an opportunist streak was first brought to the fore in the Disney comedy, *$1,000,000 Duck* (1971), but he seemed to be going nowhere fast after the dismal Neil Simon effort, *Star Spangled Girl*, the same year until he was rescued by the first of his films for Allen.

In *Play It Again, Sam* (1972), he was a yuppie before the word had been coined, a WASP achiever married to Diane Keaton, driving around in expensive cars, and relaying his telephone number at every port of call. Even poor Diane had to be 'pencilled in' for an appointment, making it little wonder that she ended up caring for nebbish Woody with more than maternal affection. Roberts' engaging features, athletic build and hearty, confident personality made him the perfect foil to Allen, and he lodged in the subconscious image bank of casual cinemagoers in five further films with Woody, stealing the odd scene and playing a major role, as did each member of the six-star ensemble, in *A Midsummer Night's Sex Comedy* (1982), as the raffish, womanising dentist.

But, as a cursory glance at his filmography will confirm, Tony Roberts has been less fortunate outside his roles for Allen. He has filled in much of the interim with stage and TV work and, while thoroughly likeable in his angst-ridden insularity, he seems destined to be connected with too narrow a type of role to see his screen career develop, at this late stage, beyond its limited margins.

1965 The Beach Girls And The Monster **1971** $1,000,000 Duck; Star Spangled Girl **1972** Play It Again, Sam **1973** Serpico **1974** The Taking Of Pelham One Two Three **1975** Le Sauvage (France) **1977** Annie Hall **1979** Just Tell Me What You Want **1980** Stardust Memories **1982** A Midsummer Night's Sex Comedy **1983** Amityville 3-D **1985** Key Exchange **1986** Hannah And Her Sisters **1987** Radio Days **1988** 18 Again! **1991** Switch

Roddam, Franc

Director

Born 29 April 1946

Stockton-On-Tees, England

Franc Roddam's career in films hasn't as yet had the success that has come to contemporaries from a similar advertising background like Alan Parker and Ridley Scott. He hasn't 'found' America in the way that they have; hasn't shown that he can absorb its rhythms and dialects. He is an interesting test case for measuring the culture gap between film (international) and television (particular, parochial). Roddam's work for British TV has been outstandingly successful. He created the long-running ITV series *Auf Wiedersehn, Pet*, and his documentary epics like *The Family* broke new ground and won prestigious prizes. He recognises the great cultural cohesiveness of the medium: 'the wonderful thing about England,' he has said, 'is that if you have something on TV everyone will see it.'

Why, therefore, one might ask, the lure of Hollywood, with all its compromises and indecisions and tendency towards playing safe? Roddam arrived on the West Coast in the wake of the disaster that befell *Heaven's Gate* (1980). For months he couldn't get any projects off the ground. At the time he spoke to the press bitterly. 'They try to break you. They tie you up in deals.' He read something like 300 scripts before alighting on and agreeing to direct *The Lords Of Discipline* (1983), a story after his somewhat left-wing heart about racism in an elite Southern military academy. (Ironically enough, the film was three-quarters made in England because of budgetary considerations – Wellington College standing in for the real-life academy in South Carolina which refused to open its doors.) Like *Quadrophenia* (1978), Roddam's first film, set in the mod-rock milieu of the 1960s, the film showed excellent use of the available big screen technology; but it was hard to detect deeper or more personal drives. The political intelligence of the director's television work seems to become clamorous and strident when pumped up into expensive spectacle. There is the problem of the artist whose real interests are social and serious, trying a bit too hard to be an entertainer – and yet lacking the populist touch of an Alan Parker to guide him.

Roddam's next film, *The Bride* (1985), a remake of the famous 1930s horror film *Bride Of Frankenstein*, was a humourless disaster. He directed a sequence of the compilation opera film *Aria*; and, following this, an action picture with political overtones about American Indians, *War Party* (1989), that once again failed to draw plaudits. Still very successful in television, it remained to be seen if, during the 90s, he would be able to extricate himself from the impasse which his film-making seemed to have reached.

1978 Quadrophenia **1983** The Lords Of Discipline **1985** The Bride **1987** Aria (section) **1989** War Party **1991** K-2

Roeg, Nicolas

Director

Born 15 August 1928

London, England

Neither Nicolas Roeg's appearance – that of a favourite uncle – nor his background in mainstream British cinema, prepare one for the surprise of his narrative approach. Entering films as a clapper boy in 1950 at MGM's British studios, he worked his way up to cinematographer by 1959, photographing films as diverse as Corman's *The Masque Of The Red Death* (1964), Truffaut's *Fahrenheit 451* (1966), Richard Lester's *Petulia* (1968) and Schlesinger's *Far From The Madding Crowd* (1967, one of the most visually beautiful British films ever made), as well as a Michael Winner movie and second unit for *Lawrence Of Arabia* (1962). He also collaborated on some routine scripts.

His first film as a director (in collaboration with Donald Cammell) set the agenda for much of his later work. Starting off as a strikingly authentic and graphic crime thriller, *Performance* (1970) slowly mutated into an examination of the transference of identity between a criminal on the lam (James Fox) and the ex-rock star (Mick Jagger) whose haven from reality he initially invades but, through a mixture of drugs, sexuality and mind games, ultimately takes him over. Much cut and delayed by the censor, the film gave the first bold example of Roeg's habit of courting controversy and redefining the boundaries of British cinema, both in style and in content. *Walkabout* (1971), shot in the Australian outback by the director himself, was another collision of opposites, the two children abandoned in the desert and the Aborigine who helps them, the city and the desert and their respective cultural gulfs of time and space. Sensual and at times almost surreal, it began the development of Roeg's stream-of-conciousness style of film-making where everything connects, despite initial appearances to the contrary, through intricate and, at its most pronounced, almost hallucinogenic editing and a complex narrative structure that renders his work inaccessible to many.

At its best in *Don't Look Now* (1973) (especially in its shocking finale in which a premonition of danger is fatally misinterpreted as a message of hope by the one person apparently least likely to believe it but who most wants to) Roeg's style can embrace a wide emotional range – and his films are emotionally rather than intellectually structured and motivated. Certainly there is no more revealing or accurate study of the psychology of grief in English-language cinema *than Don't Look Now*, and that it could be conveyed within the framework of a strong, compelling narrative made it all the more of an achievement, which he failed to repeat with *The Man Who Fell To Earth* (1976), in which the idealism of David Bowie's alien was ultimately destroyed by the forces of consumerism which he himself unleashed.

Roeg's characters all harbour the seeds of their own destruction, a theme that dominates his films and was dealt with most intriguingly in his only two major films of the 80s. In *Bad Timing* (1980) the attraction of opposites – Art Garfunkel's psychiatrist who needs, but constantly fails, to control the emotions of those around him and Theresa Russell's spontaneous free spirit – leads to their destruction, he only able to assume dominance over her when he ravishes her unconscious body after she takes an overdose. The film caused an outrage and was only passed by the censors after one scene was cut and, despite being produced by the Rank Organisation, was barred from their own cinemas, dubbed 'a sick film made by sick people for sick people' by their head of booking. *Eureka* (1982), despite giving Roeg his largest budget and an impressive cast (Hackman, Rutger Hauer, Russell again), also suffered from distribution problems, and was rapidly withdrawn from release for many years, ostensibly for legal reasons. In many ways Roeg's most ambitious and personal film, it's a Kane-like odyssey from poverty to riches and a long wait for death, with a highly stylised and less than perfectly integrated third act in which its millionaire prospector's daughter (Russell again, by now Mrs Roeg and later a frequent star of his films) finds the sense of peace that eluded her father.

Perhaps cowed by the film's failure, Roeg seemed to become its hero, Jack McCann, a man who struck gold too soon and had no dreams left. There was a definite sense of marking time with the rest of the decade's offerings, all boasting his distinctive style but without the sense of revelation, almost copies of his own work. It was not until the overtly commercial *The Witches* (1990), 'a film I could take my children to' and which earned him the enmity of Roald Dahl, that his creative juices seemed to reawaken, adopting a clearer narrative line but keeping the darker undercurrents of his best work, and heralding a return to *Don't Look Now* territory with *Cold Heaven* (1991).

1970 Performance (co-director) **1971** Walkabout **1973** Don't Look Now **1976** The Man Who Fell To Earth **1980** Bad Timing aka Illusions **1982** Eureka **1985** Insignificance **1987** Castaway **1988** Aria; Track 29 **1990** The Witches **1992** Cold Heaven

Rogers, Mimi

Actress
Born 27 January 1956
Coral Gables, Florida

The daughter of a civil engineer who was constantly on the move with his family, Mimi Rogers had lived in Virginia, Arizona, Michigan and England before settling in Los Angeles. She graduated from high school at the inordinately early age of 14 and busied herself with community work and, later, working with drug addicts, Vietnam veterans and the mentally retarded. Theatre was simply one of many interests and it was not until her early 20s that she turned to acting.

She made her feature film debut in *Blue Skies Again* (1983), playing the manager of a girl who wants to join a baseball team. Although a good-natured little romantic comedy, in which Mimi was courted by the team's wealthy owner, Harry Hamlin, the film made no impact. The actress passed similarly unnoticed in Ron Howard's comedy of ethnic clashes, *Gung Ho* (1986), but had a good supporting role as an intelligent young New York professional woman who is journalist Christopher Reeve's live-in girlfriend in *Street Smart* (1987). Until then, Rogers, who was well-known on TV for regular roles in series (*Paper Dolls, The Rousers*), guest appearances in *Hart To Hart, Magnum P.I., Quincy* and *Hill Street Blues*, and a handful of TV movies, was just a heathily nice-looking young woman with a modern, middle-class persona.

Then, in 1987, came Ridley Scott's *Someone*

To Watch Over Me, about an upper-crust Manhattan heiress who accidentally witnesses a murder and thus herself becomes the intended victim of the killers. It was a slick, glossy and intelligent film, and Mimi, co-starring with Tom Berenger, was transformed into an expensive-looking beauty, exuding class, culture, and discreet but unmistakable sexuality. She also managed to make of Claire Gregory something sensitive and sympathetic. Her image now adult and sophisticated, she wasn't short of offers, but her next movies did nothing to advance her career. A fairly meaty co-lead (opposite Gary Busey) as the menaced wife in *Hider In The House* (1989) was wasted because the movie was no good, and her supporting role – another sophisticated beauty – in *The Mighty Quinn* the same year was enigmatic and irrelevant.

Nonetheless, Mimi Rogers, her three-year marriage to Tom Cruise over, entered the 1990s with her credentials proved and a string of contracts for her services. Subsequently, her performance in the apocalyptic psychodrama, *The Rapture* (1992) – as a frustrated sexual swinger who finds God and takes her new-found faith to a chilling extreme – was a revelation.

1983 Blue Skies Again **1986** Gung Ho **1987** Street Smart; Someone To Watch Over Me **1989** Hider In The House; The Mighty Quinn **1990** The Desperate Hours; **1991** The Doors (cameo); To Forget Palermo **1992** White Sands (unbilled); Dark Horse; The Player (cameo); The Rapture; Timebomb **1992/93** Shooting Elizabeth

Romero, George A.

Writer, director
Born 4 February 1940
New York

One of the most important film-makers of his generation, George A. Romero (the A is for Andrew) is still a fringe figure. The low-budget horror movies he makes tend to be independently financed and consequently receive only limited (and very mixed) critical attention. His work *is* of variable quality, but it ranges from the merely efficient to the inspired. His themes include (in)humanity, racism, sex, religion, death . . . why shouldn't his films be scary?

Romero made his own Super-8 movies from the age of 14. In one, he threw a dummy off the top of an apartment building and found himself the subject of a police inquiry. He went to college in Pittsburgh, The Carnegie College Of Technology, studying painting and design. In the summer breaks he worked as a grip on various films, including *North By Northwest* (1959), then switched courses to the theatre school and appeared in a number of workshop productions. After graduation he formed the Latent Image company with friends in Pittsburgh, to make commercials and industrial films. A feature soon followed.

Strongly influenced by the EC Horror comic books, *Night Of The Living Dead* (1968) turned the Hollywood conception of a horror movie on its head (it even begins with a jokey reference to Boris Karloff). Shot cheaply in grainy black and white, the film has a contemporary, 'realistic' edge and a Pennsylvania setting a million miles away from the gothic piles of Bela Lugosi or Vincent Price. With a black 'hero' and a traumatised 'heroine' desperately fighting off cannibalistic zombies and equally dangerous, bigoted humans, and ultimately failing, the film has no truck with Hollywood conventions. It is also graphically visceral. It did not come out of nowhere – independent genre films like *Carnival Of Souls* (1962) and *Blood Feast* (1963) predict its ambience and gore – but *Living Dead* was the best of them, a devastating study of mankind in the worst possible circumstances. It was also an unexpected box-office hit.

Romero's next two films were tentative experiments outside of the horror genre. Although he opted to stay independent of the mainstream, *There's Always Vanilla* (1972) was 'an imitation of a Hollywood film' by Romero's own admission. A romantic comedy, it was counted a dismal failure and has since well-nigh vanished. *Jack's Wife* (1973) is a more interesting failure; an attempt to link Bergmanesque psycho-drama with horror fantasy in the tale of a bored housewife who turns to witchcraft for liberation. The director was clearly at a crossroads, torn between the art film where his social concerns might be expressed most explicitly, and a genre film where they must be worked out internally. *The Crazies* (1973) and *Martin* (1976) vindicated the latter course. Both subtly refract a repressive society through the cracked looking-glass of horror. Romero's films are as notable for their sly humour as for their suspense (perhaps because both disciplines require a cynical detachment), but, bloodied and unbowed, he remains a humanist despite everything (witness the sympathy for the adolescent 'vampire', Martin).

Like Hitchcock, Romero tends to direct interviews away from serious study of his work: 'Just because I'm showing somebody being disembowelled doesn't mean that I have to get heavy and put a message behind it'! However, his shooting script for *Dawn Of The Dead* (1978) tells a different story: 'Stores of every type offer gaudy displays of consumer items . . . at either end of the concourse, like the main altars at each end of a cathedral, stand the mammoth two-storey department stores, great symbols of a consumer society . . . They appear as an archaeological discovery, revealing the gods and customs of a civilisation now gone.' An irony in this brutal satire on consumerism is Romero's own need to cater to it, even outside the studio system. The zombie films are a trilogy, not cash-in sequels, and if 1990's *Night Of The Living Dead* (which Romero wrote and produced for his collaborator Tom Savini to direct), is arguably the most intelligent remake to come out of America in a decade, nevertheless the parameters of Romero's career have been restricted by commercial questions. This was particularly apparent in the early 80s, as it was with most Hollywood film-makers. After the failure of a personal project, *Knightriders* (1981), *Creepshow* (1982) and the *Tales From The Darkside* TV series which he produced seemed complacent and uninvolved. Romero did not quite have the measure of his ambitions in *Dawn Of The Dead* or *Knightriders*; his immediate reaction was to scale down the ambition. His short films, including his script contributions to *Creepshow 2* (1987), *Tales From The Darkside: The Movie* and his segment in *Two Evil Eyes* (both 1990), pay off debts to friends and influences without furthering his own *oeuvre* in anyway.

None of this was evident in his last two feature films. *Day Of The Dead* (1985), released to deafening silence without an MPAA certificate, was a tight, nihilistic black comedy, the third masterpiece of the trilogy, and, despite a tacked-on ending for the distributor, *Monkey Shines* (1988) was another provocative Darwinian exploration of the primitive within a brilliantly simple suspense film.

As writer-director unless stated otherwise: **1968** Night Of The Living Dead (director, co-writer) **1972** There's Always Vanilla aka The Affair (director only) **1973** Jack's Wife aka Season Of The Witch aka Hungry Wives; The Crazies aka Codename: Trixie **1977** Martin **1978** Dawn Of The Dead aka Zombies, Dawn Of The Dead **1981** Knightriders **1982** Creepshow (director only) **1985** Day Of The Dead **1987** Creepshow 2 (writer only) **1988** Monkey Shines **1990** Night Of The Living Dead (writer only); Tales From The Darkside: The Movie (co-writer only); Two Evil Eyes (w/d, part one only). **1992** The Dark Half

Rooker, Michael

Actor
Born 1956
Alabama

With an intensity in his eyes that cuts deep, the hulking, somewhat squareheaded frame and the soft gravelled voice of a man barely disguising his rage at the world, Michael Rooker is the most impressive and powerful new face to have emerged in American cinema in the late 80s. Born in Alabama, when he was 13 his family moved to Chicago where he studied at the Goodman School of Drama and appeared in regional theatre productions. Moving to Los Angeles, he worked his way through psycho-of-the-week roles on TV shows like *The Equalizer*, *Crime Story* and *Lady Blue* as well as similarly disposable bit parts in films. It was only as one of the baseball players who throws the world series in John Sayles' *Eight Men Out* (1988) that he had something to work with, albeit just a disillusioned presence in the corner of a frame or glimpsed over another player's shoulder, and it was up to his role in *Mississippi Burning* (1988) to really make his presence felt.

As police deputy and KKK killer Frank Bailey he was the very venom of racism itself, consumed with a hatred that seemed so real that people who later met him in real life disliked him on sight: 'They figured I was some thug the casting people picked up in Mississippi or somewhere.' In *Sea Of Love* the following year he managed to turn a part that at first seemed throwaway, but which later ran the risk of turning into a rent-a-rant, into something infinitely more memorable, then turned audience expectation of him on its head to appear, the same year, slimmed down, bearded, bespectacled, likeable and loving as a simple steelworker whose father is accused of war crimes in *Music Box*. There was anger here too, but directionless and passionate, a far cry from the terrifyingly controlled precision of his own crimes in *Henry: Portrait Of A Serial Killer* (1989). Even though this controversial film's subject was later discredited, Rooker's restrained performance was faultless as he dispassionately played back his victims' screams as the backdrop to the daily chores of his otherwise mundane life. Uncomfortable to watch but too compelling to ignore, here was a man who could scare you – partly and frighteningly thanks to his seeming 'niceness' – without even having to try.

Back in the ranks of the supporting players, he almost walked away with *Days Of Thunder* (1990). For all Tom Cruise's talk of his lust for speed, Rooker's rival racedriver Rowdy Burns *is* that need. His whole being, body and soul, was an expression of that craving, a barely restrained force of nature ultimately thrown away by the producers in favour of a substitute rival with none of his passion or power. Rooker's ability to draw you to a character, to make their obsessions real is amazing, but his unromantic, albeit not unpleasing, looks seemed destined to limit the parts he would be offered – although he started to break the mould, playing the good cop in George A. Romero's *The Dark Half* (1991) and Kevin Costner's sidekick in *JFK*.

1984 Streets Of Fire **1987** Light Of Day aka Born In The USA aka Just Around The Corner From The Light Of Day **1988** Rent-a-Cop; Above The Law aka Nico; Eight Men Out; Mississippi Burning **1989** Sea Of Love; Music Box; Henry: Portrait Of A Serial Killer **1990** Days Of Thunder **1991** JFK **1992** The Dark Half **1992/93** Cliffhanger

Ross, Herbert

Director, choreographer
Born 13 May 1927
New York City

In 1982 Herbert Ross directed a misfiring Neil Simon comedy, *I Ought To Be In Pictures*. The question remains whether Ross, for all his distinguished Broadway achievements and his success during the 1970s, ought in fact to have been in pictures himself. The tactful screen amanuensis of Neil Simon, he is conscientious and craftsmanlike but lacks any flair for the truly cinematic. As a man of the theatre, he has spent much of his Hollywood career opening out stage properties for the screen, a task which always carries with it inherent risks.

Ross began as an actor and dancer, rising to become resident choreographer at the American Ballet Theatre (he married ballerina Nora Kaye), and went on to make his mark on Broadway and in Hollywood: he handled the choreography on *Carmen Jones* (1954), lent some all-American zip to the routines in two Cliff Richard romps, *The Young Ones* (1961) and *Summer Holiday* (1962), and choreographed *Inside Daisy Clover* (1966), *Doctor Doolittle* (1967) and the Barbra Streisand hit *Funny Girl* (1968); during those years, he also directed for the Broadway stage: *House Of Flowers, Finian's Rainbow, I Can Get It For You Wholesale* (which saw Streisand's Broadway debut) and *Kelly*.

Not surprisingly, Ross' first foray into screen directing was a musical (of sorts) – a dire remake of *Goodbye, Mr Chips* (1969), starring a disgruntled Peter O'Toole as the doddering public school pedagogue made famous by Robert Donat in 1939. He was more at ease with the screen adaptation of a Broadway comedy, *The Owl And The Pussycat* (1971), a tart, sub-Pygmalion pairing of George Segal and Barbra Streisand as a stuffy intellectual and a semi-literate whore; then the director scored a big hit with the film of Woody Allen's stage success, *Play It Again, Sam* (1972), with Woody as the schlemiel film critic taking advice from a spectral Humphrey Bogart in his never-ending quest for love and true happiness.

After deftly steering a raft of stars through the quirky murder mystery *The Last Of Sheila* (1973), Ross (and just about everyone else concerned) found Streisand just a bit too much for him on *Funny Lady* (1975), the sequel to *Funny Girl*, and went on to play safe with *The Sunshine Boys* (1975). This Neil Simon comedy paired Walter Matthau and George Burns (in his first starring role since the 1939 *Honolulu*) as a couple of crotchety ex-vaudevillians reunited for a TV show; then Ross displayed a rare ironic touch with *The Seven-Per-Cent Solution* (1976), a wry Sherlock Holmes send-up, adapted by Nicholas Meyer from his own novel.

Then, with sadly disastrous results, Ross returned to his first and greatest love, the world of dance, with *The Turning Point* (1977), a movie about friendship, the conflict in women's lives between home and career and, above all, about ballet. The film starred Anne Bancroft and Shirley MacLaine, giving performances of the kind which are described as 'virtuoso' (if you like this kind of thing) or toe-curlingly over the top (if you don't), and offered a heart-on-the-sleeve treatment of women's relationships which was merely patronising. The whole treacly mess was ameliorated by some splendid ballet sequences – Ross' forte, after all – and marked the screen debut of the great Russian dancer Mikhail Baryshnikov. *The Turning Point* managed an astonishing 11 Oscar nominations and the humiliation of failing to convert a single one of them into the award itself.

The Goodbye Girl (1978) and *California Suite* (1979) marked a return to the Neil Simon production line – altogether a better bet – with the first producing an Oscar-winning performance from Richard Dreyfuss as the most insufferable young actor ever to infest off-off-Broadway; and the second providing Maggie Smith with one of her best screen vehicles as a tetchy English actress in Hollywood for the Oscar ceremony. So far so good, but then Ross, falling prey once again to passions that he seems unable to translate satisfactorily to the screen, delivered two massive failures: *Nijinsky* (1979) was an overblown and soapy farrago about the relationship between the legendary dancer of the title (George de la Peña), and his florid Svengali, the impresario Serge Diaghilev (a deeply un-Russian Alan Bates); *Pennies From Heaven* (1981), an Americanisation of Dennis Potter's superb British TV mini-series, had Steve Martin stepping into the original shoes of Bob Hoskins as a sheet-music salesman in the Depression whose bleak life is mocked by the relentlessly cheery songs he peddles. One part Busby Berkeley, two parts Edward Hopper, the movie lost its small-screen impact despite magnificent photography (by Gordon Willis), Ken Adam's atmospheric sets and pleasing performances from Martin and Bernadette Peters.

Ross continued to work steadily throughout the 80s (and, indeed, showed no signs of letting up in the early 90s) but a little of the spring had gone from his stride: there was more brisk Neil Simon in *Max Dugan Returns* (1983); an attempt to get hip in *Footloose* (1984), a teen pic starring Kevin Bacon which tried to combine *Rebel Without A Cause* (1955) with the high-voltage routines of *Flashdance* (1983); *Secret Of My Success* (1987), an amiable if overlong outing for fresh-faced Michael J. Fox as a young man from the sticks making his way in corporate New York; *Dancers* (1987), a botched reunion with Baryshnikov which is best forgotten; a soggy journey through the emotional wringer of *Steel Magnolias* (1989) in which no amount of salty one-liners from the likes of Dolly Parton, Olympia Dukakis and Shirley MacLaine could cut through the sentimental gloss; and *My Blue Heaven* (1990), a less than convincing vehicle for Steve Martin as an ex-mobster who turns State's evidence, then brightens up an enforced suburban exile by returning to the rackets.

Herbert Ross is nothing if not a stayer. A true man of the theatre and a committed devotee of the art of dance, his films are eclectic, old-fashioned and uneven, but he has nonetheless provided a share of pleasurable entertainment across two decades or so of film-making.

1969 Goodbye Mr Chips **1970** The Owl And The Pussycat **1971** T.R. Baskin **1972** Play It Again, Sam **1973** The Last Of Sheila **1975** Funny Lady; The Sunshine Boys **1976** The Seven-Per-Cent Solution **1977** The Turning Point; The Goodbye Girl **1978** California Suite **1979** Nijinsky **1981** Pennies From Heaven **1982** I Ought To Be In Pictures **1983** Max Dugan Returns **1984** Footloose **1987** The Secret of My Success; Dancers **1989** Steel Magnolias **1990** My Blue Heaven **1991** True Colors

Rossellini, Isabella

Actress
Born 18 June 1952
Rome, Italy

One of the beautiful twin daughters of two cinema greats, Italian director Roberto Rossellini and Swedish actress Ingrid Bergman, Isabella Rossellini was hesitant to commit herself to acting if it meant living in the shadow of her celebrated parents, particularly the mother she undeniably and hauntingly resembles, albeit in a dark-haired version.

Raised in Italy and France, Rossellini spent summer vacations assisting in the costume departments for her father's films and at 19 moved to New York to study costume design. She also attended Finch College and taught Italian when Italy's RAI television engaged her as a New York correspondent. In 1976 she made her film debut as a nun in *A Matter Of Time*, which starred her mother. On her return to Italy she became a popular TV personality on a weekly live comedy show and appeared in two features, one of them, *The Meadow* (1979), for the Taviani Brothers. Rossellini then took up modelling, with spectacular success: her face has graced the covers of more than 500 international magazines and since 1982 she has appeared under an exclusive, highly lucrative contract with Lancôme in the company's high profile cosmetic campaigns in more than 150 countries.

Rossellini's film career began in earnest after the end of her first marriage, to director Martin Scorsese, with a principal role as Gregory Hines' sweet Russian wife in the dance drama *White Nights* (1985). Her follow-up proved a sensation with a brave, distressing performance as the masochistic, off-key cabaret singer tormented by a crazed Dennis Hopper in David Lynch's audacious *Blue Velvet* (1986). Her most assured and appealing performance to date, however, was in *Cousins* (1989), Joel Schumacher's delicious sophisticated American remake of the French comedy romance *Cousin, Cousine* (1975), in which she was radiant as the cousin-by-marriage and soulmate to a charming Ted Danson. More recently she turned in a raunchy cameo with a startling blonde wig in *Wild At Heart* (1990) for David Lynch. Twice married, Rossellini enjoyed a well-known relationship with Lynch, now severed.

1976 A Matter Of Time **1979** Il Prato/The Meadow (Italy) **1980** Il Pap'occhio/The Pope's Eye (Italy) **1985** White Nights **1986** Blue Velvet **1987** Siesta; Red Riding Hood; Zelly And Me; Tough Guys Don't Dance **1989** Cousins **1990** Wild At Heart **1992** Death Becomes Her; The Pickle (cameo) **1992/92** The Innocent **1993** Joy Ride

Rourke, Mickey

(Philip Rourke)

Actor

Born September 1955

Schenectady, New York

Depending on whose opinion one follows, Mickey Rourke is either one of the most admired or one of the most ridiculed leading men of his generation. After a decade of work ranging from the acclaimed to the reviled, the off-beat star has his fervent following, is an icon in France and has made more loss-making movies than are generally considered reasonable in the film industry for one of his top-billed status.

Born Philip but dubbed Mickey (after Disney's mouse) Rourke grew up in Florida as one of a tough tribe under a police detective patriarch, his stepfather. He spent four years fighting as an amateur boxer in Miami before moving to New York, where he worked in night-clubs and as a pretzel vendor while studying acting. A move to Los Angeles brought him small roles in a few TV movies in 1980, and he made his film debut with a small role in *Fade To Black* the same year. It was with his second released film, Lawrence Kasdan's steamy thriller, *Body Heat* (1981), that he alerted viewers to something special in a brief but memorable appearance as the professional arsonist to whom love-crazed lawyer William Hurt turns for criminal advice.

An effective if chopped performance in the fiasco that was *Heaven's Gate* (1980) did Rourke no harm and in Barry Levinson's debut as a director, the impressive 50s nostalgia piece *Diner* (1982), he shone in a strong young ensemble as a hustling hairdresser. While seeming to inhabit most comfortably roles as sleazeballs, bikers, hoods and hard guys (including his first major lead, working again for Michael Cimino, as a curiously unlined but grey-haired cop in the dynamic and brutal *Year Of The Dragon* in 1985), Rourke throbbed masochistic female hearts in Adrian Lyne's controversial sex movie, *9½ Weeks* (1986). Poorly received in America, the film's success in Europe was phenomenal, pairing Rourke with Kim Basinger for a slick misogynistic tale in which he appeared unusually attractive, well-dressed and charming, and initially the answer to a maiden's prayers before descending into the dangerously seductive character of a disturbed and deeply disturbing sexual adventurer.

Subsequently the actor, who seems wilfully to have cultivated a boorish, Bohemian image as an unshaven, unwashed, uncompromising artiste, has chosen mainly to play boozers, brawlers and bad dudes, with the wildly curious exception of St Francis of Assissi for Liliana Cavani in *Francesco* (1989), which passed (mercifully) almost unremarked.

Fond of fighters, women and his Harley Davidson bike, Rourke retains his appeal for those who like 'a bit of rough' and the element of danger he brings to the screen. His choice of roles, however street-credible, does want for more career-oriented realism, perhaps. *Homeboy* (1989), for example, a boxing drama he scripted himself and spent nine years on, went straight to video hell in the US; while the ludicrous *Wild Orchid* (1990), something of a 'Son of 9½ Weeks', saw him back in smart suits as a suave seducer, but also failed to turn on a mass audience. In 1990, he reteamed with Michael Cimino for an ill-conceived re-make of *The Desperate Hours* in the role originally played by Humphrey Bogart, inviting unfortunate comparisons. Rather mystifyingly, by the early 90s, Mickey Rourke seemed still to be in a position to make whatever he likes – at any rate, for as long as he can get away with it – yet his role in the unsuccessful thriller, *White Sands* (1992) was so ambiguous, it was impossible to know what to make of it, or him.

1980 Fade To Black; Heaven's Gate **1981** Body Heat **1982** Diner; Eureka **1983** Rumble Fish **1984** The Pope Of Greenwich Village **1985** Year Of The Dragon **1986** 9½ Weeks **1987** Angel Heart; Barfly; A Prayer For The Dying **1989** Francesco; Homeboy **1990** Wild Orchid; Johnny Handsome **1990** The Desperate Hours **1991** Harley Davidson And The Marlboro Man **1992** White Sands

Rowlands, Gena
(Virginia Rowlands)

Actress
Born 19 June 1934
Cambria, Wisconsin

Whether playing a good broad, a neurotic, or a middle-class mom, Gena Rowlands has an inherent elegance that has always marked her out as a leading 'quality' actress of her generation. Loved and admired by her peers in theatre, television and film, she could doubtless have attained wider commercial recognition in her career but chose to channel her energies and talent into her remarkably happy marriage and artistic collaboration with the late actor-writer-director John Cassavetes.

Rowlands (whose first name is pronounced as Jenna, *not* as Gina) briefly attended the University of Wisconsin before enrolling at the American Academy of Dramatic Arts. A recent graduate of AADA, Cassavetes, came to a production in which Rowlands appeared, presented himself backstage after and, she recalled, 'That was it.' Before she was out of her teens Rowlands was engaged as understudy for the female lead in the Broadway production of *The Seven Year Itch*, later assuming the role. Other major parts followed and she made her feature film debut in 1958 in Jose Ferrer's romantic comedy *The High Cost Of Loving*. The most memorable film in which she appeared in her early days in Hollywood was the superior contemporary cowboy drama *Lonely Are The Brave* (1962).

Disenchanted with studio film-making after *A Child Is Waiting* (1963), the first of his films to feature Rowlands (in a supporting role), Cassavetes went about his own unique, independent work. An important feature in his films was the involvement and improvisation of his actors, and Rowlands delivered a powerful and involving presence in most of them, exploring marriage, love and sexual politics. She was most touching as lonely Minnie, enlivened by a kooky romance with Seymour Cassel in Cassavetes' most light-hearted film, *Minnie And Moskowitz* (1971), and received an Oscar nomination for her intense portrayal of a woman on the edge of a nervous breakdown in his *A Woman Under The Influence* (1974). In 1978 she won the Best Actress award at the Berlin Film Festival for her absorbing account of an actress in crisis in *Opening Night*. In arguably her most unlikely role (in her husband's most unlikely film), that of a gangster's mistress on the run with a small child from mob hit-men in *Gloria* (1980), her tough-talking, gun-toting, only slightly tongue-in-cheek characterisation elevated an otherwise rather meandering and heavy-handed piece. Her two best roles in recent years demonstrated the contrasting extremes of which this actress is capable: in the last film she and Cassavetes made together, *Love Streams* (1984), in which they played out an intensely close brother-sister relationship, hers was a demanding woman for whom love, dramatic and emotive, was all; in *Another Woman* (1988) for Woody Allen, hers was a tightly controlled woman fearful of being touched by love or emotion.

In addition to a considerable body of stage work, the statuesque and authoritative Gena Rowlands has numerous television credits and in recent years was particularly strong as the anguished mother of an AIDS victim in *An Early Frost*. Since Cassavetes' premature death from cirrhosis of the liver in 1989, Rowlands has made *Once Around* for Swedish director Lasse Hallström and *Night On Earth* for Jim Jarmusch.

1958 The High Cost Of Loving **1962** Lonely Are The Brave; The Spiral Road **1963** A Child Is Waiting **1967** Tony Rome **1968** Faces **1971** Minnie And Moskowitz **1974** A Woman Under The Influence **1976** Two-Minute Warning **1978** Opening Night; The Brink's Job **1980** Gloria **1984** Love Streams **1987** Light Of Day **1988** Another Woman **1991** Once Around **1992** Night On Earth; Crazy In Love

Rudolph, Alan

Director, writer
Born 18 December 1943
Los Angeles, California

Like his mentor Robert Altman, Alan Rudolph has attempted to make personal films outside the Hollywood mainstream, refusing to pander to the more commercial tastes of producers. Unfortunately, his single-minded pursuit of excellence has seldom brought him much financial success, despite a cult following, and he has had to resort, from time to time, to directing products instigated by others.

Rudolph had made *Premonition* (1972), a low-budget hippy horror movie, before serving as assistant director to Altman on *The Long Goodbye* (1973). After working closely with the older director on a number of other films, Rudolph made *Welcome To LA* (1977) or 'The City Of One-Night Stands', produced and greatly influenced by Altman in its quirkily oblique attitude to narrative. Featuring members of the Altman stock company, including Keith Carradine and Geraldine Chaplin, it was about the fouled-up love lives of the denizens of Tinsel Town, but the aimless characters and plotless screenplay did not appeal to either critics or the public. Chaplin then turned up as a wronged woman in the gripping but far-fetched revenge movie *Remember My Name* (1978), an updated psychological version of a 40s Joan Crawford-type vehicle. Because of its disastrous reception, producers pulled the plug on Rudolph's next project, *The Moderns*, which was to star Keith Carradine and Mick Jagger. It was ten years before it came to the screen with John Lone replacing Jagger.

For the next few years, Rudolph took on a few directing chores such as *Roadie* (1980), a coarse-grained comedy on the rock 'n' roll business, and *Endangered Species* (1982), a crude conspiracy thriller, until *Choose Me* (1984) enabled him to return to his own idiosyncratic manner of story-telling. This witty, bittersweet romance dealing with a group of loners (including Rudolph regulars Keith Carradine and Genevieve Bujold) around a singles bar, pursuing their various dreams of love and sex, made splendid use of stylised studio sets, which created a slightly surreal world. More accessible, *Trouble In Mind* (1985) also revolved around a single self-contained set, and again was less concerned with plot than with the interplay of the sad but sympathetic characters – a world-weary ex-cop (Kris Kristofferson) just out of prison, his ex-lover (Bujold), who runs a café in Rain City, and an innocent couple (Carradine and Lori Singer). Unhappily, this poetic, urban fairy-tale flopped and Rudolph was back on the commercial stuff with *Made In Heaven* (1987), a saccharine fantasy of the after-life starring Timothy Hutton and Kelly McGillis.

The long-planned *The Moderns* (1988), about American expatriate artists, art dealers and forgers in the Paris of 20s, was an intelligent, evocative, delicate and stylish work, beautifully played by the Rudolph regulars, Carradine, Bujold and Chaplin. *Love At Large* (1990), set in a mythic urban landscape, was a thriller with *noir* overtones, cleverly playing intricate games with its three enigmatic leading characters, a private eye (Tom Berenger), his client (Anne Archer), and a woman detective (Elizabeth Perkins) paid to track *him*. But the exercise was too self-conscious for most tastes, and the film failed to gain an audience. With a big-budget production and popular married stars Bruce Willis and Demi Moore, *Mortal Thoughts* (1991) held the best possibility to help Alan Rudolph, one of the most gifted of Hollywood directors, to finance further projects close to his heart.

As writer-director unless stated otherwise: **1972** Premonition aka The Impure **1976** Buffalo Bill And The Indians (co-writer only) **1977** Welcome To LA **1978** Remember My Name **1980** Roadie **1982** Endangered Species (co-writer, director) **1983** Return Engagement (docu) **1984** Choose Me **1985** Songwriter (director only); Trouble In Mind **1987** Made In Heaven **1988** The Moderns (co-writer, director) **1990** Love At Large **1991** Mortal Thoughts **1992** Equinox

Russell, Kurt

Actor

Born 17 March 1951

Springfield, Massachusetts

An extremely good, constantly under-rated actor with great comic timing, Kurt Russell is one of the few actors to effect a complete change of screen image, going from blue-eyed, mop-haired child performer and Disney star to the cynical, macho hero of John Carpenter films which also offered him an opportunity to show his fine line in straight-faced self-deprecating humour. The son of baseball player turned actor Bing Russell, he only became interested in acting when he found out two of his baseball idols, Mickey Mantle and Roger Maris, were about to make a movie, but despite work in TV shows such *The Fugitive* and *The Man From UNCLE* and being in and out of movies from the age of nine, he always looked on it as a part-time job. He only took it seriously when, two steps short of the major leagues, a damaged shoulder ended his dreams of a baseball career.

As well as keeping occcupied with his TV work he became one of the 'Walt Disney stock company' in a string of family comedies that, along with lead roles in three TV series of his own, ensured him fairly constant employment. But it was not until 1979 and his surprisingly effective and melancholy Elvis Presley (who he had kicked in the shin in his second film, *It Happened At The World's Fair* in 1963) in John Carpenter's TV movie opposite his father that he was able to escape juvenile roles completely. It was through Carpenter that Russell was able to establish a new image, exchanging fresh-faced innocence for the muscular seen-it-all cynicism of Snake Plisken in *Escape From New* York (1981) and his down-to-earth hero in *The Thing* (1982), giving vent to their more humorous asides with the blowhard truck driver battling oriental demons in *Big Trouble In Little China* (1985).

With a rowdy blue-collar appeal that is often exploited well to comic effect – never more so than as the rough-hewn carpenter of *Overboard* (1987) who convinces spoiled heiress Goldie Hawn (his real-life love since they met on the set of 1984's *Swing Shift*) that she is the amnesiac mother of his unruly kids – Russell has managed to avoid the kind of typecasting and lousy films that damaged the not dissimilar Burt Reynolds' career. Showing a more gentle side as the widowed father in *Winter People* (1989) and making the most of his straight dramatic roles, especially in *Silkwood* (1983) and the otherwise disappointing *Tequila Sunrise* (1988), this extremely good-looking and powerfully built actor has worked his way up in audiences' affections and the profession's esteem enough to topline the impressive cast of Ron Howard's firefighting drama, *Backdraft* (1991), and to cement his leading-man status with *Unlawful Entry* (1992).

1960 The Absent-Minded Professor **1963** It Happened At The World's Fair **1966** Follow Me Boys! **1968** Guns In The Heather; The One And Only Genuine Original Family Band **1969** The Horse In The Gray Flannel Suit; The Computer Wore Tennis Shoes **1970** The Barefoot Executive **1971** Fools Parade (GB: Dynamite Man From Glory Jail) **1972** Now You See Him, Now You Don't **1974** Charley And The Angel; Superdad **1976** The Strongest Man In The World **1980** Used Cars **1981** Escape From New York **1982** The Thing **1983** Silkwood **1984** Swing Shift **1985** The Best Of Times; The Mean Season **1986** Big Trouble In Little China **1987** Overboard **1988** Tequila Sunrise **1989** Winter People; Tango And Cash **1991** Backdraft **1992** Unlawful Entry; Captain Ron

Russell, Theresa
(Theresa Paup)
Actress
Born 20 March 1957
San Diego, California

Once hailed as one of the most promising actresses of her generation, like many before her Theresa Russell seems to have suffered in career terms from being too closely associated with her husband's films, although with Nicolas Roeg for a husband (and her classy, sensual looks) she has at least been assured of some meaty roles. A model from the age of 12, she studied at the Hollywood branch of the Actors' Studio for two years before making her feature film debut in Elia Kazan's low-key adaptation of *The Last Tycoon* (1976), easily overshadowing the film's vacuous nominal leading lady and holding her own against the formidable supporting cast with her confident, believable and very natural performance as the mogul's daughter in unrequited love with the title character. She similarly stole much of Dustin Hoffman's limelight in *Straight Time* (1978), before giving a performance that genuinely shocked (although it was also at times perilously close to mannered) as the destructive free spirit Milena in Roeg's controversial *Bad Timing* (1980). The furore surrounding the film's finale may have taken Roeg out of the mainstream but earned Russell much praise and proved the foundation of her subsequent screen career, as well as being the first, and in many ways the most extreme example of her tendency to exhibit the more desperate, unappealing aspects of carnality in her performances – most particularly in Roeg's films, but also in Ken Russell's horrendous *Whore* (1991).

Russell has had more mixed results away from Roeg: she was fine as the dipsomaniac in Bill Murray's zonked-out remake of *The Razor's Edge* (1984) and gave her best performance as the enigmatic killer (intriguingly co-starred with Debra Winger) in Bob Rafelson's *Black Widow* (1986) – a woman who becomes the identities and personalities she adopts to kill the rich husbands she, somewhat perversely, genuinely loves. But her weakness away from a suitably strong director was made alarmingly apparent with her stilted performance in Michael Crichton's *Physical Evidence* (1989): in the absence of strong dramatic material her talent seems to go into hibernation with surprisingly little charisma to replace it. Following an unsuccessful move towards the mainstream, Russell seems to have accepted that her true forte is in character roles, with both *Cold Heaven* and *Kafka* (1992) offering her the dementia, destructive sexuality and inability to differentiate between emotional, and psychological, torment and reality that drives her best work.

1977 The Last Tycoon **1978** Straight Time **1980** Bad Timing aka Illusions **1983** Eureka **1984** The Razor's Edge **1986** Insignificance **1987** Black Widow **1988** Aria; Track 29 **1989** Physical Evidence aka Smoke **1990** Impulse **1991** Whore **1992** Cold Heaven; Kafka

Ryan, Meg

Actress
Born 19 November 1961
Fairfield, Connecticut

Yet another of the blonde-haired, blue-eyed brigade – very pretty rather than beautiful and with an effervescent personality – Meg Ryan graduated to star status with the phenomenal success of Rob Reiner's *When Harry Met Sally* (1989), as the 'modern' girl who believes men and women (in this case she and Billy Crystal) can be friends without becoming lovers. Her unselfconscious *savoir faire* allowed her to demonstrate a fake orgasm in a deli restaurant with such humour and expertise that the scene has already passed into the canon of memorable moments from the movies.

However, this daughter of a casting agent – her mother got her her small debut role as Candice Bergen's daughter in *Rich And Famous* (1981) – was in fact pursuing a career in journalism, paying for her night course at New York University by a lucky acting job in a daytime soap called *As The World Turns*. The world turned for her, thanks to a performance of such appeal and conviction that they continued to run her character for two years. Then Meg toured Europe, returned to college, took part in a short-lived TV series, took a couple more small roles, and landed the effective featured role of Anthony Edwards' wife (he was the flyer who is killed) in the blockbusting *Top Gun* (1986).

Meg Ryan's excellence in the Tom Cruise movie led to Spielberg giving her the female lead (appropriately enough, that of an investigative journalist) in *Innerspace* (1987), which is how she met Dennis Quaid, the film's star, who she eventually married on Valentine's Day, 1991 and opposite whom she also starred in *DOA*. (1988), a reasonably efficient remake of the unusual 1949 thriller. Her co-starring role, playing three different women, opposite Tom Hanks in *Joe Versus The Volcano* (1990) promised much but the movie disappointed and Ryan's filmography to date, with the exception of the Reiner hit, has largely failed to do justice to her potential. In Oliver Stone's *The Doors* (1991) she did as much as possible with the cypher role of Jim Morrison's wife, but the lead opposite Alec Baldwin in the screen version of the acclaimed play, *Prelude To A Kiss*, seemed more appropriate a vehicle for her gifts.

1981 Rich And Famous **1983** Amityville 3-D **1986** Armed And Dangerous; Top Gun **1987** Innerspace **1988** DOA; Promised Land; The Presidio **1989** When Harry Met Sally **1990** Joe Versus The Volcano **1991** The Doors **1992** Prelude To A Kiss **1992/93** Sleepless In Seattle

Rydell, Mark

Director, actor
Born 23 March 1934
New York City

Mark Rydell trained to become an actor at New York's Neighborhood Playhouse and at the famous Actors' Studio. This led the short, dark and handsome Rydell into six years in the popular daytime TV soap *As The World Turns* and a role as a juvenile delinquent in Don Siegel's *Crime In The Streets* (1956). He subsequently turned to direction, initially for television, where he churned out episodes of *Ben Casey* and *Gunsmoke*.

His first two features were good-looking, faithful adaptations of minor works by D.H. Lawrence and William Faulkner. They were *The Fox* (1968), filmed in Canada, which told, without sensationalism, of a lesbian relationship (between Anne Heywood and Sandy Dennis) disturbed by a man (Keir Dullea); and *The Reivers* (1969), a folksy, family movie despite the presence of golden-hearted whores. *The Cowboys* (1972) was also meant for the family, although its story, of how youngsters between the ages of nine and 15 learn to become killers after their protector John Wayne is murdered, was less than edifying. *Cinderella Liberty* (1974), another commercially successful enterprise, starred James Caan as a sailor on leave falling for a prostitute (Marsha Mason). Caan and Elliott Gould played the title roles of mediocre vaudevillians in *Harry And Walter Go To New York* (1976), a painfully unfunny period comedy. Fans of raunchy, gutsy singer Bette Midler were well catered for in *The Rose* (1978), based on the life of Janis Joplin, but the story came over as the usual 'star is born' stuff.

Switching genres again, Rydell did a fine job in handling Katharine Hepburn and Henry Fonda (both winning Oscars) plus Jane Fonda in *On Golden Pond* (1981), a moving study of love and old age, which was sentimental without being mawkish. Mel Gibson and Sissy Spacek did what they could as a couple of impoverished farmers battling against nature and a land baron in the old-fashioned rural drama, *The River* (1984). With no discernible style or theme, Mark Rydell continues to tackle any subject as long as it has heart, as demonstrated by his first film after a seven-year gap, *For The Boys*, starring his old favourites Caan and Midler.

As director only unless stated otherwise: **1956** Crime In The Streets (actor only) **1968** The Fox **1969** The Reivers **1972** The Cowboys **1973** Cinderella Liberty; The Long Goodbye (actor only) **1976** Harry And Walter Go To New York **1978** The Rose **1981** On Golden Pond **1984** The River **1988** Punchline (actor only) **1990** Havana (actor only) **1991** For The Boys **1993** Intersection

Ryder, Winona

(Winona Horowitz)

Actress
Born 29 October 1971
Winona, Minnesota

Named for her birthplace, Winona Ryder had an upbringing that was more than a little unconventional. Her parents, intellectual hippies, and editors by profession, hob-nobbed with figures such as poet Allen Ginsberg and appointed drug guru Timothy Leary Winona's godfather. Her early childhood was passed variously in Haight Ashbury then, for three years, in a commune (where she became an avid reader), before the family settled for suburban stability in Petaluma near San Francisco. Noni, as she is called by intimates, was sent to junior high school, but it proved an unhappy experience for she suffered at the hands of class bullies.

As an antidote, her parents sent her to acting classes at the well-known American Conservatory Theatre School in San Francisco. There, she caught the attention of a talent scout, was given a screen test, and, by the age of 15, was in the movies. In only her second film, *Square Dance* (1987), she co-starred as Jane Alexander's semi-abandoned daughter, grown unhappy down on the farm, who arrives to live with her mother and stepfather in a sleazy Texas town. Hidden behind spectacles and shyness, she gave a performance of convincing vulnerability. Only two years later, having blossomed into a tall, dark and glamorous 18-year-old, she became a star in *Heathers* (1989), recapturing bad memories of her own childhood to fuel her enigmatic portrayal of Veronica Sawyer, the girl persuaded by her coolly sociopathic boyfriend (Christian Slater) to murder her odious upper-crust classmates. The director of *Heathers*, Michael Lehmann, said of her, 'She's not only intelligent and serious, she's also blessed with the ability to be good-natured . . . she will be a genuine movie star when she grows up . . . And she's a dream to work with.'

What Lehmann presumably means by 'a genuine movie star' is that she gives every sign of bringing true weight and a measure of versatility to her work. Certainly, she's already earned her colours – as the punky daughter in *Beetlejuice* (1988), exchanging her first screen kiss with Kiefer Sutherland in 1969 the same year, and giving a memorable performance, filled with impressive emotional shading that embraced both innocence and sensuality, as the 13-year-old child bride of Jerry Lee Lewis (Dennis Quaid) in *Great Balls Of Fire* (1989).

However, at 18, the young star was pushing a punishing schedule and was almost in danger of burning herself out from sheer exhaustion. While co-starring as Cher's daughter in *Mermaids* (1990), she was flying back to LA on her only day off each week for post-production on *Edward Scissorhands* (1990), in which she co-starred with Dianne Wiest and Johnny Depp. At the close of filming, escorted by boyfriend Depp, she arrived in Rome to start filming in *The Godfather Part III*, but became immediately ill – the result of overwork. She was laid off on doctor's orders and replaced by Coppola's daughter Sofia, but not without the threat of lawsuits and other difficulties. It was an early and salutary brush with the pitfalls of her profession, but the vital signs for Winona Ryder remained positive.

1986 Lucas **1987** Square Dance **1988** Beetlejuice; 1969 **1989** Great Balls Of Fire; Heathers **1990** Edward Scissorhands; Mermaids; Welcome Home Roxy Carmichael **1992** Night On Earth; Bram Stoker's Dracula **1992/93** The Age of Innocence

S

San Giacomo, Laura

Actress
Born ? 1962
New Jersey

Few feature film debuts have been as provocative and assured as that of dark-haired, diminutive Laura San Giacomo. Her role as the sexually voracious Cynthia in Steven Soderbergh's acclaimed *sex, lies and videotape* (1989), aside from winning her rave reviews, also guaranteed her a head start in becoming a bankable actress.

A third-generation Italian-American, San Giacomo grew up in suburban New Jersey, the eldest of three children. After setting her sights on an acting career while still at high school, she enrolled at the Carnegie Mellon Institute where she studied drama for four years. A stint in regional theatre followed, before a traditional progression to off-Broadway productions and occasional parts in TV shows such as *Miami Vice* and *The Equalizer* led to her first film role. Earthy rather than glamorous, San Giacomo's most distinctive physical feature is her husky voice. Since her sultry Louisiana drawl in *sex, lies and videotape*, she continued to put it to effective, albeit brief, use in three movies during 1990: she was Julia Roberts' rough-edged prostitute room-mate in *Pretty Woman*, a doctor's wife in *Vital Signs*, and the younger sister of Holly Hunter in *Once Around*. Her role as Crazy Cora, opposite Tom Selleck, in the mediocre Australian-set adventure yarn, *Quigley Down Under* (1990) was noteworthy for being her first leading-lady part.

To date, San Giacomo, who is married to actor Cameron Dye, has had limited screen opportunities to make full use of the talent revealed in her debut and a leading role opposite Liam Neeson in the thriller, *Under Suspicion* (1991), disappointed with its ludicrous script and was poorly received. However, her rapidly accruing credits and the increasing importance of her roles by the time the 1990s were under way, indicated that a successful career was almost certainly just a matter of time.

1989 sex, lies and videotape **1990** Pretty Woman; Vital Signs; Once Around; Quigley Down Under **1991** Under Suspicion **1992** Where The Day Takes You

Sands, Julian

Actor
Born 1958
Otley, West Yorkshire, England

A nicely mannered and nicely spoken blue-eyed blonde with the precise speech of a latterday Ronald Colman, Julian Sands would seem to be the quintessential screen Englishman. Since portraying a high-strung Percy Shelley in Ken Russell's hallucinogenic *Gothic* (1986), however, Sands has worked in films just about everywhere *but* Britain and has played Italians, Swiss, Americans, a Hungarian but almost no pale, public-school-educated Brits.

Born and raised in Yorkshire, Sands had his interest in acting stirred by the cinema and from the age of six was an enthusiastic participant in nativity plays, pantomimes and school productions. After training at London's Central School of Speech and Drama he formed a company that played in schools, youth groups and on the fringe. An early mentor, Derek Jarman, provided him with his first screen role – as the devil – in the short *Broken English*. Soon after he had television work and a one-line bit as a soldier in the screen adaptation of Peter Nichols' play *Privates On Parade* (1982). A supporting role as *Sunday Times* photographer Jon Swain in Roland Joffé's *The Killing Fields* (1984) provided a memorable experience filming in Thailand, leading Sands to shift from theatre to full-time film work. He has scarcely stopped working since, cheerfully taking on everything from leads in arty European work – Tolstoy's haunted Father Sergio in *Night Sun* for the Taviani Brothers, C.G. Jung in *Cattiva* (both 1991), a hopeless schizophrenic in the Swiss production *After Darkness* (1985) – to supporting roles like the cranky entomologist in the Hollywood horror comedy *Arachnophobia* (1990), camp druggy Carlton who turns into a monster in David Cronenberg's screen adaptation of *The Naked Lunch* (1991) and pianist-composer Franz Liszt in the romantic comedy about George Sand, *Impromptu* (1991). The most popular successes in which he has participated have been Merchant-Ivory's pretty *A Room With A View* (1986), as the ardent but inarticulate rival to Daniel Day Lewis for Helena Bonham-Carter's affections, and *Warlock*

(1989), in which he was the titular satanic, pony-tailed menace.

1982 Privates On Parade (bit) **1984** The Killing Fields; Oxford Blues **1985** After Darkness; The Doctor And The Devils **1986** A Room With A View; Harem **1987** Gothic; Siesta **1988** Vibes; Gdzieskolwiek Jest, Jeslis Jest/ Wherever You Are aka Wherever She Is (Poland) **1989** Warlock; Manika: Une Vie Plus Tard/Manika: The Girl Who Lived Twice (France); Tennessee Waltz **1990** Arachnophobia **1991** Impromptu; Night Sun (Italy) Cattiva/Wicked (Italy); The Naked Lunch **1992** Villa Del Venerdi/Husbands And Lovers (Italy) **1992/93** Tale Of A Vampire; The Turn Of The Screw; Boxing Helena; Warlock II: The Armageddon

Sarandon, Susan
(Susan Tomaling)
Actress
Born 4 October 1946
New York City

Without quite achieving the peaks of stardom, Susan Sarandon has had a successful and consistent film career, with strong and varied performances across a variety of genres. Something of a cult figure due to her appearance as the innocent and twice-seduced Janet in *The Rocky Horror Picture Show* (1975), she exudes a sexiness that has indeed something just a bit camp and comic about it. She is an actress who has not been afraid to take her shirt off – most notably in *Atlantic City* (1980) in the scene that everyone remembers where, under the lustful gaze of Burt Lancaster, she bathes her breasts lovingly in lemon water.

She was a whore in Louis Malle's *Pretty Baby* (1978) – playing Brooke Shields' mother – and, later, was lustily vampirised by Catherine Deneuve in Tony Scott's meretricious but amusing *The Hunger* (1983). Seducer and seducee equally, she enters her roles generously, with little coquetry or out-of-reach snobbery. The reward in a number of films is a surprising depth and vulnerability of performance. In the late 80s and early 90s, her career took on a sudden and welcome second wind. Memorable in the rather lightweight *Witches Of Eastwick* (1987), she is absolutely rivetting in Ron Shelton's highly original and entertaining baseball movie, *Bull Durham* (1988) as the classy groupie setting her sights on – and getting – Kevin Costner, but not before teaching Tim Robbins the arts of poetry, music, sex, and how to be a champion pitcher! In *The January Man* (1989), she is a predatory and jealous New York bitch trying to regain Kevin Kline's affections; while in the worthy (but slightly disappointing) *A Dry White Season* (also 1989), about injustice in South Africa, she is polished and effective as a crusading left-wing journalist. *White Palace* (1990), another strong picture, saw her as an older, sexy working-class woman bewitching young yuppie James Spader.

A tall, squirrel-eyed angular beauty, Sarandon was first seen to effect in Billy Wilder's fey comedy *The Front Page* (1974); then, briefly, before falling off the wing of a biplane, in *The Great Waldo Pepper* (1975). She was Ariel in Paul Mazursky's version of *The Tempest* (1982) – and took the lead opposite Richard Dreyfuss in an under-rated comedy *The Buddy System* (1984). Her life has not been entirely a bed of roses. The breakup of her marriage to actor Chris Sarandon was followed by a painful nervous breakdown, in 1976. But she recovered with resilience, forming a happy personal liaison with Tim Robbins, and her career has subsequently flourished. Deservedly – for she is a true original in the Hollywood canon – she got a hefty break and a Best Actress Oscar for her marvellous double act, with co-nominee Geena Davis, in *Thelma And Louise*, finally gaining the wider recognition that had slightly eluded her.

1970 Joe **1971** La Mortadella/Lady Liberty (Italy) **1974** Lovin' Molly; The Front Page **1975** The Great Waldo Pepper **1976** One Summer Love aka Dragonfly **1977** The Other Side Of Midnight; The Last Of The Cowboys **1978** Pretty Baby; King Of The Gypsies **1979** Something Short Of Paradise **1980** Atlantic City **1982** The Tempest **1983** The Hunger **1984** The Buddy System **1985** Compromising Positions **1987** The Witches Of Eastwick **1988** Sweet Heart's Dance; Bull Durham **1989** The January Man; A Dry White Season **1990** White Palace **1991** Thelma And Louise **1992** The Player (Cameo); Light Sleeper; Bob Roberts (Cameo); Lorenzo's Oil

Savage, John
Actor
Born 25 August 1949
Old Bethpage, New York

Despite his appearance in a number of highly interesting films that have offered him strong roles, John Savage continually seems to be the actor who gets left behind while his co-stars go on to better things. Active in New York theatre, where he organised a childrens' theatre group that performed in public housing, as well as working both on and off-Broadway (winning a Drama Circle Award for his performance in *One Flew Over The Cuckoo's Nest* in LA and Chicago) his initial film career, which included prominent supporting parts in *Bad Company* (1972) and *Steelyard Blues* (1973) came to a four-year halt (filled with TV work) after taking the lead in *The Sister-In-Law* (1975, for which he also composed the score and sung several ballads). It began in earnest with his unsentimental performance as one of the small-town volunteers who comes back from Vietnam as a bitter, foul-mouthed cripple in *The Deer Hunter* (1979), which was quickly followed by his straitlaced Midwesterner saved from a similar fate in *Hair* and an impassioned portrayal of the tortured survivor of *The Onion Field* the same year. Yet despite the strength of his performances, the films did more for the careers of Meryl Streep, Christopher Walken, Treat Williams, Ted Danson and James Woods, while Savage quickly became typecast in the role of angst-ridden professional victim – an impression his crippled failed suicide in *Inside Moves* (1980) and his impotent demobbed soldier in *Maria's Lovers* (1985) did little to dispel.

Throughout the 80s he showed poor judgement in his commercial films, often appearing as little more than an overseas sales face in Hungarian, Australian or Israeli films, while his good roles in genuinely hard-hitting films – such as his cynical photographer who only truly comes to life when there is some new atrocity to shoot in *Salvador* (1986) – have become fewer and further between. His one scene, as the unpopular white owner of a brownstone in Spike Lee's *Do The Right Thing* (1989) was little more than a strong cameo, while his role as the absent Robert Duvall's son in *Godfather III* (1990) was so brief that it seemed most of it must have hit the cutting-room floor – a rather depressing reflection of the way this actor's genuine, albeit admittedly uncommercial, talents have been discarded by the industry.

1970 Love Is A Carousel **1972** Bad Company **1973** Steelyard Blues aka The Final Crash; The Killing Kind **1975** The Sister-In-Law (also music) **1979** The Deer Hunter; Hair; The Onion Field **1980** Inside Moves; Cattle Annie And Little Britches **1982** The Amateur **1984** Brady's Escape aka The Long Ride **1985** Maria's Lovers **1986** Soldier's Revenge; Salvador **1987** Hotel Colonial; The Beat; Beauty And The Beast **1988** Caribe **1989** Do The Right Thing **1990** Any Man's Death; Point of View (Israel); Hunting; The Godfather Part III **1992** Primary Motive **1992/93** Flynn; Notti Di Paura/Across The Red Night (Italy)

Sayles, John

Writer, director, actor
Born 28 September 1950
Schenectady, New York

A witty, ingenious writer, John Sayles established himself with clever screenplays for exploitation movies, but despite the success of the personal projects he has directed himself, his liberal treatment of radical subject matter – lesbians, racism, capitalist corruption – has proved too much for Hollywood.

The son of two teachers, Sayles attended Williams College, Massachusetts, then spent several years as a nursing home orderly, a construction worker and meat packer. He had always written in his spare time, and in 1975 his first published short story, *I-80 Nebraska*, won an O. Henry award. During six months unemployment he wrote his first novel, about a dwarf private detective playing baseball in drag. Its author wanted to call it *Balls*, but it was published as *Pride Of The Bimbos* (1975). This was followed by *Union Dues* (1977), introducing two of his favourite themes – labour history and 60s radicalism – and was nominated for a National Book Award. As an actor and director in summer stock, Sayles adapted Eliot Asinof's *Eight Men Out* into a screenplay and his agents sent it to Hollywood as a sample of his work. Roger Corman's New World Pictures expressed an interest, and Sayles headed West.

A notoriously quick writer, Sayles had soon sold New World three scripts: *Piranha* (1978); *The Lady In Red* (1979) and *Battle Beyond The Stars* (1981). His exploitation work for Corman was funny, tight, and lightly subversive. The best examples are *Alligator* (1981) and two witty horror movies directed by Joe Dante: *Piranha* and *The Howling* (1981). In the latter, Sayles made a cameo appearance as a morgue attendant. Determined to direct, but with no technical film experience beyond hanging around the *Piranha* set, he took approximately $50,000 he had earned from his writing and made *The Return Of The Secaucus Seven* (1980).

Sayles wrote, directed, edited and acted in this charming ensemble comedy about the reunion of a group of 60s radicals. Its confines were largely dictated by the limited budget, but Sayles turned these to his advantage and *Secaucus Seven* hit a nerve with the 60s generation; a sort of precursor to Kasdan's *The Big Chill* (1983), it became the independent hit of the year, grossing over $2 million in the States. Its maker won the Best

Screenplay Award from the Los Angeles Film Critics. Despite this, no one in Hollywood would touch his previous script *Lianna* (1983), a sensitive account of a mature wife and mother discovering that she loves another woman. Independently financed, *Lianna* was far from perfect, but its low-key observation is still a vast improvement on mainstream attempts to address gay issues (as in *Making Love* and *Personal Best*, both 1982). Sayles cast himself in a showy role as a cool, West Coast colleague of Lianna's husband ('I'm from California – that kind of stuff doesn't faze me').

Originally planned as a studio film, *Baby It's You* (1983) was a 60s teenage romance that faced up to the hangover of growing up, unfulfilled dreams and failed relationships. It was financed independently, but at nearly $3 million the budget was four times that of *Lianna*, and Paramount distributed it. Set in Hoboken, New Jersey, where the director lives, the film featured music by local boys Frank Sinatra and Bruce Springsteen – Sayles went on to direct promo videos for Springsteen's 'Born In The USA', 'I'm On Fire' and 'Glory Days'. If this was his most mainstream project, difficulties with the studio over the film's downbeat second half left him adamant he'd never again direct without the right to final cut. His next picture was a return to shoestring budgets: $200,000 for *The Brother From Another Planet* (1984). A quirky social satire with sci-fi trappings, the film starred Joe Morton as an extra-terrestrial who crash-lands in Harlem. He's dumb, he has web-feet, and otherwise he looks exactly like a black resident of New York city. Fatally discursive, with a heavy-handed drugs message, *Brother* was over-ripe with clever ideas – a reaction against the studio system's emphasis on linear narrative, perhaps.

While he continued to accept writing assignments from the studios, and took acting jobs when they were offered (he was praised for his casual villainy in the independent film *Hard Choices* in 1986, and for his portrayal of Tom in *The Glass Menagerie* on stage at Williamstown opposite Joanne Woodward and Karen Allen, though a wider audience saw him in a cameo as a motorcycle cop in Jonathan Demme's *Something Wild*, 1986), Sayles concentrated on getting two of his pet projects onto the screen. *Matewan* (1987) and *Eight Men Out* (1988) were similar in a number of ways. They both detailed true stories of capitalist scandals from the 20s (or 1919 in the latter case); and they were both ensemble pieces open to generic treatment. *Matewan* is Sayles' finest film. Based on a miners' strike in West Virginia, Sayles coopts the style and mythology of the Western to make a gripping political testament to the nascent labour movement. *Eight Men Out* was a spry chronicle of the infamous 1919 White Sox baseball scandal, when the team threw the World Series at the behest of gamblers. Although less comfortable in its period, this was equally committed and mature film-making . . . Sayles' literate, liberal scripts were growing in scope, and more, they were beginning to *move* – as was amply demonstrated in his ambitious, funny, hip and ultimately distressing take on contemporary urban society in *City Of Hope* (1991).

As writer only unless otherwise stated: **1978** Piranha **1979** The Lady In Red **1980** The Return Of The Secaucus Seven (also director, actor) **1981** Battle Beyond The Stars; Alligator; The Howling (also cameo) **1982** The Challenge (co-writer) **1983** Enormous Changes At The Last Minute (co-writer); Lianna (also director, actor); Baby It's You (also director) **1984** The Brother From Another Planet (also director, actor) **1986** Something Wild (cameo only); Hard Choices (actor only); The Clan Of The Cave Bear **1987** Matewan (also director, actor) **1988** Eight Men Out (also director, actor) **1989** Breaking In **1990** Little Vegas (actor only) **1991** City of Hope (also director, actor) **1992** Straight Talk (actor only)

Scacchi, Greta

Actress

Born 18 February 1960

Milan, Italy

Greta Scacchi's international background – born in Milan to an Italian father and an English mother, completing her education in Australia and making her film debut in Germany (learning her dialogue phonetically as she did not speak the language) – seems to have been the ideal preparation for a predominantly continental career. Ballet school, university dramatic society and the Bristol Old Vic led her to Merchant-Ivory and *Heat And Dust* (1983) and almost overnight acclaim for her first major film, in which she instilled an unforced sexuality into the usually passionless perfection of the Merchant-Ivory *ouevre*. Despite the wildly variable quality of her subsequent films, she has managed to keep in the public eye partially through volume of work, including much prestigious television, but largely through sex appeal (as witnessed by the preponderance of nudity in her screen roles). She is one of the few actresses allowed to be both sexy and smart on screen.

Although no more than adequate as an actress, Scacchi has made just enough good films (on average one every two years) such as *Defence Of The Realm* (1985) and *Good Morning Babylon* (1987) to maintain her position in the industry despite often playing roles that demand little of her. She has also appeared in a plethora of outstandingly bad films, such as *The Coca-Cola Kid* (1985, a notoriously unpleasant experience for her as she revealed at a Cannes press conference, much to the discomfort of star Eric Roberts and director Dusan Makavejev) and the elegant but turgid *Three Sisters* (1988). The latter seem to have done little harm, with 1990's *Presumed Innocent* marking a concerted and well-received move from the arthouse into the American mainstream, where she impressed with a toughness (and a convincing accent) hitherto concealed. Her cool, superior demeanour stood her in good stead in *The Player* (1992), in which her weird painter made her the Tinsel Town outsider whose kookiness wins the heart of Tim Robbins' studio exec power player.

1982 Das Zweiter Gesicht/Second Sight (Germany) **1983** Heat And Dust **1985** Burke And Wills; The Coca-Cola Kid; Defence Of The Realm **1987** Good Morning Babylon; A Man In Love; White Mischief **1988** Paura e Amore Three Sisters (Italy); La Donna Della Luna The Woman In The Moon (Italy) **1990** Presumed Innocent **1991** Fires Within; Shattered **1992** The Player; Turtle Beach (Australia) **1992/93** Salt On Our Skin

Scarwid, Diana

Actress
Born 1955
Savannah, Georgia

After a strong start, Diana Scarwid failed to make as much of her career as her early promise implied she would – which is possibly due to her unconventional (albeit blonde) looks or her choice of films, but is certainly no reflection on her talent. Having attended the American Academy of Dramatic Arts and become a member of the National Shakespeare Conservatory in New York, she moved to Hollywood and parts in often lurid or just downright silly TV movies before making her film debut as one of the prostitutes in *Pretty Baby* (1978).

She was Oscar-nominated for her touching and credible performance in *Inside Moves* (1980), propping up emotionally scarred Vietnam vet John Savage, but seemed unable to break out of supporting roles. Her attempt to change that with her Christina Crawford role in *Mommie Dearest* (1981) proved little short of disastrous, although she did try her best to bring a touch of realism to lines like 'You'd better tie me up again before mommie wakes up or she might get angry at you.' She regained some ground with a small role as Cher's mortician lover in *Silkwood* and the 'girl' interest in Coppola's *Rumble Fish* (both 1983), but after the failure of *Strange Invaders* the same year – in which she played Paul Le Mat's extraterrestrial ex-wife – and appearing as yet another of the women in Norman Bates' life in *Psycho III* (1986), her career began to stutter to a halt with progressively smaller roles in progressively worse films (some remaining on the shelf for several years) and lurid TV movies and she has failed to make a significant place for herself in either field.

1978 Pretty Baby **1980** Inside Moves; Honeysuckle Rose aka On The Road Again **1981** Mommie Dearest **1983** Rumble Fish; Silkwood; Strange Invaders **1984** The Ladies Club (released 1986) **1985** The Sisterhood **1986** Extremities; Psycho III; Brenda Starr (released 1992) **1987** Heat

Schatzberg, Jerry

Director
Born 26 June 1927
New York City

A former New York fashion photographer-turned-film-maker who spends most of his time with his wife (actress Maureen Kerwin), breeding racehorses at his upstate New York farm, Jerry Schatzberg is difficult to define. He is not fully, eclectic, neither is he 'political' in the manner of, say, Sidney Lumet; he lacks high-octane commercialism and cinematic sweep – and, indeed, in a 20-year period, Schatzberg has only a dozen films to his credit. If there is one ingredient which links all of them to their maker, be they good or bad, it is an intelligent eye that zones in on his protagonists: Schatzberg's films are about *people*.

Schatzberg has a predilection for low-life subjects and 'real' locations – he turned Willie Nelson's Texas ranch into a movie set in *Honeysuckle Rose* (1980) – but his career has flickered fitfully and he has not imposed himself emphatically on a film. Too often he has been let down by slack scripts or a habit of sliding into the glibly self-conscious chic of the fashion layout.

He made his directing debut with *Puzzle Of A Downfall Child* (1970), starring Faye Dunaway at her most unsympathetic as a former top model trying to piece together the shards of a disordered life. Then he oversaw Al Pacino's first leading role as a junkie in *Panic In Needle Park* (1971), an unrelenting account of drug adiction, very hard-hitting for its time, which ran into censorship problems before it was released. The psychological canvas of the film was too limited to be illuminating, but it was nonetheless an excellent piece of New York-style verité, with Pacino a mesmeric bundle of nervy energy. The rising star was teamed with Gene Hackman for the director's next, *Scarecrow* (1973), very much a vehicle for its actors, who played a couple of drifters bumming across America. Hackman described the movie as 'a combination of *Of Mice And Men* and *Midnight Cowboy*', which may explain why the public stayed away and Schatzberg had to console himself with a Golden Palm award at the Cannes film festival.

Schatzberg's fascination with the sleazy underbelly of American society resurfaced in a new form in *The Seduction Of Joe Tynan* (1979), an entertaining, albeit somewhat trite and earnest, tale of a young senator (Alan Alda) facing the inevitable moral dilemmas as he climbs the greasy pole on Capitol Hill. The director finally hit commercial paydirt with his sixth attempt, *Honeysuckle Rose* (1980), sustained by strong performances from Willie Nelson and Dyan Cannon as a wayward country-and-western singer and his put-upon wife. Their intimate scenes carry a considerable erotic charge, but a film of irritating sentimentality clings to *Honeysuckle Rose*, which cries out for a more hard-edged treatment of love lost and regained.

Thereafter, Schatzberg seemed to mark time until *Street Smart* (1987), based on a somewhat far-fetched but slick and interesting idea – journalist Christopher Reeve fabricates an expose of New York pimpdom which a DA investigating a murder takes for the truth – and enlivened by high-voltage performances from Morgan Freeman as a vicious king-pimp and Kathy Baker as a hooker. The following year came *Clinton And Nadine*, an unexceptional thriller in which Ellen Barkin played a high-class whore tangled up in a Latin-American gun-running scam, and which was fairly swiftly consigned to the shelves of video stores.

Then the director stepped up a class with *Reunion* (1989), scripted by Harold Pinter in sub-Proustian mood, and starring Jason Robards as an elderly New York Jew returning to the scenes of his childhood in Nazi Germany and reliving them through flashback. This is territory in danger of being picked dry by film-makers, but once *Reunion* hits its flashback stride and shrugs off the shades of *Cabaret* (1972), Jerry Schatzberg contrives some precisely melancholy period evocation in both *mise-en-scène* and camerawork.

1970 Puzzle Of A Downfall Child **1971** Panic In Needle Park **1973** Scarecrow **1976** Sweet Revenge aka Dandy The All American Girl **1979** The Seduction Of Joe Tynan aka The Senator **1980** Honeysuckle Rose **1984** Misunderstood; No Small Affair **1987** Street Smart **1988** Clinton And Nadine **1989** Reunion

Scheider, Roy

Actor

Born 10 November 1935

Orange, New Jersey

The tall, lean Roy Scheider had to work long and hard before making it as a movie star in his own right, shifting out of the shadow of Gene Hackman *(The French Connection*, 1971), Dustin Hoffman (*Marathon Man*, 1976) and Bruce, the Shark (*Jaws*, 1975), having played second fiddle to all of them.

His usually tough screen characterisations have benefited from a broken nose sustained in boxing during his high school days, although his professional debut in 1961 was as Mercutio in *Romeo And Juliet* at the New York Shakespeare Festival. He continued in scores of productions on the New York stage while making his first big screen appearance, billed as Roy R. Sheider, in *The Curse Of The Living Corpse* (1964), a low-budget 'old dark house' horror movie. Scheider started his film career proper in the role of a Mafia heavy in *Stiletto* (1969), a lame thriller. More rewarding was his New York businessman involved with fashion model Faye Dunaway in Jerry Schatzberg's *Puzzle Of A Downfall Child* (1970). His first large role, which gained him an Oscar nomination, was as Hackman's cop partner Buddy Russo, cracking a drug ring in William Friedkin's *The French Connection*. Cashing in on the success of this exciting movie, 20th Century-Fox then trusted Scheider with the lead in *The*

Seven-Ups (1973), in which he again played a New York cop, this time called Buddy Manucci.

In an attempt to get away from the hard-man image, Scheider was cast in the comedy *Sheila Levine Is Dead And Living In New York* (1975), as the doctor with whom the frumpish girl of the title (Jeannie Berlin, Elaine May's daughter) becomes smitten. Unfortunately, the film died in New York and elsewhere and, in the same year, the actor was back playing a cop in Steven Spielberg's mega-hit *Jaws*, doing sterling work as the chief of police of the holiday resort of Amity (which is under threat by a person-eating shark), a role he played with little variation in *Jaws 2* (1978).

It was in 1979, as the government agent recovering from a nervous breakdown and trying to find the origin of a death threat to him in Jonathan Demme's Hitchcock homage, *The Last Embrace*, and in Bob Fosse's autobiographical *All That Jazz*, that he demonstrated a depth of feeling and a more complex persona than hitherto. In the latter, which earned him the Golden Palm at Cannes and another Oscar nomination, Scheider also sang and danced as a director-choreographer fantasising while undergoing open heart surgery.

An outing with Meryl Streep in *Still Of The Night* (1982), a failed thriller, did nothing for either of them. Then a souped-up helicopter in *Blue Thunder* (1983), which he flew as a Vietnam vet cop, and the spectacular spaceship in *2010* (1984), on which he was a scientist on a mission to Jupiter, somewhat obscured his new-found maturity. But back on terra firma, he was excellent as Cohen, the jaded, taciturn hit man partnered with the younger, unstable and violent Adam Baldwin in the gripping, low-budget *Cohen And Tate* (1988), and as a hard-bitten American colonel on the Czech-West German frontier opposed to his Russian opposite number, Jürgen Prochnow, in John Frankenheimer's plodding and dated *The Fourth War* (1990). Never flashy, Roy Scheider continues to bring his discreet professionalism to every role he plays.

1964 The Curse Of The Living Corpse **1968** Star! **1969** Stiletto **1970** Puzzle Of A Downfall Child; Loving **1971** Klute; The French Connection **1973** The Seven-Ups; L'Attentat/Plot aka The French Conspiracy (France); Un Homme Est Mort/The Outside Man (France) **1975** Sheila Levine Is Dead And Living In New York; Jaws **1976** Marathon Man **1977** Sorcerer (GB: The Wages Of Fear) **1978** Jaws 2 **1979** The Last Embrace; All That Jazz **1982** Still Of The Night **1983** Blue Thunder; In Our Hands **1984** 2010 **1986** The Men's Club; 52 Pick-Up **1988** Cohen And Tate; Night Game **1989** Listen To Me **1990** The Fourth War; The Russia House **1992** The Naked Lunch

Schepisi, Fred

Director, Writer
Born 26 December 1936
Melbourne, Australia

One of only a few antipodean directors to have successfully made the transition to major international productions, Fred Schepisi is a quality workhorse, respected by actors and attentive to handsome production values. While he can turn his hand to drama, comedy or thriller, it is apparent that he is most engaged by pieces that offer a moral challenge, thus suggesting he has an intellectual ambition for his work.

Schepisi's first feature, *The Devil's Playground* (1976), offered a sharp script, but was an only slightly better than routine coming-of-age tale, set in a Catholic boarding-school; but the director, however, established that he was a skilled technician, adept at cast and setting. *The Chant Of Jimmie Blacksmith* (1978) was a definitely superior work, based on a true story and picturing quite tragically the dilemma of a part-Aborigine youth trapped helplessly between white Australian and Aboriginal cultures.

His American film-making debut with the off-beat, atmospheric Western *Barbarosa* (1982), centred on country-and-western star Willie Nelson's larger-than-life outlaw and his relationship with hick acolyte Gary Busey, was also to be admired though it received little other than elite critical attention. Schepisi was in danger of remaining in the classy cult ghetto when his first-rate treatment of the science-fiction study *Iceman* (1984) – in which John Lone's frozen caveman is revived by scientists and subjected to the cruelties of their detached curiosity – and of David Hare's irritating character study *Plenty* (1985) – in which Meryl Streep's World War II underground agent cannot adjust to the banality of her post-war life – both failed at the box office.

Commercially, Schepisi got a new lease on life with Steve Martin's update of *Cyrano De Bergerac*, *Roxanne* (1987), a surprising assignment for the director but a sweet and delightful winner in which he encouraged a restrained, charming performance from Martin and conjured a perfect smalltown atmosphere. For arguably his best film to date, *A Cry In The Dark* (1988), he returned to Australia, reteamed with Meryl Streep and Sam Neill for a self-penned, highly-charged and impassioned account of the notorious 'Dingo Baby Case' that tore Australia apart when a devout religious couple, the Chamberlins, were accused of killing their baby and Lindy Chamberlin went to prison for murder. As well as being an absorbing docu-drama style courtroom tearjerker, the film was a pointed and deeply disturbing indictment of media manipulation and mass hysteria. It was all the more disappointing then, that for the financially more successful *The Russia House* (1990) Schepisi demonstrated less vigour. A handsome, expensive package, with a script by Tom Stoppard from the John Le Carré novel, A-grade stars (Sean Connery, Michelle Pfeiffer and the sadly underused Klaus Maria Brandauer) and marvellous location work in Russia, the espionage thriller-cum-love story was frankly dull.

As director only unless stated otherwise: **1973** Libido (director of segment) **1976** The Devil's Playground (w/d) **1978** The Chant Of Jimmie Blacksmith (w/d) **1982** Barbarosa **1984** Iceman **1985** Plenty **1987** Roxanne **1988** A Cry In The Dark (also co-writer) **1990** The Russia House **1992** Mr Baseball

Schlesinger, John

Director
Born 16 February 1926
London, England

The son of a paediatrician, John Schlesinger got his first taste of show business as a teenager when he entertained troops with a magic act during World War II. At Oxford, he performed in student plays, and continued to act after graduation. The prematurely bald, softly-spoken Schlesinger can be seen in small roles in a few films, including two Michael Powell-Emeric Pressburger productions, *Oh Rosalinda!* (1955) and *The Battle Of The River Plate* (1956), made before he joined BBC TV in 1957, for whom he directed a number of documentaries. In 1961, his 45-minute film *Terminus*, 24 hours in the life of London's Waterloo station, won acclaim and a prize at the Venice Film Festival, and allowed him to break into feature films at the time of the British New Wave.

A Kind Of Loving (1962) and *Billy Liar* (1963) introduced fresh young players such as Alan Bates, Tom Courtenay and Julie Christie in modest films set in accurate working-class surroundings. As the 'kitchen sink' sank to be replaced by Swinging London, Schlesinger moved into the upper echelons with *Darling* (1965), a not altogether successful attempt at a cynical morality tale. Starring Julie Christie and Dirk Bogarde, it dealt with a chic and amoral society which the director seemed to rather relish, but it earned him an Oscar nomination. Although *Far From The Madding Crowd* (1967), which seldom got beyond a handsomely picturesque illustration (Nicolas Roeg photographed it) of the Thomas Hardy novel, made little impact in the USA, United Artists felt that the 42-year-old Englishman would be able to make a good job of the essentially New York story of *Midnight Cowboy* (1969). The screenplay focused on the incongruous and interdependent friendship between a dimwitted stud (Jon Voight) and a tubercular, crippled conman (Dustin Hoffman), touchingly and humourously portrayed. But Schlesinger, through his foreign eyes, saw New York as a rotten Big Apple, over-emphatically capturing the city's brashness and indifference. However, the movie won Oscars for Best Picture and Best Director, as well as earning more than $16 million at the box office.

Over-emphasis was also a flaw in *Marathon Man* (1976), a rather tawdry thriller with each image heavily emotive and significant and a plot with as many holes as in Dustin Hoffman's teeth after Laurence Olivier's Nazi dentist is through with him. Schlesinger also applied his steamroller technique to Nathanael West's satirical novel of Hollywood in the 30s, *The Day Of The Locust* (1975).

Schlesinger's later English films have generally been more controlled and stylish than his American ventures. Peter Finch and Glenda Jackson suffer exquisitely in *Sunday, Bloody Sunday* (1971) because they're both in love with the same vapid boy; *Yanks* (1979), an old-fashioned but attractive boy-meets-girl in wartime England story, might have been better in five half-hour episodes on TV; and in an equally old-fashioned picture, Shirley MacLaine is *Madame Sousatzka* (1988), a possessive music teacher in a London boardinghouse filled with lovable eccentrics. Back to the States in search of another hit after a number of flops, Schlesinger found it in *Pacific Heights* (1990), a frightening horror story for home owners in which a Yuppie couple, Matthew Modine and Melanie Griffith, rent out a room to psychopath Michael Keaton.

1962 A Kind Of Loving **1963** Billy Liar **1965** Darling **1967** Far From The Madding Crowd **1969** Midnight Cowboy **1971** Sunday, Bloody Sunday **1973** Visions Of Eight (episode) **1975** The Day Of The Locust **1976** Marathon Man **1979** Yanks **1981** Honky Tonk Freeway **1985** The Falcon And The Snowman **1987** The Believers **1988** Madame Sousatzka **1990** Pacific Heights

Schrader, Paul

Director, writer
Born 22 July 1946
Grand Rapids, Michigan

The cinema was forbidden to the young Paul Schrader by his strict Calvinist parents. Nonetheless, when he was 17, he guiltily saw his first film. He was hooked, abandoned his divinity studies, went to film school and became a critic, screenwriter and director. However, he has always retained an ambivalent puritanical streak, and many of his movies have themes of children reacting strongly against repressive parents.

His second film as director, *Hard Core* (1979), concerned the search of a Calvinist Midwesterner (George C. Scott) for his missing teenage daughter, who has become a porn star. The overheated screenplay followed the pained father through the sleazy world of LA, pictured with a jaundiced eye. *Patty Hearst* (1988) told of the heiress who joined the gang of urban guerillas who kidnapped her in 1974, and embedded in *Light Of Day* (1987), a pop musical, was a bitter daughter-versus-religious mother conflict.

American Gigolo (1979) was a well-designed yet hollow morality play about a high-class LA stud (Richard Gere) who satisfies rich women but not himself. The final sequence was copied from Robert Bresson's *Pickpocket* (1959), but its message of redemption through love (culled from the French film) lacked conviction. (Schrader's influences are to be found in his book, *Transcendental Style: Bresson, Ozu, Dreyer.*) The director's fascination with Japan – the setting of *The Yakuza* (1974), his first screenplay – was evident in *Mishima: A Life In Four Chapters* (1985). Unfortunately, although it would seem virtually impossible to make a boring film from a subject as rich as the narcissistic, bisexual, fascist Japanese writer who ritually disembowelled himself, Schrader achieved it by opting for an awkward structure, mixing black-and-white realism and coloured theatrical sets against which the stylised, often operatic scenes are played.

'As reality becomes more depressing, we regress into fantasy,' Schrader said to justify the making of *Cat People* (1982) about an incestuous brother and sister (Malcolm McDowell and Nastassia Kinski) who turn into killer leopards at sundown. Full of lurid images, it hinted at hidden sexual fears, but was less effective than Jacques Tourneur's subtle 1942 movie of the same title. In *The Comfort Of Strangers* (1990), Natasha Richardson (who had played Patty Hearst) and Rupert Everett become involved in obscure, erotic Byzantine games with a perverse couple (Christopher Walken and Helen Mirren) in an ever-photogenic Venice–fantasy of a sort, but disturbing and cold as ice. *Light Sleeper* (1992), which starred Willem Dafoe as an ageing drug peddlar in mid-life career and life crisis, returned to Schrader's existential forte – the loner adrift, seeking a purpose.

Although Paul Schrader often reveals a portentousness and his high ambitions are seldom realised, he has proved to be a director and writer who remains slightly outside the Hollywood mainstream and continues to fascinate due to his exploration of complex sexual and philosophical themes derived from his upbringing. It was perhaps no accident that he penned the screenplay for Scorsese's highly controversial *The Last Temptation Of Christ* (1988)

1975 The Yakuza (co-writer only) **1976** Taxi Driver (writer only); Obsession (writer only) **1977** Rolling Thunder (co-writer only) **1978** Blue Collar (also co-writer) **1979** Hardcore (w/d) (GB: The Hardcore Life); American Gigolo (w/d); Old Boyfriends (co-writer only) **1980** Raging Bull (co-writer only) **1982** Cat People (director only) **1985** Mishima: A Life In Four Chapters (also co-writer) **1986** The Mosquito Coast (co-writer only) **1987** Light Of Day (w/d) **1988** Patty Hearst (director only); The Last Temptation Of Christ (writer only) **1990** The Comfort Of Strangers (director only) **1992** Light Sleeper (w/d)

Schumacher, Joel

Director, writer
Born 29 August 1942
New York City

Few (if, indeed, any) film directors in contemporary Hollywood can claim so comprehensive and multi-faceted a creative background to their work as Joel

Schumacher. He quietly beavered his way into the higher echelons of mainstream moviemaking via costume design (where his credits include two for Woody Allen, *Sleepers*, 1973, and *Interiors*, 1978), screenwriter and writer-director. By the 1990s he was making a distinctive mark with the freshness of his work, some of which has a youthful air that belies his age. It must also be said that, while he ranges impressively wide in subject matter and style (a comparison between the brash *St Elmo's Fire*, 1986, and the elegant, sophisticated *Cousins*, 1989, for example, is instructive), the results of his often ambitious (*Flatliners*, 1990) endeavours are not always successful.

Born in a very poor New York neighbourhood and raised in a family which couldn't afford a television, Schumacher spent most of his youth in the local cinema behind his house. Not surprisingly, he grew to love movies perhaps more than most. As a young man, the lean and angular Schumacher worked his way through the prestigious Parson's School of Design, earning his money as a display artist for the exclusive Henri Bendel department store. After graduating, he went into the fashion industry where he created clothing and packaging for Revlon, and opened his own boutique for which he also designed. With a solid background in design, he expanded into art direction for television commercials and then moved into feature films as a costume designer.

He began writing screenplays of which *Car Wash* (1976), a comedy starring Richard Pryor, was the first to be made. Given its loose and superficial structure, it was surprisingly successful but, before then, its writer had already made his directing debut with a TV movie, *The Virginia Hill Story*, in 1974, which he also wrote; then, in 1979, he wrote and directed *Amateur Night At The Dixie Bar & Grill*, which proved an award-winner. His feature film debut came with the Lily Tomlin vehicle *The Incredible Shrinking Woman* (1981), a pleasant excursion into slapstick which demonstrated Schumacher's assurance with comedy, albeit with a satirical angle that was distinctly fuzzy. But it was *St Elmo's Fire* (1986) that put him on the mainstream map. Much maligned in certain critical quarters, but liked in others, this slick, slightly over-hysterical post-college youth movie enjoyed popular success, was certainly not without merit, and made excellent use of its collection of Brat Packers, all of whom have proved durable (Rob Lowe, Demi Moore, Judd Nelson, Emilio Estevez, Andrew McCarthy, Ally Sheedy). But *The Lost Boys* (1987), a hip retelling of the old vampire legend designed for the MTV generation, didn't enjoy the success expected of it, although it has since acquired some cult status.

After directing David Mamet's *Speed-The-Plow* on the Chicago stage in 1988, Schumacher returned to make his first 'serious' comedy-drama, *Cousins* (1989). A remake of Jean-Charles Tacchella's French film, *Cousin, Cousine* (1975), it deals with two sets of married cousins (Ted Danson and Sean Young, William Petersen and Isabella Rossellini) who meet at a family wedding and, via what is initially a series of misunderstandings, fall for each other's partners. Funny, romantic and bittersweet, it was beautifully played amid breathtaking settings in British Columbia, was far superior to its French model and proved that Schumacher had come of age. Ironically, this is the least known of the director's work, though, at the time of writing, undoubtedly his best film. He took a fall with the ambitious, unusual, visually sumptuous but over-inflated and badly misjudged *Flatliners* (1990), but went into 1991 with a full calendar, including a sequel to *The Lost Boys*, and *Dying Young*, a clinker which reunited him with his *Flatliners* star Julia Roberts.

1976 Car Wash (writer only); Sparkle (writer only) **1978** The Wiz (writer only) **1981** The Incredible Shrinking Woman **1983** D C Cab (w/d) **1986** St Elmo's Fire (w/d) **1987** The Lost Boys **1989** Cousins **1990** Flatliners (director only) **1991** The Lost Boys II; Dying Young (w/d)

Schwarzenegger, Arnold

Actor

Born 30 July 1947

Graz, Austria

So brilliantly has Arnold Schwarzenegger plotted his course from puny youth through Mr Universe to superstar, it is something of a relief that he chose film stardom as his destiny. Had he determined to become world ruler, we might have been in trouble.

Born in Austria to police chief father Karl Schwarzenegger, Arnold grew up in a backwater, reportedly without such modern conveniences as a toilet or a fridge. In search of the American Dream, the boy seized on the idea of making himself into a perfect physical specimen as his stepping-stone to becoming Somebody. He arrived in the US, a muscle-bound youth, in the late 60s, started a bricklaying business dubbed Pumping Bricks to finance more intensive training and had won seven Mr Olympia and five Mr Universe titles before retiring from bodybuilding. Along the way he also earned a degree in business and economics from the University of Wisconsin. In 1969 Schwarzenegger's body-building celebrity landed him the toga-sporting title role as *Hercules In New York*, although his heavily-accented voice was dubbed over. Between pumping iron and displaying his pectorals he worked his way stolidly and determinedly from bit parts (a heavy sans dialogue in *The Long Goodbye*, 1973) and bombs (the Western spoof *The Villain*, 1979). He made an impression in Bob Rafelson's eccentric comedy-drama *Stay Hungry* (1976), however, in the role of a bodybuilder, and he positively wowed both muscle devotees and the uninitiated in George Butler's engrossing documentary centred on Schwarzenegger's title pursuit, *Pumping Iron* (1977), in which he was charming, amusing and charismatic.

The cult of Arnold was developing and he became a leading writer and chat show guest on the subject of bodybuilding. In 1980 he gave an acceptable performance as Mickey Hargitay in the fluffy TV biopic *The Jayne Mansfield Story*, and he turned the corner to big action star as *Conan The Barbarian* (1982), in which he wielded a mean sword and bit the head off a vulture. The film took $50 million and action fans took Arnold to their hearts. Through the 1980s the locations changed but his character was ever the brawny beefcake, slaughtering his way through lesser warriors, alien monsters or ruthless villains in *Conan The Destroyer* (1984), *Red Sonja* (1985), *Commando* (1985), *Raw Deal* (1986), *The Running Man* (1987) or *Predator* (1987). These were invariably noisy, bone-shattering affairs affording Schwarzenegger such witty quips as 'I like you; that's why I'm going to kill you last.' By 1990 Big Arnie's films had grossed a billion dollars and he was reputedly making around $50 million a year. The best of his capers of the decade, *The Terminator* (1984), was also arguably the best and certainly one of the most influential action hits in years, a simply spiffy low-budget sci-fi adventure from director James Cameron in which the star was perfect as an android assassin sent from the future to kill a seemingly insignificant waitress and thus alter history. As an implacable 'droid, the six-foot-two-inches tall, 210-pound wooden wisecracker was atypically a completely unloveable bad guy, but love him people do.

Naturalised as a US citizen in 1983, Schwarzenegger consolidated his image as the embodiment of the American dream by marrying an offspring of the Kennedy clan, NBC reporter Maria Shriver (with whom he has two children) and throwing his bulk into George Bush's 1988 Presidential campaign, leading to his appointment as chairman of the US Council for Fitness. Still bent on global box-office domination he turned to more cuddly screen characterisations and enjoyed smashes with the puerile *Twins* (1988), as Danny DeVito's innocent giant genius genetic twin, and as the resolute *Kindergarten Cop* (1990). Meanwhile, the sci-fi comic strip adventures just kept getting bigger, with the futuristic Martian epic *Total Recall* (1990), budgeted at over $50 million and sweeping aside most competition in a summer season of blockbusters, and the long-awaited *Terminator 2*, which cost nearly $100 million, earned twice that, and saw the actor's price-tag rise to upwards of $15 million a picture. Already a self-made millionaire property developer before he became the world's biggest box-office attraction, there seemed to be no stopping this cigar-chomping, Hawaiian-shirted, self-marketing genius. And if Arnold Schwarzenegger's suspected political aspirations do indeed motivate him, who is laughing? Meanwhile, 1992 saw his directorial debut in Hollywood, with a TV movie, *Christmas In Connecticut*

1969 Hercules In New York **1973** The Long Goodbye **1976** Stay Hungry **1977** Pumping Iron **1979** The Villain aka Cactus Jack; Scavenger Hunt **1982** Conan The Barbarian **1984** The Terminator; Conan The Destroyer **1985** Red Sonja; Commando **1986** Raw Deal **1987** The Running Man; Predator **1988** Twins; Red Heat **1990** Total Recall; Kindergarten Cop **1991** Terminator 2: Judgement Day **1992/93** The Last Action Hero

Sciorra, Annabella

Actress

Born c 1964?

Connecticut

Born and raised in Connecticut Annabella Sciorra enrolled at the HB Studio in New York at the age of 13 going on to the American Academy of Dramatic Arts and extensive stage work in small productions punctuated by those mainstays of the acting profession waitressing and secretarial work. Answering an ad in *Backstage* she was able to talk her way into her first screen role the lead in the low budget *True Love* made in 1989.

In this debut film as the disillusioned bride left to cope with organising her wedding single-handed she avoided cliche with a performance that seemed devoid of technique but absolutely natural and entirely believable. While the film's success on the festival circuit may not have been mirrored at the box office it did bring her to the attention of several agents. In quick succession she played Sophia Loren's daughter in the TV miniseries *The Fortunate Pilgrim* the trusting wife of corrupt cop Richard Gere in *Internal Affairs* a sophisticated New York lawyer in *Reversal Of Fortune* and the secretary from Queens (with a refreshingly under-played accent) whose husband goes berserk in *Cadillac Man* (all 1990). As with her role as James Woods' romantic interest in *The Hard Way* (1991) there was little substance beyond her performance to most of these and it was not until Spike Lee's *Jungle Fever*, later the same year, that she really had the opportunity to come into her own once more.

Sciorra dark and attractive stood out in Lee's crowded and confused narrative as the Italian-American secretary who has a contentious affair with her married black boss lending the film's tone of manifesto a more human and sympathetic face that gave it perhaps more depth than it deserved. Amid an ensemble of often overtly 'Method' or theatrical performances she alone seemed to belong in the real world and quietly stole the acting honours. As a result she earned top billing and her first big hit with *The Hand That Rocks The Cradle* (1992). While Rebecca De Mornay's killer nanny may have won the plaudits it was Sciorra's down to earth performance in the dangerously idealised role of the threatened mother that gave the film the anchor in reality it needed in order to work. And work it did proving a box-office hit. As with all her performances its success was down to her absolute honesty on screen – she is never seen to be acting her delivery of dialogue giving the impression that she has only just thought of it. This honesty sometimes puts her at risk of having no easily recognisable screen persona for the paying public to latch on to but while this may preclude her from becoming a major box-office force it should stand her in good stead as a character actress and ensure a longer career than many of her contempories.

1989 True Love **1990** Internal Affairs; Cadillac Man; Reversal Of Fortune **1991** The Hard Way; Jungle Fever **1992** The Hand That Rocks The Cradle; Sessions **1993** Romeo Is Bleeding

Scorsese, Martin

Director, actor, writer
Born 17 November 1942
New York City

Martin Scorsese, perhaps the most physically exhilarating film-maker alive, is also the film-maker who has done more to capture his native city in the raw than any other. These two characteristics – the pulsating vitality of his most memorable films, which whirls the spectator through to their climaxes with unstoppable filmic energy, and his feeling for the underbelly of New York in all its sordid fascination – are often, but not always, closely related. Though, indeed, it may be true to say that the best Scorsese films – *Mean Streets* (1973), *Taxi Driver* (1976), *Raging Bull* (1980), and the epic *GoodFellas* (1990) foremost among them – are also among the city's best, he has taken care to avoid being considered a single-subject, single-style creator. *Alice Doesn't Live Here Any More* (1975), the tender portrait of a West Coast widow building herself a new life, is one example of this director's regular attempts to vary his styles and choice of subjects; the controversial *The Last Temptation Of Christ* (1988), a lengthy, ambitious and sincere, if not entirely coherent, attempt to portray on film the 'human' Jesus of Nicos Kazantzakis's novel, is another; and his *The Last Waltz* (1976), a record-plus-report of The Band's final concert, is a third – a pop-music documentary of rarely-equalled vividness and eloquence. *Cape Fear* (1991), a deliberately overwrought re-make of the 1962 cat-and-mouse thriller, was a commercially sensational success that seemed undertaken to prove Scorsese could dispense horrific fright and suspense with the same virtuosity and style he brings to psychological study and internal drama. (Not everyone, however, agreed that its shocking violence and over-the-top central performance from De Niro was an improvement on the restrained and sinister 1962 original).

This director always takes chances, and even if they don't come off, a Scorsese failure can be relied upon to have more red blood in it than the vast majority of Hollywood 'successes'. The linking factor in all his work, which gives it such a powerfully distinctive and personal flavour, is a fascination with obsessive characters, whether violent, sexually tortured, creatively driven, or simply freakish. Scorsese is, self-admittedly, an obsessive himself: a sickly child restricted indoors by severe asthma and addicted to movies from an early age (his parents acquired their first television set when he was six). The family was of Italian-immigrant origin, and the Little Italy quarter of New York, later to be depicted with such unflinching authenticity in Scorsese films, was their native territory; having decided at the age of 14 to become a Catholic priest, he was kept out of theological college by a poor academic record, and turned instead to film studies. While attending the course at NYU he made (and wrote scripts for) several award-winning shorts, among them *The Big Shave* (1968); at this time he was also germinating the script for a first full-length feature, *Who's That Knocking At My Door?* (1969). A low-budget piece, jerkily paced – it had been made discontinuously and crudely joined up – and characterised, it bursts with revelations of the youthful director's artistic enthusiasms (for, among other things, the work of the European New Wave), his personal absorptions (in Little Italy, friendship, sexual guilt) and above all his excitement over the technical possibilities of film-making.

It was a highly promising start, pregnant with talent. After working as assistant director and editor on the celebrated pop-music documentary *Woodstock* (1970), he followed it up with a first commercial feature, produced by Roger Corman: *Boxcar Bertha* (1972), a Depression-era adventure of Arkansas union misfits turned train-robbers led by Barbara Hershey in the title role, which Scorsese made far more quirkily interesting than its basic B-movie premises would suggest. But it was with *Mean Streets* that the wider world was first alerted to the existence of an important new talent. This is the first 'signature' Scorsese film, a Little Italy tale of casual violence, guilt, and betrayal, of mobsters bonded by ties of friendship, of street smells and sounds (backed by a loud rock soundtrack) that hit the viewer with a wallop. The camera moves nervily fast; as acted by Harvey Keitel and Robert De Niro, the young Italian-American New Yorker who would subsequently become the incarnation of the Scorsese obsessive, the characters breathe a 'felt life' that is the hallmark of creative accuracy.

After this came a period of respite in the form of *Alice Doesn't Live Here Any More*, in which the performance of Ellen Burstyn (who won the 1974 Best Actress Oscar) showed, as that of Barbara Hershey had done in *Boxcar Bertha*, that Scorsese can deal as sympathetically with leading actresses as with actors. But then it was back to New York, in perhaps the most hellish of Scorsese's city visions: *Taxi Driver*, in which the tormented ex-Vietnam marine Travis Bickle is driven by his pathological fears and hatreds to the film's culminating outburst of crazed violence. De Niro as Bickle and the very young Jodie Foster as an under-age junkie prostitute are the principal players in this nightmare of urban paranoia, which takes to the limits its maker's 'physical' cinema – much of the film verges dangerously on the over-emphatic – in ways that he later toned down or else mastered more fluently. This said, the impact of the film as a whole, and of De Niro's graphic portrayal of urban alienation, remains astonishing, a veritable cinematic detonation.

It was in *Raging Bull*, the film biography of the New York boxer Jake La Motta, that lessons learnt from *Taxi Driver* were put to most effective use. This is probably the bleakest boxing film ever made: Scorsese allowed himself none of Hollywood's traditional triumphalist or sentimental rhetoric in dealing with the genre, but achieved instead a virtuoso depiction of the brutalising effect of violence, emphasised by the magnified sound of punches and heartbeats in the ring sequences, that spared the viewer no detail of physical or psychological horror. La Motta is one of the classic Scorsese obsessives – wild in the ring, riven with irrational jealousy in his personal relations – and his downfall is horrible to watch, the more so because of the avoidance of special pleading in the film and in De Niro's magnificent leading performance (for which he worked himself up to amateur boxing status; in the course of making the film he deliberately gained at least 60lbs). It was a tribute to the actor, but also to the director's new discipline, that a film of such virtuoso camerawork should seem at heart so lean, so muscular. De Niro's La Motta won the 1980 Best Actor Oscar, but – not for the first or last time – the Academy shied away from giving Scorsese himself his due. (However, critics on both sides of the Atlantic later voted it the best film of the 1980s.)

Scorsese's New York, as a handful of films made before and after *Raging Bull* so aptly demonstrate, is not just a place of violent people: it's also a city of the driven, whose obsessions shade into farce or romantic drama rather than melodrama. Even if these Scorsese films – the musical *New York, New York* (1977), and the comedies *King Of Comedy* (1983) and *After Hours* (1985) – failed at the box office, that does not make them any less original or compelling. The musical, which was first released in a badly truncated version, couples De Niro as a self-absorbed jazz saxophonist and Liza Minnelli as a love-him-then-leave-him band singer; while the mixture of highly stylised sequences and strong performances from both leads may have failed to gel, the film is full of pleasures. *King Of Comedy*, with De Niro as would-be comedian Rupert Pupkin, who kidnaps the star of a television comedy show (Jerry Lewis, brilliantly 'straight') to ransom some screen fame for himself, is an even more startling mixture. Fast-moving, surreal in its comedy and cynical in its message, it was probably too abrasive to achieve large-scale audience popularity, but holds a special place in the affections of all Scorsese admirers. So, to a lesser extent, do *After Hours*, with Griffin Dunne as an uptown yuppie unwillingly embarked on a mad series of nocturnal downtown adventures with some of the weirdest weirdos in Manhattan, and Scorsese's 'Life Lessons' (in *New York Stories*), a richly off-beat little comic fable about a famous artist (Nick Nolte) who draws new inspiration from his own emotional crises.

One side of the Scorsese argument says that after *Raging Bull* the director tended to tread water. The other says that in all of these 1980s entertainments (in the Graham Greene sense) the widening of his range in choice and handling of subjects has been constant. (To the list of those entertainments can be added *The Color of Money* (1986), a slick, unexpectedly conventional sequel to Robert Rossen's 1961 pool-room drama *The Hustler*, with Paul Newman playing the same character 25 years later opposite Tom Cruise as a rising pool star.) Both sides can find justification, and perhaps also mutual reconciliation, in the epic of New York gangster life with which Scorsese closed this particular period. *GoodFellas* is a long, enthralling interweaving of biography (the real-life tale of Henry Hill, who grew to manhood in the Mafia and eventually ratted on his former associates), social observation, black-comic incident, and scenes of horrific but always strictly justifiable violence. The huge cast list is a galaxy of New York character-acting at its athletic, up-front best: Ray Liotta as Henry Hill, De Niro, the electrifying Joe Pesci (whose Tommy DeVito, a manically violent cocksparrow, won him the 1990 Best Supporting Actor Oscar), Paul Sorvino, Lorraine Bracco as Hill's middle-class Jewish wife and others too numerous to name. Scorsese's ability to sustain the tempo of film-making at once dazzlingly and honestly fast has never seemed more exciting, particularly as the final climax approaches; and for all the physical impact of the film, the underlying moral issues are delineated in all their troubling complexity. To end an old decade and start a new one with one of the masterpieces of modern American cinema augured well, to say the least, for Scorsese's movie-making future – a future that went on to enbrace the elegant literary high ground of Edith Wharton's *The Age Of Innocence*.

1968 Who's That Knocking At My Door? aka I Call First (w/d, also cameo) **1972** Boxcar Bertha (also cameo) 1973 Mean Streets (w/d, also cameo) **1975** Alice Doesn't Live Here Any More (also cameo) **1976** Cannonball (cameo only); Taxi Driver (also actor) **1977** New York, New York **1978** The Last Waltz **1979** Hollywood's Wild Angels (actor only) **1980** Raging Bull **1981** Triple Play (actor only) **1983** The King Of Comedy (also cameo); Pavlova – A Woman For All Time (GB/USSR, actor only) **1985** After Hours (also cameo) **1986** The Color Of Money; Round Midnight aka Autour De Minuit (US/France, cameo only) **1988** The Last Temptation Of Christ **1989** New York Stories ('Life Lessons' episode) **1990** GoodFellas; Akira Kurosawa's Dreams (actor only) **1991** Guilt By Suspicion (actor only); Cape Fear **1992/93** The Age Of Innocence

Scott, Ridley

Director

Born 1939

South Shields, England

Despite having made barely a handful of films, Ridley Scott has established himself as one of modern cinema's unique and most imitated visual stylists, as well as one of the few directors to come from commercials who is successful in injecting substance into the look of his films and shaking off the televisual parochialism of most of his English contemporaries. Studying at the Royal College of Art in London (he still draws many of the production sketches and storyboards for his films himself), he joined its newly formed film school to make his first short film, graduating with both First Class

Honours and, more importantly, the prize of a one-year travelling scholarship to America where he worked for Time-Life Inc., alongside top documentary film-makers D.A. Pennebaker and Richard Leacock. In 1964 he secured a job as production designer at the BBC and within a year was directing episodes of *Z Cars* and *The Informer*. After three years he felt strait-jacketed and left to start his own commercials company (still active as one of the most successful in the industry) but it was not until ten years, numerous awards and more than 2,000 commercials later that he was able to make his first feature.

The Duellists (1977), a striking adaptation of a Joseph Conrad short story about an obsessive, long-running duel that spans much of the Napoleonic era, was a project filled with all the traditional pitfalls of costume drama, one of the great elephants' graveyards of British cinema, yet managed to turn most of them on their heads. More of a mood piece than an emotional one, the film had a supreme visual beauty that was true painting with light, with Scott's eye drawn not by a re-creation of the classical paintings of the day but by an imagination of how their artists would portray this story. Yet despite winning the Special Jury Prize at Cannes, it was his commercial work which earned him the surprise hit *Alien* (1979).

Aware of the limitations of the much rewritten screenplay, and somewhat over-reliant on his excellent cast for a human focus, he managed to turn this Sci-Fi blockbuster into another visual tour de force, inspiring the stylistic emphasis of the next two decades of genre films. His image of a dirty, run-down future where nothing works and humanity comes a poor second to commerce came into its own with the 'more human than human' replicants of *Blade Runner* (1982), one of the key films of the decade and certainly one of the most under-rated at the time. (It has become a guaranteed audience draw over the years.) Many critics felt its hellish, overcrowded world of minority wealth – lavish neon pyramids with large, classically designed interiors and artificial animals – and mass poverty – decaying art deco buildings, walls and passing airships constantly bombarding a desensitised public with commercials – overwhelmed the film, but Scott showed a gift for creating strong, empathetic characters (played by Harrison Ford, Rutger Hauer and Sean Young among others) between the lines of dialogue, and redeemed its air of fatalism (his original ad-line was 'no-one gets out of life alive') with a powerful humanism previously unequalled in screen science fiction.

With an original, sparing use of narration turned into a virtual series of monologues and an unconvincing happy ending tacked on at the last minute, the film was one of the severest cases of studio interference in his work, an experience largely repeated on *Legend* (1985). Clearly inspired by Cocteau, this simple fairy-tale (and Scott's most lyrical film) exists in various versions with various different musical scores and seemed to end his desire to become 'the John Ford of sci-fi and fantasy'; yet his move into thriller territory with *Someone To Watch Over Me* (1987) and *Black Rain* (1989) by no means marked a change in style. Both continued his themes of cultural and social divides, more interestingly between uptown and downtown lives and loves in the former, which played more emotional cards than thrills in what was perhaps a riposte to criticism that Scott was better at directing special effects than actors.

The gulf between the penthouses and the suburbs proved greater and more alien than that between East and West in the latter, very much a more commercial package, albeit skilfully delivered against overwhelming odds. With plenty of his trademarks and a plot that in various guises has been a constant of his career – a monstrous protagonist (Michael Douglas) triggering a morally ambiguous conflict in an alien environment (Tokyo) – its modest commercial success following the initial box-office disappointments of his post-*Alien* films helped to maintain his position among the major studios, allowing him the liberty of a pet project. *Thelma And Louise* (1991) finally gained him critical acceptance and his biggest commercial success since *Alien*, albeit amid controversy as to whether this exhilarating feminist adventure was a genuinely mould-breaking portrayal of women, or simply a female variation of *Butch Cassidy And The Sundance Kid*. He brought a foreigner's appreciative eye to the stunningly filmed landscapes of America's Southwest, and drew superb, Oscar-nominated performances from Susan Sarandon and Geena Davis, showing a welcome focus on character. He went on to tackle the most ambitious of the Columbus quincentennial projects, working with Gerard Depardieu and a prestigious supporting cast.

1977 The Duellists **1979** Alien **1982** Blade Runner **1985** Legend **1987** Someone To Watch Over Me **1989** Black

Rain **1991** Thelma And Louise **1992** 1492: Conquest Of Paradise

Scott, Tony

Director
Born 21 July 1944
Newcastle, England

Like his more famous and infinitely more talented brother, Ridley, Tony Scott worked his way through art school into a career in TV commercials, winning Cleo and Cannes Awards, but has no vision of his own. Since his graduation to feature films – via short films for the British Film Institute – he has proved to be one of the screen's worst offenders when it comes to turning movies into a succession of commercials. His background has taught him visual shorthand but little about character building or storytelling, with the result that his first major feature, *The Hunger* 1983), was all style (albeit strikingly so) but no substance, wasting a good cast (Catherine Deneuve, Susan Sarandon, David Bowie) and an intriguing premise and throwing in an incomprehensible finale that looks like out-takes from a heavy metal video. Depressingly, it was precisely this MTV 30-second attention-span style that was to prove so commercially successful with bland, pre-packaged entertainments, turning the product into its own commercial – in the case of *Top Gun* (1986) for the US Airforce and Tom Cruise's sunglasses, while the director sold Eddie Murphy's smile and braying laugh in *Beverly Hills Cop II*, a film so devoid of the original's thrills, laughs, plot or entertainment value that it leaves you waiting for the trademarks to appear.

Ironically, it was with his attempts to expand his range that Scott fell from grace. *Revenge* (1990) had all the makings of a pleasingly dark thriller, but Scott seemed unable to understand the demons that drove his protagonists or the demands of his audience (the film has no real climax and just fizzles out) and managed to rack up an expensive flop despite the presence of Kevin Costner. The surprise failure of *Days Of Thunder* (1990) was an altogether sadder affair. Here, the director had learned to match his flashy visuals to the simple psychology of his characters, and turned in a much under-rated modern-day Howard Hawks-type film that was finely tuned commercial cinema at its best (although much credit is undoubtedly due to Robert Towne's excellent written-on-the-lam screenplay). Tony Scott is unlikely to be remembered as a great director and must rely on a reputation for commercial viability built on two films – but with two back-to-back disappointments, he began the 1990s with that viability dented and his artistic reputation far from enhanced. That did not change with the derivative action comedy thriller, *The Last Boy Scout* (1991) starring Bruce Willis, but the movie at least made a respectable showing at the box office.

1972 Loving Memory (one-hour feature) **1983** Author of Betrraffio; The Hunger **1986** Top Gun **1987** Beverley Hills Cop II **1990** Revenge; Days Of Thunder **1991** The Last Boy Scout **1993** True Romance

Seagal, Steven

Actor
Born 1950
Detroit, Michigan

Steven Seagal was in his 30s when he moved to Los Angeles and set up a martial arts academy. A friend and bodyguard to super agent Michael Ovitz (reputedly the most powerful man in Hollywood), Seagal saw that there was a market for his skills in the movies and persuaded Warners that he was the best man to exploit it. Picking up a routine cop project, Seagal and Andrew Davis reworked the script (sharing a story credit) and co-produced *Above The Law* (1988). Davis directed, and Seagal starred as Nico – a cop with friends in the CIA and the Mafia, a Vietnam history, and a black belt in aikido. A clever first film, *Above The Law* worked as a showcase for its star by juggling elements designed to appeal to as wide a constituency as possible (with the exception of drug pushers and corrupt government agents, that is). With the sleek look of a Clint Eastwood thriller rather than a simple action exploitation movie, and almost too much plot, the movie took nothing for granted and consequently pulled in excellent box-office takings. Charles Bronson, Chuck Norris, Jean-Claude Van Damme et al looked sleepy in comparison.

Tall, slim and lanky, with hair slicked back from a high forehead, a prominent nose and strong eyebrows, Seagal might be caricatured as a vulture or an eagle. His life story smacks of myth: at 17 he left the States for Japan, where he supported himself by teaching English while studying the martial arts, and eventually earned black belts in aikido, karate, judo and kendo. He became the first non-Asian to open his own 'dojo', or martial arts school, in Japan, and he choreographed fight scenes for the movies, coaching the likes of James Mason, Sean Connery and Toshiro Mifune. Diversifying, he went into the security business, mounting special security operations, and setting up 'safe houses'. At one point he even tried his hand at bounty hunting, and he has hinted at CIA connections. After 15 years in Asia, Seagal moved to Los Angeles. Apart from establishing his academy, he served as a personal bodyguard for celebrities including his future wife and co-star, actress Kelly Le Brock. Then came *Above The Law*.

As you would expect from a man who refers to himself as 'a warrior', Seagal looks absolutely at ease during the film's many stunt scenes. He seems unsure of himself at other times however. He has a tendency to play cute, and his inexperience is obvious when he slightly misreads a camera angle or over-emphasises a throwaway gesture. What is surprising about the movie – apart from its entertainment value – is the liberal slant evident in plot *and* treatment. Covert CIA operations are behind the bad guys, while left-wing political refugees from South America are accorded a sympathetic hearing. Nico's entirely natural working relationship with a black female partner is also appealing. As violent action thrillers go, this is the quality end of the market.

Hard To Kill (1990) was essentially more of the same; a predictable revenge plot is produced with some care and attention to detail. Again it did well at the box office. By *Marked For Death* (1990) – another lone cop film – it seemed Seagal himself was ready for a change. 'In a lot of ways this is not the kind of movie I wanted to make again,' he admitted. 'I realise that it's not the deepest film in the world, and I like to make deep films. But you've got to start somewhere and build your core audience. You gotta take the shit with the sugar.'

1988 Above The Law aka Nico **1990** Hard To Kill; Marked For Death **1991** Out For Justice aka The Price Of Our Blood aka The Night **1992** Under Siege

Sedgwick, Kyra

Actress
Born 1965?
From ?

With the looks of a young Janis Joplin (albeit prettier) and a rather fetching smile, Kyra Sedgwick seems to have surmounted therather inauspicious and inconsequential nature of her early work and moved on to more challenging parts. From her work in the daytime soap *Another World* when she was 16, she went into small roles in undistinguished TV movies but it was in Dino De Laurentiis' production of *Tai Pan* (1986) that she first had much to do, as the daughter of John Stanton's over-protective villain (he has one early suitor castrated) who falls in love with the hero's son. Although she could not be said to have performed with an excess of distinction, the film was such an appalling mess that even its most accomplished cast members were left high and dry, and it took the part of Muriel in a 1988 Broadway revival of Eugene O'Neill's *Ah Wilderness*, which won her a Theatre World Award, to give a better idea of her talents and lead to her first substantial role in a film people would actually see.

As Tom Cruise's girlfriend in *Born On The Fourth Of July* (1989) many people criticised her role as a token female in Oliver Stone's misogynist vision, but neither charge was true. She begins the 60s as the archetypal girl next door but when Cruise returns from Vietnam, his body shattered but still clinging to his gung-ho patriotism, she has changed and become much more aware of the world around her; and it is through her – as the one dissenting voice his memories won't let him dismiss – that the first seeds of his politicisation are sown. There were similarities in her role as the errant daughter of *Mr And Mrs Bridge* (1990), evolving as those she should be closest to remain set in their ways, although here her character proved singularly unable to change those she loved or even herself, let alone the world. Starting off with romantic dreams of becoming an actress but discarding them with an underachieving Bohemian lifestyle, she at once embodies and fails to fulfil the forgotten hopes she awakens in her mother as completely as she goes against her father's strait-laced respectability that her brother ultimately embraces.

Despite her credits being slightly off-the-beaten-track films in a formula industry, they focused enough attention on the noticeably talented Sedgwick (who is married to Kevin Bacon) to secure her a prominent role in Cameron Crowe's ensemble piece *Singles* (1991).

1985 War And Love **1986** Tai-Pan **1988** Kansas **1989** Reise In Die Unterwelt (Germany); Born On The Fourth Of July **1990** Mr And Mrs Bridge **1992** Singles

Seidelman, Susan

Director

Born 11 December 1952

nr Philadelphia, Pennysylvania

A graduate of Drexel University where she studied design and took film classes, Susan Seidelman began her working life as a producer's assistant on a show called *Community Bulletin Board* for a local TV station, and rapidly decided that her future lay elsewhere. She enrolled at New York University's Graduate School of Film and TV and, while there, wrote, directed and edited three short films. By the time she left NYU, Seidelman had become a committed New Yorker. She lives in Greenwich Village, has shot all her films in the city, and is on record as saying, 'I've rejected the idea of working in Hollywood. It's like being on Valium. You can float away for a while, but I don't feel real there, whereas New York keeps you down to earth. Simply by living there, it ends up in your movies somehow.'

Certainly, the brio, energy and choice of material which has informed her work confirms her attitude. Her first feature, *Smithereens* (1982), was made on a shoestring, payments deferred. It concerned the relationship between a naive young out-of-towner living in his camper van on a derelict site, and a lost-cause rock groupie with whom he becomes involved. Although looking at the sleazy underside of trendsville, the movie had freshness, spontaneity and a gritty reality which added up to a pleasing package, and earned it the honour of being the first American independent feature ever to be accepted in competition at the Cannes Film Festival.

But it was the director's next movie, three years later, that put her on the map. *Desperately Seeking Susan* (1985), imaginative, off-beat and enchanting, starred Madonna and Rosanna Arquette in a tale about mistaken identity and yuppie marriage. The script was full of surprises and the film turned out to be the sleeper of the year. Her next venture, *Making Mr Right* (1987), starred the charismatic John Malkovich as a scientist who creates a robot in his own image, but which malfunctions to display all the emotion the living man lacks. Described by one critic as a romance masquerading as science fiction, and by its maker as 'both a rejection and an embracing of pop culture', it, too, offered charm and originality, but was more self-conscious and less successful than its predecessor. The small-scale, cute *Cookie* (1989) was a well-observed diversion showcasing Emily Lloyd as the daughter of Peter Falk's genial Mafia man, and was rich in the resonances of Manhattan's garment district and Little Italy, but it was too ephemeral an exercise to really take off.

Seidelman entered the big-budget big time with *She-Devil* (1989), starring Maryl Streep and Roseanne Barr. The movie displayed a firm directorial control over its New York locations, its pace and its crazy plot about crazed people. Clearly, the director is not fazed by Hollywood money, and the movie should have moved her up a notch or two in the Hollywood hierarchy. Unfortunately, the critics took agin it, pilloried Meryl Streep's long-awaited excursion into high comedy, and attacked the screenplay for its departure from Fay Weldon's original novel.

Nonetheless, Susan Seidelman has made her mark, no doubt holding on to her view that 'a script is a skeleton that I like enough to, well, hang my skin on.' With five feature films to her credit in the course of eight years she seemed in little danger of burning herself out. And if she has not consistently lived up to her early promise, she is nonetheless a noticeable original among the few women directors who have managed to break in to the mainstream.

1982 Smithereens (also co-writer) 1985 Desperately Seeking Susan **1987** Making Mr Right **1989** Cookie **1990** She-Devil **1993** Yesterday

Selleck, Tom

Actor

Born 29 January 1945

Detroit, Michigan

Moustachioed beefcake Tom Selleck is still most widely known as television private eye Magnum. Despite his action-man looks, he has a gentleness and a twinkle that endear him, particularly to women. These same qualities make him better suited to light comedy, as is reflected by his personal success in the box-office smashes *Three Men And A Baby* (1987) and its sequel, and the relative failure of his more brutal fare like *An Innocent Man* (1990).

Although born in Detroit, Selleck was raised in the San Fernando Valley and attended the University of Southern California. Signed to a seven-year contract with Fox he did countless TV roles, including several appearances as a recurring character in the popular James Garner series, *The Rockford Files*. Several TV movies later he was starring in *Magnum P.I.* from 1980 to 1988, a show that brought him an Emmy, a Golden Globe and a star on Hollywood Boulevard's walk-of-fame pavement.

Parallel with his television success Selleck's film career got off to a shaky start with a bit as one of Mae West's stud line-up in the legendary debacle *Myra Breckinridge* (1970), and many blink-and-you'll-miss-him spots in more ho-hum fare. In 1977 he was one of the prime physical specimens murdered for his organs in the solid hospital chiller *Coma* and in 1981 he suffered a huge disappointment when he was cast as Indiana Jones by Lucas and Spielberg for *Raiders Of The Lost Ark* but couldn't get released from *Magnum P.I.*, which had become a ratings hit.

Later attempts at big-screen stardom – such as the tame action adventure *High Road To China* (1983) and the fairly feeble *Lassiter* (1984), in which he played a burglar roped into espionage – were greeted with indifference until *Three Men And A Baby* (1987), a cute one-joke movie which saw him give the most delightful of three charming performances as chief fancy-free bachelor gone gooey over the squealing bundle. Selleck then rescued the dubious comedy *Her Alibi* (1989), pitted against a beauteous but hopeless Paulina Porizkova, with an amiable performance as the thriller writer falling for murder suspect number one. *An Innocent Man* (1990) saw him earnest, sympathetic and awfully macho as a framed fellow brutalised in prison, but audiences shunned it as a downer, and an attractive Western he had long dreamed of making, *Quigley Down Under* (1990), set in Australia, was handsome but routine. Inevitably, *Three Men And A Little Lady* (1990) put him back in the box-office stakes, with fans evidently wanting to see Selleck only as a big, cuddly sweetie. For an astute businessman Selleck's worst piece of misjudgement was accepting the role of King Ferdinand in the Salkinds' epic boo-boo *Columbus*, his very entrance, eyes a'twinkling beneath a silly wig, raising laughs

Married to English dancer Jillie Mack, with whom he has a little girl, Selleck is also a successful television producer and helped revive the fortunes of Burt Reynolds with the TV series *B.L. Stryker*.

1970 Myra Breckinridge **1971** Seven Minutes **1972** Daughters Of Satan **1973** Terminal Island aka Knuckle-Men **1974** The Washington Affair **1976** Midway aka The Battle Of Midway **1977** Coma **1983** High Road To China **1984** Lassiter; Runaway **1987** Three Men And A Baby **1989** Her Alibi; Hard Rain **1990** Quigley Down Under; An Innocent Man; Three Men And A Little Lady **1992** Christopher Columbus: The Discovery; Mr Baseball; Folks!

Shatner, William

Actor

Born 22 March 1931

Montreal, Canada

Before undertaking his apparently endless mission to 'go boldly where no man has gone' as James T. Kirk of the 'Starship Enterprise', William Shatner was a good young actor with some interesting work behind him.

A Canadian, Shatner was educated at McGill University and gained experience in repertory before coming to New York, where he worked in live television drama and on Broadway before making his film debut in *The Brothers Karamazov* (1958), a prestigious production in which he delivered a sympathetic portrayal of the devout Alexei, a substantial role. *Judgement At Nuremberg* (1961) offered a five-star follow-up, if a slighter screen presence, as an assistant prosecutor in the Nazi war crimes trials. Among his more notable or unusual roles was that of the charismatic white supremacist fomenting race hatred in a small Southern town in Roger Corman's powerful social message movie *The Intruder* (1961), Angie Dickinson's bank-robber partner in *Big Bad Mama* (1974), and the lead in a now-disappeared film made in Esperanto, the invented universal language of which Shatner was once an enthusiast. Pre-*Star Trek*, on TV he is remembered for his performance as the panic-stricken plane passenger in a *Twilight Zone* favourite – *Nightmare At 20,000 Feet*.

Post-*Star Trek*, Shatner starred in two more television series, *Barbary Coast* and *T.J. Hooker*, between largely unexciting films, but he was back in charge of the re-designed 'Enterprise' for the hugely popular series of *Star Trek* motion pictures from 1979 on. Attempting to emulate the directorial success of his colleague Leonard Nimoy, however, drew down the wrath of critics and Trekkies alike when *Star Trek V: The Final Frontier* (1989) proved the lamest entry in the ever-continuing adventures. Not only directed by Shatner but scripted from a story partly conceived by him, he took most of the blame for the unseemly antics the by now pensionable crew were seen to get up to. Shatner didn't need to worry: a millionaire, he writes novels, breeds horses and is active in conservation and environmental causes.

1958 The Brothers Karamazov **1961** Judgment At Nuremberg; The Explosive Generation; The Intruder aka The Stranger aka I Hate Your Guts! aka Shame **1964** The Outrage **1966** Incubus **1968** Hour Of Vengeance; White Comanche (Spain) **1974** Big Bad Mama; Dead Of Night **1975** The Devil's Rain; Impulse **1977** A Whale Of A Time; Kingdom Of The Spiders **1978** The Third Walker; Land Of No Return aka Snowman aka Challenge To Survive **1979** Riel; Star Trek – The Motion Picture **1980** The Kidnapping Of The President **1982** Star Trek II: The Wrath Of Khan; Visiting Hours; Airplane II: The Sequel **1984** Star Trek III: The Search For Spock **1986** Star Trek IV: The Voyage Home **1989** Star Trek V: The Final Frontier (also director) **1991** Star Trek VI: The Undiscovered Country

Shaver, Helen

Actress
Born 24 February 1951
Ontario, Canada

A steady supporting player, Helen Shaver became an actress by accident – her ex-husband wanted to be an actor, but she was the one who kept being asked to read for parts. She built up a stage and screen career in her native Canada but was somewhat hindered by the local film industry's penchant for outright turkeys (few countries can boast a worse sci-fi film than *Starship Invasions*, 1977) in which her roles were mostly decorative. Moving to LA in 1978, her appearance in *In Praise Of Older Women* (1978, one of many in her career that did not overly trouble the wardrobe department) attracted enough attention to secure her the role of Beau Bridges' spouse in the short-lived TV series *Married*, and a supporting role in the enormously successful *Amityville Horror* (1979).

For a while, the attractive, husky-voiced actress commuted between the States and Canada, gradually working her way up to a better class of flops (for example, as Dennis Hopper's drug-addicted wife in Sam Peckinpah's *The Osterman Weekend*, 1983) until her career was given a surprise boost with the lead in the lesbian drama *Desert Hearts* (1986), in which she took a less glamorous role as an ageing academic who comes to Reno for a divorce only to find herself being drawn to a younger woman (Patricia Charbonneau). Despite following this with the role of Paul Newman's girlfriend in Scorsese's *The Color Of Money* (1986), in which was excellent and moving, she was unable to capitalize effectively on her successes, going on to the much-delayed epic *Bethune* (1987-90), Schlesinger's disappointing supernatural thriller *The Believers* (1987) and the disastrous *Tree Of Hands* (1988). Always a confident, competent actress, Shaver remains a busy and familiar face without ever quite hitting the bullseye.

1976 The Supreme Kid; Shoot **1977** Starship Invasions; Outrageous!; Who Has Seen The Wind? **1978** High Ballin'; In Praise Of Older Women **1989** The Amityville Horror **1980** Off Your Rocker **1981** Gas **1982** Harry Tracey:Desperado; **1983** The Osterman Weekend; Coming Out Alive **1984** Best Defense **1985** The War Boy **1986** The Mens Club (uncredited); Desert Hearts; The Color Of Money **1987** The Believers **1988** Walking After Midnight; Tree Of Hands **1989** No Blame **1990** Bethune, The Making Of A Hero **1992** Zebrahead; That Night **1992/93** Change Of Heart

Sheedy, Ally
(Alexandra Sheedy)

Actress
Born 13 June 1962
New York City

With her strong jaw, dark red-brown hair and confrontational brown eyes, Ally Sheedy is attractive rather than pretty, with a personality that is characteristic of her age and background. The daughter of a literary agent mother, Ally wrote and published a children's book, *She Was Nice To Mice*, when she was 12, and later contributed articles to various publications including the *New York Times*. She was introduced to the cameras at 15 when she began making TV commercials, and appeared in a number of stage productions while still in high school. She went west to attend the University of Southern California, and managed to combine her studies with roles in several television films such as *Splendor In The Grass* before making her feature film debut.

She began her movie career at the age of 21, looking and playing younger than her age in her first three films. In *Bad Boys* (1983), she was the sympathetic girlfriend of Sean Penn, who ends up being raped by the leader of his rival gang. In John Badham's *WarGames* the same year, she was a teenager again, accompanying computer whiz-kid Matthew Broderick on the hair-raising adventures that ensue when he hacks into the Pentagon circuit. Then, like her friend and contemporary Molly Ringwald, she was corralled by John Hughes into *The Breakfast Club* (1985) as one of a bunch of high school kids suffering rebellion and teenage angst during a Saturday detention. Emilio Estevez and Judd Nelson were there too, and all three entered the post-college stratum of the Brat Pack later that year with the much-maligned *St Elmo's Fire* in which Ally, as the nearest thing to the heroine of the piece, more than held her own as Nelson's improperly treated fiancée who leaves him for Andrew McCarthy.

In between these two films, Ally was Gene Hackman and Ellen Burstyn's daughter in *Twice In A Lifetime* (1985), an 'adult' drama about divorce, before returning to John Badham to co-star with a robot in the mediocre *Short Circuit* (1986). In fact, her future didn't look good at all that year, reunited with *St Elmo's Fire* star Rob Lowe for the puerile and inept *Oxford Blues*, an attempt to make a teen romance in the venerable quads of ancient learning; and, worse still, back with Judd Nelson in *Blue City*, a low-grade crime-revenge movie in which Sheedy was as undistinguished as everything else. Her career, in fact, gives the impression of someone going around in circles for, in Alan Alda's *Betsy's Wedding* (1990), there she was again with Molly Ringwald and, again, playing a daughter (to Alda and Madeline Kahn). Nonetheless, she was the agent of a fairly amusing and charming subplot, playing a New York cop who loves her work and is courted by a young Runyonesque crook. Her only lead to date, and perhaps her most challenging role, was in *Maid To Order* (1987) the somewhat whimsical tale of an impossibly spoiled Beverly Hills brat who ends up on the streets, sniffing cocaine and losing her identity, but pulls through by becoming a maid to Wallace Shawn and Valerie Perrine. Sheedy was fine in the role but the movie, although pleasing, was lightweight and soon wafted away, leaving its competent and pleasing young leading lady not much further on than she had been before.

1983 Bad Boys; WarGames **1985** The Breakfast Club; Twice In A Lifetime; St Elmo's Fire **1986** Short Circuit; Oxford Blues; Blue City **1987** Maid To Order **1989** Heart Of Dixie **1990** Fear; Betsy's Wedding **1991** Only the Lonely **1992** The Pickle; Tattle Tale

Sheen, Charlie (Carlos Estevez)

Actor

Born 3 September 1965

New York City

Martin Sheen's third son, Charlie always wanted to follow in his father's footsteps ('I grew up in Hollywood and there was really nothing else I ever thought about doing'). He made his debut at the age of nine, appearing with his father in the acclaimed TV movie *The Execution Of Private Slovik* (1974). After finishing high school he took up his father's stage name and went straight into John Milius' gung-ho teen movie *Red Dawn* (1984). (His older brother, Emilio Estevez, had made *The Outsiders* the year before.)

If he is a touch stockier than Martin Sheen physically, Charlie's features are his spitting image, and the resemblance is often accentuated by facial expressions and gestures that precisely reflect his father's. They share an air of earnest intelligence beneath an easy, almost casual relationship with the camera. A wild, fast-living kid, Charlie (ironically) incurred his father's displeasure personally and professionally when he made Penelope Spheeris' low-budget *The Boys Next Door* (1985). Ten years after *Badlands*, this was a brutally unflinching, unromanticised look at two young men on a killing spree (a double bill would be most instructive). Some critics balked at what struck them as exploitation, others welcomed its honesty and uncompromising stance. Sheen himself gives what is still one of the best performances of his career, as a working-class kid with nothing to look forward to and a fatally undeveloped sense of morality.

It was surely no coincidence that Charlie Sheen then starred in the most important Vietnam movie since *Apocalypse Now*. Like Martin before him, Charlie drily narrates a personal journey through the war, climaxing in the assassination of a fellow American soldier. If Coppola saw this as the stuff of myth, Oliver Stone treated it as a growth experience. Martin ends up a nihilistic godhead, Charlie becomes a *man*. Although *Platoon* (1986) is more schematic than it at first seems, it was widely heralded as the real thing, Vietnam without blinkers on, vital and perhaps definitive. At a stroke, young Sheen was established as a star, and might have felt unlucky not to win an Oscar nomination. A witty cameo as a punk philosopher in John Hughes' *Ferris Bueller's Day Off* (1986) also reflected well on him.

Other projects were less well chosen. *The Wraith* (1986) was sub-standard car schlock, *Three For The Road* (1987) sank without a trace, and even the best of these efforts, *No Man's Land* (1987), miscast Sheen as a flashy, charismatic entrepreneur who really should have been much older. It was Oliver Stone again who provided a role with some impetus to it. As the yuppie stockbroker seduced by the fast buck in *Wall Street* (1987) Sheen is in his element. A callow but gifted youth torn between two fathers (once more, good and evil), the character might have been written for him – especially with Martin Sheen cast as the voice of integrity. Stone is careful to make a virtue of Charlie Sheen's youthful looks, and appreciates that he is essentially a *reactive* actor, not an active one. The film was naked melodrama with an 80s facelift, but it attracted prestige and audiences all the same. Two supporting roles in ensemble movies suggested Sheen was re-evaluating his career (*Eight Men Out*, and *Young Guns*, both 1988), but subsequent roles lacked direction. The wild baseball punk of *Major League* (1989) and the upright suitor in the Heidi adaptation *Courage Mountain* (1989) showed that he is game for anything, but both were equally pointless exercises. And neither *Stockade*, directed by Martin Sheen, nor *Men At Work* directed by Emilio Estevez (both 1990), did him any favours. He fared better as a lantern-jawed, straight-faced, prat-falling aviator in the absurd *Top Gun* parody, *Hot Shots*.

1984 Red Dawn **1985** The Boys Next Door **1986** The Wraith; Wisdom (cameo); Ferris Bueller's Day Off (cameo); Lucas; Platoon **1987** Three For The Road; No Man's Land; Wall Street **1988** Eight Men Out; Young Guns **1989** Major League; Courage Mountain **1990** Navy Seals; Catchfire aka Backtrack; The Rookie; Men At Work; Stockade aka Cadence **1991** Hot Shots **1992/93** Fixing The Shadow; Hot Shots II **1993** Deadfall

Sheen, Martin
(Ramón Estevez)

Actor
Born 3 August 1940
Dayton, Ohio

The seventh of ten children, Martin Sheen was raised Ramón Estevez, the son of a Spanish father and an Irish mother. He was a strict Catholic until his early 20s, but had dropped out of school in his senior year to commit himself to acting. His idol was James Dean. A local priest lent him a couple of hundred dollars to make his way to New York, and he arrived there in February 1959. While earning a living as a stock boy for American Express, Estevez would sneak out for readings and auditions. To avoid typecasting he changed his name to Martin (after an agent friend) Sheen (after Bishop Fulton J. Sheen). He joined the Actor's Co-op (alongside Barbra Streisand), whose members each chipped in a few dollars a month to rent a loft and do showcase productions for agents. Fired by American Express, he worked as a curtain-puller and propman at the Living Theatre, where Al Pacino held a similar position. Later they both began to pick up acting parts with the company. During this period he met his wife, Janet, and their son Emilio was born in 1962. Two more sons and a daughter followed. Meanwhile, his career began to take off. He made his television debut in *East Side, West Side* in 1963 and later became a regular on the soap opera *As The World Turns*. He made his Broadway debut in 1964 (*Never Live Over A Pretzel Factory*) and had his first substantial success later that year in Frank Gilroy's *The Subject Was Roses*.

Sheen and family moved to Hollywood in 1970, but his first feature credits proved false starts, and it was on television that he began to get a name for himself. Terrence Malick's *Badlands* (1973) was exceptional however. The ironic chronicle of a mass murderer on the run with his simple teenage sweetheart (Sissy Spacek), the film establishes a complex interplay between banal 50s teenage rebellion and the mythical iconography of the time. Sheen's intense, denim-clad youth consciously evokes the laid-back alienation of James Dean. He's a killer without a cause, a five-foot-eight-inch giant on the flatlands of the Midwest. It was a great performance, charismatic, amoral, unknowable, in one of the finest films of the 70s ('It's the only thing in my life I'm entirely proud of' says Sheen). Despite rave reviews the movie was not a commercial success, and Sheen failed to consolidate his personal success. He returned to the small screen and made some outstanding TV films: *That Certain Summer* (1972), *The Execution Of Private Slovik* (1974), *The Story Of Pretty Boy Floyd* (1974).

That might have been it for the ageing, boyish-looking actor, but for a chance airport encounter with Francis Ford Coppola in 1976. Coppola was worried that Harvey Keitel was not working out as the lead in his new picture, *Apocalypse Now*. Virtually every major star had been considered for the part, from De Niro and Pacino to Jon Voight and Steve McQueen, but either they were unsuitable, or they balked at the prospect of a long shoot in the Philippines. Coppola convinced Sheen to come aboard, and they spent the best part of two years exploring the heart of darkness together. An infamously traumatic production – beset with hurricanes and creative storms too – climaxed with Sheen's near-fatal heart attack in 1977. The experience led the actor to re-evaluate his life, put his career in perspective, and go back to God. Consequently, when *Apocalypse Now* was finally released in 1979, Sheen did not exploit his acclaim as he might have earlier. His Captain Willard is a pilgrim bearing arms to Hell, bewildered and aghast. It is impossible to measure how much of the film's spellbinding, phantasmagoric effect derives from Sheen rather than Coppola (when a huge close-up of the actor's eye fills the screen who is the author of that image?), but the measured, even tone of his voice-over narration is well-nigh perfect, and his receptive, low-key style never unbalances the film the way a more highly charged Method actor (Keitel or De Niro) might have.

It was a markedly older Martin Sheen who resumed his feature film career in the 1980s. He worked more steadily now, though not in the choicest roles, for the message (*In The King Of Prussia*, 1982), the money (*Firestarter*, 1984), or the fun of it (*Da*, 1988). He donated his fee from *Gandhi* (1982) to charity, and played JFK on television in *Kennedy* (1983). He also watched over an increasingly productive acting dynasty. His brother Joe Estevez played with him in the TV movie *The California Kid* (1974) and recently re-emerged in *Soultaker* (1990) and *Limited Time* (1991). Emilio Estevez and Charlie Sheen both became stars in the 1980s, Ramón Estevez has moved from writing and dancing to acting in *Beverly Hills Brats* (1990) and *War Song* (1990), and daughter Renee Estevez rose gradually up the cast lists in the likes of *Heathers* (1989) and *Marked For Murder* (1990). It has been said of his offspring that they none of them look alike, but they all look like Martin. In 1990 he followed in Emilio's footsteps, and turned to directing and writing with the modest liberal drama *Stockade*.

1967 The Incident **1968** The Subject Was Roses **1970** Catch-22; When The Line Goes Through (unreleased) **1971** The Forests Are Nearly All Gone (unreleased); No Drums, No Bugles **1972** Rage; Pickup On 101 aka Echoes Of The Road **1973** Badlands **1975** The Legend Of Earl Durand **1977** The Cassandra Crossing; The Little Girl Who Lives Down The Lane **1979** Eagle's Wing; Apocalypse Now **1980** The Final Countdown; Loophole **1982** Gandhi; That Championship Season; Enigma; In The King Of Prussia **1983** Man, Woman And Child; The Dead Zone **1984** Firestarter **1987** The Believers; Siesta; Wall Street **1988** Judgement In Berlin; Da **1989** Beverly Hills Brats; Personal Choice; Cold Front (Canada) **1991** Stockade aka Cadence (also director, writer); The Maid (France)

Shelton, Ron

Writer, director
Born 15 September 1945
Whittier, California

By 1991, ten years after he began making features (starting as an associate producer), it was still early days for Ron Shelton, but on the basis of his two films as writer and two as writer-director, he looked set to provide a vital, spicy ingredient to the Hollywood melting pot. His work comes out of left field. It's sophisticated but not artificial, raunchy but not sexist, political but not rhetorical. Thriller writer Elmore Leonard's three dictates for good writing are Get It Right, Make It Natural and Let It Happen. Shelton would surely concur. His screenplays are grounded in his own experience or in historical research; the dialogue comes fresh as a milkshake and his stories reflect an unusually mature perspective on the world.

Shelton won a sports scholarship (in baseball and basketball) to Westmount College. After graduation, he played second base for the Baltimore Orioles farm team for five years, then played in the international league in Rochester, New York. Doubting that he would make the majors, he quit and studied sculpture at the University of Arizona – earning an MFA in 1974. He moved to LA and supported his family in a variety of odd jobs. And he began to write; screenplays and some published fiction. His script *A Player To Be Named Later* impressed producer Jonathan Taplan and director Roger Spottiswoode, and they signed him to write (with Clayton Frohman) *Under Fire*, about American journalists covering the revolution in Nicaragua in 1979. The film eventually came to fruition in 1983, with Nick Nolte, Joanna Cassidy and Gene Hackman starring. *Under Fire* bravely took issue with American foreign policy in central America, dramatising the birth of a new political consciousness in its initially cynical heroes as they come to understand the revolutionary impetus of the Sandinistas. A polished and thought-provoking thriller, it was excellently played, with Joanna Cassidy making the most of Shelton's first gutsy, independent female character (there would be several more). Shelton also served his directing apprenticeship on this picture, on the second unit.

The Best Of Times (1986), again directed by Spottiswoode, was the first of Shelton's original screenplays to make it to the screen. Robin Williams starred as a hapless individual who, 20 years on, still has not lived down a crucial error in the town's annual football grudge match. Although the balance between farce and more sober reflections is a little uneasy here, and the plot is all too predictable, there are any number of compensations in the writer's dry treatment of sexual politics, with Williams' wife (Pamela Reed) refusing to take second place to a ball game, and our hero guiltily sneaking glances at the big match on the TV set in the middle of their reconciliation dinner. Again, Shelton was second unit director.

Another sports movie, *Bull Durham* (1988), marked his debut as director. In fact, this was the old *Player To Be Named Later* script re-drafted. Loosely based on Shelton's own experiences in the minor leagues, it was the story of a veteran ball player, Crash Davies (Kevin Costner) brought in to the Durham Bulls to knock some sense into their young hotshot pitcher, 'Nuke' Laloosh (Tim Robbins), and their affairs with passionate Annie Savoy (Susan Sarandon), a connoisseur of baseball, sex and poetry. *Bull Durham* is a fine sports movie; the chronicle of the Bulls' season rings true, it's good on the vicissitudes of the life, experience, psychology and superstition of the sport, and the game sequences are beautifully choreographed, often to hilarious effect. Even so, it is more important as a sex comedy. This is where Shelton is really out in front. The battle of the sexes has not inspired better dialogue since the Tracy and Hepburn days, the Kanins' script for *Adam's Rib* (1949), or the Howard Hawks comedies, from *Bringing Up Baby* (1938) right through to *Hatari!* (1962). Hawksian themes of professionalism, quiet integrity and the glorious anarchy of sex are clearly central to *Bull Durham*. Crash Davies might have been played by Cooper or even Wayne, Annie by Bacall or Stanwyck. What distinguishes Shelton's picture is its explicit but genuinely liberating vision of sex based on mutual gratification. There is nothing voyeuristic about it. It is shocking to consider how rare that is in contemporary cinema.

Blaze (1989) – about Louisiana's Governor Earl Long and stripper Blaze Starr – confirmed Shelton's generous, even promiscuous, vision. A tall story that happened to be true (Long, released from an institution, campaigns for re-election under the slogan 'I ain't crazy'), and a pointed equation of politics and showbiz, the film was also a simple love story, touchingly played by Paul Newman and Lolita Davidovich. Sexy, funny and immensely colourful, *Blaze* is good company, but somehow it does not come off. Perhaps it is too raucously entertaining, too busy scoring points, to just Let It Happen.

As writer-director unless stated otherwise: **1983** Under Fire (co-writer only) **1986** The Best Of Times (writer only) **1988** Bull Durham **1989** Blaze **1992** White Men Can't Jump

Shepard, Sam
(Samuel Shepard Rogers)

Writer, actor, director
Born 5 November 1943
Fort Sheridan, Illinois

Sam Shepard is a real hero for the hip. In virtually separate careers this handsome, rangy man is a prolific, Pulitzer Prize-winning playwright whose provocative dramas include *True West, Fool For Love, A Lie Of The Mind* and *Buried Child*; a screenwriter whose credits embrace *Zabriskie Point* (1970) for Michelangelo Antonioni and *Paris, Texas* (1984) for Wim Wenders; the writer and director of his own film, the tedious *Far North* (1988); an attractive leading man on screen for leading ladies including Ellen Burstyn, Kim Basinger, Diane Keaton and even Dolly Parton, and the consort of Jessica Lange off-screen as well as on.

A military brat become farm boy, Shepard took off for New York City in his late teens. His first two plays were staged there when he was 20, and he has written more than 40 since, winning multiple awards including ten Obies. By the time he made his screen acting debut in the 1970s he had spent several years living and working in London, acted and directed for the stage, played drums in his band The Holy Modal Rounders (who toured with Bob Dylan's Rolling Thunder

Revue in 1975) and collaborated with punk poetess Patti Smith.

After an appearance in Bob Dylan's shambling *Renaldo And Clara* (1978), Shepard made his film debut proper as the lonely, consumptive young rancher ill-used by drifters Richard Gere and Brooke Adams in Terrence Malick's exquisite *Days Of Heaven* (1978). Never very expressive, Shepard's lean, impassive cowboy look and languid presence have best suited him to roles as drifters, grifters and small-town drinkers, although he was particularly sympathetic as the union organiser who becomes friend, lover and confidante to Jessica Lange's tormented Frances Farmer in *Frances* (1982); and he was a most compelling laid-back superhero as legendary test pilot Chuck Yeager in Philip Kaufman's thrilling aviation homage sequences of *The Right Stuff* (1983), a performance that received an Academy Award nomination. Always scrumptious as 'the sub-plot lover', Shepard was surprisingly light-hearted support to Diane Keaton in the amusing *Baby Boom* (1987) as her smitten, kindly veterinarian, and achieved a new power as Volker Schlöndorff's enigmatic *Voyager* (1991). Previously married to O-Lan Johnson Darke, by whom he has a son, Jesse, Shepard has had children with Lange in the course of a long relationship.

As actor only unless stated otherwise: **1967** Me And My Brother (co-writer only) **1970** Zabriskie Point (co-writer only) **1971** Ringa Leevio (co-writer only) **1972** Oh! Calcutta! (contributor only) **1978** Renaldo And Clara (also co-writer); Days Of Heaven **1980** Resurrection **1981** Raggedy Man **1982** Frances **1983** Joe Chaikin Going On; The Right Stuff **1984** Country; Paris, Texas (writer only) **1985** Fool For Love (also writer) **1986** Crimes Of The Heart **1987** Baby Boom **1988** Far North (w/d only) **1989** Steel Magnolias **1990** Bright Angel **1991** The Ballad Of The Sad Café; Voyager (Germany/France); Defenseless **1992** Thunderheart **1992/93** Silent Tongue (w/d)

Shepherd, Cybill

Actress
Born 18 February 1950
Memphis, Tennessee

The big and beautiful blonde Cybill Shepherd, in effectively two film careers, has never really cracked it, but gets top marks for tenacity and effort.

As Miss Teenage Memphis, Shepherd found herself in demand as a teen model in New York, where she was sporadically attending a selection of colleges before her discovery by director Peter Bogdanovich (with whom she had a live-in relationship for several years) put her in the limelight as pretty, petulant Jacy Farrow, resident unattainable dream girl in *The Last Picture Show* (1971). To the advantage of neither, Bogdanovich starred his protegée in two expensive flops for which she was ill-equipped, *Daisy Miller* (1974) and a musical with Burt Reynolds, *At Long Last Love* (1975). She was more useful playing the elusive WASP princess she essentially was in Elaine May's *The Heartbreak Kid* (1972) and Martin Scorsese's *Taxi Driver* (1976). The latter still stands as the best film she has had the fortune to participate in – as the object of Robert De Niro's cringe-making advances – but she did reveal a natural flair for comedy as a screwy artist in the entertaining heist caper *Special Delivery* (1976). Her career seemed to have all but evaporated when she was reduced to a supporting role in a tired sci-fi yarn, *The Alien's Return* (1980), but she went home to Tennessee, regrouped, tackled stage work in regional theatre to gain some credible experience and returned to Hollywood a few years and a broken marriage later. There she was informed she couldn't get arrested, but she hung on and landed a shortlived TV series (*The Yellow Rose*) before *Moonlighting* provided her with a sensational comeback vehicle. Cast as model-turned-sleuth Maddie Hayes opposite wild and crazy Bruce Willis' David Addison, Shepherd became a prime-time darling and won a Golden Globe Award. To the sorrow of its devoted following, the show's clever take-offs on *noir* and screwball films began to falter badly after a couple of choice seasons, and it ended a four-year run in 1989, by which time Shepherd's success in that and a well-received TV version of *The Long Hot Summer* gave her another shot at the big screen.

Unlike her *Moonlighting* thorn-in-the-flesh Willis, however, Shepherd has yet to score a feature hit despite the work she has put into her acting since her debut 20 years ago. She was very appealing in the under-rated comic fantasy *Chances Are* (1989), and a welcome presence reteamed with Jeff Bridges and Timothy Bottoms in Bogdanovich's latter-day sequel to *The Last Picture Show, Texasville* (1990). A pleasant if tentative singer, Shepherd has also recorded two albums.

1971 The Last Picture Show **1972** The Heartbreak Kid

1974 Daisy Miller **1975** At Long Last Love **1976** Taxi Driver; Special Delivery **1977** Silver Bears **1979** The Lady Vanishes **1980** The Alien's Return aka The Return **1989** Chances Are **1990** Texasville; Alice **1991** Married To It **1992** Once Upon A Crime

Shields, Brooke

Actress
Born 31 May 1965
New York City

The phenomenal success of Brooke Shields as the world's most famous starlet belongs in the nature of things more to fashion and social history than it does to the history of acting. For years, her young life was ruled by her extraordinary ex-actress mother, Teri, who dedicated herself from the word go to constructing her daughter in an image of unattainable desire. At one year old, Brooke was declared 'the most beautiful baby in America' after her appearance in Ivory soap commercials. In due course, the child graduated to commending Breck shampoos and also Colgate toothpaste (the latter in some celebrated ads photographed by Richard Avedon). Marketed by her mother under the logo 'Brooke Shields & Co', her break into bigtime cinema came when she was taken up, aged 12, by French director Louis Malle to act as a child prostitute in a film about New Orleans brothels at the turn of the century, *Pretty Baby* (1978).

The movie set the pattern for Brooke's subsequent roles, in most of which her body has been pruriently offered to the public gaze while denied, off-screen, to be sexual. In her private life, such as it is (or was) she was almost fanatically encouraged to go in for the image of the healthy, sports-loving all-American maiden who would only lose her virginity on marriage. Heaven knows how these manoeuvres must have tempted the fates, but she seems, to date, to have avoided the grosser types of tragedy that lie in wait for incipient hypocrisy – at what cost can only be known to her and her mother. (An unpleasant lawsuit in 1983 revolved round some nude photographs taken of her at the age of ten.) She is undoubtedly pretty in a lean, leggy, modelish sort of way, like a young Elizabeth Taylor with dark eyebrows. Her body had wide exposure in *The Blue Lagoon* (1980) and the following year in Zeffirelli's *Endless Love*. On the set of *Sahara* (1983) she is reputed to have quarrelled publicly with her mother. The mid-80s saw her enrolment in Princeton University whence she graduated, in 1987, with a BA thesis entitled 'From Innocence to Experience in the work of Louis Malle'. (It is not her only literary work: in 1985 a ghosted autobiography came out poignantly entitled *On Your Own*.) Closely supervised by bodyguards (there is a reputed blacklist of 300 strangers with designs on her) she resides in a Californian mansion with a high fence and guard dogs, where she practises gymnastics for two hours a day. Her name has been linked romantically at different times with pop and film stars George Michael, Michael Jackson and John Travolta. Despite lack of critical success in her more recent movies, she has continued to harbour serious ambitions – among which, to be taken up by an important director like Coppola, or Polanski.

1977 Alice Sweet Alice aka Communion aka Holy Terror **1978** Pretty Baby; Just You And Me, Kid; King Of The Gypsies **1979** Wanda Nevada **1980** The Blue Lagoon **1981** Endless Love **1983** Sahara **1989** Brenda Starr **1990** Backstreet Strays **1992** Brenda Starr (made in 1989)

Shire, Talia
(Talia Rose Coppola)

Actress
Born 25 April 1946
Jamaica, New York

The only daughter of composer-arranger Carmine Coppola and the sister of Francis, Talia Shire was raised on the road since her father's career demanded that he tour with Broadway musicals. Educated at the Yale School of Drama, she moved to Hollywood and participated in small film and television productions until her break came through the good offices of her brother, who cast her as Connie, Michael Corleone's sister, in *The Godfather* (1972). Charges of nepotism were inevitable but, whether those were justified or not, Talia won an Oscar nomination when Connie resurfaced in *The Godfather Part II* (1974); and she was nominated again for her first appearance as the ever-faithful Adrian in *Rocky* (1976), a performance which also netted her the New York Film Critics Award for best actress.

Shire subsequently made a career out of playing the archetypal Italian-American woman on stage, television and the screen for almost two decades, but her claim to fame largely rests in *The Godfather* and *Rocky* series, each of which have earned upwards of $800 million and account for the only notable strand in her filmography (unless one counts her appearance as the girl's mother in her brother's ill-fated contribution to *New York Stories* in 1989). She took a break from her career to raise a family with second husband Jack Schwarzman (her first marriage in 1970 to composer David Shire ended in divorce). In the 80s, she and Schwarzman co-produced Sean Connery's Bond-revival film, *Never Say Never Again* (1983), and *Lionheart* (1986); by 1990, however, Talia Shire was back in harness with *Rocky V* and *The Godfather Part III*, the latter demonstrating that she had matured into an actress of some stature.

1968 The Wild Racers **1970** The Dunwich Horror; Gas-s-s-s **1971** The Christian Licorice Store **1972** The Godfather **1974** The Godfather Part II **1976** Rocky **1979** Old Boyfriends; Rocky II; Corky; Prophecy **1980** Windows **1982** Rocky III **1985** Rocky IV **1986** Rad **1989** New York Stories **1990** Godfather III; Rocky V **1992** Bed And Breakfast; Cold Heaven **1993** Deadfall

Short, Martin

Actor
Born 26 March 1950
Hamilton, Ontario, Canada

Like fellow comic actor and Canadian Dan Aykroyd, Martin Short was catapulted into a movie career thanks to the high visibility accorded him on the anarchic TV show *Saturday Night Live* – and his obvious talent. However, unlike the big, bulky Aykroyd, Short is, true to his name, a diminutive man of slight build who has rapidly established himself as a character actor specialising in (but not limited to) nerds and weedy types.

The son of a steel company executive father and a violinist mother, he attended Toronto's McMaster University, where he met Eugene Levy and Dave Thomas, his future Second City TV acting partners, who helped him develop his comic skills. Five years of stage, cabaret and revue work in Toronto, including a stint in the musical *Godspell*, followed before Short eventually joined SCTV's comedy troupe, where he created the popular character of lounge lizard Ed Grimley (which later became the cartoon series *The Completely Mental Misadventures of Ed Grimley*). The actor appeared in various TV movies and the series *The Associates* before heading over the border and rapidly gaining cult status with his impersonations of the likes of Katharine Hepburn and Jerry Lewis on *Saturday Night Live*.

It was with people formerly associated with that show that Short went on to make his film debut. Directed by Belushi-Aykroyd collaborator John Landis, *Three Amigos!* (1986) was a spoof musical Western featuring a trio of silent movie stars summoned to a besieged Mexican town through a series of comic misunderstandings. Steve Martin and Chevy Chase (both of whom had appeared regularly on *Saturday Night Live*) played two of the eponymous amigos; Short was the third. As Ned Nederlander, the most delicate and serious of the three, Short, with his odd features and goofy smile, held his own admirably against the more seasoned and frantic Martin and the laid-back Chase. In the following year's *Innerspace*, however, he was given much greater scope to reveal the full range of his comic style and myriad expressions in the part of a wimpy, neurotic hypochondriac who is accidentally injected with a shrunken-down Dennis Quaid. Managing to be simultaneously charming and ridiculous, the actor succeeded in outshining the charisma of both Quaid and Meg Ryan, no mean feat.

Partly due to his small size and his frequent use of effeminate gestures, Short often has the on-screen air of a hapless victim, a quality put to effective use in *Three Fugitives* (1989), a remake of the French hit *Les Fugitifs*. In it he plays a bungling bank robber who, because of his latest botch-up, is forced to take hostage ex-con Nick Nolte. An adequate if manipulative buddy movie, *Three Fugitives* cleverly traded on the contrasting little-large, sweet-gruff characters of Short and Nolte and proved that the comic actor was more than capable of sharing top billing. Equally, his uncredited and all-too-brief performance in *The Big Picture* (1989), where he sported a frightful bubbly auburn wig as Kevin Bacon's camp, cross-eyed, spaced-out Hollywood agent, was the best and by far the most hilarious thing in the movie, and confirmed the actor's versatility. Despite the setback of the inane *Pure Luck* (1991), which shamefully wasted the talents of both Short and his co-star, Danny Glover, the actor was back in scene-stealing form for the otherwise rather pointless remake of *Father Of The Bride* the same year.

1986 Three Amigos! **1987** Innerspace; Cross My Heart **1989** Three Fugitives; The Big Picture **1991** Undercover; Pure Luck; Clifford; Father Of The Bride **1992** Captain Ron

Shue, Elisabeth

Actress
Born 1964
South Orange, New Jersey

Elizabeth Shue began acting in commercials at the age of 17 while still in high school, and then went on to study English and Political Science at Wellesley College. It was during this time that she was put under contract to ABC television as part of their talent search programme, which brought her first role in 1983 in the pilot for a TV series, *Airforce*. This, in turn, led to a part in the series *Call To Glory*, which earned her recognition and the part of the girlfriend to youthful hero Ralph Macchio in the successful *The Karate Kid* (1984). Although two sequels to the movie were made, Shue was not invited to appear in them, so she returned to her education, this time studying Political Science at Harvard.

After a two-year absence, she returned to the big screen in the ill-fated British horror film *Link* (1986) with Terence Stamp. A little-seen TV movie, *Double Switch* (1987) followed, and then the actress got her first big break with the lead in *Adventures In Babysitting* (1987) playing a teenager left to baby-sit a group of kids, who ends up combing the city (with the brats in tow) trying to help her best friend out of a jam. Although it was a low-budget piece of fluff, Shue carried it off and was certainly one of the reasons for the film's modest success. More importantly, it brought her to the attention of director Roger Donaldson, who cast her as Tom Cruise's girlfriend in *Cocktail* (1988). In her numerous roles as 'the girlfriend', this was the only one where her character had the chance to stand up for herself and reject the hero (although she takes him back before the final credits), and also earned the distinction of being the only person to empty a bottle of ketchup and a plate of spaghetti in Tom Cruise's lap.

Although the film was a major box-office success, the spotlight was positioned firmly on her co-star, Cruise, and the actress' subsequent roles did little to increase her status. She played Jennifer, Michael J. Fox's girlfriend, in *Back To The Future Part II* (1989), donning a dark wig to match the hair of the brunette who played the role in the original. Unfortunately, it was a minor part, with Shue drugged and unceremoniously dumped on a doorstep within the first 15 minutes, leaving the 'boys' (Michael J. Fox and Christopher Lloyd) to have the real adventures. Despite this meagre part, she returned at the end of *Back To The Future Part III* (1990) – still asleep on the doorstep – to be rescued by her hero, Marty McFly. It was to be hoped that this attractive and intelligent actress would be rescued from more roles like that of Jennifer during the 1990s.

1984 The Karate Kid **1986** Link **1987** Adventures In Babysitting **1988** Cocktail **1989** Back To The Future Part II **1990** Back To The Future Part III; Soapdish **1991** The Marrying Man

Siemaszko, Casey (Kazimierz Siemaszko)

Actor
Born 17 March 1961
Chicago, Illinois

A likeable young supporting actor who seems permanently on the verge of big things, Casey Siemaszko is the son of a Polish concentration camp survivor and an English dancer. His father headed The Kosciuszko Dancers, a folk-dance group with whom Casey made his performing debut at the age of five. Polish is a second language to him, and he was active in the Ref-Ren Polish community theatre from his early days. He can ride a unicycle and juggle knives.

A graduate of the Goodman School of Drama in Chicago with a degree in fine arts, Siemaszko (pronounced Sheh–MA–shko) abandoned steady work in Chicago theatre for Los Angeles. He had an agent, plenty of auditions, but no feature film roles for four years. He finally made his debut in *Class* (1983). Robert Zemeckis cast him as '3-D' in *Back To The Future* (1985), which brought him to the attention of producer Steven Spielberg. Attracted by his open face and goofy humour, Spielberg starred him in his *Amazing Stories* episode 'The Mission', which in turn led to the leading role in the high school comedy *Three O'Clock High* (1987), directed by Spielberg protégé Phil Joannou, with Siemaszko as weedy Jerry Mitchell, facing a showdown with the class heavy. Meanwhile, the young actor continued to take supporting roles. He was in Kiefer Sutherland's gang in *Stand By Me* (1986), in Billy the Kid's in *Young Guns* (1988) – as Charley Bowdre – and he had some funny scenes as recruit Donald Carney in Mike Nichols' *Biloxi Blues* (1988), a prominent supporting role. Although he is a natural clown and most of his work has had a comic orientation, Siemaszko played another recruit in Francis Ford Coppola's sombre Vietnam elegy, *Gardens Of Stone* (1987), when he replaced Griffin O'Neal as Private Wildman after the latter's involvement in the tragic accident that killed Gio Coppola, the director's son. Of his famous directors, Siemaszko says: 'Spielberg is highly technical, and you learn from that – what a particular lens means, so when you see that lens you tone down your scale. Nichols sets the camera up and turns the actors loose. Coppola paints pictures: "This is how you guys move, then the music comes in here." Forsyth is more into the subtle absurdities of a situation.'

Bill Forsyth's *Breaking In* (1989) is Siemaszko's best showcase to date. A sublime, low-key comedy about two forlorn, lonely burglars, Mike and Ernie (Burt Reynolds), who meet in somebody's living-room one night. They team up, Ernie teaches Mike the trade, and then the law intervenes. Playing against Reynolds' best performance in years, Siemaszko does a marvellous turn as a hapless romantic schmuck ill-equipped to deal with the conflicts of modern urban life. The two of them are funny and ultimately very sad in this badly under-rated comedy, scripted by John Sayles.

1983 Class **1984** Back To The Future **1985** Secret Admirer **1986** Stand By Me **1987** Three O'Clock High; Gardens Of Stone **1988** Biloxi Blues; Young Guns **1989** Breaking In **1991** The Big Slice (Canada) **1992** Of Mice And Men; The Paint Job

Silver, Micklin Joan

Director, writer
Born 1935
Omaha, Nebraska

Joan Micklin Silver has been a role model and inspiration not only to women directors but to independent film-makers in general. With a determination shared by her husband Raphael (Ray) Silver she became a well-regarded artist as well as a commercial success, demanding the respect of the film industry.

A graduate of Sarah Lawrence College, Joan Micklin, the daughter of Russian Jews, married Silver and moved to Cleveland, Ohio, where she indulged her passion for cinemagoing in her spare time while bringing up the couple's three daughters and writing plays for a local theatre group. In 1972 she sold a screenplay to Universal Pictures, which became *Limbo* (1972), co-written by James Bridges, directed by Mark Robson, and one of the first films about the effects of the Vietnam War as felt back at home. Unable to obtain a directing assignment by any of the usual, male-dominated routes, Micklin Silver and her husband formed their own company, Midwest Film Productions. He raised the finance – $40,000 – and she wrote and directed *Hester Street* (1975), a poignant and joyful evocation of Jewish immigrant life in New York at the beginning of the century, filmed in black and white, and with a wonderful performance from Carol Kane as a timid wife, scorned by her Americanised husband, who finally comes into her own. When no distributor would touch it Ray Silver went to exhibitors himself and got the film into cinemas. It took $5 million and won Carol Kane an Oscar nomination for Best Actress.

After writing and directing a screen adaptation of the F. Scott Fitzgerald story *Bernice Bobs Her Hair* for television, Micklin Silver turned up another delightful sleeper in *Between The Lines* (1977), an ensemble picture about the staff of an underground newspaper whose cast of newcomers included John Heard, Bruno Kirby, Jeff Goldblum, Lindsay Crouse and Jill Eikenberry. Her low-key adaptation of an Ann Beattie novel, *Chilly Scenes Of Winter* (1979), subsequently re-titled *Head Over Heels*, was charming but less successful, and an unpleasant introduction to studio film-making for the director, who fought with United Artists and finally saw her own final cut of the film released in 1982.

There was a long gap before her next feature – *Crossing Delancey* (1988) – during which she worked in theatre and television. *Delancey*, her most popular film, with all her characteristic warmth and affection for the characters, was a fresh and charming romantic comedy rooted in a New York Jewish ethos in which Amy Irving's dreamy intellectual snob resists the wooing of Peter Riegert's Lower East Side pickle-maker and the marital schemes of her aged grandmother and an outrageous matchmaker (Sylvia Miles). Its success brought Micklin Silver her first directing offer from a major for a project she had not herself developed, and she turned the potentially tacky knucklehead comedy *Loverboy* (1989), starring Patrick Dempsey, into a not unpleasant if slight and forgettable amusement. Unfortunately, her next – *Stepkids* – looked to be even more of a retrograde move, and alarmed admirers hoped that Micklin Silver would reclaim her talent with another self-generated, self-penned project.

As director only unless stated otherwise: **1972** Limbo (co-writer only) **1975** Hester Street (w/d) **1977** Between The Lines **1979** Head Over Heels aka Chilly Scenes Of Winter (w/d) **1988** Crossing Delancey **1989** Loverboy **1992** Stepkids

Silver, Ron
(Ron Zimelman)
Actor
Born 2 July 1946
New York City

An aggressive, highly charged and electrifying stage actor (he began at Joseph Papp's Public Theatre in New York and, in 1989, won the Tony and Drama Desk Awards for his performance in David Mamet's *Speed-The-Plow* on Broadway), Ron Silver has the persona of the archetypal (Jewish) New Yorker: clever, pushy, neurotic and unexpectedly vulnerable. He has enjoyed, too, an extremely successful television career but, although he began appearing in feature movies back in 1971, he was largely confined to supporting roles, often very small and – being short and unglamorous – would never have been tipped for movie stardom. By 1990, however, he had broken the rules, landing four major screen roles in a row – three of them in major productions – and delivering the goods with virtuosity and power.

Silver is a man of surprises. After studying languages at New York University in Buffalo, he went to Taiwan where he obtained a master's degree in Chinese history at the College of Chinese Culture. Far from using these qualifications to make a career in academe or the diplomatic service, he returned to New York and enrolled for acting classes with Herbert Berghof. His first big opportunity in the theatre came when he was cast in the hit satirical show *El Grande De Coca-Cola* in 1976, after which he moved to California and found his first TV job in the series *Rhoda*. From then on, Silver was never unemployed, dividing his time between TV, theatre and, increasingly, film, where his first major role co-starred him with Anne Bancroft in *Garbo Talks* (1984). As the son who tries to humour his dying, Garbo-obsessed mother, he gave a funny, poignant and convincing performance; unfortunately, the movie itself was one of Sidney Lumet's less distinguished efforts and audiences stayed away in droves. It was the British director Philip Saville who gave Silver the break that brought him attention from film critics on both sides of the Atlantic. *Fellow Traveller* (1989) starred the actor as a Hollywood screenwriter forced to leave family, friends and career and flee to London to escape the clutches of the McCarthy hearings. As a political retrospective and moral examination it was an ambitious muddle, but one that has many admirers, and it certainly brought Silver the big screen status he had thus far failed to attract.

Stardom began to creep up with his next outing, Paul Mazursky's heartfelt version of the Isaac Bashevis Singer novel *Enemies, A Love Story*, later the same year. He played Herman Broder, an immigrant Jew who has survived the Holocaust and is living in New York, ghost-writing speeches for an upmarket rabbi. Married to the Polish girl (Margaret Sophie Stein) who adores him and saved him from the Nazis, he also runs a mistress (Lena Olin), and has his dual existence further complicated by the arrival of his first wife (Anjelica Huston), previously believed to have perished. The actor delivered a tour de force as a small-time Lothario whose looks belie his magnetic charm. Passionate yet scheming, cruel but caring, sexy, rueful and finally powerless, he was more than a match for the three women. His range and versatility was revealed in his next two movies: the famed legal expert Alan Dershowitz, intense, energetic and arrogant, defending Jeremy Irons' Claus von Bülow in *Reversal Of Fortune*; and, in a complete change of type and pace, the cold, smooth, bearded psychopath ensnaring Jamie Lee Curtis in Kathryn Bigelow's *Blue Steel* (both 1990). Then it was on to another lead, for Arthur Hiller in *Married To It* (1991), his status as a leading man firmly established 20 years after he first appeared in a Hollywood film.

1971 Semi-Tough **1976** Tunnel Vision **1981** The Entity **1982** Silent Rage; Best Friends **1983** Lovesick; Silkwood **1984** Garbo Talks; Welcome To LA; The Goodbye People; Oh God! You Devil; Romancing The Stone **1987** Eat And Run **1989** Fellow Traveller **1989** Enemies, A Love Story **1990** Reversal Of Fortune; Blue Steel **1991** Married To It

Singer, Lori

Actress

Born 4 November 1962

Corpus Christi, Texas

Blonde-haired, blue-eyed Lori Singer, who looks like a sort of cross between a youthful Farrah Fawcett and Daryl Hannah, is invariably called pretty in movie reviews. And so she is, but how far her acting talent would take her was not yet clear by the early 1990s.

The daughter of an orchestra conductor, Lori played the cello as a teenager, before going to study at the Juilliard School. No doubt it was her musical background which led to her role as the cello-playing Julie Miller in the TV series *Fame*. She made a passable feature film debut in *Footloose* (1984) as the confused daughter of a rigid Baptist preacher out in the sticks, who upsets her father by taking up with city boy Kevin Bacon; in *The Man With One Red Shoe* (1985), she did her best as the girl laid on by the CIA to vamp Tom Hanks, but, like the rest of the cast, was sabotaged by the silly script; and in *The Falcon And The Snowman* the same year, her serious role as Timothy Hutton's girlfriend was too tiny to make an impression. It was as Georgia, the rural innocent mistreated by Keith Carradine and rescued by Kris Kristofferson in Alan Rudolph's dark tale of violence, love and redemption in the underbelly of Rain City (otherwise Seattle), *Trouble In Mind* (1985), that Lori Singer displayed real quality which promised better things. That promise was not fulfilled in the supposedly steamy *Summer Heat* (1987), in which she was blank and vapid, but she did bring the right light touch to Kassandra, the waitress cursed by the *Warlock* (1989).

1984 Footloose **1985** The Man With One Red Shoe; The Falcon And The Snowman; Trouble In Mind **1987** Summer Heat; Made In USA **1989** Warlock; Salute Of The Jugger **1992** Sunset Grill; Equinox **1993** Short Cuts

Skye, Ione

(Ione Skye Leitch)

Actress

Born 1971

London, England

The daughter of folk singer Donovan, Ione Skye grew up in California without ever meeting her father. Aged just 15, she came to the attention of director Tim Hunter when he spotted some photos of her in a fashion spread in the *LA Weekly*. He then cast her in her debut role as a troubled teenager in his chilling story about adolescent alienation, *River's Edge* (1986). Shortly afterwards, the budding young actress dropped her father's name (Leitch) and proceeded to drop out of high school.

With her long, tousled brown hair and sulky, bee-stung lips, Skye seemed perfectly suited to play River Phoenix's rich lover in *Jimmy Reardon* (1988) and the privileged, sexually mature object of Dexter Fletcher's infatuation in *The Rachel Papers* (1989), adapted from Martin Amis' best selling novel. Her role opposite John Cusack in *Say Anything* (1989) was more of a challenge, and one of which Skye proved worthy; she is convincing as the brainy, uptight college-bound girl whose romance with unambitious Cusack threatens both her father's relationship with her and the path of her future.

Skye appeared to be making a smooth and successful transition from post-Brat Pack movies to more prestigious roles with *Gas, Food Lodging* (1992), in which she essayed a sullen brat of another kind: an abrasive drop out who grows up through tragedy and self-confrontation.

1986 River's Edge **1988** A Night in the Life of Jimmy Reardon aka Jimmy Reardon **1988** Stranded **1989** The Rachel Papers; Say Anything **1990** Mindwalk **1991** Samantha **1992** Gas, Food Lodging; Gun Crazy; Wayne's World

Slater, Christian

(Christian Hawkins)

Actor

Born 18 August 1969

New York City

The son of a stage actor (Michael Hawkins) and a casting director (Mary Jo Slater), Christian Slater was bent on becoming an actor from childhood. He was only seven when his mother cast him in a TV soap called *One Life To Live*, and nine when he appeared on the Broadway stage with Dick Van Dyke in *The Music Man*, staying on the Great White Way for productions of *Macbeth* and *David Copperfield*. Educated at the Dalton School and the Professional Children's School in Manhattan, by the time he turned 21 the young actor had chalked up a body of credits in the theatre, on television and, indeed, in movies which would be the envy of many men his senior.

Slater's big-screen debut passed without comment, but he made a major impression in his second movie, in tandem with no less than Sean Connery whose apprentice monk he played in *The Name Of The Rose* (1986). As the youthful witness to the perversion and corruption within a medieval monastery, who crosses the boundaries of his future calling to lose his virginity to an outcast, he exuded sincerity, innocence, fresh looks and undoubted competence. As Jeff Bridges' eldest son in Coppola's *Tucker: The Man And His Dream* (1988), and then the anti-social skateboarding fanatic who undergoes a transformation of character protecting his adopted Vietnamese brother in *Gleaming The Cube* (1989), he was progressing very nicely in the ranks of late-teen actors. But none of his earlier work really hinted at what was to come with Michael Lehmann's anarchic black satire *Heathers* (1989). Paired with another fast-rising young star, Winona Ryder, Slater played J.D., a charming, clever, bike-riding sociopath who masterminds the murders of a clutch of the couple's high school mates, staging them to look like suicide. The style of his characterisation was reminiscent of Jack Nicholson, his self-confessed idol, and the cool, laid-back conviction and sick cynicism of an audaciously exaggerative performance demonstrated that Christian had grown up (albeit with an alcohol problem he now claims to have overcome), and was ready to move into the 90s capable of major roles.

By then resident in Los Angeles, the budding star didn't have long to wait. Now matured into a handsome, noticeably well-built young man, he was given the substantial lead in *Pump Up The Volume* (1990). As the shy, frustrated high school loner who finds release in broadcasting a pirate radio programme in the guise of the anarchic 'Hard Harry', becoming a cult hero and unleashing chaos as a result, Slater was called upon to give a virtual one-man show for the best part of two hours. It was a demanding challenge which he met with impressive strength and energy before plunging into a mixed bag of successive movies, including Kevin Costner's *Robin Hood: Prince of Thieves* (1991), in which he was cast as Will Scarlett.

1985 The Legend Of Billie Jean **1986** The Name Of The Rose **1988** Tucker: The Man And His Dream **1989** Gleaming The Cube; Heathers; Personal Choice **1990** Tales From The Darkside; Pump Up The Volume; The Wizard; On The Prowl; Young Guns II **1991** Robin Hood: Prince Of Thieves; Beginner's Luck; Mobsters: The Evil Empire; Crooked Hearts; Star Trek VI: The Undiscovered Country; Kuffs **1992** Where The Day Takes You; The Baboon Heart

Smith, Dame Maggie

Actress
Born 28 December 1934
Essex, England

The daughter of a pathologist, Maggie Smith trained for the stage at the Oxford Playhouse and began her career as a revue performer, making her London debut in 1952 and her New York debut in *New Faces of 1956*. One of the warmest and most outstandingly gifted stage comediennes of her generation, later to mature into a fine dramatic and Shakespearean actress, she has been garlanded with awards and critical praise, but has never quite captured moviegoers in the way she has charmed theatregoers on both sides of the Atlantic. She has always enjoyed a happy rapport with her legions of adoring theatre fans, coaxing them into affectionate complicity with her mannerisms; but the camera has a baleful eye, seeking out the anxiety of a brilliant actress fearful that, on screen, her angular beauty will be flattened and her technical skill reduced to a battery of irksome tics.

Like Katharine Hepburn, the screen actress she most closely resembles, Maggie Smith has a mannered style which is not merely winsome but a signal of her courage and personality. Unlike Hepburn, however, she has never consistently committed herself to films. She made her screen debut as a socialite hiding Yank-on-the-run George Nader in Seth Holt's under-rated, *noir*-ish *Nowhere To Go* (1958), one of the last films made by Ealing Studios. When Ealing bit the dust her contract was taken up by MGM and Associated British, but while she established herself as a star of Britain's then nascent National Theatre, the studios dithered over what to do with her. She, meanwhile, married Robert Stephens, one of her National Theatre co-stars. (They later divorced, and she married the playwright Beverly Cross.)

After a featured role in a feeble film comedy, *Go To Blazes* (1962), the actress gave an acute performance as Richard Burton's mousy secretary in *The VIPs* (1962), stealing every scene in which she appeared. The theatre continued to claim most of her time, but there was a wickedly funny cameo in *The Pumpkin Eater* (1964) as Anne Bancroft's talkative, lazy lodger, and a less successful outing in *Young Cassidy* (1965), in which Rod

Taylor impersonated Sean O'Casey (none too convincingly) and Smith was his timid beloved. She was Desdemona to Laurence Olivier's Othello in the embarrassing screen version of their stage triumph, and then there was a two-year gap until *The Honey Pot* (1967), an updated borrowing from *Volpone*, in which she competed with Capucine, Edie Adams and Susan Hayward for a fraudulently moribund Rex Harrison.

Smith's first full-length screen role came in 1968 with *Hot Millions*, a wry caper movie in which she played another secretary, this time helping Peter Ustinov to fleece a big corporation with some computer wizardry. Then came the chance to sink her teeth into a role worthy of her talents in *The Prime Of Miss Jean Brodie* (1968), an adaptation of a Muriel Spark novel in which Vanessa Redgrave had starred on stage. As the 1930s schoolmarm, mesmerising her 'gels' with lectures on the life force, but inwardly frigid and authoritarian, Smith suggested a calculating phony rather than Spark's hysterical virgin high on Fascism, but she carried the film and carried off the Best Actress Oscar.

She then returned to the National Theatre, but contributed a telling cameo to Richard Attenborough's *Oh! What A Lovely War* (1969), playing a musical soubrette urging the boys onto the stage and into the arms of the recruiting sergeant with the promise of 'I'll Make a Man of You' – a distant figure of glamour who turns into a raddled old whore in close-up. Her commitments to the National Theatre (and the occasional foray into the commercial theatre of Shaftesbury Avenue) kept her off screen until Alan J. Pakula's modest comedy *Love And Pain And The Whole Damn Thing* (1972). Then, the same year, she buried her sharp, sensible features under ludicrous make-up for the title role in *Travels With My Aunt*, but turned in a fussy, shrill performance which threatened to bring a premature end to her film career.

Four years later she worked her way back in *Murder By Death* (1976), a Neil Simon spoof of fiction's great detectives, joining debonair David Niven in a tartly brittle parody of William Powell and Myrna Loy as Nick and Nora Charles. Then came another neat supporting performance as Bette Davis' bitch spinster companion in *Death On The Nile* (1978), one of the interminable Hercule Poirot series, groaning with stars, exotic locations and Peter Ustinov. Also in 1978, however, she stole the honours, and her second Oscar, for Neil Simon's episodic *California Suite*, cast, wryly enough, as a nominated actress in Tinseltown for the Oscar ceremony.

Smith then took a plunge into cod Greek mythology in *Clash Of The Titans* (1981). After *Quartet* (1982), a James Ivory film based on a Jean Rhys novel in which Smith played the downtrodden wife of Alan Bates, she coasted through *Evil Under The Sun* (1982); was reunited with an ailing David Niven in *Better Late Than Never* (1982), a comedy-drama of which Better Never might serve as an epitaph; played a randy Victorian aristocrat in *The Missionary* (1983); and, in *A Private Function* (1985), gave a richly comic performance as a tight-arsed, social-climbing provincial memsahib in austerity Britain. But it was as cousin Charlotte, the regretful spinster chaperone in James Ivory's *A Room With A View* (1986) that Maggie Smith surpassed herself, revealing her substantial qualities as an actress, never more than slyly hinting that Charlotte has an inkling of how life has passed her by - and laying a blueprint for a much sadder spinster, Judith Hearne, the following year. Her appearances as Granny Wendy in *Hook* (1991), and as a rigid Mother Superior in *Sister Act* (1992) were much more routine, but the Whoopi Goldberg-goes-to-a-convent comedy proved the sleeper smash of summer '92.

1958 Nowhere To Go **1963** The VIPs **1964** The Pumpkin Eater **1965** Young Cassidy; Othello **1967** The Honey Pot **1968** Hot Millions **1969** The Prime Of Miss Jean Brodie; Oh! What A Lovely War **1972** Travels With My Aunt **1976** Murder By Death **1978** California Suite **1981** Clash of The Titans; Quartet **1982** Evil Under The Sun **1983** Better Late Than Never; The Missionary **1985** A Private Function; Lily In Love **1986** A Room With A View **1987** The Lonely Passion Of Judith Hearne **1991** Hook **1992** Sister Act **1992/93** The Secret Garden

Snipes, Wesley

Actor
Born ?1963
Orlando, Florida

Tall, well built and graceful, Wesley Snipes has presented plausible athletes in several variable sports-themed films, from student football player in *Wildcats* (1986) to con-artist basketball hustler in *White Men Can't Jump* (1992). But he has rightly captured critical and popular attention – and vaulted to leading man status – with a string of more intense portrayals in a remarkably short time.

Born in Orlando, Snipes was educated primarily in New York City, where he spent two years at the celebrated *Fame* High School of Performing Arts before returning to Florida. In 1980 he entered State University of New York at Purchase for a degree in Theatre Arts and also pursued his training in dance, fencing and martial arts before embarking on a stage career. Snipes' theatre credits include Broadway roles in *Boys Of Winter*, *Death And The King's Horsemen* at Lincoln Center and *Execution Of Justice*.

In 1989 the actor made an impact on the small screen in HBO's *Vietnam War Stories*, winning the ACE Award for Best Actor. He subsequently featured as the heavy, a gang leader, in Michael Jackson's mini-drama music video *Bad*, directed by Martin Scorsese. Meanwhile, Snipes had made his film debut as one of Goldie Hawn's unruly *Wildcats*, donned boxing gloves for *Streets Of Gold* (both 1986) and demonstrated an engaging capacity for physical and fast-talking comedy in the mediocre but popular baseball comedy *Major League* (1989), in which he played the kooky wannabe Willie Mays Hayes. For Spike Lee, Snipes was first Denzel Washington's superb rival sax player in *Mo' Better Blues* (1990) and then the troubled protagonist of *Jungle Fever* (1991), Flipper Purify, a buppie architect whose adulterous fling with Annabella Sciorra sparks family and community conflicts. In between he was a chillingly charismatic crack dealer in Mario Van Peebles' controversial *New Jack City* (1991). Enjoying a hit with the comedy *White Men Can't Jump*, Snipes also opted for a character role in marked contrast – as one of the bitter paraplegic ensemble in Neil Jiminez's unsentimental, award-winning study of men coming to terms with paralysis, *The Waterdance* (1992), before turning to an action thriller and top billing in *Passenger 57*. By 1993, he had unquestionably risen to the top rank of black actors, spearheaded by Denzel Washington.

1986 Wildcats; Streets of Gold **1987** Critical Condition **1989** Major League **1990** Mo' Better Blues; King Of New York **1991** New Jack City; Jungle Fever **1992** White Men Can't Jump; The Waterdance **1992/93** Passenger 57; Rising Sun

Soderbergh, Steven

Director, writer
Born 1963
Georgia

Having sprung, seemingly, from nowhere to write and direct the hippest hot movie of 1989, *sex, lies and videotape*, Steven Soderbergh became the most wanted man in Hollywood. His debut effort put him, at the tender age of 26, on the receiving end of the kind of acclaim and hype seldom seen since Orson Welles burst on the scene as a wunderkind.

A thin, bespectacled, mild-mannered young man raised in the South, Soderbergh was obsessed with movies from childhood and began making his own short films when he was 13. Rather than attending film school he set straight to work from school, writing and editing other people's shorts. When he was 21 years old he met rock group Yes through a friend and was engaged to shoot a documentary of the band on the road in the US. The resulting feature-length film, *9012 Live* (1986) received a Grammy nomination.

Soderbergh seemed on his way, was taken on by an agent and commissioned to write a musical film for Tri-Star Pictures that never got as far as production. His career stalled, and in 1987 he sought catharsis from a disastrously failed personal relationship by writing *sex, lies and videotape*. It took him only eight days. Producer Morgan Mason (son of actor James) received the script from Soderbergh's agent and embarked on what proved a lengthy and complex quest for finance, raising the miniscule – by Hollywood standards – budget of $1.2 million from several sources. The result, shot in Louisiana, proved a remarkably self-assured, original work, full of humour, insight, sex appeal and, from one so young, astonishing perception of women, men and contemporary mores. Bowled over, jurors at the 1989 Cannes Film Festival awarded Soderbergh the top honour, the Palme D'Or, critics compared him to Woody Allen, and Soderbergh calmly predicted 'It's all downhill from here'.

Certainly the furore had exhausted itself by the time the Oscars rolled around, with the movie receiving a nod only for Soderbergh's original screenplay; the Academy, however, is not noted for its support of independent films outside the Hollywood mainstream. Certainly *sex, lies and videotape* made a handsome profit in release and ensured that the young director had no difficulty getting backing for his next project. Very aware of the so-called 'second-picture syndrome' which has seen film-makers from Welles to Spike Lee reviled after a heady debut, Soderbergh trod cautiously, eventually electing to make (on location in Prague) the ambitious *Kafka*, a psychological thriller starring Jeremy Irons as the famous novelist. Predictably it was indifferently received on its US release but fared somewhat better in Europe on the strength of its visual panache, well sustained 'Kafka-esque' tone of bewilderment and menace, and Irons' smart central performance.

1989 sex, lies and videotape **1992** Kafka **1993** King Of The Hill

Spacek, Sissy
(Mary Elizabeth Spacek)

Actress

Born 25 December 1949

Quitman, Texas

Blonde, blue-eyed, button-nosed and freckled, the waif-like Sissy Spacek looks like the kind of woman to whom a feather could cause grievous bodily harm, a major contributing factor to her early career as flakes and natural victims as well as one of Hollywood's eternal teens – she was still playing 13 at 30 – before her Oscar allowed her to grow up into slightly more resilient roles.

After winning a singer-songwriting contest, Spacek stayed with her cousin Rip Torn and his wife Geraldine Page in New York while hoping to break into the music industry, but instead studied with Lee Strasberg for eight months and broke into movies via modelling and TV work (although her screen debut was as an extra in Andy Warhol's *Trash*, 1970). She soon cornered the market in disturbed teenagers via her unnerving performances as the small-town cheerleader who goes on a killing spree with her boyfriend, Martin Sheen, in *Badlands* (1973), and the bullied ugly duckling turned bloody telekinetic avenger in *Carrie* (1976). She impressed in both, but it was not until *Coal Miner's Daughter* (1979) that she really established herself as an actress of weight.

Offered her first fully developed role as country-and-western singer Loretta Lynn, she credibly matured from the shy 13-year-old too ashamed to leave her motel room after her wedding night and dominated by her weak husband (Tommy Lee Jones) to a more confident adult via coping with the relationship and a nervous breakdown, a rite of passage that earned her an Oscar. She was again outstanding as the wife whose husband goes *Missing* (1982) in Chile, bringing to life much of his character to his initially disapproving father (Jack Lemmon) as they search for his body, but her moment was to prove short-lived.

Although sweetly comic as the voice of Ann Memelmahay's disembodied brain in *The Man With Two Brains* (1983), her strong-willed farmer's wife (to Mel Gibson) in the well-crafted *The River* (1984) was overshadowed by Jessica Lange and Sally Field's farm movies of the same year; her powerful and moving divorced mother fighting corruption on the state parole board in *Marie* (1985) failed to excite any box-office interest; and, despite an Oscar nomination, she proved irritatingly one-note as the young woman who shot her husband 'down South' in *Crimes Of The Heart* (1986). Subsequent films sank without trace, with Spacek's weak replacement for Broadway's Kathy Bates as the suicidal daughter in the film version of *'night, Mother* (1986) leading to a four-year sabbatical from movies. Her return in the racial drama *The Long Walk Home* (1990) showed that although she was still capable of making something memorable of almost any role, she was lacking the box-office pull to secure the kind of scripts that serve her best. Certainly, she was sadly wasted as the wife – no more than a cypher – of Kevin Costner's Jim Garrison in *JFK* (1991).

1972 Prime Cut **1973** Ginger In The Morning; Badlands **1976** Carrie **1977** Welcome To LA; Three Women **1979** Heartbeat; Coal Miner's Daughter **1981** Raggedy Man **1982** Missing **1984** The River **1985** Marie **1986** Crimes Of The Heart; Violets Are Blue; 'night, Mother; **1990** The Long Walk Home **1991** Hard Promises; JFK **1993** The Mommy Market

Spader, James

Actor

Born 1961

Boston, Massachusetts

With his blandly pretty, rather soft WASP looks, James Spader wouldn't appear to be sexy, but somehow he is. A thoughtful and already skilful actor he has almost always – in more than a dozen films in ten years – made viewers sit up and take notice of his characterisations, no matter how slight his role and whether the character is good, evil or merely confused.

Born in Boston into a teaching family, Spader is a graduate of the elite prep school Phillips Andover. Eschewing university, he moved to New York, where he worked as a truck driver and freight loader to finance his studies at the Michael Chekov Studio. Like Tom Cruise, he made his film debut in Franco Zeffirelli's disastrously received *Endless Love* (1981), playing Brooke Shield's brother. After theatre and TV work, he got his next film and has scarcely stopped since his succession of preppie curs in 1985. He was a stand-out as Andrew McCarthy's venomously insidious rich friend in *Pretty In Pink* (1986) and embodied yuppie greed in *Baby Boom* (1987) and *Wall Street* (1987).

Spader's breakthrough performance came as the intriguing, truth-telling, video-making Graham, whose impotence and candour have a far-reaching effect on an erstwhile friend and the women in his life, in Steven Soderbergh's fresh, perceptive debut feature, *sex, lies and videotape* (1989). It was a portrayal at once languid, opaque and intense that won Spader the Best Actor prize at the Cannes film festival.

While he was sometimes close to being arch and mannered in his earlier snoot roles, and was certainly miscast in the modern-day Jack the Ripper video fodder, *Jack's Back* (1988), post-*sex, lies* the actor seemed to grow in conviction and thought with every performance. In the otherwise preposterous *White Palace* (1991) he held his own with a terrific and sexy Susan Sarandon by delivering a spot-on observation of a numbed Jewish American Prince in the throes of a sexual obsession. Given provocative roles, Spader has shown the promise to emerge as one of the real quality actors of his generation.

1981 Endless Love **1985** Tuff Turf; The New Kids **1986** Pretty In Pink **1987** Baby Boom; Mannequin; Wall Street; Less Than Zero **1988** Jack's Back; Fresh Horses **1989** sex, lies and videotape; The Rachel Papers **1990** Bad Influence; True Colors **1991** White Palace; **1992** Bob Roberts (cameo); Storyville **1992/93** The Music Of Chance **1993** Dream Lover

Spano, Vincent

Actor
Born 18 October 1962
Brooklyn, New York

At a time when most actors his age were relegated to teen parts in movies of the John Hughes school, Vincent Spano had the advantage of appearing in more distinctive roles, even though these didn't gain him quite the wide recognition they might have done.

He began acting in elementary school, but it wasn't until he was 14 that he made his stage debut – in the 1977 production of *The Shadow Box*, first appearing at the Long Wharf Theatre and then on Broadway. After this auspicious debut, Spano won his first small film role two years later in *The Double McGuffin* (1979) and immediately followed it with a larger part, alongside Matt Dillon, as one of a group of disillusioned kids in *Over The Edge* (1979). A couple of TV movies and a break to resume his studies followed before he reappeared in a small role in Francis Ford Coppola's youth film *Rumble Fish* (1983), in the company of Dillon again, plus Mickey Rourke, and the director's nephew Nicolas Cage.

It was his next role, co-starring with Rosanna Arquette in John Sayles' *Baby It's You* (1983), that pushed Spano nearer the spotlight. As the Irish-Catholic boy nicknamed 'The Sheik' who pursues a Jewish girl in 60s New Jersey, he was singled out for praise and bright predictions were made for his future, but his next few performances failed to bring him equal success. He played a hoodlum in *Alphabet City* (1984), a naive student to Peter O'Toole's eccentric teacher in *Creator* (1985), and was relegated to a blink-and-you'll-miss-him part in *Maria's Lovers* (1985). It was not until the Taviani Brothers' *Good Morning Babylon* (1987) that his career seemed to be back on track, as one of two brothers from an artisan family in Italy, who go to America in 1915 and work for D.W. Griffith on the sets of the epic film *Intolerance*.

Then Spano had the misfortune of appearing in Roger Vadim's remake of his own . . . *And God Created Woman* (1988) which was universally (and deservedly) panned, in spite of the best efforts of Spano and his co-star, Rebecca De Mornay, to rise above the risible screenplay. His next two films were little seen, but his appearance with Sylvester Stallone in *Oscar*, and a reunion with director John Sayles for a substantial part in the impressive *City Of Hope* (both 1991), brought every chance that the promise of Vincent Spano's early career would be confirmed.

1979 The Double McGuffin; Over The Edge **1983** Rumble Fish; Baby, It's You; The Black Stallion Returns **1984** Alphabet City **1985** Creator; Maria's Lovers **1986** Il Cugino Americano/Blood Ties (Italy) **1987** Good Morning Babylon **1988** . . . And God Created Woman;

High Frequency aka Aquarium **1989** Rouge Venitien/Venetian Red (France/Italy) **1991** Oscar; City Of Hope **1992/93** Alive **1993** Tamakwa

Spheeris, Penelope

Director, writer
Born 1945
New Orleans, Louisiana

Penelope Spheeris could well claim to be the toughest woman director in (or around) Hollywood. Her films, often violent and explicit, show a preoccupation with outsiders and social misfits, subjects that condemn her to the outskirts – of Hollywood, feminism, and, apparently, good taste.

Spheeris went to film school at UCLA and gravitated towards documentaries. After the obligatory shorts, she went into production. Later, she became a producer on the TV show *Saturday Night Live* (later still, she served as a script consultant on the blue-collar comedy series *Roseanne*). Her first feature credit came as the producer of *Real Life* (1979), comedian Albert Brooks' film debut as writer and director, in which he also starred – as a documentary film-maker hoping to capture the typical American family. Her directing breakthrough was a 'true' documentary: *The Decline Of Western Civilization* (1981). Made independently, but attracting considerable attention, it is considered the definitive film record of the LA punk scene as it straggled into the 1980s.

Spheeris stayed in this downtown milieu of punk rebellion, drugs and rock music, and retained her non-moralistic stance for her first feature film, *The Wild Side* (1983). Typically, the film combines elements of the Corman exploitation youth picture (explicit violence, shock tactics, *and* social comment) with a convincing realism that has its roots in the documentary form. Raw, powerful film-making, very much on the side of the kids, *The Wild Side* is an 80s equivalent to *Rebel Without A Cause* (1955).

The Boys Next Door (1985) observes two disaffected teenagers (Maxwell Caulfield and Charlie Sheen) who take off for a joyride into the big city. The weekend begins with petty theft, then degenerates into an all-out murder spree. A demanding, explicit, even brutal film, again it inhabits a disturbing area midway between exploitation and social criticism. In many ways it anticipates John McNaughton's coldblooded *Henry: Portrait Of A Serial Killer* (1990). Both this film and its predecessor have been attacked as tasteless and gratuitous, chiefly by American critics. It might be pointed out, however, that a 'tasteful' film about a murder spree is itself distasteful. One suspects that much of the criticism is engendered by Spheeris's necessarily low-budget aesthetics and her reluctance to moralise.

Unfortunately, Spheeris' subsequent attempts to move into the mainstream were marked failures (A situation which was to change dramatically with *Wayne's World*, 1991). Both *Hollywood Vice Squad* (1986) and *Dudes* (1987) attempted comic variations on exploitation/punk themes, but the former looked simply tacky and played up the stereotypes Spheeris usually undercuts, while the latter failed to develop the radical critique of the Western its director clearly intended. Crucially, neither were particularly funny.

In this context, *The Decline Of Western Civilisation Part II: The Metal Years* (1988) signified a retrenchment, a return to essentials and ground principles, and the results were much more encouraging. Concentrating on remarkably outspoken interviews with a fair cross-section of the American heavy metal scene (from groups to groupies) with only a few musical interludes, the film presented a fascinating, funny and tragic insight into a subject not generally considered worthy of note. As usual, Spheeris herself refrained from comment on what was her biggest commercial success to that date. Then came *Wayne's World* (1992).

On the face of it, Spheeris may have seemed an odd choice for what proved a blockbusting hit comedy. However, bearing in mind that the film's origins lay in the 'Wayne and Garth' characters, presenters of a fictitious home-made TV programme, who featured regularly on the cult TV comedy show, *Saturday Night Live*, where Spheeris cut so many of her teeth, the choice becomes less surprising. And then, of course, the counter-culture of metalheads is what *Wayne's World* is all about. Where a more mainstream director would have capitalised on the 'star' appearances (Rob Lowe, Lara Flynn Boyle, Donna Dixon *et al*), and perhaps smoothed out the movie's ramshackle plot and hodge-podge of styles, Spheeris opts for allowing the engaging leads (Mike Myers, Dana Carvey) to revel to the full in their anarchic adolescent humour and peculiar jargon. The results, though patchy, are also delightfully spontaneous, wacky, and occasionally downright hilarious.

1981 The Decline Of Western Civilisation **1983** The Wild Side aka Suburbia **1985** The Boys Next Door **1986** Hollywood Vice Squad **1987** Dudes **1988** The Decline Of Western Civilisation Part 2: The Metal Years **1992** Wayne's World

Spielberg, Steven

Director
Born 18 December 1947
Cincinnati, Ohio

The most spectacularly successful Baby Boomer in cinema, Steven Spielberg infuses his films with the excitement, colour and sentiment that betray a childhood spent in Saturday matinees, nurtured on Walt Disney movies and thrilling to epic adventures. While his sensibility is frequently scorned by critics who view his work as glossy and middlebrow, there is no disputing his achievement in enrapturing international audiences with several of the biggest-grossing films in screen history.

Spielberg, intent on a cinematic career from childhood, was a veteran home-movie maker by the age of 12, churning out his own scripts and marshalling casts. At 13 the *auteur* won a competition with *Escape To Nowhere*, a 40-minute war adventure. At 16 he finished his first full-length effort, *Firefight*, which ran nearly two-and-a-half hours. While studying film at California State College in the mid-60s he completed five more films and bowed professionally in 1969 at the Atlanta Film Festival with a short, *Amblin'*, for which he later named his independent production company, Amblin Entertainment.

Landing a contract with Universal, Spielberg gained experience with considerable television work, including an episode of *Columbo*, culminating in several strong TV movies – among them *Something Evil*, *L.A. 2017*, *Savage* – and the superior, inventive suspense film *Duel* (1971), which earned a theatrical release. Very simply the nightmare of a travelling businessman, played by Dennis Weaver, who is by turns overtaken, teased, menaced and relentlessly pursued in a chase to the death by the never-seen driver of a juggernaut diesel truck, scripted – one might say sketched – by Richard Matheson, *Duel* alerted the industry to Spielberg's potential at setting up thrills and chills.

His regular feature debut came with *The Sugarland Express* (1974), a pleasing combination of a character-driven true-life tale (Goldie Hawn as the young wife of an escaped con attempting to retrieve their baby from adoption) and a screwball chase as the couple collect an ever-lengthening tail of cops across Texas. What no one could have foreseen was Spielberg's ability to parlay a hokey yarn – beach community terrorised by monster shark – and a solid but at the time scarcely glittering cast (Roy Scheider, Richard Dreyfuss, Robert Shaw) into an experience that tested the bolts on cinema seats as it smashed box-office records: the sensational scream-fest *Jaws* (1975). Abetted by Oscar-winning editing from Verna Fields, Spielberg played masterfully with primal fears to ingeniously startling effect. For his next trick he took on another theme that would seem to have been played out in the 50s – the 'they came from outer space' picture – retold it for adults (writing the story himself), and, investing it with childlike wonder and big bucks for breathtaking special effects, turned *Close Encounters Of The Third Kind* (1977) into another must-see. Spielberg himself would acknowledge that the film lost its way in the middle (when Richard Dreyfuss' unnerved Everyman obsesses on his UFO 'close encounter'), which prompted his tinkering with the middle and extending the end for the 'Special Edition' released in 1980. But the appeal of *Close Encounters* always lay in the universal yearning it conveyed so touchingly: with the simple musical call from another world, with the homage to Disney touches, and with the gasp-inducing image of The Mother of Spaceships appearing over the mountain providing one of the biggest thrills in cinema.

The industry's glee was scarce concealed when Spielberg's expensive Big Comedy, *1941* (1979), featuring a cast that ranged from John Belushi to Toshiro Mifune, flopped. Despite some spectacular set-pieces, the film lost laughs in a noisy, chaotic affair over which Spielberg seemed to impose little control. *Raiders Of The Lost Ark* (1981) was scarcely more restrained but better scripted. Concocted by a team of Saturday serials buffs (George Lucas producing, Philip Kaufman as story developer, Lawrence Kasdan providing the screenplay) *Raiders* was a blatantly no-holds-barred celebration of cliff-hanging, stunt-packed escapades of yesterday wedded to state-of-the-art SFX, and Spielberg directed it into the cinematic equivalent of a loop-the-loop roller-coaster ride, leaving audiences screaming with delight. The resulting sequels – the meaner-spirited *Indiana Jones And The Temple Of Doom* (1984) with several quite revolting elements and the more satisfactory *Indiana Jones And The Last Crusade* (1989) – made the *Raiders* trilogy the most popular film series of the 1980s, rivalled in box-office history only by Lucas' *Star Wars* adventures.

Spielberg has regularly revisited the kind of material that diverted him in his own youth, acting as executive producer and sometime writer-director on *Amazing Stories* for television; co-producing and directing one of the segments of the film marred by tragedy *Twilight Zone – The Movie* (1983); playing mentor to directors such as Robert Zemeckis and Joe Dante in executive-producing films like *I Wanna Hold Your Hand* (1978), *Poltergeist* (1982), *The Goonies* (1985), *Gremlins* (1984) and *Young Sherlock Holmes* (1985). But his most remarkable success came with the last 'kids' stuff' tale he originated, *E.T. The Extra-Terrestrial* (1982), the top-grossing film of all time. Scripted by Melissa Mathison, *E.T.* has been interpreted by analytically minded pundits as everything from a Christ allegory to a political statement, but it charmed family audiences as a thoroughly lovely, funny and tearjerking love story about a boy and his alien. As was now par for the course for a Spielberg film, *E.T.* took Oscars (for John Williams' score, and sound and visual effects) while the director's mantelpiece remained bare.

Spielberg's subsequent forays into more 'grown-up' subject matter have met with as many sneers as kudos. *The Color Purple* (1985), a film people really do either love or hate, aroused controversy, with cooler critics charging it with the betrayal of the Alice Walker novel from which it was adapted. Unashamedly emotional, it cannot be denied that the film's glories include beautiful cinematography, excellent music and performances from a superb black ensemble including Whoopi Goldberg, Oprah Winfrey, Danny Glover and Adolph Caesar. *The Color Purple* shares with one other film (*The Turning Point*, 1977) the dubious distinction of a record 11 Oscar nominations without a single win. An even more striking snub to Spielberg was the failure of the American Academy to nominate him for Best Director, an award he did win from the Directors Guild. *Empire Of The Sun* (1987), adapted from J.G. Ballard's riveting account of a boy coming of age in a Japanese prison camp in World War II, was just as handsome and even more ill-received as being emotionally overwrought but unmoving. For a man who initially showed an uncanny sympathy with what audiences want, Spielberg's decision to remake the 1940s supernatural romance *A Guy Named Joe* as *Always* (1989) was ill-judged. Slick but saccharine, it is his least successful picture since *1941*.

Apparently back on safer ground, the director retreated into a lavish revisiting of Peter Pan with *Hook*, and his recent production interests include director Martin Scorsese's *Cape Fear*. Divorced from actress Amy Irving, with whom he has a son, Spielberg subsequently married actress Kate Capshaw.

1971 Duel **1974** The Sugarland Express **1975** Jaws **1977** Close Encounters Of The Third Kind (also writer) **1979** 1941 **1981** Raiders Of The Lost Ark **1982** E.T. The Extra – Terrestrial **1983** Twilight Zone – The Movie **1984** Indiana Jones And The Temple Of Doom **1985** The Color Purple **1987** Empire Of The Sun **1989** Indiana Jones And The Last Crusade; Always **1991** Hook **1992/93** Jurassic Park

Spottiswoode, Roger

Director, writer
Born 1945
Canada

Roger Spottiswoode had shown every sign of being a director who peaked too early, with one superb film and several that were lucrative and formulaic, albeit highly professional, to his credit in the years that followed. The son of Raymond Spottiswoode, former producer and technical planning officer with the National Film Board of Canada, Roger was raised in England where he became an editor of TV ads and documentaries before graduating to feature film editor with a trio of Sam Peckinpah films, *Straw Dogs* (1971), *The Getaway* (1972) and *Pat Garrett And Billy The Kid* (1973). The partnership ended after the extensive re-editing of the latter (although Spottiswoode was to supervise its restoration in 1988) and after two more films – Karel Reisz's *The Gambler* (1974) and Walter Hill's excellent *The Streetfighter* (1975) – he filled out the wait to his first directorial credit with more TV work.

When the debut came with *Terror Train* (1980), a routine Jamie Lee Curtis slasher film, the world was less than impressed, although the direction, if uninspired, was more professional than the norm for the genre. His contribution to *The Pursuit Of D.B. Cooper* (1981) is much harder to gauge since at least two directors worked on the film before him and another apparently refilmed the ending; so is his contribution as co-writer of Walter Hill's *48 HRS.* (1982). There was no doubt about his next, however, which he was able to see through initial development for the first time: *Under Fire* (1983), a political thriller set against the Nicaraguan revolution where everybody lies, including the camera (its photographer hero finds himself taking sides, and fakes photos of a dead Sandinista, only to find that he is inadvertently being used by the CIA in the form of an apparently comically indiscreet French spy). The film, both a well-crafted piece of storytelling and a convincing examination of American foreign policy was a revelation in terms of Spottiswoode's directorial touch which belied the modest budget and used an involving but unostentatious style which favoured long takes to create a false sense of security (in a long scene when a sniper's talk of baseball is stopped short by his murder) or unease (when a journalist approaches soldiers in the street for directions). Considerably more successful in Europe than in Reagan's America, *Under Fire* marked Spottiswoode as a director who could work issues into a commercial framework without compromise, but it still took him three years to get another film.

The Best Of Times (1986) was a Capraesque small-town comedy with genuine affection for its characters but it felt disappointingly stretched with none of its predecessor's tight control of narrative. *Shoot To Kill* was by comparison a great improvement, a gripping thriller with a superbly handled opening sequence that showed much directorial imagination and promised greater things, but simply led to the director becoming a hired gun, taking over the canine-cop buddy movie *Turner And Hooch* (1989) mid-production from Henry Winkler and inheriting *Air America* (1990) from Bob Rafelson. The latter, a black comedy about a covert CIA airline in Laos with more plane crashes than politics seemed to conjure up Brando's taxicab speech from *On The Waterfront* rather than the achievements of *Under Fire*: while slick and highly polished, it is hard to believe it is what Spottiswoode really wanted to do. Even worse was yet another attempt by Sylvester Stallone to be funny, with *Stop Or My Mom Will Shoot* (1992), Spottiswoode investing what pace and slick action sequences he could in a wretchedly unfunny script for the wrong leading man. Spottiswoode may yet be a contender, but as long as Hollywood keeps asking him to take dives he may never take the brass ring.

1980 Terror Train **1981** The Pursuit Of D.B. Cooper **1983** Under Fire **1986** The Best Of Times **1988** Shoot To Kill aka Deadly Pursuit **1989** Turner And Hooch **1990** Air America **1992** Stop Or My Mom Will Shoot

Stallone, Sylvester

Actor, writer, director
Born 7 July 1946
New York City

The product of a poor, broken home, Sylvester Stallone grew up in the Hell's Kitchen neighbourhood of Manhattan (later to provide the background for his film *Paradise Alley*). He spent several years in the homes of foster parents in Maryland and Philadelphia and was expelled from 14 schools in 11 years. Nevertheless, thanks to his muscular physique he was able to attend the American College in Switzerland on an athletics scholarship. He went on to study drama at the University of Miami but left for New York before graduating. There, he spent many years writing, picking up minor parts (in a porno film, *A Party At Kitty And Stud's Place*, 1968, later distributed as *The Italian Stallion*; and in *Bananas*, 1971), and supporting himself in a string of jobs: cinema usher, truck driver, bouncer, zoo attendant, short-order cook. He made his off-Broadway debut in the nude drama *Score*, and landed a more significant role in *The Lords Of Flatbush* (1974), but frustrated by his lack of momentum he moved to Los Angeles shortly afterwards.

Legend has it that Stallone wrote the original script for *Rocky* (1976) in three days. The story of a boxer from the streets who gets a million-to-one championship bout, it was basically an old B-movie scenario, a crowd-pleasing celebration of the underdog, but written from the inside; its depiction of the crumbling tenements of Philadelphia is convincing, and the emphasis on training and hard work merits the big emotional pay-off Stallone contrives. The producers wanted another actor to play Rocky, but Stallone would only give them his project on his terms.

His acting is often ridiculed, but within an obviously limited range he is actually quite expressive. Most of his characters have been inarticulate, but it is to the actor's credit that we nevertheless identify with them as much as we do. Physically he may be the most striking male star since John Wayne; with his curled lower lip (the result of a childhood accident) and the slight slur and often mumbled delivery it results in, the man doesn't look or talk like a movie star. This has been the making of him – and also his Achilles' heel. Sly, as he is widely called, embodies a blue-collar heroism that stems from his background and his looks as much as from the roles he plays (it is in the nature of America that blue-collar heroism should consist of quickly becoming very wealthy). The public so closely identified Stallone with Rocky that they would not accept him in other roles, and quite worthy films; Norman Jewison's *F.I.S.T.* (1978) and Stallone's own *Paradise Alley* (1978), bombed at the box office.

Rocky II (1979) was an unimaginative rerun of the first film, but it revived Stallone's fortunes, and prove him a capable, if overemphatic, director. The third sequel in 1982 was a more interesting affair, a conscious attempt to reflect Stallone's own mixed success in his boxing alter-ego. Again the direction was slick and manipulative, but the movie stands up as a serious sports film, convincingly identifying fear and desire as the real opponents. Rocky's relationship with black fighter Apollo Creed is particularly well handled, re-enforcing his appeal to a working-class constituency.

John Rambo, too, is of that ilk. *First Blood* (1982) was a violent action film about a Vietnam veteran who goes to war with the society that marginalised him. Although the film, directed by Ted Kotcheff, addressed some of the alienation of the Vietnam experience, it sacrifices credibility when it builds Stallone's former green beret into an invincible superman. It's a film that requires a martyr, but opts for a hero instead. *Rambo* (1985), the epic and immensely popular sequel, went further down the same road, swapping alienation for rampant patriotism, red-bashing, and gung-ho machismo. In the process, Rambo, riding the Reaganite tide, became a cultural phenomenon on a scale Rocky never approached. Intriguingly, *Rambo III* (1988), budgeted at more than $50 million, flopped – perhaps because its star had strayed so far from his original underdog status that audiences were beginning to sympathise with the enemy.

Stallone has increasingly complained that he is trapped by his two most famous characters, that he is really an intellectual (aside from the various screenplays he has penned, he has also written novelisations and TV scripts under the pseudonym Q. Moonblood), typecast by studio and public alike as a bruiser. He even tried to kill Rocky off at the end of *Rocky V* (1990) (another partial return to form after the crude propaganda of 1985's *Rocky IV*). His comedies to date, starting with Dolly Parton in *Rhinestone* (1984), have been disastrous and significantly the failure of the first preceded his two most crassly commercial movies: *Cobra* (1986) was Rambo on the right side of the law, and *Over The Top* (1987), for which he was paid a reported $11 million, was essentially Rocky arm-wrestling. Whether or not he can successfully change his image, Sylvester Stallone appears increasingly relaxed in such unpretentious genre films as *Lock-Up* and *Tango And Cash* (both 1989), and in the early 1990s his past achievements were gradually being re-evaluated in a more positive light.

As actor except where stated otherwise: **1968** A Party At Kitty And Stud's Place aka The Italian Stallion **1971** Bananas (bit) **1974** The Lords Of Flatbush **1975** The Prisoner Of Second Avenue (bit); Capone; Death Race 2000; Farewell, My Lovely; No Place To Hide **1976** Cannonball aka Carquake; Rocky (also writer) **1978** F.I.S.T. (also co-writer); Paradise Alley (also w/d), **1979** Rocky II (also w/d) **1981** Nighthawks; Victory aka Escape To Victory **1982** First Blood (also co-writer); Rocky III (also w/d) **1983** Staying Alive (director only) **1984** Rhinestone (also co-writer) **1985** Rambo: First Blood Part II (also co-writer); Rocky IV (also w/d) **1986** Cobra (also writer) **1987** Over The Top (also co-writer) **1988** Rambo III (also co-writer) **1989** Lock-Up; Tango And Cash **1990** Rocky V (also writer) **1991** Oscar **1992** Stop! Or My Mom Will Shoot

Stanton, Harry Dean

Actor

Born 14 July 1926

Irvine, Kentucky

Hands-down winner of the title busiest actor of his generation, the multi-talented (he also sings and plays the harmonica, bass and guitar) narrowfaced Harry Dean Stanton has proved a godsend for casting directors in search of losers and eccentrics, working with most of the major directors in the business in many classic films punctuated by the occasional dud that is easily qualified by the sheer quantity and almost universal quality of his work.

Following his service in the US Navy in World War II, during which he saw action in Okinawa, he studied at the university of Kentucky on a GI Bill and started acting there, winning notice as cockney dustman Alfred Doolittle in *Pygmalion* (his rather less-than-convincing accent was dusted off in

1988 for his American butler masquerading as an English one to get higher pay in *Mr North*). After graduating he spent four years at the Pasadena Playhouse and toured in several shows, ending up in LA where he played bit parts in movies and TV westerns as Dean Stanton. By the late 60s he had become a recognisable face, but his career really took off in the 70s with small roles in cult movies like *Two Lane Blacktop* (1971), *Pat Garrett And Billy The Kid* (1973) and *Rancho Deluxe* (1975), even performing a song with Bob Dylan and Joan Baez in the endless *Renaldo And Clara* (1978) before his monumentally silly I-know-there's-a-monster-on-the-loose-but-I'll-just-go-into-this-dark-room-on-my-own-and-get-killed-looking-for-the-cat scene in Ridley Scott's *Alien* (1979) brought him more prominent roles. Soon he had more than one or two scenes and the odd line of dialogue to work with and chalked up an impressive array of losers, con-men, misfits and sleazeballs, most of whom had more than a passing acquaintance with proscribed substances or worse ('There are over 100 bodily fluids,' he announces in 1982's *Young Doctors In Love* 'and I have tasted each and every one of them.').

He was outstanding as the pathetic dog-napper in *The Black Marble* (1980) and suitably off-kilter as the career *Repo Man* (1984) passing on his philosophy of life to his protégé, but has proved his greater range: with *Paris, Texas* (1984) – a role written for him and relying heavily on body language, most notably when his initially mute character mimics his estranged son's movements as a way of establishing common ground with him – and showed a more tender side with two surprisingly sweet and gentle performances, as a guardian angel in *One Magic Christmas* (1985) and as Molly Ringwald's burnt-out father in *Pretty In Pink* (1986), and has even voiced a *Care Bears* cartoon! There have been some bad performances – most notably his atrocious impersonation of Robert Mitchum in *The Fourth War* (1990) – and some strange choices, but Stanton has continued to be one of the most welcome and interesting of American character actors.

As Dean Stanton: **1956** The Wrong Man **1957** Tomahawk Trail **1958** The Proud Rebel **1959** Pork Chop Hill; A Dog's Best Friend **1962** Hero's Island; How The West Was Won **1963** The Man From The Diner's Club **1966** The Hostage; Ride In The Whirlwind **1967** Cool Hand Luke; A Time For Killing **1968** Day Of The Evil Gun; The Mini-Skirt Mob **1970** Kelly's Heroes; Rebel Rousers As Harry Dean Stanton: **1971** Cisco Pike; Two Lane Blacktop **1972** Count Your Bullets **1973** Dillinger; Pat Garrett And Billy The Kid **1974** The Godfather Part II; Where The Lilies Bloom; Zandy's Bride **1975** Farewell My Lovely; Rancho Deluxe; Rafferty And The Gold Dust Twins; Win, Place Or Steal; Born To Kill; 92 In The Shade **1976** The Missouri Breaks **1978** Straight Time; Renaldo And Clara **1979** Alien; The Rose; Wiseblood **1980** The Black Marble; Deathwatch; Private Benjamin **1981** UFOria (released 1986); Escape From New York; **1982** One From The Heart; Young Doctors In Love **1983** Christine **1984** The Bear; Repo Man; Paris, Texas; Red Dawn **1985** Fool For Love; One Magic Christmas **1986** Pretty In Pink **1987** Slam Dance **1988** Mr North; Stars And Bars; The Last Temptation Of Christ **1989** Dream A Little Dream; Twister; Jackal's Run **1990** Wild At Heart; The Fourth War **1991** Stranger In The House **1992** Man Trouble; Twin Peaks: Fire Walk With Me

Steenburgen, Mary

Actress

Born 1953

Newport, Arkansas

Tall, sweet-faced and with a (sometimes irritating) voice that seems to break even as she speaks, Mary Steenburgen must have always seemed an unlikely prospect for a successful acting career. Star-struck to this day, she tap-danced from the age of three, going on to study drama with Sanford Meisner at the New York Neighborhood Playhouse before an improvisational troupe, Cracked Token, and community theatre led to a TV scout bringing her to the attention of Jack Nicholson, for whom she made her refreshingly off-beat debut in the comedy Western *Goin' South* (1978), a film that did more for its supporting cast than its star director.

Her real breakthrough was as H.G. Wells' modern-day love interest in *Time After Time* (1979) – which turned into a real-life love story when she married (albeit later divorced) co-star Malcom McDowell – winning the role over director Nicholas Meyer's original intention to cast a fast-talking Jean Arthur type. Her soft-spoken, slow delivery couldn't have been further away, but her delightfully appealing performance was a real star-maker, a status she confirmed with a Best Supporting Actress Oscar as Melvin Dummar's down-to-earth stripper first wife in Jonathan Demme's *Melvin And Howard* (1980), and with roles for Milos Forman, Woody Allen, Martin Ritt and Arthur Penn.

She was very restrained and controlled as the Mother in *Ragtime* (1981), quietly ringing in the changes and making a difference more effectively than Coalhouse Walker's terrorism, one of the most pronounced of the still-waters-run-deep contradictions of her characters. Interestingly, her roles, generally seemingly serene and strong, often take the sexual initiative, nearly raping her male leads in *Time After Time* and Woody Allen's hauntingly Bergmanesque *A Midsummer Night's Sex Comedy* (1982). After a series of disappointing mid-80s films (with only Disney's *One Magic Christmas*, 1985, providing a hit) in which her career took a backseat to raising her children and occasional stage work, she came back into the mainstream with supporting roles as Steve Martin's believable wife in *Parenthood* (1989) and, in a wry reflection of her *Time After Time* role, as time traveller Doc Brown's romantic interest in *Back To The Future Part III* (1990). Steenburgen was delightful, too, in support as the choir director who longs to be a cabaret singer in *The Butcher's Wife* (1991), a film which received a less than enthusiastic response.

1978 Goin' South **1979** Time After Time **1980** Melvin And Howard **1981** Ragtime **1982** A Midsummer Night's Sex Comedy **1983** Cross Creek **1984** Romantic Comedy **1985** One Magic Christmas **1987** End Of The Line; Dead Of Winter; The Whales Of August **1989** Miss Firecracker; Parenthood **1990** Back To The Future Part III **1991** The Butcher's Wife **1992** Clifford

Stern, Daniel

Actor
Born 28 August 1957
Bethesda, Maryland

A tall, beaky, mostly comic actor with a richly nasal voice and a sardonic attitude, Daniel Stern made an impact in only his second film, the acclaimed youth movie *Breaking Away* (1979). As Cyril, Stern is dryly funny and refreshingly self-effacing. He was already acting on the New York stage and had been for a year, but 1980 brought his best theatre role, as Lee in Sam Shepard's *True West*. In the movies, he played a Krishna in *One-Trick Pony* (1980), and an aspiring artist in Woody Allen's *Stardust Memories* (1980).

In *Diner* (1982), with the benefit of an outstanding script by Barry Levinson, Stern and his young co-stars, Mickey Rourke, Kevin Bacon, Ellen Barkin and Steve Guttenberg, light up the screen. As 'Shrevie', Stern shares a wonderful scene with Ellen Barkin, when he tries to explain the order of his beloved record collection. It's funny, but it's also poignant; we are always aware of Shrevie's painful immaturity. Stern's gifts do not commend him to straight drama, and he had not made much impression in the likes of *Blue Thunder* (1983), or playing an ambivalent character in *D.O.A.* (1988). Nor has his choice in comic vehicles worked to his advantage. Only his energetic slapstick turn with Joe Pesci in *Home Alone* (1990) – a colossal hit from John Hughes – and a terrific cameo as a philistine pop star (in the market for big paintings, as long as his interior decorator approves) in Woody Allen's *Hannah And Her Sisters* (1986) do justice to his timing and precision. Stern has narrated the nostalgic TV comedy series *The Wonder Years* since it started in 1988, as well as directing occasional episodes and, in 1991 with *City Slickers*, appeared on course for more substantial vehicles in keeping with a man in his 30s.

1979 Starting Over; Breaking Away **1980** It's My Turn; One-Trick Pony; Stardust Memories; A Small Circle Of Friends **1981** Honky Tonk Freeway **1982** Diner; I'm Dancing As Fast As I Can **1983** Blue Thunder; Get Crazy **1984** C.H.U.D. **1985** Key Exchange **1986** Hannah And Her Sisters; The Boss' Wife **1987** Born In East LA **1988** The Milagro Beanfield War; D.O.A. **1989** Leviathan; Crazy Horse; Little Monsters **1990** Friends, Lovers And Lunatics; Home Alone; Coupe De Ville; My Blue Heaven **1991** City Slickers **1992** Home Alone 2: Lost In New York; Family Prayers **1993** Rookie Of The Year (director)

Stockwell, Dean

Actor
Born 5 March 1936
North Hollywood, California

Dean Stockwell is one of only a handful of Hollywood child stars to make a significant acting career in adulthood, and he is arguably the finest of any of them, then and now, having started with an uncanny instinct for acting, to which he later added – after a not altogether happy period more or less in the wilderness-hard experience.

Born to Broadway artists, Stockwell and his younger brother, actor Guy, made their stage debuts in 1943 and at the age of nine Dean made a delightful screen bow in the MGM Gene Kelly musical *Anchors Aweigh* (1945). The archetypal pretty moppet with curly hair, Dean was also refreshingly natural and free of 'the cutes', attributes that made him in demand for more than a dozen films before he reached adolescence. Among his most memorable performances of this period were the war orphan of the title role in Joseph Losey's fine fantasy with a social message, *The Boy With Green Hair* (1948), the lonely, petulant invalid boy in *The Secret Garden* (1949) and Rudyard Kipling's *Kim* (1950).

Stockwell did not enjoy being a child performer, recalling years later his resentment at being exploited and treated 'like a piece of meat', but he remained an actor. Grown into a handsome and intelligent young leading man he was underused as a romantic lead but turned in excellent performances when given the opportunity: partnered with Bradford Dillman in Richard Fleischer's *Compulsion* (1959) he was plausible and disturbing as one of the youths who commit murder for a thrill, a story inspired by the chilling Leopold-Loeb case; in the first-rate adaptation of D.H. Lawrence's *Sons And Lovers* (1960) he affected one of the best British accents ever delivered from an American mouth on film.

Always good in his increasingly sporadic film roles, Stockwell began to work more often on television and has won an Emmy for his work in the popular series *Quantum Leap*. In 1982 he wrote and directed, in collaboration with rock star Neil Young, the flipped-out anti-nuclear comedy *Human Highway*, featuring the duo and longtime Stockwell buddies Russ Tamblyn and Dennis Hopper but, by the mid-80s, now grey-haired and rougher hewn, he found himself as sought-after by film-makers as he had been in boyhood. A string of showy supporting roles revealed him as one of the most versatile and compelling character actors in the business: among his many later credits are *Dune* (1984), *Paris, Texas* (1984), *Blue Velvet* (1986) – in which he out-weirdo'd even Dennis Hopper as a sadistic club owner drugged to the eyeballs and miming to Roy Orbison's 'In Dreams' – *Beverly Hills Cop II* (1987) and *Married To The Mob* (1988), in which he was a delight as the horny Mafioso in pursuit of Michelle Pfeiffer.

1945 Anchors Aweigh; Valley Of Decision; Abbott And Costello In Hollywood **1946** The Green Years; Home Sweet Homicide **1947** The Arnelo Affair; The Mighty McGurk; Song Of The Thin Man; The Romance Of Rosy Ridge; Gentleman's Agreement **1948** Deep Waters; The Boy With Green Hair **1949** Down To The Sea In Ships; The Secret Garden **1950** The Happy Years; Kim; Stars In My Crown **1951** Cattle Drive **1957** The Careless Years; Gun For A Coward **1959** Compulsion **1960** Sons And Lovers **1962** Long Day's Journey Into Night **1965** Rapture **1968** Psych-Out **1970** The Dunwich Horror **1971** The Last Movie **1972** The Loners **1973** The Werewolf Of Washington **1975** Win Place Or Steal aka Another Day At The Races; Won Ton Ton, The Dog Who Saved Hollywood; The Pacific Connection **1977** Tracks **1982** The Man With The Deadly Lens aka Wrong Is Right; Human Highway (also co-writer, co-director); To Kill A Stranger **1983** Alsino And The Condor **1984** Citizen Soldier; Dune; Paris, Texas **1985** Papa Was A Preacher; To Live And Die In L.A.; The Legend Of Billie Jean **1986** Banzai Runner; Blue Velvet **1987** The Time Guardian; Beverly Hills Cop II; Gardens Of Stone **1988** Buying Time; Palais Royal; Blue Iguana; Married To The Mob; Tucker: The Man And His Dream **1989** Limit Up; Jorge, A Brazilian **1990** Catchfire aka Backtrack; Sandino (Spain) **1992** The Player

Stoltz, Eric

Actor

Born 1961

Whittier, California

Pale, slim and distinctively red-haired, the versatile Eric Stoltz began his acting career at school, appearing in high school theatrical productions as well as playing piano accompaniment (he learned the instrument from the age of six) in school musicals. Deciding to pursue an acting career, he studied theatre arts at USC, but dropped out to train with the *crème de la crème* of acting teachers – Stella Adler, William Taylor and, finally, Peggy Feury. Accustomed to travelling (although born in California he had also lived in American Samoa in the South Pacific as a child), he went to Europe and played a season with an American rep company in Edinburgh.

Returning to the States, Stoltz made brief appearances in TV series before winning a role in *Fast Times At Ridgemont High* (1982), with up-and-coming actors Sean Penn, Jennifer Jason Leigh and Judge Reinhold. The film, about teenage life at a Californian high school, was praised for its performances and came to be recognised as seminal to the youth movie genre. He also appeared in the follow-up with Sean Penn's brother Christopher, *The Wild Life* (1984), and a series of minor films with young actors like James Spader. It was not until he was cast as drug-taking biker Cher's tragically disfigured, gentle son, Rocky Dennis, in Peter Bogdanovich's Oscar-nominated *Mask* (1986) that Stoltz began to be a name to look out for. Restricted by make-up that made his head look twice his normal size and his face unrecognisable, Stoltz, as John Hurt did in *The Elephant Man* (1980), broke the chains of his disguise to create a rounded and almost unbearably poignant character.

Changing direction, Stoltz played the lead in the John Hughes-scripted *Some Kind Of Wonderful* (1987), as a poor kid who falls in love with a beautiful rich girl (Lea Thompson). Although the film was a blatant re-working of Hughes' earlier *Pretty In Pink* (1986), it was popular with the teen market and scored a moderate success theatrically and on video. A couple of minor parts in forgettable films (the worst being the 20s farce *Manifesto* in 1989) followed, the most notable being the role of the poet Shelley in Ivan Passer's *Haunted Summer* (1988). Following this, the actor teamed up with friend John Cusack for a cameo role in the very successful *Say Anything* (1989). Keen-eyed viewers spotted Stoltz in rooster costume, throwing a graduation party early in the film, and showing another side to his acting persona with his wild gyrations.

A more serious assignment came next with the lead in the horror film *The Fly II* (1989), playing the son of the original 'fly', Seth Brundle (Jeff Goldblum), doomed to grow up as half-man, half-insect. Then he co-starred with other young actors (Sean Astin, Billy Zane, Matthew Modine, Harry Connick Jr) in the World War II drama *Memphis Belle* (1990); he was Danny Daly, the idealistic Irish-American radio operator aboard the B-17 bomber of the title, that flew bombing missions from Britain during the war. An accomplished actor, Stoltz now divides his time between films and the New York stage where, after a flourishing off-Broadway career (including Horton Foote's *The Widow Claire*), he made his Broadway debut in 1988 in the revival of Thornton Wilder's *Our Town*, for which he earned Tony and Drama Desk nominations.

1982 Fast Times At Ridgemont High aka Fast Times **1984** The Wild Life; Surf II; Running Hot aka Highway To Hell **1985** The New Kids; Code Name: Emerald; Mask **1987** Lionheart; Some Kind Of Wonderful **1988** Sister, Sister; Haunted Summer; Manifesto **1989** Say Anything; The Fly II **1990** Memphis Belle **1991** Money (France/Canada/Italy) **1992** The Waterdance **1992** Foreign Affairs **1992/93** Bodies, Rest, And Motion

Stone, Oliver

Director, writer
Born 15 September 1946
New York City

Few film directors have taken on the mantle of conscience of their generation so determinedly as Oliver Stone, a child of the 60s. Regarding film as a poet's vision and as valid as a piece of literature, he uses his work to try to understand 'and reshape the world through movies', frequently returning to themes of drugs, greed, music, masculinity and Vietnam – particularly Vietnam. A rich, unhappy kid and a Yale University drop-out, Stone had a troubled family life which gave him a strong death wish and a belief that the world had nothing to promise him, leading him to volunteer for the infantry as a private and to request posting to Vietnam because he wanted to see war 'from the lowest level'. The war, which caused him to be twice wounded and decorated, ironically gave him a strong commitment to life and shaped both his politics and the nature and substance of his visceral screen work.

On his return home, Stone was jailed for drugs offences; on his release he enrolled in the New York University film programme to study writing and directing (Martin Scorsese was one of his classmates there). His first film as writer and director, the low-budget and extremely oddly cast shocker *Seizure* (1973) was quickly (and best) forgotten and it was not until 1978 that he made the grade with his hard-hitting screenplay for *Midnight Express*, set in a Turkish prison. Despite winning an Oscar, the Writers' Guild of America Award and a Golden Globe (earning much notoriety when the organisers tried to herd him off-stage mid-speech only for presenter Richard Harris to slug it out with them) he was accused of playing fast and loose with the facts, an allegation that resurfaced with *Born On The Fourth Of July* (1989), which Stone attempted to film that year–1978–only for the financing to collapse when Al Pacino pulled out at the last minute. Although Stone does not deny specific inaccuracies of detail, he does admit to often combining a series of real events with imaginative ideas to convey the greater truth of his subject. Following his much rewritten screenplay for *Conan The Barbarian* (1981) – his first draft proved too expensive for even Dino De Laurentiis to film – he returned to directing with the confused and contrived horror movie *The Hand* (1981). It was his first major-budget picture and far too overtly commercial a genre piece for him, with some interesting details wasted amid a misjudged, rehashed *Beast With Five Fingers* (1946) script for which Stone (who played the first of his many cameos as a murdered tramp) had no one to blame but himself.

He returned to the typewriter amid allegations of racism and excessive violence with both *Scarface* (1983, updated for Brian De Palma with Cuban 'refugee' villains, Al Pacino, and a prominent part for a chainsaw), and *Year Of The Dragon* (1985), directed by Michael Cimino. Although both were conceived on an epic scale, only the latter, enabling Stone to bring the war home to the streets of New York via Asian drug dealers ('It's like Vietnam', cries Mickey Rourke's cop at one point. 'No one wants to win this thing.'), showed a clear sense of purpose. Stone claimed that producer De Laurentiis reneged on a deal to bankroll a low-budget film for Stone as director and took him to court to sue him into making it; unsuccessful, he eventually raised the money in Britain and the result, *Platoon* (1987) – the first Vietnam film to be made by a veteran – made Stone the hottest director around and its producers $100 million, leaving De Laurentiis looking very silly. Originally only a small arthouse release, the film struck a chord with American audiences, partially because its moral debate – two sergeants, one good, one evil, battling for the soul of a young 'grunt' based closely on Stone – and moments of religious symbolism were at times so lightly defined that the film appeared all things to all audiences: one man's anti-war film, another man's action pic.

Far more impressive, though less commercially successful, was *Salvador* (1986), a veritable emotional and political sledgehammer to the solar plexus of a film that hit hard at America's 'backyard' policies which allowed Central American dictatorships to flourish while death squads freely committed atrocities. It featured powerful recreations of the murder of Archbishop Romero and the sickening aftermath of the murder of several American nuns, committed with US approval though as much through incompetence as intent. By then, Stone was getting into his stride 'shaking cages' and took on the uneven conflict between the value of productivity of his father's generation versus the unfettered greed of that which followed it with *Wall Street* (1987). Structurally it was a slick and accomplished remake of *Sweet Smell Of Success* (1957) that at times seemed to wallow in the trappings of its irredeemable villain, Gordon Gekko (Michael Douglas), and turned his phrase 'Greed is good' into the mantra of a generation of entrepreneurs and insider traders.

Talk Radio (1988) seemed to indicate that Stone, who always identifies strongly with his central characters, was aware that he might in fact be becoming what he beheld: the movie's confrontational talk-show host simply exploits issues for gain, clouding them in his role as devil's advocate without making any attempt to resolve them. There was, however, certainly no confusing the intent of the much-lauded *Born On The Fourth Of July* when Stone finally brought it to the screen in 1989. His biggest picture, moving from vivid romanticism (the director has always had a good visual eye and shown a tendency towards lush orchestral scores for his most political films), it was his most deeply felt and painfully emotive reflection of the experience and legacy of the Vietnam War on both those who went and those who stayed at home, told through the cathartic experiences of crippled veteran Ron Kovic (Tom Cruise), convincingly portraying both the confusion of the time and the accidental nature of the atrocities inherent in war.

Since, Stone has been able to write his own ticket and, in his capacity as a producer, has helped punch through both *Blue Steel* (1989) for Kathryn Bigelow and *Reversal Of Fortune* (1990) for Barbet Schroeder. But he chose to remain in the 60s with his film *The Doors* (1991), pre-empting the inevitable criticism that greets any rock biopic (this one about Jim Morrison) by delivering a portrait as much of what the music meant to his generation as of the 'Lizard King' himself, impressively impersonated by Val Kilmer.

His next as director was the highly controversial *JFK* (1991), whose breathtaking cast ranged from Jack Lemmon, Walter Matthau and Kevin Bacon to Oscar-nominated Tommy Lee Jones, Joe Pesci and lead star Kevin Costner; and whose screenplay (by Stone and Zachary Sklar), embracing the wildest, most paranoic byways of assassination conspiracy theory, managed simultaneously to enrage and enthral. Sensational, and disturbingly well-made in the skill with which it seamlessly interweaves fact with fiction, Stone's insistent presentation of John F. Kennedy as the King of Camelot whose murder precipitated all of America's international woes, particularly Vietnam, was, to many, historically indefensible but undeniably cinematic. This nose-thumbing at conservative opinion was rewarded with Oscar nominations for Best Picture, Best Director and Best Screenplay.

As writer-director unless stated otherwise: **1973** Seizure **1978** Midnight Express (writer only) **1981** Conan The Barbarian (co-writer only); The Hand **1983** Scarface (writer only) **1985** Year Of The Dragon (co-writer only) **1986** Eight Million Ways To Die (writer only); Salvador (co-writer/director) **1987** Platoon; Wall Street (co-writer/ director) **1988** Talk Radio (co-writer/director) **1989** Born On The Fourth Of July **1991** The Doors **1991** JFK (co-writer/director) **1993** Heaven And Earth (w/d)

Stone, Sharon

Actress
Born 1958
Meadville, Pennsylvania

Blonde, husky-voiced and beautiful, Sharon Stone spent a decade going unremarked in a succession of bimbo and siren roles before her performance as an ice-cold bitch in the controversial *Basic Instinct* (1992) sent temperatures soaring and catapulted her to stardom.

A small-town girl, Stone won several local beauty contests before enrolling in Pennsylvania's Edinboro University, but the academic life held little appeal and by the age of 19 she had signed up as an Eileen Ford model and was soon on her way to Italy. After a few successful years in front of the cameras, she decided to return to New York and join the model-turned-actress queue. She didn't have long to wait: at an extras audition she was hand-picked by Woody Allen for *Stardust Memories* (1980). The tiny part, credited only as 'pretty girl on train', was to prove a helpful foot in the door for the budding actress, but it also marked the beginning of a blonde-bombshell pigeonholing that would continue to plague her throughout the 80s. The roles that followed, in feature films and TV movies ranging from mediocre to out-and-out schlock, demanded little from her other than good looks and some semblance of 'girly' sexiness, which Stone supplied with no effort and little distinction.

It took Dutch director Paul Verhoeven to identify the actress' real forte. Casting her in a supporting role opposite Arnold Schwarzenegger in the futuristic blockbuster *Total Recall* (1990), Verhoeven extracted a performance from Sharon Stone that had less to do with blowsiness than balls; pummelling and lunging at Arnie, she gave real meaning to the term 'killer bimbo'. Having thus tapped the actress' potential for oozing on-screen danger, Verhoeven offered her the perfect vehicle for fully exploiting this talent: the role of Catherine Tremell, a bisexual author who seduces men who serve as inspiration for characters in her novels, in the Joe Eszterhas-scripted *Basic Instinct*. An arch manipulator and possible serial killer tangling with cop Michael Douglas, Stone's Tremell perfectly combines chilling control with smouldering sexuality, to fascinating effect. While the film was rightly trashed by critics (less for its alleged homophobia and sexism than for its undeniable triteness and absurdity), the actress was internationally lionised and her star was firmly in ascendence.

However, despite the massive boost of the Verhoeven association, Stone is still more notable for her looks and presence than for the range or skill of her acting abilities – a distinct disadvantage in the talented climate of the 1990s.

1980 Stardust Memories **1981** Deadly Blessing **1982** Bolero (France) **1984** Irreconcilable Differences **1985** King Solomon's Mines **1987** Cold Steel; Allan Quatermain And The Lost City Of Gold; Police Academy IV **1988** Above The Law (GB: Nico); Action Jackson **1989** Personal Choice; Sangre Y Arena (Spain) **1990** Total Recall **1991** Year Of The Gun; He Said, She Said; Scissors **1992** Basic Instinct; Where Sleeping Dogs Lie; Diary Of A Hit Man **1993** Sliver

Streep, Meryl
(Mary Louise Streep)

Actress
Born 22 June 1949
Summit, New Jersey

Meryl Streep is one of the most highly accomplished of contemporary actresses, peerless in technique, although she herself would claim (against her quite numerous detractors) that technique has never been an especial priority. 'Acting isn't really mysterious,' she has said. 'There is a process involved, one that I don't wholly understand. To me, it doesn't feel psychologically complex. It just feels like this is what I do.' Acting with Shirley MacLaine in *Postcards From The Edge* (1991) she said she was amazed at the older woman's 'professionalism', glossed as the 'ability to carry out a director's instructions faultlessly'. Her own approach is much more spontaneous; 'The more I go on with this craft, the less I know, and the more I'm in awe of people who do it well.' This is admirably modest and probably not disingenuous. Certain critics, such as Pauline Kael on *The New Yorker*, hate her, and taunt her with the epithet 'android' (it is the substance of Kael's review of *Postcards*). Against which, it might be argued that the films Streep has appeared in have been, almost without exception, interesting and adult works of art; and it is not unreasonable to assume that some of their artistic success might be owing to the integrity and emotional intelligence of their star.

There are tricky films to get out of the way first. Streep won the Best Actress Oscar for her part in *Sophie's Choice* (1983). The film is powerful but meretricious at the same time, with a falsity issuing out of the original novel. The famous dilemma of the title – surrender or not of her child – is bogus, and vulgarises the tragic Jewish-Nazi subject matter from which it springs. (Oddly enough, such objections don't hold against an earlier television series Streep starred in, *Holocaust*, 1978, which is populist, but all of a piece. There her performance – as a young Aryan German woman trying to save her Jewish husband – had a genuine and memorable poignancy.)

Kramer vs. Kramer (1979) was also slightly stupid in retrospect, for all its popularity and Oscar successes (Meryl won Best Supporting Actress). The film is Dustin Hoffman's not Streep's; an antidote to previous 'feminist' movies like *An Unmarried Woman* (1978, directed by Paul Mazursky). Streep plays the bitchy wife in the divorce proceedings – rather well. Elegant, aloof and somewhat dangerous women were thought, at that early period of her career, to suit her. She is handsome and aristocratic – beautiful skin, clear blue eyes – and looks as if she can hold her end up in battle (her stores of 'vulnerability' were to be tested later). In *Manhattan* (1979), a Woody Allen comedy of New York manners, she leaves her husband coldly for another woman – as she did with conscience in *Falling In Love* (1985), magically paired with De Niro in a 'Brief Encounter' for 80s New York. She is excellent, too, as the Senator's PA in a film by Alan Pakula, *The Seduction Of Joe Tynan* (1979). Along with Michael Ritchie's *The Candidate* (1972, starring Robert Redford) this film was one of the best pictures of politics-in-action to emerge out of the 1970s. Sleek in attire, seductively sexy in her command of Southern vowels (Streep is famous for being able to 'do' any accent), smoothly calculating as to the ultimate advantage or disadvantage of pursuing an affair with her colleague, hers is as flawless a portrait of ambition as one has come across in post-war American cinema.

In *The French Lieutenant's Woman* (1981, Karel Reisz) she played the eponymous heroine, a real pre-Raphaelite beauty. The film is delectably pictorial. The flaw is not in the acting, but in the adaptation by Harold Pinter of the original John Fowles novel. The film is split into two different stories that are supposed to interact, but in fact they remain resolutely separate – sketches towards a life rather than the picture of a complete life itself. In the longer, Victorian, episode we are troubled by our inability to see into the heart of the heroine, this ravishing redheaded governess. Is she in love with the hero (Jeremy Irons, a geologist)? Or is she in the grip of a mania (the memory of her vanished French officer)? To known whether she is *serious* or *mad* would alter our view of her character. But the film-maker himself is unsure, so that, in the end, the magnificent performance of Streep becomes merely a species of melodrama.

One of the strengths of Meryl Streep as an actress is an ambiguity as to whether she is confident or shy. At times she is as shy as an animal: she seems like one of those timid, aristocratic gazelles at their waterhole who take flight at the first sight of danger. She is like this in Michael Cimino's powerful Vietnam drama, *The Deer Hunter* (1978), for which she received her First Academy Award nomination. In a film about men at arms, Streep's is the residual womanly presence. Her doom and her destiny is to keep a place in her heart for a lover who will never come home to her. Her consciousness is finer than the consciousness of the men she is involved with. Brave, abandoned and weeping, jabbing at the supermarket goods with her price marker, she communicates the dignity of a woman gracefully unaware that she is superior to her surroundings.

All things considered, no contemporary actress has a stronger, more commanding presence. And this may be because (despite the talk of 'spontaneity') she really *is* an actress, trained on the classical boards. Streep (the origin of her name is Dutch) was raised in a middle-class family. Her father was a pharmaceuticals executive, her mother a commercial artist, and she herself was educated at Vassar and Dartmouth. The decisive moment of her career came immediately after, at Yale, where she enrolled at the University's famous drama school. The plays she performed in her three years at New Haven – numbering an impressive 40 in all – gave her a sense of the classical, and a basis in the European tradition, that has animated all her subsequent film work.

Her films of the 80s and early 90s kept up, maybe even improved upon, her previous high standards. Sidney Pollack's *Out Of Africa* (1986) is one of those movies that might have been critically damned as middle-brow but in fact are highly affecting works of drama. Streep plays the famous Danish writer Karen Blixen, married to a syphilitic baron (Klaus Maria Brandauer) and in love with a charming but feckless white settler (Robert Redford). One ought not really to care about these rich spoiled people, yet the scene where Streep reads the poem by Housman beside her lover's grave is, against the odds, one of the most beautifully moving in modern cinema.

Similarly, *A Cry In The Dark* (1989) could have been merely documentary and exterior in its retelling of the notorious case in Australia when a child was (or wasn't) abducted by a dingo; but film-maker Fred Schepisi's decision to go for a subjective vision of the mother's torment is triumphantly vindicated in the actress' authoritative performance. (Here she added perfect Australian to the Polish, English and Danish already achieved.)

Schepisi had directed her in an earlier film, *Plenty* (1985), an adaptation of the stage play by David Hare. Though the film is – like all Schepisi's work – handsomely mounted with fine widescreen effects and period detail, and although Streep's acting (as a neurotic upper-class Englishwoman at the time immediately after the Second World War) is more than adequate technically, the dreary bitterness of Hare's world view scuppers audience identification, so that one would not think of it as a film to return to. Not so *Silkwood* (1984), Mike Nichols' chilling account of the Karen Silkwood case in which the actress played the nuclear-contaminated factory worker – a small-town, chain-smoking, working-class Texan – with a raw conviction that many consider to be her best performance.

Two last, somewhat unsuccessful, films are worth mentioning for the record. *Heartburn* (1988), from a novel and script by Nora Ephron, was glib and sub-standard, but Streep bravely rose above it as a betrayed wife (husband: Jack Nicholson). Though she can be an engaging light actress, a detour into black comedy with *She-Devil* (1990) didn't, for one reason or another, come off, and critics castigated her with what amounted to glee, happy to pounce on what they perceived (unfairly) as a weakness in her armoury.

With *Postcards From The Edge* (1991), however, the fictional recounting of *Star Wars* actress Carrie Fisher's stormy relationship with her mother (magnificently played by Shirley MacLaine) Meryl Streep was once again triumphantly at the top of her form, even breaking into song on screen and revealing a fine singing talent. Her Best Actress Oscar nomination made her ninth Academy Award nomination in all – a staggering acknowledgement of a career which still had a long run ahead of it – almost equalling Katharine Hepburn's lifetime record of 12. But her desire to play comedy was ill-served by the unfocused script of *Death Becomes Her.*

In private life, Meryl Streep is married to sculptor Donald Gummer. The couple have four children and live far from the tarnished glitter of Hollywood, on the Eastern Seaboard.

1977 Julia **1978** The Deer Hunter **1979** Manhattan; Kramer vs. Kramer; The Seduction Of Joe Tynan **1981** The French Lieutenant's Woman **1982** Still Of The Night **1983** Sophie's Choice **1984** Silkwood **1985** Falling In Love; Plenty **1986** Out Of Africa **1987** Ironweed **1988** Heartburn **1989** A Cry In The Dark **1990** She-Devil **1991** Postcards From The Edge; Defending Your Life **1992** Death Becomes Her

Streisand, Barbra
(Barbara Joan Streisand)

Actress, singer, director
Born 24 April 1942
Brooklyn, New York

Like Fanny Brice, the Ziegfeld singer-comedienne she portrayed to such effect in *Funny Girl* (1968), Barbra Streisand had a Jewish upbringing in Brooklyn, and was considered something of an ugly duckling because of her gawky physique and long and prominent nose; and both she and Brice could put over a song with gusto and make audiences laugh and cry. However, Streisand came from a middle-class household – her father, who died while she was still a baby, taught English and psychology at the local high school, and her mother had harboured acting ambitions. She also differs from her predecessor in that, thanks to modern film, she has reached a far wider audience and, through her dynamic personality, has made herself attractive enough to make more conventional beauties seem insipid and characterless.

While doing various odd jobs such as waitress, usherette and switchboard operator in New York, she studied acting and won a nightclub talent contest in Greenwich Village. In 1962, she landed the small role of Miss Marmelstein, a frumpy office clerk with man problems in the Broadway musical *I Can Get It For You Wholesale*. She literally stopped the show and, a year later, married its leading man, Elliott Gould. She was soon offered the starring role in the Jule Styne-Bob Merrill musical *Funny Girl* on Broadway, a triumphant success which she repeated in the film version directed by William Wyler.

The movie is full of self-conscious references to Streisand's unclassical features, the large nose and mouth, the eyes a little too close together (in fact, cat-like, startlingly blue and beautiful), and her mother deplores the fact that 'If A Girl Isn't Pretty', she hasn't much chance in show business; but when Barbra sang in her throbbing, soaring voice 'His Love Makes Me Beautiful' with conviction, nobody argued with her. She emerged in the 60s, a period of alternative lifestyles and alternative looks, and she was one of those stars – Dustin Hoffman was another – who forced audiences to reassess their preconceived notions of beauty. Her debut screen performance won her an Oscar, shared with Katharine Hepburn for *A Lion In Winter*, the only Best Actress tie in the Academy's history to date. At the same time she divorced Elliott Gould.

Fresh from her huge success in *Funny Girl*, 20th Century-Fox chose Streisand to play the matchmaker Dolly Levi in the film version of the Jerry Herman hit musical, *Hello Dolly*! (1969), directed by Gene Kelly. Although she was far too young for the middle-aged widow, she had the right comedic style and vocal quality, and managed to convince through the sheer infectious energy of her performance. The film, however, proved an expensive flop, as did Vincente Minnelli's *On A Clear Day You Can See Forever* (1970), demonstrating that the traditional Hollywood musical, the natural home for artists like Liza Minnelli and Streisand who were, alas, born too late, was a dying form.

Adapting herself easily to comedy of the screwball variety, Streisand demonstrated that she didn't have to burst into song to establish her star quality. She played an endearing Jewish kook-cum-hooker opposite nebbish intellectual George Segal in *The Owl And The Pussycat* (1970), then varied the role only slightly in Peter Bogdanovich's *What's Up Doc?* (1972), with Ryan O'Neal, and in a few other less amusing vehicles. However, Sydney Pollack's radical chic *The Way We Were* (1973) gave the star the chance to show that her acting talents were not limited to playing dotty, loud-mouthed accident-prone women, and got her an Oscar nomination. The chemistry between Robert Redford, as a politically uninvolved WASP, and Streisand's Jewish left-wing activist, whom he marries, was dynamic enough to draw huge audiences. Both in *Funny Lady* (1975), the reasonably entertaining sequel to her Oscar-winning first picture, and in *A Star Is Born* (1976), produced by Jon Peters, her former hairdresser and then inseparable companion, her singing and acting encompassed a vast range. In fact, the versatile performer earned a second Oscar as composer of the song 'Evergreen', which she sang in the latter film, a second remake of the story of a wife's show-business success in direct contrast to her husband's (Kris Kristofferson) declining career.

It took Streisand almost ten years to set up *Yentl* (1983), her first film as director. Finally, with the actress starring, co-producing, co-writing, and singing all 17 of Michel Legrand's schmaltzy songs, it got off the ground and gathered healthy box-office returns. Based on the Isaac Bashevis Singer story of a Jewish girl in Eastern Europe at the turn of the century, who spends most of the time disguised as a boy in order to pursue rabbinical studies, it was directed with admirable tact, with the feminist message allowed to emerge subtly. In the title role, Streisand was both moving and comic as an intelligent girl with a lust for learning.

Whatever she does as actress, singer or director, Barbra Streisand always arouses intense interest, no more so than when it was announced she would produce, direct, and take part in the screen adaptation of Pat Conroy's massive, sprawling novel, *The Prince Of Tides* (1991). This multi-talented mega-star is nothing if not ambitious but, although her efforts garnered a clutch of

Oscar nominations, she was not honoured with a treasured director's statuette from the Academy – the only major award she had yet to win in a deservedly award-laden career.

1968 Funny Girl **1969** Hello Dolly! **1970** On A Clear Day You Can See Forever; The Owl And The Pussycat **1972** What's Up, Doc?; Up The Sandbox **1973** The Way We Were **1974** For Pete's Sake **1975** Funny Lady **1976** A Star Is Born **1979** The Main Event **1981** All Night Long **1983** Yentl (also director, co-writer) **1987** Nuts (also music) **1991** The Prince Of Tides (also director)

Sutherland, Donald

Actor
Born 17 July 1934
St John, Canada

The lanky, shambling, enigmatically smiling, fish-eyed Donald Sutherland has brought his disturbing and unconventional presence to bear on dozens of films (good and bad) since his breakthrough role of Hawkeye Pierce, the irreverent army surgeon in Robert Altman's *M*A*S*H* (1969). It marked him out as an iconoclastic figure of the 60s generation, but he matured into an actor who has made a speciality of portraying taciturn, self-doubting characters. This was best seen in his roles as the weak, concerned middle-class father of a guilt-ridden teenage boy (Timothy Hutton) in Robert Redford's *Ordinary People* (1980), and as the tormented parent of a drowned girl, seeking solace in Venice in Nicolas Roeg's *Don't Look Now* (1973). He so admired the director of the latter film that he named one of his two sons (by French-Canadian actress Francine Racette) Roeg.

As a result of a highly-praised performance in a college production of James Thurber's *The Male Animal*, Sutherland abandoned his engineering studies at the University of Toronto and took up acting. After a stint as a disc jockey at a Nova Scotia radio station, he enrolled as a student at the London Academy of Music and Dramatic Art, but was considered too tall and ungainly a specimen to get anywhere. However, he obtained a year's work as a stage actor with the Perth Repertory Theatre, and got occasional parts in TV series like *The Saint* and *The Avengers* in London. It was producer Warren Kiefer (after whom Donald's eldest son was named) who put him in an Italian-made horror film, *The Castle Of The Living Dead* (1964), but the actor had to wait three more years until he made any impression on audiences.

Curiously enough, it was Sutherland's big ears which led Robert Aldrich to choose him as one of *The Dirty Dozen* (1967), which led to *M*A*S*H* and stardom. He was at his most laconic, verging on the soporific, in the title role of Alan J. Pakula's *Klute* (1971), an ex-policeman investigating the disappearance of a friend, and getting deeply involved with a prostitute (Jane Fonda). At the time, he and Fonda were in love, and had participated together in the anti-Vietnam War troop show F.T.A. (Free The Army), the film of which Sutherland co-scripted, co-produced and co-directed. His political activism has remained strong since the 60s – his second wife Shirley was arrested in 1970 for having supplied hand-grenades to the Black Panthers – although it only surfaces occasionally in his films, many of them being run-of-the-mill comedies and thrillers. Exceptions have been his two Italian excursions in 1976: Bernardo Bertolucci's *1900*, in which he was a broadly caricatured Fascist thug, and in Fellini's *Casanova*, he coldly calculated seduction under extraordinary make-up. Hugh Hudson's *Revolution* (1986) saw him playing a complex and sadistic British officer, and *A Dry White Season* (1989) gave him the role of a South Africa Afrikaner schoolteacher beginning to understand the brutal realities of apartheid. Donald Sutherland's career reveals a man walking a tightrope between undemanding parts in potboilers and those in which he is willing to take exceptional risks, and his performance in *JFK* (1991), holding the screen with an extended monologue as he spills the conspiracy beans to Kevin Costner, was a tour de force.

1963 Pussycat Alley (GB: The World Ten Times Over) **1964** Castle Of The Living Dead **1965** The Bedford Incident; Dr Terror's House Of Horrors; Fanatic aka Die! Die! My Darling **1966** Promise Her Anything **1967** The Dirty Dozen; Billion Dollar Brain; Sebastian; Interlude **1968** Oedipus The King; The Split; Joanna; Start The Revolution Without Me **1969** M*A*S*H **1970** Kelly's Heroes; Alex In Wonderland; Ace Of The Heart; Little Murders **1971** Klute; Johnny Got His Gun **1972** F.T.A. (doc, co-director, co-swriter); Steelyard Blues **1973** Lady Ice; Don't Look Now; Alien Thunder aka Don Candy's Law **1974** S*P*Y*S **1975** End Of The Game; The Day Of The Locust **1976** Novecento/1900 (Italy); Casanova aka Fellini's Casanova (Italy); The Eagle Has Landed **1977** The Kentucky Fried Movie (cameo); The Disappearance **1978** Les Liens De Sang/Blood Relatives (French-Canadian); National Lampoon's Animal House (cameo); Invasion Of The Body Snatchers; The First Great Train

Robbery; A Man, A Woman And A Bank aka A Very Big Withdrawal **1979** Murder By Decree; Bear Island; Eye Of The Needle; Nothing Personal **1980** Ordinary People; Threshold **1981** A War Story **1982** Max Dugan Returns **1983** Crackers **1985** Ordeal By Innocence **1985** The Trouble With Spies; Revolution **1986** Catholic Boys aka Heaven Help Us; Oviri; The Wolf At The Door; The Rosemary Murders **1987** Bethune **1989** A Dry White Season; Apprentice To Murder; LockUp; The Road Home aka Lost Angels **1990** Eminent Domain **1991** JFK; Buster's Bedroom (Canada); Scream Of Stone (French Canadian) **1992** The Railway Station Man (GB); Buffy The Vampire Slayer **1993** Younger And Younger

Sutherland, Kiefer

Actor

Born 21 December 1966

London, England

Strongly resembling his father, Donald, and intent on being an actor himself since childhood, Kiefer Sutherland made his film debut at the age of 18. Within seven years he had made an astonishing number of films, married and divorced older actress Camilia Kath and embarked on his highly publicised, abruptly called off engagement to actress Julia Roberts.

Born in London where his Canadian parents (his mother is successful stage actress Shirley Douglas) did their drama training, and named for the writer Warren Kiefer, the younger Sutherland was taken to California at the age of four when his parents separated – he to join Jane Fonda and the anti-Vietnam War campaign, she to engage in radical activism with groups like the Black Panthers. Aged ten, the boy was transplanted to the relatively subdued environment of Toronto, where he participated in local theatre workshops, unhappily attended several boarding-schools and dropped out at 16. With some stage work behind him he won the lead in *The Bay Boy* (1984), a coming-of-age drama set in the rural Canada of the Depression, for which he received a Canadian Academy award nomination. After moving to New York he rejected one offer of a soap opera and spent the next year unemployed and broke. A chance assignment modelling jeans provided the wherewithal to get to Los Angeles, where he was hired for an episode of *Amazing Stories* within six weeks and soon after embarked on one movie after another.

Bad boys and crazy, mixed-up youths became his stock in trade, as in Rob Reiner's *Stand By Me* (1986) and Joel Schumacher's *The Lost Boys* (1987). One of his better, largely overlooked, performances was as the lonely misfit who falls in with wild, punky Meg Ryan with tragic consequences in *Promised Land* (1988); one of his lamest was as a gentle hippy in the clinker *1969* (1988), in which, admittedly, he was handicapped by dialogue like 'We don't have to work man, naked people will feed us'. As part of the rootin' tootin' ensemble of *Young Guns* (1988) Sutherland was the nice, poetic one and survived for the 1990 sequel, also a hit. He was more persuasive than lead Michael J. Fox as a coke-snorting yuppie in *Bright Lights, Big City* (1988) but in starring roles he has yet to establish that he can carry a film himself, particularly when it is garish nonsense of the order of *Chicago Joe And The Showgirl* (1990), in which he played a World War II GI deserter in London running amok on a Bonnie-And-Clyde-type spree with the equally at sea Emily Lloyd. Back in an ensemble with Kevin Bacon, Julia Roberts and William Baldwin for Joel Schumacher's intriguing supernatural weirdie *Flatliners* (1990), he fared better again on screen and at the box office. A favourite with young cinemagoers, Sutherland has, through his apparent maturity for his age and his commitment to volume of work, indicated he was in it for the long haul, and he should survive it with little effort if his range expands as he ages.

1984 The Bay Boy **1986** At Close Range; Stand By Me; Crazy Moon **1987** Killing Time; The Lost Boys **1988** Promised Land; 1969; Young Guns; Bright Lights, Big City **1989** Renegades **1990** Chicago Joe And The Showgirl; Young Guns II – Blaze Of Glory; Flatliners; Flashback **1992** Article 99; Twin Peaks: Fire Walk With Me; A Few Good Men **1992/93** The Vanishing

Swayze, Patrick

Actor

Born 18 August 1952

Houston, Texas

Swivel-hipped hunk Patrick Swayze is an all-American bundle of contrasts. In personality he is essentially a 'good ole boy' from Texas, long and happily married to the sweetheart of his adolescence, and crazy about his horses. It comes as no surprise that he was a football star and went to university on a gymnastics scholarship, nor that he has a colourful past as a heavy-drinking, motorcycling hellraiser. What is interesting is that he is a sensitive, sentimental man who cries easily, and, highly-trained from childhood by his dancer-choreographer mother Patsy, spent time with two of America's most prestigious ballet companies – the Harkness and the Joffrey – and was a principal dancer in the Eliot Feld company.

Swayze made his professional debut as Prince Charming in *Disney On Parade* before settling in New York to dance. Ironically, an old football injury necessitated periodic knee surgery and Swayze turned to acting, realising his dancing days were numbered. After dancing in a Broadway musical he assumed the role of Danny in the long-running hit *Grease*. Removing to LA to further his acting studies, he made his film debut with a small role in the roller-disco fluff, *Skatetown, U.S.A.* (1979). In the four years before he got another and better movie part he put in some useful appearances as teens and toughs on TV and made a touching, brave young soldier dying of leukemia in *M*A*S*H*.

The cast list of Francis Ford Coppola's *The Outsiders* (1983) reads like a Brat Pack Who's Who, and at this distance it's interesting to note that while it was Matt Dillon who drew most of the attention at the time, only Tom Cruise – who played one of the smallest roles – has become a bigger box-office star than Swayze, who played big brother Darry. All that the film led to for Swayze, however, was a succession of ordinary military/youth/athletic fare in features, but his television work culminated in the flashy, heroic lead in the Civil War epic mini-series *North And South* in 1985 – followed by the continuation, *North And South Book II*, a year later. Handsome in uniform, he cut sufficient dash as a lover and a fighter to keep the series' diverted multitudes dewy-eyed and drooling. No one, including the actor, however, was prepared for the *Dirty Dancing* (1987) phenomenon. An extremely low-budget ($5 million) period romance aimed at teens, it took back many times its cost in the US and was as successful internationally, thanks to female audiences slavering over the gyrating star. While it started off promisingly as a coming-of-age comedy well set in the Catskills mountain resort scene of the early 60s, *Dirty Dancing* degenerated into melodramatic piffle. No one cared because leading lady Jennifer Grey gave an utterly charming performance, Swayze's body was breathtaking, and the skimpy plot gave him an opportunity to dance on film – possibly for the last time, since the old knee injury again troubled him and he had another operation in the middle of filming.

An overnight sensation, Swayze now had plenty of offers but the films he did were disappointing. He was signed for *Total Recall* but the project fell through, to reappear several years later snapped up by Arnold Schwarzenegger. Although Swayze was pleasing as the macho beefcake bouncer of *Road House* (1989) – 'It's my way, or the highway!' – he was in danger of becoming history with the risible *Next Of Kin* (1989).

Then, unheralded in a season prepared for a stream of expensive action films, *Ghost* (1990) took audiences and the industry unawares. Swayze may be nobody's idea of a yuppie investment banker, but once he got his shirt off and got down all was well, the film's cute mix of supernatural slush, romance and suspense (bolstered by a sharp comic performance from Whoopi Goldberg) proving so captivating it took over $200 million to become the top-grossing film of the year. All Swayze needed to do now was hold out for good movies. His casting as a Zen surfer/crime mastermind in *Point Break* (1991) was settled before *Ghost* materialised, but a serious role as a troubled American doctor finding new purpose in life in the slums of Calcutta, in Roland Joffé's ambitious *City Of Joy* offered him his first real stretch in a prestige project; and he could be proud of his work in the troubled, not entirely successful production. Swayze, who is also a singer-songwriter and had a Top Five hit with a single from *Dirty Dancing*, has expressed hopes to do a good, last dance film with his dancer wife Lisa Niemi.

1979 Skatetown, U.S.A. **1983** The Outsiders; Uncommon Valor **1984** Grandview U.S.A. (also choreographer); Red Dawn **1986** Youngblood **1987** Dirty Dancing; Steel Dawn **1988** Tiger Warsaw **1989** Road House; Next Of Kin **1990** Ghost **1991** Point Break **1992** City Of Joy

T

Tandy, Jessica

Actress
Born 7 June 1909
London, England

To win an Oscar at any age is an achievement, but to win it at 81, more than half a century after one's film debut, is remarkable. Jessica Tandy's Best Actress award for *Driving Miss Daisy* (1990) was not given for sentimental reasons, but for her superb rendering of the obstinate, wealthy Jewish widow, who gradually develops a close friendship with her black chauffeur (Morgan Freeman). Like her almost exact contemporary, Don Ameche, she was discovered by a whole new generation of moviegoers, while much older people renewed their acquaintance with an actress they remembered in a number of films some decades earlier. However, it was to the theatre that this English-born actress devoted most of her career, and where she was best known.

She studied for the stage at the Ben Greet Academy of Acting, and made her debut at the age of 16. Her first film appearance, in *The Indiscretions Of Eve* in 1932, coincided with the year of her marriage to British actor Jack Hawkins. One more film, a whodunnit, *Murder In The Family* (1938), was all she could manage in her busy schedule, which included several Shakespeare productions. Two years after her divorce from Hawkins in 1940, she met and married Canadian-born stage and screen actor Hume Cronyn, and the couple settled in the USA, where they became a popular husband-and-wife team in plays such as *The Fourposter* (1951) and *The Gin Game* (1978), for which she won a Tony. But, in a distinguished stage career, her most celebrated performance was as the original Blanche Dubois in Tennessee Williams' *A Streetcar Named Desire* on Broadway in 1947.

Tandy's film work has been sporadic, but she is remembered for her performances as Gregory Peck's spiteful sister in *The Valley Of Decision* (1945), the supportive wife of Rommel (James Mason) in *The Desert Fox* (1951), and as Rod Taylor's possessive mother in Alfred Hitchcock's *The Birds* (1963). She began to appear in movies with more regularity in the 80s, notably as a member of the rejuvenated elderly community in *Cocoon* (1985) and *Cocoon: The Return* (1988), and as dotty Faye, the wife of gruff Frank (Hume Cronyn), whose New York brownstone is saved from demolition by tiny flying saucers from outer space in *batteries not included* (1987).

1932 The Indiscretions Of Eve **1938** Murder In The Family **1944** The Seventh Cross **1945** The Valley Of Decision **1946** The Green Years; Dragonwyck **1947** Forever Amber **1948** A Woman's Vengeance **1951** September Affair; The Desert Fox **1958** The Light In The Forest **1962** Hemingway's Adventures Of A Young Man **1963** The Birds **1974** Butley **1981** Honky Tonk Freeway **1982** Best Friends; Still Of The Night; The World According To Garp **1984** The Bostonians **1985** Cocoon **1987** batteries not included **1988** Cocoon: The Return; The House On Carroll Street **1990** Driving Miss Daisy **1991** Fried Green Tomatoes At The Whistle Stop Café **1992** Used People

Taylor, Elizabeth

Actress
Born 27 February 1932
London, England

By the 1980s, Elizabeth Taylor's feature film career, which had begun almost 40 years previously, was fading from sight; by the 90s it appeared to have gone forever, her appearances confined to TV movies of glitz, gloss and drivel, but which showcased her not inconsiderable gifts and her legendary and perennial beauty.

Undoubtedly the last of the Great Movie Stars in a tradition which goes back to Theda Bara and Gloria Swanson in the silent era, Taylor has remained one of the world's most famous women, with every detail of her romances, illnesses, and fabled jewels, commanding the attention of the public the world over.

Born in England to American parents who courted high society, her fate was changed by the outbreak of World War II which took the family back to the US. There, Frances Taylor, an art dealer, set up shop in Beverly Hills, thus developing a network of influential contacts in the movie colony. Elizabeth's mother, herself a former actress of disappointed aspirations, decided that her raven-haired, violet-eyed daughter, already exceptionally pretty, should fulfil the destiny she had denied herself. At that time Hollywood was in the grip of Anglophilia, and there was a demand for children with authentic English accents. Elizabeth was offered a contract by Universal, who cast her in *There's One Born Every Minute* (1942), then left her idle and declined to renew her contract, believing she would never be a star.

The following year, MGM hired her to play opposite Roddy McDowall in *Lassie Come Home*; they gave her a bit in *The White Cliffs Of Dover* and loaned her to Fox for a small part in *Jane Eyre* (both 1944). In 1943, she had been seen by MGM producer Pandro S. Berman, about to make *National Velvet* (1945), the story of a horse-mad child who trains a Grand National winner. Berman felt the girl was too short for the role of Velvet Brown but decided to wait for her to grow into it. The film proved the turning point of Elizabeth's life, cementing her lifelong love of animals, bringing her a contract with Hollywood's most powerful studio, and making her a star with a capital 's' at the age of 13.

As the vicissitudes of Taylor's life and career were to prove with monotonous regularity, her early and astounding success was bought at a heavy price. The first instalment paid was the loss of her adolescence for, like other studio children (notably Judy Garland), she was literally owned by MGM, educated in the studio schoolroom, working to order, her freedom curtailed, her friendships monitored. The high school prom, the parties, the first tentative dates with boys so essential to growing up, were experiences she had only on screen, never in reality. Little wonder then that her private life became a catalogue of doomed love affairs and failed marriages beginning, when she was an inexperienced 17-year-old, with her first marriage to Nicky Hilton, son of the multimillionaire hotel magnate. Ill-equipped to recognise that Hilton's boorish behaviour was a sign of deeper disturbance, she left him after seven months of misery – but not before the studio had capitalized on her nuptials by starring her in the hugely successful romantic comedy *Father Of The Bride* (1950).

Shortly afterwards, on loan-out to Paramount, George Stevens directed her in *A Place In The Sun* (1951), a dark tragedy that presented her with new challenges to her acting range, and began an intimate friendship with her troubled co-star, Montgomery Clift, that lasted until his death. It was doubtless her feeling for Monty (and her later friendship with Rock Hudson) which shaped her sympathetic attitudes to homosexuality and resulted in her becoming a tireless and influential campaigner and major fundraiser on behalf of AIDS sufferers some 35 years on.

The early MGM years kept the young actress very busy, but the movies themselves were largely forgettable, although she played Meg in Mervyn LeRoy's remake of *Little Women* (1949), and it's worth noting *Conspirator* (1950), made on location in London, because it evidences her extraordinary physical maturity, playing Robert Taylor's sexy wife though still in her teens.

In 1952, Elizabeth married the English actor Michael Wilding, extracting five relatively happy years and two children from the liaison before it ended in divorce. Professionally, one can draw a veil over the next eight or nine films, which included such deathless titles as *Callaway Went Thataway* (1951), and some mediocre period blockbusters such as *Ivanhoe* (1952) and *Beau Brummel* (1954), as well as the ill-fated *Elephant Walk* (1954) opposite Peter Finch, in which she replaced an ill Vivien Leigh halfway through shooting in Ceylon. Matters improved when she co-starred, again for George Stevens, with Rock Hudson and James Dean (killed towards the end of shooting) in *Giant* (1956), an epic melodrama from Edna Ferber's novel about an oil tycoon, in which Taylor shone. Indeed, throughout her career, although hampered by lack of formal training and a voice whose scratchy quality has proved a liability, this highly intelligent woman has excelled in weighty roles, giving the lie to detractors who considered her just a pretty face.

She will be remembered for her Maggie the Cat, with Paul Newman in *Cat On A Hot Tin Roof* (1958), all the more extraordinary because it was filmed immediately after the tragic death of her adored third husband, the flamboyant showman Mike Todd. For him she converted to Judaism (a faith she has retained) and they had a daughter, but he was killed after barely a year of marriage. She was splendid in *Suddenly Last Summer* (1959), holding her own against Katharine Hepburn; creditable in the mess of *Butterfield 8* (1960), for which she got the Best Actress Oscar, an odd choice, reflecting Hollywood at its most sentimental and causing co-nominee Shirley MacLaine to remark that 'I lost out to a tracheotomy.' But Taylor's major and lasting achievement was for her uncompromisingly honest, Academy Award-winning portrayal of Martha, the unhappy virago of

Who's Afraid Of Virginia Woolf? (1966), opposite her then husband, Richard Burton.

This superb film was also the professional high point of the Burton years. In 1960, Taylor began filming *Cleopatra* (1963) in England, co-starring Stephen Boyd, when she was taken gravely ill and nearly died in the London Clinic. (It was the first of several major illnesses.) The film was abandoned, but was resuscitated two years later in Rome where it became one of the most costly and well-publicised screen catastrophes of the age. Not the least of its notoriety came from the love affair between the married Burton (replacing Boyd) and Taylor, then the wife of crooner Eddie Fisher, whose desertion of his wife, Debbie Reynolds, for Elizabeth, had heaped scandal and opprobrium on the couple's head.

Burton was the great love of Elizabeth's life, but it was a destructive relationship. They divorced in 1974, after several years of alcoholic turbulence, remarried on an African river bank in 1975, and were divorced again a year later. During those years, in the quest for togetherness and money, they co-starred in a string of really poor films such as *The Sandpiper* (1965), of which, aside from *Virginia Woolf*, only Zeffirelli's rumbustious version of *The Taming Of The Shrew* (1967) showed them off to any advantage. And Elizabeth, too, commanding an uprecedented $1 million per picture, fell into the money trap, making a lot of movies solo which did nothing to enhance her career (*Secret Ceremony*, 1968, *Zee & Co*, 1972, are just two examples).

The sorry list of flops continued throughout the 1970s and, more sadly still, was added to by films that were released barely at all or never: *The Blue Bird* (1976), *A Little Night Music* (1977) and her last feature to date, playing an operatic diva for Zeffirelli in *Young Toscanini* (1988). With Burton, she rather foolishly exposed herself to the rigours of the live theatre, appearing with him in *The Little Foxes* in New York and London, and Coward's *Private Lives* in New York.

Another marriage, to US senator John Warner, took place in 1976 and, for a while, grown fat and falling prey to illness, alcohol and pills, Elizabeth played the central role of a campaigning politician's wife. Needless to say, the marriage lasted only a short while, but the actress pulled herself together at the Betty Ford clinic, emerging older but as lovely as ever. By the 1990s, it was impossible to predict whether or not she would grace the screen again in a role worthy of her but, like Garbo and Monroe, she was already a legend.

The long career and extraordinary life of Elizabeth Taylor have unsurprisingly, several filled biographies, most notably a long but very readable tome by Kitty Kelly and a comprehensive and gripping account by Alexander Walker.

1942 There's One Born Every Minute **1943** Lassie Come Home **1944** Jane Eyre; The White Cliffs Of Dover **1945** National Velvet **1946** Courage Of Lassie **1947** Cynthia; Life With Father **1948** A Date With Judy; Julia Misbehaves **1949** Little Women **1950** Conspirator; The Big Hangover; Father Of The Bride **1951** Quo Vadis (unbilled cameo); Callaway Went Thataway (cameo); Father's Little Dividend; A Place In The Sun **1952** Love Is Better Than Ever; Ivanhoe **1953** The Girl Who Had Everything **1954** Rhapsody; Elephant Walk; Beau Brummel; The Last Time I Saw Paris **1956** Giant **1957** Raintree County **1958** Cat On A Hot Tin Roof **1959** Suddenly Last Summer **1960** Scent Of Mystery (unbilled cameo); Butterfield 8 **1963** Cleopatra; The V.I.P.s **1965** The Sandpiper **1966** Who's Afraid Of Virginia Woolf? **1967** The Taming Of The Shrew; Doctor Faustus; Reflections In A Golden Eye; The Comedians **1968** Boom! Secret Ceremony **1970** The Only Game In Town **1971** Under Milk Wood **1972** Zee & Co aka X, Y & Zee; Hammersmith Is Out **1973** Divorce His, Divorce Hers; Night Watch; Ash Wednesday **1974** That's Entertainment (on-screen co-narrator); The Driver's Seat aka Identikit **1976** The Blue Bird; Victory At Entebbe **1977** A Little Night Music **1980** The Mirror Crack'd **1981** Winter Kills **1988** Young Toscanini

Taylor, Lili

Actress

Born 1966 or 67

Chicago, Illinois

Gutsy young Lili Taylor, who thus far has eluded being type cast, already had ten years' acting experience behind her when she made her feature film debut at 20 in *Mystic Pizza* (1988). One of a trio of ingénue female leads in the well-received 'girls coming-of-age' sleeper, Taylor not only held her own but made a strong impression as the plucky, independent, unpredictable pizza-slinging JoJo where a less-assured film debutante might have been lost between the more experienced, vulnerable appeal of Annabeth Gish and the obvious charm of ravishing Julia Roberts.

Taylor, raised in the pleasant Chicago suburb of Glencoe, is the second youngest of six children and, although a self-characterised loner at school, began appearing in local theatre as a child. A graduate of Rock Hudson and Ann-Margret's alma mater, New Trier High School, she studied drama briefly at DePaul University in Chicago before moving to New York in 1988. (Before leaving Illinois she was engaged for a fleeting appearance in John Hughes' Chicago-set *She's Having A Baby* 1988.) There she made her off-Broadway debut in *What Did He See?* and won several television roles before entering films. Taylor's other theatre credits include work with Chicago's Northlight Repertory Theatre, the Actors Theatre of Louisville and a drama group tour of Czechoslovakia.

Following *Mystic Pizza*, the young actress made a bright and funny supporting player in Cameron Crowe's fresh, original teen comedy-drama *Say Anything* (1989) as a guitar-strumming, dirge-wailing buddy of John Cusack's, and delivered a moving cameo as the young widow of the soldier killed by Tom Cruise's Ron Kovic in Oliver Stone's *Born On The Fourth Of July* (1989), adding to her growing reputation as a girl who can deliver the goods. She was duly considered up to leading roles and was cast as a tough, restless Canadian drifter in *Bright Angel* opposite Dermot Mulroney and Sam Shepard in 1990, followed immediately by *Dogfight*, in which she plays River Phoenix's entrant in an 'ugliest date' competition. Between film assignments, Taylor continues to do theatre work, mainly contemporary plays with avant-garde young companies in New York, where she continues to live.

1988 Mystic Pizza **1989** Say Anything; Born On The Fourth Of July **1990** Bright Angel **1991** Dogfight **1992** Watch It **1992/93** American Dreamers **1993** Short Cuts

Thompson, Lea

Actress
Born 31 May 1961
Rochester, Minnesota

A small, delicate-looking but perky actress, Lea Thompson showed much promise in her first feature roles, but appeared regularly in downmarket teen fare. She is best known for her multiple roles in the *Back To The Future* series.

Raised without television, Thompson was encouraged by her parents to study dance. She was so successful that she was dancing professionally by the age of 14, and won scholarships to the Pennsylvania Ballet, American Ballet *and* the San Francisco Ballet. She gave up the discipline because she felt her height would prevent her from becoming a prima ballerina. Instead, she moved to New York, became a waitress, and pursued a career in acting. Her first break involved a series of more than 20 commercials for Burger King. Within a year she made her feature film debut, in *Jaws 3-D* (1983). She followed it immediately with *All The Right Moves* (1983). This unusually gritty, working-class teen picture, directed by Michael Chapman, was probably Thompson's best showcase after her recurring Lorraine Baines McFly role. As the home-town girlfriend of school football jock Tom Cruise, Thompson stole the movie. She's touchingly vulnerable in the central sex scene, sassy and determined elsewhere.

These qualities are also evident in *Red Dawn* (1984), where she joined Patrick Swayze, Charlie Sheen and the boys in repelling the Reds, and *The Wild Life* (1984) – a feeble follow-up to *Fast Times At Ridgemont High* (1982) that nevertheless convinced Robert Zemeckis to cast Eric Stoltz as Marty McFly and Thompson as his amorous mother in *Back To The Future* (1985). Stoltz was replaced by Michael J. Fox two weeks into shooting, but Thompson found the right light touch, with a hint of caricature, in her dowdy, whiney 1980s characterisation, and a fresh, flirtatious sexiness in the 1950s sequence. This was surface acting, but it suited the surroundings while Zemeckis pulled the strings. In *Back To The Future 11* (1989) she added two more variations to the role, at 77 years old, and as a distorted version of her 1985 self, this time married to Biff Tanen, complete with physical accoutrements ('Mom, you're so – big!'). The third instalment (1990) introduced her as Marty's great-great grandmother Maggie McFly. No matter that her presence here was illogical and her piping Irish accent wobbly, the series was all about recognition by this time.

Unfortunately, none of Thompson's subsequent pictures have gone beyond the artificial. Lightweight vehicles like *Space Camp* (1986) and *Casual Sex?* (1986) did nothing to stretch her as an actress, and she coasted on her lithe body and pert charms in *Some Kind Of Wonderful* (1987), in which Eric Stoltz takes her – Miss Amanda Jones – on the ultimate date, only to go off with tomboy Mary Stuart Masterson at the end. Meanwhile, she was unfortunate to find herself in a sex scene with *Howard The Duck* (1986), a colossal flop from producer George

Lucas. Her character roles in the television movies *Nightbreaker* (1989), *Montana* (1990) and the PBS Playhouse co-production *The Wizard Of Loneliness* (1988), suggested that Thompson was ready for a change, and quite capable of it.

1983 Jaws 3-D; All The Right Moves **1984** Red Dawn; The Wild Life **1985** Back To The Future **1986** Howard The Duck; Space Camp **1987** Some Kind Of Wonderful **1988** Casual Sex?; Going Undercover; The Wizard Of Loneliness **1989** Back To The Future 2 **1990** Back To The Future 3 **1992** Article 99

Thurman, Uma

Actress
Born 1970
Boston, Massachusetts

'Uma', according to the myth, is an ethereal form of the Hindu female divinity Siva-Shakti. A more banal interpretation suggests it is an Americanised Swedish name. Presumably it depends on whether you ask Thurman's father, a professor of Buddhism and comparative literature, or her Swedish-born mother, a psychologist and former model (previously married to LSD guru Timothy Leary). Appropriate parents for this Pre-Raphaelite beauty, with her beguiling mixture of the other-wordly and the down to earth.

Thurman grew up on the Amherst College campus and at her family's bohemian retreat in Woodstock, New York. When she was 12, her father took the family to India for a two-year sabbatical and her mother tutored her. Back in the States, she went to a New England boarding-school, then, determined to become an actress, attended the Professional Children's School in Manhattan. At 15 she was washing dishes. At 16 she was modelling. A year later, she had her first film behind her, *Kiss Daddy Good Night* (1987), an independent 16mm thriller. Thurman played the lead, a vamp who seduces then robs men. She does not talk of the project fondly. Nor of her second film, the crude teen comedy *Johnny Be Good* (1988), in which she took on the thankless and implausible task of playing Anthony Michael Hall's girlfriend. 'People kept telling me that *Johnny Be Good* would be important for me, and I kept saying, "It's *not* important",' she reflects.

Dangerous Liaisons (1988) changed everything. The prestigious mainstream film of the year, it was cast with the cream of American actors: John Malkovich, Glenn Close, and Michelle Pfeiffer. As Cecile de Volonges, a virgin corrupted by Malkovich's Valmont, Thurman earned reviews as good as any of them. She is poised yet vigorous, and her transformation from virtuous ingenue to uninhibited teenager is wickedly amusing; it tapped into the dichotomy that both her next two major films focused on. Here is a woman so beautiful she is almost untouchable; unknowable certainly. Yet it transpires she is no goddess, but a woman more in need of intimacy than worship. This was the essence of her role in *The Adventures Of Baron Munchausen* (1989). Terry Gilliam – with his artist's eye – presented her as Botticelli's Venus, adored by Oliver Reed's Vulcan king, but all too ready for a dalliance with the Baron. Thurman's part was too brief here to get much beneath the surface – a waltz through the air and she's gone – but it distilled an impression of her as the most captivating face of the young actresses, the only one who might usefully follow von Sternberg's advice to Dietrich: 'Don't just do something, stand there!.'

Philip Kaufman's *Henry And June* (1990) (her third major costume film) saw her once more as an object of beauty struggling to become a subject. Her June Miller obsesses both Henry (Fred Ward) and Anaïs Nin (Maria De Medeiros). Thurman gives the role a curious, abstruse hard-headedness and thick New Yorkese accent that contrasts bluntly with the effete sensuality espoused by Nin. Not her fault that Kaufman's bathetic script and self-conscious visuals left her stranded in a fog of vaseline.

The actress was almost thrown away in the Hitchcockian *Final Analysis* which centred on the relationship between her shrink (Richard Gere) and her sister (Kim Basinger), but she certainly seized her moments as the disturbed but cunning schemer. Next, Thurman took on romantic comedy in company with Robert De Niro and Bill Murray (*Mad Dog And Glory*), and another thriller (*Jennifer 8*), co-starring with Andy Garcia and John Malkovich.

1987 Kiss Daddy Good Night **1988** Johnny Be Good; Dangerous Liaisons **1989** The Adventures Of Baron Munchausen **1990** Henry And June; Where The Heart Is **1992** Final Analysis **1992/93** Mad Dog And Glory; Jennifer 8 **1993** Even Cowgirls Get The Blues

Tilly, Meg

Actress
Born 14 February 1960
California

Oscar-nominated for *Agnes Of God* (1985), in which she played a disturbed young nun who murders a baby, Meg Tilly very quickly established herself in the ranks of those younger screen actresses who have real class and weight. And yet it was the ballet for which Tilly thought she was destined and for which she began training at the age of 14. However, the shattering of some lumbar vertebrae while dancing led to her rethinking her future. Although California-born, she grew up in British Columbia and, at 16, left Canada for New York where, among other things, she got a part in *Hill Street Blues* and made her movie debut as a bit player in *Fame* (1980). In 1982, Meg moved to Los Angeles where, within six months, she landed her first featured role as Matt Dillon's sympathetic girlfriend in the critically well-received *Tex* (1982), a story of contemporary teenage problems, set in Oklahoma.

Another accident was to befall her, but with a fortunate outcome: cast as Constanze in *Amadeus*, she tore her ligaments just as shooting was about to commence and had to relinquish the job, thereby being available for *Agnes Of God*. By then, she had survived the idiocies of *Psycho II* (subbing for Janet Leigh as a victim) and *One Dark Night* in 1983, and distinguished herself in the wonderfully intelligent *The Big Chill* the same year (as the young, spaced-out but somehow worldly-wise girlfriend of the dead man whose funeral is the focus of the film); and it is a mark of her quality that the co-lead in the silly and fairly nasty horror thriller, *Impulse* (1984), did nothing to halt her progress.

Tilly ended the decade with *Valmont* (1989), Milos Forman's version of *Dangerous Liaisons*, in which she played the tormented innocent, Madame De Tourvel (Michelle Pfeiffer in the rival movie). It was a role perfectly suited to her pale, oval, period face and reticent delivery, and helped erase memories of *Masquerade* the previous year, a romantic thriller of unutterable drivel; and it was the long-awaited Jack Nicholson-directed sequel to *Chinatown* (1974), *The Two Jakes*, which launched this unusual actress into the 1990s.

1980 Fame **1982** Tex; One Dark Night **1983** Psycho II; The Big Chill **1984** Impulse **1985** Agnes Of God **1986** Off Beat **1988** Masquerade **1989** The Girl In A Swing; Valmont **1990** The Two Jakes **1992** Leaving Normal **1992/93** Body Snatchers

Tomlin, Lily
(Mary Jean Tomlin)

Actress

Born 1 September 1939

Detroit, Michigan

One of America's finest stage and TV comediennes, Lily Tomlin has fared less successfully with film, her few successes overshadowed by her more colossal misjudgements. Dropping out of pre-med studies at University to perform in local cabaret (incorporating characters she invented while at college) and study mime with Paul Curtis, she arrived in New York in 1966 and while playing on the coffeehouse circuit got her first short-lived TV exposure on *The Garry Moore Show* the following year. Her big break came with Rowan And Martin's *Laugh-In* (1969–72), where she created two of the mainstays of her live act, Ernestine the garrulous telephone operator and the demonic five-year-old Edith-Ann.

Despite the success of her own TV specials, records and shows, it was not until 1975 that Tomlin made her film debut with a touching dramatic performance as a troubled gospel singer in *Nashville* that won her a New York Critics Award; and she gave a remarkably detailed comic performance two years later as a woman who hires an ageing private eye to find her cat in *The Late Show*. But there really was no excuse for *Moment By Moment* (1978) in which the narrow-faced performer would still have been unconvincing as the older woman seducing John Travolta even if her longtime relationship with the film's director, Jane Wagner, was not becoming increasingly public knowledge. *Nine To Five* (1980), co-starring Jane Fonda and Dolly Parton, though hugely successful at the box office, was similarly dire, but at least Tomlin was allowed one great comic set-piece in which to shine when her downtrodden secretary turns into Snow White and poisons her boss with the aid of some Disneyesque animated animals.

Her own production of *The Incredible Shrinking Woman* (1981) is best described as a travesty, replacing its male predecessor's humanistic philosophy with crude blasts at consumerism and corporate ambition, while Tomlin's three roles were easily overshadowed by Rick Baker's performance as a skateboarding gorilla called Stanley. She came up aces at last with *All Of Me* (1984), as a rich invalid so mean that only orthopaedic bed companies send telegrams to her funeral, but spent much of the film occupying the right-hand side of Steve Martin's body, thus relegating her part to a glorified voiceover. However, *Big Business* (1988), in which she and Bette Midler each played a pair of twins, was another mess where the jokes got lost in the high concept. Although Lily Tomlin's live act is truly outstanding, her lack of conventional looks and her inability to adapt her comedy to the screen have time and again proved an insurmountable obstacle to her film career.

1975 Nashville **1977** The Late Show **1978** Moment By Moment **1980** Nine To Five **1981** The Incredible Shrinking Woman **1984** All Of Me **1988** Big Business **1992** Shadows And Fog; The Player (Cameo) **1993** Even Cowgirls Get The Blues; Short Cuts

Townsend, Robert

Actor, writer, director
Born 6 February 1957
Chicago, Illinois

After finding his thespian feet performing stand-up comedy at Chicago's fabled Second City comedy revue among other places, there was no way to stop the all-encompassing talents of Robert Townsend. The Windy City native attended Illinois State University and Hunter College and intended to pursue a career in baseball before he caught the acting bug.

A veteran of improvisational and experimental theatre, television commercials, stage and screen, it was *Hollywood Shuffle* (1987), his debut foray into directing (as well as producing and writing) that made this skilled performer a talked-about name in Tinseltown. Indeed, Townsend's cunning in getting this semi-autobiographical satire on black actor's problems in Hollywood made at all was remarkable. With $60,000 of his own savings and a cast of friends, Townsend used a mass of credit cards to scrape together another $40,000 to finish the film. He even furnished his crew with UCLA T-shirts so he could claim they were shooting a student film! The Samuel Goldwyn Company liked the result: they paid off the actor's debts and footed *Hollywood Shuffle*'s heavy post-production bill. The film – released the same year as Eddie Murphy's provocative stand-up comedy routine, *Raw* (1987), also directed by Townsend – was a critical and popular success.

Robert Townsend made his feature debut in the hilarious inner-city spoof of *American Graffiti*, *Cooley High* (1974); and, on a totally different, serious note, convinced in Norman Jewison's screen version of *A Soldier's Story* (1983). After a small role in the blazing rock 'n' roll tale *Streets Of Fire* (1983) and an impressive performance in the respectable *American Flyers* (1985), his acting career consisted of solid performances in less-than-notable works: *The Mighty Quinn* (1989) was a stupid, near 'blaxploitation' film in which his performance as the spaced-out prime suspect in a Caribbean murder case investigated by Denzel Washington was one of the few quality ingredients on offer. He began the 90s as producer, writer, director and actor of *The Five Heartbeats*. It flopped miserably, a fate this tale of a black singing group from doo-wop 60s to soul stardom to decline, did not deserve, albeit Townsend lost his grip on the multi-faceted material. Inviting comparison with the young Woody Allen, if Townsend can capitalise on his early success and a positive, if limited, following, his gift for delivering serious points in a comic metier could bear rich fruit.

As actor only unless stated otherwise: **1974** Cooley High **1980** Willie And Phil **1983** A Soldier's Story; Streets Of Fire **1985** American Flyers **1986** Ratboy **1987** Odd Jobs; Hollywood Shuffle (also director, co-writer, producer); Eddie Murphy Raw (director only) **1989** The Mighty Quinn **1991** The Five Heartbeats (also w/d) **1992/93** The Meteor Man

Travis, Nancy

Actress
Born ?
New York City

To play alongside three of the most desirable men in Hollywood in your film debut must certainly be regarded as something of an achievement, and Nancy Travis managed just that, when she was cast in *Three Men And A Baby* (1987) with the handsome starring trio of Tom Selleck, Steve Guttenberg and Ted Danson.

Her acting career began much earlier, however, when she attended New York University and earned a degree in drama before studying with the Circle In The Square repertory company. Her ability was first evident in a touring production of Neil Simon's play *Brighton Beach Memoirs*, and from this auspicious beginning Travis landed a few small roles in TV movies like *High School Narc* and *Malice In Wonderland*. From here, she won the lead role in the mini-series *Harem* (1986), playing an American damsel in distress sold to a Turkish sultan (Omar Sharif), who finds herself part of his harem. It was a very poor series but, unlike many actresses who find themselves confined to TV roles, she was able to step up to her feature film breakthrough as the baby Mary's English mother in *Three Men And A Baby*, Touchstone Films' major box-office success of 1987.

Supporting roles in critical successes *Eight Men Out* (1988) and *Married To The Mob* (1988) followed, topped by a major role in the thriller *Internal Affairs* (1990), opposite Richard Gere and rising star Andy Garcia. As the wife of Internal Affairs officer Ray Avila (Garcia), Nancy Travis was one of the few convincing characters in a film filled with stereotypical women who were portrayed as either lesbians, whores or victims. Within days of completing her work in that film, she boarded a plane for Thailand to appear in the Mel Gibson-Robert Downey Jr comedy, *Air America* (1990). Although third-billed, her part as the peace-corps worker in Laos who is friendly with the Air America pilots who ship goods 'Anytime, anything, anywhere', was slight and a waste of her abilities. Preferring to play characters who know their own minds and who are in charge of their emotions, it was a surprise to see Travis return to play Sylvia again in the poor sequel to *Three Men And A Baby, Three Men And A Little Lady* (1990) albeit with her original role expanded.

In between her film appearances, Nancy Travis remains active in the New York theatre, where she joined the award-winning Broadway run of *I'm Not Rappaport* with Judd Hirsch, and is a founding member of The Naked Angels, a successful off-Broadway theatre company.

1987 Three Men And A Baby **1988** Eight Men Out; Married To The Mob **1990** Internal Affairs; Loose Cannons; Air America; Three Men And A Little Lady **1992** Passed Away **1992/93** The Vanishing

Travolta, John

Actor
Born 18 February 1954
Englewoo, New Jersey

Happily timed to coincide with the disco craze of the mid-70s, *Saturday Night Fever* (1977) rocketed to stratospheric success fuelled by the delirious screams of teenagers (and even many adults!) who fell prey to the physical charms of its leading man, John Travolta. Although tall, dark, blue-eyed and dimpled, the actor's good looks are attractively blue-collar rather than Ivy League, and his lissom body, gyrating sensuously in a white three-piece suit, made him a star overnight. For his portrayal of Tony Manero, a poor Brooklyn boy who finds fame on the dance floor, he earned an Oscar nomination in only his third film.

The youngest of six children, Travolta quit school to pursue an acting career, and managed to find work both on and off Broadway before he was chosen to join the ensemble cast of the TV sitcom, *Welcome Back, Kotter*, in which he popularised the character of smart-ass Vinnie Barbarino. After an unremarked debut in an unremarked film, *The Devil's Rain* (1975), De Palma cast him as the high school rough-neck who douses Sissy Spacek in pig's blood in *Carrie* (1976). It was an efficient performance but gave little hint of his imminent rise to fame. *Grease* (1978), the movie version of the Broadway musical, capitalised on the success of *Saturday Night Fever*, and confirmed his image as a dancer. The same year, however, he switched gear to co-star, fairly disastrously, with Lily Tomlin in *Moment By Moment*, a somewhat old-fashioned and unconvincing love melodrama about a liaison between a good-looking layabout and an older woman estranged from her husband. He did rather better paired with Debra Winger in *Urban Cowboy* (1980) which, once again, allowed him to swing those hips of his in the context of a Texas honky-tonk bar.

But the 1980s were less kind to John Travolta, whose bright star grew dimmer with each successive movie until the phenomenally successful *Look Who's Talking* at the end of the decade. The reason is really to be found in the films themselves rather than in the quality of their star who, in fact, proved that he's capable of some range and doesn't need to dance in order to make an impression. De Palma's *Blow Out* (1981), for example, cast him as a sound engineer who accidentally finds himself embroiled in trying to save Nancy Allen from a psychopathic murderer. It's a slick enough thriller and showcased Travolta to advantage, but the critics and the public just didn't buy the movie and, although the tough-minded Pauline Kael gave Travolta the thumbs up, he failed to get the recognition he was seeking as a 'serious' actor. *Staying Alive* (1983), a sequel to *Saturday Night Fever*, was a botched effort from Sylvester Stallone wearing his director's hat, and nobody had a good word to say for *Perfect* (1985), in which John played a *Rolling Stone* reporter attempting to expose the aerobics industry, represented by Jamie Lee Curtis. Once again, there was nothing wrong with his performance: nobody believed the screenplay.

Displaying a penchant for easygoing, deft romantic comedy in *Look Who's Talking* (and its less popular sequel), John Travolta found himself a big star for the second time around, but *Chains Of Gold* (1990), in which he essayed a caring social worker, was a failure, leaving him still in search of a vehicle which would properly tap his dramatic potential.

1975 The Devil's Rain **1976** Carrie **1977** Saturday Night Fever **1978** Grease; Moment By Moment **1980** Urban Cowboy **1981** Blow Out **1983** Staying Alive; Two Of A Kind **1985** Perfect **1989** The Experts; Look Who's Talking **1990** Look Who's Talking Too **1991** Midnight Rider; Shout

Turner, Kathleen

Actress
Born 19 June 1954
Springfield, Missouri

Statuesque, strong, and so sexy men find her disturbing, Kathleen Turner emerged as the most ambitious, bold and classy of 80s screen goddesses, switching back and forth between spiderwoman and comedienne.

The daughter of a diplomat, Turner spent much of her childhood in Venezuela, Cuba (where she was once treated to sweets by Fidel Castro), and Canada before a period in London in her teens turned her on to theatre and an acting career. After training at Southwest Missouri State University and the University of Maryland she moved to New York, where her first break was a 20-month gig as Nora Aldrich on the popular daytime soap *The Doctors*. Simultaneously, she graduated from off-off-Broadway roles to nine months in the Broadway hit *Gemini*.

In 1981 Turner made a sizzling big-screen debut as the duplicitous femme fatale seducing William Hurt's Southern lawyer into murder and ruin in Lawrence Kasdan's labyrinthine and steamy *noir* homage, *Body Heat*. She was another gold-digging bitch to Steve Martin's *The Man With Two Brains* (1983) before her charmed screen partnership with Michael Douglas confirmed her as a real star in *Romancing The Stone* (1984). In a welcome carry-on from *Raiders Of The Lost Ark*, this canny romantic caper saw the actress at her most appealing as plain Joan, wistful spinster author of trashy love stories who blooms in travail into the heroine of a wild fantasy.

Bravely turning from family fare to arguably the filthiest adult 'mainstream' feature in memory, the blonde bombshell offered an uninhibited performance as the repressed designer by day and reckless prostitute by night, self-destructively enacting female stereotypes from nun to whip-cracker, in Ken Russell's rampant, controversial and frankly compelling *Crimes Of Passion* (1984) – not a major box-office hit but subsequently concealed near many a video machine. Despite her reluctant participation in the crass sequel to *Stone, The Jewel Of The Nile* (1985), and a glowing, Oscar-nominated outing in Coppola's otherwise unsatisfying fantasy *Peggy Sue Got Married* (1986), Kathleen Turner has evidently been more engaged by the dark side, whether it has come in psychological thriller form, as in *Julia And Julia* (1987), in which she was absorbing as a woman leading two lives, or in very black comedy. She was another superior sexpot and a plausible hit-woman in John Huston's savagely wry *Prizzi's Honor* (1985), and a powerhouse as the-mouse-that-roared vindictive wife in the genuinely shocking, sour and highly effective marriage and divorce satire, *The War Of The Roses* (1989), her third screen teaming with Michael Douglas as the 'Tracy and Hepburn of the 80s'. She was also bravely porky and unpleasant as the wife you wish would get lost in *The Accidental Tourist* (1988) for Lawrence Kasdan, but was altogether too much and trying too hard in a conventional comic piece, the noisy, strained update of *His Girl Friday* (1940), *Switching Channels* (1988). Restless during her pregnancy, she was able to fall back on her distinctively smoky, throaty voice to record the dialogue for voluptuous Jessica Rabbit in *Who Framed Roger Rabbit?* (1988) before retaking Broadway with her highly-acclaimed, flagrant Maggie the Cat in *Cat On A Hot Tin Roof*.

Shrewd and driven, Turner is anxious to produce, and acquired the rights to a Robert Stone novel, *A Flag For Sunrise*, as a potential vehicle. Married to estate agent and property developer Jay Weiss, with whom she has a daughter, Turner lives on Long Island.

1981 Body Heat **1983** The Man With Two Brains **1984** A Breed Apart; Romancing The Stone; Crimes Of Passion

1985 Prizzi's Honor; The Jewel Of The Nile **1986** Peggy Sue Got Married **1987** Julia And Julia **1988** Switching Channels; The Accidental Tourist **1989** The War Of The Roses **1991** Warshawski aka V. I. Warshawski **1992/93** House Of Cards; Cloak And Diaper

Turturro, John

Actor
Born 28 February 1957
Brooklyn, New York

One of the most impressively gifted young character actors to emerge in the 80s, John Turturro possesses the sort of riveting on-screen volatility that has made stars out of the likes of Robert De Niro and John Malkovich, though he has neither the physicality and good looks of De Niro nor the sex appeal of Malkovich. Dark-haired and brown-eyed, Turturro has an unromantic curved nose and a goofy, slightly askew mouth and is therefore unlikely to become a 'star', but he has been used to increasingly good effect, in increasingly substantial roles, by some of the industry's most respected film-makers, a career pattern which in the 90s showed no signs of abating.

A native of New York, Turturro grew up in the working-class area of Queens, where his father worked as a builder. He fell in love with movies at an early age and, after graduating from the State University of New York at New Paltz, he won a scholarship to study drama at Yale. Regional theatre and off-Broadway productions followed, with his starring role in *Danny And The Deep Blue Sea* bringing him an Obie award; he made his Broadway debut in 1984 in *Death Of A Salesman*. From there the actor moved into feature films with roles ranging from the truly tiny to the merely modest in such variable fare as the excruciating *Exterminator II* (1984), the cult hit *Desperately Seeking Susan* (1985), Woody Allen's *Hannah And Her Sisters* (1986, in which he had only a couple of lines as an irate TV scriptwriter), and Martin Scorsese's slickly made *The Color of Money* (also 1986). However, it was two films in 1987, Michael Cimino's *The Sicilian*, and, in particular, *Five Corners* that really displayed the actor's combustible potential. The former, a rambling, uneven epic about real-life Sicilian bandit Salvatore Giuliano, cast him as a tough comrade in arms, while the latter saw him as a troubled ex-con subject to unmotivated, shocking fits of violence. His grasp of hard-hitting characterisations was put to further test by writer-director Spike Lee, who cast him in two unlikeable roles: first as Danny Aiello's brazenly racist Italian-American son Pino, in *Do The Right Thing* (1989), followed by his inflexible Jewish club owner Joe Flatbush in *Mo' Better Blues* (1990, a role which contributed to controversial accusations of ethnic stereotyping being brought against Lee). Continuing the ethnic typing, he played Mafia mobsters twice in 1990 (*Men of Respect*, a dull update of *Macbeth*, and *Catchfire*), and another Jew, this time for the Coen brothers, in *Miller's Crossing* the same year. As the double-dealing homosexual Bernie Bernbaum, dangerously, chillingly sharklike in an armchair in one scene, blubbering and beseeching ('Look into your heart' he begs his would-be killer) in the woods in the next, he gave an astonishing performance in a superb film. It is testament to Turturro's mastery of his craft that his characterisation never for a second slides into the potential hamminess of the role but is instead elevated to heights of memorable pathos.

An impressive array of edgy, unpredictable and even psychopathic film personas aside, John Turturro is an actor of great range and was deservedly voted the 'hot actor' of 1990 by *Rolling Stone* magazine; he was a touching, lovelorn Pauley in Spike Lee's *Jungle Fever* (1991); his little-seen gift for comedy was revealed in his short-lived role as an affable, bungling hit-man in *Catchfire*, by far the best thing in the movie; and he was recognised for his lead in the Coen's *Barton Fink* with the Best Actor award at Cannes. In 1992, Turturro extended himself into directing with *Mac*, the story of which was drawn from his father's life, and the screenplay for which he wrote himself.

1984 Exterminator II; The Flamingo Kid **1985** Desperately Seeking Susan; To Live And Die in LA **1986** Gung Ho; Off Beat; Hannah And Her Sisters (cameo); The Color Of Money **1987** Five Corners; The Sicilian **1989** Do The Right Thing **1990** Mo' Better Blues; Miller's Crossing; Men of Respect; Catchfire aka Backtrack; State of Grace **1991** Jungle Fever; Barton Fink **1992** Brain Donors; Mac (also w/d) **1993** Joy Ride

V

Van Damme, Jean-Claude

Actor
Born 1961
Brussels, Belgium

Jean-Claude Van Damme is the popular Belgian star of numerous martial arts movies. He took up karate at the age of 11 (small for his age, he was being bullied at school). He proved a natural at the sport, and also trained with weights to build up his physique. After earning his black belt in Shotokan, Van Damme studied with karate world champion Dominique Valera and soon turned professional. Within a year, he had won the European Professional Karate Association's middleweight championship. Before he was 20, Van Damme was running a successful gymnasium business and earning even more money for his product endorsements and as a model. He studied ballet (hence his unusual grace in the choreographed fights) and acting. Always a keen movie fan, he appeared in the French film *Rue Barbar* (1981), then resolved to try his chances in Hollywood. He sold his gym, flew to Los Angeles, and spent three years in a variety of jobs – chauffeur, bouncer, carpetlayer, martial arts instructor – while he studied English and auditioned. In 1985, he finally got his first break, playing a Russian heavy in the lacklustre attempt to revive the spirit of Bruce Lee, *No Retreat, No Surrender* (1985). He made the most of the chance, and stood out for his energetic performance if nothing else. He played the alien monster in Arnold Schwarzenegger's *Predator* (1987), but this did not turn out to be the 'Battle of the Bulge' Van Damme hoped for. He was unrecognisable throughout, and indeed often invisible.

Determined that he should play a hero, the budding actor took the old-fashioned step of applying to a studio mogul in person – Cannon boss Menahem Golan. Impressed by his blond good looks as much as his evident combat skills, Golan gave him the lead in *Bloodsport* (1987). Based on the life of Frank Dux, the first Westerner to win the international martial arts tournament, the Kumite, this was a violent, low-budget action movie that met with surprising success in America and – especially – abroad. Coinciding with a renewed interest in the martial arts, notably in kickboxing, Van Damme found a market ready to accept crude storytelling in return for high calibre action scenes. Van Damme, still struggling with his English through a strong continental accent, proved an inexpressive actor, but his handsome Aryan features and physical prowess were compensations enough; he became 'the Muscles from Brussels'. There followed a string of what the star himself wearily dismisses as 'karate-shit movies': *Black Eagle* (1988), *Cyborg* (1989) and *Kickboxer* (1989). This last (and most popular) is typical. Van Damme is a responsible, sensitive, professional karate expert who is motivated to withdraw his restraint when his brother is brutally paralysed in the ring and subsequently kidnapped, his girl is raped and his dog knifed (the last straw!). Training in the manner of The *Karate Kid* (1984) is topped off with an extremely vicious showdown. This is not a process of dehumanisation, but of mythification: the fascistic tale of the making of a man, the 'white warrior', virgin-avenger, Jean-Claude Van Damme.

A.W.O.L. (1991), for which Van Damme came up with the story, marks an altogether more positive exercise. It sets up a revenge plot but then resists it; instead, Van Damme becomes in effect a modern-day gladiator, making his way in America the only way he can, with his fists. Technically crude, the film nevertheless invites intriguing parallels between the exploited but well-meaning immigrant hero and Van Damme himself. It also showed the first hints of a performance from the star – something he credits not to an improvement on his part, but to the attention of the director, his friend Sheldon Lettich. With the steady increase in his audience, and his experience, Van Damme insisted that a good project was now more important to him than the size of his own salary. The 90s saw a cinematic duel with Dolph Lungren, *Universal Soldier*, and *Double Impact*, a thriller produced by Michel Douglas with Van Damme as twins which evidenced a step on the way to improved material.

1981 Rue Barbar (France) **1985** No Retreat, No Surrender **1987** Predator; Bloodsport **1988** Black Eagle **1989** Cyborg; Kickboxer **1990** Death Warrant **1991** A.W.O.L. aka Lionheart; Double Impact (also co-writer) **1992** Universal Soldier

Verhoeven, Paul

Director
Born 1938
Amsterdam, Holland

Not a subscriber to the less is more school of thought, Paul Verhoeven is one of the few European directors to have made a place for himself at the top of the American commercial mainstream. He has done so through a combination of straightforward technical proficiency, off-centre black humour and the universally marketable commodity of outrageous (in the dictionary sense of the word) violence. The violence, often merciless in its excess, comes from his wartime childhood in the Hague, witnessing, at ground level, the continuous German bombing and its aftermath, and few film-makers have seemed so driven to show the fragility of the human body with such regularity.

Verhoeven began making films during his six years at the University of Leiden, going on to work as a teacher and to serve in the Dutch navy as a documentary film-maker before going into TV. Although he made his first feature in 1971, it was *Turkish Delight* two years later that first brought his obsession with depravity to an international audience. Released outside Holland with an Emmanuelle-style upmarket porn advertising campaign, it was closer to *Last Tango In Paris* (1973), but without the restraint, as Rutger Hauer's character drowned his malaise in a succession of progressively more unspeakable sexual acts. The director's association with the actor continued with the huge domestic success of the surprisingly restrained (by Verhoeven standards) wartime epic *A Soldier Of Orange* (1978, much cut overseas), and the teenage drama *Spetters* (1980), and eventually facilitated his American movie debut.

Flesh + Blood (1985) was set in the 16th Century at its most repugnant, with dead babies buried in the mud and wells poisoned with plague meat, that made *The Virgin Spring* (1959) look like a Disney film, yet simply used its period as a backdrop for an all-action romp of rape, pillage and torture that had nothing to say. It was up to the surprise hit *Robocop* (1987) to prove to international audiences that while Verhoeven may fill the screen with brain tissue there are also brain cells at work. On the surface a comic-strip revamping of the Frankenstein story with some fairly unrestrained splatter effects, in Verhoeven's hands the material became a cutting satire on rampant capitalism where the same corrupt corporations run both the police and the criminals and regard death simply as an opportunity to upgrade the hardware, while still keeping an emotional centre in the bewildered half-man, half-machine's attempts to remember his human past.

Staying with action (uncomfortable with dialogue in a second language, he finds it easier to communicate his ideas by acting them out somewhat aggressively) the sci-fi thriller *Total Recall* (1990) was an accomplished return to the dream vs. reality conflicts of *The Fourth Man* (1979). Here, Arnold Schwarzenegger negotiated a labyrinthine plot of alternative identities and realities but, despite a high body count and the presence of various deformed mutants, Verhoeven was persuaded to tone down his love of graphic violence in the final cut, raking up his biggest box-office hit in the process. Any impression that he was mellowing out, however little, was immediately dispelled by his insistence on explicit sex scenes in the psychological thriller *Basic Instinct* (1991) that caused its $3m screenwriter Joe Eszterhas and producer Irwin Winkler to leave the project before it had even started shooting – a move that cemented the director's position as one of American commercial cinema's newest and most prominent bad boys for the 90s. But the distinctive duality of character and situation that is the key to Verhoeven's American films proved less acceptable to the politically correct lobby *vis à vis Basic Instinct*. The objections were to the use of Sharon Stone's sexual desires as a mirror of her evil/good sides, although most criticism chose to overlook the fack that it was her lesbian relationship which was the loving one, and her 'normal' side destructive.

Holland: **1971** Wat Zien Ik/Business Is Business **1973** Turks Fruit/Turkish Delight **1975** Keepie Tippel/Cathy Tippel **1978** A Soldier Of Orange **1979** Die Vierde Man/The Fourth Man (released in US and GB in 1984) **1980** Spetters

USA: **1985** Flesh + Blood **1987** Robocop **1990** Total Recall **1992** Basic Instinct

Voight, Jon

Actor
Born 29 December 1938
Yonkers, New York

Before Jon Voight burst onto the screens as Buck, the dumb Texan hustler hoping to service the women of New York in John Schlesinger's *Midnight Cowboy* (1969), the blonde, six-feet-two eyes of blue actor had made three films. In 1967, he had a small part as a daytime cowboy in John Sturges' *Hour Of the Gun*, and was given the title role in *Fearless Frank*, Philip Kaufman's first solo feature, in which he played a country bumpkin who comes to Chicago, is shot by mobsters, and wakes up to find he has the power of a superman. In *Out Of It* (1969), Voight portrayed a stupid high school football hero. There was an element of Buck in all these roles, and he was experienced in the wearing of Western gear because he had also been featured in the TV cowboy series *Cimarron Strip* and *Gunsmoke*.

Of Czech descent (his father was a professional golfer) Voight was an avid participant in amateur dramatics at his Yonkers high school and at Catholic University, from which he graduated in 1960. Although many of his films cast him as a likeable but none-too-bright hunk, his stage work included a role in *The Sound Of Music* on Broadway in 1961, in which the baby-faced 22-year-old sang 'Sixteen Going On Seventeen' to Laurie Peters, who was to become his wife; he played Romeo and Ariel at the California National Shakespeare Festival, and won a Theater World award for his performance opposite Irene Papas in *That Summer, That Fall* in March 1967. He first got know his *Midnight Cowboy* co-star, Dustin Hoffman, in 1965 when Hoffman was assistant director on the off-Broadway production of Arthur Miller's *A View From The Bridge* in which Voight played Rudolpho. Their friendship had always been tinged with rivalry, something which helped them bounce effectively off each other's characters in the movie. Actually, Voight was rather too old for the role of Buck, and overdid the wide-eyed innocence, but he made enough impact to be nominated (with Hoffman) for the Best Actor Academy Award.

Fresh from his triumph in *Midnight Cowboy*, he adopted rimless spectacles and a shabby raincoat for his role as *The Revolutionary* (1970), providing an excellent portrait of a middle-class student who becomes a left-wing political activist. Playing opposite him was Jennifer Salt (the daughter of Oscar-winning screenwriter Waldo Salt), with whom the by-then-divorced Voight was living. It was not a film that was much seen, unlike John Boorman's *Deliverance* (1972), in which he was the one survivor of the four urban buddies terrorised by mountain men in the Appalachians. The actor's interest in liberal causes was well served by Martin Ritt's touching *Conrack* (1974), in which he was splendid as the white teacher assigned to an all-black school in South Carolina, and by Hal Ashby's *Coming Home* (1978), in which he starred as a paraplegic Vietnam vet. For brilliantly negotiating the difficulties of the role, in which he had to move from bitterness and self-pity to liberating romance with Jane Fonda, he was awarded the Best Actor Oscar.

In Franco Zeffirelli's tearjerker, *The Champ* (1979), Voight gave a good imitation of Marlon Brando in *On The Waterfront*, a man who drinks and is a bit soft in the head from the punches he took when he was a boxer, but in another weepie, *Table For Five* (1983), the star, playing an errant father, seemed gloomily lost amid the soap-opera suds. He was far better showing a tougher side as a hardened con on the lam in Andrei Konchalovsky's exciting *Runaway Train* (1985), for which he was once again Oscar nominated. He also gave a well-observed performance in *Desert Bloom* (1985) playing a traumatised World War II veteran stepfather of a 13-year-old girl (Annabeth Gish) at the time of the A-bomb test in the Nevada wastes. Jon Voight, who has a surpringly short filmography, has matured into a fine character actor of weight and presence.

1967 Hour Of The Gun; Fearless Frank aka Frank's Greatest Adventure **1969** Out Of It; Midnight Cowboy **1970** The Revolutionary; The All-American Boy; Catch 22 **1972** Deliverance **1974** Conrack; The Odessa File **1976** End Of The Game aka Getting Away With Murder **1978** Coming Home **1979** The Champ **1982** Lookin' To Get Out **1983** Table For Five **1985** Runaway Train; Desert Bloom **1990** Eternity (co-writer only)

Waits, Tom

Singer, composer, actor
Born 7 December 1949
Pomona, California

Tom Waits is a flamboyant, gravel-voiced singer whose *noir*-hued songs of tawdry lives, romantic losers, booze, brawls and dreams made him a cult figure. His first album, 'Closing Time' (1973), was a melancholy affair in which the influence of beat writers like Burroughs and Ginsberg was as evident as the musical reference points: jazz, bar-room blues and early rock 'n' roll, as well as more experimental figures, like Frank Zappa, who Waits supported on tour. In the albums that followed, 'The Heart Of Saturday Night', 'Small Change', 'Foreign Affairs', 'Blue Valentines', 'Heartattack And Vine', the Waits persona became as colourful as his songs. The live recording 'Nighthawks At the Diner' reveals an artist whose surreal humour and wonderfully evocative vision permeates every sensibility.

Towards the late 70's Waits became involved in the film business. A longtime Los Angelino, he often figured movies in his lyrics, either directly or by suggestion (he even covered 'Somewhere' from *West Side Story*, 1961). In 1979, he played the piano on screen in Sylvester Stallone's *Paradise Alley*, and the next year he contributed the theme song to *On The Nickel* (1980). He was at the piano again for *Wolfen* (1981), then embarked on a unique collaboration with Francis Ford Coppola. His Oscar-nominated soundtrack to *One From The Heart* (1982) acted neither as theme music nor as a traditional musical score for the actors to sing. Instead, Waits and Crystal Gayle – duetting like Beauty and the Beast – narrate and comment on the action as it unfolds before us rather like a Greek chorus. (Waits can be glimpsed playing the trumpet in a brief cutaway.)

Coppola's experiments in form and content corresponded with Waits' own direction. It afforded him a new lease of life creatively, with the bizarre orchestrations of 'Swordfishtrombones' (1982) and 'Rain Dogs' (1985) inspiring increasingly expressionist flourishes from the extravagant, larger-than-life artist. In this context his move into acting looks less like the traditional rock star's ego-trip than a natural progression into the realms of celluloid myth. He has become his own most wonderful creation, and this is what his choice of roles – and more importantly, films – reflects.

Coppola cast him in a one-line cameo as a bar owner in *The Outsiders* (1983), and then in a more extended role as Benny, who runs the poolroom in *Rumblefish* (1983), and looks on dismayed as the kids tear themselves apart. The MC in *The Cotton Club* (1984) represented their fourth consecutive movie together. Waits – unusually suave in a tuxedo – is rather like Coppola's stand-in, directing the actors on stage and off. At the climactic gun play, it is Waits who growls 'It's all part of the show, folks, all part of the show!'.

Rejecting frequent offers to play psychopaths and crazies in mainstream pictures, Waits has concentrated mostly on independent productions. He is a lucked-out disc jockey in Jim Jarmusch's *Down By Law* (1986), swapping dry one-liners with John Lurie and Roberto Benigni behind bars. He took the role, he claimed, when they told him he got to wear a hairnet. Jarmusch also uses two of his songs on the soundtrack. (In a neat joke, Waits was the voice of the disc jockey heard in each episode of *Mystery Train,* 1989 and contributed to the score for *Night On Earth* (1992). Jarmusch later directed a video promo with Waits for the 'Red, Hot and Blue' AIDS project). For Robert Frank and Rudy Wurlitzer, Waits became an unlikely golfer in plusfours (*Candy Mountain*, 1987). *Cold Feet* (1989) did cast him as a psycho, but this was a full-blooded comic turn. Here is a killer who sincerely believes he is executive material. As usual, Waits exhibits special care in his wardrobe – his penchant for fancy head and footwear is abundantly indulged. It is an exuberant, confident performance, rich in detail and invention.

Back in the mainstream, *Ironweed* (1987) was the sort of story Waits might have written himself: all down-and-outs, ghosts, city streets, love and survival. As Jack Nicholson's down-and-out pal, Waits shows himself to be a memorable charactor actor in the Elisha Cook mould, a fitting member of what the Spanish call 'los segundos'.

The concert movie *Big Time* (1988) is a monument to how linked Waits the actor and Waits the singer-songwriter have become. It grew out of his stage musical, *Frank's Wild Years*, which he performed with Chicago's Steppenwolf theatre to much acclaim. The show produced an album that plays like a narrative, which in turn led to a tour, 'Big Time', that became a movie and a live album. In the film, concert footage is cross-cut with odd scenes of Waits the bored box-office manager, the usher, the lighting grip; meanwhile, Waits the artist takes on the guises of a born-again preacher, a Vegas crooner, and an irascible raconteur. . .this in a teasingly ramshackle home-movie format that delivers much more than it promises. It is a take-it-or leave-it, all-or-nothing affair – like the man himself.

Songs only: **1980** On The Nickel **1982** One From The Heart **1984** Streetwise **1989** Sea Of Love **1990** On A Moonlit Night **1992** Night On Earth

As actor: **1979** Paradise Alley **1981** Wolfen **1983** The Outsiders; Rumblefish **1984** The Cotton Club **1986** Down By Law **1987** Candy Mountain (Canada/France/Switzerland); Ironweed **1988** Big Time **1989** Cold Feet; Bearskin **1991** Queen's Logic; At Play In The Fields Of The Lord **1992** Bram Stoker's Dracula **1993** Short Cuts

Walken, Christopher (Ronald Walken)

Actor
Born 31 March 1943
New York City

Christopher Walken, the son of a baker, has been acting most of his life, having made his Broadway debut under the name of Ronnie Walken at the age of 16 in Elia Kazan's production of Archibald Macleish's *J. B.* in 1959. After graduating from Hofstra University, he returned to the New York stage, appearing (as Ronald Walken) in the musicals *Best Foot Forward* (1963), *High Spirits* (1964) and *Baker Street* (1965). Then transformed into Christopher Walken and into a leading dramatic actor, he won acclaim in the role of King Philip of France in *The Lion In Winter* (1966). After some years playing several Shakespearean parts, including Romeo and Lysander at Stratford, Ontario, in 1968, the fair-haired, boyish Walken started to make a name in films, while never completely deserting the theatre.

He was good as the young ex-con helping Sean Connery rob an entire apartment block in Sidney Lumet's *The Anderson Tapes* (1971), but his small role in Woody Allen's *Annie Hall* (1977) as Diane Keaton's apparently normal WASP brother who has a desire to drive into other people's cars, made a huge impact. In the same year, trading on his spoilt-boy good looks, the actor was twice perfect as a gigolo: in James Ivory's *Roseland* and in Tennessee Williams' *Sweet Bird Of Youth* on Broadway. Then he landed his most celebrated film part, in Michael Cimino's *The Deer Hunter* (1978), winning the Best Supporting Actor Oscar for his sensitive performance as one of the three bright-eyed Pennsylvania steel-worker friends sent to Vietnam, who gradually hardens and then deteriorates until his death in a Saigon gambling den.

The now-established star was cast again by Cimino in *Heaven's Gate* (1980), but he could do little in the role of a hired killer out West in the confusing and rambling screenplay of one of cinema's legendary disasters. The soft-featured Walken had an uphill task convincing as a tough, battle-scarred mercenary in *The Dogs Of War* (1981), but was better employed as a man who emerges from an accident with psychic powers in David Cronenberg's *The Dead Zone* (1983). On entering his 40s, Walken developed toughness, and a charismatic aura of the sinister, as he moved into more mature character roles such as Sean Penn's outlaw psychopath father in *At Close Range* (1985), Matthew Broderick's sadistic drill sergeant in *Biloxi Blues* (1987), and the petty crook who gets boxer Mickey Rourke involved in crime in *Homeboy* (1988). Christopher Walken continues to bring his stylish professionalism and polish to bear on even the most unpromising parts, and combined all of his gifts for a virtuoso lead as the title-role gangster in Abel Ferrara's much-maligned *King Of New York* (1990).

1969 Me And My Brother **1971** The Anderson Tapes **1972** The Happiness Cage **1976** Next Stop, Greenwich Village **1977** Annie Hall; Roseland; The Sentinel **1978** The Deer Hunter **1979** Last Embrace **1980** Heaven's Gate **1981** Pennies From Heaven; The Dogs Of War; Shoot The Sun Down **1983** The Dead Zone; Brainstorm **1985** At Close Range; A View To A Kill **1987** Biloxi Blues; Deadline (GB: War Zone) **1988** Homeboy; The Milagro Beanfield War **1989** Communion **1990** King Of New York; The Comfort Of Strangers **1991** McBain **1992** Batman Returns; Mistress; All-American Murder **1992/93** Day Of Atonement

Walsh, J. T.

Actor
Born?
San Francisco, California

Had he not decided to become an actor, it is easy to believe that J.T. Walsh could have been any of the straitlaced figures of petty authority (either by the book or somewhat dodgy) that he specialises in portraying. Born in San Francisco and growing up in Newport, Rhode Island, and in Europe, Walsh worked in sales until joining an off-Broadway theatre company at the age of 30. Following his Tony nomination for David Mamet's *Glengarry Glen Ross* and a number of other impressive stage credits, including supporting Al Pacino's Richard III, his still-born movie career took off in 1987 thanks to two small roles in Barry Levinson films, playing Danny De Vito's boss in *Tin Men* and, more prominently, Robin Williams' uptight superior in *Good Morning, Vietnam* (inspiring the quip 'I've never seen a white man in more desperate need of a blow job.')

He suddenly became a recognisable face in mainstream movies such as *Tequila Sunrise* (1988, as an uptight cop), *Crazy People* (1990, a morally bankrupt ad executive) and *Narrow Margin* (1990, a smooth mob lawyer who makes some unauthorised withdrawals). He was at his best as the lowest-common-denominator producer who needs original ideas translating into stereotypes before he can deal with them in *The Big Picture* (1989), and seems so firmly established on screen as a bottom-line capitalist that not even the role of Bob Woodward in the disastrous *Wired* (1990) was able to do his career much harm – indeed, he had a splendid featured appearance in *The Grifters* (1990, as Annette Bening's former partner-in-crime) and made the most of it.

1982 Eddie Macon's Run **1984** Hard Choices **1986** Power; Hannah And Her Sisters **1987** House Of Games; Tin Men; Good Morning, Vietnam **1988** Tequila Sunrise; Things Change **1989** Dad; The Big Picture **1990** Wired; Crazy People; Narrow Margin; Why Me?; The Russia House; Misery; The Grifters **1991** Iron Maze; True Identity; Defenseless **1992** Red Rock West **1992/93** Hoffa

Walsh, M. Emmet

(Michael Emmet Walsh)

Actor

Born 22 March 1935

Ogdensburg, New York

Despite earning a degree in business and administration, the cinematically omnipresent M. Emmet Walsh, with his wide girth and lived-in looks, has earned a screen niche as the past two decades' greatest living exponent of the kind of characters more usually to be found crawling out from under rocks. Breaking into the acting profession in the late 1960s, he worked his way up to character parts more through guest roles on classic TV shows such as *McMillan And Wife*, *Little House On The Prairie* and *The Rockford Files* than the early bit parts he got as an 'interesting face' in films (although Peter Bogdanovich was among the first to realise that face's comic possibilities).

He developed a talent for seediness that, by the 80s, was to stand him in good stead in both comedy and more menacing drama – the latter most effectively in the Coens' low-budget and superb *Blood Simple* (1984), his most memorable role and the closest he has had to a lead. His pathetic private eye, so short on morals that he regards going from watching an unfaithful wife to murdering her for her cuckolded husband as little more than an opportunity for overtime, not only dominates the film but is the cinematic embodiment of all the soulless human debris that inhabits Jim Thompson novels: *film noir* incarnate in all its decay. A series of small parts in cult movies such as *Blade Runner* (1982) and *Raising Arizona* (1987) as well as much production-line fodder have reinforced the impression of Walsh as every fly's favourite gathering place, yet he was even better cast against type in *Clean And Sober* (1988) as the soft-spoken family man and recovering alcoholic helping Michael Keaton through his addiction with quiet authority and an unsentimental warmth. Casting directors took little note and Walsh – who has played cops crooked and clean, winos, strike-breakers, arms dealers and even vampires – began the 90s with his customary aptitude, filling in spaces as required in a variety of productions.

1969 Stiletto; Midnight Cowboy; End Of The Road; Alice's Restaurant **1970** Loving; The Travelling Executioner; Cold Turkey; Little Big Man **1971** They Might Be Giants; Escape from The Planet Of The Apes **1972** Get To Know Your Rabbit; What's Up Doc? **1973** Kid Blue aka Dime Box; Serpico **1974** The Gambler **1975** The Prisoner Of Second Avenue; At Long Last Love **1976** Nickelodeon; Bound For Glory; Mikey And Nicky **1977** Straight Time; Slap Shot; Airport '77 **1979** The Jerk; The Fish That Saved Pittsburgh **1980** Brubaker; Wildcats; Raise The Titanic; Ordinary People **1981** Back Roads; Reds; Fast Walking **1982** The Escape Artist; Cannery Row; Blade Runner **1983** Silkwood; Scandalous **1984** The Pope Of Greenwich Village; Blood Simple; Missing In Action; Grandview USA; Courage **1985** Fletch; The Best

Of Times **1986** Back To School; Critters **1987** Raising Arizona; Bigfoot And The Hendersons aka Harry And The Hendersons; Broken Vows; No Man's Land; **1988** Sunset; War Party; Thunderground; Clean And Sober **1989** Out Cold; The Mighty Quinn; Red Scorpion; Catch Me If You Can; Chattahoochee **1990** Narrow Margin; Sundown: The Vampire In Retreat **1992** Wilder Napalm; White Sands; Equinox

Wang, Wayne

Director, writer
Born 12 January 1949
Hong Kong

The son of a Chinese engineer-cum-businessman, Wayne Wang combines an understated directorial technique with a deft writing ability which has resulted in some of the most sharply etched but gently observed and evocative films of the 80s. Wang is most comfortable among settings and people he knows well – Chinese communities throbbing with life and a mix of traditional and modern cultures – where he can chart and understand the interplay of his well-drawn characters as they make their way through intriguing narratives which are often spiked with subtle humour.

Wang attended an English language school run by Jesuits in Hong Kong, after which he travelled to the US to study photography at the College Of Arts And Crafts in Oakland, California. He returned to the city of his birth with a Master's degree in film and TV firmly in his pocket and, once there, worked on TV comedy series until 1974, when he embarked on his first film, *A Man, A Woman And A Killer* (which he also wrote). During this period, he also worked as an assistant director for the Chinese sequences of the unsuccessful action picture *Golden Needles*.

After making an award-winning short called *1944*, and lured by the promise of bigger and better things that *A Man, A Woman And A Killer* offered from its heady success in Europe, Wang returned to the US. Winning a grant from the AFI and the National Endowment For The Arts, the young director made a huge impression with his American debut film, *Chan Is Missing* (1982). The tale, set in San Francisco's Chinatown and dealing with the mysterious disappearance of a taxi driver, was written, produced, directed and edited by its creator, and cost no more than a ridiculously unheard-of $2,200. But the result of this low-budget, one-man band operation, filmed in black-and-white, was an endearing comedy-detective story which had a million dollars worth of ideas and style coursing through its frames. Three years passed before *Dim Sum* (1985) emerged. This languidly comic study of a mother-daughter relationship possessed the same charm as *Chan*, but it was regarded as more entertaining than its predecessor, attracting a larger audience and more lasting success.

Wang lost his golden boy appeal with a doomed foray into mainstream Occidental American cinema: *Slam Dance* (1987) starred Tom Hulce, Mary Elizabeth Mastrantonio, Virginia Madsen and Harry Dean Stanton. But this vague tale of a terrorised cartoonist, confused and overwrought, never got off the ground. He returned to welcome form and familiar ground with the much-liked *Eat A Bowl Of Tea* (1989), a pointed ethnic comedy, and followed that with *Life Is Cheap . . . But Toilet Paper Is Expensive* (1990). Benefiting from an intriguing (if unattractive) title, it proved a favourite at several festivals.

Much of the public has tended to marginalise Wayne Wang's films, obviously regarding them as 'foreign' due to their Oriental flavour. There was hope that the 90s would see a change in that parochial view.

As writer-director: **1975** A Man, A Woman And A Killer **1982** Chan Is Missing **1985** Dim Sum **1987** Slam Dance **1989** Eat A Bowl Of Tea **1990** Life Is Cheap . . . But Toilet Paper Is Expensive **1992/93** The Joy Luck Club

Ward, Fred

Actor
Born 1943
San Diego, California

Fred Ward may have the looks of a lumberjack (which he once was) but he has successfully managed to extend his range beyond the reliable, macho outdoors types he embodied in the days when he helped Clint *Escape From Alcatraz* (1980). Becoming an actor after three years in the US Air Force, he studied in New York and in Rome (where he worked in mime by night and dubbed Italian movies by day, as well as appearing in two Roberto Rossellini films), before returning to America and much experimental stage and conventional TV work.

His screen career really took off in 1983 with a series of major roles – the Vietnam vet who puts his torment into twisted metal sculptures in *Uncommon Valor*, the union activist in Mike Nichols' *Silkwood* and, best of all, as ill-starred astronaut Virgil 'Gus'

Grissom in *The Right Stuff*. Effortlessly moving from the good humour of the early scenes to the anguish and domestic strife that followed the loss of his capsule, Ward's role offered the widest range of the film's formidable ensemble and his portrait of a simple, good man disgraced when he is unable to live up to the image NASA's marketing men created, gave the film a human heart and seemed to herald better things. Yet none of his subsequent films fulfilled commercial expectations, while his first starring role as *Remo Williams* (1985), in what was intended as the first of a series of Bond-style action films, failed badly at the box office.

Finding himself back in supporting roles in a series of misfires for the rest of the decade, Ward came back into the limelight with a vengeance in 1990. His superb, self-deprecating comic timing was at its considerable best in the tongue-in-cheek monster movie *Tremors* and his complete lack of vanity made itself apparent in his own production of *Miami Blues* – where his near-destitute cop loses not only his badge and his gun to a psychotic but also his false teeth! – and *Henry And June*, for which he shaved his head and gave one of his most restrained performances as writer and sexual adventurer Henry Miller for *Right Stuff* director Philip Kaufman – a role he took over at the last minute from his *Miami Blues* co-star Alec Baldwin. Once again, Fred Ward's efforts were rewarded with box-office failure and, despite being one of the most likeable and unforced of American screen actors, he had not had a single hit. Though constantly in demand, he seemed just as constantly nudged towards just-outside-the-mainstream movies and character roles, but finally got deserved status with a featured role in *The Player* (as the scene-stealing security chief).

1978 Tilt; **1980** UFOria (released 1986); Carny; Cardiac Arrest; Escape From Alcatraz **1981** Southern Comfort **1983** Timerider; The Right Stuff; Uncommon Valor; Silkwood **1984** Swing Shift **1985** Remo Williams: The Adventure Begins aka Remo: Unarmed and Dangerous; Secret Admirer **1987** Train Of Dreams **1988** Saigon aka Off Limits; The Prince of Pennsylvania; Big Business **1990** Catchfire; Tremors; Miami Blues; Henry And June **1991** Dark Wind **1992** The Player; Bob Roberts (cameo); Thunderheart; Equinox **1993** Short Cuts

Ward, Rachel

Actress
Born 1957
Chipping Norton, Oxfordshire

Even the most charitable of observers would have to admit that few actresses have gone further faster with less talent than Rachel Ward. The daughter of the Earl of Dudley, the 'sex symbol from Chipping Norton' attended the Byram Art School in London then became a top fashion model, appearing in television commercials before becoming an actress. Despite later studying with Stella Adler and Robert Modica she remained consistently poor in performance, unable to use her husky voice beyond a slightly bewildered sub-Jacqueline Bisset monotone and unable to even walk naturally on screen. It was purely on her good looks – she was voted one of the ten most beautiful women in the US in 1983 – that her career was built.

After a couple of undistinguished slasher films that quickly disappeared from her CV, she was officially launched amid much fanfare as a high-class prostitute in Burt Reynolds' *Sharky's Machine* (1981) and followed it with an equally shallow performance as Steve Martin's client and romantic interest in *Dead Men Don't Wear Plaid* (1982), but it was television that was to give her her biggest role. The mini-series *The Thorn Birds* (1983) introduced her (and her husband Bryan Brown) to the millions who didn't go to the cinema and was met with critical acclaim for almost every member of the cast except Ward, whose jarring English accent as the young Australian girl who falls in lust with a priest was as convincing as the rest of her performance. Nonetheless, her glowing beauty and evident sincerity won her some affection from viewers and another trip to Hollywood where, after proving a hollow centre to *Against All Odds* (1984) people began to catch on that there was less to her than met the eye. The result was a pronounced absence from the big screen.

Three years and some study later she finally gave a reasonable performance opposite her husband in the low-budget *The Good Wife* (1987), only to find that no one was interested anymore. Subsequent roles were at best competent (she is no worse than anyone else in the uncontrolled *How To Get Ahead In Advertising*, 1989), but with the advent of the 90s her career seemed to be fading as fast as the looks that once got her better parts than she deserved, albeit that she landed – and coped better that usual with – the female lead in *After Dark, My Sweet* (1990), another steamy steal from the Jim Thompson library of weird thrillers. This proved a respite before her unintentionally 'jolly hockey sticks' appearance in *Columbus: The Discovery*, which cruelly miscast her as Queen Isabella of Spain.

1981 Night School aka Terror Eyes; The Final Terror aka Campsite Massacre aka Three Blind Mice **1981** Sharky's Machine **1982** Dead Men Don't Wear Plaid **1984** Against All Odds **1987** The Good Wife; Hotel Colonial **1989** How To Get Ahead In Advertising **1990** After Dark, My Sweet **1992** Christopher Columbus: The Discovery; The Wide Sargasso Sea

Warren, Lesley Ann

Actress
Born 16 August 1946
New York City

A considerable and under-valued actress, unusual to look at and with a special combination of strength and vulnerability, Lesley-Ann Warren can point to a couple of outstanding performances in an admittedly chequered career.

She attended the Professional Children's School and the Music and Art School in New York, learning acting and ballet. Later she studied with Lee Strasberg and Stella Adler at the famed Actors' Studio. At the age of only 17, Warren made her Broadway debut in *110 In The Shade*. This led to her playing Rodgers and Hammerstein's Cinderella in a popular 1964 television special – where a Disney scout picked up on her. In 1966 she won a Theatre World award for *Drat! That Cat!*, and a year later she made her film debut in Disney's *The Happiest Millionaire* (1967). She also got married, to future producer Jon Peters (then a hairdresser). The marriage was to last ten years, until Peters became involved with Barbra Streisand. Despite all this early success, Warren did not make much impact in the movies and found steadier employment in the theatre and on television – including a season on *Mission Impossible* (1970–71) and numerous TV movies. A Golden Globe for *79 Park Avenue* in 1978 improved her standing a little, but it wasn't until *Victor/Victoria* (1982) that people really took notice.

Cast as James Garner's moll, Norma, the actress came up with the platinum wig and Brooklyn accent herself. Norma is a bimbo *par excellence* – a stereotype to be sure, but a brilliantly detailed comic creation nonetheless. She was Oscar-nominated for it. Warren followed it with her two finest performances, both for director Alan Rudolph. In *Choose Me* (1984) she was the hardbitten but deeply lonely owner of Eve's bar. It is a beautifully shaded piece of work: calm and sensible beside Genevieve Bujold's hyper Dr Love; delightfully acute in scenes with Keith Carradine's disarmingly honest madman. *Songwriter* was in a more throwaway vein – Rudolph inherited the project at the last minute, and cast Warren as up-and-coming country singing star Gilda. It was not a leading role, but she made it seem crucial in comparison with the laidback *bonhomie* of Kris Kristofferson and Willie Nelson.

Unfortunately, since then, the films and the roles have both been sparse. She was Miss Scarlet in *Clue* (1985) and a bewilderingly unconvincing feminist bookseller in *Cop* (1987), though this was probably due more to writer James Ellroy's conception of a feminist than any inadequacy on the part of Warren.

1967 The Happiest Millionaire **1968** The One And Only Genuine Family Band **1971** Pickup On 101 **1976** Harry And Walter Go To New York **1982** Victor/Victoria **1983** A Night In Heaven **1984** Race For The Yankee Zephyr aka Treasure Of The Yankee Zephyr; Choose Me; Songwriter **1985** Clue **1987** Burglar; Cop **1991** Life Stinks **1992/93** Pure Country

Washington, Denzel

Actor
Born 28 December 1954
Mount Vernon, New York

By 1990, with eight feature films behind him, Denzel Washington had become established as the undisputed leader of the younger pack of black actors. Tall, athletic and very handsome, this intelligent actor of no small ability found himself touted in magazines as a sex symbol, to which his characteristic reaction was, 'I haven't changed. I don't do anything different. I struggle to resist it in order not to be affected by it.'

Washington holds a BA in Journalism from Fordham University, and studied acting at the American Conservatory Theatre School in San Francisco, breeding ground for so much of the country's talent. He was already becoming a familiar face to TV audiences in the popular hospital series *St Elsewhere*, which began in 1982, before the release of his Hollywood debut film, *Carbon Copy*, the same year. He acquitted himself with aplomb as white George Segal's black illegitimate son in this comedy which, given the delicate nature of its racial subject matter, worked surprisingly well (though Washington himself loathes it and prefers to forget about it). Racism was also the theme of his next film, Norman Jewison's *A Soldier's Story* (1984), set in an all-black army barracks during World War II. As a young private who, with his fellow rookies, is part of a murder investigation, Washington simmered effectively with anger at the subservience of his position. It was a striking performance in what was essentially on ensemble line-up, and led him to a strong supporting role in Sidney Lumet's superficial but energetic *Power* (1986). As a man with questionable Middle East connections, acting as advisor to J.T. Walsh's would-be candidate for the Senate, Washington was as tough as nails, smooth and convincing.

But it was Richard Attenborough's *Cry Freedom* (1987) that seriously put Denzel Washington on the map as a screen actor, bringing him international recognition. Though the film itself opted for glossy commercialism by dwelling on the heroics of newspaper editor Donald Woods' (Kevin Kline) escape from South Africa, it nonetheless brought the struggle against apartheid to life for a wide audience. As the strong-willed and sophisticated black activist Steve Biko, murdered in detention by the South African police, Washington put on 10lb in weight and removed the caps from his teeth, the more closely to resemble the real Biko, whom he portrayed with incisive truth and integrity, and a convincing accent. He was Oscar-nominated as Best Supporting Actor, and won in that category for his embittered but courageous runaway slave in *Glory* (1989). An actor of stylishness and control, he proved his versatility in 1989, starring in *For Queen And Country* as a disillusioned British paratrooper struggling with Thatcher-era racism and social conditions (although the accent missed the mark this time); in the otherwise unworthy *The Mighty Quinn*, as an alienated and up-market police chief of a Caribbean island; and, in 1990, as a selfish, gifted jazz musician in Spike Lee's *Mo' Better Blues*.

He followed these with another comedy about racism, *Heart Condition* (1990) opposite Bob Hoskins, the inter-racial love story *Mississippi Masala* (1991) and the surprisingly tasteless and violent thriller, *Ricochet* (1991), before returning to Spike Lee for the biggest and most controversial challenge of his career to date: the title role in *Malcolm X*.

Also a stage actor of some ambition, he gave a highly original, if not entirely successful, interpretation of Shakespeare's *Richard III* in New York's Central Park in 1990, and also played *Othello* earlier in his career.

1982 Carbon Copy **1984** A Soldier's Story **1986** Power **1987** Cry Freedom **1989** For Queen And Country; The Mighty Quinn: Glory **1990** Mo' Better Blues; Heart Condition **1991** Mississippi Masala **1992** Ricochet **1992/93** Malcolm X; Much Ado About Nothing (GB)

Waters, John

Director, writer
Born 1946?
Baltimore, Maryland

Like Barry Levinson, Baltimore film-maker John Waters is a celebrant of the old home town, which he characterises as 'The Hairdo Capital of the World'. His body of Baltimore work could not be further apart from Levinson's, however, with Waters a camp underground favourite for years, famed for bad taste, causing outrage and showcasing the late transvestite Divine before his wacky 60s dance movie *Hairspray* took the fancy of a more mainstream audience.

Waters, who describes his ambition as wanting to be 'Walt Disney for peculiar children' was a nice Catholic schoolboy longing to be different, whose grandmother presented him with an 8mm camera for his 17th birthday. He spent one year applying himself to his grades at the University of Baltimore, transferred to NYU, and was expelled for smoking marijuana after only a few months in the film programme. Undeterred, he took to guerrilla film-making, rechristening one of his chums, Glenn Milstead, Divine and transforming him into the trash queen of the screen. *Hag In A Black Leather Jacket* (1964) centred on a man who carried his beloved about in a dustbin. *Eat Your Makeup* (1968) told the tragic tale of kidnapped girls made to model themselves to death (and is believed to be the earliest film to re-enact the JFK assassination – with Divine as Jackie!). Waters' first feature-length film, *Mondo Trasho* (1969), starred Divine as a wannabe Jayne Mansfield and was made for $2,000. His most famous early work, *Pink Flamingos* (1972), with a heady budget of $10,000, is a legend for the scene in which Divine eats dog poo. Described as everything from the funniest to the sickest film ever made in America, *Pink Flamingos* was acclaimed as Buñuelesque in Europe, has made a fortune and is still playing on repertory, late-night and art-house circuits.

The 1981 release of *Polyester*, starring Divine and Tab Hunter, was an entry of sorts into the mainstream for Waters. Like all his best work, it sent up, quite hilariously, American middle-class kitsch, and though it was strictly for the not-easily-offended it offered extra amusement in 'scratch-and-sniff' cards distributed to audiences to experience the film in 'Odorama'. *Hairspray* (1988) caught straight critics off guard with its good-natured, totally inoffensive satire, nostalgic dance numbers and fabulous soundtrack. Hollywood duly noted its resounding success and Universal Pictures obliged Waters with $8 million to make *Cry-Baby* (1990), a punkier, wittier variation on *Grease* (1978) starring Johnny Depp alongside Waters regular Mink Stole, Patty Hearst and ex-porno star Traci Lords.

Ever the iconoclast, Waters has written a frankly funny memoir/chronicle/treatise, *Shock Value*, and taught a course entitled *How To Laugh At A Life Sentence* to inmates of Maryland's Patuxent Institute.

1969 Mondo Trasho **1972** Pink Flamingos **1974** Female Trouble **1977** Desperate Living **1981** Polyester **1988** Hairspray **1990** Cry-Baby (also writer)

Waterston, Sam

Actor
Born 15 November 1940
Cambridge, Massachusetts

Sam Waterston is a likeable, modest man with an engagingly intelligent sense of the screen actor's vicissitudes. Twice in his career he has moved into the orbit of megastardom only to discover that, in his case, the accolade was temporary. Appearing as the narrator, Nick Carraway, in *The Great Gatsby* (directed by Jack Clayton in 1974), Waterston was for a brief period after the film's release the most sought-after screen actor in America. And again ten years later, this time as the *New York Times* reporter Sidney Schanberg in Roland Joffé's searing exposé of Cambodia's ills, *The Killing Fields*, he put in a magnificent performance universally praised by critics and remembered by filmgoers.

Yet for all that, he is not in the Redford class of fame: perhaps a little too earnest, a little too intellectual, a little too 'British' in character and reserve. His father in fact was of English nationality, and Waterston, as well as being educated at top US schools Groton and Yale, has spent much time on the Continent, picking up, among other accomplishments, a fluent command of French. Theatre was his first love, yet for a man primarily of the stage he has appeared in a remarkable number of movies – roughly one a year since the beginning of his career (in 1965). Getting off to a good start, his postgraduate year at the Sorbonne was spent as part of the American Actors Workshop under the aegis of legendary theatre director and refugee from McCarthyism John Berry. Thereafter he got small parts in Broadway plays before a movie debut in 1965 in the underground film *The Plastic Dome of Norma Jean*.

Keeping with the theatre connection, an important part of his career has been in association (an association shared among other screen actors by Meryl Streep, Richard Gere and Kevin Kline) with (the now late) Joseph Papp's annual Shakespeare Festival programmes – the high point of which was his Obie and Drama Desk-awarded performance as Benedick in the 1972 staging of *Much Ado About Nothing*. (1972 to 1973 seems in fact to have been a remarkable period for him: he followed up *Much Ado* with an Emmy-nominated performance in Tennessee Williams' *The Glass Menagerie* opposite Katherine Hepburn; after which came *Gatsby*.)

In general, Waterston has tried intelligently to alternate between stage, big screen and television, with considerable success in all three modes. As far as TV is concerned, his most memorable role is probably that of the atomic physicist Robert Oppenheimer in the well-scripted seven-part BBC series *Oppenheimer* of 1980. Back with the big screen, he has had sometimes small but always effective roles in Woody Allen movies (*Hannah and Her Sisters*, 1986, *September*, 1987). In Allen's finest and most serious film to date, *Crimes and Misdemeanors* (1990) Waterston plays a calm blind rabbi whose spiritual insight is depicted in contrast to the moral murkiness of Martin Landau losing his. Waterston on the whole is good at these 'upright' roles, although this very uprightness can be turned round skilfully to make his characters seem strained and sinister. He has had his share of playing villains, too, like the mercenary leader Frank Canton in Cimino's flawed masterpiece, *Heaven's Gate* (1982).

Acting, at any event, in any medium, is in Waterston's blood: he was first on the stage at the age of six. His British father (also from a theatrical family) set up and ran high school drama programmes. Waterston – whose quiet, well-dressed manner and suave good looks could have him mistaken in private for a banker or a high-grade academic – wouldn't have it any other way. He likes the vicarious sense of danger that is constantly provided by his profession. 'It's like sword-fighting', he has said, 'except with blunt instruments!' He is amused by its ups and downs. Despite a long and successful career he feels in his bones that its triumphs are transitory. His modest ambition has been to work hard and prosper.

1965 The Plastic Dome Of Norma Jean **1967** Fitzwilly **1969** Three; Generation aka A Time For Giving **1970** Mahoney's Estate; Cover Me, Babe **1971** Who Killed Mary What'ser Name? **1972** Savages **1974** The Great Gatsby **1985** Rancho Deluxe **1976** Journey Into Fear; Dandy, The All-American Girl **1978** Sweet William; Capricorn One **1979** Eagle's Wing **1980** Hopscotch; Heaven's Gate **1984** The Killing Fields **1985** Warning Sign **1986** Hannah And Her Sisters; Just Between Friends; A Certain Desire/Flagrant Desir (France) **1987** September; The Devil's Paradise **1989** Welcome Home; Crimes And Misdemeanors **1990** The French Revolution; Mindwalk **1991** A Captive In The Land; Man In The Moon

Weaver, Sigourney
(Susan Weaver)
Actress
Born 8 October 1949
New York City

Tall (five foot, 11 inches) and definitely handsome, Sigourney Weaver is a classy theatre actress who, ironically, is most respected in Hollywood as the leading lady with a proven ability to carry a tough action blockbuster. Starting out playing in the Greek classics of Aristophanes with Meryl Streep at Yale, Weaver became best known internationally as astronaut Ripley, clad in vest and knickers to combat the grossly horrific *Alien* in 1979 and its two sequels.

Born to ex-NBC president Sylvester 'Pat' Weaver and English actress Elizabeth Inglis in New York, Weaver attended Stanford University and after the almost obligatory 60s Israeli kibbutz experience resumed her studies in the drama department at Yale. Struggling in New York for much of the 70s, she was constantly told she was too tall for roles, although she worked in some very arty pieces off-off-Broadway. In the late 70s she found employment in a daytime soap, *Somerset*, and she is to be glimpsed fleetingly from a distance at the end of Woody Allen's *Annie Hall* (1977). Spotted off-Broadway by the makers of *Alien* (1979), she found herself starring as the indomitable heroine of a formulaic sci-fi horror picture, directed to spectacularly shocking effect by Ridley Scott to become a smash hit.

More at home, one would have thought, in roles as cultivated ladies, Weaver made less impact in *Eyewitness* (1981) as the snotty TV newswoman caught up in a murder mystery opposite William Hurt, or in *The Year Of Living Dangerously* (1983), in which she was not overly persuasive as an English embassy employee but enjoyed one of the sexiest clothed moments in 80s cinema with Mel Gibson in Peter Weir's romantic political drama. Not obviously gifted at comedy, she may well have been surprised to find herself the leading lady to the wacky Bill Murray-led gang in the huge hit *Ghostbusters* (1984) and its 1989 sequel. Retaining her interest in theatre work (appearing as Portia off-Broadway and on Broadway opposite William Hurt in *Hurlyburly* among other credits) and starting a family with husband Jim Simpson, a stage director, Weaver has seldom seemed hell-bent on getting her most lucrative roles. *Aliens* saw her wooed by 20th Century-Fox with a promised ten per cent of the profits and *Aliens*^{3} – deemed unthinkable without her – could proceed only with her input on the screenplay.

Apart from her most successful commercial outings, Weaver's most substantial and impressive work to date came in her brave, intelligent portrayal of aggressive, abrasive and obsessed murder victim Dian Fossey, whose desperate championing of the dwindling gorilla population in Rwanda made for intense, absorbing viewing in Michael Apted's *Gorillas In The Mist* (1988). She was also scorching in a supporting role as the Bitch Boss from Hell in Mike Nichols' charming contemporary Cinderella tale, *Working Girl*, in the same year. Following her shaven-headed appearance in the critically and commercially disappointing *Alien*^{3}, Weaver was pleased to join Ridley Scott's ambitious Columbus epic, *1492*, as an elaborately curled and costumed Queen Isabella.

1977 Annie Hall (bit) **1979** Alien **1981** Eyewitness aka The Janitor **1983** The Year Of Living Dangerously; The Deal Of The Century **1984** Ghostbusters **1985** Une Femme Ou Deux (France) **1986** Aliens; Half Moon Street

1988 Gorillas In The Mist; Working Girl **1989** Ghostbusters II **1992** Alien^3; 1492: Conquest Of Paradise

Weir, Peter

Director, writer
Born 21 August 1944
Sydney, Australia

Entertainment magazine once said that Peter Weir could make a trip to the toilet look like a mystical experience, yet he manages to temper his sensual lyricism with a control of narrative and a commercial sensibility that renders his films both substantial and accessible. The son of a real-estate agent, Weir studied arts and law at Sydney University, briefly travelling through Europe before landing a job with Australian TV in 1967, when he also began to make short films.

After joining the government-sponsored Film Australia to make a number of award-winning documentaries, his recurring interest in the apocalyptic – murder, wars, revolutions, even Armageddon itself – was very apparent in his feature debut as writer-director, *The Cars That Ate Paris* (1974), an outback variation on the Japanese ghost story *Onibaba* in which a town that preys on passing motorists is ultimately destroyed by the victims' cars. But it was the unnerving and atmospheric mystery *Picnic At Hanging Rock* (1975) that made the most impact as one of the most important films of Australia's New Wave of the 1970s. Like his subsequent end-of-the-world thriller *The Last Wave* (1977), it graduated from a believable, recognisable world into an ancient pagan one, exploiting the unease Australians felt for the Aboriginal culture they had deposed without ever making an effort to understand, through highly impressive, dreamlike visual passages that conveyed feeling rather than information.

Weir continued to take the less trodden path with *Gallipoli* (1981) which, despite its huge budget, was more about people than war, Heavy on characterisation, it took its two young heroes, Mark Lee and Mel Gibson, on a long journey across Australia to join up only for their lives and youthful ideals to be pointlessly thrown away in a stunning final shot obviously inspired by Robert Capa's classic photo of a soldier in the Spanish Civil War at the moment of death. *The Year Of Living Dangerously* (1983), set against the fall of Sukarno's regime in 1965 Indonesia, was by comparison a genuine disappointment, with Weir's inability to generate much enthusiasm for the political elements of the film (themselves somewhat neutered by the decision to film in another dictatorship, Marcos' Philippines) and leaving an undeveloped romance between Gibson and Sigourney Weaver mitigated only by Linda Hunt's extraordinary performance as a disillusioned local newsreel cameraman. There were no such qualms about his first American venture, *Witness* (1985) which he took over at short notice and turned from a standard fish-out-of-water thriller into an extraordinary study of different worlds – that of a homicide cop and a pacifist Amish widow and her son, forced together – with some of his most accomplished visuals. His next collaboration with its star, Harrison Ford, *The Mosquito Coast* (1986), fared less well, with the actor's heroic persona crumbling into insanity and delirium as his dream of creating a utopia in the jungle ends in disaster failing to find much critical favour and alienating an audience acclimatised to happy endings.

Dead Poets Society (1989) revived the director's fortunes on both counts and marked the beginning of a move away from mysticism to a firmer emphasis on relationships and words. It still encompassed plenty of his trademarks (synthesised, slightly other-worldly score and visual symbolism, most notably in a heavy-handed and protracted suicide scene) but sugared the darkness of the script this time with a hopeful, if not unequivocally happy ending. Similarly, his romantic comedy *Green Card* (1991) ended more hopefully than happily despite being in a more commercial vein than any of the other projects he initiated himself (although as with all of his films, it relied heavily on collaboration with both cast and crew); and though creating a near-literal urban jungle for its characters, it relied less on the visual element than any of Weir's previous films. Peter Weir's style, while still highly distinctive, continues to show signs of evolution, even if in a more mainstream direction, ensuring that he remains a director who is consistently interesting even if only intermittently successful.

As director only unless stated otherwise: **1974** The Cars That Ate Paris aka The Cars That Ate People (w/d) **1975** Picnic At Hanging Rock (w/d) **1977** The Last Wave (w/d) **1981** Gallipoli **1983** The Year Of Living Dangerously **1985** Witness **1986** The Mosquito Coast **1989** Dead Poets Society **1991** Green Card (w/d) **1992/93** Joy Ride

Weller, Peter
Actor
Born 24 June 1947
Stevens Point, Wisconsin

Peter Weller has gone to star status by hiding his lean good looks rather than exploiting them as the Frankensteinian law enforcer *Robocop* (1987), yet seems to be less lucky without the mask. Coming from a theatrical background – he studied with Uta Hagen, is a member of the Actors' Studio and has enjoyed a distinguished stage career – he made his film debut as the unstoppable lawman Joe Lefors pursuing *Butch And Sundance* in their *Early Days* prequel (1978). First glimpsed (in an echo of his character's symbolic presence in the first film) only by his straw hat, Weller had the chance to flesh out the part as one of those well-dressed, well-spoken moustachioed characters who thinks the law is whatever he decides to do: an oasis of menace in a slapstick environment. A more romantic side to his talents, comforting Ali McGraw and Diane Keaton when their screen husbands became intolerable in *Just Tell Me What You Want* (1980) and *Shoot The Moon* (1981) respectively, gave him the boost he needed for lead roles, most importantly as the *Buckeroo Banzai*. W.D. Richter's 1984 neurosurgeon, physicist, rock singer, inventor and government troubleshooter graced a desperately confused sci-fi satire that initially did little for Weller's career – despite allowing him some good one-liners – consigning him to a couple of menacing roles in unconvincing dramas, but the film's later cult following among fans of the genre helped him land the title role in *Robocop* (1987).

Chosen by Paul Verhoeven because of his 'expressive lips' (all that is visible under his helmet for much of the film) he managed to inject flashes of humanity into the role with moments of emotion skilfully expressed in dazed monotones as his mechanised hero pieces together memories of his life. It was more a director's film than an actor's, but it led to a marginally successful run of thrillers (*Shakedown*, 1988, *Cat Chaser*, 1989) and genre items (*Leviathan*, 1989) although, sensing imminent typecasting and feeling there was nothing more he could do with the role, Weller left the series after *Robocop 2* (1990) in an attempt to broaden his repertoire. Taking the very different role of the hallucinating writer, uncertain of his sexuality, in a surreal landscape that mirrors his state of mind in David Cronenberg's *The Naked Lunch* (1991), he had some real dramatic meat to get his teeth into. But, despite earning much critical acclaim for his efforts, the film failed commercially, leaving Weller yet to bring his more serious ambitions into the mainstream.

1979 Butch And Sundance: The Early Days **1980** Just Tell Me What You Want **1981** Shoot The Moon **1983** Of Unknown Origin **1984** The Adventures Of Buckeroo Banzai Across The 8th Dimension; Firstborn **1985** A Killing Affair (released 1988) **1987** Robocop **1988** Shakedown aka Blue Jean Cop; The Tunnel **1989** Cat Chaser; Leviathan **1990** Robocop 2 **1992** The Naked Lunch; 50–50; Sunset Grill

Wenders, Wim (Wilhelm Wenders)
Director
Born 14 August 1945
Düsseldorf, Germany

'The Yanks have colonised our subconscious,' says one of the itinerant friends in *Kings Of The Road* (1976). Wim Wenders is more aware than most contemporary German directors of the American cultural influence on post-war German youth. His films do not condemn this, nor do they wholly embrace it. He was brought up on the music and movies of the American occupiers, being diverted from becoming a Catholic priest by the discovery of rock 'n' roll and pinball machines. His isolated and emotionally stunted characters are often resensitised by jukeboxes, pinballs and hitting the road. Wenders takes the word 'movie' more literally than most; his people are 'movies' who move from town to town, city to city.

In *Summer In The City: Dedicated To The Kinks* (1970), his first feature after leaving Munich Film School, a newly-released prisoner goes from one gloomy German town to the next trying in vain to contact his old friends. An almost wordless journalist, numbed by recent assignments, journeys down the east coast of America with a nine-year-old girl in *Alice In The Cities* (1974). This gently amusing and melancholy road movie foreshadowed themes more deeply explored in *Paris, Texas* (1984). Although the wide open spaces of the USA seemed the natural home for Wenders' odd odysseys, his first Hollywood movie, *Hammett* (1982), shot against atmospheric sets at Francis Ford Coppola's Zoetrope studios, frustrated the director's forte for long takes and outdoor movements. The troubled film (two-thirds of which was abandoned in rough cut and re-shot), self-consciously filled with *film noir* references and actors from the 40s, told of how the writer Dashiell Hammett (Frederic Forrest) gets involved in a crime that forms the basis for his fiction.

Paris, Texas was archetypal Wenders, in which a man (Harry Dean Stanton), lost in an empty landscape and speechless for the first 20 minutes, is shell-shocked by the separation from his wife (Nastassia Kinski) and wanting to become a father to his seven-year-old son. The extraordinary calm intensity of Stanton's performance, the superb colour camerawork by Robby Müller (Wender's constant cameraman) and the haunting music by Ry Cooder, gave the film the mythic dimension of a Western.

Having seemingly got America out of his system, Wenders, who had been living in the USA for seven years, returned to Germany in the mid-80s, where he made the overly whimsical *Wings Of Desire* (1987), featuring his French girlfriend Solveig Dommartin, and in which Peter Falk turns out to be a fallen angel. However, the cosmopolitan, wanderlustful Wenders can never settle anywhere for very long, and the self-indulgent *Until The End Of The World* (1991) is the ultimate road movie, following four people who pursue each other through 17 countries.

1970 Summer In The City: Dedicated To The Kinks (W. Germany) **1972** Die Angst Des Tormanns Beim Elfmeter/ The Goalkeeper's Fear Of The Penalty aka The Anxiety Of The Goalie At The Penalty (US: The Goalie's Anxiety At The Penalty Kick) (W. Germany); Der Scharlachrote Buchstabe/The Scarlet Letter (W. Germany) **1974** Alice In Den Städten/Alice In The Cities (W. Germany) **1975** Falsche Beweguna/Wrong Movement (W. Germany) **1976** Im Lauf Der Zeit/Kings Of The Road (W. Germany) **1977** Der Amerikanische Freund/The American Friend (W. Germany) **1980** Lightning Over Water **1982** Hammett; The State Of Things **1984** Paris, Texas **1986** Tokyo-Ga (docu) **1987** Der Himmel Uber Berlin/Wings Of Desire (W. Germany–France) **1989** Aufzeichnungen Zu Kleidern Und Stådten/Notebook On Cities And Clothes (docu) **1991** Until The End Of The World **1992/93** Far Away So Close/In Weiter Ferne, So Nah (Germany)

Whitaker, Forest

Actor
Born 1961
Longview, Texas

Soft-spoken, with the manner of a teddy bear in the body of a full-grown grizzly, Forest Whitaker is a slightly different kind of black actor from the narrow norms of mainstream Hollywood – not hip and funny like Pryor and Murphy, not a Morgan Freeman or Denzel Washington-like personification of integrity, nor any of the sleazeball pimps, muggers and junkies so beloved of casting directors. Despite an apprenticeship in buddy parts, he has avoided the Hollywood shuffle to create realistic, likeable characters by fleshing out small roles while appearing to do very little.

Winning a football scholarship to college, he soon transferred to USC and got two more scholarships, to study classical music and theatre (the two initially linked by his interest in opera). Small roles in film and (mostly) television passed by almost unnoticed until he pulled off an extraordinary double-header in 1986 as one of Oliver Stone's *Platoon* and, more notably, as the seemingly dull-eyed simpleton who hustles Paul Newman in Scorseses's *The Color Of Money*. A perfect showcase for his adept brand of scene-stealing, it is the exactitude of his amateurishness that tips us and Newman off; we know nothing about him, but we know exactly what he's doing. Soon he was essaying amiable, convincing characters in the margins of hits like *Stakeout* and *Good Morning, Vietnam* (both 1987) before Clint Eastwood chose him for the role of his life as the drug-addicted jazzman Charlie Parker in *Bird* (1988).

The film's observational rather than judgemental tone gave Whitaker the room he needed to achieve a performance of astonishing variety with harrowing moments of torment, violence and deep despair – among them, his endless whacked-out telegrams to his wife when their child dies, filled with a pain that is far too real for comfort – rubbing shoulders with moments of joy and humour that showed why those he abused still loved him. The actor even surmounted the twin pitfalls of biopic acting, playing both his death scene and his saxophone with surprising verisimilitude. An uncompromising performance that won him the Best Actor award at Cannes, despite upping his profile it failed to earn him the kind of roles it proved he could handle. Nonetheless, he was impressive in Neil Jordan's *The Crying Game* (1992), as a cricket-loving British soldier (with a convincing accent) kidnapped by the IRA.

1982 Fast Times At Ridgemont High **1985** Vision Quest aka Crazy For You **1986** Platoon; The Color Of Money **1987** Bloodsport; Stakeout; Good Morning, Vietnam **1988** Bird **1989** Johnny Handsome **1990** Downtown **1991** A Rage In Harlem **1992** The Crying Game (GB); Article 99;

Diary Of A Hitman; Body Snatchers 3 **1992/93** Consenting Adults

Wiest, Dianne

Actress
Born 28 March 1948
Kansas City, Missouri

Lacking conventional glamour but offering an appealing and interesting face that is striking in its mobility of expression, Dianne Wiest has steadily raised her profile to become a jewel in the crown of Hollywood character actresses.

A highly intelligent woman who was educated at the University of Maryland, she had studied for a career in ballet but abandoned it in favour of the theatre. She joined the American Shakespeare Company, with whom she toured, before moving to New York and then to Washington, DC., as a member of the Arena Stage Theatre there. Her stage credits are immensely impressive including, as they do, Shaw's *Heartbreak House, The Dybbuk, Hedda Gabler* and *Agamemnon*. She toured the Soviet Union with Arena, worked with other regional groups, performed with the New York Shakespeare Festival company, and played Desdemona opposite James Earl Jones' Othello on Broadway. In the mid-80s she added theatre directing to her accomplishments, scoring a notable success with her off-Broadway production of the British play about Wilfred Owen and Siegfried Sassoon, *Not About Heroes*.

Little wonder, then, that Wiest came to the movies relatively far on in her career, and even less surprising that her finely honed and intelligent gifts, her distinctive personality and evident intelligence have now brought her wider recognition. A succession of very small supporting roles, often thankless in themselves (Meryl Streep's office friend in *Falling In Love*, 1984, for example), were immediately eye-catching thanks to her gift for getting to the heart of a character, no matter how marginal to the action, but it was to Woody Allen that she owed her eventual recognition. Having given her a tiny part in *The Purple Rose Of Cairo* (1985), he cast her that same year as Holly, the most mixed-up and vulnerable of the three who made up *Hannah And Her Sisters* (Mia Farrow and Barbara Hershey were the other two). It was a wonderful role, calling for depths of poignancy as well as a show of humour and Wiest did full justice to it, thus winning the Best Supporting Actress Oscar. Since then, she has continued to deliver performances of subtle nuance and powerful presence, demonstrating her versatility as the outrageous mutton-dressed-as-lamb Bronx kook who is Emily Lloyd's unmarried mother in *Cookie (1989)*; while her divorced mother of two disturbed teenagers in *Parenthood* the same year was a standout portrayal of a lonely, put-upon woman bravely fighting off self-pity. She had been a single parent, too, caught in somewhat bizarre circumstances and lending credibility to drivel in *The Lost Boys* (1987).

But it was, perhaps, in her fourth film for Woody, *September* (1989), that Dianne Wiest's particular stock-in-trade – perfectly judged nervous intensity and almost unbearable vulnerability, combined with a deep core of courage and grit – came most tellingly into its own. As Mia Farrow's best friend, painfully and unwillingly attracted to the object of Mia's desire (Sam Waterston), she gave one of the memorable performances of 1989, almost eclipsing Farrow's brilliantly uncompromising neurotic and Elaine Stritch's flamboyant faded movie star. Alas, the film was very ill-received and Wiest's achievement thus robbed of its due. However, she went on to Tim Burton's *Edward Scissorhands* (1990, playing a kindly housewife-cum-cosmetics-saleswoman) and looked set for a long run.

1980 It's My Turn **1982** I'm Dancing As Fast As I Can **1984** Footloose; Falling In Love **1985** The Purple Rose Of Cairo; Hannah And Her Sisters **1987** The Lost Boys; Radio Days **1988** Bright Lights, Big City **1989** September; Cookie; Parenthood **1990** Edward Scissorhands **1991** Little Man Tate **1993** Yesterday

Wilder, Gene

(Jerry Silberman)

Actor, director, writer
Born 11 June 1935
Milwaukee, Wisconsin

Gene Wilder, the curly-headed comic who has made hysteria hysterical, is the son of a Russian Jewish immigrant who prospered in the USA by manufacturing miniature whiskey bottles. At the University of Iowa, Wilder began attending drama classes and appeared in summer stock during vacations. On his graduation, determined to make acting his profession, he left for England, enrolling at the Bristol Old Vic Theatre School. However, he became dissatisfied with traditional English teaching methods (though he did become an expert fencer, which enabled him to teach the sport in America), and returned to New York where he joined the Actors' Studio.

His first film role was in *Bonnie And Clyde* (1967), in which he played the jumpy undertaker whisked off on a perilous joyride by the eponymous couple. But Wilder's career really took off when his friend Mel Brooks cast him in *The Producers* (1968), for which he was Oscar nominated. His wildly funny performance as the nervous accountant emmeshed in stage producer Zero Mostel's schemes to make money illegally from a flop, established his screen persona; an initially well-balanced individual transformed by even the most minor crisis into a whining bundle of neuroses. Variations on this character were offered in a number of films, including Woody Allen's *Everything You Always Wanted To Know About Sex* (1972), in which he was the doctor who falls in love with a sheep; and in his popular comedy partnership with the ostensibly cooler Richard Pryor in *Silver Streak* (1976), *Stir Crazy* (1980), *See No Evil, Hear No Evil* (1989) and *Another You* (1991).

As a departure from the urban neurotic nebbish, Wilder portrayed the Waco Kid, an alcoholic ex-gunfighter, in *Blazing Saddles*, and a descendant of the god-playing doctor in *Young Frankenstein*, two 1974 Mel Brooks parodies. His own first two films as director-star, *The Adventures of Sherlock Holmes' Smarter Brother* (1975) and *The World's Greatest Lover* (1977) were school of Mel Brooks, but they had a quirky humour all their own and were stylishly made, although they, too, couldn't resist the cheap laugh. *The Woman In Red* (1984), a vulgar and shallow remake of the less crass French comedy *Pardon Mon Affaire* (1976), and *Haunted Honeymoon* (1986), an unfunny old dark house pastiche, both featured Wilder's wife, the gifted Gilda Radner, who died in 1989, aged 42. It seems that this very funny man needs the discipline of a director other than himself.

1967 Bonnie And Clyde **1968** The Producers **1970** Start The Revolution Without Me; Quackser Fortune Has a Cousin In The Bronx **1971** Willy Wonka And The Chocolate Factory **1972** Everything You Always Wanted To Know About Sex . . . But Were Afraid To Ask **1974** Rhinoceros; Blazing Saddles; Young Frankenstein (also co-writer); The Little Prince **1975** The Adventure Of Sherlock Holmes' Smarter Brother (also w/d) **1976** Silver Streak **1977** The World's Greatest Lover (also w/d) **1979** The Frisco Kid **1980** Stir Crazy; Sunday Lovers (France/Italy; segment: actor and director) **1984** The Woman In Red (also w/d) **1986** Haunted Honeymoon (also w/d) **1989** See No Evil, Hear No Evil **1990** Funny About Love **1991** Another You

Williams, JoBeth

Actress
Born 1953
Houston, Texas

A mature, sympathetic and apparently instinctive actress, JoBeth Williams made her mark in her very first film in little more than a cameo role. Her Phyllis Bernard wanders naked through Ted Kramer's apartment and is horrified to walk straight into his young son. It is a delightful moment; certainly an entrance to remember.

Before *Kramer vs. Kramer* (1979), Williams acted with repertory companies in Rhode Island, Philadelphia, Boston and Washington DC, among others. A Texan, she was educated at Brown University, and was one of *Glamour* magazine's Top Ten College Girls Of 1969–70 (!). In the late 70s she spent more than two years in the New York daytime serials *Somerset* and *The Guiding Light*. After *Kramer*, she played on Broadway in *A Coupla White Chicks Sitting Around Talking* (1980). She acquitted herself well as the female lead in the Gene Wilder-Richard Pryor vehicle *Stir Crazy* (1980), and impressed in the television drama *The Day After*, but her best work came in Tobe Hooper's *Poltergeist* (1982) and Lawrence Kasdan's *The Big Chill* (1983). In both films, different as they are, Williams is a suburban housewife with a refreshing streak of independence. Diane Freeling in the horror film runs the gamut from child-like joy when she first witnesses the supernatural at work, to terror and anguish later on. What is notable about the performance, and the film, is the lively grounding of the character in the early stages: smoking dope with her husband Craig T. Nelson; watching through the kitchen window as her daughter deals with wolf-whistles from the pool men; depositing the dead canary before her youngest daughter sees it. In *The Big Chill* Williams again switches easily between comedy and drama. Her hesitant flirtation with Tom Berenger is lovingly nuanced.

Roles in *Teachers* (1984) and *American Dreamer* (1985) suggested she was perhaps a little soft for star material – there is no cutting edge to her – but she was as sensitive and fine as ever in *Desert Bloom* (1986, beside the very edgy Ellen Barkin) and the sentimental drama *Welcome Home* (1989).

1979 Kramer vs. Kramer **1980** The Dogs Of War; Stir

Crazy **1982** Poltergeist; Endangered Species **1983** The Big Chill **1984** Teachers **1985** American Dreamer **1986** Poltergeist II; Desert Bloom **1989** Welcome Home **1991** Switch; Driving Me Crazy **1992** Stop! Or My Mom Will Shoot; Me, Myself And I

Williams, Robin

Actor
Born 21 July 1952
Chicago, Illinois

A quick-fire virtuoso comedian with a verbal dexterity comparable to that of the late Danny Kaye, Robin Williams became a huge Hollywood star with *Good Morning, Vietnam* (1987). As the anarchic US forces disc jockey Adrian Cronauer (in real life a quiet man, very different from Williams' portrayal), the actor dazzled with his comic pyrotechnics but, more than that, he conveyed a depth of feeling beneath the manic surface which lent the movie an emotional resonance. The performance won him a Best Actor Oscar nomination and exported the popularity he had already won at home as Mork in the TV series *Mork And Mindy*.

Not that Williams and the big screen were strangers to one another and, indeed, his debut in the title role of Robert Altman's *Popeye* (1980) was a triumph of characterisation. Unfortunately, the film bombed at the box office, as did *The World According To Garp* two years later. Three out of the next four of his movies made no impression and the fourth, and best, *Moscow On The Hudson* (1984), in which Williams was touching and funny as a Russian wallowing among the consumer riches at Bloomingdale's, proved only moderately successful.

Williams studied acting, first at Marin College in California and then with the late, great John Houseman at Juilliard, which he helped to pay for by performing as a street mime. On completing his studies, however, this individualistic performer with a pronounced gift for improvisation elected to follow the comedian's rather than the actor's circuit. He did things the hard way: 'I started working in some real rough places – beer and wine houses in San Francisco. You had to, through sheer speed, force them not to throw things at you. So I developed this idea of jumping from one idea to another. It was a matter of survival.' The experience paid dividends. He went to LA and appeared at the famous Comedy Store, which led to his TV debut in Rowan and Martin's *Laugh-In*, then a guest spot in *Happy Days* as the extra-terrestrial Mork. So popular was this appearance that it resulted in the *Mork And Mindy* series which, in turn, launched his movie career. Meanwhile, he continued to excel as a stand-up comic, one of the top three in the US alongside Eddie Murphy and Billy Crystal.

After *Good Morning, Vietnam*, Robin Williams emphasised his new-found weight in Peter Weir's *Dead Poets Society* (1989). Once again he essayed an anti-Establishment figure, this time as a schoolmaster dedicated to instilling a love of literature and poetry into over-privileged and previously uninterested private-school boys. The teacher's unconventional approach leads to tragedy, but also an affirmation of spiritual values, and Williams' performance, encompassing his full range of gifts, won him his second Best Actor Oscor nomination. His follow-up film, *Cadillac Man* (1990), about a car salesman, was an inferior piece, but then came Penny Marshall's *Awakenings* (1990) in which he co-starred as the doctor who wakens Robert De Niro's patient from a 30-year sleep-like state. Based on Dr Oliver Sacks' account of his own medical experiences, this ambitious, Oscar-nominated film was given a mixed reception and Williams, effacing himself in a fully serious role, was perceived as second banana to the more showy De Niro. To the *cognoscenti*, however, his meticulous performance was one to treasure and served to demonstrate that this versatile performer is capable of real depth as well as range – an observation emphatically reiterated by a remarkable performance as the disturbed, marginalised poet-beggar in Terry Gilliam's *The Fisher King* (1991). Deservedly Oscar-nominated, many felt he should have won, and probably would have but for competing with Hannibal Lecter (Anthony Hopkins).

In his private life, Robin Williams had a period of struggle with drugs from which he emerged stronger and wiser. A man of wide-ranging interests and concerns, including politics, he is twice-married, a father of two and lives in California.

1980 Popeye **1982** The World According To Garp **1983** The Survivors **1984** Moscow On The Hudson **1985** The Best Of Times **1986** Club Paradise **1987** Good Morning Vietnam **1989** Dead Poets Society **1990** Cadillac Man **1990** Awakenings **1991** The Fisher King; Hook; Dead Again (cameo); Shakes The Clown **1992** Toys **1992/93** Being Human

Williams, Treat
(Richard Williams)
Actor
Born 1 December 1951
Rowayton, Connecticut

With rugged, dark, Irish-American good looks (which have, when required, doubled convincingly for Italian-American) and a terrifying similarity to Colonel Oliver North, Treat Williams took up drama studies after going to college on the strength of his football prowess. He played Shakespeare during vacations with Pennsylvania's Fulton Repertory Company before understudying the lead in the Broadway production of *Grease*, a show he subsequently returned to in a lead role. He made his screen debut as the handsome private detective whose impossibly high voice causes obvious misinterpretations in Richard Lester's gay bath-house comedy *The Ritz* (1976), a film that was the first, and least subtle, example of the way in which his bulky footballer's physique is often used against itself while still suggestively offsetting intimations of sensitivity or neurosis in his most effective screen roles.

In *Hair* (1979) this combination, plus the physical energy of his table-top dance during the hippies' invasion of the rich family's home, lent his characterisation rather more force than the script was able to provide. Similarly, the actor's rugged aspect helped to convey the desperate need for redemption of the compromised narcotics detective in Sidney Lumet's powerful police corruption drama *Prince Of The City* (1981), talking to IAD officers through the night in an act of confession that leaves his voice a hoarse whisper, while on the other hand, in Joyce Chopra's *Smooth Talk* (1985) his handsomeness was cleverly subverted in his portrayal of the sinister interloper, making manifest the growing sexual awareness of teenage heroine Laura Dern.

Subsequent films, including his much trimmed part as a before-and-after Jimmy Hoffa-style union organiser in *Once Upon A Time In America* (1984), tended to usher him towards the sidelines, and personal problems pushed him into increasingly (and depressingly) downmarket films that stifled his career's momentum (he reputedly made 1987's *Night Of The Sharks* purely to pay off a rather pressing debt). Indeed, despite an unassuming versatility that deserves to prosper, it has only been recently that Treat Williams has been able to find his way back to halfway decent screen roles, but seemed relegated to part of an ensemble rather than the kind of lead he has shown he is capable of handling.

1976 The Ritz; Deadly Hero; The Eagle Has Landed **1979** 1941;Hair **1980** Why Would I Lie? **1981** Prince Of The City; The Pursuit Of D.B. Cooper **1982** Stangata Napoletana – La Trastola/Neapolitan Sting (Italy) **1984** Flashpoint; Once Upon A Time In America **1985** Smooth Talk **1986** The Men's Club **1987** La Notti Degli Squali/ Night Of The Sharks (Italy) **1988** Dead Heat; Russicum **1989** Heart Of Dixie; Sweet Lies **1990** Beyond The Ocean **1993** Where The Rivers Flow North

Willis, Bruce
Actor
Born 19 March 1955
Germany

Although born in Germany, Bruce Willis grew up in New Jersey from the age of two. His first outing as an entertainer saw him playing the harmonica in a band called Loose Goose, and he acted in a production of *Cat On A Hot Tin Roof* while studying at Montclair State College in his home town.

Built to the specifications of a javelin thrower, his strong head well able to serve as a battering ram, Willis earned his living as a New Jersey security guard before becoming a professional actor. His decision to take acting lessons in the mid-1970s led him to a small part in a forgotten production off-Broadway, after which he followed the familiar path of the aspiring actor: considerable periods of unemployment relieved by an occasional theatre engagement and a commercial or two (including one for Levi 501s), and supplementing his meagre income by working in a bar. He snuck into movies as little more than an extra in a Frank Sinatra potboiler, *The First Deadly Sin* (1980), and two tough Sidney Lumet films, *The Verdict* (1982) and *Prince Of The City* (1981), all New York-based. He then moved to Los Angeles where he was offered the part of David Addison in a TV sitcom with Cybill Shepherd called *Moonlighting*, and the actor became a household name.

Willis, who was simultaneously pursuing a recording career for a while with some success, made his Hollywood movie debut co-starring with Kim Basinger in *Blind Date*, (1987), not brilliant but a palpable success. Blake Edwards' unsuccessful Western, *Sunset* (1988), did little for him, but *Die Hard* the same year rocketed him to stardom. As John

McLane, the New York cop on a visit to LA who, like a metropolitan Tarzan, fends off villains in a jungle of concrete and elevator shafts, Bruce Willis' traditional tough-hero persona came into its own. Such was his popularity that he was hired as the unborn baby's 'voice' for *Look Who's Talking* (1989) – a cute idea, but it could have been anybody. Although Willis proved his 'serious' credentials as the Vietnam veteran in Norman Jewison's rather plodding *In Country* (1989), he seemed an odd choice for the role of the drink-sodden English journalist in *The Bonfire Of The Vanities* (1990) (during the making of the film the part was tailored into an American), and *Die Hard 2* (1990) served to emphasize the popularity of the invincible McLane, this time taking on airport terrorists. *Hudson Hawk* (1991), a self-indulgent, very costly project conceived by its star, was not without its comic moments, but was reviled by critics and rejected by audiences. In the flop gangster film, *Billy Bathgate* (1991), his quickly extinguished rival to Dustin Hoffman's Dutch Shultz again saw Willis playing on one flip, wisecracking note – a tone which met with a warmer box-office reception in the violent action caper, *The Last Boy Scout*.

In private life, Willis is married to Demi Moore, with whom he appeared in Alan Rudolph's *Mortal Thoughts*.

1987 Blind Date **1988** Sunset; Die Hard **1989** In Country **1990** Die Hard 2: Die Harder **1990** The Bonfire Of The Vanities **1991** Mortal Thoughts; Hudson Hawk; Billy Bathgate; The Last Boy Scout **1992** The Player (cameo as himself); Death Becomes Her **1992/93** Three Rivers

Winger, Debra

Actress
Born 17 May 1955
Cleveland, Ohio

Perceived variously as a kook or one tough cookie, Debra Winger is a thoroughly contemporary actress with a vivid screen presence. Undeniably a major talent and set fair in the early 1980s to rival the biggest-named stars, Winger has arguably been undermined in her career by questionable judgement.

Born into an orthodox Jewish family, she moved with them from the Midwest to California in childhood. Gifted and precocious, she finished high school at the age of 15 and travelled to Israel, where she followed a stint on a kibbutz by enlisting in the Israeli army. On her return to the States a few years later she was seriously injured in a fall while working in an amusement park and temporarily paralysed. During a painful and gutsy recovery Winger determined to become an actress and tackled the business of show with the same bloody mindedness. After a few TV commercials and bit parts she was cast as Lynda Carter's sister in the series *Wonder Woman*, loathed the experience and broke her contract to leave the show after only two episodes. She was still not 20.

Several sexy teeny roles typical of the time followed, with her breakthrough coming in James Bridges' *Urban Cowboy* (1980), cast opposite John Travolta and shining as a down-to-earth honky-tonk girl. She seemed to have made it as the small-town factory worker aspiring to a better life and capturing Richard Gere in *An Officer And A Gentleman* (1982), an old-fashioned but steamy romance, but she very publicly poured scorn on the film, its director, Taylor Hackford, and Gere. Nonetheless, it made her a star – audiences loved it and it became one of the biggest hits of the year. *Terms Of Endearment* (1983) was a more personal triumph for the dark-haired actress with a distinctively husky voice, and although it was Shirley MacLaine who took the Best Actress Oscar, Winger won a nomination and raves for her performance as the outspoken daughter going down fighting with cancer.

After that things started to go wrong. *Cowboy* director Bridges was sufficiently keen to work with her again to tailor a vehicle for her, the dreadful and little-seen thriller *Mike's Murder* (1984), but her reputation for being 'difficult' made others wary. She was appealing opposite a charming Robert Redford in the slight legal comedy thriller *Legal Eagles* (1986), but the movie was a big financial loser and the packaging of it created a rift between Winger and her agents at powerful CAA. Her most successful performance since was as the frustrated justice department paper pusher determined to catch Theresa Russell's seductive serial murderess in Bob Rafelson's *Black Widow* (1987), although she was just as good as the duplicitous, guilty and vulnerable FBI agent in Costa-Gavras' somewhat dubious, unlikeable *Betrayed* (1988).

During her brief marriage to actor Timothy Hutton, Winger played a startling cameo as his male guardian angel in *Made In Heaven* (1987) and, owing to her pregnancy with their son, lost the role that went to Holly Hunter in *Broadcast News*. Since then, two on-paper prestige projects bombed: Karel Reisz's film of Arthur Miller's first original screenplay since 1961's *The Misfits*, *Everybody Wins* (1990) in which Winger played a demented hooker opposite Nick Nolte (her co-star in *Cannery Row*, 1982), and Bernardo Bertolucci's big disappointment, *The Sheltering Sky* (1990). Winger subsequently signed for the lead in *A League Of Their Own*, but was replaced by Geena Davis and left still looking for a vehicle that would restore the momentum of a decade earlier to her career.

1977 Slumber Party '57 **1978** Thank God It's Friday **1979** French Postcards **1980** Urban Cowboy **1982** An Officer And A Gentleman; Cannery Row **1983** Terms Of Endearment **1984** Mike's Murder **1986** Legal Eagles **1987** Black Widow; Made In Heaven **1988** Betrayed **1990** Everybody Wins; The Sheltering Sky **1992/93 Leap Of Faith**

Winter, Alex
(Alexander Winter)
Actor
Born 17 July 1965
London, England

This distinctive-looking actor with curly hair and wide eyes seemed typecast in his role as Bill, one half (Keanu Reeves was the other) of the weird pair in *Bill And Ted's Excellent Adventure* (1989), the way-out story of two 'cool dudes' who believe in 'partying on down', think that Joan Of Arc was Noah's wife, and have their own language and mannerisms typical of those in the San Fernando Valley area of Los Angeles. This hilarious film certainly made Winter's name, but his acting career had begun quite some time before.

It isn't surprising that Alex Winter became an actor, given his theatrical family background. His parents (Gregg Mayer and Ross Winter) were both modern dancers, and his older brother is a composer and musician. Alex began his career aged four, training as a dancer at a London school before he and his family moved to St Louis, Missouri. Once settled, at the age of seven he began to attend an improvisation workshop founded by members of Chicago's famous Second City group, and this led to work in regional productions and, later, to Broadway.

Winter spent six years on Broadway, making his debut in a production of *The King and I*, and also appearing in *Peter Pan* and Simon Gray's *Close Of Play*. He then returned to school, and studied film production, writing and editing at New York University before making his big-screen debut in Michael Winner's *Death Wish III* (1985). It was hardly a distinguished start (the film was universally panned), and he returned to University until 1987, when Joel Schumacher cast him in a supporting role in his vampire movie, *The Lost Boys* (1987). As one of the vampires following gangleader Kiefer Sutherland, Winter had the distinction of suffering one of the most grisly deaths in the film, his skin eroded by a bathful of garlic and holy water. The movie was a success, and Winter subsequently appeared in a series of TV commercials, and also guested on CBS's series *The Equalizer*, before returning to the big screen in the little-seen *Haunted Summer* (1989). Expressing a preference for slightly off-the-wall roles, he appeared in Percy Adlon's *Rosalie Goes Shopping* (1989), as one of the weird sons of Brad Davis and Marianne Sägebrecht, and then went on to co-star in *Bill And Ted's Excellent Adventure*, his biggest and funniest role to date, and so successful that a sequel was ordered within days of the original's theatrical release.

1985 Death Wish III **1987** The Lost Boys **1988** Haunted Summer **1989** Rosalie Goes Shopping; Bill And Ted's Excellent Adventure **1991** Bill And Ted's Excellent Adventure II aka Bill And Ted's Bogus Journey **1992** hideous mutant FREEKZ (also co-writer, co-director)

Woods, James
Actor
Born 18 April 1947
Vernal, Utah

One of the most explosive of contemporary screen actors, James Woods spent years playing wimps, weirdos and psychotics before being given the opportunity to carry a film. An actor's actor, he proved early in his career that he could steal a film from under the nose of more glamorous stars, but his lack of traditional leading-man looks limited the roles offered to him. It was a serious misjudgement, for, as any number of women will aver, Woods' look of a lean, hungry wolf is wildly sexy.

The son of a soldier father and teacher mother, he had a well-travelled childhood, raised in Utah, Illinois, Virginia, the island of Guam and New England. Exceptionally brainy, he won a full scholarship to that prestigious scientific hothouse, The Massachusetts Institute of Technology, where he took his degree in political science. While there, however, he was drawn to acting, performing in 36 plays not just at MIT but also at neighbouring Harvard and with the Theatre

Company of Boston. Repertory summer stock at Rhode Island's well-regarded Provincetown Playhouse followed and, soon after leaving university, he made his Broadway debut in Brendan Behan's *Borstal Boy*. He followed that with a leading role off-Broadway, in Edward Bond's controversial *Saved*, for which he received an Obie – the off-Broadway equivalent of an Oscar or Tony – and the Clarence Derwent Award, given to the most promising actor of the year. He continued to distinguish himself on the New York stage and made his film debut for Elia Kazan at the age of 24 in *The Visitors* (1972), a disastrous Vietnam vet drama.

A bit part in *Hickey And Boggs* (1972) did little more for his career, but he managed, in the company of Robert Redford and Barbra Streisand, to catch the eye in *The Way We Were* (1973) in the role of Streisand's political activist university boyfriend. The roles duly grew bigger and the actor drew raves for his performance as the cold-blooded and crafty killer Gregory Powell in Harold Becker's film of Joseph Wambaugh's *The Onion Field* (1979). At the same time, Woods was developing stature in television work. *All The Way Home*, with Joanne Woodward, led to his major role in one of the television events of the 1970s, *Holocaust*, in which he was heart-wrenching as Meryl Streep's husband, a Jewish artist sent to his death in Buchenwald. His more than 40 TV appearances include *Raid On Entebbe*, *The Disappearance Of Aimee*, and *Badge Of The Assassin* and he won two Emmys, one for a brilliant portrayal of the schizophrenic brother of James Garner in *Promise* (1986), for which he won as Best Supporting Actor, and the other for *My Name Is Bill W.* (1989), for which he was named Best Actor.

It was with Oliver Stone's *Salvador* (1986), as sleazy journalist Richard Boyle, that Woods finally 'arrived', his electrifying performance earning an Oscar nomination and top billing thereafter. The intensity of his playing, as a violent, cunning Jewish gangster in Sergio Leone's *Once Upon A Time In America* (1984) might have done the same for him earlier, had the film not been butchered for American distribution. His nervous energy and intensity have since been at the fore in always watchable if not always successful projects: the killer-turned-informer in the suspenseful *Best Seller* (1987); the obsessed hunter of a serial killer in the otherwise awful *Cop* the same year; the drug-crazed dreamer who self-destructs in *The Boost* (1988 – unfortunately better known as the scene of an alleged affair between Woods and co-star Sean Young, whom he subsequently took to court for harassment), and the brilliant defence attorney whose youthful ideals are revived by a seemingly hopeless fight for justice in *True Believer* (1989). Thus far, James Woods has not shown himself to equally strong advantage in a more sentimental vehicle, hence a poor reception for the rather sickly surrogate mother melodrama *Immediate Family* (1989) with Glenn Close and the slight romantic comedy, *Straight Talk*, in which his rather novel co-star was Dolly Parton. But for manic, driven characters on the edge (a type he self-parodied hilariously in 1991's *The Hard Way*), he has few equals.

1972 The Visitors; Hickey And Boggs **1973** The Way We Were **1975** Night Moves **1976** Alex And The Gypsy **1977** The Choirboys **1979** The Onion Field **1980** The Black Marble **1981** Eyewitness aka The Janitor **1982** Fast-Walking; Split Image **1983** Videodrome **1984** Once Upon A Time In America; Against All Odds **1985** Cat's Eye; Joshua Then And Now **1986** Salvador **1987** Best Seller; Cop **1988** The Boost **1989** True Believer aka Fighting Justice; Immediate Family **1991** The Hard Way **1992** Straight Talk; Diggstown; Bitter Moon

Woodward, Joanne

Actress
Born 27 February 1930
Thomasville, Georgia

A woman of great warmth and intelligence, and an articulate champion of liberal causes, Joanne Woodward describes herself as an actress rather than a movie star. She once told a reporter: 'I used to have great traumas about not presenting a star image. But I'm not a star. A star is someone whose personality transcends everything. Mine doesn't transcend anything. That's why I like acting – so I won't have to come on as myself.'

In her early screen career she specialised in Deep Southern slatterns, prowling hungrily around the old plantation, but her real and occasionally transcendent genius is for less exotic characters, ordinary women drifting through the backwaters of life, trying none too successfully to cope in a man's world. Arguably, her long and happy marriage to Paul Newman has had an inhibiting effect on her for long stretches of her career. She has co-starred with him in very many mediocre movies, in critic David Thomson's memorable phrase, 'like a dutiful wife who goes along on the husband's fishing trips'. But the brilliant exceptions almost make amends for all the disappointments. We would be much the poorer without *Rachel Rachel* (1968) – in which Newman decisively switched from co-star to director – and *Mr And Mrs Bridge* (1990), in which they both distilled a lifetime's personal and professional experience.

She was brought up in the South and gained her first acting experience at Louisiana State University and a small community theatre in South Carolina. Then she packed her bags for New York, where she studied at the Neighborhood Playhouse and the Actors' Studio. While still a student she understudied on Broadway in *Picnic*, meeting Newman around this time (they were married in 1958) and becoming a prolific TV actress in the 'Golden Age' of live television. She was spotted on TV by Buddy Adler, then head of production at 20th Century-Fox, and signed to a long-term contract.

Woodward made her movie debut in a modest Western, *Count Three and Pray* (1955), as a strong-willed orphan taken in hand by pastor Van Heflin. She lasted only 20 minutes in Gerd Oswald's under-rated *A Kiss Before Dying* (1956) before being bumped off by smiling psychopath Robert Wagner, and then played the schizophrenic with three personalities and three separate lives in Nunnally Johnson's *The Three Faces Of Eve* (1957). It was a leaden film but the subject was fashionable and Woodward's Oscar-winning performance a remarkable *tour de force*. She then embarked on a string of Southern roles: trapped in suburbia in *No Down Payment* (1958); co-starring with Newman for the first time in *The Long Hot Summer* (1958) as Orson Welles' wilful daughter; struggling to shake off the suffocating ties of a very odd family in another Faulkner adaptation, *The Sound And The Fury* (1959); and as a radiant outcast heroine opposite Marlon Brando in *The Fugitive Kind* (1959), adapted from Tennessee Williams' *Orpheus Descending*.

During the same period the actress revealed a flair for comedy as Paul Newman's neglected wife in the sprightly social satire *Rally Round the Flag Boys* (1958), but from the early 1960s her career was undermined by a series of flops: *From The Terrace* (1960) and *Paris Blues* (1961), both with Newman; unsuccessfully imitating Doris Day in *A New Kind Of Love* (1963); marvellously blowsy as the ageing showgirl in *The Stripper* (1963), a part originally slated for Marilyn Monroe; and reduced to near B-movie status in *Signpost To Murder* (1965). She was earthy and funny as mad poet Sean Connery's waitress wife in *A Fine Madness* (1966), but was now considered 'box-office poison'. Before eclipse became total, Newman persuaded Warners to back *Rachel Rachel*, his directing debut, in which Woodward gave an acutely observed and intensely moving performance as a middle-aged schoolmarm embarking on a final affair. It was proof of her uncanny ability to capture the social, sexual and psychological pressures afflicting an unremarkable woman and produce a 'heightened ordinariness' which went to the very heart of a blighted life. She repeated this discreetly tender form of anatomy in the appallingly titled *The Effects Of Gamma Rays On Man-In-The-Moon Marigolds* (1972), again directed by Newman, as a slovenly widow raising two strange daughters (one of them her own daughter, Nell Potts); and in Gilbert Cates' *Summer Wishes, Winter Dreams* (1973), playing a menopausal woman riven by the death of her mother and her son's homosexuality.

In the last 20 years Woodward's screen appearances have been infrequent, as television has often provided her with the chance to stretch herself and she is famously hostile to the Hollywood movie colony. But she was wryly effective as a Dr Watson to George C. Scott's Sherlock Holmes in *They Might Be Giants* (1971); co-starred with Newman in a Lew Archer thriller, *The Drowning Pool* (1974); and submitted herself to his direction again in *Harry And Son* (1984), a meandering family saga, and a respectful version of Tennessee Williams' The *Glass Menagerie* (1987) in which she was ideally cast as Amanda Wingfield.

It took the combination of director James Ivory and screenwriter Ruth Prawer Jhabvala to realise the potential of the Woodward-Newman partnership with *Mr And Mrs Bridge* (1990), in which they were a middle-class Kansas City couple leading largely uneventful lives in the interwar years. Newman was magnificent as a successful lawyer, correctly attentive to the women in his life but uncomprehending of their real needs. Woodward matched him as his wife, submissive but occasionally mischievous, seemingly one step behind everything but nevertheless pursuing her own agenda, caring for her family, lacking any form of censoriousness but imbued with a highly developed moral sense. It was an Oscar-nominated performance, glowing with the tact, discreet technical skill and humanity which are the hallmarks of Joanne Woodward at her finest.

1955 Count Three And Pray **1956** A Kiss Before Dying **1957** The Three Faces Of Eve; No Down Payment **1958** The Long Hot Summer; Rally Round The Flag Boys! **1959** The Sound And The Fury **1960** The Fugitive Kind; From The Terrace **1961** Paris Blues **1963** The Stripper; A New Kind Of Love **1965** Signpost To Murder **1966** A Big Hand For The Little Lady; A Fine Madness **1968** Rachel Rachel **1969** Winning **1970** King (docu); WUSA **1971** They Might Be Giants **1972** The Effect Of Gamma Rays On Man-In-The Moon Marigolds **1973** Summer Wishes, Winter Dreams **1975** The Drowning Pool **1978** The End **1984** Harry And Son **1987** The Glass Menagerie **1990** Mr And Mrs Bridge **1992** Foreign Affairs

Wright, Amy

Actress

Born 1950

Chicago, Illinois

Most familiar on film as plain, prim or peculiar supporting characters (specialty: sisters), Amy Wright has been offered more scope in her stage work, ranging from roles in Shakespeare and Strindberg to Dylan Thomas and Lanford Wilson.

Born and raised in Chicago, she took up acting while still at school and continued drama studies at Beloit College, after which she spent two years directing and teaching acting classes at The Stockbridge School. She subsequently joined a fledgling theatre company founded by a friend in Rockford, Illinois, where she spent a year performing in ten plays in repertory. Her long and continuing association with New York's Circle Repertory Theatre began in 1978, when Lanford Wilson wrote a part for her in the acclaimed *Fifth Of July*, in which she appeared off-Broadway, in Los Angeles, and ultimately on Broadway in 1980.

Wright made her film debut in a documentary, *Not A Pretty Picture* (1978), before winning bit parts which gradually allowed her to create an impression. A fleeting role in Claudia Weill's uneven *Girlfriends* was followed by a small but good part in the ensemble of Michael Cimino's multiple-Oscar winner, *The Deer Hunter* (both 1978), and she has done nice work in John Huston's acclaimed *Wise Blood* (1979), a turn in Woody Allen's *Stardust Memories* (1980), and has played characters in comedies, dramas and horror, proving especially able and moving as the drug-addicted no-hoper clinging to John Savage in *Inside Moves* (1980). She was particularly memorable as the fastidious sister among the eccentric siblings in *The Accidental Tourist* (1988). Deceptively colourless, Wright is a thoughtful actress capable of telling performances that arrest in mediocre pieces, as she demonstrated in the role of an acid-tongued Southern belle beauty contestant in *Miss Firecracker* (1989), and as the spinster who at last has nabbed a groom in *Love Hurts* (1990).

1978 Not A Pretty Picture (docu); Girlfriends; The Deer Hunter **1979** Wise Blood; Breaking Away; The Amityville Horror; Heartland **1980** Stardust Memories; Inside Moves **1986** Off Beat **1988** The Accidental Tourist; The Telephone; Crossing Delancey **1989** Miss Firecracker **1990** Love Hurts **1991** Hard Promises

Yates, Peter

Director
Born 24 July 1929
Aldershot, England

Peter Yates was the first of a number of British directors such as John Boorman and John Schlesinger, and much later, Adrian Lyne and Tony Scott, who made a successful transition to Hollywood. Paving the way was *Bullitt* (1968), a huge box-office hit, starring Steve McQueen as the eponymous police lieutenant at odds with a crooked politician (Robert Vaughn). The famous climax was a thrilling car chase up and down the streets of San Francisco, which proved that Yates could beat the Americans at their own game. Like McQueen, Yates had been a motor-racing driver at the same time as he was working in theatre and films.

He trained as an actor at RADA before directing a couple of plays at the enterprising Royal Court Theatre in London. (He returned to the stage in 1985 to direct Ronald Harwood's *Interpreters*.) It was Tony Richardson, a colleague at the Royal Court, who gave Yates a chance to enter films as his assistant on *The Entertainer* (1960) and *A Taste Of Honey* (1961).

Yates' early films were a mixture of typical British fare, from *Summer Holiday* (1962), a clean-cut Cliff Richard youth musical, through *One Way Pendulum* (1964), an absurdist comedy based on N.F. Simpson's Royal Court play, to *Robbery* (1967), a competently realised drama about the famous Great Train Robbery of 1963, which had a fair share of car chases. This led to *Bullitt* and a Hollywood career. The director's other movies on wheels were *The Hot Rock* (1972), an amiable heist comedy with Robert Redford and George Segal as a couple of inept jewel thieves; *Mother, Jugs And Speed* (1976), a hit-and-miss black comedy about rival ambulance drivers (Bill Cosby and Harvey Keitel) and, best of all, *Breaking Away* (1979), an amusing and ingratiating comedy centred on a 19-year-old cyclist who creates an Italian persona as an escape from the small American town that inhibits him.

Away from cars, bikes and heists, Yates showed an adult side to his nature in two thrillers, *The Friends Of Eddie Coyle* (1973), an intriguing cops-and-cons yarn with Robert Mitchum at his most seedy, and *Eyewitness* (1980), an above-average Hitchcockian homage, starring William Hurt. Like Hitchcock, Yates has a fine sense of place as in the San Francisco of *Bullitt*, Bloomington, Indiana, in *Breaking Away* or Boston in *The Friends Of Eddie Coyle*.

The eclectic and erratic Yates, who admits to being happy working within the commercial cinema in any genre – *Krull* (1982), an unoriginal *Star Wars* – type sci-fi movie; *Eleni* (1985), a creaky story about a journalist obsessed with finding out who executed his mother in Greece after World War II, and *Suspect* (1987), an underrated courtroom/conspiracy drama – was nonetheless very comfortable with the more modest world of 40s British theatre in *The Dresser* (1984), which allowed Albert Finney as a ham Shakespearean actor, and Tom Courtenay as his camp dresser (both Oscar-nominated) to display their considerable talents. And there was not a car in sight!

1962 Summer Holiday **1964** One Way Pendulum **1967** Robbery **1968** Bullitt **1969** John And Mary **1971** Murphy's War **1972** Hot Rock (GB: How To Steal A Diamond In Four Uneasy Lessons) **1973** The Friends Of Eddie Coyle **1974** For Pete's Sake **1977** Mothers, Jugs And Speed; The Deep **1979** Breaking Away **1980** Eyewitness (GB: The Janitor) **1982** Krull **1984** The Dresser **1985** Eleni **1987** The House On Carroll Street; Suspect **1989** An Innocent Man **1992** The Year Of The Comet

Young, Sean

Actress
Born 20 November 1959
Louisville, Kentucky

Slinky brunette Sean Young has attracted more attention off screen than on, and despite several supposed 'breakthrough' roles, by 1990 she was still waiting in the wings for A-list star status. She has had both bad luck and bad press: a broken collarbone from a riding accident saw her replaced by Kim Basinger in *Batman* (1989); Warren Beatty dumped her from *Dick Tracy* (1990) in favour of Madonna; and, most notoriously, she was the subject of a lawsuit from actor James Woods following allegations that she was behind harassment of the *Fatal Attraction* kind – the case was resolved out of court. But

Young is sufficiently shrewd, tenacious and able to have kept the roles coming. And for every past colleague who has labelled her kooky or difficult another has praised her for serenity and ability.

Educated at Michigan's Interlochen Arts Academy, she trained as a dancer and has a fluid, graceful bearing on screen. After a modelling stint in New York she was signed by the powerful ICM agency, where her mother, Lee Guthrie, worked in the literary division. She made her film debut in the modest Merchant-Ivory production *Jane Austen In Manhatten* (1980) and proved decorative as a soldier in the army comedy *Stripes* (1981) before her first major role saw her touted as a new star – as the cool but tremulous android for whom Harrison Ford's 'droid-hunter falls in Ridley Scott's eyeful, *Blade Runner* (1982). A few box-office clinkers followed, however, before she was tantalising Kevin Costner in the back of a limo in *No Way Out* (1987). The same year her part as Michael Douglas' wife in *Wall Street* dwindled to insignificance. It is unfortunate that the tabloid furore surrounding *The Boost* (1988) obscured what was a powerful contemporary anti-drugs film, and a first-rate performance from Young as the gentle wife dragged down into the cocaine-crazed hell of the husband played by James Woods. A change of pace as a gung-ho military helicopter pilot in the dud *Firebirds* (1990) did nothing for her, but she had more challenging work cut out for her playing very different twins wooed by a psychotic Matt Dillon in James Deardon's remake of Ira Levin's thriller *A Kiss Before Dying* (1991), before embarking on her busiest ever year with half-a-dozen movies in 1992.

1980 Jane Austen In Manhattan **1981** Stripes **1982** Blade Runner; Young Doctors In Love **1984** Dune **1985** Baby – Secret Of The Lost Legend **1987** No Way Out; Wall Street **1988** The Boost **1989** Cousins **1990** Wings Of The Apache aka Firebirds **1991** A Kiss Before Dying; **1992** Love Crimes; Once Upon A Crime; Forever; Hold Me, Thrill Me, Kiss Me; Blue Ice

Z

Zeffirelli, Franco

Director
Born 12 February 1923
Florence, Italy

Cultivated, flamboyant Italian director Franco Zeffirelli has had a remarkably diverse career, mounting grand opera at La Scala, Covent Garden and New York's Met and plays at the Old Vic and Britain's National Theatre, the Comédie Française, and in Paris, Vienna and Moscow. His film career has been more chequered, but with three commendable screen adaptations of Shakespeare to his credit he is the most successful interpreter of the Bard's classics for cinema since Laurence Olivier's trio in the 40s and 50s – and, arguably, has done more to popularise them.

Zeffirelli, who had a traumatic but exceptionally cultured childhood in Florence, was already an Anglophile and passionate Shakespeare devotee when he saw Olivier's *Henry V* (1944) at the end of World War II (in which he fought with the partisans) and decided to abandon the architectural studies he had begun before the war in favour of the film industry. His first break into films was as set designer and protégé to the great Italian director Luchino Visconti. By the 1960s he was a theatre and opera director of international repute, noted for his lavish productions and his work with great and temperamental artists such as Maria Callas and Anna Magnani, and he filmed an acclaimed production of *La Bohème* in 1965. Reacting to the catastrophic floods in his beloved Florence with a documentary, *Florence – Days Of Destruction* (1966), he helped galvanise international efforts to restore the city's damaged treasures. Then, in 1967 he delighted audiences with a lusty, vibrant film of *The Taming Of The Shrew*, directing Richard Burton and Elizabeth Taylor in one of their most pleasing, sumptuous and successful screen pairings. In 1968 he defied purists by casting two beautiful children – Leonard Whiting and Olivia Hussey – in his adaptation of *Romeo And Juliet*, rather than using experienced Shakespeareans, and produced one of the top-grossing films of the year. Breathtakingly photographed in Italian locations, the film thrilled young audiences, and if some of the poetry and power of language was lost, the beauty and palpable adolescent passion of the piece were served well.

Moving away from Shakespeare, Zeffirelli was less successful. His celebration of St Francis of Assisi, *Brother Sun, Sister Moon* (1973), was again lovely to look at and had some delightful moments but, ill-served by a weak young lead and a hippy-dippy script, was poorly received. *The Champ* (1979) fared better at the box office with Jon Voight, Faye Dunaway and terminally cute Ricky Schroder as principals, but this remake of the old Wallace Beery vehicle was desperately sentimental. *Endless Love* (1981), starring Brooke Shields and now best remembered as the film debut, in a small role, of Tom Cruise, was simply a disaster, derided by critics and ignored by audiences.

Zeffirelli was on much safer territory with his two spectacularly beautiful opera adaptations, *La Traviata* (1982), distinguished by a brilliant performance from Teresa Stratas, and the presence of Placido Domingo at the height of his vocal powers, and *Otello* (1986), again starring Domingo. While he is always knee-deep in opera and theatre engagements, and has brought opera well to television – most notably his La Scala production of *Pagliacci* with Domingo – Zeffirelli's more recent film projects have been ill-fated, with *Young Toscanini*, actually filmed in the late 80s with C. Thomas Howell and Elizabeth Taylor, yet to see release. Zeffirelli was back with a creditable *Hamlet* (1990), however. While the film was not as inspired as his first two Shakespearean outings, his unexpected choice of Australian action-man heart-throb Mel Gibson for his Great Dane was vindicated by a vigorous, attractive performance that did, as hoped, lure people in who were not previously partial to William Shakespeare.

1965 La Bohème **1966** Florence – Days Of Destruction (docu) **1967** The Taming Of The Shrew **1968** Romeo And Juliet **1973** Brother Sun, Sister Moon **1979** The Champ **1981** Endless Love **1982** La Traviata **1986** Otello **1988** Young Toscanini (unreleased) **1990** Hamlet

Zemeckis, Robert

Director, writer
Born 14 May 1951
Chicago, Illinois

Robert Zemeckis is one of the most prominent of the post-Spielberg school of Hollywood directors riding high on the renewed confidence of American film-making that began in the late 1980s. His films – which include *Romancing The Stone* (1984), *Back To The Future* (three parts, 1985, 1989 and 1990) and *Who Framed Roger Rabbit?* (1988) are pacy, subversive and immensely popular at the box office. He belongs to a modern generation of film-makers for whom script and story-telling are paramount: 'Good directing is good writing and good casting – that's all!' he has said in an interview. Of course it's more complicated than that; for one thing, this leaves out the visual side of his movies which is rich and arresting, veering to the epic, or mock-epic (*Romancing The Stone*). A protégé of Spielberg (who gave him his first break by employing him and partner Bob Gale to write *1941* in 1979) and a longtime admirer of David Lean ('for me, those are the two guys'), he shows in his own work a natural ability to handle large-scale projects with verve and brilliant visual inventiveness. Above all, he has – for success – extraordinary energy and persistence. He is one of those rare directors whose sequels are better than the original. *Back To The Future Part II* may have been something of a disappointment to fans; but it's widely agreed that *Part III* is best of the lot.

Zemeckis has needed that persistence and optimism at different times of his career, for his first three films all crashed at the box office, and in the early 1980s he had the greatest difficulty in finding support for his projects. (The script for *Back To The Future* was rejected by every major studio.) *Romancing The Stone* – the sleeper of 1984 – was his salvation; yet up to its opening night Fox executives had been prophesying failure. His major film to date has been *Who Framed Roger Rabbit?*, an extraordinary comic combination of live action and animation that re-intro duced a sort of sexy subversiveness – an adult humour – into the cosy world of full-length cartoon creation. 'Walt Disney never made his cartoons exclusively for children', he said. 'The Warner Brothers guys certainly didn't!' This delightful movie has the distinction of being at one and the same time utterly mainstream and extraordinarily experimental.

Zemeckis was educated at the University of Southern California film school (contemporaries include directors John Carpenter and Matthew Robbins, writer-director W.D. Richter and screenwriter Dan O'Bannion). This institution was always less 'intellectual' and more 'industry-directed' than its famous rival, UCLA at Berkeley, origin of such luminaries as Coppola. Drive, optimism and – as stated – meticulously crafted stories are Zemeckis' contribution to contemporary cinema. The optimism is essential: he only likes movies where characters have dreams and ideals. Thus, for Zemeckis, Capra's *It's A Wonderful Life* (1946) is 'the most perfect movie ever made'. His own films are marked by their humour and their relentless pace – he began his career as an editor and knows all about rhythm. Very few fades, or dissolves, or *temps morts*: instead, a quick cut and on with the action. A film style, you could say, whose punctuation is not the full stop but the dash. His starring vehicle for Meryl Streep, Goldie Hawn and Bruce Willis, *Death Becomes Her* (1992), marked a change of tone, if not style, and was anything but a success. Nonetheless, he holds the record for the highest-grossing Hollywood director between 1982 and 1992.

As director only unless stated otherwise: **1978** I Wanna Hold Your Hand (also co-writer) **1979** 1941 (co-writer only) **1980** Used Cars **1984** Romancing The Stone **1985** Back To The Future (w/d) **1988** Who Framed Roger Rabbit? **1989** Back To The Future II **1990** Back To The Future 3 **1992** The Looters (co-writer only); Death Becomes Her

Zucker, David

Director, writer
Born 16 October 1947
Milwaukee, Wisconsin

(See Jim Abrahams)

Zucker, Jerry

Director, writer
Born 11 March 1950
Milwaukee, Wisconsin

(See Jim Abrahams)

Zuniga, Daphne

Actress
Born 1963
Berkeley, California

Brunette Daphne Zuniga left a promising future after college to pursue an acting career, but her decision at the age of 21, when she was spotted by a talent scout, seemed to pay off. Certainly, many people would envy the actress some of her leading men. In only her second screen role she was performing alongside up-and-coming young actor Matthew Modine in *Vision Quest* (1985), a tale of a young wrestling champ and his love for an older woman (Linda Fiorentino). Although Daphne's role was small (and most of the attention was directed towards singer Madonna, who appeared in a cameo role), it brought her to the attention of director Rob Reiner, who gave her the co-lead opposite John Cusack in his romantic comedy *The Sure Thing* (1985). The film, which was regarded by many critics as one of the funniest teen movies of the 80s, paired Cusack and Zuniga as two college students, one reckless and the other (Zuniga) a rule-following good girl, forced together on a cross-country trip from New England to Los Angeles. Cusack, who seems happiest when playing the goofy guy who means well, excelled in his role, and Zuniga proved an equal match for her co-star, playing the strait-laced, brainy heroine with aplomb.

From this auspicious start, she went on to a lead in *Modern Girls* (1986), with other young actresses Virginia Madsen and Cynthia Gibb. Unfortunately, this story of three free spirits roaming the LA punk club scene was widely regarded as a complete disaster, and was barely released to the general public. Dusting herself down, Zuniga returned to comedy in the Mel Brooks spoof of the Star Wars saga, *Spaceballs* (1987), playing the Royally Spoiled Princess (modelled on Princess Leia, Carrie Fisher's character in *Star Wars*). One suspects that she was chosen more for her resemblance to Fisher than for her comic ability, which was rarely noticed amid the onslaught of silly jokes and sight gags typical of Mel Brooks.

From playing the slightly dowdy 'brain' in *Vision Quest* and *The Sure Thing*, the actress did a complete about-face in her next role, switching to portray the stunning beauty who seduces Tom Berenger's priest in the thriller *Last Rites* (1988), and proving in the process that she could be just as convincing in serious drama as in lighter fare. Unfortunately, the film was not a great success, and neither was her subsequent outing, *Gross Anatomy* (1989), in which, reunited with her former co-star Matthew Modine, she played a medical student. The film suffered mainly from the fact that other hospital comedy-dramas (including the superior *Vital Signs*) were released within weeks of *Gross Anatomy*'s premiere.

Although some of her films have been relegated to almost instant video release, Daphne Zuniga established herself as an attractive, versatile and pleasing screen presence, too seldom utilised.

1981 The Dorm That Dripped Blood **1984** The Initiation **1985** Vision Quest aka Crazy For You; The Sure Thing **1986** Modern Girls **1987** Spaceballs **1988** Last Rites **1989** Gross Anatomy; Staying Together aka A Boy's Life; The Fly II **1992** Mad At The Moon **1992/93** Chameleon

ENTRIES ARRANGED BY CONTRIBUTOR

RONALD BERGAN Abraham, F. Murray; Abrahams, Jim (and the Zuckers); Adams, Brooke; Alda, Alan; Altman, Robert; Ameche, Don; Ann-Margret; Apted, Michael; Arkin, Alan; Ashby, Hal; Avildsen, John G.; Badham, John; Bancroft, Anne; Bartel, Paul; Beatty, Warren; Benjamin, Richard; Benson, Robbie; Bergen, Candice; Black, Karen; Bogdanovich, Peter; Brando, Marlon; Bridges, Beau; Broderick, Matthew; Bronson, Charles; Brooks, Mel; Bujold, Genevieve; Caan, James; Cage, Nicolas; Caine, Michael; Carpenter, John; Carradine, David; Carradine, Keith; Cassavetes, John; Chaplin, Geraldine; Cimino, Michael; Clayburgh, Jill; Coburn, James; Connery, Sean; Coppola, Francis Ford; Corman, Roger; Costa-Gavras, Constantin; Crichton, Michael; Cronenberg, David; Danson, Ted; Dennehy, Brian; Depp, Johnny; Derek, Bo; Dern, Bruce; DeVito, Danny; Divine; Dreyfuss, Richard; Dunaway, Faye; Duvall, Robert; Duvall, Shelley; Edwards, Blake; Falk, Peter; Forman, Milos; Fosse, Bob; Gallagher, Peter; Gere, Richard; Gilliam, Terry; Grodin, Charles; Hawn, Goldie; Hemingway, Mariel; Hill, Walter; Hoffman, Dustin; Jarmusch, Jim; Kane, Carol; Konchalovsky, Andrei; Landau, Martin; Lone, John; Lucas, George; Malle, Louis; Mamet, David; May, Elaine; Mazursky, Paul; Milius, John; Moore, Dudley; Nicholson, Jack; Nielsen, Leslie; Peckinpah, Sam; Penn, Arthur; Poitier, Sidney; Polanski, Roman; Reeve, Christopher; Ritchie, Michael; Rudolph, Alan; Rydell, Mark; Scheider, Roy; Schlesinger, John; Schrader, Paul; Streisand, Barbra; Sutherland, Donald; Tandy, Jessica; Voight, Jon; Walken, Christopher; Wenders, Wim; Wilder, Gene; Yates, Peter.

JOANNA BERRY Alonso, Maria Conchita; Barrymore, Drew; Davis, Geena; Dempsey, Patrick; Feldman, Corey; Haim, Corey; Kidder, Margot; Kurtz, Swoosie; Lundgren, Dolph; McNichol, Kristy; Madonna; Matlin, Marlee; Mayron, Melanie; Modine, Matthew; Moranis, Rick; Murray, Bill; Pasdar, Adrian; Ramis, Harold; Rickman, Alan; Robbins, Tim; Shue, Elizabeth; Spano, Vincent; Stoltz, Eric; Travis, Nancy; Winter, Alex; Zuniga, Daphne.

TOM CHARITY Assante, Armand; Aykroyd, Dan; Baker, Joe Don; Baker, Kathy; Balaban, Bob; Baldwin, Adam; Baldwin, William; Boyle, Peter; Brown, Clancy; Cameron, James; Cates, Phoebe; Cattrall, Kim; Caulfield, Maxwell; Cheech and Chong; Chong, Rae Dawn; Clark, Candy; Cort, Bud; Cryer, Jon; Cusack, John; Dante, Joe; Davidovich, Lolita; De Niro, Robert; Dillon, Kevin; Dillon, Melinda; Down, Lesley-Ann; Downey, Robert Jr.; Edwards, Anthony; Elizondo, Hector; Elliott, Sam; Estevez, Emilio; Fonda, Peter; Gertz, Jami; Glover, Crispin; Glover, Danny; Gossett, Lou Jr.; Grant, Lee; Hackman, Gene; Hall, Anthony Michael; Harmon, Mark; Heckerling, Amy; Howard, Ron; Howell, C. Thomas; Jones, James Earl; Kellerman, Sally; Kidman, Nicole; Krabbé, Jeroen; Lane, Diane; Lurie, John; Lynch, Kelly; Mann, Michael; McTiernan, John; O'Connor, Kevin J.; Olmos, Edward James; Pacula, Joanna; Paré, Michael; Patton, Will; Penn, Christopher; Phillips, Lou Diamond; Place, Mary Kay; Quaid, Randy; Reinhold, Judge; Romero, George A.; Sayles, John; Seagal, Steven; Sheen, Charlie; Sheen, Martin; Shelton, Ron; Siemaszko, Casey; Spheeris, Penelope; Stallone, Sylvester; Stern, Daniel; Thompson, Lea; Thurman, Uma; Van Damme,

Jean-Claude; Waits, Tom; Warren, Lesley-Ann; Williams, JoBeth.

ROBIN CROSS Baldwin, Alec; Bisset, Jacqueline; Bridges, Jeff; Burstyn, Ellen; Cannon, Dyan; Craven, Wes; Dickinson, Angie; Englund, Robert; Fawcett, Farrah; Hooper, Tobe; Ivory, James; Jason Leigh, Jennifer; Lumet, Sidney; MacLaine, Shirley; Miles, Sylvia; Minnelli, Liza; Norris, Chuck; Pacino, Al; Redgrave, Vanessa; Ross, Herbert; Schatzberg, Jerry; Schumacher, Joel; Smith, Maggie; Woodward, Joanne.

ANGELA ERRIGO Aiello, Danny; Allen, Karen; Alley, Kirstie; Bacon, Kevin; Barkin, Ellen; Beals, Jennifer; Beresford, Bruce; Bergin, Patrick; Bochner, Hart; Bridges, James; Brooks, Albert; Busey, Gary; Byrne, Gabriel; Capshaw, Kate; Cassidy, Joanna; Coen Brothers; Cruise, Tom; Davison, Bruce; Dillon, Matt; Douglas, Michael; Garner, James; Gish, Anabeth; Glenn, Scott; Goldberg, Whoopi; Goldblum, Jeff; Goodman, John; Grey, Jennifer; Guttenberg, Steve; Harris, Ed; Hawke, Ethan; Heard, John; Hershey, Barbara; Hines, Gregory; Hopper, Dennis; Hoskins, Bob; Hughes, John; Hulce, Tom; Hunter, Tim; Hutton, Timothy; Irons, Jeremy; Johnson, Don; Kasdan, Lawrence; Kaufman, Philip; Kilmer, Val; Kirby, Bruno; Ladd, Dianne; Lahti, Christine; Lambert, Christopher; Lancaster, Burt; Lee, Spike; Levinson, Barry; Lithgow, John; Lowe, Rob; Lynch, David; MacLachlan, Kyle; Mahoney, John; Malkovich, John; Martin, Steve; Masterson, Mary Stuart; Murphy, Eddie; Neill, Sam; Newman, Paul; Nimoy, Leonard; Oldman, Gary; Olin, Lena; Patinkin, Mandy; Pesci, Joe; Quaid, Dennis; Raimi, Sam; Redford, Robert; Riegert, Peter; Ritter, John; Rossellini, Isabella; Rourke, Mickey; Rowlands, Gena; Sands, Julian; Schepisi, Fred; Schwarzenegger, Arnold; Selleck, Tom; Shatner, William; Shepard, Sam; Shepherd, Cybill; Silver, Joan Micklin; Snipes, Wesley; Soderbergh, Steven; Spader, James; Spielberg, Steven; Stockwell, Dean; Sutherland, Kiefer; Swayze, Patrick; Taylor, Lili; Turner, Kathleen; Waters, John; Weaver, Sigourney; Winger, Debra; Woods, James; Wright, Amy; Young, Sean; Zeffirelli, Franco.

ROBYN KARNEY Alexander, Jane; Allen, Nancy; Andrews, Julie; Archer, Anne; Arquette, Rosanna; Basinger, Kim; Bedelia, Bonnie; Bening, Annette; Bernsen, Corbin; Biehn, Michael; Blades, Ruben; Bracco, Lorraine; Cher; Close, Glenn; Costner, Kevin; Cox, Alex; Crystal, Billy; Curtis, Jamie Lee; Cusack, Joan; Daniels, Jeff; Danner, Blythe; Day Lewis, Daniel; De Mornay, Rebecca; Dennis, Sandy; De Palma, Brian; Dukakis, Olympia; Ferrara, Abel; Fisher, Carrie; Ford, Harrison; Fox, Michael J.; Frankenheimer, John; Freeman, Morgan; Friedkin, William; Greist, Kim; Hagerty, Julie; Hamilton, Linda; Harper, Tess; Hauer, Rutger; Hunter, Holly; Hurt, Mary Beth; Irving, Amy; Kotcheff, Ted; Lloyd, Emily; McDormand, Frances; MacDowell, Andie; McGillis, Kelly; Madigan, Amy; Malick, Terrence; Mastrantonio, Mary Elizabeth; Moore, Demi; Neeson, Liam; Parton, Dolly; Penn, Sean; Perkins, Elizabeth; Pfeiffer, Michelle; Phoenix, River; Roberts, Eric; Roberts, Julia; Rogers, Mimi; Rollins, Howard E. Jr.; Ryan, Meg; Ryder, Winona; Seidelman, Susan; Sheedy, Ally; Silver, Ron; Singer, Lori; Slater, Christian; Taylor, Elizabeth; Tilly, Meg; Washington, Denzel; Wiest, Dianne; Williams, Robin; Willis, Bruce.

KATHRYN KIRBY Belushi, John; Burton, Tim; Chase, Chevy; DeLuise, Dom; Dourif, Brad; Hamill, Mark; Headly, Glenne; Hutton, Lauren; Kahn, Madeline; Kavner, Julie; Keaton, Michael; Kristofferson, Kris; Landis, John; Lloyd, Christopher; Macchio, Ralph; Marshall, Garry; Marshall, Penny; Nelson, Judd; Peters, Bernadette; Pitt, Brad; Quinn, Aidan; Reeves, Keanu; Reiner, Carl; San Giacomo, Laura; Short, Martin; Skye, Ione; Stone, Sharon; Turturro, John.

KAREN KRIZANOVICH Blair, Linda; Channing, Stockard; Coleman, Dabney; Dern, Laura; Gardenia, Vincent; Hanks, Tom; Herman, Pee

Wee; Hunt, Linda; Keach, Stacy; Kirkland, Sally; Lehmann, Michael; Liotta, Ray; McCarthy, Andrew; O'Neal, Tatum; Patric, Jason; Perrine, Valerie; Plimpton, Martha; Reiner, Rob; Shire, Talia; Townsend, Robert; Travolta, John; Wang, Wayne.

MARK LeFANU Benton, Robert; Cohen, Larry; Eichhorn, Lisa; Huston, Anjelica; Jaglom, Henry; Jewison, Norman; Kaplan, Jonathan; Le Mat, Paul; Parker, Alan; Pryor, Richard; Ritt, Martin; Robards, Jason; Roberts, Tony; Roddam, Franc; Sarandon, Susan; Shields, Brooke; Streep, Meryl; Waterston, Sam; Zemeckis, Robert.

MAX LOPPERT Allen, Woody; Brandauer, Klaus Maria; Farrow, Mia; Finney, Albert; Fonda, Jane; Frears, Stephen; Garr, Teri; Hill, George Roy; Hiller, Arthur; Hurt, William; Jackson, Glenda; Keaton, Diane; Kline, Kevin; Lemmon, Jack; Lester, Richard; Nolte, Nick; O'Toole, Peter; Scorsese, Martin.

TREVOR WILLSMER Bates, Kathy; Beatty, Ned; Begley, Ed Jr.; Belushi, James; Berenger, Tom; Bigelow, Kathryn; Boorman, John; Bottoms, Timothy; Brooks, James L.; Candy, John; Coyote, Peter; Crouse, Lindsay; Dafoe, Willem; D'Angelo, Beverly; Davis, Brad; Demme, Jonathan; Donaldson, Roger; Donner, Richard; Douglas, Kirk; Dunne, Griffin; Durning, Charles; Eastwood, Clint; Fahey, Jeff; Field, Sally; Forrest, Frederic; Foster, Jodie; Garcia, Andy; Gibson, Mel; Gould, Elliott; Grant, Richard E.; Griffith, Melanie; Haas, Lukas; Hannah, Daryl; Hopkins, Anthony; Hurt, John; Hyams, Peter; Jones, Tommy Lee; Julia, Raul; Keitel, Harvey; Kinski, Nastassia; Kotto, Yaphet; Kubrick, Stanley; Lange, Jessica; Leachman, Cloris; Locke, Sondra; Loggia, Robert; Long, Shelley; Lyne, Adrian; Mantegna, Joe; Mason, Marsha; Matthau, Walter; McGovern, Elizabeth; Metcalf, Laurie; Midler, Bette; Mitchum, Robert; Nichols, Mike; O'Neal, Ryan; Pakula, Alan J.; Peck, Gregory; Petersen, William; Pollack, Sidney; Rafelson, Bob; Remar, James; Remick, Lee; Reynolds, Burt; Ringwald, Molly; Roeg, Nicolas; Rooker, Michael; Russell, Kurt; Russell, Theresa; Savage, John; Scacchi, Greta; Scarwid, Diana; Sciorra, Annabella; Scott, Ridley; Scott, Tony; Sedgwick, Kyra; Shaver, Helen; Spacek, Sissy; Spottiswoode, Roger; Stanton, Harry Dean; Steenburgen, Mary; Stone, Oliver; Tomlin, Lily; Verhoeven, Paul; Walsh, J.T.; Walsh, M. Emmet; Ward, Fred; Ward, Rachel; Weir, Peter; Weller, Peter; Whitaker, Forest; Williams, Treat.